The Encyclopædia of WREXHAM

Revised Edition

W. Alister Williams

bridge books

First published in Wales in 2001
by
BRIDGE BOOKS
61 Park Avenue
Wrexham
LL12 7AW

© 2001 W. Alister Williams
© 2010 W. Alister Williams

Reprinted 2002
Revised edition 2010

All Rights Reserved
No part of this publication may be reproduced,
stored in a retrieval system, or transmitted
in any form or by any means, electronic, mechanical, photocopying,
recording or otherwise, without the prior permission
of the Copyright holder.

A CIP entry for this book is available from the British Library

To Sue
For all her patience, hard work
and faith in this project over so many years.

ISBN 978-1-84494-067-7

Printed and bound
by
Gutenberg Press Ltd
Malta

INTRODUCTION

The popularity and success of the first edition of this work in 2001 surpassed my wildest expectations. Within a matter of weeks, the original print run had been exhausted and a second printing became available during 2002. I am delighted that the *Encyclopaedia* so quickly entered the stock of standard published works on the Wrexham area and has been used by so many people from every walk of life.

With any such work, errors slip in and such has been the case with the *Encyclopaedia* although, thankfully, they have been few and far between. Some were corrected at the second printing and others have been corrected for this revised edition. Many individuals have also drawn my attention to what can best be described as omissions from the original edition and, where deemed necessary, these have been researched and added. Due to the restrictions of space, it has not been possible to pursue every possible new entry and I apologise to those individuals who raised the issue. I would like to express my sincere thanks to all those people who have contacted me with comments on the *Encyclopaedia* and who have been responsible for persuading me to bring out this revised edition.

The idea behind the publication of this book goes back a number of years to when I was compiling a series of illustrated books *Old Wrexham — a collection of pictures*. Whilst researching the background to the pictures, I found that there was not one obvious source of information and what was available tended to focus on either the more prominent features of the town's history or dealt with facts that were at least 100 years old as in the case of the wonderful series of books researched and written by Alfred N. Palmer. The phenomenal growth of the interest in local history, particularly since the explosion in family history research during the last twenty-five years, suggested a need for a new history of the town. When I reflected upon the innumerable requests for information that I have received over the years, I gradually became aware that the need was not for a detailed history, telling the story of the town and its people, but instead, for a collection of facts which answer those questions that arise every day and to which there is no readily available answer.

Once the decision had been made to embark upon the project which has culminated in the publication of this encyclopædia, a number of problems arose.

The first was a question of scale. How large a volume should such an encyclopædia be? This led to further questions, not least of which was what should be included and perhaps, most important of all, what geographical area needed to be covered?

The original townships of Wrexham established in the Middle Ages did not provide an acceptable boundary for research. If one confined the work to the two 'urban' townships of Wrexham Regis and Wrexham Abbot, as Palmer did in his *History of the Town of Wrexham*, a substantial part of the modern town would not be dealt with. If the scope was extended to include all of the thirteen 'country' townships then material would have to be produced on places as far away as Brymbo and Minera — clearly the canvas would be too large to be manageable within an acceptable time limit. The same was true of the original parish of Wrexham which covered the same area as the combined 15 townships.

My final decision was to roughly follow the post-1886 parish boundaries of Wrexham and Rhosddu which gave a boundary fairly similar to that of the present day town. In addition, it was necessary to include those houses and estates located outside the 'parish boundary' e.g. Pant yr Ochain, Erddig and Wynnstay, which have had a significant role to play in the history of the town.

Similarly, the trawl for notable individuals had to be cast wide enough to include those individuals from further afield who would have regarded Wrexham as their local town and where they would have had a significant influence; this included citizens from places as far away as Marchwiel, Gwersyllt, Coedpoeth, Rhosllannerchrugog and Ruabon as well as Maelor Saesneg.

The second major problem came with the realisation that a town is constantly changing and developing. When I began my task, the entry on the Midland Bank building in High Street seemed reliable and stable, carved in stone like the building itself. Then along came the Hong Kong and Shanghai Banking Corporation and the name Midland Bank disappeared from every High Street in the land. No sooner had this change been effected than the HSBC moved its premises to Regent Street and then the building in High Street was converted into licensed premises which has had three names in the last nine years. I have encountered changes such as these all over the town, for the 1990s were probably the period of greatest change in Wrexham for 100 years. Not since the construction of the Wrexham–Ellesmere railway line in the 1890s, which drove right through the town centre, has so much disappeared so quickly. I could not have chosen a more difficult time in which to try and compile an encyclopædia, but nor could I have found a time when such a work of reference was more necessary in an effort to record the changes as they occurred.

The decision on what to include has been mainly governed by the availability of data. Where possible, I have tried to use original sources but in many cases these were no longer available. The works of Palmer have been invaluable and provided a solid foundation upon which to base my own research. I have not always agreed with his findings and as a consequence, have introduced my own theories and claims where necessary. I have been privileged to be allowed access to the research of many other local historians, to the deeds of private houses, to family papers, photographs and memories that are not held in public collections. I have endeavoured to examine as much data held in public collections as possible and, in doing so, have uncovered one or two gems of local history as a result of simply looking at the information from a different perspective.

Rudyard Kipling once wrote a short verse which I have always found to be an invaluable guide in my work as an historian:

I kept six honest working men,
They taught me all I knew.
Their names were What and Why and When
And How and Where and Who.

Wherever possible, I have tried to answer these six basic questions with historically accurate information that will meet the needs of the lay-historian, interested in the town of Wrexham, be that individual an experienced student of local history or a pupil embarking upon a school project. I have included information that falls into the following general categories: people, places, events, buildings and organisations. I must, however, admit my failings. To attempt a book of this nature is to set oneself up to be knocked down. There are people who should have been included among the great, the good and the infamous of Wrexham; there are street names whose origins I have failed to uncover but which are common knowledge to others; there are companies that are missing and interesting facts that have not been included. All of these have been omitted not because they were not worthy of inclusion but simply because I did not know about them. I would ask those who do know the answer to the previously unanswered questions to either contact me through the publisher or to place their knowledge on record with the Wrexham Museum or the Wrexham Library & Information Service.

There is a need to explain one or two features in the body of this book.

Many streets and buildings in Wrexham have Welsh place names which are often either misspelt or have a variety of ways of being written down e.g. Llwyn Issa (rather than Isaf). Wrexham has also had introduced in recent years a peculiar spelling for the Welsh word for street viz 'stryt'. Such a word does not exist in the language and is a dialectical word peculiar to Rhosllannerchrugog. The correct word is 'stryd'.

A note on census material relating to Wrexham. Since the first edition was published all the census returns from 1841–1911 have become very much easier to access via the internet. The Wrexham Registration district, however, is unfortunate in that the 1841 census is missing and all that is available is a printed section (discovered by the late Miss Mollie Preen*) for the town centre which was been transcribed and published by the Clwyd Family History Society.

Readers will note a variation in the spelling of the name of the Royal Welch Fusiliers. This is not an error as during the period *c.*1880–1920, the Army decreed that the name should be written as 'Welsh' but, following pressure from within the regiment, the name officially reverted to the old English spelling 'Welch' after the First World War (the same is true of the Welch Regiment).

In the interest of brevity, certain names have been simply written as initials e.g. RWF for Royal Welch Fusiliers; WBC for Wrexham Borough Council; WRDC for Wrexham Rural District Council; WMBC for Wrexham Maelor Borough Council and WCBC for Wrexham County Borough Council.

An asterisk positioned after a name indicates that there is a further entry dealing with that topic.

Wrexham is regarded by many as the unofficial capital of north Wales and is the largest town in the principality north of the Brecon Beacons. Historically, it was the largest town in Wales until the advent of the Industrial Revolution brought about the expansion of Cardiff and the other heavily industrialised towns of south Wales.

The origins of Wrexham are concealed by the fog of history but we can be certain that it was founded at the crossroads of two major trading routes, that its role always has been that of a market town. The north–south link along the Welsh March ran through the town and the east–west route from the uplands of Wales to the more heavily populated areas of England breached the hills at Bwlchgwyn and on to the Midlands over the river Dee at Holt. Cattle, sheep and other livestock reared in north Wales passed through Wrexham and resulted in the growth of an animal market, which in turn led to the establishment of other trades closely linked to it. The survival of place names such as Tenter's Square, is evidence of a once important cloth trade on the edges of the town, close to the river Gwenfro. This was gradually replaced by the leather industry, but both were dependant on the steady local supply of animal products. It is no coincidence that, throughout its history, one of the most important features of the town has been the *Forum Bestiale* or Beast Market. It was only the development of new routes into north Wales (the A5 and A55 roads), linking London with the port of Holyhead (and thence Dublin) that caused a decline in the importance of Wrexham.

The town was also the focal point for an educated and cultured local society, originally centred on the Parish Church, which, in the mid 16th century, Bishop Parfew wanted to make the centre of his diocese in place of St Asaph (had his plans gone ahead, Wrexham would have been an ecclesiastical city for the last four hundred and fifty years). It was a town where the local gentry built their town houses in the area which we now call Mount Street. If the evidence of place names is any guide, then Wrexham was also a strongly Welsh town with streets, houses, farms and fields — almost without exception — carrying Welsh names. Historically, therefore, the town was always a place that attracted the attention of the people of north Wales.

The advent of the Industrial Revolution brought a new importance to the Wrexham area. Its hinterland abounded in mineral wealth, not only coal and iron ore but also limestone and lead and it was not long before the leading entrepreneurs of the day began to focus their attention on east Denbighshire. Men such as the Wilkinsons who bought and expanded the Bersham Iron Works into a key manufactory without which it seems likely that the advent of the 'Steam Age' would, at the very least, have been retarded. When asked to consider the coal industry in Wales most outsiders (and residents of south Wales) would probably overlook the contribution of north Wales but to do so would be a great error as some of the most significant mines were located here, mines such as Llay Main, at one time the deepest mine in Wales, employing the largest number of men.

Such was the growth in the population of Wrexham during the 19th century that, in common with many other centres throughout Britain, it developed major problems in the realm of public health. No sooner had the Board of Health Report been published than the forward-sighted citizens of Wrexham began to campaign for borough status. Without corporate control there would be no means of stopping the proliferation of poor quality housing and the accompanying scourge of disease and high mortality figures. Despite opposition from many who saw the incorporation of the Borough as merely a means for some of the citizens to line their own pockets and a new expense on the public purse, common sense prevailed and the Borough of Wrexham came into being in 1857. The predicted extravagant spending on public buildings did not come about, instead the Council immediately set about tackling the problems of poor sanitation and highway control, improving the quality of life for its citizens. By the end of the century, they had provided a clean water supply, paved the streets, laid out a new cemetery, taken control of the electricity and gas supplies and built public baths. In the 20th century, as soon as central government passed laws to allow local authorities to assume greater responsibilities for the environment, Wrexham placed itself at the forefront with award-winning developments such as the Acton Park Housing Estate of 1920, the clearance of slum housing and the redevelopment of derelict industrial sites.

Today, with the establishment of a good road network (transport travelling to Holyhead from the Midlands is once again directed via Wrexham), the town has managed to reconstruct its economic base so that, despite the demise of heavy industry, it is once again attracting companies from all over the world to its industrial estates. The expansion of education facilities in the town, even the growth of night life in the area of High Street, has also led to the regeneration of Wrexham as a social and cultural regional centre. Gone are the 'bomb sites' and the derelict industrial buildings, Wrexham has fought its way back to being the capital of north Wales, the premier town in Wales north of the Brecon Beacons.

No work of this nature is ever the efforts of one individual. Many years ago, I was fortunate to be invited into the homes of many people in and around Wrexham who have shared their knowledge and experiences with me. To name them all would be impossible but there are a few who cannot be left out. Derrick Pratt, doyen of local historians in the Wrexham area was more than generous with his information. Deri and Beryl Jones, a rare combination of a husband and wife team ploughing through the field of local history, have given me the benefit of their advice, knowledge and friendship over the years since I first came to Wrexham. Joy Thomas, the Local Studies Librarian was generous with not only her time, but also her patience, and her knowledge of the data in her care is unsurpassed.

Many individuals and organisations granted me access to their photographs and, where possible, they have been acknowledged in the caption. I must, however, extend my gratitude to the Librarian and staff of the Wrexham Library & Information Department, the Museum Officer and staff of Wrexham County Borough Museum, the County Archivists and staff of both the Denbighshire and Flintshire County Record Offices and the Librarian and staff of the National Library of Wales, Aberystwyth.

I would like to express my sincere thanks to Gwynne Belton who has been supportive of everything I have tried to do in the realm of local history.

Whilst acknowledging my indebtedness to all who have assisted me with this work, I must also accept full responsibility for the opinions expressed within it and for any errors that may appear.

W. Alister Williams
Wrexham
March, 2010

The Encyclopædia of WREXHAM

A

Abbot Leather Works, Pentre Felin
See Hugh Price & Company.

Abbot Street
Named after the township of Wrexham Abbot in which it is located. Its Welsh name is Stryt yr Abad, which is a direct translation, and it was once known as Butchers Street. It was claimed at one time that Abbot Street had more public houses than any other comparable street in Wrexham including The Sun, The Bull, The Cannon, The Harp, The Goat, The Cymro Arms, The Hand, The Cross Foxes, The Old Swan. In the period before 1970 a large number of the premises on the north side of the street were owned and operated by the Birkenhead Co-operative Society with shops selling confectionery, groceries, provisions, boots and shoes, drapery, men's wear, fish and fruit. On the south side, in the building that has since been the venue of various nightclubs, the Co-op operated a cash and carry.

Abbot Street Welsh Calvinistic Methodist Chapel
Land was bought for £100 at the rear of the properties on the south side of Abbot Street, where a church was built in 1821 at a cost of c.£1,100 (loaned by Mrs Jones, widow of Richard Jones* of High Street), by the Nailor's Yard* congregation. The building, named Seion, was accessed via a narrow passage alongside the Swan Inn and used until 1867 when the congregation moved to Seion* in Regent Street. A number of the congregation, who were more comfortable worshipping through the medium of English, broke away and formed their own chapel in Bank Street* in 1845. The chapel building was later used as a factory and as a warehouse by Powell Brothers of Town Hill. It was demolished in c.1984. Sadly, there are no known surviving photographs of this building other than a view of its roof which can be seen in several photographs of the Ellesmere railway viaduct. In 1847, the Sunday school attached to this church had 136 pupils.

Abbot's Mill, Pentre Felin
Located in Pentre Felin* (*trans*. mill village) this served as the flour mill for Wrexham Abbot and was also known as the Town Mill. On the 1802 Wynnstay Estate map of the Manor of Wrexham Abbot [DRO/DD/WY/8352] this mill is clearly shown located on the north side of Pentre Felin opposite the entrance to Pearce's Square.* This map also shows the mill as having two mill wheels and a water reservoir extending north-eastwards along Pentre Felin and Watery Road. In the 19th century the site became the premises of the Zoedone Mineral Works* and Hugh Price & Company's* Pentre Felin leather works.* The site was redeveloped again in 1998/9 as part of the Island Green Shopping Precinct.*

The interior of Abbot Street Welsh Calvinistic Methodist Chapel, c.1892 when it was used by Powell Brothers* as a fireplace warehouse.

Abbotsfield, the architect's drawing.

Abbotsfield, Grosvenor Road
Designed in the 1860s as a private residence by the Wrexham architect J. R. Gummow* in the neo-Gothic style, Abbotsfield was the first house to be built at the Rhosddu end of Grosvenor Road. In 1895 it was the home of local surgeon John Arthur Eyton-Jones, MD. It became the Wrexham Area Divisional Education Headquarters for Denbighshire County Council* and in 1974 Clwyd* County Council's Wrexham Area Education Office before being sold in 1981 when it became a hotel. In October 2000, it was converted into Graffiti, an Italian restaurant and is now the Lemon Tree, Italian restaurant and hotel.

Abenbury

The two mediæval townships of Abenbury Fechan (*Trans.* lesser or little Abenbury) and Abenbury Fawr (*Trans.* greater Abenbury) were amalgamated in 1884.

Abenbury Fechan lay to the east of Wrexham Regis* and the river Gwenfro, west of Cefn Road and north of the river Clywedog, roughly the area now occupied by the southern end of the Queen's Park Housing Estate* and the land south of Abenbury Road. In addition, it had some detached portions namely the area around Five Fords (where Pumrhyd Mill once stood) and Woodbine Farm* (at the entrance to the present day Ysgol Morgan Llwyd*), making a total of only 130 acres. (See Flintshire detached)

Abenbury Fawr, with over 1,103 acres, lay to the east of Abenbury Fechan and north of the river Clywedog. It included a large part of the eastern section of the Queen's Park Housing Estate* (around Churchill Drive*) and the land east of Cefn Road as far as the Wrexham Industrial Estate, to the east of Bridge Road.

According to the historian Palmer, Abenbury Fawr formed part of the mediæval manor of Abenbury which also included the townships of Eyton, Sontley and Erbistock. Abenbury Fechan was part of the manor of Faborum. The most important estate in Abenbury today is Cefn Park.*

Abenbury Brickworks

Located on the south side of Abenbury Road, this brickworks was opened on land bought in 1892 by the Davies Brothers company. primarily to make red and blue bricks for the construction of the Wrexham & Ellesmere Railway.* The initial projected output was 100,000 bricks per week. The first manager was Mr Ames. Clay was transported from the pit to the works (which covered 8,500 square yards) by a rope-hauled tramway. The works were extended in 1894/5 and also manufactured copings, chequered tiles, ridge tiles, finials, floor tiles, chimney pots and vases. The company went bankrupt in 1909 and the brickworks was closed down. Reopened in 1912, the works was owned by Oughtbridge Silica Company during the 1920s. The site was requisitioned for military purposes in both world wars. In 1947, it was bought by Thomas Marshall & Co to manufacture refractory blocks for the steel industry. In 1949 the site was merged with the King's Mills Brickworks and remained in operation until closing in 1981. The site was redeveloped for private housing during the early years of the twenty-first century, the main contractor being the local firm of Gordon Mytton. See also 'The Bricky'.

Abenbury Cottage

See Coed Aben.

Abenbury Forge

Abenbury Forge was located in the Clywedog valley, to the south-east of the King's Mills. In 1881, it was occupied by Edward Minshall, an agricultural labourer and butcher.

Abenbury Lodge

A house which stood on the edge of the area known as the Dunks,* west of Cefn Road* and south of Hullah Lane,* roughly where Hafod-y-Wern School is sited today. In 1881 it was occupied by John Devereux-Pugh (a solicitor in practice at 13 Temple Row*).

Abenbury Road

An ancient routeway, this linked the main Wrexham–Ellesmere road at King's Mills* with the Cefn area of Wrexham. It lay wholly within the parish of Marchwiel. Until the late 19th century, there were a number of dwellings located alongside this road but, with the growth of the Abenbury Brickworks* and the building of the railway line to Ellesmere, these were demolished leaving only a few cottages clustered around the King's Mills and the Red Lion* public house. Today, the road forms the southern boundary of the Queen's Park* housing estate and in the late 1990s, residential development began to the south of the road.

Abenbury Quarry

A sandstone quarry located close to the Abenbury Brickworks*, on the south side of the Wrexham–Ellesmere railway line. This was operating in the late nineteenth/early twentieth century.

Abenbury Street

Located off Bryn-y-Cabanau Road,* Abenbury Street appears on plans of 1895 and a number of dwellings were built on it.

Acton Township

The name is generally believed to be a corruption of 'Oak Town'. Madog ap Gruffydd Maelor granted land in this area to the monks of Valle Crucis in 1202 and the charters of Valle Crucis Abbey for 1200 and 1222 mention abbey lands at 'Actun' but by 1236 they appear to have reverted to secular ownership. In the 1289 survey, the list of Wrexham townships includes 'Actone vachan' (Acton Fechan – 103 statute acres) and 'Acton vaur' (Acton Fawr –953 statute acres). At some time after the Edwardian conquest of Wales, the township was made part of the lordship of Bromfield and Yale.* By the late 16th century, much of the township had became part of one estate, Acton Park,* which was the property of the Jeffreys family.* Most of the township lay outside of the original municipal boundary of the Borough of Wrexham until 1935 when the boundary was extended up to the edge of the parish of Gresford.

The township* of Acton covered an area of just under 900 acres to the north of Wrexham Regis and the eastern, detached section of Wrexham Abbot. To the north, Acton was bounded by the parish of Gresford and to the west by Wat's Dyke.* In modern terms, the approximate boundaries of the township are the Wrexham–Chester railway in the west; a line running from just south of Sandway Road linking New Road (Rhosddu) with Chester Road, Derwent Crescent, Overton Way, Central Avenue, the northern end of Park Avenue, Plas Gwyn (in Maes y Dre), Hullah Lane, Deva Way, Anthony Eden Drive, Cefndre and Abenbury Road; a line linking the northern side of Abenbury Road, Cefn Road, Jeffreys Road, Smithy Lane, Plas Acton Road (in Pandy) and the Wrexham–Chester railway.

Acton Colliery

See Wrexham & Acton Colliery.

Acton Estate

See Acton Park Housing Estate.

Acton Gardens

This road, laid out during the 1920s, is located close to the kitchen gardens of Acton Hall. At one time, this street was known as Acton Park Gardens.

Acton Gate

This street, laid out in 1914 as part of the Garden Village* development, was planned to house the senior management of Gresford Colliery. It was laid out on land that was previously part of Croes Eneurys Farm.* It takes its name from the nearby main gate to Acton Hall.* Only the first five houses were built as part of the Garden Village scheme, the other properties being built later by private developers. The original plan for Garden

Village included an avenue leading from Chester Road (at the point that is now the site of St Margaret's Church*), across Acton Gate and through to Haytor Road.* This would have formed the central feature of the Village with a symmetrical development taking place on the south side.

Acton Grange
This house, built in the grounds of Acton Hall, close to the kitchen garden, was the home of William Aston.* The site later formed part of the WCBC depot in Acton Park (Municipal)* until it was sold for private residential development in the 2000s.

Acton Grange, Pandy
The site of Gresford Colliery is sometimes referred to as Acton Grange but there is no evidence that any property in this area was ever called this. It is likely to have been an error in *Collieries of Denbighshire*, committed once and then repeated, and the area should have been called Plas Acton.*

Acton Grove, Chester Road
In 1881 this house was occupied by auctioneer John Jones. It was placed on the market in 1973 by the Church Missionary Society, having been the home of their area secretary, the Revd V. Alban Jones. The sale particulars described the house as comprising: entrance hall, inner hall, lounge, dining room, morning room, five bedrooms and dressing room with large gardens and outbuildings.

Acton Hall
See Acton Park.

Acton Hill
Acton Hill is the name generally applied to the section of Chester Road from the Rhosnesni Lane/Price's Lane junction to the Box Lane junction. Until well into the 20th century, the whole length of road, from the junction with Rhosnesni Lane to the junction with Smithy Lane, was always referred to as Bryn Acton. The east side of the road is edged by the old sandstone boundary wall of the Acton Park* estate. In 1932, there was an application from Border Breweries to buy land from WBC on the junction with Price's Lane as a site for a new 'country' hotel with bowling green and tennis courts. The brewery proposed to apply for a transfer of the licence from the Rose & Crown in Chester Street. In January 1933, the required four-acre site was offered to the brewery for £800 but was not taken up. It was not until the 1970s that the licence of the Rose & Crown was transferred to a new Border public house – the Cunliffe Arms* on Jeffreys Road. (See also Chester Road and Bryn Acton)

Acton House
See Little Acton Farm.

Acton Kennels
Located on the west side of Box Lane, just north of the junction with Smithy Lane, on the site now occupied by Heol Dafydd* and Ffordd Owain.

Acton–Llan-y-Pwll Link Road
This road, designed to improve access to the Wrexham Industrial Estate* was opened on 29 March 1982 by Stephen Gray, Chairman of the Welsh Development Agency. It took 14 months to build at a cost of £1.9 million and was constructed by F. G. Whitley. Work to convert this single-lane road into a dual carriageway commenced in September 2001.

Acton Nursery, Jeffreys Road
See Borras Nursery.

Acton Hall as it appeared in c.1785, viewed from the original Chester Road (Box Lane). [NLW /S950]

Acton Park
The Acton Park estate is located in Acton township. In the 13th century the land may have been the property of Valle Crucis Abbey and later, part of the lordship of Bromfield and Yale.* In the late 16th century, it was the property of the Jeffreys family* Nominal links with this early history of Acton Park survived in the name of a house, Acton Grange,* which was located in the area of the kitchen garden of Acton Hall and in Grange Close,* off Herbert Jennings Avenue.* In Norden's Survey of 1620, John Jeffreys (son of Jeffrey ap Huw), a judge, lived here, and it was at Acton Hall that his grandson, the infamous Judge George Jeffreys,* was born on 15 May 1645 (see Jeffreys Family). George's father, John Jeffreys of Acton, was High Sheriff of Denbighshire in 1655, and his nephew, Sir Griffith Jeffreys of Acton, held the same position in 1683. The Hearth Tax Returns of 1670 show the hall as having 11 hearths and it was one of the largest houses in the Wrexham area. The last member of the Jeffreys family to live here was Robert who died in 1714 when the property passed to his sister, Elizabeth, the wife of John Robinson of Gwersyllt. For some years, the house was occupied by her brother-in-law, Philip Egerton. Following the death of John Robinson in 1732, the property passed to their son William who was drowned at sea in 1739, leaving great debts to his widow and infant daughter, Elizabeth. Elizabeth senior would appear to have moved into Acton Hall and three of her daughters are on record as having died there. By 1747, the estate's financial affairs led to it being sold by Act of Parliament (dated 1745), via trustees (namely Sir Watkin Williams Wynn – see Williams Wynn Family – and Mathew Bacon). It was bought by a family member, Ellis Yonge of Bryn Iorcyn, Hope, High Sheriff of Flintshire in 1750, and son-in-law of John and Elizabeth Robinson.

The demesne land of Acton Park at this time included the following fields: *south of the house* – Cae Clomendu (*Trans.* pigeon house field), Cae Ithen (possibly an error, it should probably have been Cae Eithin, *Trans.* gorse field), Cae yr Uchan (possibly an error, it may have been Cae Ychain (*Trans.* oxen

Sale particulars of the Acton Hall estate, 1782.
Terms and conditions for the sale of the capital mansion house call'd Acton Hall in the County of Denbigh with the estates in the parishes of Wrexham and Gresford, thereunto belonging, advertised to be sold by auction, at the Eagles in Wrexham, on Thursday, the thirty-first day of October, 1782.
In the following lots:
Lot 1. The said mansion-house with out-houses, stables, gardens, hot-houses, &c together with the demesne lands, containing 194 acres or thereabouts, be the same more or less [£858-13-10]
Lot 2. Part of a field, the R— belonging to Mrs Travers, containing 2a 2r 22p or thereabouts, be the same more or less.
Lot 3. A tenement, held by Roger Mason, containing 7a 3r 11p be the same more or less. [£20-8-0]
Lot 4. Ditto by John Barker (Part in lease for the life of Elizabeth his wife, aged 33 years) containing 64a 1r 39p be the same more or less [£118-1-2]
Lot 5. Ditto by Charles Harrison, containing 86a 0r 29p be the same more or less. [£97-4-4]
Lot 6. Ditto by Hugh Hughes, containing 4a 0r 10p be the same more or less. [£3-4-0]
Lot 7. Ditto by Thomas Davies (lease expires in 1785) containing 122a 3r 30p, be the same more or less. [£133-4-4]
Lot 8. A field called Cae ron (with a garden held by Mrs Ithell) containing 7a 1r 10p, be the same more or less.
Lot 9. A field called Maes-y-Dreisa, held by ditto, containing 4a 3r be the same more or less.
Lot 10. A field called Caeron, held by ditto, containing 3a 0r 30p be the same more or less.
Lot 11. A field held by Edward Jones, called Maes-y-dre (excepting some quillets in the same, for which is paid £6-9s) containing 21a 2r 23p be the same more or less.
Lot 12. A field held by Mrs Mary Edwards, called Frenchman's Field, containing 5a 1r 20p be the same more or less.
Lot 13. A field held by ditto, called Hill Field, containing 3a 0r 20p be the same more or less.
Lot 14. A barn, stable and croft, held by ditto, containing 3r 25p be the same more or less.
Lot 15. A field held by Mr Buttall, containing 1a 3r 10p be the same more or less.
Lot 16. A tenement called Croes yn Iris, held by Thomas Jones, containing 56a 3r be the same more or less.
Lot 17. Ditto held by J. Valentine (in lease for 14 years) containing 63a 2r 28p be the same more or less. [£143-6-10]
Lot 18. Ditto held by J. Thomas (in lease for the life of the said John Thomas, aged 50 years) containing 185a 0r 4p be the same more or less. [£555-18-0]
Lot 19. Ditto held by J. Pugh (in lease for the life of said John Pugh, aged 40 years, containing 75a 4r 18p be the same more or less. [£61-12-2]
Lot 20. A moiety of the great tythes of Wrexham Regis and Wrexham Abbot.
Lot 21. All the great tythes of the township of Acton.

Sir Foster and Lady Cunliffe portrayed in front of the new Wyatt wing of Acton Hall.

Acton Hall showing the Wyatt front added by Sir Foster Cunliffe in 1786–7. The original house can be seen on the left. A watercolour, almost certainly by Moses Griffith. [NLW]

field) or Uchaf (*Trans.* higher field); *south-east of the house* – Cae Buchan (it should probably be Cae Bychan, *Trans.* little field); *east of the house* – Coed (*Trans.* wood); *north-north-west of the house* – Cae yr Skybor (*Trans.* barn field); *north-west of the house* – Cae Marle (*Trans.* marl field); *west of the house* – Big and Little Wern (*Trans.* water meadow field), Maes Acton (*Trans.* Acton field); *south-west of the house* – Cae Wad (*Trans.* Wad's field), Higher Paddock. [FRO/D/AH/24] During this time, some additions were made to the estate. Yonge then appears to have become financially embarrassed, so much so that he was obliged to put the estate up for sale in October 1782, at the Eagles Hotel (see Wynnstay Arms Hotel), Wrexham, but it does not appear to have been sold until shortly after the death of Yonge in 1785 when Sir Foster Cunliffe* bought it for £27,000.

> The house was much in want of repair, and the place as ugly and disagreeable as possible, but the estate desirable & cheap. The ground about it lay well, and it was easy to see that it might be made cheerful and handsome. The country was beautiful, and the society desirable. I agreed to give £27,000 for it. The then rent was £1100 a year, with reversions to the amount of £300 a year more. Timber (supposed to be worth £2,000) and many other valuables were thrown in, to the value perhaps of £1,000 more, reducing the purchase to about 22 years value exclusive of reversions. On taking possession of the house in 1785 I immediately began to make alterations, so many large and useless buildings were pulled down that I found materials sufficient for every repair or alteration in the old part; all my expenses from first to last amounted in the whole to about *viz*:
>
> | | |
> |---|---|
> | Repairs to the old building including new offices | £ 500 |
> | New building | £3000 |
> | Additional furniture | £ 600 |
> | Laid out on Grounds | £ 700 |
> | Total: | £4800 |

The first stone (in the south-east corner of the plinth) of the new part of the house was laid in May 1786 and was finished the following year. I have not been able positively to ascertain at what time Acton house was built. No mention is made of a family residing there when Churchyarde wrote his *Worthynesse of Wales* in Q. Elizths time therefore (as he takes notice of Pant-y-Ocin [sic]) it is probable there was no house there then. Mr Yorke of Erddig told me that his house was built in 1620, and that Acton was built by the same Architect soon after. If so, it was built by Sir Griffith Jeffreys. It is commonly said that it was built by Judge Jeffreys, or by his mother, with his money. This is a mistake, but the Lady here alluded to was the widow of Sir Griffith Jeffreys. She survived her husband many years and was a remarkably clever, active, and benevolent woman. In Jany 1786 the house was in such a state of forwardness that I removed my family into it from Chester …'

The architect for the new west wing is believed to have been James Wyatt (1746–1813) of Weeford, completing the work in 1797. At the time of the sale, the house, stables, outbuildings, gardens and demesne totalled 194 acres. Within two years, Sir Foster having become established in local society, was appointed High Sheriff of Denbighshire.

In 1801, Sir Foster purchased a small field in Acton 'at the south-west corner of Little Acton [Farm],* between the 2 roads from Chester to Wrexham for £195 – 2a-2r-0p'. It was undoubtedly this purchase that led to the re-alignment of Box Lane.* At the same time, he bought '2 fields in Wrexham Regis from Mr Jones of Belian Place for £1,164 including Land Tax redeemed 10a 2r 0p. This was a very dear purchase but, as the land lay within sight of the house and possibly might have been built upon, it would not have been prudent to have refused it. The history of this purchase will show the rapid advance of land in the vicinity of Wrexham. In 1785, Mr Jones bought these fields for £400 and offered them to me for £600 but as he had let them for 20 years at £17 I declined. 12 years afterwards, his successor asked me £800 – 4 years after £1,000 and 3 years after £1200. But after some negotiation the price was fixed at £1164.' These two fields were almost certainly those shown in Palmer's 'Map of Wrexham Regis and Wrexham Abbot in A.D. 1844' [*History of the Town of Wrexham*] as fields 388 and 399, running along the north side of Rhosnesni Lane from Chester Road to the present day Central Avenue. The purchase of these two fields completed the acquisition of the parkland around Acton Hall and, at some time after 1801, Sir Foster had a sandstone wall constructed around the boundary, extending the length of Rhosnesni Lane (from Chester Road to Borras Road) along Borras Road (from Rhosnesni Lane to Dean Road) along Jeffreys Road (from Dean Road/Borras Road to Box Lane), along Box Lane (from Jeffreys Road to Chester Road) and along Chester Road (from Box Lane to Rhosnesni Lane), a total length of 2·3 miles. Some sections of this sandstone wall have survived.

A ha-ha (a sunken fence designed to prevent animals entering a park or garden which was almost invisible when viewed from one side, usually the side of the main house) was constructed right across the park from Chester Road (opposite Eneurys Road) to Jeffreys Road (opposite Warrenwood Road). The lake in Acton Park is shown on 19th century maps as a 'fish pond'. The lake was originally much longer and extended as far as Jeffreys Road, almost opposite the junction of Warrenwood Road. At its narrowest point it was crossed by a Chinese style footbridge and at it widest point (at the northern end) it had a small island. Today, the surface area of the lake is much reduced although the dried out section can still be identified by a hollow in the grass, running roughly parallel with Jeffreys Road and a number of old trees still lean over awaiting the return of the water. The narrow strip of water between the northern end of the lake and the island has now been filled in although occasionally, during periods of heavy rainfall, the ground is still prone to flooding. By

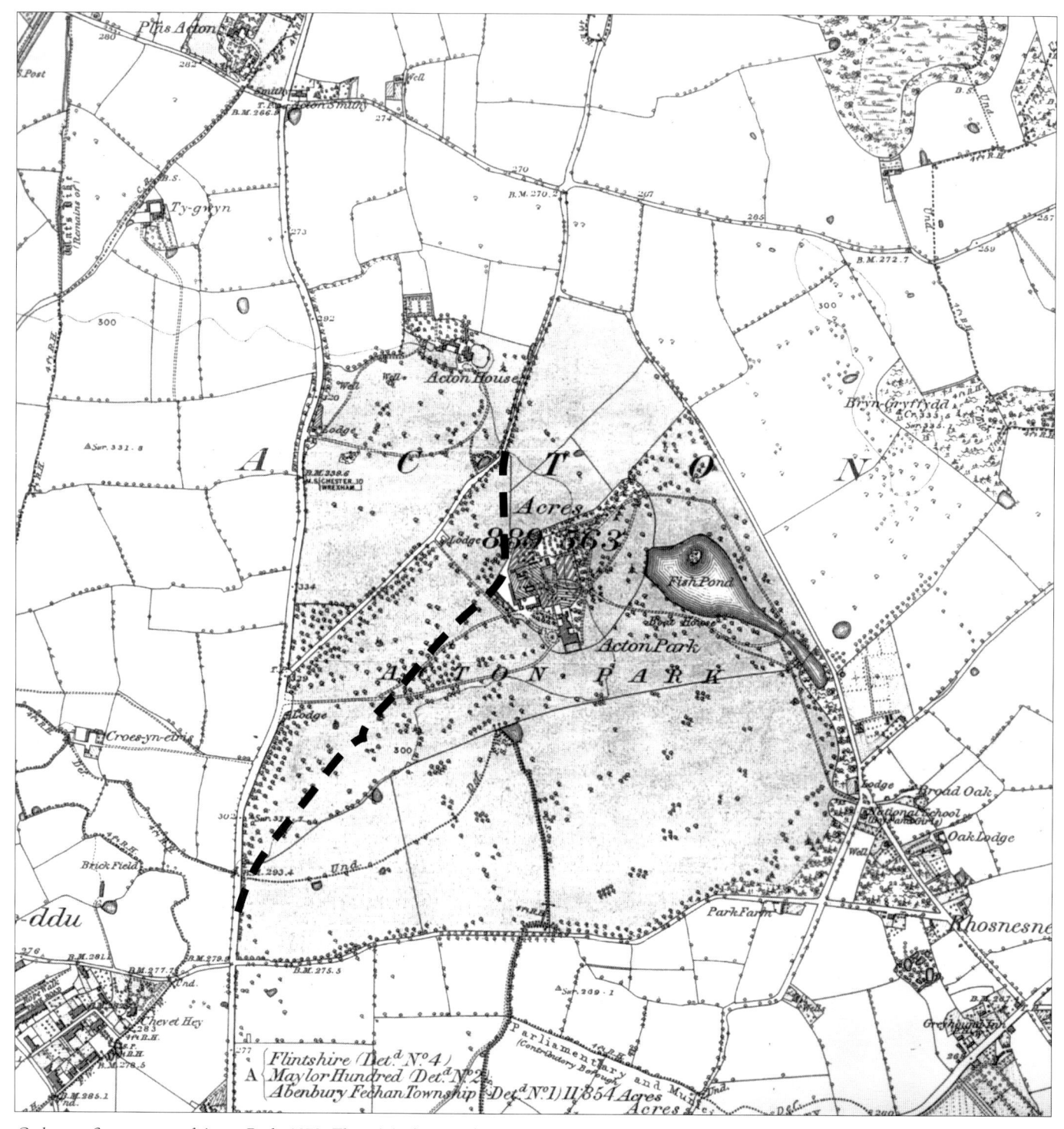

Ordnance Survey map of Acton Park, 1872. The original route of the old Chester Road (Box Lane) would almost certainly have followed the course shown by the broken line.

1807, the estate rental was bringing Sir Foster an annual income of £2,420.

The Four Dogs gateway was erected in 1820 to a design by Thomas Harrison (1744-1829). In October 1969, WBC made an application to demolish the gateway, despite the fact that it was a Grade 2 listed structure: 'The piers are defaced, and in a poor condition, the ornamental dogs which surmounted the gate piers have been damaged beyond repair and removed. Appear as an ungracious feature'. After much deliberation, the overall application was rejected in October 1970, although permission was granted for the demolition of the curved railings and stonework linking the main gateway to the Chester Road. The original dogs that sat on top of the gateway were made of wood, carved by James Edwards of Lavister and represented the greyhound crest on the Cunliffe arms.* One dog disappeared when the US Army left Acton Hall in 1944 and a second was destroyed by vandals in 1964. The surviving wooden dogs were used to create moulds by students at the Wrexham College of Art* and four new dogs were made from glassfibre and concrete. The refurbished gateway was officially opened in April 1982. One wooden dog survives in the Wrexham Museum collection.

When General Sir Robert Cunliffe came into possession of the Acton estate he discovered that 'numerous repairs were necessary [to the house], and having a large family, I desired it better to build nurseries over the back entrance. I also converted the large entrance hall into the Library and changed the Chief entrance from the South to the West and entering into what had been the Library. I also added a Terrace on the South side'.

By the time of the 1872 Ordnance Survey, lodges had been built at the gates on Chester Road (Greyhound Lodge), Box Lane (for many years this served as the home of the caretaker of Acton Park School and stands just inside the school main gate) and Dean Road/Borras Road (Rhosnessney Lodge). The latter bears the inscription R.A. – C. – E.S.E. (Robert Alfred and Eleanor Sophia Egerton Cunliffe) 1876. In addition, a fourth lodge stood close to the site of the present day Cunliffe Arms. Known as the Bailiff's Lodge this was adapted into Home Farm, part of the Acton Park Holdings* scheme, and was demolished in the 1960s. A number of estate houses were built on Acton Road (now Dean Road*), and Borras Road* during the latter part of the 19th century.

On 30 March 1878, Acton Park played host to an unusual and historic event when the first ever Football Association of Wales Cup Final was held in the grounds. For many years it was believed that this occurred on the area which is still reserved for soccer, between Rhosnesni Lane and Herbert Jennings Avenue. This would now appear to be incorrect. In fact, the most likely venue would seem to be the field now used as the playing field of Acton School. The game kicked-off at 4 p.m. in front of a crowd of 1,500 spectators, between Wrexham (see Wrexham Football Club) and Druids. Wrexham won the game 1–0. The captain of the Wrexham team was Charles Murless, proprietor of the Wynnstay Arms Hotel.* The match had been in danger of being abandoned due to the lack of a ground. The game had originally been scheduled for the Racecourse on 23 March but problems with the semi-finals caused a one week delay and the Racecourse had been booked for a cricket match. Sir Robert Cunliffe's offer of the field at Acton Park, although far from satisfactory, was readily accepted. At a later date, a Welsh Cup semi-final match was played on Chester Road which would clearly suggest that the same pitch was used. It is unlikely that there were two suitable pitches in Acton Park and the area between Herbert Jennings and Rhosnesni Lane could not in any way be described as Chester Road, whereas the Acton School playing field lies within 150 yards of the junction of Box Lane and Chester Road. Of additional interest with regard to the 1878 final is the claim made by Charles Murless that the match was the first in which a team (Wrexham) featured a centre half (previously, teams had played with two centre forwards and two half backs).

On 24 August 1889, Queen Victoria visited Acton Park. A large party of invited guests formed up in the grounds where an oval enclosure with seating had been set up. Included among the dignitaries were the Mayor (Evan Morris*), the Corporation of Wrexham, the Borough Magistrates, past Mayors, Lords Lieutenant, High Sheriffs, Members of Parliament, Mayors of other north Wales towns, the local aristocracy, the bishops and local clergy, military commanders, judges, a choir of 410 voices and Sunday School members (12–14,000, all of whom were presented with a commemorative medal). The royal party arrived shortly after 5 p.m. Security was in the hands of the police, a squadron of the Denbighshire Hussars* (commanded by Colonel Mesham), the RWF and the Cheshire Regiment.

Men of the Denbighshire Yeomanry marching down the drive at Acton Park, 1916.

Following the death of the 5th Baronet in 1905, Acton Hall was vacated by the Cunliffe family and was rented out to Sir William Hope Nelson, Bt.*

During the First World War, the house was used for training by the military, most notably the 3rd Battalion, Welsh Border Mounted Brigade (Denbighshire Hussars Imperial Yeomanry). Following the death of Sir Foster H. E. Cunliffe* in 1917, the estate was put up for sale; 224 acres (roughly the area bounded by Chester Road, Rhosnesni Lane, Borras Road, Jeffreys Road and Box Lane) were bought by the Belgian diamond merchant, Sir Bernard Oppenheimer who immediately sold 60 acres (along the north side of Rhosnesni Lane*) to WBC for housing (see Acton Park Housing Estate). He then gifted an area of 125 acres to a trust called the Sir Bernard Oppenheimer Trust for Discharged Soldiers and Sailors, generally known locally as the Acton Park Holdings* and eleven small-holdings were laid out within the park as housing for ex-servicemen, part of the so-called 'Lloyd George's Homes for Heroes'. An area bordering along Box Lane, he retained as the site for a National Diamond Factory* (where disabled servicemen could be employed in diamond polishing. The factory was not a success and it was sold, along with Acton Park house, stables and some of the parkland, to Denbighshire County Council. They converted the factory building into Acton Park School* and sold 23 acres, including Acton Park house, stables, *etc*, to local businessman William Aston for the sum of £1,500. Aston opened the grounds, including a rock garden, to the public. The house was used as a furniture store and, occasionally, members of the public were permitted inside to view the furniture. At one time Denbighshire County Council used the upper rooms of the hall as a drawing office. In 1938, Aston conveyed part of the gardens (including the walled garden) to Denbighshire County Council in return for a

Acton Park Rock Gardens, c.1930.

15

An RAF reconnaissance photograph of Acton Park taken on 22 November 1948. Acton Hall can be clearly seen in the centre foreground with Acton Grange to the left, then the stables and, finally, Acton School — with Acton Gardens just above and Box Lane heading northwards towards the Flash in the middle distance. The hedgerow crossing the picture left–right marks out Jeffreys Lane (Road) with Acton Park Lake just below it on the right. The line cutting off the bottom right-hand corner of the photograph is the ha-ha. [National Assembly for Wales]

peppercorn rent, retaining only the Acton Hall itself and Acton Grange and stables.

There was a small farm located just inside the main gate on the site of the Four Dogs* public house. In the 1930s, this was tenanted by Sam Jones who lived in the lodge where he had an ice cream stand in the garden and a butcher's shop on the corner of Box Lane.*

During the Second World War, the house and grounds were again used by the military and in the early days of the conflict Indian cavalry were billeted there. Later, detachments of the Royal Marines trained in the grounds. On 19 February 1944, 'B' Company, 33rd Signal Corps Construction Battalion of the U.S. Army arrived at Liverpool aboard HMS *Andes* and was immediately transferred to Acton Hall where they remained until 26 June 1944 when they moved to Downton (see United States Army). Photographs of the US troops at Acton Hall show traces of the temporary wooden buildings that were erected around the house.

By 1952, Sydney Aston (son of Alderman William Aston) was considering the demolition of Acton Hall and opposed efforts to have the building listed. In June, Sydney Aston wrote again to Messrs Edmund Kirby & Sons: '… it has always been our intention to give the site of Acton Hall to the Corporation to add to the Park which my Father gave some years ago, and in the course of conversation the other day with the Borough Surveyor he made it clear that he personally would favour our giving the Hall in its present condition to the Corporation for them to demolish and keep the land. … I rather favoured this idea myself, as the Corporation would then have to stand any criticism for pulling the place down'. In a letter dated 28 July, 1950, Messrs Edmund Kirby noted that there was little of merit in the building: 'The writer has few subjects nearer to his heart than the preservation of those heirlooms which our ancestors have handed down to us, nevertheless, this suggestion [that Acton Hall should be scheduled as a building of special architectural or historic interest] fills him with dismay. Without being anxious to betray ignorance, we should like you to tell us one feature either of architectural or historic interest possessed by Acton Hall – apart from some bawdy murals on the top floor left by the licentious soldiery in the last war. … This is a somewhat plain and not particularly shapely house, faced with stone and in a truly dilapidated condition after a long period of

Left: Acton Hall, c.1935, when it was the property of the Aston family. The frontage shown here is the original Jeffreys family house with rather grotesque modifications carried out by General Sir Robert Cunliffe who also moved the front door back to its near original position. For some reason Sir Robert appears to have made no attempt to balance the face of the house. The centre and right-hand sections have been embellished with Romanesque arches while the left-hand section has retained its rectangular 17th century windows. The whole of the front has been clad in stone.

Right: The interior of what appears to be part of the entrance hall at Acton Hall, photographed in c.1900. A typical Victorian decor, complete with stuffed tiger (undoubtedly a relic of General Cunliffe's service in India) and a cabinet of stuffed birds.

Below: An unknown room at Acton Hall which, if the heavily decorated door and cabinet are any guideline, may well have been called the Oak Room.

Above & below: Two views of the library at Acton Hall, c.1900. This room was located in the Wyatt wing. In the lower photograph the dining room can just be seen through the open door.

Right: Acton Park gates, c.1910, viewed from Chester Road with what appears to be the Cunliffe motor car turning towards Wrexham.

Acton Park in the early 19th century, showing the position of the house and the lake (bottom right-hand corner).

by Sir Foster Cunliffe, Bart. With additions by Sir Robert Henry Cunliffe Bart. Copied, and Illustrated, by his Sister Emma Cunliffe, [copies held by Wrexham Museum].

Acton Park (Municipal)

The grounds of Acton Hall were opened to the public as a pleasure garden by Alderman William Aston shortly after he had bought the land in the 1920s. During the Second World War much of the park was requisitioned for military purposes. Sometime post-1945 the area of the lake was reduced. The declaration ceremony for the 1977 National Eisteddfod of Wales was held here in 1976 and the Gorsedd circle of stones remains there as a reminder of that event. Close to the Gorsedd stones is a carved sandstone block which was removed from the Parish Church during the restoration programme of the early 20th century. There are rumours that this block has magical powers and that anyone climbing onto it will be unable to get off. On the north-east side of the park, to the rear of the Cunliffe Arms Hotel* there are public tennis courts and a bowling green which were laid out by the Borough Council in the 1970s. Two public football pitches have been laid out between Herbert Jennings Avenue and Rhosnesni Lane.

A totem-pole style sculpture, carved from an existing tree, by Andy Hancock, Wrexham Groundwork's artist in residence was commenced in February 2001. The completed carving is 42 feet high.

Acton Park Holdings, Acton Park

Following his purchase of Acton Park, the Belgian diamond merchant Sir Bernard Oppenheimer created a trust (in April 1918) for 'disabled or discharged officers and men of His Majesty's Royal Navy, Army or Air Force (primarily those disabled in the present war [First World War]), or their dependants ... for the establishment or instruction ... in agricultural horticulture or any skilled or unskilled labour, handicraft, art or work or otherwise, for their care, treatment or training.' Trustees were to be appointed by the Minister of Pensions to administer a deed of gift of 120.329 acres (including two lodges called Greyhound Lodge and Bailiff's Lodge – then in the occupation of Frederick Darlington and Emily Thomas respectively). Eleven smallholdings, each of approximately two acres with common grazing on the parkland, were laid out in various locations, part of the famous Lloyd George 'Homes for Heroes' scheme. The original trustees were: Rt Hon John Hodge and Sir Arthur Sackville Trevor Griffith-Boscawen. Hodge died in 1937 and Reginald Armitage Ledgard and Roderick George Fenwick Palmer* were apppointed trustees. In 1949, Ledgard died and Goronwy Owen Roberts and Charles Henry Newble were appointed to serve with Colonel Fenwick Palmer. Newble retired in 1952 and was replaced by John Henry Francis Ludgate. In 1955, the Trustees decided to sell the smallholdings and grazing land to WBC for £35,000 as they could no longer 'profitably be let for agricultural purposes'. Of the original eleven

requisition and use as a furniture store. It certainly has nothing to commend it aesthetically .... It is full of rot, both wet and dry and, if left to itself, will form a constant attraction to the juvenile delinquents of the neighbourhood who will gradually pull it to pieces. ... Please do not think us Philistines – we are not.' The Council agreed in principle to the demolition in June 1951 subject to the condition that they might preserve the 'older portion of the building on the south'. Had this condition been insisted upon, they would actually have preserved the newest part of the house, the wing built by Sir Foster Cunliffe, and the oldest section, built by the Jeffreys family, had been mistakenly identified as the newest section. As things transpired, however, they decided not to preserve any part of the house and the contractors commenced demolition of the domestic quarters at the rear, and the northern end of the Jeffreys wing, in September 1953. By January 1956, the house was gone although the stonework from the porch was initially retained for use elsewhere. All trace of the building had disappeared and the site, possibly the finest in Wrexham in terms of position, was occupied by a Civic Amenity Centre (a rather grand euphemism for domestic waste skip) from the 1980s until sold to a developer.

In 1958, the Ministry of Pensions sold the 119 acres of land that had previously been utilised by Acton Park Holdings to WBC for £35,000, thereby completing the transfer into public ownership of the whole block sold to Oppenheimer in 1918.

In the mid 1960s, work commenced on a substantial expansion of the Acton Park Housing Estate,* covering much of the land previously owned by the Ministry of Pensions and in the late 1960s, some 12 acres were sold for 'Box Lane Building Estate' (officially known as the Acton Park Farm Estate) – what was then described as a 'a private building estate of £6,000+ executive houses'. These were to be built at a density of 5–6 plots per acre and today comprise Ffordd Elan,* Ffordd Tudno,* Ffordd Elwy* and Heol Dinas* as well as the houses facing onto Box Lane* between Jeffreys Road* and Acton Gardens.*

The remainder of Acton Park is now a public leisure area, a much needed green lung in the midst of an area that has been dramatically transformed from a rural into an urban landscape during the last 50 years.

[DRO/DD/GA/1766. Documents in Liverpool Record Office, Edmund Kirby Collection; *Family Records, Collected and written*

holdings, eight still survive as part of the Acton Park Housing Estate:* N° 30 Herbert Jennings Avenue; N°s 90 & 92 Jeffreys Road; N°s 6 & 8 Ffordd Jarvis; N°s 9 & 11 (The Holding) Elm Grove Way; The Holding (off Tapley Avenue). The other smallholdings were located on the site of the Cunliffe Arms, Jeffreys Road and at Lees Farm (on the site of the present day Derwent Crescent). The house known as The Holding (located close to Tapley Avenue) is the only remaining building that gives an impression of what the smallholdings originally looked like, standing in the park and complete with it outbuildings.

Acton Park Hotel, Chester Road
Built shortly before the Second World War, the Acton Park Hotel is a typical example of the 'road house' style of public house that was popular between the wars. The layout of the premises, complete with a large car parking area, was designed to attract motorists and an off-licence was part of the main building. The Acton Park was intended to service the new Garden Village* community and the plans met with considerable opposition when first announced. The licence of the Town Hall Vaults* in Back Chamber Street* was transferred to these premises which remained little changed until 1980 when it was renovated and 2000 when the whole building underwent a major modernisation programme.

Acton Park Housing Estate
A copy of the Acton Housing Estate Sale catalogue showing plans and dated 1918, has survived in the Denbighshire Record Office [DRO/1085]. Initially, WBC proposed buying the whole of the Acton Park estate and had allocated £20,000 for the purchase but it was not enough. Instead, sixty-nine and a half acres of land along the north side of Rhosnesni Lane were bought from Sir Bernard Oppenheimer* (a Belgian diamond merchant who had recently purchased 224 acres of land from Sir Neville Cunliffe – comprising the whole of the old Acton Park* estate, including the Nine Acre Field) for £6,808.

The Acton Park housing estate was the first corporation housing development in the Borough of Wrexham. The programme to build 118 houses at a cost of £100,000 commenced in 1920. On 30 July 1920 commemorative plaques were placed on the first houses by the Mayor, Thomas Sauvage, JP,* (N° 10 Cilcen Grove*) and the Chairman of the Health Committee, Cllr Edwards-Jones, JP,* (N° 9 Cilcen Grove). It was intended that the original neo-Georgian style houses and crescents would form only a small part of a much larger award-winning plan which was to be centred on Marsh Crescent* and Neville Crescent.* The area in front of each crescent was originally laid out with a pond. The designer of the estate was Professor Sir Patrick Abercrombie of the University of Liverpool, who became one of the most influential British town planners of the 20th century, the prime mover behind the 'green belt' concept and the father of the development plan for London. Many of his ideas, reminiscent of the garden village concept – varying sizes of houses; front and rear gardens; indoor sanitary facilities; play areas and tree-lined avenues and vistas – are to be found in the layout of the original Acton Park Housing Estate. Unfortunately, the plan was only partially completed before the depression of the inter-war period led to drastic cut-backs in local government spending. The main contractor for this estate was John Laing & Sons. A second phase, to the east of Elm Grove, was begun in the mid 1930s and followed the style of the original scheme. In 1955, Wrexham Borough Council bought a total of 119.1 acres of land in Acton Park from the Ministry of Pensions for £35,000 (see Acton Park Holdings) but further development of the area did not occur until the mid 1960s when a number of new streets were laid out, but with houses built to totally different designs. Attempts to allow further residential housing development in Acton Park during the late 1990s were met with strong local opposition.

Acton Park housing estate, 1928. Chester Road can be seen in the foreground with the Rhosnesni Lane and Cilcen Grove junction bottom right.

Acton Park housing estate, 1928. Rhosnesni Lane can be seen left–right in the foreground. Also clearly visible are a number of the Acton Park Holdings' 'farms' and in the centre distance, St. Margaret's Church under construction. Two of the private houses on the south side of Rhosnesni Lane have their own tennis courts.

Acton Park Schools
Acton Park School
Opened in the grounds of Acton Hall* in 1923 in a converted diamond polishing factory building (see Oppenheimer's Diamond Factory), built by Edward W. Gittins & Sons, with Cris Davies* as headmaster, the school very quickly gained a reputation for high levels of achievement. In 1967 the school was split into two– Acton Park Infant School and Acton Park Junior School. *A History of Acton Park School* by Dennis Perrin was published in 1998.
Headteachers:
1923–46   Ald. Christopher 'Cris' Davies
1947–67   Ronald Hadlington

Acton Park Infant School
Formed in 1967 from the infant classes of Acton Park School.* It was housed in purpose-built accommodation (at a cost of £55,000), designed to accommodate 240 pupils. It was officially opened on 28 November 1967 by Alderman Eric McMahon,* chairman of the Divisional Executive. The school merged with Acton Park Junior School in September 2009 to become Acton Park County Primary School. *A History of Acton Park School* by Dennis Perrin was published in 1998.
Headteachers:
1967–78   Miss Enid Jones
1979–95   Mrs Vera Rees Jones
1995–   Mrs Linda Jane Williams

Acton Park Junior School
Formed in 1967 from the junior classes of Acton Park School* in whose old school buildings it was housed. Between 1994 and 1996 the buildings underwent major renovation. In 2001, the school had 276 pupils. The school merged with Acton Park Infant School in September 2009 to become Acton Park County Primary School. *A History of Acton Park School* by Dennis Perrin was published in 1998.
Headteachers:
1967–80   Ronald Hadlington
1980–6   Richard 'Dick' J Owen
1986–99   John R. Evans
1998–9   Mrs Denise Edwards (Acting)
1999   Mrs Denise Edwards

Acton Park County Primary School
This was formed in September 2009 by the merger of Acton Park Infant School and Acton Park Junior School. In 2010 there were 186 pupils on the role.
Headteachers
2010   Mrs S. Edgar

Acton Park Way
Built in the 1960s as part of the Acton Park Housing Estate development, this street was named after Acton Park.*

Acton Road, Rhosnesni (now Dean Road, c.1912, looking towards Rhosnesni School, Borras Road junction and Acton Park lodge.

Acton Road, Rhosddu
Named after the Acton Park* estate on whose land the road was laid out in 1901 and extended to link up with Spring Road the following year. The back fences of the rear gardens of the properties on the western side of the road follow the line of the original Municipal Boundary of the Borough of Wrexham. Not to be confused with Acton Road,* Rhosnesni.

Acton Road, Rhosnesni
The road leading from the one time village of Rhosnesni in the direction of Acton Park was originally called Acton Road but, when the village was absorbed into the Borough of Wrexham shortly before the Second World War, its name was changed to Dean Road* to avoid confusion with the Acton Road* in Rhosddu.

Acton Smithy, Smithy Lane
The earliest records of a smithy at Acton date from 1746, although one may have existed on the site long before then. Part of the Acton Park* estate, the smithy was tenanted by the Roberts family from c.1800 to 1965, through five generations. In 1881, the blacksmith was Robert Roberts who was assisted by his sons Robert William and Thomas. In 1904, when Robert Roberts died, the stock in trade was valued at £7-10s-0d, which was bought by the new tenant Robert William Roberts who agreed to an annual rental of £14. The terms of the tenancy included: 'The Tenant to keep the inside of the House and Smithy in good order and repair, and the Garden clean and properly cultivated and the fences properly trimmed. Only one Family to reside in the Cottage, and the Tenant not to underlet any part thereof or the Smithy or take in a Lodger without leave first obtained in writing

Acton Smithy — the low building on the left was the blacksmith's shop which was attached to the stables (with the large double door) – with tack room behind. To the right of this is the original cottage with, on the extreme right, a hay barn that was later added to the cottage. To the right (the area which is now the bungalows in Smithy Close) was a barn and an orchard, and to the rear was the garden. [Nat Cargius]

from the Landlord's Agents [Jones & Sons]. The Rates and Taxes to be paid by the Tenant'. The building has since been put to other uses and is currently Saneller, a hairdressing business with a private residence.

Examination of the present building would suggest that the original house was single-storey with a second storey added at a later date.

In front of the building was a pond which survived until the 1980s when it was filled in. A memorial stone in the wall surrounding the area of the pond records Joey a 'much loved swan' which died in February 1952. Smithy Lane and Smithy Close take their names from this building.

Acts of Parliament relating to Wrexham
Roads
25 Geo. II (1751–2)
An Act for repairing the Roads from the Town of Shrewsbury through Ellesmere in the County of Salop, and Overton in the County of Flint, to Wrexham in the County of Denbigh.

29 Geo. II (1755–6)
An Act for amending, widening and keeping in Repair, the several Roads from the Town of Pool in the County of Montgomery, to Wrexham in the County of Denbigh; and also the Road from Knockin in the County of Salop, to Llanrhaiader in Mochnant in the County of Denbigh.

29 Geo. II (1755–6)
An Act to enlarge the Term and Powers of an Act for repairing the Road from Shrewsbury to Wrexham in the County of Denbigh, and to repair and widen several other Roads therein mentioned, and the Road from Wrexham to Chester, and from thence to Pen Fordd-y-Waen in the Parish of Whitford, and also the Road from Broughton to Mold in the County of Flint.

30 Geo. II (1756–7)
An Act for amending, widening and keeping in Repair the Roads from the Town of Wrexham, in the County of Denbigh, to Pentre Bridge, in the County of Flint; and from the Town of Mold to Northop, Holywell and Rhuddlan, in the same County; and from thence to the Ferry House opposite to the Town of Conway, in the County of Carnarvon; and from Ruthin to the said Town of Mold.

32 Geo. II (1758–9)
An Act for repairing and widening the Roads from the Town of Mold to the Town of Denbigh, and from thence to Tal-y-Cafn and Conway; and from the Town of Wrexham to the Town of Ruthin, Denbigh and the Town and Port of Ruthland, in the Counties of Denbigh, Flint and Carnarvon.

2 Geo. III (1761–2)
An Act to enlarge the Term and Powers, and also to render more effectual an Act for amending, widening and keeping in Repair the several roads from the Town of Pool in the County of Montgomery, to Wrexham in the County of Denbigh; and also the road from Knockin in the County of Salop, to Llanrhaiader, in Mochnant, in the County of Denbigh, and to repair and widen several other roads therein mentioned.

3 Geo. III (1762–3)
An Act for repairing, widening and keeping in Repair, the Road leading from the Turnpike Road, between Oswestry and Wrexham, at or near Whitehurst's House, through Llangollen to most proper and commodious joining of the Turnpike Road leading from Wrexham to Ruthin, at or near Tavern Dwyrarch; and from Llangollen aforesaid, through Acre Fair Colliery to the Finger Post, at the joining of the Road leading from Oswestry to Wrexham, in the County of Denbigh.

19 Geo. III (1778–9)
An Act for enlarging the Term and Powers of so much of an Act made in the Thirtieth Year of the Reign of His Majesty King George the Second, instituted, An Act for amending, widening and keeping in Repair the Roads from the Town of Wrexham, in the County of Denbigh, to Pentre Bridge, in the County of Flint; and from the Town of Mold to Northop, Holywell and Rhuddlan, in the same County; and from thence to the Ferry House, opposite the Town of Conway, in the County of Carnarvon; and from Ruthin to the said Town of Mold; as relates to the District of Road from the Town of Wrexham in the County of Denbigh, to Pentre Bridge, in the County of Flint.

20 Geo. III (1779–80)
An Act for continuing the Term and Powers of so much of an Act made in the Thirty second Year of the Reign of His late Majesty, for repairing the Roads from Mold to Denbigh, and from thence to Tal-y-Cafn and Conway; and from Wrexham to Ruthin, Denbigh, and Rhyddlan, in the Counties of Denbigh, Flint, and Carnarvon, as relates to the Road from Wrexham to Denbigh.

22 Geo. III (1781–2)
An Act for amending, widening and keeping in Repair, the Road from Wrexham, in the County of Denbigh, to Barnhill, in the County of Chester.

28 Geo. III (1787–8)
An Act for more effectively repairing the Roads leading from Pool, through Oswestry, to Wrexham; from Knockin to Llanrhaiader; from Whitehurst's House, in the Road between Oswestry and Wrexham to Llangollen; and several other Roads therein mentioned, in the Counties of Montgomery, Salop and Denbigh; and for discharging the Trustees for repairing the Bala and Dolgelley Roads from the Care of the Road between Llangollen and the Confines of the county of Denbigh, and for making provision for the future Repair of the said Road.

28 Geo. III (1787–8)
An Act to enlarge the Term and Powers of an Act passed in the Twenty ninth Year of the Reign of King George the Second, for repairing the Road from Shrewsbury to Wrexham, in the County of Denbigh, and from Wrexham to Chester, and also from Broughton to Mold, in the County of Flint, and several other Roads therein mentioned; and for making and repairing a Road from the said Wrexham and Chester Road to the Wrexham and Ruthin Road, in the said County of Denbigh.

39–40 Geo. III (1798–1800)
An Act for continuing for Twenty one Years, and from thence to the End of the then next Session of Parliament, the Term, and altering the Powers of two Acts passed in the thirtieth year of the Reign of His late Majesty King George the Second, and in the nineteenth Year of the Reign of His present Majesty, for amending, widening and keeping in Repair several Roads therein mentioned, so far as the said Acts relate to the Road leading from the Town of Wrexham in the County of Denbigh to Pentre Bridge in the County of Flint.

41 Geo. III (1800–01)
An Act for maintaining the twenty one Years, and from thence to the end of the next Session of Parliament, the Term, and alter and enlarge the Powers of two Acts passed in the thirty second Year of the Reign of His late Majesty King George the Second, and in the twentieth Year of the Reign of His present Majesty, for repairing and widening several Roads therein mentioned, so far as the said Acts relate to the Road leading from the Town of Wrexham to the Towns of Ruthin and Denbigh, in the County of Denbigh, and amending widening, altering, improving and keeping in repair, the Road leading from the said Town of Ruthin into the Turnpike Road from Corwen to Llanrwst, at or near a certain House called Cernioge Mawr, in the Parish of Llanfydd, in the said County.

42 Geo. III (1801–2)
An Act for for continuing the Term and altering and enlarging the Powers of an Act, passed in the twenty second Year of the Reign of His present Majesty, entitled, An Act for amending, widening and keeping in repair the Road from Wrexham in the County of Denbigh to Barnhill in the County of Chester; and for making, amending and keeping in repair the Road branching out of the said Road at a place called Pwll yr Rhywd in the said County of Denbigh to the Borough of Holt in the said County.

48 Geo. III (1807–8)
An Act for continuing the Term, and altering and enlarging the Powers of two several Acts of His late and present majesty, for amending the Road from Shrewsbury to Wrexham, in the County of Denbigh, and from Wrexham to Chester, and several other Roads therein mentioned so far as respects the Chester District of the Road.

53 Geo. III (1812–3)
An Act for enlarging the Term and Powers of an Act of King George the Second, and an Act of His present Majesty for repairing the Road from Shrewsbury to Wrexham, and several other Roads in the Counties of Denbigh, Chester and Flint so far as relates to the Road in the County of Flint called the Mold District.

56 Geo. III (1815–6)
An Act for continuing the Term and altering and enlarging the Powers of several Acts passed for repairing the Roads from Shrewsbury through Ellesmere in the County of Salop and Overton in the County of Flint, to Wrexham in the County of Denbigh and other Roads in the said Acts mentioned so far as relates to the Ellesmere District of the said Roads.

58 Geo. III (1817–8)
An Act for continuing the Term and enlarging the Powers of Two Acts of the eleventh and Thirty-seventh Years of His present Majesty, for repairing the Road leading from Wem in the County of Salop to the Lime Rocks at Bron-y-Garth and several other Roads in the Counties of Salop and Denbigh; for repairing and diverting the Roads leading out of the said Road from Wem to Bron-y-Garth into the Turnpike Road leading from Ellesmere to Wrexham; and for repealing so much of the said Acts as relates to certain Parts of the said Roads.

59 Geo. III (1818–9)
An Act for continuing the Term and enlarging the Powers of Three Acts of the Reign of His late and present Majesty for amending several Roads therein mentioned so far as relate to the Road from Wrexham in the County of Denbigh to Pentre Bridge in the County of Flint; and for making a new Branch of Road from the said Road at a Place called Abermorddu to Mold in the said County of Flint.

1 Geo. IV (1820–1)
An Act for more effectually repairing and improving the Road from the Town of Pool in the County of Montgomery through Oswestry, in the County of Salop, to Wrexham in the County of Denbigh and several other Roads therein mentioned, in the said Counties, and in the County of Merioneth; and for making several new Branches of Roads to communicate with the said Roads in the Counties of Salop, Montgomery and Denbigh.

3 Geo. IV (1822–3)
An Act for continuing the Term and enlarging the Powers of several Acts passed for repairing the Roads therein mentioned, in the Counties of Denbigh, Flint and Carnarvon so far as relate to the Road from Wrexham to Denbigh in the County of Denbigh, and for amending the Road from Ruthin to Cerniogemawr, in the Parish of Llanyfydd in the County of Denbigh.

4 Geo. IV (1823–4)
An Act for making and maintaining a Turnpike Road from the Turnpike Road between the Town of Mold in the County of Flint, and the Town of Wrexham in the County of Denbigh to the Turnpike Road between the Town of Ruthin in the said County of Denbigh and the Town of Wrexham aforesaid and also Two several Branches of Road therefrom.

4 Geo. IV (1823–4)
An Act for more effectively amending the Road from Wrexham in the County of Denbigh to Barnhill in the County of Chester; and for making and keeping in repair the Road branching out of the said Road at Pwll-y-Rhwyd to the Borough of Holt in the said County of Denbigh.

9 Geo. IV (1828–9)
An Act to alter, amend and enlarge the Powers and Provisions of several Acts relating to the Road from Chester to Wrexham, in the City and County of Chester and the Counties of Flint and Denbigh.

1–2 Vict. (1837–8)
An Act for repairing, amending, and maintaining the Road from Shrewsbury, through Ellesmere, in the County of Salop, to Wrexham in the County of Denbigh, and other Roads branching out of the same.

Railways

7–8 Vict. (1843–5)
An Act for making a Railway from the River Dee in the County of the City of Chester to Wrexham in the County of Denbigh, to be called 'The North Wales Mineral Railway'.

48–49 Vict. (1884–6)
An Act for making a Railway from Wrexham in the County of Denbigh to Ellesmere in the County of Salop; and for other purposes.

51–52 Vict. (1887–9)
An Act to extend the time for the purchasing of Lands and for the completion of the Wrexham and Ellesmere Railway; and for other purposes.

52–53 Vict. (1888–90)
An Act to authorise Agreements between the Barry Dock and Railways Company, Alexandra (Newport and South Wales) Docks and Railway Company, Brecon and Merthyr Tydfil Junction, Neath and Brecon, Pontypridd, Caerphilly and Newport, Swansea and Mumbles, Cambrian, Wrexham and Ellesmere, Wrexham, Mold and Connah's Quay, Manchester, Sheffield and Lincolnshire, Cheshire Lines Committee, Wirral, Seacombe, Hoylake and Deeside, Mersey, Liverpool, Southport and Preston Junction, Southport and Cheshire Lines Extension, West Lancashire and Blackpool Railway Companies or some of them for the purpose of Through Traffic; to authorise the appointment of a Joint Committee and for other purposes.

53–54 Vict. (1889–91)
An Act to extend the time for the purchase of Lands for and for the completion of the Wrexham and Ellesmere Railway and for other purposes.

58–59 Vict. (1894–6)
An Act to confer further powers upon the Wrexham and Ellesmere Railway Company and for other purposes.

59–60 Vict. (1895–7)
An Act to confirm a Provisional Order made by the Board of Trade under the Railway and Canal Traffic Act 1888 relating to the Classification of Merchandise Traffic and Schedule of Maximum Rates and Charges of … the Wrexham and Ellesmere Railway Company …

24–25 Vict. (1860–2)
An Act for making a Railway from Wrexham to Minera and other Purposes.

28–29 Vict. (1864–6)
An Act to enable the Wrexham and Minera Railway Company to make and maintain new Lines of Railway and for other Purposes.

29–30 Vict. (1865–7)
An Act to vest in the Great Western Railway Company and the London and North-Western Railway Company jointly a Portion of the Wrexham and Minera Railway; and for other purposes.

25–26 Vict. (1861–3)
An Act for incorporating a Company for making and maintaining the Wrexham, Mold and Connah's Quay Junction Railway; and for other Purposes.

27–28 Vict. (1863–5)
An Act for the Extension of the Wrexham, Mold and Connah's Quay Railway to Whitchurch and Brymbo; and for other Purposes.

28–29 Vict. (1864–6)
An Act for the Extension of the Wrexham, Mold and Connah's Quay Railway to Farndon; and for other Purposes.

28–29 Vict. (1864–6)
An Act to enable the Wrexham, Mold and Connah's Quay Railway Company to extend their Railway to Connah's Quay; and for other Purposes.

29–30 Vict. (1865–7)
An Act to enable the Wrexham, Mold and Connah's Quay Railway Company to raise additional Capital; and for other Purposes.

29–30 Vict. (1865–7)
An Act for confirming certain Articles of Agreement between the Buckley Railway Company and the Wrexham, Mold and Connah's Quay Railway Company.

29–30 Vict. (1865–7)
An Act for the Extension of the Wrexham, Mold and Connah's Quay Railway to Buckley; and for other Purposes.

29–30 Vict. (1865–7)
An Act to enable the Wrexham, Mold and Connah's Quay Railway Company to extend their Railway to Connah's Quay; to make a Deviation in their authorized Railway; and for other Purposes.

30–31 Vict. (1866–8)
An Act to extend the Time for the Purchase of Lands and for the Completion of a Portion of the Wrexham, Mold and Connah's Quay Railway.

32–33 Vict. (1868–70)
An Act to authorize the Wrexham, Mold and Connah's Quay Railway Company to raise a sum of Money for their undertaking; and for other purposes.

36–38 Vict. (1872–5)
An Act for leasing the Buckley Railway to the Wrexham, Mold and Connah's Quay Railway Company; and to make certain arrangements with reference to the Capital of the Wrexham, Mold and Connah's Quay Railway Company; and for other purposes.

45–46 Vict. (1881–3)
An Act to enable the Wrexham, Mold and Connah's Quay Railway Company to make new Branch Railways, Roads, Streets and other Works, to raise further Capital and for other purposes.

46–47 Vict. (1882–3)
An Act to enable the Wrexham, Mold and Connah's Quay Railway Company to make new Railways to raise further Capital and for other purposes.

46–47 Vict. (1882–3)
An Act to enable the Wrexham, Mold and Connah's Quay Railway Company to consolidate their debenture and other stocks and share Capital and to raise a further sum of money for their undertaking, and for other purposes.

51–52 Vict. (1887–9)
An Act for conferring further powers on the Wrexham, Mold and Connah's Quay Railway Company; and for other purposes.

52–53 Vict. (1888–90)
An Act to authorise the transfer of certain portions of the Undertaking of the Wirral Railway Company to the Manchester, Sheffield and Lincolnshire and the Wrexham, Mold and Connah's Quay Railway Companies and for other purposes.

53–54 Vict. (1889–91)
An Act to extend the time for the purchase of Lands and for the completion of certain portions of the Undertaking of the Wirral Railway Company by the Manchester, Sheffield and Lincolnshire and Wrexham, Mold and Connah's Quay Railway Companies and for other purposes.

56–57 Vict. (1892–4)
An Act to confer powers upon … the Wrexham, Mold and Connah's Quay Railway Company … and for other purposes.

58–59 Vict. (1894–6)
An Act to confer further powers upon … the Wrexham, Mold and Connah's Quay Railway Company …

63–64 Vict. (1899–01)
An Act to enable the Great Central Railway Company to make new railways and other works to acquire additional lands to extend the time for the compulsory purchase of certain lands for the completion of certain railways and for the sale of superfluous lands to raise additional capital to define and regulate the existing capital of the Company to confer further powers upon the Wrexham, Mold and Connah's Quay Railway Company …

Utilities
27–28 Vict. (1863–5)
An Act for better supplying the Borough of Wrexham and Neighbourhood thereof with Water; and for other Purposes.

61–62 Vict. (1897–99)
An Act to confirm certain P.Os. made by the B.o.T. under the Gas and Water Works Facilities Act 1870 relating to … Ross Water … and Wrexham Water.

33–34 Vict. (1869–71)
An Act for incorporating the Wrexham Gaslight Company, with powers to supply the town of Wrexham and its neighbourhood with Gas; and for other purposes.

37–38 Vict. (1873–5)
An Act for confirming certain P.Os. made by the B.o.T. under The Gas and Water Works Facilities Act, 1870, Amendment Act, 1873, relating to … Wrexham.

37–38 Vict. (1873–5)
An Act to authorise the Wrexham Waterworks Company to make new Reservoirs; to extend their limits of supply; to raise more money; and for other purposes.

43–44 Vict. (1879–81)
An Act to authorise the Wrexham Waterworks Company to make new Service Reservoirs and Filter Beds; to further extend their Limits of Supply; to raise additional Capital; and for other purposes.

49–50 Vict. (1885–7)
An Act for the granting of further powers to the Wrexham Gas Light Company.

53–54 Vict. (1889–91)
An Act to confirm certain P.Os. made by the B.o.T. under the Electric Lighting Acts, 1882 and 1888, relating to … Wrexham.

60–61 Vict. (1896–8)
An Act to confirm certain P.Os. made by the B.o.T. under the electric Lighting Acts 1882 and 1888 relating to … Wrexham.

Urban Tramways
36–37 Vict. (1872–4)
An Act to authorise the construction of the Wrexham District Tramways, and for other purposes.

62–63 Vict. (1898–00)
An Act to confirm certain P.Os. made by the B.o.T. under the Tramways Act 1870 relating to … Wrexham.

37–38 Vict. (1873–5)
An Act to confirm certain P.Os. of the L.G.B. relating to the Districts of … Wrexham

Enclosures
48 Geo. III (1807–8)
An Act for inclosing Lands in the Township of Minera in the Parish of Wrexham, in the County of Denbigh.

Adderley Bank/Glan-y-Wiber, Chester Roa
A new development of private houses constructed in 2001. It takes its name from the house Adderley which used to stand close to this site.*

Ael-y-Bryn
(*Trans.* brow of the hill) Built as part of the first phase of the Garden Village* development.

Ainsdale Grove, Acton Park
Built in the 1980s on land that had once been part of the Acton Park* estate. The name has no known local significance.

Air Training Corps
Established in March 1953 at the Drill Hall* in Chapel Street* and designated No. 2279 (Wrexham & District) Squadron. It catered for forty boys aged from 14–17½ years of age. The first instructors were Flying Officers N. Etchells, RAFVR and C.R. Butler, RAFVR. In later years the ATC moved to a site alongside the RAFA Club on Ruthin Road.

Albany Terrace, Price's Lane
Developed in the latter part of the 19th century on land that had been part of Walnut Tree Farm.* The origin of the name is unknown.

Albert Street, Hightown
Built in the late 19th century and demolished during the 1960s to make way for the Napier Square* flats, this street was almost certainly named after Albert Bury, a member of the family who developed this area of the town. It is possible, however, that it was also named in honour of Prince Albert (1819–61), the husband of Queen Victoria.

Albert Place/Court, Beast Market
A small 19th century court development of low quality housing located behind the central houses on the north-west side of the Beast Market and was accessed via a passage between these houses. It appears on the 1872 survey. It was demolished in 1932 as part of the Borough Council's slum clearance programme.

Albert Villa, Grove Road
See Fern Bank.

Albion Brewery,
Originally Thomas' Brewery* the Albion, in its heyday in the mid 19th century, was owned by John Beirne.* The buildings were located below the Parish Church alongside the River Gwenfro and were accessed through an arch on Bridge Street at the foot of Town Hill. They were demolished during the construction of the Albion Car Park. Prior to being a brewery, this site was occupied by a house, yard and dye-house.

Albion Hotel, Pen-y-Bryn
(See also The Light Dragoon) In the immediate post Second World War period, this was the headquarters of the Wrexham branch of the Royal Air Force Association.*

Aldford Way
Developed in the 1960s on land that was previously part of the Acton Park estate.* It was almost certainly named after the Cheshire village of Aldford.

Alexandra Road
This street was developed in the 1880s on a field that had previously been known as Cae March Ddu (*Trans.* black horse field) and was part of the Plas Power estate. Although the road was adopted by the Borough Council in 1891, there were still plots being built upon as late as 1901. The road was named after Princess Alexandra (1844–1925), wife of the Prince of Wales (later King Edward VII).

The Albion Brewery, c.1895. The small dray wagon carries the name Beirne.

Alexandra Schools, Holt Road.
This school, built at a cost of £14,500, took its name after Queen Alexandra, consort of King Edward VII. The first pupils were admitted on 16 June 1910. Following the passing of the Education Act 1944, Alexandra became a Secondary Modern School catering for girls who had failed the 11-plus entrance examination for Grove Park Grammar School. This in effect meant that there were three schools operating at the same time in the Alexandra Schools building. The implementation of the 1944 Act led to the building of two new Secondary Modern Schools in Wrexham – St David's* and Bryn Offa – which became comprehensive schools in 1972 and took all the senior girls from Alexandra leaving only the infant and junior schools. In 1996 these schools were amalgamated

Headteachers:
  Boys
  1910–40   H. P. Williams
  Girls
  1910   Miss S. J. Jones
  1930s   Miss Annie Elizabeth Wordsworth, OBE
  1940   Miss L. E. Leonard
  Secondary Modern for Girls
  1950   Miss H. M. S. Griffiths
  1966   Miss V. I. Samuels (acting)
  1967   Miss Mary C. Jones (acting)
  1970   Mrs Raynor Pope

1972	*reorganisation for comprehensive education*
Juniors	
1941	Aneurin Williams
1966	T. Fred Jones
1978	Gareth Evans
1994	Emyr Evans (acting)
1995	Mrs Beverley Payne
1996	*Juniors and infants amalgamated*
Infants	
1910	Miss Florence E. Jones
1928	Miss Blanche Osborne
1952	Miss Esther Lloyd Roberts
1962	Miss Enid Jones
1967	Mrs Gwyneth Williams
1979	Mrs Gloria M. Belton
1994	Mrs Beverley Payne
1996	*Infants and juniors amalgamated*
Special	
1921	Mrs Marion Jones
1927	Miss E. Wynne Green

The original school buildings were demolished in January/February 2000 as part of a deal between WCBC and ASDA Stores. As part of the development, ASDA paid for the construction of a new school on part of the site. The new Alexandra School opened in September 2000. The current head teacher (2010) is Mr R. Lloyd and there are 247 pupils on the roll.

Alexandra Vaults, Yorke Street
Very little information is known about these premises which were undoubtedly named after Princess (later Queen) Alexandra, consort of King Edward VII.

Allington Drive, Queen's Park
Built in the immediate post Second World War period as part of the first phase of WBC's Queen's Park housing development. Named after the local settlement of that name (*Trans.* Trefalyn).

Alma Grange, Rhosddu
See Stansty Issa.

Alma Terrace
Located on land to the east of Madeira Hill, this terrace took its name from the opening battle of the Crimean War, fought on 20 September 1854, when British and French forces defeated the Russians who held a commanding position on the heights above the River Alma in what is now the Ukraine.

Almond Grove
This area of the Cefn Park* estate was requisitioned during the Second World War and temporary housing built in 1941 to accommodate Royal Ordnance Factory* workers in 'T'-shaped cul-de-sacs. When the war was over these houses were utilised by WBC as temporary corporation housing and, in some cases, survived until the mid 1950s when they were known locally as 'Cardboard City'. During in the 1950s and 1960s these cul-de-sacs were linked together to form streets and the pre-fabs were replaced by permanent houses, built by W. D. Stant on behalf of WBC.* Most of the streets in this area were given the names of trees and shrubs. The land was bought by means of a compulsory purchase order from Lt-Col R. G. Fenwick-Palmer.*

Alyn Close
Named after the nearby Alyn valley.

Alyndale Road, Little Acton
Named after the nearby Alyn valley.

Ancient British Fencible Cavalry
Following the declaration of war made by France on Britain on 1 February 1793, the British government announced that it wished to form 30–40 regiments of Fencible Cavalry (which derives from the Latin *defensible personis*, meaning a person capable of bearing arms). These were to be recruited from volunteers willing to take up arms for the defence of their locality, a form of mounted 'Home Guard'. Sir Watkin Williams Wynn resolved that one regiment should be raised in Denbighshire and appealed for men to volunteer. It was to consist of six troops with Sir Watkin as the colonel. On 14 March 1794 the following officers were gazetted to the corps:

Col Sir Watkin Williams Wynn, Bt; Lt-Col Robert Watkin Wynne; Maj Richard Puleston; Capt Thomas Cumming; Capt Gwilym Lloyd Wardle; Capt Edward Lloyd Lloyd; Lt & Capt Thomas Boycott; Lt Sir Henry Goodricke, Bt; Lt Edward Read; Lt W.M. Dodd; Lt Joseph Maddocks; Lt Thomas Case; Cornet [2Lt] Burton; Cornet Burganey; Cornet Jones; Chaplain Crew Davies; Adj Jones; Surg Edward Granger. Later additions to the officers were: Robert Wynne; George F. Barlow; Charles Spencer; John Edwards; Archibald Paxton; John Groom Smyth; Sir Richard Steele, Bt; Charles James Apperley;* Thomas Skelding; John Lewis; Francis Evatt; Augustus Gifford; Thomas Mason; Adolphus Gifford; Thomas Jones; Joseph Airdell Sparkes; John Waring; Thomas Foulkes; Thomas Zouch; C. Spencer; F. Stocker; ? Barlow.

The first recruit to join was James Witnal (22 March 1774) and by 1 June the regiment had 17 officers, 6 quartermasters, 7 sergeants, 12 corporals and 291 privates. The original sergeants were: John Barlow; John Kennedy; John Read; Thomas Edisbury; John Stodhart; John Davies; John Zachary; J. Hale. The original corporals were: Peter Jones; James Percy; Peter Jones; John Ball; Humphrey Williams; Thomas Miller; Edward Pearce; Thomas Burrows; William Harrison; John Edwards, William Gouldsbown.

The surnames of the privates were: Ankers, Allen, Arthur, Bellis, Baxter, Burgess, Buckley, Barlow, Billingham, Batten, Barnet, Brookfield, Brown, Barber, Bithill, Beckett, Cross, Catherall, Conway, Clarke, Chatterton, Carter, Coffack, Davies (23), Dickinson, Daley, Evans (16), Eaton, Ellis (4), Moses, Foulkes,(2), Fryer, Fithian, Fletcher, Faulkner, Griffiths (5), Gittins, Gill, Grindley, Hughes (13), Nat Hesketh, Helgrove, Hartshorn, Huddleston, Hodgkinson, Heath, Hall, Jones (38), John (9), Edward (9), Jarvis, Ibell, Lewis (4), Lightbound, Lyon, Lloyd (6), Lee, Leadbeater, Moss, Matthews, Morris (5), Mold, Owen (3), Mossham, Oldfield, Pattison, Price (3), Parry (7), Pritchard (3), Prince, Pinches, Potts, Poole, Prisk, Parbont, Partington, Piers, Pemberton, Peacock, Rodden, Rogers, Roberts

One of the pre-fabricated houses built on Almond Grove in 1941. [J. Murphy]

(9), Rigby, Rothwell, Read, Rowland, Richards, Smith, Sillers, Smathers, Stone, Stocker, Soloman, Starkey, Sanaiford, Thomas, Latham, Tomkins, Trudent, Tilston, Witnal, Williams (13), Woolley, Woodward, Ed Wynn, Wilson, Williamson, Whistle.

The regiment was to have been called the Denbighshire Light Horse but has gone down in history as the Ancient British (or North Wales) Fencible Cavalry. They were dressed in a scarlet coatee with yellow facings and gold lace and buttons, white leather breeches and high boots, black leather light dragoon helmet adorned with a feather.

On 3 June, the regiment left the Wrexham area and marched to Gloucester and then to the south coast of England. By April 1795, they were in Yorkshire from where they went to Carlisle. On 10 March 1797 they were ordered to move to Belfast where they played a prominent role in suppressing the Irish Rebellion. At Prosperous, a number of troopers were caught in a barn which was set on fire and several were killed. There was also a rumour that the regiment was involved in the death of a catholic priest, Father Michael Murphy, a matter which was vehemently denied but which earned them the nickname 'The Bloody British' and the lasting enmity of the Irish republicans.

At the battle of Newtown Barry, they recaptured a field gun that had been taken by the rebels and at Arklow they made a 'dashing charge' and lost several men killed and wounded. At Coree they lost a further 26 men killed in a charge including W. Bellis and Edward Jones of Wrexham. They returned to Denbighshire in November 1799 and, despite efforts to have the regiment recognised as a regular unit of the British Army, were disbanded on 2 April 1800.

A memorial to those members of the regiment who died on service in Ireland was placed in Nant-y-Belan Tower on the Wynnstay estate. Sadly this was severely damaged by a landslip in the 1970s. The names recorded were: Capt John Burganey; Lt Adolphus Giffard; Cornet & Adj John Davies; QM Joseph Goldsby; QM John Davies; Cpls Edward Roberts; John Bellis; Joseph Tilstone; George Chalener; Ambrose Tarling; Trumpeters Edward Edwards; Anthony King; Ptes Edward Jackson; William Lucas; John Davies; Thomas Edwards; David Burgess; David Roberts; Robert Matthews; John Parry; John Powell; Richard Williams; William Roberts; Robert Roberts; Thomas Davies; Robert Jones; Hugh Davis; James Houghson; Edward Jones; John Hughes; William Leadbetter; Robert Griffiths; George Owen; John Parry; Randle Roberts; Samuel Dunn; Thomas Lee; Michael Bellis; Boas Hughes; John Parish, Thomas Chadwicke; William Jones; James Patterson.

For fuller details see *Historical Records of the Denbighshire Hussars Imperial Yeomanry*, Appendix IV.

Anchor, Mount Street
Situated at the eastern end of Mount Street, close to the junction with Caia Road,* this public house was demolished in 1975 (to make way for the southern end of the Eagles' Meadow flyover) and the licence was transferred to The Caia.*

Anglesey Close, Borras Park
As with other streets on this private housing development of the 1960s, known as Hillcrest Estate,* this road takes its name from one of the old, pre-1974 counties of Wales, in this case, Anglesey.

Ansell Road
Laid out in the late 1970s on land that had previously been part of Plas Goulbourne Farm. This street was named after Ansell's Brewery, owners of the nearby Goulbourne public house.

Anthony Eden Drive
Laid out in the 1950s as one of the access roads of WBC's Queen's Park* housing estate but, for many years, there were no houses on this street. It was originally named, Eden Drive after Sir Anthony Eden, Foreign Secretary and Prime Minister. The name was later changed to avoid confusion with Eaton Drive.

Robert Anthony Eden was born in 1897, the son of Sir William Eden, Bt, of Windlestone, Co. Durham. He was educated at Eton and Christ Church, Oxford, served in the Great War with the King's Royal Rifle Corps and was awarded the Military Cross. He later served in the Territorial Army rising to the rank of Honorary Colonel. He was elected Conservative MP for Warwickshire in 1923 and held the seat until 1957. He became Foreign Secretary in 1935, a post which he held until his resignation in 1938 following the government's policy of appeasement with Nazi Germany. When Churchill became Prime Minister in 1940 Eden was re-appointed to the post of Foreign Secretary which he held until 1945 and again in Churchill's peacetime government of 1951–5. On Churchill's resignation in 1955, Eden was appointed Prime Minister and First Lord of the Treasury but resigned in 1957 following the disastrous Suez War of 1956. He was created a Knight of the Garter in 1954 and Earl of Avon in 1961. He was married twice, firstly to Beatrice Beckett and then to Clarissa Spencer-Churchill. He died in 1977.

Apperley, Charles James 'Nimrod' *sports writer*
Born at Plas Gronow, Wrexham in 1779, the second son of Thomas Apperley. His maternal grandfather was the Revd William Wynn of Llangynhafal. He was educated at Rugby School. During the Irish Rebellion of 1799, he served as a cornet (2nd lieutenant) in the Ancient British Fencible Cavalry.* He married Winifred Wynn of Peniarth, Merionethshire in 1801 and was employed for some years as an agent to his brother-in-law, residing at Tŷ Gwyn, Llanbeblig, Caernarfon. He then lived at various locations in England, earning his living from farming and hunting, eventually losing all his money. He first wrote for *The Sporting Magazine* in 1822, using the pen name 'Nimrod' (the Mighty Hunter), but despite his great popularity as a writer he had to flee to France to escape his creditors. He returned to England in 1842 and died in Upper Belgrave Place, London on 19 May 1843. His best known books are: *My Life and Times* (1842); *The Chase, the Road and the Turf* (1837); *Memoirs of the Life of John Mytton* (1835); *The Life of a Sportsman* (1852); *Hunting Reminiscences* (1843); *The Horse and Hounds* (1858); *My Horses and Other Essays* (1828); *Nimrod Abroad* (1842); *Nimrod's Hunting Tours* (1835); *Nimrod's Northern Tour* (1838); *Remarks on the Condition of Hunters, the Choice of Horses and Their Management* (1831); *Sporting* (1838). He had two sons.

Charles James Apperley.

Ar-y-Bryn Terrace
(*Trans.* on the hill) This terrace of houses faced onto Earl Street and backed onto Poplar Road, opposite the western extremity of the grounds of the modern St Giles School.* The noted Wrexham historian, A.N. Palmer* lived at Nº 3 for a number of years when he first moved to Wrexham in 1880.

Ar-y-Bryn Terrace.

Aran Road
This road was laid out in the 1960s by WBC as part of the Maes-y-Dre Housing Estate. It was built on land that had once been part of the Acton Park* estate. This is almost certainly named after the Aran mountain in Snowdonia.

Arc, The/Y Bwa, Lord Street
This piece of street sculpture, the work of Scottish artist David Annand, was unveiled by the Mayor of Wrexham, Cllr Michael Morris on 2 February 1996 and was sponsored by the Welsh Development Agency, the Iron and Steel Trades Confederation, the Arts Council of Wales and WMBC. It depicts a steel worker and a coal miner, representing the heavy industrial past of Wrexham County Borough. On the base is a poem *Y Bwa* by the modern bard, Merddyn ap Dafydd of Llanrwst.

> *Y Bwa*
> *Uwch-y-waedd, drwy'r gawod chwys – a helynt*
> *Y morthwylion stormus,*
> *Heibio'r awr sy'n bwyta brys,*
> *Mae tynfa yma at enfys.*

> Trans.
> *The Arc*
> *Above the cry, through streaming sweat – and the storm*
> *Of angry hammers,*
> *Past the hour that devours haste,*
> *We are drawn towards rainbows.*

Archer's Way
The generally held belief that this street was named as a link with the Royal British Bowmen* of Acton Park* is almost certainly incorrect as the name was originally written with an apostrophe before the 's' suggesting that it was a personal name. There is no evidence to suggest that the Royal British Bowmen met in this area but instead, held their meetings at Acton Park and in the grounds of other large houses in the neighbourhood. The street was laid out in 1933 as part of the second phase of WBC's Spring Lodge* housing development.

Arenig Road
This road was laid out in c.1955 by WBC as part of the Queen's Park housing development. It was built on land that had previously been part of the Cefn Park* estate. It is named after the mountain in the Bala area of Gwynedd.

Argyle Buildings, Regent Street
See Westminster Buildings.

Argyle Street
This street was laid out by the local mining engineer and mine owner, William Low* (his monogram appears over the centre of the arch). The street linked Hope Street with the site of the Wrexham Agricultural and Scientific Society Exhibition of 1876. The arched building, generally known as Argyle Buildings, but more correctly Westminster Buildings, was built by Low, reputedly as a dowry for his daughter. The row of small shops which stood on the south side of the street were demolished at the end of the 1970s. Low was born in Rothesay, Argyllshire, and was first employed as a surveyor by the Duke of Argyll, hence the name of this street, which adopts the archaic spelling which also appears in Argyle Street, Glasgow.
[Plans DRO/DD/DM/188/33]

Arms of the Borough of Wrexham
Upon the incorporation of the Borough of Wrexham an application was made to the Royal College of Heralds for the grant of arms. This was given on 26 November 1857 and was described: Ermine, two crosiers in saltire or, on a chief dancette, per pale, gules, and or, two lions passant, guardant, counterchanged, and for the crest in a wreath of the colours upon a mount vert, a dragon gules, resting the dexter claw upon a shield or charged with the character of Mars sable. The lions represent the manor of Wrexham Regis and the croziers the manor of Wrexham Abbot. The crest is the Red Dragon of Wales with the symbol of Mars on its shield representing the mineral resources of the area.

Motto: Fear God Honour the King.

Arms of the Borough of Wrexham.

Arms of the Borough of Wrexham Maelor
The Arms of WMBC were largely derived from the arms of the former authorities of WBC and WRDC. It was designed by H. Ellis Tomlinson, MA, FHS and is described as: Vert semée of ermine spots argent, two crosiers in saltire, on a chief wavy or a lion passant guardant azure. (The shield combined a green 'field',

Arms of the Borough of Wrexham Maelor/ Wrexham County Borough.

ermine spots and gold croziers with the blue lion of the Hanmers of Maelor and a wave for the river Dee in a heraldic map of the new area).

Crest: On a wreath or and vert, out of a mural crown gules masoned argent a mount vert, therein in front of an oak tree proper fructed or, a dragon passant gules resting the dexter forefoot on a lozenge sable fimbriated or. (The crest is based on a red mural (walled) crown symbolizing brick-making and Madog ap Meredydd's castle at Overton. The Red Dragon rests a foot on a black diamond edged with gold, for coal and other mineral wealth, and the tree stands for forestry and the rural areas.)

Supporters: On either side a dragon gules gorged with a collar dancetty and supporting with the interior forefoot a staff erect or, flying therefrom a forked pennon vert, the dexter dragon charged on the shoulder with the astronomical symbol for Mars and the sinister with a cogwheel or. (The supporters are Welsh dragons holding a green pennant for agriculture; one dragon is charged with a gold symbol of Mars for iron founding and the other with a gold cogwheel for engineering.)

Motto: *Labor omnia vincit* (Hard work overcomes all things).

Arms of the County Borough of Wrexham
The Arms of the County Borough of Wrexham are the same as the Arms of the Borough of Wrexham Maelor.*

Arundel, Earls of
Edmund Fitzalan, fifth earl of Arundel, inherited the lordship of Bromfield and Yale* from his maternal uncle, John, Earl of Warren. In 1375, Edmund, sixth Earl of Arundel inherited the lordship which he held until his execution on the instruction of King Richard II in 1398. For one year the lordship was granted to William de Scrope, Lord Scrope and Earl of Wiltshire, before it reverted to Thomas Fitzalan, seventh Earl of Arundel. He died in 1421 without a male heir and the land passed to his three nephews, John, second Duke of Norfolk, William, Lord Abergavenny and Sir Rowland Lenthall. By 1489 the lordship had reverted to the Crown.

Ash Grove, Queen's Park
This area of the Cefn Park* estate was requisitioned during the Second World War and temporary housing built in 1941 to accommodate Royal Ordnance Factory* workers. When the war was over these houses were utilised by WBC as temporary corporation housing and, in some cases, survived until the mid 1950s when they were known locally as 'Cardboard City'. The temporary houses were replaced by permanent dwellings, built by W.D. Stant on behalf of WBC, between the 1950s and 1960s. Most of the streets in this area were given the names of trees and shrubs. The land was bought by means of a compulsory purchase order from Lt-Col R.G. Fenwick-Palmer.*

Ashburn Way, King's Mills
A 1970s private housing development.

Ashfield House, Stansty
A large house built by John Foulkes of Charles Street on part of the land of Stansty Issa during the mid 19th century. In 1842, the house was occupied by solicitor William Bennion (the father-in-law of Foulkes) of Plas Grono before Foulkes himself moved in. By 1871, following the death of Foulkes, the house was rented to John B. Barker, the adjutant of the Royal Denbigh Militia. In 1881, it was occupied by timber merchant, William Thomas (who had business premises in the GWR Station) and his son, Charles Thomas, manager of a saw mill. In the early 1900s, the house was occupied by Capt (later Maj) G.F. Hutton, RWF. In 1920, the 50-acre estate was bought by WRDC for use as a playing field with the house itself becoming a maternity home. Nine acres were utilised as the Ashfield Recreation Ground (most of which has now disappeared under the development of the North Wales Tennis Centre) and twenty-four council houses were built along the boundary of Crispin Lane and Stansty Road. The first eighteen houses (probably the first Council Houses built by WRDC) were started on 20 July 1920, at the same time as the Acton Park Housing Estate on Rhosnesni Lane.

The opening of the Wrexham & District War Memorial Hospital in 1926 meant that a maternity home at Ashfield was not needed and the house and gardens were sold to local builder, George Fleming Sumner (*c.*1888–1947) in *c.*1930. He divided it into two, letting one half and living in the remaining half himself. Part of the grounds were used as his builder's yard. In about 1937, the Sumners moved to live at Chevet Hey* while retaining the ownership of Ashfield. George Sumner built a number of houses in the garden of Ashfield, alongside Plas Coch Road and Ashfield was demolished by G.F. Sumner & Sons in the 1960s. The sons laid out a small development of private houses in the former garden of Ashfield which they named Fleming Drive* after their father. All that remains of the house today is part of the boundary wall and gateway along Plas Coch Road, near the North Wales Tennis Centre and Ashfield Road,* off Crispin Lane, is named after it.

Ashfield Road, Stansty
Named after Ashfield,* a large house which once stood on Plas Coch Road.* Eighteen terraced houses which originally stood in this road were included in the 1959 slum clearance area and the road and council houses were then built on the site.

Aston, CBE, Alderman William *businessman & local politician*
Born in Wolverhampton in 1869, William Aston began his working life as an errand boy in his family's furniture retailing business in 1885, rising to managing director and, eventually, company chairman, when Aston & Son had twenty-five branches throughout north Wales and the Midlands. He served as a member of WRDC from 1911 until 1913 when he was elected a county councillor for Denbighshire and was chairman of the County Education Committee. He was elected a member of WBC

Alderman William Aston, Mayor and Freeman of Wrexham.

in 1926, became mayor of Wrexham in 1930, was elected an alderman in 1935 and an honorary freeman on 27 September 1944. His particular areas of interest were education and housing. He played a major role in the establishment of Acton School* in 1923 and the Denbighshire Technical College* (in Regent Street and later, 1953, on Mold Road) and was chairman of the governors of the Technical College and Grove Park School.*

During his 18-year period as chairman of the Borough Housing Committee, great advances were made in public housing in Wrexham and he was instrumental in establishing the Huntroyde, Maes-y-Dre, Spring Lodge, Bronydre, Whitegate, Acton and Queen's Park housing estates. In addition to the above, William Aston also established the first Child Welfare Clinic, the Wrexham Civic Guild for Help and was an ardent supporter of adult education, enabling the WEA to become established in Wrexham. He retired from WBC in 1949 and died on 26 June 1962 at his home, Acton Grange. He is buried in Wrexham Cemetery.

During the early 1930s, Aston converted one of his company's warehouses into the Wrexham Joy Centre, providing facilities for the young people of the town. Through his company, he also presented Acton Hall* and part of Acton Park* to the people of Wrexham.

His wife, Agnes Ann Powell of Prees, Shropshire served as a magistrate in Wrexham for many years. They had three sons and one daughter. One son, Frank, was killed serving with the King's Shropshire Light Infantry in 1916, aged 19. The family resided at Bodlondeb,* Grove Road and Acton Grange.* Mrs Aston died on 31 July 1952.

William Aston was awarded the CBE in 1949 and the hall at the Technical College was named after him. In later years, the whole college came to be known as the William Aston College.* Aston Grove* was also named after him.

At the time of his death he was described by Alderman William Dodman* as 'The greatest driving force the town ever had. No man has ever done more for Wrexham'.

Aston & Son, *Furniture Manufacturers and Retailers*
Samuel and Ann Aston of Wolverhampton moved to Wrexham in 1870 when Samuel found work at the Rhosddu Foundry and Ann rented a house and began to take in lodgers. Shortly afterwards, they rented premises in Hope Street, next to the Horse & Jockey* public house, where they opened a boot shop which was run by Ann. Samuel then began to deal, part-time, in second-hand furniture which he sold by auction in the arch below Westminster Buildings,* opposite their shop. So successful was the furniture trade that they moved from Hope Street to larger premises in Tenter's Square* in 1878. Two years later, Sam rented Bryn-y-Ffynnon Lodge* in Regent Street where he established Aston's Auction Mart, selling furniture, china, drapery and small ironmongery. In 1885, their son William* joined the business as an errand boy then a salesman and by 1900, they had six shops scattered throughout the region. A 'Model Furniture Factory' was opened at Aberderfyn, Johnstown in 1903 employing over 100 staff with its own GWR halt at Aberderfyn and Ponkey Crossing on the Legacy–Ponciau line (opened 1905–closed to passengers 1915). In 1909, the firm acquired the former Maelor Hotel* in Regent Street as their main Wrexham store (on the site of the present day Waterstones bookstore). By 1962, the firm had 25 shops throughout north Wales and the Midlands and claimed in its advertising to be the 'largest furniture makers in Great Britain supplying the public direct'. Shortly afterwards, it was taken over by Great Universal Stores.

The first premises of Samuel Aston was the small shop located next door to the Horse & Jockey public house.

Aston Grove
Proposals to lay out this road were first approved by WBC in 1931 and was to form the second phase of the Maes-y-Dre housing estate.* The land was bought from Mrs E. Wolff of Whitegate Lane. The houses were built in two stages; the even-numbered houses in *c*.1935 and the odd numbered houses during 1936 (by E.W. Gittins & Sons). These were larger than average council houses and are the only properties of their type built in Wrexham. The street was originally meant to be called Aston Avenue (after William Aston*) but was changed to Aston Road and then to Aston Grove in November 1932.

Avon Close
Developed as part of the WBC Acton Park Housing Estate* in the mid 1960s, this street was named after the Warwickshire town of Stratford-upon-Avon to celebrate the 400th anniversary of the birth of William Shakespeare in 1964.

B

Back Chamber Street
This name is first recorded in 1820. Palmer records that in 1712, the street was referred to as Black Chamber Street which appears to fit in as a translation of *Y Siambr Ddu*, a nickname often given to the lord of the manor's prison which, in the 16th century, was part of the old Shirehall which stood on the south side of this street. The remains of the street survive in the form of the raised pavement on the northern side of Town Hill, between Abbot Street and Hope Street.

Bader Court
This street was built during the 1980s on land that was formerly part of Plas Goulbourne Farm and was named after Group Captain Sir Douglas Robert Stuart Bader, DSO and Bar, DFC and Bar, CBE, Legion d'Honeur, Croix de Guerre, the noted RAF fighter pilot of the Second World War. Other than the street's proximity to the site of the former RAF Wrexham, there is no known connection between Bader and the area.

Bagshaw, John *local historian*
Born in Caerwys, John Bagshaw spent most of his childhood in New Broughton. Educated at the Victoria School and the Junior Technical School, Wrexham, he was employed as a draughtsman by the North Wales Power Company before serving with the Honorable Artillery Company in north-west Europe during the Second World War. In the 1950s, he joined the BBC in London as a senior draughtsman and retired as a chief draughtsman (Transmitter Capital Projects) in 1976. After a short period in Lincoln he moved to live in Pentre Broughton in 1983 where he was a founder member of the Broughton & District Local History Group. He was the author of *Broughton Then and Now* and *A Glimpse into the Past*, and was well known for his illustrated maps of the Broughton area. He died in 1993.

Bala Road
This road was laid out in *c*.1955 by WBC as part of the Queen's Park* housing development. It was built on land that had previously been part of the Cefn Park* estate. It is named after the town of Bala in Gwynedd.

Balmoral Close
See Balmoral Road.

Balmoral Road
Built in the 1960s (from Sandway Road as far as Balmoral Close) on land that had formerly been part of Croes Eneurys Farm,* by local builders Parker, Davies & Johnson Ltd. (see also Croes Eneurys Estate). Most of the roads on the development were given the names of royal palaces, in this case, Balmoral Castle, the monarch's holiday residence in Scotland.

Bamford, Thomas *footballer*
Born in Port Talbot, south Wales on 2 September 1905, Tommy Bamford first played soccer in Cardiff and Bridgend before joining Wrexham as a centre forward in April 1929. Originally signed as an amateur, he scored 6 goals in his first 7 games and went on to become the most successful goal scorer in the club's history (in one season, 1933–4, he scored 44 goals). In 1934, he was transferred to Manchester United where he remained until 1938 when he signed for Swansea Town. After retiring from soccer, Tommy settled in Wrexham where he was employed at Brymbo Steelworks. He had five international caps for Wales between 1931 and 1933. Married to Jane Thomas, he died in Wrexham on 12 December 1967 and is buried in Wrexham Cemetery.

Bank Street
Originally called Kenrick Street, this narrow street linking Hope Street* and Henblas Street* was laid out by James Kenrick, the founder of Kenrick's Bank, and first appears in the rate books in 1818. As all the properties on this street were once owned by Kenrick, it was for many years classified as a private street and public access could be denied by means of a chain. By the mid 19th century, with the closure of Kenrick & Bowman's Bank* and the opening of the National Provincial Bank in the same premises, the street name had become Bank Street. The Welsh Wesleyan Methodist cause was established in 1859 in the Bank Street dining rooms of Gomer Jones before moving to Brook Street* in 1862.

Until the 1980s, the Horseshoe* public house was located on the left-hand side of the street, just before the junction with Henblas Street. There are a number of references to this street being known locally as 'Little Soho' apparently because of its appearance and because of the number of foreign businessmen operating here at one time. Today, one of the oldest and best known business located in this street is Marubbi's Café which was founded by Armando Marubbi who arrived in Wrexham from Italy in 1896 and opened a Temperance Bar in Abbot Street* before moving to Bank Street in the mid 1930s. The small building on the north corner of Bank Street and Hope Street was originally Barclays Bank.

Bank Street Presbyterian Church
This congregation was formed when a group of Presbyterians broke away from the Welsh Presbyterian Church in Abbot Street in 1845. A first floor room in a warehouse on the corner of Bank Street and Henblas Street was leased at an annual rental of £12. The room, which could accommodate 150 worshippers on wooden benches (with a further 30 standing) was officially opened on Christmas Day, 1845, with a membership of 12. In its early days, the chapel had no resident minister although many services were conducted by the Revd William Hughes. In 1849, Charles Hughes (the 'Son' of Hughes & Son,* printers) joined the congregation and applied his organisational skills to help the group thrive. In 1855, the Revd Joseph Jones of Liverpool was invited to become the chapel's first minister and immediately put in motion plans to build a new church. At the time, membership of the church stood at only 16, but it had a large and very healthy Sunday school. Land in Bryn-y-Ffynnon was presented to the

church by Richard Davies, a coach-builder of Wrexham, and the new Hill Street English Presbyterian Church* was opened on 10 April 1857. The Bank Street chapel was then closed down.

Baptist Chapel, Chester Street – 'The Old Meeting'.
See Chester Street English Baptist Chapel.

Barker's Lane
The origin of this name is uncertain but, a family named Barker were certainly tenants of the Acton Park* estate in the late 18th and early 19th centuries and may well have held land in this area. (See Acton Hall – 1782 sale details, Lot 4).

Barker's Lane County Primary School, Borras Park
Built to accommodate the expanding population of children in the Borras Park and Smithy Lane area of the town, the first pupils arrived in 1977 but it was not until 9 May 1978 that the school was officially opened by Cllr J.E. Brown. Designed as an open-plan building, the school was extended to accommodate up to 225 pupils. One-third of a hectare was sold for the building in 2003 of nine houses by Michael Nield Homes and outline planning was granted for ten further houses.
Headteachers:
    1977   Mrs Shirley F. Cleverley
    1996   Terry Walker (Acting)
    1997   Mrs Helen Andrews
In 2010, there were 200 pupils on the roll.

Barn, The, (I) Hope Street
The Barn was the name given to the building which stood at the rear of the Talbot Inn in Hope Street where Wrexham's religious dissenters (Presbyterians, Independents and Baptists) met after 1672. In 1692, the Presbyterians left this venue and began to meet in a shop in College Street before again moving, this time to a house in Chester Street. Some time afterwards, the Independents left the Barn and began to meet in a disused factory in what is now Chapel Street. The Baptists finally moved to Chester Street where they established a chapel known as the Old Meeting (on the site of the present day English Baptist Chapel*).

Barn, The (II), Spring Lodge
An area of Spring Lodge. It takes its name from a barn belonging to Spring Lodge Farm* which was adapted for use as an 'institute' in 1934.

Barn Croft
Referred to in a document dated 1826 but its location is not pinpointed. It may be a reference to the Barnfield.*
[DRO/DD/HB/350-2]

Barnfield (Barn Field)
The Barn Field was an area of land, located on the south-east side of Madeira Hill,* belonging to Willow House.* In 1771, the Barn Field, formerly the property of the Revd Thomas Pulford, passed to Mary, Sarah, Dorah and Elizabeth Thompson, the heirs of Thomas Thompson and Charles Poyser of Wrexham. The 1833 survey shows the land belonging to a Mrs Ellis. By the time of the 1872 survey, the area had been developed and the name applied to a street leading from Madeira Hill to Alma Terrace.* Some of the properties in this street were demolished in 1932 as part of the Borough Council's slum clearance programme. [DRO/968]

Barn Field
See Barnfield.

Barons Road, Smithfield
Named after Barren's (or Baron's) Farm,* this was a late 19th century development running between Manley Road* and Dale Street.*

Barrens (or Baron's) Farm, The, Smithfield
According to Palmer, the name Barrens was an unofficial 17th century nick-name for a farm which was located between Crescent Road and Smithfield Road. In later years, when the property belonged to the Meredith family of Pentrebychan,* the house was demolished and the land leased to the landlord of The Feathers Inn* in Chester Street. In 1875, two acres of this farm, namely a field known as Cae Cigydd (*Trans*. butcher's field) were sold to Wrexham Council for the site of a new Smithfield.* The link between the historical name for this field and the purpose for which the land was bought by the Council would suggest that it had already been serving the purpose of a holding area for animals being bought and sold in the nearby Beast Market. See also Baron's Road.

Barter Court, Hightown
This street was laid out in the 1980s on land that had previously been the property of C.T. Clark, proprietor of the King's Mills Garage. Built by the Wales and West Housing Association, all the streets were named after RWF that had been awarded the Victoria Cross. This street was named after Company Sergeant Major Frederick Barter, VC, MC, who was born in Cathays Cardiff in 1891 and enlisted in the RWF in December 1908. He was mobilised into the 1st Bn, RWF, on 5 August 1914 and served in France 1914–15 as a company sergeant major. He was awarded the Victoria Cross for his action at Festubert on 16 May 1915, the citation for which reads:

For most conspicuous bravery and marked ability at Festubert on 16th May, 1915. When in the first line of German trenches, Company Sergeant Maj Barter called for volunteers to enable him to extend our line and with eight men who responded he attacked the German position with bombs, capturing three

Poster advertising the civic reception for Sergeant Major Fred Barter, VC, RWF. [Wrexham Museum]

WREXHAM WELCOME
TO
SGT.-MAJ. BARTER
V.C., R.W.F.

SERGT.-MAJOR BARTER will arrive at G.W.R. STATION at 6 o'clock this Evening.
    PROCESSION through Town, headed by the BAND of the R.W.F. and RHOS-DDU PRIZE BAND.
    PRESENTATION OF A PURSE OF GOLD at Imperial Hotel at 7 p.m.
    All are invited to give him a Right Royal Welcome.
                         S. G. JARMAN,
                          Mayor of Wrexham.

German officers and 102 men and 500 yards of their trenches. He subsequently found and cut eleven of the enemy's mine leads, situated about twenty yards apart.

Barter received a civic welcome in Wrexham on 15 July 1915. He was commissioned as a second lieutenant in August 1915 and served as a bombing instructor before returning to France in 1916–17. He served with the 2/3rd Gurka Rifles in North-West India and Palestine where, as a captain, he was awarded the Military Cross for gallantry. Returning to civilian life after the war, he was employed as a labour manager with AEC in Middlesex. During the Second World War, he was the major commanding the 4/7 Company of the Middlesex Home Guard. He died in Poole, Dorset in 1953. See also Barter Road.

Barter Road, Hightown
See Barter Court.

Barton Close, The Ithens
Built in the 1980s as part of the Ithens residential development, this street takes its name from the village of Barton in Cheshire. (See Ithens Farm)

Basham, Johnny *boxer*
Born in Newport, South Wales on 13 September 1889 (not 1890 as commonly believed), the son of John Michael Basham and Ellen (née Mahoney), Johnny Basham came to Wrexham in 1911 as a recruit in the RWF (eventually rising to Sergeant).* In December 1914, he defeated Johnny Summers to become the British Welterweight Champion and went on to become outright holder of the Lonsdale Belt and, in 1916, European Champion at the same

Johnny Basham is welcomed to Ruabon in 1921.

weight. Moving up to middleweight, he became European Champion in 1921. He had 91 professional fights, winning 68, drawing 6 and losing 17. He eventually lost his title to 'Kid' Lewis. He trained at Hightown Barracks and the Nag's Head in Mount Street. His 'honorary' manager and trainer was Alderman William Dodman.* For many years, he lived in Whitegate Road.* He died in Newport on 7 June 1947.

Bates' Square, Madeira Hill
A small 'court' development which could be accessed from either Tuttle Street or Foundry Road.

Bath Street, Bryn-y-Ffynnon
Bath Street was a short, narrow street which linked Brook Street with Well Square, and took its name from the 'bath' which was located next to the Town Well.* The street was built over during the construction of the railway viaduct for the Wrexham & Ellesmere Railway Company* in the 1890s. One short piece of it remains, outside the Old Three Tuns* public house (now the Railway Club*) and is today called Well Place. On the west side of Bath Street was a building called the Queen's Head which Palmer found recorded in 1817 and 1828 which, by 1833, had become the New Mitre, which appears on the 1833 survey. Along with so many other buildings in this area of the town, this public house was demolished to make way for the railway viaduct.

Bath Road, Pen-y-Bryn
A short road which links Pen-y-Bryn to Erddig Road. The origin of the name is unknown.

Baugh, JP, Samuel Thomas *local politician*
Born in 1815, the son of Wrexham shoemaker Joseph Baugh and his wife Martha, Samuel Baugh was a devout Wesleyan Methodist. He was employed as a clerk to local solicitor Thomas Hughes (the father of J. Allington Hughes*) before becoming a partner to Thomas Jones in Baugh & Jones auctioneering business in Temple Row in *c*.1859. He was elected as a Liberal member of Wrexham Borough Council and served as Mayor in 1884. He was appointed a Justice of the Peace, a member of the Wrexham Board of Guardians and of the Rural Sanitary Authority. He was a director of the Gas, Water and Public Hall Companies and was a lay preacher for 60 years. He married twice (1) Elizabeth Edisbury of Bersham Hall in 1840 (died 1887); (2) Elizabeth, the widow of his brother-in-law, James Edisbury in 1886. He lived at Plas Penyddôl, Bersham and died on 31 July 1902 at 63 Cambridge Road, Hammersmith, London, while staying with his son Alfred, an architect. He is buried in Wrexham Cemetery.

Bayley, George *publisher*
George Bayley set up the *Wrexham Register** at 14 Hope Street. This monthly newspaper first appeared in August 1848 and ran for seventeen issues until December 1849 when it was replaced by a weekly newspaper, *The Wrexham Advertizer** which was also published at the same address. In 1857, the newspaper offices were moved to Bank Street.* (See also Newspapers)

George Bayley.

Beaconsfield, Holt Road
A large house built in 1881 by Edmund Mason on open fields which had previously been owned by the Merediths of Pentrebychan.* It stood on the left of Holt Road, roughly on the site of the present day Capel-y-Groes.* The only remaining evidence of this house is the stone retaining wall close to the roundabout junction with Bodhyfryd. In its latter years it became a residential home for unmarried mothers and girls with family problems and the name was changed to Llanelwy. It was demolished in 1979.

Beale, John *local politician*
Born in Longdon, Worcestershire in *c*.1810, John Beale moved to

The weekly market held on the Beast Market in 1970. The large building on the right is the former Salvation Army Citadel (originally the National School).

Wrexham in 1826 where he was employed by the pharmaceutical chemist, Walter Henry Johnson, in High Street. He set up his own pharmacy business in Yorke Street which he later moved to premises on the corner of High Street and Hope Street. He was elected a Tory councillor and was Mayor in 1870. He was appointed a Justice of the Peace in 1879 and was a member of the Wrexham Board of Guardians and a churchwarden. He presented a reading desk as a gift to the Parish Church. He was married three times. His first two wives were sisters, the daughters of Mr Wainwright of Sontley and his third wife was the daughter of W. H. Johnson, his former employer. John Beale resided at Egerton Lodge* and died on 16 January 1887. He is buried in the Ruthin Road Burial Ground.

Bear, The Beast Market
Located on the north-west side of the Beast Market at the entrance to Farndon Street,* it is recorded by this name in 1728. The name was changed to 'The Green Dragon' in 1742 and 'The Griffin' in 1774. It appears to have ceased to be a public house by the end of the 18th century.

Bear Court, High Street
An open area at the rear of the White Bear Inn (from which it undoubtedly took its name), the site of the present day Butchers' Market, which was accessed via a passage from Yorke Street. The 1872 survey suggests that there may have been two dwellings in this court.

Bear Inn, High Street
A half-timbered building which stood on the site now occupied by the Market Hall. This was also known as *The White Bear*.

Beast Market
The earliest reference to this area of Wrexham is in a deed dated in the third year of the reign of Edward IV (1463/4) when it was referred to in Latin as *Mercatus averriorum* (Trans. bird market). By the time of Norden's survey of 1620 it is called *Forum Bestiale* (Trans. beast market). In 1893, Wrexham Corporation paid an annual rent of £10 to the Crown for its use. Originally a large open area that extended well beyond its present day boundaries, it is today limited to the area bounded by St George's Crescent and Farndon Street and was the venue for the weekly Smithfield meat market. It was also the venue for other notable public events such as fairs and executions (see St Richard Gwynn). At the lower end of the Beast Market was a large pool which, if its Latin reference in Norden's survey of 1620 is accurate, was of stagnant water (i.e. was not supplied by either a stream or spring). In 1937, following complaints from local traders who thought the name unappealing, the Beast Market was officially re-named St George's Crescent.*

During the mid 19th century an annual Wild Beast Show was held in the Beast Market. In 1898, WBC bought the Beast Market from the Commissioners of Woods and Forests for £318. In latter years the Beast Market was the site of the regular Monday market (until that moved to Eagles' Meadow in 1975) before being converted for use as a car park. In November 1975, 25 traders with businesses in the Beast Market area took proceedings against WMBC claiming that moving the Monday market and the building of a road across the Beast Market itself infringed ancient charters. The matter was not settled until 1979 when Mr Justice Browne Wilkinson decided that, while the local authority owned the rights to markets elsewhere within the ancient town of Wrexham, the Beast Market was exempt. In 1632, Charles I had made a grant to William Collings and Edward Fenn of London of 'All that tenement *etc.*, And all those the Tolls and Tollage of the Town and *within* the Town of Wrexham with their rights members and appurtenances whatsoever.' The key word in this grant being 'within' and the High Court's decision confirmed that the Beast Market was actually *without* the town of Wrexham, *i.e.* outside of its ancient boundaries. By 1643, the rights *within* the town had been bought by Kenrick Edisbury of Erddig and from him eventually passed, via the Yorke's of Erddig, to WBC.

Travellers were permitted to set up their temporary camps just off the Beast Market. On the night of the 1881 census, there were eight itinerant families camping here, most of whom were recorded as being tinkers. Of interest are two very well-known surnames, Fossett and Chipperfield, which might both be connected to 20th century circus families.

The original line of the road along the south side of the Beast Market was disrupted by the construction of the Eagles' Meadow fly-over in the 1970s. It would appear that, due to some error in the original calculations, the fly-over was constructed so that it reached the Beast Market end several feet below the level of the existing roads. As a consequence, the south-eastern corner of the Beast Market had to be lowered by several feet and a new road was constructed from the fly-over to the Charles Street/Market Street junction. The remains of the original road can still be seen in front of the business premises in St George's Crescent and is now in regular use as a car park.

Beast Market Mission Chapel
Mentioned in 1881.

Beast Market Primitive Methodist Chapel
This chapel was built in 1857 and had 170 members by 1870. In

1879, it moved to a new chapel in Talbot Road.

Beast Market Street
This was the pre-19th century name for Charles Street.*

Beating the Bounds
An old custom practised during Rogation Week, it served as a means of asking for Divine blessing on the earth and also established the correct boundaries of the parish of Wrexham. Parish officials and members of the clergy would walk around the boundaries accompanied by parishioners and their children, the latter being given a symbolic 'thrashing' at certain points in order to impress upon them the parish limits.

Beech, James *minor poet*
James Beech (sometimes referred to as Thomas Beech), a wine merchant of Wrexham, was twice mentioned in connection with Dr Samuel Johnson. *Gentleman's Magazine* described him in June 1737, as a 'Man of learning, great humanity and easy fortune, and was much respected but was blameable for his notions of religion, which 'tis thought were the occasion of his despair. He had an eloquent taste of poetry and has published some pieces of poetry that have been admired'. In Boswell's *Life of Johnson* it is recorded that 'When Goldsmith produced some very absurd verses which had been publicly recited to an audience for money, Dr Johnson said… 'I can match this nonsense. There was a poem called *Eugenio* which came out some years ago, and concludes thus' and then the Doctor quoted, imperfectly, four-lines of *Eugenio*.' This was a poem published by Beech shortly before he committed suicide on 17 May 1737. Johnson also mentions it in a letter to Cove in April 1738.

> Say now, ye fluttering, poor assuming elves,
> Stark full of pride, of folly, of—yourselves,
> Say where's the wretch of all your impious crew
> Who dares confront his character to view?
> Behold Eugenio, view him o'er and o'er,
> Then sink into yourselves, and be no more.

Beech committed suicide by cutting his own throat and it was reported that his self-inflicted wound was so severe that his head was half taken off. According to A. N. Palmer,* Beech is supposed to have 'hanged' himself 'in a barn near Chester Road', the building survived well into the 19th century and was known as 'Beech's Barn', located in what is now the Nine Acre Field. Beech is believed to have resided on the west side of Hope Street in a house which he may have built himself. Palmer gives a more detailed description of some of his poetry on p.55 of *The History of the Town of Wrexham*.

Beech Gardens
The origin of this street name is uncertain but seems likely to have been a variation on 'Beechley' and was laid out in the grounds of Beechley House.*

Beechley House
A fine example of a substantial early 18th century town house. To the rear of the building is an extension which dates from about the 1830s. This house was originally known as 'Dursley's House' after a Mr Dursley who is on record as having lived on the site in 1715–17. The property was later owned or occupied by:

c.1720	Thomas Jones (during whose time the 'new house' is first mentioned in the rate books for 1726).
1742	Vacant
1747	George Ravenscroft
1749–82	William Jones (owner) of Wrexham Fechan, later of Plas Gwern* and High Sheriff of Denbighshire.*
1780	Maj Bell (tenant)
1781	Mr Hughes (tenant)
1784	George Warrington
1786	Mr Hodgkins
1793/4	Thomas Bennion (owner), attorney at law, partner of George Kenyon, who had an office in the property adjoining. He died in 1829.

The house passed to Thomas Bennion's daughters and, at the time of her death in 1866, was the property of Miss Mary Ann Bennion. Both the house and grounds were bought for £1,800 by a Mr Hawkins during the sale of part of the Beechley Estate in June 1894 (the tenant at the time was a Mr John Lewis). It had a kitchen garden on the opposite side of Bennion's Road, next to the Green Dragon Inn* (part of this now forms the pub car park and the remainder was absorbed in a road widening scheme). [DRO/DD/G/2838] The furniture and library of the house were sold at auction in April 1896. The house still stands facing down Salop Road at the junction with Salisbury Road and is a Grade II listed building. [DRO/DD/G/2847] (See also Beech Gardens, Beechley Road and Bennion's Road).

Beechley Road
Named after Beechley House.* The Beechley and Kingsland Estates were the property of Mrs Mary Ann Bennion who died in 1866. It was not until 1895 that the estate was sold off as a number of separate building lots. The sale particulars show that all the land between Beechley Road and Bryn-y-Cabanau Road had already been sub-divided and streets laid out and named *viz*: Beechley Road, Saxon Street,* Norman Road*, Stuart Street* and Tudor Street (Road).* Beechley Road was adopted by the Council in 1895 when a rateable value was set on the houses. There were, however, still eight houses being built here as late as 1901.

Beirne, John *local politician*
Born in Chester, c.1828, the son of Timothy and Jane (née Travers) O'Beirne, John Beirne came to Wrexham as a young man and established himself as one of the town's leading businessmen, being engaged as a chandler, maltster and brewer. He was best known as the proprietor of the Albion Brewery.* He was elected a member of WBC in c.1865. A Roman Catholic, he was organist at St Mary's Cathedral and became the first non-Protestant Mayor of Wrexham in 1876. Married to Jane Griffiths of Wellington Road, he had three sons and six daughters. He built Plas Derwen,* Sontley Road. He died on 25 December 1890, aged 63 years and was buried in Wrexham Cemetery.

Belgian Refugees
In November 1914, 102 wounded Belgian soldiers arrived in Wrexham and were admitted to Croesnewydd Military Hospital.* These were the first of a number of Belgian refugees who came to Wrexham during the First World War. A group of Belgian civilian refugees from Antwerp and Malines were

Belgian civilian refugees arrive at the General Station, 1914.

accommodated in the former Waifs and Strays Home in Chester Street (see the Old Registry*) until they returned to their homeland in April 1919. There are also reports that some refugees were accommodated at Wingett House in Chester Street. During the course of the war the people of the Wrexham area donated a total of £5,350-8s-2d to support the Belgian refugees.

Belgrave Road
This road appears to have been laid out by 1889 when land at its junction with Percy Road was sold for building to Job Mason [DRO/DD/G/2330]. Named after the hamlet of Belgrave near Chester where the Duke of Westminster's home, Eaton Hall, is located.

Bell Court, Mount Street
Shown on the 1833 survey, this was located behind the houses on the north side of Mount Street, near to the public house known as the White Lion which was demolished and not to be confused with Bell Court* in Hightown.

Bell Court, Hightown
Not to be confused with Bell Court,* Mount Street. This street was laid out in the 1980s on land that had previously been the property of C. T. Clark, proprietor of the King's Mills Garage. Built by the Wales and West Housing Association, all the streets were named after RWF who had been awarded the Victoria Cross.

Captain Edward William Derrington Bell was born in 1823/4 and was brought up at Kempsey, Worcestershire the son of Lt. General Edward Bell. Educated at Sandhurst School and the RMA Sandhurst he was commissioned into the 23rd Regiment of Foot (Royal Welch Fusiliers) in 1842. He served with distinction in the Crimean War and was present at the battles of the Alma and Inkerman and at the siege of Sebastopol. He was awarded the Victoria Cross in February 1857: 'Recommended for his gallantry, more particularly at the Battle of the Alma, where he was the first to seize upon and capture one of the enemy's guns which was limbered up and being carried off. He moreover, succeeded to the command of that gallant regiment which he brought out of action; all his senior officers having been killed or wounded.'

Bell later served in the Indian Mutiny where he received a Mention in Despatches. He died in 1879 and was buried in Kempsey Churchyard, Worcestershire.

Bellevue Farm
A farmhouse located on the north side of the junction of the present day Bellevue Road* (to which it gave its name) and Bradley Road.* The house appears in both the 1833 and the 1872 surveys and still survives as N°ˢ 25–27 Bellevue Road. The development of the land adjoining this farmhouse, as far as Watery Road,* was approved by WBC in 1897 and work began almost immediately on Jubilee Street (Road*). The land facing onto Watery Road had been built upon before the end of the century. [DRO/994]

Bellevue Road
This road appears in the 1872 survey when it extended from Pentre Felin to Ruthin Road (part of it was later absorbed into Bradley Road). At that time the only properties of any significance on the road were The Red House* (now Glantz's dental technicians on Bradley Road) and Bellevue Farm* (now N°ˢ 25–27 Bellevue Road, after which the road is named) and a malthouse (part of which survives as N° 28 Bellevue Road). The chapel schoolroom for the Welsh Presbyterian Church was built

The junction of Bellevue Road and Bradley Road, c.1935.

in 1896 (it was sold in 1923 to the Cambrian Lodge of the Independent Order of Oddfellows for £825, and is now occupied by the Bellevue Christian Fellowship) and most of the houses appeared at about the same time. The Pool Bank Dairy at the junction with Watery Road was built in 1906. The properties on the corner of Bellevue Road and Pentre Felin were the subject of a compulsory purchase order in 1942 as part of the Borough's slum clearance programme.

Bellot, Hugh *bishop*
Hugh Bellot, a Fellow of Jesus College, Cambridge, was the son of Thomas Bellot of Moreton, Cheshire and Burton, near Rossett. He was the rector of St Giles (1571), rector of Doddington (1572), vicar of Gresford and sinecure rector of Caerwys (1585), bishop of Bangor (1585–95) and bishop of Chester (1596). He died at his home, Tŷ Bellot (Plas Power), Bersham, in 1596.* His funeral took place in Chester but, in accordance with his wishes, he was interred at Wrexham. He assisted Bishop William Morgan with his masterly translation of the Bible into Welsh. His badly damaged effigy, showing him in the post-Reformation attire of a doctor of divinity of the University of Cambridge (a scarlet chimere robe with ermine tippet and ruff), can be seen below the Cunliffe Memorial Window in the chancel of the Parish Church.*

Belmont Road, Ruabon Road
The origin of this name (*Trans*. pretty mound) is uncertain but it seems likely that it is a reference to the 'Fairy Mount'* in the garden of the house of the same name in Fairy Road.

Benjamin Road, Smithfield
This street was laid out in the mid 1890s by developer Ebenezer Pike, and was named Benjamin Road in 1897 after Benjamin Piercy* of Marchwiel Hall, a pioneer of railways in Wales who had owned the Caia Estate until it was broken up into lots and sold for development after his death. Sale papers dating from April 1904 show that up to that time there had been no developments on the south side of the road. [DRO/DD/G/2870]

Bennion's Road (Lane), Beechley
Named after Thomas Bennion who lived at Beechley House.* It was still being referred to as Bennion's Lane in 1889. A building plot on the corner with Percy Road was sold in June 1889. [DRO/DD/G/2330] The road was widened during the late 1890s following the sale of the Beechley and Kingsland estates and the development of new streets in the area.

Beresford, Eric John *local politician*
Born at N° 5 Albert Street, Hightown on 13 August 1929, John Beresford was educated at Acton and Gwersyllt Primary Schools. His working life was spent in the railway industry where he was employed as a signalman. He was married to Molly (herself a

Wrexham councillor) and had two children. He was elected as the Labour candidate to represent the Grosvenor Ward on WBC in 1971 and in May 1977 was elected to represent Cefn on Clwyd County Council. He was Mayor of Wrexham in 1986–7, a year when the Maelor Hospital and Tŷ Mawr Country Park were opened. John Beresford lived at Nº 32 Spring Road, Rhosddu.

Bernard Road, Smithfield
This area of Wrexham was known as the Caia Estate until it was broken up into lots and sold for development after the death of Benjamin Piercy. Sale papers dating from April 1904 show that up to that time there had been no developments on part of the east side of the road. [DRO/DD/G/2870] Named after Edward B. Bernard, a trustee of the Benjamin Piercy Estate.

Berse Drelincourt, Broughton
This fine Queen Anne-style house was built in c.1715 by Pierre Drelincourt, Dean of Armagh, and his wife, Mary. Pierre (1644–1722) was the second son of Charles Drelincourt, a French Huguenot divine. His daughter, Anne, married Hugh, 3rd Viscount Primrose and, when he died in 1741, she became associated with Prince Charles Edward Stuart, the Young Pretender. She died in London in 1775 and is buried with her husband in Wrexham Parish Church.* The house then passed to the diocese of St Asaph and was used variously as a vicarage, school and orphanage until it was sold in the 1960s.

The house underwent considerable restoration during the 1990s and a Millennium Maze of beech trees was planted in the grounds. It is now Grade II listed.

Bersham Colliery
Bersham Colliery was sunk in 1867 by the Bersham Colliery Company (owned by the Barnes family of Liverpool) who sold out to the Broughton and Plas Power Company Ltd in 1910. The mine was originally designed for operation in conjunction with a brickworks. Nine men were killed in an explosion in 1880 and there is a memorial to them in Rhostyllen Church. In 1901, it employed 675 men underground with a further 94 surface workers. By 1914, the workforce had risen to 862 underground and 117 on the surface. Following the demands of the First World War and the depression in the coal industry which followed, this workforce fell to 550 underground and 140 on the surface by 1938. The outbreak of war in 1939 boosted production and the numbers rose to 600 underground and 200 on the surface, producing 300,000 tons annually. The mine was nationalised in 1947. In 1963 Bersham and Hafod* collieries were linked underground and, from 1968, the latter was operated from Bersham. The mine remained in production until 1986 when it was closed on the grounds that it was no longer economic. This was the last working mine in the Wrexham area of the coalfield.

Bersham Iron Works, Bersham
There is ample evidence of the existence of iron works in the Wrexham area in the 17th century, if not earlier. The first recorded operator of a furnace at Bersham is Charles Lloyd in 1725. In 1730, the furnace was owned by John Hawkins who died in 1739, after which time it was operated by his widow. In 1750, the owner was a Mr Harvey.

In 1754 the Bersham furnace was leased to Isaac Wilkinson of Cumbria. He was assisted in the business by his sons, John* and William. The business was not a success and Isaac ceased trading in 1761 and moved to Bristol. The following year, John and William Wilkinson took over the furnace and established the New Bersham Company which, using the newly-developed method of using coke to heat the furnace, quickly became a success. By the 1770s, John Wilkinson was producing the cylinders of steam engines for Messrs Boulton and Watt, using the patented cannon boring machine developed by the family at Bersham. John soon converted the works to steam power and was producing iron products for both the British and overseas markets. John and William soon fell out and William gathered together '… a great number of men in the town of Wrexham … and marched with them to the large iron works at Bersham, and there, using sledge hammer and other instruments, began to break up the expensive machinery. … John Wilkinson … collected a still greater number of men, and followed exactly his brother's example, so that in a very short time the famous Bersham Iron Works became a great wreck' (James Stockdale *Annales Carmoelenses*, 1872). The partnership at Bersham was then dissolved, the violence being perhaps, as A. N. Palmer* suggested, a means of resolving the ownership of the ironworks without recourse to law! At about this time, John Wilkinson bought the Brymbo Hall Estate, rich in deposits of both coal and iron ore and built a new iron works there. His original Brymbo furnace 'Old Nº 1' began production in 1796 and survives today as a Listed Building. It may be that Bersham Iron Works had become too small by the 1790s and that its location in a narrow valley meant that it was unsuitable for expansion. A description of the iron works at the time of the Wilkinson brothers was published after their deaths in the *Cambrian Traveller's Guide* of 1813: 'The mechanism employed is exceedingly ingenious, and his [John Wilkinson] works may be ranked among the first in the kingdom. Besides the smelting furnaces, there are several air-furnaces for re-melting the pig iron, and casting it into cylinders, water pipes, boilers, pots, pans of all sizes, cannon and ball, etc. The cannon are cast solid and bored like a wooden pipe. There are also forges for making the cast-iron malleable, and a newly erected foundry. At a short distance is a mine of lead ore which is smelted upon the spot.' After the departure of the Wilkinsons, the Bersham works were converted for agricultural and domestic use as part of the Plas Power* estate. The iron works site was taken over by Clwyd County Council in the 1980s and opened as an open-air museum.

Bersham Road
This is the road which leads from Victoria Road to the village of Bersham. Most of the houses at the Wrexham end (before the road crosses the railway bridge) were built during the late 19th century. The Wrexham historian, A. N. Palmer,* lived at Inglenook for many years and died there in 1915. He is commemorated by a small plaque on the house. Edward Hughes,* the local entrepreneur, politician and historian resided at Glyndwr. Gwylfa, Nº 4, on the corner of Alexandra Road* also belonged to A. N. Palmer. Later, both houses were used as Miss Stainton's School. The site which is now part of Yale College was previously allotments backing onto railway sidings.

Bersham Road English Presbyterian Church.
Established on the corner of Edward Street and Bersham Road by the Hill Street Congregation in 1892 and called Immanuel. A new schoolroom was opened in 1901. The chapel closed before the outbreak of the Second World War when the congregation joined Trinty Church* in King Street. The Religious Census of 1904 showed: Capacity 220; attendance (AM & PM) 193.

Bertie Road, Smithfield
This area of Wrexham was known as the Caia Estate until it was broken up into lots and sold for development after the death of Benjamin Piercy. Sale papers dating form April 1904 show that up to that time there had been no developments on the east and west sides of the road although the road itself had been laid out. The origin of the name is unrecorded. [DRO/DD/G/2870]

Berwyn View, Queen's Park
Laid out in the late 1940s as part of WBC's Queen's Park* housing development, on land that was previously part of the Cefn Park* estate. It takes its name from the Berwyn mountains, to the east of Bala.

Betsi Cadwaladr University Local Health Board
This local health board, the largest health organisation in Wales, was established on 1 October 2009 and employs around 18,000 staff and has a budget of around £1.1 billion. It has responsibility for three district general hospitals (Ysbyty Gwynedd in Bangor, Ysbyty Glan Clwyd in Bodelwyddan, and the Maelor Hospital in Wrexham), 22 acute and community hospitals, 90 health centres, clinics, community health team bases and mental health units. It also coordinates the work of 121 GP practices and the services provided by dentists, opticians and pharmacies.

It was named after Elizabeth Cadwaldr of Llanycil, Bala, who was born in the 1790s. She spent her early life in domestic service in Bala, Liverpool and London before sailing to the West Indies in the service of a sea captain in 1820. She later went into service with another sea captain's family, this time in Tasmania via the circuitous route of Cape Town, Sydney and Calcutta. She later travelled to India, Singapore, China, New Zealand, Peru, Argentina, Brazil and the Mediterranean before eventually returning to London where she remained for a number of years. Following the death of her employer she trained as a nurse at Guy's Hospital and in December 1854 embarked for service with the British Army in the Crimea War. Determined not to be confined to the hospital at Scutari in Turkey and having serious disagreements with Florence Nightingale over the latter's bureaucratic methods and deprivation of basic necessities to the wounded, she made her own way to Balaclava in the Crimea. There she set up her own facilities to care for the wounded and the sick and eventually Nightingale came to recognise the invaluable contribution she had made. Despite contracting both cholera and dysentry, Betsi Cadwaladr remained in the Crimea until 1856. She died in 1860.

Biddulph, Robert Myddelton *politician*
Born 1805 and educated at Eton and Oxford, the son of Robert Biddulph of Ledbury and Charlotte Myddelton of Chirk Castle. He served as a Justice of the Peace, Lord Lieutenant of Denbighshire and Colonel of the Denbighshire Militia. He represented the Denbigh Boroughs as Member of Parliament (Liberal) from 1830–32 and the county of Denbighshire between 1832–35 and 1852–68. He married Fanny, the daughter of William Mostyn-Owen of Woodhouse, Shropshire and was the father of Richard Myddelton of Chirk Castle. He died in 1872.

Bieston
One of the thirteen country townships of the old parish of Wrexham, Bieston had an area of just over 530 acres. It included much of the land now lying to the south of Holt Road, west of Sandy Lane/Erlas Lane and north of Llwyn Knottia Farm. Parc-y-Cwning* was located here. along with Ty'n Twll Farm* and Bryn Estyn Hall.*

Bieston Close, Borras Park
Built in the 1980s, this road takes its name from the township of Bieston.*

Birch Street, Salop Road
Laid out on land that was formerly part of the Beechley House* estate in the late 1890s, the first 11 houses were built on this street in c.1900. It was named after Mrs Lousie Done (née Birch), the wife of Alderman R. H. Done.*

Bird, JP, Norman Douglas *local politician*
Born in Wrexham, the son of Samuel Henry and Lucy Bird, Norman Bird was educated at Grove Park School and articled to Wrexham solicitor J. Hopley Pierce. He was admitted as a solicitor in 1905 and became a partner in 1909, eventually rising to be the senior partner in Hopley Pierce & Bird. During the First World War, he was commissioned into the Royal Garrison Artillery and served in France.

Elected to WBC in 1934, representing Erddig Ward, Norman Bird served as Mayor in 1945 and became an alderman in 1955. He was the chairman of the Estates Committee and the Memorial Hall Management Committee. He was a founder member of the Rotary Club of Wrexham* and its president in 1937, a governor of Grove Park School,* chairman of the Wrexham Civic Guild of Help, president of Wrexham Golf Club,* captain of the Wrexham Lawn Tennis Club and president of the Wrexham Operatic Society. As mayor, he was responsible for launching the appeal to raise funds for the building of the Memorial Hall.*

He married Edith Mary Austin Lee of Newport in 1926 and had two sons. They resided at Brooklands,* Salop Road, where he died on 7 November 1957.

Birkdale Road, Goulbourne
Named after the Royal Birkdale golf course, near Southport, this road was built during the 1980s on the land of Plas Goulbourne Farm.

Birkett Evans, JP, Evan *local politician*
Evan Birkett Evans was born at Victoria Terrace, Minera on 10 June 1856. He was educated at the local school and the British School* in Brook Street, Wrexham. He became an apprentice grocer and was employed by his brother Jabez at Bersham Post Office. By 1883, he was running his own shop at Oxford House, Nº 10 Talbot Road. He married Jane (Jennie) Price, the daughter of the late Hugh Price, on 8 April 1885 at the Hirdir Primitive Methodist Chapel. They were both Welsh speakers. Jane was a partner in Hugh Price & Company* and Evan joined her in the business. By January 1900, they were living at The Wrest,* Percy Road and by 1902 at The Gables, Percy Road. In 1914, at the time of their retirement, they moved to Derwen Lodge,* Ruabon Road and bought Shirley, Marine Drive, Rhyl, as a holiday home.

Evan was elected as an Independent member serving the South Ward of WBC and was mayor in 1903–05, the last unpaid holder of that office. He eventually lost his seat on the Council in 1910. and died on 9 July 1930 at his Rhyl house and was buried in Wrexham Cemetery.* His wife died on 5 December 1930.

In addition to his business and political interests, Evan Birkett Evans was also a lay preacher, a Borough Magistrate and a trustee of the Chester & Wrexham District Savings Bank. When General Booth, founder of the Salvation Army, visited Wrexham in August 1905, he stayed with Evan Birkett Evans. Jane Birkett Evans laid the foundation stone of the new Wrexham Library* on 1 January 1906.

Birmingham Hall
Following the sale of the nearby Birmingham Square* in about 1820, some of the traders who had been in business there moved to this new location on land which had previously been known as Plas-y-Kiln, sited between Lambpit Street and Henblas Street and gave it the name New Birmingham Square. In the 1833 survey, it bears the rather grandiose name of Royal Birmingham Square. By the time of the 1872 survey both the prefixes 'New' and 'Royal' appear to have been dropped. This square had a gallery and shops on all sides, with a central block comprising seventeen galleried shops. It was bought by the Borough Council in 1898 and was eventually re-developed as the Vegetable

Market,* the site of which is today occupied by the Bhs store* and Tŷ Henblas. At one time during the late 19th century, serious consideration was given to building a Guildhall on this site.

Birmingham Square
Built by hardware dealers from Birmingham for their use during the annual March Fair, this commercial square was sited on the garden of the Hen Blas, following that house's demolition in the early 19th century. It could be accessed from Queen Street via the Rainbow Passage. In April 1813, the Square formed part of the freehold estate of Mrs B. Jones which was sold at the Lion Inn. At that time it comprised 47 shops 'which are fully occupied during the Wrexham Fairs'. [DRO/DD/G/2827] Whether the building was sold at this time is unrecorded but by about 1820, the Birmingham and Yorkshire traders had combined to buy Birmingham Square which was renamed New Yorkshire Square or the New Union Hall. Originally comprising a number of shops with a gallery, it was eventually roofed over and became the Public Hall which opened in 1873.* It later became the site of the Hippodrome Cinema.*

Bishops of Menevia
1898–1921	Francis Mostyn*
1927–35	Francis John Vaughan*
1935–40	Michael Joseph M'Grath*
1940–46	Daniel Joseph Hannon*
1947–72	John Edward Petit, MA
1972–81	Langton D. Fox* (Auxilliary Bishop 1965–72)
1981–83	John Aloysius Ward* (later RC Archbishop of Wales 1983)
1983–87	Mgr. James Hannigan*
1987	Daniel Mullins

The residence of the bishop was originally the Presbytery attached to the cathedral then, for a short period, Ricmond House on Grosvenor Road and then, after 1926, Bishop's House (formerly Plas Tirion*), Sontley Road, Wrexham.

Bishops of Wrexham
1987–94	Monsignor James Hannigan*
1994	Edwin Regan*

The residence of the bishop is Bishop's House (formerly Plas Tirion*), Sontley Road, Wrexham.

Bithell's Farm
This small farm or tenement was located between Bryn Gruffydd and Box Lane, at the northern end of what is now the Borras Park* estate, and is described in the survey of the Acton Park* estate prepared for Sir Foster Cunliffe in 1786. 'Now part of the Bryn Griffith sheep walk & pt of Davies farm. Erw pen-y-coed [Trans. end of the wood acre], Erw Fynnon [Trans. well acre], Erw Ganol [Trans. middle acre], Bryn Griffith [Trans. Griffith's hill], Erw tan-y-bryn [Trans. acre below the hill]; Erw Las [Trans. green acre], Erw tû kefn-y-tû [Trans. acres behind the house], Peter's croft in Acton, Erw Lloci [penfolds acre], Erw Rhawl [possibly an error, it may have been Erw yr hewl –Trans. road acre], Cae Vallen [Trans. apple tree field], Cae Derwen [Trans. oak field], Ty'n-y-Fynnon oer [Trans. house in the cold well], Cae cefn-y-dwr [Trans. field behind the water], Tŷ Wad [Trans. Wad's house], Cae tan-y-Wern issa and ucha [Trans. field below the water meadow, higher and lower], Erw wrth kefn-y-tû [Trans. acre behind the house], Erw ganol [Trans. middle acre], Erw Fawr [Trans. big acre], Bryn-y-Gwlan [Trans. wool hill], Cae Jenkins [Trans. Jenkin's field], Derwyn-y-Boom [this should be Derwen-y-Bwn, Trans. bittern's oak], Coed Nessa [Trans. nearest wood], Cae Pwll [Trans. field in the hollow or pool field]. The rights to three seats in Wrexham Parish Church belonged to this property. [FRO/D/AH/24]

Black Boy, The
A public house, the location of which is unrecorded but is believed to have been in the area of High Street* and owned by Joseph Critchley in the late 17th century.

Black Horse, Yorke Street
Formerly the Hop Pole Inn,* it is shown in the 1833 survey as being located on the west side of Yorke Street. This was originally a town house belonging to the Puleston family of Hafod-y-Wern. In 1836, the landlord, John Davies, died and was buried in the Burial Ground,* Ruthin Road. Also called the Old Black Horse, these premises became the Royal Ship Inn* when the Black Horse moved to its present day location on the opposite side of the street.

Black Lion, Hope Street
The public house was first recorded under this name in 1775 and appears in both the 1833 and the 1872 surveys. It was the meeting place of the Senior Society,* a local friendly society. There was a serious fire at this public house on 18 July 1895 resulting in the death of D. Dobie.

Blackwell, Herbert Stewart *genealogist*
Born in Wrexham in 1918, Stewart Blackwell was educated at Victoria and Grove Park Schools and was first employed as a sorting clerk at Wrexham Post Office. After service in the RAF during the Second World War, he joined the civil service and became an Executive Officer in the Ministry of Works in the Midlands. After retiring in 1978, he returned to live in Belvedere Drive, Wrexham and became one of the founder members of the Clwyd Family History Society and its first chairman. He was a noted expert on family history and a regular lecturer on the subject. He died in 1995 and is buried in Gwersyllt Cemetery.

Blantern Way, Goulbourne
Developed in the 1980s on land that was part of Plas Goulbourne.* The street is named after Mr & Mrs Blantern, the last people to farm at Plas Goulbourne.

Blew, Horace Elford *footballer & local politician*
Born in Bersham in January 1878, Horace Blew was educated at Grove Park Boys School. He became a professional footballer with Wrexham in 1897 and is described in the *Who's Who of Welsh International Soccer Players* as 'probably the finest Wrexham footballer of the pre-1914 era. His fearless tackling, accurate distribution and utter dependability made him an automatic choice for Wales for several years'. He reverted to being an amateur player in 1902 and in 1905 became the tenant of the Raglan Arms* in Lampit Street.* He had many offers to join

*Horace Blew (standing second from the right) in the Wales soccer team, 1907. Second from the left is Billy Meredith.**

major English clubs but turned them all down, although he did play one match each for Manchester United and Manchester City. In 1910, Wrexham organised a benefit match for Blew which attracted the attention of the Football Association of Wales* who declared that it would be contrary to his amateur status. Blew immediately turned professional, received the financial benefit due to him, and then reverted to his amateur status. He was capped 22 times for Wales between 1899 and 1910.

Retiring from soccer, Blew worked for the Erddig estate agents and as a match reporter for the *Daily Dispatch* before becoming a publican in the town. He was elected a Wrexham Borough councillor in May 1919, became Mayor in 1923 and an alderman in February 1927. He resigned from the Council on health grounds in October 1948 and was made a freeman of the Borough 9 November 1948. He was chairman of the Financial Policy Committee from 1922-46 and of the Rating and Valuation Committee. He also served as a governor of Grove Park School and was a trustee of the Dame Dorothy Jeffreys and Elizabeth Roberts Charity.

In later years, he was the proprietor of the Bowling Green,* Pen-y-Bryn, a director of Wrexham Football Club* and chairman of the Wrexham branch of the Conservative Association. Horace Blew's wife, Mary Alice, died in 1951 and he died at Nº 6 Kerry Place, Wrexham, on 1 February 1957 and is buried in Wrexham Cemetery.* He was placed in the Welsh Sports Hall of Fame in 1999.

Blore, Hannah *world champion sailor*
Born in Wrexham in 1985, the second daughter of Nick and Isabel Blore, Hannah was educated at Victoria Junior School, Bryn Offa and Yale VI Form College, before becoming an undergraduate at the University of Plymouth where she read politics and economics, graduating in 2007 going on to complete her masters at Exeter in 2009. She now lives Plymouth and works in the Launceston for a major food manufacturer.

Hannah was introduced to sailing at the age of seven and became a member of Gresford Sailing Club*, sailing and competing at the Flash. In 1994, she was the youngest competitor in the Mirror Class European Championships (when she sailed with her father) and won the Super Crew Cup. She won her first competition, at the age of nine, sailing in an Optimist dinghy.

She was a member of both the Welsh and the Great Britain junior and youth sailing squads and competed throughout the UK and Europe. In 2004 she began competing in the Olympic women's single-handed class, finishing third in the UK ranking.

In 2002, she came second in the UK National Byte Class Championships and first in 2001 and 2002 in the Inland Championships. In 2005, she won five of the six races to become national champion. That year, at the Byte Class World Championships at Lake Garda in Italy, despite a difficult start, she became the Women's World Champion and won the title again in 2008 when the World Championships were held at Weymouth.

Blossoms Hotel, Charles Street
Palmer* found evidence of a Thomas Stringer 'innkeeper and carpenter' residing at this address in 1732. The earliest reference to the name 'Blossoms' is 1780. This public house was located at the rear of the Wynnstay Arms Hotel* into which it was incorporated in the 1920s. In 1881, the licensee was named Richards. The building was demolished at the time of the Wynnstay Hotel's redevelopment. It was shown in both the 1833 and the 1872 surveys.

Blue Bell, Town Hill
Located on the north side of Town Hill where the railway bridge later stood, the Blue Bell is recorded in about 1791. After the success of the British Army against Napoleon, the name was changed to the Waterloo Tavern sometime after 1815. By the early 1820s, the premises appear to have been converted into a shop. It was demolished in the 1890s. [DRO/964]

Blue Books
The Report on the State of Education in Wales was published in 1847 and, because of the damning nature of its reports on teaching in Wales, particularly its unsympathetic treatment of the Welsh language, became known as *Brad y Llyfrau Gleision* (*Trans.* the Treason of the Blue Books). The reports on the various schools in Wrexham are included with the entry for each establishment but it may be of interest to include here the inspectors overall comments on education in Wrexham.

> There are many valuable endowments for the education and relief of the poor in the parish of Wrexham. The Commission for inquiring respecting charities having discovered that a considerable portion of the funds were misapplied, the charities in question were certified to the Attorney-General, in consequence of which a new distribution of the rents and profits of the several estates has been directed, in accordance with a scheme set forth for that purpose by one of the masters of the Court of Chancery.
>
> According to this scheme eight-twentieths of the income of the charities are to be applied for the maintenance of a school, under the charge of a master and mistress, in the district of Brymbo, and six-twentieths for the maintenance of a similar school in the district of Minera. The children in each school are to be taught English grammar, reading, writing, spelling, and arithmetic, and such other things as the trustees shall direct. The payments of the children are to be fixed by the trustees. The children of dissenting parents are to be at liberty (if required) to accompany their parents to a place of worship on Sunday.
>
> The trustees are to have power to lay out in the purchase of school sites, and in the erection of school-houses and master's and mistress's residences, any sum of money not exceeding £800; the same to be built in suitable places in the districts of Brymbo and Minera.
>
> This scheme is dated July, 1845, and the order, made in the cause of further directions, is dated the same month. But at the time of my visit, January, 1847, no steps had been taken in pursuance of the directions. The schools at Brymbo were held in two miserable cottages, inadequate to contain half the children who were members, while in the distant and populous district of Minera no school was provided for the poor.

The schools covered by this report were: Wrexham Grammar School,* Dame Dorothy Jeffreys Free School,* British School (Brook Street),* British School (Chester Street),* Wesleyan Day School,* Workhouse School,* Wrexham Infant School.* [DRO/NTD/761]

Blue Triangle Club
See Young Women's Christian Association

Bluebell Lane, Pandy
Believed to have taken its name from the Bluebell Farm (later Bluebell public house) that once stood close to the A483 roundabout. The local mining historian Ithel Kelly (the last manager of Gresford Colliery) lived at Transvaal House (which was built by a local miner named Jones who had worked for some years in the coal and gold mines of the Transvaal). The memorial to the Gresford Disaster* of 1934 stands on the left

hand side of the road close to the Gresford roundabout. The eastern end of the lane was truncated by the building of the A483 Wrexham bypass (1970s) and the Gresford roundabout (1980s).

Bodhyfryd
This road was laid out in the mid 1970s as part of Wrexham's inner ring road, linking Powell Road* to Holt Road.* It cut across Park Avenue* and the fields which had formerly been used by Grove Park Schools. The name is also used for the adjacent area of civic buildings (including the Divisional Police Headquarters,* the Magistrates Courts,* the Crown Buildings* and Water World*) and is taken from the Bodhyfryd House* which was located nearby.

Bodhyfryd House
Referred to by Palmer in 1893 as 'the house which in recent years has been called 'Bodhyfryd', this property once belonged to the Dymock family of Little Acton and was occupied by a William Dymock until his death in 1764 when he was High Sheriff of Denbighshire. Elizabeth, his daughter and heir, married Robert Wynne Esq of Garthewin in 1766 who had occupied the house from 1755–9. From 1801–4, it was leased to Capt Thomas Lee, an 'African trader' (possibly a slave ship captain) after whom it was leased to Joseph Cooper a timber merchant, coach builder and property owner. He died in 1856 and is buried in Gresford. The property passed to his heirs who retained the lease at the end of the 19th century. It is likely that Cooper's Lane (now Park Avenue*) took its name from Joseph Cooper as he owned all the fields to the east of Bodhyfryd as well as two others near the area of the present day Maes-y-Dre housing estate on the east side of Cooper's Lane. [FRO/D/AH/15]

The house was hidden from the street behind dense shrubs and railings but these were eventually removed to widen the street and revealed an attractive 18th century property. By the 1930s the house and the surrounding land was the property of WBC and was let out to various tenants. For many years it housed the Surveyor's Department of WBC. During the Second

Bodhyfryd House, once one of the most important houses in the town, gave its name to the area of civic buildings between Chester Street, Powell Road and Holt Street.

World War, Bodhyfryd was taken over by the Women's Voluntary Service as a canteen for members of the armed forces. A large hut erected in the grounds was a venue for local dances for a number of years during and after the Second World War. The house was demolished in the early 1960s to make way from the present Crown Buildings office block.

Bodlondeb, Grove Road
(*Trans.* satisfaction). Located near the junction with Rhosddu Road, this substantial villa (built for the printer Thomas Painter) was the first house to be built in Grove Road. By 1881, the house was occupied by William Overton.* It was located next door to Holm Oak (Rhosddu Road) and opposite Abbotsfield. The name of the house was later changed to Carlton Grange and it was divided into flats before eventually being demolished and replaced by a block of flats bearing the same name. In 1916 it was the home of William Aston* and later, his son Sydney.

Bonc, The Poplar Road
The Bonc (*Trans.* the mound) was a courtyard, lined on two sides by about six houses, located on Poplar Road, close to the junction with Erddig Road. There was a dame school here for 40 years in the mid 19th century, run by Mrs John Griffiths, the wife of Wrexham's last flaxdresser and parish bellman. Mrs Griffiths died in 1860. Charles Dodd was educated at this school (see Dodd Family).

The Bonc, Poplar Road.

Bonc, The Watery Lane
See Butler Square.

Bonsall, William *colliery manager*
William Bonsall was appointed assistant manager at Gresford Colliery in 1914, having previously worked at Hinckley in Leicestershire. In 1917, he succeeded to the position of Colliery Manager, a post which he held until the Gresford Disaster* of 1934. There can be little doubt that, despite his experience, Bonsall was not a competent manager. He was not the right personality to stand up to the dominant characters who controlled the company, most notably Henry Dyke Dennis.* At the Board of Trade Enquiry, the lawyers acting against the management painted a picture of a man who was a 'ruthless, cynical, slave-driving villain' and implied that his action/inaction was the main reason for the disaster. It seems, however, that the truth was closer to being that he was a 'weak man, driven beyond his capabilities, losing control of events, and ultimately paying the penalty, partly of his own incompetence, and partly of the intractable circumstances in which he was obliged to operate'. [*Gresford: The Anatomy of a Disaster*, Stanley Williamson] During the course of the enquiry, Bonsall was asked nearly 4,000 questions and gave evidence for 20 hours. Bonsall was removed from the position of manager in 1935.

Bont Bren, Tuttle Street
(*Trans.* the wooden bridge) – probably the predecessor of the

bridge in Tuttle Street, it is mentioned in Norden's survey of 1620. See the illustration of Willow House.

Border Breweries
Formed on 27 June 1931 by the amalgamation of Island Green,* F. W. Soames* and Dorsett Owen breweries. The first chairman was Francis Huntley (who served until 1944) and the company traded throughout north Wales and the west Midlands using the slogan 'The Wine of Wales'. In 1984, Border Breweries was taken over by Marston's Brewery of Burton-on-Trent and all brewing operations in Wrexham ceased shortly afterwards. In 1998 Marston's Brewery was in turn taken over by Wolverhampton & Dudley Breweries. The company had a large bottling store on Holt Road which was demolished in May 2001 to make way for the Border Retail Park (the name of which preserves the name of the brewery). See also Soames' Brewery and Nag's Head Brewery)

Border Press, Egerton Street
Located behind the Lloyds Bank building and opposite the former GPO building this business was sold in March 1921. [DRO/DD/G/2897]

Borras Farm
Located mainly between Barker's Lane,* the Llan-y-Pwll link road and the extension of Borras Road leading towards Borras Head. The house was built in the early 18th century for Robert Jeffreys, the son of Dame Dorothy Jeffreys* and great nephew of Judge Jeffreys,* (a date stone above the porch gives the date 1707). When Robert died in 1714 the property passed to his sister Elizabeth Robinson of Gwersyllt and so the last property in the Wrexham area to belong to the Jeffreys family passed into other hands. It was bought by Ellis Yonge of Bryn Iorkin in 1780 and was later sold to Sir Foster Cunliffe of Acton Park.*

The farm was detailed in the survey of the Acton Park* estate, produced in 1786. The field names were: *in Borras Riffrey township* – Pwll-y-Warren [*Trans.* warren pool], Ga ? Las [*Trans.* ? green], Twll-y-dur [*Trans.* iron hole], Twll yr ucha [*Trans.* highest hole], Twll buchan or nessa [*trans.* little or nearest hole], Cae nessa yr tû [*Trans.* field nearest to the house], Cae vechan [*Trans.* small field] or Crabtree Field, Cae Llyn buchan [*Trans.* small lake field], Cae Llyn Ganol [*Trans.* middle lake field], Cae Llyn Mawr [*Trans.* big lake field], Cae Pwll [*Trans.* pool field], Cae Bedwen [*Trans.* birch field]. Cae Glas [*Trans.* green field], Cae Derwyn [*Trans.* oak field], Cae Skybor [*Trans.* barn field], Cae Gwyn [*Trans.* Gwyn's field or white field], Morass, Cae kefn

Borras Farm, 1975, pre modernisation. Note the Jeffreys date stone above the door arch.

The arms of Robert Jeffreys and his wife, Mary Griffiths at Borras Farm.

tû [*Trans.* field behind the house]; *in Acton township* – Cae fynnon [*Trans.* well field], Bryn Ithell [*Trans.* Ithell's hill], Berth gelart [*Trans.* Gelert's hedge]. Much of the timber on this farm was felled after 1803 to pay for the purchase of Maes Daffy Farm in Gresford by Sir Foster. In 1881 the main part of the farm, 280 acres, was tenanted to Thomas Meredith who employed two labourers and two boys.

Following the death of Sir Foster H. E. Cunliffe in 1917 the farm passed to the tenants, the Griffiths family, who later sold it to the McAlpines. The original house has survived, but in a much inferior condition, with many of its finest features removed. [FRO/D/AH/24]

Borras Hall, c.1900.

Borras Hall, Borras Hall Lane
Griffri ap Cadwgan, Lord of Borras and Erlas, built Plas-ym-Mwras (Borras Hall) in about 1200. He was succeeded by his son Llywelyn and grandson Madog (whose effigy can be seen in Gresford Church). In 1988, local resident Charles Cater discovered a red wax seal buried outside the house which displayed a sun or star of eight rays and which is believed to have been Madog's seal. The family inter-married with other local landowning families and by 1500 had assumed the surname 'Burras'. In 1580, William Burras sold the estate to Owen Brereton, High Sheriff of Denbighshire, who lived at the Hall until his death in 1595. The house remained in the Brereton family until Leonora Brereton (née Robinson) sold the estate (including Borras Lodge, Pwll Warren and Llyn Mawr) in 1770 to John Twigge of Derbyshire for the enormous sum of £40,000. Interestingly, Twigge just managed to out-bid Sir Robert

41

Cunliffe, Bt, of Saighton (the father of Sir Foster Cunliffe, Bt, of Acton Park*) by £1,000. Twigge appears to have had some financial difficulties and sold the estate off piecemeal. In 1789, he sold Borras Hall and the land lying immediately around it, to Lord Kenyon for £24,000. At this time, one wing of the house was demolished and the hall became a farmhouse which was let to tenant farmers. By the mid-19th century, the tenants were the Parry family (1881 – Robert Thomas Parry was farming 167 acres and employing three men and three boys) who rented the property until c.1956 when it was sold to them by the Gredington Estate. The farm lost a substantial part of its land at the beginning of the Second World War when it was requisitioned by the Air Ministry as part of the future RAF Wrexham.* In 1999, the present owners, Mr & Mrs William John Parry, began an extensive programme of restoration. The property was surveyed by the Royal Commission on Historic Buildings in Wales and their report clearly indicates the importance of the house.

> Borras Hall … is one of the most significant late mediæval houses to have come to light in recent years. [It] belongs to a small group of of ambitious gentry hall houses in north-east Wales that were distinguished by box framing (rather than cruck framed), large halls and projecting wings. Indeed, the west wing at Borras Hall appears to be the largest surviving timber solar wing in Wales. The surviving timber work at Borras is lavish but rather plain, although traces of early painting in the solar Wing indicate that the house may have been elaborately decorated. Borras Hall can now be identified with Plas ym Mwras, so named in documentary sources. The hall belonged to the Brereton family which was celebrated for its hospitality in numerous sixteenth-century Welsh poems.

The restoration work has now been completed and this superb house has been saved for the future.

Borras Head Farm
This belonged to the Puleston (later Cooke) family in 1722 and was sold in 1803 to Lord Kenyon of Gredington for £7,050. It appears on the 1767 Gwysaney estate map [FRO/D/GW/661]. In 1834, it was a farm of 154 acres and was tenanted by the Roberts family for several generations. In 1881, when it comprised 160 acres, it was tenanted by John Milligan (who had a 14-year lease commencing in 1871) who employed six men and one boy.

Borras Higher Farm
Sometimes referred to as Borras Head Farm, this is located on the left of the road leading from the Llan-y-Pwll link road towards Borras Head. This property was formed by the joining together of four small-holdings and totalled 158 acres in 1839. Between 1721 and 1802 (and perhaps earlier) it was the home of the Roberts family (who also lived at Borras Head) and was part of the Puleston/Cooke estate until bought in 1802 by Sir Foster Cunliffe of Acton Park* for £6,600 from Bryan Cooke of Gwysaney. [FRO/D/GW/272, 283 & 535] It appears on the 1767 Gwysaney estate map [FRO/D/GW/661] when it had an area of over 167 acres and had an annual rental value of £300. In order to pay for it, Sir Foster sold his estates at Saighton and Pickhill (see also Cunliffe Family). The 1786 survey of the Acton Park estate includes details of all the field names: Further Cae Eithen (*Trans.* gorse field), Long Cae Eithen, Cae Eithen, Nearer Cae Eithen, Pant-y-Gwali bychan (*Trans.* little fenced hollow), Pant-y-Gwali Mawr (*Trans.* large fenced hollow), Cae Newydd (*Trans.* new field), Tyr-y-Wheat (*Trans.* wheat land), Cae Pant (*Trans.* hollow field), Smithy Field, Brickiln Field, Coppice, Barn Field, Pit Field, Pant Rûg Field (*Trans.* hollow of the barrow field), Pant Rûg Wood, Weans, Meadow, Hesketh's Tenement, George's Tenement, Coed-y-Vicar Tenement (*Trans.* vicar's wood tenement), Bryn Coch (*Trans.* red hill), Cae dû (*Trans.* black field), Puleston's Meadow. The last two were to the east of Borras Road, opposite Borras House. In later years, the farm became known as Walnut Tree Farm and, after the dispersal of the Acton Park* estate in the 1920s, was owned by Denbighshire County Council and McAlpines who bought the former RAF Wrexham* airfield. In recent years, it has been divided into two properties. Just opposite the farm gate is the only surviving machine-gun pill-box which formed part of the defences of RAF Wrexham.

Borras House
Also originally called Borras Head* and sometimes New House Farm, this was originally two farms that had been joined together and was owned by Samuel Sidebotham in 1742. It does not appear on a 1767 map of the Gwysaney estate [FRO/D/GW/661] because it was still in the possession of Mr Sidebottom. Pre 1826 it was the property of William Johnson Edensor and by 1857 belonged to a Dr Marsh. By the 1890s, it was part of the Acton Park* estate.

Borras Lodge
This small farm was part of the Borras Hall* estate until it was sold off by John Twigge in the late 18th century. Palmer records that a family named Matthews lived here between 1738 and 1805, farming 234 acres (they were related to William Edensor of Borras House*). In later years, it was tenanted by the Parry family (who were also tenants of Borras Hall*). Most of the farm was requisitioned by the Air Ministry for the building of RAF Wrexham* and the house and buildings (which stood on the right of the road between the Llan-y-Pwll Link Road and the Royal Observer Corps Headquarters) were demolished.

Borras Nursery, Jeffreys Road
In the early 1870s, a plant nursery was established in Cae Aderyn-y-Bwn (*Trans.* bittern's field), on the land which was sited between the present day Warrenwood Road,* Norfolk Road,* Borras Park Road* and Jeffreys Road,* which was part of the Acton Park* estate. When the field was being prepared, a small hoard of twelve Bronze Age implements was discovered in what is now the garden of Nº 15 Jeffreys Road. The hoard consisted of seven bronze palstaves, each about 6' long. Six of these were cast in the same mould but the seventh, which was broken, was of a different design; four bronze celts, 6" long (one of which was broken); one small dagger, about 3" long. The finds were retained by Sir Robert A. Cunliffe (see Cunliffe Family) and

Borras Head Farm, 1993.

then passed to his son, Sir Foster E. E. Cunliffe, then to Sir Neville Cunliffe who presented them to the National Museum of Wales in 1918.

Borras Park
A large private housing estate developed during the 1960s and 1970s on land that had once been part of the Acton Park* estate. The land, located between Jeffreys Road, Box Lane, Barker's Lane, the Acton–Llan-y-Pwll Link Road and Borras Park Road, was sold by Sir Neville Cunliffe in 1920. It passed through various owners until 1958 when the area to the south and east of Farm Side, which had been the property of former Mayor of Wrexham William Clarke,* was sold to developers Spinks & Denning of Colliers Wood, London who developed all the roads between there and Borras Park Road. The development was originally called Bryn Gryffydd Heights. The north-western section of the estate, originally known as the Park View Estate (between Barkers Lane, Jeffreys Road and Norfolk Road), also the property of William Clarke, comprised 125 houses priced at £2,500 and upwards, developed by E.G.M. Cape of Canada with G. Raymond Jones, Anderson & Associates of Wrexham as consultant architects. The showhouse was opened by local MP James Idwal Jones* in August 1965. During the Second World War much of this area was requisitioned and used by the RAF as a site for the residential camp for RAF Wrexham.* Later, at the end of hostilities, the Bryn Gryffydd area was utilised as a tank depot.

Borras Park Evangelical Church, Jeffreys Road
Plans to build a new evangelical church to serve the new Borras Park area of Wrexham were announced in November 1971. Previously, the congregation had met in the Little Acton Senior Citizens Centre. The first minister was the Revd Glyndŵr Jenkins.

Borras Park Road
Originally part of Borras Road, this road changed its name following the development of the Borras Park housing estates during the 1960s. The name comes from Parc-y-Cwning,* an ancient rabbit warren which was located in the area. Nº 19 Borras Park Road, a building on the north-west side of the road, opposite the present day junction with Caernarvon Road, is believed to have served as a school for the children of the area before the building of Rhosnesni School.* During the Second World War, this road and the surrounding fields became a restricted area and was the main approach to RAF Wrexham.* There was a small guardhouse and barrier sited close to the junction with Jeffreys Road. The site of Borras Park School was occupied by RAF accommodation hutments. As recently as the late 1950s, the only property located on this road was Cherry Hill.* Most of the other properties along the road were built in the late 1950s and 1960s. See also Broad Oak Farm. [FRO/D/AH/24]

Borras Park Schools
The school opened in 1971 to serve the expanding area of Borras Park and absorbed the former Rhosnesni Church school. Initially a combined infant and junior school and a new building to accommodate the infant school was opened in 1975 when the two schools were separated.
Headteachers:
   Primary School
   1971   Meirion Wyn Thomas
   Juniors
   1975   Meirion Wyn Thomas
   1982   Glyn Owen Jones
   2001   Brendan McDonald
   Infants
   1975   Mrs Doreen Lee
   1981   Miss Susan Jones

The current (2010) headteacher of the infants school is Mrs S. Dickson and there were 178 pupils on the roll with a further 244 in the junior school.

Borras Road
This was one of the ancient roads leading from Wrexham to the townships of Burras Hovah* and Burras Riffri.* Until the area was developed in the mid 20th century, the stretch of the road from Holt Road to Rhosnesni Lane was known as Back Lane and had a sharp dog-leg bend near what is now the side gate to Rhosnesni High School.* This bend was straightened out in the early 1960s. On a site which is now just inside the gate of Rhosnesni High School there used to stand two cottages, known as Bleak Cottages, the foundations of which would appear whenever the pupils dug over what was once the school garden area. The road from Rhosnesni Lane to Dean Road* was known as School Lane (it led to the Rhosnesni Primary School*).

The land to the west of Borras Road, part of the present day soccer fields and the site of St John's Church was known as Morgan's Tenement in the 18th century. [FRO/D/AH/24] The land on the west of Borras Road, between Camberley Drive and Rhosnesni Lane was part of Park Farm* and was sold to WBC by Philip Clarke. In 1955–6, this land was sold to Thomas Warrington & Sons who built the detached houses on the site (priced at £2,950).

Bottle Street
See Guildhall Street.

Borough of Wrexham
The Royal Charter creating the Municipal Borough of Wrexham was granted on 13 May 1857 and took effect from 23 September 1857. The new borough included the whole of the townships of Wrexham Regis* and Wrexham Abbot* as well as a small part of Esclusham Below.* Elections were to be held for the election of 12 town councillors, 4 aldermen and these were then to elect a mayor from within their number. All ratepayers were given a vote in the municipal elections. The list of eligible voters (burgesses) was produced on 15 September and contained 646 names of whom only 206 could stand for election having the necessary £15 rating valuation qualification. Polling stations were opened on 5 November at the Town Hall* and in the National School* on the Beast Market. There were fifty-two candidates and each burgess could vote for twelve councillors (with the sheet clearly showing the voter's name and address). The candidates were categorised as either White (Liberal) or Red (Tory) and had their headquarters at the Lion Hotel in High Street and the Wynnstay Arms Hotel respectively. The successful candidates at the election were:

Thomas Edgworth*	(371)	White
John Bury*	(324)	White
Daniel Jones	(321)	White
George Bayley*	(304)	White
Edward Griffiths	(302)	White
Charles Hughes*	(291)	White
John Clarke*	(286)	Red
Thomas Painter*	(268)	Red
William Rowland*	(267)	Red
Joseph Clarke*	(265)	Red
Meredith Jones*	(260)	White
Thomas Rogers	(233)	White

At the first meeting of the new Council on 9 November 1857 at the Music Hall* in Henblas Street, Thomas Edgworth was appointed Mayor of Wrexham and John Clarke, Thomas Painter, William Rowland and Dr Edward Williams (not a councillor) were appointed aldermen. This left three vacancies for councillors and in the ensuing by-election John Taylor, John Parry Hughes and Thomas Rowland* were elected. The next meeting took place on 27 November and it was resolved to rent part of Bryn-y-Ffynnon House* as a Council Chamber and the first meeting was held there on 16 December, 1857. Solicitor John James* was appointed as the first Town Clerk (part-time), solicitor Edwin Wyatt was Borough Treasurer and architect Michael Gummow* was Borough Surveyor.

On 1 April 1935, the boundaries of the Borough of Wrexham were extended to incorporate Acton, Stansty and parts of the parishes of Gwersyllt, Broughton and Bersham, an area of 1,611 acres with an additional 6,000 residents. By this time, the Council was made up of 36 members. The Borough Council moved from Bryn-y-Ffynnon House to the old Grammar School* building on Chester Street which was bought in 1883 for £2,500 (which was designated The Guildhall) and to the present Guildhall* on Llwyn Isaf* in 1961.

WBC was amalgamated with WRDC* in 1974 to become WMBC.*

Boundary Street, Rhosddu
The location of this street is uncertain but it may have been an alternative name for either Spring Road or Cunliffe Street in Rhosddu. In 1881, a Miss Edmunds is recorded as running a private school there.

Bowman, FLS, FGS, John Eddowes *entrepreneur & scientist*
Born in Nantwich, Cheshire on 30 October 1785, John Bowman was a well-known amateur botanist and scientist. He became a partner with Samuel Kenrick in Kenrick & Bowman's Bank* in Hope Street.* He died in Manchester on 4 December 1841 and there is a memorial to him in the Upper Brook Street Free Church. He was the father of Sir William Bowman, Bt, MD, LLD, a distinguished London physician and Professor John Eddowes Bowman who held the chair of chemistry at King's College, London.

Bowen, Keith *artist & writer*
Keith Bowen was born in Wrexham in 1950 and was brought up at 9 Gardd Estyn, Garden Village. He was educated at Acton Park School and Grove Park School, followed by a pre-diploma course in art at the Denbighshire Technical College before studying graphics at the Manchester Polytechnic. In 1982 and 1986 he won awards from the National Portrait Gallery. In 1983 he won the joint First Prize at the National Eisteddfod of Wales and in 1986 the First Prize.

In 1988, he was the designer of the Royal Mail stamps for the 400th anniversary of the Welsh Bible and in 1992 designed the *Wintertime* stamps. In 1991 he published his first book *Snowdon Shepherd* which became an instant bestseller and won the Frank Herring Award at the Pastel Society Exhibition in London. His second book *Snowy* appeared in 1993 and won the Federation of Children's Book Groups Picture Book of the Year award. By this

One of Keith Bowen's Wintertime stamps.

Keith Bowen's William Morgan stamp.

time, Keith was spending a year living with the Amish community in the United States which resulted in a touring exhibition and a book *Amongst the Amish*. He used to live in Minera but, in the mid 1990s, moved to live in Lanarkshire, Scotland. He was made an honorary fellow of the NEWI and a member of the Royal Cambrian Academy.

Bowen's Court, Beast Market
Located off the Beast Market.

Bowling Green, Pen-y-Bryn
One of Wrexham's oldest surviving licensed premises, the Bowling Green, sited between Pen-y-Bryn and Erddig Road is shown on the 1802 Wynnstay Survey of the Manor of Wrexham Abbot. [DRO/DD/WY/8352] and in the 1833 and 1872 surveys with a bowling green in the rear extending as far as Erddig Road. The present building was constructed in the late 19th century.

Box Lane, Acton
This was originally the main route from Wrexham to Gresford and then Chester. Part of the road was re-routed by Sir Foster Cunliffe when he reorganised Acton Park* in the early 19th century. Previous to this time, the original Chester Road had run from The Plough at Gresford (where it is still called the Old Wrexham Road), past the Flash and the Pant-yr-Ochain,* on along what is now called Box Lane* and via the present Chester Road into Chester Street. The exact route taken by the road in the vicinity of Acton Park is unrecorded but there are a number of clues which lead to an obvious and logical conclusion.

Today, Box Lane runs straight from the junction with Smithy Lane, up the hill then, close to the junction with Little Acton Gardens, turns sharply right, a turning for which there is neither a geographical nor a logical reason. If one traces an almost straight route from immediately before this bend on towards Wrexham town centre you will link up with Chester Road somewhere close to the junction with Rhosnesni Lane.

The illustration of Acton Hall in one of the 'extra illustrated' editions of Pennant's *Tours in Wales* [see Acton Park] held by the National Library of Wales shows the front of the house viewed from a gate located at the end of the drive. Careful examination of this picture leads one to the conclusion that the gate was located almost exactly on the south boundary fence of the present day Acton Park School. When he painted this picture, the artist was undoubtedly standing on the old Chester Road from where the house was clearly visible. Today, if one stands by the gate from Acton Park into Acton Park School there are a number of tall trees nearby which would certainly have been standing in 1800 and could very possibly have formed the edge of the original route. Also, close to the junction of the path at the rear of Acton School and Acton Gardens there are several lengths of sandstone wall which were probably part of the original Chester Road boundary wall of Acton Park. Sir Foster, having recently bought Acton Park, was known to be concerned about the privacy of his home and in 1801 bought a small area of land 'at the south-west corner of Little Acton, between the two roads from Chester to Wrexham'. This land was on the north side of 'Box Lane' and the east side of Chester Road. Having bought it, Sir Foster could then reposition the road along its northern edge, away from the sight of his house. This resulted in the addition of the sharp bend in Box Lane and the acute angle at which it joins Chester Road. A careful study of the 'Map of Wrexham Regis and Wrexham Abbot in A.D. 1844' published in A. N. Palmer's *History of the Town of Wrexham* shows a narrow road departing from the line of Chester Road, north of the junction with Rhosnesni Lane, almost exactly at the spot where there is a bend in the otherwise straight route. This may have been the south-western end of the vanished section of the old Chester Road or it could be evidence of the realignment of the 'new' Chester Road (see map).

Many of the houses on the north-west side of Box Lane were built between the two world wars – those opposite the Acton School field by H. V. Parker, developer of the Croes Eneurys Estate.* The houses between Jeffreys Road and Acton Gardens were built on land released by WBC during the late 1960s and early 1970s.

At the beginning of the 19th century the main turnpike road was the 'new' Chester Road but it seems likely that a barrier was placed across Box Lane to prevent travellers circumventing the toll gate at Acton Smithy. This barrier would not have justified the erection of a toll-keeper's cottage but may well have had a small 'sentry-box' style structure for the attendant to sit in. If this were the case, it would explain the introduction at this time of the term 'Box Lane'. The road has also been known as Little Acton Lane after Little Acton Farm* which stood nearby.

Brades' Court, Hope Street
A small court of houses located on the north side of Hope Street behind Ebeneser Chapel (Queen Street). This small development was the main reason why the building line of the properties in Hope Street does not match up with those in Regent Street.

Bradley, JP, George *publisher & local politician*
Born in 1825, George Bradley was a native of Cefn and began his working life as an apprentice to Edward Davies of Oswestry before working in various businesses in Rhos-y-Medre and Cefn. He became a partner to C.G. Bayley of Oswestry in an earthenware manufacturing business but it was not until he began to have articles published in local newspapers that he found his true vocation. On the death of George Bayley of the *Wrexham Advertiser** he was invited to become a partner in the business and to take on the role of managing editor in 1863. This he did with great success for the remainder of his working life.

Bradley was elected to represent the North Ward as a Liberal councillor on WBC in November 1877 and, three years later, was elected Mayor. He became a Borough JP in 1881, the same year that Bradley Road* was opened and named after him. His wife

Bradley Road Bridge. The view looking towards St Mark's Church and Central Station.

died in 1882 and the following year he resigned from the Council on the grounds of ill health. In 1888 he became a member of the new Denbighshire Council. A member of the Liberal Party he was Vice President of the Wrexham Liberal Association and 'Liberal Prime Minister' in the Wrexham Parliamentary Debating Society.

A member of the Square and Compass Lodge of the Order of Freemasonry, he resided at N° 3 Grove Park Road during his latter years. He died at his home on 25 April 1890 and is buried in Wrexham Cemetery.* His obituary appeared in the *Wrexham Advertiser* on 3 May 1890.

Bradley Road, Newtown
Named after George Bradley,* Mayor of Wrexham, this road was laid out by Wrexham Corporation in 1881 between Mold Road and Ruabon Road, allowing for the further development of the town into the area often referred to in the 19th century as 'Newtown'.*

No sooner had the road been laid out than alterations were required following the approval of plans to extend the Wrexham, Mold and Connah's Quay Railway from the Exchange Station* through to a new town centre terminus at Central Station* in 1887. This meant that a large railway bridge had to be built to carry Bradley Road over the new lines. In 1891, the road was extended further south, across Cae Dicas (*Trans.* Dicas' field) to reach as far as Ruthin Road. [Plans for extension, dated 1885–91, DRO/1043]

On a private plan of 1894, the main residence appears to have been the Red House* which stood opposite the junction with Belle Vue Road.* The terraced houses between the junctions of Bright Street* and Villiers Street* had been built by 1895 but other properties appear to be of a later date. The building on the eastern junction with Watery Road was the North Wales Miners Association until the closure of Bersham Colliery* in the 1980s. N° 11 was the Army Information Office until it was sold in 1963.

Bradley Road English Baptist Chapel.
The Chester Street congregation laid the foundation stone of this chapel in 1898 and the chapel was opened the following year. The Religious Census of 1904 showed: capacity 150; attendance (AM & PM) 60.

Bradley Road Evangelical Baptist Church
Built in 1991–95 at a cost of £80,000, with much of the manual work being carried out by members of the congregation.

Braeside, Abenbury
Part of a private housing development of the 1990s. The name, which is the Scottish term for a hillside, has no significance other than an allusion to the slope down to the river Clywedog.

Brecon Close, Borras Park
As with other streets on this private housing development of the early 1960s, known as Hillcrest Estate,* this road takes its name from one of the old, pre-1974 counties of Wales, in this case, Breconshire.

Breese, JP, Alderman Ethel Claire *local politician*
Born in Leicester (her family was originally from Northumberland) Ethel married Wrexham printer Alfred Breese and had one son, Cyril. She was elected a Conservative councillor for the Erddig Ward in 1927, Mayor in 1943 and an Alderman in 1945. She was also a Denbighshire County Councillor for the Erddig Ward and was appointed a Justice of the Peace, Wrexham Borough, in 1935. She lived at Nº 63 Ruabon Road where she died in December 1955 and was buried in Wrexham Cemetery.*

Breese Family
Printers, with premises at 3 Church Street and 29 Rivulet Road, founded in 1894 and taken over by Woodalls in 1954.

The noted politician Rt Hon Enoch Powell, MP,* was the son of Ellen Mary Breese. The Rivulet Road premises are now occupied by printers Ron Bentley & Sons.

Breese brothers printing works in Rivulet Road, 1909. [Wrexham Museum]

Brewery Place, Pentre Felin
Named after the Island Green Brewery which was located here.

Bricky, The, Abenbury
Whenever comment is passed on the red-brick buildings of Wrexham the word 'Ruabon' is invariably added to the description as in 'Ruabon red brick'. This is very often a mistake as many of the red bricks used in the local area were actually produced at the Abenbury brickworks which was located on either side of Abenbury Road, above the east bank of the river Gwenfro and the north bank of the river Clywedog. The works on the north side of the road were officially called the King's Mills Brickworks while those to the south were the Abenbury Brickworks. Both works were linked to the Wrexham–Ellesmere railway by their own sidings. The clay used in the manufacture of bricks was excavated on both sites and fired in the works. In addition to bricks, various other brick-associated products were manufactured to a very high standard. In 1912, the King's Mills works were owned by the Wrexham Brick & Tile Co. The site was offered for sale in March 1922. [DRO/DD/G/2905]

In later years, both works were the property of Davies Brothers and, finally, Marshalls. Both sites are currently (2001) being developed as private housing estates.

Bust of John Bright produced at Davies Brothers Abenbury Works. [Mr & Mrs Ken Jones]

Bricky, The, Meredith Street
The recreation ground off Meredith Street, known locally as the 'Bricky', was laid out sometime in the early 1920s when Wrexham Borough Council bought land from The Court* estate. It gained this name as it was the site of a large brickworks, possibly established by John Bury* in the early nineteenth century. In February 1852, local architect and builder, Michael Gummow,* leased the land from Henry Meredith of Pentrebychan Hall. By 1863, the works were leased by Edward Bramley and it remained in his family's control until the 1890s.

A more significant company operating as brickmakers in this area was that established in 1863 by Edward Meredith Jones (a builder's merchant at 12 Charles Street and a relative of the family that owned the Cambrian Leather Works*) on a site previously operated by Edward Williams. When this site became exhausted in 1882, Meredith Jones leased additional land from the Pentrebychan estate and in 1887 produced 1,222,530 bricks, albeit of an inferior quality. In 1895, the brickyard was taken over by Whitehouse & Co (which became the Wrexham Brick & Tile Co in 1903) who operated there until 1905 when it was sold.

This yard produced bricks that were used in the construction of Roseneath,* the Lager Brewery* and Hightown Barracks.* Meredith Jones also established Abenbury Brickworks* on Llwyn Onn land. Clay was extracted from both sides of the driveway leading to The Court and was transported via a tramway which ran through a short tunnel under the drive. The clay pits, which can be seen on the 1872 Survey, were eventually filled in to form part of the recreation ground. The private housing developments of Green Park and Maes Tomos were both located on part of the brickworks site.

Bridewell
The original Bridewell was a palace built for Henry VIII in London in 1515–20. In 1553, it was given to the City of London 'for the reception of vagrants and homeless children and for the punishment of petty offenders and disorderly women' and was soon turned into a prison. When it became necessary for other towns to have some form of secure building for the detention of offenders, it became fashionable to adopt the same name. Wrexham's first Bridewell (which dated back to at least 1698, and probably much earlier) was located in Wrexham Fechan on the north bank of the Gwenfro, to the east of Salop Road, on the site of Havelock Square,* very close to the present day Wrexham Musical Society building. The building had 14 cells. Traces of this Bridewell (which appears in the 1833 survey) were visible until after the Second World War. A.N. Palmer* quotes entries in the

The Bridewell, Tenters Square, c.1975.

parish register relating to persons 'employed' at the Bridewell:

Jan. 1625–6	William ap William, the und[er] [under] gaoler, was buried the xiith daie.
Aug. 18, 1702	Lowry, wife of Richard Williams, of W. A. [Wrexham Abbot] hangemon [hangman], poor, was Buryed.
Dec. 18, 1709	David Owen, whipper, of Bridewell, was Buryed.

Masters of the House of Correction

Edward Ducker	? – 1790
George Oldfield	1790–2
John Alcock	1792–1800 (and possibly late). He was also Sheriff's Baliff for Wrexham.

A second Bridewell was built in 1849–50 by Michael Gummow,* architect and builder, on behalf of the Clerk of the Peace of the County of Denbigh at a cost of £1,203. It was located on Tenters Field near Tenters Square,* Pen-y-Bryn, land that had previously belonged to Sir Watkin Williams Wynn. The bond for building what was then referred to as a 'new lock-up and police station' was signed on 16 October 1849 and was to be completed by 'December next'. Prisoners were marched through Regent Street and Hope Street for their trials at the Town Hall.*

In 1879, the police moved from the Bridewell to the County Buildings on Regent Street and long-term prisoners were housed in the County Gaol in Ruthin. In later years, when it was known as Ael-y-Bryn, the building was taken over by Denbighshire County Council as the headquarters of the County Surveyor's Department until sold in 1969. [DRO/QSA/AE/10/26] The building appears in plan form in the 1872 survey. The Pen-y-Bryn Bridewell was demolished in the 1980s, although part of its sandstone outer wall still forms part of the wall on Tenters Square.

Bridge House, Wrexham Fechan (Salop Road)
The first mention of a house of this name is in 1768 but, according to Palmer, the house was built in 1742 or earlier.

Ownership/Residence:

1776	William Jones I, died 1776 (son of the Revd William Jones of Beechley House*).
1780	William Jones II, died 1782 (son of the above William Jones I).
1793	John Jones (brother of the above William Jones II).
1794	John Mellor of Gatewen Hall and later living in the Town Hall.*
1818	Revd William Browne (Presbyterian minister) who let it as an inn and converted the part alongside the river Gwenfro into a 'skin-yard' for his son William.
1857	Michael Gummow.*

The house is shown on the 1833 survey. Palmer believed that the later house, an interesting neo-gothic building, known as Bridge House was designed and owned by local architect Michael Gummow* in the 1850s but appears to have always been used as an inn. Like its predecessor, this house was located on the south corner of Willow Road with Salop Road. During the latter part of the 19th century, a brewery (Bridge House Brewery), owned by the Eyton family, operated behind this house. The whole building was demolished during the 1960s. It appears in both the 1833 and the 1872 surveys as a public house.

Bridge House, c.1969, just before its demolition.

Bridge Street
Named after the Horns Bridge which crosses the River Gwenfro at this point. The 1812 Wynnstay Survey of the Manor of Wrexham Abbot shows this street to have been named Pont Liana.* There is an interesting portrayal of this bridge in a painting by the Wrexham artist Downman*.

Some of the houses here are timber-framed and date from at least the 17th century. One property, located down an alleyway off Bridge Street had a decorated stone panel, of possible Elizabethan origin, above the door.

The buildings on the east side of the street were demolished (as far back as the old Cambrian Yard*) in 2004 to make way for a multi-million pound development which, to date, has not materialised.

Bridge Street (probably by Downman) showing the river Gwenfro flowing under the Horns Bridge, with Town Hill on the left.

The decorated panel discovered off Bridge Street in the 1950s.

Bright Street, Newtown
Bright Street was first laid out in 1894 following the death of Benjamin Piercy* whose Red House* estate property was divided into numerous building plots and put up for auction in September of that year. When further lots were sold the following year, there was no evidence of any building having taken place in Bright Street. By 1900, however, most of the houses on both sides of this street had been built. The street was named after the anti-Corn Law campaigner John Bright (after whom the noted school in Llandudno was also named).

Bright was a founder member of the Anti-Corn Law League in 1839 and was soon regarded as the movement's chief orator. He was elected a Liberal MP for Durham in 1843, Manchester in 1847 and Birmingham in 1857. He was an opponent of trade protection and an ardent supporter of parliamentary reform. He died on 27 March 1889. He once visited Wrexham in the company of Richard Cobden (Cobden Street*) and spoke to a large crowd gathered in Yorkshire Square.* Most of the streets around Bright Street provided housing for the employees of the Cobden Flour Mill* in Watery Road, hence the choice of names of leading Anti-Corn Law League campaigners.

Briscoe, DD, BA, BD, **Dr Thomas** *cleric & scholar*
Born in Wrexham on 30 June 1813, the son of Richard Briscoe, a local druggist, Thomas was educated at Ruthin School and Jesus College, Oxford where he gained a First Class Lit.Hum. BA in 1833, followed by an MA in 1836, a BD in 1843 and a DD in 1868. Ordained in 1836, he became a Fellow of Jesus College (1834-59) and a tutor there from 1835 and was appointed Vice-Principal in 1849. He became curate of Henllan, near Denbigh in 1830, vicar of Holyhead in 1858 and Chancellor of Bangor Cathedral in 1877. He died on 16 February 1895. A great linguistic scholar, he was proficient in several ancient and modern languages and carried out a great deal of translation work from Hebrew into Welsh. His library was donated to Bangor Cathedral on his death.

Britannia Inn, Mount Street
See Dolphin Inn.

British Schools
The British Schools operated from several premises in Wrexham commencing at the Friends Meeting House* in Holt Street in the mid 18th century from where they moved to the Chester Street Presbyterian Church.* In 1832, they again moved, first to a room at the rear of Mr Francis' shop in Hope Street, then to the Town Hall (where they accommodated 100–150 pupils) where they operated with a headmaster and two assistants. In 1844, they were given notice to quit the Town Hall. Local entrepreneur Alexander Wylde Thornley donated to the school part of an old tanyard that he had bought on Brook Street and a new school was designed by local architect Thomas Penson.* Thornley donated a further £400 towards the cost of building the school and his wife Mary Ann Thornley (see Mary Ann Square) donated a further £50. The total building costs were approximately £1,200.

Known as the Victoria Schools, this new building accommodated 300 boys and 300 girls (it seems unlikely that these figures were ever achieved) 'only of the labouring, manufacturing and other poorer classes in the Parish of Wrexham and its vicinity'. Internally the classrooms had brick walls washed with lime and a galvanised iron bucket in the corner serving as a toilet. Outside, the children had an unflagged playground which turned to mud in wet weather. The 1847 *Report on the State of Education in Wales* stated:

A school for boys and girls, taught respectively by a master and a mistress, in separate rooms of a school built for the purpose. Number of boys, 143; of girls, 83; number employed as monitors, 33. Subjects professed to be taught – Holy Scripture, reading, writing, arithmetic, English grammar, geography and history. Fees, 1d. and 2d. per week, varying according to age. Master's salary, £80; mistress's salary, £40.

I visited this school on January 21, during a heavy fall of snow. Only 64 boys and 19 girls were present; 30 of these could read with ease; and of 36 who could answer Scripture questions, 19 were well acquainted with the history of the New Testament, and 9 with that of the Bible generally. Among 82 copy-books, 52 were legibly written, and 7 contained good writing; 45 scholars were learning arithmetic; 9 of these could apply the Rule of Three. 2 could work a sum in Compound Subtraction, and the rest were learning the first rules; a class of 14 were learning mental arithmetic, and 2 could solve difficult questions with great readiness. There were 6 who excelled in geography out of a class of 18; 3 in English grammar out of a class of 16; and among 16 learning the history of England, I found 5 who could answer many questions intelligently; 12 receive instruction in drawing.

The master and the mistress are English people, and have both been trained at the Borough-road. The mistress's control over her pupils appeared defective; but she is only 20 years of age. Both teachers were superior, and their questions were very intelligent. The alphabet is taught from words, the master considering this method better calculated than the old system to fix the relative value of letters in the minds of the children.

The building is large and handsome. It was built at a cost of nearly £1200 by voluntary contributions, unaided by Government, and is well furnished with fixtures, and all other apparatus except copy-books, which the children are required to provide, and for want of which many are compelled to write upon slates. A play-ground is being formed for gymnastic exercise. The girls receive instruction in needle-work daily.'

In 1875, Latin and mathematics were added to the curriculum, due greatly to the efforts of teacher Charles Dodd (see Dodd Family*). Parents were obliged to pay a fee of 1d or 2d per week according to the age of the pupil. The Master still received an annual salary of £80 and the Mistress £40. Evening classes were started at the British Schools by Charles Dodd in 1896.

Following the establishment of the Wrexham School Board* in 1871 regular detailed examinations were made of the educational facilities in the town and, in 1897, while praising the work carried out at the British Schools, the report condemned the standard of the buildings. The school managers agreed to place the school under the care of the School Board and, as a consequence, the Board put in motion plans to build new schools in Poyser Street to be known as the Victoria Board Schools which opened in 1901 (see Victoria Schools). The Brook Street premises were immediately offered for sale in January 1901 and by 1902 were known as the Victoria Hall.* [DRO/DD/G/2862] (See also Dodd Family)

Headteachers:
Boys:
1767(?)–83	Revd Thomas Davies
1783–00	Revd William Browne
1800–20	Revd James Parry
1820	Revd John Pearce
1832–50	Joseph Langton
	Mr Ryder
	George Haden
18 ? –54	Mr Hawkins
1855–84	Alexander Fyfe
1884–1901	Charles Dodd

Girls:
	Miss Mary Jones (Mrs Evan Powell, see Powell Brothers & Whitaker)
	Miss Tucker (Mrs Edward Jones)
	Miss Coghill (Mrs Lumsden Hull)
	Miss Drummond (temp)
c.1863–85	Miss Jane Jones (Mrs Richard Phennah)
1885–1901	Miss Winifred Griffiths

Infants:
1872–91	Miss Alice Fyfe (Mrs Snaith)
1891–94	Miss E. Kennan (Mrs Cornes)
1894–1901	Miss A. Harris-Jones

In recent years the building has been used as a warehouse by Aston & Son,* as retail premises and as a night-club. The premises are currently (2010) vacant. [DRO/ED/LB/101/1–3 & ED/X/101/14]

British Workman Public House Co Ltd
This was a non-sectarian and non-political organisation established to set up temperance rooms where working class men could go to relax without having to resort to alcohol. In Wrexham, cocoa rooms were officially opened by Sir Robert Cunliffe, Bt (see Cunliffe Family) on 31 December 1878 'facing Henblas Street and the Green Market' (between Nos 12 and 14 Henblas Street, next to the Lion Yard*– which was alongside the Old Vaults* public house – managed by G. Black in 1881). The ground floor accommodation comprised a large public room and canteen where food was provided. On the first floor was a gentlemen's lounge (with newspapers) and a large room with a piano, which could be used for concerts. It was not a charity but a commercial venture and the major shareholder in the company was Osborne Morgan, MP, with Edward Evans acting as chairman. The British Workman offered copper tokens for sale which could be bought by affluent people who would then give them to the needy. As the tokens could only be exchanged at the British Workman, the donor was assured that the recipient could not spend the gift on alcohol. In 1881, the secretary was W. H. Tilston. At the same time, cocoa rooms appear to have been opened at Nº 32 High Street, listed as 'The British Workman Public House', run by David Davies. [FRO/D/AH/38]

Broad Oak Farm, Rhosnesni
This smallholding was located on the corner of Dean Road and Borras Park Road. In 1786 it was part of the Acton estate and was known as Matthew's Tenement. In 1881 it was the tied house where the Acton Park coachman lived. It was put up for sale in 1918 when it comprised 8 acres. The farm buildings were later demolished and a new house, Oak House, was built on the site. [FRO/D/AH/24]

Broderick, David *local politician*
David Broderick was born in Liverpool in 1920 and was educated at the local primary school and St Elizabeth's Central School. As a member of the Territorial Army Royal Artillery, he was mobilised in Liverpool on the outbreak of war in 1939. As a forward artillery spotter, he saw active service in Libya, Greece and Crete and was taken prisoner in 1942. He spent two years in a PoW camp in Italy before escaping from a working party and made his way to Switzerland where he was interned. Six months later he left Switzerland and travelled through France until eventually meeting up with the advancing Allied forces and returning to the UK. His mother and the rest of his family were evacuated to Llay in 1940 and were still there when the war ended in 1945. Obtaining a job as an administrative officer with the National Coal Board, he settled in Llay where he married and had three children.

In 1965 he was appointed clerk to Llay Community Council. He was elected a member of Clwyd County Council in 1977 and served until the re-organisation of 1996 when he was elected a Labour member of the newly formed WCBC, representing the Llay Ward. He became Mayor in 1997, when he hosted HM The Queen on her visit to Wrexham to open the new Wrexham Water World. In recent years, Cllr Broderick has served as an Independent Labour candidate. He lives at 32 First Avenue, Llay.

Bromfield and Yale, Lordship of
The lordship of Bromfield and Yale was created by King Edward I (from territories previously held by the rulers of Powys Fadog) and granted to John de Warren as the first English lord. It then passed to his son William in 1284 and then to his grandson, John,* in 1285. It was then inherited by: Edmund Fitzalan, Earl of Arundel; William, Lord Scrope (1398); Thomas, Earl of Arundel (1399). After Thomas' death in 1421, the lordship was divided into four parts. One part went to the dowager Countess of Arundel, a second to John, Duke of Norfolk (nephew), a third to William, Lord Abergavenny and the fourth to Sir Rowland Lenthall. Eventually, by 1489, the lordship reverted to the Crown and was granted by King Henry VII to Sir William Stanley who held it until his execution in 1495. In 1534, King Henry VIII granted the lordship to his illegitimate son, Henry Fitzroy, Duke of Richmond and Surrey, on whose death in 1536, it again reverted to the Crown. During the reign of Edward IV, the lordship was held for a short time by Thomas Seymour, Admiral of England until his execution during the reign of Queen Mary. It is likely that in 1588 Queen Elizabeth granted the lordship to her favourite Robert, Earl of Leicester before it again reverted to the Crown where it has remained ever since (with the exception of the period of the Commonwealth 1649–60).

Bromfield & Yale Court Leet
Courts Leet were established to enquire into all offences (under the degree of High Treason) committed against the dignity of the Crown. The name 'Leet' comes from the Anglo Saxon word *leatan* meaning censure or *lathian* meaning to assemble. There were two levels of Leet, public and private. The public leets, under the jurisdiction of the sheriff or steward, met in turn in each hundred of a county and all the residents of that hundred were bound to attend. A private leet was created by a grant from the Crown to a lord of the manor or the head of a religious institution and took precedence over the public leets. In private leets, the lord of the manor performed the duties of the sheriff and was allowed to charge a fee, or leet money, on the residents by way of compensation for his inconvenience. Every Court Leet had a *connor* or ale taster who was responsible for ensuring the *assize and goodness* of the ale and beer. It was customary in most areas for residents to meet in a convenient building to pay their fees to the Court Leet which would involve dancing and the drinking of Leet Ale (spiced, hot ale). Before the Norman Conquest, the Court Leet was often the sole tribunal for the administration of criminal justice. Gradually, the powers of the

Courts Leet were replaced by other legal bodies, in particular the magistrates' and county courts.

The jurymen for a Court Leet were generally given 15 days notice to attend and were made up of between 12 and 25 men taken from 'the best inhabitants'. They were under instruction to ensure that the routes to the mill, church and market were kept clear, that all disturbers of the peace were impounded; that all water courses, culverts and landmarks were kept in order and to supervise all weights and measures used in local trade. Anyone contravening the regulations relating to these matters, could be brought before the Court Leet to answer for their actions.

In Wrexham, there were two Courts Leet, one serving Wrexham Regis and the other Wrexham Abbot, which usually met at Easter and Michaelmas. The position of steward was usually given to a leading local landowner and that of deputy steward to another notable local citizen e.g. at the end of the 19th century, the steward of the Abbot Leet was Sir Watkin Williams Wynn of Ruabon with J. Allington Hughes* (a Wrexham solicitor) as his deputy. The Abbot Court Leet covered the areas of Eglwysegle, Llantysilio (Llangollen), Stansty Isaf and Ruabon.

The Regis Court Leet met at the old Town Hall and the Abbot Court Leet met at the Bowling Green Inn until 1856 when it moved to the Old Swan, Abbot Street where it held its last meeting on 5 December 1894. By this time, neither of the Courts Leet had any real power having been superseded by the Justices of the Peace, the Quarter Sessions, the Assizes and the establishment of the Borough of Wrexham in 1857. The Regis Court Leet continued to meet until the turn of the 20th century when it lapsed.

Silin quoted in the *Wrexham Leader* in September 1972, a case brought before the Wrexham Regis Court on 13 May 1778:

> Danvers Gartside ... doth present John Davies, chandler, for laying 13 large hogsheads in and upon the common highway called Hope Street and continuing the same ranged before the front of his distilling house whereby the said street straitened and obstructed to the great damage and annoyance of the said inhabitants and others his liege subjects passing and repassing that way.' The same court also heard the case against Pryce Bithel who was charged with enclosing a part of Rossett Green and John Boydell with digging a saw-pit on the King's waste at Rossett Green 'to the great danger of His Majesty's subjects.

The Regis Court was revived briefly in 1911 by Alderman Edward Hughes of Glyndwr with a jury of 30 members who met in the old Town Hall. Alderman Hughes was Steward of the Manor to the Lord of the Manor, HM King George V. The object of the Court at this time was declared to be 'to uphold the law and secure the good of the community. To appoint constables, boroheads, tithingmen, pound keepers, bread weighers, market lookers, town scavengers, sealers of leather, clerks of wheat and dog muzzlers', although in reality it served little or no real function other than ceremonial. Alderman Hughes proposed that the Court should meet annually. There appears to be no evidence of how long this revival persisted.

Bromfield Grove, Acton
Built in the early 1920s as part of the first phase of the Acton Park housing estate.* This street was named after the lordship of Bromfield and Yale. (See Lordships of Bromfield and Yale)

Bromfield High School, Pen-y-Maes Avenue
In 1972, following the adoption of comprehensive education by Denbighshire County Council, Grove Park County Grammar School for Girls* merged with Grove Park County Grammar School for Boys* to form two new mixed-sex comprehensive schools – Grove Park School and Bromfield High School. Bromfield was accommodated in the buildings of the former girls school and served the Chester Road, Maes-y-Dre and Queens Park areas. (See also The Groves High School)

Headteachers:
　　1972　Miss Violet Brown
　　1978　Thomas Davies

Bron Haul Farm, King's Mills
A smallholding located on the north side of the main Wrexham to Marchwiel road. The farmhouse was situated opposite the King's Mills Hotel* and was up for sale in June 1913 and in 1929. [DRO/D/G/2881] In the 1660s, this land was the property of David Phillips, a chandler with premises at Nº 16 Charles Street.* After his death the property passed to his son William, followed by a second David Phillips and then, before 1780, it was bought by Roger Kenyon (probably of Cefn). Sometime after 1810, it was sold to Joseph Cooper of Bodhyfryd* who built a new farmhouse which had been demolished sometime before the end of the 19th century. A large private house was built on the site and took the name Bron Haul (*Trans.* sunny crest). In latter years, this was the property of the National Coal Board and was a senior manager's house. The house was demolished in the 1980s and the Orchards, a small private housing development, was built in its grounds. To the east of Bron Haul, on Rose Bank, was a row of half-timbered, thatched cottages which were demolished by 1912 when the present house, also called Rose Bank, was built.

Rose Bank Cottages, Bron Haul Farm, King's Mills. A special excursion stagecoach passing en route to the races at Bangor, c.1910.

Bron Llwyn, Grosvenor Road
Designed by J. R. Gummow* and completed in 1872 for Edward Jones (hatter and outfitter of Nº 1 Hope Street), this substantial

Bron Llwyn, Grosvenor Road, photographed in 1872.

private residence (originally Nº 8 Grosvenor Road) eventually became the Holy Family Convent School.* It was located to the east of Gerald Street, on part of the site now occupied by the offices of the Department of Social Security. The house was demolished in c.1972. The name (*Trans.* the edge of the grove) is an association with the Groves, the traditional name of this area.

Bron-y-Coed, Coed-y-Glyn
Part of the Coed-y-Glyn* development of the 1970s. The name (*Trans.* edge of the wood) is a reference to its location next to the woodland of Erddig Park.*

Bron-y-Dre, Ruabon Road
(*Trans.* edge of the town). This small corporation housing project, located opposite the Ruabon Road Cemetery, was built on a former garden that had been bought by WBC from a Mr Humphreys in 1931. The nearby Recreation Ground, commonly known as The Bricky* was laid out in the 1920s on land that had previously been part of the Court* estate.

Bron-yr-Efail, Little Acton
A small cul-de-sac on the private housing development built by Caergwrle Investments Limited (CIL) in the 1960s. The name (*Trans.* close by the smithy) refers to its location behind the Acton Smithy.*

Bron-y-Nant, Croesnewydd
Located opposite the main Maelor Hospital building off Croesnewydd Road, Bron-y-Nant (*Trans.* the brook side) takes its name from its proximity to the river Gwenfro. It was built in the 1980s as accommodation for medical staff at the hospital.

Bronwylfa Hall, 1970s.

Bronwylfa Hall, Esclusham
Originally a small farm of 28 acres, belonging to Samuel Egerton in the late eighteenth century and to John Beardsworth of Wrexham in 1805. It was sold in 1871 to Edward Evans, JP, LLD, a drug wholesale merchant of Rockferry, who rebuilt the house in a neo-gothic style, complete with castellated turret. In 1995, following a £2.5 million win on the National Lottery, the house (which had eleven bedrooms and six bathrooms) was bought by Mel and Pat Edison. They sold it a few years later.

Brook Close, Abenbury
Built as part of a private housing development in the 1990s, Brook Close takes its name from its location close to the river Clywedog.

Brook Street, presenting a very different appearance to that of today. A variety of small shops line the opposite side of the street, with a motorcycle, motor bus, charabanc and motor car drawn up at the kerb. In the distance, in front of the entrance to the Albion Brewery, two electric trams are passing each other. Evidence of the culverted nature of this street can be seen in the levels of the road and the pavement on the right, in front of Mary Ann Square.

Brook Square, Brook Street
This court of poor-quality industrial housing was located behind Mary Ann Square* off the south side of Brook Street.* It was demolished during the early 1930s and the site became the location for the Odeon Cinema.*

Brook Street
This thoroughfare takes its name from the river Gwenfro which, until the late 19th century flowed along its course. In 1881, under the supervision of Isaac Shone,* the Gwenfro was culverted and the surface of Brook Street laid over the top of it. In 1700, a public brew-house was located in Brook Street, close to Town Hill, where local people could, for a small charge, take their own malt and hops and use the brewing equipment provided. It was sold at the turn of the 19th century. Many of the poor-quality industrial houses located on the south side of Brook Street were demolished during the early 1930s and the site was occupied by the new Odeon Cinema.* For many years Brook Street served as the terminus for buses operating between Wrexham and the Rhos, Ruabon, Penycae and Coedpoeth areas. In 1953 the buses were moved to the new bus station on King Street, a decision that many shopkeepers felt was the ruination of business on Brook Street. The large, red-brick premises on the corner of Bridge Street were built by William Jonah Williams* as the Central Stores and after a variety of retail uses are now a restaurant and night-club. The premises latterly occupied by Scotts night-club was originally the British School.* [See photograph on page 56]

Brook Street House, Pentre Felin
Despite its name, this house appears to have been located in Pentre Felin, on the east side of the entrance to Pearce's Square* and was once occupied by Thomas Edisbury, proprietor of the Zoedone Mineral Works* which was located on the opposite side of the street.

Brook Street Welsh Wesleyan Chapel
Founded in Wrexham 1859 in the dining rooms belonging to Gomer Jones in Bank Street,* the Welsh Wesleyan Methodists bought an old chapel in Brook Street in 1862. This was rebuilt in 1867. It was sold to the Wrexham & Ellesmere Railway Company in 1882 and the congregation moved to a new chapel, Jerusalem,* on Egerton Street. The Religious Census of 1881 showed: Capacity 168; attendance (AM & PM) 162.

Brooklands, Salop Road
This house on the west side of Salop Road, just south of the junction of the present day St Giles Way, was also certainly built by Wrexham architect, James Reynolds Gummow* for the local pharmacist William Rowland* and was later the home of the Bird family until it was sold in the early 1960s and demolished in the early 1970s. (See also Norman Douglas Bird) The site was later used as a lorry park and storage area by Thomas' Removals.

Broom Grove, Queen's Park
This area of the Cefn Park* estate was requisitioned during the Second World War and temporary housing built in 1941 to accommodate Royal Ordnance Factory* workers. When the war was over these houses were utilised by WBC as temporary corporation housing and, in some cases, survived until the mid 1950s when they were known locally as 'Cardboard City'. The temporary houses were replaced by permanent dwellings, built by W. D. Stant on behalf of WBC, between the 1950s and 1960s. Most of the streets in this area were given the names of trees and shrubs. The land was bought by means of a compulsory purchase order from Lt-Col R. G. Fenwick-Palmer.*

Broughton Buildings, Abbot Street
Located on the north side of Abbot Street in what was later the rear of the Marks & Spencer store, this small 19th century tenement development was demolished in 1932 as part of the Borough Council's slum clearance programme.

Broughton Family of Marchwiel
The first member of this family recorded as living in Wales was *Ralph Broughton* of Plas Isa, Is-y-Coed who lived in the 16th century. His son *Valentine*, was an alderman of Chester and possibly the founder of the Wrexham Grammar School. *Morgan Broughton* (c.1544–1614) gained the Marchwiel Hall estate by his marriage to the daughter of Henry Parry of Basingwerk and Marchwiel. He was high sheriff of Denbighshire in 1608. His son *Edward* was knighted at Hampton Court in 1618 and was a Commissioner of Array for Denbighshire. He served as a major in the Royalist army and was captured (along with two of his sons) at Marchwiel Hall in October 1643. He is known to have still been alive in 1648.

Robert Broughton, of Stryt-yr-hwch, Marchwiel was the younger brother of Sir Edward Broughton (senior). He was a captain commanding 150 Denbighshire men who served in the second Bishops' War against the Scots in 1640. By 1641, he was a colonel commanding 1,000 Denbighshire men sent to serve in Ireland. He returned to Chester in January 1644 and from there was part of Prince Rupert's force sent to relieve Newark and then Liverpool. He led the Royalist attack on Bolton and fought in the decisive battle at Marston Moor. He was made governor of Shrewsbury in August 1644 and was wounded and captured at Montgomery in September of that year. Despite his being a major-general, he was released and saw active service in north Wales in 1645 and at Naseby. He was compounded as a delinquent and fined £76. During the period of the Commonwealth, he again took up arms in Booth's Rebellion of 1659 and was captured.

Lt-Col Sir Edward Broughton, Bt., the son of Maj Sir Edward Broughton of Marchwiel Hall. On the outbreak of the Civil War, he went to Ireland as a captain of foot under the command of his uncle, Col Robert Broughton, before returning with the rank of major in the Royalist Army. Wounded at Wem in Shropshire and captured at Rowton Moor, Chester in 1645. During the period of the Commonwealth he again took up arms in support of Prince Charles and commanded the foot soldiers at the Battle of Winnington Bridge in Booth's Rebellion. He was captured at Worcester in 1651 and may well have fled abroad to serve with the Royal Guards at Ypres in the service of the King of Spain. He

Brooklands, Salop Road. [Peter Bird]

was certainly back in Britain by August 1659 when he was again captured as one of the garrison at Chirk for which he was specifically excluded from the Articles of Surrender and nearly lost his life. Imprisoned at The Gatehouse, Westminster, he married Mary Wyke the daughter of his gaoler. On the restoration of the monarchy, he was knighted in 1663 and died of wounds sustained in a sea battle with the Dutch two years later. He was buried in Westminster Abbey. He was created a Baronet at the time of his death. The Committee for the Compounding of Delinquents described him as 'a bloody delinquent'.

When the family died out the estate passed to Aquila Wyke of Llwynegryn Hall, Mold in 1743.

Broughton, Urban Hanlon *engineer*
Educated at Grove Park in the 1870s, Urban Broughton graduated from the University of London and became a civil and mining engineer. After a period of employment on railway, drainage and dock works in Britain he went to the USA in 1887. There he was engaged in engineering, manufacturing, mining, railways and finance before becoming president of various companies including the Virginia Railway Company and the Utah Mining Company. In 1906, he married Cara Huttleston Rogers, the daughter of one of Rockefeller's partners. He returned to Britain and was elected MP for Preston from 1915–18 and was offered a peerage but died on 30 January 1929 before he could take his seat. His son was created Lord Fairhaven, whose family home was Anglesey Abbey, Cambridgeshire.

Browne's Court, Mount Street
One of the many unsavoury 19th century developments in the Mount Street area of the town, Browne's Court lay parallel to Jones' Square, between Mount Street and the bowling green that was located on Eagle's Meadow. This street was demolished in 1932 as part of the Borough Council's slum clearance programme.

Broxton Road, Queen's Park
Built in the immediate post Second World War period as part of the first phase of WBC's Queen's Park housing development. It is named after the parish of Broxton in Cheshire.

Brwmffild, Matthew, *poet*
A native of Maelor, Matthew Brwmffild was alive between 1520 and 1560. He wrote poems in praise of Rhisiart ap Rhys of Gogerddan, of Rhys ap Howel of Porthamyl, of Lewis Gwynn and of Siôn Wynn of Gwydir.

Brymbo Beaker Man
The remains of an early Bronze Age man in a burial cist were discovered in the village of Brymbo in August 1958 by a group of workmen digging a trench at N° 79 Cheshire View. One of them, Ron Pritchard, realised that they had discovered something of significance and called in the authorities. The cist measured 3' 3" by 2' 3" and was covered by a capstone measuring 5' 6" by 3' 3" (9" thick) made from sandstone. It contained a partial human skeleton of a man who had been about 5' 7" tall and aged between 35 and 40 years. Also inside the cist was a flint knife and a beaker which would certainly have contained liquid refreshment to sustain the deceased on his journey to the next world. The find was deposited in the National Museum of Wales, Cardiff where it remained until May 1998 when it was returned to Wrexham and placed on display in the Wrexham Museum. Fittingly, the remains were transported from Cardiff in an undertaker's hearse. A reconstruction of the 'Beaker Man's' skull was carried out at Manchester University in 2001 and the resulting wax model of his head was unveiled at Wrexham Museum on 18 June, 2001.

Brymbo Hall, Brymbo
Built *c*.1624 for John Griffiths, owner of the estate which was considerably older than the house. Substantial additions were made to the house in a highly ornamented Baroque style which, according to Thomas Lloyd (*Lost Houses of Wales*) was unique in Wales. The last member of the Griffiths family, Mary, the daughter of Robert Griffiths, married Robert Jeffreys of Acton Park* in 1713 and secondly Richard Clayton in 1716/7. She married a third husband, Arthur the son of Sir Robert Owen of Brogyntyn, Selattyn in 1727/8. After her death, the house passed to her daughter Alethea, the wife of Dr James Apperley. When she died, it passed to her sister Jane Wynne of Foelas and through her to Elizabeth, the wife of Thomas Assheton Smith of Faenol, near Bangor. Local legend has it that Elizabeth's ghost haunted the house for many years after her death.

In 1792, the 500-acre estate was sold to the ironmaster John Wilkinson* of Bersham for £14,000 who added some 400 acres at a later date. Unfortunately, from a historical viewpoint, the house sat on rich deposits of coal and iron ore and Wilkinson built a number of pits and furnaces in the grounds. The house passed to John Wilkinson (junior) in 1808 and was sold to James Kyrke (son of Richard Kyrke of Gwersyllt Hill*) in 1829 when it was described as including '… a valuable ironworks, collieries and mines. The capital mansion house of Brymbo Hall and several compact farms and lands containing nearly 900 acres. The situation of the mansion house commands one of the most beautiful and extensive views in the kingdom'. The house was the residence of Samuel Smith Adams for a short period and then, in 1834, William Legh. Later occupiers were Sir George Osborne Morgan, MP,* and Peter Williams* (managing director of Brymbo Steel Works pre-1914). The growth and expansion of the Brymbo Iron Works* (later the Brymbo Steel Works*) led to the gradual deterioration of the house throughout the 19th century and was eventually used to accommodate pigs, chickens and other animals. In its latter years, it was the property of Percy Evans and was finally demolished in 1973 to allow for open-cast coal excavation. A detached chapel which stood in the grounds was ascribed in the sale catalogue of 1829 as having been designed by the great 17th century architect, Inigo Jones, but there is no evidence to support this claim.

Brymbo Iron Works
(See also Brymbo Hall and Bersham Iron Works)). John Wilkinson (1728–1808)* had owned and operated a successful iron works at Bersham before buying the Brymbo Hall estate in 1792 and transferring his operations to the new location shortly afterwards. He built two major blast furnaces there with the intention of producing 4,000 tons of pig iron each year. The first of these furnaces, known as Old N° 1, still survives and is a listed building. By 1796, it was producing 884 tons and remained in production until 1894.

For many years, the works was managed by William Rowe. After the departure of the Wilkinson family, the Brymbo Iron Works was bought by a Mr Reid in 1830 and, in 1841, by Scotsman, Robert Roy, who brought in some new partners in the form of Henry Robertson,* William Betts and Alexander Mackenzie Ross, with whom he founded the Brymbo Mineral and Railway Company. In 1872, Roy's share of the Brymbo works was bought by Henry Robertson. By this time the management of the works was in the hands of Charles Edward Darby and W. H. Darby, members of the Darby family of Ironbridge.

Brymbo Steel Works
The Brymbo Steel Company was incorporated in June 1884 with Colonel Wilson as chairman of the board. N°1 Furnace produced

the first basic open hearth steel to be produced in Britain in January 1885. A three-high, 28" rolling mill was installed in the same year. Wilson died in 1891 and was succeeded by Sir Henry Beyer Robertson (the son of Henry Robertson*) who held the position until his death in 1948. The first by-product coke oven plant to be operated in conjunction with a steel plant was introduced at Brymbo by John Henry Darby. In 1908, Peter Williams, the son of a local farmer, was appointed managing director of Brymbo Steel Works and in 1914 moved on to become General Manager of the new Normanby Park Steel Works at Scunthorpe. He was succeeded by J. Spencer Hollings who was managing director until 1930.

In 1931, the world recession led to the shutdown of the steel works and the plant did not re-open until 1934 (mainly due to the efforts of Sir Henry Robertson) under the joint managing directorship of J. P. Bowman and W. L. Venables. In 1939, a new electric melting shop was opened which, on the outbreak of war, resulted in Brymbo being chosen to supply high quality steel to the Air Ministry. In addition, four arc furnaces were installed. In 1940, the works came under the control of Thomas Firth & John Brown Ltd. and Esmond Morse was appointed managing director.

On the restoration of peace, the company was acquired by GKN who owned it until nationalisation in 1951. Four years later, in 1955, the steel industry was de-nationalised and GKN once again became the owners of the works. In 1957, H. W. A. Waring took over as managing director and a second electric melting shop was opened two years later at the same time the old open hearth furnace department was shut down. Waring was tragically killed in an aeroplane crash at Luxemburg Airport in 1962 and his position was taken by Emrys Davies, a locally born man who had worked at Brymbo since 1920. He in turn was succeeded by Neville Davies.

In 1969, the Labour government again nationalised the steel industry and de-nationalised it again in 1974 and reverted to the ownership of GKN. In 1976, work commenced on a new billet and bar mill which entailed the demolition of part of the village of Lodge. The new mill cost £47.5 million and began production in 1980, making Brymbo one of Europe's leading manufacturers of specialist steels. In 1983, Frank Winter was appointed managing director, a position which he held until 1987.

In 1986, a new company was formed – United Engineering Steels Ltd – by the merging of several independent companies. This heralded the beginning of the end for Brymbo and in May 1990, the company announced that all steelmaking would cease in four months' time, shortly after the company had declared Brymbo to be operating at improved levels of profitability.

The works finally closed on 27 September 1990 and the new billet and bar mill was eventually sold to China. In recent years, the site has been redeveloped for residential purposes.

Bryn, Tuttle Street
The 17th century town house of Sir Richard Trevor of Trefalyn, Bryn was situated at the rear of the present day Nags Head* public house, off Tuttle Street.*

Bryn Acton, Chester Road
The Garden Village houses on Chester Road, north of the Garden Village shops were officially named Bryn Acton. (See also Acton Hill).

Bryn Castell, Tenters Square
(*Trans.* castle hill) This house was located on the south-west corner of the junction of Tenters Square* and Pen-y-Bryn.* It was a large two storey double-fronted, brick house facing onto Pen-y-Bryn across a small front garden with a larger garden on the south-west side. It was once the home of the governor of the Bridewell* which stood nearby.

Bryn Draw Terrace, Chapel Street
Bryn Draw Terrace, a small development of four houses with sizeable front gardens, is located off the north-eastern side of Chapel Street. Built in the 19th century they are good examples of superior small terraced houses. The literal translation means 'Yonder Hill'. The terrace does not appear on the 1859 sale plans for the Cambrian Brewery but is shown in the 1872 survey.

Bryn Estyn Hall
Originally a small farm close to Clay's Farm, Bryn Estyn was part of the Erlas Hall estate (belonging to the Davies family). It passed by marriage into the Kyffin family until 1783 when Sir Thomas Kyffin sold it to Wrexham banker, Richard Lloyd* who, shortly afterwards, built the first Bryn Estyn Hall in the Regency style. The architect was probably Joseph Turner. It was the birthplace and later the home of Richard's son, Major Sir William Lloyd.* In 1881 the house was the property of Emily Fitzhugh of Plas Power* who married Captain Charles Rumney Godfrey. Following her death in 1893, her son sold it to Frederick W. Soames,* the Wrexham brewer. The house was demolished in 1905 and Soames built a new house nearby in mock-Tudor style which bore the same name. When sold in 1928 (when it was the property of Mrs F. W. Soames), Bryn Estyn was described as 'a replica of a Cheshire Manor House' with 20 bedrooms and dressing rooms, 2 bathrooms, a billiard room, 5 reception rooms, garage for 5 cars, stabling for 11 horses, stud grooms and other cottages, a fitted laundry, central heating, telephone, electric light, two tennis and croquet lawns, an ornamental lake, a walled kitchen garden, a home farm and timbered parkland extending to 95 acres, 'for sale at half its original cost'. [DRO/DD/G/2858 & 2916, DRO/DD/WY/5452.] During the inter-war period, the house was leased to a number of private individuals before eventually becoming a local authority Approved School until its closure in the 1970s. It was taken over by Clwyd County Council Education Department (later WCBC) as its Information Technology Centre and the name was changed to Erlas House (later Erlas Centre).

Bryn Estyn Hall, built by Richard Lloyd in the 1780s and demolished in 1905.

In the late 1990s, the house became the focus of a national scandal following allegations that pædophiles had operated there during its latter years as an Approved School. After the ensuing investigations and trials, Peter Howarth (a former deputy headmaster) and Stephen Norris were convicted of sex offences and both received lengthy prison sentences. Paul Bicker Wilson was convicted of assault and received a suspended sentence. A detailed account and analysis of the events *The Secret of Bryn Estyn: the making of a modern witch hunt*, by Richard Webster, was published in 2005.

Bryn Estyn Road (Lane)
This road, running through the township of Bieston, links Rhosnesni with the Wrexham Industrial Estate and takes its name from Bryn Estyn Hall.* Much of the land, and two cottages, on the west side belonged to the Wrexham Parochial Charities.* These cottages had 1 rood 27 perches of land and generated an annual rent of £2 10s and £3 12s. In 1891, they were occupied by Thomas Blythen and Thomas Moody (the Blythens were the ancestors of the Liverpool-born entertainer Cilla Black). Most of the charity land was sold and developed as part of the Fairways* estate.

Bryn Grove, Queen's Park
Developed immediately after the Second World War by WBC as part of the first stage of the Queen's Park* housing estate. The street was built on land that had previously been part of the Cefn Park* estate, bought by means of a compulsory purchase order from Lt-Col R.G. Fenwick-Palmer.* The origin of the name is probably a reference to its position overlooking the remainder of the estate.

Bryn Gryffydd
Bryn Gryffydd (*Trans.* Griffith's hill) is an ancient place name and used to refer to a smallholding located just outside of Acton Park in what is now the Borras Park estate (see Bithell's Farm). There is evidence to suggest that land in the area of Acton was once owned by Madog ap Gryffydd, Prince of Powys, and was given by him to the newly founded monastery of Valle Crucis in the 13th century. This land certainly included Acton Park and it is possible that the reference to Gryffydd came from this source. The smallholding was the property of the Wynnstay estate in 1715 and was sold by Sir Watkin Williams Wynn to Ellis Yonge of Acton Park in 1772 for £1,470. Today, the name survives as the name of a street in Borras Park developed by Spinks & Denning during *c*.1968. The original name for the street was Min-y-Coed (*Trans.* edge of the wood).

Bryn Gwiail
This was an area of land located at the eastern end of the Beast Market. It was owned by John Ellis, surgeon and High Sheriff of Denbighshire in 1784, who died at Bangor-is-y-coed in April 1791. In 1844, Capt Henry Ellis is shown as the owner. The name literally means the hill of twigs. It is not mentioned on the 1872 survey.

Bryn Hafod, Queen's Park
Laid out in the early 1960s by Wrexham Borough Council as part of the Queen's Park* housing estate. The name, which translates literally at summer grazing place on the hill, is undoubtedly a reference to Hafod-y-Wern* farmhouse which stood on this site.

Bryn Isaf Terrace, Bridge Street
A small development of five terraced houses, Bryn Isaf Terrace was located below the gardens of Bryn Draw Terrace, facing across the valley of the Gwenfro towards the Parish Church. They were accessed from an entry alongside Bryn Issa House* on Bridge Street. The terrace does not appear on the 1859 sale plans for the Cambrian Brewery but is shown in the 1872 survey.

Bryn Eglwys Road, Queen's Park
(*Trans.* church hill) Developed in the late 1950s as part of WBC's Queen's Park housing estate, this road takes its name from its hillside location alongside St Mark's Church.*

Brynhyfryd, Grosvenor Road
Designed by Wrexham architect J. R. Gummow,* Brynhyfryd was the first house to be built in Grosvenor Road, *c*.1868. In 1881, it was the home of Charles Hughes, deputy chairman of the Provincial Insurance Company.* The house became the office of the Registrar of Births, Marriages and Deaths during the 1990s and later underwent a major refurbishment and conversion into private offices.

Bryn Issa, Bridge Street
(*Trans.* lower hill) Located on the east side of Bridge Street, Bryn Issa was the surgery of Dr Gwilym E. Morgan and was sold in the 1930s for £700. It was later used as a printing works and was demolished in the 1990s. The site is now occupied by Bryn Issa House. [DRO/DD/G/2923]

Bryn Offa
In the late 1860s, Bryn Offa was the home of John Bernard Murless, the father of Charles Murless,* and mayor of Wrexham (see Mayors of Wrexham). By 1881 it was the residence of Edward Rowland the Wrexham chemist. Sale particulars for August 1919 described the house as having an entrance porch, hall, dining room, drawing room, morning room, back kitchen (with wash boiler), pantry, store room, 4 bedrooms, bathroom, WC, good cellarage, 2 stall stable, saddle room, trap house (or garage), croquet lawn. Prior to this date, it had been occupied by Charles Davies, JP. In the 1930s, it was the home of Miss Marian Owen and her sister. In 1956, the house was bought by the Royal Air Force Association as their Wrexham clubhouse (N° 436). [DRO/D/G/2888]

Bryn Offa Housing Estate
This housing estate was first developed along the south side of Ruthin Road,* between Bryn Offa* and Bryn Offa School, by WBC in the 1950s on land that had previously been occupied by Bryn Offa Terrace, a row of houses that were demolished as part of the Borough Clearance programme. It was extended southwards to link up with Bersham Road in 1957 and this new

Bryn Offa Terrace (sometimes called Offa Terrace), 1950s.

road was given the name Centenary Road (to commemorate the anniversary of the incorporation of the Borough of Wrexham). Despite the presence of name plaques bearing the name Centenary Road, this street has always been grouped together with the properties on Ruthin Road and the whole development is simply referred to as Bryn Offa.

Bryn Offa High School, Bryn Offa
Designed by Denbighshire County Architect, R.A.C. Macfarlane, work commenced on building this school in 1959 and it was originally suggested that it be called the Emyr Cyfeiliog School in honour of Alderman Dr Emyr Williams. It opened in 1960 with an intake of 510 pupils drawn from Victoria Boys Secondary Modern School,* St David's Secondary Modern School* (within the town) and Penygelli School, Coedpoeth. Built at a cost of £176,224, the school had 16 classrooms, 2 laboratories, an art room, general purpose room, 2 domestic science rooms, a library, hall, stage, gymnasium, and changing rooms. It became a comprehensive school in 1974. It closed in July 2003 as part of the local authority's reorganisation of secondary education within the county borough and the site was taken over by the new Ysgol Clywedog. The school motto was Goreu Arf, Arf Dysg (Trans. the best weapon is the weapon of learning). An illustrated history IYsgol Bryn Offa School – a collection of pictures by Roland Humphreys was published in 2003.

Headteachers:
    1960 – Cerdyn Lloyd Thomas
    1974 – Mrs Ruth Wills (had been Deputy Head since 1972)
    1983 – James Bevan
    1994 – Miss Linda Webb
    2000 – Terry Wales (acting headteacher)
    2000 – Paul Roberts
    2003 – Julia Thomas (acting headteacher)

Bryn-y-Cabanau Road, Hightown
Literally translated as the hill of the cabins, the origin of the name Bryn-y-Cabanau is not known although local legend has it that the name derives from a time when there was an outbreak of 'plague' in Wrexham and wooden huts were erected in this area to accommodate those afflicted with the illness. The road appears on early 19th century maps and was widened during the late 1890s following the development of several new streets in the area. Land on the west side near the junction with King's Mills Road was part of the Gatefield estate and was sold in June 1889. [DRO/DD/G/2831] By 1927, this was the property of Brigadier General J. H. Lloyd of Ellesmere who sold it to WBC, and thirty-two council houses were built on the site, the majority

Bryn-y-Cabanau Road with the junction of Nelson Street on the extreme right.

in the newly-created Haig Avenue.* On the eastern corner of the junction with King's Mills Road stood Gatefield* which was demolished in the late 1960s to make way for the block of council flats which bears the same name.

Bryn-y-Ffynnon
This name was applied to the whole area around the old town well* and included all properties north of Brook Street,* west of Vicarage Hill,* east of St Mark's Road* and the south side of Hope Street* and Regent Street.* The name is also applied to the narrow road that links Hill Street* and Priory Street* which formed the northern boundary of the garden of Bryn-y-Ffynnon House.*

The second Bryn-y-Ffynnon English Methodist Church, with St Mark's Terrace and the spire of St Mary's Cathedral on the right.

Bryn-y-Ffynnon English Methodist Church, Regent Street
By the mid 19th century, due to the expanding congregation and the growth in the prosperity of the town, the Green Chapel* in Salop Road was no longer found to be suitable for the needs of the English Wesleyan congregation and, on 24 July 1855, Ada Bealy laid the foundation stone of a new, and much grander chapel on what had been the Orchard Field* of Bryn-y-Ffynnon House.* The first sermon was preached in the new chapel by the Revd Francis A. West on 27 June 1856. The building was designed by James Simpson and built by James Reynolds Gummow of Wrexham. Its gable end faced Regent Street* and the building comprised two aisles, a schoolroom and a vestry. The total cost of construction was £1,645-18-0^{1}/2. The Minister's House was at Pen-y-Bryn* until 1865, when the congregation purchased Epworth Lodge* on Grove Road* which became the manse. The chapel was closed on 25 May 1889 prior to its

demolition and replacement by a much enlarged and grander edifice.

The second Bryn-y-Ffynnon Chapel was designed by William Waddington and Sons of Manchester and Burnley. John Gethin of Shrewsbury was the contractor and the builder was James Davies of Wrexham. Five foundation stones were laid on 5 July 1889 (by Sir Robert Cunliffe, Bt; Miss Morris; G. W. Taylor; T. C. Jones and Mrs John Hopley Pierce). The cost of building was £4,993. The first sermon was given in the new chapel on Friday 5 September 1890. A detailed description of the interior of this building is to be found in Palmer's *History of the Town of Wrexham* (p73–4). The cost of re-building was met by the establishment of a building fund based upon £1,000 left in the will of James Ollerhead,* a local businessman, who had died in 1876. The fund raised sufficient monies in twelve months to build the new chapel.

The church was demolished as part of the Grosvenor Shopping Centre* re-development of the 1960s and replaced by the Methodist Church located above the present day shops. This was designed by G. Raymond Jones & Associates and John Laing Design Associates. The interior was designed by the Design Group Partnership of Chester. This is generally regarded as one of the less attractive modern buildings in Wrexham's town centre although it must be said that it tackles the problem of high land values and the commercial re-development of Regent Street in a novel manner with a free-standing staircase giving access from street level to the chapel itself which is on the first floor.

The Religious Census of 1881 showed: Capacity 520; attendance (AM & PM) 486. The Religious Census of 1904 showed: Capacity 650; attendance (AM & PM) 392. [DRO/ND/1 & ND/12/1–7 & ND/1/59, 64, 74–6, 86–9, 91–100, 102]

Bryn-y-Ffynnon Gatehouse
See Priory Gatehouse.

Bryn-y-Ffynnon Hill
This narrow road extended from the southern end of Priory Lane (Street) to Well Square, at the rear of the Bryn-y-Ffynnon Vicarage. It disappeared as part of the redevelopment of the area during the building of the Central Station in the 1890s. There were no properties shown on this road in the 1872 survey, the land to the west being the gardens of Bryn-y-Ffynnon House* and those to the east being the gardens of the Vicarage.*

Bryn-y-Ffynnon House
Bryn-y-Ffynnon was the largest house in the old town of Wrexham, standing in its own gardens on the west side of Priory Street on the site now occupied by Yales café bar and the Victoria Youth Club.

The origins of the house are unrecorded although Palmer believed that it was built in the early 17th century by Thomas Trafford (died 1645). The land upon which it stood was described in some detail in Norden's survey of 1620 but there was no mention of the actual house. It may be that a much smaller house stood on the site which did not merit any detailed mention. By the 1640s, it would appear that Sir Richard Lloyd* (the defender of Holt Castle during the Civil War*) of Esclus Hall* was living at the house although probably as a tenant. On 7 October 1642, King Charles I on his visit to Wrexham is said to have called on Sir Richard at Bryn-y-Ffynnon. It is believed that at one time, Colonel John Jones,* the regicide, was the owner of Bryn-y-Ffynnon (possibly shortly after the death of Thomas Trafford) and in 1647, the dissenting minister Morgan Llwyd* made it his home and held dissenting meetings there. The house was certainly a substantial property by 1670 when it was taxed for 14 hearths.

By 1699 it had become the property of Sir William Williams of Glascoed and the tenant at that time was Sir Henry Bunbury, Member of Parliament for Chester. In about 1716, Sir William's son, Watkin Williams, indicated that he was planning to live at Bryn-y-Ffynnon with his new bride but, shortly afterwards, inherited the Wynnstay* estate at Ruabon along with the baronetcy and became Sir Watkin Williams Wynn (see Wynn Family). By the end of the 17th century, the house appears to have been subdivided, one part being used as a school by the Revd John Evans, an Independent minister.

By 1808, John Parry was renting the main part of the house and converted it into a school which he left in the following year and it became a young ladies school run by the three daughters of John Kenrick of Wynne Hall, Ruabon who remained there until the 1830s (they are shown to be in residence in the 1833 survey). In 1841, Miss Sarah Humble was the tenant but the house was still being used as a school which appears to have had 15 resident pupils.

In 1844, the house and grounds were sold to the Shrewsbury & Chester Railway Company who were proposing to bring the railway into the centre of Wrexham. This plan, however, was not proceeded with and the station was built on the site of the present Wrexham General Station.

In 1857, when the landlord is recorded as being a Mr Griffith, part of Bryn-y-Ffynnon was leased to the newly incorporated Borough of Wrexham as a municipal building (at an annual rental of £35), a role which it served until 1883 when the Council purchased the old Grammar School building on Chester Street. A brief description of the house when it was under consideration for use by the Borough Council has survived:

> In front there is a spacious courtyard, and the entrance hall is a fine room covered from floor to ceiling with antique oak panelling which when cleaned would be exceedingly appropriate. On the right is a large apartment which will be used as a council chamber and a smaller room on the left will serve as a committee room. A smaller room alongside will

Bryn-y-Ffynnon House, c.1850.

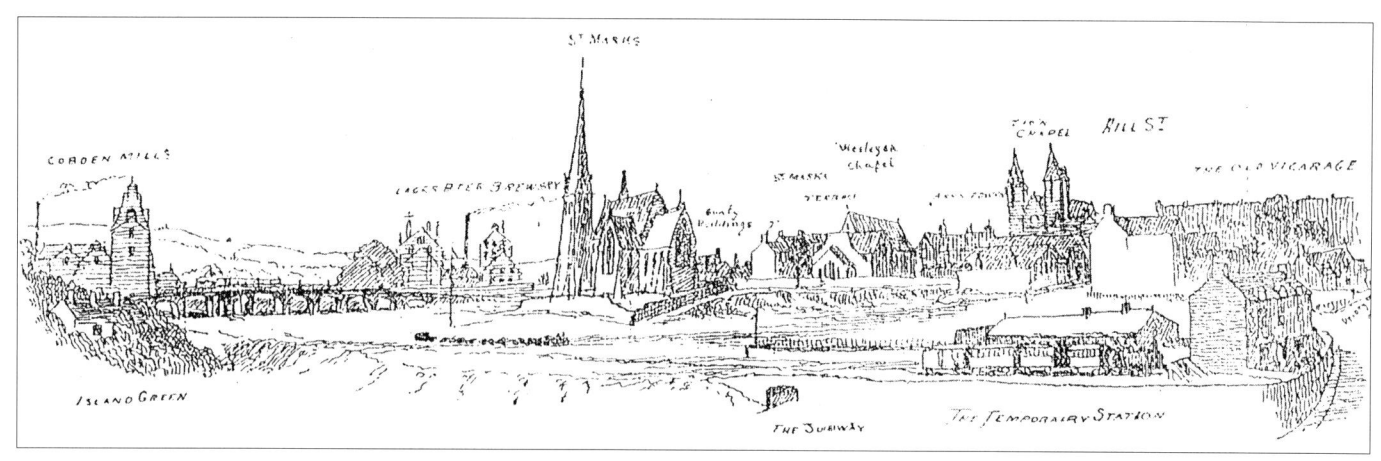

A panoramic drawing of the Bryn-y-Ffynnon area, c.1885, before the building of the Wrexham–Ellesmere railway. This rare illustration shows the original Bryn-y-Ffynnon Methodist Church and a subway beneath the railway. The presence of the Lager Brewery dates it to post 1882. [Derrick Pratt]

accommodate the Inspector of Nuisances. From the hall, a wide staircase led up to the sessions room ... which is now undergoing re-furbishing.

Wrexham's first Jewish* congregation met at Bryn-y-Ffynnon in 1894 and the house survived the railway developments of the 1890s only to be demolished in about 1915.

Palmer quotes a detailed description of this building given by Hugh Davies, sanitary inspector, produced in the mid 19th century:

[The gatehouse] had its front as at present, with a cumbrous oak door to the entrance, and a small door inserted in it for convenience. The ground in front of the lodge was open to Priory Street. After going through the opening through the lodge there was a broad gravel walk ... to the front door of the 'house' [Bryn-y-Ffynnon] and on the right a raised embankment, covered with grass, with clumps of trees and shrubs and flower beds; on the left hand was a flat lawn with a small fish pond in it; this lawn reached as far as the lime trees. At the back of the embankment on the right was a kitchen garden, covering the whole of the ground from the lodge [gatehouse] to Regent Street and [what is now] Hill Street, in which [garden] was a large number of choice fruit trees, one or two of which still remain in Mr Turner's garden ... from the lodge along Priory Street, and up Regent street as far as Hill Street, was a stone wall about 12 feet high and 2 feet thick ... At the end of Hill Street was the back entrance, and the whole of Hill Street was a common yard.

The site of the present day Little Theatre* in Hill Street* (formerly the Hill Street Chapel Schoolroom) was vacant (apart from a small group of very tall trees) until 1857. To the south of the main house stood a double coach house and stables which were converted for use by Wrexham's first Ragged School* before a purpose built school was constructed in the grounds sometime after 1881.

On the south side of Regent Street and to the west of Hill Street was Bryn-y-Ffynnon orchard which amounted to some 5.25 acres and contained Bryn Edwyn where the Bryn-y-Ffynnon Chapel was built in 1855/6. The orchard was separated from Regent Street by a wall, behind which was a gravel footpath which was raised above ground level of the orchard. In the early 17th century, the orchard was one of the town fields of Wrexham, known as Maes Estome (or Maes Ystum) which translated as the field above the river bend. It extended from what is now Brook Street to Regent Street and was bought by Thomas Trafford of Bryn-y-Ffynnon in about 1620. In 1812, there was a kiln sited in the corner of the orchard close to Well Square.* Today, the modern retail premises facing onto Regent Street (between Hill Street and St Mark's Road), Roxburgh House and the Grove Park Little Theatre occupy the site.

Recorded owners/tenants of this property were:

c.1644	possibly Thomas Trafford of Esclus
c.1645	Richard Lloyd of Dulasau (later Sir Richard Lloyd)
1659	Maj John Manley
1682	Thomas Lloyd, gent. (probably of Plas Madoc, Llansannan) pre-1699 Sir William Williams of Glascoed – divided into three tenements
	1. 1699 – Sir Henry Bunbury (of Stanney and Bunbury, Cheshire)
1. 1699	Kenrick Eyton – left 1708
1. 1715	Richard Weaver (probably of Abenbury Hall)
2. 1699	Lady Eyton–died 1701
2. 1701	Madam Morton, daughter of Kenrick Eyton above
2. 1715	Dr John Davies
3. 1699	Revd John Evans, Independent minister – used as a school – (buried in the Dissenters Burial Ground* 1700)
3. c.1705	Thomas Pulford
3. pre-1713	William Anwyl
1716	2 & 3 & gatehouse – Henry Conway of Bodrhyddan
1716	2 & 3 & gatehouse – Watkin Williams (later of Wynnstay and first Sir Watkin Williams Wynn)
1730	Robert Williams (son of first Sir Watkin Williams Wynn)
1746	Madam Trygan
1751	George Warrington (see also Gresford Cottage)
c.1770	Thomas Boycott (of Rudge, Boycott and Hinton, Shropshire)
c.1790	Mrs Puleston (until c.1798)
c.1808	John Parry (used it as a school)
1818	Misses Kenrick (three daughters of John Kenrick of Wynne Hall, Ruabon) used it as a young ladies' school
c.1844	Shrewsbury & Chester Railway Company*
1857	WBC (used as the municipal buildings)

Bryn-y-Ffynnon Lodge, Regent Street

Located on the north side of Regent Street between the junctions of Priory Street and Hill Street. This house was known to exist in 1699 and in 1716 was the town house of Richard Clayton of Brymbo Hall. It is shown on the 1833 survey but appears to have been demolished, or at least considerably altered in shape, by the time of the 1872 survey. Palmer would suggest the latter and states that by 1893, it was being used as Aston's Auction Mart (see Aston & Son). [DRO/1014]

Residents (for most of its history the house appears to have been the property of the Wynnstay estate):

1699	John Wynn
1704	John Wynn

1705   Revd Nathaniel Long (Presbyterian Minister, Chester Street)
1716   Richard Clayton (of Brymbo Hall)
1727   Arthur Owen
pre 1751 William Henry (dancing master)
c.1751   Thomas Payne (bookseller)
1765   Mrs Payne
1774   William Durack (dancing master)
1779   Thomas Durack
1841   James Jones (blacksmith)

Bryn-y-Ffynnon School
Part of Bryn-y-Ffynnon House* was converted into a school by John Parry in 1808. In 1809, it became a school for young ladies, run by the daughters of John Kenrick of Wynne Hall, Ruabon. Recorded in the 1841 Census as having 15 girl boarders.

Bryn-y-Glyn, Rhosddu
This cul-de-sac of former police houses was built very close to the point where the original Rhosddu Road* was truncated by the building of the Chester–Wrexham railway line. The houses were sold off by the Police Authority in the 1980s.

Bryn-y-Grog Hall
(*Trans.* hill of the gibbet or cross) This house, which was built in the mid 18th century, was purchased in 1772 from John Jones, grocer of Wrexham, by Philip Yorke of Erddig. It was later sold to the Marchwiel Hall Estate from whom it was purchased by the Edgworth family who were lawyers in Wrexham. The first of that family to live here was John Edgworth (1712–98), followed by his son John (1765–1826) who may have bought the house in 1800. After the death of his widow, the property passed to his nephew, Thomas Edgworth,* the first Mayor of Wrexham (1807–68). His son, the Revd Roger Edgworth sold the estate between 1880 and 1885. In the early part of the 20th century, the house was the residence of Leonard Cookson (died 29 November 1918). At the time of writing (2010), the owner is William Paran Price.

Bryn-y-Grog Hill
Now part of the A525 between King's Mills and Marchwiel. There was a row of thatched cottages on the west side of the road, just after the turning for Abenbury, which were certainly standing after the First World War.

Bryn-y-Pys Hall, Overton
Bryn-y-Pys Hall was the home of the Price (or Prys) family who were closely related to the Puleston's of Emral Hall. The Prices also owned the Croesnewydd estate in the 18th century. The bulk of the later house was probably built in 1739 as a square, brick structure to which two bowed features were later added. In 1807 what was described as 'a new mansion', but more likely a remodelled house, was opened on 31 December. The last of the Prices, Francis Richard, died in 1853. Bryn-y-Pys then became the property of the Peel family who significantly altered the house in 1883 to a design by John Douglas, whereby the house was encased in stone and an unusual rather Germanic-looking entrance tower built on a new east entrance front, quite out of character with the remainder of the house.

The first member of the Peel family to settle here was Edmund Ethelston – who assumed his mother's maiden name of Peel in 1851 (1826–1903). He is reputed to have owned 5,779 acres in Wales as well as land in Cheshire, Devon, Shropshire and Norfolk. The last of the male line was Maj Hugh William Jardine Ethelston Peel who was killed in action serving with the Welsh Guards in Holland in 1945 and the estate passed to his two year old daughter Sarah. Bryn-y-Pys Hall was, for a short time, a school and was demolished in 1956. Only the stables survive.

Bryn-y-Grog Hill, c.1920.

Buck, Hope Street
Located at N°s 28 & 29 Hope Street (just to the south-east of the Horse and Jockey), reference to the Buck first appears in the records for 1788. It is clearly shown in both the 1833 survey and the 1872 survey.

Buck's Barn, Borras Road
This is mentioned in the 1786 survey of the Acton Park* estate as being located close to the junction of Borras Road and Holt Road. [FRO/D/AH/24]

Buckingham Road, Croes Eneurys
Built in the 1960s on land that had formerly been part of Croes Eneurys Farm,* by local builders Parker, Davies & Johnson Ltd. All the streets were named after royal residences, in this case, Buckingham Palace in London.

Two views of Bryn-y-Pys, Overton in the early 20th century.

Bull Inn, Abbot Street
Shown in the 1833 survey. It was converted into two shops by James Lee in 1900.

Bull & Dogs, Town Hill
This public house was located at N[os] 4 & 4a Town Hill before 1755 when the building was converted into a chandlers shop. The name would certainly be an allusion to the sport of bull baiting.

Bull's Head, Farndon Street
Mentioned by Palmer as standing somewhere between the tithe barn (on the site of the present day War Memorial Club) and the Victoria Inn, this public house does not appear in either the 1833 or the 1872 surveys. In 1881 the tenant is shown as John Williams.

Burial Ground, Ruthin Road
Originally known as the New Burial Ground, this was located on the south side of Ruthin Road, east of Victoria Road. As the parish churchyard had become full, the land for this cemetery was given by Sir Watkin Williams Wynn in 1784 for all burials in the parish of Wrexham but it was not consecrated until 1793. There was considerable opposition to it being used by people who felt that their loved ones should be buried next to the church and, according to local tradition, the first burial stemmed from the granting of a free plot to a poor family from Bersham, without which they could not be persuaded to allow their young son, Edward Harrison (who died on 6 November 1783), to be buried there. The cemetery was enclosed in 1822 and an extension added in 1872. With the rapid growth in the town's population, the burial ground very quickly filled up and a new, landscaped, cemetery was opened in Ruabon Road in 1876 (see Wrexham Cemetery). The last burial at Ruthin Road was in 1915. The burial ground was taken into local authority control and converted into a Garden of Rest in 1959. It was later 'landscaped' and converted into a public park which opened on 1 May 1963. The headstones were moved and placed along the perimeter wall (only the obelisk memorial to Peter Walker* survives in situ). Part of the Burial Ground is now used as a play area for the Victoria Schools* and it has been fenced off. Although most of the headstones are either badly weathered or damaged beyond repair, the remaining ones give a clear indication of the area of the old parish with burials from as far away as Rhostyllen, Minera, Brymbo and Southsea. The headstones also illustrate the nature of 19th century Wrexham society with burials of brewers, solicitors, innkeepers, schoolmasters, printers, surgeons, veterinary surgeons and churchmen identified from their inscriptions. A computer database of the surviving headstones is available at Wrexham Library.

Among those buried here are: Revd George Cunliffe* (vicar of Wrexham); Samuel Jones (mining engineer of Brymbo); Peter Walker* (brewer and Mayor); Thomas Penson I* (architect); John Burton (industrialist of Minera Hall); Richard* and Ann Jones (pioneer Methodists of Coed-y-Glyn),* Railton Potter (printer of High Street).

A chapel was built at the eastern end of the cemetery in 1794 which served as a mission church with regular services until 1912 when St Michael's Church,* Poyser Street (now All Saint's Church) was built. In later years, the building was used as a mortuary chapel and was eventually demolished. The Religious Census of 1904 showed that Ruthin Road Mission Church had a capacity of 200 and a total daily attendance (AM & PM) of 114. [DRO/DD/WY/8352]

Burma Bell, Bodhyfryd
See Memorial Hall.

Burma Garden, Bodhyfryd
See Memorial Hall.

Burnham, Eleanor *politician*
Eleanor Burnham was born in Wrexham and brought up in Gwnodl Fawr, Cynwyd. Her early career was in social services management. She served as a magistrate in Wrexham and was a member of Denbigh Hospital Mental Health Tribunal. A fluent Welsh speaker, she is a qualified aromatherapist and her hobbies include gardening, cycling and swimming. She is also a Llangollen International Eisteddfod soprano prize-winner. She succeeded as Liberal Democrat AM for the North Wales region on 22 March 2001 upon Christine Humphreys' resignation due to ill-health. She is the Welsh Liberal Democrat Assembly champion for Culture, Welsh Language and Sport.

Burnham Gardens, Queen's Park
Built in the immediate post Second World War period as part of the first phase of WBC's Queen's Park housing development. The origin of the name is unknown.

Burras Hall
See Borras Hall.

Burras Hovah Township
The most north-easterly township of the old Parish of Wrexham, Burras Hovah was originally called Burras Hwfa and may have taken its name from Hwfa ap Iorwerth of Hafod-y-Wern. In 1851 the township became part of the Parish of Gresford. It covers just over 160 acres and was the property of the Pulestons of Hafod y Wern. Today, the township is the area covered by Borras Head* and Borras Higher* farms. Most of the land was sold to Lord Kenyon (see Kenyon Family) in 1803 and some was later the property of the Cunliffes of Acton Park.*

Burras Riffri Township
One of the townships surrounding Wrexham, Burras Riffri was probably named after someone named Griffri, possibly Griffri ap Cadwgan and was part of the Parish of Gresford. It covers 341 acres in the area which is today covered by Borras Hall* and most of the old RAF Wrexham. Most of the township was the property of the Kenyon family* until the mid 20th century.

Burton Brewery, Bridge Street
This brewery and malting house, comprising a three-storeyed, red-brick brewhouse on the west side of Bridge Street, dates back

Burton Brewery, 1913.

to the mid 19th century when it was owned by W. Williams. By 1859, it was the property of Charles Evans. It was bought by Julius H. Chadwick in 1875 for £541. The brewery specialised in the production of stout and also bottled Guinness and Burton ales.

The original building was demolished in 1897 and replaced by a new brewery and malt kiln on the site of what later to be Sergeant Pepper's night-club. The Burton Brewery closed in 1922 (the year that Hubert Chadwick took it over from his father) and was converted into a bottling store for Walker & Homfrays of Manchester. All the pubs belonging to the brewery were sold to F.W. Soames' brewery. [DRO/DD/DM/286/1–21]

Burton Buildings, Bridge Street
This red-brick and terracotta building, built in 1896, takes its name from its location next-door to the former Burton Brewery.*

Burton Drive
A street of private houses, begun in the early 1950s, it takes its name from the village of Burton near Rossett.

Bury Family
A 'dynasty' of civic administrators who served Wrexham well during the late 19th and early 20th centuries. John Bury, a native of Shrewsbury, moved to Wrexham where he had a house on Town Hill. He was the father of John and Thomas Bury.
John Bury, JP – son of John Bury and brother of Thomas Bury,* was born in c.1819. He was appointed an assistant to Thomas Edgworth, the first Clerk to the Wrexham Board of Guardians.* In 1857, he was appointed Clerk, a post which he held until his retirement in 1907 at the age of 88. He was succeeded in the post by his son, J. Oswell Bury,* and his grandson, J. Bagnall Bury. He was elected a member of the first Borough Council in 1857 (see Borough of Wrexham). Among the other positions which he held in 1881 were: Borough Magistrate; Clerk to the District Highways Board; Superintendent Registrar. He lived Hillbury.* It is believed that he was the original developer of the village of Johnstown which was named after him. He died at Hillbury on 26 December 1909 and is buried in Wrexham Cemetery.

Thomas Bury – born in 1844, Thomas Bury became a law student and qualified as a solicitor. He joined T.B. Acton in partnership, then T.A. Acton after which the partnership was dissolved. He served as the second Town Clerk (part-time) of Wrexham from 1879–1906 and clerk to the Engineer Volunteers of the County of Denbighshire, clerk to the Commissioners of Taxes, clerk to the Wrexham & Bersham School Boards and clerk to the Wrexham Charities, secretary of the Wrexham Gas and Coke Company and a qualified accountant. He became he first Honorary Freeman of the Borough of Wrexham (created 28 March 1906). He was a Freemason.

Thomas Bury lived for a period at Claremont Cottage,* Stansty, before marrying Miss Phillips of Carmarthen. They had one son (who died in 1890) and lived at Oaklands, Sontley Road. Thomas Bury died on 8 January 1931 and is buried in the Wrexham Cemetery.* He was the brother of John Bury.*

John Oswell Bury, JP – the son of John Bury,* was born c.1841. He was appointed secretary of Wrexham Infirmary in 1876, a position which he held for 16 years, and chairman of the governors of Wrexham Infirmary from 1892 until his resignation in 1918. In 1898, he pressed for the purchase of Roseneath,* as a site for a new hospital. He was appointed clerk to the Wrexham Board of Guardians, as successor to his father and in 1908, became president of the Wrexham Infirmary. He was made a Justice of the Peace in 1886. He was the father of John Bagnall Bury and resided at Kingscroft,* King's Mills Road. He served as a borough councillor and was appointed an alderman for the East Ward. Among the other posts which he held in 1881 were: clerk to the Rural Sanitary Authority; Registrar of Births, Marriages and Deaths; secretary to the Market Hall Company. In the 1912 will of John Jones* of Grove Lodge, he is recorded as being an 'insurance agent'. He died at Kingscroft in December 1928 and is buried in Wrexham Cemetery.

John Bagnall Bury – was born c.1879, the son of John Oswell Bury,* whom he succeeded as Clerk to the Wrexham Board of Guardians. He was also the secretary of the William & John Jones Charity Trust* 1913–61. Married to Phyllis Brown Bury, MBE, JP, he lived at N° 7 Grove Road and died on 28 January 1961. He is buried in Wrexham Cemetery.*

Bury Street, Hightown
Laid out in the late 19th century, this street was named after the Bury family* who lived at Gatefield,* a house located on King's Mills Road.

Butchers' Arms, Abbot Street
Shown in both the 1833 and 1872 surveys. One of the 19th century landlords, William Eyton, died in 1879 and is buried in the Burial Ground,* Ruthin Road. The premises were located on the south side of the street, opposite the Cross Foxes.

Butchers' Market, High Street
The first of Wrexham's three indoor markets, the Butchers' Market, designed by Thomas Penson,* was built by the Wrexham Market Hall Company and opened on 16 March 1848. The entrance from High Street and the Market Hall offices were built on the site formerly occupied by the Oak* and the Bear* public houses and a shop. Penson's design allowed for 13 shops around the walls of the market with 31 stalls in the centre. The entrance was used by women selling butter, eggs and poultry. Previously, the butchers had occupied stalls in High Street, Church Street and Abbot Street.

Butchers' Street
See Abbot Street.

Butler Square, Watery Road
Originally known as The Bonc (*Trans.* the mound), this comprised a number of small cottages which once belonged to the Ambrose Lewis family. In 1764 the cottages were sold to John Jones of the Miners' Arms,* College Street. At the beginning of the 20th century this became the property of his grandaughter, Mrs Butler, from whom the name derived. The houses were demolished to make way for the dairy development on the junction of Bellevue Road and Watery Road.

Buttall, James
Builder of Grove Park* in the 1760s. A wealthy London

Butler Square, Watery Road, c.1890.

ironmonger, he was married to Elizabeth (died 13 March 1767) See *Hel Achau* Sept 1989. He was a relative of the Master Buttall, who was painted by Gainsborough as 'The Blue Boy'.

He died on 15 November 1794 and is buried in the Dissenters Burial Ground, Rhosddu Road.* [DRO/DD/WY/5452].

Butter Market, Henblas Street
Also known as the General Market, this site was originally occupied by a smaller building which housed the Potato Market* and the Music Hall.* This was demolished in the 1870s and the present red brick and terracotta building erected in its place by the Market Hall Company, was opened in 1879.

C

Cae Siac (Shack)
Trans. Jack's field. Until well into the 20th century, Cae Siac was the commonly used name for the area bounded by Ruabon Road, Victoria Road and Poyser Street. Palmer refers to the area as Cae Siacman (*Trans.* Jackman's field) and suggests that it was only shortened to Cae Siac sometime during the 19th century. The origin of the name is unknown but is often semi-Anglicised as Cae Shack. The land was the property of local solicitor Hampden Poyser who developed it as a residential area in the late 1890s. By 1898 Poyser Street* and Hampden Road* had been laid out and houses were built, a few at a time, over the next 5–10 years. The third street in the development was Edward Street.*

Cae Shack
See Cae Siac.

Cae'r Cleifion (*Terra Leprosorum*)
Trans. the field of the sick. Cae'r Cleifion/Cae Clivion (1802) was located within the township of Wrexham Regis and a large part of it was utilised as the town's new Burial Ground (see Wrexham Cemetery) in the 19th century. It was probably the mediæval area, outside of the actual town itself, where individuals suffering from leprosy and/or the plague were accommodated. It is referred to by the Latin name *Terra Leprosorum* in a lease from the bishop of St Asaph in November 1840. [DRO/DD/WY/8352]

Caernarvon Castle, Bridge Street
An inn is recorded on this site as early as 1710. For a short period in the 1980s, it was renamed Smiley's Bar but later become The Caernarvon. Landlords: Robert Done 1869 (father of R. H. Done*), Josef Wassman 1886. The premises were demolished as part of the Bridge Street redevelopment in the early 2000s.

Caernarvon Road, Borras Park
As with other streets on this private housing development of the early 1960s, known as Hillcrest Estate,* this road takes its name from one of the pre-1974 counties of Wales, in this case Caernarfonshire.

Caia Farm
The name Caia is a distortion of the Welsh word *caeau* (*Trans.* the fields). This farm was located on the site of the present day Caia House public house and was once part of the Hafod-y-Wern* estate. In 1790, it was leased to John Valentine. It appears on the 1833 survey when it was the property of William Jones (1782–1841) and his wife Maria (1788–1856), the parents of William* and John Jones.* Maria established a small brewery at the farm and, after her death, her sons established the Island Green Brewery* in Pentre Felin. By the late 19th century, when it was owned by Walter Jones, it had ceased to function as a farm and was gradually swallowed up by the growth of Wrexham. This Walter Jones may well have been a brother or relative of William and John Jones as the house seems to have reverted back to their ownership and, following the death of John Jones in 1913, became the property of their nephew, Frederick William Morris and for many years, it was rented out to tenants. In 1912, the tenant was Lt-Col Carden. It is now the Caia House* pub. (See also Piercy Estate)

Caia House, Caia Road
The Caia House pub, which opened in the mid 1970s in the premises that were once Caia House Farm,* took over the licence that had previously been held by the Anchor in Mount Street.

Caia Park Estate
The Caia Park Estate was the property of Benjamin Piercy* until his death in 1888 after which it was bought for development by Ebeneser Pike. His plans for a number of streets were delayed and then dramatically changed by the building of the Ellesmere railway line in the mid 1890s. Some of the plots were sold in the early 1890s to local builder Charles Huxley. [Sale details of plots, dated 1918, DRO/1083]

Caia Park
This is the official name for the WBC housing development commonly (and originally) known as Queen's Park.*

Caia Park 'Riots'
During the evening of 22 June 2003, following a disturbance between some local youths and Kurdish immigrants who were residing in Caia Park, a violent confrontation developed between a mob of 150–200 youths and the North Wales Police which spread over two nights. This led to 70 arrests and considerable damage being caused to the Red Dragon* public house.

Caia Road
Named after Caia Farm* (the farmhouse which is now the Caia House* public house), this road does not appear to have existed at the time of the 1833 survey. In the early 1890s, the road had been laid out and named but was undeveloped. All the land on both sides of the road was the property of developer Ebenezer Pike. Until the 1980s, the south side of the road was bordered by the Wrexham–Ellesmere railway* embankment with sidings for the Cambrian Leather Works* alongside. Following the total closure of this line, the embankment was redundant and was eventually partially removed and the site used for a development of senior citizens' bungalows. The premises now occupied by Colour Supplies was originally the Caia Road Mill (later the

Caia Road in the middle distance, separated from Mount Street by the Anchor public house, with Eagle Street to the left. The Wrexham–Ellesmere railway line has now disappeared.

Brolac Paint Store) which contained timber and masonry in its structure which had been removed from the old Town Hall* in High Street. The Anchor Inn* stood at the junction with Mount Street and was demolished in the mid 1970s to make way for the Eagle's Meadow flyover.

Camberley Crescent
Built in the 1930s as a private development, some of the houses, viz N°s 6 & 8 and the former police houses, were not built until the 1950s. (See also Camberley Drive)

Camberley Drive
This road was laid out shortly before the Second World War on land that had previously been part of Park Farm* and the Acton Park* estate. The developer was local businessman William Clarke* who built N°s 2, 4, 5, 6, 7, 8, 9, 10, 12, 14, 16 & 18 pre 1939 but most of the houses were not built until the 1950s. N° 3, Ingle-Nook, was built by Donald Dutton in 1949. The reason for the name is unknown but is presumed to be a reference to the town of Camberley in Surrey, supposedly a suggestion made by the architect, F. A. Roberts of Mold. N°s 11, 13 & 15 were formerly police houses and the police station at N° 11 is still identifiable as part of the present day private residence.

Cambrian Brewery, c.1880.

Cambrian Brewery
First established as the Clark & Orford Brewery, sometime in the mid-19th century, the earliest surviving record shows it being sold by auction at the Lion Hotel on 16 March 1859 on the instructions of its owner, Joseph Clarke (see Mayors of Wrexham and White Lion, Hope Street) of Plas-y-Bryn,* who had previously owned it in partnership with Jonathan Orford. The sale particulars described the brewery as having 'been established for many years, an extensive trade carried on, and the name has acquired great celebrity. The Premises have been erected with great judgement for economising the working expenses in every possible manner consistent with a due regard to the efficient working of the Brewery and are scarcely to be surpassed, if equalled, in the Principality.' There was a house for the owner/manager at the Bridge Street entrance. Between the brewery and Chapel Street, there was 'fine old dry pasture' valuable as building land.

In 1874, the brewery was taken over by William John Sisson (see Sisson family), a wine and spirit merchant, who reconstructed the brewhouse which was located below the Parish Church with access from Tuttle Street.

The brewery was closed in 1922 and its forty-eight pubs were leased to Island Green Brewery. In recent years, the vacant premises were bought by local businessman Bob Gray and demolished in the early 2000s as part of the proposed Bridge Street development.

Cambrian Iron Works
Originally the premises of Powell Brothers and Whitaker,* the Cambrian Iron Works were located in the area beyond the General Station yard. (See also Rogers & Jackson)

Cambrian Leather Works
John Peers is on record as owning a sheep tannery in Salop Road in 1770. Through a chance meeting with John Smalley, a cotton mill owner of Holywell and an associate of Richard Arkwright, he was able to develop the important market of providing leather rollers for the cotton industry and the business became nationally known for the high quality of the leather produced.

In 1822, the leather works was sold to Evan Morris, one of Peers' former employees who developed the business and considerably extended the works. In 1858 the works were again sold, this time to Charles Rocke (who appears to have made his fortune in the Australian goldfields) and his partner, John Meredith Jones (born 21 September 1832; died 14 June 1892), who had already bought a small tannery owned by the latter's father in Charles Street,* Wrexham. They developed the leather works by building on adjoining land and turned it into the largest commercial concern in the town, renaming it The Cambrian Leather Works and adopted the Prince of Wales' feathers as their trade mark.

In 1888 they dissolved their partnership (Rocke becoming the principal of Rocke & Sons, Colonial merchants in London) and the business continued as J. Meredith Jones & Sons (with John's sons Frank Meredith Jones and A. Seymour-Jones as new partners). The business continued to expand and opened warehouses in Liverpool and Manchester and depots in 18

Left: John Peers' tannery, Salop Road, c.1770.

Below: The Cambrian Leather Works, Salop Road, 1858, showing the developments over nearly 90 years.

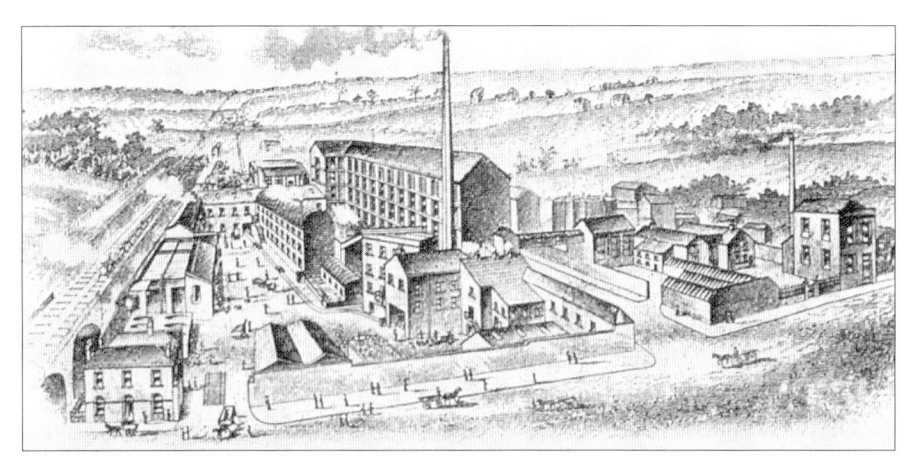

J. Meredith Jones & Sons, Cambrian Leather Works, 1895. Salop Road runs left–right in the foreground. The Wrexham–Ellesmere railway is on the left.

countries. At its peak, the Cambrian Works employed over 500 workers and installed the first leather industry laboratory in the country. The Cambrian was badly affected by the Depression of the 1930s and closed in 1934.

It re-opened in 1946 under the ownership of the Gomshall Group (still trading under the name J. Meredith Jones & Sons) and employed 200 staff. Perhaps its most noted contract post-1945 was the supply of nearly 1 million skins for the bindings of the 11th edition of *The Encyclopædia Britannica*. In 1968/9, the company's annual sales topped £2 million and the works produced over 10 million square feet of leather each year.

In 1972 the business was sold to the Garner Group of tanneries and eventually closed down in 1975. [DRO/DD/DM/763/1–4]

Cambrian Vaults, 9 Townhill
Originally called the *Miners Arms*, this public house appears in both the 1833 and 1872 surveys under its former name. The name Cambrian first appears on these premises in 1876 and therefore cannot have any connection with the building of the Cambrian Railway in the 1890s.

Cambridge Square, Tŷ Gwyn
A development by local builders H.R.&E. Roberts of private houses completed in the 1960s. The name follows the pattern of naming streets on this estate after English counties.

Cambridge Terrace, Talbot Road
Located on the west side of Talbot Road, this row of houses had been built by 1881. Many of the houses in this terrace (if not all of them) were owned by John Jones* the co-founder of the Island Green Brewery,* at the time of his death in 1912.

Camps (Wrexham) Ltd
This motor car business, located at 15 Hill Street, was founded by a Mr Norton shortly after the end of the Great War. The manager, Arthur G. Camp, eventually took over the business. It closed in April 1980.

Cannon Inn, Abbot Street
This inn stood on the north side of Abbot Street, next door to the Sun Inn, on a site that is now part of the New Look store. It appears in the 1872 survey. [Plan DRO/1066].

Capel-y-Groes, Bodhyfryd
The congregation of Seion Church,* Regent Street, decided in 1978 to build a new church and bought the house named Llanelwy,* the former Church in Wales Girls Home, in May 1979. The house was demolished and Colwyn Bay architects, Bowen, Dann & Davies were commissioned to design a new church and schoolroom for the site. Work began in January 1981 at an estimated cost of £325,000, the builders being M‘Alpine. The first service was held in Capel-y-Groes on 7 February 1982 and it was officially opened six days later.

While the former Seion congregation had been without their own chapel, they had been accommodated at their 'daughter' church, Ebeneser,* in Price's Lane, Rhosddu. During this period the congregation of Ebeneser decided to sell their church and to combine with Seion in the new church.

Carden Park Way
Developed in 2001 by Harwood Homes (Redrow) as part of the Fairways development between Holt Road and Bryn Estyn Road. The land was formerly the property of the Wrexham Parochial Charities.

Cardigan Road, Borras Park
As with other streets on this private housing development of the early 1960s, known as Hillcrest Estate,* this road takes its name from one of the old, pre-1974 counties of Wales, in this case, Cardiganshire.

Carlson Drive, Tŷ Gwyn
A development by local builders H. R. & E. Roberts of private houses completed in the late 1960s. Four of the bungalows were originally bought by the Health Authority as temporary accommodation for doctors moving into the area. The origin of the name is unknown.

Carlton Grange, Grove Road
See Bodlondeb, Grove Road.

Carnarvon Hall, Mount Street
A house located on the northern side of Mount Street, opposite The Mount.* It was assessed for tax at 2 shillings in 1742.

Carrington, Thomas *hymn writer*
Born at Gwynfryn, Bwlchgwyn on 24 February 1881, the son of John and Winifred Carrington, Thomas was educated at Bwlchgwyn School and was apprenticed to Hughes & Son, printers of Wrexham. In 1905 he married Mildred Mary Jones of Minera and the couple lived in Coedpoeth where he was in business as a printer and music publisher.

His talent as a musician showed through very early in his life and, aged only 9, he became the organist of the Wesleyan Methodist Church at Bwlchgwyn, a position which he held for 15 years before becoming the organist at Rehoboth Church, Coedpoeth, for 50 years. He studied music in his free time and became music editor of *Y Winllan* and *Eurgrawn*. He was the secretary to the committee that produced *Llyfr emynau and thonau y Methodistiad Calfinaidd a Wesleaidd* in 1929. He was the general secretary of the 1933 National Eisteddfod* in Wrexham. He wrote *Hen Weddi Deuluaidd fy Nhad* (1910); *Concwest Calfari* (1912); *Gwynfryn*; *Bryn-du*; *Doniau Da* (1955); *Yr Ysgol Gân* (1957).

He died at his home in Coedpoeth on 6 May 1961. There was a memorial plaque to him in Rehoboth Church, Coedpoeth. He was given two 'bardic' names – Alaw Maelor (Swansea, 1907) and Pencerdd Gwynfryn (Llangollen, 1928). Ffordd Maelor* is almost certainly named after him.

Carter-Jones, CBE, MP, **Lewis** *politician*
Born in Gilfach Goch, south Wales on 17 November 1920, the son of Tom Jones of Kenfig Hill, a former miner. Lewis Carter-Jones was educated at Kenfig Hill Council School, Bridgend County School and gained a BA honours degree in economics and a diploma in education at the University College of Wales, Aberystwyth (when he represented both the university and the county as captain of hockey). He served as a flight sergeant navigator in the RAF during the Second World War and taught at the Denbighshire Technical College and Yale Technical Grammar School,* Wrexham, where he was head of Business Studies until he was elected to Parliament.

Carter-Jones joined the Labour Party in 1940 and was a member of the Transport & General Workers Union. He contested Chester for Labour in the by-election of 1956 and the General Election of 1959 and was elected MP for Eccles in 1964, a seat which he held until retiring in 1987. A passionate campaigner for the disabled, he was chairman of the Committee for Research for Apparatus for the Disabled (1973–80), the Possum Charity Foundation, Committee of the National Listening Library and the British Limbless Ex-Servicemen's Association. He once said: 'If you want to know why I am obsessive about the disabled and the injured, it is partly that I have a guilty conscience about dropping bombs, injuring innocent people. When I was young, I did not realise what havoc I was helping to create for civilians in German cities – now, I wish to atone for what I have done.' He is on record as having played a significant role in the passing of the Chronically Sick and Disabled Persons Act of 1969. He was awarded an Honorary MA by Salford University for his work with the disabled. He was the secretary of the Indo-British Parliamentary Group from 1965–85. He was awarded the CBE in 1995.

Outside of parliament, he was an avid rugby fan and acted as a referee for many years.

He married Pat Bastiman of Scarborough in 1945 and they had two daughters. They lived at 5 Cefn Road, Rhosnesni. He died on 26 August 2004.

Cartrefle College, Cefn Road
Following the end of the Second World War there was a major shortage of qualified teachers. In an attempt to overcome this difficulty the government introduced emergency one-year teacher training schemes aimed primarily at ex-servicemen. Cartrefle College, founded in 1946 as part of this scheme, was accommodated in the former Ministry of Supply Hostel on Cefn Road (which had been built during the war to house workers from the Royal Ordnance Factory, Marchwiel*). By 1949, the college, funded by Denbighshire County Council, was providing full teacher training facilities for female students qualifying for the Certificate in Education. By the mid 1960s some mature male students were being admitted and the college became dual gender in 1969. The college became part of the North East Wales Institute in September 1975. In April 1993, it ceased to be under the control of Clwyd County Council and came under the direct funding control of the Welsh Office.

Principals:
1946–49	T. C. H. Parry
1949–52	Miss Magdalen Morgan
1953– ?	Miss E. M. Gwynn
c.1965–?	Miss Mary Taylor (a memorial garden dedicated to her memory was laid out at the college)
?	Frank Lloyd (acting)
?–1975	Howel Evans

The college moved to the Plas Coch site in 1994–95 and four years later some of the vacant premises on Cefn Road (including many of the original hostel buildings) were demolished in preparation for the site's conversion into the new premises for Ysgol Morgan Llwyd.* The former administration offices of the college are now the offices of Caia Park Community Council.

Cartrefle College, c.1960. This aerial photograph clearly illustrates the origin of the college buildings, built as a hostel for workers at the ROF, Marchwiel during the Second World War.

Castle, Pentre Felin
See Pentre Felin Welsh Wesleyan Church.

Castle Close, Tŷ Gwyn Lane
Part of a Wain Homes development of 1989/90, this small cul-de-sac may have been named after Caergwrle Castle which could be seen from this location when the houses were built (trees lining the edge of the bypass have since grown to obstruct the view). The castle was granted to Prince Dafydd ap Gruffydd in the late 13th century. (See also Prince's Close and Heol Dafydd)

Castle Square, Pentre Felin
Located on the southern side of Pentre Felin, just east of Pierce's Square*, it undoubtedly took its name from the house called The Castle* which was located nearby.

Cathrall's Lane, Regent Street
See Union Street.

Cattle Market, Smithfield
In 1872, the cattle market or Smithfield was a purpose-built area containing cattle and sheep pens, located on the north-east side of the Beast Market behind the Primitive Methodist Chapel in the area now occupied by part of the Tesco car park. It was closed and moved to a new Smithfield* in 1877.

Cavendish Square, Little Acton
A development of private houses completed during the early 1960s on an estate that was originally known as the Edgby Park Estate (named after the developer). The land was once part of Cae'r Hen Dy (*Trans.* old house field) and Erw Coed Mawr (*Trans.* big wood acre), fields belonging to Little Acton Farm* and later, to the Acton Park* estate.

Caxton Place, Regent Street
Laid out during the late 19th century on land that was formerly the site of a regular gypsy encampment, this street took its name following the establishment of the Principality Press of Messrs Hughes & Son, publishers, in premises on its west side in 1895. When Hughes & Son moved to Cardiff in 1920, the premises became the offices of the *Wrexham Leader*. The upper floor of the building was let to M.M. Johnson Ltd, a clothing firm, and it is believed that an electrical fault in their premises led to the disastrous fire which broke out in the early hours of a June morning in 1949.

It was common for printers to associate their premises with the name of William Caxton who, in the 15th century, established a press at Westminster in London and introduced printing to Britain. The premises were re-built and were re-opened in 1950. In February 1974 the newspaper moved to Centenary Buildings in King Street.* In the 1970s and 1980s the Principality Press premises were used as a shop and then a solicitor's office. The west side of this street was demolished during the early 1990s and is now an apartment block.

Cedar Close, Borras Park
Developed in the late 1960s as part of the development of the Borras Park estate. The name has no particular significance and follows the practice of naming streets after trees.

Cefn
See Cefn Park.

Cefn Park
(*Trans.* ridge park, being a reference to the escarpment on which the house stands). In the mid 18th century, the Cefn (Park) estate belonged to the Griffith family who had a town house in Hope Street, Wrexham. From them, the estate passed to the Kenyons of Gredington. In 1794 the house itself was burned down and the present house was built shortly afterwards. The estate became the property of the Revd Nathaniel Roberts, probably following the sale held at the Wynnstay Arms Hotel on 30 June 1830, when it was described as comprising 'an excellent mansion, desmesne and pleasure grounds; together with several farms and lands containing upwards of nine hundred acres of excellent land (lying in a ring fence)'. The Revd Roberts married Frances, the daughter of John Matthews, attorney of Chester. Sometime after the death of Mrs Roberts in 1850, the estate passed to Sir William Henry Roger Palmer, Bt, of Kunure Park, Dublin who had married Eleanor Matthews (the sister of Frances) in April 1828.

The house was again burned in 1830, leaving little standing apart from the walls, and the core of the present building dates from this period. An artificial boating lake and gardens were laid out during the 19th century. Sir William had one son, Roger William Henry Palmer* who was born in 1832 and succeeded to the title on the death of his father. In the 1881 Census, the house is shown as being staffed by a live-in butler, valet, footman, groom, servant, housekeeper, laundry-maid, two house-maids, kitchen maid and a scullery maid. At the lodge lived a coachman and there was also a gardener living on the estate.

Cefn Park, c.1900.

Sir Roger died childless in 1910 and, after the death of Lady Palmer in 1929, the estate passed to his nephew Roderick George Fenwick of Plas Fron who adopted Palmer as an additional surname.

Lt-Col Fenwick-Palmer* was in possession of Cefn Park during a period of great upheaval and change. At this time, the estate included: Cefn Park, Llwyn Knottia,* Plas Issa,* Erlas Hall, Old Llwyn Onn, Little Llwyn Onn,* Hafod-y-Wern,* Dunks Farm, Abenbury Lodge,* Hullah Farm,* Abenbury Cottage,* Woodbine Farm,* Little Erlas, Coed-y-Bint, Cae Mynach, Cacca Dutton Farm. In 1942 a substantial acreage in Abenbury was sold by compulsory purchase to the Ministry of Aircraft Production to provide a site for what became the Rubery Owen* factory, which was erected to manufacture aircraft wings. Further land was taken in the area of Cacca Dutton for the Royal Ordnance Factory,* Marchwiel (much of this was returned after the end of the Second World War) and, in conjunction with this, land was taken for the construction of barracks and other facilities for the workers at the ROF on what had been Hullah Farm (which later became Cartrefle College* and is now Ysgol Morgan Llwyd*). In c.1948, much against the wishes of Lt-Col Fenwick-Palmer, WBC made a compulsory purchase of c.145 acres (roughly the remaining estate area located between Holt Road* and the southern end of Vyrnwy Way,* which were then developed as the first stage of the Queen's Park* housing estate. A further 127 acres were bought at a later date enabling the Queen's Park estate to be extended as far as Abenbury Road in the south.

Lt-Col Fenwick-Palmer died in 1968 and the estate passed to his cousin, Roger Graham, who also adopted the surname Palmer. In recent years, additional property has been added to the estate (most notably Llwyn Onn*) and large areas of the Wrexham Industrial Estate have been sold for industrial development. Roger Graham-Palmer was the Conservative candidate for Wrexham in the 1987 General Election. [Sale particulars, dated 1830 – DD/DM/233/2] (See also Palmer Family)

Cefn Road
An ancient roadway skirting the edges of the townships of Acton, Erlas, Abenbury Fawr and Abenbury Fechan, it is named after the Cefn Park* estate and marks the eastern boundary of the Queen's Park* estate and, in 2001, the main building line of the town itself. The road, which originally passed in front of Cefn Park, was diverted further west to its present position in 1825. Located on the road are the entrances to Llwyn Knottia Farm,* Cefn Park,* Llwyn Onn* and Five Fords. Twenty-four flats were built in 1959 which were originally to be called Churchill Crescent but, to avoid confusion with the nearby Churchill Drive,* the name was changed to Beeston Terrace. The section of road between Cartrefle College* and Churchill Drive was widened in 1968.

Cefndre, Queen's Park
(*Trans*. town ridge) Developed c.1955 as part of WBC's Queen's Park* housing estate. It takes its name from the ridge on which it stands overlooking the town of Wrexham.

Ceiriog Road, Queen's Park
Built in the late 1940s as part of the first phase of WBC's Queen's Park housing development, it is named after the Ceiriog valley.

Cemetery
See Cae'r Cleifion and Wrexham Cemetery.

Centenary Road, Bryn Offa
Laid out in 1957 as part of WBC's Bryn Offa housing development, it was named to commemorate the Borough Centenary in that year. (See also Bryn Offa)

Central Arcade, Hope Street
This was built in 1891 (the date appears on the decorative gable) on the site of Nº 58 Hope Street which was a public house, The King's Head* from c.1711 until c.1745 when the name was moved to premises across the street. In the mid-19th century it was the premises of John Clark, tailor, who served as Mayor of Wrexham in 1860–1. The shop was demolished to make way for the entrance. The arcade was developed by the Wrexham Arcade Company which had Cllr George Bevan, a local accountant, as secretary. The arcade provided 18 lock-up shop premises, offices and one photographic studio, generating an annual income of £1,080. The shops either side of the entrance had an annual rental of £250 and £150.

Central Avenue, Acton
Part of the WBC Acton Park housing estate* development of the early 1920s.

Central Road, Bradley Road
See St Mark's Road.

Central Station
Opened in 1887 with the extension of the Wrexham, Mold & Connah's Quay Railway* from Wrexham Exchange Station into the town centre. The original plan was to build a new, very palatial station to be named Wrexham Jubilee (in honour of Queen Victoria's 50 years on the throne) but this never materialised and the buildings erected were some second-hand church buildings purchased from mid-Wales. The ecclesiastical origin of the buildings is evident on examination of the windows in the few surviving photographs.

In 1895, the Wrexham & Ellesmere Railway* reached the Central Station and added extra platforms and a few small buildings to the complex. To make way for this development, the

Central Station, c.1910. A clear view of the length of the station. The tracks on the right were laid by the Wrexham & Ellesmere Railway while those on the left (where the trains are standing) were laid by the Wrexham, Mold & Connah's Quay Railway.

Central Station, c.1915. A troop train is moving out of the station, passing the engine sheds.

Central Station, 1959.

Wrexham & Ellesmere Railway demolished the old Wrexham Vicarage* which they had bought from the Benjamin Piercy* Estate in 1896 to serve as their company office.

The redevelopment of the Island Green* site in the 1990s gave an opportunity to build a new Central Station in another location. Despite opposition from many quarters, including local Member of Parliament, Dr John Marek, the station was re-sited about 150 yards further west, in the centre of the Island Green shopping precinct and given access to the town centre via St Mark's Road.* The first phase of the re-development was completed in 1998 and the station was completed and officially opened in 1999 with the bilingual name Wrexham Central/Wrecsam Canolog.

Stationmasters: (these are only some of the Stationmasters and the dates are not their date of appointment)
- 1881   Isaac A. Roberts
- 1895   Arthur Edgecumbe (died 1918, aged 84)
- 1913   R. Rainford (retired 1919)
- 1931   W. Harris
- 1938   W. Inch
- 1951/4 R.A. Webster

Central Station, c.1900. The station staff of the Wrexham, Mold & Connah's Quay Railway pose in front of a Cambrian Railways tank engine.

Challoner, Arthur, *local politician*
Born c.1878, the son of Samuel and Emma Challoner of Greenfield Terrace, Gwersyllt, Arthur Challoner was educated at Gwersyllt School and took up employment at the Wilderness Brick & Terra Cotta Company in Gresford before setting up his own business as a builders merchant. He was also a partner in the Cooke's Explosive Works at Penrhyndeudraeth and was involved with several local collieries. Elected an Independent (Wrexham Ratepayers Association) member of WBC in 1932 he became Mayor in 1940, chairman of the Highways Committee and a Denbighshire County Councillor for the Grosvenor Ward. He was appointed a Justice of the Peace in 1939. During the Second World War, he was an Air Raid Warden and was a supporter of the Air Training Corps. He was an active member of the North Wales Asylum Board, the Committee for the After-care of Tuberculosis Patients, the Town & Country Planning Committee, the Denbighshire Assessment Committee, the Assistance Board Advisory Committee, a trustee of the Dame Dorothy Jeffreys Charity and Hon Treasurer of the Wrexham Civic Guild of Help. A founder member of the Rotary Club of Wrexham* he was its President in 1932 and was the Worshipful Master of the Square & Compass Lodge of Freemasons. A keen sportsman, he played football for Wrexham, was a cricketer and President of the East Denbighshire Bowling League.

Arthur Challoner married Victoria, the daughter of John Davies of Leeswood (the sister of Alderman 'Cris' Davies, JP*), who was also a Borough Councillor and County Councillor. They had two children. He died at his home, Aingarth, Gerald Street, on 20 February 1942.

Chanticleer Farm, Holt Road
Captain William M. Kington, DSO, the son-in-law of F.W. Soames* of Bryn Estyn,* was severely injured serving in the Royal Welsh Fusiliers during the First World War and opened a small poultry farm on Holt Road which he named Chanticleer (French for cockerel). He was the father of Bill Kington (a director of Border Breweries) and the grandfather of journalist, broadcaster and writer Miles Kington (see Wrexham Links). Capt Kington died in the early 1930s and his widow moved to live at Whybro House.* The farm then became a market garden belonging to the Thomas brothers (who moved here in 1934 from Croes Eneurys Farm*).

Chanticleer Close, Holt Road
Built in the 1970s as a small private housing development on the site of a smallholding named Chanticleer Farm.

Chapel Buildings, Wrexham Fechan
A small block of four terraced dwellings located just to the south-east of Mount House* with access from Salop Road* almost opposite the junction with Rivulet Road.* They appear on the 1872 survey. Before the Second World War, Jack Jones' blacksmith shop was located here.

Chapel Square, Pentre Felin
This was located on the northern side of Pentre Felin, behind the

Wesleyan Methodist Chapel and near the site of the present day Mitre Inn.

Chapel Street, Pen-y-Bryn
Also known as Stryt Draw (*Trans.* yonder street). The English name comes from Pen-y-Bryn Chapel (Chapel Street English Congregational Chapel) which was built in 1789, Wrexham's oldest surviving Non-conformist religious building. This street was probably first laid out during the 18th century. The other major building in this street is Plas-y-Bryn,* now a medical centre but originally a private house.* In 1872, the south-western side of the street was dominated by private gardens belonging to Plas-y-Bryn and other substantial houses in the area. Charles* and Sarah Dodd, the parents of Professor A. H. Dodd* and Dr C. H. Dodd* lived at Clavelly Cottage, Charles dying there in 1928. From about 1880 until after the Second World War, there was Drill Hall located on the corner of Chapel Street and Poplar Road (now part of St Giles' School playing field). In 1912 this was the headquarters of the Denbighshire Hussars Imperial Yeomanry.* After the First World War it became the headquarters of the local Territorial Army artillery battery (Denbighshire Yeomanry) and during the Second World War it was used by the Home Guard.

Chapel Street English Congregational Chapel
This congregation was formed by a break-away group from the 'Old Meeting' in Chester Street. They first met in a pin factory in Stryd Draw,* Chapel Street before being given the adjoining land build a chapel. The chapel was opened in 1789 (although a Sunday school had been opened five years earlier) and remodelled in 1881. On the opening of Salisbury Park Church,* the Chapel Street building was sold to the Welsh Baptists (See Chapel Street Welsh Baptist Chapel). In the 1833 survey it was shown as the Independent Chapel. The building is Grade II listed. In 1847, the chapel had a Sunday school with 165 pupils. The Religious Census of 1881 showed: Capacity 200; attendance (AM & PM) 240.

Chapel Street Welsh Baptist Church
Members of the congregation at Garden Road Welsh Baptist Chapel* established a 'daughter' church in rooms above Stanford's Café in Hope Street in 1895. Two years later they bought the former Chapel Street English Congregational Church.* The Religious Census of 1904 showed: Capacity 300; attendance (AM & PM) 209. (See also Hope Street Welsh Baptist Chapel)

Charity School
Located beside the Tenterfield above Pentre Felin, the Charity School is shown on the 1833 survey. (See National School, Tenters Square)

Charles Street
The origins of this street's name are unknown but, according to Palmer, it was known as Beast Market Street until late in the 18th century (and in the Middle Ages it was regarded as an extension to High Street). It is a commonly held belief that Charles Street is named after King Charles I but this seems very unlikely as the first mention of the name in a surviving document does not appear until 1788 and on gravestones in the 1830s. Dr Jonathan Edwards* was born at N° 15, a house that dates back to at least 1650. The large building on the left when approaching from High Street (formerly Bumbles shop and coffee shop) was built by Thomas Penson* who lived here. Later, the house became the offices of the Wrexham Water Works Company.* At the end of the 19th century this building was the property of William Bernie, who had a pawnbrokerage on the ground floor. It was built on the site of a property which, from 1715–30, was the home of Edward Hanmer, postmaster of Wrexham. Near this site was a narrow passage between two buildings known as Cutler's Entry – after the trade of the occupant on the house on Charles Street.

Behind N° 22 stood the tannery belonging to Meredith Jones (died 1888) the father of John Meredith Jones of the Cambrian Leather Works.* N° 22 is the premises of Fletchers, the last wooden clog-maker in Wrexham (founded by Alfred and James Fletcher in the mid 19th century). At N° 23, stood the Blossoms* –next door but one to the Wynnstay Arms Hotel– which had been an inn since at least 1723 and which appears on the 1872 survey.

N° 18, now a taxi office, was found to be a wattle and daub building dating back to at least the 17th century.

The last public house in the street, the Elephant & Castle, first appeared in the rate books in 1788. It lost its licence in *c.*1999 and is now Dao Siam Thai restaurant.

At the rear of the premises adjoining the Beast Market, on the south side, was the saw mill belonging to Edward Meredith Jones in 1881.

A timber and thatch building, next door to the Elephant & Castle, and formerly known as the Hat Inn,* is now the premises of Schwarz Opticians and contains a beam dated 1621. At the end of the 19th century, another half-timbered building stood between The Hat and Market Street;* in its latter years this was T. C. Crump's fish and chip shop which was burned down when a stray firework landed in the thatch on bonfire night. The fire spread to the Hat and seriously damaged the roof and upper floor. Considerable alterations took place in 1998, including the building of new premises and a pedestrianisation scheme, turning what had been a rather run-down street into one of the more attractive small retail streets in the town centre.
[Deeds for properties in this street DRO/DD/DM/218/1–38. Plans DRO/1053]

Chelston Avenue, Barker's Lane
Built in the late 1970s by Broseley Homes. The origin of the name is unknown.

Cherry Hill, Borras Park
Built in 1936 for Charles Llewelyn Thomas, this is one of the finest inter-war houses in Wrexham. Designed by Edgar Beresford in the Arts and Crafts style, it remains almost unchanged and is a Grade II listed building. Following the opening of RAF Wrexham in 1941, the house was requisitioned as officer's quarters. Both of C. Ll. Thomas' sons were killed while serving in the RAF during the Second World War (Flying Officer Charles Raymond Delauny Thomas, 236 Squadron (Blenheims), died France 18 July 1940, buried Quiberville Churchyard, Seine-Maritime; Pilot Officer Anthony Delauny Thomas, 37 Squadron (Wellingtons), RAFVR, died 7 March 1941, buried Phaleron War Cemetery, Greece) and the house eventually passed to Ursula Thomas of Cambridge who sold it to Denbighshire County Council Children's Department in *c.*1960 for use as a children's home. The property is now a private children's day nursery.

Cherry Hill Drive, Borras Park
A private housing development of the early 1960s by London developers Spinks & Denning on land that had formerly been the property of William Clarke* of Oak Lodge.* The street takes its name from the nearby house, Cherry Hill.*

Cheshire View, Spring Lodge
Built in the 1930s as part of WBC's Spring Lodge* housing scheme which re-housed people from the Pentre Felin* area of the town. The name refers to the aspect from the street when it was built, looking eastwards towards Cheshire.

An RAF reconnaissance photograph of Wrexham town centre, taken on 17 November 1948. The railway network between the Wrexham Lager Brewery and Cobden's Mill on the left, passing under Bradley Road bridge and into Central Station on the right gives a clear indication of the continued importance of railways, as does the congestion of carriages and engines in and around the Central Station. Also visible in this photograph are the railway goods sheds (with St Mark's Church behind), Bryn-y-Ffynnon and Seion Churches and, in the distance, the Wrexham & East Denbighshire War Memorial Hospital. In the distant centre background is Garden Village. [National Assembly for Wales]

Chester Lane
See Chester Street.

Chester Road
The original route of Chester Road (until the late 18th century) was very different from that which we know today and followed part of the course of the present day Box Lane* towards Gresford. It seems very likely that the road took a course across what later became Acton Park from somewhere between Rhosnesni Lane and Hazel Grove, linking up with Box Lane somewhere near the bend by the junction of Acton Gardens.

The present day Chester Road, west and north of the junction with Powell Road, was first developed in the latter years of the 19th century when land which had once been part of the Grove Park estate was released for building. Among the significant houses here were St John's* and Plas yn Llwyn,* Grove Lodge* (now part of Plas Darland flats on Grove Road) and Greystones.* Trevose, Oak Dene, Woodlands and Acton Grove* were built on land that was formerly part of the Acton Park* estate, as was all the land, on both sides of the road, from the Prices Lane/Rhosnesni Lane junctions to the Gresford roundabout.

Heading north up Acton Hill, the land on the west side of Chester Road, from Prices Lane to Tŷ Gwyn Lane, part of Croes Eneurys Farm* and Tŷ Gwyn Farm,* was sold in 1913 to the Welsh Town Planning & Housing Trust Ltd. for the development of the proposed Garden Village* scheme. The outbreak of the First World War and the introduction of corporation housing in the immediate post-war period meant that less than half of the scheme was built and, consequently, much of the land was sold again and developed by different builders. The houses on the bank (backing onto Eneurys Road* as far north as Sandway Road*) were built in the late 1920s and early 1930s. Those between the two entrances to Acton Gate* in the late 1920s/early 1930s were built by H.V. Parker (see Croes Eneurys Estate). The houses between the northern entrance to Acton Gate and the Garden Village shops were built as part of the Garden Village* development, with certain exceptions *e.g.* Dorville (opposite the Acton Park public house) which was privately built by Alderman

Roger A. Dutton* in the 1930s. Just beyond the Garden Village shops are the first houses to be built as part of the first phase of the Garden Village Estate and the date '1914' appears on a plaque between N°s 187 & 189. From just beyond this terrace to Pandy Lane,* was Tŷ Gwyn Farm* which was developed during the 1960s and early 1970s by H.R.&E. Roberts. Finally, on the west side, the houses between Pandy Lane and the Gresford roundabout were built at various times between the 1930s and the 1980s. Returning towards the town on the eastern side of Chester Road, the houses between the roundabout and Acton Smithy* were individually built at various dates between the 1920s and the 1980s. A house named Adderley previously stood on this site and a new private housing scheme in a previously undeveloped field nearby is called Adderley Bank. The Little Acton housing estate was built by H.R.&E. Roberts for WBC in the early 1950s and the houses on either side of Newbrigg Road* were built between the wars. Between Little Acton Drive and the Acton Park* public house, the houses were mainly private developments for individual owners. The Acton Park* was built just before the outbreak of the Second World War and the Four Dogs* in the late 1970s. The Acton Park housing estate between the Four Dogs and Hazel Grove* was built in the 1960s by WBC, Hazel Grove in the 1930s and Cilcen Grove* in the early 1920s. The Nine Acre Field,* bought by WBC from the Acton Park estate after the First World War was tenanted to Park Farm* during the 1920s and was then used for allotment type cultivation during and after the Second World War, after which it became the playing fields for Grove Park Boys School* (later Bromfield School* and latterly the Groves High School*). Some of the land between Westminster Drive* and Pen-y-Maes Avenue* was the property of brewer and philanthropist, John Jones* of Grove Lodge,* at the turn of the 20th century. The most northerly section of the land between Pen-y-Maes Avenue and Powell Road* was owned by Wrexham solicitor Hampden Poyser* who built the two semi-detached houses that now form Strathmore Surgery (N° 20, originally named Coed Derw, was occupied by his two spinster sisters). N°s 14 & 16 were built by Wrexham architect, Michael J. Gummow,* in 1901, on land which he had bought from the Acton Park estate.

Chester Road (Ebeneser) Welsh Congregational Church,
Chester Road
Built to replace Ebeneser Church in Queen Street on land that was formerly the site of Whybro House,* this chapel was designed by Raymond Jones of G. Raymond Jones & Associates, Wrexham. A totally unconventional wedge-shaped building, it is one of the more interesting modern buildings to be found in the town centre. Built at a cost of £182,000 it was consecrated on 14 January 1976. It contains a pulpit in memory of the Revd T. Glyn Thomas, minister at the old Ebeneser Chapel for 34 years.

Chester Street
Sometimes referred to as Chester Lane, this street, along with Lambpit Street and Holt Street, formed an area of Wrexham known as The Lampit/Lambpit.* The former Feathers* public house, on the corner of Charles Street,* is one of the most significant buildings in Chester Street, and is now the Tessuti men's clothing shop. Opposite the old Grammar School* site, on land now occupied by the People's Market,* stood Tŷ Meredith, which was probably the town house of the Merediths of Pentrebychan until they acquired the Court.* The Post Office was located at what is now the site of *The Old Vaults** between 1786 (or earlier) and 1814, before being transferred to N° 36 Chester Street.

Between the entrance to the Guildhall and the Rose & Crown* (which stood on the southern corner of the Lambpit Street* junction) was a row of tall terraced properties, the most significant of which was the Bromfield Hotel. These houses were demolished in *c*.1970. On the northern corner of Lambpit Street stands the Seven Stars* public house, built in 1904 by Jack Scott who also built the adjoining premises. The Registrar's office was housed at N° 23, Chester Street House, an early 18th century town house (see the Old Registry). N° 25 (now Wingett House) was the home of William Harrison, cashier of Lloyds Bank,* from *c*.1811–60, who bought it from Richard Lloyd almost as soon as it had been built.* Harrison's initials can still be seen in some of the stonework in what is now the wall of the car park at the rear of this building. Harrison's Court (Chester Street) was named after him. During the 20th century, N° 25 Chester Street became the home, and later the offices, of Frank Wingett, the founder of Wingetts Estate Agency and Auction Rooms and the Frank Wingett Cancer Appeal. For a short time from 1991–96, this building was the offices of Bridge Books and is now a Grade II listed building.* N°s 26 & 27, now solicitor's offices (Humphreys & Co. and Tudor Williams) are examples of early 19th century small town houses and are both Grade II listed buildings. N° 28 is the last house in Chester Street still in use as a dwelling. N° 29, now the premises of Francis Opticians, was built about 1830 and, according to CADW, was probably intended to have office accommodation on the ground floor from the outset. It is also a Grade II listed building. Alongside N° 29 is a modern office block, built in 1991 on the site of the former Chester Street English Baptist Chapel.* The last building on this side of the road is the former chapel schoolroom which was converted into the chapel in the late 1980s. In the early 20th century, there was one other building on this side of the street, a small stone-built lodge at the end of the drive leading to Llwyn Isaf.* The boundary wall and entrance to Llwyn Isaf survives as the entrance to the Library car park and just beyond it, is the old Wrexham–Chester milestone which originally stood on the opposite side of the road. Between this and the inner ring road stands the former premises of Grove Park County School,* opened in 1902 and now part of Yale College.*

The land on the opposite side of the road to Grove Park was, in the 1860s, used as a plant nursery which was opened to the public on Sundays and provided the town's first unofficial park. At this time there was also a skating rink located in this area. Bodhyfryd House* stood on the east side of the street, on the site now occupied by Crown Buildings.* Next door, in the early 20th century, was a domestic staffing agency run by Miss Johnson. N° 35, formerly the office of Bartlet & Co (solicitors), now the office of NACRO Cymru (National Association for the Care and Resettlement of Offenders), was built in *c*.1840 and is a Grade II listed building. Next to this house was another attractive town house which was demolished by W. Higginson to build the Wrexham Motor Company Garage (which eventually became the Lucas Garage until the 1980s when the premises was converted into shops). The Red Lion* stood on the corner of Chester Street and Holt Street and was re-built and re-named the Welch Fusilier.*

Chester Street British School
This school for the children of Non-conformists in Wrexham was opened with a bequest from the will of Dr Daniel Williams* who died in 1716. It was first housed in the Friends' Meeting House in Holt Street before moving to the Presbyterian – later Congregational Chapel – in Chester Street in 1781. The *Report on the State of Education in Wales, 1847* stated:

> A school for boys, taught by a master, in a room in the Presbyterian chapel. Number of scholars, 69; number employed as monitors, 7. Subjects taught – the Scriptures,

reading, writing, arithmetic, English grammar and etymology, geography, history, and music. Fees 1d. per week, and from 6s 6d to 10s per quarter. Endowment, £35.

I visited this school, in company with Mr Thomas, on the 22nd January. There were only 39 scholars present; 10 of these could read with ease; and out of 15 who could answer Scripture questions, 4 excelled: 29 copy-books were shown, but only 3 specimens were good. I examined 20 boys in arithmetic, and 3 of these excelled in the Rule of Three and upwards; 12 had commenced English grammar, 10 English history, and one was learning geography. Some of these scholars had made good progress; but the information of the majority appeared desultory and unconnected. They all understand English.

The master has been 4 years a teacher, and received some preparation at a school in Glasgow.

The principal defect in the organization of the school was, that while one class was being examined the rest did nothing.

The school-room was built with the aid of a Government grant. It forms the cellar, as it were, of a handsome Presbyterian chapel, being 7 feet below the level of the street. The out-buildings were in an atrocious condition. The master states that there is a debt of £700 upon the chapel, which accounts for the deficiency of apparatus, which the Committee should provide. There were no books on geography, and only 6 grammars for 15 pupils. The fixtures were deficient for the British system.

The endowment, £35, is derived from Dr Daniel Williams's* Charity, the terms of which require that the Assembly's Catechism shall be taught in the school. The master and the minister of the chapel informed me that no Cathechism is taught. Only one scholar has been taught free within the master's recollection. The majority belong to an Independent congregation.

The school closed in 1848 and the charitable bequest eventually passed to the running of the Dr Williams School in Dolgellau. One of its most notable local pupils was the surgeon Thomas Taylor Griffith.* (See also Blue Books, Dr Daniel Williams' School and the British School, Brook Street)

Chester Street Congregational Church
Originally a break-away group of Presbyterians (who later took the name Congregationalists) who had set up a chapel in a shop premises in College Street* in the 17th century. In 1697 they were given the lease of land in Chester Street* on a peppercorn rent. Work on the first chapel commenced in 1698 and ended in 1700 but the building was destroyed by mob violence in 1715. This was replaced the following year by another small building located on the corner of Guildhall Street* and Chester Street which appears on the 1833 survey in front of the Manchester Hall.* This was demolished in 1840 –during the ministry of the Revd John Pearce of Ysbyty.*

The last chapel on this site, a much larger neo-classicalbuilding, was opened in 1841. It was built at a cost of approximately £2,611 to a design by local architect Michael Gummow* and was demolished in the early 1960s following the collapse of its roof. A Sunday school, catering for 172 pupils, was being held here in 1847. The Religious Census of 1881 showed: Capacity 550; attendance (AM & PM) 340. The Religious Census of 1904 showed: Capacity 400; attendance (AM & PM) 238.

Chester Street English Baptist Church
In 1747, land which had once been the property of Lady Dorothy Jeffreys,* and which extended for 240 feet along Chester Street, was bought for £40. A chapel was first built here in 1762 which came to be known as the 'Old Meeting'. This building (and two adjacent houses) was demolished in 1875 and a new, larger, chapel was built the following year, with a schoolroom alongside, at a total cost of £2,200. A new schoolroom was opened in April 1936. The chapel was demolished in 1987 and the services were transferred to the schoolroom. The original chapel site was then sold and a new office block (N° 30 Chester Street) was built on the land. [DRO/ND/1] In 1847 this congregation had a Sunday school catering for 79 pupils. The Religious Census of 1881 showed: Capacity 350; attendance (AM & PM) 246. The Religious Census of 1904 showed: Capacity 300; attendance (AM & PM) 205. For further details see *The Old Meeting*, G.V. Price.

Chester Street House
See the Old Registry.

Chester Street Presbyterian Church
See Chester Street Congregational Chapel.

Chevet Hey, Price's Lane
Built in the mid 19th century as a private house (quite possibly to a design by J.R. Gummow*), it had a number of owners and residents until the time of the First World War. The Studio School (see The Studio) took the property over in the late 1920s and remained there until c.1938. At the start of the Second World War it became the home of local builder, George F. Sumner, until the National Fire Service took it over and the family did not return until the end of hostilities. It was George Sumner who built N°s 40a–46 Price's Lane in the garden of Chevet Hey. The Sumner family sold the house in about 1953 and it became a children's home. It was demolished for re-development in 2000. [Sale of furniture documents, 1912. DRO/1024]
Residents:
1871   John Thomas Trotter Pilkington, civil & mining engineer.
1881   Thomas Evans Jackson, coach-builder (still living here in 1893).
1913   Ll. Hugh-Jones.
1940   G.F. Sumner.

*Chevet Hey, c.1950
[Don Sumner]*

Cholera Outbreaks
When Cholera first broke out in north Wales in 1830 Wrexham was fortunate and no recorded cases were discovered. In 1866, however, the town was less fortunate but the spread of the disease was kept under control. The town fire engine was used to pump diluted carbolic acid into affected houses, cottages were lime-washed (with free lime being provided by the Borough Council), ash pits were covered and pig sties were moved away

An aerial photograph of Wrexham town centre which clearly illustrates the changes that have taken place in the fifty years since it was taken. The bottom left-hand quarter of the picture has changed beyond all recognition. Gone are Ebeneser Chapel (Queen Street), Lambpit Street, the Vegetable Market, the old Guildhall (Grammar School), the Hippodrome Cinema, nearly all the buildings along Chester Street, the Public Hall and the Congregational Church. Also gone are the railway, the horse repository on Eagles' Meadow, most of Mount Street, the Cambrian Leather Works, much of Bridge Street and the Cambrian Brewery. In their place there are now the Eagles Meadow precinct, the numerous barn-like shopping outlets along Salop Road and the St Giles Link Road.

from houses. Bedding used by those who had contracted the disease was burned. An isolation unit was constructed on stilts close to the Union Workhouse.

Church Army, Hill Street
The Religious Census of 1904 showed: Capacity 500; attendance (AM & PM) 233.

Church of Christ, King Street
First recorded in Wrexham in 1837 when some members of the Chester Street English Baptist Church formed a new congregation that met in Bank Street. In 1858 they took over the former Roman Catholic Chapel of St David in King Street.* Meetings of this church are recorded in the Religious Census of 1881 which showed: Capacity 120; attendance (AM & PM) 78. The Religious Census of 1904 showed: Capacity 120; attendance (AM & PM) 86. In 1912 they moved to the former Primitive Methodist Church in Talbot Road.

Church House, Regent Street
Opened in 1910 on the corner of Regent Street and St Mark's Road, this Tudor style brick building provided administrative and social facilities for the Anglican church in Wrexham. It achieved national fame in the 1930s when it was the location of the public enquiry into the Gresford Colliery disaster of 1934. In its latter years Church House was well-known as a venue for Saturday night dances. It was demolished in the 1960s as part of the re-development of Regent Street.

Church Street
This name first appears in Norden's survey of 1620. The property currently used as a wine bar (N°s 7–10) is possibly the oldest in Wrexham and may pre-date even the Parish Church by 100–150 years (despite the information on the plaque on the front of the building). According to local historian, the late D. Leslie Davies (who made a particular study of Wrexham's timber-framed buildings), the property is an excellent example of a mid-mediæval hall house to which a number of alterations have been

The gable-end of N°s 7–10 Church Street, exposed during building work next door, clearly shows the cruck-frame of the original building.

An artist's impression of what N°s 7–10 Church Street may have looked like when first built. The Church Street frontage is on the left. [RCHBW]

made over the years. As a hall house, the building would have had only one floor with the space above open all the way to the roof. The building has a timber cruck frame (which resembles a wooden ship turned upside down) and would originally have had a thatched roof. The wall panels would have been in-filled with wattle and daub. The hall would probably have had a raised platform at one end where the owner and his family would have dined. A floor was added to the building in the mid-17th century, creating the two storeys which we see today and the gables which now face onto Church Street may have been added at the same time in order to provide windows for the upper floor. At the top of the stairs is the date 1681 which may well be a record of the date when the alterations were carried out. The earliest documented reference to this building is, surprisingly, 1723, when an indenture was drawn up between Thomas Collins, a glover of Wrexham, and John Taylor. The building is now Grade II* listed. The street was referred to as Church Yard Street in the early 18th century.

On the opposite side of the street are N°s 3–4 which are basically 17th century buildings with 18th century additions when the premises incorporated N° 6 Temple Row* and was divided into two houses and shops by Samuel Edwards. The buildings have a timber frame and N° 3 has a fine 19th century shop window. They are now Grade II listed.

The premises on the corner of Church Street and Town Hill were demolished in 1961 and an unsightly concrete building put in its place. This was badly damaged by fire in the 1990s and was eventually remodelled to form part of the 1–5 bar/restaurant on Town Hill.*

The building on the corner of Church Street and College Street, which was for many years the premises of Horton's pawnbrokerage was, despite much opposition from many individuals and organisations (including WBC) demolished *c*.1972 and the new building erected on the site was designed by the Wrexham firm of G. Raymond Jones & Associates. At the same time, plans were submitted for the demolition of the building on the corner of Church Street and Temple Row but, fortunately, these were refused permission and the building was renovated.

Churchill Drive, Queen's Park
This was built in the immediate post Second World War period as part of the first phase of WBC's Queen's Park housing development. It was named after the statesman and prime minister, Sir Winston Leonard Spencer Churchill (1874–1965).

Churton Drive, Spring Lodge
Built in the 1930s as part of WBC's Spring Lodge* housing scheme to re-house the residents of the Pentre Felin* slum area. The road was named after the parish of Churton by Farndon in Cheshire.

Cilcen Grove, Acton
Built in the 1920s as a major thoroughfare of WBC's Acton Park Housing Estate.* The original intention was that this road was to be named Corporation Avenue but, almost immediately, the Borough Council changed its mind and it was named (but incorrectly spelt) after the village of Cilcain in Flintshire – probably by the chairman of the Health Committee and former Mayor, Dr Edwards-Jones* (1910–11), who had family connections with the village. There is a plaque on N° 15 to commemorate F/Lt David S. A. Lord, V.C., D.F.C.,* who lived there during the 1920s and 1930s. There are foundation stones on N°s 9 & 10.

City Status
The suggestion that Wrexham should be considered for city status was first aired by Town Clerk Philip Walters in December 1950 when he suggested that it might be a fitting way of commemorating the 100th anniversary of the incorporation of the Borough of Wrexham.

The issue was again raised in 1998 with a view to Wrexham becoming a city in 2000. The grounds for the application were:

Wrexham was the premier administrative, commercial and industrial centre in north Wales;
Wrexham had a growing educational sector and was hoping that NEWI* would achieve university status within two years;
Wrexham had the largest hospital in north Wales;
Wrexham had St Mary's Cathedral* and the highly regarded St Giles Parish Church;*
There was no civic city in north Wales;
Wrexham was already a unitary authority;
Wrexham had an enviable record for economic regeneration

red dragon rampant which were the gift from the RWF in recognition of their having been given the Freedom of the Borough of Wrexham in 1946.

The Mayoress' Chain – This was purchased in 1902 and was manufactured by Wrexham jeweller A. W. Butt. The 15ct gold chain 'is twenty-four inches in length, composed of links formed by enamelled Tudor roses at intervals, with larger links bearing the Prince of Wales plumes on enamelled escutcheons (blue and white) and Borough devices *i.e.* lions and crosiers, as on the Wrexham achievements, also enamelled red and white respectively, the tablets or shields being surmounted by mural coronets; these links alternated with the initial letter of the Borough name, the 'W' being of an antique pattern. The centre link will display the Royal Cypher 'E.R. VIII' surmounted by the Royal crown and supported by the lions of England (*passant guardant* in gold)'. From this link is suspended a pendant bearing a miniature portrait of Queen Alexandra within a circlet of diamonds surmounted also by the Royal crown and a pair of sceptres in saltire – the whole to form a coronation badge. The badge is supported and held in position by a smaller chain, known as the Prince of Wales pattern, attached to the links of the larger chain in four festoons, with small gold knobs on either side of the badge. The coronation badge and festoon chain also supports the Corporation jewel which has in the centre the Borough Arms on a Louis XVI shield, resting on a goat's head,

Chains of office of the Mayor and Mayoress of Wrexham. [WCBC]

following the decline of the heavy industries of the region.

The application was unsuccessful and work commenced on a second application for a grant to be made in 2002, the fiftieth anniversary of the accession to the throne of Queen Elizabeth II. On this occasion, the successful application was that of Newport in Gwent.

A further bid is likely to be made to coincide with the Queen's Diamond Jubilee in 2012.

Civic Regalia

The Mayor's Chain – This was purchased from N. S. Scotcher of Birmingham in 1872 and cost £193. It was worn for the first time at the Mayor's Banquet in 1873. The chain is made up of twenty-four hollow links of 18ct gold on each of which is engraved the name and year of office of a Mayor of Wrexham. Suspended from the chain is a heart-shaped 18ct gold pendant with an enamel heraldic shield depicting the arms of the Borough of Wrexham and the motto 'Fear God, Honour the King'. Above the shield is a closed helmet in silver and the pendant is surmounted by a gold Welsh dragon passant supporting a heraldic shield with the symbol for Venus embellished upon it. On the rear of the pendant is engraved 'Presented to the corporation of Wrexham for the use of the Mayor for the time being by the present and several former members of the Town Council, 1st March 1873'. Three links back from the pendant, on both sides, is suspended a silver gilt heraldic shield on which is displayed a champleve

Chain of Office of the Deputy Mayor of Wrexham. This was originally the Chain of Office of the chairman of WRDC. [WCBC]

75

correctly emblazoned. Above the shield, on a wreath of the colours (white and red) the Borough crest, with the motto 'Fear God, honour the King' entwined below on an enamelled ribbon. On the dexter side is a sword of justice, with a leek set in emeralds, while on the sinister side is a copy of the civic mace and a branch of laurel in emeralds. The whole springing from the Welsh goat's head at base and enclosed with a framework of scrolls.

Deputy Mayor's Chain – This was originally the chain of office of the chairman of WRDC Manufactured *c*.1950, it is a silver gilt collarette in the form of thirty-one rectangular step effect plaques engraved with the names and dates of the Chairmen of WRDC and sixteen quartre foil open work plaques with inner lozenges enclosing the double line block letter 'W'. At the apex is a heraldic shield with a daffodil on a green ground surmounted by a castellated coronet. Suspended from this shield is a silver gilt medallion with a crest in green ground basse-taille depicting two bulls heads caboshed, two lozenges and crossed croziers, all surmounted by a helmet. The supporters are a green and yellow enamel floral design with an enamel red dragon passant supporting a heraldic shield representing the brick industry. At the bottom of the pendant is a scroll bearing the motto in red enamel 'Sum Cuique Tribvere'. On the reverse is the inscription 'Presented by Iorwerth Williams, Esquire'.

Deputy Mayoress' Pendant – A modern hallmarked silver gilt pendant bearing the arms of WMBC. This was manufactured in 1983 by Thomas Fattorini of Birmingham as a replacement for an earlier pendant which was lost. The original was presented to WMBC by the Wrexham branch of NALGO in 1976.

The Mace – In 1866, a large silver mace was presented to WBC by the then Mayor Joseph Clark. This was seen as a symbol of the Council's authority and measures 5 feet 8 inches. Manufactured in London it has an ebony staff with a silver top that is engraved

The Deputy Mayoress' Pendant. [WCBC]

The Civic Mace of Wrexham. [WCBC]

with leaves, leeks, goat masks, the Arms of the Borough of Wrexham and a Welsh harp. This is surmounted by a dragon holding a shield. The decorations in the middle and at the foot of the staff also feature leeks and goat masks.

Since 1866, when the post of Sergeant at Mace was instituted, the mace has been carried in front of the Mayor on all civic occasions. The first person to hold this post was David Higgins (Borough Inspector of Nuisances, he resided in Slaughter House Cottage, Holt Road in 1881), who was still in post in 1885 when he made a formal request for a new uniform. Quotes for replacing the uniform were again provided in March 1951 when it was estimated to cost between £38 and £41. Since the 1970s the role of Macebearer has been one of the duties carried out by the Mayor's chauffeur.

Civil War

Wrexham, the largest town in north Wales, had no castle and was open to attack. But it was seen as a convenient centre for assemblies and, only a few miles away, stood Holt Bridge, a key defended crossing point of the Dee. According to Dr Thomas Richards, Wrexham was a hotbed of Puritanism and 'bred a numerous crop of cornets and captains.' Despite this, the local gentry seems to have been a major source of officers for the Royalist army and, in August 1642, the gentry of Denbighshire and Flintshire met in Wrexham and unanimously resolved to raise a regiment of volunteers for the King and to subscribe £1,500 for that purpose. The regiment was to be commanded by Sir Thomas Salusbury of Lleweni, Denbigh.

On 27 September 1642, King Charles came to Wrexham and addressed the townspeople from the old Shire Hall* and returned on 7 October when he was a guest at Bryn-y-Ffynnon,* the town house of Richard Lloyd* whom he knighted. Sir Richard Lloyd was the Attorney General for north Wales, and is buried in the Parish Church – 'a loyal and devoted subject and servant of the Royal Martyr, Charles I, whom he received at Bryn-y-Ffynnon in this town in the year 1642'.

Following the fighting at Holt Bridge (where the Royalists were commanded by Lt-Col John Robinson* of Gwersyllt Hall*) on 7 November 1643, the victorious Parliamentary forces (under the command of Sir William Brereton, marched into Wrexham – 'About six o'clock Thursday evening we entered Wrexham. The enimy [sic] fly apace and begin to remove all their goodes out of these partes, but Holt Castle holds out, butt is beseidged'. The following morning, Brereton led a force to Hawarden which surrendered without a fight. Colonel John Booth and Sir Thomas Myddelton were left in Wrexham with 900 men, some of whom sheltered in the Parish Church where they 'broke in pieces one of the best pair of organs in the King's dominions, which Sir Thomas Myddelton took for proper pillage, to make bullets out of'.

The arrival of a Royalist army from Ireland (under the command of, amongst others, Robert Broughton* of Marchwiel) changed the whole situation in north Wales and the Marches so that the Parliamentary army was forced to consolidate and appears to have left Wrexham. This reverse was, however, only short-lived and at the end of January 1645, Brereton and Myddelton crossed the Dee and recaptured Wrexham which had reverted to the King. Colonel John Owen marched to relieve the town which he made his headquarters after being appointed a major general with instructions to drive the Parliamentarians out of north Wales. In March, the Parliamentarians, under Colonel Michael Jones captured Holt Bridge (defended by John Robinson* of Gwersyllt) but Sir John Owen quickly re-captured it. When Prince Rupert visited Holt on 19 March, he witnessed the execution of 24 Parliamentary supporters.

In December 1645, Wrexham again fell into the hands of Parliament and became the headquarters of General Mytton and the Parliamentary County Committee for Flintshire. At this time Plas Teg was plundered by Parliamentary forces, an action that undoubtedly offended its owner, Parliamentarian Sir John Trevor. Following the fall of Chester to Parliament, Sir John Owen was ordered to rendezvous at Wrexham on 23 February which would suggest that Mytton's forces had withdrawn from the town. The declining fortunes of the King meant that by late 1646 the focus of military attention – and conflict – had moved away from the Wrexham area.

In about 1647, Thomas Edwards of Cilhendref was appointed Parliamentary Governor of Wrexham.

The Second Civil War broke out on 9 May 1648. Sheriffs, Justices of the Peace and other leading Parliamentarians met at Wrexham to put the county of Denbigh in a defensive state to withstand any Royalist attacks but the area remained peaceful, even after the death of the King in 1649. There then followed the period of the inter-regnum, of rule by the army, by Parliament and by the Lord Protector, Oliver Cromwell (whose brother-in-law, Colonel John Jones,* is reputed to have owned property in Wrexham). The death of Cromwell resulted in a dramatic change of opinion throughout the Commonwealth, so much so that Charles Stuart was invited to return to London as King Charles II. In Wrexham, the new king was proclaimed by the 80-year-old Sir Thomas Myddelton of Chirk Castle. (See also Broughton Family of Marchwiel, Edisbury Family of Marchwiel, Edwards Family of Stansty, Robert Ellice, Gwersyllt Hill, Gwersyllt Park and Jeffreys Family of Acton Park)

Claremont Cottage, 29 Stansty Road
This was built in 1842 by John Foulkes of Ashfield as a residential property investment.* In 1861, it was occupied by accountant John Wyke. Ten years later, it was the home of solicitor Thomas Bury,* and by 1881, Miss Martha Francis and her brother Absalom, a civil and mining engineer, were living here. It was later the manager's residence for the Wrexham & Acton Colliery.* The house has changed very little since the mid 19th century and still has Gothic-style tracery windows, similar to those manufactured by John Wilkinson at Bersham.

Clarence Road, Croes Eneurys
Built in the 1970s, along with other streets, as an extension to the Croes Eneurys* development. The names of these new roads continued the theme of royal residences, in this case, Clarence House, the London home of Queen Elizabeth the Queen Mother.

Clark, John *local politician*
Originally from Aspatria, Cumberland, John Clark established a tailoring and outfitting business in Hope Street, Wrexham (on the site of the Central Arcade*). He served on the Borough Council as a Conservative and was elected to serve as Mayor in 1860. He married Miss Chaloner of Holt and had four sons and two daughters. He was the brother of Joseph Clark.* The family name is often spelled as Clark but the burial records and headstones show it to have been written Clarke.

Clark, Joseph *local politician*
Born in c.1804 at Aspatria, Cumberland, Joseph Clark established a successful wine, spirit and brewing business at Nº 59 Hope Street, Wrexham. He later entered into partnership with Jonathan Orford in the Cambrian Brewery* off Bridge Street. He was elected a Tory councillor and served as Mayor in 1864. He died at Plas-y-Bryn,* Chapel Street on 7 December 1881. He presented the Borough with £50 with which the Corporation bought the Mace. The family name is often spelled as Clark but the burial records and headstones show it to have been written Clarke.

Clarke, JP, William *local politician*
A master baker and confectioner, William Clarke was a member of the noted local firm of Clarke Brothers. He was elected an Independent Borough Councillor for Acton Ward in March 1935 and served until 1954. He was Mayor in 1950, the last to automatically become the chairman of the Wrexham Magistrates Bench due to the Borough losing its separate Commission of the Peace. He also served for a period on the WRDC and was a Denbighshire County Councillor.

For a short time, William Clarke lived in Pennsylvania, USA. He bought up a great deal of land in Rhosnesni and Acton and was responsible for much of the development of those areas between the 1920s and 1960s. His wife, Mrs Lily Maud Clarke was a native of Pentre Broughton. They lived at a number of addresses including: Stoneycroft (Rhosnesni Lane), Beech Court (Marford), Anerley (Gresford), Oak Lodge* (Rhosnesni) and, finally, Woodside (Pulford). William Clarke died on 13 November 1967 as is buried in Gresford Cemetery. His brother and business partner, Philip, lived at Park Farm* and was responsible for developing much of the land between Rhosnesni Lane and Pen-y-Maes Avenue* and Maes-y-Dre.*

Clarke Road, Borras Park
Built in the early 1960s by London developers Spinks & Denning on land that had previously belonged to local businessman William Clarke* of Oak Lodge.* The land had originally been part of the Acton Park* estate.

Clwyd County Council
Clwyd County Council was created in 1974 by the amalgamation of the old counties of Denbighshire and Flintshire. Many people

77

The opening of the Wrexham Co-operative Society's 'flagship' store in Hightown, 1923. This is now a Farm Foods store.

felt that the county town should have been Wrexham but the county headquarters was established at the Shirehall in Mold. Clwyd was abolished with effect from midnight on 31 March 1996 and Wrexham became a unitary authority in its own right. (See WMBC and WCBC).

Clwyd Wen, Whitegate
Built by WBC shortly before the Second World War on land that was previously part of Whitegate Farm.* The name is a literal translation of 'white gate'.

Co-operative Societies
The Wrexham Co-operative Society was established in 1890 by the management and staff of the Cambrian Leather Works,* with J. Meredith Jones as president and Edward Hughes* as secretary. The first shop was opened in Abbot Street* on 5 May 1890. Edward Hughes resigned as secretary in May 1890 and his duties were taken over by J. G. Crompton. The Society later had stores at: Nos 23 & 24 Abbot Street (Central Premises); Hightown (opened in 1909 on the corner of Newton Road. New, purpose-built premises were opened here in 1923 which operated as the Co-operative Society shop until it was taken over by lingerie manufacturer Dennis Ginsberg in the 1980s (Sylvia Jeffreys – before moving to a site on Queensway*) when the Hightown premises were taken over by Kwiksave; Rhosddu (opened 1904 on the corner of Newton Street), Bradley Road (opened 1896, which had a bakery alongside); 19b Abbot Street (opened as a drapery store in 1911) – later a large number of the premises on the north side of Abbot Street were owned and operated by the Birkenhead Co-operative Society with shops selling confectionery, groceries, provisions, boots and shoes, drapery, men's wear, fish and fruit. On the south side of Abbot Street, in the building that has since been the venue of various nightclubs, the Co-op operated a cash and carry. The last significant Co-op premises in Wrexham was the large shop which opened in the New Regent Street shopping development of the 1960s. Eventually changing its name to Living, this shop operated until the mid 1990s.

Coach & Horses, High Street
This was located at Nº 25 High Street from the mid 18th century until the late 19th century and appears in both the 1833 and the 1872 surveys. At one time this building was the property of the Langford family, notable tradesmen and retailers in the town.

Coach & Horses, Church Street
Located c.1770 at Nos 1 & 2 Church Street.

Cobden Street, Newtown
This street was laid out in 1894 on land which had been part of the Red House estate. On the death of Benjamin Piercy* the land was sold off as building plots and most of the terraced houses here appear to have been built by 1900. The close proximity of these streets to the Cobden Flour Mill* undoubtedly attracted the developers to using the names of anti-Corn Law campaigners. Both the street and the mill were named after anti-Corn Law campaigner Richard Cobden (1804–65) who, in the company of John Bright, visited Wrexham and spoke to an appreciative audience gathered in Yorkshire Square.*

Cobden Flour Mill, Watery Road
This was built sometime after the repeal of the Corn Laws in 1846 and named after William Cobden the great anti-Corn Law campaigner (see Cobden Street). The mill was located alongside the GWR and LNER railway lines on a 2 acre site, just to the east of the level crossing in Watery Road. In 1879 was owned by J. Davies & Co, the manager was Mr Goodier and they employed over 150 men. The grain was imported through Liverpool and Connah's Quay and then transported to Wrexham by the Wrexham, Mold & Connah's Quay Railway* in 12-ton long-wheelbase wagons (built in Rhosddu in 1904). By the early 20th century, all the grain coming through the port of Connah's Quay was destined for the mill. The mill building was a major feature of the Wrexham skyline, being the largest commercial premises in the town, consisting of a basement and five floors covering 68,000 square feet. The tower contained a grain silo. The company was taken over by Rank Millers and the Wrexham plant was closed as part of a rationalisation programme and the site was offered for sale in May 1930 with the proviso that it could not be used for flour milling. WBC expressed an interest in purchasing the site but it eventually became part of the Wrexham Lager Brewery complex. The graded flour (Sunbeam, XL and Super) produced at the mill was distributed over a very large area by means of a fleet of steam lorries.

Cobden Flour Mill, Wrexham.

Cobham Close, The Ithens
Built in the 1980s, on land that had previously been part of the Erddig estate, this street takes its name from either the town of Cobham in Surrey, from the noted aviator Sir Alan Cobham who brought his noted Flying Circus to Wrexham during the 1930s (there is no evidence to suggest that he used land in this area for his flying display) or, more likely, after Sir Ralph de Cobham who held lands throughout Bromfield in the early fourteenth century e.g. Cobham Almer and Cobham Isycoed. (See Ithens Farm)

Cock, The, Farndon Street
Palmer notes that in the late 17th century this public house was owned by the Rosindale family. It took its name from the brutal sport of cock fighting of which the Rosindale family were avid supporters (see the Cockpit). It is shown on the 1802 survey of the Manor of Wrexham Abbot, when it appears to have been the property of the Wynnstay Estate [DRO/DD/WY/8352]. It also appears on the 1833 survey. By the time of the 1872 survey, the name had been changed to The Victoria (the change is likely to have taken place to commemorate the accession to the throne of Queen Victoria in 1837). The pub survived as The Victoria Inn* until 2000 when it was demolished during the redevelopment of the area by Tesco. It stood on the site of the present day roundabout at the junction of Holt Road and Farndon Street. (See also Victoria Brewery)

Cockpit, The
This was built 'for the fighting of cocks' by Dr Michael Rosindale, sometime around 1700, on land leased next to the garden of his house in Chester Street, in what is now Lion Yard.* The Cockpit eventually passed into the ownership of the Trustees of the Presbyterian Chapel,* Chester Street, who leased it out to successive tenants of the Lion Hotel* in High Street. When cockfighting was banned in 1849 the pit was turned into a cooper's shop. It was demolished in 1884 and a chapel schoolroom was built on the site.

The Cockpit.

Coed Aben, Queen's Park
Coed Aben was once the most important farm in the old township of Abenbury Fawr. It appears in Saxton's map of 1577 and in Norden's survey of 1620 when it was occupied by Edward Puleston of Llwyn Knottia and described as 'a messuage or tenement, orchard, garden, and divers closes of land ... lately of Robert Sontley, Esq., containing by estimation 70 [customary] acres [148 statute acres]'. At times the property is called Coed Abynt, Coed Abint and Coed Abimbury. By the early 18th century it had become the property of Sir William Williams, Bt, and through him became part of the Wynnstay estate. (See Williams Wynn Family). By the end of the 18th century it seems to have been bought by Edward Lewis and, shortly afterwards, became part of the Cefn* estate belonging to George Kenyon. It was then bought by the Revd Nathaniel Roberts from whom it passed to the Palmer family of Cefn Park.* For most of the 18th and 19th centuries the farm was tenanted by the Taylor family. By the 1880s, the farm amounted to 104 acres and was occupied by Lt-Col Alfred Stowell Jones, VC* (manager of the Wrexham Sewerage Works).

Coed Derw Skating Rink, Chester Road
Recorded in *Crocker's Wrexham Directory*, 1881. The location was on Chester Street, close to Bodhyfryd House.*

Coed-y-Glyn
Located in the area once known as Glyn Park.* The earliest record that Palmer* found of this property was the burial entry for Philip Griffith of Coed-y-Glyn on 5 July 1688/9.

Residents:
1729	Richard Jones, the agent of the Erddig estate who died there in 1741.
1741	John Jones I. His daughter Ann was the wife of Richard Jones,* a leading Wrexham Calvinistic Methodist.
c.1793	John Jones II (the son of John Jones I).
1817	Mrs Penelope Jones (the widow of John Jones II).
c.1827	Revd Robert Myddelton.
1841	Ms Harriet Eyton
1843	Thomas Wynne Eyton.
1857	Miss Eyton.
c.1860	Peter Walker.*
1882	Sir Robert Eyles Egerton, KCSI.* Still living there in 1912. Lady Egerton living there at time of her death in 1918.

During the Second World War the house was requisitioned for use by the army and the Women's Land Army. In its latter years, Coed-y-Glyn became a farm house and was part of the Erddig Hall* estate. The last tenants were Mr & Mrs Cheetham. The land was sold by Philip Yorke in order to endow the Erddig Estate with a capital sum which would enable the National Trust to take over and maintain the house. The house, which stood approximately on the site of Maes Celyn, was demolished in the mid 1970s. The driveway to the house led off Erddig Road and (along with some trees) is now all that now remains of an important Wrexham house.

Coed-y-Glyn
This private housing estate, built in the main by Parry Homes during the 1970s and 1980s, takes its name from Coed-y-Glyn,* a house which stood on the site.

Coleman, OBE, Warren *local politician*
Born in Chirk Castle, Warren Coleman was brought up in Rhos-y-Medre, Cefn Mawr and Acrefair. Educated at Ruabon Grammar School, he worked for the Co-operative Society for ten years before becoming a mature student at Padgate College, Warrington. Qualifying as a teacher, he was appointed to the staff of Grove Park School and, after 1974, Grove Park Comprehensive School and The Groves School until his retirement in 1993.

Elected to WBC to represent Cefn Mawr in 1973 (Labour), he was Mayor of WMBC 1984, Leader of WMBC for 9 years and Leader of WCBC from 1996–7. He lives in Acrefair and is married to Glenys and they have three children.

An RAF reconnaissance photograph taken on 17 November 1948. A number of features can be identified including: Longueville bungalow (bottom left), Coed-y-Glyn (centre foreground), Plas Derwen (right centre ground) with Hillbury just above, the Parish Church centre background. The inverted 'V' shape roads are Erddig Road (left) and Sontley Road (right). St Mark's Church (top left). [National Assembly for Wales]

Colemere Street, Ruabon Road
Land between Erddig Road and Ruabon Road, belonging to J. Colemere Gittins, (an ironmonger with premises in Hope Street) was developed for residential purposes in the late 1890s. The name Colemere Street was sanctioned by the Borough Council in 1899.

College, The
Several documents refer to 'The College' and 'College Field' in the Berse area of Wrexham. This may be a link with College Street* and College House* and the references to Wrexham Parish Church being a collegiate church. If there were plans to create such an establishment during the 16th century, it is likely that land was designated for the maintenance of this enhanced status which might be the origin of the use of the name 'College' in the Berse area. [DRO/DD/PP/894–6, DRO/QSD/DC/4]

College House, Parish Church of St Giles
College House, located in the churchyard at the Parish Church, is currently used as the Parish Office. See also The College and College Street.

College Street
Probably named after College House,* it is thought that there were once plans to make Wrexham Parish Church a collegiate church but there is no evidence that this ever actually occurred.

College Street, c.1950s before any of the original properties were demolished, giving the street a very Dickensian feel. [RCHBW]

It may have been that the events of the Reformation put paid to any plans before they were actually implemented. The Welsh name for this street was Camfa'r Cŵn (The Dog's Stile) after the stile which was situated by the churchyard. It has also been known as Cefn-y-Cwm which was undoubtedly a distortion of Camfa'r Cŵn. There was once a kiln located at the foot of the present day steps. The Blue Bell Inn* (later the Commercial), one of the oldest licensed premises in Wrexham, and the Cambrian Vaults are located here. It is claimed to be in a premises in this street called Hughes' Yard that the first Wesleyan Methodist sermon was preached in 1773 by Samuel Bradburn of Chester.

Colliery Road, Rhosddu
This road, as its name would suggest, was laid in the 1870s as housing for coal miners employed at the nearby Wrexham & Acton Colliery.* By 1881 it had 22 occupied houses. The terraced cottages were demolished by the local authority in 1978.

Collins Court, Hightown
This street was laid out in the 1980s on land that had previously been the property of C.T. Clark, proprietor of the King's Mills Garage. Built by the Wales and West Housing Association, all the streets were named after RWF who had been awarded the Victoria Cross.

A/Cpl John Collins was born in Taunton (or West Hatch) in Somerset in 1877 and his family moved to Merthyr Tydfil when he was about 10 years of age. He enlisted as a Driver in the Royal Horse Artillery in 1895 and served in the South African War and in India before being discharged as time served. On the outbreak of war in 1914 he enlisted in the Welsh Horse which became the 25th Battalion, Royal Welsh Fusiliers in March 1917. He served in Gallipoli, Syria, Palestine, France and Flanders and was awarded the Victoria Cross for his action at Wadi Saba, Beersheba, Palestine on 31 October 1917. His citation reads:

> For most conspicuous bravery, resource and leadership when, after deployment, prior to an attack, his battalion was forced to lie out in the open under heavy shell and machine-gun fire which caused many casualties. This gallant non-commissioned officer repeatedly went out under heavy fire and brought wounded back to cover, thus saving many lives.
>
> In subsequent operations throughout the day, Corporal Collins was conspicuous in rallying and leading his command. He led the final assault with the utmost skill in spite of heavy fire at close range and uncut wire. He bayonetted fifteen of the enemy and, with a Lewis gun section, pressed on beyond the objective and covered the reorganisation and consolidation most effectively although isolated and under fire from snipers and guns.
>
> He showed throughout a magnificent example of initiative and fearlessness.

Collins was promoted to sergeant in October 1917 and while serving in France was awarded the Distinguished Conduct Medal. He was wounded in October 1918 and discharged. After the war he was employed as a tip labourer at Dowlais and later as a security guard at Dowlais Steel Works. Married with six sons and two daughters. John Collins died in 1951 and was buried in Pant Cemetery (Roman Catholic Section), Merthyr Tydfil.

Commercial, The, College Street
Originally called the Blue Posts, this is one of the oldest pubs in Wrexham. Recorded as existing in the 1690s it appears in both the 1833 and 1872 surveys. At some stage (probably in the 18th century) it absorbed the Ship Inn which was located next door. In the mid 1990s the name was changed to Scruffy Murphys when the premises were converted into an Irish style public house, but has now reverted to the Commercial.

Concorde Row, Goulbourne
Developed in the 1980s on land that was previously part of Plas Goulbourne Farm, this street was named after the world's first supersonic airliner, the BAe/AS Concorde, which has no connection whatsoever with Wrexham. The name was probably chosen, illogically, because of the close proximity of the street to the former RAF Wrexham* airfield at Borras.

Congregational Chapel, Chester Street
See Chester Street English Congregational Chapel.

Congregational Chapel, Queen Street
See Queen Street (Ebeneser) Welsh Congregationalist Church.

Congregational Free Church, Lord Street
See Lord Street Congregational Free Church.

Coningsby Court, Goulbourne
Developed in the 1980s on land that was previously part of Plas Goulbourne Farm, this street was named after RAF Coningsby in Lincolnshire, which has no connection with Wrexham. The name was probably chosen because of the close proximity of the street to the former RAF Wrexham airfield at Borras.

Connor Crescent, Whitegate
This WBC housing development was laid out just before the Second World War, in the wake of the 1936 Housing Act.

Named after Maj-Gen Sir Luke O'Connor, VC, KCB, (1831–1915) who, as Sgt O'Connor was the first RWF to be awarded the Victoria Cross. Born at Elphine, Co. Rosscommon, Ireland, he enlisted as a private on 21 July 1849. He served in the Crimean War and the Indian Mutiny. As a reward for his services at the Battle of the Alma, 1854, O'Connor was commissioned (without purchase) in his own regiment and retired an hon major-general in 1887. He was appointed Colonel of the RWF in 1914. He died in London on 1 February 1915 and is buried at St Mary's RC Cemetery Kensal Rise. Luke O'Connor House on the Barrackfield estate, is also named after him. His citation reads:

> Was one of the centre Sergeants at the Battle of the Alma between the officers carrying the colours. When near the Redoubt, Lieutenant Anstruther, who was carrying a Colour, was mortally wounded and he was shot in the breast at the same time and fell, but recovering himself, snatched up the Colour from the ground, and continued to carry it till the end of the action although urged by Captain Granville to relinquish it and go to the rear on account of his wound; was recommended for and received his commission for his services at the Alma (September 20, 1854). Also behaved with great gallantry at the assault on the Redan 8th September 1855, where he was shot through both thighs.

Maj-Gen Sir Luke O'Connor, VC.

81

Convent Grammar School, Grosvenor Road.

Convent Grammar School, Grosvenor Road
Following a request by the Vicar General of the Shrewsbury Diocese, three sisters of the Rock Ferry Convent of the Sisters of the Holy Family (the education section of which is called the Sisters of St Joseph of the Immaculate Conception) came to Wrexham in March 1877 and moved into a small house on Pen-y-Bryn.* They were asked to take charge of the parish schools, as a consequence of which they established a convent school in the town in March 1879. At the time of the 1881 Census they are shown as being resident in the 'Convent High School' at 22 Regent Street.

In the early years of the 20th century they moved into the house formerly known as Bron Llwyn* on the corner of Grosvenor Road* and Gerald Street* where they established a private school. In 1914, as the school's population grew, they built an annexe in the grounds, known as the Bungalow. By 1923 they had bought the adjacent property, N° 17 Grosvenor Road and in 1937, N° 2 Gerald Street. In 1949, a canteen and domestic science room were built. In 1951 the Nursery and Junior School moved to premises at N° 6 Gerald Street, thereby allowing the main school to carry out major alterations to its Grosvenor Road buildings. As a result of these changes the school was recognised as a Grammar School and Preparatory School by the Ministry of Education in August 1954.

Throughout its history, the Convent School had been supported by the Holy Family Convent at Rock Ferry but, by the late 1960s, it was becoming obvious that this support would not be available indefinitely – 'The Congregation has done its utmost over the years to support the school, both in finances and in personnel, but we have come to a point now when we are drained to the maximum in our resources and rather than continue to 'hang on' inadequately and inefficiently I feel we should close down our Independent School in 1970'. The closure was, however, delayed until July 1972 when it coincided with the reorganisation of education in Denbighshire and parents were given the option of sending their children to St Joseph's* (which had just become a Roman Catholic comprehensive school) or of sending them to any of the other comprehensive schools in the district.

Headmistresses:
  Independent School
  1951   Sister M. Imelda
  Grammar School
  1963–72 Sister Enda
  Preparatory School
  1951   Sister M. Clarissa

Conway Drive, Queen's Park
Built in the immediate post Second World War period as part of the first phase of WBC's Queen's Park housing development. The street is named after the Conwy valley (the old Anglicised spelling was Conway).

Cooper, JP, Frank *local politician*
Born in Yorkshire, Frank Cooper spent many years at Ilkeston, Derbyshire and Spondon before moving to Wrexham in 1947 as chief clerk to the engineering department at British Celanese. In 1958 he was appointed bursar at Cartrefle College, a post he held for twenty-one years. The last three years of his working life were spent at the BICC factory on Wrexham's Industrial Estate.

He served as the Labour councillor for the Caia Ward from 1952–67 and became Mayor in 1965. His wife, Evelyn M. Cooper, JP, was the headmistress of Is-y-Coed School. They had one son and one daughter. At the time of his term as Mayor, Frank Cooper lived at School House, Bowling Bank, but later moved to N° 209 Herbert Jennings Avenue. He died in December 1974.

Cooper's Close, Rhosnesni
Cooper's Close, a small 1960s corporation housing development in Rhosnesni, built by H.R.&E. Roberts, takes its name from Cooper's market garden which was once located here. In the early 20th century, most of the land between Holt Road and Rhosnesni Lane was owned by the Acton Park* estate then, after 1918, by Mrs Clarke of the Rhosnesni Post Office.

Cooper's Lane
See Park Avenue.

Copland, OBE, JP, Margaret M. *educationalist*
Born in Liverpool in 1900, Miss Copland spent most of her childhood in south Wales where she was educated at the Girls' County School, Penarth from 1912-19. She gained a BSc (Hons) from the University College of North Wales, Bangor in 1924 and began her teaching career at Hengoed County School for Girls. She was seconded for twelve months to Beverley High School, Massachusetts, USA in 1937.

She was appointed Headmistress of Grove Park Girls' School in 1944, a post she held until her retirement in 1965. She was the President of the Welsh Secondary Schools Association, chairman of the Welsh Council for Education, a Member of the Welsh Joint Education Committee, Member of the Schools Council for Women, Member of the Broadcasting Council for Wales, Member of the Wrexham Library Committee, Vice President of the Grove Park Little Theatre and a Governor of St Christopher's School. She was appointed a Justice of the Peace to the Bromfield Bench in 1952 where she served for twenty years. She was awarded an OBE in 1963 for her services to education in Wales. Her portrait by the artist Margaret Lindsay Williams was presented to Grove Park Girls School in 1957. She died in March 1992.

Cordell, Alexander *novelist*
Born George Alexander Graber in Colombo, Ceylon, on 9 September 1914, the son of RSM Frank Graber of the Royal Engineers. He was educated by the Marist Brothers in Tianjin. Cordell served in the Royal Engineers during the Second World War, was commissioned and retired as a major. He first came to Wales in 1936 and was employed post-war as a quantity surveyor for the War Office in Monmouthshire. He wrote more than 30 books including *A Thought of Honour* (1954), *Rape of the Fair Country* (1959), *The Hosts of Rebecca* (1960), *The Race of the Tiger* (1963) *Song of the Earth*, (1969) *The Fire People*, (1972) *The Sinews of Love* (1965), *The British Cantonese* (1967), *The Dream and Destiny* (1975) *Land of My Fathers*, (1983) *This Sweet and Bitter Earth*. (1977).

He married twice (1) Rosina Wells (died 1972) and (2) Elsie May Donovan, known as Donnie (died 1995). He had one daughter. An active member of Plaid Cymru, Cordell never fitted in well with the Welsh literary 'establishment' who saw him as a poor mimic of Richard Llewellyn but, despite this, he had a large following and only the lack of film or television dramatisation of his books prevented him becoming a major figure on a world stage.

In the 1980s he moved to Railway Road, Rhosddu, hoping to write a novel based around the Gresford Colliery disaster of 1934. On 9 July 1997, his body was found beside a stream on the Horseshoe Pass near Llangollen. A coroner's inquest returned a verdict of death by natural causes.

Corn is Green, The film
This 1979 film, based upon the play by the Flintshire-born playwright, Emlyn Williams, directed by George Cukor and starring Katharine Hepburn, was partially filmed at Hafod Colliery* in 1978.

Cornish Close, Ithens
A private housing development of the 1980s, Cornish Close probably takes its name from Cornish Hall near Holt. (See Ithens Farm)

Cosford Close, Goulbourne
Developed in the 1980s on land that was previously part of Plas Goulbourne Farm, this street was named after RAF Cosford, near Wolverhampton, which has no connection whatsoever with Wrexham. The name was probably chosen because of the close proximity of the street to the former RAF Wrexham* airfield at Borras.

Cottage, The, Holt Street
Shown in the 1833 survey standing at the eastern end of the Quaker Burial Ground (now the Peace Garden). At that time it was occupied by F. J. Hughes.

County Buildings, Regent Street
Until the mid 19th century, the Denbighshire Militia Regiment used the Town Hall,* located at the top of the High Street in Wrexham as its headquarters and armoury. The social unrest which spread throughout the county and the expanding role of local government meant that the 17th century civic building was no longer suitable for the many functions which it tried to fulfil. An obvious option was for the Militia to move out into a purpose-built headquarters. The first mention of a 'Militia Barracks' in Wrexham appears in the minutes of the 1854 Michaelmas Quarter Sessions for the County of Denbigh.

> Militia Depot Ordered in pursuance of the public Notice given to the Clerk of the Peace and the representation of Robert Myddelton Biddulph Esquire, Lord Lieutenant of the County and Colonel Commandant of the Militia, that secure and suitable Stores and an orderly and guard room and magazine, and a sufficient yard or place werein the same may be mustered and also quarters for a Sergeant Major and six Sergeants of the permanent staff be provided...(and that) the plans this day be submitted to the Court by Mr Penson.

The plans were drawn up by Thomas Penson,* the County Surveyor of Denbighshire, who was assisted by the adjutant of the militia, Capt McCoy and the resulting design clearly shows the influence of both men's area of expertise. They were approved and land lying on the edge of the town, alongside Regent Street, was purchased from Thomas Bury.* A contract was signed on 3 September 1855 between Joseph Peers, Clerk of the Peace, on behalf of the County of Denbighshire and the builders Ebenezer Thomas of Menai Bridge and John Thomas of Holyhead and, it would appear, that work commenced almost immediately. By mid-June 1857, the building was nearing completion and the *Wrexham and Denbighshire Advertiser* for 13 June reported:

> This large building is now pretty nearly completed in every respect and the resident officers, one Sergeant Major and six Sergeants have taken possession of it. The rooms of the officers are very snug and commodious and are fitted with every convenience for use and comfort, especially those occupied by Sergeant Major Mr. Wright.

A study of the plans for the original building clearly show the accommodation that was available. With the appearance of a fort, the Militia Barracks was built of Cefn Mawr sandstone and was in something of a late mediæval/early Tudor style. At each corner stood a decorative turret (complete with ornamental arrow slits). The original specifications stipulated that bullet-proof shutters were to be fitted to the lower parts of the windows of the regimental store and that the guard room and magazine were to

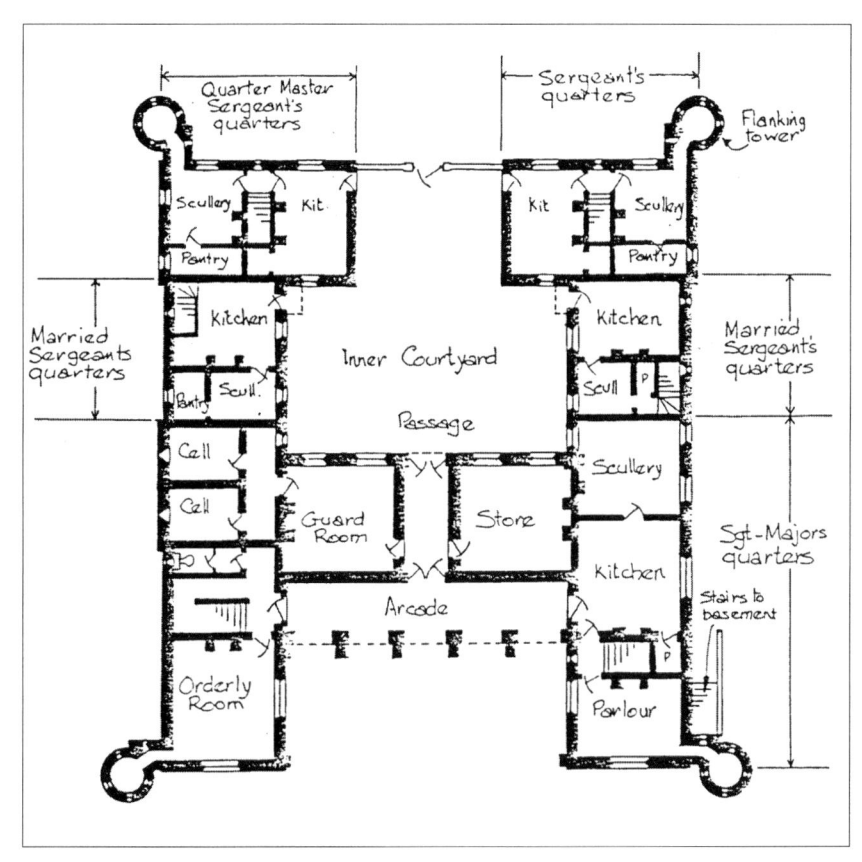

Ground floor plan of the Militia Barracks as they appeared in 1914 when used as the Police station. [Eric Wilson, Open University Architecture Project, 1980]

be constructed below ground level, but a detailed examination of the building during the 1980s failed to show any evidence that either of these features ever materialised.

The building was only used as the Militia Barracks until about 1877 when, with the completion of the new barracks for the RWF at Hightown, Wrexham, the Militia moved. The Regent Street Barracks were then converted for use by the Court of Petty Sessions and the Police Headquarters and re-named 'County Buildings'. The conversion work was completed by 6 January 1879 when the Magistrates Court was held there for the first time. After due consideration had been given in 1897 to demolishing the building to make way for a new Guildhall, it was decided to carry out further alterations which resulted in a second court room and new public entrances being built. These changes brought about a considerable alteration to the front elevation of the building as two of the original turrets were removed and a new wing was built on the eastern side.

The building was occupied by married police officers and their families until shortly after the Second World War and the last resident, the Bridewell Sergeant, moved out in 1960. In 1940, a two-storey flat-roofed building was constructed at the rear to accommodate the Wrexham ARP equipment store, garage and cleansing depot. After the war, part of this extension was taken over by the police CID department and the remainder was used as a garage for police vehicles.

The police vacated the building in January 1976 (moving to the new Police Divisional Headquarters* at Bodhyfryd) and the Magistrates on 28 April 1978 (moving to the new Magistrates Courts* at Bodhyfryd), although a special court for soccer hooligans was held there on 1 May. After a short period of use as the Wrexham Citizens Advice Bureau, the building was taken over by Aston College* (later the North East Wales Institute*) as its Art Department. In September 1995, the building was taken over by WMBC and, on 30 September 1996, opened as the Wrexham County Borough Museum.

Today, the building is undergoing a lengthy period of refurbishment to both equip it for its new role as a museum and to preserve its integrity. It was re-opened as the Wrexham Museum in 1996* and an extension was built on the back with the aid of Lottery funding.

A second Lottery award led to the museum's closure in 2010 to enable major structural alterations to be made. During this period a reduced museum service was accommodated at Bersham Heritage Centre. [DRO/QSD/AE/8–9]

County Court

In 1881, the County Court Office was in Egerton Street. In the 1950s, the County Court proceedings were heard in the County Buildings (Magistrates Courts), with administrative offices in Egerton Street. By the 1990s, the County Court proceedings were heard in the Magistrates Courts in Bodhyfryd, with administrative offices in Crown Buildings, Chester Street. After 1996 the County Court proceedings have been heard in the Crown Buildings where the administrative offices are also located. Plans are currently afoot to move the County Court to newly-built premises in the Magistrates Court* building.

Court, The, Green Park

The Court was a property located on the site now occupied by the Green Park housing development. Its origins date back to the Middle Ages when there was a manor house here belonging to the Abbot of Valle Crucis, probably known as the Abbot's Court House, which was the focal point of the township of Wrexham Abbot.* It was here that tenants came to pay their tithes to the Abbey (the Rectorial Tithes of the Parish of Wrexham were granted to Valle Crucis by Madog ap Gruffydd, Prince of Powys, in 1247). Following the dissolution of Valle Crucis Abbey in 1537, the Crown granted the lease of the manor of Wrexham Abbot to Sir William Pickering of Oswaldkirk in Yorkshire.

During the reign of Elizabeth I, the manor was leased to Edward Wotton and remained in the possession of his family until sequestered (confiscated) by Parliament in 1651. The Wottons (and the Pickerings) had been absentee landlords and in 1616, the house is shown as being occupied by Edward Meredith, draper, of London, who was the brother of Sir William Meredith of Stansty* and Hugh Meredith of Pentrebychan*. In about 1663, the Valle Crucis estate was sold by the Crown to Henry Wynn and it would seem likely that the sale included the manor of Wrexham. Certainly, at a later date, it was part of the Wynnstay estate. The house, and what came to be known as The Court estate, was the residence of John Wynne, a local barrister, before being leased to Roger Lewis (a farmer) in c.1720, followed by various members of the Meredith family including: Sir Roger Meredith of Leeds Abbey, Kent and Richard Meredith of Bristol, until about 1774 when it was leased for six years by John Wilkinson,* ironmaster of Bersham.

By 1792, it was the home of William Wilkinson,* John's brother, who remained there until about 1806. In 1802, the property, which still appears to have been part of the Wynnstay estate, is shown with the Welsh spelling *Y Cwrt* [DRO/DD/WY/8352].

By 1806, it was occupied by Philip Parry, a

The Court, c.1973, just before it was demolished. The trees behind the house are the boundary of Erddig Park. The triangle of grass in the bottom left-hand corner is now part of the garden of Nº 24 Green Park. [Mrs Dulcie Wright]

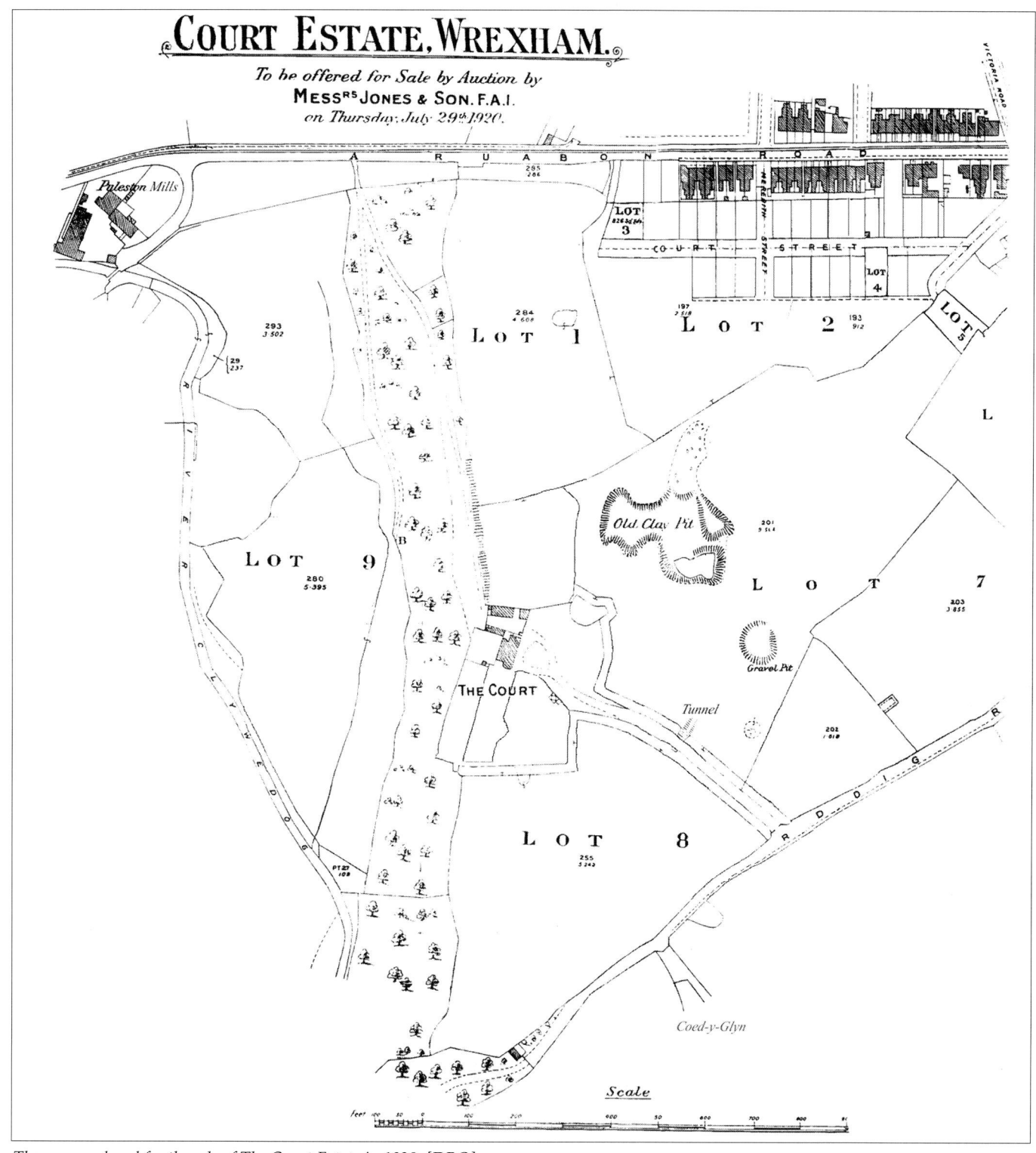

The map produced for the sale of The Court Estate in 1920. [DRO]

solicitor, and in 1817 the house was being leased by John Eddowes Bowman of Kenrick & Bowmans Bank.* The estate had certainly been sold by the time the Tithe Apportionment was recorded in 1844 and there followed a series of different occupiers commencing with Henry Warter Meredith of Pentrebychan in 1844 (the son-in-law of the noted Victorian explorer Mungo Park); Henry Southern, a farmer (1851); Elihu Southern (1861 – still there in 1870); James Dixon, curate of Wrexham (1871); John Meredith Jones,* leather manufacturer (1881); Francis James Vaughan-Williams, son-in-law of Peter Walker* (1882); William Young Craig, coalmine owner and MP for North Staffs (1901); Mrs Emily Stanley (died 1915).

In 1920, following the death of Peter Macara Meredith, the estate was put up for sale by auction but it would seem that the house itself was not included and was occupied by Duncan Robertson, son of Sir Henry B. Robertson.* After the Second World War, the house came under the ownership of the National Coal Board until 1951 when it was bought by Dennis Wright. In 1957, it was divided into two residences; the main house was known as the Court and the domestic wing, which became a self-contained unit, was called Courtwood. The Wright family lived in both properties but, gradually, found the maintenance costs of the property to be prohibitive and in 1975 the house was demolished. At the time, the Royal Commission for Historic Monuments in Wales described the house as being 'of no archaeological or architectural importance except as the successor to the house of the steward of the ecclesiastical manor of Wrexham Abbot where manorial courts were once held'.

The house site and gardens were bought by John Parry who redeveloped the land as Green Park. At the time of the house's demolition, the 'estate' comprised only nine acres, *viz* four acres of the house and gardens and five acres of woodland. The woodland was given to the National Trust and now forms part of the boundary of the neighbouring Erddig estate.

On the ground floor, the house had a large hallway and stairs, four entertaining rooms (including a large oak-panelled room which could accommodate 50 persons), a breakfast room (with French window), kitchen, scullery, housemaid's room and butler's pantry and on the first floor, five bedrooms, two bathrooms and two linen rooms and, on the second floor, five attic bedrooms. Outside was a large formal rose garden, two tennis courts and a drive that led off Erddig Road (following the line of the present roadway into Green Park). There was also a large kitchen garden, the wall of which, and a horse mounting block are the only surviving features of the house. (See also The Bricky)

Court Baron
The Court Baron was a manorial court established in mediæval times to hear minor offences committed in the manor. The usual punishment imposed was a fine which often proved a lucrative source of income for the lord of the manor. These courts began to fall into disuse after the 16th century but it would seem that in Wrexham they remained until at least the late 18th/early 19th century. In the early 19th century there was an appeal to Charles Watkin Williams Wynn, the Deputy Steward of the Lordship of Bromfield and Yale, from a number of traders in the town, requesting that the Court Baron be re-established 'for the recovery of small Debts under Forty shillings and Trespass upon the case, which Court until within a few years back was regularly held at Wrexham every three weeks and if re-established would be of great local advantage to Tradesmen and others within the said Lordship as Judgement could be obtained in much less time than in the County court according to the usual practice'. [DRO/DD/WY/6362]

Court Leet
See Bromfield and Yale Court Leet. [DRO/DD/WY/6362]

Court Road, Ruabon Road
Named after The Court,* the house and small estate which once belonged to the Meredith family of Pentrebychan.* Early plans show this development as being named Court Street.

Craig, JP, Robert Stanley *local politician*
He was born in Rhosddu Road, Wrexham, the son of James Craig, in a house which stood opposite the present day Coronation Walk. He entered the family drapery business which had been established at N° 5 Lord Street by his father, who had moved to Wrexham from Scotland. Educated at Grove Park School, Craig was a keen sportsman and, as well as being captain of the Wrexham hockey team, was goalkeeper of the Welsh national side on seventeen occasions between 1927 and 1932. He also played cricket for Wrexham.

He was elected a member of the Denbighshire County Council in 1949, became an alderman in 1964 and chairman of the County Council in 1969. He retired at the time of local government re-organisation in 1973. He was also elected to serve on WBC (representing Wats Dyke and later Bryn-y-Ffynnon Wards) from 1952–65. He became Mayor of Wrexham in 1963. He was the chairman of the Denbighshire County Planning Committee (1970), a member of the Development Corporation of Wales, a member of the North Wales Police Committee and a governor of Grove Park and Bromfield Schools.

Stanley Craig lived at N° 63 Park Avenue and later at the Craig family home, Wren's Nest,* on Rhosddu Road, which he gave to WBC to to use as a residential home.

Craig Way, Acton
This was built in the 1960s as part of WBC's expansion of the Acton Park housing estate.* Contrary to popular belief, the name is not pronounced as in the Welsh word for 'rock' but rather as in the Scottish surname Craig. The street was named after Stanley Craig.*

Craigmillar Road, Maes-y-Dre
The first house to be built on this private road was Craigmillar, which was the property of the National Coal Board and was occupied by Scotsman John Kerr an NCB manager. It seems likely that he gave the house its name after Craigmillar in Scotland and that the road took its name from the house.

Cranford Road, Queen's Park
Built in the immediate post Second World War period as part of the first phase of WBC's Queen's Park housing development. The origin of the name is unrecorded.

Crematorium, Pentrebychan
See Pentrebychan.

Crescent House, Beast Market
A large house located in the centre of the south side of the Beast Market which was probably built by John Eddowes during the late 18th century on the site of three smaller houses, one of which had been the home of John Pulford, prothonotary (chief legal clerk) of north Wales in the early 18th century.

The Eddowes family owned the house until at least the 1850s but rented it out: 1824 – Vernon Poole Royle, surgeon; John Dickenson,* surgeon; *c*.1887 – H. Venables Palin,* surgeon and Mayor of Wrexham (nephew of John Dickenson). By the turn of the 20th century there was therefore a long tradition of medical practitioners on this site and to this day the St George's Crescent surgery is located here.

Crescent Road, Smithfield
This road was laid out in the 19th century when it was called Crescent Terrace. N°⁸ 5-13, located on the north side of the road, facing the Smithfield, were demolished as part of the Borough slum clearance programme. The Wrexham abattoir was located here until the 1990s, replacing the old slaughter house in Holt Road.* During the Second World War it became the central slaughter house for a very wide area surrounding Wrexham. It was closed and demolished in the 1990s. Also located here is the Wrexham Foyer building.

Crescent Terrace
See Crescent Road.

Crispin Lane, Stansty
Crispin Lane follows the line of Wat's Dyke* between Mold Road and Stansty Road and much of the ancient earthwork was destroyed during the building of the adjacent railway. Crispin was a Roman Catholic saint of Roman origin who, according to legend settled in Gaul where he was a Christian missionary. He made shoes for the poor before being martyred in 287AD during the persecution of Diocletian. He became the patron saint of shoemakers and his saint's day is 25 October.

According to Palmer, Plas Ucha in Stansty (later the site of Stansty Hall, the property of the Edwards family) was known as Crispin Inn and another farm located nearby was known as Crispiannus and Crispinanna. He believed that this name originated from John ap John of Stansty who was known as a shoemaker and weaver.

There was also another property located on the eastern side of Wats Dyke* between what is now Rhosddu Road and Mold Road which was known as Lower Crispin* (or Crispiannus). It is from this property that Crispin Lane takes its name. In the 1960s the new Yale Technical Grammar School* was built on the west side of this lane. The original council houses were built on Crispin Lane in 1920 (G. F. Sumner & Sons being the main contractors).

A gravestone in Wrexham Cemetery records a William Jones, Sergeant Instructor to the 1st Volunteer Bn, RWF, of the Volunteer Depot, Crispin. The location of this depot is unrecorded.

Croes Eneurys
This is the area situated on the side of Acton Hill overlooking Rhosddu and Stansty. In the 1707 Survey of the Manor of Stansty, several references were made to field names which would suggest that there was once a stone cross standing somewhere in this area e.g. 'From the north end of Rhosddu to the west corner of Maes-y-Groes Vaen [*Trans.* field of the stone cross] being the late lands of Doctor James Jeffreys deceased in Gwersyllt Hall along the Hedge which divides betwixt the said Maes-y-Groes Vaen the late lands of William Jones in Acton called Cai-y-groes [Cae-y-Groes–*Trans.* field of the cross] & Doctor Rosindales Moores in Wrexham regis to Croes yn Eiries [Croes Eneurys]...' In 1881, the farm appears to have been divided into two tenancies – Hughes Hughes, 167 acres and John Hughes, 56 acres.

When council workmen were rebuilding part of the Acton Park wall along Chester Road, they removed a large stone on which was carved a cross. Close examination of this stone by local historians J.M. Cleary and D. Leslie Davies* revealed that the reverse side had been chiselled out and may have formed part of the support for the original cross. This stone still forms

A. N. Palmer's map of east Stansty. The Wrexham–Chester railway follows the line of Wat's Dyke. Rhosddu 35 is the site of Rhosddu Farm (now the Walnut Tree public house).

part of the old Acton Park* wall, on Chester Road opposite the southern junction of Acton Gate.* Local legend suggested that the engraved cross simply marked the spot where Sir Watkin Williams Wynn* died in 1749 after falling from his horse while hunting. (See also Croes Eneurys Estate and Croes Eneurys Farm)

Croes Eneurys Estate
Croes Eneurys Farm* was bought in 1934 by chartered surveyor and builder Harold Vincent Parker. In partnership with Robert Davies and John Hughes he commenced building on the land almost immediately and by the outbreak of war in 1939 had built most of Sandway Road,* Haytor Road, the east side of Sandringham Road and the west side of Eneurys Road. Development was then stopped because of the war and did not recommence until 1960 when Parker and Davies were joined by Frank Johnson (John Hughes having withdrawn from the development partnership). They developed the west side of Sandringham Road, Edinburgh Road, Buckingham Road and the upper end of Balmoral Road as far as Balmoral Close. The remainder of Balmoral Road was developed by Frank Johnson alone with a number of other builders constructing Osborne Road, Crathie Place, Clarence Road, Holyrood Crescent, Rothesay Close and, finally, in the late 1970s/early 1980s, Parker's Close (developed by Gordon Mytton and named after H.V. Parker who had died in 1971). Parker had previously been responsible for developments in a variety of locations in Wrexham including Box Lane,* Park Avenue,* Pen-y-Maes Avenue* and Chester Road.*

Croes Eneurys Farm
This was a small estate of land in the township of Acton; the house stood on the south side of what is now Sandway Road. In about 1700, the land was the property of John Jones and later

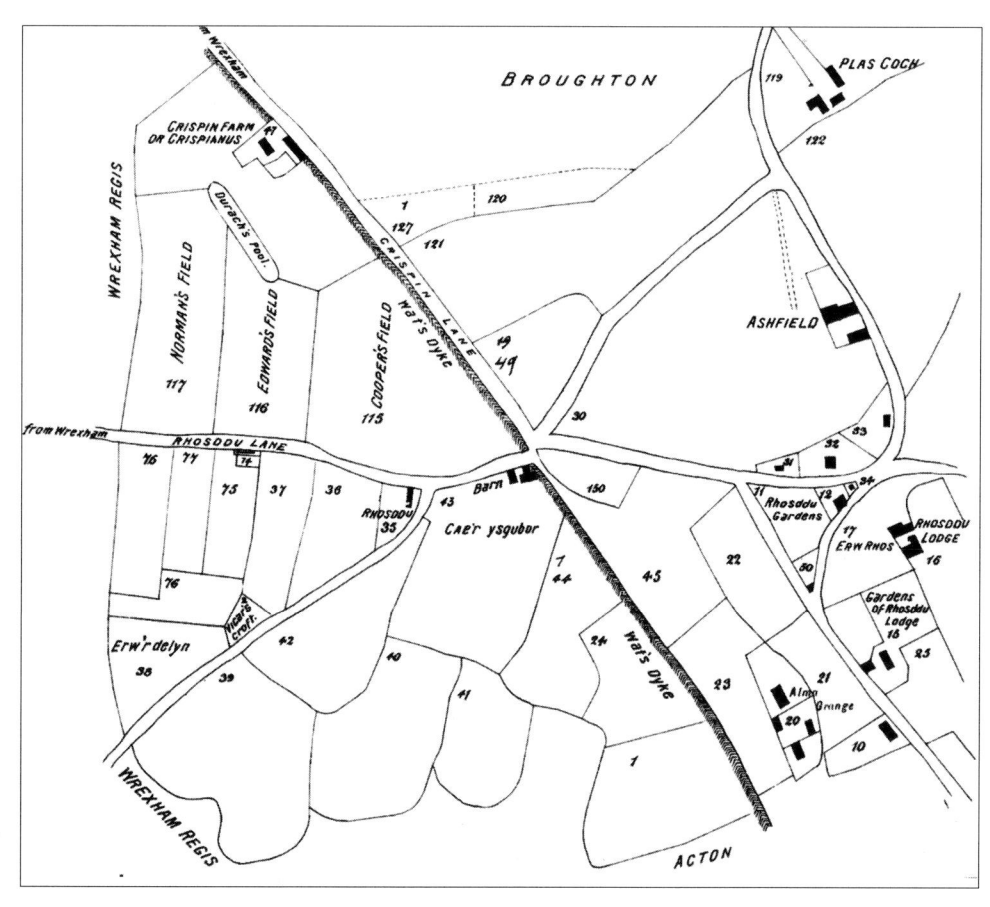

Joseph Jones (his son). At some point during the mid 18th century, the farm (which totalled just over 52 acres) was bought by John Twigge who sold it to Ellis Yonge of Acton Park* in 1770 for £1,400. The field names were: Cae Pant (*Trans.* hollow field), Cae Banadl (*Trans.* broom field), Cae Rhos dû (*Trans. black moor field*), Cae Coer (probably Cae Coed *Trans.* wood field), Erw Croft (*Trans.* croft acre), Erw Eithin (*Trans.* gorse acre). In 1785, Sir Foster Cunliffe bought the Acton Park* estate, including Croes Eneurys. Four years later he bought five additional fields for £860, which were located in the north-west angle formed by the junction of Chester Road and Price's Lane, making a total of 18 acres. The names of these fields were: Erw St Silyn (*Trans.* St Silin's acre), Erw Groes (*Trans.* acre of the cross) or Lane Field; in the township of Wrexham Regis – Cae Derwyn y Boom (*Trans.* bittern's oak field), part of which was later lost to the turnpike road, Naney & Nearer Meadow. [FRO/D/AH/24] The farm was sold to the Welsh Town Planning & Housing Trust Ltd in 1913 as part of the site for the proposed new Garden Village.* The scheme, however, fell far short of the original plan and the Croes Eneurys land was re-sold to a developer who built the houses on Eneurys Road* and Chester Road* with the remainder going to a Mr B. Thomas who sold it to Harold Vincent Parker in 1934. (See Croes Eneurys Estate). The land was developed as a residential estate between the late 1920s and the 1980s. The farmhouse was in a ruinous state by the early 1970s and was in danger of being the subject of a compulsory demolition order. It was, however, saved and rebuilt and is now N° 9 Parker's Close.

Croesnewydd Hall
Originally called Y Groes Newydd (*Trans.* the new cross), Palmer believed that the original name may well have been Y Gwas

Probably the earliest surviving image of the present-day Croesnewydd Hall, taken from 'A New Map of the Counties of Denbigh and Flint' by William Williams, 1720. [FRO DM/4/6] The map shows the house when it was the property of Robert Ellice.

Two views of Croes Eneurys Farm in the 1960s. This building still exists, albeit considerably altered, as N° 9 Parker's Close. [Mrs Isobel Taylor]

Croesnewydd Hall after restoration. (Geoffrey A. Jones)

Newydd (he believed that *Gwas* was an ancient word meaning 'hall' as well as servant). The first known person to have lived at a house called Croes Newydd was Colonel Robert Ellice,* but this was undoubtedly a much smaller house than that which survives today and was taxed for only 6 hearths in 1670. Colonel Ellice died in *c*.1660 and the estate passed to his son, Peter, although it was officially held by his widow Mary until 1674. It was this Peter Ellice who built the new Croesnewydd Hall and his initials, and those of his wife Sarah, along with the date 1696, once appeared on the west front. The evidence would suggest that the new house replaced the earlier building and was a completely new structure. The Ellices appear to have been absentee landowners almost from the start and the house seems to have been occupied by John Morgan (an attorney) and, later, by his widow. They were followed by Robert Cawley of Gwersyllt Ucha and then, by 1719, Miss Mary Myddelton until her death in 1747. All three of these later occupants were tenants of the Ellices. In 1750, part of the Croesnewydd estate became the property of the Price family of Bryn-y-Pys, Overton, through a foreclosure of a mortgage advance to the Ellice family. There is no evidence to suggest that Richard Parry Price or Francis Parry Price ever lived at the house and by 1825 it had passed into the hands of Thomas Fitzhugh of Plas Power. In 1920 (following the death of Godfrey Fitzhugh in the First World War), the property was sold by the trustees of the Plas Power estate to Alderman Edward Hughes* of Wrexham for £4,500. The close proximity of the property to the railway and the

A map of the Croesnewydd estate, c.1800. [FRO/D/BC (additional) Fitzhugh 15/22]

Croesnewydd railway yards led Hughes to believe that it was a potentially valuable industrial asset. In October 1929, the house and 104 acres were again put up for sale and the sale catalogue gives a description of the house which included a large entrance hall, panelled drawing room, morning room, dining room, servants' hall, kitchen, back kitchen, scullery, three pantries, dairy and press house, excellent cellarage and a dairy and milk house sited in the basement. A very wide and handsome antique oak staircase led to the first floor where there were five bedrooms, two dressing rooms, a bathroom and WC and a new bathroom. On the second floor were five further good bedrooms. Outside there was a wash house and an excellent walled garden, a kitchen garden, an orchard and two paddocks (totalling 14.5 acres). The house was bought by Clwyd County Council in 1984 and underwent an extensive restoration programme at the end of which it formed the central focus of the Croesnewydd Technology Park development. As a Grade II* listed building, it is a fine example of how imagination and investment can save significant historic buildings for the future.
[FRO/D/BC/Additional Miscellaneous/4/5 & 6]

Croesnewydd Hospital
The first medical establishment to be located on the Croesnewydd site was the hospital (in reality a ward) which formed part of the Wrexham Poor Law Union* Workhouse. On 2 October 1886 a 30-bed Fever Hospital was opened alongside the Workhouse on Cae Margaret Halkyn (north of Croesnewydd Road and east of the river Gwenfro) which was jointly run by WBC and WRDC. The cost of the site and the building were £6,500. In later years the two original authorities were joined by Ruthin RDC, Hiraethog RDC, Overton RDC and Llangollen RDC and the hospital was known as the Wrexham Joint Fever Hospital or the Isolation Hospital. On the outbreak of the First World War in 1914, the Fever Hospital was requisitioned and became the Croesnewydd Military Hospital, the first patients being wounded Belgian soldiers who arrived in November 1914. Handed back to the

*Plas Maelor, 1934. Built by Denbighshire County Council as a residential home for the aged, to replace facilities previously provided by the Workhouse. This now forms part of the Maelor Hospital.
{Derrick Pratt]*

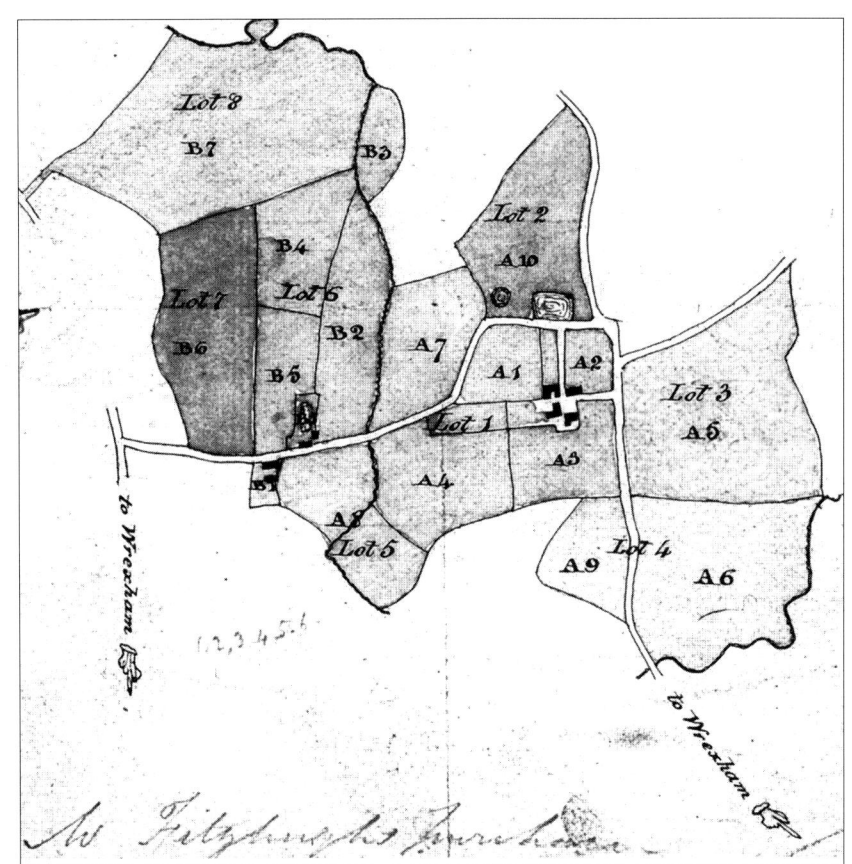

civilian medical authorities after the war, a programme of expansion was embarked upon and new buildings, known as Plas Maelor (opened by the Rt Hon David Lloyd George in 1934), were constructed on on an 11-acre site on the south side of Croesnewydd Road to accommodate the residential home for the elderly, replacing the old Workhouse facilities. During the Second World War Plas Maelor was taken over as a military hospital and this developed into the Maelor General Hospital, taking a great deal of the burden off the Wrexham & East Denbighshire War Memorial Hospital* which had been built in the early 1920s but which very quickly proved inadequate for the growing demands made upon it, particularly after the establishment of the National Health Service in 1948. In addition to providing medical facilities to the region the site was accommodating the administrative offices of the Wrexham, Powys and Mawddach Hospital Management Committee, the Isolation Hospital, the County Welfare Hospital and the General Emergency Hospital. By 1960, the Maelor Hospital had 591 beds and it was becoming increasingly obvious that there was a need for either a major re-development of the existing hospital facilities or the building of a new hospital to take over from both the Maelor and the War Memorial. (See Maelor Hospital)

Croesnewydd Road
Named after the nearby Croesnewydd Hall.*

Croom-Johnson, Henry, JP *publisher, entrepreneur and philanthropist*
He was born in Carmarthen on 5 May 1852, the eldest son of Henry Croom-Johnson, a civil engineer and friend of Isambard Kingdom Brunel. The family moved to Hereford when Harry was a small boy and, after completing his education, he was employed by the Great Western Railway before setting up a

The wedding of Harry Croom-Johnson and Elizabeth Roden, a typical late Victorian 'society' event in Wrexham. Included in the wedding group is the Revd David Howells, Vicar of Wrexham (standing sixth from the right).

business, with his brother Arthur, as a railway contractor in Hereford. He first came to Wrexham in 1882 and married Elizabeth Roden, the daughter of George Bradley,* proprietor of the *Wrexham Advertiser*. For eighteen months the couple lived in Shrewsbury before returning to and settling in Wrexham. He joined his father-in-law's business and eventually rose to be the Managing Director of Messrs Bayley and Bradley Ltd. He was also the proprietor of several quarries in Shropshire and was chairman of the Wrexham & East Denbighshire Water Company.* He lived at The Elms,* Rhosddu Road from 1893 until his death in 1923. He had four children, his youngest son Lt Brian Croom-Johnson was killed serving with the 4th Bn, RWF in France, in May 1915.

Harry Croom-Johnson was appointed a Justice of the Peace for the County of Denbighshire in 1897 and served on the Bromfield Petty Sessional Division and the Denbighshire Licensing Committee. A major part of his later life was devoted to the provision of health care in Wrexham and he served as a committee member for the Wrexham Infirmary* and was a prime mover behind the campaign to build a new hospital on the Roseneath site.* He was a member of the Building Committee of the War Memorial Hospital* and was an ardent supporter of the St Giles Boys Home* (it was his efforts that led to the building of a new home on Rhosnesni Lane), a trustee of the William & John Jones Charity Trust* convalescent homes at Rhyl and Minera, a trustee of Wrexham Parochial Charities and Vice-President of the Wrexham branch of the National Society for the Prevention of Cruelty to Children.

Harry Croom-Johnson died in March 1923. After his death, his widow moved to Stratford House* in Fairy Road.*

Cross Foxes, Abbot Street
It was shown in the 1833 survey. When it was put up for sale in September 1918 it realised £2,200. In the late 1990s, the name was changed to the Foxhound & Firkin, in 2000 to the Abbot's Bar and more recently to Last Orders. This was the first public house to be bought by the Wrexham Lager Beer Company. After the Second World War, the fledgling RAFA club held its meetings here before moving to Bryn Offa.* Part of the building was demolished in the 1970s.

Cross Keys Inn, Mount Street
Dating from the 17th century, this appears in both the 1833 and 1872 surveys, this public house was located on the north side of Mount Street, opposite the entrance to the Mount House.* In 1841, the publican was Alice Humphreys. According to Palmer, it was one of the oldest licensed premises in Wrexham in 1893 having existed as far back as 1661. It closed in 1920. It was demolished as part of the WBC slum clearance programme.

Cross Street, Rhosddu
This was laid out in the late 19th century on land that was part of the Acton Park* estate. Unlike other streets in this area built at the same time, the name Cross Street does not appear to have any connection with the Cunliffe family* and seems simply to be a description of a street that links across from Lorne Street* to Cunliffe Street.* Planning permission for the shop and attached house was granted in 1901.

Crown Buildings, Chester Street
Built in the late 1960s on the site of Bodhyfryd House,* this building originally provided accommodation for various government departments including the Inland Revenue and the County Court. Following the reorganisation of local government in 1996, Crown Buildings became offices for WCBC.

Crown Inn, High Street
Mentioned in Norden's survey of 1620 as being located on the south side of High Street.

Crown Inn, Hope Street
Located at N° 56 Hope Street, this public house appears in the records for the period *c.*1715–32. It later became a brew-house and was owned by John Brereton, a tinman and later chandler. After the death of Brereton in 1776, the building became a shop belonging to grocer and tallow chandler Samuel Kenrick, who later founded a private bank next door (Kenrick's Bank*), the site of the present day Halifax Building Society offices.* In the late 1840s, the premises were taken over by Richard Hughes* of Church Street and became the offices of the printing business Hughes & Son.* The premises later became part of Wrexham's original F.W. Woolworth shop and then part of the W.H. Smith premises until the latter burned down and was replaced by a new store.

Crown Inn, Abbot Street
This was shown in the 1833 survey.

Crusaders, rugby league football club
Founded in 2005 as the Celtic Crusaders, after pioneering work since 1996 by clubs such as the Cardiff Demons and the Bridgend Blue Bells, the team was originally based at the Brewery Field in Bridgend, where they played their first game in 2006. In their second season they won the National League 2 Championship and were promoted to League 1 in 2008. During this season they applied to become members of the Super League and were accepted for 2009. The club's facilities at Bridgend failed to meet the requirements of the Super League and plans were made for them to move to Rodney Parade in Newport. However, following a successful match at the Racecourse* in Wrexham where they attracted the support of a large crowd, the club was bought by Wrexham Village (the company that owns Wrexham FC*) in December 2009. The club is

committed to playing two matches each season at the Gnoll ground in Neath.

The club plays in red and white (home) and black and yellow, (away, the colours of the flag of Saint David). At the time of publication (2010) there are plans to change the name of the team to the Wrexham Crusaders.

Cunliffe Arms, Jeffreys Road
Plans for the building of a new public house to serve the Borras Park area of Wrexham were first announced in 1969. The closure of the Rose & Crown public house in Chester Street enabled the licence to be transferred to the new pub which was built at a cost of £45,000 and officially opened on 22 March 1971 by C.F. Huntley, Chairman of Border Breweries. The name was decided following a local competition, which was won by F. Jones of Y Wern. Other suggested names were: the Whippet Lodge; Swinging Judge; Hanging Judge; the Scaffold; the Woolsack and Borderline Case.

Cunliffe Family
The Cunliffe family is first recorded as having been granted land in the hundred and parish of Blackburn in Lancashire and in the townships of Billington, Rushton and Harwood. Near Billington stood an old house known as Cunliffe House (demolished in 1770) and the high land nearby is still called Cunliffe Moor or Cunliffe Edge. The family lost its local status at the time of the Tudors and moved to a lesser estate at Hollings where John Cunliffe, a Parliamentarian, resided during the Civil War. After the death of Charles I, John switched to support the Royalist cause and his property was sequestered (confiscated) by Parliament in 1651 when the family moved to Wycoller Hall, near Colne where they remained after the Restoration. His son, the Revd Ellis Cunliffe, was educated at Cambridge and became a Fellow of Jesus College. He was presented with the living of Newmarket where King Charles II made him one of the Royal chaplains. He married Janet, the daughter of Anthony Foster of Airton in Yorkshire and their son was christened Foster in recognition of his mother's family. King Charles was one of the boy's godparents. Ellis Cunliffe later became rector of Etwall where he died in 1712.

It was intended that Foster would follow his father into the church but he preferred a career in trade and was apprenticed to Sir James Thornhill, a great London merchant. When Sir James was declared bankrupt, the Cunliffes lost a great deal of money and Foster made his way to Liverpool where he set up his own business. He inherited the Airton estate from his mother and in 1714 married Margaret Carter of Lancaster who brought with her a fortune of £800. He was originally involved in the tobacco trade with America and the Irish Sea trade and became owner and part-owner of a number of vessels sailing out of Liverpool. He and his sons Ellis and Robert then moved into what was euphemistically called 'the Africa Trade' dealing in slaves between Africa and the Americas. During the 1730s he sent four ships to Africa each year. The family business had representatives at Oxford (on Chesapeake Bay in New England) and New Town (the present day Chestertown) in Maryland, most notably the Welshman Robert Morris (1734–1806), a signatory of the American Declaration of Independence. Morris was a member of Congress in 1776 and Secretary of Finance to the rebel American government in 1781. It was he who furnished the funds to keep the War of Independence going and was said to be wealthier than the United States government. He resigned his government post after three years and founded a national bank.

Foster Cunliffe was made an alderman of Liverpool, served three times as Mayor and was known as a 'tyrannical ruler of both the Corporation and the town'. He was, however, a great philanthropist giving substantial sums to the Liverpool Infirmary and the Blue Coat School. He was described by Dr Smith, Dean of Chester, as a man whose 'abilities were so extraordinary, that whatever station Providence had placed him, he must have risen to the height of his profession; and he scrupled not to assert that he was amongst the very first men of his time'. In Liverpool, he was known as 'Honest Foster'. He rented an estate at Saighton in Cheshire and, when he died in 1758, left a fortune valued at over £200,000. He was buried in St Peter's Church, Liverpool and Cunliffe Street in Liverpool is named after him. His epitaph describes him as 'a merchant whose sagacity, honesty and diligence procured wealth and credit to himself and his country; a magistrate who administered justice with discernment, candour and impartiality, a Christian devout and exemplary.'

Arms of the Cunliffe family.

Sir Ellis Cunliffe, 1st Baronet, the eldest son of Foster Cunliffe, was born in 1717 and became a partner in the family business. Due to ill health, he did not, however, play a prominent role in its day-to-day running and spent much of his time in the south of England and abroad. He was elected MP for Liverpool in 1755 and was knighted by King George II in 1756. Three years later he received a Baronetcy. He married Mary Bennett of Moston, Chester in 1760. He was the first member of the Cunliffe family to try to establish links with Wrexham when he tried to buy the 1,000-acre Borras estate for £39,000 but was out-bid by £1,000 by a Mr Trigge who later sold it to Lord Kenyon. He died on 16 October 1767 and is buried at Churton Heath.

Sir Robert Cunliffe, 2nd Baronet, the brother of Sir Ellis, was born in 1719 and became a partner in the family business. He married Mary, daughter of Ichabod Wright of Nottingham, in 1752, against the wishes of his father (she died in 1791). On the death of Foster Cunliffe, Robert retired from active participation in business and lived at Saighton before moving to a house which he had bought at Dee-Side in Chester. He bought the Pickhill estate with the intention of building himself a mansion there but died on 9 October 1778 before he was able to take any steps towards fulfilling his plans. He was buried at Churton Heath Chapel.

Sir Foster Cunliffe, 3rd Baronet, the eldest son of Sir Robert, was born on 8 February 1755 in Liverpool. The family moved to live in Chester when he was aged 8. He was educated at Mr Thomas Hunter's School in Weaverham, Cheshire until he went up to Trinity College, Cambridge in 1773. He was awarded his BA in 1777 after which he went to Angers in France to complete his education at the Angers Academy. He spent much of his early adult life travelling in Europe. He married Harriet, the daughter of Sir David Kinloch of Gilmerton, Scotland, on 1 October 1781 and they lived at Dee-Side, Chester with the dowager Lady Cunliffe. They had twelve children, four born at Chester *viz*: Foster (born 17 August 1782); Mary (born 28 September 1783); Robert Henry (born 22 April 1785); Harriet (born 16 June 1786) and eight born at Acton *viz*: Ellis Watkin (born 5 September 1787); Francis Kinloch (born 3 February 1789; Brooke (born 23 July 1791); Emma (born 8 February 1792); Charlotte (born 28

Portrait of Sir Foster Cunliffe, 3rd Bt. of Acton Park, Wrexham, Denbighshire (c.1787). Purchased by University of Michigan Museum of Art, USA, 2007.

September 1793); George (born 3 June 1795); a son stillborn in 1796; Thomas (born 23 November 1798). He bought the Acton Park* estate in 1785. Sir Foster introduced archery meetings to Acton Park (see Royal British Bowmen) and was High Sheriff of Denbighshire, 1787. His large memorial in Wrexham Parish Church was designed by the Chester architect Thomas Jones.* His son, Robert Henry, described him: 'To say that he was pious, humane, charitable, and generous, that he was beloved, revered and looked up to would be to give but a faint idea of the noble, just and self denying principles which through life actuated his conduct. He came nearer to perfection than any being I have ever known.' His life-size portrait, painted by Hopper, is currently located in the University of Michigan Museum of Art, USA.

Sir Robert Henry Cunliffe, 4th Baronet, the second son of Sir Foster, was born at Dee-Side, Chester on 22 April 1785. He was educated initially at Mr Lloyd's School in Warrington but, due to his father's dissatisfaction with the education he was receiving, was then taught by private tutors at Acton Hall until aged 11 when he went to school near Liverpool. His father wrote a description of him: 'Robert is 16, well looking without being handsome, tho' he carries himself so well that at first sight he is called so. He is under no embarrassment in company but finds himself perfectly at ease. His address is so manly and his manner so gentlemanlike that he seems to have been educated in the first circles. He never showed any capacity or inclination for study, but he possesses a large portion of that everyday sense, that useful sterling knowledge which will make him a valuable member of society and assist him in passing through the world with advantage to himself and others.' He was originally intended for a commission in the Royal Navy but was offered a 'cadetship in India' by a cousin and he sailed for the sub-continent in May 1800. There he joined the East India Company Army. He married Louisa Forrest in 1805 (she died in 1822) and they had two sons and three daughters. By 1817, he was Deputy Commissary General of the Bengal Army and had served as the officer commanding the Commissariat during two wars against Nepal. He was promoted to lieutenant-colonel in 1823 when he was described in a letter from the Military Department of the Bengal Army: 'Adverting to the high character, for zeal, integrity and ability, in the Deputy Commissary General, Major Cunliffe, and to the state of the irregularity into which the duties of the Military Board in all, but the Commissariat Department have generally fallen during the last 2 or 3 years, we have considered it to be a measure highly advantageous to the public interest to appoint Major Cunliffe in succession to Lieut-Col Paton, as Comy. Genl.' He married Col Paton's daughter Susan Emily in 1825 and they had three sons and three daughters (she died 11 November 1856 and is buried in Highgate Cemetery, London). Robert was knighted for his military services in 1829. He returned to Britain in May 1833, after 33 years away from home, and took up residence firstly at Overton then at Gerwyn Fawr, Bangor-is-y-coed. His brother Foster died on 17 April 1832 and, on the death of Sir Foster on 15 June 1834, he succeeded to both the title and the Acton Hall estate. He was High Sheriff of Denbighshire in 1835. He died on 10 September 1859 and was buried in Bruera Church, near Alford.

Revd George Cunliffe, MA, the sixth son of Sir Foster Cunliffe, was born at Acton Park on 3 July 1795. He became vicar of Wrexham in 1826 and Dean of St Asaph. His father recorded in July 1826 that 'I received a letter from my friend the Bishop of St Asaph [Dr Luxmore] offering *me* the living of Wrexham for my son George. The very kind manner in which the Bishop performed this act of friendship greatly enhanced the value. It was as unexpected as it was acceptable. We had been

The Revd George Cunliffe, Vicar of Wrexham.

Sir Robert Cunliffe, 5th Baronet. A political cartoon published to celebrate Sir Robert's defeat of the Hon George Kenyon in the 1872 election.

contemporaries at Cambridge.' George made little mark on the parish of Wrexham, partly because of his rather rigid personality and his aversion to the use of the Welsh language in church services which, when coupled with the growth of Nonconformity during the mid 19th century, did not endear him to a large percentage of the growing population of the town. He campaigned for a higher moral standard in the activities of the people of Wrexham, most notably by his campaigns to have the Racecourse* closed. He retired in 1875 having served as vicar for nearly half a century but, in the end, was, as were so many of the Anglican clergy, a member of the landed gentry who epitomised Gladstone's comment that the Anglicans were the Conservative Party at prayer. It was George who moved the vicarage from the 'Old Vicarage'* to Llwyn Isaf* and who later gave that house to the parish to serve as a permanent vicarage. He died at Cae Dai, Denbigh on 31 January 1884 and is buried in Wrexham. A window was placed in the chancel of Wrexham Parish Church as a memorial to him.

Sir Robert Alfred Cunliffe, 5th Baronet, the grandson of Sir Robert Henry Cunliffe, was born on 17 January 1829. His father, Robert Ellis Cunliffe had died in 1855. His mother, Charlotte Mary, was the daughter of Illtyd Howell. Sir Robert married (1) Eleanor Sophia, the daughter of Maj Egerton Leigh of Jodrell Hall, Middlewich. She was the mother of his children and died in 1898 (buried Wrexham cemetery). (2) Hon Cecelie Victoria, daughter of Lt-Col W.E. Sackville-West (married in 1901) – she later lived at River House, Tillington, Petworth, Sussex and Haslemere in Surrey (died 1955). Sir Robert served as the Liberal Member of Parliament for Flint Boroughs, 1872–4 and Denbigh Boroughs, 1880–5 and was High Sheriff of Denbighshire in 1868. He had two sons, Foster Hugh Egerton* (6th Baronet) and Robert Neville Henry* (7th Baronet) and two daughters Mary Evelyn and Kythe. He died in 1905 and is buried in Wrexham Cemetery.*

Sir Foster Hugh Egerton Cunliffe, 6th Baronet, born 17 August 1875, son of Sir Robert Alfred Cunliffe, 5th Baronet, and his first wife Eleanor Sophia. Educated at Eton (1888–95) and New College, Oxford; BA 1898, MA 1901. Foster was an athlete and cricketer, gaining a cricketing 'Blue' as a Freshman in 1895 and was later Capt of the Oxford XI. He was a Fellow of All Souls, Oxford. Foster Cunliffe was appointed a lecturer in military history at Oxford (specialising in the Napoleonic Wars) and wrote *The History of the Boer War* (2 Vols), the official government history of that conflict. In 1914, he was appointed editor of *The Times History of the Great War*, a post which he resigned upon volunteering for military service. He served as lieutenant in the 1st Cadet Battalion, Royal West Surrey Regiment before being commissioned into the Rifle Brigade and promoted to major. He was killed in action while serving in France with the 13th Bn, The Rifle Brigade, 1917 when the local press reported that he was 'The kindliest of neighbours, the most considerate of landlords and one of the county's most brilliant and accomplished sons'. He is buried in grave IG3 in the Bapaume Post Military Cemetery, Albert, Somme, France. He left an estate valued at £149,209-18s-6d.

Sir Foster Cunliffe, 6th Baronet.

Although he had not resided at Acton Hall since childhood, Sir Foster had played a role in the development of the town of Wrexham and was a member of both the Denbighshire County Council and the Denbighshire Education Committee and was a Justice of the Peace on the Denbighshire Bench. He stood as a Unionist candidate for the East Denbighshire constituency in 1906 and 1909 but was not elected.

Sir Robert Neville Henry Cunliffe, 7th Baronet, the son of Sir Robert Alfred Cunliffe, was born on 8 February 1884. Educated at Rugby School and Hertford College, Oxford, he succeeded to the baronetcy on the death of his brother Foster in 1917 and lived at 25 St James' Court, Buckingham Gate, London. It was Sir Neville who was responsible for the sale of the Acton Park estate after the First World War. He died on 1 May 1949, but had no children. Neville Crescent* was named after him.

Sir Cyril Henley Cunliffe, 8th Baronet. Born 3 March 1901, the second son of Alfred Edward Cunliffe and great-grandson of Sir Robert Henry Cunliffe* (his elder brother Robert Ellis was killed in action in 1915). He was educated at Dulwich College and Faraday House and served in the Royal Electrical and Mechanical Engineers during the Second World War. He married Eileen Clifford in 1956 and had two sons and one daughter. He died in 1969.

Sir David Ellis Cunliffe, 9th Baronet, eldest son of Sir Cyril Henley Cunliffe. Born 29 October 1957, he was educated at St Alban's Grammar School and resides in Needham, Norfolk. He married Linda Batchelor in 1983 and has three daughters. The heir to the baronetcy is Sir David's brother, Andrew Mark Cunliffe (born 17 April 1959).

Cunliffe Street, Rhosddu
This street was laid out in the late 19th century on land that had previously been part of Spring Gardens* on the Acton Park* estate and which was just outside the municipal boundary of the Borough of Wrexham. The street originally only extended from Rhosddu Road to the end of Springfield Terrace. In 1902 it was proposed to link the north-eastern end of Cunliffe Street with Acton Road by creating a new street which was to be named Neville Road (after Neville Cunliffe – see Cunliffe Family). Instead, Cunliffe Street was extended to the junction with Spring Road and Acton Road was extended south to the same point. The street was named after the Cunliffe family* of Acton Park.

Cunliffe Walk, Garden Village
Laid out as part of the original phase of the Garden Village*

development, this street was named after Sir Foster Cunliffe (6th Baronet)* of Acton Park* who was a member of the board of administrators of the Wrexham Tenants Ltd, administrators of the Garden Village project.

Cunningham Avenue, Queen's Park
Part of the Queen's Park* housing estate. A group of streets were laid out off Holt Road immediately after the end of the Second World War where pre-fabricated houses were constructed. These streets were named after leading British commanders of the Second World War.

This street, which originally had 44 'pre-fabs' (later replaced by permanent brick houses), was named after Admiral Andrew Browne, 1st Viscount Cunningham of Hyndhope (1883–1963), Commander-in-Chief of the Royal Navy's forces in the Mediterranean and Allied naval C-in-C under the Supreme Commander General Eisenhower.

Cutler's Entry, Charles Street
A 19th century development of some twelve very small dwellings located between Chester Street and Market Street and accessed from Charles Street. A house that stood on the site of the entrance to this was, from 1758, occupied by Thomas Williamson, a cutler, and was usually referred to as 'The Cutler's'. This was demolished and two houses (N°s 7 & 8 Charles Street) built in its place with a passage through to the 'entry' which then took the name of 'Cutler's Entry'. [Plan DRO/1048]

Cycle of the White Rose, The
This Jacobite 'secret' society (often referred to as simply The Cycle) was formed with the aim of restoring the House of Stuart to the throne of England. It was founded on 10 June 1710 but the first recorded meeting is that held at the Eagles Inn, Wrexham (The Wynnstay Arms Hotel*) on 1 May 1724. At the time of the coronation of King George I in 1714, Jacobite supporters attacked and badly damaged two dissenters' meeting houses in Wrexham (see Ambrose Tanner). Following the decisive defeat of Bonnie Prince Charlie at Culloden in 1746, the society gradually developed into a social club and survived as such until the mid 19th century. The Lady Patroness always appears to have been Lady Williams Wynn, a clear indication of the prominent position held within the society by Sir Watkin Williams Wynn. The society's badge was a white rose, surrounded by the word 'CYCLE'.

The Chester Courant of 30 May 1884 records details of the society in 1723:

> We whose names are underwritten do promise [to meet] at ye time and place to our names respectively affixed, and to observe the rules following *viz*:–
>
> Imp's [*imprimis*]. Every member of this society shall, for default of his appearance, submit to be censured, and shall thereupon be censured by the judg'nt of the society.
>
> 2ndly. Every member yt cannot come shall be obliged to send notice of his non-appearance by 12 o'clock at noon, together with his reason in writing; otherwise his plea shall not excuse him, if within the compass of fifteen miles from the place of meeting.
>
> 3rdly. Each member obliges himself to have dinner upon the table by 12 o'clock at noon from Michaelmas to Lady-day, and from Lady-day to Michaelmas at 1 of the clock.
>
> 4thly. The respective masters of the place of meeting oblige themselves to take down in writing each default, and to deliver the same at the general meeting.
>
> 5thly. Every member shall keep a copy of these articles by him to prevent plea of mistake.
>
> 6thly. It is agreed yt a general meeting shall be held by all ye subscribers at the house of Daniel Porter, junr., holden in Wrexham, on the 1st day of May, 1724, by 11 o'clock in the forenoon, and there to dine and to determine upon all points relating to and according to the sense of these articles.

1723   Signed
   Thomas Puleston, May 21st (of Emral)
   Richard Clayton, June 11th (of Brymbo Hall)
   Eubule Lloyd, July 2nd (of Penylan)
   Robert Ellis, July 23rd (of Croes Newydd)
   W. Wms-Wynn, August 13th (afterwards the first Sir Watkin Williams-Wynn, of Wynnstay)
   John Puleston, September 3rd, (of Pickhill Hall)
   Thomas Eyton, September 24th (of Leeswood)
   Wm. Edwards, October 15th (of Plas Newydd, Chirk)
   Thomas Holland, November 6th (of Marchwiel)
   Ken. Eyton, November 26th (of Eyton)
   Phil. Egerton, December 17th (of Acton Hall and Oulton, Cheshire)
   Jno. Robertson, January 8th, 1723-4 (of Upper Gwersyllt)
   Geo. Shackerly, January 29th (of Lower Gwersyllt)
   Robert Davies, February 19th (of Gwysanau)
   Jno. Puleston, March 14th (of Hafod-y-Wern)
   Broughton Whitehall, April 3rd (of Broughton Hall, Maelor Saesneg)
   Wm. Hanmer, April 24th 1724 (of The Fenns)'

The reference in this document to 'the house of Daniel Porter, junr., holden in Wrexham' seems to suggest that he was the landlord of the Eagles Hotel. Membership of the society in 1795 was:

   Rt. Hon. Earl Grosvenor
   T. B. S. Boycott, Esq.
   Lord Belgrave
   J. Humberston Caley, Esq.
   Wm. H. C. Floyer, Esq.
   Chas. W. W. Wynn, Esq.
   Edwd. W. Lloyd, Esq
   William Leche, Esq
   Sir Thomas Hanmer, Bart.
   Watkin Williams, Esq.
   Thos. Boycott, senr., Esq.
   Thomas Crewe Dod, Esq.
   Peter W. Davies, Esq.
   Richd. Aldersey, Esq.
   Philip H. Fletcher, Esq.
   Thos. Apperley, Esq.
   Sir Watkin W. Wynn, Bart.
   Frederick Phillipse, Esq.
   Sir Foster Cunliffe, Bart.
   Samuel Riley, Esq.
   Revd Ph. Puleston, D.D.
   Gwyllym Wardle, Esq.
   Henry E. Boates, Esq.
   Revd W. Whitehall Davies
   Revd H. W. Eyton
   Edwd. Morgan, Esq.
   Thos. Tarleton, Esq.
   Thos. Cummings, Esq.
   John Leche, Esq.
   Richd. Puleston, Esq.
   John Hill, Esq.
   John Kynaston, esq.
   John Wynne, Esq.

Membership of the society in 1825, with the dates that each individual joined were recorded on a circular card:

   Sir Watkin Williams Wynn, Bart (4/2/1822)
   T. Tarleton, Esq. (4/3/1822)
   S. Riley, Esq. (4/4/1822)
   S. Yorke, Esq. (13/5/1822)
   Sir F. Cunliffe, Bart. (3/6/1822)
   Sir John Hill, Bart. (1/7/1822)
   Hon T. Kenyon (29/7/1822)
   W.O. Gore, Esq. (26/8/1822)
   Sir Richd Puleston, Bart. (30/9/1822)
   T. Fitzhugh, Esq. (28/10/1822)
   Revd Dr Wynn (25/11/1822)

Revd H.W. Eyton (23/12/1822)
J.W. Eyton, Esq. (2/1/1823)
F.R. Price, Esq. (24/2/1823)
John Mytton, Esq. (24/3/1823)
W.Wynne, Esq. (21/4/1823)
Revd. Ph. Egerton (19/5/1823)
Lord Hill (23/6/1823)
T.N. Parker, Esq. (21/7/1823)
Revd W.W. Davies (18 /8/1823)
J.W. Dodd, Esq. (15/9/1823)
Revd R. Wingfield (13/10/1823)
J. Williams, Esq. (17/11/1823)
W.W. Wynn, Esq. (15/12/1823)
W. Lloyd, Esq. (12/1/1824)
E.Ll. Lloyd, Esq. (19/2/1824)
J. Maddocks, Esq. (15/3/1824)
W. Owen, Esq. (12/4/1824)
T. Boycott, Esq. (10/5/1824)
Wm. Egerton, Esq. (7/6/1824)
Revd P. Ravenscroft, secretary (5/7/1824)
S. Aldersey, Esq. (9/8/1824)
F.Ll. Fletcher, Esq. (6/9/1824)
Rt Hon C.W.W. Wynn (4/10/1824)
Revd G. Robson (1/11/1824)
Sir T. Mostyn, Bart. (6/12/1824)
Ph. Ll. Fletcher, Esq. (3/1/1825)
Revd R.W. Eyton (31/1/1825)
H.E. Boates, Esq. (28/2/1825)
Rd. Puleston, Esq. (28/3/1825)
J.H. Leche, Esq. (2/5/1825)
Rev W.W. Drake (30/5/1825)
Hon & V Revd G. Neville (27 June 1825)
H.W.W. Wynne, Esq. (25/7/1825)

D

Dairy, The, Market Street
This property, which stood in the middle of Market Street, is described by Dorothy Scott (later Mrs Sunter Harrison) in her memoir *Around the 'Stars'*. It was a small timber-framed hall-house with heavy beams and a through passage 'dividing the house from the service end'. At the turn of the 20th century it was the property of John Sunter who operated a successful dairy business from the premises as well as being the licensee of the Long Pull in Chester Street. The house has since been demolished.

Dale Street, Smithfield
This street was laid out on land that was part of the Cefn Park estate. Most of the houses were built in 1902–03. The street takes its name from its position above the valley of the Gwenfro.*

Dame Dorothy Jeffreys Free School & National Schools, Beast Market
The Dame Dorothy Jeffreys' School (sometimes known as the Lady Jeffreys' School for Boys) was established in about 1809 in a converted barn building that stood in the Beast Market, facing Seven Bridge Lane.* It was funded from a charitable endowment set up by Lady Dorothy Jeffreys of Acton Hall in the 17th century. The cost of the conversion of the barn was met by Sir Watkin Williams Wynn of Wynnstay.* The school operated the system of education introduced by Joseph Lancaster, whereby pupils were taught by means of the monitorial system, the first attempt at a national system of elementary education for the children of poor families. This building, close to the junction of Market Street and Beast Market, appears in the 1833 survey.

The Revd George Cunliffe* was a prime instigator behind the moving of the school to a purpose built school-room on the opposite side of the Beast Market, on a site which measured 23 yards by 12 yards. [Plan DRO/ED/SBD/41]. These proposals appear to have been only partially carried out, and a less elaborate school was constructed. By 1847, the report of the school inspectors noted that it accommodated no fewer than 308 pupils! Lack of funds to pay the teachers' salaries led to the school being closed in 1836. *The Report on the State of Education in Wales,** 1847, recorded:

This charity was founded under the will of Lady Dorothy Jeffreys, dated 1728. The income consists of rents, to the amount of £100, for teaching poor children of the parish: the number of scholars, and the subjects of instruction, are left unlimited. In the Report of the Charity Commissioners it is stated that at the date of their Report [1845] the then master was superannuated and addicted to drinking. At that time two schools were in operation, for boys and girls respectively. At the time of my visit [1847] the boys' school was in abeyance.

It appears from the statement of the Revd G. Cunliffe,* the vicar of Wrexham, that the present income of the charity is £100; that the salaries of both teachers have not together exceeded £60 per annum; that no children have been taught free, and that no subscriptions or collections have been obtained for that purpose in aid of the endowment; that the fees demanded from the poor have been the same as in schools established in parishes which derive no benefit from endowments, and in which there are no wealthy residents; that the master's salary has averaged £35 per annum, without a house, or other emoluments; and that at present no master can be obtained.

Boys' School – I visited this building January 22. The school was not in operation. The school-room is handsome and spacious, affording accommodation for 308 scholars. The fixtures are well-arranged, and the books and apparatus are sufficient and in good repair. The windows, although defended by iron rails and by a wire grating fixed outside, were broken, and the intervals filled with sticks and stones. The vicar states that previously it was impossible to approach the building, although situate in the centre of the town, by reason of the nuisances which were committed around it. The school-room contains a small library intended for the benefit of the schools supported by this charity. The books are few, but appear to have been well used.

Girls' School – Taught by a mistress in a school built for the purpose. Number of scholars, 74. Number employed as monitors, 5. Subjects taught – the Scriptures, the Church Catechism and Ritual, reading, writing, and arithmetic.

I examined this school January 22, when 27 children were present, 12 had been members of the school for more than three years, and 7 for more than four years. I found 5 who were able to read a chapter of the Bible, and to work very easy sums in arithmetic. There were 19 copy-books belonging to the entire number of scholars; only one contained good writing. When examined in Holy Scripture, 7 were able to answer very easy questions, but none possessed a competent knowledge of the subject: 7 could repeat parts of the Church Catechism. one of them perfectly.

The mistress has never been trained at any training school, but spent six months at a National School in Lancashire, to learn the National system. She has been taught to explain the collects and prayers according to the ritual of the Church of England; and in this respect has instructed her pupils carefully. She states that no one assists her to give religious instruction in the day-school, and that her school is visited by the clergymen about once in two months. Every afternoon she is employed in teaching needlework.

The school has great advantages. It is held in an excellent building, well furnished with books and apparatus. The

The former National School, Beast Market. This photograph was taken in the early 1970s, shortly after the building had been vacated by the Salvation Army. It was sold for £90,000 and demolished shortly afterwards as part of a road improvement scheme.

mistress has apartments adjoining the school-room, provided by the trustees of the education charity with every description of household furniture.

A new school was opened in the same building in 1853 under the control of the National Schools (Church of England) Society in response to the growth of the Non-conformist British Schools. The headmaster, John Haughton, a staunch Irish Protestant, was a tireless worker for the school and faced great difficulties in every aspect of his job. At one stage, there were insufficient funds for the salaries of the staff and Houghton is reported to have made up the deficit from his own pocket. On retiring, he was awarded a pension of 10/- (50p) per week, which was paid until his death in 1912.

A description of the National School in 1871 was given in *The National Magazine* for 1901:

> A thing of beauty is a joy for ever, and here beauty is conspicuous by its absence. But the school has greater drawbacks than a lack of architectural design. The site on which it stands is the worst in Wrexham so far as it affects the interest of teacher and scholar. The building contains two schools, an infant school on the ground floor over which is the boys school. Every alternate Thursday the infant school is closed on account of the fortnightly fairs and the injurious effect on the attendance of the boys is most discouraging ... how much the teachers lose in a pecuniary point of view, from the Government grant, owing to these circumstances we are unable to state.
>
> The approach to the infant school the morning after a fair day is like wading over a manure heap, and in wet weather there is a terrible fight with the miasma from the open ash-pits at the back and ozone from the neighbouring garden, the former as a rule being the victor for a considerable distance.
>
> We have heard with very great delight that there is a prospect of these school buildings being numbered with the things of the past and replaced in some more eligible site by edifices more in character with the wealthy party to whom they belong.
>
> [When the annual pleasure fair was in town] how was it possible for teachers to teach and scholars to learn amidst the noise of organs, hooters, ringing of bells, and the crys of showmen one can hardly imagine. Her Majesty's Inspector in one of his reports states that the examination was interrupted by the roaring of a lion and the squeaking of a pig. On one occasion a cow walked up the stairs into the school. But in spite of the difficulties the work was nobly carried out and many of Wrexham's leading men passed through that school.

Following severe condemnation in various inspectors' reports, a new school building was constructed at the top of Madeira Hill (the present day St Giles' School*) which opened in 1885. When the Beast Market School eventually closed, the building was taken over by the Salvation Army for use as its Citadel, a role which it fulfilled until that organisation moved out in the 1970s. Shortly afterwards, the Beast Market building was demolished and some of the sandstone blocks were recycled and used to form the retaining wall on the approach to the northern end of the Eagles' Meadow fly-over.

Headteachers:
Boys:
1812   Ralph Taylor
1836   Closed
1853   John Haughton
Girls:
?   Miss M'Coll
Infants
1881(?) Mrs Alice Parker

Darby, John Henry *industrialist*
Born at Pen-y-Garth, Brymbo in 1856, a relative of the Darby family of Ironbridge, John trained as a chemist and metallurgist at the Brymbo Iron Works and local collieries and spent most of his life in a variety of managerial positions in the steel works. He commissioned the first British basic open-hearth furnace at Brymbo and introduced the first by-product coke oven plant to be operated in conjunction with a steel plant. He designed and erected the Normanby steel works at Scunthorpe and was awarded the Bessemer Medal by the Council of the Iron and Steel Federation in 1912. He died in 1919 at Parkstone, Dorset and is buried in Wrexham Cemetery.*

Davies Family *gatesmiths*
The Davies family were renowned blacksmiths at the end of the 17th and the early 18th centuries. They lived at Croes Foel Farm* near Rhostyllen and had a smithy alongside the farmhouse.

William Davies, was the smith at Rhostyllen in the mid 17th century and may well have been the father of Hugh Davies.

Hugh Davies originally resided at the Rhostyllen smithy but, some time after 1676, moved to Croes Foel Farm. He is recorded in the Chirk Castle Accounts for 5 August 1690 as having been paid for work done at Cadwgan Mill and 'at Mrs Hall's late home'. He appears again in 1701, being paid for further work at Cadwgan Mill. He also appears as a churchwarden of Wrexham Parish Church in 1699–1700. He was buried in Wrexham churchyard on 2 September 1702 and his will mentions his widow Elinor, sons Robert, Thomas, Hugh and John and six daughters Anne, Magdalen, Jane, Sarah, Ellinor and Margaret.

Robert Davies, the eldest son of Hugh* and Elinor Davies, was baptised at Wrexham on 24 April 1676. He appears to have taken over his father's business in 1702 and married Ann Jones of Esclusham on 20 February 1706. His name appears in the accounts of the Parish Church, Erddig and Chirk Castle. Robert Davies died in 1748/9 and was buried in Wrexham churchyard on 7 February.

John Davies, the third son of Hugh,* was baptised on 24 February 1682/3. He worked with his father, and then his brother, at the Croes Foel smithy.

Gates known to have been produced by the Croes Foel smithy:

Eaton Hall, Chester; Leeswood Hall, Mold; Ruthin Parish Church; Wrexham Parish Church; Erddig Hall, Wrexham; Cholmondeley Castle; Hanmer Parish Church; Chirk Castle; Oswestry Parish Church; Abbey House, Shrewsbury; Carden Hall, Malpas; Eccleston Church; Emral Hall, Worthenbury; Mold Parish Church (removed and relocated to Gwysanau Hall near Mold, Colomendy School near Mold and Cilcain and Gwernafield churches); Aldenham Park, Bridgnorth; Newnham Paddox, Warwickshire. [DRO/1116]

Davies Court, Pentre Felin
A small court development of poor quality houses, Davies Court was located on the south side of Pentre Felin, west of Pierce's Square.

Davies Court, Hightown
This street was laid out in the 1980s on land that had previously been the property of C.T. Clark, proprietor of the King's Mills Garage. Built by the Wales and West Housing Association, all the streets were named after RWF who had been awarded the Victoria Cross. Davies Court was named after Cpl Joseph Davies of the 10th Battalion Royal Welsh Fusiliers who was awarded the Victoria Cross for his actions at Delville Wood, France, 20 July 1916. A native of Tipton, Staffordshire, Joseph Davies survived the war and died in Bournemouth in 1976. The citation for his VC reads:

> For most conspicuous bravery. Prior to an attack on the enemy in a wood he became separated with eight men from the rest of his company. When the enemy delivered their second counter-attack his party was completely surrounded, but he got them into a shell hole, and by throwing bombs and opening rapid fire, succeeded in routing them. Not content with this he followed them up in their retreat and bayonetted several of them. Corporal Davies set a magnificent example of pluck and determination. He has done other very gallant work and was badly wounded in the Second Battle of Ypres.

Davies, Arthur *tenor*
Born in Wrexham in 1941, Arthur Davies was employed as a factory draughtsman before he embarked on a career as a professional opera singer. He made his solo debut with the Welsh National Opera as Squeak in the opera *Billy Budd* in 1972. He has performed principal roles in numerous productions with English National Opera, Scottish Opera, Opera North as well as several European and American companies. He is noted for his performances of Elgar oratorios.

Davies, JP, Christopher 'Cris' *local politician*
Born in 1882, Cris Davies was the headmaster of Acton School* from its opening in 1923 until his retirement in 1947. He was elected a borough councillor in May 1919, became Mayor in 1922, an alderman in February 1927 and resigned from the Council in 1935. He served as chairman of the Parks Committee and the Public Library Committee, was a member of the Court of the University College of North Wales, Bangor and was Wrexham's representative on the Association of Welsh Local Authorities. A magistrate for many years, he served as the deputy chairman of the Wrexham Bromfield Bench before retiring in March 1957. He was made a Freeman of Wrexham on 26 March 1935. Married to Jessie Davies, he lived at Mandalay, Gerald Street* and died on 9 October 1962.

Davies, MBE, MA, David Garfield *educationalist*
Born in Ruabon and educated at Ruabon Grammar School, he served with the Welch Regiment in France during the First World War. He gained an MA from Oxford and was a teacher at Grove Park School 1922–65. For many years, he was the senior history master at the school and, from 1961–5, deputy headmaster. During the Second World War he was the officer commanding the Wrexham detachment of the Royal Observer Corps for which service he was awarded the MBE.

Davies, David Leslie *local historian*
Born in Wrexham in 1905, the son of a local retailer, Leslie Davies was educated at the Victoria School* (under the headmaster Charles Dodd*) and Grove Park County Grammar School.* In 1924 he became an undergraduate at the University College of North Wales, Bangor (reading history under Sir John Edward Lloyd) where he met A. H. Dodd.*

Upon graduating, he qualified as a teacher and taught at Whitehaven Grammar School before spending a year in London in the employ of the Royal Commission on Ancient Monuments in Wales and Monmouth. While there he completed a course on archaeology conducted by Sir Mortimer Wheeler. He then returned to Wrexham where he worked in the family grocery business in Ruabon Road. In his spare time he became a lecturer on social and economic history to the Wrexham Workers' Education Association and was a member of the Borough Library Committee. After twenty years he gave up his business and returned to teaching, joining the staff at Victoria School.

In 1960, he was appointed tutor-in-charge of the local history class in Wrexham and was responsible for organising three very successful local history exhibitions which led to the formation of the Wrexham Local History Society in 1973 of which he was the first president. He was also one of the founding members of the Wrexham Civic Society. He was responsible for saving the papers of Miss Mary Myddelton of Croesnewydd Hall* which were deposited in the National Library of Wales (Plas Power MSS). Leslie Davies was also a founder member of the Denbighshire Historical Society and was its president from 1977–84. He retired from teaching in 1970.

Leslie Davies was married to Audrey and they had one daughter. He died on 10 April 1993.

Davies, Derick (Frederick) *opera singer*
Born in Wrexham, the son of Mrs Bertha Davies of 66 Bradley Road and the nephew of bass baritone Ernest Davies,* Frederick Davies was educated at Victoria School* and Grove Park County Grammar School.* He became a professional opera singer with the Welsh National Opera and was singing at Glyndebourne when he was involved in a serious car accident which ended his career. He made many broadcasts with the BBC. Married to Ingrid, he had two sons.

Davies, JP, Alderman Edward *local politician*
Born in Rhosllanerchrugog, Edward Davies spent all his working life as an employee of Crosville Motor Services, most of the time as a bus driver, but latterly as an inspector.

He was the Labour councillor for Caia Ward from November 1946 until 1989, chairman of the Watch Committee, Mayor in 1960 and was made an alderman for Caia Ward in 1965. He was also a county councillor for the Caia Ward from March 1946 (firstly on Denbighshire County Council and then on Clwyd County Council) and was chairman of Clwyd County Council, chairman of the Clwyd Education Committee, chairman of the County Youth Committee and vice chairman of the County Grants Committee. He was also vice chairman of the Hightown Youth Committee, a trustee of the Wrexham & East Denbighshire Hospital Contributions Scheme and the Hospital Samaritans' Fund, a governor of Grove Park Schools* and a manager of St David's School.*

Edward Davies also served as a Justice of the Peace for Denbighshire from June 1957. He was married to Doris (died May 1993) and had one son, and lived at Nº 71 St John's Road, Hightown.

Davies, Ernest *opera singer*
A native of Wrexham (his father was an official with the

Wrexham Electricity Department), he was educated at Alexandra School.* His musical talent was recognised very early in his life and he was a junior member of the choir at St John the Baptist's Church,* Hightown and later, the choir of St Giles' Parish Church.

He won the John Stokes Scholarship to the Royal Academy of Music and, on completion of his course in 1934, gained the highest award that the Royal Academy could bestow. On the recommendation of Sir John Barbirolli, he was auditioned for the Sadlers Wells Opera Company by the legendary Miss Lilian Bayliss who immediately appointed him as a baritone. In 1938 he moved to the Universal Opera Company. During the Second World War he served in the Royal Observer Corps in both Wrexham and Surrey. After the war he was appointed Principal Baritone at Covent Garden where he remained until 1952. He sang at the Henry Wood Promenade Concerts on several occasions.

He gave up his stage career to return to Wrexham to care for his sick mother in their home in Farndon Street and re-joined the choir at the Parish Church. A member of the Bromfield Lodge of the Order of Freemasons, Ernest Davies died at Meadowslea Hospital on 11 January 1985. He was the uncle of Derick Davies.*

Davies, George Thomas *local politician*
Born in Rhosymedre, the son of William Davies, The Beehive, he studied to become a Wesleyan minister and was preaching at the age of 18. He decided, however, that the church was not the life for him and joined the staff of Cobden's Flour Mill* in Wrexham becoming a sales repre-sentative in Liverpool and in north and south Wales. He became a partner in the firm of Lloyd & Brearey of Liverpool and, in 1925, was appointed the General Manager of the Cobden's Flour Mill and the Hanwood Flour Mill in Shrewsbury. He was elected to serve as a Liberal councillor on WBC in 1921 and was Mayor in 1925.

A keen soccer supporter, he became a director of Wrexham Football Club*. George Davies married the daughter of Andrew Guppy of St Helier, Jersey and had one son and three daughters. He built Longueville, a bungalow in Erddig Road.

Davies, John (Jack) Arthur *local politician*
Born on 31 May 1913, the son of a farmer (his grandfather had owned Moreton Farm and the Moreton Inn, Johnstown), Jack Davies was educated at Marchwiel and Rhosymedre. He spent his entire working life in farming, firstly at Pont-y-Ffrwd Farm in Marchwiel and latterly at Pum Rhyd Farm, Sesswick.

He was first elected in 1967 as an Independent councillor for Abenbury on WRDC. In 1974 the local government reorganisation led to a change in his ward and he was returned as a councillor for Marchwiel, Sesswick and Erbistock. He remained as a member of WCBC representing Marchwiel. Jack Davies was mayor in 1983–4 when the Freedom of the Borough of Wrexham Maelor was granted to the RWF. In his latter years he was known as the 'Father of the Council'.

After retiring from farming he lived at The Croft, Cross Lanes until his death in September 2002. He had two daughters and one son.

Davies, JP, Alderman John A. *local politician*
Born in Coedpoeth *c*.1891, John Davies was the principal of the chartered accountants John Davies & Co Ltd.

He was elected a Borough councillor for Acton ward in 1930 (later Cefn ward) and became mayor in 1938 and, due to the outbreak of war, remained in office for two years. He was elected an alderman in 1948 and was made a Freeman of the Borough in 1957. He served as the chairman of the Finance Committee and of the Wrexham Council School Governors.

When his wife, Alderman Linda Davies,* was Mayor in 1954–5, he served as deputy mayor. He resided at 1 Acton Gardens and later at 57 Acton Gate. He died on 22 November 1967.

Davies, John Albert *local politician*
Born in Wrexham, John Davies was a china and hardware merchant. He served in the First World War with the 4th Dragoon Guards and was a founder member of the Wrexham Royal British Legion. When it seemed likely that the Wrexham branch would close down during the 1930s, John Davies was instrumental in keeping it going and was awarded the Royal British Legion Order of Merit and made a life vice president of the Wrexham branch. He was also chairman of the Victoria Youth Club.

He was elected to represent Caia Ward on WBC in 1945 and, in 1951 was elected Independent Councillor for Offa Ward. He served as mayor in 1956–7. He was appointed a Wrexham Borough Magistrate in 1956.

John Davies was married to Emily and had one son, John. He resided at Cartref, 15 Little Acton Drive. He died at his home in January 1960, aged 64 years, and is buried in Wrexham Cemetery.*

Davies, JP, Alderman Linda *local politician*
Born in Widnes, Cheshire, Linda Davies was elected a Liberal member of the Borough Council in 1945, representing the Wat's Dyke ward (later Acton Ward). She became Mayor of Wrexham in 1954 and was created an alderman in 1959. She was the wife of Alderman John Davies* and as such, had served as Mayoress of Wrexham in 1936–7. She was chairman of the Markets Committee, Wrexham Liberal Association, Wrexham Women's Voluntary Service, a member of the Gresford Colliery Disaster Fund Committee, President of the East Denbighshire Women's Royal British Legion and a Governor of Grove Park Schools. During the Second World War she was primarily responsible for establishing the WVS Canteen at Bodhyfryd House,* Chester Street. She had one son and one daughter.

Davies, Owen *minister*
Born in Wrexham in 1752, Owen Davies was one of the twin sons of Owen Davies a local tailor. After working in London and Brentford he became a Wesleyan Methodist and began to work and preach in the capital. On the recommendation of John Wesley he entered the ministry in 1788 and became Superintendent of the Redruth Circuit in 1798.

In 1800, he became Superintendent of the Welsh Mission and made his headquarters in Ruthin. After sixteen years in Wales he moved to Liverpool where he died on 12 January 1830.

A leading supporter of the Armenian sect he, according to the *Dictionary of Welsh Biography*, 'probably did more than any other person to lay securely the foundations of the Welsh Wesleyan Methodist Church'. He had married while living in Brentford but had no children.

Davies, Ron *local politician*
Born in Wrexham on 10 September 1937, Ron Davies was educated at New Broughton Primary School and Grove Park County School. He commenced his working life as a pupil architect with Denbighshire County Council in 1954 and then an architectural assistant with Birkenhead Borough Council in 1957. Passing his RIBA intermediate examination in 1960 he took up employment with Cheshire County Council where he remained until 1993 when he retired from the post of Property Information Manager. He married Hilda in 1960 and has three children.

Ron Davies joined the Liberal Party in 1979 and served as chairman and vice chairman. In 1985, he was elected a member of Acton Community Council and, two years later, became a member of WMBC and then Wrexham County Borough Council.

He served as the Millennium mayor in 1999–2000. He was a governor and vice chairman of both Acton Park* and St David's Schools.*

During his year as mayor he represented Wrexham at the opening of the Welsh Assembly in Cardiff and was present at the opening of the NEWI Sports Centre, the Henblas Square *shopping development and the Pryce Griffiths stand at the Racecourse.*

Ron Davies lives at N° 16 Burton Drive,* Little Acton.

Davies, Silas *local politician*
Born in New Broughton and educated at New Broughton School and Victoria School, Silas Davies spent most of his working life as the caretaker of the Denbighshire Technical College.*

A passionate trade unionist, he was awarded the Labour Party's Gold Medal in 1982. He was a Labour councillor for Cefn Ward and served as chairman of the Health Committee. He became Mayor of Wrexham in 1972 and retired from the Council in 1987 after over 30 years' service. He was appointed a Justice of the Peace in 1965.

In addition to his civic posts, Silas Davies also served as chairman of the Wrexham Multiple Sclerosis Society, chairman of the Queensway Youth Centre, and chairman of the Grosvenor Bowling Club. Married to Lily, he had two children and lived at 50 Coed Aben.* He died in January 1990, aged 79.

Davies, William (I) *highwayman*
Born in Wrexham in 1627, he moved to live in Sodbury, Gloucester where he married the daughter of a local innkeeper by whom he had eighteen children. He settled in a farm near Bagshot in Surrey and became a pillar of his local church and earned himself the nickname 'The Golden Farmer' because he would settle every bill with gold coin, never with paper money.

He later set himself up in business as a corn merchant in Thames Street, London but his good fortune seems to have been accumulated at the expense of others for he was also a noted highwayman, a fact that he kept secret even from his wife. A master of disguise, he specialised in daylight robbery and on one occasion was reported to have stolen money from his own friends but was so well disguised that he was later able to meet up with them and entertain them at their own expense without arousing any suspicions.

His criminal career began in about 1650 and he managed to avoid capture for over 40 years, a record for any British highwayman. His initial sorties were against cattle drovers returning from market across Bagshot Heath but he then expanded his targets to include almost any traveller including the Duchess of Albemarle who was protected by four men, all of whom Davies wounded before escaping with their mistress' jewels. On one occasion he paid the rent for his farm to the landlord and then, a few minutes later, stole the money back and later commiserated with the unfortunate man.

His luck eventually ran out when, during a coach robbery, he failed to search his victims and, as he left, was shot in the back. He was placed in Newgate Prison, tried, found guilty and executed on 20 December 1690 at Salisbury Court, off Fleet Street in London. His body was then hung in chains on Bagshot Heath as a warning to others.

Numerous pamphlets and one play were written about his life and his activities gained him an entry in the *Dictionary of National Biography*.

Davies, William (II) *musician*
Born in Rhosllanerchrugog on 1 October 1859, William Davies was a talented musician and chorister. He was taught music by Hugh Griffith and Richard Mills of Rhos. A graduate of the University College of Wales, Aberystwyth, Davies was appointed a music teacher in Llangefni and a chorister at Bangor. He won prizes at various National Eisteddfodau – Liverpool (1884), London (1887), Wrexham (1888) and Brecon (1889). He was appointed tenor soloist and lecturer in music at Magdalen College, Oxford in 1889 and, five years later, became assistant vicar-choral at St Paul's Cathedral in London.

Well remembered as a composer of songs, his best known being *O na byddai'n haf o hyd* and *Nant y Mynydd*. He married Clara Leighton in 1891.

He died 30 January 1907 and is buried at Abney Park, London.

Davies, Winifred *missionary*
Winnie Davies was born in Coedpoeth on 30 November 1915, the daughter of Howell and Alice Davies. Educated at Penygelli School, she was first employed as a dental clerk in Wrexham. A deeply committed Christian, she was a regular communicant at St Tydfil's Church, Coedpoeth where she also taught in the Sunday school.

She eventually enrolled for nurse training at Bootle General Hospital in Liverpool and whilst there, despite being an Anglican, joined Emmanuel Evangelical Church in Birkenhead, an establishment where she first encountered the call to become a missionary and she enrolled in the Emmanuel Bible College which specialised in training missionaries for service in the Belgian Congo.

She first arrived in Africa in 1946 where she began working as a general and maternity nurse, spreading the word of Christianity amongst the local people, particularly in Nobobongo in north-east Congo.

In 1960, the Congo was granted independence and almost immediately violence erupted as various political and tribal factions sought to assert their own authority. Early in 1964, a group calling themselves *Simba* rebelled against the government in the north-east of the Republic of Congo. As the region sank into chaos, violence and terror became the norm and many thousands of Congolese citizens were captured, tortured and executed. Despite the intervention of various foreign powers and the United Nations, the situation deteriorated.

By this time, Winnie Davies had been working in the Congo for many years for the World Wide Evangelical Crusade with the Heart of Africa Mission. She went home to Park Road, Coedpoeth for some well-deserved leave before going back to her mission station in 1964, fully aware of the dangerous situation. Shortly after her return her mission station was overrrun by the *Simba* rebels and she and many others were captured. They spent more than 2$\frac{1}{2}$ years as a prisoners/hostages, being moved around the country as the rebels sought to evade the government forces. All this time Winnie continued working as a nurse, tending the sick and injured. Eventually, on Sunday, 28 May 1967, near Opienge, as the government forces closed in on the rebel group that was holding her, she refused to abandon her patients and, as they were unable to keep up with the group, they were all killed. The Under-Secretary for Foreign Affairs announced her death in the House of Commons:

> Miss Winifred Davies ... was captured by rebels when they overran the mission station nearly three years ago. Since that time, our Ambassador has done all in his power to urge the Congolese authorities to take what steps they could to secure Miss Davies' release.
>
> We have always realised that a military rescue operation could endanger Miss Davies' life, but reports from various sources led us to hope that the rebel leader, Ngalo, might be induced to surrender if a favourable opportunity presented itself.
>
> We could not ourselves, of course, organise a relief expedition, but our Defence Attache at Kinshasa kept in touch

with the Congolese military command. On several occasions he offered to arrange the supply of material which was especially required for the particular operations they had in mind; owing to internal difficulties, however, these operations never took place as planned.

Members will wish me to convey their sympathy to Miss Davies' relatives and to the missionary society, with whom we have kept in close touch throughout.

A memorial cross to Winifred Davies was erected outside St Tydfil's Church, Coedpoeth. The inscription reads:

This cross commemorates Nurse Winifred Davies who served as a missionary in north east Congo from 1946 and died a martyr on May 27 1967.
I gofio y Genhades Winifred Davies a ferthyrwyd yn y Congo. Mawrygir Crist yn fy nghorff i pa un bynnag ai trwy fywyd ai trwy farwolaeth. Phil-1-20

Her biography, *The Captivity and Triumph of Winnie Davies*, by David Morgan Davies, was published in 1968.

Dawson, Nick *chief executive*
Served as the Chief Executive of Wrexham Maelor Borough Council from 1995–6.

Dean Close, Rhosnesni
A cul-de-sac of private houses developed by B. & G. Raw in the late 1960s and early 1970s on land that was previously Broad Oak Farm* (called Mathew's Farm or Tenement in 1786). The road takes its name from the nearby Dean Road.*

Dean Road, Rhosnesni
Known as Acton Road* until this area of Rhosnesni was absorbed into the Borough of Wrexham in the 1930s (to avoid confusion with the Acton Road in Rhosddu). The origin of the name Dean Road is unknown. (See also Broad Oak Farm)

Denbigh Close, Borras Park
As with other streets on this private housing development of the late 1960s, known as Hillcrest Estate,* this road takes its name from one of the old, pre-1974 counties of Wales, in this case, Denbighshire.

Denbighshire County Council
Created following the passing of the Local Government Act of 1888, allowing all householders to vote within the county. The county town was Ruthin although many of the Local Authority's offices were in Wrexham. The county ceased to exist with the formation of the County of Clwyd by the amalgamation of Denbighshire, Flintshire and part of Merionethshire in 1974.

Denbighshire Hussars Imperial Yeomanry
The Wrexham Yeomanry Cavalry or Wrexham Gentlemen and Yeomanry was formed on 3 June 1794 with Capt John Leache, Lt Simon Yorke and Cornet Thomas Jones being commissioned as its first officers. Command was offered to Sir Foster Cunliffe (see Cunliffe Family) of Acton Park* but he declined, preferring to serve in the new unit as a private soldier, and his place was taken by Capt Leache. The unit, of troop strength (no more than 60 men), was presented with a guidon by Mrs Lloyd of Bryn Estyn* in 1796 which was eventually laid up in St Asaph Cathedral. A second troop was raised at Denbigh in 1799 and in 1800 Sir Foster Cunliffe took command of the force with the rank of captain. In 1803 the strength was increased to 120 rank and file and Sir Foster was promoted to major. In 1807, command passed to Maj Edward Lloyd of Pen-y-Lan, Ruabon.

In 1819, two more troops were raised (at Denbigh and Ruthin) and the force became known as the Denbighshire Corps of Yeomanry Cavalry under the command of Col Sir Watkin Williams Wynn (see Wynn Family). In 1827, the Government ordered the Denbighshire Yeomanry to disband but the officers and men agreed to continue in service without pay and three years later was taken back onto the strength of the yeomanry. During the 1830s they were called out for service against rioters in Ruabon. Mold and Rhos where the infamous 'battle of Cinder Hill' occurred. On that occasion, the Yeomanry was ordered to patrol the streets to 'terrify' the mob, which soon quietened down. Sir Watkin then began to lead his men away down Gutter Hill but, as they passed a large cinder mound upon which a very large crowd had gathered, a cinder was thrown at them causing one of the horses to jump. The rider and his companion drew their pistols and fired at the crowd, but hit no-one. Sir Watkin

An officer and a trooper of the Wrexham Yeomanry Cavalry, 1803.

A group of NCOs and men of the DHIY, c.1905, showing the influence of South African service on their uniform. Seated in the centre is Sgt Brand who lived in Wrexham for many years.

quickly restored order and the crowd dispersed.

In 1862, the regiment adopted the hussar-style busby and became known as the Denbighshire Hussars Yeomanry Cavalry, a title which became official in 1876. In 1899 members of the regiment volunteered for service in South Africa as part of the 29th (Denbighshire) Company of the 9th (Welsh) Battalion Imperial Yeomanry. They arrived in Cape Town on 5 March 1900 and they did not return to Britain until 1902. During that conflict they lost 1 officer, 5 NCOs and 9 men killed or died of disease. A memorial to these men was placed in Wrexham Parish Church. After this time, the regiment wore the bush hats which had been adopted in South Africa and came to be known as the Denbighshire Hussars Imperial Yeomanry. By 1904 there were troops based at Wrexham, Ruabon, Llangollen, Mold, Denbigh, Ruthin, Rhyl, Dyserth, Bangor (Gwynedd), Beaumaris (with Amlwch), Caernarfon (with Llandudno), Porthmadog (with Llanrwst), Liverpool (2 troops), Birkenhead and New Brighton, with a strength of 579 men of all ranks. In 1912, the regimental headquarters is listed as being in Erddig Road which would suggest that it was the Drill Hall in Chapel Street.* [Documents relating to horse racing DRO/DD/GR/261]. A detailed history of this unit was published in Wrexham in 1909, *Historical Records of the Denbighshire Hussars Imperial Yeomanry From Their Formation in 1795 Till 1906*, compiled by Col Ll.E.S. Parry, DSO and Eng Lt B.F.M. Freeman, RN.

On the outbreak of the Great War the regiment mobilised and more men were recruited for active service. They were sent to Worlingham Camp in Suffolk where they remained in training until 1916. In February 1915 two members were drowned in the river Yare. Early in 1916 they were brigaded with other units to form part of the South Wales Yeomanry brigade and sailed for Egypt where their horses were taken away and they became part of the 4th Dismounted Brigade. In February 1917 they saw their first action as part of the 74th Division during the attack on Gaza and suffered their first war casualty when Sergeant Edward Rohun (of Merthyr Tydfil) was killed in action on 15 April. By the time of the 3rd Battle of Gaza, in October 1917 the regiment was known as 24th Bn, RWF (Denbighshire Yeomanry). They took part

A group of troopers of the DHIY during training in East Anglia, c.1916.

in the assault on Jerusalem and spent Christmas 1917 in Bethlehem.

On 3 April 1918, they were ordered to move to France and landed at Marseilles on 7 May. The 24th Bn, RWF was transferred to the 31st Division and went into action on 28 June. They took part in the final Allied offensive as part of the Fifth Army. At the time of the Armistice, they were advancing into Renaix in Belgium. The regiment was part of the British Army of Occupation until 1919 when most of the men were demobilised. During the Great War the regiment lost 6 officers and 192 men (including 2 officers –Captains Alyn Reginald James (of Gresford) and William Rooper– killed while serving with the Royal Flying Corps– and 27 men killed when the ship transporting them to Egypt as reinforcements for the battalion, sank on 15 April 1917).

Shortly after returning to Britain, 24th Bn, RWF reverted to

Officers 61st (Caernarvonshire & Denbighshire Yeomanry) Medium Brigade, Royal Artillery, St James' Palace, March 1931.
Front row (L–R): Capt A.T. Henderson; Capt F.S. Pollit; Capt A.J. Booth, MC (Adjt); Maj H. Johnson; Maj J.S. Barton, MC; Lt-Col R.G. Fenwick-Palmer; Maj C.B. Arnold, DSO; Maj J. Jarvis Jones; Capt H. Lloyd Pierce; Capt B. Squire; Lt G.E. FitzHugh. Back row: Lt T.K. Foulkes; Lt G. Marmion; 2Lt F. Taylor Downes; Lt D.M. Bateson; Lt C.L. Fairless; Lt D.W. Roberts; 2LT D.A. Price-White; Lt J.H. Gee; 2Lt W. Arfon Owen.

being the Denbighshire Hussars Imperial Yeomanry. As part of the re-organisation of the armed forces in 1920, they merged with the Caernarvonshire Yeomanry to form the 61st (Caernarvon & Denbigh Yeomanry) Medium Regiment, Royal Garrison Artillery, Territorial Army, based at the Drill Hall in Chapel Street,* Wrexham. The regiment was mechanised in 1927 and in c.1930 the suffix Royal Garrison Artillery was replaced by Royal Artillery. In 1939, the regiment was split into two and became the 69th Medium Regiment, RA, TA (Caernarvon, Bangor and Llandudno), commanded by Lt-Col Arnold, DSO, and the 61st (Denbighshire Yeomanry) Medium Regiment, RA, TA (Llanrwst, Colwyn Bay and Wrexham), commanded by Lt-Col Jarvis Jones.*

On the outbreak of the Second World War, the 61st Medium Regiment was mobilised and sent to France as part of the British Expeditionary Force. It saw action during the German invasion of France and the Low Countries and was evacuated from the beaches at Dunkirk. The regiment then spent four years training in Britain before returning to France after D-Day 1944 and forming part of the advance into Germany. They were in north-west Germany when the war ended in 1945.

The regiment was placed in 'suspended animation' in the spring of 1946 and re-activated in 1947, continuing as a Territorial Army artillery regiment until being amalgamated with the 372nd Light Regiment, RA, TA to become the 372nd (Flintshire, Denbighshire Yeomanry) Light Regiment, RA, TA in 1956. The name survives today as a TA battery.

Commanding Officers:
1794	Capt Leache
1800	Sir Foster Cunliffe,* Acton Park
1807	Edward Lloyd, Penylan
1819	Sir Watkin Williams Wynn,* Wynnstay
1838	Sir William Lloyd, Bryn Estyn*
1857	Charles Tottenham, Llangollen
1874	Naylor Leyland, Nantclwyd Hall, Ruthin
1886	Arthur Mesham
1892	George Mousley
1892	Henry Howard, Wigfair, St Asaph
1903	Llewelyn England Parry
There is a gap in the records until 1917	
1917	Lt-Col H. N. H. Clegg
1920	Lt-Col W. F. Christian, DSO
1924	Lt-Col W. Hesketh Hughes
1929	Lt-Col R. Fenwick Palmer of Cefn Park*
1933	Lt-Col J.S. Barton, MC
1938	Lt-Col C.B. Arnold, DSO
1939	Lt-Col J. Jarvis Jones* of Wrexham
1939	Lt-Col G.E. Fitzhugh, TD of Plas Power*
1944	Lt-Col D.M. Batson, DSO, TD of Pant yr Ochain
1945	Lt-Col J.W. Tritton
1946	*Regiment placed in suspended animation*
1947	Lt-Col Sir Owen Watkin Williams Wynn* of Wynnstay
1949	Lt-Col Trevor Foulkes
1952	Lt-Col Geoffrey Ashmore
1955	Lt-Col T.R. Leathes of Ruthin
1956	*Amalgamated*

Denbighshire Technical College, Regent Street/ Mold Road.
The Denbighshire Education Authority, aided by a grant of £10,000 from the Miners' Welfare Fund, acquired the old Infirmary building on Regent Street which was then converted for use as the Denbighshire Technical College, a successor to the Wrexham School of Science & Art.* The new college was opened on 18 October 1927 by Lord Eustace Percy, President of the Board of Education. The first chairman of governors was James Darlington of Black Park, Chirk, with William Aston* as vice chairman. A substantial extension was built in 1931 to accommodate new laboratories and workshops (at a cost of £34,000). It was opened by Sir Josiah Stamp in 1932 by which time the college had 700 students (100 of which were full-time).

By the end of the 1930s, it was becoming obvious that the demand for places at the college was exceeding vacancies and that further expansion was required. The outbreak of war in 1939 put all development plans on hold and it was to be nearly ten years before matters were put in hand for a new college building. The original intention had been to build on the nurseries site (between the Wrexham General Station* and Grosvenor Road*) but this was changed to a 30-acre site on the Mold Road, alongside the Racecourse (covering part of the area of the original horse-racing course). Designed by Saxon, Smith & Partners of Chester and built by Holland, Hanner & Cubitt, work began on the new college in 1949. The foundation stones were laid in October 1950 by the chairman of the Denbighshire Education Committee, County Councillor T.P. Roberts, and the chairman of the Board of Governors, Alderman William Aston (the silver and ivory trowel and maul used in laying the foundation stones were presented to the college and are on display in the foyer area). The completed building was officially opened by HRH the Duchess of Gloucester on 11 November 1953 (although some classes had been held in the building since September 1952) and provided facilities for nearly 3,000 students studying art, building, commerce, food technology, general education, science, mathematics, engineering and mining (the last two subjects being taught at the old Infirmary building in Regent Street). The new college cost £585,906-4s-9d to build. On 1 January 1953, the building department became the first to move into the new premises.

One of the controversial aspects of the new building was the inclusion of a 900-seater concert hall (cost £60,000) which many argued was an unnecessary luxury which would prove to be a white elephant and a drain on the college's limited resources. Named the William Aston Hall, it was felt that this building negated the plans for Wrexham to have a Victory Community Hall (see War Memorial Hall) and would result in the abandonment of the plans for the Grove Park School Amateur Dramatic Society to build a new little theatre on the Nurseries site. The first public event to be held here was a concert by the National Youth Orchestra of Wales on 31 July 1953. The first play to be performed at the William Aston Hall was *The Prodigious Snob* by Molière, which was staged on the evening of the official opening by the Technical College Drama Group.

At the same time as the new college was being built, the Education Authority purchased the former Westminster Hotel* in Grosvenor Road which provided hostel accommodation for 30 male students; female students being accommodated in lodgings in the town.

In 1956, the RIBA architectural bronze medal of the Liverpool Architectural Society area was presented to the architects for their design and the building, regarded by many as a fine example of post-war British modern architecture, is Grade II listed.

In 1954, the first steps were taken to try and make the engineering department a constituent college of the University College of North Wales but the proposal was rejected. Ten years later, plans for the art department to become a college of art, accommodated in the old Infirmary building were also rejected but, in 1968, it become the School of Art.

By 1960, the college was desperately short of teaching accommodation and new blocks were added to house the mining and engineering departments. One weakness of the college was the inadequate provision of hostel accommodation. In 1959, plans to convert the Infirmary into a hostel were turned down as being too expensive. In 1964, plans to build a new hostel for 50 girls in the grounds of the college (costing an estimated £69,000) were approved. Designed by Robert Macfarlane, the County Architect for Denbighshire, and built by H. Roberts of Coedpoeth, the building was opened on 21 November 1967 by Alderman Mrs Dorothy Dodd, chairman of the Denbighshire Education Committee (although it had actually been in use since

September). The actual cost was £63,000. In the same year plans were passed for a new £47,000 domestic science and catering block. By this time the college had over 3,800 students.

Principals:
- 1927 Dr William Thomas
- 1928 Thomas G. Samuel
- 1948 D. Cecil Morgan, BSc, FRIC
- 1966 Dr Harold Wynne Green, MSc, PhD

Denbighshire Volunteer Regiment
The demands for men brought about by the expansion of the armed forces during the First World War led to moves to form volunteer units to assist with home defence from those men unable to serve in the regular army due to age or the nature of their occupation – a concept very similar to the Home Guard* during the Second World War – with units serving on a part-time basis. The Wrexham & District Volunteer Training Corps was formed on 3 February 1915 and meetings were held at Alexandra School on Tuesdays, Wednesdays, Fridays and Saturdays, with route marches arranged for Sunday mornings. By November, the Corps had expanded sufficiently to form a regiment covering the old county of Denbighshire and consisted of two battalions. The Eastern Battalion was based at Wrexham with units in most of the surrounding towns and villages.

Denbighshire Yeomanry
See Denbighshire Hussars Imperial Yeomanry.

Denning Road, Borras Park
Built in the 1960s as part of the Borras Park* housing estate by London developers Spinks & Denning. The road takes its name from the developers.

Dennis, Henry *industrialist*
Born in Bodmin, Cornwall in 1825, and educated at the local grammar school. Henry Dennis was employed as an articled pupil to the Borough Surveyor before joining the Cornwall Railway Co as an engineer. In the 1850s he was appointed to construct the tramway from the Llangollen slate quarries to the canal at Llangollen. He returned to the Wrexham area as the manager of the Bryn-yr-Owen Colliery, Pentrebychan where he remained until 1857. A qualified surveyor and mining engineer, he sank Legacy Colliery and had a substantial interest in the Westminster, Wrexham & Acton and Hafod Collieries and was instrumental in the sinking of Gresford. He was also the founder of the brickworks at Hafod and Pant. He was a director of the Glyn Valley Tramway, chairman of the Snailbeach lead mines in Shropshire, a member of the Institute of Civil Engineers, chairman of the North Wales Coalowners Association and President of the Mining Association of Great Britain. He was elected an Alderman of Denbighshire County Council. He lived at Hafod y-Bwch* and later at New Hall, Ruabon. Henry Dennis was married to Susan Hicks and was the father of Henry Dyke.* He died on 24 June 1906 whilst on a visit to his Cornish residence and was buried in Wrexham Cemetery.*

Dennis, Henry Dyke *industrialist*
Born at Hafod-y-Bwch, Croes Foel in 1863, he was the eldest son of Henry Dennis* and became the Managing Director of the United Westminster & Wrexham Collieries Ltd after the death of his father. Married to Mabel, he died at his home, New Hall, Ruabon in June 1944 and is buried in Wrexham Cemetery.* The underground location of the Gresford Disaster* of 1934, the Dennis Section of Gresford Colliery,* was named after him.

Derby Road/Street, Hightown
The southern section of Derby Road was laid out in the mid 19th century and by the time of the 1872 survey only the houses on the west side of the road, south of Greenbank Street had been built. Of these the largest was Derby Villa, which stood on the south-west corner of the road. This had large gardens extending behind it as far as Stanley Street as well as on the opposite side of the road. The house was eventually demolished to make way for flats in the early 1970s. The section of the street between Greenbank Street and Rivulet Road was laid out and developed in the 1880s and 1890s. The former gardens of Derby Villa on the south-east section of the road were not built upon until the late 20th century. The street was named after the the Stanley family (the Earls of Derby) of Knowsley who had strong historical connections with the Wrexham area.

Dermott Court
See McDermott's Buildings/Court.

Derwen Lodge, Ruabon Road
In 1881, it was the home of Robert Parry and was later the home of the Birkett-Evans* family, proprietors of Hugh Price & Co.* At one time this house served as the Police Traffic Department Headquarters and in the 1970s the Wrexham Doll Museum, before reverting back to being a private house in the 1980s.

Deva Way, Queen's Park
Built in the immediate post Second World War period as part of the first phase of WBC's Queen's Park housing development, this street provided the link to the Spring Lodge housing estate. It was named after Deva, the Roman name for Chester.

Devon Close, Tŷ Gwyn
A development by local builders H. R. & E. Roberts of private houses completed in the late 1960s.

Dickenson, FRCS, John *surgeon & local politician*
Born in Cheshire in 1800, John Dickenson was a highly respected surgeon and general practitioner, residing at Crescent House, Beast Market and later in Chester Street (in a large Georgian style house located next to the present day Welch Fusilier public house). In 1847 he carried out what is believed to be the first operation in Wales using anaesthetics, only some four months after the procedure had been developed in Boston, USA. He was elected to the Borough Council in 1860 and served as mayor in 1861. He was married to Minnie. He died on 19 March 1887. He was the uncle of Dr H. V. Palin,* mayor in 1889 and 1890.

Diocese of Menevia
The Roman Catholic Diocese of Menevia was consecrated in 1898. On 19 March 1987 the northern part of the diocese was taken away to form the new diocese of Wrexham.* See also Bishops of Menevia.*

Diocese of Wrexham
Created 19 March 1987 from the Roman Catholic Diocese of Menevia,* the Diocese of Wrexham covers the counties and county boroughs of Isle of Anglesey, Gwynedd, Conwy, Denbighshire, Flintshire, Wrexham and the northern part of Powys (the old county of Montgomeryshire). See also Bishops of Wrexham.*

Dispensary, The Yorke Street
Opened on 1 May 1833 on the instigation of Dr Thomas Taylor. Griffith* and Sir Watkin Williams Wynn (see Williams Wynn Family) for the use of labourers, their wives and children, servants (earning less than £3 per year) and those persons unable

to pay for medical advice or medicines but who were not in receipt of poor relief. Each person was to pay one penny per week (or four pence for a family). All patients would be treated at home. The 'officials' of the Dispensary were:

Patron	Sir Watkin Williams Wynn, Bt, MP*
President	Sir Foster Cunliffe, Bt*
Vice-Presidents	Revd George Cunliffe*
	Thomas Fitzhugh
	John Madocks, MP
	F. R. Price
	E. Lloyd Williams
	John Williams (Gwersyllt)
Treasurer	R. M. Lloyd
Consulting Physician	Dr Parker
Surgeons	Hugh Hughes
	George Lewis
	T. T. Griffith
	V. P. Royle
Committee	Mr Bowman
	John Foulkes
	T. Griffith (Queen Street)
	Joseph Griffiths
	Mr Jackson (The Groves)
	Mr James
	E. Jones (architect)
	E. P. Jones (ironmonger)
	Mr Kewley (Stansty Lodge)
	Revd J. Pearce
	John Richards
	Mr Thornley
Dispenser & Secretary	Mr Durnell

Those people subscribing £1 annually were appointed governors and were entitled to recommend two patients at all times of the year. Subscribers of £20 became governors for life and could also recommend two patients at all times of the year. Subscribers of £1 or more were entitled to vote at annual meetings (ladies only by proxy). Each member of the medical staff agreed to attend the Dispensary for one day each week. The Dispenser was not permitted to take on any private work nor care for any patients not on the books of the Dispensary and could not practise within ten miles of Wrexham for five years after leaving the Dispensary. The Dispensary ceased to function after the opening of the Infirmary* in Regent Street.

Dissenters Burial Ground, Rhosddu
Palmer* claimed that this graveyard was 'of ancient date' and that 'thousands lie within it'. It was probably laid out during the period of the Interregnum of the 1650s on land given by the Puritan Daniel Lloyd of Pen-y-Bryn Farm, Abenbury (see Pilgrim's Place). Among the first to be interred here was the Puritan Morgan Llwyd who died in 1659. It is believed that the graveyard was laid out by the Independents.

By the mid 18th century, the graveyard was being used and maintained by Chester Street Baptist Church. It was enclosed by a wall in 1857 and was closed to new burials in 1888 (although the last burial did not take place until 1901). A memorial to Morgan Llwyd was unveiled by Mrs Margaret Lloyd George on 10 April 1912. The graveyard was taken over by WBC in 1960 when the headstones were moved and the ground cleared and re-opened as the Morgan Llwyd Memorial Park on 1 May 1963.

Among the notables buried here are Captain William Wynne of Ruabon (Parliamentary Commissioner for Wales), John Evans (first pastor of the Independent Church in Wrexham, he had been appointed master of Oswestry School on the personal recommendation of Oliver Cromwell), the Revd John Kenrick (of Wynne Hall, Ruabon), James Buttal* of Grove Park,* James Reynolds Gummow* (architect), Richard Hughes* (publisher), George Bayley* (founder editor of the *Wrexham Advertiser*) and William Wilkinson* (ironmaster). The graveyard was later landscaped and now serves as a public park.

Dodd Family
Dodd, Charles educationalist – born in Wrexham in 1855, the son of Edward (died 1891) and Frances Dodd (née Griffiths), a whitesmith, and brought up at 4 Brook Street.* Charles was educated for a short time at his grandmother's dame school on the Bonc* off Poplar Road (see Dame Schools) then, aged 5, was sent to the 'Brookside School' – the British School* in Brook Street. He became a monitor and, aged fourteen, began a five-year apprenticeship as a pupil teacher. By 1877, he was the senior assistant teacher at the British School, dealing with classes of varying sizes, the largest number of pupils being 88. Whilst there, he advanced his own education by studying Latin, Greek and mathematics which he then introduced into the school curriculum. He was appointed headmaster in 1884 and transferred the school to the control of the Wrexham Board of Education. In 1901 he became the headmaster of the new Victoria School in Poyser Street, a post which he retained until retiring on 30 September 1919 after 52 years as a teacher. In 1882 he married Sarah Parsonage (1854–1940), head teacher at Penygelli School, and they had four sons, Edward Ernest (an author and history teacher, later a lecturer in philosophy at Jesus College, Oxford), Percy William, Charles Harold (a theologian and Regis Professor of Divinity at Cambridge University) and Arthur Herbert (a historian and Professor of History at the University College of North Wales). In 1881, Charles Dodd lived at 31 Erddig Road and later at Clavelly Cottage, Chapel Street.* He died on 31 October 1928, aged 73 and is buried in Wrexham Cemetery.

Dodd, Arthur Herbert historian – born in Wrexham in 1891, the son of Charles Dodd,* Educated at the British School, Brook Street, Grove Park School and New College, Oxford he served in the Royal Army Medical Corps during the First World War after which he joined the Wrexham Extra-Mural Department of the University College of North Wales. Appointed a lecturer in history at Bangor in 1922, he was Professor of History from 1930 until his retirement in 1959 when the University conferred upon him a D.Litt. and the title Emeritus Professor of History. He was granted the Freedom of the Borough of Wrexham in 1963. The author of numerous works on Welsh History, Professor Dodd is regarded as one of the finest Welsh historians of the century. A number of attempts were made to induce him to take up a Chair of History at Oxford but he always declined. He died in 1975. Publications include *The Industrial Revolution in North Wales; History of Caernarvonshire; History of Wrexham* (Editor); *Studies in Stuart Wales; A Short History of Wales.*

A. H. Dodd, 1891–1975.

Dodd, CH, MA, DD, FBA, *Revd Dr Charles Harold* theologian – born Wrexham, 7 April 1884, the son of Charles Dodd and brother of Arthur Herbert Dodd,* Charles Dodd was educated at Grove Park School and University College, Oxford. He was ordained a Congregational Minister in 1912 and served as a minister in Warwick from 1912–5 and 1918–9. He became a lecturer in New Testament Greek and Exegesis at Mansfield College, Oxford (1915–30) and Ryelands Professor of Biblical Criticism, Manchester University, 1930–5. He was appointed Norris-Hulse Professor of Divinity at Cambridge University (later Regis Professor) from 1935–49. He received honorary doctorates from 10 universities in 6 countries. Dr Dodd became

General Director of the New English Bible Project (1950–65) and then served as Joint Director from 1965–9. He was created a Companion of Honour in 1961 and a Freeman of the Borough of Wrexham in 1963. He was married to Phyllis Mary (née Stockings) of Bournemouth in 1925 and had one son and one daughter. He died on 22 September 1973 and had a Service of Thanksgiving at Westminster Abbey. His biography was published in 1977: *C.H. Dodd – Interpreter of the New Testament*, by F.W. Dillistone, London. Portrait in Jesus College, Oxford.

Dodman, Alderman William Thomas *local politician*
Born in Denmark Hill, London, on 19 December 1877, William Dodman came to Wrexham in 1898 where he started a gymnasium in Erddig Road and later founded a shoe manufacturing and retailing business at N° 4 Town Hill* and a motor-car dealership. He married Frances Florence (died 1965) and, in later life, lived at Hurst Newton* on Bersham Road and Gwern Hall, Bwlchgwyn.

The *Wrexham Advertizer & Star* described him in October 1954 as a 'Boxer, sprinter, script-writer, pantomime manager, cobbler, masseur, motor salesman, businessman, sportsman and

The staff at Dodman's boot and shoe shop, Town Hill, c.1910.
[Mrs Gaynor McMorrin]

Alderman'. His passion for sport resulted in his being a director of Wrexham Football Club and a successful boxing trainer with three champions to his credit: Johnny Basham,* George Cook (European Heavyweight Champion) and Billy Mack (British Welterweight Champion). Dodman was elected a Borough councillor for the Erddig Ward in 1927 (later Bryn-y-Ffynnon Ward), became Mayor in 1931, an alderman in 1937 and was made Freeman of the Borough on 28 March 1951. He served as chairman of the Watch Committee and was also the manager of the Walter Roberts Pantomime Company. He died at Hurst Newton on 26 August 1964 and is buried in Wrexham Cemetery.*

His business premises on Town Hill was reputed to have been built in the 16th century and have been a public house, known as the Bull & Dogs* in the 18th century, and later a chandlery, a millinery shop, a toffee manufactory and a butcher's shop before becoming the premises of Dodman's shoes in the early 1900s. At one time, William Dodman claimed to be selling over 600 pairs of wooden clogs each week and, during the Second World War, had the contract for repairing the boots for the American servicemen stationed in the Wrexham area.

Dog Kennel House, Caia
Dog Kennel Farm was located on the north side of the river Gwenfro, roughly on the site of what later became Rivulet Road. Land belonging to the farm was sold to the Wrexham Gas and Coke Company in 1868 for the expansion of their premises on Rivulet Road. It appears on the 1833 survey. The origin of the name is unrecorded but is almost certainly a reference to a hunt kennels for one of the local estates. [DRO/DD/DM/404/1-15]

Dol Acton, Rhosddu
(*Trans.* Acton meadow). This name for a small cul-de-sac off Colliery Road,* is a link to the Wrexham & Acton Colliery* which was located nearby.

Dolphin Inn, Mount Street
This public house stood on the north side of Mount Street on the site now occupied by the Halfords store. At the rear of it was Jones Court.* It appears on the 1833 survey as the Britannia Inn* and the licensee in 1841 was John Jones who is shown in the census as 'butcher & publican'. By the time of the 1872 survey it had become known as the Dolphin Inn. It closed in 1920 and was eventually demolished as part of a WBC slum clearance scheme.

Dolydd Road, Croesnewydd
(*Trans.* meadows road) The houses on the west side of Dolydd Road were built in the late 19th/early 20th century. The eastern side of the road has been occupied by the offices and depot of L. Rowland & Company* since 16 June 1964.

Done, Robert Henry *local politician*
Born 1 January 1856, Robert Henry Done was the son of Robert Done, the landlord of the Caernarvon Castle Inn on Bridge Street. He was the proprietor of the Town Hall Vaults (wine and spirit merchants), had interests in the Turkey Paper Mill* at Bersham and was chairman of J. F. Edisbury & Co., mineral water manufacturers. He was a Conservative member of the Borough Council and served as Mayor in 1893 and as an alderman. In addition to his business interests, he was also steward, guarantor and clerk of the course at Wrexham Races and Worshipful Master of the Square & Compass Lodge, Wrexham. Robert Done married twice (1) Lousia Ann Birch (died 1898) and (2) Florence Maud Grey (died 1901), and lived at Wrest,* Percy Road. He died on 8 September 1901 and is buried in Wrexham Cemetery.*

Dorset Drive, Tŷ Gwyn
A development by local builders H. R. & E. Roberts of private houses completed in the 1970s on land that was previously part of Tŷ Gwyn Farm.*

Dougall, MBE, Kathleen *dancer*
Born in Wrexham, the daughter of James Dougall, photographer of the Chicago Studio, Regent Street, Kathie Dougall began her dancing career at local Scottish dancing classes and went on stage with pantomimes in Widnes and Wrexham. She became choreographer to the Walter Roberts Pantomime Company in Wrexham before going into pantomime in Liverpool at the age of 19. She eventually had her own solo cabaret act which she took all over Europe before establishing herself as a dancing teacher in the Wrexham area and founded her own pantomime company which produced a regular Christmas show in Wrexham for many years. She was awarded an MBE in the New Year Honours list of 1998. For many years she lived at Bryn-y-Grôg Cottage.

Doughty-Wylie House, Hightown
Built in the early 1980s as the community centre for the Clwyd Alyn Housing Association residential housing development next to the barracks in Hightown.

The house was named after Lt-Col Charles Hotham Montagu

Doughty-Wylie, VC, CB, CMG (1868–1915), of the RWF, who was born at Theberton, Leiston, Suffolk, the son of a barrister. Commissioned into the RWF on 21 September 1889, he served on the north-west frontier of India (where he was severely wounded), Crete, Nile Expedition, South Africa (again severely wounded), China and Somaliland. He was Acting Vice-Consul in Turkey, British Consul in Addis Ababa and staff officer to Sir Ian Hamilton at Gallipoli in 1915. He received his Victoria Cross for gallantry at Old Fort Hill, Gallipoli on 26 April 1915, during which action he was killed. He was buried nearby in an isolated grave. His citation reads:

> On 26th April 1915, subsequent to a landing having been effected on the beach at a point on the Gallipoli peninsula, during which both Brigadier General and Brigade Major had been killed, Lieutenant Colonel Doughty-Wylie and Captain Walford organised and led an attack through and on both sides of the village of Sedd-el-Bahron the Old Castle at the top of the hill inland. The enemy's position was very strongly entrenched and defended with concealed machine guns and pom-poms.
>
> It was mainly due to the initiative, skill and great gallantry of these two officers that the attack was a complete success. Both were killed in the moment of victory.

Downman, John *artist*
The exact place of Downman's birth is unknown other than that it was somewhere in the old county of Denbighshire (sometimes incorrectly shown as 'Devonshire'), in 1750.

According to Elizabeth Cust in her book *Chronicles of Erthig on the Dyke*, he was born in Ruabon. He studied art in Liverpool and at the Royal Academy Schools under Sir Benjamin West. He worked as a portrait painter in Cambridge and Exeter before returning to London where he remained for many years. He was an associate of the Royal Academy by 1795 and regularly exhibited paintings there e.g. *The Return of Orestes* in 1782. He married the daughter of William Jackson, a composer and organist of Exeter. Downman moved to Chester and then finally, by 1817, to Wrexham where his daughter (Isabella Chloe, the wife of Richard Benjamin, solicitor of Chester Street) was living and died on 24 December 1824. He is buried in the parish churchyard but, unfortunately, his gravestone was removed in the early 20th century.

He painted in both watercolour and oils and a number of his illustrations of Wrexham have survived. He is best known for his portrait drawings which were 'very delicate in style and often highly tinted with water colour'. Amongst his sitters were members of the royal family, the Duchess of Devonshire (drawn in 1787 and still held by the family) and the actress Mrs Siddons. A large collection of his work was owned by the Cunliffe family* of Acton Park.*

Dr Daniel Williams School, Chester Street
See Chester Street British School.

Drill Hall, Poyser Street
The Drill Hall was designed by Wrexham architect Michael J. Gummow* and built by the firm of Davies Brothers. The building, which is basically a large glass-roofed hall, has an interesting frontage which is a fine example of decorative brickwork and terracotta, in the form of a pseudo castle, completed with castellations and decorative arrow-slits. It was completed in 1902 and officially opened in 1903 by Field Marshal Lord Roberts of Kandahar, Pretoria and Waterford, VC, the last Commander-in-Chief of the British Army. The hall was the headquarters of the 4th (Volunteer) Battalion, RWF.* During the Second World War, the Army Cadets trained here. In recent years the hall has been the premises of Chas. R. Eames, electrical contractors.

Drinkwater, Dr Harry *physician and botanist*
Born in Northwich, Cheshire, he moved to Wrexham in 1880 where he practised medicine. He produced a collection of watercolours of nearly 500 north Wales plants, mostly from the Wrexham area, most of which he later donated to the National Museum of Wales. He remained in Wrexham until his death in 1925. He was the co-author of *Plant Portraits* (with A.E. Wade).

Drws-y-Coed, Coed-y-Glyn
(*Trans.* doorway to the woods) Built in the 1970s on land that was once part of the Coed-y-Glyn* estate. The name is a reference to its location alongside the Erddig estate woodland.

Duke Street
Duke Street was laid out in 1885 and was named after the title duke which had no direct relevance to Wrexham but was merely following on with the pattern established by the naming of King Street,* Regent Street* and Queen Street.*

Dunks, The
The name first appears as Gwern Dwnk and originally referred to an area of moorland north of the river Gwenfro and south of a line drawn west to east from the Beast Market to Churchill Drive. The Dunks was traditionally believed to have been named after a rent (*twnc*) paid by all land holders in Wales to the lord of the commote. In Wrexham's case, the Dunks was an area of marsh or moor and of little real value. Local historian, Derrick Pratt, has put forward a well-argued case for the name originating as Tonc, Tunch or Tong, a possible reference to the grange of Valle Crucis Abbey. A third alternative is that the name originates from the old 'lost' township of Midden Hill, the case for which is argued under the entry for Wrexham Townships.* The growth of Wrexham meant that the edges of the marsh were developed so that the area was gradually reduced in size and there are references to land situated at the Dunks, part of Whitegate Farm,* being sold in June 1906. By that date, the Dunks were bounded on the north by the Caia Estate and on the south by the Borough Sewage Farm.* A small terrace of five industrial cottages in the area was known as the Dunks as late as the 1930s. They were demolished as part of the Borough's slum clearance programme. Today, the name is still applied to the open area bounded by Benjamin Road, Queensway, Whitegate Road and Derby Road.

Dunks Farm
This was a farm which existed in the 18th and 19th centuries, located in the township of Abenbury. In the early 19th century it was occupied by Peter Taylor, whose family had previously been tenants of Llwyn Knottia.*

Durack's Pool
See Pwll y Wrâch.

Dutton, OBE, MSc, CEng, **Robert J.,** *Chief Executive*
Born in Chester on 30 April, 1941, Bob Dutton was educated at Victoria Road Junior School and the King's School before becoming a student at the Liverpool College of Advanced Technology. He was employed by the Cheshire Rivers Board as a trainee civil engineer (1959–60) before moving to work for Chester City Council (1960–66, resident engineer) and Cheshire County Council (1967–69, senior civil engineer on trunk roads). In 1966 he became a student at Loughborough University of Technology.

An RAF reconnaisance photograph of Wrexham taken on 17 November 1948. Of interest in this photograph are: the river Gwenfro – centre left to bottom right; Ministry of Aircraft Production factory (later Rubery Owen) – bottom left; Wrexham Gas Works – centre left;Benjamin Road – centre, with Hafod-y-Wern Sewage Works tanks below to the left; Border Bottling Stores, Holt Road – upper right, with the pre-fab houses along Montgomery Road and, extreme right, Spring Lodge. The rough ground between the sewage tanks and Spring Lodge is reputed to have been very marshy, with the consistency of quick sand. [National Assembly for Wales]

In 1969, he joined WRDC as Deputy Engineer and Planning Officer and, on the re-organisation of local government in 1974, became Director of Resources and Planning for WMBC. Three years later he was appointed Deputy Chief Executive to Sydney Tongue* and, on the latter's retirement in 1988, became Chief Executive until his retirement in 1995. During his term as Chief Executive he witnessed an expansion in the light industrial base of the Wrexham economy as well as the commencement of the re-generation of Wrexham town centre and the increased investment in leisure facilities, including the Alyn Waters Country Park, Minera Lead Mines and the North Wales Regional Tennis Centre, Plas Coch.

Bob Dutton has an MSc. in Management (Loughborough), is a Chartered Engineer, a Member of the Institution of Civil Engineers, a Member of the Institute of Management, a Member of the Institute of Directors and a former Member of the Institute of Highways and Transportation. He was awarded an OBE 1991.

After retirement, Bob Dutton commenced a new chapter of service to the Wrexham area by being elected an Independent councillor for the Erddig Ward of WCBC. He is leader of the Independent group, member of the Executive Board and Deputy Leader of the WCBC. He lives in Drws-y-Coed,* Wrexham.

Dutton, Roger Audley *local politician*
Born in Chester in 1890, the son of Harry Boulton Dutton (Sheriff of Chester 1908 and Mayor of Chester 1912). He was educated at the King's School, Chester and Deytheur College, Penrhos, Montgomeryshire. He joined the family firm of George Dutton & Co and was appointed manager of the Wrexham shop after the First World War. He became Managing Director of the company in 1947 (see Dutton's Sig-ar-ro Stores*).

During the First World War he served as a sergeant in the Army Service Corps (Mechanical Section) in East and Central Africa and during the Second World War, was a member of the Wrexham Royal Observer Corps.

He was elected an Independent (Wrexham Ratepayers' Association) councillor for Erddig Ward in 1927, and later that year Wat's Dyke Ward of WBC. He became Mayor in 1937. He was Chairman of the Transport Committee and became an alderman in 1946.

He married Gladys Briggs of London in 1919 and had one son, Donald). Roger Dutton lived at Dorville, Chester Road until his death on 1 January 1960. (See also Roger Dutton)

Dutton, Roger *judge*
Born in Wrexham in 1952, Roger Dutton is the son of Donald and Doreen Dutton and the grandson of Roger Dutton,* Mayor of Wrexham in 1937–8. Educated at Grove Park School and the University of Kent, he was called to the Bar in 1974 and served as a barrister in Chester for 22 years. He was appointed an Assistant Recorder in 1988, Crown Court Recorder in 1991 and a judge in 1996 on the Wales and Chester Circuit, and was at the time one of the youngest judges in Britain. He was the Magistrates Liaison Judge for North Wales. He now sits on the Chester Circuit, is a tutor judge with the Judicial Studies Board and honorary treasurer of HM Council of Circuit Judges. He was a member of the Board of the North-East Wales Institute since 2008 and, latterly of Glwyndŵr University. He was appointed Deputy Lieutenant for the County of Clwyd in January 2009. He is married to Elaine and has three children.

Dutton's Sig-ar-ro Stores, Hope Street/High Street
This building (now the site of the Nationwide Building Society) was described in a sale catalogue of 1777 as 'A dwelling house ... standing at the corner of the High Street, near the Market Hall [Town Hall], containing a commodious shop fronting two streets, a large dining room, a parlour, kitchen, pantry, scullery and cellar, five lodging rooms, with garrets over.'

In the 19th century, it was known as 'The Corner Shop' and was a grocery and chandlery business run by Joseph Jones between 1804 and 1828. It then became a druggist, owned by John Beale* of Egerton Lodge. In 1871, it was taken over by the Dutton family of Chester who ran a high-class grocery and off-licence business there until it was sold by Donald Dutton to the Nationwide Building Society in 1973. Of particular interest in these premises was a very fine alabaster ceiling.

'Sig-ar-ro' was the inscription on a Roman altar which was discovered in the cellar of the Dutton's shop in Chester which was adopted as the company's trade mark. (See also Roger A. Dutton* and Roger Dutton).

E

Eagle Brewery, Bridge Street
Owned by Robert Williams and specialising in strong ales, the Eagle Brewery was located in Bridge Street. It was re-built by R. Venables Williams in 1893 and a plaque to this effect can still be seen on the front of the building. The brewery was taken over by Thompson & Co (see Sun Brewery) in the late 19th century and was eventually only used as a store and for bottling Watkin's London Stout and locally produced mineral waters. When it closed in 1922, the brewery was owned by Heasman. [Lease, dated 1883, DRO/1037]

Eagle Foundry, Tuttle Street
Originally owned by Chadwick and then by Cudworth & Johnson, this foundry was capable (if its 1886 advert is to be believed) of manufacturing a very wide range of products including: water wheels, colliery plant, agricultural implements, locomotive and portable engines, girders, boilers, wrought and cast iron. In addition they could provide 'fixed and complete in any part of the country churches, chapels, conservatories, schools, greenhouses, public buildings &c heated by water'. They were also scrap iron and brass dealers. The company was previously known as Arthur Cudworth and operated at the St Mark's Engineering Works. The foundry appears on the 1872 survey. Cudworth was joined in partnership by W. E. Johnson (died 21 March 1919).

Eagle Street, Mount Street
Located on the north side of Mount Street, opposite the junction with Salop Road, this street was built *c.*1848 and comprised of some 15 terraced houses. The five houses on the west side were the subject of a compulsory purchase order as part of the Borough slum clearance programme of 1938. The remaining houses N[os] 7–16 were made the subject of a clearance order in 1959 and the street finally disappeared in the construction of the Eagles Meadow fly-over. The name, like that of Eagles Meadow, is a reference to the Eagles Hotel* in Yorke Street. The most notable resident of the street was Gunner Ernest Parry,* C de G. There was access from Eagle Street to Eagles Meadow, Smithfield Road and the horse market through Eagle Street.

Eagles Hotel, The Yorke Street
(See Wynnstay Arms Hotel)

Eagles Meadow
Takes its name from being the field behind the The Eagles Hotel* which was always let to the tenant of the hotel (now the Wynnstay Arms Hotel*). Until the 1970s, there was a street leading from The Green* to the area behind the Wynnstay Arms known as Eagle Street.* The meadow was subject to regular flooding from the river Gwenfro.

Eagles Meadow, 1975 with the Monday Market in full swing. In the background is the ASDA supermarket and the Wynnstay Arms Hotel when it was trading as The Crest Motel.

In the 19th century, there was a bowling green at the western end of the meadow and from 1874, for approximately 100 years, there were regular horse sales held on part of the meadow, behind the premises on Yorke Street,* which attracted buyers from all over Britain, Ireland and mainland Europe. The sales were established by auctioneer. Frank Lloyd of Eyton House, who in 1891 constructed stabling for 350 horses, sale rings that could cater for 2,000 people coming to either buy or sell. Alongside the sales area was a quarter-mile trotting track where horses and ponies could be exhibited. The sales were originally held in March, June, September and November. By 1892, Frank Lloyd was able to claim that 'this sale can eclipse all its rivals by more than three times the number, and without a doubt it is the largest horse sale in the world'.

The decline in the demand for horses during the 20th century led to the gradual decline of the horse sales. The area of the bowling green and the horse market was considered in 1965 as the site for a multi-storey car park but was eventually re-developed as the ASDA supermarket in the 1970s (closed 2000). The remainder of the meadow was private land until the late 20th century.

In January 1971, in order to improve traffic congestion problems, the Monday market and the Easter Fair were moved here from the Beast Market and in order to stabilise its marshy surface, rubble was brought here and used as in-fill. Ironically, and rather fittingly, when the Wynnstay Arms Hotel* was partially demolished in the late 1960s the rubble was dumped on Eagles Meadow. A road was then constructed into Eagles' Meadow from Yorke Street* and a flyover, carrying a road linking the Beast Market* to Salop Road,* over Eagles Meadow, was opened in 1976. The first ASDA supermarket in Wrexham was located here until the store moved into new premises on the Alexandra Schools* site.

During the Second World War an encampment of Nissen huts was erected on Eagles' Meadow to accommodate United States Army* servicemen.

In October 2008, the Eagles Meadow (Dol-yr-Eryrod) Shopping Centre was opened on the former open Eagles Meadow site after the demolition and clearance of the former ASDA store and the road flyover. Built by Wilson Boden Developments in partnership with WCBC as an open mall-style shopping precinct, providing 400,000 sq ft of retail and leisure premises with residential premises located above the western section. The largest retail premises were provided for Debenhams (90,000 sq ft) and Marks & Spencer (55,000 sq ft). An eight-screen Odeon cinema complex opened at the eastern end of the complex in 2009. On the ground floor and sub-ground floor is undercover parking for 970 vehicles.

The whole development was met with very mixed reactions by the public, many feeling that it presented a very bleak, windy shopping area that was too far removed from the existing centre of the town. This, coupled with the advent of a significant downturn in the national economy, caused the development to have a very unsteady start and, at the time of writing, it has yet to achieve its full potential.

Earl/Earle Street, Pen-y-Bryn
A 19th century street which appears on the 1872 survey when only part of the south-west side was developed with seven terraced houses. The north-east side consisted of the gardens of properties facing Poplar Road and a large garden fronting Erddig Road. The 1872 spelling shows Earl without the extra 'e'.

East Avenue, Rhosddu
East Avenue, linking New Road* to Croes Eneurys* was first laid out in the 1920s, probably as housing for the nearby Wrexham &

N°s 4, 5 & 6 Earle Street.

Acton Colliery.* The origin of the name is intriguing and appears to be a simple reference to the fact that the street lies to the east of the railway lines. (See West Street, Rhosddu)

Eastleigh Close, Rhosddu
Part of a small private housing development of the 1980s, comprising three streets, all partly named 'leigh' and named 'North', 'East' and 'South' according to the position of each in relation to the others.

Eaton Drive, Queen's Park
This was built in the immediate post Second World War period as part of the first phase of WBC's Queen's Park housing development. The original houses were pre-fabricated as temporary solutions to the post-war housing shortages. The street was named after Eaton in Cheshire.

Eaton, Edward *pirate*
Although only an ordinary seaman, Edward Eaton is the only known pirate to hail from Wrexham. He is recorded as being a member of the crew of a Capt Harris in the 17th century. He was captured and hanged for piracy at Newport, Rhode Island on 19 July 1723 when he was 38 years of age.

Ebeneser Welsh Presbyterian Chapel, Price's Lane
See Price's Lane (Ebeneser) Welsh Presbyterian Church.

Ebeneser Welsh Presbyterian Church, Chester Road
See Chester Road (Ebeneser) Welsh Congregational Church.

Edge Street, Beast Market
This short street led from Crescent Road to James Street and comprised seven houses on the north-east side. The site now forms part of the Tesco car park. The origin of the name is unknown.

Edgeworth, Roger *Roman Catholic divine*
Born in Holt Castle, Roger Edgeworth was educated at Oxford and graduated with a BA in 1507 and was made a Fellow of Oriel College the following year. A noted preacher, he was made Chancellor of Wells Cathedral in 1554. Unhappy with the Reformation under Henry VIII and Edward VI, he became a zealous defender of the Roman Catholic faith during the reign of Mary. He published a number of theological works. He died in 1560 and was buried in Wells Cathedral.

Edgworth, Thomas *local politician and solicitor*
Born on 30 January 1805, the only child of Thomas and Elizabeth Edgworth of Bryn-y-Grog,* he resided at Gatefield,* Fronhaulog* and Bryn-y-Grog. Articled to a legal practice in Stockport he established his own practice in Temple Row* on the east side of the churchyard. He served as Clerk to the Poor Law Guardians (1836–57) and Registrar of the County Court (a post he held until his death). He was a founder of the Wrexham Market Hall Company and a director of the Wrexham, Mold & Connah's Quay Railway Company.

Palmer* described him as being 'of fine presence, genial in manners, liberal, and cultivated, he was wonderfully popular'. Standing as a 'Red' (Radical) in the election for the first Town Council he came top of the poll and was chosen to serve as the first Mayor in 1857. He pushed hard for sanitary reform, which made him unpopular amongst those who had been opposed to the whole notion of incorporating the Borough. Nominated for a second term as Mayor, he found himself in a contested election and the matter resulted in a split vote. When Edgworth realised that his opponent had voted for himself, he gave the Mayor's casting vote in his own favour and was elected for a second term.

Thomas Edgworth, 1st Mayor of Wrexham.

He was married to Eliza Jane Roberts of Welshpool and they had two sons and two daughters. He built Fronheulog,* Bwlchgwyn. Edgworth retired from practising law in 1866 and died at Bryn-y-Grog on 7 January 1868. An oil painting of him was known to have been owned by WBC but this was 'disposed of', along with a number of other portraits, in the early 1960s.

Edinburgh Road, Croes Eneurys
This was built on land that had formerly been part of Croes Eneurys Farm,* by local builders Parker, Davies & Hughes Ltd. All the roads on the development were given the names of royal palaces, in this case, Edinburgh Castle in Scotland. The first houses were completed in 1960.

Edisbury Family of Bedwal, Marchwiel
Originally a Cheshire family, the Edisburys first appeared in Denbighshire in the mid 16th century when Richard Wilkinson (alias Edisbury) is recorded as holding Bedwal. His grandson, Kenrick Edisbury, became surveyor to the Navy Board, a post which he occupied with great efficiency during the reign of Charles I. In 1630 he bought the Pentre Clawdd estate and died at Chatham in 1638. His son John Edisbury followed him into the Navy Office and was called to the Bar in 1634. A Royalist, he was arrested at Bangor-is-y-coed by Parliamentary forces in 1643. After his release he became Steward of Chirkland under Sir Thomas Myddelton. Under the rule of Parliament, he successfully added to the family's stature in the Wrexham area and, bought the Erddig estate. He married Christian Grosvenor, the widow of Sir Roger Grosvenor of Eaton. Their son Joshua became High Sheriff of Denbighshire in 1682 and built Erddig Hall* which (in conjunction with other business speculations) brought him into financial difficulties. Joshua's brother, John, MP for Oxford University and a Master in Chancery, ruined himself trying to assist with the family's financial difficulties and it was his successor in office, John Mellor, who bought the Erddig Estate in 1718 and from him it passed to the Yorke family.

Education Report 1847
See Blue Books.

Edward Street, Victoria Road
This was developed on land that was previously known as Cae Siac* (Shack), mostly in 1903. The other streets in the development were Poyser Street* and Hampden Road.* The street was almost certainly named after King Edward VII who acceded to the throne in 1901.

Edwards Family of Stansty,
The Edwards family held Stansty from 1317 to 1783. One member of the family was John Edwards, Court Physician to King Charles I. His brother, Jonathan was Archdeacon of Londonderry in 1679. Their sister Margaret, a strict Protestant, was the first wife of Colonel John Jones* the regicide. David Edwards, a nephew of the above, served as a captain in the Royalist army during the Civil War. The family remained at Stansty until the death of Peter Edwards in 1783 when the estate passed to the Lloyds of Pengwern who eventually sold it to the iron-master Richard Thompson,* the builder of the present Stansty Hall in 1830–2.

Edwards, James Coster *industrialist*
James Edwards was born in 1828, the son of William and Diana Edwards of The Cottage, Trefynant, Acrefair. His father was originally from Llandysul, Montgomeryshire and was employed as a clerk-supervisor at the kilns along the Montgomeryshire Canal. His mother, the daughter of stonemason James Coster, came from Llanymynech. In 1836, his father took over the running of the lime kilns at Pontcysyllte Wharf where he had been previously employed by Exuperious Pickering. William gradually expanded this small business, becoming involved in the clay industry of Acrefair. James followed his father into the family business and quickly showed considerable entrepreneurial talent so that, by the time William died in 1870, they were also operating the Plas Kynaston Potteries, the Trefynant works and the Pen-y-Bont Brick & Tile works. By 1878, James had acquired the Copi Works in Rhos.

He lived at Trevor Hall and later built Bryn Howel, Trevor, as his home. He had two sons – E. Lloyd Edwards and James Coster Edwards II. He served as a Justice of the Peace and was the county councillor for Cefn on the newly formed Denbighshire County Council. In 1894 he was High Sheriff of Denbighshire and was Deputy Lieutenant for the county. He died in 1896.

His company, J.C. Edwards & Co of Acrefair had works on three sites – the Albert Works, Rhos (brick production), the Pen-y-Bont Works at Newbridge (clay) and the Tref-y-Nant Works (decorative tiles). Edwards was once described as 'Perhaps the most successful producer of terracotta in the world' and exported tiles all over the globe including tiles for a rajah's palace in India. The firm was eventually sold in 1956. The name survives on the old wall to the offices alongside the A539 road in Acrefair.

Edwards, John William *local politician*
Born on 6 December 1876, John Edwards lived in Hill Street and attended the neighbouring Ragged School.* He became a master monumental mason with premises on Ruabon Road, where he built his own house, South Grove, adjoining the workshop, in 1910. He was elected a Liberal member of WBC and served as Mayor in 1944. He was a lifelong member of the Presbyterian Church and served on the committee that organised the building of the new Trinity Church* on King Street. John Edwards was a keen supporter of Wrexham Football Club* and was a bowls

player. He died at the War Memorial Hospital on Christmas Day, 1949 and is buried in Wrexham Cemetery.

Edwards, Dr Jonathan *cleric and academic*
Born in Charles Street, Wrexham in 1629 (probably in a house that was located opposite the Elephant & Castle*). He was educated at Christ Church, Oxford from where he graduated in 1659 and became a Fellow of Jesus College in 1662 and Vice-Principal in 1668. He was rector of Kidlington, Hinton Ampner and Llandysul, and vicar of Clynnog Fawr. He became Principal of Jesus College in 1686, Vice Chancellor of Oxford University 1689–91 and Treasurer of Llandaff Cathedral. He published a number of theological works. He died on 20 July 1712 and left his money and library to Jesus College in whose chapel he was buried.

Edwards, MA, Meredith *actor*
Born in Rhosllanerchrugog in 1917, Meredith Edwards was educated at Ruabon Boys Grammar School where he first acquired a taste for acting. On leaving school he became a laboratory assistant at the Courtaulds factory at Greenfield in Flintshire where he became involved in amateur dramatics.

He eventually moved to London and became a professional thespian, quickly acquiring a reputation as a good character actor (perhaps because of the advent of early baldness when he was only 24 years of age). He had a distinguished stage career, but is perhaps best known for his film roles in: *Whisky Galore*, *Kind Hearts and Coronets*, *Dunkirk*, *The Cruel Sea* and *The Blue Lamp*.

Married to Daisy, he had two sons and one daughter and spent the latter part of his life living in the village of Cilcain near Mold. He was awarded an Honorary MA by the University of Wales in 1997. An active supporter of Plaid Cymru, he died on 8 February 1999 and is buried in Cilcain, Flintshire.

Edwards, Mike *local politician*
Mike Edwards was born on 15 April 1947 in Stratford-upon-Avon, Warwickshire where he was educated at Broad Street Primary School and later, at Warwick School. He worked from National & Grindlays Bank in the City of London before moving into hospital financial administration, working for Reading Hospitals, United Oxford Hospitals, South Warwickshire Hospitals, Cheshire Area Health Authority, Chester Health Authority and Cheshire Health Agency (where he was Assistant Director of Finance). He moved to Chester in 1975 and, two years later, to Marford.

A Social Democrat (and then Liberal Democrat) he was elected to Gresford Community Council in 1990 (chair 1995–6 and 2004–5) and became a member of WMBC in 1991 (WCBC post 1996) representing Marford and Hoseley Ward. He has held a number of posts in the Council including chair of Scrutiny Co-Chairs Co-ordinating Committee and co-chair of: Corporate Issues Scrutiny Panel/Committee; Finance Scrutiny Committee; Corporate Issues Scrutiny Committee. He has also been a member of the Welsh Joint Council (representing the employers); Community Safety Partnership; Youth Justice Service Board; Flood Risk Wales Committee; Wrexham Local Health Board. He is an active supporter of Nightingale House Hospice* and the Wrexham Maelor Hospital League of Friends. He served as Mayor of WCBC in 2005–06.

He married Kay in 1973 and has two daughters.

Edwards, Wayne *soldier*
Lance Corporal Wayne 'Eddie' Edwards, the son of John and Barbara Edwards of Cefn Mawr, was a pupil of Cefn Mawr Junior School and Ysgol Rhiwabon. On leaving school he became a apprentice motor mechanic before becoming a regular soldier serving with the 1st Bn, RWF.

Following the break-up of the old Yugoslavia and the ensuing war that raged between the newly-formed states, the United Nations agreed to send a peace-keeping force to the region. Britain agreed to supply soldiers for this force. One of the units sent to Bosnia was the Cheshire Regiment to which L/Cpl Edwards was on detachment. On 13 January 1993, a unit of the Cheshire Regiment was providing an armed escort for a civilian ambulance (carrying two Muslim and one Croat woman injured in the fighting) in a UN convoy passing through the town of Gornji Vakuf in Bosnia. The convoy came under fire from a sniper and L/Cpl Edwards, who was driving an armoured personnel carrier, was hit in the head and died instantly, the first UN soldier to be killed in Bosnia. He is buried in Rhosymedre.

Wayne Edwards' name is recorded on a memorial plaque on a dovecote at Tŷ Mawr Country Park, Cefn Mawr. The plaque was unveiled on the first anniversary of his death. There is also a plaque on the roadside at Gornji Vakuf.

Edwards-Jones, JP Alderman Dr Samuel *local politician*
Born in Cilcain, Flintshire, the son of Henry Jones of Leeswood, on 10 April 1871, Samuel Edwards-Jones was educated at Anderson's and St Mungo's Colleges, Glasgow and became an LRCP (Edinburgh), LRCS (Edinburgh), LFPS (Glasgow) and LM. He was, for a time, the senior resident surgeon at the Royal Infirmary, Glasgow and served as a medical officer to the Post Office. He later lived and practised medicine at Holt Street House.*

He was elected a councillor for WRDC in 1905 and the following year was elected a Conservative councillor representing the East Ward on Wrexham Borough Council (serving until 1927). He became chairman of the Health Committee in 1907 and a member of the Joint Fever Hospital Committee and the Board of Guardians (1905). He served as mayor during the Coronation year of 1910 and was made an alderman in 1927. He was made an honorary Freeman of the Borough of Wrexham on 9 June 1931.

Dr Edwards-Jones (standing) outside his surgery at Holt Street House. [Edward Clarke]

He was also chairman of the Wrexham Unionist Council.

Dr Edwards-Jones died on 7 March 1934, aged 64 years. His wife, Milly Edwards-Jones,* followed him into local politics.

Edwards-Jones, JP, Mrs Milly *local politician*
Milly Edwards-Jones was the daughter of Capt G.M. Marsh, RWF, of Pickhill Hall. She married Dr Samuel Edwards-Jones* (Mayor of Wrexham, 1910) in 1895 and had one son, Henry George Elliott. He was a professional soldier who was commissioned into the King's Shropshire Light Infantry in 1915 and died in 1940.

She was elected Wrexham's first lady councillor in a by-election for the East Ward on 13 February 1920 with a majority of 93. In the Council elections of 1 November 1921 she was allowed a 'walk-over' but lost her seat in 1925 only to be re-elected in 1927 when she was also elected Mayor, serving for two years. Appointed a Justice of the Peace she served as chairman of the Borough bench for three years.

She lived at Holt Street House* and died on 30 September 1940 and is buried in Bangor-is-y-coed.

Egerton, KCSI, DL, Sir Robert Eyles *colonial administrator*
Born on 15 April 1827, the son of William Egerton of Gresford, Robert entered the Indian Civil Service in 1849 and spent over 30 years working in India. During the Indian Mutiny (1857) he was chief magistrate of Lahore. From 1871–74 he was a member of the Governor General's Legislative Council after which he became Governor General of the Punjab until retiring in 1882 when he returned to Wrexham. For a short time he lived at Glan Alyn in Gresford before moving to Coed-y-Glyn.* He served as president of the Wrexham Infirmary Board of Management, a governor of Grove Park School and deputy lieutenant of Denbighshire. Married to Emily Garstone, he died on 30 September 1912 and is buried in Wrexham Cemetery.* His son, Robert Walter Egerton, lived at Stansty Lodge.*

Egerton Arms
See Egerton Lodge/House.

Egerton Lodge/House, Egerton Street
This house appears on the 1872 survey, surrounded by substantial gardens.
Residents:
  1881   John Beale
  1888   John Gittins
  1896   R. W. Evans*
  1899   Dr E. D. Davies
  1913   it was the home and surgery of Dr Richard Geoffrey Williams.
  1951   it appears to have been sub-divided into flats.

The house was offered for sale to WBC in 1932 but remained a private house until the 1950s when it was converted into a public house named the Egerton Arms. In the late 1990s the name of the public house was changed to the Thirsty Scholar, a move which many thought a cynical appeal to the students of Yale College which had just moved into new premises on Rhosddu Road. Today, Arnold's Bar & Grill occupies the premises.

Houses on the corner of Egerton Street and Lord Street, c.1900.

Egerton Street
This street took its name from Lady Eleanor Cunliffe, the wife of Sir Robert Alfred Cunliffe, Bt, who was the daughter of Colonel Egerton Leigh of West Hall, High Leigh and Jodrell Hall, Cheshire (see Cunliffe Family).

Egerton Street Welsh Wesleyan Methodist Church
See Jerusalem Welsh Wesleyan Methodist Church.

Egerton Walk, Garden Village
Laid out shortly before the Second World War as an extension to the Garden Village* housing scheme. The houses were built by Wrexham Building Estates Ltd, with prices starting from £650 freehold (inclusive of all public services and concrete roads). The street was named after Robert Walter Egerton of Stansty Lodge,* the son of Sir Robert Eyles Egerton,* one of the original administrators of the Garden Village Estate.

Eirianfa, Chester Road
Located at N° 2 (now N° 4) Chester Road, this was the home of Frederick William Morris, nephew and heir of John Jones* of Grove Lodge.*

Electricity
The WBC Electricity Undertaking was set up in 1900, generated at the Willow Street Depot.* [DRO/QSD/DL/1, 4–5, 20–1, 23] This operated until the Electricity Act of 1947 brought the Wrexham works under the ownership of the Merseyside & North Wales Electricity Board (MANWEB) who had a sub-office at Rhostyllen. In addition, a power station was erected on the Royal Ordnance Factory* site in 1941 (now the Red Wither Tower, Wrexham Industrial Estate).

Elephant & Castle, Charles Street
First recorded in the Rate Books in 1788, this public house was described as N° 13, Charles Street when Palmer was writing in the 1890s, and appears in both the 1833 and 1872 surveys. In 1881 the licensee was Mrs Ellen Birch. It lost its licence in 1999 and was converted into flats. The ground floor now operates as Dao Siam, Thai restaurant.

Ellerslie House, Grosvenor Road
Ellerslie House (originally N° 14 Grosvenor Road) was built by Joseph Jones, of N° 43 High Street, on part of what had previously been known as Oak Tree Field (the other half being the site of Hendre*) in the late 1870s. The house was first occupied by Joseph Jones himself and Anne Maria Wilson. Jones went into voluntary liquidation in 1879 and his debts (totalling over £5,700) were cleared by John Thomas Jones of Frondeg Terrace, Port Dinorwig (ship owner), William Hughes of Bodarborth, Port Dinorwig (cashier), John Hughes of Frondeg Terrace, Port Dinorwig (harbour master) and Margaret Anne Jones, the wife of Joseph Jones and the property passed to them and their heirs. (See also Grosvenor Road)

Ellesmere Road, Hightown
See King's Mills Road.

Ellice, Robert *soldier*
Robert Ellice of 'Gwasnewydd' (Croesnewydd), the son of Griffith Ellice ap Risiart, had served as a soldier under King Gustavus Adolphus of Sweden during the Thirty Years War. With the rank of Colonel, he later raised and commanded a regiment of foot in the Royalist army during the English Civil War.* A specialist military engineer, he was mainly responsible for the construction of the defensive works around Chester. He captured

Chirk Castle in January 1642 but was captured, along with 600 of his men, at Middlewich in March 1643. He was exchanged for a Parliamentary officer. He was made Royalist Commander-in-Chief of Flintshire and Denbighshire and raised a second regiment which was present at the defence of Holt Bridge but was defeated by Brereton. He then raised a third regiment and defeated Mytton at Longford near Montgomery. Joining up with Prince Rupert, Ellice marched through Lancashire and helped in the captures of Bolton, Wigan, Liverpool and Bury. He probably fought at Marston Moor and Montgomery. When Oxford surrendered to Parliament in 1646, Ellice was among those taken prisoner. He was only fined £150 by the Committee for the Compounding of Delinquents, a clear indication that he was not a wealthy man. He was the father of Peter Ellice and the brother of Thomas Ellice, the Lieutenant-Governor of Barbados. Robert Ellice died c.1660.

Ellice Way, Croesnewydd
This new road was developed in the 1990s as the main route through the Wrexham Technology Park. It is named after the Ellice family who once owned Croesnewydd Hall (see Robert Ellice).

Ellis, Gordon *local historian*
Born in Rhosllanerchrugog, Gordon Ellis spent most of his working life as a printer, first with the *Rhos Herald* and then (from 1935–70) with the *Wrexham Leader*. In his retirement, he was the author of the 'Looking Back' column in the *Wrexham Leader* which he wrote under the pseudonym 'Silin' until his death in February 1991.

Ellis, D.Litt., Revd Islwyn Ffowc
Born in 1924 at Nº 12 The Beeches, Wrexham, the home of his aunt, Islwyn Ffowc Ellis spent his childhood in Dyffryn Ceiriog. Educated at the University College of North Wales, Bangor, then theological colleges at Aberystwyth and Bala, he became a noted Nonconformist minister. He left the ministry in 1956 and became a freelance writer, broadcaster and producer with the BBC in Bangor. In 1963, he was appointed a lecturer in Welsh at Trinity College, Carmarthen and in 1968 an editor and translator with the Welsh Arts Council. In 1971, he returned to live in Wrexham (at Nº 6 Acton Gate), by which time he was a full-time writer. In 1975 he became a lecturer in Welsh at the University College, Lampeter, was appointed a Reader in 1984 and retired in 1988. His major claim to fame was in the field of Welsh literature and will be best remembered for *Cysgod y Cryman* (1953) which was nominated as the Welsh Book of the Century. He was a Prose Medal winner at the National Eisteddfod and was awarded an Honorary Doctorate of Literature by the University of Wales in 1993. Married to Eirlys he had a daughter Siân.
  Islwyn Ffowc Ellis died on 22 January 2004.

Ellis, Robert Thomas 'Tom' *politician*
He was born 15 March 1924, at Pant, Rhos, the son of Robert and Edith Ann Ellis. His father was a miner at Hafod Colliery where he was the captain of the rescue team. Tom was educated at the University College of Wales and Nottingham University. He was employed as a works chemist at the Cookes explosives factory in Penrhyndeudraeth (1944–46), coal miner (1948–50), student (1950–52), mining engineer (1953–70) and colliery manager at Bersham Colliery (1957–70). Elected a Labour Member of Parliament for Wrexham in the General Election of 1970, he was a passionate 'European' and campaigned vigorously on behalf of Britain remaining a member of the European Common Market. He was elected the Member of the European Parliament for North Wales in 1975. The results of the 1979 Westminster election were: Tom Ellis (Labour) – 30,405; Roger Graham-Palmer (Conservative) – 18,256; Martin Thomas (Liberal) 11,389; Hywel Wyn Roberts (Plaid Cymru) – 1,740. In the aftermath of Labour's defeat in the 1982 General Election, Tom Ellis was one of the founding members of the Social Democratic Party and continued to represent Wrexham until he was defeated by the Labour Party candidate in the General Election of 1987. He lived at the old Vicarage in Ruabon and was the author of *Mines and Men*. His autobiography *Dan Loriau Maelor* was published in 2003, followed by *After the Dust Has Settled* in 2004. He married Nona Williams, the daughter of the managing director of the Cookes factory at Penrhyndeudraeth, in 1949 (she died in 2009) and they had three sons and one daughter. Tom Ellis died on 11 April 2010 and was cremated at Pentrebychan,* Wrexham.

Ellis, Thomas Peter *judge & historian*
Born in Wrexham on 4 June 1873, the son of Peter and Mary Ellis, Thomas Ellis spent his early life on a farm in Glyndyfrdwy and was educated at Oswestry High School and Lincoln College, Oxford. On graduating, he went to India where he was recognised as one of the most able judicial officers in the Indian Civil Service. He married Rosetta McAlister who died in 1912 leaving him with a son and a daughter. He married again in 1915 to Hilda Broadway. He became an expert on the customary law of the Punjab and was the Attorney General of the Punjab during the First World War. Appointed President of the Defence of India Tribunal he served as an adviser on martial law during the armed rebellion of 1919. Disgusted at the leniency shown to so many prisoners convicted of very serious offences, he declined the appointment of judge of the High Court at Lahore and in 1921 returned to Wales where he settled at Llysmynach near Dolgellau. Whilst there he became an expert on the tribal life of mediæval Wales. A convert to Roman Catholicism, he made a serious study of Catholicism in Wales. Thomas Ellis died in Liverpool on 7 July 1936. He was the author of numerous legal books as well as works on Welsh history.

Elm Grove, Acton Park
The first five flats (from Marsh Crescent to Oak Drive) were built in the early 1920s as part of the first phase of the Acton Park housing estate.* Most of the streets on this estate were named after trees, although there was some concern about using the name Elm Grove as it was thought that it would be mistaken for the house called The Elms* on Grove Road. The street was extended by the addition of nine houses and 21 flats in the 1930s and was linked up with Herbert Jennings Avenue* in the 1960s.

Elms, The, Grove Road/Rhosddu Road
Originally built on the corner of Rhosddu Road and Grove Road, modern road changes have meant that it is now sited on the corner of Rhosddu Road and the inner ring road. The Elms was built in the second half of the 19th century. In 1881 it was, surprisingly, listed as the home of Edward Roberts, a coal miner. It was the residence of Harry Croom-Johnson* from 1893 until his death in 1923. Mrs Croom-Johnson remained in the house until 1925 when it was sold to Richard Geoffrey Williams, MRCS, a prominent local physician and surgeon. In August 1939 it was sold to the Wrexham & East Denbighshire War Memorial Hospital and became the accommodation for the hospital's junior doctors. After a period when it housed the Mental Health Department of the local health trust, it is now used as a centre for the treatment of adult substance misuse. Much of its garden has become part of the coach park of Yale College Wrexham.

The Elms, Rhosddu Road. [Brian Croom-Johnson]

Embassy, The, High Street
See Royal Oak.

Empire Cinema, Lambpit Street
Located alongside the Seven Stars public house in Lambpit Street, the Empire was built by John Scott of the Seven Stars* and opened in 1902 as a variety theatre, with seating for just under 600. It was designed by Thomas Price of Liverpool and Dolgarrog who incorporated many safety features that were unusual at the time *e.g.* outward opening emergency exits. In its early days, the Empire engaged artistes who were resting from the Argyll Theatre at Birkenhead, thereby securing low cost entertainment. The opening night was reported in the press:

> The Hall … will be found convenient and arranged for the purpose. Entering the Hall from Lambpit Street we pass through doors which like all those in the building open outwards. The staircase broad and handsome has an encrusted dado. In case of emergency there are two other exits, one at the rear of the building and one leading from the Gallery. The interior of the Hall is prettily decorated and well fitted. The electric light has been installed throughout. The heating is by the hot air system and the ventilation is admirable. Tip-up seats are provided for those paying the highest price of admission and the remainder of the accommodation consists of chairs with benches in the Gallery. Due regard has been given to the Public in the ample provision of fire extinguishers. Exit at the back of the stage has a twenty-one foot opening and is sufficiently large for the purpose. Scenery has been supplied by the Studio of Messrs. Wilkinson of Liverpool. The Proprietor intends to provide entertainment of the highest class. As a general manager he has secured Mr. William Gregory, a gentleman who recently filled the post of Acting Manager at the Theatre Royal, Birmingham, and who has wide experience in connection with London and Provincial Music Halls. The opening has been fixed for April 1st. A Royal Bioscope has been installed. It showed the Queen's Funeral; Opening of Parliament by the King; Battle of the Giants – Wales v. Scotland; and the Transvaal War. On the stage were Miss Eva Nelson, Mike Scott, Miss Almer Heath, George Ripley, Miss Mat Venus, well-known music hall names of the age. Orchestra Stalls 1/-, Pit Chairs 6d, Balcony 4d. Open at 7 for 7.30 pm.

As can be seen from this report, short silent movies were a major feature of the programme from the very first night until 31 October 1910 when it opened as a cinema. By 1914, the building was leased by the People's Popular Picture Company and was known as The Empire Picture Palace. During the First World War it once again became a variety theatre. Reverting to a cinema in the 1920s, the Empire had another short period as a theatre before closure on 7 February 1932. Two months later, after a refurbishment, it re-opened as a cinema showing talking films. Along with all theatres and cinemas in Britain, the Empire closed on the outbreak of war in 1939 but re-opened after only two weeks (Manager Miss K. Nutter). Little was spent on the fabric of the cinema after the war and, failing to meet the challenge of television, the Empire finally closed on 26 August 1956, by which time it was in a very poor condition. The building still survives next door to the Seven Stars public house.

Empress Road/Street, Ruabon Road
This street was laid out during the 1880s on a field that had previously been known as Cae March Ddu (*Trans.* black horse field) and was part of the Plas Power estate. It was named after Queen Victoria who was created Empress of India in 1876. Some of the land utilised had previously belonged to Sir Evan Morris.* The road was adopted by the Borough Council in 1891 but it seems likely that the section of the road between Bersham Road and Ruabon Road was a second phase and there are records of nine houses being built there as late as 1898. The delay in building this southern section may well have been the result of boundary difficulties with the Wrexham Cemetery.*

Emral House, Chester Road
Built in the early 1920s on the site of Plas-yn-Llwyn,* this was once the home of William Higginson, proprietor of the Wrexham Motor Company in Chester Street (later the Lucas Garage). It later became the home of Miss Batho who sold it to the church for use as a vicarage. During the Second World War, the house was requisitioned and for a short time was used as a motor pool by black American servicemen. (See also Wrexham Vicarage (3)). It was sold by the church in the early 1980s to a person who had previously been the landlord of the Emral Arms in Worthenbury and was later converted into a residential home.

Eneurys Road, Croes Eneurys
Built in two stages on land that was formerly part of Croes Eneurys Farm.* The eastern side was developed in the period 1930–31 while the western side was built later by local firm of Parker, Davies and Hughes Ltd. (see also Croes Eneurys Estate). Named after Croes Eneurys Farm.*

For a short period after the demolition of the Lambpit Street shops, this view of the west side of the old Empire Cinema was exposed.

Erddig Hall [Geoffrey A. Jones]

Engine House, Chester Street
This was the 'garage' for the Wrexham volunteer fire engine. It is shown in the 1833 survey sited on the west side of Chester Street, immediately in front of the Grammar School building.

English Baptist Chapel, Chester Street – 'The Old Meeting'.
See Chester Street English Baptist Chapel.

Epworth Lodge, Grove Road
This was built in 1865 as the manse for Bryn-y-Ffynnon Wesleyan Church,* Regent Street and probably designed by J.R. Gummow.* In March 1868, James Ollerhead gave a piece of land in Grove Park to add to the garden of this property. The last minister to reside here was the Revd Whitford Roberts, after whom the house was sold in 1967 to Michael Forté, the brother of Sir Charles Forté (of Trust House Forté) who owned the Steak and Claret restaurant on Regent Street. He sold it in 1975 to Mr & Mrs Armstrong, dental surgeons of Grosvenor Road. The house is a Grade II listed building. [DRO/ND/1/1]

Erddig Hall
Designed by Thomas Webb of Middlewich, Cheshire for Joshua Edisbury* of Pentre Clawdd in 1683, at a cost of £677-10s-9d. In November 1683 he agreed to 'undertake and perform the care and oversight of the contriving building and finishing of a case or body of a new house for the said Joshua Edisbury at Erthigg aforesaid ... according to the designes, compassee, manner and methodde of draughts already given by the said Thomas Webb'. The mason was Edward Price, carpenter Philip Rogers; bricklayer William Carter of Chester; Contracts were signed in March 1684 and the house finished some three years later. Edisbury had been appointed High Sheriff* of Denbighshire the previous year and probably felt that the time was right for him to build a house that was worthy of his status in society and also to develop his lead mines at Trelawnyd in Flintshire. Unfortunately, he had insufficient funds and was forced to borrow large sums from such leading local figures as Elihu Yale* of Plas Grono.* Joshua's brother, the London lawyer and Master in Chancery, Dr John Edisbury, was also in financial difficulties and both men became bankrupt.

In 1716, John Mellor, another Master in Chancery, bought the mortgage on Erddig from Sir John Trevor and it was he who completed the construction and furnishing of the house. He had no money problems and settled to a life of considerable comfort, away from London. A strong supporter of the royal house of Hanover, Mellor had settled into a strongly Jacobite locality and, consequently, treated his neighbours with some suspicion. He carried out a number of alterations at Erddig. Unmarried, John Mellor left his estate to his nephew, Simon Yorke,* in 1733, thereby establishing an unbroken line of ownership that was to

The Lodge on Erddig Road. [National Trust]

Erddig Road. These houses faced onto Poplar Road.

last for nearly 250 years.

In 1771, Philip Yorke I* began a programme of significant alterations to the house including facing the west front with stone, building a new stable-yard, kitchen and domestic offices and moving the bedrooms from the ground floor to the first floor.

In 1966, the estate passed to bachelor Philip Yorke who gave it to the National Trust and it was opened to the public in 1977.

Erddig Park
See Erddig Hall.

Erddig Road
One of the older streets in the Fairfield area of the town, Erddig Road was originally, as its name suggests, the main route from Wrexham to Erddig Hall. Beginning in Chapel Street the road led directly to Erddig via the lodged gateway which stood at the top of the hill near the present day Green Park* estate. A new lodge, built here in 1900, was demolished in the 1970s.

Many of the terraced houses in the street were far more substantial than those in other streets in Fairfield and housed lower middle class families. The street also has a number of mid-Victorian villas. Today, the only public building in the street is the Fairfield Tavern. The properties on the corner of Erddig Road and Poplar Road, sometimes referred to as The Bonc* (now forming part of the playing fields of St Giles' School), were the subject of a compulsory purchase order in 1934 as part of the Borough slum clearance programme. N°s 14, 16 & 18 (located opposite the Bonc) and N°s 30, 32 & 34 (located opposite Earle Street) were also demolished at this time.

Erlas
The mediæval township of Erlas, one of the country townships that made up the 19th century parish of Wrexham (before 1851 it was a detached part of the parish of Gresford). The township lay on the eastern side of the parish covering the area between the Dunks* (in what is now Queen's Park*) and the escarpment leading down to the present day Wrexham Industrial Estate and between Llwyn Knottia Farm in the north and Abenbury in the south. The most important house in the township was Erlas Hall.* In recent history, most of the township has been part of the Cefn Park* estate, a substantial part of which was sold to WBC for the Queen's Park* housing estate. The origin of the name is unknown but may be a distortion of the Welsh *erw las*, meaning green acre.

Erlas Grove, Queen's Park
Built in the early 1950s as part of WBC's Queen's Park* housing development. It was named after the mediæval township of Erlas in which it is situated.

Erlas Hall (or Erlisham)
Located in the township of Erlas, just to the east of Erlas Lane* near the present day Clay's Farm golf course, this house was the centre of the Erlas estate, the property of the Davies family in the 16th century, and was originally known as Plas yn Erlas. It is mentioned in Norden's survey of 1620 which also mentions that at one time the land was held by Edward Erles (alive in 1584 and taking his family name from that of the township). The Davies family was descended from the Pulestons of Emral. Ermin Davies, the daughter of Roger Davies (who was alive in 1661) married William Kyffin of Maenan and the house passed to him as part of her dowry. It remained in the ownership of the Kyffins until 1783 when Sir Thomas Kyffin sold all his property in the parish of Wrexham at which time Erlas Hall and Perth-y-Bi, along with 105 acres of land, were bought by Roger Kenyon of Cefn. After his death, the house passed to his son George Kenyon of Cefn and, in 1836, from him to George, Lord Kenyon, becoming part of the Gredington estate. [DRO/CP/652, 916]

Erlas Lane
This lane leads from Bryn Estyn Road to Red Wither Lane on the Wrexham Industrial Estate.* It takes its name from the mediæval township of Erlas* and from Erlas Hall* which is located just to the east of it.

Ernest Parry Road, Queen's Park
Built in the immediate post Second World War period as part of the first phase of WBC's Queen's Park housing development. The street is named after Gunner Ernest Parry* of Eagle Street,* the only local man to be posthumously awarded the French *Croix de Guerre* during the Second World War.

Erw Clai, Chester Road
(*Trans.* clay acre) See Nine Acre Field.

Erw Las, Maes-y-Dre
Laid out and built in 1930–31 as part of the first phase of the Maes-y-Dre housing estate. The name means green acre and has no particular significance in this location.

Esless Hall, Rhostyllen
See Esclus Hall.

Esclus Hall in the early part of the 20th century.

Esclus Hall, Rhostyllen
Located in the mediæval township of Esclusham-is-y-Clawdd (*Trans.* Esclusham below the Dyke), this timber and brick house is known to have existed in the early 17th century when it was the home of Thomas Trafford. In 1638, the Trafford family was

succeeded by Richard Lloyd* who was knighted by King Charles I in 1642. The house is sometimes called Estlys and, in recent times, Esless, but both are a corruption of the original Esclus. Through Sir Richard's daughter, Mary, the Esclus Hall estate passed to Sir Henry Conway, Bt, of Bodrhyddan, Rhuddlan. His son, Sir John Conway, inherited the estate in 1669 and, following his death in 1721, the estate passed, through the female line, to Sir Thomas Longueville, Bt, of Prestatyn who sold the house to John Humberston Cawley of Gwersyllt who in turn let it to Philip Puleston during the 1760s and 1770s. By 1781, Esclus Hall had been bought by Sir Watkin Williams Wynn* of Wynnstay, Ruabon and it remained as part of that estate until at least the end of the 19th century, being used as a farmhouse.

The house that survives today is only a small portion of the original Esclus Hall. In 1670, it was described as having 16 hearths and Palmer* records that there were steps in the middle of the lawn which once led down to the extensive cellars.

Esclus Mills, Rhostyllen
These three mills were part of the Esclus Hall* estate until 1788 when they were sold by John Humberston Cawley to Joseph Clubbe who rebuilt them. His son, Thomas Clubbe, operated the mills until he became bankrupt and they were sold in 1830 to William and Joseph Harris of Esclusham Lodge and Laurel Grove, Bersham, who converted them into paper mills. A relative, George Frederic Harris of Harrow Park, Middlesex, bought the mills in 1850 and later sold them to Ellis Phillips of Bryn Castle, Wrexham for £850. One of the mills was bought by Messrs Jones & Rocke of the Cambrian Leather Works* who used it for the manufacture of chamois-leather and was then converted into a steam laundry. By the end of the 19th century it was empty.

During the 1850s, the middle of the three mills, known as The Old Turkey Paper Mill, became the property of Henry Methold Greville of Worcester (who also lived at Laurel Grove) and became famous for the production of high quality bank-note paper. The mill was burnt down in April 1897 (see Fire Brigade) and was re-built as the Bersham Paper Mills. The Greville family then sold the mill to Alderman R. H. Done* of Wrexham.

Esclusham Township
The township of Esclusham – later the two townships of Esclusham-*uwch-y-clawdd* (*Trans.* Esclusham above the dyke) and Esclusham-*is-y-clawdd* (*Trans.* Esclusham below the dyke) – was one of the largest of the townships that made up the parish of Wrexham, totalling over 5,500 acres. The two townships were divided, as their names would suggest, by Offa's Dyke.* The name Esclusham originates from the two words and is a perfect example of a Welsh word ('Esclus') being Anglicised by the addition of the Saxon suffix ('ham'). The origin of the word *Esclus* is either a variation of the word *eglwys* (*Trans.* church) or of the word *ystlys* (*Trans.* side or flank). One section of Esclusham below the Dyke, in the area of the old Vicarage and Pentre Felin was detached from the main body of the township and was wholly contained within the town centre of Wrexham.

Esclusham Hall, Rhostyllen
Standing in a hollow close to the Pentrebychan Crematorium, this timber-framed hall house, which was originally called Upper Esclus Hall, dates back to at least the late 17th century when it was re-built by Robert Trevor. In 1757, Richard Trevor sold the house and surrounding land to John Hughes of Cilnant, Llangollen. Three years later, Hughes mortgaged the estate to Peter Ellames of Chester and from him it passed to his son Peter (mayor of Chester in 1781) and, in 1864, to Thomas Ellames Withington of Culcheth Hall. Twenty years later he sold the house to Henry W. Meredith of Pentrebychan. In 1834, the house was leased to the Puleston family. The house survives today and is located just to the south of Legacy Water Tower.

Essex Close, Tŷ Gwyn
A development of private houses by local builders H. R. & E. Roberts completed in the late 1960s/early 1970s.

Evacuees
During the weeks leading up to the outbreak of the Second World War, the Government put into action plans to evacuate children from densely populated urban areas where there was a high risk of enemy bombing to those towns and villages thought to be in comparatively safe areas. Although no exact figures are available for the numbers of children evacuated to Wrexham throughout the war period, the initial wave in September 1939 was carefully recorded in the local press.

The first parties of evacuees arrived in the Wrexham area from Liverpool and Birkenhead on 1st (two days before war was declared), 2nd and 3rd September. Six trains brought over 3,000 children and their teachers and attendants who were placed in the care of WRDC. They were taken from the station to the Majestic Cinema and from there by bus to various district centres. On 3rd & 4th September Wrexham Borough dealt with over 2,000 evacuees from Merseyside which included 128 teachers, 26 blind people and 40 expectant mothers. After walking to the Majestic, they were conveyed to the distribution centres scattered throughout the town under the control of members of the Women's Voluntary Service viz: Erddig –National Girl's School (Mrs J. Birkett Evans); Grosvenor – Trinity Schoolroom (Mrs A. Challinor) and Rhosddu Junior School (Mrs E. S. Price); Wrexham Fechan – National Boy's School (Mrs J. C. Griffiths); Wat's Dyke – Garden Village Institute (Mrs Aston) and Acton School (Mrs Gwen Lloyd); Offa – Victoria Central School (Miss Marian Owen); Acton – Grove Park (Mrs Arthur Davies) and Rhosnesni (Mrs Dudley); Caia –Church of England Infants (Mrs Hickman) and Salvation Army Citadel (Mrs Lawson); Maes-y-Dre (Mrs Wolfenden); Bryn-y-Ffynnon – St Mary's School (Mrs Price) and Victoria Junior School (Mrs Breese*).

This enormous influx of children caused considerable problems for the local schools where days were shortened so that the evacuees could make use of the buildings for their lessons. Grove Park Girls' shared its new building with the girls of Calder High School, Liverpool while Acton School had 14 children from Queens Road Infant School, Liverpool and 56 children from all over Britain, including London, West Hartlepool, Salford, Leeds, Birmingham, Burslem, Hornchurch and Surrey.

Evans, Arthur *local politician*
Born in 1916, Arthur Evans was a painter and builder by trade and served in the Royal Hampshire Regiment in the Second World War. He entered local government in 1950 when he was elected a parish councillor for Gwersyllt. He became a member of WRDC and, in 1974, WMBC and WCBC, representing Gwersyllt South, until his retirement in 1999. He was Mayor in 1987–88 and also served as chairman of the Personnel Committee and chairman of the Governors at Ysgol Bryn Alyn. His wife Mary came from Bwlchgwyn. Arthur Evans died in August 1999.

Evans, Sir (Robert) Charles *surgeon, mountaineer and university administrator*
Although not strictly a 'Wrexham man', Welsh-speaker Charles Evans and his family had strong associations with the County Borough. He was born on 19 October 1918 in Derwen, Denbighshire, the son of the late Robert Charles (a native of Bangor-is-y-coed and a partner in the legal firm of J.S. Lloyd, he was killed serving with the 15th Bn, The Welsh Regiment in August 1918) and Edith Lloyd Evans (née Williams of Plas-y-Ward, Ruthin),

and the grandson of W. R. Evans, Clerk of the Peace for Denbighshire. Educated at Shrewsbury School and University College, Oxford, he qualified in medicine in 1943 and was commissioned into the Royal Army Medical Corps. He saw active service in the Far East and was awarded a Mention in Dispatches. Demobilised in 1947, he was appointed a surgical registrar at Liverpool Regional Hospitals.

His great passion was mountaineering and had taken part in three expeditions to the Himalayas before being selected as deputy leader and quartermaster for the 1953 attempt to scale Mount Everest. On 26 May 1953, accompanied by Tom Bourdillon, Evans reached to within 300 feet of the summit of Everest when he realized that their oxygen supply was about to run out and there was insufficient daylight remaining to continue with the climb. He made the decision to turn back and was able to provide valuable information to the next pair who were attempting to reach the summit – Edmund Hillary and Sherpa Tenzing.

In 1955, he led the team that made the first successful climb of Kangchenjunga when he halted five feet short of the summit so as not to offend the people of the Indian state of Sikkim who believed it to be inhabited by the gods and was sacred spot.

In the mid 1950s, Evans was diagnosed with multiple sclerosis which ended his climbing activities. In 1957 he was appointed Principal of the University College of North Wales, Bangor, a position which he held, enduring considerable oppostion, until 1984. He was knighted in 1969. Amongst his many honours were: Hunterian Professor, Royal College of Surgeons (1953); Vice-Chancellor of the Univeristy of Wales (1965–7); President of the Alpine Club (1967–70); Cullum Medal of the American Geographical Society (1954); Livingstone Medal of the Scottish Geographical Society (1955); Founder's Medal of the Royal Geographical Society (1956).

He married fellow mountaineer Nea Morin in 1957 and had three sons. He died in Deganwy on 5 December 1995.

Evans, JP, Richard William *local politician*
Born in Wrexham in 1853, the son of Richard Evans of Willow House* who opened a brewery there which he later sold to Peter Walker* and became the licensee of the Chester Street Vaults. Richard William was educated at Holt Academy and articled to William Turner, Borough Surveyor of Wrexham. His father died in 1864 aged only 39 and left him the Chester Street Vaults.

He was elected a Conservative member of WBC in 1883 and served as Mayor in 1892. He was elected an alderman in 1889 and became a Justice of the Peace.

Outside of his work and politics he was a bellringer, President of the Wrexham Borough Brass Band, a lieutenant in the Prince of Wales' Volunteer Fire Brigade* and a Freemason* (Worshipful Master of the Square and Compass Lodge). He married Miss Parsonage of The Nelson's Arms* public house and had three daughters and one son. In his latter years he lived at Egerton Lodge.* He died on 24 April 1896 following a fall from his bicycle near Rossett and is buried in Wrexham Cemetery.*

Evans, Peter Maelor *publisher*
Born at Adwy'r Clawdd, Coedpoeth on 10 April 1817, the son of Thomas Evans, a schoolteacher and mine manager, Peter Evans was educated at his father's school in Mold and at Ruthin Grammar School. He took up a career as a printer and became a partner in the firm of Lloyd and Evans of Mold and Holywell, becoming sole proprietor in 1848. He published a number of important Welsh works including *Y Drysorfa*, *Y Traethodydd* and *Trysorfa'r Plant*. A keen Liberal, he played a prominent part in local politics in the Holywell area. He died following an accident in Aberystwyth on 29 May 1878.

Evans, Dr Samuel *industrialist*
Born at Pant-y-Garn, Plas Drain, Rhos on 10 February 1859, Samuel Evans was educated at the British School,* Brook Street, Wrexham. He was employed as a proof reader with Hughes & Son, Wrexham before joining the staff of *Y Herald Cymraeg* and later, *The Sheffield Independent*.

Appointed secretary to Lord D'Abernon, financial adviser to the Egyptian Government, he held several important offices including Head of the Egyptian Coastguard Service (1887), General Inspector of the Asian branches of the Ottoman Bank of Constantinople (1890), partner in the H. Eckstein Company, Johannesburg (1902), and Managing Director of the Crown Mine, Johannesburg (1909). During the Second Boer War he was an adviser to Field Marshal Lord Roberts and was appointed Civil Commissioner of Johannesburg. Samuel Evans was a highly respected expert on gold mining and carried through many proposals which improved the health and living conditions of the native workers in the Witwatersrand area of South Africa. He was also one of the founders of the Witwatersrand University.

He was created a commander of the Order of the Mejidieh and of the Osmanieh Order, received an Honorary LL.D from both the University of Wales and the Witwatersrand University. He married Katherine Mason in 1903 and had one son and two daughters. He died in Johannesburg on 10 October 1935.

Evans, William H. *local politician*
Born in Pickhill, the son of a farmer, William Evans joined a local firm of butchers and rose to become a partner. During the Second World War he served in the Royal Artillery.

He was elected an Independent Borough councillor for the Wat's Dyke ward in 1946 and became Mayor in 1957. He lived at 2 Stansty Road, Rhosddu, before moving to Lodge Road where he died on 7 July 1968, aged 56. Married to Edith, he was chairman of the Health Committee, a governor of Grove Park School and, from 1966 until his death, chairman of Wrexham Football Club.

Evans' Row, Farndon Street
A terrace of five houses located next to the Tiger Inn on the south-eastern side of Farndon Street. They were demolished as part of a slum clearance programme.

Exchange Club
Founded in the 19th century, the Exchange was one of the oldest businessmen's clubs in the area. It was located in Henblas Street in the premises now occupied by the Wrexham Snooker Club. One of its presidents was Hampden A. Poyser.* In 1912 the secretary was W. Rogers.

By the time of the First World War the club was in difficulties and looked as if it would close. In 1922, a consortium of local businessmen, led by Walter Roberts,* took the club over and it survived until 1980. Among the membership (which was restricted to 180) at this time were William Dodman,* Bert Murless (father of Sir Noel Murless), W.E. Samuel,* Horace Blew,* Ted Robbins (secretary of the Football Association of Wales*), Vic Dennis (son of Dyke Dennis*), F.W. Stevens (of Stevens Café), R.A. Dutton.* The secretary from 1922–49 was Joseph Wilson.

Exchange Station
See Wrexham, Mold & Connah's Quay Railway.

Executions
See Pwll-yr-Uwd and Beast Market.

F

Fairbourne Street, Stansty
Located off Crispin Lane,* nineteen houses in this street were included in the 1959 slum clearance scheme.

Fairfield House, Erddig Road
This was built c.1811 on land that was formerly the site of a tithe barn by Mrs Edwards, the widow of tanner William Edwards (see Madeira Hill). In 1819, the Revd John Hughes (brother of Richard Hughes,* the founder of publishers Hughes & Son) established a training academy here for the Calvinistic Methodists which survived until 1834. In 1827, the residents were recorded as being John and Mary Ann Hughes. In the early part of the 20th century it became the home of Alderman William Jonah Jones.* Its location is unrecorded and it does not appear on the 1833 survey. It is possible, however, that it may have been the house which is now the Fairfield Tavern.*

Fairfield Road/Street
This road was almost fully developed by the time of the 1872 OS map survey, and extended all the way from Poplar Road to Erddig Road. There did not appear to be any buildings of significance in the road, with the exception of the Fairfield Tavern.* In 1872 it was referred to as Fairfield Street.

Fairfield Tavern, Fairfield Street
This first appears as a public house in 1883 when the landlord was Richard Dykes. It has been a tied house belonging to various breweries.

Fairs
See Markets and Fairs.

Fairways, Holt Road
This private housing development was carried out by several builders on land that had previously been Church charity land which was sold off during the late 1990s, along with some land from Ty'n Twll Farm,* to fund the development of the St Joseph's Catholic and Anglican High School.* The street names on this development, all notable golf clubs or golf competitions, were probably chosen to reflect its close proximity to Wrexham Golf Club.*

Fairy Mount, 5 Fairy Road
On February 25, 1882, W.E. Samuel, who had bought a plot of land on the corner of Fairy Road* and Belmont Road,* ordered a small trench cut in the side of a mound (which measured some 1.5 metres high at the centre and some 55 metres in circumference) which was located in the proposed garden of a new house which he was building. Inside the mound they discovered a heap of decomposed human bones and a pottery urn. The discovered items were given to E.H. Acton and, after his death, passed to T.A. Acton. Historically, this burial mound (or tumulus) had been thought to be a mound where fairies danced and played and consequently became known as the Fairy Mount. The house took its name from this, as did Fairy Road and Belmont (*Trans.* pleasant or pretty mound). The oak tree which grows out of the mound has always been known as the Fairy Oak. In 1929, Fairy Mount was the home of W. H. Wright. On 20 August 2002, when it was the home of Brian and Lynn Lynes, the garden became the location of the Welsh launch of the Peter Pan set of stamps by the Royal Mail.

Fairy Road
Named after the an ancient burial chamber which stands in the garden of the house called Fairy Mount.* The Football Association of Wales* had its headquarters at Nº 3 Fairy Road until the 1980s. Most of the properties on this road date from the late 19th century.

Farmside, Borras Park
This small cul-de-sac of private houses was laid out in the late 1960s and took its name from a smallholding called Trederwen which stood on Jeffreys Road, opposite the Cunliffe Arms,* until the late 1990s.

Farndon Street
This street links the Beast Market with Holt Road and, in the early 20th century, was lined on both sides by low quality housing. At its western end stood the Victoria Inn,* next to which was the Victoria Corn Mill* and, on the corner of the Beast Market, the Tiger Inn. Behind the houses on the opposite side of the street was Brown Horse Yard. Gradually, all the houses and buildings were demolished (the last being the Victoria Inn in 2000) so that the street is now little more than an approach road to the large roundabout on Holt Road. The street was named after the village of Farndon in Cheshire.

Farndon Street, c.1930.

Feathers, The, Chester Street
Originally known as the 'Plume of Feathers' this was one of the town's most important coaching inns. According to Palmer it was, for over 200 years, the property of the Meredith family of Pentrebychan.* 'It was a good inn of the second class.' It was in the yard of the *Plume of Feathers* that the Lancashire cotton traders were first allowed to set up their stalls, a privilege which later resulted in the building of Manchester Square.* The original inn was demolished in the mid 19th century and replaced by the present building. In 1900, when the landlord was William Tickle, the hotel was described as having a smoke room, commercial room and bedrooms with stabling at the rear for 30 horses. Nº 62 Chester Street, alongside this inn and for many years used as part of it, may be an original timber-framed building. To the rear are the stables and coach-house which retain many original architectural features from the days of pre-motorised transport. The whole building is Grade II listed.

The on licence was surrendered shortly after the new millennium and the premises were offered for sale by auction on

The Feathers Hotel, c.1882.

14 March 2001 when it comprised the former public house, a lock-up shop at 62 Chester Street, coach houses, stables and a garage. Following the sale, the building was renovated, retaining the same external appearance, and is now the premises of Tessuti, a men's clothing shop.

Felin Puleston
This mill, the property of Robert Puleston Esquire, of Hafod-y-Wern, was built in 1582 on the south side of the river Clywedog at the Ruabon Road end of Erddig Park. In the 1802 Wynnstay Survey of the Manor of Wrexham Abbot the mill is clearly shown as having one large water-wheel. A small settlement grew up around the mill which, at its peak in the early 19th century, had a shop and a small inn. However, by the latter part of the century the mill was in decline and the population of the settlement began to fall. In the latter years of the 19th century and the first two decades of the 20th century, the mill was owned by the Revd C.J. Jackson but operated by a Mr Wright. The grinding of corn ceased in about 1914. After the First World War, it was taken over by the Bishop brothers who operated it under the name of Millers Supply Co (Wrexham) Ltd. By the 1920s, the settlement still had one shop but, shortly afterwards many of the houses were condemned and fifty families were re-housed in Wrexham. By the 1970s, only one house remained standing, occupied by Mr & Mrs William Gillam and their children Joyce, Terry and Billy, the others had been levelled and the land used as a parking ground for Millers Engineering Co Ltd. Most of the former residents of Felin Puleston were moved to housing on the Whitegate estate. This hamlet had its own pub and it is reputed that a row of trees was planted by the Erddig estate to block the view of people leaving.

Fenwick Drive
This area of the Cefn Park* estate was requisitioned during the Second World War and temporary housing built in 1941 to accommodate Royal Ordnance Factory* workers. When the war was over these houses were utilised by WBC as temporary corporation housing and, in some cases, survived until the mid 1950s when they were known locally as 'Cardboard City'. In 1946 there were 39 'houses' of this type in Fenwick Drive. Gradually, the temporary houses were replaced by permanent housing, built by W. D. Stant, between the 1950s and the late 1960s. The street was built on land that had previously been part of the Old Maids Farm which had been bought by means of a compulsory purchase order from Lt-Col R. G. Fenwick-Palmer* after whom it is named.

Halfway down Fenwick Drive, on the site of Ysgol Morgan Llwyd, stood the community centre. A roundabout at the junction of Fenwick Drive, Sutton Drive and Rose Grove was known locally as 'The Ring'.

Fenwick-Palmer, CBE, DL, MA, **Lt-Col Roderick George** *soldier & landowner*
Born on 30 March 1892, the son of Capt George Fenwick of Plas Fron, Roderick Fenwick was educated at Wellington College and New College, Oxford where he was awarded an MA. He joined the 2nd Life Guards in 1913 and saw active service in the First World War where he was wounded and received a Mention in Despatches. He commanded the 61st Medium Brigade, Royal Artillery (Territorial Army) from 1929–33 and the 4th Bn, RWF from 1933–37. During the Second World War he commanded the 8th Bn and 31st Bn, RWF. He inherited Cefn Park,* from his aunt, Lady Palmer (widow of Sir Roger Palmer*) on her death in 1929 and, in accordance with the terms of the inheritance, added the surname Palmer to the name Fenwick. A keen sportsman and race-horse owner, he never married and died in 1968, leaving the estate to his cousin Roger Graham. Fenwick Drive* is named after him.

Lt-Col Fenwick-Palmer.

Fernbank, Grove Road
This house (and the coachhouse which is located at the rear) was designed by J.R. Gummow* for local businessman Ezekiel Mason (clothier and pawnbroker), and was originally named Albert Villa (after Albert Ezekiel Mason, the builder's son) and was numbered 6 Grove Road. Gummow described the house as being an 'Anglo-Italian cottage'. The site was originally part of the Grove Park* estate and was sold to Ezekiel Mason by James Ollerhead for £226-16s-0d. The terms of the sale specified that a villa costing a minimum of £400 (or semi-detached villas costing a minimum of £700) had to be built on the site by 1 January 1875. The house was completed by 1873 and is featured in Gummow's book *Hints on House Building* where the drawing shows the house standing on a corner plot. This is incorrect as there has never been a roadway alongside the house although one may have been intended, in which case the layout of the house would

Fernbank, Grove Road. The architect's drawing for the house which was built in 1872 for Ezekiel Mason.

have made much more sense.

Mason died in 1885 and the house was sold by his son (Alfred Charles Mason of Liverpool) to John Griffiths, a tailor of Yorke Street* who appears to have changed the name to Fernbank. Griffiths died in 1905 leaving the house to his wife and, after her death, to her companion Miss Isabella McTavish Low of Dundee, on condition that the latter remained living at the house. It would appear that this requirement of the will was not complied with and, following the death of Mrs Griffiths, the house passed to the Trustees of the will of John Griffiths, viz Robert Stobo (draper) of Langlands, Maes-y-Dre Road, John Craig* (draper) of Wren's Nest,* Rhosddu Road and Elizabeth Ann Underwood (wife of John Bayley Underwood, boot manufacturer of Castellan, Rhosddu).

The house eventually became the property of Mrs Underwood who left it to Doris Helen Pritchard. Following her death in 1959, the house was sold to Arthur B. O. Stabler (see Garden Village) for £2,900 in 1961 and, in 1994, was bought by Mr & Mrs Ron Jones.

Ferndale, Queen's Park
It was laid out in the immediate post Second World War period by WBC as part of the first phase of the Queen's Park* housing estate. It was local authority policy at one time to name streets after trees and shrubs (See Acton Park housing estate).

Fernham Drive, Barker's Lane
Built in the late 1970s by Broseley Homes. The origin of the name is unknown.

Ffordd Alafon, Borras Park
This short street was laid out in the early 1970s and named after Owen Griffith Owen (bardic name Alafon). Originally intended to be named Alafon Way, the name was made completely Welsh following considerable wrangling in the Borough Council.

Owen Owen was born on 8 November 1847 at Pant Glas in Caernarfonshire, the son of a pub landlord. He was employed as a farm labourer and in the Dorothea Quarry before going to train as a minister at the age of 29. He studied at the Methodist College at Clynnog and Bala and spent some time at Edinburgh University (but did not graduate). He was ordained in 1885. He was the editor of Y Drysorfa and the author of Cathlau Bore a Nawn (1912) and Ceinion y Gynghanedd (1915). He died on 8 February 1916 and is buried at Bryn'rodyn, Llanllyfni.

Ffordd Aled, Borras Park
This private housing development of the late 1960s was named after the poet Tudur Aled who was born in Llansannan, Denbighshire, in the late 15th century, the son of Robert ap Ithel. Little is known of his early life but he had become an established poet by the 1490s. In 1524 he was one of the two bards responsible for arranging the eisteddfod at Caerwys which established the rules of modern Welsh poetry and where he received the chair. His patron was Sir Rhys ap Thomas of Carmarthenshire and Tudur Aled is believed to have died while visiting Carmarthen in 1526.

Ffordd Almer, Smithy Lane
A private housing development by local firm, Caergwrle Investments Ltd (CIL), in the early 1970s, it is named after the Almer family who built and lived at Pant-yr-Ochain* in the 16th century.

Ffordd Alun, Borras Park
A private housing development of the late 1960s in an area of Borras Park known as Park View. It was named after John Blackwell, a cleric and poet whose bardic name was Alun.

Born at Ponterwyl, Mold in 1797, Blackwell was apprenticed to a shoemaker at the age of eleven and through him developed a love of Welsh poetry. He began competing in eisteddfodau winning his first prizes in Mold and Ruthin in 1823. He became a mature student at Jesus College, Oxford in 1825. He was ordained and became a curate in Holywell in 1829 and became rector of Maenordeifi in 1833. He married Matilda Dear of Pistyll, Holywell in 1839 and died the following year.

His poems are regarded as the forerunners of the lyrical poetry of the romantic movement.

Ffordd Caerfyrddin, Rhosddu
A private housing development of the 1970s. Ffordd Caerfyrddin is named after the pre-1974 county of Caerfyrddin (Carmarthenshire, literally translated as Merlin's fortress).

Ffordd Cwm, Coed-y-Glyn
Developed in the 1970s on land that was previously part of Coed-y-Glyn,* a property on the Erddig estate,* it is named after the Welsh word for a valley or glen and is a reference to the Clywedog valley.

Ffordd Cynan, Borras Park
Part of a private housing development laid out in the late 1960s, Ffordd Cynan is named after Sir Albert Evans-Jones, whose bardic name was Cynan.

Cynan was born in Pwllheli on 14 April 1895 where his father was the proprietor of the Central Restaurant. Educated at Pwllheli Grammar School and the University College of North Wales, Bangor, he had a varied employment history having been an extra-mural lecturer, a lay preacher, actor and dramatist. He won the Chair at the National Eisteddfod in 1924 and the Crown on three occasions. He was the Archdruid of Wales on two occasions. Cynan died in 1970.

The street was originally meant to be named Cynan Road but, after considerable discussion in the Council, it was decided that the whole name should be Welsh.

Ffordd Dyfed, Borras Road
A street of privately developed houses which were built in the 1960s on plots sold by Wrexham Borough Council on land that was previously part of Park Farm.* It is named after the cleric and poet Evan Rees whose bardic name was Dyfed.

Rees was born on New Year's Day 1850, the son of James and Eunice Rees of Puncheston, Pembrokeshire. The family moved to Aberdare when he was a child and he began work at Blaengwawr Colliery when aged only eight. In his early twenties, Evan Rees moved to Cardiff where he became a Calvinistic Methodist minister. He also became a noted poet, winning numerous eisteddfod prizes at Merthyr Tydfil (1881), Liverpool (1884), Brecon (1889), Merthyr Tydfil (1901, Chicago (1893). He was appointed Archdruid of Wales, a position which he held for 21 years, and was the editor of Y Drysorfa. He died on 19 March 1923.

Ffordd Dylan, Acton
A street of privately developed houses which were built in the late 1950s on plots sold by Wrexham Borough Council. The land had previously been part of Park Farm.*

It is named after the poet Dylan Marlais Thomas who was born in Swansea on 27 October 1914. Educated locally, he was employed as a junior reporter on the South Wales Evening Post before moving to London to try and earn his living as a writer and poet. His first book of poetry was published in 1934 and he also published a number of short stories, including Portrait of the Artist as a Young Dog and A Child's Christmas in Wales. He was employed by the BBC as a scriptwriter and wrote his most famous work, the radio play, *Under Milk Wood*. While on a lecture tour in New York he collapsed and died on 9 November 1953. He is buried in Laugharne, Dyfed.

Ffordd Edgeworth, Maes-y-Dre
Developed by Wrexham Borough Council as part of the first phase of the Maes-y-Dre housing estate* in 1930–31.

The street was named after Thomas Edgworth,* first Mayor of the Borough of Wrexham and the spelling of the name Edgeworth on the street signage is an error.

Ffordd Elan, Acton
A street of privately developed houses which was laid out in the 1970s on land that was sold by WBC which had originally been part of Acton Park.* It is named after the Elan valley in Powys.

Ffordd Elfed, Maes-y-Dre
A street of private houses developed in the late 1950s by WBC on land that had previously been part of Park Farm.*

The street is named after Dr Howell Elvet Lewis, the hymn writer and preacher. Born in Cynwyl Elfed in Carmarthenshire on 14 April 1860, Elvet Lewis was educated at the Presbyterian College, Carmarthen and became the Minister of King's Cross Chapel in London (1898–1940). He won the Crown at the National Eisteddfod in 1888 and 1891 and the Chair in 1894 and was the Archdruid of Wales from 1924–28. He published *Caniadau* (2 Vols., 1895 and 1901). He married Mary Taylor of Buckley, and died on 10 December 1953.

Ffordd Elwy, Acton
A street of privately developed houses which was laid out in the 1970s on land that was sold by WBC, which had originally been part of Acton Park.* It is named after the river Elwy in the vale of Clwyd.

Ffordd Estyn, Garden Village
One of the original streets of the Garden Village* development, the majority of the houses in Ffordd Estyn were built before the First World War. The date '1914' appears on a lintel between N[os] 12 & 14 and between N[os] 11 & 13. It was probably one of the first post 18th century streets in Wrexham to have a Welsh name.

The street is almost certainly named after Thomas Richard Lloyd whose bardic name was Yr Estyn. He was born in Denbigh in 1820 and educated at Ruthin Grammar School and Jesus College, Oxford from where he graduated as a BA in 1839. He became the curate of Hope and was ordained in 1844 when he was appointed to the living of Llanfynydd where he remained until his death on 10 May 1891. A keen supporter of the Eisteddfod movement he was one of the organisers of the Llangollen Eisteddfod of 1858, which was in everything but name, the first 'national' Eisteddfod.

Ffordd Frondeg, Ithens
A private housing development of the 1980s. The street name (*Trans.* beautiful hill-crest way) is a reference to its location on the edge of the slope above the Clywedog valley. (See also Ithens Farm)

Ffordd Garmonydd, Little Acton
A private housing development by local firm Caergwrle Investments Ltd (CIL) in the early 1970s which is named after Humphrey Bradley Jones (bardic name 'Garmonydd'), the father of Wrexham Mayor, Cyril Oswald Jones.* Humphrey Jones was born in Rhewl near Ruthin and was a headteacher at Amlwch, Bethesda, Llanarmon, Holyhead and Tregeiriog. An ardent supporter of the eisteddfod (where he was a musical conductor) he also published a volume of Welsh and English poems. He died in March 1904.

Ffordd Gerwyn, Ithens
A private housing development of the 1980s on land that used to be the Ithens Farm.*

Ffordd Glyn, Coed-y-Glyn
(*Trans.* glen way) A private housing development by John Parry in the 1970s. This street, which is the main thoroughfare through the estate, is named after Coed-y-Glyn* the house and farm which previously occupied this site.

Ffordd Gwilym, Acton
Developed by Wrexham Borough Council as part of the Acton Park housing estate* extension of the 1960s. This street is named after local politician Gwilym Herbert Jones.*

Ffordd Gwynedd, Garden Village
Developed in the 1960s, Ffordd Gwynedd almost certainly takes its name from the cleric and *eisteddfodwr* Thomas Edwards, whose bardic name was Gwynedd.

Edwards was born at Glasinfryn, near Bangor, on 8 April 1844, the son of Henry and Jane Edwards. His father was the local schoolmaster. Educated at St Bees School in Cumbria, Edwards was ordained a deacon in 1867 and a priest in 1868. He held several livings in Caernarfonshire and was the diocesan inspector of schools and a canon of Bangor Cathedral. A passionate supporter of the National Eisteddfod, he served as treasurer to the Gorsedd of Bards from 1902 until his death in 1924.

Ffordd Hendre, Ithens
A private housing development of the 1980s on land that used to be part of the Ithens Farm. This street is named after the Welsh word *hendre* which literally means old settlement, but is historically used to describe the summer pasture for animals.

Ffordd Hooson, Maes-y-Dre
A street of privately developed houses which was laid out in the late 1950s. The land was sold to WBC by Philip Clarke of Park Farm* and then sold to local builders as part of the Park Farm Estate. It is named after the poet I. D. Hooson.*

Ffordd Jarvis, Acton
Developed by Wrexham Borough Council as part of the Acton Park Housing Estate* extension of the 1960s. This street is named after Alderman Catherine Jarvis Jones.*

Ffordd Lerry, Little Acton
A private housing development by local firm Caergwrle Investments Ltd (CIL) in the early 1970s. It is named after George Lerry,* editor of the *Wrexham Leader* and local historian.

Ffordd Llawhaden, off Smithy Lane
Named after Llawhaden Castle near Narbeth in Pembrokeshire.

Ffordd Llywelyn, Little Acton
A private housing development by Broseley Homes in the early 1970s which is named after Llywelyn ap Gruffydd, Prince of Wales, who was born c.1230, the second son of Gruffydd ap Llywelyn Fawr and Senena. He seized the throne of Gwynedd from his brother and went on to control nearly all of Wales. He allied himself with the English baron, Simon de Montfort, against King Henry III and secured his position by signing the Treaty of Montgomery in 1267 whereby he was officially

recognised as Prince of Wales by the English Crown. Following the death of Henry III, Llywelyn refused to observe his obligations to the new king, Edward I, which resulted in the outbreak of war between the two countries. Edward defeated Llywelyn and at the Treaty of Aberconwy, severely reduced the prince's power. Llywelyn married Simon de Montfort's daughter, Eleanor in 1278 and the two rulers lived in relative harmony until 1282 when Llywelyn's younger brother Dafydd ap Gruffydd attacked Hawarden Castle, thereby sparking off a national war. Llywelyn was compelled to join in the rebellion and led his forces south into Powys and was killed near Builth on 11 December in circumstances that are still the subject of debate today. His head was sent to the king in London (where it was displayed on London Bridge) and his body was smuggled away and buried at Cwm Hir. His only child, a daughter named Gwenllian, was placed in a convent at Sempringham in Lincolnshire, where she died in 1337.

Ffordd Madoc, Borras Park
Part of a private housing development laid out in the late 1960s, Ffordd Madoc is named after the local poet Madog Benfras.*

Ffordd Maelor, Maes-y-Dre
Developed by WBC in 1930–31, this street was part of the first phase of the Maes-y-Dre housing estate. The name is either a reference to the Maelor area in which Wrexham is located or to local hymn writer Thomas Carrington* of Coedpoeth who was known as Alaw Maelor.

Ffordd Meirionydd, Rhosddu
A private housing development of the 1970s. Ffordd Meirionydd is named after the pre-1974 county of Meirionydd (Merionethshire).

Ffordd Môn, Rhosddu
A private housing development of the 1970s. Ffordd Môn is named after the pre-1974 county of Môn (Anglesey), a name which was revived with the re-organisation of local government in Wales in 1996.

Ffordd Morgan, Little Acton
A private housing development by local firm Caergwrle Investments Ltd (CIL) in the early 1970s. It is probably named after the local Puritan divine Morgan Llwyd.*

Ffordd Morgannwg, Rhosddu
A private housing development of the 1970s. Ffordd Morgannwg is named after the pre-1974 county of Morgannwg (Glamorgan).

Ffordd Owain, Little Acton
A private housing development by Broseley Homes in the early 1970s.
This street is named after Owain ap Gruffydd, the eldest son of Gruffydd ap Llywelyn Fawr and Senena. He was held in the Tower of London as a hostage by the English king for many years and, later, in conjunction with his younger brother Dafydd, tried to seize the throne of Gwynedd from his brother Llywelyn, claiming that, as the eldest son, it was rightfully his. He was defeated by Llywelyn at the battle of Bryn Derwin in 1254 and spent over twenty years as a prisoner in Dolbadarn Castle. Owain was released after the disastrous war of 1277 between Wales and England and was appointed lord of Llŷn and died shortly afterwards.

Ffordd Pedrog, Borras Park
Part of a private housing development laid out in the late 1960s, Ffordd Pedrog is probably named after the poet and Congregationalist minister John Owen Williams, whose bardic name was Pedrog. John Williams was born in the Gatehouse, Madryn Castle on the Lleyn peninsula on 21 May 1853 and brought up at Llanbedrog. He began his working life as a gardener before moving to Liverpool where he was employed in the grocery trade. In 1878, despite having received no formal education, he became a Wesleyan preacher before joining the Congregationalists. Three years later, in 1884, he was ordained a minister and served as the pastor of the Kensington Church, Liverpool, until retiring in 1930. As a poet, his record of success at eisteddfodau is unequalled: Chair – Porthmadog 1887, Swansea 1891, Llanelli 1895 and Liverpool 1900; Gold Medal – Utica (USA) 1889. He was a prolific contributor to numerous learned Welsh journals and served as Archdruid from 1928–32. He died 9 July 1932.

Ffordd Tegid, Borras Park
Part of a private housing development laid out in the late 1960s, Ffordd Tegid is named after the cleric, poet and man of letters John Jones, whose bardic name was Tegid.
John Jones was born in Bala on 10 February 1792 and was educated locally before attending the Presbyterian Academy at Carmarthen and, eventually, became an undergraduate at Jesus College, Oxford, graduating in 1818. He then took holy orders and became a chaplain of Christ Church before being awarded an MA in 1823. He developed an enviable reputation as a Hebrew scholar but it is in the field of Welsh studies that he is best remembered. He was a published poet and worked with Lady Charlotte Guest in the transcription of the famous *Red Book of Hergest*. He edited the poems of Lewis Glyn Cothi and was involved with the production of a new edition of the Welsh New Testament for the Society for the Promotion of Christian Knowledge. In 1841, he was appointed Lord Chancellor of Nevern in Pembrokeshire and became a canon of St David's Cathedral in 1848. A prominent figure in the eisteddfod movement, he died on 2 May 1852.

Ffordd Tegla, Borras Park
Part of a private housing development laid out in the late 1960s, Ffordd Tegla is almost certainly named after Edward Tegla Davies who was born in Llandegla in 1880, the son of a quarryman. He was a pupil teacher for 7 years before enrolling at Didsbury College in Manchester and becoming a Wesleyan minister. He edited *Y Winllan*, *Yr Efrydydd* and *Cyfres Pobun*. A noted writer he was also a columnist for *Y Herald Cymraeg*. His autobiography *Gyda'r Blynyddoedd* was published in 1952. E. Tegla Davies died in 1967.

Ffordd Trefaldwyn, Rhosddu
A private housing development of the 1970s. Ffordd Trefaldwyn is named after the pre-1974 county of Trefaldwyn (Montgomeryshire).

Ffordd Trefin, Borras Park
Part of a private housing development laid out in the late 1960s, the street is named after the Archdruid of Wales, Edgar Phillips, whose bardic name was Trefin. He was born at Rose Cottage, Trefin, Pembrokeshire on 8 October 1889. He was brought up in a predominantly English-speaking home but developed his Welsh language skills through the local Sunday School. He qualified as a tailor and worked in west Wales and London before opening his own business in Cardiff in 1914. The following year he enlisted in the Royal Garrison Artillery and was severely wounded on active service, resulting in his discharge with the rank of Bombardier. In 1921 he became a student at Caerleon College of Education and became a teacher of

Welsh at Pengam (1923) and Pontllanfraith Secondary School (1924) where he remained until retiring in 1954. A passionate eisteddfod competitor he won 33 chairs and crowns and served as the Keeper of the Sword to the Circle of Bards from 1947–60. He was appointed Archdruid of Wales in 1960. Married three times, Edgar Phillips died on 30 August 1962.

Ffordd Tudno, Acton
A private housing development of the late 1960s/early 1970s on land that was originally part of the Acton Park* estate and which was sold off by WBC.

The street was named after Thomas Tudno Jones who was born on 28 April 1844 in Llandudno, the son of Thomas and Mary Jones. Educated locally he began his working life as a shop assistant before entering the world of journalism and becoming editor of the *Llandudno Directory*. He worked on the *Caernarvon & Denbigh Herald* and was editor of *Llais y Wlad*. He married Mary Rowland of Bodedern, Anglesey in 1879 and then trained at St Bees College and was ordained into the Church of England. He was against the disestablishment of the church in Wales and was the curate of the Welsh church in Liverpool and at Llanyblodwel. He competed and won prizes at numerous eisteddfodau. He died in Llanrwst on 18 May 1895.

Ffordd Ystrad, Coed-y-Glyn
(*Trans.* vale way) Developed in the 1970s on land that was previously part of Coed-y-Glyn* and the Erddig Park* estate, the name is a reference to the nearby valley of the river Clywedog.

Field, LRAM, Helen *opera singer*
Born in Wrexham, Helen Field was brought up in Box Lane and attended Acton Park School* and Grove Park County School.* On leaving school, she completed a four-year degree course at the Royal Northern College of Music in Manchester and two years at the Royal College of Music in London. She won the Young Welsh Singer title in Cardiff in June 1976. Gaining a scholarship, she then spent two years studying music in Germany.

As a professional opera singer, Helen Field has appeared in many of the world's leading opera houses including the Royal Opera House, Covent Garden and the Metropolitan Opera House in New York. She has appeared in many leading roles with the Welsh National Opera and has made many recordings. She currently lives in Cardiff.

Field View, Montgomery Road
Originally a terrace of six Victorian houses located at the eastern end of Crescent Road. These were demolished in *c*.1960 and new houses built as part of WBC's Queen's Park* housing development, Field View takes its name from from the street's position which once overlooked The Dunks.*

Finney Close, Stansty
See Finney Street.

Finney Street, Stansty
Laid out in the 1870s as housing for the colliers employed at the nearby Wrexham & Acton Colliery,* it had 44 housing plots by 1881 although one side of the road had very few houses built upon it. The street was truncated by the construction of the Wrexham bypass in the 1970s and the name changed to Finney Close. The origin of the name is unknown but, almost certainly, came from one of the developers of the colliery. The terraced houses were demolished by the local authority in 1978.

Fire Brigade
Provincial Insurance Fire Brigade

The original Field View, a terrace of houses at the far end of Crescent Road.

The Provincial Insurance Company* of High Street, Wrexham was the first organisation to establish an official fire brigade in the town which operated until the Prince of Wales' Volunteer Fire Brigade* was established in 1863. The 1833 survey shows a building labelled 'Engine House'* in the grounds of the Grammar School* on Chester Street. The superintendent in 1854–7 was Sgt-Maj William Bragger.

Prince of Wales' Volunteer Fire Brigade

The lack of a regular fire brigade led to the establishment of the Prince of Wales' Volunteer Fire Brigade in Wrexham in 1863. It comprised 7 members of the Provincial Insurance Company* staff, 10 local tradesmen along with a number of other volunteers and was equipped with two fire-engines. Originally housed in a building off Chester Street, it moved to a purpose-built fire station in Guildhall Square* in 1894. In 1874, the brigade captain was John Scott, licensee of the Seven Stars* public house. In 1881, the Capt was E. Evans. When the Brigade had its photograph taken on the bowling green at the rear of the Eagles Hotel* its members were: Capt Evans, Lt Vaughan, Sgt Davies, Firemen Stevens, D. Samuel, Thompson, Fisk, Jos. Lloyd, T. Samuel, Branchmen Randles, Smith, A. Davies, Loxham and Engineer Lloyd. They operated a horse-drawn fire engine named *Victoria*

Members of the Prince of Wales Volunteer Fire Brigade pose for a photograph on the bowling green on the corner of Eagles' Meadow, c.1881. The buildings in the background are the rear of the premises on Charles Street; the largest is the timber yard of Edward M. Jones. [Wrexham Museum]

which was pulled by horses loaned for the purpose by several prominent town businessmen. There is a story of the horses at Caldecott's funeral parlour being used and when the alarm went off, they were released from their stables and galloped to the fire station of their own accord, such was their delight at being given the opportunity to draw a vehicle at speed! A large fire which destroyed the Victoria Corn Mills in the Beast Market in 1895 led to open criticism of the Brigade and its members came out on strike. As a result of this the council decided to form their own brigade.

Borough of Wrexham Fire Brigade

Formed in September 1895, but still made up of volunteers. In 1898 they attended the town's largest fire of the 19th century which gutted the Central Stores, Brook Street. When the fire first broke out, the Brigade was attending another fire at Ty'n-y-Coed Farm, Adwy, and were therefore slow to respond. By the time they had reached Brook Street the blaze was out of control and threatening to spread to surrounding houses. Help was enlisted from the RWF Depot in Hightown, from the Wynnstay Hall Brigade in Ruabon and from the Chester Volunteer Fire Brigade. A new fire-engine was purchased in 1899. In 1904, the Borough Council introduced payments for the firemen and many of the volunteers resigned. The town's first motorised fire-engine (and the first in north Wales), a Morris named *Maud Elsie* (after Miss Elsie Taylor), was purchased in December 1914 (complete with a 35-foot extension ladder) at a cost of just over £1,000. A second engine arrived in 1931/2.

In 1929 WBC permitted its fire service to be used by neighbouring authorities which then contributed to the running costs. In 1938 the Fire Brigade Act made it a legal obligation for all local authorities to provide a fire brigade service and the WRDC joined WBC in operating the Wrexham Fire Brigade. In 1941 fire brigades throughout Britain were nationalised as the National Fire Service then, in 1947 the Fire Services Act placed the control of fire brigades with county councils and the Wrexham service became East Denbighshire Divisional Headquarters of the Denbighshire and Montgomeryshire Fire Brigade. At the time of writing (2010), it is part of the North Wales Fire Service.

Fire Station

Wrexham's fire-fighting equipment, such as it was, was always stored in the crypt of the Parish Church until the early years of the 19th century when a dedicated Parish Fire Engine House (shown on both the 1833 and 1872 surveys), located in a small building on Chester Street in front of the old Grammar School, was built. When the Corporation purchased the school building they also bought the fire station building; the local authority did not, however, own the freehold until 1884 when it was bought from the wardens of Wrexham Parish Church for £20 (in lieu of the annual £1 ground rent). The original engine house was demolished in 1894 and replaced by a larger fire station on the north side of what came to be known as Guildhall Square. This served the town until 25 February 1957 when the present fire station, built by W. Gittins (at a cost of £46,000), was opened on Bradley Road. When the plans for this redevelopment were announced in April 1954, the original site for the new station was the corner of Ruthin Road and Bradley Road but the landowner, Wrexham Borough Council, refused to sell. The Guildhall Square Fire Station was demolished shortly afterwards. (See also Fire Brigade)

Firgrove Corner, Borras Park

A development of private houses built *c.*1968 by the London firm of Spinks & Denning on land that had previously belonged to William Clarke* and, pre-1918, to the Acton Park* estate. The name probably comes from the three staggered rows of Scots pine trees which stood here.

Five Barn Street
See Holt Street.

A Wrexham fire engine, almost certainly a 1920s Dennis which was probably the machine bought in 1931/2.

Five Fords Farm, Marchwiel

This early 18th century house, located just outside the township of Abenbury, was once part of the Wynnstay* estate and the centre of a 210-acre farm. In 1892, part of the lease was surrendered and the property eventually came into the possession of WBC who developed it as a sewage works (see Five Fords Sewage Works) on part of the site. It was the Council that authorised the demolition of the house in 1973, a sad loss to the architectural heritage of the Wrexham area. The fine staircase was saved and re-used at Hafod-y-Bwch,* Rhostyllen.

Members of the Wrexham Auxiliary Fire Service, photographed during the Second World War.

125

Five Fords Farm.

Fleece Inn, Hope Street
Located at Nº 22 Hope Street (the site of the present day Thomas Cook travel agency), The Fleece first appears in the records in 1804. Palmer* records that a bowling green was located behind it – this appears in the 1833 survey but had disappeared by the time of the 1872 survey. In 1954–5, when owned by Bent's Brewery, the building has either demolished or a new facade was built on the existing structure.

Fleming Drive, Stansty
A small private housing development of the 1960s on the site of a 19th century house named Ashfield.* The developer was George Fleming Sumner, after whom the road was named.

Flintshire (detached)
The old county of Flintshire was unique in Wales in that it was not comprised of one unified area of land but of one large area and numerous small, detached areas scattered in eastern Denbighshire and between Denbighshire and Shropshire (the Maelor Saesneg, *Trans.* English Maelor). Until 1885 four of these detached portions of Flintshire were within the area of the present day Wrexham.

Two very small areas at Llwyn Onn* and Llwyn Knottia, a slightly larger area at what is now Ysgol Morgan Llwyd* (formerly Cartrefle*) and the township of Abenbury Fechan.* These lands had been retained by the Crown after 1282, when the lordship of Bromfield and Yale* was granted to the Earl of Surrey. In 1315 Queen Isabella (the wife of Edward II) held Abenbury Fechan which was administered as part of Maelor Saesneg. In 1331 it passed into the ownership of Ebulo l'Estrange of Knockin, Ellesmere and Overton and remained with his family for over 100 years.

Florence Street, Rhosddu
Florence Street, a short street of 19th century terraced housing which was sited at the south-western end of George Street.* It was demolished in the 1960s. The street may have been named after Florence Vanda Cunliffe, the granddaughter of Sir Foster Cunliffe (3rd Bt) who was married in 1891.

Flower-de-Luce, Pen-y-Bryn
A public house of this name is mentioned in the Quarter Sessions Rolls for 1719 when Mary, the wife of Thomas Powell (innkeeper) accused William Harvey (alias Glace) of stealing 17/6 from her house. It is described as being 'at Highgate'.*

Flynn, Katie *romantic novelist*
Katie Flynn is the pen name of romantic novelist Judith Saxon was born in Norfolk in 1936 and educated at Norwich High School for Girls. On leaving school she worked as a shorthand typist before marrying Brian Turner in 1957. When her husband's work brought him to north Wales in 1959 they lived in Mold then Rhyl before moving to Wrexham in 1972. She was successful in having several short stories published in a number of national magazines before the publication of her first full-length novel, *Raleigh's Fair Bess*, in 1972. Since then, writing as Judith Saxton, Judy Turner, Jenny Felix and Lydia Balmain, she has written 86 novels in both the romantic and the saga genre. In 1995 she was diagnosed with ME and since then has written 28 regional sagas based on Merseyside and north Wales under the pseudonym Katie Flynn. Her novel *The Blue and Distant Hills* was shortlisted for the Romantic Novel of the Year Award and her books regularly feature in the *Sunday Times* bestsellers list. Judith Saxton has two sons and two daughters and lives in Park Avenue.

Forum, The
Derived from the Latin for market-place, The Forum was a name applied in mediæval times to the crossroads of High Street,* Church Street,* Hope Street* and Town Hill* where the High Cross* once stood.

Foster Road/Street, Rhosddu
Named after Foster Cunliffe, later the 6th Baronet, of Acton Park (see Cunliffe Family) whose family owned all the land in this area of the town. This street does not appear in the 1872 survey. The first house to be built on this site was probably Greystones* but, as that house is officially listed as being on Chester Road, it will not be dealt with here. The first house to be officially built on Foster Street (as the road was then called) was Nº 2, known throughout its history as Lea Hurst. This house was built by Thomas Walker, the former manager of Wrexham Gas Works in about 1899.

The double plot of land next to Lee Hurst (now occupied by Nᵒˢ 4 & 6) was bought for £150 by Walker's son-in-law, Richard Hugh Lupus Dodd (auctioneer) who sold half of it (Nº 4) to his brother-in-law, William Lee Walker in 1901 and they jointly built two semi-detached houses there. William Walker died in 1902 and Nº 4 (which was then called Dolwar) passed to his mother. After the death of Mrs Sarah Freeman Walker (widow of Thomas) in 1906, Lee Hurst and Dolwar passed to her daughter Alice Mary Hugh Dodd and the former house became the Hugh Dodd family home for many years. In 1917, Dolwar was sold to Miss Annie Jane Jones, the headmistress of Grove Park County School for Girls (for the sum of £650) and she in turn sold it in 1943 to Wrexham solicitor William Emyr Williams for £950. In 1971, the house was sold to Mr & Mrs Sidney Arthur Minson of London.

Nᵒˢ 12 & 14 were built in 1910 by John Shone, licensee of the Royal Ship Inn,* Yorke Street. Shone had been a collier who had worked in the United States of America for some time before returning to Wrexham and setting himself up in business. He sold Nº 14 to Howel Davies who named it Bodhowel and the Shone family resided in Nº 12.

The land on the south side, belonging to High Grove (later Plas Darland* on Grove Road), was used as a garden until c.1905 when it was offered for sale 'suitable for a Villa Residence to be built' although there is no evidence that any such house was ever built here. [DRO/DD/G/2871] (See also Greystones).

Foundry Road
This road took its name from the Eagle Foundry, which was

located along its southern side. In the 1872 survey, its northern side was flanked by open land, with a brewery and the entry to Bates' Square near its junction with Tuttle Street. This road now forms part of the Albion car park, below the Parish Church.

Four Dogs, Chester Road
Standing on land that was originally part of the Acton Park* estate, this plot of land was once the site of a smallholding (see Acton Park Holdings). In 1971, plans were submitted for the construction of a three-storeyed hotel on this site but, by the late 1970s, the plans were changed to a public house which was opened on the corner of Box Lane and Chester Road. A competition was held to find a name for the new pub and the winning choice was The Four Dogs, a clear reference to the four greyhounds on top of the adjacent Acton Park gates.* The name obviously lends itself to the old saying 'Going to the dogs'.

Fox, BA, DD, Rt Revd Langton Douglas, *cleric and bishop of Menevia*
Langton Fox was born on 21 February 1917, the son of Claude Douglas and Ethel Hellen Fox (née Cox) and educated at Mark Cross, Wonersh and Maynooth. He gained a BA in 1938 and was ordained a priest in 1942. He lectured at St John's Seminary, Wonersh from 1942–55 and was a member of the Catholic Missionary Society from 1955–59. Appointed parish priest of Chichester in 1959 he became the Auxilliary Bishop of Menevia on 16 December 1965 (to assist the ailing Bishop Petit*) and succeeded to the bishopric of Menevia on 27 June 1972. He encouraged the ideas put forward by the Second Vatican Council and supported the ecumenical movement in Wales. He suffered a stroke at Lourdes in 1979 and was permanently incapacitated so that a co-adjutor bishop was appointed until he retired in 1981. He died at Nazareth House,* Wrexham in 1996.

Fox & Dog, Well Street/Well Square
This public house is shown in the 1833 survey but appears to have ceased trading by the time of the 1872 survey. The site was cleared to make way for the railway viaduct built during the 1890s. (See also Fox & Goose)

Fox & Goose, Well Square/Well Street
It would seem that this was the same premises as the Fox & Dog.* The only known reference to it as the Fox & Goose is in Palmer's *History of the Town of Wrexham*.

Foxwood Drive, Bryn Offa
The main thoroughfare of a private housing development of the 1990s. The name has no particular significance.

Frances Avenue, Little Acton
Work began on developing this street in the late 1930s when brothers R. & F. Jones (who lived for many years at N°s 35 & 37) built eleven houses. The origin of the name is unknown although it is possible that it was named after the builders' mother.

Frankland, Rose Marie *Miss World*
Born in Rhosllanerchrugog, Rose Marie Frankland moved to live in Lancashire with her parents but

Rose Marie Frankland.
[Wrexham Leader]

often returned to spend time with her grandmother Fanny Green.

She won the Miss Wales and Miss Universe beauty titles before going on to win the then much coveted Miss World title in 1961 when she was 18 years of age.

In later life, she married and went to live in Los Angeles. She was divorced and married American Warren Entner with whom she had a daughter Jessica. Rose Marie Frankland died at Marina del Rey near Los Angeles in December 2000, aged 57, and her ashes were buried in Rhos Cemetery on 9 February 2001.

Freedom of the Borough of Wrexham/Wrexham Maelor
The following have been made Honorary Freemen of the Borough of Wrexham. Biographical details of all he individuals are given in the alphabetical listing in the main body of the text.
Thomas Bury, 28/3/1906; died 8/1/1931
Alderman W. E. Samuel, JP, 8/11/ 1911; died 24/02/1918
Rt Hon David Lloyd George, OM, MP, PC, DCL 10/8/1923; died 26/4/1945
Ex-Alderman Ralph Williamson, JP, 19/9/1923; died 15/7/1932
Thomas Jones, JP, 19/9/1923; died 25/1/1924
Alderman William J. Williams, JP, 10/6/1931; died 3/3/1937
Alderman Edward Hughes, MBE, JP, 10/6/1931; died 24/12/1938
Alderman Sydney Gardner Jarman, JP, 10/6/1931; died 17/1/1949
Alderman Robert Sauvage, JP, 10/6/1931; died 25/4/1942
Alderman Dr Samuel Edwards-Jones, JP, 10/6/1931; died 7/3/1935
Alderman Christopher 'Cris' Davies, JP, 26/3/1935; died 9/10/1962
Walter Roberts, JP, 20/10/1937; died 24/10/1942
Alderman William Aston, CBE, 27/9/1944; died 26/6/1962
Royal Welch Fusiliers 15/6/1946
Past-Alderman Horace Blew, 9/11/1948; died 1/2/1957
Alderman W. Emyr Williams, Ll.B, 28/3/1951; died 11/7/1958
Alderman Cyril Oswald Jones, LlB, BA, 28/3/1951; died 7/10/1969
Alderman William Dodman 28/3/1951; died 26/8/1964
George G. Lerry, MBE, 28/3/1951; died 3/12/1971
Alderman Herbert Hampson, JP, 9/10/57; died 1982
Alderman John Davies, 9/10/57; died 22/11/1967
Joseph Parton, JP, 9/10/57; died ?/12/1976
Professor Arthur Herbert Dodd, MA, 11/11/1963; died 1975
Professor the Revd Charles Harold Dodd, CH, DD, 11/11/1963; died 22/9/1973
Philip John Walters, MBE, 1/5/70; died 6/12/1984
Trevor Lloyd Williams, OBE, LlM, 5/4/1978
North Wales Police, 15/7/1978
Royal Welch Fusiliers, 17/9/1983
The Royal Welsh, 6/9/2008

Freemasonry
Heddwch a Chymdogaeth Dda (Trans. peace and good neighbourhood) *Lodge*
Founded at Wynnstay, Ruabon on 1 October, 1795 but erased on 25 November, 1801, for failing to comply with the laws of Grand Lodge. It was re-established on 24 November, 1802 at the Eagles Inn,* Wrexham, but was again struck off on 10 February, 1809.

Square and Compass Lodge N° 1336.
Warrant 4 November 1870; Consecrated 11 March 1871. The original meetings were held at the Wynnstay Arms Hotel.* The founding members were: John Lewis, John Jones,* G. Bradley,* E. Knibbs, W. Sherratt, Walter Jones, J. W. Robertson, Y. Rushton, G. Chadwick, W. Peate, ? Wallis, T. Roberts, J. Oswell Bury,* Albert Bury, J. T. Edisbury,* William Jones,* T. Eyton Jones, J. P. Murless,* ? Wooding.

The meeting place was changed to the Public Hall* and Corn Exchange in September 1876. In November 1905, the Lodge moved back to the Wynnstay Arms Hotel temporarily and in September 1906 agreed to buy the schoolroom at the Hill Street Chapel for £800 which was designated The Masonic Hall, Hill Street (see Hill Street English Presbyterian Church). and was used for the first time in February 1907. A petition for the formation of a Royal Arch Chapter to be formed and attached to the Lodge was approved in September 1909. The Chapter was to be called the Sir Watkin Chapter. In 1914, the Masonic Hall was requisitioned by the army and the Lodge again held its meetings in the Wynnstay Arms Hotel until May 1915. In September, 1946 the first meeting was held in the new Masonic Hall at 28 High Street. In September, 1963 the Lodge held its first meeting in the New Temple at Maesgwyn Hall,* Mold Road.

Worshipful Masters:

1871	John Lewis*	1936	O. A. Davies
1872	ditto	1937	W. H. Black
1873	Walter Jones	1938	Sydney Thornton
1874	John Oswell Bury*	1939	H. V. O. Cook
1875	A. H. Reid	1940	N. W. McCord
1876	William Low*	1941	J. W. Williams
1877	John Oswell Bury*	1942	ditto
1878	Edward Smith	1943	Hughie Jones
1879	ditto	1944	Arthur Davies
1880	J. C. Owen	1945	W. G. Caldecott
1881	Howel Davies	1946	Tom Carrington
1882	J. W. M. Smith	1947	J. R. Williams
1883	John Oswell Bury*	1948	W. R. Evans
1884	C. K. Benson	1949	A. Ll. Roberts
1885	J. F. Edisbury	1950	A. H. Kelly
1886	Richard William Evans*	1951	S. A. Balsom
1887	J. Abbot Harris	1952	Dr John Reid
1888	J. E. T. Young	1953	Emrys Thomas
1889	G. P. Rowbotham	1954	Revd T. Gethyn Roberts
1890	Gwilt Cathrall	1955	Dr Wesley Hill
1891	R. H. Done	1956	Bruce Brown
1892	T. Beech Barton	1957	Bryn Roberts
1893	D. D. Pierce	1958	Colin Stubbs
1894	Howel Davies	1959	Leslie Spencer
1895	Gwilt Cathrall	1960	F. Parry Jones
1896	W. A. Fraser	1961	Haydn Ira Carrington
1897	Jos. W. Bishop	1962	James Bland Dryburgh
1898	Charles Pryce	1963	Don Ferguson Kelly
1899	Richard T, Powell	1964	Arthur Clarke
1900	Edward Jones	1965	George Sinners
1901	Thomas Samuel	1966	Leslie J. Thompson
1902	Samuel R. Johnson	1967	Eric R. Myers
1903	William E. Johnson	1968	Albert E. Jones
1904	R. W. Glascodine	1969	F. D. G. Alton
1905	John T. Morgan	1970	Clifford Williams
1906	Arthur Cudworth	1971	D. Ronald George
1907	Sir Herbert Ll. Watkin Williams Wynn, Bt, CB*	1972	G. MacLennan
		1973	N. G. Alton
1908	ditto	1974	R. R. Williams
1909	Jos. Grimshaw	1975	K. C. Taylor
1910	J. Kerrison Jones	1976	W. G. Ash
1911	J. B. Bunson	1977	E. Parry
1912	Edward Hughes	1978	E. D. Evans
1913	H. C. Armstrong	1979	G. J. Watts
1914	Charles D. Rutter	1980	D. S. Hughes
1915	Leonard Bromfield Rowland*	1981	A. Andrews
		1982	J. Marles
1916	James C. Murless*	1983	R. Griffiths
1917	David Davies	1984	H. Owen-Jones
1918	R. J. Kendrick	1985	B. Evans
1919	W. E. Eames	1986	G. McTavish
1920	W. G. Pickvance	1987	E. C. Foulkes
1921	E. Escott Wood	1988	G. R. C. Cleverley
1922	Samuel Rogers	1989	C. A. Harris
1923	H. D. Thomas	1990	G. Wright
1924	Harry Woodnoth	1991	P. Chalk
1925	Charles S. Meadway	1992	R. R. Jones
1926	Thomas A. Hayes	1993	H. L. Fisher
1927	Charles Jones	1994	J. Marles
1928	William Edwards	1995	L. F. Mitchell
1929	A. Kent Jones	1996	R. Wynne
1930	R. Hughes Jones	1997	K. H. Jones
1931	A. E. Owen	1998	G. Jones
1932	N. Woodward	1999	R. A. F. Butcher
1933	W. Harris	2000	R. A. Brown
1934	D. Affleck	2001	Q. P. S. Green
1935	W. Roberts		

Bromfield Lodge, N° 4233

Warrant December 1920; Consecrated 27 May 1921. Meetings were originally held at the Masonic Hall, Hill Street (see Hill Street English Presbyterian Church) before moving to Maesgwyn Hall* in 1963.

Worshipful Masters:

1921	Sir Leonard Bromfield Rowland, Kt.	1962	E. C. Jarvis Jones
		1963	J. Bramall
1922	W. E. Eames	1964	D. Lang
1923	F. Hughes	1965	R. S. Blackshaw
1924	H. P. Williams	1966	J. I. Edwards
1925	Dr F. Yates	1967	G. H. Balsom
1926	G. R. Knox Mawer	1968	J. R. Roberts
1927	J. W. Tucker	1969	H. Wilson
1928	D. Craig	1970	T. E. Roberts
1929	J. Jarvis Jones	1971	A. B. Tunnah
1930	P. R. Hayes	1972	L. C. Moore
1931	H. G. Davies	1973	D. F. B. Roberts
1932	N. D. Bird	1974	R. Morris
1933	D. J. Jones	1975	G. H. Husbands
1934	Dr C. I. G. Bourhill	1976	A. C. G. Gabriel
1935	G. E. Challoner	1977	C. D. Vincent
1936	J. I. Williams	1978	F. L. Stritch
1937	G. W. Turner	1979	J. Hartley
1938	I. W. Edwards	1980	G. P. Jarvis
1939	W. L. Williams	1981	P. A. Dempsey
1940	H. Bird Jones	1982	R. Davies
1941	T. W. Thomas	1983	W. F. Hooper
1942	Tudor Williams	1984	D. E. Brooker
1943	Ross Wallis	1985	J. W. Caplehorn
1944	F. G. Bell	1986	J. S. Jones
1945	Frank Bellis	1987	D. Jones
1946	Baden Caldecott	1988	J. R. Stones
1947	Herbert Howarth	1989	J. C. Stritch
1948	R. A. Parry	1990	B. J. Mackreth
1949	T. T. Evans	1991	D. Lloyd
1950	A. G. Camp	1992	R. Thomas
1951	E. W. Davies	1993	R. A. Evans
1952	J. H. Williams	1994	J. A. Dyson
1953	J. E. Williams	1995	M. C. A. Brown
1954	G. S. Turner	1996	D. I. R. Scott
1955	H. Lloyd Evans	1997	G. M. Taylor
1956	Revd C. P. Williams	1998	T. O. Hill
1957	J. Roberts	1999	T. H. Harrison
1958	R. W. O. E. Phillips	2000	A. J. Nobbs
1959	A. K. Forster	2001	I. Greenwood
1960	H. Duce Jones		
1961	H. Evans		

Yale Lodge, N° 5636

Warrant Consecrated October 1936. Originally intended to be called Plasmadoc Lodge. Meetings were originally held at the Masonic Hall, Hill Street (see Hill Street English Presbyterian Church) before moving to Maesgwyn Hall* in 1963.

Worshipful Masters:

1936	G. R. Knox Mawer	1967	Royd Davies
1937	G. V. Price	1968	W. J. Evans
1938	A. W. H. Johnson	1969	R. D. H. Jones
1939	L. A. Bellis	1970	E. Whitley
1940	A. T. Evans	1971	A. D. Jones
1941	John Roberts	1972	Leo Wilson
1942	W. D. Jackson	1973	W. C. Howell
1943	J. H. Rathbone	1974	G. A. Bacon
1944	H. Humphreys	1975	H. Edwards
1945	Edward Davies	1976	H. W. Capper
1946	H. B. Lewis	1977	D. G. Price
1947	H. A. Thomas	1978	W. J. Davies
1948	C. L. Thomas	1979	C. W. Hale
1949	G. R. Castell	1980	J. C. Evans
1950	J. E. Parry	1981	C. H. Hindley
1951	F. A. Williams	1982	C. Griffiths
1952	R. L. Davies	1983	G. Ll. Jones
1953	A. T. Samuel	1984	L. G. Hockey
1954	G. N. Rogers	1985	R. J. Ledsham
1955	E. H. Hindley	1986	W. Alun Lloyd
1956	Arthur Hughes	1987	J. Manuel
1957	L. H. Livingstone	1988	D. C. Howell
1958	J. P. Fellows	1989	D. Capper
1959	Ernest Jones	1990	J. Bennett
1960	W. J. Sutton	1991	R. D. Williams
1961	E. Wyn Jones	1992	W. Stanley
1962	Norman Parry	1993	G. O. Jones
1963	G. K. Tilston	1994	D. L. Chamberlain
1964	R. Randles	1995	A. G. Lloyd
1965	T. D. Mostyn	1996	I. Ll. Kelly
1966	J. J. Deboo	1997	R. T. L. Humphreys

| 1998 | S. P. Kelly | 2000 | R. W. Harvey |
| 1999 | D. I. Kelly | | |

Offa Lodge, Nº 6660
Warrant 5 May 1948; Consecrated 28 July 1948. Meetings were originally held at the Masonic Hall, Hill Street (see Hill Street English Presbyterian Church) before moving to Maesgwyn Hall* in 1963.

Worshipful Masters:

1948	N. Woodward	1975	G. E. B. Jones
1949	Griff H. Lewis	1976	E. Griffiths
1950	John Wilson	1977	S. J. Owen
1951	F. H. B. Derrick	1978	A. R. Brown
1952	J. G. S. Thornton	1979	G. O. Evans
1953	J. E. Davies	1980	E. S. Jones
1954	J. W. Lloyd	1981	A. G. Pope
1955	D. E. Jones	1982	G. Maddocks
1956	D. C. Morgan	1983	G. W. Ould
1957	Hughie Jones	1984	N. W. Edwards
1958	J. E. Brown	1985	N. Maddocks
1959	E. Hughes	1986	E. R. Hanmer
1960	D. J. Roberts	1987	B. R. Ayling
1961	H. E. Jones	1988	H. C. Steel
1962	W. N. Barber	1989	B. Cornes
1963	R. R. Broad	1990	G. Barnes
1964	K. R. Eldridge	1991	K. Lush
1965	D. N. Johnson	1992	M. N. Williams
1966	W. Taylor	1993	R. E. Mobbs
1967	F. W. Hughes	1994	R. E. Bird
1968	N. A. Jones	1995	M. R. Evans
1969	H. Griffiths	1996	D. Owen
1970	I. Williams	1997	D. M. Jones
1971	C. F. Dodman	1998	M. Mullen
1972	J. H. Edwards	1999	R. Rowlands
1973	J. G. Roberts	2000	D. C. Warburton
1974	J. Barnes	2001	C. L. Tilston

Wrexhamian, Nº 6715
Warrant 28 July 1948; Consecrated 30 October 1948. Meetings were originally held at the Masonic Hall, Hill Street (see Hill Street English Presbyterian Church) before moving to Maesgwyn Hall* in 1963.

Worshipful Masters:

1948	F. W. Diggory	1975	J. W. Roberts
1949	Alfred Jones	1976	Ieuan Jones, MBE
1950	John Unwin	1977	J. M. Rowley
1951	Thomas Lythgoe	1978	E. J. Buckley
1952	Hugh Jones	1979	G. R. Venn
1953	J. A. Price	1980	A. E. Jones
1954	W. D. Blythen	1981	Kenneth Hughes
1955	T. K. Lythgoe	1982	William Ffoulkes
1956	S. Kershaw	1983	R. Trevor
1957	D. Ellis Williams	1984	V. Davies
1958	W. A. Blythen	1985	R. L. Marles
1959	J. Duckworth	1986	J. A. Lloyd, MBE
1960	I. Glynne Jones	1987	H. F. Westbury
1961	Fred Roberts	1988	T. B. Kendrick
1962	Philip Crotty	1989	B. S. Jones
1963	James Ward	1990	A. B. Morris
1964	D. Emlyn Rowlands	1991	P. Marles
1965	D. Raymond Charles	1992	J. J. Jones
1966	Edward Hopwood	1993	R. D. Evans
1967	Alun Davies	1994	B. L. Williams
1968	Alfred S. Jones	1995	M. W. Pugh
1969	William H. Evans	1996	G. Binnion
1970	Bryan Jones	1997	K. R. Jones
1971	Ronald Davies	1998	W. I. D. Webster
1972	Arthur Davies	1999	K. L. Taylor
1973	Claude E. Prior	2000	P. Picken
1974	W. Edwards		

St Catherine, Nº 8577
Warrant 13 March 1974; Consecrated 13 July 1974. Meetings have always been held at Maesgwyn Hall.*

Worshipful Masters:

1974	C. Lloyd Thomas	1976	E. Elwyn Jones
1975	J. Openshaw	1977	J. Aubrey Roberts
1978	Kenneth Cawsey	1990	James W. Ward
1979	Marsden F. Street	1991	Penri Ll. Hughes
1980	Ronald M. P. Gregory	1992	William D. Sloane
1981	Thomas Henderson	1993	David Edwards
1982	K. Lloyd Thomas	1994	Philip A. James
1983	Graham D. Jones	1995	Elgan Ll. Williams
1984	Arthur D. Jones	1996	Gareth T. Downing
1985	Michael J. Worsnip	1997	Stephen Williams
1986	Bill Millington	1998	Eric R. Hart
1987	Terry G. Ross	1999	Colin Lambert
1988	Cyril Cunnick	2000	Andrew Phillips
1989	John Kirman		

Erddig, Nº 8933
Warrant 1 May 1980; Consecrated 14 June 1980. Meetings have always been held at Maesgwyn Hall.*

Worshipful Masters:

1980	D. G. Price	1991	D. B. Davies
1981	D. I. R. Brown	1992	A. G. V. Lewis
1982	J. Pilkington	1993	A. D. Pierce
1983	H. R. Pierce	1994	D. Spalding
1984	O. W. Jones	1995	J. W. Coppack
1985	K. Prosser	1996	E. W. Evans
1986	D. M. Hughes	1997	D. J. Brookfield
1987	R. M. Prys Jones	1998	A. Lloyd
1988	M. S. Marshall	1999	D. E. Meacock
1989	G. F. Thomas	2000	A. M. Jones
1990	C. Davies		

Croeso Ladies Lodge Nº 203. Meetings are held in Garden Village.

In addition to the above, two other Lodges were formed in Wrexham – Berwyn (Nº 7361) in September 1954 and Pegasus (Nº 9124) in July 1984. Both now meet in Caergwrle.

French Mills
These were located up stream from King's Mills and were also known as Melin Coed-y-Glyn. They were sited close to the Sontley Road bridge and the remains of the leet can still be seen in the field by the bridge. They were demolished during the 19th century.

Friars Close, Borras Park
A private housing development of bungalows built c.1969. As there has never been a friary in Wrexham, the origin of the name is a mystery. (See also Bithell's Farm)

Friendly Societies
Palmer quotes a memorandum dated 1841 which detailed all the Wrexham Friendly Societies of that time:
  Senior Society (1744) meeting at the Black Lion, Hope Street; Union Society (1766) meeting at the Pigeons, Hope Street;

The Independent Order of Foresters parading in Chapel Street, outside the Albion Hotel, c.1905.

Friendly Union Society (1807) meeting at the Fleece, Hope Street; Ancient Britons (1824) meeting at the Highgate Inn, Pen-y-Bryn (later the Feathers, Chester Street); Court Prince of Wales Lodge of Foresters (1840) meeting at the Carnarvon Castle, Bridge Street (later The Fleece, Hope Street); Ivorites (1836) meeting at the Three Tuns; Royal Cambrians, meeting at the Nag's Head, Mount Street; Odd Fellows (1821), meeting at the Greyhound; Cambrian Lodge Order of Oddfellows, meeting at the Coach & Horses, High Street; United (1772), meeting at the Blossoms Inn; Amicable (1769) meetings at the Blossoms Inn; Waterloo (1816) meeting at the Red Lion; Prince of Wales' Lodge, meeting at the Bowling Green, Pen-y-Bryn.

Several of these societies deposited their funds in Lloyds Bank* and, on the collapse of that business in 1849, ceased to function.

Fronheulog, Bwlchgwyn
A substantial house, built for Thomas Edgeworth,* solicitor of Wrexham (the first mayor) to a design by J.R. Gummow.* The house was sold to Richard Kyrke who sold it to his son, Richard Venables Kyrke, in 1883. The house later became a girls' school, a guest house and a convalescent home before eventually becoming the property of the Bwlchgwyn Silica Company. Their quarrying activities threatened the security of the building and it was demolished in about 1930.

G

Gainsborough Road, Borras Park
This street was laid out in the early 1960s as part of the Borras Park* estate by London developers Spinks & Denning. For some unknown reason it is named after landscape and portrait painter Thomas Gainsborough (1727–88), one of the most popular British artists.

Garages
The earliest recorded motor garages in Wrexham were:
The North Wales Motor Exchange, Rhosddu (1912);
T.A. M'Kee, motor car body maker, Regis Place Works. Established 18th century as a coach builder. Included the Duke of Westminster among its clientele (1912);
Triplex Motor Company, motor engineers and electrical contractors, Regent Street (opposite the Infirmary*). Contractors to the Royal Motor Mail Service. Repairers to the RAC, AA, MU and CTC Garage. Hire cars available (1912);
Central Carriage and Motor Works, College Street. Proprietor William Rollings. Repairs and painting, cars overhauled, petrol, oils, accessories, tradesmen's vehicles a speciality (1912);
The Wrexham Taxicab Company, Union Road. Cars for hire, repairs, electric accumulators charged (1912);
Wrexham Motor & Electrical Engineering Company Ltd, 37 & 38 Chester Street (1912).

Garden Court, Chester Road
This was developed by Bowlee Properties (Wrexham) in 1983 on land that was formerly a field belonging to the Roman Catholic church.

Garden Lane, Rhosddu
See Garden Road.

Garden Road, Rhosddu
This was originally called Garden Lane, possibly because it was located close to the former Spring Gardens.* A mission was set up by Hill Street English Presbyterian Church in two houses in this street between 1880–1882. Calfaria Welsh Baptist Chapel was opened in 1882 just to the south of the junction with Springfield Terrace but was demolished to make way for the Council flats development in Springfield.* A terrace of 19th century houses alongside Calfaria Chapel were demolished to make way for the new offices of Messrs Rogers & Jackson* which is now the Salvation Army Citadel.* The south side of the road is bounded by the William Jones Recreation Ground.* The council houses at the southern end of the recreation ground were built by WBC in the late 1950s.

Garden Road (Calfaria) Welsh Baptist Church
This chapel was opened in 1882 by a congregation which had previously met in premises at the rear of the Talbot Hotel. The chapel, and the adjacent terrace of houses, were demolished in the 1960s and the site utilised for the new Springfield flats.* In 1886 the minister was the Revd R.M. Humphreys. The Religious Census of 1904 showed: Capacity 200; attendance (AM & PM) 119.

Garden Village
Throughout the 20th century Wrexham has had an enviable reputation for innovative residential housing schemes beginning with the pre-First World War Garden Village.

Lord Davies of Llandinam, head of the Welsh Town Planning & Housing Trust of Cardiff, proposed the development of a 'Garden Village' at Wrexham in 1913, the first such scheme in Wales. The United & Westminster Colliery Company had developed a new mine at Gresford (see Gresford Colliery) which it was anticipated would provide 3,000 jobs and create a demand for quality housing on the northern outskirts of Wrexham. The original plan allowed for the building of 1,000 houses which would provide homes for everyone involved in the new colliery, from face workers to managers. The development would extend from Price's Lane in the south to Tŷ Gwyn Lane in the north.

Land totalling 200 acres was purchased from the Acton Park* estate at Croes Eneurys Farm* and Tŷ Gwyn Farm* alongside Chester Road. Prospective tenants were invited to join Wrexham Tenants Ltd by purchasing shares ranging in value from £30 to £200. The company was given a £44,000 government loan which allowed them to obtain a 999 year lease on 31 acres on the site from the Welsh Town Planning & Housing Trust and commence the construction of 249 houses. The Directors of Wrexham Tenants Ltd. were: Rt Hon Lord Kenyon,* Mrs T. G. Boscawen, Sir Foster Cunliffe, Bt,* Lt-Col David Davies, MP, H. Dyke Denis,* Arthur Evans, F. A. Sturge, Dr E. D. Evans, William John Evans, John Francis and Charles Morris. The architects for the scheme were the Welsh Town Planning & Housing Trust and T. Alwyn Lloyd.

The first 240 houses were built along Bryn Acton (later renamed Chester Road*) between 1913 and 1917 and the streets were named Kenyon Avenue, Cunliffe Walk, Ffordd Estyn, Ael-y-Bryn and Wat's Dyke Way. Each house cost from £300 upwards to build. Lack of money, the First World War, the introduction of local authority housing and the recession of the early 1920s,

Lord Davies of Llandinam, prime instigator of the Garden Village scheme.

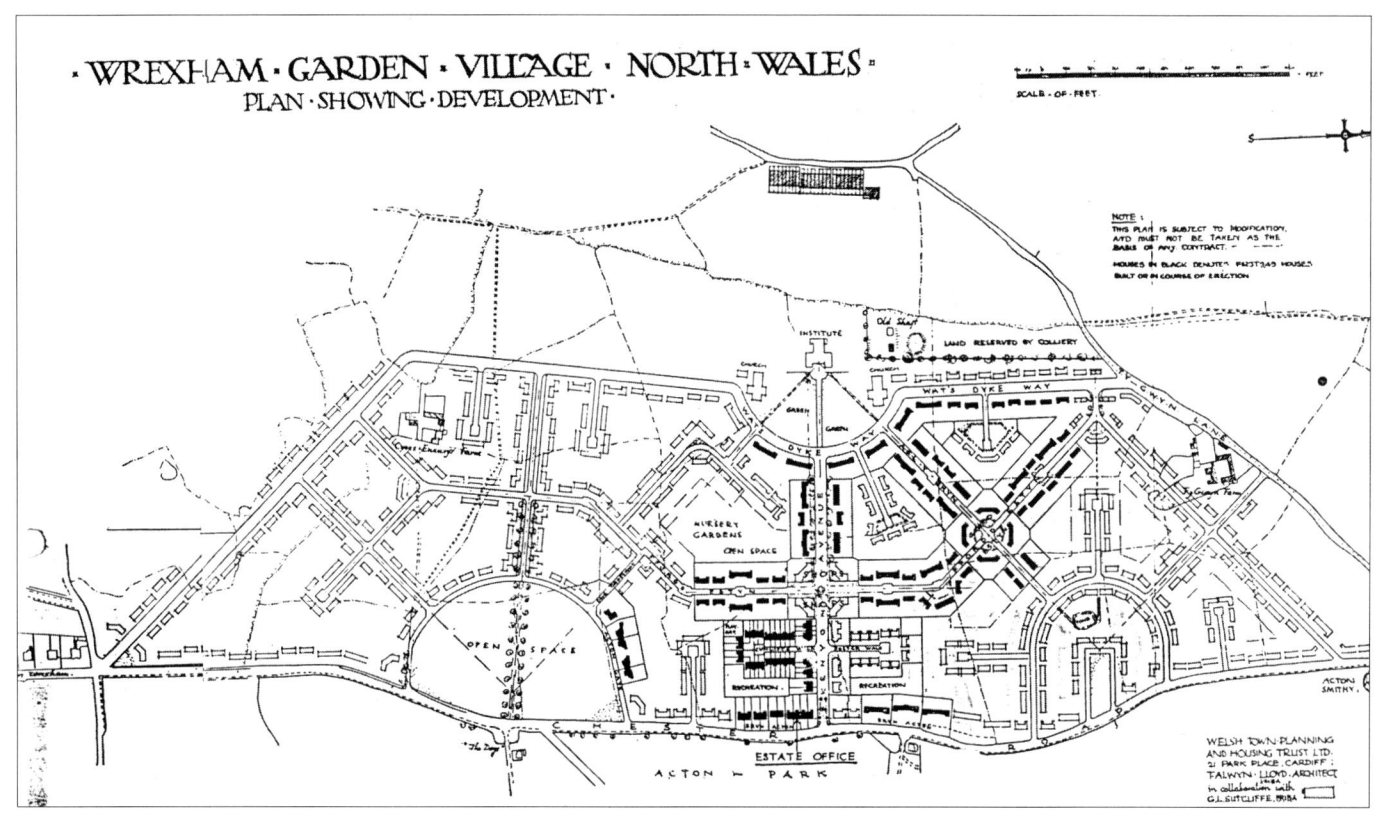

The original plan for Garden Village showing the full scope of the proposals which, had they been carried out, would have extended from Price's Lane (left) to Tŷ Gwyn Lane (right). Chester Road runs left–right across the lower part of the plan.

meant that the full scheme for development was never realised and, very quickly, plans were altered and fewer houses were built. The main roads as laid out in the original proposals were built but many of the subsidiary roads were abandoned. The grander houses, intended for the colliery management were built on Acton Gate and another crescent of similar design was planned for Tŷ Gwyn but never materialised.

Some of the housing styles were:
1. Through living-room, parlour, scullery (with bath and copper), two large bedrooms, box-room.
2. Living-room, front parlour (with bay window), scullery, hall, three bedrooms, bathroom.
3. Large living-room, lobby, scullery (with bath and copper), three bedrooms.
4. Through living-room, parlour, scullery (with gas heated copper), entrance lobby, three bedrooms, bathroom.
5. Semi-detached, with entrance hall, large dining-room, drawing-room, kitchen, scullery and usual offices, four bedrooms, bathroom, kitchen garden, lawn.

There were strict regulations regarding gardens, allotments, trees, hedges, etc. but these were gradually relaxed so that the original concept never materialised.

Facilities provided in the village were: church (St Margaret's*), tennis club (now re-developed as Village Court), village institute, Nonconformist chapel (Bethel), cricket ground, bowling greens (on Kenyon Avenue and Chester Road) and playing fields (now Wat's Dyke School*). Shops were originally opened in the front rooms of houses in Gardd Estyn before purpose-built shops were opened in Kenyon Avenue and Chester Road. Acton Park School* was opened in 1923 to cater for the children of both Garden Village and the new Acton Park housing estate. The estate office of Wrexham Tenants Ltd was the bungalow at Nº 20 Kenyon Avenue where the estate was administered by the secretary Arthur B.O. Stabler (later Alderman Stabler) after whom Stabler Crescent was named.

The government loan was eventually paid off in the early 1950s and, about 1955, Wrexham Tenants Ltd put forward proposals to sell off about 200 houses to sitting tenants for prices ranging between £250 and £400. The plan was approved and all the houses were sold off by 1957 and the communal facilities sold to WBC.

Land at the southern end of the area, part of Croes Eneurys Farm was sold off for private development in the 1920s (see Eneurys Road and Croes Eneurys) and the northern end (formerly part of Tŷ Gwyn Farm) was sold off and developed during the 1960s and 1970s by which time the rural nature of the development had disappeared. For a short time the estate was known by the grandiose title of Bryn Acton Garden City.

The whole concept was highly imaginative and forward thinking, providing Wrexham with a model upon which to base future public housing schemes. Garden Village has managed to maintain its unique identity.

Garden Village Bethel Presbyterian Church

Some residents of the newly-built Garden Village* estate set up a Sunday school at Nº 8 Ffordd Estyn at the end of the First World War. When the Garden Village Institute was built, the school moved there from Ffordd Estyn and religious services were held on Sundays. These services were discontinued in 1922 but the school carried on and in 1926 a small hall was built at a cost of £1,700 on a site donated by Lord Davies of Llandinam. The original plan included the addition of a church on the site but lack of funds meant that this never came to fruition. The hall was opened on 5 January 1927 and, at the first Sunday service 120 worshippers attended with 70 children at the Sunday school. The first minister was the Revd Ezekiel Williams (who was also pastor of the Victoria Hall in Wrexham). An extension to the church was begun in 1970 and opened on 22 June 1971 (total cost £7,000). Further alterations were carried out in 1989 including the erection of a porch. A Boys Brigade Company was established at the church.

Garden Village Tennis Club
Located on the site of the present day Village Court off Egerton Walk, Garden Village Tennis Club served this area of Wrexham for many years. With four courts and a clubhouse, it became one of the most successful in north Wales. When the club moved to form part of the new North Wales Tennis Centre at Plas Coch, the site was sold to Harvey Homes for development as Village Court.*

Garner, BSC., AKC, CEng., MICE, Mrs Isobel *chief executive*
Born in London, she gained a degree in civil engineering at King's College, London. She began her working career as an engineer in London before becoming a project manager on a major nuclear and chemical refurbishment plant with the United Kingdom Atomic Energy Authority in 1987. In 1996 she joined Bristol City Council and four years later was appointed Strategic Director of Oxford City Council. She succeeded Derek Griffin as the Chief Executive of Wrexham County Borough Council in March 2003. She is married to Ian and has one daughter.

Garner Road
This was built as part of the second phase of WBC's Spring Lodge housing development, designed to provide modern houses for those people who had previously lived in the slum houses of Pentre Felin. The road is named after John Garner Jones.*

Gas Supply
In 1827, Keay, Edwards & Co opened north Wales' second gas works on The Green,* Wrexham, and the first gas lights were operational the same year. It was, according to the press, opened with 'the ringing of bells and other demonstrations of joy' but very quickly became unpopular because of its high prices and the noxious fumes given off by the gas works.

In 1839, a group of local businessmen established the Wrexham Gas & Coke Co which opened for business in 1840 and quickly bought out Keay, Edwards & Co for £705. The W.G.&C. company built a new works on the south side of Willow Lane (Road) but, in 1869, bought part of the Dog Kennel Farm* and built a new gasholder close to the site of the present day Wrexham Musical Theatre building in Rivulet Road. In 1871, a fire at the Willow Road offices led to everything being moved to the Rivulet Road/Salop Road site and the main office entrance which still stands bears the date 1877 above the door.

The W.G.&C. company then changed its name (with the same directors) to the Wrexham Gaslight Company. Such was the demand for gas that the premises were extended in 1885 and in 1897, completely remodelled and enlarged so that by the early 20th century the Wrexham gas works was amongst the most modern in the country.

On 1 May 1949 the Wrexham gas works became part of the nationalised Wales Gas Board. Following the building of the Maelor Gas Works near Marchwiel (cost £950,000, opened 15 October 1953 by Lord Lloyd, Parliamentary Under Secretary in the Home Office and the Office of Welsh Affairs) and the intrduction of the grid system for gas distribution, the production of gas at Wrexham ceased on 16 September 1953. [DRO/DD/DM/24/6–15 & DRO/DD/DM/151/1–11, 18–85]

Gate Hangs High, Rhosnesni Lane
An unusual public house, the Gate Hangs High gives the impression of being of great antiquity but examination of tithe maps for the early 19th century gives no indication of any such licensed premises existing on this site. It first appears as a public house on the Ordnance Survey map for 1872. In 1881 it was the home of solicitor's managing clerk and bee hive keeper Thomas Woodville. It takes its name from an old sign which was a five bar gate suspended above the road, on which was written 'This gate hangs high and hinders none, refresh and pay, and travel on' which supposedly celebrates the removal of the Wrexham toll-gates.*

Gatefield (1)
Located in the angle of land formed by the junction of Bryn-y-Cabanau Road and Hightown, this substantial house, the home of Thomas Edgworth,* was sold by auction on 30 December 1889. The sale particulars provide a detailed description of the property:

> Handsome suburban residence embracing large dining room, large drawing room, servants hall with kitchen, scullery, laundry, and other out-offices, 5 bedrooms, bathroom, WC, handsome conservatory and greenhouse, two-stalled stable, coach-house, saddle room, shippons, kitchen gardens and shrubbery, also attractive large garden and pleasure ground, enclosed by a rockery wall, rendering the same quite private, and enclosing a large grass plot laid out for two lawn tennis courts, and containing two summer houses. Within the grounds also, and near the house, is a capacious, newly-erected building containing a commodious room at present used as a library, with a second room adjoining. The roof of this building is flat and commands an extensive and beautiful panorama of the surrounding country.

Some building plots fronting Shrewsbury Road (King's Mills Road*), Nelson Street* and Bryn-y-Cabanau Lane (Road*) and the proposed new street had been sold in June 1889.

The house remained isolated in the acute angle of a triangle of land bounded by King's Mills Road,* Bryn-y-Cabanau Road* and Napier Street* until the late 1960s when it was demolished to make way for a block of flats built by WBC.

Residents:
1877	Joseph William Clarke (son of Joseph Clarke*)
1881	Frank M. Jones, leather dresser
1916	William Houghton [DRO/DD/G/2831]
1931	E. H. T. Jones
1956	A. S. Deakin (Army Dental Centre)

Gatefield (2)
Following the demolition of the house called Gatefield* in the late 1960s, the name was revived as that of one of the new blocks of flats built on the site by Wrexham Borough Council.

Gatefield Lane
This appears to have been a name which was applied for a short time to Bryn-y-Cabanau Lane/Road.*

Gatewen Colliery, Broughton
Sited alongside the road leading from Rhyd Broughton towards Pentre Broughton, next to Gatewen Hall, Gatewen Colliery belonged to the Broughton and Plas Power Company. Sinking began in May 1875 and the colliery was opened in 1877. The first manager was David Pryde. In 1901, it employed 690 men (557 of whom worked underground). By 1914 this number had risen to 816 (696 underground). The demands placed upon the coal industry by the First World War, followed by the recession of the 1920s, meant that Gatewen became unprofitable and the mine was closed in 1932.

General Station (GWR)
The original station building was built for the Shrewsbury and Chester Railway (formed in 1846 and taken over by the Great Western Railway in 1854) to designs by Thomas Mainwaring Penson.* A writer of the 1860s described the General Station as looking like a small country cottage and, on the opposite side of the road, was a wooden hut serving as a refreshment room.

The original station was demolished in 1881 and replaced, on the same site, by a new building in the GWR 'French chateau' style. Built of roughly coursed and squared stone with a fishscale slate roof, the GWR building remains almost intact despite extensions being constructed between 1909 and 1912. A collision in the station led to a major refurbishment of the building which was officially re-opened by the European Commissioner for Transport, Neil Kinnock, in April 1998. The building was listed as Grade II in 1986.
[Plans DRO/DD/DM/101/29–30]

Stationmasters: (This is not a complete list, nor do the dates shown represent the date of appointment)

1850	Thomas Williams
1856	James H. W. Watts
1868	William James
1876	Mr Fryer
1878	W. Fisher
1881	Thomas Martin (resided in Spring Road)
1931	J. H. Robinson
1951	T. H. Burton
1958	W. T. Clarke
1959	G. E. Moore

George, The
A reference is made to 'The George', presumably a public house, in a document of 1727. [DRO/DD/WY/6955] Unfortunately, there is no indication of its location.

George Street, Rhosddu
Named after the Revd Canon George Cunliffe,* Vicar of Wrexham. This cul-de-sac of industrial terraced housing was built in the late 19th century and comprised only seven houses which were demolished by WBC and replaced by the Springfield* houses and flats. There are now no houses with the George Street address.

Gerald Street, Rhosddu
Laid out and developed in the 1890s as semi-detached and terraced housing for Wrexham's growing middle class. It would appear that the street was originally only intended to extend as far as the junction with Vernon Street. In 1903, plans were submitted for the extension of the street, under the name Kyrkeland Grove, but the original proposals were turned down by the Council and a second plan was drawn up which followed the line of Gerald Street more closely. This was approved and the name Gerald Street was applied to both. The street was almost certainly named after Gerald Grosvenor, the son of the 1st Duke of Westminster. (See also Convent Grammar School)

Gibbon's Court, Salop Road
A small 19th-century terrace development with access from Salop Road, Gibbon's Court was sited close to the Willow Bridge on the opposite side of the road to the Cambrian Leather Works and was demolished in 1932 as part of the Borough Council's slum clearance programme. The origin of the name is unknown.

The original Wrexham General Station with the Stationmaster, his family and staff.

Aerial photograph, c.1963, of the area between the Wrexham General Station (bottom right) and Grove Park Girls County School (centre background). The main feature of the photograph is the William Jones Memorial Recreation Ground, Garden Road. [Derrick Pratt]

Gibson Street, Newtown
Named after Thomas Milner-Gibson, a supporter of the Anti-Corn Law League. Laid out in 1895 this street was part of the Red House estate which belonged to Benjamin Piercy,* on whose death the property was divided into lots and put up for sale as building land. It seems likely that the street was built at the same time as the nearby Villiers Street,* Peel Street* and Bright Street.* Most of the properties in the street appear to have been built by 1900.

Gillett, Eric W. *life saver*
Of 3 Springfield Terrace, Rhosddu. He was awarded the *Daily Herald* Order of Industrial Heroism in November 1953 for saving the life of a British Railways fireman who had fallen from the footplate of a locomotive into the path of an oncoming train.

Gilpin, Gilbert *industrialist*
Baptised in Wrexham Parish Church in 1766, he was the son of Benjamin Gilpin, a worker at the Bersham Iron Works.* Gilbert was also employed at Bersham and rose to the position of Chief Clerk to John Wilkinson* between 1786 and 1796 when he left the Wrexham area to work for Boulton & Watt in Birmingham. For a short time he worked in south Wales before joining Botfield & Sons, Old Park Ironworks in Shropshire in 1799, where he was given the task of modernising the works. He pioneered the use of winding chains in place of ropes in collieries and eventually set up his own business at Coalport, Shropshire where he manufactured 'pit chains of a type superior to any that had been made before' receiving the medal of the Society of Arts. He settled in Dawley, Shropshire where he issued his own coins. He was compiling a Welsh dictionary when he died in 1827. Gilbert Gilpin is buried in Wrexham Churchyard.

Gladwyn Road, Little Acton
Built by H.R.&E. Roberts for Wrexham Borough Council in the early1950s this development provided housing for the growing population of Little Acton which was caused by the expansion of Gresford Colliery.* It takes its name from the house Gladwyn, located between Gresford Colliery and the village of Gresford (now a nursing home).

Glan Aber, Maes-y-Dre
Laid out and built in 1930–1. The name means the edge of the estuary or confluence which seems to have no relevance in this location.

Glan Garth, Maes-y-Dre
Laid out and built in 1930–1. The name means edge of the hill or enclosure and is a geographical reference to the street's location.

Glan-y-Pwll
This was the most important house in the mediæval township of Gourton and its name has been distorted to the present day Llan-y-Pwll.*

Glanrafon Colliery
See Bersham Colliery.

Glen Avon, Maes-y-Dre
Built by WBC in 1930–1 as part of its scheme to improve the housing stock and demolish the slums of the town. The origin of the name is unknown, but appears to be an Anglicisation of the Welsh words *glyn* and *afon* (*Trans.* valley and river) although there is no river valley nearby.

Gloucester Drive
This street of private housing was laid out in 1930s. It was named after Field Marshal Prince Henry William Frederick Albert, Duke of Gloucester, Earl of Ulster and Baron Culloden, KG, KP, PC, GMB, CGMG, GCVO, who was born 31 March 1900, the fourth son of King George V and Queen Mary, younger brother of King Edward VIII (Duke of Windsor) and King George VI.

Glyn Avenue, Little Acton
A street of individually built private houses, Glyn Avenue was laid out in the 1970s and 1980s on land that had once been a part of the Acton Park* (and previously Little Acton Farm*) estate. The origin of the name, which literally translates as valley avenue, is unknown but, as it runs off Glyndŵr Road, may have been an abbreviation of that name.

Glyn Park
(*Trans.* valley park) Now part of Erddig Park, this was originally the area of the Clywedog valley and one of the earliest recorded mentions of the name dates from September 1397 when Geoffrey Kynaston, an archer in the king's army, was appointed keeper of Glyn Clywedog Park for life. The park also appears in the 1620 survey and in *A History of Powys Fadog*, Volume III. (See also Coed-y-Glyn)

Glyndŵr Road, Little Acton
This street of private houses and bungalows was built in on land that was once part of the Acton Park* estate (and previously part of Little Acton Farm*).

It is named after the 15th-century Welsh hero, Owain Glyndŵr (*c*.1354–*c*.1416), the son of Gruffydd Fychan ap Madog ap Gruffydd Fychan, lord of Glyndyfrdwy and Cynllaith Owain in Powys. He spent some of his early life at the Inns of Court in London and took part in several military campaigns in the 1380s where he acquired a high reputation as a soldier. Following a disagreement with Reginald Grey, lord of Ruthin, Glyndŵr made an appeal to the English Crown but failed to received the support to which he thought he was entitled. On 16 October 1400 he attacked the town of Ruthin and sparked off a rebellion that soon spread throughout Wales. By 1404, he was a virtual independent monarch in Wales having gained a number of victories over the forces sent against him by the English king Henry IV. He was recognised as Prince of Wales by both the French Crown and by the Pope. Gradually, following his defeat at Pwll Melyn in May 1405, he lost control of Wales and by 1412 had vanished. It is generally believed that after moving to live near his daughter, he died at Monnington in the Golden Valley of Herefordshire in 1416. The location of his grave is unknown but is generally believed to be at Monnington Straddel in Herefordshire.

Glyndŵr University
Wrexham has made two bids to become a university town. The first, in 1883 was an attempt to become the home of the new proposed North Wales College that had been proposed by the Aberdare Report of that year. The town was in direct competition with Bangor, Caernarfon, Conwy, Denbigh and Rhyl. Wrexham's case was argued by Evan Morris.* The proposed site was 6 acres on the east side of Chester Road, where the Groves School and Powell Road are now located, which would be provided free by Benjamin Piercy of Marchwiel Hall and Henry Robertson of Brymbo Hall. On 24 August the Arbitration Committee announced that they had decided on Bangor and the Borough Council directed their efforts towards the provision of a technical college for the town and the Wrexham School of Science and Art* was founded in 1892. This led, in turn, to the establishment of the Denbighshire Technical College,* which became the North East Wales Institute.*

Wrexham's second bid for a university began in the 1990s and initially resulted in the designation of NEWI as a 'university sector college' of the University of Wales in 2003 and, five years later, was granted its own charter, becoming Glyndŵr University.

   Chancellor Lord Barry Jones
   Vice-Chancellor Prof Michael Scott
   Board of Governors
      Chair Michael Cant
      Vice Chair Robert Hill
      Professor Bim Bhowmick
      Mervyn Cousins
      His Honour Judge Roger Dutton*
      Derek Griffin*
      Brian Heath
      Pam Hope
      David Howard
      Judge R. Philip Hughes
      John Kenworthy
      Ian Morris
      Lynda Powell
      Bruce Roberts
      Professor Michael Scott
      Malcolm Thomas
      Professor Peter Toyne
      Ian Williams
      Julia Grime
      + 1 student governor

For full details of the first bid, see *Transactions of the Denbighshire Historical Society*, Vol. 38 (1989), 'Wrexham's Attempt to Become a University Town', by Anita M. Thomas.

Glynn Cinema
Built on land owned by the Borough Council as a 'temporary' cinema (on the site now occupied by the Guildhall Lambpit Street car park), it took its name from Glynn Hill who, with his partner G. E. Bulford, owned the Glynn Animated Picture Company which operated a small circuit of cinemas in the border area. Opened on 23 September 1910, it was claimed that the Glynn was the first purpose-built cinema in north Wales. The first manager was Charles Bayley and the last, Kate Nutter, the daughter of William Henry Nutter, musical director at the Hippodrome.* The management was involved in the commissioning of local newsreel films for showing at the Glynn and one of these, showing the Co-op Parade of 1912, is the oldest surviving piece of moving film of Wrexham (which has now been preserved in the video *Wrexham – a journey through time*). The Glynn became the second talking-picture house in Wrexham. When the 50-year lease for the land expired in 1959, it was decided not to renew and the Glynn closed on 4 November 1960 (the last film to be shown was *Hercules Unchained*) and was demolished shortly after. (*Ninety Years of Cinema in Wrexham*, Brian Hornsey, privately published 1990)

Golden Lion, High Street
Originally a private house, this was the property of the Pulford family in the mid 17th century. In 1674, it had the highest assessment for tax of any property in High Street, although it only had five hearths. It was converted into a public house c.1700 but, for a short period during the early 18th century, became two shops before reverting to a public house. It remained in the ownership of the Pulfords until 1745/6 when it passed to Robert Samuel on his marriage to Ellen Pulford. Robert was the son of William Samuel of The Lamb, High Street. It was shown in the 1833 survey. [DRO/995] In the 1990s the shop premises fronting High Street* was added to the public house but access to the building via the Golden Lion Entry* was retained.

Golden Lion Entry
One of the few such 'entries' to survive the alterations of the 20th century, the Golden Lion Entry provided the main access from High Street to the Golden Lion public house.

Gort Avenue, Queen's Park
This street of pre-fabricated houses developed by WBC in the late 1940s as part of the earliest phase of what was to become the Queen's Park Estate. With the building of brick houses in the area of Wilson Avenue, Cunningham Avenue and Portal Avenue, the 'pre-fab' houses were demolished and Gort Avenue was not re-built.
The street was named after Field Marshal Lord Gort VC, GOC of the British Expeditionary Force of 1939–40.

Gough, Matthew *soldier*
Born at Penley, Maelor, the son of Owen Gough, bailiff of the manor of Hanmer. His mother was a daughter of Sir David Hanmer and the sister-in-law of Owain Glyndŵr (see Glyndŵr Road). Matthew gained great distinction as a soldier during the Hundred Years War with France when he was present at the battles of Cravant (1423) and Verneuil (1424) and was given the command of various French towns including Laval, Le Mans, St Denis, Bayeux and Belléme. Captured by the French at St Denis he was ransomed. In 1447 he had the unpleasant task of surrendering the English territories of Anjou and Maine to the French and, after the English defeat at Formigny in 1449, returned to England where he was appointed one of the joint commanders of the Tower of London. On 5 July 1450, during Jack Cade's rebellion, Gough was killed on London Bridge while organising the defence of the City. For many years his name 'Matago' was revered by the French as the epitome of military prowess and he was used as the 'bogey man' to frighten small French children.

Goulbourne, The, Goulbourne
This public house was built by Ansells Brewery to serve the newly-developed Goulbourne private housing estate. It was built on land that formerly belonged to Plas Goulbourne* from where it takes its name.

Goulbourne Avenue, Goulbourne
Developed in the early 1980s as a street of private houses on land that was previously part of Plas Goulbourne Farm from where it takes its name.

Gourton
The mediæval township of Gourton was one of the thirteen country townships of the old parish of Wrexham. It was located between Borras Riffri and Bieston and had as its chief residence, Glan-y-Pwll, the home of the Powell family in the 17th century. The house and land eventually became part of the Borras Hall* estate which was owned by the Kenyon family until the mid 20th century.

Gourton Square, Goulbourne
Developed in the early 1980s as a street of private houses on land that was previously part of Plas Goulbourne Farm. It takes its name from the mediæval township of Gourton in which this estate is located.

Grammar School, Chester Street
See Wrexham Grammar School.

Graesser, JP, Robert Ferdinand, *industrialist & entrepreneur*
Born in Obermosel, Saxony on 5 October 1844, Robert Graesser

Robert Ferdinand Graesser.

was the youngest of twelve children. He was educated locally then spent three years at the Chemnitz Technical College studying chemistry. In 1863, he received the college's bronze medal before going to Manchester where he was employed as an industrial chemist by Calvert, manufacturers of tooth powder where he was soon promoted to works manager with special responsibility for the production of phenol. In 1867, he went into partnership with Timothy Crowther and established a chemical works at Plas Kynaston, near Acrefair, where they produced paraffin oil and wax from the local shale. Competition with the American producers meant that the company was unsuccessful and the partners soon fell out and the ensuing litigation found in Graesser's favour. The partnership was dissolved and Graesser set up in the same area as Robert Graesser (Ruabon) Ltd. and before long had taken over the old works. His company extracted tar and carbolic acid from local coal shale but again, this was unsuccessful and he switched to the production of tar acid before falling back on the production of phenol which he had been so successful with in Manchester. Because of the dangers involved in the production and transportation of phenol, Graesser made use of the local canal network and developed a new method of purification and soon became the world's leading producer.

In 1886, while travelling by train to Liverpool, Robert Graesser met Ivan Levistein, a manufacturing chemist and a founder director of the Wrexham Lager Beer Company.* Levistein explained that his company had a problem with cooling the lager and Graesser provided him with a solution to his problem – using brine coils in the cellars – and was made a director of the company.

The Acrefair company was eventually taken over by the American chemical company, Monsanto, and latterly operated under the name Flexsys. The company closed in 2010.

Robert Graesser married Mary Elizabeth and died in 1911. He is buried in Froncysyllte churchyard.

Grange Avenue, Rhosddu
One of the early streets of council houses developed by WRDC in the 1920s, this development was named after Rhosddu Grange.*

Grange Farm
(see Rhosddu Grange)

Gredington Arms, Llan-y-Pwll
Known as The London Apprentice in the period 1815–33, and forming part of the Borras Hall* estate, this public house was also a small farm. The main road from Wrexham to Holt originally passed through what is now the car park and the pub, a half-timbered building, stood to the north of the road. When the new public house was built in 1839 it was placed on the present site, to the south of the old road. The out buildings considerably pre-date the main building.

Like most properties in this area, the pub was owned by the

Fire crews fighting the fire at the Gredington Arms caused by a lorry crashing into the building.

Gredington estate from the late 18th century until 1954 and the name reflects this ownership. In 1881, the tenant of both the pub and the land (40 acres) was Edward Bellis, a descendant of the Roberts family who were reputed to have lived here for several hundred years. By the early 20th century it had been taken over by Edward's niece, Annie Bellis, who also had the tenancy of Hafod-y-Wern Farm* which was run by her half-brother, Mr Swan. In 1954 the Gredington Estate sold the premises to Harold Dick Hitchcock for £2,100 and it was tied to Border Breweries. In 1962, it was sold to Mr & Mrs James Browne of Hugmore Lane. Mr Browne died in 1969 and his widow Annie Dorothy continued with the licence until 1977 when she let the ground floor of the pub to her daughters. In January 1979 the premises were bought by Hydes Anvil Brewery of Manchester who carried out considerable alterations to the premises during the 1980s. In the late 1980s one end of the building was destroyed when a lorry crashed into it at night.

A study of 19th-century Ordnance Survey maps indicates the route of the old Wrexham–Holt road, passing behind the present day Gredington Arms and rejoining the turnpike road just to the east of Llan-y-Pwll Farm.

Gredington Close, Goulbourne
Developed in the 1980s on land that was formerly part of Plas Goulbourne Farm.* This small street of private houses was named after the Gredington Estate which had owned Plas Goulbourne from the mid-18th century until the 1950s. (See also Kenyon Family)

Green, Arthur Aubrey *local politician*
He was born Pentre, Pen-y-Coed, Ruabon, c.1884, the son of John Green, a colliery manager and farmer. In 1895 he became an apprentice grocer with the Co-operative Society and rose to General Manager by 1940. During the First World War he served with the Army Service Corps in Mesopotamia.

He was elected a member of WBC in 1932, representing Maes-y-Dre Ward. He was chairman of the Transport Committee, Deputy Mayor in 1935 and Mayor in 1941. He was a Justice of the Peace and a life governor of the Wrexham & East Denbighshire War Memorial Hospital. He was also a keen thespian and Freemason.

Arthur Green married Nelly Attwell (died 1960), the daughter of Isaac Hughes, a joiner of Regent Street, and they had one son. They lived at Durbar, 69 Park Avenue. He died at his home on 13 April 1947 and is buried in Wrexham Cemetery.

Green, The, Little Acton
Built by H. R. & E. Roberts for Wrexham Borough Council in the 1950s, this development provided housing for the growing population of Little Acton which was caused by the expansion of Gresford Colliery.* It takes its name from the open recreational field sited in front of the houses.

Green, The, Wrexham Fechan
The Green was the name given to the area now known as Salop Road* and Mount Street.* It would appear that in the early 17th century, it was common land but was built upon by the end of the century when it belonged to the Pulestons of Hafod-y-Wern.*

Green Bridge
This was the bridge which carried Salop Road across the river Gwenfro* from the area known as the Green* into Wrexham Fechan.* The bridge was demolished and replaced by the Willow Bridge* in 1877. [DRO/QSD/FS/2/7]

Green Dragon, Beast Market
See The Bear, Beast Market.

Green Dragon, Salop Road
Shown in the 1833 survey, an inn of this name is mentioned as early as 1740. In 1805 it was the property of Thomas Stephenton of Willow House* after whose death it was sold to Mrs Bennion of Beechley. In 1895 it was still part of the Beechley House estate and was tenanted by John Jones of the Island Green Brewery who let it out to Edwin Pugh as the licensee. In the sale of that year it was sold for £1,575 to Thomas Roberts. The present building was constructed in the early 1900s and was a Bent's Brewery house, then a Bass Charrington's house and is now owned by Enterprise Inns. [DRO/DD/W/729–43, 746–50]

Green Lane
Green Lane was a footpath located in Stansty between Crispin Lane* and Plas Coch Road* which in the mid 19th century formed the boundary between the Racecourse* and Ashfield House,* emerging almost opposite Plas Coch* at one end and where the railway meets Crispin Lane close to the railway bridge at the other. The access was shared between John Ffoulkes of Ashfield and Sir Watkin Williams Wynn.* In April 1883 it was agreed to close the access and build a wall to divide the two properties. As Green Lane was regarded as an 'ancient thoroughfare' there was a great deal of local feeling against this closure but it was proceeded with regardless. [DRO/DD/WY/6831]

Green Man, Charles Street
See The Hat Inn.

Green Man, The Hope Street
Located at Nº 26 Hope Street, this public house was known as the Green Man from c.1788 until the late 19th century (it appears as such in both the 1833 and the 1872 surveys). By the 1890s it was an off-licence for the Town Hall Vaults.*

Green Park
Green Park is the name given to the private housing development carried out by local builder, John Parry, on land that was formerly part of The Court* estate and the Bricky,* a former brickyard operated by Meredith Jones until the 1920s. The estate is built on two levels, the lower of which was built on the land which had been stripped of its clay surface while the higher level was part of the gardens of The Court. Work commenced on the lower level in 1973 and on the upper level in 1975, after the demolition of The Court.

There does not appear to be any significance in the name Green Park. The road which is the entrance to the estate from Erddig Road follows the line of the driveway to The Court. When the brickyard was in operation, there was a tunnel under this road which allowed clay-bearing wagons to pass from one side of the brickfield to the other without affecting the access to The Court. The high brick wall inside Green Park was part of the kitchen garden wall of The Court and the horse mounting block can still be seen alongside it.

Green Wesleyan Chapel, The
This chapel was opened in Salop Road on New Year's Day 1805, with a minister's house located behind it. It remained in use until 1855 when it was sold to the Wesleyan Reformers and the congregation transferred to the newly built Bryn-y-Ffynnon Church.* In 1847, this congregation had a Sunday school catering for 114 pupils. The Wesleyan Reformers died out in Wrexham shortly afterwards and the chapel was bought by Thomas Rowland* who demolished it and built a row of houses known as Chapel Place* on the site.

Greenaway, Mrs Bronwen *local politician*
Bronwen Hughes was born in Wrexham on 20 May 1933 and spent her early life at Crispin Lane. She was educated at Rhosddu and Alexandra Schools. She married Dennis Greenaway in 1952 and had two sons and two daughters. Her working life began in a local brick-works, followed by a period in the baby unit at the local hospital, Metal Box in Gwersyllt and, finally, as a traffic warden in Wrexham for over 24 years.

She was elected a Labour member of the Brymbo Community Council in 1975 and WBC in 1984. In 1996 she became the first Mayor of the newly-formed WCBC, serving for 14 months, and was Chair of the Markets Committee. She was deselected by the Labour Party in 1999 but, standing as an Independent, held the Brymbo seat. In her latter years, despite suffering from ill health, Mrs Greenaway devoted a great deal of time and energy to campaigning for the regeneration of the former Brymbo Steel Works site. She lived at Cheshire View, Brymbo and died on 3 June 2000.

Gresford Colliery
Gresford Colliery was sunk by the United Westminster & Wrexham Collieries Ltd following the cutting of the first sods of each shaft (the most northerly, named the Dennis, or downshaft, pit being cut by Mrs Dyke Dennis and the southerly, named the Martin, or upshaft, pit by Sir Theodore Martin) at Acton Cottage on 6 November 1907 (the site is often referred to as Acton Grange but this would appear to have been a mistake on the part of George Lerry in his book *Collieries of Denbighshire*). The silver and oak spade used in this ceremony is currently on display in the foyer of Glyndŵr University.* The shafts were 50 yards apart and the Dennis was completed to a depth of 2,263 feet on 11 June 1911, followed by the Martin (to a depth of 2,206 feet) in 1912. By 1914, the colliery was employing 899 men (689 underground workers and 210 surface workers) and this grew to 2,200 (1,850 underground and 350 surface workers) by 1934 when it was the scene of the worst disaster in the history of the north Wales coalfield and the second worst mining disaster in Wales.

At 2 a.m. on the 22 September an explosion, followed by a fire, occurred in the Dennis Section. Apart from a handful of men working near the pit bottom and one deputy and five men who managed to escape from the section itself, every man on the shift was killed, a total of 261 miners. During the rescue attempts, three rescuers were killed. Determined efforts to control the underground fire came to nothing and by the evening of the 23 September all hopes were abandoned of rescuing any of the miners. Due to the dangers involved in continuing the rescue operations, the Inspectors decided to seal off the mine and allow

The names of the men who were killed in the Gresford Disaster, September 1934

John Anders, 27, Beltman, 17 Empress Road, Wrexham
John Thomas Anders, 31, Repairer, 39 Bertie Road, Wrexham
George Anderson, 67, Repairer, Old Rhosrobin, Wrexham
Alf Owen Andrews, 43, Cutter, Benjamin Road, Wrexham
John Archibald, 47, Metal, Finney Street, Wrexham
Thomas Archibald, 30, Cutter, 44 Council Houses, Pandy
David Baines, 26, Haulage, 9 Victoria Road, Brynteg
Maldwyn O. Bateman, 15, Haulage, 11 Lorne Street, Rhosddu
Edward Wynn Bather, 36, Collier, Finney Street, Rhosddu
Edward Beddows, 63, Collier, The Woodlands, High St, Gwersyllt
Arthur Bew, 45, Cutter, 13 Colliery Houses, Rhosddu
Thomas Lloyd Bewley, 58, Collier, 15 Park Street, Rhosddu
Alf Bowen, 53, Borer, 71 Langdale Avenue, Rhos
Henry Boycott, 38, Packer, 18 Offa Terrace, Wrexham
Herbert Brain, 31, Repairer, 15 Pentrefelin, Wrexham
George Bramwell, 30, Haulage, 11 Western Road, New Broughton
John Brannan, 32, Collier, Ffordd Edgeworth, Maesydre, Wrexham
William Arthur Brown, 22, Haulage, 2 Albert Street, Wrexham
John A. H. Bryan, 20, Packer, 72 Llewelyn Road, Coedpoeth
Buckley, 21, Haulage, Mountain View, Windy Hill, Summerhill
Fred Burns, 41, Collier, 33 Bennions Rd, Huntroyde, Wrexham
John A. Capper, 35, Packer, 1 Wrexhgam Road, Broughton
Albert Edward Cartwright, 24, Packer, 25 Florence Street, Rhosddu
Charles Cartwright, 24, Filler, 25 Florence Street, Rhosddu
Stephen Chadwick, 21, Filler, 8 Kenyon Street, Wrexham
Edwin Chester, 67, Fireman, Beales Cottages, Bradley
Arthur Clutton, 29, Packer, 40 Lorne Street, Rhosddu
George Albert Clutton, 20, Packer, 7 March Terrace, New Rhosrobin
John T. Clutton, 35, Haulage, 40 Council Houses, Pandy
John Collins, 62, Shot-firer, Council Houses, Pandy
Thomas R. Cornwall 30 Haulage, 23 Bennions Road, Wrexham
William Crump, 36, Cutterman, 157 Council Houses, Bradley
Thomas Darlington, 28, Ripper, 39 Mountain Street, Rhos
Arthur Davies, 24, Filler, Havelock Square, Wrexham
Edward Davies, 53, Packer, 33 Cyngorfan, Rhos
George William Davies, 26, Haulage, 29 Farndon Street, Wrexham
Hugh T. Davies, 26, Borer, Holly Bush Terrace, Bradley
James Davies, 31, Repairer, 4 Williams Cottages, Moss
James Davies, 37, Repairer, 14 Boundary Terrace, Green, Brymbo
James Edward Davies, 21, Filler, 29 Farndon Street, Wrexham
John Davies, 64, Repairer, 7 Meifod Place, Wrexham
John Davies, 45, Repairer, Fern Leigh, Rhosrobin Road, Wrexham
John E. Davies, 32, Collier, 43 Bennions Road, Wrexham
John R. Davies, 69, Repairer, Fern Leigh, Rhosrobin Road, Wrexham
Matthias Davies, 24, Filler, 4 Erw Las, Maesydre, Wrexham
Peter Davies, 50, Repairer, 8 Newtown, Gresford
Peter Davies, 25, Filler, 6 March Terrace, New Rhosrobin
Peter Davies, 21, Borer, 7 Glanllyn, Bradley
Robert Thomas Davies, 34, Collier, 4 Mountain View, Caego, Wrexham
Samuel Davies, 35, Filler, 14 Woodland View, New Rhosrobin
Thomas Davies, 31, Repairer, Erw Cottage, Caergwrle
William Davies, 33, Repairer, 14 Acton Terrace, Rhosnesni
Thomas Dodd, 39, Ripper 5 Maeseinnion, Rhos
Fred Duckett, 29, Collier, 7 Beech Terrace, Ruabon
John Edge, 28, Haulage, 62 Nelson Street, Hightown, Wrexham
T. Samuel Edge, 30, Collier, 17 South Street, Rhos
Albert Edwards, 62, Repairer, Nr King's Road, Moss
Ernest Edwards, 16, Haulage, 31 Green Road, Brymbo
E. Glyn Edwards, 23, Haulage, 13 Woodland View, New Rhosrobin
Ernest Thomas Edwards, 53, Ripper, 4 Queen Street, Rhos
Frank Edwards, 23, Pipeman, Chestnut Avenue, Acton
James Sam Edwards, Haulage, Top Road, Moss
John Edward Edwards, 39, Collier, 6 Glan Afon, Maesydre, Wrexham
John C. Edwards, 30, Packer, 9 Coronation Cottages, New Road, Southsea
Thomas David Edwards, 40, Ripper, 6 New Street, Rhos
William Edwards, 32, Ripper, 20 Church Street, Rhos
John Edwardson, 41, Beltman, High Street, Gresford
George Edward Ellis, 43, Collier, 35 Council Houses, Pandy
Fred Evans, 50, Collier, 1 Grange Avenue, Rhosddu,
John Evans, 32, Cutterman, Ness Cottage, Park Wall, Gwersyllt
Norman Evans, 45, Doggie, 14 Grange Avenue, Rhosddu
Ralph Evans, 37, Cutter, 135 Pentre Lane, Llay
Len Fisher, 30, Haulage, 44 Maple Avenue, Acton, Wrexham

Irwin Foulkes, 21, Haulage, 15 Cyngorfan, Rhos
Richard George Gabriel, 61, Collier, Crispin Lane, Wrexham
John Henry Gittens, 42, Repairer, 11 Abenbury Street, Wrexham
John Goodwin, 51, Packer, 6 Chapel Road, New Broughton
Edward Griffiths, 21, Filler, Brandy Cottages, Ruabon
Ellis Griffiths, 50, Packer, 68 Cyngorfan, Rhos
Emmanuel Griffiths, 53, Packer, 14 High Street, Penycae
E. C. Griffiths, 25, Repairer, 6 Gardd Estyn, Garden Village
John Francis Griffiths, 57, Repairer, 14 Oxford Street, Wrexham
Walter Griffiths, 50, Repairer, 53 Victoria Road, Brynteg
Walter Hall, 49, Packer, 4 Church Road, Brynteg
Thomas W. Hallam, 32, Packer, 3 Railway Terrace, Gwersyllt
Arthur Hamlington, 62, Repairer, Yew Tree Cottage, Little Mountain
Frank Hampson, 32, Repairer, 78 Ruabon Road, Rhostyllen
Arthur Harrison, 21, Collier, 30 Moss Hill, Moss
Charles Edward Harrison, 15, Haulage, 19 James Street, Wrexham
Phillip Hewitt, 56, Repairer, Poplar Avenue, Rhos
William Henry Higgins, 27, Haulage, 12 Finney Street, Rhosddu
Alfred F. Holt, 31, Cutter, 15S, Pentre Lane, Llay
John Henry Houlden, 21, Haulage, 25 2nd Avenue, Llay
Cecil Hughes, 23, Packer, Tanygraig, Minera
Francis O. Hughes, 60, Repairer, 7 Acton Terrace, Rhosnesni
Harry Hughes, 44, Cutterman, 3 Hill Crest, Spring Lodge
John Hughes, 58, Repairer, 59 Percy Road, Wrexham
Peter John Hughes, 27, Collier, Tanygraig, Minera
Robert John Hughes, 29, Collier, 14 Lorne Street, Rhosddu
Walter Ellis Hughes, 24, Packer, Rosemary Crescent, Rhostyllen
William Hughes, 43, Collier, 4 Long Row, Brymbo
Ben Humphreys, 34, Collier, 50 Vernon Street, Rhosddu
John Humphreys, 30, Cutterman, 22 Edward's Road, Brynteg
Thomas Husbands, 40, Collier, 18 Manley Road, Wrexham
Ernest Jarvis, 41, Cutterman, 7 Vownog, Bersham
William T. Jenkins, 25, Collier, 14 Heol Offa, Vron, Wrexham
Percy Johns, Packer, 27 Ffordd Edgeworth, Maesydre, Wrexham
Albert Edward Jones, 31, Borer, 25 Nelson Street, Wrexham
Azariah Jones, 37, Header, 50 Westminster Road, Moss
Cyril Jones, 26, Collier, Main Road, Old Rhosrobin
Dan Jones, 33, Repairer, 14 Western Road, New Broughton
David L. Jones, 36, Cutterman, 9 Colliery Road, Rhosddu
Edward Jones, 64, Repairer, 5 Woodland View, High Street, Gwersyllt
Edward Jones, 56, Repairer, Queen Street, Cefn
Edward George Jones, 23, Haulage, 29 Ruabon Road, Wrexham
Eric Jones, 23, Filler, 116 Rosemary Crescent, Rhostyllen
Ernest Jones, 36, Packer, 35 Glan Garth, Maesydre, Wrexham
Evan Hugh Jones, 55, Repairer, Marion House, New Brighton, Minera
Fred Jones, 30, Packer, 4 Woodland View, New Rhosrobin
Frederick H. C. Jones, 31, Borer, 1 Bridge Street, Holt
Francis O. Jones, 27, Haulage, 21 Council Houses, Berse
George Jones, 47, Beltman, 18 Glan Garth, Maesydre, Wrexham
George Humphrey Jones, 22, Haulage, 24 Russell Street, Cefn
Gwilym Jones, 52, Repairer, 16 Glan Garth, Maesydre, Wrexham
Henry Jones, 59, Collier, 1 Gordon Terrace, Rhosddu
Idris Jones, 37, Haulage, 59 Nant Road, Coedpoeth
Iorwerth Jones, 52, Haulage, Bryn Dolwar, Rhosrobin Road
Jabez Jones, 43, Haulage, 1 Morgan Avenue, Rhosddu
John Dan Jones, 42, Repairer, 3 Williams Cottages, Moss
John Richard Jones, 33, Repairer, 6 Mostyn View, Coedpoeth
John Robert Jones, 55, Repairer, 119 Pentre Lane, Llay
Llew Jones, 49, Repairer, 3 Windsor Road, New Broughton
Llew Jones, 40, Haulage, Yew Tree Bungalow, Gresford
Llew Jones, 38, Collier, 3 Bersham Road, New Broughton
Neville Jones, 30, Beltman, Ffordd Maelor, Maesydre, Wrexham
Richard Henry Jones, 21, Haulage, 5 Bryn Terrace, Ruabon
Richard J. Jones, 34, Repairer, 3 White Houses Lodge, Brymbo
Robert Jones, 57, Fireman, Drefechan, Penycae
Robert Jones, 49, Packer, Hillock Lane, Gresford
Thomas Jones, 55, Packer, 28 Council Houses, Gresford
Thomas E. Jones, Collier, Poolmouth Valley, Moss
Thomas John Jones, 58, Haulage, Bryndedwydd, Marford Hill
Thomas O. Jones, 59, Collier, Penllyn, Trevor
William Jones, 51, Haulage, 16 Lorne Street, Rhosddu
William Jones, 21, Filler, 2 Lloyd Street, Rhos
James Kelsall, 30, Haulage, 34 Florence Street, Rhosddu
John Kelsall, 37, Packer, Rose Cottage, Common Wood, Holt
William Lawrence, 43, Haulage, 9 Nelson Street, Hightown, Wrexham
John Thomas Lee, 30, Repairer, 10 Heol Offa, Coedpoeth
Thomas Lee, 16, Repairer, 10 Heol Offa, Coedpoeth
David Lewis, 44, Repairer, 6 Merlin Street, Johnstown

David Thomas Lewis, 46, Cutterman, 3 Middle Road, Coedpoeth
Joel Lilley, 41, Repairer, Main Road, Old Rhosrobin
Thomas Lloyd, 55, Packer, 14 Colliery Road, Rhosddu
Willianm Lloyd, 59, Collier, 22 Finney Street, Rhosddu
William Sidney Lloyd, Haulage, 172 Pentre Lane, Llay
John Lucas, 59, Collier, 153 Council Houses, Glanllyn, Gwersyllt
John McKean, 30, Repairer, 15 Cheshire View, Spring Lodge, Wrexham
Colin V. Maggs, 17, Haulage, Talwrn House, Talwrn
Albert Mannion, 29, Filler, 12 Hill Crest, Spring Lodge, Wrexham
Thomas A. Manuel, 33, Repairer, 31 Meadows Lane, Spring Lodge
William Henry Martin, 37, Ripper, Newtown, Gresford
William V. Matthews, 18, Haulage, 22 Hill Street, Penycae
Samuel Matthias, 42, Fireman, 6 Eagles Place, Moss
William Meade, 39, Packer, 22 St. John's Road, Wrexham
George Mitchell, 23, Haulage, 35 James Street, Wrexham
Ernest Monks, 23, Haulage, Glan Afon Bwlchgwym
Edward Morley, 57, Repairer, 89 Council Houses, Bradley
Alfred Morris, 20, Haulage, 20 High Street, Penycae
Harry Nicholls, 32, Repairer, 3 Ashfield Road, Crispin Lane, Wrexham
John Nicholls, 29, Collier, 18 Beast Market, Wrexham
William Henry Nicholls, 25, Collier, 34 Farndon Street, Wrexham
Evan Henry Owens, 54, Packer, 22 Cunliffe Walk, Garden Village
Alex Palmer, 20, Haulage, Kingstown, Maesydre
Isaac Parry, 40, Repairer, 41 Western View, Wrexham Road, Lodge
Joseph Parry, 65, Repairer, 41 Western View, Wrexham Road, Lodge
John E. Parry, 31, Haulage, 19 Pisgah Hill, Pentre Broughton
John Richard Parry, 21, Haulage, 37 Manley Road, Wrexham
Stephen Penny, 23, Filler, 10 Stansty View, New
William H. Penny, 32, Ambulance Man, 60 Council Houses, Pandy
Frank C. Perrin, 23, Haulage, Finney Street, Rhosddu
Henry Peters, 38, Packer, 114 Pentre Lane, Llay
George Phillips, 22, Haulage, 75 Trevenna Way, Spring
Herbert Phillips, 30, Filler, 27 Haig Road, Hightown,
John Phillips, 40, Filler, Wrexham
John Frederick Pickering, 22, Haulage, Sycamore Terrace, Old Rhosrobin
Charles Powell, 57, Railman, 24 Dale Street, Rhosddu
Ernest Price, 27, Cutterman, 31 Moss Hill, Moss
Samuel Price, 37, Cutterman, Oldfield Terrace, Gresford
John Pridding, 32, Haulage, 19 Oxford Street, Wrexham
Mark Prince, 59, Repairer, Manley Road, Wrexham
William Prince, 30, Repairer, 23 Meadow Lea, Spring Lodge, Wrexham
Isiah Pritchard, 54, Repairer, 11 Woodland View, New Rhosrobin
Ernest Pugh, 49, Doggie, 5 Quarry Road, Brynteg
Thomas Pugh, 54, Collier, 61 Vernon Street, Rhosddu
John Ralphs, 53, Cutterman, Market Street, Wrexham
Thomas R. Rance, 21, Haulage, 11 High Street, Pentre Broughton
Albert Rees, 56, Pipeman, 3 Gatewen Road, New Broughton
Lloyd Reid, 20, Haulage, Engine Driver, 11 Bryn Gardden, Rhos
Arthur A. Roberts, 63, Repairer, Wire Mill Cottage, Bradley
Edward Roberts, 35, Collier, Bryn Estyn Cottages, Rhosnessney
Edward C. Roberts, 42, Collier, 12 Council Houses, Gresford
Ernest Roberts, 26, Filler, Little Penybryn, Abenbury, Wrexham
Frank Roberts, 26, Haulage, 3 Bury Street, Wrexham
George W. Roberts, 28, Filler, 12 Glan Afon, Maesydre, Wrexham
Idris Roberts, 16, Haulage, Pump Houses, Highfield, Stansty
John David Roberts, 47, Collier, 14 Lorne Street, Wrexham
John H. Roberts, 33, Packer, 2 Patison Row, Coedpoeth
Olwyn Roberts, 24, Filler, 32 Hill Street, Penycae
Percy Roberts, 26, Haulage, The Bungalow, Llydiart Fanny, Coedpoeth
Robert Roberts, 33, Repairer, 6 Off Brook Street, Rhos
Robert John Roberts, Filler Market Street, Wrexham
Robert Thomas Roberts, 57, Rail man, Crispin Lane, Rhosddu
Robert William Roberts, 38, Packer, 5 Forge Road, Southsea
Thos James Roberts, 19, Filler, Kendrick Place, Beast Market, Wrexham
William Roberts, 45, Packer, 41 Princess Street, Wrexham
William T. Roberts, 40, Collier, 165 Pentre Lane, Llay
William Robertson, 41, Cutterman, Spring Road, Rhosddu
Edward Llew Rogers, 20, Haulage, 18 New Houses Lane, Buckley
Grenville Rogers, 29, Repairer, 19 Wheatsheaf Lane, Gwersyllt
Harry Ross, 34, Collier, 45 Nelson Street, Wrexham
John Rowlands, 36, Cutterman, 85 Holt Road, Wrexham
John David Rowlands, 17, Haulage, Old Cross Foxes, Minera
William Salisbury, 36, Fireman, 48 Victoria Road, Brynteg
George Shaw, 63, Collier, Ashwood, Wrexham Road, Brynteg
John Shone, 34, Packer, Gresford, Wrexham
Richard Shone, 49, Doggie, High Street, Gresford
Arthur Slawson, 22, Haulage, Crescent Road, Wrexham
Leonard Smith, 20, Haulage, 25 Bennions Road, Huntroyde, Wrexham
Richard T. Stevens, 22, Haulage, 27 Pisgah Hill, Pentre Broughton
Albert Strange, 25, Collier, 21 Nelson Street, Wrexham
Stanley Stratford, 39, Packer, 9th Avenue, Llay
John Tarran, 59, Repairer, 77 Liverpool Road, Buckley
William Henry Taylor, 53, Cutter, Church Street, Holt
Berwyn Thomas, 26, Haulage, 2 Kent Road, Lodge, Brymbo
John Elias Thomas, 29, Repairer, 5 Queen's Terrace, Gwersyllt
Robert Thomas, 32, Haulage, Pant Hill, Rhos
Tec Thomas, 26, Collier, 51 Council Houses, Pandy
John Thornton, 24, Repairer, 6 Coronation Cottages, New Broughton
Edward Tittle, 44, Repairer, Smithy Lane, Acton, Wrexham
Ernest Trow, 41, Collier, 13 Huntroyde Avenue, Wrexham
Fred A. Valentine, 24, Haulage, 20 Glan Dwr, Acrefair
John Edward Vaughan, 28, Repairer, 15 Alford Street, Wrexham
John White, 38, Beltman, Chapel Cottages, Gresford
George Williams, 31, Collier, 3 Garden Terrace, Summerhill
Harold Williams, 37, Collier, 2 Osborne Terrace, Claypit Lane, Gresford
Hugh Ll. Williams, 43, Collier, Park Street, Rhosddu
John Williams, 62, Repairer, Cheetham's Lodging House, Mount Street, Wrexham
John Williams, 44, Repairer, 28 Dale Street, Wrexham
John Williams, 66, Repairer, 1 Council Houses, Brynteg
John D. Williams, 29, Repairer, 2 Vulcan Cottages, New Road, Southsea
John Thos Williams, 33, Packer, 12 Bryn-y-ffynon, Brymbo
Morris Williams, 24, Electrician, Pentre Lane, Llay
Reg Williams, 29, Electrician, Old Rhosrobin
Thomas Williams, 57, Repairer, Park View Stores, Bradley
William A. Williams, 29, Cutterman, 9 Gatewen Road, Pentre Broughton
John Walter Wilson, 32, Haulage, 5 Victoria Terrace, Coedpoeth
Henry Witter, 56, Repairer, The Mount, Gresford
Edward Wynn, 68, Repairer, 32 Bradley Road, Wrexham
William Walter Wynneyard, 47, Repairer, New Inn, Cefn-y-bedd
Morgan, J Yemm, 28, Repairer, 39 7th Avenue, Llay

Rescue Team
Dan Hughes, 56, Rescue, 23 1st Avenue, Llay
William Hughes, 54, Rescue, Jackson's Houses, New Rhosrobin
John Lewis, 48, Rescue, 9 Railway Terrace, Cefn-y-bedd

Killed by further explosion on 25.9.34
John George W. Brown, 59, Surface labourer

the fire to burn itself out. Despite this being done immediately, further underground explosions resulted in the seal being blown off the Dennis shaft on 25 September and one additional surface worker being killed by the flying debris. Only eleven bodies were ever recovered. Disaster appeals were launched almost immediately and a total of £566,871-4s-2d was collected. This money was placed in a fund which was to assist the dependants of those men who had lost their lives (there were 166 widows, 229 children, 194 partial dependants and 130 pensioners).

In the ensuing Board of Trade enquiry, which opened at Church House in Regent Street on 25 October 1934, considerable blame was heaped upon the mine manager William Bonsall* but the general opinion now is that he acted as a scapegoat for the mine owners who had failed to provide sufficient safety measures in the colliery. Legal proceedings were instituted against the owners, the manager, the under manager and some deputies and shot firers by the Director of Public Prosecutions in April 1937. Some of the charges were dismissed or withdrawn and the others resulted in fines totalling a derisory £140. Costs were set at £350.

The mine remained sealed for six months and an air-lock was built over the Martin shaft and specially trained men re-entered the shaft and commenced clearing and restoring the underground sections and production of coal was resumed in January 1936. By 1938 there were 1,370 people employed at Gresford (1,088 underground and 282 on the surface). The outbreak of war led to an expansion in the workforce to 1,588 by 1941 (1,265 underground and 293 on the surface). In 1939, pit-

Gresford Disaster, 1934. Crowds outside the colliery awaiting news of the trapped miners.

head baths were installed at a cost of £29,000, paid for by the Miners' Welfare Fund. The mine was nationalised on 1 January 1947 and continued in operation until closed in 1974. The Dennis headgear remained in position for some years after the closure but was eventually removed when the site was cleared for redevelopment as a small industrial estate in the 1980s. The actual wheel from the Dennis shaft was used as part of the Gresford Disaster Memorial.*

The known managers of Gresford Colliery were:
    G. H. Groves
    W. Bonsall*
    T. S. Charlton
    W. J. Charlton (1942)
    T. Jameson (1944)
    I. Kelly* (acting at time of closure)

Gresford Cottage
Situated in the Alyn valley, this was a small, ornamental thatched cottage built in the mid 18th century by George Warrington of Bryn-y-Ffynnon House.* After his death in 1770, the property passed to his widow and then his daughter, wife of John Parry, MP, who built the nearby Gresford Lodge.*

Gresford Disaster Memorial, Pandy
The memorial to the 265 men who lost their lives in the Gresford Disaster* of 1934 was unveiled at Pandy by HRH The Prince of Wales on 25 November 1982. Built of slate blocks it features the wheel from the headgear that once stood over the Dennis shaft. The names of all 266 miners are recorded on the memorial.

Gresford Lodge
This house was designed by James Wyatt of Weeford for John Parry (MP for Caernarfonshire) c.1790 and built close to Gresford Cottage* in the Alyn valley. John Parry was originally from Wernfawr, Llanbedrog, Caernarfonshire and was Attorney General for North Wales and Constable of Conwy Castle. In about 1820, the property was bought by William Egerton, the father of Sir Robert Eyles Egerton.* After the death of Lady Egerton in 1872, the house was sold to a number of individuals each of whom only remained there for a short time. In the 1930s, John Woolan, English amatuer golf champion lived there for a period followed by Colonel Lloyd Wadle.

The house was seriously affected by mining subsidence caused by the nearby Gresford Colliery* and was demolished as unsafe in 1956. All that remains today is the garden boundary road alongside the Llay–Gresford road, close to the bypass.

Gresford Sailing Club, Pant-yr-Ochain
This sailing club was established in 1958 by Arthur E. Jones (proprietor of the Pant-yr-Ochain Farm) and Reg Gibbs, utilising the Flash, one of the glacial kettle holes, located alongside the Old Wrexham Road. Although operating on what can only be described as a small area of water (approximately 10 acres) the club has thrived and has hosted a number of dinghy classes over the years including Heron, Graduate, Albacore, Snipe, Moth, Fireball, Topper, Enterprise, GP14, Mirror, Solo and Optimist (only the last five classes are currently sailed). A number of members have gone on to be very successful dinghy racers, perhaps the most successful being Hannah Blore,* a world champion in 2005. The club has had European champions in the Mirror Class (Graham and Martyn Ellis, Ben Dutton and Alex Brereton) and five boats in the Great Britain team which won the Mirror World Championship at Milford Haven.

The club operates a complete sailing programme from mid March until early December. It has encouraged children to take up sailing and since 1982 courses are run in conjunction with Gresford School and a junior section sails on Friday evenings. In November 2010, former club commodore, Rodney Evans, was presented with the Royal Yachting Association Volunteer Award in recognition of a lifetime commitment to the sport, in particular the work he has done with local youngsters.

In recent years the club has established a model-boat section.

Presidents:
	–70	Jack Jones
	1970–2010	Arthur Jones
	2010–	Keith Jones

Commodores
1959–65	R.W. Gibbs
1965–70	A.E. Jones
1971	S. Jones
1972	J. Beattie
1973	K. Ellis
1974	H. Bainbridge
1975	A.S.T. Smith
1976	A. Valentine
1977	L. Tucker
1978	D.T. Hawkey
1979	J.A. Wright
1980	R.R. Willcock
1981	Mrs M.L. Bainbridge
1982	R.S. Evans
1983	K. Ellis
1984	C.G. Jones
1985	P.J.R. Caldwell
1986	Miss R.M. Cook
1987	N.H. Bloor

Gresford Lodge. Note the effects of subsidence on the right of the verandah.

1988	K.A. Forbes
1989	G.E. James
1990	Mrs D.W. Turtle
1991	A. Rogerson
1992	R.W. Shires
1993	T.G. Ward
1994	O. Parry
1995	P.A. Sharples
1996	B.C. Cooper
1997	D.G. Morris
1998	I.T. Ware
1999	D.J Turtle
2000	C.G. Jones
2001	R. Norton
2002	L. Tucker
2003	S. Price
2004	Miss R.M. Cook
2005	G.N. Blore
2006	G.N. Blore
2007	R. Bendon
2008	Mrs S. Stapley
2009	R.S. Evans
2010	D.J. Turtle

Gresford Way, Little Acton
Built by H.R.&E. Roberts for Wrexham Borough Council in the early 1950s this development provided housing for the growing population of Little Acton which was caused by the expansion of Gresford Colliery.* It takes its name from the village of Gresford.

Greyhound Inn, High Street/Yorke Street
Shown in the 1833 survey as being located between High Street and Temple Row. In the 1841 census, it is recorded under Yorke Street with William Evans as the innkeeper. [DRO/DD/PL/90]

Greyhound, Holt Road
Taking its name from the crest on the arms of the Cunliffe family of nearby Acton Park,* the Greyhound was originally located on Holt Road, about 50 yards from its present site in a building which was also the blacksmith's shop of the village of Rhosnesni. This house was later used as accommodation for students at Cartrefle College* and was demolished in 2000 when a terrace of five small houses was built on the site. In 1881, the premises were occupied by Charles Edwards a tinplate worker and publican. The present Greyhound was built in c.1900.

Greyhound, The, Town Hill
Despite its name, there is no evidence that the Greyhound was ever a public house or inn. It was a large town house, probably built in the 17th century, set back from Town Hill on the site later occupied by N⁰ˢ 20, 22 and 23, just a little higher up the hill than the site of the present day Town Hill Post Office. It had many gables, incorporated a great deal of carved oak and was fronted by railings. By 1818 a new shop had been built on the site and the frontage was brought into line with the street by Hugh Davies (sometime before 1852) who then divided the property. This was probably the building that was eventually occupied by Ralph Williamson (a pork butcher, who died in 1873 and is buried in the Burial Ground* on Ruthin Road) and which was demolished in the early 1980s.

Greyhound Court, Yorke Street
Situated off Yorke Street and named after the Greyhound Inn,* High Street, it consisted of three poor quality houses.

Greystones, Chester Road
On 1 December 1875, Sir Robert Cunliffe, Bt, (see Cunliffe Family) sold half an acre of building land to the north of Grove Lodge* to John Thomas Trotter Pilkington (of Chevet Hey*), Colonel Charles Henry White and John Barnet (of Ashfield*). The house was almost certainly built as a children's home and, very shortly

Greystones, c.1965. Dr Brock is painting in the garden. [Noel Parry]

afterwards, Greystones was operating as Mrs White's Orphan Home. It accommodated 19 children of both sexes, aged between birth and 14/15 years, living as a single family unit, a quite revolutionary establishment for the late 19th century. In 1881 the headmistress was Miss Caroline E. Spicer (who is listed on the Census as being an 'Industrial teacher') who was assisted by Miss Julia Macgrath. [See the *Report of Charitable Endowments*, 1893, p. 514]. The house comprised an entrance hall, drawing room, library, large dining room (20' x 15'), kitchen, 10 bedrooms, 2 attic bedrooms and a bathroom. The house was sold by authority of the Board of Charity Commissioners on 21 October 1880. By 1914, the house was the property of the Misses Pickering of Grove Lodge* and was rented to John Ogwen Jones, the assistant manager of the Midland Bank. Later, Mr Jones bought the house and re-named it Preswylfod. In 1932/3, the house was sold to medical practitioners Dr R.S. and Mrs E.M. Brock (surgeon) who opened two surgeries, and the Jones family moved to N⁰ 6 Maes-y-Dre Road.* When the Brocks retired from medical practice the house (which had reverted to the name Greystones) was sold to the Wrexham & District Handicapped Children's Society on 10 April 1967 for £10,500 and converted into a residential home at a total cost of £42,500. The home was then handed over to Denbighshire Social Services Department and catered for 20 residents and provided two respite care beds. The advent of Care in the Community legislation during the 1980s and 1990s made it increasingly difficult for the home to continue to function and, eventually, the building regulations were such that it would have been impossible to adapt the building to meet the statutory requirements while remaining an economically viable project. The home closed in 1995 and was sold to the Corbanhill company for redevelopment. The house was demolished to be replaced by

Greystones, c.1965 — the junction of Foster Road and Chester Road. [Noel Parry]

a block of private flats using the same name. After demolition, the dressed stones of Greystones were shipped to Japan for use in a new building there.

Griffin, The, Beast Market
See The Bear, Beast Market.

Griffin, BEng, MSc, Derek *Chief Executive*
Born in Swansea on 12 May 1950, Derrick Griffin was educated at Dynevor Grammar School, the University of Wales Institute of Science and Technology, Cardiff and the University of Aston, Birmingham, gaining a BEng in industrial engineering and an MSc. in environmental planning and design. He was a Research Fellow at Aston from 1975–78, was then appointed an Industrial officer with Staffordshire County Council/Staffordshire Development Association (1978–80); County Industrial Officer, Mid Glamorgan County Council (1980–84); Director of economic and Community Development, Clwyd County Council (1984–90); Director of Corporate Services, Clwyd County Council (1990–92); Director of Personnel Administration, Liverpool City Council (1992–95); Chief Executive WCBC Shadow Authority (1995–96); WCBC (1996–2003). He was appointed National Health Service Regional Director for North Wales in 2003. He was appointed Chief Executive of the Children and Family Court Advisory and Support Services in Wales (CAFCASS CYMRU) in April 2008. He is a Fellow of Glyndŵr University and was appointed to the Board of Governors of the university in 2009. Married to Joyce, Derek Griffin has one daughter and lives in Mold.

Griffith, FRCS, Thomas Taylor *surgeon & antiquary*
One of eleven children of Thomas Griffith, surgeon of Wrexham, Thomas Taylor Griffith was born on 11 December 1785. He was the great grandson of John (Siôn) Griffith, a noted genealogist and herald whose collections he inherited. Educated at Dr Daniel Williams' School,* Chester Street and Wrexham Grammar School,* he became an apprentice to his father before furthering his medical training at Guy's and St Bartholomew's Hospitals in London and then Leeds and Paris, becoming a MRCS in 1817 and an Honorary Fellow of the RCS in 1844.

He joined his father in partnership in Wrexham in 1820 before setting up his own practice at Chester Street House* six years later. He married Mary Ann Robertson of Keavel, Fifeshire in 1826 and they had three children. In 1832, he attended to Princess Victoria who was staying at Wynnstay with her mother, the Duchess of Kent. He was a leading light behind the establishment of the north Wales branch of the British Medical Association of which he was elected President on two occasions.

He helped found the Dispensary* in Yorke Street* and, in 1838, the Wrexham Infirmary* and was an ardent supporter of the incorporation of the Borough in 1857. He endowed the new corporation with a special trust fund, but declined the offer of becoming the first Mayor. He helped to found the Ragged School* (later the Free School) in 1852.

His collection of Welsh documents was placed in the National Library of Wales in 1910 and included the famous *Black Book of Basingwerk*. He died on 6 July 1876 and is buried in the Ruthin Road Burial Ground.

Thomas Taylor Griffith, FRCS

Griffiths, Arnold 'Arnie' *local politician*
Born in Tan-y-Fron on 24 January 1935, the son of a steel worker, Arnold Griffiths was brought up in Coronation Terrace, New Broughton. He was educated at New Broughton and Penygelli Schools. After leaving school he was employed for a short time by Rogers & Jacksons in Wrexham before joining Brymbo Steel Works in the early 1950s. He became a crane driver in Electric Melting Shop 2 and the trade union branch officer, eventually rising to become the chairman of the Joint Union Committee at the works.

He was elected a Broughton community councillor in 1974 and a Labour member for the Brynteg Ward of WMBC in 1983, twice serving as chairman of the Council and became Mayor in May 1994. He was the area chairman for the Royal National Lifeboat Institution and a passionate supporter of Wrexham AFC. Married to Sheila, he lived at Windsor Road, New Broughton. Arnold Griffiths died on 22 October 2000.

In March 2001, Mrs Sheila Griffiths was elected to serve as the County Borough councillor for New Broughton.

Griffiths, David John *local politician*
Born on 25 February 1953, David Griffiths was educated at Gwersyllt Council Primary School and Bryn Alyn Secondary Modern School. He has worked for 37 years in the National Health Service.

After joining the Labour Party he became a community councillor for Gwersyllt and then a Wrexham County Borough councillor. He has been the chair of Gwersyllt Community Council (2009–11), the Labour Group on WCBC and the Environmental Licensing Committee and vice-chair of the Licensing Committee. He served as Mayor of Wrexham in 2008–09.

During his mayoral year the Eagles Meadow Shopping Centre* was opened, the Royal Welch Fusiliers* were given the Freedom of the Borough, NEWI* was officially chartered as Glyndwr University and the Mayor of Wrexham was granted an honorary fellowship.

David Griffiths married Denise in 1975 and they have two sons, David and Gavin.

Griffiths, Harold *local politician*
Born in the Lodge, the son of coal miner Robert Price Griffiths, Harold Griffiths moved to Wrexham when he was two years old.

He was elected Labour councillor for the Cefn Ward of WBC in 1952 and served for 20 years. A pattern maker by trade, he eventually set up a small foundry in Rhosddu, in partnership with his son. He was also the proprietor of a small grocery shop. He became Mayor in 1964 and an alderman on 27 June 1967.

He and his wife, Mary Elizabeth, were among the first people to move into Tower View on the new Queen's Park Housing Estate. At the time of his death in May 1991, he was living in Ffordd Dyfed.*

Griffiths, (Susan) Lesley *politician*
Born in Glasgow in 1960, Lesley Griffiths moved to north Wales as a child and to Wrexham when aged eleven. Educated at Ysgol-y-Grango and Ysgol Rhiwabon, she completed a medical secretarial course at the North-East Wales Institute before being employed for twenty years as an administrator at the Maelor

Hospital. She became a constituency assistant to the Wrexham MPs, Dr John Marek and Ian Lucas and served as a member of Coedpoeth Community Council for eight years. She has also been a school governor.

First selected to fight the Wrexham constituency for Labour in the 2003 National Assemby elections, she won the seat in 2007. She has served on three standing committees viz: Communities and Culture; Sustainability and Audit, as well as the Scrutiny Committees for Legislative Competence on Vulnerable Children, Affordable Housing and the Welsh Language. She is also a founding member of the Assembly's Cross-Party Group on Hospices and Palliative Care.

In December 2009 Lesley was appointed deputy minister for Science, Innovation and Skills.

Grosvenor Lodge, Grosvenor Road
Often known as Nº 1 Grosvenor Road, Grosvenor Lodge was built in 1869, in the Italianate style, for Isaac Shone,* engineer and local politician, who had previously resided at The Castle* in Pentre Felin.* Designed by the Wrexham architect J. R. Gummow* the house is built of brick with ashlar decorations. In the early 1880s, Thomas Eyton Jones, MD, JP, a surgeon, lived here, followed in the 1890s by Dr Drinkwater.

In 1924, the house was bought from the executors of Isaac Shone by Wrexham Borough Council and became the offices of the Surveyor's Department. This led to some very unsympathetic extensions being added to the property during the inter-war period.

The RWF War Memorial* was originally located in front of the house, on the corner of Regent Street and Grosvenor Road, and the curved wall which stood behind the memorial still survives. In addition, the Wrexham War Memorial* was sited inside the porch of the house. Both memorials were eventually moved to Bodhyfryd. The memorial to David Lord, VC* was also originally located here.

During the latter part of the 20th century, following the removal of the Surveyor's Department to Bodhyfryd House in Chester Street, Grosvenor Lodge became a health clinic and, following the establishment of the Wrexham Museum Service, the Museum office was housed in the red brick extension on Grosvenor Road with the reserve collection housed upstairs in the main house. By the 1990s, the house was in dire need of repair and renovation and was standing empty until bought by

Unveiling of the RWF Memorial outside Grosvenor Lodge, on the corner of Regent Street and Grosvenor Road, 15 November 1924.

Grosvenor Lodge – Nº 1 Grosvenor Road, with possibly members of Isaac Shone's family in the garden.

property developers Taymove who began a major refurbishment, commencing in 2001. The house is a Grade II listed building.

Grosvenor Road
This road takes its name from the Grosvenor family of Eaton Hall, Chester (later the Dukes of Westminster). The road was laid out at the end of the 1860s through open land known as Oak Tree Field and following a path known as the Rope Walk. The road was originally private and is believed to have been accessed by gates at each end. If this was the case, there is no surviving evidence of the gates, either documentary or structural. Palmer* believed that the first house to be built in the road was Brynhyfryd* with the house opposite, Grosvenor Lodge,* being the second.

Many of the large, Victorian houses in the street were designed by the local architect J.R. Gummow* for the new 'middle class' businessmen emerging in the town. At Nº 1 Grosvenor Road lived Isaac Shone* (see Grosvenor Lodge). Some of the houses, most notably Abbotsfield* (on the junction with Rhosddu Road) are in the neo-gothic style which was very fashionable in the mid 19th century. The Knox Mawer family lived at Nº 26 Grosvenor Road (now part of the offices of Gwilym Hughes & Partners) during the early part of the 20th century.

By 1881, most of Grosvenor Road had been developed and the original names, numbers and occupants were: *north-west side*– Grosvenor Lodge* (Nº 1), Thomas Eyton-Jones, JP, MD, FRCS, surgeon; Irvon Villa (Nº 2) Mrs Mary Powell; Irvon Villa (Nº 3) Mrs Elizabeth Frimston; Belgrave House (Nº 4) James F. Edisbury, chemist; Nythfa* (Nº 5) George W. F. Robbins, a student at Brasenose College, Oxford; Roslyn Villa (Nº 6) Yeoman Strachan, seed merchant and nurseryman; Kelso Villa (Nº 7) Mrs Harriet Elias; Bron Llwyn* (Nº 8) Edward Jones, hatter; (Nº 9) James Stevens, baker; Ellerslie House (Nº 10) Maj Augustus Bolle-de-Lasalle, paymaster staff; four vacant plots; (Nº 14) Mrs Anne Maria Wilson's ladies school; Hendre (Nº15) Joshua Broughton, farmer; Richmond Villa (Nº 16; this was the residence of the Bishop of Menevia* for short time in the early 20th century) Edward Taylor Fitch, wine merchant; Abbotsfield* (Nº 17) Revd George Turner Birch. *South-east side* – Brynhyfryd* (Nº 29) Charles Hughes, publisher; Plas Darland* (Nº 28) Edward Davies, MD, medical practitioner; (Nº 27) Simon Jones, confectioner and Baptist preacher; Melton Villa (Nº 26) James C. Morrell, railway and corporation stock holder; Trevor Villas (Nºˢ 1&2) Mrs Sarah Pryce-Jones's school and Moses Wright, draper;

Ilar Villa (N° 21) William Jones, boot & shoe dealer; Oak Villas (N° 20) Edward Ll. Lloyd, insurance secretary; Oak Villas (N° 19) Louis Frederic Scott, dental surgeon; (N° 18) Ishmael E. Evans, solicitor's managing clerk.

By 1951, Grosvenor Road had become a street of offices with very few of the houses still in residential use and the new numbers and occupants were: *north-west side* – N°s 1 & 3 (Grosvenor Lodge) were WBC and WRDC offices; N° 5 (Irvon Villas) was a Welsh Board of Health office; N°s 7 & 9 (Belgrave House and Nythfa*) were the Westminster Temperance Hotel; N° 11 (Rosslyn Villa) was the National Health Service office; N° 13 (Kelso Villa) was the Ministry of Pensions office; N°s 15 & 17 (Bron Llwyn* and Ellerslie House) were the Roman Catholic Convent Grammar School;* N°s 21 & 25 were dental surgeries. *South-east side* – N° 2 was the Assistance Board Area Office; N° 4 was divided into a wholesale confectioner's premises, the Workers' Educational Association, the Wrexham Trades Council and the Labour Party Headquarters; N° 6 was shared between the Mine Workers' Institute,* the Gresford Colliery Disaster Relief Fund office and the Ministry of Fuel and Power office; N° 8 was a dental surgery; N° 12 was the premises of a masseur; N° 16 was the Denbighshire Medical Officer of Health's office and School Clinic; N° 18 was a site occupied by two new buildings *viz* the King Edward VII Welsh National Memorial Tuberculosis Institute and the Telephone Exchange*; N°s 20 & 22 were the Wrexham Nursing Home; N° 24 was the Ministry of National Insurance office; N° 30 was the Welsh Board of Health and Regional Medical Officer's office. [DRO/DD/DM/1050/1–26]

The Department of Social Security offices were built in the mid 1970s (opened by 1978) for £1.25 million, on the site previously occupied by the Roman Catholic Grammar School. This building had originally been intended to accommodate the Wealth Tax Inspectorate but, when plans to establish that department came to an end when the government Bill was quashed, the offices remained empty for three months until taken over by the Department of Health and Social Security and the Pay As You Earn (PAYE) department of the Inland Revenue.

Grosvenor Shopping Centre, Regent Street
This was designed by local architects G. Raymond Jones, Anderson & Associates in association with John Laing Design. This large shopping-centre development, covering the whole block between Hill Street* and St Mark's Road,* was co-ordinated and funded by Grosvenor Estates and was completed in 1972. The major construction problem was the re-location of Bryn-y-Ffynnon Church* which stood on a freehold site in the centre of the block. A 'flying lease' on a new chapel on the first floor of the development was offered to the Methodists but, as an entrance between the shop premises was unacceptable to Grosvenor Estates, a new entrance was built in the middle of the pavement with a bridge connection to the chapel at first floor level.

Grove House, Chester Street
Between 1762 and 1765, James Buttall,* a retired but wealthy London ironmonger, bought land in Pant-y-Crydd (*Trans.* shoemaker's hollow) and Pant-y-Glofer (*Trans.* clover hollow), which had formerly been some of the town fields lying along the west side of Chester Road (they had previously been the property of Thomas Meredith of Pentrebychan) – where he began to build a house. The house was located between Chester Street* and Rhosddu Road* in the area now occupied by Yale College.* In 1793, the property passed to his grandson Jonathan Buttall (who may have been the subject of Gainsborough's famous portrait 'The Blue Boy'), although there is no evidence that he ever lived here. In 1823, the house was converted into a private

The main entrance to Grove House which later became the Groves Academy then Grove Park School.

boarding school known as The Groves or The Groves Academy.*
Owners and residents:
    1762   James Buttall
    1793   Jonathan Buttall
    *c.*1797 Mrs Fryer (widow of John Fryer of Aldermanbury, London who bought a great deal of the surrounding land giving the house grounds amounting to some 22 acres)
    *c.*1817 Epharim Parkins (who later leased it out as a school)
    1823   James Jackson (converted the house into the Groves Academy*)

Grove Lodge, Grove Road
The home of John Jones, co-founder of the Island Green Brewery.* The house appears on the 1872 survey and was designated N° 17 Grove Road. In 1913, Jones left the house, and that adjoining (Preswylfod – possibly Plas Darland), to his nieces, Elizabeth and Harriet Roberts of Eyton (on condition that they lived there for at least six months of every year) for the term of their life, thereafter to go to his nephew, Frederick William Morris and, after him, to his heirs. Grove Lodge was the home of the Sumner family from mid way through the Second World War until just after the restoration of peace when they moved to Chevet Hey.* Dr Martin Cecil Shirley Stephens then moved into Grove Lodge and remained there until the mid 1960s. In 1968, various plans were put forward for the house, all of which involved its demolition. These included:
– building 36 flats on the site
– building 26 town houses on the site
– building a new Jerusalem Welsh Methodist chapel, schoolroom and offices on the site.

Grove Park County School for Boys, c.1900.

The house was eventually demolished and the site was used for the construction of an extension to Plas Darland flats. The red-brick wall and gate posts on Chester Road are all that remain of Grove Lodge, other than the name which has been used as the name of a small close off Foster Road.

Grove Lodge Close, Foster Road
This close was built in the 1990s on land that would have originally been part of the garden of Grove Lodge.*

Grove Park
See Grove House.

Grove Park Academy
See the Groves Academy.

Grove Park County School for Boys, Chester Road
Founded in 1895 from the school which had previously been known as The Groves Academy,* Grove Park provided grammar school education to a high standard for boys from Wrexham and the surrounding area. Originally, the school was housed in the old Groves Academy buildings. The sale of the old Grammar School buildings to WBC provided the basis of a fund totalling £11,500 which led to the construction of new red brick buildings facing Chester Road which were opened in 1902.

By this time girls, albeit in small numbers, were also being educated at Grove Park. In 1939 the girls moved out into a new, purpose-built school on the opposite side of Chester Road.

In the late 1950s and early 1960s there were large extensions built in the form of a new gymnasium, science block and additional classrooms. A new domestic science block was built in preparation for the introduction of comprehensive education throughout Denbighshire in 1972 when the school became a mixed-sex comprehensive.

The new school retained the name Grove Park until its closure in 1983 when its pupils and staff were absorbed into the Groves High School. The buildings were then empty for some years before being used as part of the NEWI School of Art. With the transfer of resources between NEWI* and Yale Sixth Form College in the early 1990s, the Grove Park School site was absorbed into the new Yale College. A short illustrated history of the school was written by ex-pupil Gwynne Belton in 1997 *Grove Park Schools – a collection of pictures*.

Headmasters:
  1895 William James Russell
  1913 Frank P. Dodd
  1931 J. R. Edwards
  1935 D. J. Lloyd
  1946 Jonathan Jones
  1950 E. Haddon Roberts
  1966 Nathaniel White
  1969 John H. Marwood (acting headmaster)
  1970 Neville H. Newhouse
  1978 Jim Bevan

Grove Park County School for Girls, Chester Road
Founded in 1896 as part of the Grove Park School for Boys, the school was accommodated in the old Grove Park School buildings. By 1925 the school had some 300 pupils who were accommodated in the north end of the school, close to Grove Park Road.*

In 1939 the school moved into new, purpose-built accommodation on the opposite side of Chester Road and by the end of the Second World War, had 580 girls on the roll. By the late 1960s it was obvious that comprehensive education was coming to Denbighshire and, despite strong campaigns to maintain single-sex schools in Wrexham, Grove Park County School for Girls was amalgamated with Grove Park County School for Boys in 1972 and two new mixed gender comprehensive schools emerged.

The old 'Girls School' was originally designated Park Avenue Comprehensive but this was eventually changed to Bromfield High School. In 1983, Bromfield High School merged with Grove Park School to become The Groves High School, both accommodated on the former Grove Park County School for Girls site.

Headmistresses:
  1896 Miss Annie Jane Jones
  1925 Miss Alicia Gower Jones
  1944 Miss Margaret M. Copland
  1965 Miss Violet Brown

(See also Grove Park County School for Boys, Grove Park Comprehensive School, The Groves High School and Bromfield High School)

Grove Park Little Theatre
This was formed in 1925 as the Grove Park Old Boys' Amateur Dramatic Society. The first plays to be performed were *Thread of Scarlet* (by J.J. Bell) and *Motoring* (by Harry Tate) which were put on in the Victoria Hall, Brook Street, on 12 October 1925, the funds raised going to the YWCA and YMCA. The next performance was Sheridan's *The Rivals* at the Church House* in November 1927. In 1936, it was decided to merge the society with the Grove Park Old Girls' Dramatic Scoiety to form the Grove Park Amateur Dramatic Society with Dr John Reid being elected its first President. Originally accommodated in the billiard room at Bodlondeb* the society was given land in Caxton Place* by its President where a wooden building was erected in 1939 at a cost of £180. Almost immediately, the hut was requisitioned for the war effort and it was not returned to the society until 1945. It moved to its present premises, the former Hill Street English Presbyterian Church,* in April 1954. The new theatre opened on 21 November 1954 with three one-act plays.

In the 1970s, the Wrexham Youth Theatre was established and given free use of the theatre on Hill Street and in 1975 the society joined the Little Theatre Guild of Great Britain, changing its name to Grove Park Little Theatre.

In 1981 the society staged the first of its regular pantomimes.

The auditorium, which can accommodate 170 people, was refurbished in 1999 and further front of house projects were commenced in 2010.

Grove Park Road
This road linked Rhosddu Road with Chester Road and was laid out in the 1860s. The two houses still standing on the corner of Grove Park Road and Rhosddu Road (N°s 9 & 11 Grove Park Road) were built in about 1862 by George Simpson who let N° 9

to George Bradley* and Nº 11 to Isaac Shone.* In 1869, Bradley bought both houses for £1,204-19s-0d. In 1900 they were sold to Robert Stobo of Park Lodge* for £1,400 and, following the death of his widow in 1961, they were bought by his nephew James Stobo. In 1994 they were bought by Hawksmere Properties Ltd. The other significant residence in this road was Roseneath,* built by William Low* in 1864/5.

Grove Park Road also provided access to Grove Park County School for Boys* and the War Memorial Hospital Casualty Department. Following the construction of the inner ring road link from Rhosddu Road to Chester Road and Powell Road, Grove Park Road was closed to traffic and now forms the main thoroughfare through the Yale College campus.

Grove Park School, Grove Park Road
This school was established in 1972 as a mixed-sex comprehensive following the merger of Grove Park County School for Boys* and Grove Park County School for Girls.* The school was accommodated in the premises of the former boys school. In 1983 as part of the re-organisation of secondary education in Wrexham, the school merged with Bromfield School and the Grove Park Road premises were closed. The buildings now form part of Yale College.*
Headteachers:
    1972   N. Newhouse
    c.1978 James Bevan

Grove Road/Street
In 1760, land just outside the town centre, to the west of Chester Road, known as Pant-y-Crydd (*Trans.* shoemaker's hollow) and Erw Row (*Trans.* acre row) was bought by William Dymock of Bodhyfryd* and Little Acton Farm.* By 1798, it appears to have been the property of Arthur Bolton of Half Moon Street, Piccadilly, London who left it in his will to a number of trustees. The following year, the land to the north-west of Grove Road, bordering onto the property of Sir Foster Cunliffe of Acton Park,* was divided into 18 lots and sold at public auction to a number of buyers, including George Kenyon and Ann Fryer, the latter being one of the trustees of Bolton's will. By 1815, both Grove House and the surrounding land were owned by her and the area had assumed the English name of Grove Park. Some of the land was sold for development in 1854 to Ephraim Parkin, the terms of sale stipulating that any villas that were to be built 'must not be seen from Grove House'. Three years later, James Parkin sold four plots of building land to Robert Thornley of Birkenhead for £620 and in 1860, he sold the plots to James Ollerhead. By 1873, Ollerhead had built two semi-detached houses (now the White House nursing home) and sold one plot, alongside Epworth Lodge, to Ezekiel Mason (where Albert Villa* was built). In 1880, the remaining vacant plot was owned by Thomas James Ollerhead, a surgeon, of Minehead, the great-nephew of James Ollerhead, and he sold it to Wrexham plasterer and slater, Gwilt Cathrall who built Ivy Grove* on the site. The street that was originally laid out was called Grove Street before becoming Grove Road by 1880. Some of the houses here were certainly built by 1866, the first being Bodlondeb* (located on the north corner of Grove Road and Rhosddu Road and the second High Grove* (later re-named Plas Darland). The last house to be built on the north-west side was Ivy Grove. An Italianate villa named Romano was built on the south-east side sometime after 1881.

In 1881 the houses were named, numbered and occupied as follows: *North-west side* – Bodlondeb* (Nº 1) William Overton, ironmonger; Leeswood House (Nº 2) Tubal Cain Jones, draper; (Nº 3) Thomas Bennion Acton, solicitor; (Nº 4) vacant site; Albert Villa* (Nº 5) Ezekiel Mason, tailor; Epworth Lodge* (Nº 6) Revd E. Evans, minister; High Grove (Nº 7) Alexander Wilson Edwards, JP; Grove Lodge* (Nº 8) John Jones, brewer. *South-east side* – no properties.

In 1951, the houses were named, numbered and occupied as follows: *North-west side* – Carlton Grange* (Nº 1) flats; Plas Gwilym* (Nº 3) Dr W. Glynn-Evans; (Nº 5) J. T. Wright; (Nº 7) J. Bagnall Bury; Nythva* (Nº 9) Raymond Gill; Ivybank* (Nº 11) Mrs E. A. Underwood; Epworth Lodge* (Nº 13) Revd J. C. Jones; Plas Darland* (Nº 15) flats; Grove Lodge* (Nº 17) Dr M. C. S. Stevens. *South-east side* – (Nº 2) Nurses Home;* Romano* (Nº 4) nurses home.

A nurses home for the Wrexham & District War Memorial Hospital,* named Plas yn Llwyn,* was built on the south side of Grove Road (it was demolished to make way for the Nightingale House Hospice*). Also on the south side of the road, opposite 'Nythfa', the Wrexham Red Cross Society had its headquarters for many years.

Groves Academy, Chester Road.
Shortly after 1823, James Jackson leased the Groves House,* made several additions to the buildings, and converted it into a private boarding school for boys which appears in the 1833 survey. In the 1841 census the school and household are shown as having a headmaster (Jackson), a matron (Mrs Jackson), seven female servants, one male servant, two teachers –James Floater and Abraham Little and 50 pupils aged between 8 and 15. This school was also known as Grove Park Academy.

By the 1860s, the school had become the principal school for the education of the sons of many prominent men of Wrexham and was posing a serious threat to the long-established Wrexham Grammar School.* In 1895 the premises were sold by Mrs Pryce-Jones to the new Denbighshire County Council and the school became a County School under the terms of the Welsh Intermediate Education Act. At the same time, The Groves also took over what remained of the Grammar School. The new school was officially named the Wrexham County School but to the pupils and the people of Wrexham it was Grove Park County School.*
Headmasters:
    1823   James Jackson
    1824   Matthew Sibson
    1836   James Parkins (a relative of the owner of the house)
    1841   James Jackson
    1861   John Pryce-Jones
    1877   William James Russell

Groves High School, Pen-y-Maes Avenue.
In 1983, Bromfield High School changed its name to The Groves. Although occupying the same site as the former Grove Park County School for Girls, the main entrance has been moved to Pen-y-Maes Avenue.
Headteachers:
    1985   Thomas Davies
    1985   Terry Wales

Guildhall, The, Chester Street
WBC, which had previously been accommodated in part of Bryn-y-Ffynnon House,* purchased the old Wrexham Grammar School* building in Chester Street in 1883 for £2,500 and adapted it for use as a municipal building, giving it the name of the Guildhall. Many prominent townspeople and councillors saw this as an extravagance that was ill-afforded. It was mentioned at the time that the building might eventually be demolished and the site used for the construction of a new, purpose-built Guildhall. A comment in 1897, when the council was considering the demolition of the County Buildings in Regent Street and the building of a new Guildhall on that site, described the Chester Street building as, 'grotesque, not strikingly handsome and incapable of fulfilling its obligations'. An extension was built to the premises in 1894 which housed the Wrexham Fire Brigade on

the ground floor with the Wrexham School of Arts and Sciences* on the first floor. Behind this building, at the northern end of the old Grammar School was the Wrexham Free Library (until the new library was opened in Yspyty in 1907). To commemorate the death of Queen Victoria in 1901 a statue was placed in front of the Guildhall, facing Chester Street (see Queen Victoria Statue). During the Second World War an air raid shelter was built in front of the Guildhall. It took until 1960/61 for the Council to build a new Guildhall on Llwyn Isaf* and the Chester Street premises were not demolished until the 1970s. For most of the 1970s, 1980s and 1990s the site of the Guildhall was used as a public car park. Today, it is the site of the T.J. Hughes store and part of the Henblas Square* shopping precinct.

Guildhall, Llwyn Isaf
WBC had deliberated for many years over the possibility of building a new, purpose-built Guildhall and various sites were considered including, as early as the 1890s, the County Buildings* in Regent Street. In 1939, plans were produced for a new Guildhall, assembly hall and fire station on Bodhyfryd, but the proposal for a ten-penny rate to cover the £99,000 cost was rejected by the government. The outbreak of war in September meant that matters were then put on hold and it was not until 1951 that the former vicarage and grounds at Llwyn Isaf* were bought and the site for the new Guildhall was cleared.

Based on a neo-Georgian design the new Guildhall was built by E.W. Gittins & Sons at a cost of £150,000 and was opened on 25 May 1961 by HRH Princess Alexandra. Following the creation of WMBC in 1974, plans were drawn up for the extension of the Guildhall, the cost of which would be offset by the sale of the old Imperial Hotel* which had been the offices of Wrexham Rural District Council* for many years. While plans and building work progressed, the new Council made use of the old WRDC offices at Rhostyllen.

A large brass lantern was presented to WMBC by Lt-Col Mike Burkham of the RWF in 1977. Previously, the lantern had been one of two that stood in the RWF Headquarters at Hightown Barracks. Also displayed in the Guildhall are various documents and artefacts relating to the Honorary Freemen of the Borough, portraits of several Mayors and the Colours of the 1st Bn RWF.

Guildhall Square, Chester Street
See Guildhall, Chester Street.

Guildhall Street
Named after the original Wrexham Guildhall which stood alongside it, facing Chester Street. This street was once known as Bottle Street. It has now disappeared under the Henblas Square* shopping precinct.

The Guildhall on Chester Street. This building was formerly Wrexham Grammar School. The Fire Station stands on the right. This site is now occupied by the T. J. Hughes store in Henblas Square/Chester Street.

The Guildhall, Llwyn Isaf [WCBC]

Guildhall Square, Chester Street with the statue of Queen Victoria.

Gummow Family

Benjamin Gummow – architect
Born c.1766, Benjamin Gummow trained with S. P. Cockerell, who employed him as a clerk of works on St Margaret's Church, Westminster (1799–1802). In 1803, he was appointed supervising architect at Eaton Hall, near Chester and afterwards appears to have remained resident in north Wales. In 1827, he was employed by Sir Watkin Williams Wynn at Wynnstay, Ruabon, and appears to have had a house on the estate. He died in Ruabon in March 1844.

Michael Gummow – architect & Borough Surveyor
Born on 24 January 1802, he was the nephew of Benjamin Gummow.* Officially recorded as a builder, he served as the first Borough Surveyor of Wrexham from 1858–61 at a salary of £25 per annum. He married Sarah (1800–84) and was the father of James Reynolds Gummow. He may be the Mr Gummow that is shown as living in Wrexham Fechan* in the 1833 survey and was certainly the Michael Gummow living at Bridge House* in 1857. He died on 21 May 1876 and is buried in the Dissenters Burial Ground.*

James Reynolds Gummow – architect
The son of Michael and Sarah Gummow* and great-nephew of architect Benjamin Gummow,* James Reynolds was born on 24 January 1826. He practised as an architect in Wrexham and was responsible for many of the Victorian villas built in Grosvenor Road and Sontley Road including Abbotsfield,* Plas Tirion,* Brooklands* and Grosvenor Lodge*, as well as Fronheulog* in Bwlchgwyn and Stoneleigh Hall, Rossett. He was the author of *Hints on House Building* which was published in Wrexham in 1874, containing plans and photographs of some of the houses

Stoneleigh Hall, Rossett, designed by J.R. Gummow.

which he had built in the town. James Gummow resided at N° 3 Salisbury Park, Wrexham (possibly Oteley House*) and died on 25 February 1877 and is buried in the Dissenters Burial Ground* on Rhosddu Road. [DRO/DD/DM/357/2].

Michael John Gummow – architect
Born in Wrexham c.1856, the grandson of architect James Reynolds Gummow.* He lived at N° 3 Salisbury Park. He was articled to William Turner of Wrexham and designed the Drill Hall* in Poyser Street and Salem Independent Chapel in Bank Street, Rhosllanerchrugog as well as two houses on Chester Road (N°ˢ 14 & 16). His brother, William H. Gummow, was a coal merchant in King Street.

Gummow's Building, Brook Street
Recorded on the 1841 census, it provided living accommodation for five families. Its exact location is unknown.

Gwenfro, river
This small river, which forms the boundary between Wrexham Fawr* and Wrexham Fechan,* takes its name from *gwen fro* (*Trans.* fair vale or country). On 1 December 1874, WBC approved the culverting of the Gwenfro (referred to in the Council Minutes as 'the Town Brook') from Pentre Felin to Bridge Street, a task which was completed by 1879. The prime mover behind the scheme was Isaac Shone.*

Gwenfro Schools, Queensway.
Plans for the building of a second primary school in Queen's Park were announced in 1954. In September 2007, the infant and junior schools merged to become Gwenfro County Primary School. In 2010 the school had 259 pupils on the roll.

Headteachers:
Juniors:
1958–76	Emrys Charles
1976–83	Herbert Tunnah Williams
1983–97	Russell Jones
1997–2007	Dominic Coope

Infants:
?	Miss Williams
?	Miss Glenys Roberts
?	Miss Beryl Williams
?	Mrs Nancy M. Davies
?	Mrs Monica Wynn
?	Mrs Jean Lewis
?	Mrs Janice Ashford

Primary
2007	Mrs Janice Ashford

Gwern Alyn, Percy Road
This substantial Italianate style villa on the corner of Hillbury Road, bears a remarkable resemblance to the houses designed by James Reynolds Gummow.* In 1919 it was the home of the Johnson family. In recent years it has become a residential home for the elderly.

Gwersyllt Hall, Gwersyllt
See Gwersyllt Park.

Gwersyllt Hill, Summerhill
This was the home of Captain Ellis Sutton who served in the Civil War in Lord Byron's Foot and commanded Colonel Robinson's* own company. He was present at the siege of Chester and was fined £75 by the Committee for the Compounding of Delinquents. Impoverished, he was forced to sell his house to Colonel Sir Jeffrey Shakerley, Bt.* The house was later the property of ironmaster Richard Kyrke after whom it passed to his son-in-law Thomas Penson II* who carried out extensive alterations and enlargements to the house in 1841.

Gwersyllt Hill, c.1910.

During the latter decades of the 19th century, the house was occupied by James Sparrow, ironmaster and colliery owner who, in 1881, employed 'on average 420 men'. The house declined rapidly during the 20th century and ended its days as a nightclub, becoming known locally as 'Dracula's Castle'. It was demolished in *c*.1980.

Gwersyllt Park, c.1720.

Gwersyllt Park, Gwersyllt
This house (also called Gwersyllt Hall), which stood just to the north of the main Gwersyllt to Cefn-y-Bedd road, in what is now the Alyn Waters Country Park, belonged to a family named Sutton but was sold to Dr Nicholas Robinson, Bishop of Bangor, in the mid 16th century. In Norden's survey of 1620, the estate (of 199 acres) is shown as being owned by William Robinson, the bishop's son. William's son, John Robinson,* served in the Royalist army during the Civil War* and the estate was sequestered (confiscated) by the Committee for the Compounding of Delinquents and leased to Captain Roger Sontley of Common Wood, Holt, a Parliamentary officer. In 1651, the property was bought by Piers Robinson who built a new house called Plas Newydd.

On the restoration of the monarchy in 1660, the estate was returned to John Robinson and it was held by his direct descendants until William Robinson drowned in 1739, leaving debts of over £12,000 and the property was put up for sale in 1745 (see also Acton Park). It was bought by Gwin Lloyd of Hendwr, Merionethshire. In 1775, the estate was again sold, this time to John Humberston Cawley, the nephew of the late William Robinson, who resided at Upper Gwersyllt. He later sold it to John Atherton of Liverpool who was living at Gwersyllt Park by 1805. Sometime around the turn of the 19th century the house was 'remodelled' into that which is shown in the enclosed

Gwersyllt Park, c.1900.

photograph. By the end of the 19th century it was the residence of Mr Humble then of Colonel M. J. Wheatley.

The house, like so many others around Wrexham, was badly affected by mining subsidence and was demolished in about 1910. Much of the landscape around the house was changed during the 1980s when the park became a corporation rubbish tip. The grounds have now been turned into the Alyn Waters Country Park. The only remaining evidence of the house is the boundary wall alongside the A541 and the entrance gate to the stables. Park Wall in Gwersyllt is a reference to Gwersyllt Park.

Gwydyr-Jones, DSO, OBE, DL, **Brigadier Llewellyn** *soldier*
Born in 1900 the son of Evelyn Gwydyr-Jones of Richmond, Surrey, Llewellyn Gwydyr-Jones was educated at Marlborough School and the Royal Military College, Sandhurst. He was commissioned in the RWF in 1920 and served in Madagascar and Burma during the Second World War, becoming a lieutenant-colonel in 1942 and a brigadier in 1945. He retired in 1952. He was a deputy lieutenant of Denbighshire, a county councillor and High Sheriff of Denbighshire in 1966. He died in 1986. He lived at River House, Erbistock, Wrexham. Gwydyr Way was named after him.

Gwydyr Way, Hermitage
Developed by WBC in the 1970s on land that had previously been part of the Hermitage* army camp/farm, this street was named after Brigadier Llewellyn Gwydyr-Jones.*

Gwyn, St Richard *Roman Catholic martyr*
Born at Llanidloes, Montgomeryshire, *c*.1557, Richard Gwyn was brought up as a Protestant and was educated at Oxford and St John's College, Cambridge. He was appointed a schoolmaster at Overton in 1562 and later worked in Wrexham and in other schools in Wales. He acquired a considerable reputation as a Welsh scholar, and married Catherine by whom he had six children. The arrival of seminary priests in Wales led to his conversion to Roman Catholicism and he was arrested at Wrexham in 1579 and incarcerated in Ruthin gaol where he was offered his freedom if he would conform to the Anglican church, which he declined to do. In 1580, he was again arrested and transferred to Wrexham where he was interrogated, persecuted and forcibly carried into the Protestant services at the Parish Church before being brought before several assizes. In May 1583, he was brought before the Council of the Marches and was tortured at Bewdley and Bridgnorth before being sent back to Wrexham where he was held prisoner in the Black Chamber* until the autumn assizes. He was brought to trial on 9 October, found guilty of treason and the following day was sentenced to be executed. He was offered his life if he acknowledged Elizabeth I as the Head of the Church but, again, refused to do so.

On 17 October, 1584 he was taken from the gaol and spoke to the crowd outside, saying 'Weep not for me, for I do but pay the rent before the rent day' and then gave 5 shillings in silver to the poor. He then gave his wife 11 shillings and his beads before saying farewell to her and their baby. His arms were then tied behind his back before he was laid on a hurdle and drawn through the streets to the place of execution. Traditionally, this place is believed to have been the Beast Market but it may have been a little further out of the town, closer to Pwll yr Ywd* or possibly somewhere on the site of the present Tesco car park. There, a triangular gallows had been erected. As Gwyn was dragged through the streets, the sky is reported to have clouded over and rain began to fall.

On reaching the gallows, Gwyn was untied and climbed the ladder unaided. The executioner kneeled to ask his forgiveness and Gwyn replied 'I do forgive thee before God and I wish thee no more harm than I wish mine own heart'. The charges on which he had been found guilty were then read out and he denied any treason to which the vicar of Wrexham asked, 'Dost thou acknowledge the Queen to be the Supreme Head of the Church?' Gwyn replied 'I acknowledge her to be the lawful Queen of England, and otherwise I never said; and I beseech you all to be witness hereof, that they belie me not when I am dead'. He then made a lengthy speech and the executioner was ordered to carry out his duty. Having again asked for, and received forgiveness, the executioner placed the noose around Gwyn's neck and twisted the ladder away. Swinging on the rope, Gwyn beat his chest with both hands until he passed out when the Sheriff ordered him cut down and carried to the hurdle and, as the executioner prepared to cut off his 'secret parts', Gwyn recovered consciousness. A small hole was then made in his stomach through which his guts were pulled piecemeal. The executioner then 'mangled his [Gwyn's] breast with a butcher's axe to the very chine, most pitifully; then tearing his entrails he threw them into the fire before his face, whereat the servant of God never shrunk, nor once shewed any sign of impatience, but still continued knocking his breast, until the sheriff's men held his arms back by force. He then lifted his head and shoulders, looked at what was being done and said 'O Dduw gwyn, pa beth ydyw hwn?' ('Good God, what is this?') The gaoler replied 'It is an execution for the Queen's majesty' and Gwyn called out 'Jesus have mercy upon me' and his head was struck off, lifted up and the executioner declared 'This is White's head!' but did not declare him a traitor. Gwyn's torso was then quartered. One quarter and his head were sent to Denbigh and displayed above the town gateway. A second quarter was sent to Ruthin and third to Holt. The final quarter was displayed on the gallows in Wrexham.

On Christmas Eve, 1584, the remains in Wrexham and Holt were stolen and the armed search party that was sent out on Christmas Day failed to find any trace of them. One bone, reputed to have been from Gwyn's arm, eventually turned up in Manresa Jesuit House in London from where it was transferred to St Mary's Roman Catholic Cathedral,* Wrexham in 1950.

Regarded as the first Welsh Catholic martyr, Richard Gwyn was beatified by Pope Pius XI on 15 December 1929 and canonised by Pope Paul IV on 25 October 1970. Until the late 1990s, on the Sunday nearest the anniversary of his execution, an annual procession of Roman Catholics made its way to the Beast Market.

In 2000 the cathedral of St Mary's, Wrexham, commissioned an icon of St Richard Gwyn which was created by iconographer Sister Petra Clare at the monastic skete at Cannich in Scotland. The icon depicts Richard Gwyn himself with nine scenes from his life and death. The icon was consecrated by Bishop Edwin Regan* on 15 October, 2000. A detailed account of his life was published in 1970 – *Richard Gwyn – Man of Maelor: Martyr or Traitor?* by Thomas Dempsey, Bolton.

H

Hackett, Edward Stanley *local politician*
The son of a railway foreman, Edward Hackett was born in Shifnal, Shropshire where his father was the station master. In 1896, the family moved to Blaenau Ffestiniog and then, when Edward was aged 6, to Acrefair, followed by Ruabon and Coedpoeth before returning to Shropshire in 1923 and finally, in 1925, moving to Wrexham. He was educated at Acrefair School and joined the railway in 1909, working in Llangollen, Bala, Frongoch and Wrexham. During his various placements he learned to speak Welsh and was secretary of the Wrexham Branch of the National Union of Railwaymen from 1937–47. In 1935 he was elected a Labour councillor for Wrexham Fechan Ward (later Erddig Ward) and served as Mayor in 1946. In 1947, he left the railway and joined the accounts department of British Celanese where he worked for 15 years before retiring in 1961. At British Celanese he served as chairman of the Welfare Association and secretary of the Staff Council. Appointed a Justice of the Peace in 1939, he became chairman of the Wrexham Borough Magistrates in 1952, a position which he held for 14 years. A founder chairman of the Hightown Youth Club he also served as a governor of various schools and was awarded the Gold Medal and bar of the St John's Ambulance Brigade. He married schoolteacher Ethel May Jones, the daughter of the headmaster of Minera School in 1919, and they had two children. Ethel died in 1956 and, four years later, he married Ada. He retired from the Council on the grounds of ill-health in 1951. At the time of his death in 1964, he was living at 22 Saxon Street, Wrexham.

Hackett Court, King's Mills Road
This street was laid out in the 1980s on land that had previously been the property of C. T. Clark, proprietor of the King's Mills Garage. Built by the Wales and West Housing Association, all the streets in this development were named after RWF who had been awarded the Victoria Cross.

Lt-Col Thomas Bernard Hackett, VC, 1836–1880 was born in 1836, the son of Thomas Hackett of Moor Park, King's County, Ireland. He was commissioned (by purchase) into the 6th Foot on 7 June 1854 and transferred into the RWF a few months later. He served in the Crimean campaign, the Indian Mutiny (awarded the Victoria Cross) and the Ashanti War before retiring on 1 April 1874 when he returned to Ireland. He was accidentally shot dead while out shooting partridge on 5 October 1880 and was buried at Lockeen, County Tipperary. His Victoria Cross citation reads:

> For daring gallantry at Secundra Baugh, Lucknow, on the 18th November 1857, in having, with others, rescued a Corporal of the 23rd Regiment who was lying wounded and exposed to a very heavy fire. Also for conspicuous bravery in having, under a heavy fire, ascended the roof and cut the thatch off a Bungalow to prevent it being set on fire. This was a most important service at the time.

Hafod-y-Bwch, Rhostyllen
Originally a late medieval timber-framed hall-house (which

Hafod-y-Bwch, mid 1970s.

A watercolour landscape showing Hafod-y-Wern located amidst open countryside with Wrexham Parish Church in the distance. [NLW PA9250]

survives as the west range), Hafod-y-Bwch was built by Hugh Roberts (died 1607), of Croes Foel.* It had various features added, particularly a timber-framed cross-wing on the south end of the hall (which was later extended by the addition of two short, parallel, gabled wings on the east side in the early 17th-century. At that time, Edward Lhuyd described Hafod-y-Bwch as the second most important of the chief houses of the parish of Wrexham. It was the home of the Roberts family until the early 18th century when it passed to the Parrys of Pwll Halawg, Dyffryn Clwyd. By the 1780s, it was part of the estate of William Lloyd of Plas Power*. The house has a fine 17th-century staircase that was brought from Five Fords, Marchwiel in about 1970.* Hafod-y-Bwch is a Grade II Star listed building.

Hafod-y-Wern

This house, a large timber-framed building, stood on roughly the site of Bryn Hafod* and was, for many years, the single most important estate in the immediate vicinity of Wrexham. According to Palmer, the first recorded resident of Hafod-y-Wern was Hwfa ap Iorwerth, who was living in the mid-13th century, whose son was vicar of Wrexham in 1294. The estate passed in a direct line to Hwfa's great-great grandson Hywel ap Goronwy and then, in the female line by marriage to John Puleston of Berse in the 15th century. A detailed description of this family genealogy, complete with tabulated pedigrees is given by Palmer in *A History of the Town of Wrexham*. (See also Puleston Family of Hafod-y-Wern)

In 1620, Norden's survey described Hafod-y-Wern as comprising (transcription by A.N. Palmer*): 'one capital messuage called Havod-y-werne, barn, stables, orchards, gardens, and closes or parcels of land to the same pertaining, being arable, meadow and pasture land, called by these names:– Kae Stacie (*Trans.* Stacy's field), Kae Cor (*Trans.* the stall or pen

The only known photograph of Hafod-y-Wern shows it after a substantial section of the house had been demolished.

151

field), Lloyn-y-Cocksuite (*Trans.* probably the cockshoot grove), Y Cae Mawr (*Trans.* the big field), Cae Vallen (*Trans.* the apple tree field), Dole Dda (*Trans.* the good meadow), which should probably be 'Dol ddu' the black meadow. Grost-y-kerddorion (*Trans.* evidently 'Grost-y-cerddorion' the singers croft), Kaer groise (*Trans.* field of the cross), The field beyond the mill, Errow vechan (*Trans.* little acre), Y wern vechan (*Trans.* the little aldermarsh), the Coppie (*Trans.* the top), One close of land beyond the river … two cottages, a garden and … by the New Mill, and … and garden in Pentre velyn yr Abbat (Pentre Felin yr Abad– *Trans.* the abbot's mill village), and one parcel of land adjacent to the same, containing in all, y estimation, one hundred [customary] acres.' [211.5 statute acres]. In 1841 it was tenanted by James Matthews. By the late 1890s, the Hafod-y-Wern estate had been reduced to about 84.5 acres. In the late 1860s, the old house was let to WBC as part of a sewage farm and it was for a time the residence of Lt-Col Alfred Stowell Jones, VC, Manager of the Borough Sewerage Works.*

A picture of the old house was reproduced by Palmer in his *History of the Town of Wrexham* but the house was demolished in two stages *c*.1829 and *c*.1880 when a new house was built on the site by Mr Davies-Cooke of Gwysanau, the heir to the Puleston estate. Part of the land was sold to the Wrexham & Ellesmere Railway Company.* The estate was bought by Sir Travers Twiss, QC, of Fulham in September 1895 for £17,000. It eventually became part of the Cefn Park* estate and was the subject of compulsory purchase orders when it was bought by Wrexham Borough Council and developed as the eastern part of the Queen's Park* Housing Estate during the 1940s and 1950s. [FRO/D/GW/921]

Hafod-y-Wern Farm
Also known as Swan's Farm (after the family who lived there in the early 20th century), this farm was located behind the present day Red Dragon public house on roughly the same site as the original Hafod-y-Wern* house.

Hafod-y-Wern Schools, Deva Way
Built very close to the site of Abenbury Lodge* by Edward W. Gittins & Sons Ltd. Plans for the building of a new infant and junior school, accommodating 240 pupils, in the Queen's Park Housing Estate* were revealed in 1951. The foundation stones were laid on 1 August 1952 by Alderman Mrs E.A. Cross, MBE, JP, (chairman of the Denbighshire Education Committee) and County Councillor A.J. Jenkins. By this time the school was planned to accommodate 560 children and would cost £107,000. The infant school (the first to be built in Wrexham since 1910) opened on 1 February 1954 with 203 children enrolled but teaching was not to start until the following September. The suggested names for this school were: Cefn Parc/Cefn Park and Berwyn. The name Hafod-y-Wern was the suggestion of Lt-Col Fenwick Palmer of Cefn Park but was originally rejected due to its association with the local sewage farm. In 2001 the junior school had 243 pupils on the roll and the infant school had 168. In 2010, the merged primary school has 236 pupils on the roll.

Headteachers:
Juniors
1954   W. Elward Parry
1977   John O. Roberts
1988   W. Trefor Roberts
          Mrs Jan Smith
Infants
1954   Miss M. Beryl Jones
1970   Miss Minnie Jones
1982   Miss Della Price-Roberts
1995   Mrs Julia Botterell
          Mrs Rhian Hughes
Primary
2007   Simon Edwards

Haig Road, Hightown
In 1927, Wrexham Borough Council received an offer of three acres of land behind the Travellers' Rest* public house and along Bryn-y-Cabanau Road* from Brigadier-General J.H. Lloyd, DSO, of Ellesmere. The land was available for £400 which Brigadier General Lloyd wished to use to fund a scholarship for a child in Flintshire. The offer was accepted and plans were drawn up to build 32 houses on the site, most of them behind the Traveller's Rest on a new street that was to be called Lloyd Avenue. Whether the Council changed its mind or whether Brigadier General Lloyd objected, is unknown but the name Lloyd Avenue was discarded in favour of Haig Avenue. The houses were built by Broughton builder George Fleming Sumner at a cost of £10,817. A foundation stone was laid in Nº 1 Haig Road by the Mayor of Wrexham, Cllr Milly Edwards-Jones,* and her husband, Alderman Edwards-Jones* (chairman of the Housing Committee) in October 1928.

The street was named after Field Marshal Earl Haig of Braemersyde, GCB (1861–1928), Commander-in-Chief of the British forces in France 1915–19.

Hall of Pleas
See Town Hall.

Halton Cottage, Poplar Road
Shown on the 1833 survey as standing on what was to become Poplar Road, on a site which is now part of the St Giles' School grounds.

Hampden Road, Cae Siac
This late 19th century street of terraced houses was named after Hampden Poyser of Gwersyllt who developed this area in the 1890s in a field that was called Cae Siac.* An 'iron' chapel was built here by the Welsh Wesleyans in 1899 (see Victoria Road Welsh Wesleyan Methodist Church and Poyser Family).

Hampshire Drive, Tŷ Gwyn
The final part of the Tŷ Gwyn development by local builders H.R. & E. Roberts, completed in the early 1970s. Tŷ Gwyn* farmhouse stood on what is now the corner of Hampshire Drive and Snowdon Drive.*

Hampson Avenue, Whitegate
Built just before the outbreak of the Second World War by WBC, following the passing of the 1936 Housing Act, this street was named after Alderman Herbert Hampson,* Mayor 1933–4 and an Honorary Freeman of Wrexham.

Hampson, Alderman Herbert *local politician*
Born at Overton Bridge in 1885, his family moved to Wrexham when he was aged 10. He was educated at the National School and became a baker's apprentice at Stevens Bakery. Qualifying as a master baker, he opened his own business when he was aged 26 and acquired the Charles Street Bakery in 1913. During the First World War he was awarded the contract to supply bread to the Royal Welsh Fusiliers in Hightown Barracks which meant the production of 30,000 lbs of bread each week. At the Wembley Exhibition of 1924–25 Hampson's bread was awarded both the gold and silver medals. He retired in 1947.

Hampson was elected a member of WBC in 1927, representing the Offa Ward and was elected Mayor in 1933. Following the Gresford Disaster he invited the Lord Mayor of London to visit Wrexham (although it was only the Deputy Lord Mayor who came) and was instrumental in establishing the Gresford Disaster Fund. Herbert Hampson was chairman of the Highways Committee, the Wrexham Playing Fields Association and

Wrexham Boys Clubs. He was also vice chairman of the Borough Housing Committee for 18 years. He was made an alderman in 1937 and an Honorary Freeman in 1957. In March 1956, following the death in office of William Shone, Herbert Hampson became Mayor for a second time. Appointed a Justice of the Peace in 1935, he became a vice chairman of the Wrexham Borough Bench until his retirement in 1960.

He married Mary in 1911 and they had two sons and two daughters. For many years he lived at 15 Charles Street, then 6 Chester Road (the house which is now named Hampson House after him) and, for a period, at Plas Acton.* At the time of his death in 1982, he was living at 64 Park Avenue. Hampson Avenue* is named after him.

Hampson, Joseph *clockmaker*
See Thomas Hampson.

Hampson, Thomas *clockmaker*
Thomas Hampson was probably the best known Wrexham clockmaker. He lived and worked in a half-timbered house in High Street *c*.1728–48, known as 'The Clock' on the site now occupied by the Market Hall.* He was buried in Wrexham churchyard on 12 April 1755. He may have been the father of Joseph Hampson. For a time the North & South Wales Bank public house in High Street was named the Thomas Hampson.

Hand Inn, Town Hill
The Hand Inn was located at the rear of the Town Hall between Back Chamber Street, Abbot Street and Town Hill with its main door facing the latter. A building on this site was described in Norden's survey of 1620: 'Edward Davies holds … one fair tenement with two shops and curtilage, at the west end of the Shirehall'. There would appear to have been a building, probably an inn of some description, on this site in the 16th century. An inn, named the *Black Lion*, was built here in *c*.1715 and it would seem likely that some of the timbers from the 16th century building were used in the 18th century construction. By 1788, the inn had changed its name to the *Bulls Head* and, by 1801, was known as *The Hand*. Like most of the buildings on Town Hill and High Street, the Hand was entered by way of steps which meant that the ground floor level was above that of the street. The landlord in the mid 19th century was Joseph Bate who died in the 1870s and was buried in the Burial Ground* on Ruthin Road. It appears in both the 1833 and the 1872 surveys.

The Hand Inn, Town Hill. This building was demolished shortly after this photograph was taken and a new Hand Inn was built on the same site. Abbot Street and Back Chamber Street on the left, Town Hall on the right.

Photographs showing the building were taken shortly before it was demolished by the owner, John Scott, at the end of the 19th century, in order to widen the entrance to Abbot Street. These show the old timbers and early style of the architecture. Some of these timbers were preserved and still survive in the National Museum of Wales and are clearly of 16th century origin. They have been decoratively carved with the crowned portcullis (the symbol of King Henry VII) and three rabbits. Once the site had been cleared, John Scott built another *Hand Inn* on the same site, albeit slightly smaller than its predecessor. This had an appearance of a Tudor or Jacobean stone building. The *Hand* was offered for sale in July 1929 (but was withdrawn having only gained a bid for £5,100). Along with the Town Hall, the *Hand Inn* was demolished in April 1940 as part of the Town Hill road improvement scheme. The name was then transferred to a new public house built on Holt Road.*

Hand Inn, Holt Road
Built at the beginning of the Second World War this public house took both the name and the licence of the old Hand Inn* on Town Hill which was demolished in April 1940.

Hannigan, Rt Revd James *Bishop of Menevia*
Born in County Donegal, Ireland, in 1928, James Hannigan was ordained a priest in 1954 and came to Wrexham in 1958 when he was secretary to Bishop John Petit.* Between 1958 and 1983 he served as diocesan treasurer, chancellor and secretary of education at Wrexham. He was an administrator of the Diocesan Welfare Fund and vicar general to Bishop Langton Fox* and Bishop John Ward.* In 1983, he was appointed Bishop of Menevia and, on 24 March 1987, on the reorganisation of the diocese of Menevia, he became the first bishop of Wrexham. He served as chairman of the Catholic Education Council (1985–91) and was an ardent worker for the Catholic Children's Society. He died aged 65 at the Countess of Chester Hospital on 6 March 1994, following heart surgery.

Hannon, DD, Rt Revd Daniel Joseph *Bishop of Menevia*
Born in Rotherham, Yorkshire on 12 June 1884, the son of Patrick and Elizabeth Hannon (née McGlynn), Daniel Hannon was educated in Cardiff, Valladolid (Spain), Oscott and Rome. He was Bishop's Agent in Rome before being appointed curate of St David's Cathedral, Cardiff. He was then appointed the Administrator of St David's and was the parish priest in Aberafan and Penarth. He was consecrated as Bishop of Menevia on 1 May 1941. He was a fluent speaker of Spanish, Italian and Welsh. He died at Bishop's House on 26 April 1946.

Happy Valley, Rivulet Road
This was an area where summer concerts were held in the late 19th century. It was located at the eastern end of Rivulet Road on the site of what was, during the second half of the 20th century, McDermott's scrap yard.

Harp Inn, Abbot Street
Also known as the Welsh Harp, it had once been known as the Fox & Goose. It appears in the 1833 survey.

Harrison's Court, Chester Street
Accessed by way of a passage on the north side of 25 Chester Street, this backed onto Llwyn Isaf. It was named after William Harrison a cashier at Lloyd's Bank* who lived at 25 Chester Street* between *c*.1811 and 1860. The housing here was condemned as unfit for human habitation in the 1890s and, when the owner declined to take any action, was the subject of a compulsory demolition order which was executed in 1898.

Harrison's Court, Farndon Street, 1933.

Harrison's Court, Farndon Street
A small court development of eight poor quality industrial dwellings located behind the houses on the western side of Farndon Street. It took its name from John Harrison (church warden 1791–2), a glazier who lived next door to the Cannon Inn* in Abbot Street. These houses were demolished as part of the Borough's slum clearance programme following the Housing Act of 1930. It appears in the 1872 survey.

Hat Inn, Charles Street
This was located on the north side of Charles Street, next door to the Elephant & Castle,* very close to the junction with Market Street and may have dated back to the 17th century. It was once known as The Green Man* and had changed to The Hat by 1808. Shown in both the 1833 and 1872 survey, the licensee in 1881 was Thomas Lester. Originally a timber-framed building roofed in thatch, it still survives as the premises of Schwarz Opticians who carried out a major renovation and restoration programme on the building during the 1980s.

Havard Way, Queen's Park
Built by WBC in 1949 as part of the Queen's Park housing estate on land that had previously been part of the Hafod-y-Wern Farm (part of the Cefn Park* estate). This street was named after the Rt Revd William Thomas Havard, MC, TD, DD, MA, Surrogate Bishop of St Asaph. He became Bishop of St David's in 1950.

Havelock Square, Salop Road. The Cambrian Leather Works can be seen in the background.

Havelock Square, Salop Road
This development of poor quality industrial housing was located in the elbow of the river Gwenfro and accessed via a passageway from Salop Road. Although numbered from 1–7, there does not appear to have been a dwelling number 2. The six houses were demolished under the Borough's slum clearance programme of 1938. It appears in the 1872 survey.

Hawthorns, The, Acton Park
Laid out in 1932 as part of the second phase of the Acton Park housing estate,* it was built by G.F. Sumner of Ashfield.*

Haytor Road, Croes Eneurys
Laid out in the 1930s and developed on land that was previously part of Croes Eneurys Farm.* The origin of the name is unknown. See also Croes Eneurys Estate.*

Heap Terrace
Located in Wrexham Abbot, 1881.

Heber, Bishop Reginald *theologian & hymn writer*
Born in 1783 in Malpas, the son of the rector, Reginald Heber was educated at Brasenose College, Oxford where he gained a reputation as something of a poet. After ordination, he was a Fellow of All Souls' College before being appointed rector of Hodnet in 1808. He soon acquired a reputation as a popular priest and hymn writer. While at Hodnet he wrote his best loved hymn *Holy, Holy, Holy, Lord God Almighty*. He married the daughter of Dean Jonathan Shipley, the vicar of Wrexham.

Bishop Reginald Heber, taken from his memorial window in the Parish Church.

While on a visit to his father-in-law in 1819, Heber was to preach at the Parish Church on the subject of missionary work. While preparing his sermon, reputedly lodging at Mary Rowland's shop on the corner of High Street and Church Street (as the Vicarage had been let), he decided to write a new hymn which would emphasise his message. The result was the famous hymn *From Greenland's Icy Mountains*. He was appointed a canon of St Asaph Cathedral in 1812. In 1823, he became Bishop of Calcutta where he died of a seizure on 3 April 1826 and was buried in the Anglican cathedral which he had founded. A memorial window, recording Heber's link with Wrexham and the 'Wrexham' hymn can be seen on the north side of the Parish Church and, in 1926, a memorial plaque was placed on Vicarage Hill, close to the site of the early 19th century vicarage. A biography entitled *Bishop Sahib: Life of Reginald Heber*, by D. Hughes was published by Churchman in 1986. The Bishop Heber School in Malpas was named after him. (See also Royal British Bowmen)

Heber Mount, Queen's Park
Built in the immediate post Second World War period as part of the first phase of WBC's Queen's Park housing development. This cul-de-sac was named after Bishop Reginald Heber.*

Helicopter Service, Plas Coch
The world's first scheduled helicopter service was inaugurated by

One of the Westland helicopters that flew out of Plas Coch.

British European Airways between Liverpool–Wrexham–Cardiff on 2 June 1950. Flights operated from a concrete pad on the site of the present day Homebase store at Plas Coch (now Plas Coch Retail Park). The only structure on the site was a small glass-fronted cabin which served as a waiting room. The Westland helicopters had a limited passenger capacity but operated a service six days each week. The fares were Wrexham–Liverpool (return) £1; Wrexham–Cardiff (return) £5. The capacity of the helicopters was such that the flights were uneconomic and the service ceased on 31 March 1951, by which time they had carried only 219 passengers.

Hen Blas
(*Trans.* old hall) This was a building which, in the early 18th century, stood on Queen Street,* next to the Rainbow Inn,* with Henblas Street* running along its north side. It was demolished before 1808 and replaced by three separate houses. Its garden was developed as Birmingham Square* which was used by hardware dealers during the March Fair (see Markets and Fairs). The house was built of brick with some stone decoration and alongside it stood a stable and coach-house, surrounding a cobbled yard. It gave its name to the nearby Henblas Street and Henblas Square,* built in the late 1990s, was also named after it.

Owners/Occupiers:
1748–61	John Myddelton, apothecary
1764–*c*.71	Miss Anne Maria Powell (formerly of Plas Gwern*), a member of the Broughton Hall family.
c.1772	John Jones (stationer)

Henblas Street, c.1935 showing the Music Hall at the eastern end.

1780	Revd John Jones *c*.20 years (formerly rector of Knockin and vicar of Llansantffraid-ym-Mechain)

Henblas Square
Built in 1998/9 and opened in October 1999 this retail development was the culmination of over 10 years of wrangling and debate. Built by Centros Miller, Henblas Square occupies the site that was formerly the Vegetable Market,* the Guildhall*/ Wrexham Grammar School* (Chester Street), the south side of Lambpit Street,* the Rose & Crown* public house, the Congregational Chapel* (Chester Street) and the north side of Henblas Street.* A previous development plan to build a shopping precinct on this site failed to materialise due to the collapse of the developers, Warrington, in 1991.

Two views of Henblas Street.
Above, c.1985, showing the entrance to the Vegetable Market.
Below: Henblas Street looking towards Queen Street, c.1975.

Henblas Street
First described in 1620, it named after the Hen Blas* which once stood in the area. In the 1833 survey, Henblas Street is shown as running in a virtually straight line from Queen Street to Chester Street. It would appear that the building of the Public Hall and the Congregational Chapel, considerably narrowed the eastern half of the street so that it became in effect a footpath leading alongside the old Grammar School and that the name Henblas Street was then transferred to the road leading around the Potato Market (now the Butter Market) and into the Chester Street end of Kenrick Street (from the bottom of the present Bank Street to

Chester Street). There was surviving evidence of the old Chester Street end of Henblas Street until the construction of Henblas Square and the present day T. J. Hughes store which resulted in the old cobbled road surface finally being removed.

Henry, Matthew *theologian*
Born at Broad Oak, Maelor, on 18 October 1662, Matthew was the son of Philip Henry, the renowned Presbyterian minister. Educated at various Nonconformist academies and Gray's Inn in London, Henry is most famous for his published commentaries on the Old and New Testaments. He was a preacher in Chester before moving to Hackney in 1712. He died in Nantwich on 22 June 1714. (See also Warburton Lee)

Henry, FRS, Thomas *chemist*
Born on 26 October 1734, the son of a Wrexham schoolmaster, Thomas Henry was apprenticed to an apothecary in Oxford and later set himself up in business in Manchester. He was the author of several papers on both chemistry and medicine which resulted in his becoming a Fellow of the Royal Society in 1775. He died on 18 June 1816. He was the father of the chemist William Henry who formulated Henry's Law.

Heol Dafydd, Little Acton
This street forms part of a residential development by the Broseley building firm in the early 1970s and was named after Dafydd ap Llywelyn, Prince of Wales, brother of Llywelyn ap Gruffydd and grandson of Llywelyn the Great.

Dafydd was born in *c*.1236. In 1241, he and his brother Rhodri were taken as hostages by King Henry III as part of a treaty between the King and Dafydd's mother Senena. He fought for his brother Owain against their brother Llywelyn in 1255 as a consequence of which he was imprisoned for a year. In 1263, he joined Henry III against Llywelyn and once again his brother forgave his treason. In 1276, he joined with the English king, Edward I, against Llywelyn and, following the treaty of Aberconwy was granted lands in north Wales, including Caergwrle Castle. Dafydd, however, was not satisfied and felt that he had been short-changed by Edward and, on Palm Sunday 1282, attacked Hawarden Castle and sparked off the great uprising that was to result in Llywelyn's death in December. At last, Dafydd succeeded his brother and became the leader of the Welsh forces. Sadly, it was too late. Edward I had too strong a grip on Wales and Dafydd was driven into hiding in Snowdonia. In June 1283, he was betrayed by his own supporters and taken to Shrewsbury as a prisoner where he suffered death by the horrific method of hanging, drawing and quartering on 3 October, possibly one of the first men to be executed by this barbaric method. Dafydd's daughters were locked away in nunneries. His son, Llywelyn, died a prisoner in Bristol in 1288 and his second son, Owen, was last heard of still a prisoner there in 1305.

Heol Llawhaden, Little Acton
This street forms part of a residential development by the Broseley building firm in the early 1970s and was named after Llawhaden Castle in Pembrokeshire which was built in the early 12th century by the bishop of St David's. In 1192 the castle was attacked and destroyed by the Lord Rhys and, during the 13th and 14th centuries, the earth and wood castle was transformed into a great stone fortified mansion suitable for use as both a residence and a military stronghold.

Heol Pwll-y-Kiln, Little Acton
(*Trans.* kiln pool road) This road is now known as Smithy Lane* but was originally named after a small private estate of the same name. The estate had lands, not only in Acton township, but also extending into Gresford, Gwersyllt, Dutton Diffaeth and Brymbo and included the farm known as Tŷ Gwyn.*

The exact site of the main estate house is unrecorded but a row of cottages alongside Acton Smithy on the north side of Smithy Lane were known as 'Ubitykil Cottages', name is probably a distortion of the *oddeutu y kiln*, meaning 'about the kiln' which would suggest that the kiln, and therefore the house, may well have been located nearby. Also, south of Smithy Lane* on the land now occupied by Windermere Road and Kendal Way, was a field known as Cae'r Hen Dy [*Trans.* field of the old house) which may have been a reference to it. The *pwll* was probably a reference to the pool which was, until the latter part of the 20th century, sited in front of Acton Smithy.

In the mid 17th century the estate was owned by Hugh Kendrick who was succeeded by his son, John Hughes (John ap Hugh). The land then passed to John Hughes II, then to his son-in-law, John Jones of Hope, then to John Jones II and then John Jones III who sold much of his land to Ellis Yonge of Acton Park* in the late 18th century. The remaining land then passed to Edward Ellis of Wrexham whose family sold it during the 1820s to Sir Foster Cunliffe of Acton Park. The land remained part of the Acton Park estate until the 1920s and, shortly afterwards, the first houses were built in this area.

Herbert Jennings Avenue
Named after Alderman Herbert Jennings,* this street in the Acton Park housing estate* was laid out by WBC in the 1960s on part of the grounds of Acton Park.*

Hermitage Camp
Hermitage Camp was established during the Second World War on land that was previously part of the Hermitage Farm.* Located in the area between Percy Road and Hightown barracks, it was a training camp for the Auxiliary Territorial Service, the Pioneer Corps and, for a time, the Commandos. After the war,

Two indistinct views of Hermitage Camp, taken in the early 1960s after Ysgol Morgan Llwyd had taken over the buildings.
[Ysgol Morgan Llwyd]

activity at the camp was wound down until it was re-activated during the Korean War, again as a training camp for the Royal Pioneer Corps, becoming the Royal Pioneer Corps Training Battalion Depot. The Hermitage Camp remained operational until the end of National Service in 1963. All that remains of the camp today is the small cul-de-sac of houses on the north side of Hermitage Drive which was the officers' married quarters and the avenue of trees on Hermitage Drive which was the site of one of the camp's entrances.

Ysgol Morgan Llwyd,* Wrexham's first Welsh-language secondary school was developed on the site of the camp in 1963/64 (the school moved to the former Cartrefle College* site in 2000 and the Hermitage buildings now accommodate St Christopher's School*). The remainder of the camp has been developed as both private and public housing estates.

Hermitage Drive
Hermitage Drive was laid out as one of the entrances to Hermitage Camp.* Following the closure of the camp the street was developed as part of WBC's Hermitage private housing estate in which all the street names have military connections (Stockwell Grove,* Gwydyr Way,* Waterloo Close* and Trafalgar Close*).

Hermitage Farm
Hermitage Farm was located to the south of Wrexham between Sontley Road and Bryn-y-Cabanau Road. It was originally called Ithens Farm. During the Second World War the farm was requisitioned for use as an army camp (see Hermitage Camp).

Hermitage Park
A private housing development of the 1990s, built on land that was previously part of the Hermitage* army camp. Three of the streets have names that are taken from the legend of King Arthur viz: Avalon Court, Pendragon Court and Bedevere Court.

Hickman, Charles Edward *local politician*
Born in Northampton and educated at Dr Morby's School, Charles Hickman began his working life by going to sea and was employed in the catering section of White Star shipping lines. He came to Wrexham in *c*.1900 when he was employed by local caterers T. Hughes & Co. In 1914, he joined the Royal Navy and served as a petty officer in the armoured car section. He was promoted to warrant officer in 1915 but declined a commission. He took part in the seaplane expedition to relieve the besieged British forces at Kut in Mesopotamia and then served in France. He was de-mobbed in 1919 and returned to Wrexham where he was one of the founder members of the Wrexham War Memorial Club.

Elected a councillor in 1920, he became Mayor in 1924.

He married twice (1) Alice, the daughter of Police inspector Lindsay of Wrexham (died 1925) and (2) Emily Adelaide Moore of Liverpool, who was also a Wrexham councillor (died 1956). He lived at Linsdell, Rivulet Road and died at the War Memorial Hospital in November 1944 and is buried in Wrexham Cemetery.

High Cross
The High Cross stood in front of the Shire Hall* at the end of High Street, near to the junctions of Church Street and Hope Street. Palmer* first found a mention of it in a deed dating from the 15th century and it was also mentioned in Norden's survey of 1620. By the time Palmer was carrying out his research in the final quarter of the 19th century, there was no trace of the High Cross remaining although he does mention that 'old people still speak of the space in front of the hall [Town Hall*] as 'The Cross''.

High Grove, Grove Road
A substantial private house which was the property of William Pritchard, JP. In 1881 it was the home of A. Wilson Edwards, JP, a deputy chairman of the Provincial Insurance Company.*

The 1905 sale particulars provide a detailed description of the property: 'Containing entrance hall, lobby, drawing room, dining room, morning room, smoke room, butler's pantry, larder, large kitchen, scullery, wash-house, boot-house, excellent dry cellarage, 6 bedrooms, dressing room, box room, bathroom (with H&C water) separate WC, pleasure grounds, tennis lawn, summer-house, conservatory, two large yards, servants WC, kitchen gardens, coach-house, saddle room, two stall stable, approached by carriage drive. electric light cable is laid along Grove Road'. The property also comprised land fronting onto Foster Road 'used as a garden by Edwin Butcher suitable for a villa residence to be built' which was also offered for sale. [DRO/DD/G/2871]

In *c*.1936 the house became the property of Dr J.E.H. Davies, DSO who had formerly lived at Plas Darland* on Grosvenor Road. He had sold his previous home to the Mine Workers Institute and brought the name to his new home in Grove Road. The house had been converted into flats by 1951 before being demolished and the site used for purpose-built private flats bearing the same name. These flats were later extended to incorporate the site of Grove Lodge.* [DRO/DD/G/2927]

High Sheriffs
The post of High Sheriff for the county of Denbighshire has been held by many men from the town of Wrexham and the surrounding area. Since 1974 the posts of High Sheriff of Denbighshire and High Sheriff of Flintshire have been combined into that of the High Sheriff of Clwyd. A High Sheriff is the monarch's representative and chief officer in a county/sheriffwick. Originally elected, they then became royal appointments through the Exchequer and, by way of qualification, have to be the owners of sufficient land which could be confiscated by the Crown should they abuse their position. The position of High Sheriff is an honorary one and the holder of the office does not obtain any financial benefit. Their role has been gradually reduced and today they administer (*via* the office of Under Sheriff) all High Court enforcements within the sheriffwick and entertain judges attending the Crown Court at Mold.

1543	Sir John Puleston of Hafod-y-Wern*
1556	Thomas Bellot of Burton Hall, Rossett
1558	Edward Almer of Pant Iocyn,* Gresford
1559	Robert Puleston of Hafod-y-Wern*
1566	Hugh Puleston of Bersham
1570	Robert Puleston of Hafod-y-Wern*
1571	Edward Almer of Pant Iocyn,* Gresford
1576	Edward Jones of Plas Cadwgan*
1581	Owen Brereton of Borras [Hall]*
1582	Edward Hughes ap Fowke of Holt Castle
1587	William Almer of Pant Iocyn,* Gresford
1588	Owen Brereton of Borras [Hall]*
1589	Edward Eyton of Watstay, Ruabon
1591	Thomas Powell of Horsley Hall,* Gresford
1598	Edward Brereton of Borras [Hall]* (died in office)
1598	Robert Sontley of Sontley, Marchwiel
1603	Edward Eyton of Watstay, Ruabon
1608	Morgan Broughton of Marchwiel Hall
1610	Sir Richard Trevor of Trevalyn Hall,* Rossett
1616	Thomas Powell of Horsley Hall,* Gresford
1620	William Vaughan of Eyton, Bangor-is-y-coed
1621	Hugh Meredith of Pentrebychan*
1626	George Bostock of Plas Bostock, Holt
1629	Edward Meredith of Stansty
1630	William Robinson* of Gwersyllt Park*
1639	Sir Thomas Powell, Bt, of Horsley Hall,* Gresford
1640	Richard Langford of Trevalyn House,* Rossett
1642	John Bellot of Burton Hall, Rossett
1647	John Kynaston of Plas Kynaston, Ruabon
1648	Robert Sontley of Sontley, Marchwiel

1649	Thomas Ravenscroft of Pickhill Hall,* Bangor-is-y-coed
1652	Thomas Ball of Ball's Hall, Rossett
1654	William Edwards of Eyton, Bangor-is-y-coed
1655	John Jeffreys* of Acton Park*
1657	Sir Thomas Powell, Bt, of Horsley Hall,* Gresford
1663	Roger Puleston of Emral,* Worthenbury
1674	Sir John Wynn, Bt,* of Watstay, Ruabon*
1677	John Langford of Trevalyn House,* Rossett
1678	Edward Brereton of Borras [Hall]*
1682	Joshua Edisbury* of Erddig*
1683	Griffith Jeffreys* of Acton Park*
1684	Thomas Powell of Horsley Hall,* Gresford
1685	Robert Griffith of Brymbo Hall*
1686	William Ravenscroft of Pickhill Hall,* Bangor-is-y-coed
1689	Roger Mostyn of Plas Mostyn, Brymbo
1690	William Robinson* of Gwersyllt Park*
1697	John Hill of Sontley, Marchwiel
1698	Sir Edward Broughton of Marchwiel Hall
1704	Elihu Yale* of Plas Grono,* Wrexham
1705	John Roberts of Hafod-y-Bwch,* Ruabon
1718	John Jones of Llwyn On,* Wrexham
1719	Eubule Lloyd of Pen-y-Lan,* Ruabon
1724	John Puleston of Hafod-y-Wern*
1727	Humphrey Brereton of Borras [Hall]*
1731	Thomas Salisbury of Erbistock Hall
1732	Robert Ellis of Croes Newydd*
1739	Cawley Humberston Cawley of Upper Gwersyllt
1743	Aquila Wyke of Marchwiel Hall
1752	John Jones of Llwyn On,* Wrexham
1753	Kenrick Eyton of Eyton Hall, Bangor-is-y-coed
1760	Griffith Speed of High Street, Wrexham
1764	William Dymock of Chester Street, Wrexham
1773	Edward Lloyd of Royden Hall, Bangor-is-y-coed (died in office)
1774	William Jones of Wrexham Fechan
1776	John Humberston Cawley of Upper Gwersyllt
1783	Charles Goodwin of Burton Hall, Rossett
1784	John Ellis of Eyton, Bangor-is-y-coed
1785	John Twigge of Borras
1786	Philip Yorke* of Erddig*
1787	Sir Foster Cunliffe, Bt,* of Acton Park*
1789	Charles Brown of Marchwiel Hall
1793	Edward Eyton of Eyton Hall, Bangor-is-y-coed
1794	Brian Cooke of Hafod-y-Wern*
1795	John Wynne of Gerwin Fawr, Bangor-is-y-coed
1796	John Hughes of Horsley Hall,* Gresford
1798	John Jones of Pen-y-Bryn, Wrexham
1799	John Wilkinson of Brymbo Hall*
1803	Henry Ellis Boates of Rose Hill, Erbistock
1805	Samuel Riley of Marchwiel Hall
1806	Richard Jones of Belan Place, Ruabon
1807	Simon Yorke* of Erddig*
1813	Thomas Murhall-Griffith of Holt Street House,* Wrexham
1814	Edward Rowland of Gardden Lodge, Ruabon
1822	Samuel Newton of Pickhill Hall,* Bangor-is-y-coed
1824	Richard Myddelton Massie Lloyd of Chester Street, Wrexham
1825	William Egerton of Gresford Lodge*
1826	Thomas FitzHugh of Plas Power*
1829	Sir William Lloyd* of Bryn Estyn*
1835	Sir Robert Henry Cunliffe, Bt,* of Acton Park*
1840	Townshend Mainwaring of Marchwiel Hall
1841	Lt-Col Henry Ellis Boates of Rose Hill, Erbistock
1843	John Townshend of Trevalyn House,* Rossett
1844	Henry Warner Meredith of Pentrebychan Hall*
1848	Simon Yorke* of Erddig*
1849	Thomas Griffith of Trevalyn Hall,* Rossett
1850	John Burton of Minera Hall
1852	Francis James Hughes of Little Acton House*
1854	Richard Jones of Belan Place, Ruabon
1859	Thomas Lloyd FitzHugh of Plas Power*
1860	James Hardcastle of Pen-y-Lan,* Ruabon
1864	Boscawen Trevor Griffith of Trevalyn Hall,* Rossett
1868	Sir Robert Alfred Cunliffe,* Bt, Acton Park*
1872	Samuel Pearce Hope of Marchwiel Hall
1873	James Hassall Foulkes of Llay Place, Gresford
1886	Colonel Henry Warter Meredith of Pentrebychan Hall*
1889	Charles William Townshend of Trevalyn House,* Rossett
1890	Sir Herbert Lloyd Watkin Williams Wynn, Bt,* of Wynnstay, Ruabon
1891	John Robert Burton of Minera Hall
1894	Edward Evans of Bronwylfa Hall*
1895	Philip Yorke of Erddig*
1908	George Hunter Finlay Robertson of Gladwyn,* Gresford
1909	Alfred Ashworth of Horsley Hall,* Gresford
1910	Godfrey FitzHugh of Plas Power*
1911	Alfred Hood of Strathalyn, Rossett
1913	Philip Henry Ashworth of Horsley Hall,* Gresford
1914	Arthur Ernest Evans of Bronwylfa Hall*
1916	Oliver Ormrod of Pickhill Hall,* Bangor-is-y-coed
1922	Henry Dyke Dennis* of Hafod-y-Bwch,* Ruabon
1923	Sir Alfred David McAlpine* of Marchwiel Hall
1931	Sir Edmund Fleming Bushby, Bt, of Bronwylfa Hall*
1932	Godfrey Edmund FitzHugh of Plas Power*
1934	Ronald Stewart Brown of Bryn-y-Grog,* Marchwiel
1937	Simon Yorke* of Erddig*
1940	William Rimington Glazebrook of Manley Hall, Erbistock
1948	Sir Watkin Williams Wynn, Bt,* of Belan Place, Ruabon
1959	Lt-Col Sir William Guy Lowther, Bt, of Erbistock Hall
1962	Maj Peter Charles Ormrod of Pen-y-Lan,* Ruabon
1966	Brigadier Llewellyn Gwydyr-Jones* of River House, Erbistock

1974 The Sheriffwick of Clwyd

1974	Philip J. Warburton-Lee* of Broad Oak, Redbrook
1977	Capt Sir John Hanmer, Bt, Mere House, Hanmer
1980	David Foulk Myddelton, Caeaugwynion, Chirk
1982	Lt–Col Arthur David Bentley Brooks, Iscoed
1986	Hon Lloyd Tyrell Kenyon, Gredington, Hanmer*
1993	Philip Godsall, Iscoed
1996	Roger Henry William Graham-Palmer, Cefn Park*
1997	Colonel Sir Charles Douglas Lowther, Bt, Erbistock Hall
1999	Peter Rosselli, Ashgrove, Overton

In addition, the following Wrexham and district men have served as High Sheriffs of Flintshire:

1750	Ellis Yonge of Bryn Iorkin, Hope and Acton Park
1816	George Boscawen of Marford
1962	Alastair Stewart Durward Graesser of Glasfryn, Gresford

High Street

The earliest reference to a street here is made in the 1562 survey which records '… the king's highway leading from the old cross of the said town [Wrexham] to the beast market' and later names the highway as 'High Streate', although it may well have existed long before then. It is evident, therefore, that High Street originally extended from the Old Town Hall building to the Beast Market,* along the present day High Street and Charles Street. There are also references to the section of Town Hill between Abbot Street and Church Street being included in High Street. At its highest point, in front of the Shire Hall stood the High Cross* which Palmer* saw mentioned in a document which he dated as being from the reign of Edward IV.

In the 17th century, much of the south side of the street was occupied by Tŷ Mawr which had a rentable value three times that

High Street, c.1832. The buildings and people are out of proportion to each other but this image does provide the earliest view along High Street.

High Street, c.1895.

of any other premises in High Street. It was demolished in 1738. John Rowland, apothecary, lived at Nº 6 during the 1780s which house (along with Nº 7) became the Northern and Central Bank of England in 1834 until that company failed in 1836.

By the 19th century, and well into the 20th century, High Street was the retail hub of the town. The removal of the buses from High Street to King Street changed the whole focus of Wrexham and the street declined as a retail thoroughfare. Instead, by the 1960s it had became the commercial centre of the town with several banks and insurance companies occupying the buildings.

The re-development of the town centre during the latter part of the 1990s, led to the active promotion of High Street as a 'wining and dining quarter' and a number of licensed premises opened here, particularly during 1998 and 1999. The street was finally closed to through traffic and pedestrianised in 2000 (access being given only to buses and disabled drivers). In 2001, a further £50,000 was spent on reducing the width of the pavements to allow easier access for buses travelling along High Street in both directions.

Perhaps the most interesting of the houses that have now been demolished was Nº 1, which occupied the site which is now the premises of the Nationwide Building Society. From 1871 until their demolition in the 1970s, these premises housed Dutton's Sig-ar-ro Stores,* one of Wrexham's leading grocery businesses. Before then, however, the premises had almost certainly been a town house of some significance. At the time of its proposed demolition the building was described as 'A quite extraordinary building ... now in three storeys with a flat roof; it is of two

High Street, c.1900. The east view with the Wynnstay Arms Hotel in the distance. The centre of the street was used as a cab rank.

High Street (south side), c.1960. The premises of Woodalls Printers and Hughes & Son. [RCHBW]

periods visibly, the latter section (on the corner) possibly casing or replacing a timber-framed building' which was 'of at least two storeys, rectangular in plan with the High Street corner cut off. In the first floor is the decorated plaster ceiling, in two decorative sections, but possibly intended as decoration for a single room.' Planning permission for its demolition was granted subject to the proviso that efforts were made to remove and preserve the decorated ceiling.

Nºˢ 36–37 High Street: This was an early 18th century building with an even earlier wing at the rear positioned at right angles to the street line. On the ground floor were two 19th century shops which were once occupied by Woodalls & Hughes & Son.

The building on the corner of Church Street was built in 1897 as new premises for Parr's Banking Company Ltd. This later became the Westminster Bank (until the 1960s), the Trustee Savings Bank (until the 1990s), and was converted into licensed premises named Harveys (in 2001) and is currently the Bank wine bar and bistro.

Highfield (Cae Bryn)
Located off the Wrexham – Summerhill Road at the junction with Pump House Road (now the site of Stansty Nursing Home). Originally called Cae Bryn, this 17th century house. It was sold to the Kyrke family of Bryn Mali in 1814. Richard Kyrke turned the house from a modest farm house into a modernised country house and changed the name to Highfield. In 1839, the house was inherited by the Wrexham surgeon, John Dickenson,* and his wife, Margaret, daughter of Richard Kyrke. In 1881, the small Highfield estate was sold to Sir Evan Morris,* the Wrexham solicitor and Mayor. It was sold by auction on 12 August 1895 when it was described as being 'of modern design'. It was surrounded by ornamental gardens and tennis courts. The new proprietor was Walter Pen Dennis who changed the name to Pendine Hall. Some of the land was sold off for building and the residential area today known as Highfield was built in the 1890s. Plans were also submitted for selling off some of the land on the Wrexham side of the house for building but nothing came of this. [Plan DRO/DD/DM/188/33] See also Pendine Hall.

Highgate Inn, Pen-y-Bryn
One of the oldest public houses in Wrexham, the Highgate Inn stood on Pen-y-Bryn, opposite the junction of Chapel Street. Palmer* found records dating from 1680 which made reference to this property. In its latter years, when it was known as Highgate

159

The Highgate Inn, c.1910.

House, this building was a private residence. The house was timber-framed with a cruck in the south wall. The building was occupied until a few weeks before its demolition in 1953. Edward Matthews of the Highgate Inn died in 1859 and Thomas Lloyd, of Highgate in 1869. Both are buried in the Burial Ground on Ruthin Road. It was demolished in November 1953. (See also Flower-de-Luce)

Hightown
Hightown was the name given to the late nineteenth century development bounded by Rivulet Road in the north, Bryn-y-Cabanau Road in the west and Hightown Barracks* in the south and east. A number of streets of terraced houses were built south of King's Mills Road, alongside Bryn-y-Cabanau Lane (Road).*

Most of these houses were demolished in the late 1960s to make way for the blocks of flats at Gatefield* and Napier Square.* Bury Street,* Albert Street,* Stanley Street* and Derby Road were laid out in the early 1890s.

Hightown Barracks
Building work on the barracks to serve as the 23rd Brigade Depot was finished in 1877, the whole having cost £30,000. The first soldiers, members of the 23rd Regiment of Foot (RWF) moved in to the barracks on 17 August 1877. The barracks were the focus of RWF life until the headquarters was moved to Caernarfon Barracks in 1968. During both the First and Second World Wars, recruits reported to Hightown Barracks where basic training was carried out. During the Second World War the barracks were also used by a Commando unit. The first intake of National

The Sergeants' Mess, Hightown Barracks, c.1910.

Aerial view of Hightown taken in 1963. Of particular interest is the triangle of open land on the left, between Bryn-y-Cabanau Road, King's Mills Road and Napier Street. At the top corner of the triangle is Gatefield which was demolished, along with Napier Street, Trafalgar Road and Nelson Street to make way for the council flats. Also clearly visible is the Rivulet Road gas works and the Cambrian leather Works. [Derrick Pratt]

The Parade Ground, Hightown Barracks, c.1910.

Servicemen arrived in January 1952. In recent years the barracks have served as the Depot for the RWF Territorials and, at the time of writing (2010)), the only military presence is a A Company of the 3rd Bn, Royal Welsh (TA) and the Battalion HQ and HQ Company of 101 Force Support Bn, Royal Electrical &Mechanical Engineers.

Part of the barracks has been taken over by the Department of Transport as the Wrexham Driving Test Centre and a developer has converted part of the site into apartments. In addition, a new block of apartments, named Corunna Court (after the 1809 battle where the RWF fought), has recently been built overlooking Kingsmill Road by Hawk Group of Wem.

Hightown English Wesleyan Methodist Chapel, Nelson Street
A Calvinistic Methodist mission was established in Hightown in 1884 and, in 1890 a substantial chapel was opened in Nelson Street* with a membership of 35.

Hightown Halt
This small railway halt was located on the south-west side of the Wrexham – Ellesmere railway line and was accessed by steps leading down from Whitegate Road,* alongside Connor Crescent.* Opened in July 1923, it was the first stop for trains after leaving Wrexham Central and was regularly used by children attending Grove Park Schools* and commuters travelling to Wrexham town centre.

Hightown Halt, 1950s.

Hightown Iron Church
This church was located on the north-west corner of the Whitegate Road/King's Mills Road junction. It was moved to make way for the Church of St John the Baptist* which was built on the site and opened in 1910. The Iron Church was reassembled behind the new church and served as a schoolroom and vestry. The Religious Census of 1881 showed: Capacity 200; attendance (AM & PM) 214.

Hightown Road
Hightown Road was laid out in the early 1890s by Ebenezer Pike through what had previously been the Caia Park Estate, between Smithfield Road and Rivulet Road. Most of the houses along this road appear to have been built in 1898/99. It was crossed by a bridge carrying the Wrexham–Ellesmere railway just below the junctions of Caia Road and Benjamin Road.

Hill Court, Hightown
This street was laid out in the 1980s on land that had previously been the property of C. T. Clark, proprietor of the King's Mills Garage. Built by the Wales and West Housing Association, all the streets in this development were named after RWF who had been awarded the Victoria Cross.

Hill Court is named after Pte Albert Hill, VC, of the 10th Bn, RWF. A native of Hulme in Manchester, Albert Hill was a collier before volunteering for service on the outbreak of war in 1914. He was awarded the Victoria Cross for his action at Delville Wood on 20 July 1916. He also received the Croix de Guerre from France. The citation for his VC reads:

> For most conspicuous bravery. When his battalion had deployed under very heavy fire for an attack on the enemy in a wood, he dashed forward, when the order to charge was given and, meeting two of the enemy suddenly, bayonetted them both. He was sent later by his platoon sergeant to get in touch with the company and, finding himself cut off and almost surrounded by some twenty of the enemy, he attacked them with bombs, killing and wounding many and scattering the remainder. He then joined a sergeant of his company and helped him to fight the way back to the lines. When he got back, hearing that his Company Officer and a scout were lying out wounded, he went out and assisted to bring in the wounded officer, two other men bringing in the scout.
>
> Finally, he himself captured and brought in as prisoners two of the enemy. His conduct throughout was magnificent.

Hill emigrated to the USA in 1923, living in Rhode Island. He died on 17 February 1971 and was buried in Highland Memorial Park, Johnston, Rhode Island.

Hill Crest, Spring Lodge
This street was laid out in 1933 as part of the second phase of the Borough Council's Spring Lodge housing estate.* The name is a reference to the geographical location of the street.

Hill Street
This was originally the rear entrance to Bryn-y-Ffynnon House* and provided access to the coach house and stables. The street ended just below the English Presbyterian Chapel* – the present day Little Theatre* – and was only extended round into Vicarage Hill* following the opening of the Central Station.*

Hill Street English Presbyterian Church
Originally housed in an old warehouse on the corner of Bank Street,* this congregation had been established in Wrexham in 1845. Land alongside the drive leading to the stables of Bryn-y-Ffynnon House* (now Hill Street) was presented to the Bank Street church by local coach-builder Richard Davies and a new church and schoolroom was built there at a cost of £650. The new

church was opened on Good Friday, 10 April 1857. The congregation in Abbot Street had been a very small one but, as soon as they moved to Hill Street, it grew quite dramatically and by 1860 had trebled. A schoolroom and vestry, which had been built alongside the chapel on land bought from Sir Watkin Williams Wynn, at a cost of £688-10s-4d, was opened in 1873.

The congregation here was responsible for establishing three missions, the first at Garden Lane [Road],* Rhosddu in 1880 (closed 1882); the second in the schoolroom of the Rhosddu Welsh Methodist Chapel* and the third on the corner of Bersham Road* and Victoria Road* which opened in 1892.

By the early years of the 20th century, church members were becoming dissatisfied with the Hill Street premises which were bounded to the south by the railway, and had electric trams passing the front door. Properties were bought in Roxborough Place* with a view to expanding the church there. Eventually, however, they bought a site on the south-west corner of King Street* and Rhosddu Road* and work commenced on the building of a new church and schoolroom which was to be named Trinity.* The old Hill Street church was sold and the congregation moved into the new, but as yet incomplete, church in November 1907.

The Hill Street church schoolroom was sold to the Freemasons* for £800 and the chapel itself (and the Chapel House) to the Temperance Hall Trustees for £1350. The former schoolroom now houses the Grove Park Little Theatre.* A history of this church *A Few Notes on the origins and progress of Hill Street English Presbyterian Church*, by Edward Jarman, was published in 1908 and further details appeared in 1988 in the book *Trinity A Town Centre Church* by Joan M. Hughes. The chapel building, with seating for 300, is shown on the 1872 survey. The Religious Census of 1881 showed: Capacity 320; attendance (AM & PM) 240. The Religious Census of 1904 showed: Capacity 400; attendance (AM & PM) 265.

Hillbury, Hillbury Road
Located on Hillbury Road, this was the home of the Bury family. The house was built in the early 1860s by John Bury (possibly to a design by J. R. Gummow*) in a field which was called Cae'r Garnedd (*Trans*. field of the cairn) at the time of the 1620 survey. In later years the field was called Cae Bryn (*Trans*. hill field). In December 1862, workmen laying out the kitchen garden began to level out a mound (about 30 metres in diameter and 4 metres high in the centre) when they discovered a burial chamber containing human bones and fragments of pottery believed to have been a food vessel and a cinerary urn (which would have contained incinerated human bones). In 1907 the urn fragments were presented to Wrexham Public Library where they were exhibited; they have since disappeared. The house was named Hillbury after this mound and the Bury family. During the early years of the 20th century Hillbury was the home of George A. S. Mowat, (co-proprietor of the Island Green Brewery*). In later years it was the home of Frank Crowe (wholesale fruiterer) who sold it in 1966 to the Congregation of the Poor Sisters of Nazareth and its name was changed to Nazareth House.* In 2005 the nursing home was sold to the Kreft family and merged with Gwern Alyn residential home.

Hillbury Road/Lane
This was named after Hillbury* the home of John Bury,* a member of the original Town Council. The house named Wrest* stood at the junction of Hillbury Road and Percy Road. This road originally extended from Percy Road to Sontley Road but now only has footpath access beyond the entrance to Nazareth House.*

Hillcrest Estate, Borras Park
Hillcrest was the name given to the housing estate built in the 1960s on the south-east side of Borras Park Road, comprising Brecon Close,* Caernarvon Road,* Cardigan Road,* Anglesey Close,* Denbigh Road,* Denbigh Close, Pembroke Road* and Monmouth Road. The land on which these houses were built was bought by William Clarke* and sold to the Blantern family of Plas Goulbourne who were responsible for the development.

Hilltop View Road, Borras Park
A small development of private houses built in c.1965 by the London firm of Spinks & Denning on land that had previously belonged to William Clarke* and, pre-1918, to the Acton Park* estate. The name relates to the position of the street.

Hilly View
A small terrace of houses located between Erddig Road and Fairfield Street and between John Street and Earl Street.

Hippodrome Cinema
This was built in 1909 as the Opera House or New Public Hall on the site of the old Public Hall* in Henblas Street which was destroyed by fire in 1906. It had seating for 800 and opened on 2 August 1909 with the musical comedy *Sergeant Brue*. In July 1913, the building became known as the Hippodrome and was owned by The Wrexham Hippodrome Ltd (which later became Wrexham Entertainments Ltd) which continued with live plays and variety shows until 9 September 1929 when, after conversion to a cinema, it showed *The Donovan Affair*, the first talking film to be seen in Wrexham.

The cinema closed in November 1959 and remained so until 13 June 1961 when it was re-opened by Barry Flanagan. In addition to films, the Hippodrome was also a venue for professional wrestling and rock concerts. In 1988, the cinema was divided into two, following the trend for multi-screen cinemas.

After the opening of a new multi-screen cinema at Plas Coch in 1997, the Hippodrome closed in the autumn only to re-open for a few weeks over the Christmas period. The building was empty for over ten years (suffering a fire on 16 August 2008) and, despite a local campaign for it to be granted listed status, was demolished on 6 April 2009 and the site is currently vacant, awaiting redevelopment. (*Ninety Years of Cinema in Wrexham*, Brian Hornsey, privately published 1990).

Hippodrome Theatre
See Hippodrome Cinema.

Holly Bank, Ruabon Road
A pair of semi-detached houses on the corner of Ruabon Road and Wellington Street. One of these (Nº 17 in 1881) was the childhood home of Sir Leonard Rowland.*

Holly Grove, Queen's Park
This area of the Cefn Park* estate was requisitioned during the Second World War and temporary housing built in 1941 to accommodate Royal Ordnance Factory* workers. When the war was over these houses were utilised by WBC as temporary corporation housing and, in some cases, survived until the mid 1950s when they were known locally as 'Cardboard City'. The temporary houses were replaced by permanent dwellings, built by W.D. Stant on behalf of WBC, between the 1950s and 1960s. Most of the streets in this area were given the names of trees and shrubs. The land was bought by means of a compulsory purchase order from Lt-Col R.G. Fenwick-Palmer.*

Holly Walks, Pen-y-Maes Avenue
Laid out in the grounds of the large house called Pen-y-Maes,* these houses were a speculative development by local builder Norman Rogers in the 1980s.

Holm Oak, Rhosddu Road
A private dwelling located opposite Abbotsfield,* close to the corner with Grove Road. [DRO/DD/G/2919]

Holt Court
Located between Regis Place and Market Street.

Holt Road
The site of the Wrexham gallows was in Holt Road, just below the roundabout at the junction of Holt Road, Bodhyfryd, Holt Street and Farndon Street.

On the north side of the road, in the area now occupied by the grounds of Wrexham Water World* and the inner ring road, stood Holt Street Terrace* (9 houses) and Park View* (4 houses). Next to these, on the site now occupied by Capel-y-Groes* was a large private house, built in the late 19th century, named Beaconsfield. After the Second World War this house was bought by the Church in Wales and was converted into Llanelwy, a home for unmarried mothers. It was demolished in the 1970s and all that remains of it is the boundary wall along the Holt Road footpath. The Alexandra Schools were built here in 1910 and, along with St Christopher's School, served the area until demolished in 2000 to make was for the new ASDA building. Further along was the British Celanese Club, the Maes-y-Dre Community Centre and the Religious Society of Friends Meeting House, all built in the 1950s and 1960s. Between Aston Grove (laid out in the 1930s) and Borras Road, WBC developed the Maes-y-Dre* Housing Estate in the early 1930s. The shop premises on the junction of Borras Road was built by Alderman Herbert Jennings* in the late 1930s. The Hand Hotel* was built in the early years of the Second World War. There was once a tollgate situated close to the junction with Borras Road which, in 1841, was occupied by Ann Edwards (gatekeeper) and her son Price. The estate of private houses (Moorhead Close, Bickley Wood Drive and Halstonwood Close) was built in the early 1990s on land that had previously been part of the playing fields of St David's School.* The commercial building (now the premises of PHS) was a NAAFI building during the Second World War providing various facilities to the servicemen billeted in the area. Post war it was taken over by Hollis & Vines as a sewing-machine factory then by clothing manufacturer Chester Barrie and, in 1978, Jaeger clothing and now (2010) Denbighshire Stair Lifts. The former police station just beyond St David's Court was built as the village police station for Rhosnesni. To the north-east of the police station stood a small farm which was the property of Ernest Owens who, in the 1930s, built two pairs of semi-detached houses (Nos 81, 83, 85 & 87) on part of the land fronting onto Holt Road. Approaching the crossroads by the Greyhound public house, set back from the road, are two of the old cottages of the village of Rhosnesni (N°s 197 & 199) and the last building on the north side of Holt Road is the old tollgate house, known locally as the Old Bar.

Travelling along the south side of Holt Road from the roundabout junction with Farndon Street there is now little to observe for the first 200 yards. However, this was originally the site of the Victoria Inn* and James Edwards' garage. In 1888, James Edwards (died 1900) is listed in the trade directories as a cab proprietor and licensed victualler of the Victoria Inn. The garage was founded on vacant land next to the inn and continued to serve as a motor agency (originally British Leyland then Ford) until demolished in 2000 to make way for the new Tesco Extra store. Next to this stood the former Border Bottling Store which was demolished in 2001 when the profile of the land was completely changed to accommodate the Border Retail Park. Land to the east side of this site, belonging to Edward Hollis, was sold in June 1892 as ten building plots and the row of red-brick terraced houses (at one time known locally as Pig Tail Row because of its proximity to the slaughter house) were built on the site shortly afterwards. The Borough Depot and slaughter house were built in the area of Pwll-yr-Uwd* in 1863, close to the present day Hill Crest Surgery. A disused sand hole, belonging to John Bithell and much of land surrounding the depot was used as the town rubbish dump from 1898 until after the Second World War, when it became the site of corporation housing in the area of Montgomery Road.* The Spring Lodge* Housing Estate was built on the site of Spring Lodge Farm* in the early 1930s. The Tan-y-Dre Housing Estate was laid out in the 1960s as part of the larger post-war Queen's Park estate. On the site of the present day Chanticleer Close* was Chanticleer,* a market-garden smallholding and the two houses named Ladysmith and Natal (N°s 182 & 184) were built by Mrs Nancy Taylor who had been born in South Africa. Drawing closer to Rhosnesni, Brooklands Garage was named after the world famous Brooklands motor racing track in Surrey. Just to the east of Brooklands Garage, at N°s 196 & 198 Holt Road, are two private houses which used to be one. The linking building, which was demolished in 2000, was part of the original house of the Old Maids' Farm* and part of the farm orchard survives as the garden.

In 2001, five new cottages were built (N°s 1 – 5 Smithy Court) on the site of what had been the village blacksmith's shop for Rhosnesni. This cottage was also the original Greyhound public house (the tenant was a blacksmith by day and a publican by night). Finally, the present Greyhound* public house was built c.1900.

Beyond the Holt Road/Dean Road/Bryn Estyn Road/Cefn Road roundabout, the flats at Langford Close were built in the 1970s and the Goulbourne private housing estate was developed on land that had been the fields of Plas Goulbourne* Farm. Mile Barn Cottage,* on the north side of Holt Road just before the Llan-y-Pwll Link Road* roundabout was once a farm in its own right with what was probably a tithe barn nearby. The houses on the south side of the road were built at various times after the end of the First World War with Old Gardens being built in 2000–01. Work commenced in 2000 on the large private Fairways* housing estate on the opposite side of Holt Road to the Goulbourne estate. Most of the land on which it was built, known as the Poor Ground,* was previously the property of local church charities and one small section was part of Ty'n Twll Farm.* The street names on this new estate show an almost total lack of local association and are taken from the names of golf courses and golfing events, because of the proximity of Wrexham Golf Club.*

Holt Street
Named after the village of Holt. This street appears on early surveys of the town as Lower Lampit Street [DRO/ DD/WY/8352] and Palmer* refers to it as having been called 'Five Barn Street' in 1749 and that the name 'Holt Street' did not come into use until the end of the 18th century. The Friends (Quaker) Meeting House* stood to the west of the Quaker Burial Ground (now the Peace Garden), on the site now occupied by the Wingett offices. The burial ground was laid out here sometime after 1708. To the east of the burial ground, roughly the site of the entrance to the present day Bodhyfryd Car Park, was for many years an area of open meadow. Alongside this was Holt Street Cottage* which was still standing at the end of the 19th century and can be seen on both the 1833 and 1872 surveys. Holt Street House* stood near the junction with Market Street [plans for cottages in this street,

dated 1912, DRO/1078]. The properties opposite the junction with Farndon Street consisted of a terrace of poor quality housing with the White Horse* public house in the centre. Some of these were demolished as part of the Borough's slum clearance programme of 1938 and the remainder were levelled when the inner ring road and swimming baths were constructed at Bodhyfryd.* [Plans DRO/1053]

Holt Street Buildings
A terrace of houses on the southern side of Holt Street* near to its junction with Farndon Street.*

Holt Street Cottage
Built in about 1726 as the home of William Jones, the Parish Clerk, this house was located on the north side of Holt Street, roughly where the entry to the Bodhyfryd Car Park is now located. It was later bought by Thomas Hayman, an attorney and he was followed in ownership by the Griffith family of Hafod-y-Bwch* and Great Ash, Whitchurch, and by Joseph Cooper of Bodhyfryd House.* Between 1806 and 1814, Thomas Edgworth, a solicitor, lived here and he was followed in 1826 by Edwin Wyatt, another solicitor, and then by Owen Owen Williams, whose widow was still living here in the 1880s.

Holt Street House
Built in the mid 18th century, probably by Thomas Hayman (whose daughter was Privy Purse to Queen Caroline and built Glasfryn in Gresford). The house was located on the south side of Holt Street between Market Street and Farndon Street, opposite the gate to the present day Peace Garden.* It was for many years the surgery of various doctors. The house was demolished in the 1960s. [DRO/958]
Owners and residents:
- c.1759 Thomas Hayman, attorney (of Tŷ Meredith* and Yspyty*)
- c.1788 Robert Griffith (of Hafod-y-Bwch, died 1795)
- c.1795 Thomas Murhall Griffith [I] (High Sheriff of Denbighshire, 1813, died 1820)
- c.1820 Thomas Murhall Griffith [II] (of Great Ash, Whitchurch)
- c.1820–25 various tenants
- c.1825 Joseph Cooper (of Bodhyfryd*)
- c.1856 Dr Edward Williams, surgeon (son-in-law of Joseph Cooper above), although he had lived in it as a tenant for many years previously. He was still living here in 1888.
- c.1912 S.E. Jones, surgeon.
- c.1952 D. Livingstone, surgeon.

Holt Street Terrace.

Holt Street Terrace
A terrace of houses on the northern side of Holt Road, almost opposite the Victoria Inn.

Holy Family Convent, Sontley Road
See Plas Derwen.

Holyrood Crescent, Croes Eneurys
It was built on land that had formerly been part of Croes Eneurys Farm.* In common with the other roads on this development, the road was named after a royal palace, in this case, Holyrood House in Edinburgh.

Homestead
Located on the northern side of Bersham Road, between the Homestead housing estate and Centenary Road, this house would appear to have been built during the 1860s, possibly to a design by the local architect Gummow (see Gummow Family). In 1881 this was the house of the Revd George Bewsher, MA, (died 1888) and, between 1902 and 1912, was the home of R. Lyons. At one time, it was the home of Henry Robertson (son of Sir Henry B. Robertson*). Described in the 1902 sale brochure as 'a charming freehold family residence', it had four bedrooms, one dressing room and a bachelor bedroom. The house and grounds were bought in the late 1920s by D.T. Roberts & Sons Ltd, butchers, who converted the outbuildings into a meat processing factory and abattoir. The company closed down in the 1970s and the land sold for development. The house was demolished in the mid 1980s. It gave its name to The Homestead, a small private housing estate that was built in the late 1970s/early 1980s.

Homestead Lane
Named after the house 'Homestead'* which stood nearby.

Hooson, MA, **Isaac David 'I.D.'** *poet*
Born in Rhosllanerchrugog in 1880, Isaac David Hooson was the son of Alderman Edward Hooson, JP, a grocer and draper and former chairman of Denbighshire County Council of Victoria House,

Holt Street House. The surgery was located in the annexe on the right of the photograph. [RCHBW]

I.D. Hooson.

Market Street, Rhos. Educated at Ruabon Grammar School he became a trainee wholesale grocer before becoming an articled clerk to the Wrexham legal firm of Hopley Pierce. Admitted as a solicitor in 1909, I.D. Hooson went into partnership with Oswald Hughes of Wrexham. For twenty years he was the Official Receiver for Chester and North Wales. He served as chairman of the Appeal Tribunal of the Assistance Board, the Wrexham Public Library Committee and was a governor of both the Ruabon and Wrexham Grammar Schools. He was also the legal adviser to Wrexham Football Club and President of the Rhos Chess Club.

I.D. Hooson was the author of many ballads and lyrics and was recognised as one of the foremost poets of Wales in the 20th century. His translation of the Pied Piper of Hamelin is generally regarded as a Welsh classic. A member of the National Eisteddfod Council and a poetry adjudicator, he received an honorary MA degree from the University of Wales in June 1947.

A lifelong bachelor, he died on 18 October 1948. A three-ton granite memorial to him was unveiled on the Panorama Walk, above the Dee valley in September 1952, close to the spot where his ashes were scattered. A painting 'The One-Man Band' by Leonard Applebee, captures the mood of his early poem *Y Band Undyn* (The One-Man Band), and hangs in the Miners Institute in Rhosllanerchrugog.

Hop Pole Inn, Yorke Street
According to Palmer,* the public house that is now known as the Black Horse Inn* in Yorke Street 'was aforetime 'The Old Hop Pole''. This would seem to indicate that there was an actual inn called 'The Old Hop Pole' but the evidence would suggest otherwise. What appears to have happened is that a public house called 'The Hop Pole' moved premises from half-way down the east side of Yorke Street to a site next to the Wynnstay Arms Vaults.* The vacated premises then took on the new name of 'The Black Horse' but, for a time, were referred to as the 'Old' Hop Pole to differentiate them from the 'New' Hop Pole. It does not appear in the 1833 survey but is in the 1872 survey.

Hope Cottage/Villa, Regent Street
This house, which is now the premises of the Lager Club on Union Road appears in the 1841 census as 'New Cottage' and was the home of the Cathrall family. Thomas Cathrall was a slater and was followed into the business by his son Gwilt who, towards the end of the 19th century, became an important builder in the town. It is this family home that gave the original name Cathrall's Lane to Union Road. In 1859 the resident was Mr Wood. A James Davenport of Hope Villa died in 1884 and is buried in the Burial Ground* on Ruthin Road. This house is sometimes referred to as Hope Villa, and was bought in the 1890s and converted for use as a nurses' home for the Wrexham Infirmary.

Hope Road
See Regent Street.

Hope Street
All the older street names in the town appear to refer to the towns and villages that they lead towards. Thus Hope Street (Stryt yr Hôb) takes its name from the village of Hope in Flintshire. Palmer* found a reference to this street being called 'stryd yr hopp' in 1553. The name originally applied to the whole road from the High Cross* to Wat's Dyke* (roughly the railway bridge at the end of Regent Street*). It was only during the 19th century that the name became restricted to the road from the High Cross to the junction with Priory Lane (now Priory Street*). The regular vegetable market was held in Hope Street until the opening of the Market Hall* in 1841. On the corner of Priory Street* stood three thatched cottages, two of which were demolished in 1889 and the remaining one was converted into the Horse & Jockey public house.*

James Kenrick had a grocery business at N° 56 Hope Street in the early 19th century and built a private bank on the southern side of the entrance to Bank Street. After Kenrick's death in 1824, his nephew continued the business and went into partnership with John Eddowes Bowman to form the Kenrick & Bowman Bank.* In 1849, the business went into bankruptcy and the building was taken over by the National Provincial Bank of England who later built the present building on the same site. In the 1960s, the National Provincial Bank merged with the Westminster Bank and the District Bank to become the National Westminster Bank and remained on this site until the property was sold to the Halifax Building Society. The former Lion Hotel*

Hope Street, c.1905.

Hope Street, c.1935.

at N° 57 was demolished in the 1930s and became the site of Wrexham's first F.W. Woolworth store. After the building of the new Woolworth store in Regent Street in the 1970s, the shop had a number of occupants, culminating in W.H. Smith and various retail outlets. The building was badly damaged in a fire during the night of 22/23 October 2001 and the site was cleared and a new store built. The Central Arcade was built between this site and Dutton's Sig-ar-ro Stores* on the corner of High Street in 1891.

Hope Street House, Regent Street
Located on the north side of Regent Street this half-timbered house was demolished by Thomas Hughes, to provide a site for the building of N°s 31 & 32 Regent Street. His son, the solicitor Allington Hughes, had his office in the new building and the company remained there until it moved to its present offices in Grosvenor Road. In 1869, this was the home of William Davies, dental surgeon.

Hope Street Welsh Baptist Chapel
Founded in a room of Stanfords Café in Hope Street by 54 members of Capel Calfaria. They remained here until 1897 when they moved to Chapel Street. (See Chapel Street Welsh Baptist Church)

Horns Bridge
Named after the Horns Inn which stood on its south end. In 1585/6 the bridge is recorded as being named Pont-y-Llianeu and the spelling changed over the years to Pont-y-Lleaney (1665), Pont-y-Llyana (1707). The word *'lleianau'* is Welsh for nuns suggesting that there may at some time have been a religious house located in the area.

Horns Inn, Bridge Street
Shown in the 1833 survey, this was a favourite haunt of the cattle drovers as they passed through Wrexham. It had been re-named the King's Arms by 1890 (when its former landlord, John Smith, was buried in the Burial Ground* on Ruthin Road) but retained its earlier name amongst the local population.

Horse & Jockey, Hope Street
Despite appearances to the contrary and the popular belief that the *Horse & Jockey* is one of the oldest public houses in Wrexham, Palmer* makes no mention of it being a public house in his 1893 *History of the Town of Wrexham*. Instead, he refers to three old cottages located in Hope Street, between the *Buck* public house and Priory Lane (Street), of which only one remained standing in 1893, the one on the actual corner. The name was given to the public house in recognition of the famous jockey Fred Archer. Town re-development plans produced in the late 1950s included the demolition of this building but, thankfully, neither they, nor a fire in the 1980s, have managed to remove this last example of a timber and thatch building from the Wrexham streetscape.

Horse Sales
See Eagles' Meadow.

Horseshoe, Bank Street
This public house is first recorded in 1755 and was located on the north side of Bank Street on the site now occupied by an amusement arcade. Originally licensed to sell only beer it obtained a full on-sales licence in 1963 and was a Wrexham Lager house. It closed in 1985.

Horsley Drive, Little Acton
Built by WBC on land that was previously part of Little Acton Farm.* It is named after the township of Horsley in the parish of Gresford.

Horsley Hall, Marford
Originally Plas-yn-Horsli, this property dates back to before the Norman Conquest and is mentioned in the Domesday Book. By the late Middle Ages the estate was the property of the Powell family, descendants of Howell ap David ap Gruffydd Fychan. In the mid sixteenth century, Thomas Powell built a large half-timbered manor house on the site which was described in Norden's survey of 1620. When the Powell line became extinct with the death of Sir Samuel Powell in 1707 it passed to the family of his sister, Winifred Lloyd. In 1792 it was sold to John Hughes of Wrexham and after him to Frederick Potts, agent to the Grosvenor Family of Eaton Hall. Potts demolished much of the original house and built a new hall in the neo-Tudor style. His son sold the estate to cotton manufacturer Alfred Ashworth in the early twentieth century. In 1917 it was sold to William Hall Walker, MP for Widnes (1900–19) who was made 1st Baron Wavertree in 1919 and he spent a great deal of money on restoring and developing the gardens. Walker was the son of the Liverpool brewer Sir Andrew Barclay Walker and a nephew of Peter Walker,* the Wrexham brewer and mayor. His father was a benefactor of Liverpool University and founded the Walker Art Gallery to which Lord Wavertree later also made a sustantial bequest in his will. He was a passionate polo player and horse breeder, founding the stud which later became the Irish National Stud. On his death in 1933 Horsley Hall was sold to a developer. During the Second World War it was taken over by the military and was demolished in 1963.

Above & below: Horsley Hall, c.1910.

Howell, BD, Dean Davidj *theologian*
David Howell, perhaps the most outstanding religious figure to hold the living of vicar of Wrexham, was born at Tre Oes, Llangan in Glamorgan on 16 August 1831, the son of John Howell, a farmer, poet and Calvinistic Methodist elder. He was educated at the Eagle School, Cowbridge and then the Llandaff church training college at Abergavenny. He was ordained a deacon in 1855 and a priest the following year. David Howell was curate at Neath from 1855–61, vicar of Pwllheli and St John's, Cardiff before being appointed vicar of Wrexham during a period of great change in the Anglican church both nationally and within the town. When he was appointed in 1875, Wrexham had only two churches (St Giles and St Marks), the latter serving as a chapel-of-ease. When he left to become vicar of Gresford in 1891 the town boasted nine Anglican churches. Howells was awarded the degree of Bachelor of Divinity by Lambeth Palace in 1877, became Rural Dean of Wrexham in 1882, an Hon Canon of St Asaph, Prebendary of Meliden and Treasurer of St Asaph in 1885 and Archdeacon of Wrexham in 1889. In 1897 he was appointed Dean of St David's. He married Anne Powell of Pencoed, Glamorgan in 1851 when aged only 19 (she was 16) and they had four sons and four daughters. She died in 1891 at Llwynisaf Vicarage* and was buried in Gresford. One of their sons was Brigadier-General Arthur Anthony Howell.

Howell, an ecclesiastical nationalist, would undoubtedly have welcomed the disestablishment of the Welsh Anglican Church. He was a thorn in the side of the Anglican establishment with his constant demands for a revised focus on Wales and Welshness within the Church. He lambasted the 19th century Anglicans for their almost total failure to produce a preacher of note, had there been one then there might have been a stronger counter to the Nonconformist 'reformation' that was sweeping through the land. He believed that the Anglicans had deliberately overlooked churchmen who were fluent in Welsh in favour of the appointment of outsiders with greater political and social power. The ability to preach well through the medium of Welsh was, he said, almost certainly to result in an individual career coming to an abrupt halt. 'The Church has ignored Wales. Think of conditions in the last century when a Bishop of Bangor could hold the see without so much as setting his foot within his diocese for six years. Think of the early part of the century when the Bishop of Llandaff – regarded as a model bishop – lived as a farmer in Westmorland whither clergy of his

David Howell, Vicar of Wrexham.

diocese had to go whenever they wished to consult with him.' It was little wonder therefore that the mass of the people of Wales felt that the Church was an alien force within their land. In Wrexham, his campaign to make the Church more tolerant towards the Welsh language resulted in the establishment of St David's Welsh Church on Rhosddu Road.* Howell was twice considered for a bishopric but had too many enemies within the Anglican church. The fact that he had married only five months before the birth of their first child was held up as evidence of his unsuitability for high office and when this fact was pointed out to the naïve Queen Victoria, any hope he may have had of advancement to a see vanished. His sixteen years in Wrexham endeared him to everyone in the parish, both Anglican and Nonconformist. Even those who, like the congregation of St Mark's Church, criticised him in his early days, spoke highly of him when he departed and he certainly left his mark upon both the religious and social life of the town. Survey figures show that when he arrived in 1875 there were only seven Anglican services conducted at various locations each Sunday by three clergymen and at Easter, there were 128 communicants. In 1895, there were twenty-one services, conducted by ten clergymen with 835 Easter communicants.

In addition to his church duties, Howell was also a poet of some repute, writing under the bardic name of Llawdden. He died in St David's on 15 January 1903 and is buried in the St Nicholas Chapel of the cathedral. He is remembered on a memorial tablet in St David's Cathedral and a memorial window in St Giles' Parish Church, Wrexham was unveiled by Canon Fletcher in 1904. In recognition of Howell's great power as a preacher, the window depicts the Sermon on the Mount.

Canon Fletcher spoke of Howell in 1904: 'The ministry of Dean Howell ... in this town, was, characterised by three great points. First of all there was his tremendous industry ... seen in his indefatigable labours. ...the colliers as they went to work in early morning would often see the Vicar's gas lighted in his study, and knew that he had begun to work for them, perhaps on his knees, before they went forth to their daily toil. Secondly, there was his pastoral visitation ... his deep earnestness, his true sympathy, his large heartedness, won for him a ready entrance into the homes, aye more, into the hearts of his parishioners. And then, last of all, there was his preaching; ... his fervent eloquence drew thousands to the Saviour's side. None of them could forget the last occasion when he preached within those walls. The sight of the great crowd, and the remembrance of how hundreds were turned away from the Church's door. He stepped out in their lives and was a revelation to them of what human nature could be. He made them ashamed of themselves, and was a summons to them to rise ... to higher things.'

An excellent biography of Howell was published in 1998: *David Howell – A Pool of Spirituality. A Life of David Howell (Llawdden)*, Roger R. Brown, Gee, Denbigh.

House of Correction, *Salop Road*
See Bridewell.

Hugh Price & Company, Bridge Street & Pentre Felin
At the beginning of the 19th century the Bridge Street tannery was owned by E. Beardsworth who lived at 7 Bridge Street. It was located behind the houses on the east side of Bridge Street and on the south side of the river Gwenfro and appears in the 1833 survey. There is no reference to Beardsworth after about 1868 and, by 1870, the tannery is shown to be in the possession of Hugh Price who first appears in the 1841 census as an apprentice skinner, aged 17, living in Salop Street.* By 1871, Price is shown as a master leather dresser employing 11 men and 2 boys. By 1885, Price's tannery is one of only three shown to be operating in Wrexham.

Above: Hugh Price & Company's Bridge Street Tannery.

Below: Hugh Price & Company's Trade Mark.

Hugh Price died in 1884 and the business passed to his children, Hugh, David and Jane. Hugh died the following year and David and Jane set up a partnership under the name Hugh Price & Company. In 1885 Jane married Evan Birkett Evans* and set up home at Nº 10 Talbot Road and her husband joined her in the business. The partnership with David was dissolved in 1889 and Evan and Jane Birkett Evans became the joint owners of the company which specialised in the manufacture of leather (made exclusively from sheep skins) for use in the manufacture of rollers in the cotton industry, boots, shoes, bookbinding, belts, gloves and bags.

In 1900, the business was described as being 'laid out on an extensive scale, and the various departments are replete with machinery and appliances of the most improved and effective type, though as far as possible all the work is done by hand labour, and Messrs Hugh Price & Co. are almost the only firm who adhere to the old oak bark system of tannage. This is the only tannery in the Wrexham district where the process is carried through completely, from the rough hide to the finished article.

'Upwards of eighty workpeople find regular employment at the Bridge Street Tannery, and ... strikes are unknown to them, and there has never been a labour dispute since the works have been in existence.'

In 1903, Evan Birkett Evans bought the former Zoedone Mineral Works* in Penre Felin* for £2,050. This building had originally housed the water mill for the township of Wrexham Abbot.* In 1904 the company moved from the Bridge Street premises into what was to be known as the Abbot Leather Works. Evan retired in 1914 and the running of the company was taken over by his sons Hugh and Joseph (who were later joined by their younger brothers Harold and Ralph).

On 13 August 1928, the Abbot Leather Works was destroyed by one of the largest fires in Wrexham's history, with damage estimated at £25,000. The works had been closed for the annual

Hugh Price & Company's Pentrefelin Leather Works which were built following the fire of 1928.

holiday and was due to re-open the next morning when the fire began in a small building at the rear of the works. It was already out of control when it was discovered at 11.40 p.m. and fears for the safety of the firemen meant that efforts to save the building were abandoned shortly after midnight. Such was the demand for water by the fire brigade that the mains were unable to cope and the nearby Island Green Brewery* and cottages were threatened. Despite rumours to the contrary, the Chester fire brigade was not called to assist. While the site was cleared and a new works constructed, the company (which employed a staff of 50) moved into a small tannery in Maentwrog.

The new works, built on the same site as the old works, was opened at the end of 1931 and had 36,000 square feet of floor space on three floors. Shortly afterwards, a film was made showing the whole process from the arrival of the skins to the departure of the finished leather (extracts from this were incorporated into the video *Wrexham – a Journey Through Time*). Hugh died in 1956 and Joseph and Harold in 1963. The surviving brother, Ralph, was joined in the company by his son David and, in 1966, they established their own sales company, Hugh Price & Co (Leather) Ltd. Ralph retired in 1967, In 1970 the company won the British National Export Council award. At this time the company also entered the leather waste products industry and the works was fully re-equipped and expanded with a workforce of 120. Nearly 40% of its output was exported to 25 countries.

Unfortunately, like so many other British companies at the time, Hugh Price & Co had suffered from chronic under-investment and David Birkett-Evans sold the company (which had a staff of 125) to the British Chrome Tanning Co Ltd in 1975 and the operations were moved to Northampton two years later. The works buildings were left empty for many years and were finally demolished to make way for the Island Green shopping precinct in the late 1990s.

The company Trade Mark was a cat and monkey with the Welsh motto *Dal Vi Os Medri* (*Trans.* catch me if you can).

Hughes, Charles *publisher*
Born in Wrexham on 3 March 1823, the son of Richard* and Anne Hughes, Charles Hughes was educated at the Fairfield School (established by his uncle John Hughes) and Bridgnorth Grammar School. He was an apprentice publisher with the London firm of Simpkin & Marshall from 1844–8 before joining his father's business in Wrexham. He married Catherine Lewis of Penucha, Caerwys.

As well as his business interests he was a member of Wrexham's first Borough Council, a magistrate for both Wrexham and Denbighshire, played a prominent role in establishing the English Presbyterian Churches in both Abbot Street and Hill Street and was President of the Wrexham Liberal Association. He died at his home, Brynhyfryd,* Wrexham on 24 March 1886. His daughter Adelaide was the first wife of Sir John Herbert Lewis, Member of Parliament for Flint Boroughs (1892–1906), Flint County (1906–18) and the University of Wales (1918–22).

Hughes, Clifford *local politician*
The grandson of Ralph Williamson,* a former Mayor and Freeman of Wrexham, Clifford Hughes was born in Wrexham on 28 April 1907 and was educated at Victoria School and Grove Park Grammar School. His working life was spent in the family pork butchery business, R. Williamson Ltd, on Town Hill. He was eventually appointed the company's Managing Director. He served as the President of the Master Butchers Association for North Wales and for Wrexham.

Elected an Independent Borough Councillor in 1955, representing the Erddig Ward, he was Mayor in 1970 and Vice-chairman of the Markets Committee. He married Nora Griffiths in 1968 and lived at Derby Villa,* Derby Road, until 1971 when he moved to Westminster Drive. Clifford Hughes was a member of the Rotary Club of Wrexham,* Wrexham Probus Club, Grove Park Amateur Dramatic Society and Norman Road Tennis Club. He died in August 1982.

Hughes, Edward *trade unionist*
Born at Trelogan, Flintshire, the son of an agricultural labourer, he was educated at the local school before leaving, aged seven, to work at Trelogan mine. After various mining jobs in both north Wales and in County Durham he became known as a miners' leader during an industrial dispute at Easington Colliery. In 1887 he returned to Flintshire where he worked as a face worker at Point of Ayr colliery. The following year he successfully led a three week strike which resulted in his being appointed the colliery's first checkweighter. In 1891 he was appointed financial secretary of the Denbighshire and Flintshire Miners Association and, six years later, general secretary of the North Wales Miners Association. In 1898 he was elected permanent agent and secretary to the NWMA and moved to live in Wrexham. During his twenty-seven years in office the membership of the NWMA grew from 2,732 to 15,229 and he was elected a member of the executive of the Miners Federation of Great Britain. Elected a county councillor for Stansty in 1901 he was a county alderman from 1907–18. He married Elizabeth Hughes of Lloc in 1877 (died 1932) and they had three children. Edward Hughes died on 10 March 1925 and is buried in Wrexham Cemetery.

Hughes, MBE, JP, Alderman Edward *local politician & antiquarian*
He was born in Oswestry on 12 October 1862, the son of Joseph and Jane Hughes. He was apprenticed as an accountant in Oswestry and on qualifying became a cashier to draper Robert Lloyd. In 1884 he moved to work as a book-keeper at Jones and Rocke, Cambrian Leather Works, Wrexham. In 1888 he became chief clerk and head of the office. In 1902 he became company secretary and had a seat on the board from 1905. In 1910 he was appointed joint managing director a position which he held until internal company politics led to his resignation in 1924. Hughes was also a founder of the Yale Motor Company of Brook Street, a director of S. Aston & Son, secretary to the Wrexham Steam Laundry and a manager of the Savings Bank.* He was elected to WBC in 1898 and served as chairman of the Finance Committee 1908–19, Borough Electricity Committee 1919-38, Mayor 1906–07, alderman and Freeman of the Borough 1931, Denbighshire county councillor and Deputy Mayor of Wrexham 1911. He was quartermaster to the Denbighshire Volunteer Regiment during the First World War and was awarded the MBE in 1931 for his public service. He played a leading role in the organisation of the National Eisteddfod in 1912* and 1931.*

He married Margaret Armstrong of Oswestry in 1888 and they had three daughters. The family lived at Glyndŵr, Bersham Road, (on the corner of Princess Street). He was an avid local antiquarian and his enormous collection of local documents and ephemera form the Glyndŵr Collection held at the Denbighshire Record Office. *A Wrexham Collection* by Kevin Matthias and W. Alister Williams, an illustrated book dealing with this collection, was published in 1998. Edward Hughes died at his home on Christmas Eve, 1938 and is buried in Wrexham Cemetery.*

Hughes, Edwin 'Balaclava Ned' *soldier*
Born Wrexham 12 December 1830, the son of William Hughes, tin-plate worker of Mount Street. He was employed as a shoemaker until his enlistment as a private (N° 1506) in the 13th Light Dragoons on 1 November 1852.

On 25 October 1854, he rode in the 'fifth file, front rank, right of the first line' in the famed Charge of the Light Brigade during which he was wounded. He served throughout the Crimean campaign and remained in the army until discharged on 24 November 1873 with the rank of Troop Sergeant Major.

He then enlisted in the Worcestershire Yeomanry Cavalry, serving as a Sergeant Instructor until 5 January 1886, living at Park Cottage, Alcester then Moseley, Birmingham. He married Hannah and had 2 sons and 2 daughters. In 1910, a widower, he went to live with his unmarried daughter, Mary, in Blackpool. He was a member of the Balaclava Commemoration Society. In 1923, he became the last survivor of the charge of the Light Brigade. He died on 18 May 1927 at 64 Egerton Road, Blackpool and was buried with full military honours at Leyton Cemetery, Blackpool.

Edwin Hughes.

His grave was restored by his old regiment in 1992. In October 1992, on the anniversary of the Charge, Wrexham businessman Bob Gray, placed a plaque on N° 2 Mount Street to commemorate him. (See also Sir Roger Palmer)

Hughes Charity
This was set up in 1812 by the will of Joshua Hughes, a wealthy merchant in Jamaica, and administered by the church wardens of Wrexham parish. It was money from this charity, £1,500, that was loaned to enable the new St Giles National Schools* to be built in 1885.

Hughes Court, Pentre Felin
Located on the south side of Pentre Felin close to the junction with Lea Road,* Hughes Court consisted of four poor quality industrial houses. They were demolished as part of the Borough's 1938 slum clearance programme.

Hughes, John *minister*
Born at Adwy'r Clawdd, Coedpoeth on 11 February 1796 the son of Hugh and Mary Hughes. His father was a carpenter. He was a brother to Richard Hughes.* He began preaching in 1813 and, two years later opened his first school.

In 1819, he opened a school at Fairfield in Wrexham which soon acquired a good reputation and expanded to take in students intending to go into the Calvinistic Methodist ministry. Ordained in 1829, John Hughes, after the closure of his school in 1834, became a shop keeper at Adwy'r Clawdd and then Liverpool where he eventually became the Calvinistic Methodist minister.

He was the author of several Welsh language books including *Methodistiaeth Cymru* a three volume history. He died in Abergele on 8 August 1860. A biography of him by Roger Edwards and John Hughes was published in 1864.

Hughes, Ll.B, John Phillips *Town Clerk*
John Phillips Hughes, a native of Llanrwst, was appointed Deputy Town Clerk of the Borough of Wrexham in 1957, having previously been employed by Crosby Borough Council. He succeeded Philip Walters as Town Clerk on 1 April 1970 and was appointed Chief Executive of Aberconwy Borough Council on re-organisation in 1974. Leaving to take up his new post in the Shadow Aberconwy authority, his position as Town Clerk of Wrexham was taken, temporarily, by his deputy, John Clive Hall. Married to Rhiannon, John Phillips Hughes had three children and lived at 29 Jeffreys Road. He died in August 1985.

Hughes, John Allington *solicitor*
Born 4 June 1836 at Higher Berse, the son of Thomas Hughes, a solicitor of Wrexham and grandson of Thomas Hughes of Plas Newydd Llandegla. He was educated at Shrewsbury School and began his articles in Mincing Lane, London before joining his father who had founded a practice at 4 Regent Street in 1831. He was admitted as a solicitor in 1859 and worked in London before moving back to his father's firm in 1861 where he was made a partner and the company's name was changed to Thomas & John Allington Hughes. His father died two years later and John continued the practice alone until 1899. On 2 January, he was joined by a new partner, Joseph Henry Bates, his former pupil. He retired from legal practice on 31 December 1905.

John Allington Hughes was appointed Clerk to the Wrexham Borough Justices on 29 October 1862, succeeding John Lewis (who had retired on becoming Mayor) and remained in the post until retiring on 1 January 1906. He was a council member of the Incorporated Law Society, a member of the Chester and North Wales Law Society and founded the John Allington Hughes Prize which was awarded annually to clerks serving their articles in the area. He was also a member of the Solicitors' Benevolent Association, deputy registrar of the Wrexham County Court and an ardent supporter of the Wrexham Infirmary. He was appointed a Denbighshire County magistrate in 1908 and served as the chairman of the Gresford Parish Council, chairman of the Gresford Unionist Association, was a manager of the Gresford Endowed School, a member of the Restoration Committee of Wrexham Parish Church and a prominent member of the Wrexham Court Leet.*

On the business front, as well as his legal interests, John Allington Hughes was a director of the Wrexham & East Denbighshire Water Company.*

He married Emily Sykes of Croes Howel and they had one daughter, Kathleen.* In later years, the Allington Hughes family lived at Bryn-y-Groes, Gresford. He died on 5 April 1913 and was buried in Gresford Parish Churchyard.

Hughes, MBE, JP, Kathleen Frances Allington, *public benefactress*
Born in 1879, the only child of John Allington Hughes* and his wife, Emily (née Sykes). She was deeply involved in various aspects of the community throughout her life, serving as a Justice of the Peace, member of the Wrexham Juvenile Advisory Committee, District Commissioner for the Girl Guides Association, the British Red Cross Society. She also devoted a great deal of time to the Parish Church in Gresford. She was awarded the MBE. She lived at Bryn-y-Groes, Gresford (a house designed by James Reynolds Gummow*), and died on 22 May 1946.

Hughes, Richard *printer & publisher*
Born in 1794 at Adwy'r Clawdd, Coedpoeth, the son of Hugh and Mary Hughes, Richard was the brother of John Hughes the noted Methodist minister (see above). He was educated at Evans' School, Minera, and was employed by Kendrick's Bank* in Hope Street before being appointed an accountant at the Bersham Paper Mill. When the mill's proprietor died, Richard took over the business under the name of Hughes & Phillips. He opened a paper store in Bank Street in 1820 and, by 1823, had established a bookshop and printing press at N°s 1 & 2 Church Street. He married Anne Jones and their son Charles* joined him in the business in 1848 (two other children died young). They specialised in the publication of books and sheet music and the firm of *Hughes ai Fab* (Hughes & Son*) became well-known throughout Wales. Richard Hughes died at Brynhyfryd,* Wrexham on 12 January 1871 and is buried in the Dissenters Burial Ground,* Rhosddu Road. A history of his company, *Braslun o Hanes Hughes ai Fab*, was published in 1946.

Hughes, William *murderer*
Born in Denbigh, William Hughes enlisted in the Cheshire Regiment and served in India. He was discharged and obtained employment at various collieries in the Wrexham area. He was married to Siân and they had 2 children. He deserted his family and was prosecuted by the Wrexham Board of Guardians in an effort to recover the costs of maintaining his family and, as a result, was sentenced to 3 months in Shrewsbury Prison from where he was released on 6 November 1902. Returning to Wrexham, he discovered that his wife was living with a man named Tom Maddocks of Rhosrobin and, on 10 November 1902, he went to the house and shot and killed his wife with a shotgun. Maddocks was working at the Wrexham & Acton Colliery and was on the night shift or he would almost certainly have also suffered the same fate. After the shooting, Hughes gave himself up to the police. Tried on 29 January 1903 and sentenced to death, Hughes became the only man to be executed at Ruthin Gaol when he was hanged at 8.00 a.m. on 17 February 1903.

Hughes & Son, *publishers and printers*
Located in 1843 at N°s 2, 3 & 7 (opposite) Church Street until they moved to N° 56 Hope Street (part of the site of the present day W. H. Smith store). Hughes & Son was probably the best known Welsh publishing house of the late 19th and early 20th centuries. Perhaps their best known publication was *Llyfr Mawr y Plant* which introduced Welsh children to the character Wil Cwac Cwac. The company were the Welsh pioneers of the 48-hour working week which they introduced in 1896. In the company's latter years in Wrexham, when they were part of Woodalls Printers (The Principality Press) they had premises at N° 36 High Street (next to the Royal Oak*).

Hullah Farm
Located on Cefn Road, the farmhouse was sited on the east side of the road, almost opposite the junction of Hullah Lane and still survives as a private house. The farm was offered for sale in October 1849 when the particulars were: 'All that excellent farm house and offices, and capital Meadow, Arable, and Pasture Land, containing 47A 3R 15P or thereabouts ... in the Township of Abenbury Fawr and Wrexham Abbot, in the said Parish of Wrexham, in the occupation of Mr John Bythell'. The field names given were Ucha Flint (26), Barn Field (27), Pit Field (28 & 38), Plantation (29 & 34), Garden (30), Field over Road (31), Brewis (32), Long Field (33), Bottom Field (35), Middle Field (36), Sandhole Field (37), Rhos Field Shone (39), Cae Samuel (40). At the time of the 1849 sale the name was spelt Holloa Farm. [DRO/DD/CP/840 & 729–30 & 732] By 1881, the farm is shown as being 96 acres in the occupation of William Edwin Jones.

Hullah Farm, Cefn Road, with the tenant William Edwin Jones. [Miss Gwendoline Sheppard]

Hullah Lane
Named after Hullah Farm.* It was sometimes referred to as Holloa Lane.

Huntroyde Avenue, Huntroyde
Named after Huntroyde (N° 32 Percy Road), the residence of J. A. Chadwick (Burton Brewery*), who named it after an estate of that name in Heywood, Lancashire. This was developed by the Borough Council in 1930.

Huntroyde Estate
The first house to be completed by WBC on this estate was N° 21 Bennions Road which has the date plaque '1930' on its front wall. The estate comprised 57 houses built on part of Bennions Road,* Huntroyde Avenue* and Mason Avenue.* The houses were built by W.F. Humphreys Ltd of Acrefair and cost a total of £19,386. (See Huntroyde Avenue).

Huntsmans Corner, Borras Park
Developed c.1968 by the London firm of Spinks & Denning on land that had been part of the Acton Park* estate, which had been bought by William Clarke* of Oak Lodge. The name is a reference to a local nickname for this area of Bryn Gryffydd.*

Hurst Newton, Bersham Road
Hurst Newton, a large private house was offered for sale by the executors of the late W. N. Capper in June 1927. It was the home of William T. Dodman.

I

Imperial Buildings, Regent Street
See Imperial Hotel.

Imperial Hotel, Regent Street
Located on the corner of Regent Street and King Street, work was started on this hotel in 1899 and completed in 1901. Funded by a consortium of local businessmen (including Walter Roberts*), the Imperial was intended to compete with the Wynnstay Arms as the town's premier hotel. Like the Wynnstay, it had its own private bus service to transport guests to and from the railway station. The Imperial was never a great success and was requisitioned in January 1918 for use by the military. In 1929 it was taken over by WRDC who occupied the building until shortly after the creation of WMBC in 1974 when it was demolished and the site was taken over as the Department of Employment's Wrexham office. The building is currently the premises of Town & Country estate agents.

Island Green Brewery, Brewery Place, Pentre Felin
Founded in 1856 by brothers William* and John Jones* with premises just off Brook Street, drawing on water from the Town Well. The brewery took its name from the nearby Island Green House.* There had been earlier breweries on this site, including Thomas Evans in 1822. Some of the buildings were extended and others re-built in c.1890. Following the death of William Jones in 1904, the business was sold the following year to Francis Huntley and George Mowat and, by 1925, had twenty-three tied houses and leased a further forty-eight from the Cambrian Brewery.* On 27 June 1931, Island Green merged with F.W. Soames* and Dorsett Owen of Oswestry to form Border Breweries* with Francis Huntley becoming chairman. Brewing operations were then transferred to the company's site in Tuttle Street (see Nag's Head Brewery) and the Island Green site became a major storage area for wines, spirits and tobacco, although it was not a bonded warehouse.

Part of the brewery buildings accessed from Brewery Place were used as a creamery in the period immediately before the Second World War. For much of the 1990s the brewery was empty until it was converted into private apartments.

The brewery/malthouse complex is the best surviving example of a Wrexham brewery. The malthouse is a Grade II listed building.

Island Green Cottages
This small 19th century development was demolished in 1932 as part of the Borough Council's slum clearance programme.

Island Green House (Ireland Green)
Located on the west bank of the Gwenfro, it appears in the 1833 survey. Palmer found the first mention of this property to have been in 1715 when it was an undeveloped area of land called Ireland Green. In 1742 it was still being described as simply a barn and a meadow and a house first appears in the rate books in 1762 which belonged to Edward Tomkies whose father (John Tomkies) had apparently developed a tannery on the Island Green site. By the 1780s the tannery was owned by William Edwards of Pen-y-Bryn and he was followed by his sons Watkin and Robert. In 1825 the house and tannery belonged to Mrs Thompson. The house appears to have been rebuilt shortly after this date as the sale records of December 1850 indicate:

> Lot 1. All that capital mansion-house called 'Island Green' … with the gardens and appurtenances thereunto belonging, together with a piece of meadow land in front, containing about four acres, one rood and 34 perches, or thereabouts, now in the holding or occupation of Mrs Bennion.
>
> The house which has been recently built at a considerable expense, contains a bold Entrance Hall, Breakfast, Dining, and Drawing Rooms, light good Bed-rooms, Kitchen, Back Kitchen, Wine and Ale Cellars, Laundry, Wash-house, and other conveniences. The Out-buildings consist of two good Stables, Saddle and Harness Rooms, excellent Coach-house, Shippons, Piggeries, etc. The walled Garden is exceedingly good, well stocked with choice Fruit Trees and the Lawn is very fine Pasture Land, and may be made most ornamental.
>
> There is an excellent pew in the middle aisle of Wrexham Church appurtenant to this Lot.

The house was approached by a curving drive from Pentre Felin, the gateway being sited opposite the junction with Belle Vue Road. A second driveway appears to have led to the house from a road leading off Well Square. Island Green survived until the building of the extensions to the Wrexham, Mold & Connah's Quay Railway in 1887. It appears in the background of a photograph showing the construction work of the Central Station, but does not appear in the rather grandiose plans for the Wrexham 'Jubilee Station' published in the *Wrexham Advertiser* on 25 June 1887. [FRO/D/BC/ ADDITIONAL FITZHUGH/14/16]

Island Green Shopping Precinct
This shopping precinct, car park and railway station on the site of the former Hugh Price & Company* leather works, Central Station* and part of the Island Green Brewery,* was developed by Trinity Investments and opened in the summer of 1999.

Isle of Man, Pentre Felin
This row of small terraced houses was located between the Hugh Price & Co* leather works and the Island Green Brewery.* Recorded on the 1841 census, it appears in the 1872 survey.

Isle of Man.

Ivy Close, Rhosddu
See Ivy Cottage.

Ivy Cottage, Rhosddu
This house is shown standing alongside Rhosddu Road* in the 1842 tithe survey of the parish. The site and name survive today as Ivy Close, Rhosddu. The original Rhosddu Road was severed by the railway line just south of this house. (See New Road)

Ivy Grove, Grove Road
See Nythfa.

J

Jackson, Clifford *local politician*
A native of Tan-y-Fron, Cliff Jackson was educated at Grove Park County School.* He was employed for many years in the Personnel Department of the BICC factory in Wrexham.

Elected a member of WBC in 1957 he was the last Mayor of the Borough of Wrexham in 1973–74. He married twice (1) Joyce and had one daughter (2) Jennifer. He lived at 89 Norman Road and latterly at Longview Road, Pentre Broughton when personal difficulties caused him to withdraw from public life. He died in December 1995 and is buried in St Paul's Churchyard, Pentre Broughton.

Jackson, James *educationalist*
Founder of Grove Park Academy* in 1823.

James, George D. *local politician*
Born in Brecn on 3 January 1949, George James was educated at St Mary's* and St Joseph's* Schools in Oxford. He was employed by Wales Gas. He became an Independent community councillor in 1986, then a member of Clwyd County Council and finally a Wrexham County Borough Councillor. He is currently the co-chair of the Social Affairs, Health and Housing Scrutiny Committee. He served as Mayor of Wrexham in 2006–07 and is the first councillor to serve as the Chair of the Standing Advisory Council for Religious Education in Wrexham.

George James is married, with five children, and lives on Stockwell Grove.

James, John *solicitor and Town Clerk*
He was born in Wem, Shropshire, the son of Thomas James (who established a legal practice in King Street, Wrexham and who died on 2 September 1850, aged 86, and is buried in the Dissenters Burial Ground*) and his wife Petronilla (died 1 October 1871). Details of his education are unknown but he followed his father into the legal profession. He set up in practice in 1828 and remained on the Roll of the Law Society until retiring in September 1880. For a time he lived and practised in the Old Vicarage (in partnership with a James Charles Owen) before moving to Elwy House on King Street and finally to offices in Bryn-y-Ffynnon Gatehouse, Priory Street. In his latter years he lived at Plas Acton,* a house that he built.

He married three times (1) Mary Anne, the second child of John Painter* the well-known printer of High Street. After her death (26 November 1836, buried in the Dissenters Burial Ground), he married (2) Catherine, the daughter of Thomas Hilditch of Wem, in 1838 (died 5 January 1843, buried Dissenters Burial Ground*). By 1850, again a widower, he married (3) Anne Elizabeth, whose father, John Farrer (originally of Higher Broughton, Manchester), was the manager of Kenrick &

John James, first Town Clerk of Wrexham.

Bowman's Bank in Hope Street and later of the Northern & Central Bank of England in High Street. Anne died *c*.1875.

John James was a member of the Old Meeting in Chester Street. He played a prominent part in the campaign for the incorporation of Wrexham and, in 1857, when the town was granted borough status, was appointed the first Town Clerk (part-time), a post which he held until 1879. He was a County magistrate and also served as a deputy chairman of the Provincial Insurance Company.* He died at Plas Acton, on 1 May 1888 and was buried in Gwersyllt churchyard. His legal practice was inherited by his sons Thomas Reginald James (died 1932) and Richard Percy James (died 1935). He had one daughter, Sarah Jolson James.

James, Tom *Olympic rower*
Born in Cardiff on 11 March 1984, the son of Michael and Julia James, Tom lived for most of his childhood at Bron Offa, Ffordd Rhedyn, Coedpoeth. Educated at the King's School, Chester and Trinty Hall, Cambridge, he gained a BSc in engineering in 2007. He represented Cambridge University in the Varsity Boat Race four times between 2003 and 2007 (winning at the fourth attempt) and was president of the University Boat Club in 2006–07. In 2001 he won a bronze medal in the junior rowing eight event at Duisburg and, the following year, a silver in the rowing four at the World Junior Championships. In 2003, selected for the Great Britain men's rowing eight at the World Championships in Milan, he competed in the finals and gained a bronze medal. He represented Great Britain in the 2004 Olympic Games in Athens, where he was handicapped by illness and the team failed to gain a medal. In 2007, he won a bronze medal in the men's rowing eight at the World Rowing Championships, followed by a silver medal in the men's four at the World Cup. He competed at the 2008 Olympics in Beijing in the men's four (his team mates being Andy Hodge, Peter Reed and Steve Williams), winning the coveted Olympic Gold Medal at the Shunyi Olympic Rowing Park.

James Street
Located at the end of Edge Street and almost certainly named after John James* the first Town Clerk of Wrexham. N[os] 2-7 were cleared during the 1930s as part of the Borough slum clearance programme. The site is now part of the Tesco car park.

James, James & Hatch
Until recently, the oldest legal practice in Wrexham, James James & Hatch was founded in 1788 by Thomas James of Wem (1764–1850). The son of Mary James, Thomas was sponsored through his education by his aunt's employer, the Revd Samuel Garbet of Wem (who was almost certainly his father). The firm passed in 1828 to his son John James* and was located in the Old Vicarage* (Vicarage Hill), Elwy House* (King Street) and finally Bryn-y-Ffynnon Gatehouse (Priory Street). In 1847 John was joined by a partner James Charles Owen who left the practice in 1865. In 1880, John's son Thomas Reginald James (1855–1932) joined the firm (having qualified in 1878) and, two years later a second son, Richard Percy James (1859–1935) also joined. The firm continued as James & James until 1909 when the brothers were joined by Francis Frederick Hatch who had been in practice on his own since 1901. In 1916, Frank Hatch left the practice only to rejoin in 1919 (possibly following the death of Alyn James in the Royal Flying Corps). Both the James brothers retired from the firm on 31 December 1926. The firm of James, James & Hatch took over the practice of Evan Morris & Co in 1928. This well-known firm had been established by Evan Morris* (later Sir Evan) in 1872 and eventually had offices in Wrexham, Ruabon and Overton. It was not until 1948 that Frank Hatch was joined by William Neville Cromar (retired 1976). In 1936, Frank Hatch further expanded the firm by taking over the practice of Jagger & Clement Jones which had been established in Wrexham in 1890. In 1953 the firm expanded to a third partner when Samuel Kenyon Jonathan joined (retired 1982).

During the 1960s, Bryn-y-Ffynnon Gatehouse was demolished and the firm built new premises on the same site in Priory Street. In 1971, a fourth partner John Philip Glyn Evans joined from the rival firm of Edmund Pickles & Upton. In 1979, the vacant partnership of Mr Cromar was taken up by David Spalding. In 1984, James, James & Hatch amalgamated with the practice of Bowen Jones, Parry & Rogers of Wrexham and Ruabon. It was eventually bought by Steggles and closed down in the mid 2000s.

Jarman Avenue, Huntroyde
Built by WBC in the early 1930s as part of the Huntroyde Estate,* it was named after Alderman Sydney Jarman.*

Jarman, JP, Alderman Sydney Gardner *local politician*
Born in Devon, Sydney Jarman began his working career as a reporter on the *Tiverton Gazette & Bridgewater Mercury* before coming managing partner of the *Huntingdonshire County Guardian*. He moved to Wrexham in 1894 when he bought the *North Wales Guardian*ic* and took up the position of editor. He published a number of books including *A History of Tiverton Castle* (being a romance in rhyme) and *a History of Bridgewater*. A keen local historian he also published works on Gresford, Caergwrle, Rossett and Marford. He was elected a Conservative member of WBC and served as chairman of the Highways Committee, chairman of the Public Library Committee and vice chairman of the Education Committee. He served as Mayor in 1913–14, was created an alderman and an Honorary Freeman of Wrexham in 1931. He retired from politics in 1945.

He married Mary Hooper of Tiverton and they had five sons, one of whom, Percy, succeeded him as proprietor of the *North Wales Guardian* newspaper. He served as a Justice of the Peace on the Borough bench from 1915 until 1942, was an honorary member of the 1st Vol Bn, RWF (during the First World War was a prime mover behind the foundation of the 13th Bn, RWF – the Pals Battalion). At this time, both he and his wife worked hard with the Belgian refugees who arrived in Wrexham for which Mrs Jarman was later awarded the Medal of Queen Elizabeth of Belgium.

His other interests were many and varied and included: Churchwarden, St James' Church,* Rhosddu; Governor Grove Park School*; Member Independent Order of Oddfellows*; President Wrexham Peripatetic Society*; President Wrexham Branch of the Fellowship of Freedom and Reform; chairman North Wales District of the Institute of Journalists.

Sydney Jarman died, aged 92, at his home Oakdene, Haytor Road, on 17 January 1949, and is buried in Wrexham Cemetery.*

Jarvis Jones, Catherine and Joseph *local politicians*
Catherine Jarvis Jones was born in Bangor, Gwynedd, the daughter of a local Post Office official. She was educated at Garth Elementary School, Bangor and the Bangor County School before becoming a teacher and took up her first appointment at her old school in Garth in 1914. On 15 April 1914, she married Joseph Jarvis Jones, a native of Rhosllanerchrugog, who was a teacher at Glan Adda School, Bangor. Almost immediately, her husband was appointed headmaster of Birtle School in Bury and they moved to Lancashire. In 1915, he volunteered for military service and joined the Royal Field Artillery. Commissioned in 1916, he saw active service in France while his wife returned to her parents home in Bangor. In 1921, Joseph was appointed headmaster of the National School (St Giles*) in Wrexham. As a member of the Wrexham branch of the Civic Guild of Help Catherine Jarvis Jones carried out valuable service in the town, particularly during the General Strike of 1926. In 1929, she fought the Bryn Offa Ward on behalf of the Liberal Party and, against all the odds, was elected a Borough Councillor. She became Mayor in 1947 and served an extraordinary term of eighteen months as the date for 'Mayor Making' was changed to May during her term of office. She was made an Alderman for the Maes-y-Dre Ward in 1949. She served as chairman of the Child Welfare Sub Committee.

In addition to her political service, Catherine Jarvis Jones was the President of the Wrexham branch of the Royal College of Nursing, a member of the House Committee of the Wrexham War Memorial Hospital, chairman of the Managers of St David's School and Bodhyfryd Welsh School, a governor of the Denbighshire Technical College and a member of the Court of Governors of the University College of North Wales, Bangor. In 1939, she was the local organiser of the Women's Voluntary Service. She had one daughter, Gwynna (later Mrs Powell) who was Head Girl of Grove Park Girls Grammar School.

Her husband remained as headmaster of the National School until 1930 when he was appointed to the headship of the Victoria Senior Boys School.* Between the wars, he served as an officer in the Territorial Artillery and commanded the 224 Medium Artillery Battery (Wrexham) of the 61st Medium Artillery Regiment until 1938 when he succeeded Lt-Col Fenwick Palmer to the command of the regiment. He took them to France in 1939 and led them through the events which culminated in the Dunkirk evacuation of 1940. In the same year he was given command of the 224 L.A.A. Training Regiment, Royal Artillery at Aberystwyth, a post which he held to the end of the war. Lt Colonel Jarvis Jones died in December 1966. Catherine Jarvis Jones, one of the most popular local politicians of the 20th century, died on 15 September 1971, at her daughter's home in Amlwch, Anglesey. Lt-Col and Mrs Jarvis Jones lived at 9 Ruthin Road and, in their latter years, at The Flat, Pen-y-Maes Avenue.

Jarvis Jones, TD, RA, Lt-Col Joseph *teacher & soldier*
See Catherine Jarvis Jones.

Jarvis Way, Acton
Built in the 1960s, it was named after Alderman Catherine Jarvis Jones.*

Jeffreys Family of Acton
See also Acton Park.
The Jeffreys family first appear as the owners of land in the townships of Acton and Borras in the early 17th century. Churchyarde does not mention either them or Acton in his book *Worthynesse of Wales* which was published in the late 16th century but Norden does mention both the family and the house in the 1620 survey.

John ap Jeffrey (assumed the Anglicised surname of Jeffreys), a son of Jeffrey ap Hugh ap Robert ap Richard ap Ieuan ap Adda of Trevor. He was admitted a member of Lincoln's Inn in 1587, elected a Bencher in 1611 and became a judge on the north Wales circuit. In 1618 he bought land in Acton which was later part of Tŷ Gwyn Farm.* He is recorded as having died at Acton on 19 May 1622 and was buried in Wrexham Parish Church. At the time of his death he held land totalling 800 acres. He married Margaret, the daughter of William Lloyd of Halghton.

John Jeffreys of Acton, the son of John ap Jeffrey, was born 22 May 1608. He served in the Royalist army during the Civil War and was captured near Sir Gerard Eyton's house at Eyton by Colonel Mytton in 1644. He was living at Acton by 1631 and became High Sheriff of Denbighshire in 1655. He is on record as having bought land from the Crown in both Acton and Wrexham Regis townships in 1666 and inherited land at Eyton. He also bought land near Shrewsbury and was a member of that town's council in 1638. He married Margaret, the daughter of Sir Thomas Ireland of Bewsey, Lancashire, a noted lawyer, Sergeant-at-Law and editor of *Coke's Report*. He was buried at Wrexham on 2 April 1691. The father of Judge George Jeffreys.

Edward Jeffreys, second son of John ap Jeffrey, was a captain in the Royalist army during the Civil War, serving in Maj-Gen Sir John Owen's Regiment of Foot. He later lived at Broughton, Denbighshire. He was buried in Wrexham on 11 May 1680.

George Jeffreys, 1st Baron Wem and Loppington – Born at Acton Hall, Wrexham on 15 May 1645, the sixth son of John and Margaret Jeffreys. His grandfather (also named John ap Jeffrey) had been Chief Justice of the Anglesey circuit of the Great Sessions. George was educated at Shrewsbury School from 1652–59, St Paul's School, London 1659–61 and Westminster School 1661–2 before becoming an undergraduate at Trinity College, Cambridge in March 1662. He left university after a year and was admitted as a member of the Inner Temple in May 1663. He married Sarah Neesham on 23 May 1667 and they lived at 79 Coleman Street near the Guildhall in London (she died in 1678 and in 1679 he married Lady Ann Jones, the widow of Sir John Jones of Fonmon, Glamorgan and daughter of Sir Thomas Bludworth). In 1671 he was appointed Common Serjeant in the City of London and then Solicitor General to the Duke of York in 1676. He was knighted in 1677 before becoming Recorder of London the following year. In 1680 he was appointed Chief Justice of the Chester Circuit, Counsel for the Crown at Ludlow and JP for Flintshire. In 1681 he was created a Baronet. By 1683 he was Lord Chief Justice and a Privy Councillor to King James II. In 1685 he became Baron Wem and Lord Chancellor and was rumoured likely to be created Viscount Wrexham and Earl of Flint had he adopted the Roman Catholic faith of the King. He is best remembered for the Assizes which he held at Shaftesbury in Dorset following the rebellion of the Duke of Monmouth. On instruction from the King, he dealt with the rebels with great severity earning him the nickname Bloody Jeffreys and the undying hatred of the people. On the accession to the throne of William and Mary in 1688, Jeffreys was placed in the Tower of London for his own safety and died there on 18 April 1689. He was buried in the Chapel at the Tower, close to the grave of the Duke of Monmouth, but, in November 1693, his body was exhumed and re-buried in St Mary's Aldermanbury without a memorial. In the 19th century a plaque was placed in the church: In memory of George Baron Jeffreys (of Wem) Recorder of London, Chief Justice of the King's Bench, and Chancellor of England, 1685, formerly a resident of this parish, and whose remains are buried in this church – The Lord seeth not as man seeth. I Sam. xvi. 7.' The church was bombed in December 1940 and now forms a memorial garden. There is no indication of the location of George Jeffreys' grave. He was the youngest ever Chief Justice of England. His son John succeeded to the title.

Sir Griffith Jeffreys, grandson of John and Margaret Jeffreys and son of John Jeffreys of Ruyton. Due to the premature death of his father, he succeeded to the Acton estate on the death of his grandfather in 1691. He rebuilt the house at Acton and gave it the name 'Acton Militis' (Knight's Acton). He served as High Sheriff of Denbighshire in 1683 and was knighted in 1687. Following the 'Glorious Revolution' of 1688, Griffith Jeffreys became well-known as a supporter of the Stuart monarchy and was believed to be in regular communication with the 'Old Pretender'. He was married to Dorothy Pleydell. Sir Griffith was buried at Wrexham on 19 March 1694.

Dame Dorothy Jeffreys, the daughter of Robert and Elizabeth Pleydell of Holyrood Amney, Gloucestershire. She married Sir Griffith Jeffreys* of Acton Hall* in 1683. A great benefactress and supporter of the church, Dame Dorothy was an advocate of the

A crude 18th century depiction of the arms of the Jeffreys family. [NLW CR4672A]

Lord Chief Justice George Jeffreys, 1st Baron Wem.

establishment of a Welsh church in Wrexham. She bequeathed £400 'to be laid out to interest on land security and the interest thereof applied for the teaching and instructing and putting out apprentices such and so many poor children of the said parish ... as the Vicar or Minister and Churchwardens of the said parish of Wrexham shall direct and appoint.' Her daughter, Margaret Jeffreys also left £120 for the schooling of poor children in Wrexham. These two bequests were allowed to earn interest before the compounded sum of £822-7s-0d was used in 1753 to purchase land in the parish of Holt. The profits from this land purchase were by the early 19th century, divided equally between the Boys National School in the Beast Market* and the Girls School in Tenters Field.* When the new National School was built* the money from the Dame Dorothy Jeffreys Charity was used to pay the some of the interest on £1,500 which had been borrowed to pay for the building and to gradually repay the capital sum. She was buried in Wrexham 21 July 1729.

Robert Jeffreys, second son of Sir Griffith and Lady Dorothy Jeffreys. He married Mary, daughter of Robert Griffith of Brymbo. He was buried in Wrexham 30 December 1714.

Elizabeth Jeffreys, second daughter of Sir Griffith Jeffreys, was born on 8 June 1689. She married John Robinson of Gwersyllt. On the death of her brother Robert, the Acton estate passed to her husband. Following the death of John Robinson on 2 November 1732 the property passed to their son William who was drowned at sea in 1739, leaving his widow and infant daughter, Elizabeth, with great debts. In 1745, the estate (which comprised Acton Park* and Pant-yr-Ochain*) was sold by Act of Parliament to their brother-in-law, Ellis Yonge of Bryn Iorkin (the husband of Dorothy Robinson).

Jeffreys Road
This is one of the old roads of the township of Acton which appears in various 18th and 19th century maps. It extended from Borras Road to the original Chester Road (now Box Lane*) and skirted the boundary of Acton Park. It was named Jeffreys Road in the 20th century after the Jeffreys family* who lived at Acton Park between the 16th and 18th centuries. It seems likely that the course of the road was changed by Sir Foster Cunliffe* in the early 19th century as the boundary wall of Acton Park was moved several hundred yards to the east (part of the original wall can still be seen inside the present day park. With the development of the Borras Park estate during the 1960s, Jeffreys Road was changed from a small rural lane to an urban road, carrying an ever-increasing volume of traffic. This also led to the development of new houses along its north-eastern side so that today, very little of its pre-urbanised character remains.

The oldest surviving houses on the road are: the Lodge on the junction with Borras Road which was built by Sir Robert Alfred Cunliffe* in 1876. On the gable are the initials of Sir Robert and his wife (see Cunliffe Family); the former Borras Nursery,* now Nº 15 Jeffreys Road, once had grounds which extended between the junctions of Warrenwood Road* and Borras Park Road.* In the early 1870s a small hoard of Bronze Age implements was discovered in the grounds. In 1881 the nursery comprised 5 acres and was occupied by John Farquhason who employed four men and four boys.

The land between Warrenwood Road* and Bryn Gryffydd* was developed as individual private plots between 1938 and 1947.

A smallholding, with one field in front of it, stood on the site now occupied by Nº 99 until the 1990s and is recalled in the naming of a nearby cul-de-sac Farmside.

The Cunliffe Arms* public house was built in 1970-1 and the Borras Park Evangelical Church* in 1972. Despite considerable local opposition, WBC laid out the recreation area at the back of the Cunliffe Arms in 1973, which comprised 1 bowling green, two tennis courts, a pavilion and a small car park.

In 1970, plans to build a petrol station on the junction of Jeffreys Road and Box Lane were considered and rejected.

Jennings, Alderman Herbert *local politician*
Born in Golbourne, Lancashire, c.1901, the son of Alfred Jennings a former master painter and coal miner. Herbert received an elementary education before emigrating to Canada, aged 22 where he worked in an engineering works in Windsor, Ontario before moving to similar work in Chicago and Detroit. In the latter city he changed careers and became a grocer and was appointed manager of a large business with shops throughout the state of Michigan. He returned to Britain in 1932 and came to Wrexham the following year. He bought land on the junction of Holt Road and Borras Road where he built a shop and a flat and ran a successful grocery business.

He was elected as Liberal councillor for Maes-y-Dre in February 1943 and developed a passion for housing issues, becoming chairman of the Borough Housing Committee. He became Mayor of Wrexham in 1953 and was created an Alderman on 26 November 1957.

He died at his home, 87 Holt Road in October 1979 and is buried in Wrexham Cemetery.* Herbert Jennings Avenue in Acton was named after him in recognition of his great contribution to the development of corporation housing in Wrexham.

Jerusalem Welsh Wesleyan Chapel, Egerton Street/Pen-y-Maes Avenue
Built in c.1882 to accommodate the congregation of the Brook Street chapel* which was demolished in the 1890s, this building was demolished and the chapel moved to Keston Lodge, a large private house on the corner of Pen-y-Maes Avenue* and Chester Road. This house, originally named Kumara Lodge, was built in the late 1930s by local consultant Dr Ray Aiyar and was designed to have the appearance of an Indian country house with verandahs. In 1949, the house was sold to Mr John Spalding, a consultant surgeon, who renamed it Keston Lodge after Keston Park in Kent. He in turn sold it to Dr J. E. Wilson. In 1970 it was placed on the market with the agent's comments that it was suitable for conversion to an hotel. The house then comprised an entrance hall, cloakroom, study, drawing room, dining room, kitchen and seven bedrooms. It was sold to the Welsh Wesleyan

Jerusalem Church, Egerton Street

Church who converted the ground floor into Jerusalem chapel, with the minister's accommodation upstairs.

The Religious Census of 1904 showed: Capacity 300; attendance (AM & PM) 254.

Jewish community
Wrexham has a small Jewish community but no significant buildings associated with the religion.

Bryn-y-Ffynnon House*: There is a belief that Wrexham's small 19th century Jewish community held their religious services in Bryn-y-Ffynnon House, although there does not appear to be any documentation to support this.

King Street: Mr Ruben, a qualified solicitor who operated a clothing business in the Vegetable Market, owned the corner building on the junction of King Street and Rhosddu Road. The ground and first floors were occupied by Dr Elgan Evans and the second floor was used for Jewish religious services although it was not classified as a synagogue.

Beechley Road: The house once occupied by Dr Jenkins as his surgery, had two kitchens which were used by its Jewish inhabitants to prepare meat and dairy produce.

John Jones Park, Chester Street
This small (2 acre) park was the proposal of local philanthropist John Jones* of Grove Lodge. In his original will (of 1912) he proposed leaving the land opposite his house (Grove Lodge) on Chester Street to the Corporation of Wrexham for use as a public park. This was to be endowed with £500 to cover the costs of laying out pathways, planting shrubs and flowers and the building of a wall, gate and memorial fountain. Unfortunately, by the time of his death in April of the following year, he had changed his will, and the land was left to his nephew Frederick William Morris, with the restriction that it must be used as pasture and could not be built upon for 40 years after his (John Jones') death. It would appear, however, that this restriction was removed and the land was built on soon after the First World War.

Jolly Drovers, Pen-y-Bryn
Shown in the 1833 survey, this public house was located on the west side of Pen-y-Bryn opposite the junction with Chapel Street.* It was almost certainly the building which was also known as the Highgate.*

Jolly Tavern, High Street
A short-lived public house, the Jolly Tavern was located in High Street during the early 1980s on the site of the former Conservative Club.

Jones, Albert Edgar *local politician*
Born in Tan-y-Fron in 1913, Edgar Jones was the son of a worker at Brymbo Steel Works. He was educated at Tan-y-Fron School and worked as a driver with Crosville. In 1938 he married Nancy Beryl Smallwood and they had one daughter and one son. He established his own drapery business in the Vegetable Market in 1947 (which later moved to the People's Market).

He was elected to WBC as an Independent member for the Bryn-y-Ffynnon Ward in May 1969. He was Mayor of WMBC in 1977, a year which included a very busy programme to celebrate the Silver Jubilee of Queen Elizabeth II. He was also elected to serve as a Clwyd County Councillor and became chairman for 1981–2. In addition to his duties in local government, Edgar Jones was the president of Brymbo Cricket Club, a governor of Yale VI Form College and chairman of the Friends of Greystones House Committee.

Edgar Jones lived at 27 Windsor Drive, Maesgwyn and died in August 1991.

Jones, Arwel Gwynn *local politician and teacher*
Born in Wrexham on 5 November 1934, Arwel Jones is a proud native of Rhosllannerchrugog and was educated at Rhos C.P. School and Ruabon Grammar School. Following three years training as an accountant, he became a student at Bangor Normal College in 1953 and began his career as a teacher at Acrefair C.P. School two years later. Appointed to the staff of Gwenfro Junior School in 1959, he was seconded for twelve months to complete an Advanced Diploma in Education at Liverpool University. In 1965 he was appointed Head Teacher of Pentre Celyn C.P. School where he remained until 1976 when he became Head Teacher of Ysgol Bodhyfryd (Welsh Medium) School in Wrexham. From 1970–2 he was seconded to the Schools Council in Pontypridd to act as Field Officer and Language Advisor and, in 1973, visited schools in Canada to report on the provision of bilingual education there. In 1989–90 he attended Keele University to follow an advanced certificate course in education management. During his career as a teacher Arwel Jones was president of the National Association of Head Teachers in Clwyd, chairman of Clwyd Urdd Gobaith Cymru, chairman of the Rhos Orpheus Male Voice Choir (for ten years), a church organist for 30 years and a lay preacher. A qualified Estyn inspector, he has represented WCBC for many years on the Welsh Joint Education Committee where he is currently the vice-chairman and chairman of the Audit Committee.

On the political scene, he has served as a parish councillor in both Rhos (1960–5) and Llanfair D.C. (1967–85) and as a community councillor for the Pant ward, Rhos (1998–2010. He was elected a county councillor for the Pant ward of WCBC in 1998, serving on the executive board and as lead member for Children and Young People's Services. He served as Mayor in 2009–10 when his wife, Mair, was the Mayoress. During his year of office he raised a record £39,000 for the Mayor's Charity Fund and is proud to have used the Welsh language at every official function, irrespective of where it was held.

Arwel Jones has been the chairman of Mudiad Ysgolion Meithrin (2006–10). He was awarded the Fellowship of Glyndŵr University in 2010 and is Hon President of the National Eisteddfod of Wales – Wrecsam & District, 2011.

He married Mair Jones in 1961 and they have two children: Yale College teacher and harpist Llinos Ann Roberts and Aberystwyth University lecturer Dr Dylan Gwynn Jones.

Jones' Court, Brook Street
This small 19th century development was demolished in 1932 as part of the Borough Council's slum clearance programme. It appears in the 1872 survey.

Jones' Court, Hope Street
It was situated at the rear of the properties in Hope Street.

Jones' Court, Mount Street
This was a very poor, slum development of four houses located behind the Dolphin Inn on Mount Street. In 1872, there was an iron and brass foundry immediately to the north of Jones' Court. It was the subject of a compulsory purchase order as part of the Borough slum clearance scheme of 1932.

Jones' Court, Pentre Felin
This was located on the north side of Pentre Felin, almost opposite Lea Road. N°s 1-6 Jones Court were the subject of a compulsory purchase order in 1938 as part of the Borough slum clearance programme.

Jones, LIB, BA Cyril Oswald *local politician*
Born in Llanarmon-yn-Iâl on 20 December 1880, the son of local

schoolteacher Humphrey Bradley Jones (bardic name Garmonydd), he was educated at Cybi British School, Holyhead and Denbigh Grammar School before becoming an under-graduate at Dublin University. He was articled to Frederick Llewellyn Jones of Holywell (his brother) and after qualifying, set up as a solicitor in Holyhead in 1905. He was elected to serve as an Urban District Councillor in Holyhead.

Moving to Wrexham he set up in practice in Egerton Street. He was elected a Labour councillor for the Cefn Ward, in 1920, an alderman in 1929 and became Mayor in 1936. He was chairman of the Health Committee.

Outside of local politics he stood as a Labour parliamentary candidate in three elections, was chairman of the Wrexham Divisional Labour Party, secretary of the Poor Persons Committee of the Chester & North Wales Law Society (a forerunner of the Legal Aid system). During the First World War Cyril Jones was commissioned into the Royal Welsh Fusiliers and was later president of the Wrexham branch of the Royal British Legion. He was president of the Law Society of Chester & North Wales in 1953.

A devoted supporter of the National Eisteddfod, he acted as a guarantor for the 1933 Wrexham Eisteddfod. He was made an Honorary Freeman of the Borough of Wrexham on 28 March 1951. Cyril Jones married Margaret J. Roberts of Holywell (daughter of the bard Mynyddwr) and had three sons and three daughters. They lived at Annefield, Gresford.

Oswald Way* on the Acton Park Housing Estate* was named after him.

Jones, Daniel *poet*
Born in Ruabon in *c*.1725, Daniel Jones received no formal education and lived much of his life in poverty. He received some patronage from the Myddelton family of Chirk and the Lloyd family of Trefor. Some of his work was published in *Cynulliad Barddorion i Gantorion sef Carolau, Cerddi ac Englynion* which he published in 1790. He was buried in Ruabon on 10 March 1806.

Jones' Day & Boarding School, Mr
Chestnut House, Chester Street. Mentioned in the *Wrexham Advertiser* 1 July 1851.

Jones, Edward *conspirator*
The son of Edward Jones of Plas Cadwgan, Bersham and Cornhill, London, his father was a tailor to Mary Tudor and Master of the Wardrobe to Elizabeth I. He entered the service of the Earl of Leicester and became a close friend of Thomas Salusbury of Lleweni who persuaded him to turn against the Protestant faith of the late 16th century. He then opposed Leicester and became involved in the Babington Plot to depose Elizabeth and replace her on the throne with Mary Queen of Scots. Both he and Salusbury were denounced in 1586 as preparing to raise Denbighshire on behalf of Mary and they fled to Cheshire in August. Jones was arrested and sent to London for trial where he admitted knowledge of the plot and helping Salusbury to escape but denied any disloyalty to Elizabeth, saying that he had made every effort to dissuade his friend from becoming involved. He was found guilty of high treason and beheaded on Tower Hill on 21 September 1586 and his estate, which included Plas Cadwgan, was forfeited to the Crown.

Jones, FRS, DSc, PhD, MA, FRIC, Sir Ewart Ray Herbert *chemist*
Ewart Jones was born in Wrexham on 16 March 1911 and educated at Victoria School and Grove Park School, Wrexham, UCNW Bangor (1st Class Hon Chemistry, 1932) and the University of Manchester. After completing his Diploma in Education Ewart Jones gained a PhD at Bangor in 1935. He had a distinguished career in the field of chemistry: Fellow University of Wales 1935–37; Lecturer Imperial College 1938; Reader in Organic Chemistry, University of London and Assistant Professor 1945; Sir Samuel Hall Professor of Chemistry Manchester University 1947–55; Arthur D Little Visiting Professor of Chemistry Massachusetts Institute of Technology 1952; Karl Folkers Lecturer at Universities of Illinois and Wisconsin 1957; Member of the Council for Scientific and Industrial Research; chairman Research Grants Committee 1961–65; Member SRC and chairman University Science and Technology Board 1965–69; member Science Board 1969–72; Chemical Society Tilden lecturer 1949; Pedler lecturer 1959; Award in Natural Product Chemistry 1974; Meldola Medal, Royal Institute of Chemistry 1940; Davy Medal Royal Society 1966; Fritzsche Award, American Chemical Society 1962; President of the Chemical Society 1964–66; Royal Institute of Chemistry 1970–72; founder President of the Royal Society of Chemistry (1980–2); Fellow Imperial College 1967; Foreign Member American Academy of Arts and Sciences 1967; Hon DSc: Birmingham 1965; Nottingham 1966; New South Wales 1967; Sussex 1969; Salford 1971; Wales 1971; Hon LlD Manchester 1972. Author of numerous papers in the *Journal of the Chemistry Society*. Knighted 1963; FRS 1950; Waynflete Professor of Chemistry University of Oxford 1955–78; Fellow of Magdalen College. He married Frances Mary Copp in 1937 (she died in 1999) and they had one son and two daughters. He lived in Kidlington, Oxford and died in 2002. His portrait hangs outside the Council Chamber and Library of the Royal Society of Chemistry, Burlington House, London.

Jones, JP, Alderman Glyn Ellis *local politician*
Glyn Jones began his working career with Barclays Bank in 1912. He served on active duties in France during the First World War and, on the restoration of peace, rejoined Barclays. He came to Wrexham in 1943 when he was appointed the manager of the town branch of Barclays Bank where he remained until his retirement in 1954.

He was elected an Independent councillor for the Maes-y-Dre Ward in 1946, became Mayor in 1959 and was created an Alderman. In addition to his civic duties, Glyn Jones was a member of the Wales Tourist Board, a governor of Grove Park School, a manager of Bryn Estyn Approved School and a member of the Denbighshire Education Divisional Executive.

His passion was football and he served as President of the Welsh Football League and Treasurer of the Football Association of Wales and Treasurer of the Wrexham Football Club Supporters' Association. Married, he lived at Tan-y-Coed, 28 Acton Road. He died in 1965.

Jones, JP, Gwilym Herbert *local politician*
Gwilym Jones was born in Rhosrobin in 1897. During the First World War he served with the Denbighshire Yeomanry and was reported missing, believed dead following the Battle of Cambrai. Fortunately, he had only been captured and returned home at the end of hostilities. In 1920, he opened a road haulage business which he ran until 1933 when he opened a motor garage in Rhosddu (now the Spar shop and garage opposite Spring Road). During the Second World War he worked for the Ministry of Information and served with the local Royal Observer Corps.

Elected a Liberal councillor for the Grosvenor Ward in 1952, he became chairman of the Transport Committee of WBC and mayor in 1966. He was appointed a Justice of the Peace in the same year.

A Welsh speaker and keen amateur artist, Gwilym Jones was also deeply involved with local amateur dramatics and was vice president of the Grove Park Amateur Dramatic Society. He married Mary Louise of Minera in 1922 and they had two daughters, Eunice and Isobel. In their latter years, he and his wife lived at The Cottage, 8 Stansty Road, Rhosddu. He died on 7 July 1969, aged 72. His business, Rhosddu Garage, was carried on by his son-in-law Ralph Lawson until 1988 when it was bought by Burmah Oil. Ffordd Gwilym* was named after him.

Jones' Hall, Queen Street
It was located in Queen Street,* opposite the junction of Lambpit Street, for the sale of linen and fancy goods. It was built by John Jones towards the end of the 18th century. Originally intended for use during the March Fair, the hall was 'open in the middle, with a covered gallery around three of its sides, having shops in the gallery and on the ground floor below them'. It was later referred to as the New Linen Hall (1796), the Irish Hall (1818) and Manchester Square/Hall (1827) – although there was already another building in Chester Street with this name. It is shown in the 1833 survey, still existed in 1841 but does not appear on the 1872 survey.

Jones, BSc, MP, James Idwal *politician*
Born in Rhosllanerchrugog on 30 June 1900, the son of coal miner James Jones and his wife Elizabeth Bowyer. James Idwal was educated at Ruabon Grammar School and the Normal College, Bangor. As a certified teacher in 1922 he took up his first appointment at Holt School before moving on to Glyn Ceiriog and Penycae. During his early years as a teacher he successfully completed an external BSc. degree in Economics with London University. In 1938, he was appointed Headmaster of Grango Secondary Modern School in Rhos where he worked until 1955. He was the author of several educational books and political works including: *An Historical Atlas of Wales/Atlas Hanesyddol o Gymru* and *An Atlas of Denbighshire.* He married Catherine Humphreys and they had one son.

James Idwal Jones joined the Labour Party in 1918 and was deeply involved with socialist politics throughout his life (his brother Thomas William Jones,* later Lord Maelor, became the Labour MP for Merionethshire). He was Chairman of the Rhos Labour Party in 1932–36 and 1950–54 and was later President of the Rhos Labour Party. In 1951, he stood for Parliament as the Labour candidate for West Denbighshire but was unsuccessful until 1955 when he was elected Labour MP for Wrexham, a seat which he held until retiring in 1970. In 1980, he was created a Knight of Mark Twain for his services to education.

A fluent Welsh speaker he had a great interest in Welsh affairs, social justice and education. A member of the Bardic Circle he was also a Scotch Baptist lay minister. He lived at Maelor, Ponciau and died on 18 October 1982.

Jones, James Meredith *businessman*
James Meredith Jones and his partner Charles Rocke bought the Cambrian Leather Works* from Evan Morris in 1858. He was an ardent campaigner against the incorporation of the Borough of Wrexham. When the Charter of Incorporation was granted he stood for election and came 11th in a poll of 52 candidates–the first twelve forming the first Town Council.

Jones, Colonel John *soldier & regicide*
Born in about 1597, John Jones was the son of Thomas Jones of Maes-y-Garnedd, Merionethshire and his wife Elin, daughter of Robert Wynn of Taltreuddyn, Merionethshire. As a youth, John Jones is recorded as being in London in the service of the Myddelton family of Chirk. By 1639 he was employed by Sir William Myddelton, having had a good education which may have included some legal training. He married Margaret, the daughter of John Edwards of Stansty, sometime before 1639 (see Edwards Family). In addition to his Merionethshire property, John Jones is also believed to have owned Bryn-y-Ffynnon House in Wrexham (which he had probably inherited from his brother Edward). He and his wife lived at Stansty, Uchlaw'r Coed, Llanenddwyn and Plas Uchaf Eliseg, Llangollen. In June 1644 he was commissioned as a captain in the forces raised by Sir Thomas Myddelton in support of Parliament and saw active service in north Wales as paymaster then in south Wales as a captain of foot. He was present at the storming of Laugharne Castle in December 1644 and, in April 1645, was with the forces laying siege to Chester. By 1646 he had been promoted to colonel of horse and was one of the envoys sent to negotiate the surrender of Anglesey to Parliament. On 23 September 1647 he became the Member of Parliament for Merioneth and, on the outbreak of the second Civil War, rejoined the army and served in Denbigh and in Anglesey. He attended the trial for treason of King Charles I and was one of the signatories of the King's death warrant.

In 1649, he was appointed one of the council of six set up by the Rump Parliament and was created an Alderman of Denbigh. He was a keen member of the Commission for the Propagation of the Gospel in Wales and was sent to Ireland in 1650 as one of the three civil administrators of that country. His wife Margaret died while he was serving in Ireland. In 1655 he was appointed Commissioner for North Wales during the rule of the major-generals and the following year married a widow, Katherine Whetstone, the sister of Oliver Cromwell. Appointed to the Lord Protector's Council of State he was elected to represent both Denbighshire and Merionethshire (and chose the latter). In 1657 he was elevated to the House of Lords and was later again appointed as a Commissioner for Ireland. Following the death of Cromwell, Jones served as a member of both the Committee for Safety and the Council of State and was Governor of Anglesey. As the tide of public opinion swung back in favour of the monarchy, Colonel Jones was arrested in January 1660 and taken to London. After a period on parole, when he is reported to have visited Wrexham to put his affairs in order, he returned to the capital to face trial as a regicide. He was found guilty and beheaded on 17 October 1660 and his body dragged through the streets of London. The diarist John Evelyn wrote: 'October 17, 1660. Scott, Scrope and Jones suffered for reward of their iniquities at Charing Cross. I saw not their execution but met their quarters mangled and cut and reeking carried from the gallows in buckets…' Jones was a devout Protestant and a regular correspondent with Morgan Llwyd* (who resided at Bryn-y-Ffynnon) and Vavasor Powell.

Jones, John *local politician*
He was born in Wrexham in 1822, the son of Robert Jones, a partner in Jackson & Jones, coachbuilders of Hope Street. He joined the family business as an apprentice on leaving school but very soon realised that this was not the route that he wished his life to take and began training as a teacher at the Borough Road College in London. He was employed in the schoolroom below the Chester Street Congregational Chapel,* at the Normal School of the National Society, Westminster Bridge (1847), in Warrington and in Ruabon (2 years). Again deciding on a change of career, he became articled to a Mr Parker then John Lewis and in 1857 qualified as a solicitor with an office at N° 1 Henblas Street. His nephew, R.J. Kendrick was articled to him in 1879 and, upon qualifying, became his partner.

John Jones was the Clerk to the Broughton, Brymbo and Stansty School Boards and was elected a Liberal member of WBC in 1857. He was created an alderman in 1864 but resigned in 1870. In 1886, he was created an alderman from outside of the Council

179

(a position which he held until his death) and was elected Mayor in 1887. During his year of office, the National Eisteddfod was held in Wrexham. He was also an alderman of the newly-formed Denbighshire County Council, a Borough Justice of the Peace, and a member of the Wrexham Board of Guardians. He was the Vice-President of the Wrexham Liberal Association for 25 years and was political agent for Colonel Biddulph, Watkin Williams, Sir George Osborne Morgan and Sir Robert Cunliffe.

He was the author of a number of books including: *Wrexham & Its Neighbourhood* (1868); *The Maid of Caergwrle & Other Poems* (1871) – reprinted as *Winifred Meredith* (1885); *Wrexham & Thereabouts Eighty Years Ago* (1883). He built St John's House* on Chester Road where he died on 3 April 1892 and is buried in Wrexham Cemetery.*

Jones, John *brewer and philanthropist*
Born on 23 November 1825, at Caia Farm,* Wrexham, the second son of William (1782–1841) and Maria Jones (1788–1856), John Jones was educated locally (possibly at Wrexham Grammar School) before being apprenticed to a chemist in Corwen. He worked in Liverpool before returning to Wrexham in about 1850 where he began brewing at the existing Caia Brewery. Shortly afterwards, in about 1856 (possibly following the death of his mother), he joined his brother William Jones,* in founding the Island Green Brewery* in Brook Street, where he was the brewer. The company was very successful and the two brothers were among the most affluent businessmen in the area. Following the death of William in 1904, John sold the business in 1905.

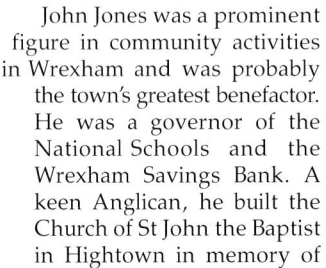

John Jones was a prominent figure in community activities in Wrexham and was probably the town's greatest benefactor. He was a governor of the National Schools and the Wrexham Savings Bank. A keen Anglican, he built the Church of St John the Baptist in Hightown in memory of his wife, Jane (daughter of William Roberts, farmer, of Eyton, who died 22 October 1908) at a cost of £8,500, placed a window in the Parish Church and endowed a bed at the Infirmary in memory of his brother William. Also in memory of his brother, he gave the Borough of Wrexham the William Jones Recreation Ground in Rhosddu and paid for laying it out. He established a scholarship for Grove Park pupils to go to Oxford or Cambridge to study theology. A fervent supporter of the Infirmary,* he funded the first X-ray department and served as the hospital's Vice-President. He bequeathed the Roseneath* property in Wrexham, and the surrounding land, as a site for a new hospital and endowed the foundation with a substantial sum of money from his estate. Today he is best remembered for setting up the William & John Jones Charity* which financed the building and operation of convalescent homes for coal miners in Rhyl and Minera (the latter became Pen-y-Nant residential home in November 1952 and has recently been converted into private appartments). The charity still has substantial funds which are distributed to needy persons in the Wrexham area.

John Jones lived at Grove Lodge* but owned property all over Wrexham and district including premises in Cambridge Terrace, Pentre Felin, Chester Street, Chester Road, Jones Court, Abbot Street, Bank Street, King Street, Foster Road, Caia, Rhosddu, Rhos, Acrefair, Sutton, Pickhill, Overton, Gwernymynydd, Ellesmere, Minera, Gresford, Ruabon and Bangor-on-Dee. He also owned land in Hilgay, Norfolk. He died on 6 April 1913 and was buried in the Wrexham Cemetery.* His estate was valued at £304,763-7s-3d and, as he had no children, was left to numerous nephews and nieces, with the largest part going to various charitable bequests in the local area as well as the John Jones Trust at the Royal Orphanage, Wolverhampton. He stipulated in his will that his portrait should be hung in the Infirmary (this now hangs in the Maelor Hospital).

(See also William Jones; William & John Jones Charity Trusts; John Jones Park; Roseneath; Wrexham Infirmary; Wrexham & East Denbighshire War Memorial Hospital; William Jones Recreation Ground; Caia Farm; St Giles Home for Waifs and Strays; Wrexham Infirmary Trust)

John Jones of the Island Green Brewery

Jones, John Garner *local politician*
He was born in Llanarmon-yn-Iâl in 1878, the son of John and Harriet Jones. He was educated at the local school before becoming an apprentice to Mr Woodward, a butcher with premises in Bridge Street, Wrexham. He eventually established his own business at 35 Yorke Street. He was elected to serve on Denbighshire County Council and, in 1929, on WBC, becoming Mayor in 1935.

John Garner Jones married Harriet Moss Jones, the daughter of Enoch and Elizabeth Jones of Graianrhyd, Llanarmon-yn-Iâl and had six children. He died at 174 Chester Road in February 1940 and is buried in Wrexham Cemetery.

Jones, MP, Martyn David *politician*
Born 1 March 1947 in Crewe, Cheshire, the son of Vernon Pritchard Jones (a railway-engine driver) and his wife Violet. The family moved to Wrexham when Martyn was 18 months old and he was educated at Victoria School,* Grove Park Grammar School,* the Liverpool College of Commerce, Liverpool Polytechnic (gaining a CIBiol) and Trent Polytechnic (gaining a MIBiol). He was appointed a microbiologist at the Wrexham Lager Beer Company* in 1968 and, while there became involved in union politics.

He was elected a member of Clwyd County Council in 1981 and in 1987 was elected Labour Member of Parliament for Clwyd South West, which he held until the boundary changes of 1997 when he became MP for Clwyd South. He was a Labour Whip in the House of Commons from 1988–92 and Opposition Spokesman on Food, Agriculture and Rural Affairs 1994–95 and has chaired the Select Committee on Welsh Affairs. He retired as an MP at the dissolution of Parliament in May 2010. He married Rhona Bellis in 1974, they have one son and one daughter.

Jones, JP, Miss Mair Megan *local politician*
Megan Jones was born in 1917, the daughter of John Peter and Elizabeth Jones. A schoolteacher, she taught at Rhosddu Infant School before being appointed Headmistress of Holy Trinty Infant School in Gwersyllt (later Bryn Golau Infant School). She was a member of the national Executive of the National Union of Teachers and a passionate member of the Campaign for Nuclear Disarmament.

Elected as the Labour representative for Caia Ward on WBC in November 1964, Megan Jones continued with her political service to Wrexham after the creation of WMBC in 1974 and became Mayor in 1980. She was appointed a Justice of the Peace and eventually became Chairman of the Wrexham Bench

(1980–3). She lived at 6 Court Road. Megan Jones died on 23 June 1984 and is buried in Wrexham Cemetery.

Jones, Morgan *local politician*
Born at Ffynnongroew, Flintshire, on 30 September 1906, Welsh speaker Morgan Jones was the son of a collier. He began his education at the local Ffynnongroew School then attended Rhosddu School, Wrexham, after his father commenced work at Gresford Colliery in c.1916 (his father was killed in the Gresford Disaster of 1934). On leaving school he trained as an electrician in the coal industry, an occupation in which he remained all his working life.

Elected a WRDC Labour councillor for Llay, he also served on the Parish Council and later the Community Council. In 1974 he became the first Mayor of WMBC. When he retired from public life, Morgan Jones had given 50 years of service to his community as a councillor and was the 'Father of the Council'.

He married Minnie May Wilkes of Gwersyllt in 1931 and they had one daughter. He died on 17 February 1981.

Jones, Richard *Methodist pioneer*
Richard Jones of Llanddyn Farm, Llangollen left Wales in the mid 18th century to seek his fortune in London. There he met and married a fellow Methodist, Ann Jones of Coed-y-Glyn,* Wrexham. The couple returned to Wrexham where they opened an ironmongery shop in High Street and re-joined the Methodist congregation at Adwy'r Clawdd, Coedpoeth. Richard became a trustee of the new Methodist chapel being built in Rhosllanerchrugog in 1770 (Capel Mawr). By the time Ann Jones died in 1793, the Wrexham Methodists were meeting in a room at the rear of a house in Pentre Felin called The Castle.* In 1797, the congregation acquired property in the Naylor's Yard* area of Pentre Felin which they converted into a chapel and of which Richard Jones was a trustee. Richard Jones and his second wife were well known for the hospitality which they showed to visiting preachers at their substantial High Street home. After the death of Richard in 1805 this hospitality was continued by Mrs Jones and it was she who provided the finance for Wrexham's first purpose-built Methodist chapel in Abbot Street in 1821.*

Jones, Samuel *mining engineer*
Locally born in about 1806, Samuel Jones began his working life as a collier in one of the Brymbo pits. His natural engineering talent was recognised by William Rowe, chief manager of the Brymbo Colliery, and he was soon promoted to pit manager. In 1843–4 he sunk the Brymbo furnace pits and by 1846 was being employed by the Westminster Colliery Company as designer of their underground workings. In this capacity he was responsible for the sinking of the Moss pits. In 1850 he was approached by Henry Robertson* to form the Ruabon Colliery (the Brandie Pits) which eventually sank the Glan-yr-Afon Colliery (later re-named Hafod) in 1863. In the late 1850s he bought the Broughton Colliery on behalf of the Brymbo Iron Company and was appointed a director and part owner. He was one of the prime movers behind the establishment of the Brymbo and Broughton British Schools. He died at Broughton Farm in 1866 and was buried in the Ruthin Road Cemetery.*

Jones, Dr Samuel Edwards
See Dr Samuel Edwards-Jones.

Jones' Square, Mount Street
This short, straight row of buildings, located on a cul-de-sac passage leading from Mount Street, does not appear to have had any reason for using the adjective 'square'. It was demolished during one the Wrexham Borough Council slum clearance programmes. Not to be confused with Jones' Court.*

Jones, Thomas *architect*
Born c.1794, he had an office in Chester. He was County Surveyor of Flintshire from 1827–55. He specialised in the neo-Tudor and neo-gothic Perpendicular architecture that was popular in the mid-19th century. The only example of his work in Wrexham is the memorial to Sir Foster and Lady Cunliffe in Wrexham Parish Church (1835). Elsewhere, examples of his work include: the Deanery, St Asaph (1830); Llwynegrin Hall, Mold (1830); County Hall, Mold (1833–4); Grosvenor Lodge, Eaton Hall, Chester (1835); Llanferres Church (1843); Llanarmon DC Church (1846). He died in Barmouth on 2 October 1859.

Jones, Thomas (Taliesin o Eifion) *poet*
He was born 13 September 1820 at Llanystumdwy, Caernarfonshire. A plumber and decorator by trade, he became a well-known poet and his strict metre poems are among the finest recorded. He won the chair at the National Eisteddfod* held at Wrexham in 1876 but, when the result was announced, it was realised that he had died on 1 June that year and the chair was ceremonially draped in black.

Jones, JP, Alderman Thomas *local politician*
He was born in Trevor in September 1845, the son of Thomas Jones, a local quarryman. He began his working life in the local quarry before becoming a farm labourer and then a grocer's assistant in Cefn Mawr. In 1864 he was employed by Mrs Phillips of Queen Street as a shop assistant. In 1866 he left Wrexham and went to work in Bollington and Stockport in order to improve his English before returning four years later to set up his own grocery and provision business on the corner of High Street and Chester Street, in partnership with his brother Benjamin. One month later, Benjamin died and Thomas took his brother Hugh as a new partner. Their business prospered and they built a new warehouse in Chester Street where they opened a wholesale business. In 1883, they bought the Lion Hotel in Hope Street which they re-opened as H.&T. Jones, Ltd, groceries and provisions.

Thomas Jones was elected a borough councillor in 1889 and served as Mayor in 1899 and 1900. He became an alderman in 1901 and served as chairman of the General Purpose Committee (1917–20). He was also chairman of the Managers of both the Council School and the British School and a governor of Grove Park County Schools. He was appointed a Justice of the Peace on the Wrexham Bench in 1902 and the Bromfield Bench in 1912. He retired from the Council in 1920 and was made an Honorary Freeman of the Borough on 19 September 1923. In 1881 he was living at N° 3 Queen Street and later at Bryn Melyn, Grosvenor Road. He died on 25 January 1925. (See also Wrexham Corn Mills)

Jones, OBE, CBE, Thomas 'Tom Spain' *trade unionist*
Born in Lancashire in 1908, Thomas Jones was brought up in Rhosllanerchrugog and was a fluent Welsh speaker. During the Spanish Civil War he volunteered for service with the International Brigade which had been formed to assist in the fight against the Fascist forces of General Francisco Franco. On 30 September 1938, while serving on the Aragon Front, Tom took part in the battle of Ebro where, along with other members of the Brigade, he was captured by officers of a light machine-gun company. Almost immediately, they were all shot and left for dead and a death certificate was sent to his parents. Fortunately, however, he had only been wounded, albeit seriously, and was imprisoned at Zaragoza and Burgos for two years before it was

181

announced that he was still alive and had been sentenced to 30 years imprisonment. The public outcry which ensued led to demands from the British Government that he be released and Spain demanded a ransom payment of £2 million which was paid in 1941 and he returned to Britain.

Still politically minded, Tom Jones devoted his life to trade union activities and eventually rose to become the General Secretary of the Transport and General Workers Union in Wales. He was a member of the Economic Development Council for Wales, treasurer of the North Wales Education Authority and a member of the Welsh Industrial Estates Co-operative. He was awarded the OBE in 1962 and the CBE in 1974. In recognition of his service to Spain, the Spanish Government in exile created him a Knight of the Order of Loyalty in 1974. At the time of his death in June 1990, he was living in Blackbrooke Avenue, Hawarden. His biography *A Most Expensive Prisoner* was written by Jane Pugh and a TV drama *Hen Elynion* (Trans. old enemies), based on his story, was produced in 1996.

Jones, MD, FRCS, JP, Dr Thomas Eyton local politician
Born in Corwen in c.1832, Welsh-speaker Thomas Eyton Jones moved to Wrexham in 1848 where he was articled to Dr T. T. Griffiths. In 1853 he moved to London to train at St Bartholomew's Hospital where he gained the midwifery 1st prize in 1855 and the surgery 1st prize in 1856 and became a member of the Royal College of Surgeons. He studied in Paris for a short time before returning to Wrexham as a partner to his former mentor. In 1859, he was appointed a surgeon to the Volunteers and to the Wrexham Infirmary* and was made a governor of the Ragged Schools.

He was elected a Wrexham borough councillor in 1864 and became chairman of the Sanitary Committee. In 1867 he was appointed president of the north Wales branch of the British Medical Association and a Justice of the Peace. He was also appointed as surgeon to the Denbighshire Yeomanry (1870), fellow of the Obstetrical Society (1872), Poor Law guardian (1873), president of the Corwen Eisteddfod (1874), honorary secretary of the North Wales Medical Association (1875), MD (1875), fellow of the Royal College of Surgeons (1875). He was elected Mayor of Wrexham in 1875, a year when the town hosted the National Eisteddfod.*

He married twice (1) Miss Mortimer Maurice of Oak Lodge* and (2) Miss Long, a native of Manchester. He had four sons and two daughters and resided at Grosvenor Lodge,* N° 1 Grosvenor Road.

Jones, RA, Thomas H. artist
See the Studio.

Jones, MP, Thomas William (Lord Maelor) politician
Born in Rhosllanerchrugog on 10 February 1898, the son of James Jones, a collier, Thomas Jones was educated at Ponciau Boys School before starting his career at Bersham Colliery. A life spent underground was not for him, however, and he quickly obtained a position as a pupil teacher in his old school before leaving to follow a teacher training course at the Normal College, Bangor.

During the First World War he was a conscientious objector but volunteered to serve in a non-combatant corps. While in the army he was courtmartialed for refusing to obey an order and sentenced to 6 months hard labour which he was later proudly able to boast led to his incarceration in not only Wormwood Scrubs but also Dartmoor Prison. A passionate socialist, he first stood for Parliament in 1935 but was not elected. He was appointed a Justice of the Peace in 1937, serving on the Ruabon Bench (of which he was the chairman for 20 years). During the Second World War he was the Welfare Officer for the North Wales Power Board. He was elected Labour MP for Merioneth in 1951 and was responsible for persuading the CEB to build the Tan-y-Grisiau Pump Storage Station and the Trawsfynydd Nuclear Power Station. He retired from Parliament in 1966 and was created Baron Maelor, a Life Peer, being sworn in on 29 June. He had also served as chairman of the North Wales Labour Federation and chairman of the Wrexham Trades Council.

Outside of politics his interests were in the field of literature (he wrote a number of books, mostly in Welsh, including a biography of Thomas Jefferson and his autobiography entitled *Fel Hyn y Bu*). He was a poet and was appointed to the Gorsedd of Bards of the National Eisteddfod in 1982. He was President of the Llangollen International Eisteddfod. At the Investiture of Charles as Prince of Wales in 1969, Lord Maelor carried the crown and ring. He married Flossy Thomas of Birkenhead in 1928 and had one son and one daughter. Lord Maelor died in a fire at his home, Ger-y-Llyn, Ellis Street, Ponciau in November 1984.

Jones, William entrepreneur
Born on 8 October 1819, the eldest son of William and Maria Jones of Caia Farm,* Wrexham. After the death of his father, William's mother established a small brewery at Caia Farm and it seems likely that both he and his brother John would have assisted in the running of this in their very early days. William was articled to local solicitor Edwin Wyatt (with offices in Wrexham and Overton) and, after qualifying, became an auditor of the Wrexham Gas* and Wrexham Water* companies, the Wrexham Savings Bank* and the Wrexham Poor Law Union.* He was appointed agent to the Bryn-y-Pys* estate and Clerk to the Justices of the Maelor Bench and the Tax Commissioners at Overton. He resided at Quinta in Overton but appears to have had an office at 8 Temple Row, Wrexham in 1899. In about 1856, he joined his brother John in establishing the Island Green Brewery* in Pentre Felin, probably acting as Company Secretary. The company was highly successful and both brothers became very wealthy. After his death on 7 August 1904, his brother gave the William Jones Recreation Ground* in Rhosddu to the people of Wrexham in his memory. He left effects to the value of £213,359. (See also John Jones and John & William Jones Charity)

Jones' Yard, Bridge Street
A small 'court' development which appears on the 1872 survey, Jones' Yard was located on the north-west side of Bridge Street opposite Bryn Issa House. It was accessed via a passage which ran alongside the malt house belonging to the Eagle Brewery.

Joy Centre, Willow Road
Housed in part of the old Peter Walker Brewery building, behind the Bridge House Inn,* the Joy Centre was established in the 1930s by William Aston* and provided a dance floor and rooms where the unemployed could practise various crafts.

Jubilee Road/Street, Newtown
This land was originally part of the nearby Bellevue Farm.* Plans for laying out the street were passed by the Council in 1897 and work began almost immediately on building houses and continued until at least 1903. The street was named after Queen Victoria's Diamond Jubilee which occurred in 1897 and was first of all referred to as Jubilee Street but by 1912 was called Jubilee Road.

Juniper Close, Borras Park
A small cul-de-sac of private houses developed c.1967 by the London firm of Spinks & Denning on land that had previously belonged to William Clarke* and, pre-1918, to the Acton Park* estate. The name has no particular significance.

K

Keeper's Cottage, Llan-y-Pwll
Located on the south side of the Holt Road as it drops down the hill towards the Gredington Arms,* this was the gamekeeper's cottage for the Gredington estate property in the Wrexham area.

Kelly, James A., KSG *local politician*
James Kelly was born in Wexford, Ireland on 30 September 1936. He was educated by the Irish Christian Brothers before beginning his working career with the Irish Post Office in Wexford in 1956 when he transferred to Dublin. Two years later he moved to Manchester as a clerical officer in a packaging company, eventually becoming production manager. He moved to Wrexham in 1964 to help set up a plastics packing company on the British Celanese site on the Wrexham Industrial Estate.

James Kelly has served as a community councillor for Acton for twenty-five years and was elected a county councillor on WCBC in 1999. He was a member of the Standards Committee for six years and co-chair of the Children's Scrutiny Committee for six years. He is a member of the Standing Advisory Council for Religious Education committee and a past member of the Planning Committee. He was elected Mayor of Wrexham for the year 2010–11.

He was installed as a Knight of Saint Gregory the Great by Pope John Paul II in 1988 in recognition of his service to the Roman Catholic Church and the community at large.

Cllr Kelly married his wife, Lily, in 1959 and they have three daughters, Angela, Patricia and Paula.

Kelsey, Tom *murderer & housebreaker*
Tom Kelsey was born in Holborn, London but moved to Wrexham as an infant when his parents inherited property in the town. At the age of 14 he ran away from home, intending to make his way to London but, *en route*, was hired to look after some horses and was dismissed for pilfering. On reaching the capital he found life harder than he had expected and became a petty thief. He was eventually captured and tried for the theft of money and silver and would very likely have been hanged had his father not travelled from Wrexham to plead for mercy and he was released. Returning to Wrexham he was apprenticed to a weaver but very soon ran away again and returned to London, accompanied by his cousin David Hughes who, within the short period of six days, was caught picking pockets, tried and hanged at Kingston. Undeterred by David's fate, Tom continued with his criminal career and was eventually identified as a burglar of some repute and was forced to flee to Flanders to escape the law. There he is reported to have robbed a number of items from the tent of King William and fled to Amsterdam where he sold his ill-gotten gains to a wealthy Jew whom he then burgled and sold the same items to a second buyer in Rotterdam before returning to London.

Breaking into a linen-draper's house in Cheapside, Tom Kelsey was caught and imprisoned in Newgate where he stabbed a gaoler named Goodman in the belly. The man died of his injuries and Tom was charged with murder, tried and sentenced to death at the Old Bailey. He was hanged in Newgate Street, aged 19, on Friday 13 June 1690.

Kelso House, Grosvenor Road
This was a small private school during the early part of the 20th century. The school was owned and run by Miss Harriet Simons until it was passed to Miss M. Moore. Prior to the opening of Kelso House School, Miss Simons had run schools at Leeside (in Rhosddu), King Street and Elm Grove (probably The Elms* in Rhosddu Road).

Kendal Way, Little Acton
A development by local builders H.R.&E. Roberts of private houses completed during the late 1950s on an estate that was originally known as the Edgby Park Estate. The land was once part of Cae'r Hen Dy (*Trans.* old house field) and Erw Coed Mawr (*Trans.* big wood acre), fields belonging to Little Acton Farm* and later, to the Acton Park* estate.

Kendrick's Row/Place, Farndon Street
A row of seven sub-standard dwellings close to Harrison's Court,* Kendrick's Row was demolished in 1932 as part of the Borough Council's slum clearance programme.

Kenrick Family
Of Wynn Hall, Ruabon. The family were early members of the 'Old Meeting'* in Chester Street when that church was established by Morgan Llwyd and they provided premises for the worshippers from 1672 until the chapel was built ninety years later. When a breakaway faction split from the 'Old Meeting' in 1691, one of the prime movers was Samuel Kenrick.

John Kenrick (1684–1745), the son of Samuel, was ordained by Matthew Henry and became pastor of the 'New Meeting' from 1707 until his death. He inherited Wynn Hall through his wife's family. His sons, Samuel and Edward were the co-founders of Kenrick's Bank at Bewdley in 1776.

James Kenrick (born 1757) a former grocer and chandler in Wrexham, established a bank in the town. He died as a result of a fall on 26 September 1824 and is buried in the Dissenters Burial Ground.*

Samuel Llewelyn Kenrick (1848–1933) was educated at Ruabon Grammar School and eventually qualified as a solicitor opening a practice in Ruabon. He served as clerk to the Magistrates at Ruabon and was coroner for East Denbighshire. A keen footballer, he played for Plasmadoc and was instrumental in transforming that club into the legendary local club Druids. He was the founder of the Football Association of Wales in 1875. He established the Welsh Cup competition and arranged the first inter-national match between Wales and Scotland in March 1876. As full-back, he made five appearances for Wales including both the first international and the side that beat England in 1881 (on that occasion, he was called in as a substitute at the last minute and had to play in his everyday clothes). He went on to become the first chairman and honorary secretary of the Football Association of Wales. He died on 29 May 1933 and is buried in Ruabon.

Kenrick Street
See Bank Street.

Samuel Llewelyn Kenrick.

Kenrick & Bowman's Bank, Hope Street
Founded by James Kenrick, a former grocer and chandler of Nº 56 Hope Street, it was located in a building on the southern corner of Bank Street (which was named after it). After Kenrick's

death in 1824, his nephew Samuel Kenrick took over the business and went into partnership with John Eddowes Bowman. The business became bankrupt in 1849 and the site was taken over by the National Provincial Bank of England. It appears in the 1833 survey. The building was later demolished and a new bank, built by the National Provincial Bank, was opened on the site. After the amalgamation of the National Provincial, Westminster and Martins banks, this was the main premises of the National Westminster (NatWest) in Wrexham until they moved to the old Tesco building on the corner of Lord Street and Rhosddu Road and the Hope Street premises were re-furbished and opened as the Halifax Building Society (later bank).

Banknote issued by Kenrick & Bowman's Bank.

Kenrick's Bank, Hope Street
See Kenrick & Bowman's Bank.

Kenrick's Farm
Located on the land between Holt Road and Borras Road (now occupied by Moorhead Close, Bickerley Wood and Halstonwood Close) and between Borras Road, Park Avenue and Aston Grove (now occupied by the Maes-y-Dre* housing estate). The farm was detailed in the 1786 survey of the Acton Park* estate, prepared for Sir Foster Cunliffe. The fields were called: Erw Glas or Cae Glas (*Trans.* green acre or green field), Bryn-y-glan (*Trans.* hillside), Berth-y-Benglog (*Trans.* fine skull), Cae Mawr Nesa (*Trans.* nearest large field), Cae Mawr Ganol (*Trans.* middle large field), Cae Mawr Pelle (*Trans.* smallest big field), Cae yr Groes (*Trans.* field of the cross), Gweierglodd (*Trans.* meadows). [FRO/D/AH/24]

Kenricks' Row/Place
A terrace of six houses located in a small entry off Farndon Street. The southern gable end of the row stood against the wall of the cattle market.

Kent Drive, Tŷ Gwyn
A development by local builders H. R. & E. Roberts of private houses completed in the early 1970s.

Kenyon Avenue
This was the first street to be laid out in the Garden Village estate before the First World War. Plaques between N[os] 23 & 25 and N[os] 35 & 37 bear the date '1914'. The street is named after Rt Hon Lord Kenyon,* KCVO, chairman of the Wrexham Tenants Ltd which developed the Garden Village estate. One of the gateposts which stood at the entrance to the estate can still be seen close to the junction with Chester Road.*

Kenyon Family
Baronetcy created 1784. Title created 1788.

Lloyd Kenyon Born 1696, the eldest son of Thomas and Catherine Kenyon. Educated St John's College, Cambridge. He married Jane Eddowes, whose father had purchased Gredington from Sir John Hanmer and they moved into the house sometime after the Revd Eddowes' death in 1706.

Lloyd Kenyon, KC, MP, Bt, *1st Baron Gredington* – Born at Gredington 5 October 1732, Lloyd Kenyon was educated at Ruthin Grammar School, admitted to the Middle Temple in 1750 and called to the Bar in 1756. He became a renowned lawyer and, through his links with the Lord Chancellor, was appointed a King's Counsel in 1780. Later that same year, he was appointed Chief Justice of Chester, Flint, Denbigh and Montgomery, raised to the bench of the Middle Temple and elected MP for Hindon in Wiltshire. In 1784 he became MP for Tregony. In March 1782, he was appointed Attorney-General and, two years later, became Master of the Rolls. On 12 April 1784 he was made a Privy Councillor and created a baronet on 28 July. In 1788, he became Chief Justice of the King's Bench and created Baron Gredington on 9 June. He was involved in the trials of Lord George Gordon and Warren Hastings. He was Lord Lieutenant of Flintshire 1796–98 and custos rotulorum from 1796 until his death. He married his cousin Mary Kenyon of Peel, Lancashire and had three sons. He died in Bath on 4 April 1802.

George Kenyon, MA, Bt, *2nd Baron Gredington* – Born at Gredington in 1776, he was educated at Harrow and Christ Church, Oxford, gaining a BA in 1797 and an MA in 1801. He became a barrister of the Middle Temple in 1793, a bencher in 1811, reader in 1815 and treasurer in 1823. He was a vice-president of the National Society and was responsible for building the Madras School in Penley, the first National School in Wales. He married Margaret Emma Hanmer in 1803 and had three sons and three daughters. He died at Gredington 25 February 1855.

Lloyd Kenyon, MA, MP Bt, *3rd Baron Gredington* – Born at Gredington 1805, he was educated at Harrow and Christ Church, Oxford from where he graduated with a BA in 1826 and an MA three years later. He was the Tory MP for St Michael's in Cornwall 1830–32 and unsuccessfully fought the election for Denbighshire in 1833. He married Georgina de Grey, daughter of Lord Walsingham, in 1833 and had five sons and five daughters. He died in Eastbourne in 1864.

Lloyd Kenyon, KCVO, Bt, *4th Baron Gredington* – Born 1864, the son of the Hon Lloyd Kenyon and grandson of the 3rd Baron Kenyon and the 1st Lord Harlech. He was President of the University College of North Wales 1900–27; Senior Deputy Chancellor of the University of Wales; Pro-Chancellor of the University of Wales 1920–7. Married Gwladys Julia, daughter of Colonel H.R. Lloyd Howard, CB. He died on 30 November 1927.

Sir Lloyd Tyrell-Kenyon, BA, LLD, CBE, FSA, DL, JP, Bt, *5th Baron Gredington* – of Cumbers House and Gredington, Wrexham. Born 13 September 1917, the only son of the 4th Baron Kenyon, he was educated at Eton and served as a 2nd lieutenant in the Shropshire Yeomanry from 1937. He was commissioned as a lieutenant in the Territorial Artillery in 1940 but retired on the grounds of ill-health in 1943, with the honorary rank of captain. He gained a BA at Magdalene College, Cambridge in 1950. He was a director of Lloyds Bank (1962) and the National Provident Institution; president of the University College of North Wales (1947–82); president of the National Museum of Wales (1952–8); Trustee (1953) and chairman National Portrait Gallery (1966); member Royal Commission on Historical Manuscripts (1966); Chairman of the Friends of National Libraries (1963); Chairman Wrexham, Powys and Mawddach Hospital Management Committee (1960–74); chairman of Clwyd Health Authority

(1974–8); Chief Commissioner Wales, Boy Scouts Association (1948–65); Chairman of the Ancient Monuments Board of Wales; Provincial Grand Master North-West Province of the Freemasons. Lord Kenyon was a member of Flintshire County Council from 1945–54 (and served as its chairman in 1954–5). He was made an honorary doctor of law by the University of Wales in 1958. He was appointed a Justice of the Peace on the Maelor Bench (1943), Chairman 1962–74, Chairman of the Wrexham Maelor Bench 1984–7, Deputy Lieutenant of Flintshire 1948. Order of St John. Married to Leila Mary Cookson 1946, two sons Lloyd and Thomas, one daughter Kate. Died in May 1993.

Lloyd Tyrell-Kenyon, Bt, BA, 6th Baron Kenyon – Born 13 July 1947. Educated Eton and Magdalene College, Cambridge. Married Sally Carolyn, daughter of J.F.P. Matthews in 1971. Two sons. Member of WMBC and WCBC, European Union Committee of the Regions (1994–7), High Sheriff of Clwyd, 1986. Lives at Gredington, Hanmer.

Hon George Thomas Kenyon, JP, MP (1840–1908). The second son of the 3rd Lord Kenyon. Educated at Harrow and Christ Church, Oxford. Called to the Bar 1865. Justice of the peace for three counties, deputy lieutenant of Flintshire, steward of the Lordship of Bromfield and Yale,* captain in the Shropshire Yeomanry, 1873–78. Married Florence Anna Leche of Carden. Conservative Member of Parliament for Denbighshire. Author of *The Life of Lord Justice Kenyon*.

Dame Kathleen Mary Kenyon, DBE, MA, DLitt, DLit, LHD, FBA, FSA, Daughter of Sir Frederic G. Kenyon, GBE, KCB, Director of the British Museum. Educated St Paul's Girls School and Somerville College, Oxford She was the leading field archæologist of her time and had been the Director of the Viroconium Roman dig near Shrewsbury (1936–37) and Wrekin (1939). She led expeditions to Southern Rhodesia (now Zimbabwe), Palestine and Jerusalem and made significant discoveries in Jericho in 1952. CBE (1954), DBE (1973). Author of numerous publications on the subject of archaeology. Lived at Rose Hill, Erbistock. Member of the Erbistock Parochial Church Council. Died in Wrexham, August 1978, aged 72.

Kenyon Street, Farndon Street
Located off Farndon Street, this street appears in the 1872 survey.

Kerry Place
This street was laid out by WBC. The origin of its name is unknown, but it seems likely to have been named after the area of Kerry, near Newtown, in Montgomeryshire.

Keston Lodge, Chester Road
See Jerusalem Welsh Wesleyan Chapel.

Key to the Millennium, Llwyn Isa
This ambitious work of art on the wall of the Wrexham Library & Arts Centre was produced by children from eight local schools *viz*: St Giles Infant and Junior Schools, Victoria Infant and Junior Schools, Erddig Nursery, Rhostyllen County primary School, Bwlchgwyn County Primary School and St Mary's Aided School Overton. The project was co-ordinated by Mrs Anne Edmunds (Headteacher of St Giles Infant School) and relied heavily upon ceramic tile artist Penny Hampson. The tiles were fired by Dennis Ruabon and the project was funded by the Arts Council of Wales Lottery Fund with support from several local organisations and businesses. The ceramic mural depicts a variety of aspects of life in the Wrexham area, both historical and up-to-date, and the design shows a strong Celtic influence with links to local features such as the wrought-iron work on Westminster Buildings.*

Kilfoil, Geoffrey E. *judge*
Born in Acrefair in 1939, he was the son of Thomas and Hilda Kilfoil. His father was an engineering pattern-maker at the Hughes & Lancaster factory in Acrefair. His mother (nee Johnson) was a schoolteacher. He was educated at Acrefair Junior School, Ruabon Grammar School and Jesus College, Oxford where he gained an honours degree in jurisprudence and an MA. After leaving university in 1960 he worked underground in Gresford and Hafod collieries, taught as head of the English Department at Ysgol Bryn Alyn, Gwersyllt and lectured in law at the Denbighshire Technical College, Wrexham.*

He was elected (Labour) to the WRDC, representing Acrefair and Penybryn, in May 1964 and served as vice-chairman of the Housing and Finance Committees. In May 1967 he was elected to Denbighshire County Council (Labour) and Chairman of the Cefn Mawr Parish Council. In 1965 he was selected as prospective Labour candidate for Ludlow.

Called to the Bar by Gray's Inn and elected to the Wales & Chester Circuit in 1966, he entered barristers' chambers in Chester as a pupil of Robin David (Head of Chambers) – eighteen years later becoming Head of Chambers himself.

He was appointed Deputy Circuit Judge in 1976 and then Recorder in the Wales & Chester Circuit. In 1987 he was sworn in as a Crown Court Judge by Lord Chancellor Havers in the House of Lords in the Welsh language by special dispensation upon request. He served on the Circuit bench in North, Mid & South Wales, Cheshire and London. He retired in March 2004.

He is married with one daughter and one son.

Kiln Cottages, Poplar Road
Located off Poplar Road on what is now part of the playing fields of St Giles' School, this terrace of very poor quality houses was the subject of a compulsory purchase order in 1934 as part of the Borough slum clearance programme.

King Street
This was the first 'planned' street in Wrexham and was almost certainly named in honour of King George IV who had been the

King Street, c.1910, looking towards the County Buildings and St Mark's Church. The junction with Lord Street is on the left.

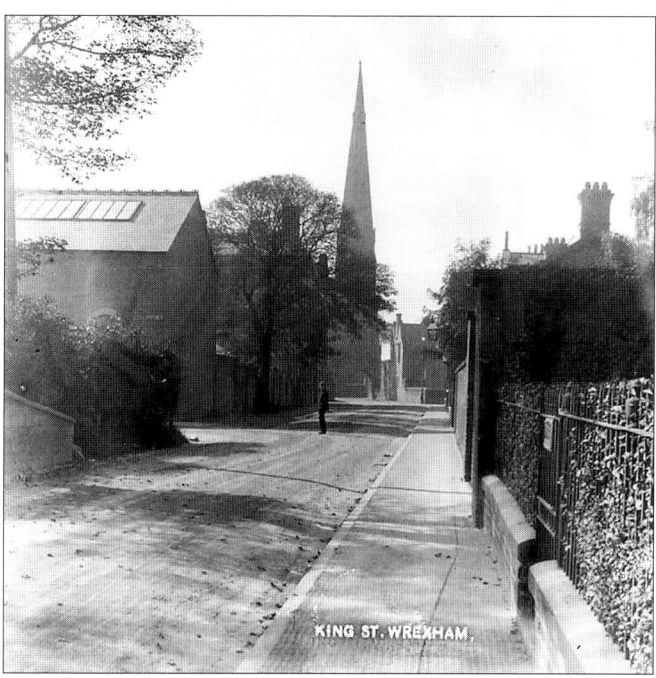

Prince Regent until 1820. It is first mentioned in 1828 and is shown in some detail (including the names of residents – Mrs Watson, Miss Mathews, K. Jones, Thomas Evans, Mr Gibbons, Mr Brett, Mr Rowland, Edward Jones) in the 1833 survey. The field on which the street was built was called Cae-ron and was the property of Miss Potts.

The two buildings on the western corner of Regent Street were known as Wynnstay Place at the end of which stood the Roman Catholic Chapel* and Elwy House. The next block of houses (now the site of Centenary House) was known as Wellington Place and those nearest to Rhosddu Road (opposite Trinity Church) were called Gwersyllt Place (after Gwersyllt Hill* the home of Richard Kirk who owned the seven houses). All of these properties were originally fronted by private gardens.

Most of the east side of King Street was, in 1833, the property of Thomas Griffith and was later taken up with private tennis courts which were bought by the Borough Council in 1924 for £5,500 with a view to the site being used for a new Guildhall. Instead, they were re-developed as a new bus station and taxi stand in the early 1950s. This served Wrexham until September 2002 and a new station was developed on the same site by WCBC and Thornfield Properties of Leeds at a cost of £3 million.

Most of the alterations to the original King Street houses were carried out during the 1920s by local builder Charles Caldecott when they were converted to retail premises. Wellington Place was demolished in the mid 1950s to make way for Centenary Buildings, one of the poorest examples of 20th century architecture in the town centre, which was developed by local solicitor Hywel Glyn Jones and opened in 1957 and named after the centenary of the Borough of Wrexham. This led to other new developments in the street, including the premises of T. E. Roberts. The premises on the corner with Rhosddu Road, once the surgery of Dr D. B. Evans, had an elaborate portico until it was demolished in 1956.

King Street Baptist Chapel
Shown in the 1872 survey as being located at the rear of the former St David's RC Chapel.*

King's Arms, Bridge Street
See The Horns.

King's Croft
Built in c.1895/6, King's Croft was the home of John Oswell Bury* before the First World War. It was the property of J. S. Oakes when it was put up for sale in June 1970 and comprised: a drawing room, dining room, wine cellar, reception hall, five bedrooms on the first floor and two on the second floor. Outside there were extensive gardens and a tennis court. During the latter years of the 20th century it became a private nursing home and is now apartments.

King's Head (I), 26B Hope Street
The King's Head first appears in the records c.1808 although records show that the premises were occupied by an 'innkeeper' as early as 1770. It appears as *The Old King's Head* in the 1833 survey but as the *King's Head* in the 1872 survey. The surviving memorials in the Burial Ground* on Ruthin Road include a headstone for Joseph Davies, King's Head Vaults, who died on 10 February 1889. The building was demolished in the 1960s.

King's Head (II), 58 Hope Street
Located on the site of the present day Central Arcade, this site was an inn as early as 1711. When the landlord, Rowland Samuel moved premises across the street to the Old Raven, he took the name with him. The premises then became an ironmonger's shop, then a grocer's shop and finally a tailor's shop (occupied by John Clark,* Mayor of Wrexham). It was demolished to make way for the Central Arcade.

King's Head (III), 6 Bridge Street
This is shown in the 1833 survey. The frontage of these premises were considerably altered as part of a road widening and improvement scheme in 1898. It was closed in the 1980s and re-opened as the Amble Inn. It was demolished in June 2003 as part of the proposed Bridge Street Regeneration Strategy. At the time of writing (2010) the site is undeveloped. [DRO/986]

King's Mills
Known at various times in history by a variety of names including: Lord's Mill, Queen's Mill, Prince's Mill and Crown Mill (a reference to the ownership of the Lordship of Bromfield and Yale), this was the flour mill for Wrexham Regis. All the tenants and residents of Wrexham Fawr,* Wrexham Fechan* and Stansty had to have their corn ground here and paid $1/16$th of the total value of the flour to the miller. Freemen of Wrexham could take their corn elsewhere but were obliged to contribute to the maintenance of the mill building and machinery. It is located on what was the main road from Wrexham to Marchwiel on the bank of the river Clywedog. There has been a mill on this site for nearly 700 years and from 1495 until 1790 it was the property of the Crown. In addition to the actual mill building the property also comprised an adjacent farm (now the King's Mills Hotel*) and was usually let to tenants and sub-tenants.

1562	Katherine Puleston
1573	Thomas Bellot of Plas Bellot (Plas Power*)
1576	Roger Puleston (sub-tenant)

Roger Puleston's father, Piers, had built a new mill on his own land alongside the King's Mill which would suggest that the older building was in need of repair and therefore unable to cope with the demand for milling. Consequently, customers were in danger of being turned away. The presence of this second mill led to a series of protracted legal disputes between the tenant of the King's Mill and the Puleston family which lasted until well into the 18th century.

1594	Roger Bellot
1620	Robert Puleston (sub-tenant) of Hafod y Wern
1626	Roger Myddelton (sub-tenant) of Plas Cadwgan. He expanded the mill to compete with the Puleston mill next door.
1631	Jointly held by Sir William Russell, Bt., William Collins and Edward Fenn (all of London).
1633	Jointly held by Thomas Hughes of Middlesex and John Davies of Kent.
1634	Kenrick Edisbury of Deptford and Marchwiel
1658	Sir Thomas Delves, Bt, (sub-tenant) of Cheshire.
1662	John Edisbury of Erddig.
1677	Joshua Edisbury.
1714	John Mellor of Erddig.
1733	Simon Yorke I of Erddig.
1770	Philip Yorke I (who gained control of the adjacent Puleston mill by exchanging land in Bryn-y-Cabanau and the Nag's Head, Mount Street for the mill, making a holding of some 40 acres).
1772	John Lowe (sub-tenant) of Mold, a miller.
1790	Philip Yorke I purchased the Crown title to the mill.
1815	Joseph Cooper (tenant)
1816	John Williams (tenant)
1834	Edward Davies (tenant)
1846	Charles Griffiths (tenant)
1875	Thomas Minshall (tenant)
1917	Wrexham & District Farmers Co-operative Society Ltd. From this time the farm and the mill were let as separate units by the Erddig estate.
1927	Wrexham & District Farmers Co-operative Society Ltd. & Co-operative Wholesale Society of Manchester as joint tenants.
1931	Co-operative Wholesale Society of Manchester.
1932	Stanley Thomas (tenant).
1940	Closed
1973	The National Trust/ WBC.

King's Mills, c.1905. The mill building is directly opposite the bridge and Rose Bank Cottages can be seen on the right of the picture.

In the Middle Ages this mill was referred to as the 'New Mill' and gave the name to the small settlement of Pentre'r Felin Newydd (*Trans.* new mill village) which developed alongside it (in the area around the present day Red Lion public house). A detailed article on the King's Mill was published by local historian Derrick Pratt in the *Transactions of the Denbighshire Historical Society* (Vol. 29, 1980).

In 1991, the mill building was opened as a mill museum by HRH The Princess of Wales on behalf of WMBC. Unfortunately, the museum closed a few years later.

King's Mills Bridge
This late 18th century stone bridge once carried the main Wrexham–Whitchurch road across the river Clywedog until the corner was bypassed in 1971. The nearby thatched half-timbered cottages were demolished in 1919 to make way for Rose Bank.

King's Mills Hotel, Kings Mills
This was originally the site of the farmhouse that was part of the King's Mills property. In the 19th century the house was re-built as King's Mills House and was converted into a guest house then, in the early 1990s, a public house.

King's Mills Road
Named after the flour mill located on the Clywedog River, near the town boundary. It was originally known as the Ellesmere/Shrewsbury Road and was the route used by the mail and passenger coaches travelling to Shrewsbury and London. Land opposite Derby Road, part of the Gatefield Estate, was sold for development in June 1889. The most important buildings still to be seen on this road are the Traveller's Rest* Wrexham Barracks* and King's Croft.* Until its demolition in the 1980s, St John the Baptist's Church,* on the corner of Whitegate Road, was a significant feature of the area.

N[os] 35 & 37: In 1980, Revd Owen Hardwicke, a Roman Catholic priest in Wrexham, bought these two houses as a home and to provide an office for both the LIFT project (designed to help young male adults) and for the area's peace movement. In 1981 the houses became the registered offices for the charity Wrexham Concern Trust. Six years later, three sisters from the order La Sainte Union des Sacrés Coeurs arrived in Wrexham to work for the Trust and then bought the building which was converted into the Wrexham Peace and Justice Centre. [DRO/DD/G/2831]

A controversial plan to build a new road linking Salop Road (from the present day junction of St Giles' Way) with King's Mills Road (cutting through Bury Street, Albert Street and Stanley Street) was approved by Denbighshire County Council in 1973 but was never implemented. The £110,000 bypass of King's Mills was opened in 1971.

Kingston House Ladies School, Salisbury Park
An 1881 advertisement for this school records that the principal was a Miss Humphreys of the Home and Colonial College, London, assisted by Miss Farquharson (University of Edinburgh) and a full staff of teachers – 'School healthily situated. Teaching on the newest and most approved methods. Best masters in attendance, Boarders enjoy all the comforts of home. References to the clergy, Her Majesty's Inspector of Schools and the parents of past and present pupils. Pupils prepared for the University Local Examination and for the College of Preceptors.'

Kington, Miles *journalist, wit and jazz aficionado*
Born in Downpatrick, Ireland, 13 May 1941, the son of William Kington (a director of the Border Breweries in Wrexham) where his father was serving with the RWF. He was the grandson of Edith Kington (née Soames, of Brynestyn,* Wrexham). He recieved his first formal education at Acton Park School* until he became a pupil at Bilton Grange, Rugby and Trinty College, Glenalmond, Scotland. He graduated in Modern Languages from Trinty College, Oxford.

He joined the satirical magazine *Punch* in 1965 and became its literary editor in 1973 where he created a successful comic sketch series that lampooned the British inability to master second languages. This developed into a number of books in the series *Let's Parler Franglais!* He later wrote humorous columns in the *Times* and the *Independent*, broadcast on BBC radio, presented a number of television documentaries and wrote several stage shows and one stage play.

Kington played several musical instruments, most notably the double-bass, and performed as a member of the jazz quartet Instant Sunshine.

Married twice, Miles Kington had two sons and a daughter. He died at Limpley Stoke, Wiltshire on 30 January 2008.

Knowle's Hotel, Regent Street
Located on Regent Street, it was sold for redevelopment in March 1901.

Knox Mawer, June *broadcaster & writer*
Born on 10 May 1930, June, the daughter of Wrexham accountant Frank Ellis, spent the early part of her life living at 94 Park Avenue. She was educated at Acton Park School and Grove Park Grammar School. Leaving school in 1947, she took up a career as a journalist, obtaining her first job with the *Chester Chronicle*. She married barrister Ronnie Knox Mawer* in 1951 and went to live in Aden where he had been appointed Chief Magistrate. From there she moved to Fiji and devoted much of her time to

writing travel books and became a part-time broadcaster on Radio Fiji. Her early books included: *The Sultans Came to Tea* (1961) and *A Gift of Islands* (1965) *A South Sea Spell* (1975).

Returning to Britain in 1971, she was given a job by the BBC and became presenter of the long-running *Woman's Hour* on the radio and, gradually, added television work to her portfolio. She published her first novel, *Marama*, in 1982 which was followed by *Marama of the Islands* (1986), *Sandstorm* (1992, Romantic Novel of the Year), *The Shadow of Wings* and *A Ram in the Well* (2001). During the 1990s she also presented a regular BBC radio programme on classical music.

June Knox Mawer had one son and one daughter. She died on 19 April 2006.

Knox Mawer, Ronald *judge & writer*
Ronald (Ronnie) Knox Mawr was born 3 August 1925, the son of George and Clara Knox Mawr. His father was a prominent chemist and became managing director of L. Rowland & Son.* The family lived at Resthaven, Nº 26 Grosvenor Road (now part of the offices of GHP Legal. Educated at Acton Park School and Grove Park Grammar School, Ronnie won a Denbighshire County Scholarship to Emmanuel College, Cambridge where he gained an M.A.

After service in the Royal Artillery during the Second World War, he was called to the Bar, Middle Temple, and served on the Wales and Chester Circuit before being appointed Chief Magistrate and Acting Chief Judge of Aden in 1952. In 1958 he was appointed Senior Magistrate and Puisne Judge, Justice of Appeal and Acting Chief Justice of Fiji and Chief Justice of Naura and Tonga. He returned to Britain in 1971 and practised on the Northern Circuit before being appointed a metropolitan stipendiary magistrate in 1975 and a deputy circuit judge in London in 1979. He retired from the law in 1984 and began a second career as a writer of humourous books and articles, many of which are autobiographical: *Tales from a Palm Court* (1984), *Islands of Hope and Glory* (1985), *Wretchedness in Wrexham* (1986), *More Tales from a Palm Court* (1987), *Tales of a Man Called Father* (1989), *A Case of Bananas and other South Sea Trials* (1992), *Land of My Father* (1994) and *Are You Coming or Going – My Sixty Years on the Run* (1999). In retirement, although living for much of the time at his cottage, Hafod, in Pentredwr, near Llangollen, he devoted a great deal of his time helping the homeless in Westminster, London.

He married Wrexham girl, June Ellis in 1951 and they had one son and one daughter. He died on 7 February 2009. (See also June Knox Mawer)

Korean War Memorial, Bodhyfryd
Located in a concealed spot behind the RWF Memorial at Bodhyfryd is the memorial for the Korean War 1950-3. This was unveiled on the 50th anniversary of the outbreak of the war.

Kumara Lodge, Chester Road
See Jerusalem Welsh Wesleyan Chapel.

L

Labour Exchange
Wrexham became one of the first towns in Britain to set up a Labour Exchange. The former Welsh Chapel on Lord Street* was adapted for use as offices serving both the counties of Denbighshire and Flintshire.

Lake View, Borras Park
A small development of private houses built in the early 1960s by the London firm of Spinks & Denning on land that had previously belonged to William Clarke* and, pre-1918, to the Acton Park* estate. The name is a reference to the nearby lake in Acton Park.

Lamb, The, Charles Street
In 1784/5, the site of the house which Palmer described as Nº 6 Charles Street* was a public house called 'The Lamb'.

Lamb, The, High Street
This property, which may have been a public house or tavern, was located on the north side of High Street between Hope Street and what was later to become the Market Hall entrance. In 1742, it was occupied by William Samuel and in 1760 was sold by Revd Edward Hughes of Radway, Warwickshire to Peter Taylor of Llwyn-y-cnottié (Llwyn Knottia*). By 1780, it was owned by William Taylor, of Coed Aben. In 1791, it was the property of William Taylor, a surgeon, who appears to have sold it to Richard Jones,* an ironmonger. One should not confuse occupation with ownership and the tenants are known to have been:

1780	Mr Prosser – surgeon
c.1786	John Rowland – apothecary
c.1789	Mr Thomas Griffith – surgeon
1790	Mr William Taylor–surgeon (owner)
c.1797	Richard Jones–ironmonger

In 1834, the house was converted into a branch of the Northern & Central Bank of England and had served as such for two years before the company failed.

Lambpit, The
This was an area of the town which incorporated Chester Street,* Lambpit Street* and Holt Street.* Although there is no evidence to confirm the origin of the name, which Palmer believed may once have been Loampit and is often written as Lampint and Lampit, it would seem likely that it originally referred to a lime pit, possibly located in the general area of the junction of the above three streets. Crushed limestone was regularly used in the production of building mortar and, particularly after the mid 18th century, as an agricultural fertiliser. There is ample evidence of lime kilns scattered all over the town (as there were in almost every pre-19th century community) and one was, according to Palmer, located in Lambpit Street itself.

Lambpit Street
This took its name from the area known as the Lambpit.* As the other streets in this area were easily identified by the names of the places to which they led, it would have been natural for this street, which served as a link between Chester Street and Queen Street/Rhosddu Road, and did not lead directly anywhere, to take its name from a significant local feature. It might have been the means of access to the 'Lambpit' or 'Lime Pit'. During the 18th century, the street seems to have had a number of sizeable houses in it which were occupied by gentlemen of some substance e.g. attorneys and doctors but, by the 19th century, it had become a street of shops and small cottages. In the late 1890s, the Borough Council began to take steps to redevelop the area and, following the purchase of the original Queen Square building in 1898, the cottages along the south side of Lambpit Street were demolished in preparation for the expansion of what was to become the Vegetable Market.*

The properties between the Raglan Arms and the Rose & Crown on Chester Street were demolished in the early 1970s. All the other properties (apart from the Seven Stars* and the old Empire Cinema*) were demolished in the late 1980s in preparation for the St Giles Shopping Precinct re-development but, when this fell through, the south side formed part of the

Henblas Square* development. The north side of the street was re-developed at the same time and the extension to the Guildhall now occupies most of the area (officially opened by Barry Jones, MP for Alyn & Deeside, on 16 September 1992). The only pre-1980s buildings remaining in the street are the Seven Stars* public house (including the building which was once the Empire Cinema*) on the junction with Chester Street.

Lancastrian School, Beast Market
See Dame Dorothy Jeffreys Free School, Beast Market.

Land Valuation Office
In 1921 this was located at N°2 King Street. [DRO/1097]

Langlands, Maes-y-Dre Road
Built shortly before the First World War as a family home by Robert Stobo, a well-known local Scotch (credit) draper. Robert's son, John Stobo, lived here until c.1970 when the house was sold. It later became the property of the Lacey family (including noted gardening journalist and writer, Stephen Lacey).

Larch Grove, Queen's Park
This was built in the immediate post Second World War period as part of the first phase of WBC's Queen's Park housing development. It was local authority policy at one time to name streets after trees and shrubs (See Acton Park housing estate).

Larchwood Road, Borras Park
A street of private houses developed c.1968 by the London firm of Spinks & Denning on land that had previously belonged to William Clarke* and, pre-1918, to the Acton Park* estate. The name has no particular significance.

Larkfield
A large, red brick house built during the closing years of the 19th century on the southern side of the junction of Bersham Road and Victoria Road. This house was part of the estate of Sir Evan Morris.* In 1895 it was occupied by Benjamin Owen.

Laurel Grove, Bersham
Offered for sale in May 1923. it was later the home of Brigadier F. Peter Barclay, DSO, MC, and Field Marshal Viscount Montgomery stayed there in October 1953, when Deputy Chief of NATO forces. [DRO/DD/G/2902]

Laurel House, Egerton Street
Lease 1911. [DRO/1071]

Laurels, The, Acton Park
Built in the early 1930s as part of the second phase of the Acton Park housing estate,* this street was originally going to be called the Ring.

Law Courts, Bodhyfryd
Built by W.G. Curtin & Partners with work beginning in June 1975, the Law Courts (also known as the Magistrates' Courts) were opened by Colonel G.E. Fitzhugh, OBE, TD, JP, MA, (of Plas Power*) on 1 September 1978, although courts had been sitting there since 8 May. The Law Courts replaced the old magistrates courts in the County Buildings* on Regent Street and cost £711,000 to build. The building received the 1982 Certificate of Merit by the Brick Development Association. The building houses five courts and, until the summer of 2010, all the ancillary support services required by the modern legal system. At that time, the administrative staff moved to Mold to enable the County Court to be moved from Crown Buildings* into the Law Courts. At the time of publication, this move has not taken place. The Law Courts building is linked directly to the Police Headquarters by a first-floor bridge corridor.

Lawson Close
A late 1970s extension to Lawson Road, built on land that had previously been part of the gardens of the St Giles Boys Home* on Rhosnesni Lane.

Lawson Road
Most of the houses in this road had been built by 1969. It was named after Lawson Taylor, third Town Clerk of Wrexham.*

Lea Road
Plans for laying out this road were passed by WBC in 1897 but, despite the fact that the original notion was for a road linking Pentre Felin to Tenters' Square, the road was never linked right through. Following the publication of A.N. Palmer's* *History of the Town of Wrexham* in 1893, information about the history of the area became available to the public and, consequently, the street may well have been named after Michael Lea of London who, along with his partner John Lawson, bought the manor of Wrexham Abbot* from Parliament following the sequestration (confiscation) of Lady Wotton's estate in 1651.

Leadbetter, Major Thomas John *police officer*
Born at Alder Bank, Bothwell, Lanarkshire, Thomas Leadbetter was commissioned in the King's Own Scottish Borderers (25th Foot). On leaving the army he became attached to the Metropolitan Police and, in 1878, was appointed Chief Constable of Denbighshire. He was in charge of the force during the period of the Tithe Riots (during which he was injured when thrown from his horse) and the visit of Queen Victoria in August 1889. When he retired in 1911, he was the senior Chief Constable of England and Wales and lived at Netherby, 4 Gerald Street. He died at his son's home in Bowden, Cheshire on 26 November 1915 and is buried in Rossett.

Leech, Chris *chief executive*
Chief Executive Wrexham Maelor Borough Council 1996.

Leeswood House, Grove Road
See Plas Gwilym.

Lerry, MBE, George G. *journalist & local historian*
Born in Oswestry in 1883 and educated at Oswestry Grammar School, George Lerry was apprenticed to Mr Woodall, the editor of the *Oswestry & Border Counties Advertiser*. His choice of a career in journalism is not surprising as his grandfather was a journalist and his father, as well as being a lawyer's clerk, was also a part-time journalist. He became a junior reporter on the paper and in 1903 moved to cover the Wrexham area. On the outbreak of the First World War he tried to volunteer for the Royal Welsh Fusiliers but was rejected as being unfit for military service. He then obtained a position as a member of the Denbighshire War Pensions Committee at Bodhyfryd House* in Chester Street and was its secretary from 1916–20. He was also the secretary of the Joint Disablement Committee for North Wales and was the only north Wales representative on the Ministry of Pensions Advisory Committee. For his services towards the rehabilitation of ex-servicemen Lerry was awarded the MBE.

In 1920 Woodall, Minshall & Thomas launched the new *Wrexham Leader* weekly newspaper and George Lerry was appointed its first editor. In addition to his news journalism, he also wrote columns for children (under the pen name 'Uncle Jeff'), a football and cricket column (under the pen name 'XYZ') and a drama column (under the by-line 'GGL'). In addition to his activities with the *Wrexham Leader* he was also a member of the Mayor's Committee for Unemployment, the Wrexham Borough Library Committee, the East Denbighshire Industrial Savings Council, the Wrexham National Savings Committee, the organising committee of the National Eisteddfod of Wales (1912 and 1933) and the Council of the Football Association of Wales. He was also chairman of the Denbighshire and Flintshire Drama Festival and a Welsh international soccer selector. During the Second World War he was the honorary Emergency Information Officer for Wrexham. In later life he was made a director of Woodall, Minshall & Thomas Ltd. After retiring as editor of the *Wrexham Leader* in 1948, George Lerry was able to devote more time to his passion for local history, a field in which he had already published a number of books: *Association Football in Wales (1870–1924); Links With the Past; Alfred George Edwards, Archbishop of Wales; Collieries of Denbighshire*. He was made an honorary freeman of the Borough of Wrexham on 28 March 1951 and an honorary member of the Rotary Club of Wrexham in 1960. In 1968 he was appointed chairman of the governors of the Denbighshire Technical College.

Married to Bertha, George Lerry lived at Nº 16 Gerald Street, Wrexham. He died on 3 December 1971 and is buried in Wrexham Cemetery.* In his will, he made a major bequest to Wrexham Parish Church.

Lewis, John *solicitor and local politician*
Born in 1816, John Lewis was the son of Moses and Lydia Lewis of old Llwyn Onn.* He qualified as a solicitor and set up in practice at Yspytty* and was clerk to the Wrexham Borough Magistrates until 1862. He lived at Rhosddu Lodge, then Beechley House.* He was elected a Tory councillor on WBC and was Mayor in 1862 and 1863. He was eventually struck off the roll of solicitors in April 1896 having been convicted at Denbigh Assizes of 'converting to his own use the proceeds of a cheque for £450, which had been entrusted to him' (despite being 80 years of age, he was sentenced to twelve months hard labour). He died in Hope and is believed to be buried in Wrexham Cemetery* although his name does not appear in the register of burials.

Lichgate House
Located at Nᵒˢ 3 & 4 Church Street in the 18th century. Its name is a direct reference to the lych-gate which once stood at the entrance to the parish churchyard before the construction of the present gates by the Davies* family of Croesfoel.

Light Dragoon, Pen-y-Bryn
Located on the corner of Pen-y-Bryn and Chapel Street, this public house is now known as the Albion Hotel.* Appears in the 1833 survey. The landlord in 1859 was Thomas Rogers.

Lilac Way, Maesgwyn
A development by WMBC on land that was previously the site of pre-fabricated houses, erected after the Second World War. (See Pre-fabs)

Limbo, Holt Road
This delightfully named smallholding is detailed in the 1786 survey of the Acton Park* estate. It was comprised of only two fields, Frenchman's Field and Hill Field, and was located on the west side of Holt Road in the area of the present day Friends' Meeting House. It was bought by Ellis Yonge of Acton Park from a Mr Benjamin in 1765. [FRO/D/AH/24]

Linden Avenue, Whitegate
The land on which this street was built was sold in *c*.1932 and was called the Charleston estate.

Linen Hall, Queen Street
See Jones's Hall.

Linley Place, Tŷ Gwyn
A development by local builders H. R. & E. Roberts of private houses completed in the early 1960s. This close was named after Viscount Linley, the eldest child of Lord Snowdon and Princess Margaret, who was born on 3 November 1961. (See also Snowdon Drive)

'Lion' *dog*
The dog belonging to Dean Howell.* It died in 1889 and was buried in the garden at Llwyn Isaf, close to Rhosddu Road. The gravestone was moved for preservation in March 1953.

Lion Hotel, 57 High Street
Also known as *The Red Lion*. This was once Wrexham's leading inn and in 1670 was assessed for tax as having fourteen hearths (only Bryn-y-Ffynnon House had more). It is recorded as having being an inn as far back as 1663. At one time it belonged to the Myddelton's of Chirk Castle and later to their relative, the Hon Frederick West (*c*.1844) and was well known as a meeting place of the local Whigs. The Lion Yard,* which was located at the rear, was accessed from Chester Street and was the site of the cockpit which was rented by the *Lion Inn* from the trustees of the poor of the Presbyterian Chapel, Chester Street. It is believed that J. M. W. Turner painted his view of High Street while staying at this hotel. Shown in the 1833 survey. At one time, Wrexham FC used the hotel as its headquarters. The hotel was demolished in the early 20th century and occupied the site of the present day North & South Wales Bank public house.

Lion Hotel, Hope Street
Located at Nº 57 Hope Street, on the site now occupied by the W. H. Smith store, *The Lion* replaced an earlier hotel known as *The (Old) Three Pigeons* (*c*.1699–*c*.1843). The Italian patriot Garibaldi visited this hotel in April 1864 during his tour of

The Lion Hotel, High Street.

The Lion Stores, Hope Street (formerly the Lion Hotel).

Little Acton House.

Britain, coming to Wrexham to visit his friend, Benjamin Piercy* of Marchwiel Hall. It did not survive as the *Lion Hotel* for very long and by 1893 was the Lion Stores.

Lion Yard, Henblas Street
Entered from Henblas Street, via an alleyway alongside the Old Vaults* public house, this gave access to the rear of the Lion Hotel* (in High Street) and through to Chester Street. It is shown, but not named, on both the 1833 and the 1872 surveys and survives today, still without an official name. It was the location of the cockpit.*

Lisburne Grove, Barker's Lane
Built in the late 1970s by Broseley Homes. The origin of the name is unknown, although, despite the spelling, it would almost certainly have some connection with Lisburn in Ireland.

Little Acton Drive
This followed the line of the driveway to Little Acton House* from which it takes its name. The first house, Little Acton Lodge, was built in 1887 and displays the initials R.A.C. and E.C. on the gable (Sir Robert Alfred Cunliffe and Lady Eleanor Cunliffe – see Cunliffe Family).

Little Acton House/Farm/Hall
Sometimes called Acton House, the earliest recorded resident here was John Dymock (died 1706). The property then passed to his son, also named John. In the mid 18th century, when Ellis Yonge was the owner of the Acton Hall estate, Little Acton Farm was in the occupation of Mary Jones. In 1772, the farm was tenanted to the Revd George Warrington and, in 1796, to John Hughes. He was succeeded to the tenancy by his son, Dr Francis James Hughes, HSD, JP.

In the 18th century, this property was a farm of some 89 acres located on west side of Box Lane,* extending from what is now the Acton Park Hotel* to the Llan-y-Pwll Link Road.* There was a small, detached part of the farm on the west side of Chester Road. The actual farmhouse and outbuildings stood on the site of the present day Llwyn Kensington.* Almost all the fields had Welsh names and one, located south of Smithy Lane* on the land now occupied by Windermere Road and Kendal Way was known as Cae'r Hen Dy [*Trans.* field of the old house) although which house this was is unrecorded (it may have been Pwll-y-Kiln*). The land was bought by Sir Robert Cunliffe in December 1885 for £9,000 and remained part of the Acton Hall estate until after the First World War when most of the land was sold off for development along Box Lane,* Glyndŵr Road* and Smithy Lane. The narrow angled piece of land, located between Chester Road and Box Lane, a little over 2 acres in area (now the site of a motor vehicle service station), was bought by Sir Foster Cunliffe in 1801 for £195. The property was sold at the time of the sale of the Acton Park estate in 1918.

For a time the house became a children's home, taking many of the children formerly accommodated in Chester Street House.* In 1970, an educational assessment centre was built in the grounds at the cost of *c*.£100,000. By 1976, part of the property was being used as a teachers' centre belonging to Clwyd County Council.* The house was demolished in the 1990s to make way for the private housing development, Llwyn Kensington.*

Little Llwyn Onn
In 1881 a farm of 48 acres in the tenancy of John Viggars.

Little Vawnog, Bersham Road
A small private housing estate, built on land that was previously a smallholding of the same name. In 1881 it was the home of corn miller Thomas Breese.

Llan-y-Pwll
This area undoubtedly incorrectly named. As there is no record of either a church or a churchyard in the area the name should be Lan-y-Pwll, meaning the edge of the pool. In the late 19th century the settlement comprised the Gredington Arms,* a smithy and several small farms.

Llan-y-Pwll Link Road
See Acton–Llan-y-Pwll Link Road.

Llanelwy Hostel for Adolescent Girls, Holt Road
This house, located close to the site of the present day Capel-y-Groes (part of the garden wall can still be seen below the chapel on Holt Road), was the property of the diocese of St Asaph and was administered by a board of governors. It provided a home for unmarried mothers during an era when that condition was socially frowned upon. It closed in April 1977 and there were plans for it to be converted into a hostel for the homeless but the project was rejected by WMBC and the house was demolished.

Lloyd, Daniel *puritan*
See Pilgrim's Place.

Lloyd, Jacob Youde William *historian*
Born in 1816, the son of Jacob and Harriet Hinde of Langham Hall, Essex, Jacob Lloyd was educated at Wadham College, Oxford and became Curate of Llandinam, Montgomeryshire in 1839. He later resigned and was accepted into the Roman Catholic Church. In 1856 he inherited his mother's estate which included Plas Madog and Clochfaen. In 1868 he changed his name from Hinde to Lloyd in deference to his mother's ancestors who came from Clochfaen, Montgomeryshire. He joined the Pontifical Zouaves who were pledged to protect the temporal power of the Pope and was created a Knight of the Order of St Gregory by Pope Pius IX in 1870, giving him the title of Chevalier. He gradually became disillusioned with the Church of Rome and in 1877 went to live at Clochfaen. He was the author of numerous learned articles but will be best remembered for his six volume *History of Powys Fadog*. He died on the Isle of Wight on 14 October 1887.

Lloyd, Colonel Sir Richard *soldier, politician & judge*
The son of Evan Lloyd of Dulasau, Caernarfonshire. He entered the Inner Temple in 1631 and, after a number of visits abroad on behalf of the Crown was given the office of Prothonotary and Clerk to the Crown in Denbighshire and Montgomeryshire. He was with the King during the Scottish campaign of 1639 and was subsequently made Attorney General of North Wales. He resided at Esclus near Wrexham. He was present in Wrexham when the King visited the town on 27 September and 7 October 1642 and was knighted on the latter occasion. The following year he was active in raising local support for the Crown during the siege of Chester and was made Governor of Holt Castle which he held until 13 January 1647 when he was forced to surrender to Thomas Mytton. He was allowed by Parliament to go abroad and he refused to waver in his support for the Crown and, consequently, was unable to return until the restoration of the monarchy in 1660 when he was elected to Parliament for both Cardiff and Radnorshire. He also served as Justice of Glamorgan, Brecknock and Radnor and Chief Justice of Wales. He married Margaret, the daughter of Robert Sneyd of Bradwell and Keele in Staffordshire on 4 September 1632 and died on 5 May 1676. He was buried in Wrexham Parish Church on 12 May 1676 and his memorial can be seen behind the organ.

Lloyd, Richard *banker*
A Wrexham mercer and flannel merchant, he founded his own bank *c.*1785. He was the brother of Sir Richard Lloyd of Bryn Estyn.* He was the father of Richard Myddelton Massie Lloyd* and Sir William Lloyd* and built Bryn Estyn Hall* sometime after 1785. He died in 1817. (See also Henblas Street/Chester Street/Lloyd's Bank/Wrexham & North Wales Bank)

Lloyd, Richard Myddelton Massie *banker*
R. M. M. Lloyd was one of the most prominent figures in Wrexham society during the early years of the 19th century. He was the son of Richard Lloyd,* the founder of Lloyd's Bank* in Chester Street and the brother of Sir William Lloyd of Bryn Estyn Hall. He followed his father into the family banking business and, despite financial difficulties, managed to maintain the support of the leading local families. He became High Sheriff of Denbighshire in 1824 and was later appointed a deputy lieutenant of the county. He was Vicar's Warden at the Parish Church and a Justice of the Peace. When his bank collapsed in 1849 he was completely disgraced and left Wrexham. He died in a terraced house in Birkenhead on 22 May 1860. (See also Lloyd's Bank)

Lloyd, Robert *local politician*
Born at Ysceifiog in Flintshire, Robert Lloyd was the proprietor of a drapery business in High Street (later the site of Phillips Tea Merchants). He served as an Independent member of WBC and was Mayor in 1873 and 1874. He became an alderman in 1877 but resigned the position the following year when he moved to Rhyl. He was the prime mover behind the establishment of the new Wrexham Cemetery* on Ruthin Road. Robert Lloyd died in Llandudno, aged 91, on 22 July 1919.

Lloyd, Thomas *cleric & lexicologist*
He was born *c.*1673, the son of Thomas Lloyd, an attorney of Wrexham. The family were related to the Lloyds of Plas Madog and the Myddeltons of Chirk. Educated at Jesus College, Oxford he matriculated on 25 February 1688 and gained his BA in 1692 followed by an MA in 1695. He served as a curate in Wrexham and was a tutor to the Myddelton family at Chirk Castle before becoming chaplain to Mary Myddelton of Croesnewydd Hall.* In her will, Mary Myddelton bequeathed Plas Power to him and it was there that he died in 1724, being buried in Wrexham. He is best remembered for his work in amending the *Dictionarium Duplex* of John Davies (a Welsh–Latin/Latin–Welsh dictionary published in 1632), to which he added many additional words and definitions.

Lloyd, Kt., Col Sir William *soldier*
Born in Wrexham in 1782, the son of Richard Lloyd of Bryn Estyn. He was educated at Ruthin School and obtained a cadetship in the East India Company army in 1798. Joining the Bengal Infantry he was a lieutenant by 1800 and, two years later, saw action in command of a body of Royal Marines in Sumatra. He then served for some 20 years as the commander of the Residency Guard at Nagpur before retiring with the rank of major in 1825. In 1821, Lloyd went on an extensive tour of the foothills of the Himalayas and recorded what he saw in a memoir which was later published as *Narrative of a journey ... to the Boorendoo Pass in the Himalaya Mountains ....* His father had died in 1817 and he returned to Wrexham to take up his inheritance as the master of Bryn Estyn. There is no record of his ever having married in India but he certainly had a son, George, and a daughter, Mary, both of whom appear to have been of mixed-race. It seems

Sir William Lloyd, Kt.

likely that the presence of George at Bryn Estyn may well have led to the exclusion of his father from the local 'Society'. William Lloyd served in the Denbighshire Yeomanry* and in 1838 became its lieutenant-colonel. Had the family's reputation not have been tarnished beyond repair by the collapse of the Wrexham & North Wales Bank (see Lloyd's Bank) in 1849, Sir William would probably have been elected to serve as the first Mayor of Wrexham in 1857. As it was, however, he died at his seaside residence, Plas Trevor, Llandudno, shortly after the incorporation of the Borough of Wrexham and is buried in St Tudno's cemetery on the Great Orme.

Lloyd Williams, Regent Street
Wrexham's home-grown department store, Lloyd Williams was located on the corner of Regent Street and Egerton Street (the site is now the location of the McDonalds fast-food outlet). It closed in September 1977. The last owner was Charles Lacy. There was a sister store in Llangefni, Anglesey from 1961 until 1977.

Frontage and interior of Lloyd Williams' store on Regent Street.

Lloyd's Bank, Chester Street
Shown on the 1833 survey as R.M. Lloyd's Bank (Richard Myddelton [Massie] Lloyd*). It was located in the house that is now known as Tŷ Meredith,* on a site set back from Chester Street where the present day main entrance to the People's Market is located. It later became known as the Wrexham & North Wales Bank. It survived until 1849 when it failed with liabilities of £49,000 and many of the bank's depositors were ruined. Two of the biggest losers were the Wrexham Friendly Union Society (£6,000) and the Wrexham Infirmary* (£196). The

Banknote issued by R. M. Lloyd.

liquidators eventually cleared the bank's debts at a rate of 2/6d (12.5p) in the pound.

Llwyd, Morgan *theologian & writer*
Born in 1619 at Cynfal, Maentwrog (hence his being known as *Morgan Llwyd o Wynedd* (*Trans.* Morgan Llwyd of Gwynedd). He was probably educated at Wrexham Grammar School* in about 1634/5 where he came under the influence of the puritan Walter Cradoc. During the English Civil War, he may have served as a chaplain in the Parliamentary Army and returned to Wrexham at the end of hostilities. He was appointed non-episcopalian vicar of Wrexham and, although he toured north Wales extensively preaching to many Nonconformist congregations, it is doubtful whether he ever actually preached in Wrexham Parish Church.

Credited with being the first Nonconformist minister in Wrexham, he is also recognised as a classic Welsh writer and his works include *Llyfr y Tri Aderyn, Gair o'r Gair* and *Llythyr at y Cymry Cariadus*. In addition to his religious and literary work, Morgan Llwyd was also deeply involved in the politics of the Commonwealth period and was a stern critic of Oliver Cromwell's adoption of the title 'Lord Protector'. He died on 3 June 1659 and was buried in the Dissenters' Burial Ground,* Wrexham, where the Morgan Llwyd Memorial* to him was unveiled in 1912.

Llwyn Isaf/Llwynisaf/Llwyn Issa
Also known as Yspytty Ucha or Upper Yspytty. A house of this name stood here as far back as the 17th century. The ownership of the property during the late 18th century is well-recorded, passing from George Ravenscroft (1780) to Mary Puleston of Hafod y Wern* and then to Bryan Cooke of Owston (1802). By 1827, the rate books show the owner as being the Revd John Pearce. Sir Thomas Longueville lived here at the time of his death in 1759, followed by the Revd John Salusbury, then George Ravenscroft, Mrs Mary Puleston and the Revd Canon George Warrington. After the latter's death in May 1830, the Revd George Cunliffe,* vicar of Wrexham, came to live in the house the lease of which he later bought for £2,500 and, at a later date, the freehold (with the exception of one small plot which remained leasehold until purchased by the Church in the 1880s). It was Cunliffe who changed the name to Llwyn Isaf.

The house stood in 8 acres and the buildings comprised the house (with three principal reception rooms, kitchen and offices, five bedrooms and a bathroom on the first floor and six bedrooms on the second floor), some cottages, a conservatory, hot houses, stables, a coach house, cowhouse and a piggery. When Cunliffe retired in 1875, the house was valued at £12,000 and he presented the whole property to the parish of Wrexham for use as a vicarage, with the stipulation that Mrs Cunliffe was

The rear view of Llwyn Isaf, c.1930, when it was the vicarage.

to have a life interest (in 1880 this was exchanged for an annuity of £70). Full of dry rot and in need of many urgent repairs, Llwyn Isaf was quite unsuited for use as a vicarage by a parish that was short of money. To help pay for the cost of repairs, the Old Vicarage* was sold for £1,300. A portion of the grounds at Llwyn Isaf was donated by the Revd David Howell* as a site for the construction of St David's* church.

The Borough Council first made approaches to the Church in Wales, expressing a wish to buy Llwyn Isaf, in 1931 but the offer they made was seen as derisory. It was eventually purchased by the Council in 1951 for £6,436 and provided temporary accommodation for Wrexham Public Library while an extension was built on the library in Queen Square. Llwyn Isaf was eventually demolished to make way for the present Guildhall* building.

Certain members of the Council suggested that the name Llwyn Isaf would be too difficult for non-Welsh speakers to pronounce and that the grounds should be re-named Vicarage Grounds. Fortunately, the original name was preserved.

Llwyn Kensington/Kensington Grove
This road was developed by Redrow in the late 1990s on the site of Little Acton House*. The name does not appear to have any connection with Wrexham.

Llwyn Knottia Farm
This was the largest estate in the township of Erlas and extended into the township of Abenbury. The name has had various spellings *e.g.* Llwyn-y-knottie, Llwyn-y-knottye and Llwyn-y-knottia. The origin of the name is somewhat obscure but Palmer* believed that it came from Llwyn-y-cnottié, meaning the grove of the hillocks. The land was owned by various families and individuals including: Cynwrig ap Rhiwallon; the Lloyds of Llwyn Onn (until Hugh Lloyd who was alive in 1543); the Pulestons of Llwyn Onn (inherited from Margaret Lloyd, the daughter of Hugh Lloyd, who married Hugh Puleston and died in 1606) who held the land until the late 17th century when the house and land were sold. A description of the house at the time of the sale in 1662 was cited in Palmer's *History of the Thirteen Country Townships of the Old Parish of Wrexham*.

The property comprised 'hall, out-houses, gardens, and orchards [which] were valued at £20 a year. Some of the names of the fields are worthy of being preserved: 'Hwla hir' (Long Hullah), 'Hwla Vawr (Great Hullah), 'Cyvie mawr', 'Cyvie buchaine' (that is the great and little joint-field), 'Gwaith y gwr mawr' (The big man's work, the extent of land a man could deal with in a day being often called *gwaith y gwr*), 'Bryn-y-fittas' (nest of the vetches), 'y Lawnt', 'Gwernydd Nest' (Nêst's alder-marshes), 'Cae-y-walke' (referring doubtless to some walk-mill or fulling house), and 'Gwern dunke' [in Wrexham] (see The Dunks). In 1672, John Puleston left the estate to his brother-in-law, Simon Thelwall. In the early 18th century, Wrexham apothecary David Thelwall sold it and by 1715 it was part of the Wynnstay estate and was rented out to a family named Taylor who remained there for about 100 years. In 1859 the farm was occupied by a Mrs Lewis. Today, the farm is part of the Cefn Park* estate. On 8 May 1941, a Heinkel 111 bomber of 6/KG 55 was shot down by a Defiant night-fighter and crashed into the edge of woodland at Llwyn Knottia. All the crew were killed – *Oberfeldwebel* Walter Hottenrot (pilot), *Unteroffizier* Paul Götze, *Oberfeldwebel* Karl Gerstle and *Oberfeldwebel* Hermann Reese.

Llwyn Onn Hall, Cefn Road
Also called New Llwyn Onn and Llwyn Onn Park. In 1881 the house was staffed with a maid, cook, parlour-maid, housemaid and groom.

Among the residents were:
c.1870	Revd F. G. Tippinge
1881	Thomas Parry Jones Parry, JP
1885	John Boliver (died in 1885 and buried in the Burial Ground in Ruthin Road)

Now part of the Cefn Park* estate, the house became the Llwyn Onn Hotel in the 1980s and reverted to a private residence some ten years later. [DRO/DD/LP/1–10]

Llwyn Onn Cottage
Resident during the 19th century was the Revd Twycross, D.D., who is buried in the Burial Ground,* Ruthin Road.

Llwyn Onn Hall, c.1920.

Llyn Tro, Bersham.

Llwyn Onn Mill
The only reference to this mill appears in 1881 when Thomas Minshall was shown as being the 'corn miller'.

Llyn Tro, Bersham
All that now remains of this small moated house is the moat (approx 6m wide, 2m deep and now partially filled) which can be seen opposite Bersham Cricket Ground. The two-bedroomed timber-framed house was still standing in the 1930s.

Llewellyn, MA, John Desmond Seys *judge*
He was born in Cardiff in 1912, the son of Charles Ernest and Hannah Margritta Llewellyn. Educated at Cardiff High School and Jesus College, Oxford, he joined the Inner Temple in 1936, saw active service with the Royal Tank Regiment (1940–6) and was called to the Bar in 1945. He was part of the British prosecution team at the Nuremberg Trails before setting up a practice as a barrister in Chester in 1947. He practised on the Wales and Chester Circuit (1947–71) and was, from 1957–62 the Clerk to the Magistrates on the Wrexham Petty Sessional Divison Bench after which he set up his own chambers in White Friars, Chester. He was deputy chairman of the Cheshire Quarter Sessions, was appointed a County Court judge and then, in 1971, a Circuit judge. He retired in 1985.

He contested the Chester constituency for Labour in 1955 and 1956. Judge Seys Llewellyn lived in Gresford. He was married to Elaine Porcher in 1939, he had three sons. He died on4 April 2003.

Llys David Lord
(*Trans.* David Lord's court) This housing association development was built in the 1990s and named after Flight Lieutenant David S.A. Lord, VC, DFC.*

Long Pull, Chester Street
See Chester Street Vaults.

Longueville
This small residential development occupies land that was once part of the Court* estate until sold at public auction in 1920. Longueville was the name originally given to the first house to be constructed here, a bungalow, built by Mr & Mrs George Thomas Davies* and named after the village of Longueville in Jersey, the childhood home of Mrs Davies. In the late 1970s, the land surrounding the bungalow was sold for development by the owner, Neville Scott, and the whole cul-de-sac took the house name as its address.

Lord, VC, DFC, F/Lt David Samuel Anthony *airman*
Born at St Mary's Avenue, Cork (where his father was stationed with the RWF) on 18 October 1913, the son of Samuel Beswick Lord, MSM, and Mary Ellen Lord. When his father retired, the family moved to Wrexham where they lived at 15 Cilcen Grove and later 22 Sandringham Road. He was educated at Lucknow Convent School, Lucknow, India; St Mary's RC School,* Wrexham; St Mary's College, Aberystwyth and the English Ecclesiastical College, Valladolid, Spain. On leaving school, David Lord began to train as a Roman Catholic priest in Spain but returned to Wrexham in 1934 where he was employed as a photographer's assistant by Francis & Co.* before trying to earn his living in London as a freelance writer.

Enlisting in the RAF on 6 August 1936 as an aircraftsman (2nd class), he became a sergeant pilot on 5 April 1939 and was posted to 31 Squadron at Lahore, India. He served in Burma and North Africa and received a Mention in Despatches. He was commissioned as a pilot officer on 12 July 1942 and was awarded the DFC on 16 July 1943 for his service in the Western Desert and re-supplying Chindit units in the Burmese jungle. Joining 271 Squadron as a Dakota pilot, he took part in the D-Day Operations in June 1944 and in the Arnhem operations on 17, 18 and 19 September 1944. He was killed in action over Arnhem on 19 September 1944 and is buried in grave 4B5 at the Arnhem Oosterbeck Military Cemetery, Gelderland, Holland. His VC citation reads:

Flt Lt David S.A. Lord, VC, DFC.

> Flight Lieutenant Lord was the pilot and captain of a Dakota Aircraft detailed to drop supplies at Arnhem on the afternoon of September 19th, 1944. Our airborne troops had been surrounded and were being pressed into a small area defended by a large number of anti-aircraft guns. All crews were warned that intense opposition would be met over the dropping zone. To ensure accuracy they were ordered to fly at 900 feet when dropping their containers.
>
> While flying at 1,500 feet over Arnhem, the starboard wing of Flight Lieutenant Lord's aircraft was twice hit by anti-aircraft fire. The starboard engine was set on fire. He would have been justified in leaving the main stream of supplying aircraft and continuing at the same height or even abandoning his aircraft. But, on learning that his crew were uninjured and that the dropping zone would be reached in three minutes, he said he would complete his mission, as the troops were in dire need of supplies.
>
> By now the starboard engine was burning furiously. Lord

David Lord's aircaft makes its approach to the Drop Zone. A painting held at RAF Down Ampney.

came down to 900 feet where he was singled out for the concentrated fire of the anti-aircraft guns. On reaching the dropping zone he kept the aircraft on a straight and level course while the supplies were dropped. At the end of the run he was told that two containers remained. Although he must have known that the collapse of the starboard wing could not be long delayed, Flight Lieutenant Lord circled, rejoined the stream of aircraft and made a second run to drop the remaining supplies. These manoeuvres took eight minutes in all, the aircraft being continuously under heavy anti-aircraft fire.

His task completed, Flight Lieutenant Lord ordered the crew to abandon the Dakota, making no attempt himself to leave the aircraft which was down to 500 feet. A few seconds later the starboard wing collapsed and the aircraft fell in flames. There was only one survivor who was flung out while assisting other members of the crew to put on their parachutes.

By continuing his mission in a damaged and burning aircraft, descending to drop the supplies accurately, returning to the dropping zone a second time and, finally, remaining at the controls to give his crew a chance to escape, Flight Lieutenant Lord displayed supreme valour and self-sacrifice. [*London Gazette*, 13 November 1945]

There are memorials to David Lord outside the Memorial Hall,* Wrexham; outside 15 Cilcen Grove inside St Mary's RC Cathedral,* Wrexham; in St Mary's RC School,* Wrexham; in the Air Cadets* headquarters in Wrexham; in Down Ampney Church, Gloucestershire and an RAF VC-10 aircraft (XR810) of 10 Squadron was named *David Lord, VC*. The Lord Trophy (RAF Transport Command) was presented by his family to the RAF squadron that was most proficient in the air supply role. His VC, DFC and medals were brought in 1997 by the Ashcroft VC Collection for a then world-record price of £110,00. The most detailed account of his career appears in *Heart of a Dragon, the VCs of Wales and the Welsh regiments, 1914–82* by W. Alister Williams.

His brother, Wing Commander Frank E. Lord, was awarded the AFC in the 1952 New Year's Honours List.

Lord Street
The first reference to a street on this site is in the WBC Minutes of August 1891 when planning permission was sought for a new street from Argyle Street to Egerton Street. In order to conform with the street-naming pattern of the centre of Wrexham (Duke Street,* Regent Street,* King Street* and Queen Street.*), this street takes its name not from an individual but from the title Lord. Originally, Lord Street was very much a secondary street in the town centre and was not used for retail premises. One of the earliest buildings here was the Lord Street Congregational Free Church* which was opened in 1901. The premises at the junction with Rhosddu Road (now the site of the NatWest Bank) was Turner's wholesale warehouse and the remainder of north side, up to the corner of Egerton Street, was the Dee Mineral Water Company works. In the mid 1960s F. W. Woolworth moved into new premises on Regent Street which extended through and occupied much of the south side of Lord Street. In 1967, the north side was demolished and new retail units were built by Laing Development Co Ltd (architects G. Raymond Jones, Anderson & Associates), at a cost of £400,000, which opened in late 1968. The major feature of this new development was the Tesco store on the corner of Rhosddu Road (which later became Timberland and, finally, after major alterations, NatWest Bank). The street was pedestrianised in 1979 and re-modelled with raised flower beds in 1995 and the sculpture Y Bwa/The Arc* was unveiled the following year.

Lord Street Congregational Free Church.
Formed from ex-members of the Chester Street congregation, who first met in the Assembly Rooms in High Street, this church aimed to appeal to working-class people who had no particular affinity with any organised church in Wrexham. Their chapel (with a vestry and lecture room) was opened in Lord Street in 1901 at a cost of £2,200. It amalgamated with Salisbury Park after only eight years and the building was sold in 1910 for £1,200. It later became Wrexham's first Labour Exchange.* It was bought by L. Rowland & Co in 1958 and the ground floor was converted into a shop. It was demolished in 1976 during the redevelopment of Lord Street. The Religious Census of 1904 showed that the church had a capacity of 360 with an attendance (AM & PM) of 194.

Lorne Street, Rhosddu
Lorne Street was one of the older streets of Rhosddu and was developed during the 19th century, leading off Rhosddu Road. It was a street of poor quality housing and much of it was demolished as part of a WBC slum clearance programme and replaced by flats. The origin of the name is unknown and there does not appear to have been any link between Lorne in Scotland and Wrexham other than the civil engineer William Low* who was originally employed by the Duke of Argyll. Low named Argyle [sic] Street* after the Duke whose secondary title was Marquess of Lorne and Kintyre.

Love Lane
See Mount Street.

Low, JP, William *civil engineer*
Born in Rothsay, Argyllshire in 1815, Low came to Chester as the Senior Engineer of the Chester to Holyhead Railway.

In 1851, he bought Lloft Wen a property at Adwy and became the joint owner of the Vron Colliery. He served as a consultant engineer on the construction of both the Ceiriog and the Dee viaducts. He married Elizabeth, a native of Knutsford. By 1864 he had built himself Roseneath, a substantial house on the site of the present day Yale College* in Wrexham from where he practised as a civil engineer.

In the 1860s, Low formed the Channel Tunnel Company which received the support of the Emperor Napoleon III, Queen Victoria and John Bright (the President of the Board of Trade – see Bright Street). He spent over £50,000 of his own money buying up land at Dover and Calais and commenced tunnelling on the British side. However, the outbreak of the Franco-Prussian War in 1870 turned people against the project and Low found himself in financial difficulties. By 1875, he was compelled to join forces with his main rivals the Anglo-French Submarine Railway Company. This did not, however, save the scheme and the project was abandoned shortly afterwards. He served as a magistrate on the Bromfield Divisional Bench.

In 1882, Low left Wrexham and moved to live in London where he died

William Low.

four years later. Low built Westminster Buildings in Regent Street which spanned the entrance to Argyle Street as a dowry for his daughter Alison at the time of her marriage to Dr Edwards Jones. A ceramic memorial to William Low was unveiled under the arch in Argyle Street. A commemorative plaque to William Low was unveiled by Richard Low at Yale College on 21 October 2002, close to the site of Roseneath. [DRO/NTD/234]

Lowe, Joan M. local politician
Mrs Joan Lowe represents the Penycae & Ruabon South ward on WCBC. She is deputy leader of the Liberal Democrat/Independent Alliance group and is a member of the Executive Board where she is lead member for Social Care and Health. She served as Mayor of Wrexham in 2007–08.

Lower Crispin
This property is first referred to in 1699 as Crispianus and is mentioned in the survey of the manor of Stansty Issa, drawn up on 13 December 1707: '... the said lane along the hedge that divides Mr Ambrose Lewis's Lands called Crispiana alias Tŷ ar Clawdd Watt (*Trans.* the house on Wat's Dyke) in Stansty Issa from the lands of one Daniel Nicholas in Wrexham Regis called Erw Goiedog (*Trans.* ?)'. From *c*.1700 to *c*.1810 it was the property of the Ambrose Lewis family after when it was bought by Thomas Durack (who gave his name to Durack's Pool*) who re-named it Bryn-y-Llyn. The farm appears to have lost many of its fields in *c*.1829/30 and Palmer* clearly shows the property on his map of the 'Eastern Part of Stansty in 1844'. In 1865 the farmhouse was used as the Stationmaster's house for the Wrexham Exchange* station (using the name The Crispins) and, in 1868, became the Wrexham, Mold & Connah's Quay Railway offices (which were moved there from 56 Hope Street). The house was demolished *c*.1870 during the construction of the railway and the site utilised for a railway signal-box. Crispin Lane* takes its name from this house.

Lower Hope Street
See Queen Street.

Lower Lampit
See Holt Street.

Lower Minster, Borras Park
A private housing development of bungalows built *c*.1969. As there has never been a minster anywhere in Wales, let alone Wrexham, the origin of the name is a mystery. (See also Bithell's Farm)

Lucas, MP, Ian politician
Ian Lucas was born in Gateshead, Tyneside, 18 September 1960, the son of Colin and Alice Lucas. His father was a process engineer. He was educated at Harlow Green Primary School, Greenwell Junior High School, Gateshead and Newcastle Royal Grammar School. He is a graduate of New College, Oxford University (BA Jurisprudence, 1982) and Chester Law College (1983). He worked in London for two years and was admitted as a solicitor in 1985 when he moved to live in Marford and practised with Percy Hughes and Roberts in Chester (until 1987), Lees Moore & Price, Birkenhead (until 1989), Roberts Moore Nicholas Jones in Wrexham (until 1992) and Crawford in Oswestry (until 1997) where he went into partnership to form Crawford Lucas. From 2000–01 he was a partner in Stevens Lucas. His most noted case was when he represented Trevor Rees-Jones, the bodyguard of Princess Diana, in a case against Mohamed Al-Fayed, the owner of Harrods. His specialisation was criminal law and personal injury claims.

He joined the Labour Party in 1986 and was a member of Gresford Community Council from 1987–91 and stood for election to Parliament as the Labour member for North Shropshire in 1997 before being selected as the candidate for Wrexham, following the decision by Dr John Marek* not to serve as both Member of Parliament and Assembly Member. Ian Lucas won the Wrexham seat in the General Election of 2001. He has been a member of the Environmental Audit Select Committee and the Transport Committee and Parliamentary Private Secretary to the Minister of State for Lifelong Learning, Further and Higher Education. He resigned from the latter post in 2006 in protest against the Prime Minister, Tony Blair's refusal to announce a date whe he would stand down. He was appointed assistant chief whip in 2008 and Parliamentary Under Secretary of State for Business and Regulatory reform the following year. He is married to Norah, formerly the head of music at Ysgol Bryn Alyn (then Ysgol Dinas Brân). They have one son and one daughter.

M

Mᶜ Alpine Family
The Mᶜ Alpine international civil engineering company is in fact two companies. The first was founded by *Sir Robert Mᶜ Alpine, Bt.* Sir Robert was joined in the family business by his sixteen-year-old son *Alfred* (later Sir Alfred) who was sent to north Wales in 1911 to supervise the Dolgarrog contract. So taken was he with the region that in 1916 he bought Marchwiel Hall and lived there until his death. On the death of Sir Robert Mᶜ Alpine in 1944 the company was divided into two and a new company, Sir Alfred Mᶜ Alpine & Son was established, headed by Sir Alfred and his son *James 'Jimmy'* (later Sir James).

The company gained numerous contracts to build factories (including part of Brymbo Steel Works and the BICC factory at Wrexham – now Prysmian) airfields (including RAF Wrexham* and Gatwick), Hydro-Electric schemes (including Trawsfynydd and Ffestiniog) and motorways (including parts of the M1, M4, M6 and M62). The company had a subsidiary in United Gravel which opened pits at Llay, Borras and Gresford and ran the giant Penrhyn Slate Quarries at Bethesda in Gwynedd.

When Sir Alfred died in 1944, Jimmy Mᶜ Alpine succeeded to the title and took the reins of the company. He in turn was joined in the business by his son *Robert (Robin) James Mᶜ Alpine* (later Sir Robin). In addition to his business interests, Sir Alfred had a passion for cricket, racing and shooting (on an estate in Llanarmon DC which he had bought from the Duke of Westminster in 1922). He enlarged the cricket ground at Marchwiel Hall and built the pavilion. He was President of Wrexham Football Club* and High Sheriff of Denbighshire in 1923. Sir Jimmy McAlpine shared his father's passion for cricket and was captain of Denbighshire and vice chairman of Lancashire Cricket Club. He lived at Gerwyn Hall, Marchwiel. His other main interests were golf (captain of Wrexham Golf Club*), vintage cars and shooting. Five times married, the last time to Cynthia Greenaway, a local beauty queen, he retired from the company in 1985 and died in 1991. He is buried in Llanarmon DC.

Sir Robin Mᶜ Alpine, FICOB, was born on 6 May 1932, and educated at Harrow. He was the Chairman of Sir Alfred Mᶜ Alpine & Son from 1983–92, and the Captain of Marchwiel Cricket Club.

Mᶜ Conville, Mrs Agnes local politician
Born in Liverpool, the daughter of a Scotsman, Agnes married Tom Mᶜ Conville. They moved to live in Ponciau in 1941 and,

eighteen months later, to the Royal Ordnance Factory* bungalows. After ten years there they moved to the newly-built houses on Ceiriog Road and finally to 77 Hullah Lane.

She was elected a member of WBC in 1965 as the Labour councillor for the Caia Ward. She became Deputy Mayor in 1974 and Mayor in 1975. A lifelong socialist, Agnes McConville was a founder member of the Wrexham Fabian Society and the Christian Socialist Group and was a Parochial Church Council member at St Mark's, Queen's Park. She died in February 1988.

McDermott's Buildings/Court, Yorke Street

A small 'court' development to the east of Yorke Street and accessed via a passage a little lower down than the Black Horse Inn. This was demolished in 1932 as part of WBC's Clearance Area 8. This development may have been named after P. McDermott, an iron and brass founder who had premises in Mount Street and Yorke Street in the late 19th century or after Martin McDermott who is shown in the Census of 1881 and 1891 as a lodging house keeper who resided there. P. McDermott is shown as the proprietor of the Bee Hive Foundry in Mount Street in 1874.

McGrath, DD, MA, LID, Rt Revd Michael Joseph *cleric and bishop of Menevia*

Born in Kilkenny, Ireland on 24 March 1882, Michael McGrath was educated at Rockwell College, Co. Tipperary and University College, Dublin (degree in Celtic studies) and spoke English, French, German, Irish, Welsh and Italian fluently. He was ordained in 1908 and became an assistant priest in the Diocese of Clifton in Bristol where he remained until 1919. In 1920 he was appointed Rector of Flint and in 1927 Rector of the Diocesan College, Aberystwyth (where one of his students was David S. A. Lord* of Wrexham). He became Bishop of Menevia in 1935 (the first bishop to be consecrated in the Pro-Cathedral) and Archbishop of Cardiff in 1940. He died on 28 February 1961.

McMahon, Alderman Eric *local politician*

The son of Michael McMahon, Eric followed his father into the family fishmongery business. He was elected a member of WBC in 1944, representing Bryn-y-Ffynnon Ward. He served as Mayor in 1952 and became an Alderman. He served as chairman of the Finance Committee and retired in 1974 on the creation of WMBC. He was elected a Denbighshire County Councillor in 1948 and became a County Alderman in 1961. He continued his service with Clwyd County Council, serving as its chairman in 1971–72. He was also the chairman of the Clwyd Education Committee. Outside of local politics, he was a director (and chairman) of Wrexham Football Club*; chairman of Wrexham Catholic Club and a Governor of St Mary's RC School.* Married to Phyllis, Eric McMahon lived at 23 Pen-y-Maes Avenue, Wrexham. They had three daughters. He died at his home in November 1986 and is buried in Wrexham Cemetery.

Machine (I), The, Hope Street

Despite its name, this property, at N°s 16 & 17 Hope Street (located on the site of the present day QD Stores), was never licensed. A private residence, it took its name from a weighing machine which stood outside it from *c.*1786 until late in the 19th century. It can be clearly identified in the 1872 survey by the weighing machine which is on the road in front of it.

Machine (II), The, Pen-y-Bryn

See The Red Cow.

Madeira Hill

The origin of this street name is unknown but it appears on the 1833 survey with the same spelling. The land to the west of the road was then an open field, belonging to Charles Edwards, known as Cae Deintyr (*Trans.* tenters' field] which would clearly indicate that it was an area used for the manufacturing of cloth. At the foot of the hill stood a small terrace of houses built in the 18th century by William Edwards, a tanner, of Y Palis, Pen-y-Bryn (later known as Bryn Issa*). At this time the land to the east of the road was the property of the Willow House* estate. The west side of this street was demolished in 1932 as part of the Borough Council's slum clearance programme.

Madeira Hill was closed to traffic in 1997 and the new St Giles' Way link road was built across the bottom of the hill, covering the former Cae Deintyr and Willow Road.* (See also Tuttle Street)

Madocks, John, *politician*

Born 1786 of Glan-y-Wern, he was educated at Oxford and served as High Sheriff of Denbighshire. He was the Liberal Member of Parliament for Denbighshire from 1832-1835.

Madocks, MP, William Alexander *politician & entrepreneur*

Born in London on 17 June 1773, W.A. Madocks was the son of John Madocks, KC, MP, and his wife Frances (née Whitchurch) of Llay Hall, Gresford and Vron Iw. He was educated at Charterhouse and Christ Church, Oxford, was called to the bar at Lincoln's Inn and became a Fellow of All Souls. He married Mrs Elizabeth Anne Gwynne (née Hughes) of Tregunter, Talgarth, Brecon-shire in 1818.

A passionate supporter of the new developments in transportation he bought land in south Caernarfonshire and built the model village of Tre Madoc with a view to the new route from London to Dublin passing through the area en route to Porthdinllaen where it was proposed to build a packet station for Ireland. He also went on to build the Cob across Traeth Mawr and the Glaslyn estuary which resulted in the construction of Porthmadog. He died at 109 Faibourg Saint-Honoré, Paris on 15 September 1828, while on the grand tour of Europe.

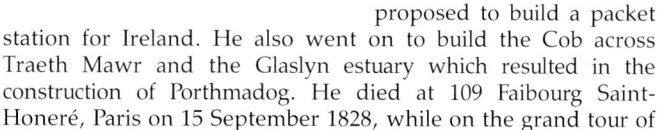

William Alexander Madocks.

Madog ap Gruffydd *prince*

Madog, the eldest son of Gruffydd Maelor I and Angharad *ferch* Owain Gwynedd, succeeded to the throne of Powys Fadog with his brother in 1191 and became sole ruler six years later. He became an ally of King John against Llywelyn Fawr before eventually coming over to the side of the Welsh leader in 1215. He granted land in Wrexham to his newly founded abbey of Valle Crucis. These lands later became known as the manor or township of Wrexham Abbot. He died in 1236 and was buried in Valle Crucis.

Madog Benfras *poet*

Madog Benfras ap Gruffydd ap Iorwerth of Marchwiail (Marchwiel) was one of three brothers who were poets. He is believed to have won the bardic chair and wreath at an eisteddfod during the reign of Edward III. He was a close friend of Dafydd ap Gwilym, for whom he wrote an elegy. His dates of birth and death are unknown but he was certainly alive in the period 1320–60 and his name appears in several legal documents of cases tried in Wrexham in 1340.

Maelor, Edward *poet*
An itinerant bard of east Denbighshire, Edward Maelor flourished in the period 1580–1620. He wrote verses in praise of Edward and Owen Brereton of Borras, Dafydd Hanmer, David Powell of Ruabon and James Eyton of Eyton Isaf.

Maelor, Lord
See Thomas William Jones, MP.

Maelor General Hospital
See Croesnewydd Hospital and Maelor Hospital.

Maelor Hospital
The notion of a new general hospital serving Wrexham and north-east Wales was first mooted in the early 1960s but the plans were not drawn up until 1979. Located on a 9-acre site alongside the old Maelor General Hospital* and designed by Wrexham architects, TACP, the first section of the new 284-bed hospital came on-line in March 1985 having cost £14.3 million to build and was officially opened by HRH The Duchess of Kent on 26 October 1986. The services provided at the Wrexham & East Denbighshire War Memorial Hospital were then transferred to the new facility. The second phase of the building was partially in use by 1994 and was officially opened by HRH The Duke of Kent on 23 July 1998. The hospital is now part of the Betsi Cadwaladr Univeristy Health Board.*

Maelor Hotel, Regent Street
Often referred to as the Temperance Hotel, this occupied the premises which later became the Aston furniture store. It was owned at one time by Wrexham coachbuilder, Richard Davies, a leading member and benefactor of the English Presbyterian Church in Bank Street and later Hill Street. It was a favourite hostelry for itinerant ministers and was regarded as an unofficial 'Chapel House' in the 1880s.

Maes Tomos, Erddig Road
This private housing development, completed in 2000/01 by Taymove Ltd, was on land that was once part of The Court* estate and, until the 1920s, was part of Meredith Jones' brickworks known as The Bricky.*

Maesgwyn, Mold Road
(*Trans.* white field) In 1881, Maesgwyn was the home of Edward Tench, a deputy chairman of the Provincial Insurance Company,* and retired land agent who was also farming 140 acres.

Sale particulars published in May 1916 provide a detailed description of the house and grounds.

> 7¼ acres. Basement: arched cellarage, dairy, larder. Ground floor: Entrance hall, sitting room, drawing room, floral house, dining room, glass lounge leading to greenhouse, housekeepers room, house-maids' pantry, lavatory, cloak room, kitchen, back kitchen. 1st floor: 4 best bedrooms, bathroom, WC, good servant's bedroom, secondary stairs. Outside: Laundry, servants' WC, boothole, coal house, bake oven. Gardener's cottage (4 rooms), open shed, piggery, 2 stall stable with fruit room over, cottage WC, potato cellar, potting shed, mushroom house. Pleasure grounds, full size tennis court, lawn, woodland walks, greenhouse, walled kitchen garden. [DRO/DD/G/2883]

From 1916, Maesgwyn was the home of A.A. Hawkins, General Manager of the Wrexham & District Transport Company. It was offered for sale in June 1925. [DRO/DD/G/2907]

Maesgwyn Hall
Maesgwyn,* a large house off Mold Road was bought by the various Freemasonry Lodges in Wrexham and converted for use as a Masonic Temple. The first meetings were held here in September 1963. (See Freemasonry) [DRO/DD/DM/1032/3–14]

Maesgwyn Road
Maesgwyn Road was named after the house named Maesgwyn* which stands nearby. The land was part of the Maesgwyn Estate and was the property of Benjamin Piercy. In 1894, after Piercy's death, the land was divided into building plots and four new roads were laid out. The previous year, in order to facilitate access to this road, the estate bought the Toll Bar House which stood at its junction with the Mold Road. The new road which became Maesgwyn Road extended from Mold Road to the boundary with the Wrexham Union Workhouse. Plans were in place for the river Gwenfro to be diverted in order to permit the building of another road to the south of the river (on the Wrexham side of Maesgwyn Road) and two further roads forming a cross roads with Maesgwyn Road on the northern side of the river. The sale of the building plots did not go as well as anticipated and in the end only Maesgwyn Road was built. The first houses to be built were the first five dwellings on the western side of the road as you enter from Mold Road. Close to these, between N°s 14 & 20, is a former dance-hall (which had once stood in Lord Street as part of the St James' Hall). The eastern side of the road, close to Mold Road, is dominated by the large brick building which was originally the depot of the Wrexham Electric Tramway Company.* Further down the road, also on the eastern side, is a red brick building which was once the premises of the North Wales Coal Owners Association which also accommodated the Mines Rescue Service.*

Maes-y-Dre
Maes-y-Dre Issa (*Trans.* lower town field) was the area bounded by Chester Road, Rhosnesni Lane, and Holt Road, outside of the built-up area of the town. It comprised some of the common fields of the town and remained undeveloped until the late 19th century. Maes-y-Dre Ucha (*Trans.* upper town field) was also originally common land and lay to the west of Chester Road and included the Llwyn Isa grounds. This was built upon at an earlier date than the area east of Chester Road.

Maes-y-Dre Housing Estate
The Maes-y-Dre housing estate was laid out in 1930 on 27.584 acres that had been bought from Philip Clarke of Park Farm* and Ernest Owen of the Old Maids' Farm (it had been part of the Acton Park* estate until 1918). It was bought by the Borough Council for £3,500 and the first phase of 173 houses (built to the same design as those on the Huntroyde estate*) were let in 1931. (See Kenrick's Farm). An unusual feature of this estate is what is commonly called the Power House, a two-storey mock Tudor building at the junction of Plas Gwyn and Glan Garth which houses an electricity sub-station with a community office above. Unlike other estates of the inter-war period, there was no cohesion in the names chosen for the streets of this development. The original names proposed were: Glan Garth,* Llwyn Derw, Lime Grove, Ash Grove, Cherry Grove, Beaconsfield Square, Gladstone Square and Macdonald Square. The next suggestions were perhaps even stranger: Glan Garth,* Cefn View, Cae'r Delyn, Shelbrooke Road, Loch Leven, Kingstown, Cae Glas and Glan Aber.* In the end, only the first and last of these survived, the other names adopted being Plas Gwyn,* Glan Aber,* Erw

The Maes-y-Dre housing estate in 1932. The track cutting across the bottom right-hand corner is the future Aston Grove. In the far distance Holt Road and Hullah Lane can be seen without a house in sight.

Las,* Ffordd Edgworth,* Ffordd Maelor* and Russell Grove.*

In 1931, plans were passed for the second phase of the estate which was to be built along Aston Grove, a new road linking Park Avenue* and Holt Road.* The final phase of the estate comprised Aran Road,* Kerry Road* and The Mount.*

Maes-y-Dre Road
This road name (*Trans.* town field), is a reminder of the fact that the area on either side of Chester Road from the end of Chester Street to Rhosnesni Lane once comprised the old town fields of Wrexham (*Meusydd-y-Dre*). The first houses to be built on this road were N°s 4, 6 and 8, commencing in 1911. All three were built by J. H. Swainson (formerly of Fairy Road). He lived in N° 6 and built N° 4 (Langlands) for local Scotch draper Robert Stobo; N° 8 was a speculative venture. On Swainson's death, N° 6 was left to Charles Griffiths and in 1932/3 was sold to John Ogwen Jones, manager of the Midland Bank. On Robert Stobo's death, his widow sold Langlands and moved into a new house called Eildon on the corner of Pen-y-Maes Avenue and what is now Craigmillar Road (the present day Pinfold). The houses on the west side of the road were built as follows: N° 1 (Hartfield) for Wrexham photographer Algernon Smith (later the home of the Lloyd Williams family, owners of the department store on Regent Street); N° 3, late 1920s, the home of pawnbroker J. Horton of Church Street; N° 5 (Gorwydd) built sometime before 1933 for the Hugh Dodd family of auctioneers and later the home of Town Clerk Philip Walters* until the 1980s; N° 7 was built in the 1930s by Kenneth Hugh Dodd and substantially extended in 2001.

Magistrates Courts
Wrexham was granted its own Commission of the Peace on 26 March 1858, shortly after the incorporation of the Borough. The first magistrates to be appointed were:

    Sir Watkin Williams Wynn, Bt*
    Sir Robert Henry Cunliffe, Bt*
    Edward Williams
    Henry Walter Meredith
    Thomas Lloyd Fitzhugh
    Paul Griffith Panton
    Simon Yorke*
    James Hassall Ffoulkes
    Thomas Jones Parry
    William Langford Ffoulkes
    Daniel M'Coy
    Charles Hughes*
    Tubal Cain Jones
    Anthony Dillon
    Edward Fench
    Thomas Taylor Griffith*
    William Rowland*

The Mayor of Wrexham was always appointed an ex-officio Justice of the Peace for his year of office and, from 1892, the Judge of the County Court of Denbighshire was automatically made a Borough Magistrate.

In 1881 & 1912, the Bromfield Petty Sessional Division sat on alternate Tuesdays in the County Buildings* in Regent Street, while the Borough Petty Sessional meetings sat every Monday and Friday in the Guildhall,* Chester Street.

In October 1951, following the Justices of the Peace Act, 1949, the Borough Commission (which had previously sat in the Guildhall*) was abolished and became part of the Division of the County of Denbighshire.

  Chairmen
    Wrexham Borough
      For many years it was the normal practice for the Mayor of Wrexham to serve as the chairman of the Wrexham Borough bench. The last Mayor to be so honoured was William Clarke who was Mayor in 1935–6.
      John Lewis ?–1862
      Allington Hughes 1862–1906
      Charles Hughes
      Parry Griffiths, 1953
      E. S. Hackett, *c.*1954
    Bromfield Petty Sessional Division of Denbighshire
      Colonel Fitzhugh, OBE, TD, MA, 1952–74
    Ruabon Petty Sessional Division of Denbighshire
      Lord Maelor,* 1955–70
      Samuel Williams 1971–4
    Maelor Petty Sessional Division of Flintshire
      Lord Kenyon, CBE, DL, LLD, 1962–74
    Wrexham Petty Sessional Division
      Edmund S. E. Hackett 1962–4
      Aneurin Williams 1965–72
      Harold James Bennett,* 1973–4
    Wrexham Maelor Petty Sessional Division
      Colonel Fitzhugh, OBE, TD, MA 1974–5
      Harold James Bennett* 1976
      Stanley Reynolds, OBE 1977-80
      Miss Megan M. Jones 1980-83
      Lord Kenyon, CBE, DL, LLD 1984–7
      Harry Smith 1988-91
      Arthur Blackwell 1992–4
      Sir John Hanmer, Bt 1995–7
      Miss Brenda Roberts 1998-2000
      N. Malcolm Taylor 2000–03
      Edward Wardle 2003–06
      Michael Pugh 2006–09
      Dr Richard Pickles 2009–12
  Clerks to the Magistrates
    Ruabon Petty Sessional Division
      Llewelyn Kenrick* 1896–1932(3)
      Maurice Evans 1933–62
      Arthur Burt 1962–74
    Bromfield Petty Sessional Division (*offices at 16 Chester Street in 1951*)
      Llewelyn Hugh-Jones 1896–1922
      R. C. Roberts, OBE, KtStJ 1922–54
    Wrexham Petty Sessional Division (*offices at 4 Regent Street in 1951*)
      John Lewis* ?–1862
      John Allington Hughes* 1862–1906
      Joseph Henry Bates 1906–32
      C. Parry Griffiths 1932–54
      E. L. Bradley MA 1954–57
      John D. Seys Llewellyn 1957–62
      Arthur Norman Burt 1962–74
    Wrexham Maelor Petty Sessional Division (*offices in the Magistrates Courts, Bodhyfryd*)

Arthur Norman Burt 1975–88
George Tranter 1988–2002
Iolo Thomas 2002–

(See also County Buildings and the Law Courts)

Magistrates Office
Shown in the 1833 survey as being located about mid-way along the north side of Charles Street.

Majestic Cinema, Regent Street
Opened in 1910 as the Rink and Pavilion (a roller skating rink and public hall) this building, located between Regent Street and Lord Street, was almost immediately converted into a cinema which showed its first film on 17 September 1910 under the control of The Glynn Animated Picture Company. By 1 May 1911, roller skating had ceased altogether and the building was known as The Rink Theatre (complete with five-piece orchestra, directed by George Smith). Occasional variety shows were staged and, in 1914, a seasonal pantomime. Sometime around the period of the First World War, the name was changed to the Majestic Cinema and silent films were shown there until 1930 when it underwent a major renovation to turn it into the largest cinema in north Wales (1,770 seats), decorated in the fashionable art-deco style. In 1951, children's Saturday shows were started and, four years later, Cinemascope facilities were installed. The Majestic closed on 22 June 1960 and the building now houses the the Elihu Yale public house. (*Ninety Years of Cinema in Wrexham*, Brian Hornsey, privately published 1990)

Manchester Hall
See Jones's Hall.

Manley Road
It is not known when this road was laid out but the headstone of Maria Jones, who died in 1867 and is buried in the Burial Ground* on Ruthin Road, gives her address as 'Manley Road' although the road does not appear on the 1872 survey. In 1881 the street had 38 dwellings. In the early 20th century there was a girls' home in this street, the matron being Miss Owen. The houses on the west side of the street were demolished sometime after 1985. The name may be a link with the Manley family of Erbistock.

Maple Avenue, Acton Park
Laid out in 1932 as part of the second phase of the Acton Park housing estate.* Built by G. F. Sumner of Ashfield.*

Marek, BSc, PhD, MP, AM, John *politician*
Born in London 24 December 1940, of Czech origin. Educated at Chatham House Grammar School and King's College, London from where he graduated with a BSc (1962) and a PhD (1965) in Applied Mathematics and General Relativity. He was appointed a lecturer in applied mathematics at the University College of Wales, Aberystwyth (1966).

He was elected a member of Ceredigion District Council in 1979 and was chairman of the Finance Committee in 1982–3. He was chairman of the Dyfed Labour Party 1978–80. He contested the Ludlow Parliamentary constituency for Labour in October 1974 and was selected as Labour Party candidate for Wrexham in 1982 –amongst the other candidates was the then unknown Tony Blair. He won the Wrexham seat for Labour at the General Election of June 1983, defeating the Tory candidate Kay Wood by a small margin. He was the Opposition Junior Health Spokesman from 1984–87 and a Shadow Treasury Minister (with responsibility for VAT, Customs & Excise and the Civil Service) from 1987–92.

He was elected Assembly Member for Wrexham at the first elections for the National Assembly of Wales after which he declared his intention not to stand for Parliament at the 2001 General Election. He became the first Deputy Presiding Officer of the National Assembly.

In November 2002, he was de-selected by the Wrexham Labour Party for opposing the views of Wrexham County Borough Council, although he ran in the February 2003 ballot which he lost by four votes to Lesley Griffiths. On 1 May 2003, he stood as an independent candidate for the National Assembly, defeating Lesley Griffith by 6,539 votes to 5,566. He then established his own political party, Forward Wales/*Cymru Ymlaen*, but was defeated in the 2007 election. In March 2010 he joined the Welsh Conservative Party and hopes to fight for the Wrexham seat at the next Welsh Assembly elections.

Appointed a vice-president of Wrexham AFC in 2006, he is also a keen chess and bridge player.

He married Ann Pritchard in 1964 who acted as his secretary.

March Fair
See Markets and Fairs.

Market Hall
The neo-Tudor entrance to what became the Butcher's Market, along with the shops on either side and the hall above, was designed by local architect Thomas Penson* and erected in 1848. One of the first Market Hall keepers was William Jones who died in 1872 and is buried in the Burial Ground* on Ruthin Road. The site of the Market Hall had previously been occupied by three smaller properties one of which had been *The Bear** (or *The White Bear*) public house and another the High Street premises of Thomas Hampson, the Wrexham clockmaker. By 1756, the Hampson house had become *The Oak** (or *The Royal Oak*) public house. All three properties were half-timbered and can be seen on the right hand side of Henri Gasteneaux's print of High Street *c*.1832.

Market Street
Named after the Beast Market which it enters at its eastern end. It was previously known as Seven Bridge Lane,* a reference to the open drain which once flowed down the middle of the street, carrying water to the pool at the bottom of the Beast Market.* This 'stream' was crossed at regular intervals by narrow plank 'bridges'. By 1849 this open drain had disappeared into a purpose laid sewer and was perhaps the reason why the name changed during the second half of the 19th century. Palmer* objected strongly to the name Market Street, writing in *History of the Town of Wrexham*: 'I must protest against the attempt which has been made to substitute for the ancient, pleasing, and significant name of Seven Bridge Lane, the new, absurd, and meaningless name of Market Street'. It is shown under the old name in the 1833 survey and Palmer found evidence of the name being used as early as 1720. One of the town's blacksmiths' shops stood on the eastern side, opposite the rear entrance to the present People's Market. In 1872, a public urinal stood on the western side of the street near the junction with the Beast Market. N°s 2–6, 10–15, 21, 25–35 Market Street were demolished in 1938 after a compulsory purchase order had been issued as part of the Borough slum clearance programme. [Plans for cottages in this street, dated 1912 DRO/1078]

Market Street Square, Market Street
Located on the south-west side of Market Street (opposite the present People's Market), it consisted of a court of five poor-quality houses. They were the subject of a compulsory purchase order in 1938 as part of the Borough slum clearance scheme.

Markets and Fairs
Wrexham is known to have been the site of an established fair as far back as 1391 although it is not known who held the market rights. By 1489, the rights were held by the Crown, and from then until 1632 their ownership fluctuated between the Crown and a variety of private landowners. In 1620, markets were held on Mondays and Thursdays and stalls were erected in High Street, Church Street, Hope Street and inside the churchyard, the primary market day being Thursday. In 1632, Charles I granted William Collings and Edward Fenn of London 'All that tenement etc., And all those the Tolls and Tollage of the Town and within the Town of Wrexham with their rights members and appurtenances whatsoever.' By 1643, the rights had been bought by Kenrick Edisbury of Erddig and they eventually passed, through the manor of Erddig, to the Yorke family.

In 1858, the newly-formed Wrexham Corporation regularised the markets and appointed Thursdays and Saturdays as market days. Open air markets were also held on Tuesdays for potatoes and vegetables (in Henblas Street and Queen Street) – until the opening of the Vegetable Market,* meat (Church Street) and general goods (High Street and Hope Street). In 1861, the fairs were fixed to take place on the Thursday after the first Wednesday of each month (apart from the March fair which was fixed on 1–14 April. In 1875, the Council bought land for the Smithfield* market and in 1898 bought all the rights and buildings of the Market Hall Company and the Yspytty land (for £50,000) and the freehold of the Beast Market.

The main annual fairs generally began on 12 March, 5 June and 8 September. The change from the Julian to the Gregorian calendar in the mid 18th century altered the dates of the fairs to 23 March (March Fair), 16 June and 19 September (Honey Fair). In addition to these, there were smaller fairs held annually on 3rd Thursday in January, Holy Thursday (the day before Good Friday), 7 August, 29 October and the third Thursday in December (this became the Feather Market where Christmas poultry was sold until the 1960s).

The 19th century cycle of fairs in the region was always deemed to begin on 6 March at Wrexham and end on 28 November with the Sheffield Wakes.

March Fair – this was the oldest fair in Wrexham and, until the arrival of the railways in the mid 19th century when animals and produce could be transported anywhere in the country, was the largest fair of its type in north Wales. During this time the Welsh traders brought into Wrexham a wide range of goods including: flannel, linsey woolseys, coarse linens, horses, cattle and sheep. Traders from outside of Wales brought: Irish linen, woollen cloth, manufactured goods from Birmingham, Sheffield and Manchester. It lasted for two weeks with specific days devoted to different activities *e.g.* the first day was usually when cattle were sold on the Beast Market* (there being no dedicated Smithfield* in existence until 1875). Agricultural products were normally sold in Yorke Street* and, as the old name for Yorke Street was Marchnad-y-Moch (Pig Market Street), it is likely that pigs were also sold there. Meat and vegetables were sold from stalls erected in High Street. It was during the March Fair that numerous traders from the industrial towns of England moved into the town to sell their wares and, as a consequence, trade halls or markets were set up by them *e.g.* Birmingham Hall* and Yorkshire Square.* Once the retail activities and dealings were over, the Beast Market became the focal point for local people seeking entertainment in the form of hobby horses, flying boats and various side-shows. As the importance of the fair declined and the goods on offer became more readily available in the many shops opening in the town during the course of the 19th century, the fair came to be known as the Wrexham Spring Pleasure Fair.

Wrexham Spring Pleasure Fair – This developed from an annual trade fair (which dated back to the 14th century) but, with the establishment in the town itself of more permanent sales premises by the various traders, it gradually became a pleasure fair during the late 19th century. It was held annually on the Beast Market ground until it was moved to the Eagles' Meadow ground in 1976. In the 1880s, a letter to the local newspaper complained bitterly about the fair but in doing so, gave a description of the attractions:

> For how much longer must we suffer this unmitigated nuisance? Is it too much to hope that we have seen the last of it? Last week we saw too many repugnant sights and degrading influences and overheard too many disgusting conversations for the good of our souls. And many of the so-called amusements provided for the youngsters were unwise and some of them positively dangerous. It seems to be the general verdict that a fair without any pleasure can not properly be called a pleasure fair. It was as dull as the weather itself … the whole fair has been utterly tame and spiritless. Of the conglomeration of Beast Market attractions nothing can be said in its favour. A bilious-looking ghost exhorted us to pop inside the waxworks show whose chief attraction was its external appearance. A miserable peep show and a low boxing booth mad up the sum total in the way of shows, while the rest of the ground was encumbered with the customary collection of shooting galleries, dangerous swings and dizzy roundabouts and standings of all denominations.
>
> But we must not forget the African lion-faced ladies and the unwholesome collections of depraved human beings. Those who viewed the two fat ladies – 35 and 31 stone respectively – must feel grieved that the Creator's munificence should be so misapplied.
>
> The usual string of itinerant photographers were much in evidence. Their art appears chiefly to concern in cleverly concealing your identity from even your intimate friends.

The scale of charges levied by the Borough Council on the fairground operators for the April Pleasure Fair in 1896 were:

1. For Gallopers, Rockers, Gondolas, Switchbacks and other large Riding Machines – £10–0–0; Hobby Horses, per set – £8–0–0; Small sized Hobby Horses, per set – 15s–0d
2. Large Exhibition, with parading stages in front over 30 feet deep, per lineal foot – 2s–6d
3. Small Exhibitions and Side Shows of less than 30 feet deep and without parading stages in front, per lineal foot – 1s–3d
4. Shooting Galleries, per lineal foot – 15s–0d
5. Swings, per set, large size – £1–10s–0d
6. Gems, or small Swings, per set – 15s–0d
7. Photo Booths, ordinary size, other than Vans, each – 12s–6d
8. Photo Vans, each – £1–5s–0d
9. Emmas, Tubs, Cocoa Nut Shuts, Stick Stalls, American Bowling Alleys, Hot Pea Saloons, etc, per lineal foot – 1s–0d
10. Strikers, each – 2s–6d
11. Nut Stalls, per lineal foot – 10d

Markischer Kreis, Germany
The twinning agreement between Wrexham Maelor Borough and Markischer Kreis in Germany was signed at the Guildhall on 9 April 1976.

Marsh, Richard *bookseller & printer*
Born *c.*1710. The first official record of his life is the entry for his marriage on 12 February 1746 at Wrexham to Miss Mary Hurst, when he is described as 'a writing master'. In 1733 he was a bookseller (and later a printer) at Nº 42 High Street, Wrexham where he remained in business until his death on 24 May 1792.

Aerial photograph of Mold Road, c.1953. In the centre of the photograph are the streets of pre-fabricated houses, built shortly after the Second World War, which survived until 1978. To their left is Maesgwyn Hall and the Crosville bus garage. Beyond the pre-fabs is the Racecourse and the Denbighshire Technical College.

He was buried in Wrexham Churchyard. The business was then run by his son, John Marsh (1747–95) and, after his death it was taken over by John Painter.*

Marsh Crescent
This street was laid out in the early 1920s by WBC as part of the Acton Park Housing Estate.* It was named after Mrs Milly Edwards-Jones,* whose maiden name was Marsh. She was the wife of Dr Edwards-Jones* and the daughter of the Rector of Bangor-is-y-coed.

Mary Ann Square, Brook Street
One of the many 'courts' located in the Brook Street/Pentre Felin area of the town. These houses were built in 1844 by Alexander Wylde Thornley* and named after his wife. The houses were demolished in the early 1930s and the site became the location of the Odeon Cinema.*

Mason, JP, Alderman Job *local politician*
Born in Worcester in 1855, the son of Job Mason. He qualified as a teacher and was appointed to Acocks Green National School, Birmingham in 1876. He became the Headmaster of the Wrexham National School* in 1886, a position which he held until his retirement in 1921. Charles Dodd* wrote of him 'Mr Job Mason came to Wrexham with very high credentials which he has never dishonoured'. On retiring, he was elected a councillor on WBC and became Mayor in 1926 and an alderman in 1935.

He married Rachel Jane Halliley of Birmingham and they had six children. Job Mason was appointed a Justice of the Peace in 1923 and lived at Percy Lodge, Percy Road where he died on 16 May 1937. He is buried in Wrexham Cemetery.* Mason Avenue* is named after him.

Mason Avenue
Developed in 1930 as part of the Borough Council's Huntroyde housing estate,* this street was named after Wrexham Mayor Job Mason* (1926–7).

Mason's Entry
Located off the Beast Market.

Matthews, MBE, Kenneth Joseph *Olympic athlete*
Born on 21 June 1934, in Erdington, Birmingham, Ken Matthews was educated at Moor End Secondary Modern School and began his working life as a trainee electrical fitter with an interest in competitive cycling. His father was a keen competitive walker and it was he who persuaded Ken to take up walking as a means of getting fit before embarking on his National Service in 1952.

Returning to civilian life after two years with the Royal Army Ordnance Corps, Ken decided to continue walking as a sport and very soon began to achieve considerable success at local, county and then national levels. Employed by the Central Electricity Generating Board as a fitter's mate in a power station, he was able to obtain leave of absence to travel to competitions and to train in the grounds of the power station. Qualifying for the Great Britain team for the 1960 Olympics in Rome, he contracted a virus some six weeks before the competition. In the final he led the 8km walk until he dropped out due weakness and dehydration. He won the 20km walk at the World Championships in Lugano in 1961, the European Championships in Belgrade in 1962 and the World Championships in Lugano in 1963. He set unofficial records for the 7-mile road walk (48 mins 2 secs), the 10-mile road walk (69 mins 47 secs) and the 5-mile track walk (34 mins 35.6 secs). At the 1964 Tokyo Olympics he won all his heats and took the Gold Medal in a new 20-km walk Olympic Record

Britain's golden four at the Tokyo Olympics. L–R: Ken Matthews, Ann Packer, Mary Rand and Lyn Davies. [Ken Matthews]

time of 1 hr 29 mins 34 secs. Ken then retired from competitive walking and returned to his first love, cycling.

Married to Sheila Eyre in 1962 (they have one son), Ken Matthews was offered a position by Rogers & Jackson in their new sports department and he moved to Wrexham in 1965. He later moved to the firm's electrical department until 1970 when he took up employment with BICC as a quality controller. He retired in 1995. In 1978 he was awarded the MBE for his services to sport. He lives in Acton.

Matthias, BEM, Alfred *local politician*
Brymbo Steel worker, Alf Matthias, was elected as a Labour councillor in 1965, representing the New Broughton and Bryn Cefn areas on the WRDC. On the creation of WMBC in 1974 he continued to serve and became Mayor in 1988. He retired in 1996. He also served on the Parish and Community Councils. He was awarded the British Empire Medal in 1978 for his services to the local community. Married to Joan, Alf Matthias lived at Cae'r Haf, Summerhill and had one daughter. He died in 1997.

Mawddwy Avenue
Named after Dinas Mawddwy, the birthplace of D. Harding Griffiths, the builder of this private development in *c*.1900. The houses were bought for £12,000 by WBC in the late 1960s.

Mayfield Court, Garden Village
A small development of private houses built in 2001.

Mayors of Wrexham

Wrexham Borough Council
1857	Thomas Edgworth
1858	Thomas Edgworth
1859	Thomas Painter
1860	John Clark
1861	John Dickenson
1862	John Lewis
1863	John Lewis
1864	Joseph Clark
1865	William Overton
1866	Peter Walker
1867	Peter Walker
1868	Thomas Rowland
1869	William Rowland
1870	John Beale
1871	John Bernard Murless
1872	James Charles Owen
1873	Robert Lloyd
1874	Robert Lloyd
1875	Thomas Eyton Jones
1876	John Beirne
1877	James Charles Owen
1878	Isaac Shone
1879	Edward Smith
1880	George Bradley
1881	Thomas Rowland
1882	Yeaman Strachan
1883	John Bernard Murless
1884	Samuel Thomas Baugh
1885	William Edge Samuel
1886	John Prichard
1887	John Jones
1888	Sir Evan Morris
1889	Henry Venables Palin
1890	Henry Venables Palin
1891	Frederic William Soames
1892	Richard William Evans
1893	Robert Henry Done
1894	Charles Murless
1895	Charles Murless
1896	Philip Yorke
1897	Ralph Williamson
1898	Ralph Williamson
1899	Thomas Jones
1900	Thomas Jones
1901	Frederic William Soames
1902	Frederic William Soames
1903	Evan Birkett Evans
1904	Evan Birkett Evans
1905	Evan Birkett Evans
1906	Edward Hughes
1907	Edward Hughes
1908	Thomas Sauvage
1909	John Stanford
1910	Samuel Edwards-Jones
1911	William Jonah Williams
1912	William Jonah Williams
1913	Sydney Gardner Jarman
1914	Sydney Gardner Jarman
1915	Sir Leonard Bromfield Rowland
1916	Sir Leonard Bromfield Rowland
1917	Sir Leonard Bromfield Rowland
1918	Sir Leonard Bromfield Rowland
1919	Thomas Sauvage
1920	Thomas Sauvage
1921	Thomas Sauvage
1922	Christopher Davies
1923	Horace Blew
1924	Charles Edward Hickman
1925	George Thomas Davies
1926	Job Mason
1927	Mrs Milly Edwards-Jones
1928	Mrs Milly Edwards-Jones
1929	Mrs Milly Edwards-Jones
1930	William Aston
1931	William Dodman
1932	W. Emyr Williams
1933	Herbert Hampson
1934	Joseph Parton
1935	J. Garner Jones
1936	Cyril O. Jones
1937	Roger A. Dutton
1938	Mrs Milly Edwards-Jones
1939	John Davies
1940	Arthur Challoner
1941	A. A. Green
1942	John Taylor
1943	Mrs Ethel Claire Breese
1944	J. W. Edwards
1945	Norman D. Bird
1946	Edward Stanley E. Hackett
1947	Mrs Catherine Jarvis Jones
1948	Mrs Catherine Jarvis Jones
1949	William Morris
1950	William Clarke
1951	George William Turner
1952	Eric A. McMahon
1953	Herbert Jennings
1954	Mrs Linda Davies
1955	William Shone (died in office 1/3/56) Herbert Hampson
1956	John Albert Davies
1957	William H. Evans
1958	Thomas Francis Thomas
1959	Glyn Ellis Jones

1960	Edward Davies
1961	Robert Roberts
1962	Joseph Parry
1963	Robert Stanley Craig
1964	Harold Griffiths
1965	Frank Cooper
1966	Gwilym Herbert Jones
1967	Ernest Price
1968	Joseph Harold Tapley
1969	Harry Moore
1970	Clifford Hughes
1971	Gwilym H. Parry
1972	Silas Davies
1973	Clifford Jackson

Wrexham Maelor Borough Council

1974	Morgan Jones
1975	Mrs Agnes McConville
1976	Noel I. Wright
1977	Albert Edgar Jones
1978	T. M. Williams
1979	John J. Myers
1980	Miss M. Megan Jones
1981	J. R. Thomas
1982	Mrs Rose Nicholson
1983	J. A. Davies
1984	J. Warren Coleman
1985	R. W. Squire
1986	Eric John Beresford
1987	Arthur Evans
1988	R. Alfred Matthias
1989	F. V. Robinson
1990	Malcolm Williams
1991	Cyril Williams
1992	D. J. Roberts
1993	Mrs Willow Williams
1994	Arnold Griffiths
1995	Michael G. Morris

Wrexham County Borough Council

1996	Mrs Bronwen Greenaway
1997	David Broderick
1998	Barrie C. Williams
1999	Ron Davies
2000	Neil Rogers
2001	Mrs Sandy Mewies
2002	Rodney Skeland
2003	Aled Roberts
2004	David Rogers
2005	Michael Edwards
2006	George James
2007	Joan Lowe
2008	David Griffiths
2009	Arwel Gwynn Jones
2010	James A. Kelly

Mayor's Sunday
An annual event that normally takes place in mid June, Mayor's Sunday is when the newly elected Mayor, accompanied by his family, fellow councillors, local authority officials and various public figures in the Borough (and lately County Borough) visit the Parish Church. The tradition goes back to 1857 and for many years it was held in November. It was stopped for a short time in the 1970s. The event was an important occasion in the local calendar and was once seen by many as an excuse for a local celebration, so much so that in 1887 concerns were raised in the Council by a number of prominent townspeople who deplored 'the disorderly state of the town on Mayor's Sunday – It is made the occasion of much drunkenness and desecration of the Sabbath and begs that the council will suggest to future mayors that they arrange the service and procession on a week-day, thereby removing the cause of very loud and general complaints of the violation of the religious sentiments of the inhabitants.'

Meifod Place, Erddig Road
A terrace of fifteen small houses with yards at the rear which appears for the first time in the 1872 survey, facing a small, unnamed street, which led off Erddig Road* and at right angles to Wellington Road. The Victorian street has all but disappeared with the demolition of the houses and the building of modern flats on the site. It is sometimes incorrectly written as Meivor Place.

Melin Coed-y-Glyn
See French Mill.

Mellor, John *landowner*
Born in 1665, John Mellor was a barrister in the Middle Temple who succeeded John Edisbury as Master in Chancery. He bought the Erddig Hall* estate on 28 January 1714 for £17,000 and moved to live there from London. Unmarried and a fierce anti-Jacobite, he appears to have been ill-suited to the life of a country gentleman in Wrexham where his neighbours were staunch supporters of the Jacobite cause (see the Cycle). He spent a great deal of time and money enhancing the house at Erddig. He died on 23 November 1733 and is buried in Marchwiel Church. He left the Erddig estate to his nephew, Simon Yorke.*

Members of Parliament
From 1544 until 1832, Wrexham was represented in Parliament by one member who was returned for the county of Denbighshire. From 1832 until 1885, the county of Denbighshire returned two members of Parliament. From 1885 until 1918, Wrexham was represented in Parliament by a member who sat for Denbighshire East. Since 1918 Wrexham has been a constituency in its own right although the boundaries of the constituency have been changed on several occasions.

1544	Sir John Salusbury (Lleweni)	
1547	Sir John Salusbury (Lleweni)	
1553	Robert Puleston (Bersham)	
1553	Sir John Salusbury (Lleweni)	
1554	Sir John Salusbury (Lleweni)	
1554	Sir John Salusbury (Lleweni)	
1555	Edward Almer (Plas Iocyn)	
1557	Sir John Salusbury (Lleweni)	
1558	Sir John Salusbury (Lleweni)	
1562	Simon Thelwall (Plas-y-Ward)	
1571	Roger Puleston	
1572	William Almer (Pant Iocyn)	
1584	Evan Lloyd (Bodidris)	
1586	Sir Robert Salusbury (Rug)	
1588	John Edwards (Plas Newydd)	
1593	Sir Roger Puleston	
1597	John Lloyd (Bodidris)	
1601	Sir John Salusbury (Lleweni)	
1604	Sir Peter Mutton (Llannerch)	
1614	Simon Thelwell (Plas-y-Ward)	
1621	Sir John Trevor (Trevalun)	
1623	Sir Eubulus Thelwell (Plas-y-Ward)	
1625	Sir Thomas Myddelton (Chirk Castle)	
1625	Sir Eubulus Thelwell (Plas-y-Ward)	
1628	Sir Eubulus Thelwell (Plas-y-Ward)	
1640	Sir Thomas Salusbury (Lleweni)	
1640	Sir Thomas Myddelton (Chirk Castle)	
1653	*'Barebones Parliament, no local member*	
1654	Simon Thelwell (Plas Coch)	
	Sir John Cartier (Kinmel)	
1656	Colonel John Jones (Bryn-y-Ffynnon)	Resigned 1656
	Lumley Thelwell	
	Sir John Cartier (Kinmel)	
1658	Sir John Cartier (Kinmel)	
1660	Sir Thomas Myddelton (Chirk Castle)	
1661	Sir Thomas Myddelton (Chirk Castle)	Died 1663
1664	John Wynne (Melai)	
1679	Sir Thomas Myddelton II (Chirk Castle)	
1679	Sir Thomas Myddelton II (Chirk Castle)	
1681	Sir John Trevor (Brynkinallt)	
1685	Sir Richard Myddelton (Chirk Castle)	
1688	Sir Richard Myddelton (Chirk Castle)	
1690	Sir Richard Myddelton (Chirk Castle)	
1695	Sir Richard Myddelton (Chirk Castle)	
1698	Sir Richard Myddelton (Chirk Castle)	

1700	Sir Richard Myddelton (Chirk Castle)	
1701	Sir Richard Myddelton (Chirk Castle)	
1702	Sir Richard Myddelton (Chirk Castle)	
1705	Sir Richard Myddelton (Chirk Castle)	
1708	Sir Richard Myddelton (Chirk Castle)	
1710	Sir Richard Myddelton (Chirk Castle)	
1713	Sir Richard Myddelton (Chirk Castle)	
1715	Sir Richard Myddelton (Chirk Castle)	Died 1716
1716	Watkin Williams (Wynn) (Llanforda)	
1722	Watkin Williams Wynn (Wynnstay)	
1727	Watkin Williams Wynn (Wynnstay)	
1734	Watkin Williams Wynn (Wynnstay)	
1741	Sir Watkin Williams Wynn (Wynnstay)	
1747	Sir Watkin Williams Wynn (Wynnstay)	Died 1749
1749	Sir Lynch Salusbury Cotton (Lleweni)	
1754	Sir Lynch Salusbury Cotton (Lleweni)	
1761	Sir Lynch Salusbury Cotton (Lleweni)	
1768	Sir Lynch Salusbury Cotton (Lleweni)	
1774	Sir Watkin Williams Wynn (Wynnstay)	
1780	Sir Watkin Williams Wynn (Wynnstay)	
1784	Sir Watkin Williams Wynn (Wynnstay)	Died 1789
1789	Robert Watkin Wynne (Plas Newydd & Henllan)	
1790	Robert Watkin Wynne (Plas Newydd & Henllan)	
1796	Sir Watkin Williams Wynn (Wynnstay)	
1802	Sir Watkin Williams Wynn (Wynnstay)	
1806	Sir Watkin Williams Wynn (Wynnstay)	
1807	Sir Watkin Williams Wynn (Wynnstay)	
1812	Sir Watkin Williams Wynn (Wynnstay)	
1818	Sir Watkin Williams Wynn (Wynnstay)	
1820	Sir Watkin Williams Wynn (Wynnstay)	
1826	Sir Watkin Williams Wynn (Wynnstay)	
1830	Sir Watkin Williams Wynn (Wynnstay)	
1831	Sir Watkin Williams Wynn (Wynnstay)	

Great Reform Act, 1832 – first MPs elected to represent Denbighshire Boroughs

1832	Sir Watkin Williams Wynn (Wynnstay)	Con.
	R. M. Biddulph Conservative	
1835	Sir Watkin Williams Wynn (Wynnstay)	Con.
	Hon William Bagot	Con.
1837	Sir Watkin Williams Wynn (Wynnstay)	Con. Died 1840
	Hon. William Bagot	Con.
1840	Hon Hugh Cholmondeley	Con.
1841	Sir Watkin Williams Wynn (Wynnstay)	Con.
	Hon. William Bagot	Con.
1847	Sir Watkin Williams Wynn (Wynstay)	Con.
	Hon. William Bagot	Con.
1852	Sir Watkin Williams Wynn (Wynnstay)	Con.
	R. M. Biddulph	Lib.
1857	Sir Watkin Williams Wynn (Wynstay)	Con.
	R. M. Biddulph	Lib.
1859	Sir Watkin Williams Wynn (Wynstay)	Con.
	R. M. Biddulph	Lib.
1865	Sir Watkin Williams Wynn (Wynnstay)	Con.
	R. M. Biddulph	Lib.

Extension of the Wrexham Parliamentary Borough, 1867

1868	Sir Watkin Williams Wynn (Wynnstay)	Con.
	George Osborne Morgan	Lib.
1874	Sir Watkin Williams Wynn (Wynnstay)	Con.
	George Osborne Morgan	Li.b
1880	Sir Watkin Williams Wynn (Wynnstay)	Con. Died 1885
	George Osborne Morgan	Lib.
1885	Sir Herbert Lloyd Watkin Williams Wynn	Con.
1885	George Osborne Morgan	Lib.
1886	George Osborne Morgan	Lib.
1892	Sir George Osborne Morgan	Lib.
1895	Sir George Osborne Morgan	Lib. Died 1897
1897	Samuel Moss	Lib.
1900	Samuel Moss	Lib.
1906	Samuel Moss	Lib. Resigned 1906
1906	E. G. Hemmerde	Lib.
1909	E. G. Hemmerde	Lib.
1910	E. G. Hemmerde	Lib.
1910	Edward Thomas John	Lib.
1918	Sir Robert J. Thomas	Lib. Coalition
1922	R. Richards	Lab.
1923	R. Richards	Lib.
1924	C. P. Williams	Lib.
1929	R. Richards	Lab.
1931	A. O. Roberts	Lib.
1935	R. Richards	Lab.
1945	R. Richards	Lab.
1950	R. Richards	Lab.
1951	R. Richards	Lab.
1955	J. I. J. Jones	Lab.
1959	J. I. J. Jones	Lab.
1964	J. I. J. Jones	Lab.
1966	J. I. J. Jones	Lab.
1970	Robert Thomas Ellis	Lab.
1974	Robert Thomas Ellis	Lab.
1974	Robert Thomas Ellis	Lab.
1979	Robert Thomas Ellis	Lab. (joined Soc. Dem.)
1983	Dr John Marek	Lab.
1987	Dr John Marek	Lab.
1992	Dr John Marek	Lab.
1997	Dr John Marek	Lab. (became AM)
2001	Ian Lucas	Lab.
2005	Ian Lucas	Lab.
2010	Ian Lucas	Lab.

Members of the National Assembly for Wales

Following the passing of the Government of Wales Act, 1998, the National Assembly for Wales was established with 60 members who sit in *Y Senedd* in Cardiff. Under the mixed member proportional representation system 40 of the members are elected for single-member constituencies on the basis of first past the post. The remaining 20 members are elected from five regional closed lists using an alternative party vote.

Wrexham Members
Dr John Marek*	1997–2007
Mrs Leslie Griffiths*	2007–

Clwyd South Member
Karen Sinclair	1999–

Regional Members
Mrs Eleanor Burnham*	2001–

Memorial Hall, Bodhyfryd

The original proposal for a memorial hall was made in 1946 with an estimated cost of £53,000 for a building that was to be located off Regent Street. Plans for a Victory Memorial Hall, by Prof George Stephenson, were exhibited in November 1952 with an estimated cost of £57,000. The actual Memorial Hall, commemorating those who died in the Second World War was built at Bodhyfryd in 1956–7. An appeal by the Mayor led to £20,000 being subscribed by members of the public and the balance of £15,000 was provided by Wrexham Borough Council. The foundation stones were laid by Cllr John Albert Davies, JP (Mayor) and Alderman Norman Douglas Bird (chairman of the Management Committee) on 20 March 1957 and the hall was built by Edward W. Gittins & Sons. Inside the foyer are stone panels bearing the names of all those who died between 1939 and 1945. This was seriously, albeit accidentally, damaged in the early 2000s. Also located here are bronze plaques recording the names of the dead of the Great War, 1914–18 (which were previously displayed in the entrance to Nº 1 Grosvenor Road*). Also inside are two plaques recording the names of those employees of Wrexham Borough Council were were killed in the two world wars and a slate plaque referring to the Burma Star Association. A memorial stained-glass window, presented by the 'Burgesses of Wrexham' is also a feature of the war memorial. Outside the hall, in the porch, is a memorial to Flt Lt David S.A. Lord, VC, DFC,* which used to stand on the corner of Grosvenor Road and Regent Street.

In the grounds of the Memorial Hall is the Burma Garden, opened by Ron Thomas, RWF, and G. Walford Hughes of the Burma Star Association on 12 August 1995, to commemorate the 50th anniversary of the end of the war against Japan. Designed by a student at the Welsh College of Horticulture it takes the form of a circular area laid in local bricks in the shape of the Burma Star and a winding path, inlaid with railway sleepers (representing those prisoners-of-war who were forced to work on the infamous Burma Railway) leading to a seating area planted with shrubs representative of the Far East. Nearby is the Burma Bell, taken by members of the 1st Bn, RWF from the Incomparable Pagoda at

Mandalay, during the Burma War of 1885–7. Presented to WBC it was displayed outside the Guildhall on Coronation Walk until moved to its present location in 1995.

Menai Road, Queen's Park
Built in the late 1940s as part of the first phase of WBC's Queen's Park housing development, it is named after the Menai Strait which separates Anglesey from the mainland of Wales.

Mere Crescent, Goulbourne
A private development of the late 1970s on land that was previously part of Plas Goulbourne* which was once part of the Gredington Estate. The word 'mere', meaning 'lake' is used in Shropshire but is not normally found in Wales. In this instance it may be a reference to Hanmer Mere which is located alongside Gredington Hall in Hanmer.

Meredith Street
Named after the Meredith family of Pentrebychan, proprietors of the Cambrian Leather Works* and owners of the Court* estate on whose land the street was developed.

Meredith, William 'Billy' Henry *footballer*
Born at Black Park, Chirk on 30 July 1874, Billy Meredith was once described as the 'football wonder of all time'. Educated locally and coached by schoolteacher T.E. Thomas, he first began working at Black Park colliery as a pony driver where he remained for ten years until aged 26. He began to play for Wrexham before signing for Northwich Victoria (1894) – while still retaining his colliery job– before joining Manchester City (1894). He gained his first Welsh cap in 1895. He joined Manchester United in 1906 and returned to Manchester City in 1921. He had a total of 48 caps, a record that was to stand for many years, and was the oldest player to appear in an international match. A failed businessman (he was declared bankrupt in 1909 after a period as a partner in a sports outfitting business) he took on the Church Hotel, Manchester, in 1915. He won both a Welsh Cup Winners Medal and an FA Cup Winners Medal and scored 181 goals in 676 League appearances. He died at Withington, Manchester, on 19 April 1958.

Merlin Road, Little Acton
A development of private houses completed during the late 1950s on an estate that was originally known as Edgby Park Estate. The land was once part of Cae'r Hen Dy (*Trans.* old house field) and Erw Coed Mawr (*Trans.* big wood acre), fields belonging to Little Acton Farm* and later, to the Acton Park* estate. Undoubtedly, but inexplicably, this road was named after Merlin, the legendary magician to King Arthur.

Mewies, BA, Mrs Sandy *local politician*
Born at Trefalyn Hospital on 16 February 1950, Sandy Mewies was educated at Grove Park Girl's County School* and later gained a BA with the Open University. She was employed as a journalist for 20 years before becoming a voluntary service co-ordinator and is now a Lay Inspector of Schools, a director of the Wales European Centre in Brussels and a member of the North Wales Probation Board. She is married to broadcaster Paul Mewies and they have one son.

Mrs Mewies was elected a member of Gwersyllt Community Council in 1987 and a Labour member of WBC in 1988, representing Gwersyllt North. She has chaired the Social Services Committee and the European Issues Committee. She is also the chairman of the Gwersyllt Residents Environmental Action Team and a school governor. She became Mayor in 2001, the year when Wrexham made its bid for city status as part of the Queen's Golden Jubilee celebrations.

Mrs Mewies was shortlisted in 2002 as the Labour candidate for the Delyn seat in the National Assembly which she won in May 2003 and was re-elected in May 2007. She has served as chair of the Assembly's European and External Affairs Committee, as a member of the Social Justice Regeneration Committee and the Environment, Planning and Countryside and North Wales Regional Committees. A former Board member and director of the Wales European Centre in Brussels and the North Wales Probation Board. Honorary Fellow of the North-East Wales Institute* (later Glyndŵr University*).

Mile Barn Cottages, Goulbourne
These cottages stand just off Holt Road by the Llan-y-Pwll Link Road roundabout. They take their name from a large barn which stood here, possibly a tithe barn, roughly one mile from Wrexham.

Mile Barn Road, Goulbourne
Laid out in the 1980s as part of a private residential development, this street takes its name from Mile Barn Cottages.*

Millbrook Road, Abenbury
A private housing development of the 1990s which takes its name from the nearby river Clywedog which was the power source for King's Mills.*

Mills, Richard *journalist*
Born in Llanidloes in 1840, Richard Mills came to Wrexham to work as a compositor for Hughes & Son.* He married Sarah Owen of Aberderfyn, Rhos in 1876 and set up a printing business in Johnstown (later moving to Rhos) and founded the weekly newspaper *The Rhos Herald*. He was also well known as a choral conductor and composer. He is generally regarded as the founder of the Rhos musical tradition.

Militia Barracks, Regent Street
See County Buildings.

Mills
See by name e.g. King's Mills, Felin Puleston.

Mine Workers Institute, Grosvenor Road
Located at N° 6 Grosvenor Road, the North Wales Mine Workers Institute provided social, leisure and educational facilities for members who were originally drawn from the local mining community. The Institute, which opened in 1923, was funded by the miners in the form of membership fees and profits from the bars and dining facilities. A large function suite was installed at the rear of the building with a dance floor on the first floor. There was also a bowling green located alongside the main building and the building hosted snooker, domino and darts teams. In the stable block at the rear facilities were provided for the administrative offices of Gresford Colliery Disaster* Relief Fund and, in later years, the dental surgery of Mr Felix Richards.

Unable to meet the administration costs (particularly the cost of heating such a large building) with dwindling membership, the Miners Institute finally closed in July 2008 and the charitable trust put the building up for sale at a price of £1 million.

In September 2010, the Wrexham Muslim Association* finalised the purchase of the building and immediately began using it for daily prayers.

Miners Arms, Town Hill
See *Cambrian Vaults*

Mines Rescue Station, Maesgwyn Road
A purpose-built mines rescue station to serve the North Wales Coalfield was opened in Maesgwyn Road in 1913 in a building which also housed the North Wales Coal Owners Association. It served as a training centre for the various mines rescue teams in the region and a central co-ordination point at times of crisis. As well as offices and storage facilities for equipment, the building had two galleries which were used for the training of rescue teams. In the tunnel gallery specially equipped miners were given various scenarios and trained how to react to them. In addition, they were taught basic emergency first aid to enable them to safely recover injured men from underground.

The station closed in the 1980s and its functions were taken over by the Fire Service and the building was sold to local businessman, Neville Dickens, who was granted planning permission to demolish it to build apartments. Following concern that the building (and particularly the galleries) was in danger of being demolished, it was granted Grade II listed status by Cadw on 18 August 2010. Significant parts of the building were demolished two days later.

Gresford Nº 3 Rescue Team, 1935, photographed outside the Mines Rescue Station. Back row: Maj Herbert (Superintendent); W.H. Taylor; Seth Davies; T.J. Roberts (Instructor). Front row: Ben Edwards; T.A. Charlton (Manager); Tom Tilston (Captain); Dr D. Wallace; Ralph Roberts.

Minafon
(*Trans.* riverside) Built by WBC in *c*.1955 as part of the Queen's Park Housing Estate on land that was previously part of Hafod-y-Wern* farm. This street is named after its position on the northern bank of the river Gwenfro.

Mine Workers' Institute, Grosvenor Road
See Plas Darland.

Mining Accidents
In addition to the numerous individual accidents that occurred in the mines of the Wrexham area and the infamous Gresford Disaster*, a number of other accidents occurred which are worthy of being remembered as part of the heavy price paid by the mining communities for the production of coal.

Acrefair, January 1841 – six youths killed when a badly cracked chain snapped as they were descending into the British Iron Company mine. The owner, Mr Wood later reported to a parliamentary enquiry that the accident was caused by the negligence of the young men who failed to check the quality of the chain before beginning their descent.

Pentrefron, Talwrn, September 1819 – two men drowned:
    Edward Salisbury of Harwood
    John Taylor of Adwy
A third man, John Evans,* was rescued twelve days later.

Penycoed, Brymbo, March 1844 – two boys were scalded to death by a burst steam valve, one man buried and upwards of 15 seriously burned.

Minera, December 1844 – five men killed.

Minera, 20 July 1849 – nine men killed.

Westminster, Moss, 7 December 1850 – a man and two boys were burned in an underground fire. Both boys died.

Ffrwd, 19 October 1854 – seven men killed.

Bryn-yr-Owen, 1855 – seven men were drowned underground.

Brynmally, 20 September 1856 – thirteen men drowned underground.
    Edward Cunnah, age 26
    Steven Davies, age 28
    Ishmael Evans, age unknown
    Ishmael Griffiths, age unknown
    Henry Jones, age 30
    Thomas Jones, age 22
    William Jones, age 31
    Thomas Lewis, age 36
    Samuel Parry, age 15
    Evan Roberts, age 22
    Edward Thomas, age 24
    James Thomas, age 31
    John Williams, age 23

Wynnstay, 9 December 1863, thirteen men killed.
    Thomas Williams, driver, age 26
    Edward Evans, collier, age 40
    Elias Jones, collier, age 29
    Benjamin Thomas, collier, age 27
    Thomas Davies, collier, age 25
    David Jones, collier, age 41
    Samuel Thellwall, driver, age 13
    Thomas Stephens, drawer, age 22
    John Blower, collier, age 40
    William Jones, collier, age 48
    William Williams, drawer, age 17
    John Davies, collier, age 36

Wynnstay, 30 September 1868 – ten men killed
    Thomas Ward
    Henry Davies
    Moses Andrew
    David Roberts
    John Lloyd
    James Davies
    Hugh Edwards
    Edward Edwards
    Meshech Jones
    John Brown

Wynnstay, 24 April 1873 – seven men killed.
    Griffith Hughes, fireman, age 35
    Joshua Davis, collier, age 34
    George Edwards, collier, age 33
    Richard Thomas, collier, age 22
    Edward Williams, collier, age 27
    John Jones, filler, age 16
    Peter Darlington, roadman, age 18

Brynmally, 27 January 1877 – three men killed.

Brynmally, 30 May 1878 – six men killed.

Joseph Millington, aged 34
David Edwards, aged 29
Richard Powell, aged 56
Ishmael Davies, aged 28
John Powell, aged 18
John Davies, aged 20

Bersham, 3 August 1880 – nine men killed.
William Pattison, manager
Joseph Matthias, fireman
Edward Owen, fireman
John Jones, fireman
James Roberts, fireman
Thomas Evans, collier
Evan Parry, collier
Robert Lloyd, hooker
Henry Valentine, pitman

Brynmally, 13 March 1889 – twenty men killed.
James Davies, waggoner, age 14
Thomas Davies, pony driver, age 16
William Davies, filler, age 22
Edward W, Edwards, waggoner, age 14
Robert Thomas Edwards, filler, age 17
Thomas Edwards, charter master, age 40
Henry Garston, charter master, age 50
Peter Griffiths, filler, age 22
Charles Hughes, waggoner, age 14
Thomas Jarvis, filler, age 20
Hugh Jones, bye-man, age 48
Peter Jones, bye-man, age 15
Thomas Jones, collier, age 42
Samuel Millington, filler, age 18
Edward Rowland, hooker-on, age 14
Arthur Thomas, filler, age 17
Henry Tudor, jigger, age 17
Evan Williams, collier, age 53
Joseph Williams, pony driver, age 15
Thomas Williams, collier, age 33

Llay Hall, 1881 – two workers killed.
Llay Main, 5 December 1924 – nine miners killed.
Isaac Evans, of Mold, age 19
J. W. Hughes, of Llay, age 22
William Ernest Williams, of Llay, age 41
John Humphreys, of Llanferres, age 53
Edward Henry German, of Rhosddu, age 15
Joseph Reginald Evans, of Abermorddu (brother of R.P. Evans), age 35
Robert Percival Evans, of Cefynybedd (brother of J. R. Evans), age 32

An RAF reconnaissance photograph taken on 17 November 1948, looking west along Mold Road. Of interest in this photograph are: the Wrexham–Chester railway left–right in the foreground; the old Wrexham Electric Tram Company's depôt on the left, just over the railway bridge; the prefabricated houses, Maesgwyn Hall and the Crosville bus garage. On the right of Mold Road is the Racecourse with only earth banks on two sides. The field where the Denbighshire Technical College was to be built in the 1950s is empty but shows the clear trace of a track all the way round it — the last vestiges of the horse (or more accurately, pony) racing track from the early 1900s. Beyond the race track is Plas Coch Farm and, just to the left of centre in the far distance, Gatewen Colliery. [National Assembly for Wales]

Thomas Charles Fletcher, of Mold, age 43
Henry Jones, of Llay, age 36

Mission Church, Beast Market
Recorded as holding meetings in the Beast Market. The Religious Census of 1881 showed: Capacity 80; attendance (AM & PM) 39.

Mitre, High Street
A public house which was located at N° 30 High Street from c.1710 until c.1825 when the premises were converted into a shop. It was on these premises that the stalls for the High Street open-air market were stored during the 18th century.

Mitre, The, Pentre Felin
There have been two public houses in Pentre Felin bearing the name Mitre. One appears in the 1833 survey on the site of the present day Old Three Tuns* in Well Street.* The second, referred to as the Old Mitre in the 1833 survey, stands on Pentre Felin itself alongside Jones' Court.*

Mivor Terrace
See Meifod Place.

Mold Road
Undoubtedly laid out as one of the new turnpike roads leading out of Wrexham, Mold Road does not appear as a named road until the late 19th century. The section of road passing the Technical College* and the Racecourse* was widened and made into a dual carriageway in 1963. The next major change occurred with the building of the Plas Coch Retail Park development in 1990 when the junctions of Plas Coch Road and Berse Road were re-aligned and a new roundabout was built to accommodate the greatly increased flow of traffic. During the Second World War the US Army built a camp of nissen huts alongside the Racecourse, on the site that would become the Denbighshire Technical College.* These huts were used as temporary housing for some years before being demolished during the construction of the college in the 1950s.

Monger Road
This street was laid out in the 1980s on land that had previously been the property of C.T. Clark, proprietor of the King's Mills Garage. Built by the Wales and West Housing Association, all the streets were named after RWF who had been awarded the Victoria Cross.

This street was named after Drummer George Monger, VC, (1840-87) who was born at Woodmancote, Basingstoke, Hampshire on 3 March 1840. He enlisted as a Boy Soldier in the RWF on 10 November 1855 and saw active service in the Indian Mutiny. He was discharged from the army on 9 November 1868 after which he was employed as a builder's labourer and bricklayer. He died of consumption at St Leonards on Sea, Sussex and was buried in Hastings Borough Cemetery.

His citation reads: 'Private George Monger volunteered to accompany Lieutenant Hackett when he assisted in bringing in a corporal of the 23rd Regiment.'

Monmouth Road, Borras Park
As with other streets on this private housing development of the early 1960s, known as Hillcrest Estate,* this road takes its name from one of the old, pre-1974 counties of Wales, in this case, Monmouthshire.

Monslow, MP, Walter (Lord Monslow of Barrow in Furness) politician
Born in Wrexham the son of a Bersham iron moulder, Walter Monslow was brought up at 41 Trinity Street, Rhostyllen. He became a Great Western Railway apprentice at 15 years of age and soon gravitated into trade union politics, becoming organising secretary of ASLEF and chairman of the Wrexham branch of ASLEF then secretary of the Railway Machinery for Negotiation. In 1937, he was the leader of a British Trades Union delegation to the Soviet Union.

His first steps into politics were taken when he was elected a parish councillor in Esclusham and in 1924, became a member of WRDC (serving for 12 years). He was a manager of Bersham School and a Methodist lay-preacher at Bryn-y-Ffynnon Chapel* in Regent Street before moving to Leeds in the mid-1930s. In 1935, he failed in his bid to be elected as the Member of Parliament for Newcastle-upon-Tyne Central and was elected MP for Barrow-in-Furness in 1945. He was a Parliamentary Private Secretary at the Ministry of Civil Aviation in 1949–50 and Parliamentary Private Secretary in the Ministry of Food in 1950–51. He remained in Parliament until his retirement in 1966 when he was created Lord Monslow (Life Peerage).

He married (1) Mary, the daughter of Cllr Thomas Rogers (she died in 1959), one daughter, Rosemary; (2) Jean Baird McDonald. He lived at Ardbeg, Rothesay, Isle of Bute for the latter part of his life. He died on 12 October 1966, aged 71 years.

Moore, Alderman Harry local politician
He was born in Wrexham in 31 August 1923, the son of Henry and Olive Moore, and educated at Victoria School. Harry followed his father into the family painting and decorating business. During the Second World War he served in the army in North Africa and Italy. Elected an Independent councillor for Offa Ward in May 1954 he became Mayor in 1969 and hosted Prince Charles during his Investiture visit to Wrexham. Married to Gwendoline Nicholls of Dudleston, they had one daughter. He was elected an alderman for Maes-y-Dre Ward in 1970. He lived at 9 Poplar Road and died on 4 January 1980.

Moorland Avenue, Spring Lodge
Laid out and developed in the mid 1930s as part of the second phase of the Spring Lodge housing estate.*

Mold Road, c.1880, showing the roofline of the original railway station behind the hedge of Crispin Lane. In the distance can be seen the towers of Seion Church, Wrexham Parish Church, the spire of St Mary's RC Pro-Cathedral and the top of the spire of St Mark's Church. These all provide a strong guide to the date of the photograph.

Montgomery Road, Spring Lodge
This area of public housing was developed in the 1940s on open land that was known in the 18th century as Gwerglodd Groom or Gwerglodd White when it formed part of the Wynnstay Estate. [DRO/DD/WY/8352] The original houses on the western side of the road were pre-fabricated buildings which were later replaced by permanent houses. By 1951 there were 81 dwellings on this road. Following the pattern of naming streets in this area after British military commanders of the Second World War, this road was named after Field Marshal Viscount Montgomery, the most notable British general of the Second World War.

Montrose Gardens, Queen's Park
Built in the immediate post Second World War period as part of the first phase of WBC's Queen's Park housing development, on land that had previously been part of Hullah Farm* and the Cefn Park* estate. The reason for the name is unrecorded.

Morgan Avenue, Rhosddu
One of the early streets of council houses developed by WRDC in the 1920s.

Morgan, The Most Revd Dr Barry *clergyman*
Born in Neath, Glamorgan, in 1947, he was educated at University College, London, and Selwyn College, Cambridge and gained a PhD from the University of Wales in 1986. He was ordained a deacon in 1972 and priest in 1973 when he was appointed a curate in the parish of St Andrews Major, with Michaelston-le-Pit. He was then appointed chaplain and lecturer in theology at St Michael's College and the University College of Wales, Cardiff. He was subsequently appointed warden of the Anglican University Chaplaincy in Bangor and director of Ordinands and in-service training adviser in the diocese of Bangor. He was appointed Rector of Wrexham in 1984 when he was responsible for the closure of St John's Church,* Hightown and the re-arrangement of the interior of the Parish Church of St Giles, a period which proved quite controversial in the history of the parish. He became Rector of Criccieth with Treflys and Archdeacon of Meirionydd in 1986, before being appointed Bishop of Bangor in 1993 and Llandaff in 1999. Upon the enthronement of the Archbishop of Wales, the Most Revd Dr Rowan Williams, as Archbishop of Canterbury, Archbishop Morgan became Archbishop of Wales in July 2003. A Welsh-speaker, he has written books on various subjects, including the poetry of R.S. Thomas. He was appointed Pro-chancellor of the University of Wales in 2006. He is married with two children.

Morgan, QC, Bt, Sir George Osborne *politician*
Born in Gothenburg, Sweden 8 May 1826, the son of the Revd Morgan Morgan, the Vicar of Conwy; his mother was Fanny Nonnen of Gothenburg. Educated at Friars School, Bangor, Shrewsbury School and Oxford University, he was elected a Fellow of University College in 1850 and called to the Bar at Lincoln's Inn in 1853. He took silk in 1869.

He represented Denbighshire (including the Borough of Wrexham) as a Liberal in 1868 and introduced the Burials Bill of 1870 which permitted any Christian service in a parish churchyard; the Bill eventually became law in 1880. He was appointed Judge Advocate General in 1880 and was responsible for the abolition of flogging in the army. In 1886, he was appointed Under Secretary for the Colonies and took a keen interest in the Welsh colony of Patagonia. In 1885 he retained his seat and was created a Baronet in 1886.

He died on 25 August 1897 and is buried at Llantysilio, Llangollen.

Morgan Llwyd Memorial
The absence of a headstone to record the final resting place of the Puritan divine Morgan Llwyd,* led to a fundraising campaign being launched in 1905 but, despite Llwyd's importance in the story of Nonconformity in Wales, monies were not readily forthcoming and sufficient funds were not collected until 1912. Even then, there were insufficient funds to pay for a proposed railing around the memorial. The obelisk was unveiled in the Dissenters Burial Ground, Rhosddu on 10 April 1912 by Mrs Margaret Lloyd George (wife of the then Chancellor of the Exchequer, later Prime Minister). The memorial was seriously damaged by vandals in 1999.

Morris, Evan *industrialist*
A native of Montgomeryshire, he came to Wrexham in 1822 and was the proprietor of the leather works in Salop Road which eventually developed into the Cambrian Leather Works. He was the grandfather of Sir Evan Morris,* Mayor of Wrexham. He died in 1859.

Morris, Sir Evan *local politician*
Born 25 July 1842, the grandson of Evan Morris,* the proprietor of the Salop Road leather works. He was articled to J. Devereux Pugh of Wrexham and admitted as a solicitor in 1872 when he established his own practice in Temple Row.* He married Fannie Elizabeth, eldest daughter of Thomas Rowland,* on 17 September 1872 and they had six daughters and one son. In 1875 he opened a second office in Ruabon and, in 1888, was joined as a partner by Llewellyn Hugh Jones. In later years his practice was based at The Priory.* Morris lived at Highfield,* Stansty but also owned Roseneath.*

A passionate supporter of the railway developments in Wrexham he served as a Conservative councillor on the Borough Council and was Mayor in 1888, the year that Queen Victoria visited Wrexham and knighted him. He also served as an honorary major in the 1st Vol Bn, RWF.

Sir Evan retired early on the grounds of ill-health and moved to live in Eastbourne where he was reported to have died on 18 April 1890.

Morris, Michael *local politician*
Born in Wrexham on 12 January 1953, Michael Morris was educated at St Paul's Primary School, Is-y-Coed and Grove Park School. On leaving school, he was employed in the Commercial Department of BICC and attended college on a part-time basis, graduating in 1975 as a Member of the Institute of Purchasing and Supply.

He was elected a member of Is-y-Coed Community Council in 1974 (and has remained a member ever since) and was elected as a Conservative member of WMBC in 1983, representing Holt (at the time, the youngest member of the Council), and became the last Mayor of WMBC in 1995. His year of office coincided with the many celebrations marking the 50th anniversary of the end of the Second World War.

Unmarried, Michael Morris' Mayoress was local Probation Officer, Jane Tilston. He is the Director of Finance and Administration at Castell Alun School in Hope and lives in Bowling Bank.

Morris, William *local politician*
Born in Holt in 1881, William Morris began his working life as a market gardener but, in 1904, moved to Wrexham where he became a caretaker at Grove Park Grammar School.

He was elected as a Liberal councillor for the Offa Ward in 1935 and became chairman of the Markets Committee and Mayor of Wrexham in 1949 (his daughter-in-law acted as his Mayoress) and was the first Mayor to be 'made' at an evening ceremony in May (all previous holders of the office had been 'made' at a ceremony held at noon in November). He was Vice-President of the East Denbighshire Liberal Association.

He lived at 13 Chester Street, Wrexham and died in May 1951. He is buried in Wrexham Cemetery.*

Mostyn, D.D., Rt Revd Francis *Bishop of Menevia*
Born at Talacre, Flintshire, 6 August 1860, the son of Sir Pyers Mostyn (8th Baronet) and the Hon Frances Fraser (daughter of Thomas Alexander Fraser, 14th Baron Lovat), Francis Mostyn was educated at St Mary's College, Oscott (Birmingham) and St Cuthbert's College, Ushaw (Durham).

He was ordained a priest in Birkenhead on 14 September 1884 and became curate of the Church of Our Lady, Birkenhead in 1884 and rector of that parish in 1891. On 14 September 1895 he was appointed Vicar Apostolic of North Wales and came to live at St Mary's Presbytery in Regent Street and later in Grosvenor Road. Three years later, on 12 May 1898, the position of Apostolic Vicar was elevated to that of Bishop of Menevia and he remained in Wrexham until 1921 when he was appointed Archbishop of Cardiff and the see of Menevia was left vacant for six years. Appointed an Assistant to the Pontifical Throne in 1926 he was created a Knight of Malta in 1929 and died on 25 October 1939.

Mount, The, Mount Street
An *aula senescalli* (*Trans.* hall of the seneschal/steward), is mentioned in the 1391 survey as having been 'built for the Steward, *viz* a hall, chamber, kitchen, stable and barn'. The 1562 survey, making reference to a lease dated 1495, mentions a 'plas Stuarde' in Wrexham Fechan.* The records of the Parish Church stated that in 1524, Matilda, the daughter of John ap Gruffydd of Plas-y-Stiwart, presented a brass eagle lectern to the church in accordance with her father's will. This property was probably built by the Puleston's of Hafod-y-Wern* and stood on the south side of Mount Street on some rising ground and was one of the most notable houses in 17th and 18th century Wrexham.

The house then disappears from the records for over 150 years until December 1678 when, known as The Mount, it was

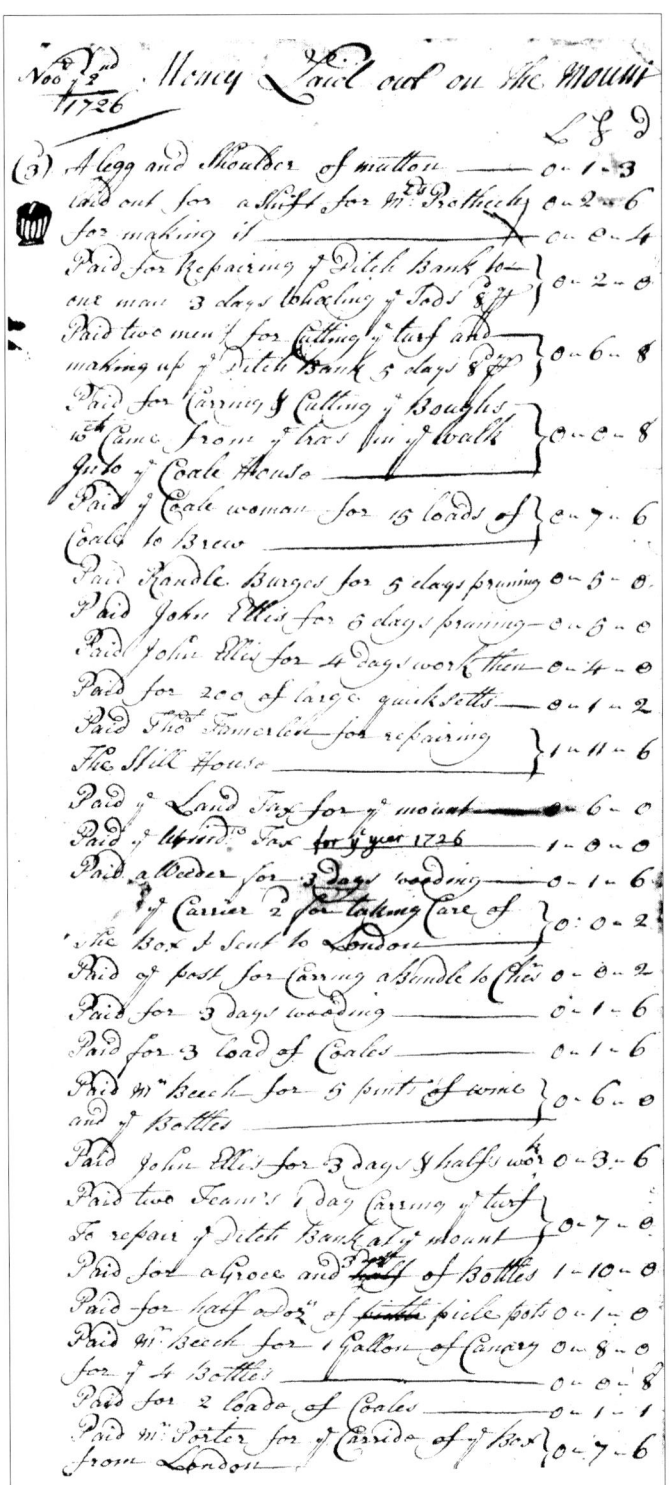

The household accounts for The Mount, 1726 [FRO/D/LE/576]

Left: This simple pencil sketch (which has been cleaned up), dating from c.1700, is the earliest known image of The Mount. [FRO/DLE/645]

A watercolour of The Mount by John Ingleby at the end of the 18th century when it still appeared to be a house of some standing. [NLW/S947]

occupied by a Kenrick Eyton and in 1699 by Lady Eyton of Eyton. Miss Anne Davies of Gwysanau came there to live in 1704 (she died in 1744) and her sister, Lady Catherine Williams (widow of Sir William Williams of Llanforda) remained there until c.1750. A clear portrayal of the house can be seen in Buck's print of 1748 although its position has been changed slightly to make for a more commercially successful picture. The house was inherited by their nephew, Thomas Eyton and on his death in 1787 it passed to his cousin, Miss Letitia Eyton. A Robert Dodd was the tenant of the Mount from 1788 until 1800, at an annual rental of £40. It was sold for £900 in 1806 by the Revd John Hope Eyton, MA, to John Samuel and Thomas Barker of Manchester after whom, it became the property of Samuel Barker (presumably the son of the latter) until his death in 1834. His estate became the subject of a law suit in Chancery and the house was sold in 1852 to help pay some of the legal costs but the buyer's name is unrecorded. In the early 1800s the house was described as comprising a mansion house, stables, coach house, and a lodge on Mount Street along with 2 acres of land.

The Mount was sold again in 1871 (for £475) to a party of Wrexham gentlemen who established a Workmens Institute in the building. The Institute was opened by the Marquess of Westminster and prominent among the subscribers were Sir Robert Cunliffe,* Simon Yorke* and Sir Watkin Williams Wynn.* The Institute was intended to be 'a centre where the working classes can meet in social intercourse in as jovial surroundings as a public house, but free from the influence of liquor'. Evidently it was not a great success and the house was again sold during the early 1880s for £1,050 and for a short time provided a home for Wrexham's Roman Catholic School before it was eventually acquired by the Wrexham and Ellesmere Railway Company who demolished it to make way for the Wrexham to Ellesmere railway line. The Mount is clearly shown on both the 1833 and the 1872 surveys. The surplus monies available after the closure of the Workmen's Institute were placed in a trust fund and used to provide books for the Wrexham Public Library. Eventually, the trust disposed of the assets by means of a donation towards the cost of building the new library* at Ysbytty in 1907.

The best image of the Mount is that which appears in the Ingleby Collection of the National Library of Wales. Dated about 1793, and described as 'the Revd. J. Hope Eyton's House', this watercolour shows a fine three-storied brick house with stone quoins and decorations. It stands above the level of the street and is approached by a stone staircase, leading to the central front door. Other records suggest that there was also a cellar which had windows above ground level at the front. The house was surrounded by a garden which was itself bounded by a high wall along the edge of Mount Street. The only image that we have of

The Mount photographed in c.1895 as the builders of the Wrexham–Ellesmere railway cut a swathe through the area of Mount Street, clearing away all the properties in their path.

A very similar view to that painted by Louise Rayner, but dated about 30 years earlier. The main difference is the brewery building which appears to be the same as that shown in the painting of the Nag's Head Brewery.

'Mount Street with St Giles Church, Wrexham'. An oil painting by Louise Rayner, c.1870. [Grosvenor Museum, Chester]
This detailed 'social' painting gives an image of a busy street that has seen better days. Visible in the picture are the Nag's Head public house and brewery, The Green Steps (leading up to Temple Row and the Church), the southern end of Yorke Street, a barber's shop and a tin-smith's wares offered for sale on the wall of his home (right).

the rear is a photograph taken at the end of the 19th century as the house was being demolished. The photograph was taken from the yard of the Willow Brewery.* A second photograph, taken at the same time, shows the partially demolished side of the house, viewed from the east.

Mount Place
A narrow street which ran roughly south-south-west from Mount Street through to Walker's Brewery*. The 1872 survey seems to indicate that there were no dwellings on this street.

Mount Street
The first reference to a street in this location appears in the 1562 survey when it is described as '... the road leading from the cemetery [churchyard] towards Wrexham Vaughan [Fechan]'.

The street is named after The Mount,* a house which stood nearby until demolished to make way for the Ellesmere Railway in the 1890s. The street has also been known as Love Lane and the eastern end of the street, nearest Salop Road, was known as The Green. The name Mount Street only appears to have been

Mount Street c.1935, shows the Dolphin Inn (extreme right) and the entrance to Jones Court (just to the right of the bus stop).

Mount Street c.1976.

used since the end of the 17th century. Originally, this area was one of the most sought after addresses in Wrexham with a number of substantial houses which served as town houses for some of the local gentry. At the western end of Mount Street were the steps leading up to Temple Row* and the Parish Church.* On the eastern corner of the junction with Yorke Street* stood the Union Vaults* (now an Indian restaurant) with the White Lion Inn,* the Dolphin Inn,* the Cross Keys* and the Goat Inn* on the corner with Eagle Street.* The Anchor Inn* faced Mount Street from the junction of Caia Road.* On the south side of the street (from west to east) were the Nag's Head Inn,* Mount Street House,* The Mount,* The Office* and Carnarvon Hall.*

Mount Street House, Mount Street
Located on the eastern side of the Nag's Head* in Mount Street, this property was first recorded in the rate books in 1699 when it was occupied by Ellis Lloyd of Pen-y-Lan. The Lloyd family later let the property and among their tenants were: James Mytton (1724–37); Mrs Mytton (1737–49); George Ravenscroft (1750–65); the Revd John Lloyd, curate of the Parish Church; the Revd John Yale (resident in 1793); George Kenyon of Cefn Park* (resident 1797). In 1782, the house was bought by John Jones and, on his death it passed to his son William. By 1808, it was owned by Samuel Jones. whose son, John, a surgeon, ran his medical practice from the house until his death in 1824. His widow remained in residence until her death some twenty years later and the house was bought by William Rowe (formerly of the White House, Bersham). Rowe was married to Margaret Elizabeth and died on 22 November 1873; there is a brass plaque in his memory in the Parish Church.

During the late 19th century the property was taken over by F.W. Soames & Co,* brewers, and used as the offices for the Nag's Head Brewery.* Various alterations were made to it during the 20th century before the site was cleared during the redevelopment of Mount Street in the 1980s.

The house was of brick construction with some decorative stone features. It was not symmetrical, having the front door on the right hand side, nearest the Nag's Head. The Hearth Tax assessment showed that the house had 12 hearths.

Murless, Charles Herbert *local politician*
Born in Canterbury in 1854, Charles Murless came to Wrexham in 1864 with his father, John Barnard Murless. The family resided at Bryn Offa.* He was educated at the Groves School* and was apprenticed to a London wine merchant before returning to Wrexham and joining his father who was the proprietor of the Wynnstay Arms Hotel.* He was elected to WBC in 1869, representing the South Ward, and became Mayor in 1894–95 (his father had been Mayor in 1871 and 1883). He retired from civic affairs in about 1901. He was responsible for the purchase of the old Willow Brewery* for use as the Council Depot.

Charles Murless became a Justice of the Peace on the Wrexham Bench in 1899. In addition to his own business at the Wynnstay Arms Hotel, he was also a director of the Wrexham Gas Company (eventually chairman), chairman of the Wrexham Steam Laundry and, in the will of John Jones* of Island Green Brewery,* is referred to as a 'railway agent'. He was a passionate supporter of horse racing in Wrexham and became chairman of the Board of Guarantors of Wrexham Races and a steward of the Pony and Galloway Society. A keen and talented footballer, he captained Wrexham against Druids in the inaugural Welsh Cup Final* of 1878, which Wrexham won 1–0. It is not surprising, therefore, that the Wynnstay Arms Hotel features so prominently in the early history of football in Wales. Murless was a breeder of greyhounds and a keen hare courser. He was also the chairman of the Trustees of the William and John Jones Charity.*

Murless married Miss Susannah Harriet Peate of Pentreclawdd, Oswestry in 1878 (the niece of John Jones* of Grove Lodge*) and they had one son and two daughters (she died in 1940). In 1881 they were living at Nº 37 Wrexham Fechan. They moved to live at Bersham Hall* in 1898, then Plas Power Home Farm (1902), Plas Tirion* (Sontley Road) and finally to Nº 1 Belgrave Road. On 25 November 1938, he was knocked over by a motor van while walking along Ruabon Road, fracturing his arm and receiving some minor facial injuries but was discharged home from hospital the same day. His condition deteriorated, however, and he was re-admitted only to die in hospital on 27 November. He is buried in Wrexham Cemetery.* He was the brother of Elizabeth Edisbury and Emilia Sophia Murless.

Murless, John Barnard *local politician*
Born *c.*1829 in Taunton, Somerset, John Barnard Murless seems to have moved around the country quite frequently as a young man. His wife Clara Amelia was born in London and their son Charles* was born in Canterbury (she died in 1883). He moved to Wrexham in 1864 from Fermoy in County Cork and became the licensee and tenant of the Wynnstay Arms Hotel* where he remained until retiring in 1888. In later life he resided at Bryn Offa.*

Elected a Tory councillor onto WBC, he served as Mayor in 1871 and in 1883 and was a member of the Wrexham School Board. He retired in 1888 and died at his home on 18 December the same year and is buried in Wrexham Cemetery.*

Murless & Loxham Brewery
Located in the Wynnstay Arms Hotel in 1881.* It had originally traded under the name of J.B. Murless, Jun.

Music Hall, The Henblas Street
Following the refusal of the proprietors of the Town Hall* to allow the Liberals to use the building for a lecture, a group of prominent local Liberals combined to build the Music Hall in about 1853 as a place where lectures and meetings could be freely held. It was built alongside the old Grammar School* and behind the Chester Street Congregational Chapel* with its main entrance facing onto Henblas Street.* By 1864, the requirements for the building appear to have declined and it was let to the *Wrexham Advertiser** who eventually bought the property. It was here that Wrexham Council held its first meeting after the incorporation of the Borough in 1857. (See photograph of Henblas Street)

Myddelton, Mary
Born in 1688 at Chirk Castle, the daughter of Sir Richard Myddelton. When her bachelor brother succeeded to the estate and title she acted as his hostess. When he died of smallpox in London the estate passed to a cousin and Mary was obliged to leave Chirk and she rented Croesnewydd Hall* where she lived until her death in 1747. She contributed money to the local churches, most notably Minera Chapel (now Minera Church). There is a fine memorial to Mary Myddelton by the sculptor Roubilliac in the Parish Church.

Following the death of her mother in 1694, Mary had been cared for by her cousin the Revd Thomas Lloyd. In later years he lived at her property Plas Power and, on her death, his son William inherited the estate. When William died the Plas Power estate passed to his son-in-law Thomas Fitzhugh of Marylebone, a director of the East India Company. Their descendants still reside at Plas Power today.

Myers, John Joel *local politician*
Born in Liverpool on 21 April 1921, John Myers was a member of an Anglo-Welsh family with strong roots in the Vale of Clwyd. He was educated at Townsend Lane School. In 1934, the family moved to live in Pentre Glyn and, later, the Old Vicarage, Llandegla. He joined the North Wales Power Company in March 1937, working in consumer accounts but left in 1940 when he volunteered for service with the RAF. Qualifying as a flying controller, with the rank of sergeant, he was stationed in Iceland and various stations in Britain before being posted to RAF Wrexham* in 1943. De-mobilised in January 1946, he rejoined the North Wales Power Company (later MANWEB) and worked at Rhostyllen and Chester, ultimately becoming the Revenue Superintendent for the North Wales area. He retired in September 1981.

John Myers was elected as a Conservative member of WBC, representing Wat's Dyke Ward, in 1970 (winning the seat by the narrow margin of only four votes). In the same year he was elected to represent Wat's Dyke ward on Clwyd County Council where he was chairman of the Social Services Development Committee and the Records Advisory Committee. He became Mayor of Wrexham in 1979.

He married (1) Mabel Lily in 1946, but she died in January 1948, and (2) Glenys in November 1953. He lives in Croes Eneurys, Wrexham. He is the brother of Sir Philip Myers.*

Myers, Kt, OBE, QPM, DL, **Sir Philip Alan** *police officer*
Born in Liverpool on 7 February 1931, the son of John and Catherine Myers, Philip Myers was brought up in Pentre Glyn, Llandegla and Gresford and attended Grove Park School.

On leaving school he completed two years National Service (1949–50) in the RAF before joining the Shropshire Constabulary in 1950. He transferred to the West Mercia Police in 1967 and became Deputy Chief Constable of the Gwynedd Constabulary in 1968. In 1970 he was appointed Chief Constable of the North Wales Police (the youngest man to head any of the UK police forces), a position he held until 1981. In 1982, he became HM Inspector of Constabulary for the North West Region. He was awarded the Queen's Police Medal and created a member of the Order of St John of Jerusalem in 1972, awarded an OBE in 1977, appointed a Deputy Lieutenant of Clwyd in 1983 and knighted in 1985.

He married Hazel Gittings in 1951, has two sons and lives in Colwyn Bay. He is the brother of John Joel Myers.*

N

Nag's Head, Mount Street
The earliest reference to this property is in 1742, when, according to Palmer,* it was described as a house in the occupation of Samuel Davies. Whether it was licensed at that

The Nag's Head Brewery, c.1850. The sign above the office door (right) reads: 'William Rowlands & Son, Offices, Nag's Head Brewery'. Although the perspective leaves much to be desired, this appears to be a very accurate depiction of the actual buildings.

Poster advertising F. W. Soames & Company's brewery, Tuttle Street. The scale of the picture has been grossly exaggerated and the north side of Mount Street omitted in order to give the impression of a much larger brewery, dominating even the Parish Church.

time is not recorded, although it would seem unlikely. Certainly, by the early 19th century, the property was being used as a public house and was sold in 1834 and formed the basis of the Nag's Head Brewery.* Shown in the 1833 survey and, as the Nag's Head Vaults, in the 1872 survey. [DRO/976]

Nag's Head Brewery, Mount Street
Developed as a major brewery following the purchase of the Nag's Head* public house by William Rowland* in 1834. He and his son Thomas* (Mayor of Wrexham), expanded the business before it was sold to Henry Aspinall for £46,300 in the 1870s. Aspinall went into partnership with William Overton,* a Wrexham wine merchant, to form the Wrexham Brewery Company in 1874 and won first prize for his beer in London the following year. He had ambitious plans to expand the brewery into the area below the Parish Church* but met a great deal of local opposition and was declared bankrupt in 1879 with debts of £50,000. The business (which included six public houses) was then bought by Arthur Soames, a brewer from Newark, who appointed his son Frederick* (later Mayor of Wrexham) as manager. In the years which followed, the brewery grew considerably and a new building was constructed between Tuttle Street* and the Parish Church which was soon the largest brewery in Wrexham.

A new brewhouse (which incorporated an earlier 19th century building) was built on Mount Street, at the foot of the steps leading to the Parish Church, and opened in 1920. The top floor of this building was used as a malt store and the third floor was where the malt was screened (to remove the dust), lightly crushed. The malt then passed to the second floor where it was mixed with hot liquor to make a mash and then allowed to stand for about an hour when the 'sweet wort' was drawn off and pumped back up to the third floor where it was placed in a 'copper' (of which there were three). Sugar solution was then added to the wort and the mixture boiled for up to two hours when the liquid was separated from the hops and cooled before being stored in a fermenting vessel (of which there were 20) for three days. The beer was then pumped under Tuttle Street to the tank rooms at the rear of the Nag's Head where it was stored at just above freezing point for several days before being filtered and sent out to the pubs. Beer for bottling was transported by tanker to the company's bottling plant on Holt Road.

F.W. Soames became a private company in 1931 under the direction of Major Evelyn Soames and John Rankin but, two months later, 27 June 1931, it merged with Island Green Brewery* and Dorsett Owen of Oswestry to form Border Breweries.*

In 1936, the company bought S.K. Williams of Colwyn Bay, manufacturers and retailers of soft drinks. This developed into an off-licensing business centred on the old Island Green Brewery.*

The Border Bottling Store on Holt Road (now the site of the Border Retail Park) was bought by the company in 1951, having originally been built as a clothing factory. Here the beer was stored, chilled, carbonated, filtered and sterilised before being bottled. In addition to its own beer, Border also bottled the products of other breweries, most notably Guinness, handling

7,200 bottles per hour. Next to the bottling plant stood a £250,000 soft drinks plant which was built in the 1960s to accommodate a plant which had previously been located on Salop Road.

The Board of Directors of Border Breweries in 1931 were: F.O.J. Huntlet (chairman, 1931–44); F.E. Soames (chairman, 1945–63); G.A.S. Mowat; M.C.D. Cordeaux; J.T. Rankin. In 1981, shortly before the company was taken over by Marstons, the directors were: A.W. Gaade (chairman, 1978–84); J. Hatton; W.C. Howell; R. Formstone; J.A. Huntley; J.D.C. Jardine; P.E. Gough; R.M. Martineau.

Border Breweries was taken over by Marstons Brewery in 1984.

Nailers' Yard, Brook Street
Named after the occupation of many of the residents, Nailers' Yard was located on the south side of Brook Street* in the area that later became known as Mary Ann Square* and was later part of the site of the Odeon Cinema. Not to be confused with Naylor's Yard.*

Nant-y-Ffrith Hall, Bwlchgwyn
This house was built in the mid 19th century as a hunting lodge for a Liverpool merchant, Thomas Fry, who almost immediately sold it to another Liverpudlian buinessman by the name of Peek, in 1851. In 1863 it was sold to Richard Venables Kyrke, a local landowner and industrialist, who enlarged it during the 1880s. Kyrke had been born in the parish of Gresford and had previously lived at Pendwyll Cottage, Gresford and Stansty Lodge.* It was reputedly used as a munitions and storage facility. The house and outbuildings were demolished at the end of the 1940s.

Nant-y-Ffrith.

Naylor's Yard, Pentre Felin
Located on the south side of Pentre Felin,* opposite the retail premises forming part of the Island Green* development, close to what is now Pierce's Square.* At the rear of the square, furthest away from Pentre Felin, was the site of the Welsh Calvinistic Methodists' chapel* from 1797 until 1821 when they moved to Abbot Street. According to Palmer, Naylor's Yard was separated from Pentre Felin by a house/shop which had once provided accommodation for the chapel's visiting preachers. Not to be confused with Nailers' Yard*.

Napier Square
This took its name from Napier Street* which was one of several streets that were demolished to make room for this late 1960s public housing development.

The impressive stables at Nant-y-Ffrith.

Napier Street
Napier Street appears to have been laid out by 1895 but plans from that date do not show any houses having actually been built. The street, along with several others, was demolished to make way for the Napier Square public housing development.

The names of the streets in this area all have nautical links (e.g. Nelson and Trafalgar) so it would seem highly likely that this street was named after Admiral Sir Charles Napier (1786–1860).

National Eisteddfod of Wales
A Festival of Bards, a forerunner of the National Eisteddfod, was held in the Town Hall, Wrexham in 1820. The Chair was won by the bard Nantglyn with an ode on the death of King George III and Ieuan Glan Geirionydd received the Silver Medal.

Wrexham's first National Eisteddfod of Wales was held in a Pavilion erected off Hill Street (at the rear of the present day Little Theatre) in 1876. In that year the chaired bard was Taliesin o Eifion who had unfortunately died on the day that he submitted his entry. As a consequence of this the 1876 Eisteddfod became known as *Eisteddfod y Gadair Ddu* (the Black Chair Eisteddfod) after the black cloth that was draped over the vacant Chair, a procedure which was repeated at Birkenhead in 1917. The 1876 Eisteddfod made a surplus of £63.

The National Eisteddfod returned to Wrexham in 1888 when the Pavilion was erected on land belonging to Roseneath,* immediately to the north of Grove Park House,* probably the site of the present day Dental Centre* and Nightingale House Hospice.* This event was attended by W.E. Gladstone, the Liberal Prime Minister. This second Wrexham National Eisteddfod made a surplus of £530.

Workmen delivering the stones to Bodhyfryd for the Gorsedd Circle for the 1932 declaration ceremony of the National Eisteddfod.

The National Eisteddfod of Wales, 1876. The Chair is draped in black to signify the death of the Bard Taliesin o Eifion. The figure standing to the left of the Chair is the Archdruid of Wales, Hwfa Môn. The actual Chair from this Eisteddfod is on display in the Wrexham Library & Arts Centre. The photograph is taken in front of N⁰ 1 Grosvenor Road.

The National Eisteddfod returned to Wrexham in 1912. The 1911 Proclamation was held in the grounds of Llwyn Isaf* (now the Library and Arts Centre Car Park). When David Lloyd George, the Chancellor of the Exchequer, visited the Eisteddfod he was stoned by a group of suffragettes. Both the Chair and the Crown were won by Dr T.H. Parry Williams. The surplus at this Eisteddfod was £1,090.

The 1933 National Eisteddfod was held in The Parciau, the Proclamation Ceremony of 1932 having been held in the school fields at Grove Park School (now the site of Wrexham Police Divisional Headquarters*) where the Gorsedd Stones were erected. These were later removed by William Aston* and re-used as part of the rock garden at Acton Park.

The 1977 National Eisteddfod was held on Borras Airfield, the Proclamation Ceremony of 1976 having taken place on 3 July in Acton Park* where the Gorsedd Stones (provided by Tarmac Roadstone Ltd from Minera Quarry) still form a major feature. The Eisteddfod Chair was presented by the Rotary Club of Wrexham.*

Wrexham formally invited the National Eisteddfod to come to the town in 1904 and in 1923 but the offers were declined on both occasions. The National Eisteddfod is, however, due to return in 2011 when the Wrexham and District National Eisteddfod will be held on the land at Lower Berse Farm, just off the Ruthin Road. The proclamation ceremony for the 2011 Eisteddfod was held on Llwyn Isaf, Wrexham on 3 July 2010.

National Schools, Beast Market
See Dame Dorothy Jeffreys School.

National School, Tenters Square
The National School for girls (and infants) was opened in 1817/19 and was located on the site now occupied by St Mary's RC School. Access to the school was by steps and a path from Pentre Felin or from Tenters Square. An internal plan of the building appears on the 1872 Survey. The school was eventually closed in 1896 and the pupils moved to St Giles School when the Tenters Square building was taken over as a Welsh school but, by 1902, most of the activities were being conducted through the medium of English.
Schoolmistresses:
    1881   Mrs Scott

National School (Infants), Hightown
The location of this school is unrecorded.
Schoolmistresses:
    1881   Mrs Rowe

Nazareth House, Hillbury Road
On 21 October 1966, Bishop Petit*opened Nazareth House for the Congregation of the Poor Sisters of Nazareth, in the house that had previously been known as Hillbury,* which they had purchased from the Crowe family. The order had been established in Bala in the early 1930s before moving to Gwynfryn, a country house outside Llanystumdwy, Gwynedd, in March 1949. They again moved, this time to Wrexham, in 1966. A modern care facility, named Plas Gwyn, was built in the grounds of Nazareth House at a cost of £215,000 (by E.W. Gittins & Sons), providing accommodation for some 65 elderly patients and 25 mothers and babies. All the funds for the building project were met through donations and legacies. It had a mother and baby unit, a nursery and a residential care unit. In danger of closure, it was taken over by Mario Kreft and re-named Hillbury House in June 2003. The last mother superior was Sister Gertrude.

Nef, Y (The Nev), High Street/Temple Row
The access to the east end of the churchyard is shown on the 1792 survey of Wrexham as Y Nef (*Trans.* heaven). The Nef was a name given to a narrow passage running from High Street to Temple Row, between the Vaults* public house and N⁰ 26 High Street. There were three houses located in the passage which were all demolished to make way for the Provincial Welsh Insurance Company* building. The 1841 census identifies three of the inhabitants as Jane Williams ('sells cakes') and Elizabeth and Phoebe Jones ('confectioners').

Nelson Family, of Acton Park
Following the death of Sir Robert A. Cunliffe in 1905, Acton Park was vacated by the Cunliffe family and the house leased to William Nelson (born 8 December 1851, the son of James and Elizabeth Nelson of Coddrinagh, Co. Kildare) until shortly before the outbreak of war in 1914. He married Margaret Hope of Garlandstown Co. Westmeath and they had three sons and five daughters. On 5 February 1912 he was created Baronet Nelson of Acton Park. He died on 7 July 1922 and the title was inherited by his eldest son, Sir James Hope Nelson (born 26 February 1883). On his death on 5 May 1960, the title passed to his nephew, Colonel Sir William Vernon Hope Nelson, OBE, (born 25 February 1914) of White House Farm, Holnest, Sherborne (died 1991) and then to Jamie Vernon Hope Nelson (born 23 October 1949).

Nelson Street, Hightown
Built in the latter years of the 19th century, this street of terraced houses was located off King's Mills Road, opposite Whitegate Road. Land on the west side (belonging to the Gatefield estate)

N⁰ˢ 58–63 Nelson Street (east side) and N⁰ 11 Bryn-y-Cabanau Road.

Neville Crescent, c.1930, looking down Bromfield Grove.

as far as Bryn-y-Cabanau Road was sold for building in June 1889 and surviving plans show that some houses had been built there by 1895. Some of the residents were re-housed by the Borough Council in 1950, many moving to the newly built houses in the area of Eaton Drive. Along with several other streets, Nelson Street was demolished during the 1960s to make way for the Napier Square* public housing development although the name was preserved in a new street. [Plans of houses DRO/1022]

The street was named after Vice Admiral Viscount Horatio Nelson (1758–1805), the hero of Trafalgar, probably the most famous and popular British sailor of all time.

N⁰ˢ 1–15 Nelson Street (west side) and N⁰ 9 Bryn-y-Cabanau Road.

Nelson Street, Rhosddu
Like its namesake, Nelson Street* in Hightown, this small street of terrace houses off Crispin Lane was named after the hero of Trafalgar. The street was located in Rhosddu and to avoid confusion its name was changed to West Street.*

Nelson's Arms Vaults, 15 Hope Street
Originally called the Ship Inn until about 1811, then the Nelson's Arms, this rather inappropriately-named public house stood on a site opposite the junction of Queen Street.* It appears in the 1833 survey. The landlord in 1855 was Timothy Parsonage.

Neville Crescent
Laid out in the early 1920s as part of the first phase of the Acton Park housing estate,* this crescent was named after Sir Robert Neville Cunliffe, Bt,* of Acton Hall,* who had owned the land until shortly before the Acton Park Housing Estate* was built. In 1931 the open area in front of the crescent was laid out as an ornamental garden with a pond. There had previously been plans to name part of Cunliffe Street* after Neville Cunliffe.

New Hall, Ruabon
Built for Charles Myddelton of Chirk Castle at the end of the 17th century, this brick, three-storeyed house was one of the most prominent residences in the parish of Ruabon. In later years the house was clad in stone. After being leased to various tenants for a number of years, New Hall was sold by Colonel Cornwallis-West (a relative of the Myddelton family) to the industrialist Henry Dennis* in 1839. In its latter years the house was a residential home for the elderly, run by Denbighshire County Council. Located on New Hall Road, just beyond the built-up area north-east of Ruabon, it was demolished in 1950.

New Hall, Ruabon

New Llwyn Onn, Abenbury
See Llwyn Onn Hall.

New Mitre, Bath Street
This public house appears in Bath Street,* off Brook Street,* in the 1833 survey and appears to have been a new name for premises previously called 'The Queen's Head'.* It was demolished in the 1890s during the construction of the Wrexham & Ellesmere Railway.*

New Road, Rhosddu
This road was laid out following the construction of the Shrewsbury–Chester railway line in 1846. The original route of

Rhosddu Road was twice intersected by the railway, once near to Walnut Tree Farm* (where the present day railway bridge is located) and once just to the north of the Railway Inn. Prior to the building of the railway bridge, the line was crossed by means of a level-crossing a situation which proved far from satisfactory and, after a campaign of protests lasting over twenty years, this was eventually replaced with the bridge. The second breach of Rhosddu Road was neither bridged nor provided with a level-crossing. Consequently, a new road had to be built between Walnut Tree Farm and Ivy Cottage. As this section of road no longer led directly into the 'centre' of Rhosddu, it became known simply as New Road, Rhosddu.

New Swan Inn, Pen-y-Bryn
Shown in the 1833 survey.

New Union Hall
See Birmingham Square.

New Yorkshire Square
See Birmingham Square.

Newbrigg Road
Laid out in the 1920s. The origin of the name is unknown.

Newspapers
The Wrexham Recorder, was Wrexham's first newspaper. The first issue appeared in March 1848 and was published on the 1st of each month at a price of 2d for 16 pages. It ran for eleven issues to January 1849. It was founded by the printer Richard Hughes.*

The Wrexham Registrar and People's Friend (*Wrexham Registrar*) first appeared in August 1848 and went through several title changes and breaks in publication between then and 1958 when it was absorbed by the *Wrexham Leader*. It was printed and published by its proprietors, William and George Bayley* at their General Printing Office in Hope Street, Wrexham. William Bayley had founded the printing press in around 1838 but by 1846 it was being run by his son George. The paper appeared on the 1st of each month at a price of 1d for 16 pages. In March 1849 the title was shortened to the *Wrexham Registrar* and the number of pages was reduced to 12. The last issue of the original paper appeared in December 1849.

In January 1850 (although the company adverts state that it was established in 1848), George Bayley published the *Wrexham Advertiser, and Register of literary, railway, local and general information*. It was a broadsheet of 4 pages, published on the 1st of each month and priced at 1d. In January 1851 the *Wrexham Advertiser* became a fortnightly publication (appearing on the 1st and 15th) but this lasted for only four months. The *Wrexham Advertiser* ceased publication in September 1852 then restarted in March 1854 under a new title – the *Wrexham Weekly Advertiser*. By 1857 the title had become The *Wrexham and Denbighshire Weekly Advertiser, and Cheshire, Shropshire, Flintshire and North Wales Register* (*Wrexham Weekly Advertiser*) a 4 page broadsheet costing 2d.

The *Wrexham Albion*, a Conservative newspaper, was first published by James Lindop in September 1854. The following year Lindop brought out the *Anglican and Conservative Wrexhamite*. In 1856 it changed its name to the *Wrexham and Denbighshire and Flintshire Reporter* and later became the *Wrexham Telegraph and Denbighshire and Flintshire Reporter* (1857–63) and then the *Denbighshire and Flintshire Telegraph, North Shropshire and West Cheshire Reporter* before closing in February 1867.

The Conservative *Wrexham Guardian and Denbighshire and Flintshire Advertiser* was published as a weekly paper in 1869. It

Offices of the North Wales Guardian *in Argyle Street, c.1880.*

was declared bankrupt five years later and was temporarily saved by leading figures in the local Conservative Party. It was relaunched as the weekly *North Wales Guardian* in February 1879 by Frederick Edmund Roe and had offices in Argyle Street.* It remained in print until 1925.

The *Wrexham Weekly Advertiser* moved its offices to Bank Street* and in 1868 to the Music Hall* in Henblas Street.* George Bradley* became editor and part-owner with George Bayley. In 1877 it published a monthly guide – the *Wrexham Advertiser Railway, Coach and Steam Packet Guide*. George Bayley died on 12 January 1863, aged forty-two and his place was taken by his widow Selina, in trust for their children. Charles George Bayley, her brother-in-law, joined the company at this time.

The newspaper changed its title several times from the *Wrexham and Denbighshire Weekly Advertiser and Cheshire, Shropshire, Flintshire and North Wales Register* (January 1857) to the *Wrexham and Denbighshire Advertiser and Cheshire, Shropshire, Flintshire and North Wales Register* (August 1857). In December 1858 the word Flintshire was dropped from the title and in February 1863 it reverted to the *Wrexham Advertiser and Denbighshire, Cheshire, Shropshire and North Wales Register*. A month later the word Shropshire was dropped. By 1864 the title again included 'Shropshire' and 'Flintshire' and six years later 'Merionethshire' was added. In September 1880 it became the *Wrexham Advertiser and North Wales News*.

The *Wrexham Trader*, a weekly free sheet which circulated in the first quarter of the 20th century, was published by Woodhall, Minshall & Thomas.

The *Wrexham Star* was established by Colenso Fletcher after the First World War and published from an office on Town Hill. Following his death in 1925, the paper was produced by his son, Charles (Chris) Hardy Fletcher (of Fletcher & Westall Ltd), and published at the Abbot Press in Abbot Street until the mid 1930s when it was bought by the *Wrexham Leader* and merged with the *Wrexham Advertiser*.

The first issue of the weekly *Wrexham Leader* was published by Messrs Woodhall, Minshall and Thomas of the Border Press, Egerton Street, on 10 January 1920, with offices at The Principality Press in Caxton Place.* In 1945 it took over *Yr Adsain* and the *Llangollen Chronicle*. The newspaper's offices in Caxton Place* were gutted by fire in June 1949. In 1958, a second paper was published on Tuesdays, replacing the *Wrexham Advertiser and Star* (which had been launched by the *Wrexham Leader* in April 1953 as a weekly). The *Wrexham Leader* moved to Centenary Buildings, King Street* in February 1974.

Editors:

1920	George Lerry
1948	Harold Lewis
1950	Glyn Griffiths
1962	H.A. (Tony) Lloyd
1980	Reg Herbert (MBE 2002, for services to journalism)
1989	Barrie Jones

The *Wrexham Evening Leader* was first published in October 1973, as a weekday, evening paper. In 2010, the paper became a daily morning newspaper.

The *Wrexham Gazette* was published by Selwyn Mattox, a director of Woodhall's Newspapers, on 9 November 1967 and continued in publication until 1971.

The *Wrexham Journal* was published by Jarman & Sons in Argyle Street until the mid 1950s.

The *Wrexham Express* was first published on 25 September 1980, the *Wrexham Advertiser* was reserected (without the suffix *& Star*) in April 1988 and the *Wrexham Mail* was published from 5 February 1988 until 7 July 1995 and the name was revived by the Chronicle Group of newspapers in the late 1990s.

Further details on the early newspapers can be found in the *Transactions of the Denbighshire Historical Society*, Vol 47 (1998).

Newton Street, Hightown
Named after Hurst Newton, Bersham Road the home of W.N. Capper, who did much to develop this area of the town in the early 20th century.

Newtown
This is an unofficial name given to the area of Wrexham which was developed on both sides of Bradley Road during the latter part of the 19th century and, in addition to Bradley Road itself, included Watery Road, Jubilee Road, Bellevue Road, Bright Street, Villiers Street, Cobden Street, Peel Street, Gibson Street, Poyser Street, Hampden Road, Edward Street, Alexandra Road, Empress Street, Princess Street and part of Bersham Road.

Nicholson, MBE, JP, Mrs Rose, *local politician*
Born in Lodge, Brymbo, the daughter of a local farmer, Rose Roberts was educated at Brymbo Church School and Grove Park Girls School.* She became a probationary nurse at Wrexham Infirmary* before marrying Joseph Nicholson and they became licensees of the Royal Oak Inn in Long Lane; her husband died in 1944.

Rose Nicholson became a Broughton Parish Councillor in 1952 and in 1958 a Labour member of WRDC. In 1974 she was elected a member of WMBC and held the seat until her retirement. She was Mayoress to Noel Wright* in 1976 and became Mayor in 1982.

A Justice of the Peace, Rose Nicholson was awarded the MBE for her community work. She died on 18 January 1997.

Nightingale House Hospice, Chester Road
This was originally established by Dr Graham Arthurs (a consultant anaesthetist) and colleagues as a pain clinic in the Maelor Hospital in the 1970s. In the 1980s, Dr Arthur's Terminal Care Fund was set up and, with a grant from the Cancer Relief Fund, the first two Macmillan nurses were employed in the

The main entrance to the Nightingale House Hospice, one of the finest modern buildings in Wrexham. [TACP]

Wrexham area. In 1986, Nightingale House Day Hospice was opened, based at the old Nightingale Ward at the Maelor Hospital. Six years later, the Wrexham Hospice and Cancer Support Centre Foundation was launched to raise £3.5 million for a new, purpose-built hospice. The general public immediately took the project to heart and generous donations and fundraising activities, coupled with three large donations from the Brdbury Trust, the Mathias Trust and the Frank Wingett Cancer Appeal enabled work to begin on a purpose-built hospice. In 1994, Plas-yn-Llwyn*, the former nurses home on Chester Road was demolished and a new building, designed by local architectural practice TACP, was erected on the site at a cost of £2.2 million. The new unit offered specialist palliative care service for patients with specific life-limiting illness in north-east Wales and the border area. The building was officially opened in August 1995 for the use of day patients. Residential patients were admitted for the first time in November 1995. In 2010, the hospice has 16 beds for in-patients and caters for 15 day-care patients. The hospice receives statutory funding for 20% of its running costs, the remainder of the annual £2.4 million (2010) running costs are raised by voluntary donations and fundraising projects.

General Manager
  1995 Duncan Miller
Chief Executive
  2005 John Savage
Matron
  1995 Lynda Johnson
        Tracey Livingstone
Director of Nursing & Patient Services
        Tracy Livingstone

Nine Acre Field, Chester Road
Formerly part of the Acton Park* estate, the area of land which now comprises the Nine Acre Field was known as Erw Clai (*Trans.* clay acre) in the 19th century. After the First World War the field was bought by WBC and let to W. H. Jones of Park Farm.* It was bought by the governors of Grove Park School in November 1950 to allow for the building of a pavilion and the laying out of two rugby pitches, two soccer pitches, a cricket field, a running track and two jumping pits.

Norden, John *surveyor*
Commissioned in 1620 (along with his son John), by Charles,

Prince of Wales, to survey all of the prince's property, John Norden was given

> authorite to survey, inquire, and finde out, Aswell by the oaths of good and lawfull Men or Tennauntes, and others, as by the relation, examinacon, Depositions & Testimony of or under Steward or understewards Bayliffs Reeves, and other ministers, Tennants, occupiers and persons whatsoever As also by other means and waies Whatsoever, by wch you may best knowe and findout ye truth in that behalf All that or Lordshipp of Bromfield and Yale, with all ye rightes members and uppur-tenancies thereof in the Countie of Denbigh or elsewhere belonging to the said Lordshipp and all and Singular, Castles Houses edifices buildings, Milles landes Tenements, feedings, pastures, parkes, woods underwoods waters fishinges piscaries, void groundes, furzes, heathes, Moores Marishes Commons proffitts Commodites and hereditaments whatsoever in the saide Countie.

This is the earliest surviving survey of the town of Wrexham and is held in the British Museum.
[Harlean MS 3696. DRO/DD/WY/8959]

Norfolk Road, Borras Park
Laid out in the early 1960s, this was the main thoroughfare through the new Borras Park* estate developed by William Clarke* of Oak Lodge* on land that had once been part of the Acton Park* estate.

Norman Road
This street was developed during the 1890s (and adopted by the Council in 1898) following the sale of the old Beechley and Kingsland estates, once the property of the Bennion family of Beechley House. It was named after the Norman dynasty of monarchs who reigned from 1066–1154.

Normandy Veterans Association Memorial
The memorial to the Normandy Veterans was unveiled on Bodhyfryd (to the rear of the RWF Memorial) in 1994.

North & South Wales Bank
In 1762, Banc-y-Llong, (*Trans.* the ship bank) probably the first commercial bank in Wales, opened in Aberystwyth. In 1790, Sankey & Company (later to become the North Wales Bank) was formed in Holywell, followed by Douglas, Smalley & Company in 1822. Fourteen years later, the North & South Wales Bank was established with a head office in Liverpool but aimed at providing a modern banking service for the whole of Wales. Very quickly, they set about opening a network of branches through the principality and immediately took over the business of both Banc-y-Llong and the North Wales Bank. By 1839, it had swallowed up Douglas, Smalley & Co. A Wrexham branch of this bank was established at Nº 43 High Street in 1843 (later referred to as Old Bank Buildings). In 1860 this branch moved into the ground floor of the Provincial Welsh Insurance Building* in High Street (shown on the 1872 survey) before moving shortly afterwards into new, purpose-built premises on the opposite side of High Street. In 1908, the North & South Wales Bank merged with the London City & Midland Bank Ltd and it was as the Midland Bank that it traded until 1992 when it became part of the Hong Kong and Shanghai Banking Corporation, eventually changing its name to HSBC in 1999. The building ceased to be a bank in 2001 when HSBC moved to new premises in Regent Street. The building was then acquired by Wetherspoons who converted it into the Thomas Hampson public house in 2001. There was a plaque on the outside wall of the High Street premises to record the origins of the building. The name of the public house has now been changed to the North & South Wales Bank.

North-East Wales Institute
The North-East Wales Institute (NEWI) was formed in September 1975 by joining together the Denbighshire Technical College,* Wrexham, the Flintshire Technical College, Kelsterton and Cartrefle College,* Wrexham. The new college was aiming to become a college of Higher Education and gradually transferred its Further Education courses to other tertiary colleges in the region (Kelsterton College in Deeside and Yale College* in Wrexham). In April 1993 NEWI became an incorporated college of Higher Education and all Wrexham based HE courses became centralised at the Plas Coch site by 1995. A major building programme was commenced in the 1990s which included a new library, sports centre and teaching facilities. In 2003, the institute became a university sector college of the University of Wales and, five years later, was granted its own charter, becoming Glyndŵr University.

Principals:
1975–92	Professor Gwyn O. Phillips
1992–00	Professor John Williams
2001	Professor Michael Scott

North Wales Mineral Railway
A railway line linking Chester, Wrexham and Ruabon had been considered as early as 1839 with George Stephenson as chief engineer. The purpose behind building a railway line was to transport coal from the mines of north-east Wales to Chester – under the pre-railway system coal was transported to Pontcysyllte where it was loaded onto canal boats and taken to Chester via Ellesmere, Whitchurch and Nantwich, a journey of over 70 miles. The plans, however, did not come to fruition and were brought to an end by the economic depression of the time.

As soon as the economy began to pick up the project was revived and plans were made for the laying of a line linking Wrexham, through the Moss valley, Caergwrle and Kinnerton to Chester but such was the opposition of the local landowners that they were abandoned. A new scheme was advocated the following year by Henry Robertson* which linked Chester to Wrexham, without a link to the industrial area west of Wrexham. Robertson proposed that the railway should have a terminus in Wrexham, close to Bryn-y-Ffynnon* (on the site of the present day Island Green Shopping Centre). Despite opposition, this scheme was passed through Parliament on 6 August 1844 and on 30 August, the North Wales Mineral Railway Company held its first general meeting in London.

The line was to be single-tracked but sufficient land was to be bought for a second track to be laid if required. In addition, all bridges were built to accommodate two tracks. Almost immediately, proposals were considered to extend the line towards Brymbo in the west and Ruabon in the south. A public meeting was held in Wrexham on 24 October where people who had supported a line terminating in Wrexham objected to a line continuing towards Ruabon, believing that any advantages which the town might benefit from the original plan would be dissipated by the extensions. In a masterly speech, Henry Robertson convinced the doubters that the town could only benefit from an expansion of the railway network to draw in all its industrial hinterland, and opposition faded away. Seven days later, the company approved the extension of the line from Wrexham to Ruabon and announced their intention to further extend to Cefn Mawr, Rhosrobin, Gwersyllt, Stansty, Broughton, Brymbo and Minera. The North Wales Mineral Railway extension Bill was passed and the railway established in 1846 linking Chester to Wrexham (General Station*), Wheatsheaf

Junction (Gwersyllt) with the Moss Valley, Brymbo and Minera, through two tunnels (Summerhill and Brymbo) and two rope-worked inclines, or brakes (Gwersyllt and Moss). Before the line could be completed to Ruabon, the company had merged with the Shrewsbury, Oswestry & Chester Junction Railway Company to form the Shrewsbury & Chester Railway Company.* The section from the Wheatsheaf to the Moss valley closed in October 1908; the Brymbo line closed in the early 1950s and the Minera branch in 1972. (See also Acts of Parliament relating to Wrexham)

Northwood, Borras Park
A small cul-de-sac of private houses developed c.1967 by the London firm of Spinks & Denning on land that had previously belonged to William Clarke* and, pre-1918, to the Acton Park* estate. The name has no particular significance.

Nythfa, Grosvenor Road
In 1898 the house was sold and John Francis moved to Ivy Grove on Grove Road which he re-named Nythva.* The house was originally Nº 5 Grosvenor Road.

Nythva, Grove Road
The land on which this house stands was originally part of the Grove Park* estate. Wrexham builder Gwilt Cathrall bought the plot (1,008 square yards) from Thomas James Ollerhead, a surgeon of Minehead in Somerset for £350 in 1880. He immediately built the house which bears the date stone 1881 above the front door and appears to have lived in it himself, calling it Ivy Grove. In 1898, the house was sold to John Francis (formerly of Nythfa,* Grosvenor Road*) for £1,365 and the name was changed to Nythva, with the English 'v' replacing the Welsh 'f'. Francis died and in 1922 his widow (Sarah) and daughter (Enid Glyn Watts) sold the house to John Johnstone, a draper, of 20 King Street.* It was again sold in 1939 to Raymond and Kathleen Gill (he was the colliery agent at Gresford Colliery*) of Longfields, Sontley Road, for £1,300. In 1961, the house was bought by Dr Thomas Anthony M‘Givern. The house was originally Nº 5 Grove Road and is a Grade II listed building.

O

Oak, The, High Street
This 18th century public house was formerly the premises of the Wrexham clockmaker, Thomas Hampson.* It stood on the site now occupied by the Market Hall.* In the 1833 survey it is shown as the *Old Royal Oak*.

Oak Drive, Acton Park
Laid out in 1920 as part of the first phase of the Acton Park housing estate,* it was extended in the 1930s as far as Oswald Way* and The Laurels* and again in the 1960s to link up with Herbert Jennings Avenue.*

Oak Lodge, Dean Close
An interesting house for which little or no early history has survived. In 1870, it was the home of Mortimer Morris and in 1881, Henry Humphreys, a solicitor with a practice at Nº 4 Temple Row. In the early years of the 20th century it was the home of Cameron Davies. In 1907, it became the home of T.A. Acton, the noted local archaeologist who excavated the Roman site at Holt. In c.1925, it became the house of Wrexham Mayor, William Clarke* (of Clarke Brothers, bakers & confectioners).

Oak Tree, Ruabon Road
Originally Oak Tree field which was recorded as being part of the Red House* estate in 1844. Three cottages were built facing Ruabon Road by Edward Ellis in c.1820, two of which form the basis of the present day public house. The first reference to licensed premises is in c.1900 when it was referred to as the Oak Tree Inn.

Odeon Cinema
Built on the site of the insanitary Mary Ann Square, the Odeon Cinema was part of the 'franchised' chain founded by Oscar Deutch (**O**scar **D**eutch **E**ntertainer **O**f **N**ations = ODEON) and operated by the Odeon (Wrexham) Company Ltd. Designed by the Harry Weedon Practice of Birmingham, it was built in the art-deco style with a seating capacity of 1,246 (958 in the stalls and 288 in the circle) at a cost of £28,000. The cinema was officially opened by the Mayor, Alderman Cyril Jones, on 13 March 1937.

Most of the films shown at the Odeon were supplied by the Rank Organisation. A wide screen was installed in 1950 and an even wider one five years later. In 1969, it received a £10,000 face-lift. In 1972, the loss of audiences to television resulted in the introduction of Bingo and films were relegated to three nights each week. On 15 May 1976, *The Man Who Would Be King* became the last film to be shown at the Odeon and the building became a Top Rank Bingo club until 2000 when the club moved into new premises in Smithfield Road. The last cinema manager was Malcolm Boothby.

The old Odeon premises remained empty until 2001 when they were acquired by Luminar Leisure for conversion into the Chicago Rock Café and the Liquid Club.

In 1997 a new Odeon cinema was opened on the Plas Coch Retail Park. With six screens, this was Wrexham's first purpose-built multi-screen cinema. This closed in 2009 and the cinema moved to new eight-screen premises at the eastern end of the Eagles Meadow* shopping complex.

Offa's Dyke
Controversy continues to surround the origins and purpose of Offa's Dyke, over 1200 years after it was constructed. Undisputed is the existence of Offa, the Saxon ruler of Mercia (Midlands) between 757 and 795 AD. Whether he actually built the dyke (an earth ridge extending for 149 miles from near Prestatyn in the north, via Mold, Coedpoeth, Bersham, Chirk and eventually to the sea at Chepstow in the south) is open to debate. It is generally accepted that the dyke was not a defensive feature but rather a boundary line that could not be missed between the Saxon kingdom to the east and the Welsh kingdoms to the west. It has an average height of 6 feet and a width (across the dyke and the ditch which was on the western side) of 60 feet. Ancient laws declared that any aliens found carrying arms on the wrong side of the dyke were liable to have their hand cut off and all trade (in both directions) could be regulated through the gaps or gates in the dyke. Good sections of the dyke can be seen alongside the footpath linking Bersham with Nant Mill and again in the grounds of Chirk Castle.

Office, The, Mount Street
The Office was a large stone and timber residence on the south side of Mount Street* between the Mount* and the junction with Salop Road.* It was first recorded in the rate books in 1663 where it was described as 'the house where the office is kept'. By 1665, it was the residence of Maj Francis Manley (later Sir Francis) of Manley Hall, Erbistock who probably used it as his town house at a date when Mount Street was regarded as a fashionable address amongst the local gentry. During the latter part of the 17th and early 18th centuries, the house was occupied by Kenrick

The Office, Mount Street. A painting by John Ingleby, c.1800. [NLW/S948]

Eyton of Eyton Isaf, Bangor-is-y-coed, as a tenant, and he was followed by his son Gerard, a Wrexham attorney, who died in the house in 1715. His widow, Anne, married John Travers of Wrexham and the house came into his possession. Travers, a Presbyterian, had been trained as a lawyer, but appears to have drifted into the drapery business and by 1717 (the time of his second marriage) was one of the wealthiest men in the town. Eventually, he became agent for the Trefalyn Hall Estate and steward of the manor of Marford and Hoseley. At the time of his death in 1748 he was resident in Trefalyn Hall. During the latter years of John Travers' life, the Office was let to various people: 1731 – Dr Rossendale Lloyd, son of Foulk Lloyd of Foxhall, Denbighshire and Aston, Shropshire; 1734–44 – Thomas Kyffyn of Maenan (the son of Sir Thomas Kyffyn) an attorney and the owner of Bryn Estyn and Perth-y-Bi, Wrexham; 1769–80 – Revd John Yale of Plas yn Iâl, Bryneglwys; 1781–1800 – Mrs Newton. By 1800, Samuel Kenrick of The Bank, Wrexham, is recorded as the owner of the property (possibly of Kenrick & Bowman's Bank*) and he divided the house into two dwellings. The last recorded resident was John Parry, a maltster and churchwarden at the Parish Church (died 1810). Shortly after this time the house was demolished and consequently does not appear on any of the detailed maps of the town produced during the 19th century. The best illustration of this house is by Ingleby and is held in the collection of the National Library of Wales, Aberystwyth.

Old Home Tenement/Farm, Borras
Bought by Ellis Yonge of Acton Park* in 1750 from John Thomas and his wife, this smallholding was detailed in the 1786 survey of the Acton Park estate. It was in two parts, located on the north side of Barker's Lane (opposite the Royal Observer Corps* headquarters) and on the east side of Borras Road (on the site of RAF Wrexham*). The field names were: Home Croft, Cae Hir (*Trans.* long field), Cae Buchan (*Trans.* little field), Higher Wood Fields, Vron (*Trans.* ridge or crest of a hill), Cae Pwll-y-ronen (*Trans.* field of the ash-tree pool), Cae Glas (*Trans.* green field), Herdyard Dwr (*Trans.* ? water), Lower Wood Fields.
[FRO/D/AH/24]

Old Hop Pole, Yorke Street
It seems unlikely that any public house existed which bore this name and that the adjective 'Old' was merely applied to a premises where the business operating under the name Hop Pole* had been moved elsewhere.

Old King's Head, 26 Hope Street
See King's Head (I).

Old Llwyn Onn
Located to the south of Cefn Road, opposite the junction with Red Wither Lane, this was, since the Middle Ages, the home of the Jones-Parry family who had once owned most of the township of Abenbury as well as lands in neighbouring parishes. By the early 17th century their estate had been reduced to less than 600 acres. In 1714 a first mention is made in the rate books of 'New' Llwyn Onn* which would suggest that a second house had been built in the area, leaving the original house to be known as 'Old' Llwyn Onn. In 1881, it was a farm of 150 acres in the tenancy of Evan Jones.

Old Maids' Farm, Rhosnesni
This farm was located in the village of Rhosnesni, to the south-east of Holt Road shortly before the Greyhound public house. The property was offered for sale in October 1849 when it was described as: 'All that Messuage or Tenement, Out-buildings, Gardens, and Farm Land, called 'The Old Maid's', situate at Rhosnesney, in the Township of Acton, in the said Parish of Wrexham, in the occupation of Mr Michael McLevie, and containing 23a 2r 30p or thereabouts'. At this time the field names were given as: Garden Field, Long Croft, Lane Field, Middle Croft, Cae Fynnon, Middle Field, Holloa Lane Field, Far Field and Plantation. It was again sold in January 1920 (31.7 acres) for £2,200 when the accommodation comprised: a sitting room, living room, back kitchen, dairy, combined wash and bake house, four bedrooms and a box room. The farmhouse had a cowshed and pig sty extending from its north-east wall. In the early 1970s the pig sty and part of the cowshed were demolished and the house extended to provide two, linked dwellings. In 1999, the remaining section of the former cowshed was demolished, thereby creating two detached houses, N°s 196 & 198 Holt Road). [DRO/DD/CP/840 & DRO/DD/G/2892]

Old Mitre, Pentre Felin
Shown in the 1833 survey as being on the site of the present day Mitre public house.

Old Registry, Chester Street
According to Palmer* the earliest record of a house existing on this site is 1727 when a property is described in the rate books as 'Mr R[ichar]d Jones' new house'. It was the residence of Dr Apperley – the father of Charles James Apperley* – from c.1740 until his death in 1772 when John Matthews, attorney-at-law, became the owner (his daughter married Sir Roger William Palmer, Bt,* thereby bringing that family to her home at Cefn Park*). In 1826 it became the home of Thomas Taylor Griffith, FRCS,* a noted local surgeon. In the early years of the 20th century this building housed the St Giles' Home for Children which later moved to Little Acton House and then, in 1915 to St Giles' Home* on Rhosnesni Lane. (Mr & Mrs Knight were master and matron at Chester Street). During the First World War the house was used, until April 1919, to accommodate Belgian refugees from Antwerp and Malines. Sometime after 1921, the office of the Registrar of Births Marriages and Deaths moved here from Temple Row, hence the building's current name. The Registrar moved to Grosvenor Road in October 1978 and the house is now the premises of Messrs Walker, Smith & Way, solicitors. The building is Grade II listed.

Old Raven Inn, Hope Street
The name of this inn was changed to The King's Head* (see King's Head (II)) in about 1743.

Old Swan Inn, Abbot Street
Shown in the 1833 survey. The landlord in 1869 was Mr Lovatt. In 1996, this building underwent major changes in the 1990s and

re-opened as Aiden Brady's Irish Bar. The Old Swan is currently closed (2010).

Old Temperance Hotel, Bank Street
Sometimes referred to as the Old Temperance House, this property was sold in the 1850s by William Penn Allcock of Birmingham to William Bayley of Wrexham (stationer) and, by the opening years of the 20th century, was the property, ironically, of John Jones* of the Island Green Brewery.*

Old Three Tuns, Brook Street
Originally called the Pen-y-Bont, this public house first appears in the records in 1670. The current premises, on the corner of Brewery Place (Pen-y-Bont*), were built in 1896 on the site of the earlier building. It ceased trading as a public house in the 1990s and the building was bought by the British Rail Staff Association Club as new premises following the re-development of the Island Green site. The building is particularly noteworthy because of the fine painted stucco panel in the roof gable.

Old Vaults, Chester Street
Known locally as 'The Long Pull', these premises stand on the site of a substantial house recorded in 1688 as being occupied by Thomas Rosindale, gentleman. This had a large garden where Manchester Square* was built. Next to this garden, at the turn of the 18th century, Dr Rosindale built a Cockpit.* The house was turned into an inn which, in 1771, was called 'The Angel' and for a time the Post Office* was located here before being transferred to Nº 36 Chester Street sometime after 1814. At some later date (after the tithe map of 1846 had been produced) the original house was demolished and the present building, a good example of a mid-19th century public house, was built on the site.

The origin of the nickname 'The Long Pull' dates back to the time when the licensee used to give extra measure to outdoor customers in order to draw in custom from other public houses. In order to give the extra measure, a long pull was made on the beer pump. Alongside the pub, in Henblas Street, was the Lion Yard.* An advert in the 1881 *Crocker's Wrexham Directory* records the owner as being R.W. Evans whose business had been established in 1750. The Old Vaults is a Grade II listed building.

Oppenheimer's Diamond Factory
Bernard Oppenheimer (1866–1921), was a South African-British diamond merchant and philanthropist. He was chairman of Pniel's Ltd, the New Vaal River Diamond & Exploration Company, and Blaauwbosch Diamonds Ltd, and managing director of Lewis & Marks Ltd of Holborn. In 1917, he established the Bernard Oppenheimer Diamond Works (National Diamond Factories Ltd) at Lewes Road, Brighton, on 1 April 1918. This was a scheme for the training of disabled soldiers in diamond cutting. In 1920 it also opened branches in Cambridge, Fort William and Wrexham. New men were referred to the company by the Ministry of Labour and received six months training, during which they were paid a maintenance allowance by the government, and were then virtually guaranteed employment at a good wage. The Wrexham branch for the polishing of diamonds, was opened in a purpose-built factory alongside Box Lane, in Acton Park. The business, however, did not do well and closed in 1923. For his work with the disabled, Oppenheimer was created a baronet (of Stoke Poges) in the 1921 New Year Honours. He died suddenly six months later at the age of 55. By 1923, the building had been converted and opened as Acton Park School.* See also Acton Park Holdings.*

Inside Oppenheimer's diamond factory, c.1918.

Orchard Field, Regent Street
Orchard Field, as its name would suggest, was once the orchard of Bryn-y-Ffynnon House* and extended from what is now Hill Street to St Mark's Road.* In Norden's survey of 1620, it is called Maes Estome (more correctly Maes Ystum – *Trans.* the field of the river meander) and extended as far down the hill as the river Gwenfro, covering the area later called The Walks* which is Island Green* today.

Orchard Gardens, Wat's Dyke
Built in the 1990s by Harvey Homes, this small private development is sited on land that was originally intended to be part of the Garden Village Estate.*

Oswald Way, Acton Park
Laid out in 1932 as part of the second phase of the Acton Park housing estate.* This street was named after Alderman Cyril Oswald Jones.* Built by G.F. Sumner of Ashfield.*

Oteley House, Salisbury Road
Located off Bennion's Road at the rear of the Green Dragon Hotel. This has the appearance of a house designed by Wrexham architect James Reynolds Gummow* and it seems likely that it was built by him as his own home. It was later (1881) the home of William Sissons, the son of William J. Sisson, owner of the Cambrian Brewery.*

Sometime after the Second World War, the house was a hostel for working men but then became empty for two years when, on 29 September 1958, the Roman Catholic order of the Little Sisters of the Assumption established a convent there. It was in a very poor state of repair when the nuns moved in but, by 11 October, they were able to hold their first Mass in the chapel. At its height, the convent had 12 sisters, 6 nurses and 1 social worker, with 4 further sisters training at the hospital. The convent's first Mother Superior was Sister Brigid Keane. The convent closed in 1998 and the remaining nuns moved into 4 Gibson Street. The house then became the Wrexham offices of the charity Dynamics and the upper floor was occupied by Chariotts a Wrexham-based charity providing transport for the physically handicapped. In recent years, known as Bradbury House, the property has been the premises of Dynamic, a charity-funded centre for children and young persons with disabilities.

Overton Arcade
In about 1818, William Overton of Charles Street bought the premises at Nº 30 High Street to where he moved his business. He was succeeded by his widow (Elizabeth) and then his son, also named William,* and it is from this family that the arcade takes its name. Built in 1868 the Overton Arcade is a glass-

covered thoroughfare leading from High Street to Temple Row. Originally designed to have small retail premises opening out onto it, the Overton Arcade provided premises for, amongst others a hairdresser, a bookshop and a restaurant. It later declined as a retailing area and the shops were absorbed into the main buildings. During the 1980s, the owner of the arcade re-opened the small shops thereby recreating the Victorian arcade atmosphere of this often overlooked area.

Overton, William *local politician*
Born in Wrexham c.1814, William Overton was the son of William Overton, a grocer and ironmonger of High Street. William Overton (junior) was a man of many business talents and in addition to being a grocer and ironmonger, was also a wine & spirit merchant, having purchased the old Town Hall* from the Crown in 1857 in partnership with his brother-in-law, Thomas Painter*. He was elected a Tory member of WBC and served as Mayor in 1865. He and his wife Elizabeth (née Johnson, whose father had been the tenant of The Eagles*) are shown in the 1881 census as living at Bodlondeb, Grove Road, with his brother-in-law, Thomas Painter.* Elizabeth died on 10 November 1882 and William on 6 January 1899. Both were buried in the Burial Ground* on Ruthin Road. They had no children. Overton was a great benefactor of the Wrexham Infirmary* and served as its President from 1879–98. He also made a gift of £500 towards the restoration of the Parish Church.

Overton Way, Acton Park
Developed by WBC in the 1960s as part of the third phase of the Acton Park housing estate,* Overton Way was probably named after the village of Overton which was the birthplace of Alderman Herbert Hampson,* for many years chairman of the Borough Housing Committee. For many years (until his death in 1995) N° 6 was the home of W.G. Sylvester, GC.*

Owen, Alfred *entrepreneur*
See Rubery Owen Group.

Owen, JP, Alderman James Charles *local politician*
Born c.1816, James Owen was the managing clerk to Wrexham solicitor John James (the first Town Clerk*) and qualified as a solicitor in 1847 and became a partner to his former employer. The partnership did not last long and Owen set up in practice at his home, Alma House on Madeira Hill.

He was elected a Conservative councillor onto WBC and twice served as Mayor (1872 and 1877). He was appointed an alderman from outside of the Council, a Justice of the Peace for the Borough and a Freemason.

He was a founder member of the Chester & North Wales Incorporated Law Society and was elected its president in 1881. Unmarried, he died at his home on 15 August 1887 and is buried in Wrexham Cemetery.* The Mayoral Chain was purchased during his year of office for £193-10s-0d.

Owen's Court, Beast market
Located off the Beast Market, two premises to the east of Market Street, Owen's Court had six dwellings. Shown on the 1872 survey.

Osborne Close, Croes Eneurys
Built in the 1970s by local builder Frank Johnson, it takes its name from the adjacent Osborne Road.*

Osborne Road
Built in the 1970s by local builder Frank Johnson, this street was named after Osborne House in the Isle of Wight, the summer residence of Queen Victoria and Prince Albert. (See also Croes Eneurys Estate)

Owen, Sir Alfred Owen *industrialist*
See Rogers and Jackson.

Owen's Cottages, Rhosnesni
These three cottages were located on the north-west side of Holt Road close to the junction with Dean Road (Acton Road).*

Owens' Court, Beast Market
A small 19th century poor quality housing development to the rear of the properties on the north-west side of the Beast Market. It was accessed via a passage between the second and third building from the corner of Market Street.

Oxford Street, Smithfield
Built in the late 19th century

P

Painter family *printers, stationers & booksellers*
In 1795, John Painter bought the printing and publishing business of Marsh which was located at N° 42 High Street. He was married to Catherine Burton of Wrexham on 3 October 1798. In about 1800 he moved the business to N°s 18 and 19 High Street. He was succeeded by his son John (married to Catherine, daughter of Hugh Burton) who ran the business until his death in a riding accident on 22 February 1828 (buried in the Dissenters Burial Ground*) and he was succeeded by his son, Thomas.* The family are best remembered for the printing of *The Royal Tribes of Wales* by Philip Yorke in 1799 and the 1813 translation by John Humphreys of Samuel Clarke's Family Bible. It was John Painter who set up and printed Bishop Heber's* hymn *From Greenland's Icy Mountains* on a Sunday morning so that it could be first sung in the Parish Church later the same day. Thomas Painter retired in 1856 and the business was taken over by Railton Potter (formerly of Carlisle).

Painter, JP, Thomas *local politician*
(See Painter Family) Thomas Painter, born 10 April 1808, was the second son of John and Catherine (née Burton) Painter. His father was a bookseller, printer and stationer of High Street, and Thomas was sent to London to work for the Whittaker company before returning to Wrexham. He succeeded to the family business in 1833 when his elder brother died after falling from his horse. He married Anne (1816–1912), the daughter of Wrexham businessman William Overton, and built Bodlondeb* in Grove Road as his home. He was elected as a 'White' (Tory) to the Borough Council in 1857 and served as Mayor of Wrexham in 1859. He was also a Justice of the Peace, the chairman of the Wrexham Gas Company* and the Market Hall Company and a director of the Provincial Welsh Assurance Company.* Palmer* described Painter as 'one of the tallest and handsomest men in the town'. In partnership with his brother-in-law, William Overton,* he bought the Town Hall* from the Crown in 1857 and set up a business as a wine merchant. He died at Ilar Villa on 16 January 1889 and is buried in the Wrexham Cemetery.*

Palin, JP, BM, BS, LRCP, LRCS, LSA Dr Henry Venables
local politician
Born on 5 March 1851 at Stapleford Hall, Cheshire, the son of William Palin and Mary Eleanor Dickenson, Henry Venables Palin was brought up at Gwersyllt Hill Hall, the house of Venables Kyrke, his maternal great-grandfather.* His paternal grandparents had lived at Llay Hall. He was educated at Birkenhead Collegiate School, Edinburgh University and St Thomas' Hospital, London. He succeeded to the Crescent House practice of his uncle, Dr Dickenson,* and served as honorary

surgeon and consultant physician to Wrexham Infirmary.* He was also Medical Officer and Public Vaccinator for the Wrexham Union and served as President of the north Wales branch of the British Medical Association in 1898–99.

On the political front he was a Conservative and an Imperialist and served as a member of WBC for many years, including two terms as Mayor – 1889 and 1890.

He was appointed a Justice of the Peace on the Borough bench in 1892. He married (1) Sarah Francis, the daughter of George Plant of Southsea, an ironmaster and had one son and three daughters, and (2) Ethel Sarah Roberts, daughter of Robert Lund Roberts. He died at Crescent House on 26 March 1924 and is buried in Wrexham Cemetery.*

Palmer, FCS, Alfred Neobard *historian*
Born in Thetford, Norfolk on 10 July 1847, the son of Alfred and Harriet (née Neobard) Palmer. His father was a coachmaker with premises on London Road. Alfred, the eldest of three children, was educated at Thetford Grammar School and Morgan Lloyd's Private Academy. He showed great promise as a Wesleyan Methodist lay preacher, but declined to follow that vocation and was apprenticed to a druggist in Bury St Edmunds, where he won the Bell Scholarship of the Pharmaceutical Society. He was employed as an analytical chemist by W.J. Coleman in Bury St Edmunds (the producer of the famed Wincarnis tonic wine) before moving to London as an assistant to Dr Attfield of the Pharmaceutical Society's laboratory in Bloomsbury. In the 1870s he moved to Manchester where he married Esther, the daughter of surveyor John Francis, a leading figure in the city's Welsh community.

Palmer was appointed chemist to the Zoedone Works* at Pentre Felin, Wrexham in 1880 and the following year set up his own practice at his home, 3 Ar-y-Bryn Terrace,* Poplar Road, before moving the business and his home to 34a Chester Street.* This was not a financial success and the following year he was appointed industrial chemist at the Brymbo Steel Works. Between 1891 and 1904 he was a consultant analytical chemist at the Cambrian Leather Works.

A.N. Palmer.

The latter years of his life (certainly post 1898) were spent at Inglenook, Bersham Road, Wrexham.

A prolific researcher and writer on local history, Palmer published numerous books and articles dealing with the Wrexham area including: *Town Fields and Folk of Wrexham in the Time of James the First* (1883); *History of Ancient Tenures of Land in the Marches of North Wales* (1885); *History of the Parish Church of Wrexham* (1886); *History of the Town of Wrexham* (1893); *Owen Tanat – a novel* – (1897); *John Wilkinson and the Old Bersham Iron Works* (1899); *History of the Thirteen Country Townships of the Old Parish of Wrexham* (1903); *History of the Townships of the Old Parish of Gresford* (1905); *The Town of Holt in County Denbigh together with the Parish of Is-y-coed* (1910); *History of Ancient Tenures of Land in North Wales and the Marches* – with Edward Owen (1910); *History of the Parish of Ruabon* (1992). Many of his articles appeared in the *Archæologia Cambrensis*, *Y Cymmrodor*, *Wales* and *Byegones*. He also published scientific articles in *The Leather Trades Review*.

In recognition of his contribution to the history of the area, Palmer was granted a small pension from the Civil List in 1904 and, in his latter years was employed by the Royal Commission on Ancient Monuments in Wales and Monmouthshire as an Inspecting Officer. He died of pleurisy and pneumonia at his home on 6 March 1915 and is buried in the Wrexham Cemetery.*

He was described by W.S. Spranton: 'Palmer's energy was boundless; he never lost an hour from business, he studied botany, collected and pressed wild flowers, he tried music and singing; at neither of which was he successful; he read history and poetry, as well as theology, and was a keen political reformer. … he was old fashioned, frank and unobtrusive, always pleased to see and welcome an old friend, open-handed and hospitable.'

A bronze bas relief memorial to his memory, paid for by public subscription, was unveiled by Lord Howard de Walden in the old Wrexham Library in November 1922. It was the work of Mr Youngman of Chelsea, a pupil of Sir Goscombe John. This was located in the Library and Arts Centre before being moved to the A. N. Palmer Local Studies Centre at Wrexham Museum in 2002. A memorial plaque was placed on his home in Bersham Road in 1994 by the Wrexham Civic Society and unveiled by W. Alister Williams.

Palmer, JP, Lt-General Sir Roger William Henry *soldier & landowner*
Born 1832, the son of Sir William Palmer, 4th Baronet of Castle Lackin, County Mayo, Ireland and Elenora (née Matthews), daughter of John Matthews of Eyarth and Plas Bostock. He matriculated at Christ Church, Oxford on 23 May 1850 and was commissioned a cornet [2nd Lieutenant] in the 11th Hussars on 22 January 1853.

The regiment embarked for the Crimea in May 1854 and Palmer was promoted to Lt in September of the same year. Sometime during October, he came across Pte Jowett of the 11th Hussars who had fallen asleep at his post. Instead of reporting him and having him punished according to the rules, Palmer merely gave him a caution.

On 25 October 1854, he rode in the famous Charge of the Light Brigade at Balaclava where his horse was shot away from under him. Pte Jowett, seeing Palmer's predicament, came to his rescue and brought him back to the British lines safely. Palmer left the Crimea in August 1855 and in January 1856 became a lieutenant in the 2nd Life Guards. He was promoted captain in July 1859 and major and lieutenant-colonel in March 1864. He became a brevet colonel in March 1869 and retired on half pay in September 1870. Promoted to major-general in March 1879 and honorary lieutenant-general in July 1881, Palmer saw no further active service.

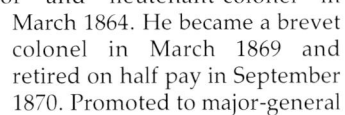

Sir Roger Palmer, Bt.

In 1883, he married Millicent, the daughter of the Revd Plumer Rooper of Abbots Ripton, Huntingdonshire at St James' Church, Piccadilly. They had no children. He became the 5th Baronet in 1869. In 1891 he was appointed colonel of the 20th Hussars, was the member of parliament for County Mayo for eight years and served as a deputy lieutenant of Sligo. His total estate in Wales, Ireland and England amounted to some 115,000 acres.

He was made colonel of the 20th Hussars in 1891 and died at his home, Cefn Park,* Wrexham, on 30 May 1910 and was buried in the Cefn vault in Wrexham Parish Churchyard.

Palmer Family, of Cefn Park
See Cefn Park, Lt-General Sir Roger Palmer and Lt-Col Fenwick-Palmer.

Palmer Street
This street was laid out in the early 1890s on land that was previously part of the Cefn Park* estate. Most of the houses appear to have been built by 1902.

The street was named after the Palmer family* of Cefn Park.

Pandy Halt, Plas Acton Road
This railway halt (also known as Rhosrobin Halt), which served the workers at Gresford Colliery, was located on the southern side of the road bridge that crosses the main Wrexham–Chester railway line on Plas Acton Road. The halt was opened on 1 September 1932 and closed on 6 October 1947.

Pandy Lane
Named after a *pandy* (*Trans.* fulling mill) which must have stood nearby. The same fulling mill gave its name to the nearby area of Pandy.

Pant-yr-Ochain Farm, Old Wrexham Road
Pant-yr-Ochain Farm was the subject of a detailed survey in 1786 when it was part of the Acton Park* estate, newly acquired by Sir Foster Cunliffe.* It had previously been the property of Ellis Yonge* who had bought it from the trustees of William Robinson of Gwersyllt Park.* The field names were: Cae Derwyn (*Trans.* oak field), Cae Coed Bychan *Trans.* little wood field), Pant-y-Gwppan Mawr and Buchan (*Trans.* hollow of the big bowl/hollow of the little bowl), Py ? Marl (*Trans.* ? marl), Bonki (*Trans.* hillocks), Cae Brichilau (*Trans.* apricot trees field), Moss, Broomy croft, Pigeon house croft, Cae Glas (*Trans.* green field), Hillcroft Clapper, Hop ground, Cae ganol or Cae Marl (*Trans.* middle field or marl field), Cae Cockshut ucha and issa (*Trans.* higher and lower Cockshut field), Tyr-y-netir (*Trans.* ? land) or Cae Pantrochan (*Trans.* Pant yr Ochain field – located on the north-east corner of the Barker's Lane/Box Lane roundabout, the site now occupied by Ranscombe Crescent and Sherwell Avenue). [FRO/D/AH/24] A William Jones of Pant-yr-Ochain is buried in the Burial Ground*, Ruthin Road. Upon the break up of the Acton Park estate following the death of Sir Foster Cunliffe* in 1917, Pant-yr-Ochain was sold to the tenant, John Edward Jones. He was succeeded by his son, Arthur and grandson, Keith. (See also Pant-yr-Ochain Hall)

Pant-yr-Ochain Hall, Old Wrexham Road
An early reference to 'Pantyrochain' occurs in 1523 when it was said to be the residence of John Aylmer 'armour-bearer and sergeant-at-arms to the most illustrious and most excellent Henry VIII, king of England'.

In 1587, the house was described as a 'place of considerable magnitude and the residence of Maister Aylmer' [*Worthynesse of Wales*, Thomas Churchyard]. In 1615 it appears to have been occupied, possibly owned, by George Lloyd, Bishop of Chester. In 1668 it was bought by Timothy Myddelton of Cadwgan Hall for £2,000. His daughter Ann (1668–93) married William Robinson (High Sheriff of Denbighshire 1690, Member of Parliament for Denbighshire 1705–7, died 1717), son of Colonel John Robinson* of Gwersyllt Hall,* and the house came to him as part of her dowry. In 1708, their son John married Elizabeth (1689–1750, the eldest daughter of Sir Griffith Jeffreys on whose death they inherited the house and the whole Acton Park* estate). In 1730 they moved to Gwersyllt and Pant yr Ochain became a farm house. In 1749 it passed to their son-in-law, Ellis Younge* of Acton Park* and, along with the remainder of the Acton Park estate, was sold to Sir Foster Cunliffe* in 1785.

In 1803 Sir Foster bought a farm called Maes Daffy in Gresford from a Mr Hughes for £1,170 and added the land to Pant yr Ochain – 'I paid for it by felling timber at Pant-y-Ochin and Borras Farms'. Two years later, Sir Foster 'began … to make alterations in the buildings at Pant-y-Ochin. This place was once one of the principal gentlemen's seats in this country but for nearly a century has been inhabited by farmers'. Sir Foster intended to leave the house to his unmarried daughters 'to secure to them the option of a comfortable residence in this neighbourhood. This I shall be enabled to do at a moderate expense by taking part of the house at Pant-y-Ochin, which is, in its present state, much too large for a Farmer, and converting it into a commodious dwelling and giving it as much land as such a residence requires'. It is this 'new' house, built in the Jacobean style, that forms the bulk of the present day pub/restaurant. The older, timber-framed building is still in use as the farmhouse and some of the timber work can be seen in part of the restaurant. On Sir Foster's death the house was left as a home for his unmarried daughters Emma and Charlotte and it was they who extended the house in 1835 (adding the large library room overlooking the garden). In an account written in the 19th century, Sir Robert Henry Cunliffe* referred to it as 'the house and farmhouse of Plas isa, now called Pant-y-Ochin'. In 1885 it was extensively damaged by a fire.

In the period following the Great War, the house, as part of Pant-yr-Ochain Farm,* was bought by the tenant, John Edward Jones, whose descendants continue to own it today. In the mid 1920s, the house was let to Liverpool stockbroker, Ernest Bateson. In the 1950s, Wrexham dentist, Reginald Rider, lived there for five years. Following a fire in the early 1960s, it became a restaurant in 1963 and was later leased to various tenants as a public house/restaurant. In 1994, the Pant-yr-Ochain became part of the Brunning & Price chain, successfully offering 'good beer, good food and good conversation'. A detailed history of the house by C.J. Williams can be found in the *Transactions of the Denbighshire Historical Society*, Vol 51, 2002.

Parc-y-Cwning
Located in the township of Bieston, this park was often mistakenly called Parc-y-Coming or Parke Conynge, but the origin of its name is almost certainly Parc-y-Cwningod (*Trans.* rabbits park) and it would have been a warren where rabbits were actively encouraged to breed as a source of food. It was mostly located to the north of the Holt Road and was, according to Palmer,* 'co-terminous with the great moor in Acton called 'Rhosnessney' on which moor the name 'Pwll Warren' should be noted, as indicating an earlier and larger warren. It ought to be added that the names Park and Prys cling still to portions both of the northern and southern areas, which were included in Park Cwning in 1620'. The warren covered much of what is now the Goulbourne and Borras Park* estates, indeed the latter may have been given the adjectival suffix 'Park' in light of its location in relation to the 'Parc'. Certainly, Warrenwood Road* in Borras Park derives its name from it.

Parc-y-Llys
Parc-y-Llys (Court Park) appears in the 1620 survey but its exact location is unrecorded. It may have been located in the area of the Parciau.* It was probably the court house of the township of Wrexham Regis and belonged, in the 15th century, to the Countess of Arundel. It would have become obsolete with the building of the Court of Pleas in the Shirehall.

The Parciau, c.1900, looking across to the Bridewell in Tenters Square. The rural nature of this side of the town at the end of the 19th century is clearly emphasised in this picture. The pool is at the bottom of a former gravel pit which was worked until the late 1870s. [RCHBW]

Parciau, The (*alias* The Parkey or Belle Vue Park)
This area of land originally incorporated, not only the present day park of the same name, but also land which was used as the old Burial Ground* and for the laying out of Ruthin Road, a total of some 20 acres. It appears in Norden's survey of 1620 as 'Parc-y-llys' (*Trans.* park of the court), probably a reference to the old court house of Wrexham Regis which is believed to have stood in this area. In the 19th century, and earlier, the whole area was part of the Wynnstay* estate.

Proposals for a town park were first made in about 1876 and it was felt that it should either form part of the new Wrexham Cemetery, or occupy the site between Erddig Road and Ruabon Road or should be alongside Chester Road. Lack of funds, however, prevented the idea from progressing any further. The site known as Belle Vue had been owned for many years by the Wynnstay estate and was normally let to the tenant of *The Eagles.** In 1878 part of it was developed as a gravel pit with some form of allotments, gardens or grazing along the north side of Ruthin Road, and was used for this purpose until 1902 when it was placed on the market by Lady Williams-Wynn. The Borough Council considered purchasing it for use as a park but decided that it was unable to afford the £4,500 asking price. In 1906, with the land remaining unsold, the Council decided to apply for a loan and it was bought in 1907 for £4,250. The Council designated that the land would be called by the unusual dual language name of 'The Parciau'.

A competition was held for the design of the new park which was won by J. Cheal & Sons of Westminster with their design called *Erica*. Cheal's proposals were somewhat more elaborate than the actual park that was finally laid out. Work commenced in 1911 and went on for a number of years, as and when money became available, and the bulk of The Parciau had been completed by the early 1920s. A bandstand was opened on 18 November 1914. Further landscaping took place between the two

The Parciau, c.1900, looking across to Ruthin Road where the town is pushing out into the countryside. [RCHBW]

A Russian cannon captured in the Crimean War (1854–56) which stood in Parciau until the government appealed for scrap metal during the Second World War.

World Wars and a full refurbishment programme was carried out by the County Borough Council commencing in 1999.

On 5 January 1920, Wrexham received a Mk 1 Tank (Nº 146) in recognition of the work of the local War Savings Committee which had collected £6 million. This was sited in The Parciau until 1928 when it was scrapped by Messrs Arthur Cudworth & Sons. An artillery piece from the Crimea was also sited here until the Second World War when it was removed during an appeal for scrap metal. In 1928, the statue of Queen Victoria was moved from Guildhall Square* onto the site previously occupied by the tank. The Parciau was the site of the National Eisteddfod of Wales* in 1933. A full and detailed article on the history of The Parciau can be found in the *Transactions of the Denbighshire Historical Society*, Vol. 47 (1998) entitled: 'Wrexham's Urban Parks: I. Bellevue (The Parciau)' by André Berry.

Park Avenue

Park Avenue was originally a short lane leading from Chester Street for about 400 yards when it degenerated into a footpath leading towards Acton. In the 18th century, the land on both sides of the road, at the Chester Street end, were the property of the Dymmocks of Little Acton Farm and from them passed to Richard Wynne of Garthewin who married Elizabeth Dymmock in 1766. By the 19th century the road was known as Cooper's Lane after coachbuilder Joseph Cooper who lived at Bodhyfryd* until his death in 1856 and who owned much of the land in the area. The road has also been known locally as Lovers' Lane. In the early 20th century a field at the town end of the road, known as Timber Croft, was dominated by a large timber yard with tall advertising hoardings on top of a stone wall, which may originally have been part of Joseph Cooper's business premises but was, by the 1930s, leased by S. Rogers, timber merchant, of Charles Street.

The first houses to be built on what was to become Park Avenue were the large semi-detached houses opposite the Groves School.* Following the sale of the Acton Park* estate the land between Pen-y-Maes Avenue/Aston Grove and Rhosnesni Lane became available for development and Cooper's Lane was extended. Liverpool architects Lockwood, Abercrombie and Saxon drew up proposals which, had they been implemented, would have resulted in the road curving sharply to the west and diagonally crossing the Nine Acre Field to emerge at the junction of Rhosnesni Lane and Chester Road, balancing the junction of Cilcen Grove. The plan was, however, rejected and Cooper's Lane was laid out with a more gradual curve so that it emerged on Rhosnesni Lane opposite Central Avenue. The first houses to be built, in the early 1930s, towards the northern end of Cooper's Lane were the present day Nᵒˢ 65, 67, 69, 71, 130, 132, followed by Nᵒˢ 61 and 63 in 1934. In 1930, WBC decided to build 14 'semi-detached villas' on the east side of the road, facing onto Cooper's Lane (Nᵒˢ 90–116). These were designed by Liverpool architects Lockwood, Abercrombie & Saxon and were intended to be let to key workers who were either already living in the town or who were moving into the area to take up significant positions with local employers. In 1954, 110 Park Avenue became the first council house to be sold in north Wales following the granting of permission by the Ministry of Housing. In September 1931, the Council was expressing concern about the name Cooper's Lane, perhaps feeling that it did not carry sufficient 'style' for what was to be an important new residential development. In February 1932 the name was officially changed to Park Avenue and by March the first two tenants – D. T. Morgan (a teacher at Grove Park) and Mrs Minnie Pickvance had been given the tenancies. In January 1932, the Council bought 152 trees (at a cost of £22-16s-0d) which were planted on either side of Park Avenue.

The small crescent of dormer-style houses between Pen-y-Maes Avenue and Westminster Drive were designed by F. A. Roberts of Mold and built between the wars by H. V. Parker (see Croes Eneurys Estate) for Philip Clarke of Park Farm* and his brother William Clarke.* One of these houses was demolished in the late 1990s to make way for a new house, Nº 39 Park Avenue.

Grove Park Boys School used fields at the town end of Park Avenue as their playing fields (these were to become the site of the Police Headquarters* in the 1970s). Throughout the early 1930s, discussions took place between the local authority and the governors of Grove Park School with a view to the provision of land off Cooper's Lane for the proposed new Grove Park Girls School.* The first offers were rejected as unsuitable and eventually the land between Chester Road,

The Parciau, c.1914. A similar view to that shown in the 1900 photograph looking towards the Bridewell. Here the hollow left by the gravel pit has been landscaped and a band stand erected as part of the overall design of the public park.

Park Avenue and Pen-y-Maes Avenue was agreed upon and the new school opened in September 1939.

Until the 1970s, Park Avenue extended from Rhosnesni Lane to Chester Street but, with the linking of the roads known as Powell Road and Bodhyfryd, and the building of the Police Headquarters,* the street was truncated and now only begins by the former Groves School (hence the absence of any lower house numbers). The 'town section' of Park Avenue has survived as the approach road from near the RWF War Memorial* to the Police Headquarters.

A druidic circle for the Proclamation Ceremony of the 1933 National Eisteddfod was erected in 1932 in the field now occupied by the Police Headquarters* and the Magistrates Courts.* This was later dismantled by Alderman William Aston and moved to Acton Park.

Sir Walter Stansfield, the Chief Constable of Denbighshire* lived at Nº 84, the broadcaster June Knox Mawer* lived at Nº 94.

Park Farm, Rhosnesni
Park Farm house and buildings stood close to the south-western corner of the junction of Borras Road and Rhosnesni Lane, on the site formerly occupied by Ray's Motors. In 1881 it comprised 39 acres and was tenanted by James Smith. In 1918, when the farm was offered for sale, it comprised 29 acres and was bought by Mr Jones of Ty'n Twll Farm* who sold it to Philip Clarke (of Clarke Brothers, bakers and confectioners) in c.1923. Following the approval of WBC to the development of 132 houses on this land in April 1954, Philip Clarke built some himself and sold a substantial part of the land to WBC who began to further develop it as the Park Farm Estate, with plots being sold off to individuals and contractors. Much of the building work for Philip Clarke was done by local builder Fred Williams and the architect was F. A. Roberts of Mold. Today, the area sold to WBC is occupied by Ffordd Hooson,* Ffordd Dylan,* Ffordd Elfed,* Ffordd Dyfed* and the eastern section of Camberley Drive.*

The land facing Rhosnesni Lane was developed as a petrol station (Ray's Motors, closed 2009), flats (Nºˢ 114 & 116, believed to have been the first business enterprise of Albert Gubay, the founder of the Kwiksave supermarket chain), retail premises and private housing.

Park Lodge, Rhosddu Road
The land on which this house was built was originally 'part of the meadow land commonly called or known as The Grove Park'. Along with an adjoining piece of land facing onto what was to become Grove Park Road, it was sold in March 1862 by George Simpson to Edward Lloyd for £174. Lloyd appears to have built Park Lodge shortly afterwards and the building restrictions stipulated that there were to be no windows on the north-facing wall (where today there appear to be three windows outlined in the brick). In 1878 the house was sold to J. Allmand for £1,225 and in 1895 it was bought by Scotch draper Robert Stobo of 27 Lambpit Street for £1,050. Stobo married Elizabeth Davidson in 1906 and they lived in and operated their business from the house. In 1914 the Stobos moved to a new house, Langlands in Maes-y-Dre Road* but continued to operate the business from Park Lodge. When Mrs Stobo died in 1961, her nephew James Stobo bought the property and it was let as business premises. It was again sold following the death of James Stobo's widow in 1992. Today it is the offices of accountants Godfrey Edwards.

Park Street English Presbyterian Church, Rhosddu
Established as a Mission church by the Hill Street congregation in 1895, the church was accommodated in a purpose-built hall in Park Street. In 1904, the 'Iron Chapel' on Bersham Road was moved to the site in order to accommodate increasing congregations. By 1911 it was necessary to build another church to accommodate the growing numbers. The Religious Census of 1904 showed: Capacity 350; attendance (AM & PM) 312.

Park View, Holt Road
A terrace of houses, next to Holt Street Terrace, on the northern side of what is now Holt Road.

Park View, Borras Park
This is the name given to the area of Borras Park* between Ffordd Alun* and Barker's Lane,* which was developed in the mid 1960s.

Parker's Close, Croes Eneurys
Built in the late 1970s/early 1980s on land that had formerly been part of Croes Eneurys Farm,* by local builder Gordon Mytton. Unlike the other streets in this development which were all named after royal palaces, this street is named after H.K. Parker, ARICS, a director of the building firm Parker, Davies & Hughes Ltd, who began the development of the Croes Eneurys Estate.*

Parry, Ernest *soldier*
Gunner Ernest Parry (Nº 1784115) 43/61st Light Anti-Aircraft Battery, Royal Artillery was posted as missing-in-action on 26 June 1942 but was eventually declared to be a prisoner-of-war of the Italians in North Africa in September 1942. He was the son of Robert and Selena Parry of 12 Eagle Street.* He died as a POW on 2 November 1942, aged 36, at the Military Hospital, Busetta, Tripoli, of dysenteric enterocolitis. In 1948/9 he was posthumously awarded the French *Croix de Guerre* for his 'exceptional services' during the fighting at Bir-Hakim in 1942. He was buried in the Commonwealth War Graves Cemetery in Tripoli, Libya (Grave 11.B.24). Ernest Parry Road* was named after him.

Parry, Gwilym Hefin *local politician*
Born in Pen-y-Groes, near Caernarfon, the son of a headmaster, Gwilym Parry worked with MANWEB as a chief cashier. He was elected as an Independent councillor for Wat's Dyke ward in 1956 and became Mayor in 1971. Married to Irene Probert, he lived at 157 Chester Road.

Parry, Alderman Joseph *local politician*
The son of William Parry of Castletown, Moss, Joseph Parry was educated at Pentre Broughton School and began his working life at the Blast Pit in Brymbo before becoming an engine man at the Westminster Colliery. In 1914, he volunteered for military service but was rejected for being under-age. Making a second application, when he lied about his age, he was accepted for service with the Royal Welsh Fusiliers. He saw active service at Ypres, Armentières and Pilkem Ridge in France and Flanders at the age of 16 and was captured only to escape in less than 24 hours. Trying to make his way back to the British lines he was severely wounded in the knee by shrapnel from a German shell and was eventually discharged as being unfit for further military service. He then returned to the Westminster Colliery until it closed in 1926 when he took up an appointment with the Highways Department of Denbighshire County Council. He remained in this job until retiring in 1962, when he was a foreman.

He was elected a Labour councillor for Caia Ward on WBC in 1947, became Deputy Mayor in 1958 and Mayor in 1961. During his year of office, the Council moved into the new Guildhall* building on Llwyn Isaf. He was elected an alderman for Cefn Ward in 1965. He retired from local politics in 1974. A lifelong trade unionist, he was a member of the General Executive of the Transport and General Workers Union and received a gold medal for his services to trade unionism. He became a member of the Grand United Order of Oddfellows in 1921 and in 1951 was appointed Grand Master of the Order.

He married Elizabeth Harriot Hughes of Summerhill in September 1920 and they had one son and two daughters. Joseph Parry lived at 6 Queensway and 140 Y Wern. He died at the Maelor Hospital on 31 August 1982.

Parry-Thomas, John Godfrey *racing driver & world land speed record holder*
Born at N° 6 Spring Road, Rhosddu, on 6 April 1884, the second son of the Revd John William Thomas, curate of Rhosddu Church. The family moved to live at Bwlch-y-Cybau near Oswestry when he was five years old. He was educated at Oswestry School and the City and Guilds College in London (where he studied Electrical Engineering).

During the First World War he was employed in the design of aeroplanes and in 1917 was appointed Chief Engineer of Leyland Motors where he was partly responsible for the design of the Leyland Eight, an eight-cylinder car fitted with servo-assisted brakes and an automatic chassis lubrication system operated by the movement of the rear springs.

He gave up his career with Leyland to become a professional motor-racing driver at Brooklands in Surrey in 1923 and lived in a bungalow inside the circuit. Known as 'Daredevil Thomas' or simply 'Tommy', he built cars under his own name. The Leyland-Thomas or Thomas Special cars were advanced vehicles for their time. He graduated from standard racing cars to specially modified vehicles which he used in an attempt on the world land speed record and to this end bought a second-hand Higham Special that had been built in 1923 by Count Louis Vorrow Zborowski and engineer Clive Gallop. Zborowski, a renowned racing driver (his most famous car being Chitty-Chitty-Bang-Bang), had been killed in the 1924 Italian Grand Prix and the Higham Special was sold for £125. Parry-Thomas put in a new engine, a 26.9 litre, 500 bhp, 4-carburatored aero engine from a First World War bomber. He also added a 4-speed chain drive Benz gearbox and a Leyland Eight front axle and steering. He improved the streamlining of the body and re-named the car 'Babs' after his niece. The chassis of the car was, co-incidentally, built by the Rubery Owen* company.

The car was ready in 1926 and, at Pendine Sands in Carmarthenshire, Parry-Thomas broke the world land speed record twice, setting 168.074 mph then 171.02 mph as the new target for his great rival Malcolm Campbell to beat. Unfortunately, the record only stood for a short time and was broken by Campbell with a speed of 174.223 mph. On 3 March 1927, Parry-Thomas was back at Pendine Sands where, in bad weather, he set out to recapture the record. During a high speed run, the chain

Parry-Thomas at the wheel of 'Babs'.

drive snapped at 170 mph, causing Babs to cartwheel three times. Parry-Thomas was killed outright, some say by the broken chain hitting him and resulting in his decapitation. His body was recovered from the wreckage and was buried at St Mary's Church Cemetery, Byfleet, Surrey (close to Brooklands).

The wrecked Babs was buried amid the sand dunes at Pendine Sands where it remained until 1969 when it was recovered by Owen Owen of Capel Curig who painstakingly restored the car which is now on display at the National Museum of Wales. A memorial plaque on the wall of his birth place was unveiled by Mayor Cyril Williams in 1991.

Parton, JP, Alderman Joseph *local politician*
Joseph Parton was born (*c*.1881) at Patshill, Wolverhampton, the son of a farm worker of the same name. He commenced his working life, aged 12, as an agricultural labourer but in 1902 obtained employment with the Great Western Railway at Wellington and in 1903 came to Wrexham as a railway shunter. In 1918 he was appointed a goods guard. He was elected a Labour member of WBC in 1927 and served as Mayor in 1934. He was made an alderman in 1944 and retired in 1955. He served as chairman of the Parks Committee from 1936–55.

A keen trade unionist, Joseph Parton was a member of the National Union of Railwaymen, a founder of the Wrexham & District Amateur Bowling Association and an avid supporter of Wrexham Football Club.* He was appointed a Justice of the Peace in 1942. His wife, Eliza, was a native of Dawley in Shropshire and they had three sons and one daughter. He lived at N° 45 Percy Road and at Melrose, Caego. He died at the Maelor General Hospital in December 1976 and is buried in Wrexham Cemetery.

Peace Gardens, Holt Street
(see Quaker Burial Ground)

Pearce's Court, Lampit Street
Mentioned by Palmer,* it seems that this was located on the south side of the street, to the east of the Raglan Arms.*

Peel Street
This street was laid out in 1895 following the death of Benjamin Piercy part of whose Red House* estate was sold off by auction in the July of that year. Most of the terraced properties in this street appear to have been built by 1900 and the area was then known as Newtown. The close proximity of the Cobden Flour Mill* led to a number of the streets being named after leading figures in the Anti Corn Law League.

This street was named after the politician Sir Robert Peel (1788, anti Corn Law campaigner and one time Prime Minister. Peel is perhaps best remembered for his service as Home Secretary when he introduced the Metropolitan Police Force to London.

Pembroke Road, Borras Park
As with other streets on this private housing development of the late 1960s, known as Hillcrest Estate,* this road takes its name from one of the old, pre-1974 counties of Wales, in this case, Pembrokeshire.

Pen-y-Bont
(*Trans.* bridge end) See Brewery Place. The name was a reference to Pentre Felin Bridge* which crossed the Gwenfro at this point until the river was culverted in the late 19th century. (See Brook Street)

Pen-y-Bont, Brook Street
(*Trans.* bridge end) A public house. (See Old Three Tuns)

233

Pen-y-Bryn
For some unrecorded reason, the main route out of Wrexham towards Ruabon and Oswestry was not named after the traveller's destination (as in Hope Street, Chester Street, Salop Road, etc.) but took the name Pen-y-Bryn (Trans. hilltop). The name Ruabon Road is only applied to that section of the road that was developed in the 19th century, extending beyond Pen-y-Bryn towards Felin Puleston. The official extent of Pen-y-Bryn is from the junction of Chapel Street, south to the junction of Ruthin Road.

Pen-y-Bryn Farm, Abenbury
(Trans. hilltop) Owned by the Eddowes family for many generations, this farm was located near to the present day Pentre Maelor on the edge of the Wrexham Industrial Estate. The grave of Daniel Lloyd* was in the field in front of the house.

Pen-y-Bryn House
In the 1833 survey, Pen-y-Bryn House (the property of Mr Edwards) is clearly shown on the north-eastern side of Tenters Square.

Pen-y-Bryn (Salisbury Park) English Congregationalist Chapel.
Opened in 1898 by the former congregation of the Chapel Street church. A memorial to local businessman Alexander Wylde Thornley* was placed in the church. A schoolroom had also been founded in 1897. The church was demolished and the schoolroom converted for use as the chapel. The Religious Census of 1904 showed: Capacity 600; attendance (AM & PM) 383. In recent years this has been the United Reformed Church.

Pen-y-Lan, Ruabon
Although an earlier building almost certainly existed on this site, the house known as Pen-y-Lan was probably built by Ellis Lloyd in about 1690 following his marriage to Elizabeth Edwards. In 1712 the estate passed to Lloyd's great nephew, Eubule Williams and, after him, to his brother Edward Williams. In 1792, it was sold to Roger Kenyon of Cefn Park,* Wrexham. In 1854, it was again sold, this time to James Hardcastle, a partner in the legal firm of Ormrod, Hardcastle & Co of Bolton. He was succeeded by his brother-in-law, James Ormrod, from whom Colonel Peter Ormrod, MC, DL, JP, (died 2007) was descended. The house underwent extensive alterations and additions in 1830 and again towards the end of the 19th century. Many of the later additions were demolished during the 1950s, reverting to the stuccoed and castellated house of 1838.

Pen-y-Lan, c.1910.

Pen-y-Maes Avenue
(Trans. the avenue at the end of the field) The town fields of Wrexham ended in this area.

The bungalow on the north corner of Pen-y-Maes Avenue and Chester Road was once the home of Dr Wesley Hill. The large house now in the centre of Holly Walks, was called Pen-y-Maes and was built in the 1930s by Dr John 'Jock' Reid (who had a surgery in Regis Place*) and his wife Mrs Doris Reid (née Moss) who was a noted amateur botanist. Following the death of Mrs Reid the house was sold to local builder Norman Rogers who built the Holly Walks development in the garden. The property to the east of Holly Walks was built in the 1930s by Mr Powell, a senior consultant at the War Memorial Hospital. Nº 23, the Dutch style house close to the junction with Park Avenue was built by Wrexham fishmonger Eric A. McMahon.*

Pinfold, the detached house on the corner of Craigmillar Road,* was originally named Eildon and was built in the 1930s by

Pen-y-Bryn, c.1890. This rather fuzzy photograph shows the area of Pen-y-Bryn opposite the Bowling Green public house. The Pentice can be seen on the right.

234

Mrs Elizabeth S. Stobo (née Davidson, who had previously resided at Langlands, Maes-y-Dre Road*).

Penadur (Penadwr) Mineral Works, Beast Market
This company, manufacturing soda water, lemonade, Vichy water, lemon squash, quinine tonic, ginger beer, etc., was founded in 1867 by J. F. Edisbury, JP, and by 1876 was located in premises on the site now occupied by the Tesco Extra store, it was taken over by Soames' Brewery* and remained in production until the 1930s when it was moved to the Holt Road premises of Border Breweries.* The Beast Market site was then acquired by WBC as a depot. A detailed account of the works in 1892 appears in *Wrexham Illustrated*.

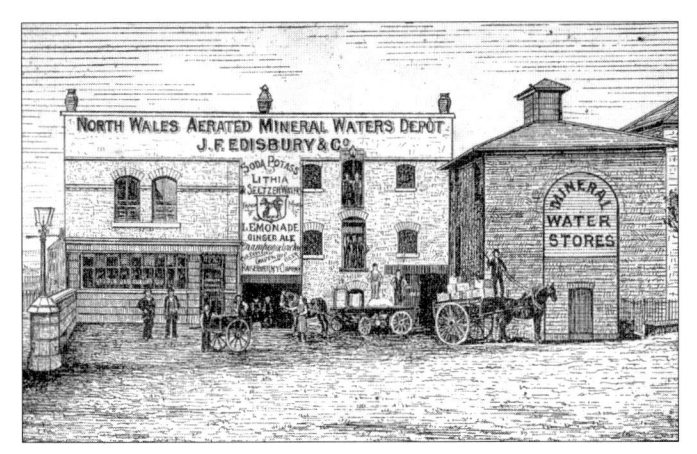

The exterior and interior of J. F. Edisbury's Penadur Mineral Works. [Derek Jones]

Pendine Hall, Little Mountain
Originally Cae Bryn, then Highfield, this property was bought by Walter Pen Dennis of New Hall, Ruabon* in t he 1890s. He carried out extensive alterations and extensions to the house and changed the name to Pendine Hall. The Dennis family lived there until 1929 when it was sold to Mr Duncan Robertson, the son of Henry Bayer Robertson*. During the Second World War, the house was the temporary home of St Monica's RC School from Croydon. In 1949 it was bought by Mr & Mrs J.W. Finch who converted it into Pendine Hall Hotel, which was described in its advertising as 'The most attractive hotel in North Wales, situated in 15 acres of parkland, fully licensed. AA and RAC 3 Star rated.' In April 1958, the property was burned down and the site is now occupied by Pendine Park, a private nursing home, belonging to health care entrepreneur Mario Kreft.

Pendine Hall, Summerhill, 1951.

Penson, Richard Kyrke *architect*
Born in 1815, Richard Kyrke was the eldest son of Thomas Penson II.* He trained as an architect at his father's office in Oswestry and was taken into partnership in 1844 before leaving to set up his own practice firstly in Shropshire then in south Wales. He became County Surveyor of Carmarthenshire and, after his father's death, County Surveyor of Montgomeryshire.

The most notable buildings designed by him in Wrexham were St Mark's Church* and the Provincial Welsh Insurance Company's* offices in High Street. Elsewhere, he designed the church at Pont Fadog and Minera School. He was also a talented watercolour artist and for over thirty years exhibited paintings at the Royal Academy. He died in 1886.

Penson [I], Thomas *architect*
Born in *c.*1760, he practised in Wrexham as a mason and an auctioneer before becoming an architect in the latter part of the 18th century. He married Charlotte Brown of Wrexham in February, 1781 (she died in 1813). Although probably unqualified, Penson served as unofficial County Architect for Flintshire for many years before being officially recognised as such in 1810. He appears to have specialised in penal buildings and was responsible for the design of the County Gaols in Caernarfon (1784) and Flint. He bought a large house for himself in Charles Street which he subsequently rebuilt.*

In Wrexham, his name is best remembered for the theatre which he designed and built on Smithfield Road, moving to live in a house that was located behind it in about 1818. In 1815 he was sacked as County Surveyor following the collapse of his new, single-arched bridge over the Dee at Overton and his failure to provide an alternative. Despite this disaster, Penson was almost immediately appointed County Surveyor for Denbighshire. Legal action was taken against him by both Denbighshire and Flintshire and lasted until shortly before his death on 30 March 1824. He was buried in the old Burial Ground,* Ruthin Road. He was also the architect of Brynmally Hall, built for Richard Kirk*.

Penson, FRIBA, MICE, [II] Thomas *architect*
Born in 1790, the son of Thomas Penson [I],* he was a pupil of Thomas Harrison, an architect with a practice in Chester. After qualifying, Penson established his own practice in Wrexham and Oswestry and married Frances, the daughter of Richard Kyrke.* He served as County Surveyor to both Denbighshire and Montgomeryshire for over 30 years and was a Fellow of the Royal Institute of British Architects and a Member of the Institute of Civil Engineers.

His greatest contribution appears to have been in the field of road building and he is often described as having 'revolutionised' the roads of Montgomeryshire. In his designs for buildings he specialised in a neo-Jacobean style which, according to Hubbard, was 'characterised by fancifully shaped gables, pedimented windows and the use of ashlar'.

In addition to many projects all over the two counties he is best remembered in Wrexham area as the architect responsible for the Market Hall* in High Street (1847), Gwersyllt Hill* (1841), the British School,* Brook Street (1844), the County Buildings* in Regent Street (1857), Holy Trinity Church, Gwersyllt (1850–1), the Parish Church at Rhosllanerchrugog (1852–3), the New Bridge over the Dee at Cefn Bychan and the Sontley Road* bridge over the Clywedog (1845). Further afield he designed: the bridge over the Severn at Llanymynech; the Flannel Market Hall at Newtown (1832); the Newtown & Llanidloes Union Workhouse at Caersws (1838–40); Pentrehelyn (1830); Vaynor Park (1840–53); Llanrhaiadir Hall (1842); Holy Trinity Church, Oswestry (1836–7); St David's Church, Denbigh (1838–40); Christ Church, Welshpool (1839–44); St David's Church, Newtown (1843–7). He resided at Gwersyllt Hill (which he re-fronted and which was demolished in the 1970s) and gave his name to Penson's Corner in Summerhill. He was the father of Thomas Mainwaring Penson* and Richard Kyrke Penson,* both architects with successful practices in Chester. He died in 1859.

Penson, Thomas Mainwaring *architect*
Born in 1817, the son of Thomas Penson (II),* Thomas Mainwaring Penson was a leading architect in Chester where he was one of the forerunners of the half-timbered revival which so characterises the centre of that city today. He was the main architect for the Shrewsbury–Chester Railway and designed many of the stations along the route including the original Wrexham General Station* (*c.*1847). He died in 1864.

Penson's Theatre, Beast Market
This theatre operated under a number of names including the Play-house, the Theatre Royal and the Theatre of the Varieties. It was rumoured that the theatre was the result of a casual meeting between Thomas Penson [I]* and George Stanton (a prominent theatrical impresario in the Midlands). The latter assured the architect that, if there were a theatre in Wrexham, he would pay an annual rent of £80 for its use on condition that he had the first refusal on any dates. Built shortly before 1818 it was located close to what is now a roundabout at the end of the Eagles' Meadow flyover. The building had seating on the ground floor with a gallery on three sides on the first floor. The stage was at the southern end of the building. Next door, was a house which was also built by Thomas Penson. Both the theatre and the house were sold to John Jones of Pwll-y-Go, Bersham, in *c.*1824 and again sold in 1837. By the 1830s, George Stanton had died and gradually the theatre went into decline so that by the 1850s it was often standing empty. In the 1860s, the licensee was Mr Aston and, shortly afterwards it was taken over by Philip Hannan and, by 1869, conditions seem to have improved. Mrs Hannan, who, in addition to being the owner's wife, had performed at the theatre, described it in 1867:

'My first impression was one of dismay. The stage was covered with damp sawdust and as I went to my dressing room I was followed by an old woman bearing an open umbrella ... because the roof ... let in the rain. The people in the pit and gallery sat with coat collars turned up and umbrellas open.' Hannan died in 1870 and the theatre thereafter only opened for occasional travelling players until 1873 when it was re-named The Theatre Royal. In 1875, the theatre was converted into a Temperance Hall and, shortly afterwards, was used by the Salvation Army.* In 1889, it was sold, along with some cottages, to Messrs Powell Brothers & Whitaker,* for £1,800 and the corner was removed as part of a road improvement scheme. Powells also altered the

The front of Penson's Theatre when it was used as a warehouse by Powell Brothers, c.1880.

Penson's Theatre, Beast Market, the east side and rear of the building, viewed from what is now Smithfield Road (it was once called Theatre Road).

frontage for use as a showroom for their agricultural implements. In 1927 it became a showroom for Messrs Rogers & Jackson* and more of the frontage was removed in 1964. The last wall was demolished in 1974 to make way for the Eagles Meadow flyover. The theatre appears in both the 1833 and 1872 surveys.

Pentice, The, Pen-y-Bryn
Located between Tenters Square and Ruthin Road, almost directly opposite the Bowling Green public house, The Pentice was one of the best known and most distinctive buildings in Wrexham until its demolition in about 1890. The name Pentice is a corruption of Penthouse which was a description of a house with an upper storey that projected over the street. The house gable bore a plaque with the initials T.E.W. (which probably stood for Thomas Whitbread) and the date 1689. Shortly before its demolition, the Pentice was being used as a common lodging house before becoming a shop owned by a Miss Davies.

Pentre, Abenbury
This was the area to the north of Abenbury Road now the site of the most southerly section of the Queen's Park housing estate,* known as Pentre Gwyn.* In 1881 it comprised Pentre Farm (40 acres, occupied by Edward Ellis) and a number of cottages. It was part of the Cefn Park* estate.

Pentre Felin
The most significant building in this ancient thoroughfare was the Abbot's Mill* which became the Zoedone Works* in the late

19th century and then Hugh Price & Company's* leather works. The mill building was destroyed by a fire in 1928 and a new leather works was built on the same site. These premises were vacated in the mid 1970s and were left empty until their demolition nearly 20 years later to make way for the Island Green Shopping Centre.*

The first properties in this street to be demolished as part of the Borough Council's slum clearance programme were taken over in 1932 and the residents were transferred to the Spring Lodge* housing estate. N°s 1–7 (partly on Pentre Felin and partly on Hughes' Court), 8–11, 30–31 Pentre Felin were subject to a compulsory purchase order in 1938 as part of the Borough slum clearance programme of Clearance Area N° 25 and N°s 14-17 Pentre Felin followed suit in 1939.

Pentre Felin Bridge
Originally a wooden structure which, according to Palmer,* stood across the Gwenfro* at the east end of Pentre Felin* (on the site of the present day junction of Brook Street,* Well Street* and Mitre Place*). This was later replaced by a stone bridge which served the area until it disappeared under the culverting of Brook Street in 1881. It is shown on both the 1833 and the 1872 surveys.

Pentre Felin Independent Chapel
This is almost certainly the chapel shown in the 1872 survey as the Wesleyan Methodist Chapel, opposite Hughes' Court. It could accommodate 120 people. [FRO/MF/363 & DRO/MFD/177]

Pentre Felin Mill
See Abbot's Mill.

Pentre Felin Welsh Congregational Chapel, Pentre Felin
Congregationalists moved from their meeting room off Queen Street to Pentre Felin in 1844. They remained there until the Ebeneser Welsh Congregational Chapel was opened in Queen Street in 1863. The noted bard Hwfa Môn (rev, Rowland Williams) was one of the early ministers of this chapel.

Pentre Felin Welsh Wesleyan Church
The first Welsh Calvinistic Methodist congregation in Wrexham met in a small room at the rear of a house called The Castle about the year 1770, as a branch of the chapel at Adwy'r Clawdd, Coedpoeth. They moved to Pentre Felin in 1797. Located on the south side of Pentre Felin, just below the present day St Mary's School, this chapel appears in the 1833 survey located on the opposite side of the street to The Mitre* public house. This seems to be contradicted by Palmer* who places it at the back of Naylor's Yard,* opposite the site of the Pentre Felin Mill. On the balance of probability it would seem that the 1833 survey is more accurate. Palmer also points out that in 1797 a 21-year lease was taken out on some existing buildings belonging to Edward Jackson, a dyer, and converted into a chapel. The trustees were

A view of Pentre Felin in the early 1930s. The cars are parked outside W. Rollings Ltd's Central Garage. The first two houses on the left are part of Hughes Court.

Pentre Felin looking east towards Brook Street. Most of the houses and courts in this area were cleared in the 1930s and the residents re-housed in the new Spring Lodge housing estate.

named as: Richard Jones (ironmonger of Wrexham);* Revd Thomas Charles (of Bala); Revd Thomas Jones (of Mold); Revd Robert Ellis (of Cymau, Hope); Revd John Edwards (of Gelli Gynan, Iâl). The chapel was closed in 1821 when a new chapel was opened in Abbot Street at the rear of the Old *Swan Inn*.*

Pentre Gwyn, Abenbury
One of the last developments by WBC on the Queen's Park* housing estate. The origin of the name is unrecorded.

Pentrebychan, Esclusham
This house was built in 1823–4 by the Meredith family, replacing a 16th century, single-story, half-timbered and thatched predecessor which had originally belonged to the Tegin family. Hugh Meredith bought the estate in 1620 and his descendants lived there until 1802 when the male line died out and the property passed to Joseph Warter (who took the surname Meredith). The three-storey, dressed stone, neo-Tudor building of 1823 was derelict by the 1960s and was demolished. The site then became the location of Pentrebychan Crematorium which opened in 1966. The walled garden, dovecot, a wild meadow and semi-woodland of the old estate have been preserved as part of the 40-acre crematorium grounds. A section of Offa's Dyke passes through the grounds which are inhabited by a wide variety of wildlife, including heron, badgers, buzzards, snakes, ducks and owls.

Pentrebychan, c.1900.

Pentre'r Felin Newydd
(*Trans.* new mill village) This was the original name for the small settlement which grew up around the King's Mills* in the area of the present day Red Lion* public house. The name was normally abbreviated to Pentre and as such the hill from the bridge over the Gwenfro passing the rear of the Red Lion, was called Pentre Hill, at the top of which, on the north side was a row of thatched cottages known as Pentre Cottages which survived until well into the 20th century.

Percy Road
This road does not appear on the 1872 survey and was probably laid down during the 1880s. In June 1889, seven lots of freehold land known as Hirdir, located between Bennions Lane (Road), Percy Road and Belgrave Road, were offered for sale but only two appear to have been sold (on the corner of Bennions Lane and Percy Road and the corner of Belgrave Road and Percy Road) –the latter to Job Mason.* [DRO/DD/G/2330] In June 1896, John Bury of Hillbury sold off seven building plots on the western side of Percy Road, comprising all the land between Belgrave Road and the junction with Bennions Lane (Road). A house called Wrest,* stood on the corner of Percy Road and Hillbury Road.

Several streets in this area (Salisbury Park, Trevor Street and Talbot Road) appear to have been named after noted late mediæval or Tudor families. In this instance the street appears to have been named after the Percy family, dukes of Northumberland.

Peter Walker Brewery
See Walkers Brewery and Peter Walker.

Petit, Rt Revd John Edward *Bishop of Menevia*
Born in Highgate, London on 22 June 1895 of Irish parentage (both parents had left Ireland during the famine of the 1840s) John Petit was educated in the Parochial School of the Passionist Parish of Highgate, became a church student for the archdiocese of Westminster and attended the English College at Valladolid in Spain from 1910–16 and St Edmund's College, Ware, Hertfordshire from 1916–18.

He was ordained a priest in the diocese of Brentwood. He graduated from Cambridge University and was appointed assistant at Custom's House in London, bishop's secretary and, in 1923, appointed pastor of Malden. The following year he returned to Valladolid as vice-rector until 1930 when he started a new parish at Dagenham in Essex and, the following year, was made pastor of Grays in Essex. In 1934 he was appointed Master of St Edmund's House, a house of residence for clergy at Cambridge University. In 1946 he was sent to Nottingham to start a junior seminary, St Hugh's College, Tollerton. On 25 March 1947 he was consecrated bishop of Menevia and came to live at Bishop's House, Sontley Road (see Plas Tirion). He was Ecclesiastical Assistant (Supreme Chaplain) of the Knights of St Columba in England, Wales and Scotland and invited the religious order of the Little Sisters of Assumption to Wrexham in 1958. Ill health caused Bishop Petit to have an auxilliary bishop appointed to assist him in December 1965. He died on 2 June 1973.

Petty Sessions
In 1951, these were held at the County Buildings* in Regent Street on the first and third Tuesday each month. The Borough Petty Sessions were held in the Guildhall every Monday.

Philips Close, Borras Park
Developed in the 1960s on land that had once been part of the Acton Nursery by London developers Spinks & Denning. This street was named after Philip Walters, fourth Town Clerk* of Wrexham.

W. Phillips & Co *tea merchants*
Founded in 1850 by William Phillips of Borras Hall, Wrexham.* The business expanded and William's sons followed him into the business although only two, William Britain Phillips, JP, and John Phillips remained with the firm all their working lives. The business was originally located in Town Hill but later moved to High Street and a second shop was opened in Hope Street. The family also opened a café known as The Yale. The premises in Hope Street and High Street were sold in March 1955 with the former site being developed by Littlewoods as a shop.

Pickhill Hall, Marchwiel
A substantial brick-built mansion with decorative stone features dating from the early 18th century, possibly to a design by Richard Trubshaw. It was one of several family homes of the Pulestons. In 1801, the estate was sold by the Revd Phillip Puleston to the Ormrod family. In the twentieth century, due to a series of tragedies during the First and Second World Wars, the

238

Pickhill Hall, pre 1914.

house went into decline and was in 'extreme disrepair'. In the autumn of 1985 the house was gutted by fire and has since been converted into apartments.

Pierce's Square, Pentre Felin
A small court style development of poor quality housing, Pierce's Square was demolished in 1932 as part of the Wrexham Borough slum clearance programme. The area was redeveloped as commercial premises and the name is one of very few 'slum' addresses to have survived.

Piercy, Benjamin *civil engineer*
Born at Trefeglwys, Montgomeryshire on 16 March 1827, the son of Robert Piercy a valuer and surveyor. Benjamin was trained by his father, qualified as a surveyor and in 1851 was employed by Henry Robertson of Brymbo* to prepare plans for the Shrewsbury & Chester Railway Bill and a railway from Oswestry to Newtown.

He became a noted campaigner for the extension of the railway network and was involved with many of the lines that later formed the Cambrian Railways network. He was appointed surveyor to the Royal Sardinian Railway Company and became a wealthy landowner in his own right. A friend of the Italian patriot Garibaldi, Piercy was created a *Commendatore* of the Crown of Italy. He was employed on a scheme to canalise the river Tiber which supplied Rome with water, and was appointed engineer-in-chief of the Napoléon–Vendée Railway in France and, in India, engineer to the Assam Railway. It is believed that Garibaldi visited Wrexham in 1864 to meet up with Piercy and that whilst there addressed a large crowd from the balcony of the Lion Hotel* in Hope Street.*

Piercy used part of his fortune to buy the Marchwiel Hall estate outside Wrexham and was responsible, both directly and indirectly, for the development of several areas of the town, including the Red House* estate. In his latter years he devoted his time to consolidating the position of many Welsh railways and founded the Marchwiel Cricket Club. He died in London on 24 March 1888 and was buried in Kensal Green Cemetery.

Pilgrim's Place, Pentre Maelor
Named in honour of Daniel Lloyd* a 17th dissenter and prominent member of the early Independent Church in Wrexham, who was buried in a nearby field on Pen-y-Bryn Farm (see also Dissenters Burial Ground). His inscription reads: 'Here is asleep Daniel Lloyd, servant of Jesus Christ, interred November 19, 1665'.

Pines, The, Acton Park
Laid down in 1920 as part of the first phase of the Acton Park housing estate.*

Pinfold
A pinfold was a pound or lock-up for stray animals, particularly cattle. There are three recorded pinfolds in Wrexham, one on the north-west side of the Beast Market* (marked on the 1833 survey but removed by 1844), serving the township of Wrexham Regis, another in Tenters Square,* off Pen-y-Bryn, serving the township of Wrexham Abbot [DRO/DD/WL/170] and a third on the corner of Plas Coch Road* and Stansty Road* (the site of the present day Stansty Close) serving the township of Stansty.*

Pinfold House, Pen-y-bryn
A document of 1812 refers to a property by this name which was located close to the pinfold in Tenters Square. [DRO/DD/WL/170]

Pioneer Corps
See Hermitage Camp.

Plas Acton
Plas Acton, a large detached house in its own 25 acre grounds with substantial stables, a carriage-house for two vehicles and outbuildings, was built by solicitor John James,* the first Town Clerk of Wrexham, in about 1860. From the appearance of the house it is possible that the architect was J. R. Gummow.* The 1881 Census shows that, in addition to the James family, the house was occupied by three servants *viz* a housekeeper, cook and housemaid. In 1929, the property was by bought by Cyril Jones & Company (solicitors), divided into two residences and leased to various tenants including Mr Woolam (a noted Wrexham butcher) and Alderman Herbert Hampson.* The front half of the house retained the name Plas Acton and the rear half

Benjamin Piercy.

Plas Acton, c.1910.

became Acton House. During the Second World War evacuee families named Stevens and Wiles occupied the house. The front half was bought for £1,000 by electrical contractor Austin Eames in 1945, and the rear half was bought by Tom Evans (later of Gresford). The house stood alongside the present day Austin Eames premises in Pandy facing south-west, and was approached by way of a gated drive from Tŷ Gwyn Lane. It was the subject of a compulsory purchase order in 1970 and was demolished shortly afterwards to make way for the A483 Wrexham bypass.* Its name survives in Plas Acton Road, Pandy and Plas Acton Close off Chester Road.

Plas Acton Close
Named after its close proximity to Plas Acton Road.*

Plas Acton Road
Named after Plas Acton* which stood nearby. The road originally linked Pandy to Chester Road but was cut off by the construction of the Wrexham bypass in the 1970s.

Plas Cadwgan, Bersham
This medieval hall house in the township of Esclusham, contained the tallest aisle truss of any that survived into the twentieth century. The great hall measured 13m x 11m. Sadly, most of it was demolished in 1967 although the original truss was preserved and moved to Avoncroft in Worcestershire.

In the 16th century, the house and estate was the property of Edward Jones who was Master of the Wardrobe to Queen Elizabeth I. His son, also named Edward, became involved in a plot to remove Elizabeth from the throne and replace her with Mary, Queen of Scots, which was masterminded by his close friend Anthony Babbington. Although a relatively periferal player in the plot, Jones was arrested and charged with high treason and sentenced to be hanged, drawn and quartered. The conspirators were executed in two groups and such was the horror exhibited by many at the death of the first group, that the Queen ordered the second to be hanged until dead before the latter parts of the sentence were carried out. It was as a result of this plot that Mary, Queen of Scots, was herself executed in 1587.

The Cadwgan estate was then forfeited to the Crown and passed into the Cure family and from them, via a marriage, became part of the Chirk Castle estate. In 1796, the Myddelton family sold the estate to Thomas Fitzhugh of Plas Power*.

Plas Coch
(*Trans.* red hall) This property appears in the 1670 Hearth Tax Returns as having 9 hearths. It was an early brick gentry house that may have been built by Sir William Meredith of Stansty (see Meredith Family) in about 1580/90, located on the site of the present day Plas Coch public house. It was one of the earliest known brick-built houses in Wales. In 1606, it was the property of William Meredith, a ward of the King. William was created a baronet in 1622 and spent most of his adult life residing at Leeds Abbey, Kent while renting out Plas Coch. By the early 18th century the property had been purchased by Sir John Wynn of

Plas Cadwgan, photographed shortly before demolition.

Plas Coch Farm, 1953. The farm is separated from the new Denbighshire Technical College (bottom left) by Plas Coch Road.

Wynnstay, Ruabon. John Harrison, a tenant in 1868, is buried in the Dissenters Burial Ground,* Rhosddu Road. In 1881 it was tenanted by Robert Harrison who was farming 108 acres (died 1902).

In its latter years, Plas Coch formed part of the Clwyd County Council sports ground on which were held various youth sports events including county athletics meetings and cricket matches. During the 1980s, when education authorities went through a period of financial difficulties, Clwyd County Council sold the Plas Coch fields and farmhouse for development as a retail park. Despite some local opposition, the house was demolished to make way for the public house which bears its name. The name is used today to refer to the whole area between Plas Coch Road and the Wrexham bypass.

The landing ground of the world's first regular helicopter passenger service, linking Liverpool, Wrexham and Cardiff was located on Plas Coch. (See Helicopter Service)

During the preparatory work for building some of the Plas Coch retail premises, remains of a Roman farm were discovered and excavated.

Plas Coch, Plas Coch Road
A public house, opened by Banks brewery as part of the Plas Coch retail park development, which was named after the Plas

Coch* farmhouse which stood very close to the same site and which was demolished to make way for the development. In 2010 the public house was extended considerably.

Plas Coch College, Mold Road.
See Denbighshire Technical College and North East Wales Institute.

Plas Coch Retail Park
This was developed during the 1990s on land that had previously been the site of Plas Coch* and the Clwyd County Council sports ground. The first store to be built on the site was Sainsbury's.

Plas Coch Road
Plas Coch Road has undergone dramatic changes at two stages of its history. Named after Plas Coch,* the farm which was located on the site of the present day Plas Coch* public house, the road originally led from the Mold Road through to what is now the northern section of New Road in Rhosddu to Rhosrobin and Tŷ Gwyn Lane.* The building of the railway cut right across this small thoroughfare so that the road in effect ended at Stansty Lodge.* Lodge Road* is the last remaining section of the old road.

Plas Darland, Grosvenor Road
Plas Darland was the original name given to the house on Grosvenor Road that is now better known as the Mine Workers Institute. The name was later transferred to High Gate, a house on Grove Road,* and later still to the flats that occupy the same site on Grove Road. It 1881 it was the home of Edward Davies, MD, a deputy chairman of the Provincial Insurance Company* (died 1897).

Plas Darland, Grove Road
This property was located close to the corner of Grove Road* and Chester Road,* next door to Grove Lodge.* Originally known as High Gate, it was offered for sale in March 1936, having been the home of Dr J.E.H. Davies, DSO. The house had been converted into flats by 1951 before being demolished and the site used for purpose-built private flats bearing the same name. These flats were extended in 1979 (at a cost of £64,000) to incorporate the site of Grove Lodge.* [DRO/DD/G/2927]

Plas Derwen, Sontley Road
The first recorded owner of this house is the noted 19th century businessman and former Mayor of Wrexham, John Beirne.* On his death it passed to other members of his family. By 1943, it was the property of the Bishop of Menevia, Rt Revd Daniel Hannon* who invited the Sisters of St Joseph of the Apparition Convent to move into the house to establish a care home for the diocese. On 25 August 1943, the Revd Mother Gabriel of St Joseph's Hospital, Whalley Range, Manchester, accompanied by three sisters, moved into the house. They remained in the house until the mid-1960s when financial difficulties compelled them to place it on the market. In 1966, it was bought by the Sisters of the Holy Family of Bordeaux who established a convent there, having previously resided in the premises of the Convent Grammar School* in Grosvenor Road.

Plas Dinas, Chester Road
A large semi-bungalow, located on the north corner of Pen-y-

The only known photograph of Plas Grono, Erddig, taken in c.1860. [National Trust]

Maes Avenue and Chester Road, Plas Dinas was the home of Dr Wesley Hill. When sold in 1967 it comprised an entrance porch, lounge, dining room, morning room, kitchen, three bedrooms, box room, bathroom and two garages. Between the mid 1950s and 1967, the house was the Manse for the Methodist Church. In 1968 permission was sought to demolish the house and build a three storey block of twelve flats on the site but, despite approval being granted by WBC, the plans were rejected on appeal. The house is now called the Groves Guest House.

Plas Goulbourne
This was part of the Gredington estate, belonging to the Kenyon family.* In 1881 it amounted to 130 acres, farmed by a tenant Thomas Griffiths. The farm was put up for sale by the Gredington estate after the Second World War and was bought by the Blantern family (see Blantern Way) who remained there until the 1970s when it was sold for development.

Plas Grono (Gronow or Goronwy)
Once known as Tŷ Cerrig yn Hafod-y-Bwch and also as Plas Newydd, it stood in the grounds of Erddig. In the late 17th century it was the home of Elihu Yale.* In 1731 it was bought by John Mellor* of Erddig and was, for a time, the home of the Wilkinson* family (ironmasters) and the Apperley family. Charles James Apperley* described the house as: 'one of humble pretensions, consisting of four sitting rooms, with other suitable accommodation for a household of 20, for such as we were, with room to spare. It stands in what in days of yore was called a court, a space surrounded on some sides by shrubberies and buildings, ornamented on others by lawns and flower beds and directed by a ha-ha from very park-like looking grounds of some extent and formed by the confluence of two limpid brooks'. The house included a library and had good stabling. It was demolished in 1876 but the name has survived in a house used as a hostel in the grounds of Erddig Hall.

Plas Gwern
Described by A.N. Palmer as 'The most important house in Tuttle Street … it stood at the back of the Nag's Head in the premises of Messrs F. W. Soames and Company. I believe the

very hill on which it was placed is now [1893] levelled. I have some reason for believing that Plas Gwern is the same house that … was, in the time of Queen Elizabeth and King James I, called 'Y Bryn'. By the 18th century the house belonged to a Mr Davies who also owned the Nag's Head. In its latter years the house was badly neglected and used as a barrel store for Soames' brewery before being demolished in 1888. Palmer also believed that Plas Gwern was once called 'Y Bryn' in the late 16th and early 17th centuries and that it was described in Norden's survey of 1620 as follows: 'Richard Trevor, knight, holds one fair tenement lately built next the mount there called Y Bryn, with garden adjacent to the same demised, with other property to Frances Lloyd dated 11 Dec., 45th year of Elizabeth [1602–24 March 1603] … Also three cottages, garden and stable together adjacent in the street leading towards 'Y Bont Bren,'* [*Trans*. 'The Wooden Bridge' in Tuttle Street*]. Sometime after 1660, the house was occupied by a Mrs Elizabeth Jones, and by 1685, is referred to a Plas Gwern and is described as being ' a house, barn and kiln'. By the mid 18th century it was part of the Nag's Head property and by the 19th century was being used as a barrel store until it was demolished in 1888. Strangely, although the shape of this house is known from a photograph and sketches in Palmer's *History of the Town of Wrexham*, no evidence of it can be seen in either the 1833 or the 1872 surveys nor is it shown in Buck's print of 1748.

Plas Gwilym, 3 Grove Road
This Italianate villa was almost certainly designed by Wrexham architect J. R. Gummow and built for S. T. Baugh in the early 1860s. It was originally called Leeswood House and designated Nº 2 Grove Road. In May 1900, when it was the property of a Miss Jones, it was sold by auction. [DRO/DD/G/2859] By 1910, it was known as Plas Gwilym and had been the home of Wrexham brewer William John Sissons. In 1951 it was the residence and surgery of Dr W. Glynn-Evans and became offices shortly afterwards. Today it is the offices of Guy Walmsley & Co, accountants. The house is a Grade II listed building.

Plas Gwyn, Maes-y-Dre
Laid out and built in 1930–1 as part of the first phase of the Maes-y-Dre housing estate,* the name means white hall, or Gwyn's hall, but does not appear to have any significance in this location.

Plas Issa, Abenbury
(*Trans*. lower hall) This was a substantial house on the Old Llwyn Onn* estate which eventually became a farmhouse.

Plas Issa, Gresford
This was a name used for a short period in the early 19th century to refer to Pant-yr-Ochain Hall (as opposed to Pant-yr-Ochain Farm).

Plas Madoc, Ruabon
The original half-timbered house, dating from the mid 15th century, was built by Madoc ap David. His descendant, John Lloyd built a replacement house on the same site and died there in 1564. In 1773 the estate passed to Sarah Edwards of Crogen, Glynceiriog, a widow, who married the Revd Thomas Youde in 1773. Her son-in-law, Captain Jacob Hinde mortgaged the estate to fund his gambling debts. George Hammond Whalley, DL, JP, a descendant of one of the signatories of the death warrant of King Charles I, a noted lawyer and later MP for Peterborough, foreclosed on the mortgage and bought the estate in 1838 to clear the debt. Whalley extended the house, building the unbalanced wing visible on the left of the photograph. He died in 1878. His son, George Hampden Whalley, served in the Royal Navy, the Militia and the Denbighshire Yeomanry.* He saw active service in the Zulu War as an officer in Lonsdale's Horse. Elected MP for

George Hammond Whalley, MP, of Plas Madoc

Peterborough, he was eventually declared bankrupt and convicted of robbery for which he served a period in prison. Emigrating to Australia, he changed his name to White.

Plas Madoc was eventually sold to the Wynnstay estate and was leased to a series of tenants. By the 1960s, the house itself was derelict and was demolished, the site and grounds being used by the local authority for corporation housing and the construction of the Plas Madoc Leisure Centre.

Plas Madoc, showing the dilapidated condition of the house shortly before it was demolished.

Plas Panton
This was the name used on registration certificates *etc*. as the address of the residents of the Wrexham Workhouse. (See also Poor Law Union and Wrexham Board of Guardians)

Plas Power, Bersham
Originally known as Tŷ Bellot, Plas Power was once the home of Bishop Bellot,* who is buried in the Parish Church.* The name change to Plas Power came when the estate became the property of the Power (originally de la Poer) family who lived there as early as 1620 (one of whom, Henry, was created Viscount Valentia in 1620). It was acquired by Mary Myddelton* who leased it to her cousin, the Revd Thomas Lloyd, and bequeathed it to his son, William Lloyd, who built a substantial brick house on the site. William's daughter Mary married Thomas Fitzhugh, of Portland Place, Marylebone, London, in 1769. He was a director of the East India Company and they came to live at Plas

Plas Power pre 1857.

Plas Power, c.1920.

Power. In 1858, the house was considerably enlarged by Thomas Lloyd Fitzhugh (to a design by John Gibson) who also built St Mary's Church, Bersham as a private family chapel. During the Second World War there was both a sizeable Italian prisoner-of-war camp in the park and, prior to D-Day, a military camp accommodating US Army medical personnel. Following the discovery of wood-rot and death-watch beetles the main house was demolished by the owner, Colonel Geoffrey Fitzhugh, in about 1952, and the family took up residence in a smaller house on the estate which assumed the name Plas Power.

Plas Steward, Mount Street
See The Mount.

Plas Tirion
Designed by Wrexham architect J.R. Gummow* in what he termed the 'Anglo-Italian style', Plas Tirion was built in 1865 for local wine merchant Thomas Williams (he died in 1879 and is buried in the Burial Ground on Ruthin Road). After the death of Williams, the house was let to Major Charles Leighton, RWF, who died in India in 1889. By 1890, Plas Tirion was the home of Albert Llewelyn Hughes (c.1891), the son of publisher Richard Hughes* of Hughes a'i Fab, Hope Street. The house was sold to Susan Murless, the wife of Charles Murless, proprietor of the Wynnstay Arms Hotel.* In 1921, the house was sold to printer and publisher Rowland Thomas of the Caxton Press, founder of tyhe *Wrexham Leader* newspaper. In 1926, the house was bought by the Roman Catholic Diocese of Menevia as a permanent residence for the Bishop and the name was changed to Ty'r Esgob (*Trans.* the bishop's house) when it became the residence of the Roman Catholic Bishop of Menevia* and later Wrexham.* The house is now a Grade II listed building. The diocesan office is housed in the stable block at the rear. *The Story of Bishop's House (Plas Tirion), Wrexham* by Kathryn Byrne, published in 2009.

Plas Ucha, Stansty
See Stansty Hall.

Plas Yollen, Ruthin Road
The only reference to this name appears in sale particulars of October 1849 when a piece of land was offered for sale 'between the Railway and the New Burying Ground on the Ruthin Road, called 'Plas Yollen' containing 3a-2r-21p in the occupation of Mr Richard Lovatt'. This is the corner site, opposite the entrance gates to Parciau, which is now occupied by a filling station. The land next to it, further along Ruthin Road, was the property of the Ruabon Poor. [DRO/DD/CP/840]

Plas-y-Bryn
In 1802, a property of this name is shown on the Wynnstay Estate map of the Manor of Wrexham Abbot* [DRO/DD/WY/8352], located on the corner of what is now Poplar Road* and Chapel Street,* a site now occupied by the playing field of St Giles' School.* It seems that this house was demolished shortly afterwards as, by the time of the 1833 survey, it appears, un-named, on the south side of Chapel Street. It also appears in the 1872 survey, with substantial ornamentally laid-out gardens both alongside and on the opposite side of the street (the site now occupied by a pharmacy). An indenture dated 25 April 1766 shows that this land (on the south side of Chapel Street) was sold by Adam Davies of Liverpool, gentleman, to Robert Samuel, builder of Wrexham. The sale included 'all that messuage or dwelling house with its appurtenents situate in Wrexham Abbot in a street or place there called Pen-y-Bryn and adjoining upon the Bowling Green and commonly called the red house and the Garden, barn, stables and buildings thereunto belonging together with those two fields those pieces or parcels of land in Penybryn aforesaid to the said messuage or dwelling house belong commonly called and known by the names of Cae Mawr and the Well-field ... now in the holding or occupation of Hugh Jones husbandman and were the estate of Joseph Davies deceased father of the said Adam Davies.' When the actual house now known as Plas-y-Bryn was built is unrecorded. When the

Plas Tirion, Sontley Road, c.1870. Now the Bishop's House.

243

land was sold by Miss Mary Ellis in 1821, the deeds refer to 'four houses and fields and a large garden at Stryt Draw and in Penybrin'. The purchaser on that occasion was a Richard Browne, an attorney-at-law in Wrexham. His will provides some detail of the property: 'I devise the dwelling house in which I reside, stable, garden and appurtenances, four houses adjoining the garden unto my wife for her natural life.' This would appear to be the property as shown in the 1833 and 1872 surveys.

Following the death of Anne Browne in 1837, the house and land became the property of John Jenkins, yeoman of Acton, who leased it to Joseph Clark* and Jonathan Orford. In 1849, a lease for eleven years for 'all that messuage or dwelling house with the Yard, Garden and appurtenances thereunto belonging and also all that Field, Close or Croft of Land adjoining a certain Tan Yard' was made out in the sole name of Joseph Clark who was a brewer and wine merchant (see Cambrian Brewery).

By the early 1880s, the property was owned by William Low* (almost certainly the Wrexham based civil engineer) whose widow sold it in 1886 to Benjamin Owen, a builder, who, two years later, sold 'Pen-y-Bryn House' to William Richard Parry-Jones, a surgeon. This would appear to have been the first time that the house was linked with the medical profession and, by 1897, it was being used as the surgery of Dr Richard Evans. Since that time the house has remained a surgery, eventually ceasing to serve any domestic purpose.

In 1996, a large extension was built on the back of the house (designed by Wrexham architects TACP) to accommodate all the services required of a fund-holding practice. It would appear that the houses standing in the former garden area, facing the Congregational Chapel, were built by Benjamin Owen during the 1880s.

Plas-yn-Llwyn Nurses Home, Chester Road.

Plas-yn-Llwyn, Chester Road
Located in Grove Park, facing Chester Road, near the present day junction with Grove Road, this house appears on the 1872 survey. In 1881, the house is recorded as being empty and was sold in about 1902. The house was demolished and Beech Grove was built on the site, probably by the Batho family. The name Plas-yn-Llwyn was given to the nurses home which was built in the grounds of this house, on the site now occupied by Nightingale House Hospice.* [DRO/1065 & DRO/DD/G/2925]

Plas-yr-Esgob
This was a large house recorded by Norden in 1620 as belonging to Lady Puleston although, unfortunately, its location is not recorded. Palmer believed that its name (*Trans.* the bishop's hall) originated from the fact that it may have been the house in which Bishops Parfew or Wharton resided during their visits to Wrexham in the 16th century. It was Parfew who tried to make Wrexham the head of the diocese in place of St Asaph. Palmer* records that Bishop Standish of St Asaph mentions his house in Wrexham in his will, and that there is no trace of it because it may have been destroyed in the great fire of 1643. An alternative suggestion might be that the house survived for considerably longer than 1643, but under another name. Might it not have been the house which, under the name Bryn-y-Ffynnon, first appears in the records in the early 17th century? If so, it was certainly conveniently located for the town centre, the Town Well* and stood close to the area which appears to have had some religious significance for many centuries, where the old Vicarage was later built. The original Plas-yr-Esgob could either have either been demolished or re-modelled at this time, so much so that it became natural to call it by its new name?

Play-house, Beast Market
See Penson's Theatre.

Plume of Feathers, Chester Street
See The Feathers.

Plygain Service
This ancient religious ceremony was a regular prelude to the Christmas activities in churches throughout Wales. In Wrexham plygain services were held in the Parish Church* until 1890 and afterwards at St David's Welsh Church* in Rhosddu Road. The service was held at 6 a.m. (or earlier, in fact any time after midnight) and usually took the form of a shortened version of matins with the singing of carols. The service was usually conducted by candlelight.

Police
Before the establishment of a regular police force, following the setting up of the Metropolitan Police in 1829, communities such as Wrexham were policed by parish constables, men who were appointed by parish vestries or the justices of the peace. They were rarely paid and acted under instructions from the local magistrates.

A Society for the Prosecution of Felons* was formed in Wrexham towards the end of the 18th century but very quickly lapsed into disuse, only to be revived in 1816.

The County Police Act, 1839 allowed the establishment of a police force in Denbighshire and, in turn, the appointment of a superintendent and four police constables in Wrexham. The superintendents were paid £100 per year and the constables 15 shillings per week (plus a uniform provided). The 1841 census shows the Superintendent of Police, Thomas Mostyn (aged 25) living in King Street and John Evans (Police Officer) and his family living in Holt Street. This small force was soon criticised for being highly selective in the areas which it patrolled and the officers were even accused of being in league with the thieves operating in the town. One critic said: 'Our police can neither catch a thief nor keep him when they do catch him. Of bone and muscle, fat and big stick there is more than enough, to give the men their due. They are docile, active and affable. What is wanted is not so much guts as brains – and these they have not got. They cost £1,000 a year and their inadequacy must be apparent to everyone.' Such was the bad feeling towards the Wrexham Police that in 1844 the Quarter Sessions only narrowly voted not to disband them. The Denbighshire Constabulary was divided into two divisions – Division A (Wrexham) and B (Denbigh). (See also Major Thomas J. Leadbetter)

In 1967, the Denbighshire, Flintshire and Gwynedd Constabularies were merged to form the Gwynedd Constabulary which, in 1974, following the creation of the new county of Gwynedd) changed its name to North Wales Police/*Heddlu Gogledd Cymru*. At the time of writing (2010), the force is divided into three divisions: Western (covering Anglesey & Gwynedd, HQ Caernarfon); Central (Conwy & Denbighsire, HQ St Asaph); Eastern (Wrexham & Flintshire, HQ Wrexham). Each division is under the direct command of a chief superintendent.

Police Divisional Headquarters, Bodhyfryd
The foundation stone for the new Police Headquarters in Bodhyfryd was laid by Colonel G. E. Fitzhugh, OBE, TD, JP, chairman of the Gwynedd Police Authority, on 25 March 1974. The Police moved into the new £770,000, 14-storey offices in January 1976 and the building became fully operational on 12 January. (See also County Buildings). In 2010 it is the Headquarters of the Eastern Division of the North Wales Police.

Pont Liana
See Bridge Street.

Pont Tuttle
(Y Bont Bren) A small wooden bridge which crossed the Gwenfro at the foot of Madeira Hill. It can be seen in Buck's print of 1748.

Pont Tuttle House, Tuttle Street
Located close to the wooden bridge over the river Gwenfro,* this house was occupied by George Blackbourne, sometime agent for the Trevalyn Hall estate, in the early 18th century. No description of this house has survived.

Poor Ground, Holt Road
See Holt Road.

Poor Law Guardians
First meeting held at the Wynnstay Arms Hotel on 31 March 1837 when they decided to build a new workhouse at Croesnewydd. (See Poor Law Union) For many years the office of the Poor Law Guardians was located at 9 & 10 Temple Row. [DRO/DD/G/2884] In 1881, they met at 11 a.m. every Thursday at the Workhouse.

Clerks:
Thomas Edgworth* resigned 1857 on being appointed Mayor of Wrexham
1857   John Bury*
1907   J. Oswell Bury* (also recorded as such in 1881)
1911   J. Bagnall Bury*

Chairmen:
1881   Capt B.T. Griffith-Boscawen
1907   Simon Jones
1912   George Cromar
1914   Dr Samuel Edwards-Jones*

Poor Law Union (see also House of Correction and Bridewell)
Wrexham Poor Law Union was formed in 1847 and covered a total of 41 parishes reaching into Cheshire and Flintshire. In later years this was reduced to 37 parishes, all in Denbighshire. Prior to this date, the poor were the responsibility of the local magistrates who appointed Overseers of the Poor (unpaid) who doled out money from the parish poor rate to worthy cases. It was to the financial advantage of a parish to have as few 'paupers' as possible and at one time it was even permitted for the paupers of another parish to be flogged back to the parish where they originated. Until the formation of the Poor Law Union, Wrexham had a small workhouse housed in a part of the Bridewell* building in Salop Road. Built sometime before 1737, it was funded by voluntary contributions. A. N. Palmer* quotes the

The only known image of the Workhouse on Croesnewydd Road is this, taken from the plans for the Jubilee Station (Wrexham Central). Ground plans of part of the building are available on most OS maps of the period.

list of subscribers towards its erection and maintenance in his *History of the Town of Wrexham*:

Lady Williams [of The Mount] – £50-0-0
Mrs Anne Davies – £50-0-0
Miss Bennett – £10-0-0 for 5 years
Miss [Mary] Myddelton (of Croes Newydd*) – £10-0-0 for 5 years
Mrs Mytton – £5-0-0 for 5 years
Robert Williams, Esq [of Bryn-y-Ffynnon] – £5-0-0 a year during pleasure
Richard Puleston, Esq (Hafod-y-Wern) – £4-0-0
Jas. Apperley, Esq – £5-0-0
Simon Yorke, Esq – £5-5-0
Mrs Williams – £1-16-0
Mrs Lloyd – £1-1-0

It was run by a master and matron who supervised the female inmates as they carried out the daily chores. The workhouse could accommodate 80 people including 'male and female lunatics, idiots and imbeciles who mixed during the day with the other inmates'. In addition to the mentally handicapped, the workhouse population was largely made up of the elderly infirm or the blind or physically handicapped. In 1795, the Master was

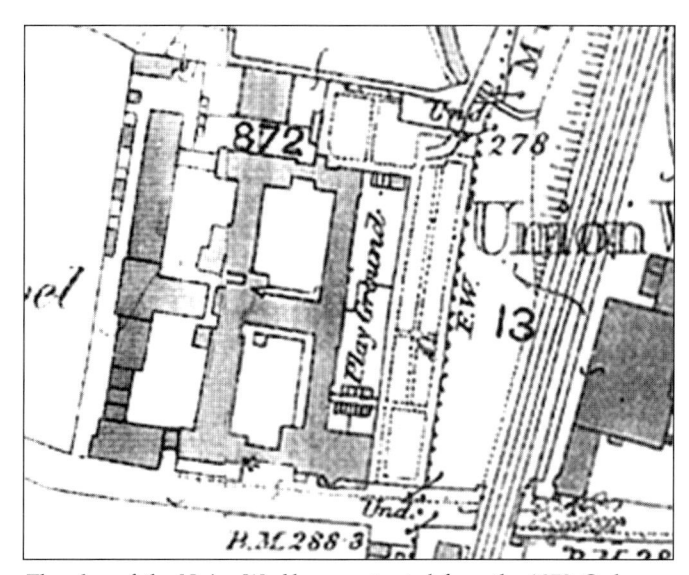

The plan of the Union Workhouse extracted from the 1872 Ordnance Survey map of Wrexham. Croesnewydd Road/Watery Road, crossed by the railway lines south of Wrexham General, runs W–E along the bottom of the map.

allowed to charge the parish 2s (10p) per week for each inmate's food and could also set all able-bodied inmates to work. The rising cost of corn (kept artificially high by the penal Corn Laws) during the early years of the 19th century meant that there was an increase in the numbers of able-bodied paupers and the old system of parish relief failed to adapt to the growing demand for localised financial support. Such were the conditions by the 1820s that magistrates in Wrexham were loath to commit people to the workhouse and there are many reports of inmates escaping. This original workhouse was probably still standing until after the new workhouse was built and part of its boundary wall formed the entry to Havelock Square* as late as 1891.

The newly-formed Poor Law Union, formed on 30 March 1837, was administered by 61 elected members of the Board of Poor Law Guardians* who held their first meeting in Wrexham on 31 March 1837. The townships which formed the Wrexham Poor Law Union were from the old counties of Denbighshire, Flintshire and Cheshire and most had one representative although four (indicated by a figure in brackets) had more. The townships were: Abenbury Fawr; Abenbury Fechan; Acton; Agden; Allington; Bangor; Bersham; Bieston; Borras Hovah; Borras Riffri; Bradley; Broughton; Brymbo; Burton; Cacca Dutton; Chidlow; Chorlton; Cuddington; Dutton Diffaeth; Dutton-y-Brain; Erbistock; Erlas; Erddig; Eyton; Esclusham Above the Dyke; Esclusham Below the Dyke; Gourton; Gresford; Gwersyllt; Llai; Holt; Hope (2); Malpas; Minera; Ridley; Marford and Hoseley; Marchwiel; Newton Juxta Malpas; Oldcastle; Overton; Pickhill; Royton; Ruabon (3); Sesswick; Shocklach Church; Shocklach Oviate; Stansty; Stockton; Sutton-is-y-Coed; Threapwood; Treuddyn; Wichaugh; Wigland; Worthenbury; Wrexham Abbott (2); Wrexham Regis (2). The Poor Law Guardians decided to build a new workhouse (or Poor-Law Institution of the Guardians of the Wrexham Union as it was officially known) on land near Croesnewydd, just to the west of Wrexham on the north side of the Croesnewydd Road, just after the present day level crossing. The new building was intended to accommodate 400 inmates (although there is some evidence to suggest that this may have been as many as 500) and cost £6,525 to build (the land costing £300). After 1838, a schoolmaster was appointed to educate the children (often this was a second position held by the Master). There were also porters, nurses (untrained) and, after 1902, one midwife.

Masters and Matrons of the Workhouse
1851–6	Daniel & Jessie Kemp
1857–63	Sgt-Maj William Bragger (ex 1st Royal Dragoons) of Deptford, & Mary Ann Bragger.
1863–8	Mr Higginson
1868–?	Luke & Elizabeth Ralph
1891–1901	George Stewart Bessell & Ellen Bessell
1901–?	Peter Cartwright & Harriet Annie Cartwright

The Board of Guardians was abolished by an Act of Parliament in 1929 by which time the Wrexham workhouse was no longer in use having been offered for sale in November 1925. The building was bought and most of it demolished to make way for Croesnewydd Hospital. The site is now occupied by part of the Maelor Hospital. All that remains today to remind us of the existence of the workhouse is the name Union Street and some of the older buildings on the Croesnewydd General Hospital site. [DRO/DD/G/2901]

A school was founded within the workhouse in 1838 and measured 28' x 17'. The *Report on the State of Education in Wales, 1847* gave report on the condition of this school:

> A school for boys and girls, taught separately, by a master and a mistress in the workhouse. Number of boys 36, of girls 40. Subjects taught – reading, writing, arithmetic, and geography, the Scriptures, and the Church Catechism. Master's salary £36 (with board and lodging), and the mistress's salary £18 (with board and lodging).
>
> There are 24 of the children belonging to this school who have attended it for periods varying from one to five years.
>
> I examined the school on the 22nd of January, when there were 31 boys and 36 girls present. Among the 67 only 8 could read tolerably, and only 6 could answer the plainest Scripture questions, and even these were very ignorant of the Bible. In the boys' school I was told that Eve was the first man and the mother of Jesus Christ. 20 copies were shown to me, 16 were very ill written, and none contained good writing. There were 9 boys learning arithmetic, but the best scholar did not understand Compound Multiplication. 2 boys were learning geography, but were very ignorant of the subject.
>
> The girls receive no instruction in arithmetic, and are not taught to write upon paper. Their education is confined to two mornings of the week, at which times they are taught reading, and writing upon slates. The mistress has not commenced to question them upon what they read in Scripture. They are taught to sew and wash. The boys were orderly, but the girls were not so.

The only known detailed plan of the Union Workhouse which only shows the eastern section of the building in 1872.

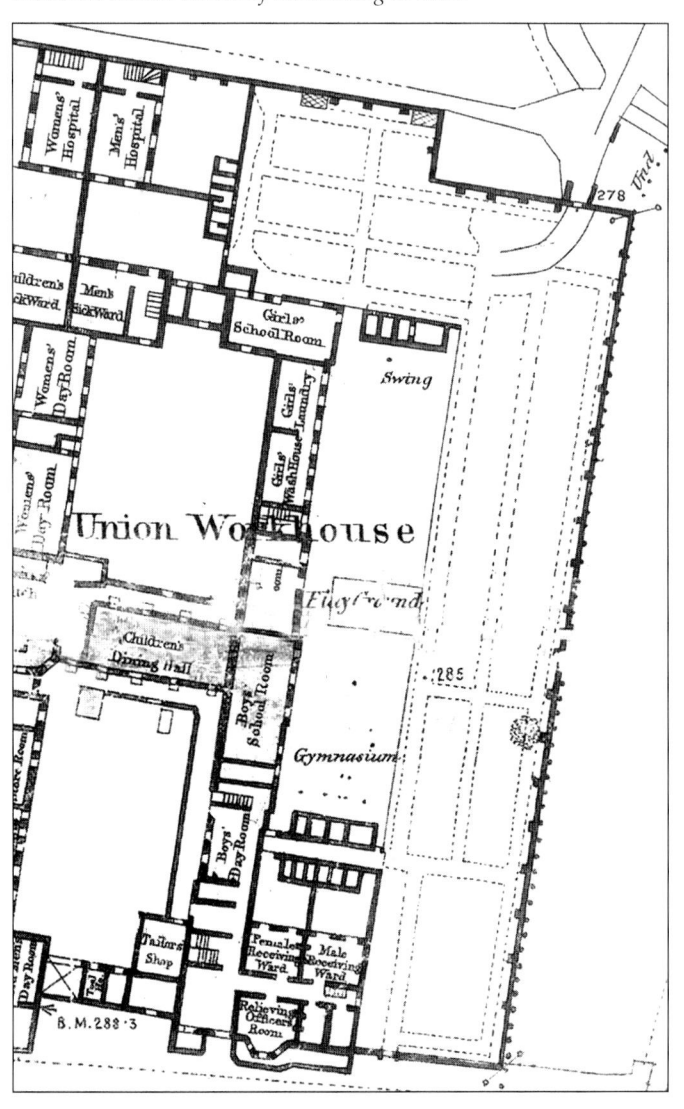

Neither of the teachers has received any kind of training.

The boys' room was dirty and oppressively close. Many of the scholars were in the sick-room. The furniture and apparatus were insufficient in both schools.

Very little good had been effected by these schools. The guardians visit them only once in two months.

The children are, for the most part, illegitimate.'

A letter written to the Wrexham Board of Guardians in 1864, described, in almost Dickensian terms, the Christmas activities in the Union Workhouse.

Gentlemen, may I on behalf of the inmates of the workhouse thank you for our Christmas treat, for the food and also for the good brown stout with which to wash it down. Thanks are due to our beloved master and matron for their kind endeavours to make everyone happy. The master played on his violin and we danced with much glee. May the master and matron live long to hold the office. After tea we had a drop more of the brown stout and some currant bread and the time was spent in friendship and amity. Gentlemen, all the children, both boys and girls, wish me to thank you from the bottom of their hearts. Many kind cheers were given at the end of the day to those kind gentlemen for their kindness to the poor but grateful paupers of Wrexham. Thanks to Mr Leader for the oranges and to the Revd Roberts for the current buns. Again many thanks to you gentlemen for everything, especially the bit of tobacco for the old men and the snuff for the old women. Your obedient servant and poor but grateful pauper, Sarah Watson.'

Among the rules of the Workhouse was one which stated that women with more than one illegitimate child were to wear a distinctive dress.

In 1881, the Workhouse was accommodating 367 inmates of whom 36 were classified as imbeciles and 1 as deaf and dumb. There were two other deaf and dumb children recorded but these were both the sons of the master and matron. The school was in the charge of George Stewart Bessell and Ellen Bessell.

An Inspector's report in 1920 gave a depressing picture of the Workhouse:

Building is roughly built, the walls unplastered and the wards badly ventilated. There are no damp courses in the walls and the floors in many parts are worn through and harbour dust and dirt. Most of the windows are of iron. The arrangements for rapid exit in case of fire are very unsatisfactory and in view of the inflammable nature of the buildings, which are full of dirt timber, this is of considerable importance.'

He went on to describe the dormitories as 'cold and badly ventilated'; the day rooms as 'very depressing, cheerless with flagged and tiled floors'; the heating as coming from 'antiquated fireplaces'; staircases 'dark and narrow, awkward, dilapidated, quite unsuitable for aged and infirm'. The residents numbered '242 inmates with 32 tramps in the vagrants section' and included '17 lunatics or feeble-minded persons' plus '50 bedridden cases in the infirmary'. The inspector recommended that £10,000 needed to be spent on the workhouse to bring it up to an acceptable standard for the time 'to give a fresh lease of life to a building which is no longer suitable for the purpose for which it was built'.

For the purposes of registration on official documents, the workhouse was usually referred to as Plas Panton to perhaps erase the stigma of being born in a workhouse. During the early years of the 20th century, families entering the workhouse were often split up with the children being taken away to a house in Chester Street (now The Old Registry*). This home was closed in 1921 and the children (totalling about 35) were sent to the Scattered Homes in Little Acton, accommodated in houses that had been bought by the Board of Guardians. When of age, the girls were found suitable jobs in domestic service and the boys were often found jobs elsewhere in the United Kingdom or, in many cases, were sent to Canada where they were settled with families and employers.

Poplar House, c.1980.

Poplar House/Cottage

Located at the top of Madeira Hill opposite the junction with Barnfield, this three-storey Georgian house was built by Edward Davies in 1817–24. Surprisingly, the house does not face towards the town and the Parish Church but, instead, overlooks Salisbury Road which had not been developed at that date. It is referred to as Poplar Cottage in the 1833 survey. There is evidence to suggest that the property was split into two occupancies very early in its history and as the Revd J. Tussell, schoolmaster, is known to have died here in 1839, it may have been a house located above a schoolroom. In latter years, the house fell into a rather dilapidated condition and in 1989 proposals were made that it should be demolished to provide a car park. Fortunately the proposal was rejected and the house was sold for £50,000 in 1993. The new owners carried out an extensive programme of refurbishment turning it into one of the most attractive properties in the area.

Poplar Road

This road appears to have been laid out during the mid-19th century to provide a link between Chapel Street and Salisbury Road. Named after Poplar House* the road does appear on the 1833 survey but has very few buildings on it and is not named. At the time of the 1872 survey there were very few buildings on the north-eastern side of the road and much of this land was later taken up by the drill-hall grounds and the construction of the National Schools* (St Giles) in 1885. The properties known as The Bonc, on the corner of Polar Road and Erddig Road (now forming part of the playing fields of St Giles' School), were the subject of a compulsory purchase order in 1934 as part of the Borough slum clearance programme.

Population Growth
Population figures for the town of Wrexham before the introduction of the national census in 1801 can only be the result of intelligent guesswork.

1801	2,575	
1811	4,524	
1821	4,795	
1831	5,484 (2,043 in Wrexham Abbot, 3,441 in Wrexham Regis; the population of the Parish of Wrexham was 11,515)	
1841	5,854	
1851	6,714	
1861	7,562	
1871	8,537	
1881	10,978	
1891	12,552	
1901	14,966	
1911	18,377	
1921	18,703	
1931	18,567	
1941	No census carried out	
1948	Unofficial census to include those areas incorporated into the Borough of Wrexham shortly before the Second World War. 29,100	
1951	30,962	
1961	35,427	
1971	38,650	(Rural 1968 – 62,190)
1981	40,357	(Rural 71,673)
1991	41,281	
2001	42,576	

Portal Avenue
Named after Marshal of the Royal Air Force Lord Portal of Hungerford (1893–1971), Chief of the Air Staff, this street was laid out and built by WBC in the 1940s when it consisted of only three pre-fabricated houses.

Post Office
The recorded names of people connected with the delivery of mail in the Wrexham area are:

Richard Lewis of the King's Head Inn (later the Greyhound Inn, Yorke Street) who was an innkeeper and postmaster in 1674 and was still alive in 1684;
John Pearce, postmaster, living in Wrexham Regis in 1665;
Robert Owen, postmaster, in 1681;
Mr Lewis, postmaster, 1684 (possibly the same man as Richard Lewis above)
Thomas Lowes (or Lewis), postmaster, died 1690;
Edward Hanmer, postmaster, 1702 (mentioned by Palmer* as living in Charles Street* between 1715 and 1730);
Mr Davies, postmaster, 1717/18;
Daniel Peers, Red Lion Inn, postmaster, died 1736;
A.H. Dodd refers to a postmistress in the 1770s;
c.1786–c.1814, Mrs Worrall, kept the post office in The Angel* public house in Chester Street;
c.1814, John Roberts kept the post office at N⁰ 36 Chester Street;
c.1823, Miss Catherine Roberts, N⁰ 36 Chester Street, postmistress (she married John William Todd Penson, the artist son of Thomas Penson* in 1823);
Richard Hughes, N⁰ 3 Church Street, 1824;
R. Mosedale, postmaster, 1837;
The 1833 Survey shows a post office located half way along the north side of Charles Street;
Richard Hughes, printer and postmaster, 3 Charles Street, 1845;
Richard Hughes, postmaster, 8 Hope Street, 1858;
There is some reference to a post office located on the corner of Lampit Street and Queen Street in the 1860s;
R. Edgar, postmaster, 1873;
R. Edgar, postmaster, 7 Regent Street, 1878 (this office was closed in 1885). In an 1881 directory, the postmaster is named as James Edgar.

A new post office was opened in Egerton Street in December 1885. Built at a cost of £2,000, it was leased to the Postmaster (R. Edgar, who retired in 1890) by the Revd T. Llewelyn Griffiths of Ruabon. The freehold to this post office, was bought by the Crown in 1904. In 1906, St James' Hall,* which was located next door, was demolished to make way for a new sorting office. A third storey was added to the post office in 1910 to house a telephone exchange which served the town until 1936, when a new purpose-built exchange was opened in Grosvenor Road.* [DRO/NTD/503]

Postmasters

1873–90	R. Edgar
1890–1904	J. Owen
1904–09	W. Paton
1909–13	C. R. Thomas
1913–22	G. J. Reay Scott
1922–27	J. B. Jones
1927–32	P. Allen
1932–33	P. Lewis
1933–45	H. Williams
1945–50	D. Davies
1950–58	T. I. Jones
1958–68	A. G. Davies
1968–71	J. T. Roberts
1971–82	L. Evans
1982–86	R. E. Hinde

The main post office was transferred to Regent Street in the 1980s and to Henblas Square in the new millennium.

Potato Market
See Butter Market.

Powell Brothers & Whitaker
Founded in about 1784 in High Street as an ironmongery business by Richard Jones. He was succeeded by his son John who later became a Calvinistic Methodist minister. In 1845, John's nephew, Evan Powell of Llangammarch (born 25 April 1814) joined the business and married Mary Jones (born Liverpool 26 November 1814, the daughter of Revd Daniel Jones; died 1 October 1897) his uncle's sister (she came to Wrexham as the first headmistress at the British School* in Brook Street). Following his death on 29 December 1874, the business, which was now an engineering and iron foundry works, was run by his sons, John Evan Powell (born c.1851, see also Powell Road) and Robert James Powell (born c.1853, married to Martha Williams of Moss Bank, Liverpool, he lived at Irvon, Grosvenor Road*). By 1879, the Powell brothers had been joined in the business by agricultural implement maker John Whitaker (born 1812) of Leigh in Lancashire (and later of Rhuddlan).

Powell Brothers & Whitaker had premises at the Cambrian Iron Works,* located next to the Wrexham General Railway Station* in what is now the yard of the Builder Center. Here they built up a successful business as manufacturers of agricultural implements, the products of which were well-known throughout Britain. John Whitaker died at N⁰ 4 Cross Street* in July 1896. His son, William, became a partner in the business. By 1914, Robert

Powell Brothers' Cambrian Works, Wrexham General Station, c.1882.

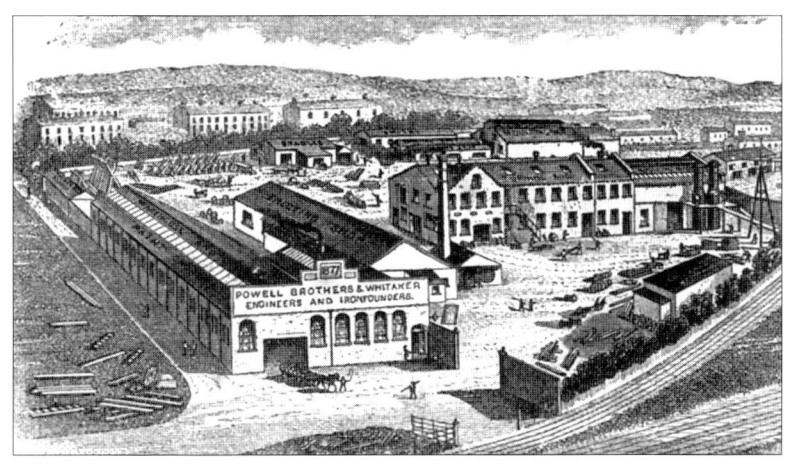

Powell Brothers' Cambrian Works, c.1916, manufacturing trench bombs.

Powell and William Whitaker had retired and the partners in the firm were John Evan Powell and his sons, J.W. Powell and Robert Glyn Powell (a third son, Lt Dafydd Emrys Powell was killed in action on 23 March 1918). The company dropped the name Whitaker and was incorporated as Powell Brothers Ltd on 16 April 1914.

During the First World War, the company converted its works into a munitions factory producing trench mortar bombs which were shipped out by rail. At this time, due to the manpower shortage caused by the war, many of the staff were women. After the war, in addition to resuming production of agricultural implements, the company began producing motor-cycles, an example of which can be seen in the Bersham Industrial Heritage Centre. *The Motor Cycle* magazine of 12 August 1920 described a pre-production model of the motorcycle (which was commercially launched in 1921):

> The new Powell machine has already proved its merit in strenuous reliability trials this season. [It] is an addition to the ranks of the single-cylinder medium weights, and a very sturdily-built machine it is. The 4 h.p. engine has a bore and stroke of 85mm and 96.5mm respectively, the capacity, therefore, being 547 c.c., so that, for competition purposes, it falls in Class D (750 c.c.). The engine impressed us as being of the 'beefy' order. It possessed great powers of acceleration, and would get away with extraordinary vigour, especially in the low gear ratios. A quality with which we were greatly impressed was the delightful steering of the machine.

Another motorcycle was introduced in 1923, the 170 c.c. lightweight, described as being 'so small and light that it is as handy as a bicycle'.

The economic recession of the 1920s led to the business going into voluntary liquidation in 1925 taken over in 1927 by Rogers & Jackson Ltd,* (part of the Rubery Owen Group). R.G. Powell remained as a director and the company became engineers' merchants. In addition to the Cambrian Works, Powell Brothers & Whitaker had premises on Town Hill (at the junction with College Street – this was destroyed by fire and rebuilt in 1891) and in the former Penson's Theatre* in the Beast Market. The Cambrian Works and the Theatre sites were later taken over by Messrs Rogers and Jackson. [DRO/DD/G/2912]

Powell Brothers
See Powell & Whitaker.

Powell Road
Powell Road was laid out in the late 1930s, probably as a service road to the new Grove Park Girl's School,* although it probably did not have a name at the time. It was originally a short cul-de-sac off Chester Road, extending only as far as the present day pedestrian underpass. It was extended to the end of Park Avenue and, with the name Bodhyfryd, through to Holt Road in the c.1976. It was named after John Evan Powell (c.1851–1926), of Irvon, Wrexham. Educated at the Liverpool Institute in the 1860s, he eventually became the senior partner in Powell Brothers & Whitaker* a passionate educationalist (he was an adviser for the Welsh Intermediate Education Act), the first chairman of the Governors of Grove Park County School* for Boys and deacon at Capel Seion.* The first house to be built here (pre-1939) was N° 2 which was the Divisional Police Commander's house, followed by N° 6 (just post-war) and N° 4 and finally, N° 8 in c.1966. All four houses lost substantial portions of their front gardens when Powell Road was widened and extended in the 1970s.

Poyser Family
Charles Poyser (mercer) of N°s 38 & 39 High Street, father of Charles Poyser (mercer) of Summerhill, and grandfather of Hampden A. K. Poyser.*

Hampden Alfonso Kusseth Poyser was born in Ellesmere on 15 March 1851, the son of Charles Poyser of Summerhill. He was articled to Wrexham solicitor J. Allington Hughes,* admitted as a solicitor in 1875 and established his own legal practice in Wrexham. He owned a fourth share of the Cae Siac* estate (off Ruabon Road) which was developed at the end of the 19th century and two of the new roads were named Hampden Road* and Poyser Street.* He also owned land on the east side of Chester Road* in the area of the present day Strathmore Surgery. Poyser was the Conservative agent for Sir Watkin Williams Wynn* and the Hon G.T. Kenyon. He chaired the Gwersyllt Conservative Committee, was Deputy Steward of the Lordship of Bromfield & Yale and President of

Powell Brothers shop at 6 Town Hill with a display of their motorcycles in the window.

the Wrexham Exchange Club. A bachelor all his life, he lived at Rose Cottage, Gwersyllt and died in September 1908.

Poyser Street
The land on which this street was laid out in 1898 was previously known as Cae Siac* (Shack). It was named after solicitor Hampden Poyser* who developed this area. The first houses appear to have been built in the years after 1900. Other than the houses, the major buildings in this street are the Victoria Schools* (opened in 1901), the Drill Hall* (opened in 1902), All Saints Church* (opened as St Michael's Church in 1912) and the Primitive Methodist Chapel (demolished 1990s).

Poyser Street Primitive Methodist Chapel
Built by the Primitive Methodists, the foundation stone for this new chapel was laid in May 1911 and it was opened by Mrs Jane Birkett Evans* and Peter Wilcock in December 1911 when the Talbot Road congregation moved here. A Sunday school was opened in 1915. The chapel was demolished in the 1990s and the site is now occupied by Chapel Place, a block of flats belonging to the Clwyd Alyn Housing Association.

Pre-fabs
Shortly after the end of the Second World War WBC built a number of pre-fabricated houses to try and quickly resolve the housing shortage problem in the town. The main developments were:
Maesgwyn: Jasmine Way, Laburnum Way, Wisteria Way, Acacia Way, Lilac Way* and Primrose Way.*
Pwll yr Uwd: Montgomery Road,* Wilson Avenue,* Portal Avenue,* Gort Avenue.*

Pre-fabs off Mold Road, 1963.

Preen, Edith Mary (Molly) *local historian*
Molly Preen was born in 1906, the daughter of Sgt-Maj Preen of the RWF. She was educated at the Convent School,* Grosvenor Road and St Mary's Church of England Teacher Training College, Bangor. After teaching in Liverpool and Gresford she was appointed to the National School,* Wrexham where she remained until retiring in 1967. During the Second World War she was a volunteer ambulance driver and a member of the Women's Voluntary Service. A keen churchwoman, Molly served as treasurer and secretary of the Parochial Church Council and as Sunday-school teacher.

Miss Preen was a founder member of the Denbighshire Historical Society, a member of the Cambrian Archæological Society and a founder member of the Clwyd Family History Society. She was a lecturer to the WEA and UCNW Extra-Mural classes in Wrexham and was elected a life member of the Wrexham Maelor Historical Society. She had lived all her Wrexham life in Ruabon Road. She died on 3 April 1998.

Presbyterian Church, Hope Street
In the 17th century, the house which stood on the site now partially occupied by the former Burton store and partially by New Look was licensed for worship and was the property of the Kenrick family of Wrexham and Wynne Hall, Ruabon. The property was sold at the end of the 18th century and was demolished shortly afterwards.

Price, Alderman Ernest *local politician*
Born in New Broughton, Ernest Price served in France with the Royal Garrison Artillery during the First World War. He married Blodwen Lloyd of Caego and they had one daughter. He set up his own bus service from New Broughton and Southsea to Wrexham but it was taken over by Crosville in the 1930s and he became an inspector with that company.

He was elected a member of Denbighshire County Council in 1946 and became a Wrexham Borough Magistrate in 1950. In 1953, he was elected as a Labour councillor for the Bryn-y-Ffynnon Ward of Wrexham but later became an Independent. He became Mayor in 1967 and an alderman in 1969 (on the death of Alderman Robert Roberts). He was a member of the North Wales Hospital Management Committee and Chairman of the Denbighshire and Montgomeryshire Joint Fire Service Authority. He lived at Nº 65 Mold Road, Wrexham.

Price, MBE, George Vernon *local historian & clerk to WRDC*
Born in Cefn Mawr in 1881, George Vernon Price began his working career as a clerk in a solicitor's office before training as an architect. He obtained a national prize for architecture and had honours in building construction. He then qualified as an art teacher and took up an appointment at the Wrexham Science & Art School.* In 1906, he entered local government service when he was appointed an assistant to J. Oswell Bury.*

During the First World War he was an interim clerk to the WRDC and in 1919 was given the permanent post, succeeding R.C. Roberts. He was a member of the National Housing and Town Planning Council, the Rural District Councils Association Executive Council and President of the National Association of Local Government Officers. During the Second World War he also held the positions of: Food Control Officer, National Registration Officer, Secretary of the Joint Fire Brigade Committee and Chief Billeting Officer. He was elected a Fellow of the Institute of Chartered Secretaries. He retired in 1946.

Vernon Price was a Freemason, a member of the Order of Knights Templar and Malta (Prior of the de L'isle Adam Preceptors and Great Bailee of the Great Priory of Malta) and president of the Rotary Club of Wrexham* (1951–2). He was awarded an MBE in 1943.

After retiring, he devoted much of his time to a study of local history with a particular slant on the religious history of the Wrexham area. His published works include: *The Old Meeting* (a history of the Chester Street Baptist Church*); *Valle Crucis Abbey*; *Service of God* (the life of Morgan Llwyd*) and a history of the Cefn Baptists.

He married Susannah Mary Noble, BSc, a science mistress at Grove Park Girls School,* in September 1920, and they lived at Arona, Wynnstay Lane, Marford.

Price, Henry *artist*
Born in Ruabon (*c*.1872), Henry Price was educated at the British School,* in Brook Street before becoming a student of the Wrexham School of Science and Art.* After graduating he set up

a studio in London and was commissioned by the Royal Artillery to produce a statue of Queen Victoria for the Royal Military Academy at Woolwich. He gave a duplicate of this statue to WBC and it was unveiled on 1 April 1905 in the square in front of the Guildhall on Chester Street.* The Woolwich statue was eventually moved to the Royal Military Academy, Sandhurst.

Price emigrated to the United States where he worked on New York Cathedral and on the Ritz Carlton Hotel as well as on the Government Buildings in Ottawa, Canada. After the First World War he was commissioned to produce many war memorials in the United States. In 1926, he was living in Chicago, employed as a superintendent (caretaker) of the Chicago Tribune Building and was commissioned to design a new statue of Abraham Lincoln but died before he could commence the work.

Price, Thomas *Prime Minister of South Australia*
Born in Brymbo on 19 January 1852, the son of John and Jane Price, Thomas Price became a stonemason in Liverpool where he met and married Anne Elizabeth Lloyd in 1881. Two years later, health problems forced him to leave Britain for Australia where he settled in Adelaide. In 1891 he was elected secretary of his trade union and, two years later, a Labour member of the South Australia House of Assembly. In 1900 he became Secretary of the Labour Party and, in 1901, its leader. In the Liberal and Labour coalition government of 1905 he became Prime Minister of South Australia. He died in office on 31 May 1909.

Price's Court, Holt Street
Located between Market Street and Regis Place. Price's Court was demolished in 1932 as part of the Borough Council's slum clearance programme. [Plans for cottages, dated 1912. DRO/1078]

Price's Lane
When Palmer was writing in 1893, he merely refers to 'the lane leading to Rhosddu' (from Chester Road) and the land to the north was known as Acton Moor or Gwaun-y-terfyn (Boundary Moor). The road began to be developed in the late 19th century following the opening of the railway sheds in Rhosddu. At the western end of the lane stood Walnut Tree Farm* which disappeared under the early development, particularly of Price's Lane itself, Walnut Street* and Albany Terrace.* The early cottages in this area had been built by the time of the 1872 survey but the developments had no street names allocated even as late as 1881. The terrace named Grange View, close to the junction with Park Street, is a reminder of Rhosddu Grange* close to the junction of Railway Road and Lodge Road, which was once clearly visible from this spot. Sackville Cottages took their name from Lady Cecelie Victoria Cunliffe (wife of the 5th Baronet of Acton Park*) whose maiden name was Sackville West (see also Cunliffe Family and West Street).

Most of the land in this area belonged to the Acton Park* estate. The only property towards the eastern end of the road in 1872 was Chevet Hey* which was surrounded by substantial gardens and was located just outside the original boundary of the Borough of Wrexham. The name Price's Lane almost certainly originates from Thomas Price, who was farming at Walnut Tree Farm* in the 1860s. The council houses on Price's Lane were built in 1939 by G.F. Sumner & Sons of Ashfield.* The present day St John's Ambulance* station is accommodated in the former Rhosddu Police Station. The playing fields were laid out in 1953.

Price's Lane (Ebeneser) Welsh Presbyterian Chapel
The Welsh Calvinistic Methodists of Seion Church* in Regent Street established a schoolroom in George Street in 1870. Its membership grew rapidly and the building was expanded, first by purchasing the house next door then, in 1873, by erecting a

Price's Lane Welsh Presbyterian Church, 1886.

purpose-built school room in Price's Lane. In 1886, when the Minister was Revd Griffith Owen, Ebeneser Chapel was erected at a cost of £1,400. The Religious Census of 1881 showed: Capacity 150; attendance (AM & PM) 199.

In 1979 the congregation of Seion, who had sold their church prior to building a new one, joined the congregation at Ebeneser where they remained until Capel-y-Groes* was opened in February 1982. In the interim period, the congregation at Ebeneser decided to sell their chapel and to unite with Seion at Capel-y-Groes. A number of groups expressed an interest in buying Ebeneser and it was sold to the Free Methodists and the congregation moved out after the last service on 31 January 1982. The church and schoolrooom are now occupied by the Community Church Centre.

Primitive Methodists Chapel, Beast Market
Shown in both the 1833 and 1872 surveys.

Primrose Way, Maesgwyn
A development by WMBC on a site that was previously occupied by pre-fabricated houses erected shortly after the Second World War. (See also Pre-fabs)

Prince Charles Road, Queen's Park
This street was laid out in 1949 by WBC as one of the access roads of the Queen's Park* housing estate but, for many years there were no houses with this address. The road was named after Prince Charles (later Charles, Prince of Wales) the eldest son of Queen Elizabeth II and Prince Philip who was born in 1948.

Prince's Close, Garden Village
Part of a Wain Homes development of 1989/90, this small cul-de-sac may have been named after Prince Dafydd ap Gruffydd who was granted Caergwrle Castle in the late 13th century. (See also Castle Close and Heol Dafydd)

Princess Street
Along with the other streets in this area, Princess Street was given its name as part of Wrexham's celebration of the reign of Queen Victoria. The name was a reference to Alexandra, the Princess of Wales. The street was laid out during the 1880s on a field that had previously been known as Cae March Ddu (*Trans.* black horse field) and was partly the property of the Plas Power estate with some of the land having belonged to Sir Evan Morris.*

Priory, The, Priory Street
The Priory was a large town house located on the eastern side of Priory Street opposite the junction with Bryn-y-Ffynnon. The

origin of the name is unclear and, according to Palmer did not appear until the end of the 18th century. The house appears in the records as far back as 1699 when it was the town house of the Edwards family of Stansty Isaf. In 1836 it was bought by Charles Poyser* and by the end of the 19th century was the offices of Sir Evan Morris & Co, solicitors. It appears in both the 1833 and the 1872 surveys. The site is now occupied by the Peacocks store at the rear of the Horse & Jockey* public house.

Recorded owners/tenants of this property were:

1661	Mrs Dorothy Edwards of Stansty Isaf
1699	Edwards of Stansty Isaf
1744	Madam or Miss Yonge of Bryn Iorcyn
1771	Madam or Miss Yonge and Miss Barbara Speed
1783	Peter Edwards
c.1808	Miss Letitia Eyton of Leeswood
c.1836	Charles Poyser
1869	Mr Eyton-Jones
1893	Sir Evan Morris & Company, solicitors

One of Wrexham's great architectural losses, the Priory Gatehouse (Bryn-y-Ffynnon) was one of very few surviving Tudor gate houses in Wales..

Priory Gatehouse, Priory Street
This late 16th early 17th century brick building was located on the western side of Priory Street on the site later occupied by James, James & Hatch (solicitors).* At one stage the building was covered in ivy but this was later cleared and at the time of its demolition in about 1966, was evidently a building of great historical interest, one of very few town gatehouses to have survived in north Wales. In the latter part of the 19th century the gatehouse was the offices of John James* (solicitor and first Town Clerk of Wrexham) and then, at the time of his sons, Messrs James, James & Hatch.* It would appear from the photographs of this building that have survived that it was more likely to have been the gatehouse to Bryn-y-Ffynnon House rather than to the Priory.

Priory Street
This was originally known as Priory Lane and believed to date back to the mid-17th century. The reason behind the name is unclear although it was believed at one time that Bryn-y-Ffynnon House had served as a Priory or that such a building, long since forgotten, had once stood on the southern side of the street. The premises on the west side of the street (now the Abbey National Bank) were formerly the Regent Tavern* and a general store. On the south side of Bryn-y-Ffynnon* stood the Priory Gatehouse* which was demolished in the 1960s and replaced by the rather inferior retail and office block that still survives. On the corner of Hill Street* is the Lloyds/TSB Bank which was built in 1928 for the Chester and Wrexham Savings Bank. The retail premises on the east side of the street, formerly the premises of Rogers & Jackson,* ironmongers and builders merchants, were destroyed by fire and rebuilt in the 2000s.

Pritchard, JP, John *local politician*
Born in Gwyddelwern, Denbighshire in c.1838, John Pritchard, was educated at the Mechanics Institute, Liverpool before joining his brother William as an employee of Shoolbred & Co, London. In 1864 they left London and became partners in Ward & Pritchard of N° 14 Hope Street (the site of the present day QD Stores). He was elected a Liberal member of WBC in 1882 and served as Mayor in 1886. He was a Justice of the Peace for the Borough of Wrexham, a director of the Wrexham Water Company and the Alliance Insurance Company. A passionate Nonconformist, John Pritchard married the daughter of the Revd John Roberts of Llanbrynmair and had three sons and two daughters. He lived at Longfields, Sontley Road (a house which took its name from the old field name 'Hirdir') where he died on 13 November 1894 and is buried in Wrexham Cemetery.*

Prospect Square, Pen-y-Bryn
A small 'court' type development which was located at the rear of the terraced houses on Pen-y-Bryn near where that street becomes Ruabon Road. Prospect Square was accessed from Pen-y-Bryn via a narrow passage.

Provincial Welsh Insurance Company, High Street
The Provincial Insurance Company Ltd was established in Wrexham on New Year's Day 1852. The company's prospectus showed that its capital totalled £100,000 made up of £10 shares. The trustees were: Sir Watkin Williams Wynn,* Sir Robert Henry Cunliffe,* Frederick Richard West, the Ven Archdeacon Clough and John Heaton. The company secretary was Anthony Dillon, the manager of the Wrexham branch of the National Provincial Bank, and the agents were John Clark and John Bury. It commenced trading on 1 April.

Originally accommodated in premises above N° 19 High Street it was soon operating throughout Britain and opened offices in London and Glasgow. By 1858, Government returns were showing that 'more farming stock insurances were effected with the Provincial Welsh Insurance Company than with any other Office in the Kingdom'. The decision was made to build new offices in High Street to allow the company to continue its programme of expansion and the foundation stone was laid by Lady Watkin Williams Wynn on 3 January 1860 on the site previously occupied by the large timber-framed building (which had been occupied by Mr Cottingham and which was painted by the artist J.M.W. Turner) and the houses in the narrow passage known as Y Nef.* The offices were located on the upper floors of the new building with the ground floor being let as two shops. On 26 October 1861 the business was transferred to the new premises. Undoubtedly one of the main architectural features of the new building was the General Office which was located on the first floor. Its 'enriched beams, panels, cornices and architraves' made it probably the finest office in Wrexham if not

Clerks busily working in the first-floor office of the Provinicial Insurance Company, High Street, c.1865. [Ken Wilson]

the whole of north Wales'.

Robert Lewis,* a Wrexham man who joined the Provincial Insurance as a clerk aged 18 in 1853 and who was transferred to the London office shortly afterwards, left in 1862 to join the Alliance Assurance Company. Within four years, aged only 31, he had become Chief Officer of the Alliance, a post which he held for 51 years. In 1874 the Alliance took over all of the fire insurance business of the Provincial Welsh and, in 1899, took over the whole company.

Secretaries:
1850	Anthony Dillon
1869	Robert Williams
1875	John Francis

On 4 January 1960, the High Street premises underwent remodelling and the ground floor re-opened as part of the insurance office. In 1973, the Alliance merged with the Sun and The London to become the Sun Alliance & London Insurance Company. In the 1990s a further merger with the Royal Insurance Company created the Royal Sun Alliance Insurance Company and, as part of that company's policy of streamlining their operations, the office in High Street was closed and is today the premises of Yates' Wine Lodge. [DRO/DD/DM/231]

Pryce, Thomas Maldwyn *racing driver*
Born in Rossett, the son of a policeman, Thomas Pryce spent much of his early life living in Ruthin and was employed as a tractor mechanic after leaving school. He was to become the most successful Welsh Formula One Grand Prix driver of all time. Having competed in 40 Grand Prix, and the winner of the 1974 Race of Champions at Brands Hatch, he was the N° 1 driver for the UOP Shadow Racing Team. His promising career was cut short when he was killed in a crash at the Kyalami circuit during the South African Grand Prix of 1977. His team-mate, Renzo Zorzi had crashed his car which burst into flames. A track marshal ran across to try and extinguish these flames but was hit by Pryce's car and killed. In the impact, the marshal's fire extinguisher was thrown into the air and hit Pryce, killing him instantly.

Public Hall, Henblas Street
Located in the centre of a block which included the old Masonic Hall and the Exchange Club, on the site of the old Birmingham Square* (later Union Square). The site was acquired by Yorkshire traders for their use during the March Fair and had a gallery with shops. The Square, which was roofed over during the early 1870s to accommodate 52 shops, was known as the Union Hall. In 1878, the hall was bought by the Wrexham Public Hall and Corn Exchange Company (offices at N° 3 Queen Street) who converted it into a hall which could be used as an assembly room and a theatre. In 1907 a fire which gutted the building was brought under control by the use of a 'steamer' engine of the recently re-formed Wrexham Fire Brigade. This site, along with that of the Rainbow Vaults* in Hope Street was under consideration for redevelopment by the Borough Council as a new Guildhall.

Puleston Family of Hafod-y-Wern
The Puleston family had played a significant role in the history of north Wales since the 13th century when Sir Roger de Puleston acquired land at Emral in *Maelor Saesneg* and was appointed as the first Sheriff of Anglesey by King Edward I. A kinsman, Richard de Puleston, was also appointed as the first Sheriff of Caernarfonshire at the same time. By the middle of the 15th century a branch of the family had land at Berse, Wrexham and, a few years later, had acquired Hafod-y-Wern through the marriage of John Puleston of Plas-ym-Mers to Aswn, the daughter of Hywel ap Ieuan ap Gruffydd. His son, also named John, fought at Bosworth Field in 1485 and was rewarded with a grant for life of twenty marks by King Henry VII and was also appointed a Gentleman Usher of the King's Bed Chamber. He was deputy-lieutenant to the chief steward of the Lordship of Bromfield and Yale* and was granted the lordship of Dyffryn Clwyd. He served in the French campaign of 1513. His son, John Puleston of Hafod-y-Wern, was High Sheriff of Denbighshire* in 1543–4. The family remained at Hafod-y-Wern until 1786 when Frances, the daughter of Philip Puleston and his wife Mary Davies (the heiress of Gwysanau), married Colonel Bryan Cooke, MP, of Ouston in Yorkshire. They died childless in 1820 and the combined Hafod-y-Wern and Gwysanau estates passed to Philip Davies Cooke of Owston.

Pwll-yr-Uwd, Spring Lodge
Pwll-yr-Uwd (*Trans.* porridge or plaster pool), a house which was the property of the Puleston family, was located in the area now known as Spring Lodge. There is no trace of the property remaining nor is its name commemorated in that of any area, street or building. The house took its name from a pool which was located near the junction of the present day Montgomery Road and Holt Road. Nearby, where Holt Road rises towards Borras Road and Spring Lodge, was reputed to be the location where public executions were carried out. The ridge, which runs parallel with Holt Road and upon which, until recently, the Border Brewery Bottling Stores was located, was called Bron Pwll-yr-Uwd (*Trans.* porridge pool brow) in Norden's survey of 1620. In the second half of the 19th century and the first half of the 20th century this area was used as the town rubbish dump until it was levelled to make way for the corporation housing in the area of Montgomery Road.* The Borough Depot was sited here until after the Second World War.

Pwll-y-Wrâch, Regent Street
(*Trans.* the witch's or hag's pool) Pwll-y-Wrâch is located between the Wrexham General Station* and Gerald Street.* Local legend has it that this was the place where nagging wives were 'ducked'. In recent years it formed part of the Grosvenor Nurseries. Palmer makes mention of a Durack's Pool (named after Thomas Durack of Bryn-y-Ffynnon Lodge* and Crispin*) near the GWR Station and it would seem likely that this is the same place. During the 17th century, the area surrounding this pond was generally

referred to as Pwll-y-Wrâch and was the property of John Jeffreys* of Acton Park.* By the 19th century, some of it was part of the glebe land belonging to the Parish Church (much of it was sold to the Chester and Shrewsbury Railway Company) and the remainder was part of the Hafod-y-Wern* estate.

Pwll-yr-Hwiad, Holt Road
(*Trans.* the ducks' pool) See Pwll yr Wydd.

Pwll-yr-Wydd, Holt Road
(*Trans.* the goose's pool) This small pond was located between Borras Road and Holt Road, close to what is now Moorhead Close although some references have been made to the name being applied to Pwll-yr-Uwd* in Spring Lodge. The 1841 census names it as Pwll-yr-Hwiad (*Trans.* the ducks' pool). In the 1841 census the name is applied to a dwelling which was occupied by farm bailiff Richard Evans and his wife Mary.

Q

Quaker Burial Ground, Holt Street
Located on the site of what is now called the Peace Garden (and which was then in an area of the town known as Lampint [sic]), this site, comprising two cottages and their gardens, was bought by the Wrexham members of the Society of Friends (The Quakers) in 1708. One of the cottages was probably used as a Meeting House and the gardens were designated a burial ground. There is no surviving record of the persons who were buried here, in fact the only recorded burials are two for which a Friends minister paid 39/- (£1.95) in 1728. By the mid 18th century, the Quaker movement in Wrexham had declined to such an extent that the Meeting House and burial ground were in the hands of others and was later let to the occupier of Holt Street House. The burial ground was landscaped in 1984 and named the Peace Garden. [DRO/957]

Quakers, The
See Religious Society of Friends.

Queen Square
The name Queen Square was given to a small development located between Queen Street and Birmingham Hall on the site which was later occupied by the Vegetable Market. It was the last surviving market square in the town and specialised in the sale of calico and table linen. It was entered from Queen Street 'through a pair of iron gates and under a covered entrance. We then reach an open square, surrounded on two sides [probably on three sides originally], with a covered gallery supported by pillars. In this gallery were shops, and beneath them, on the ground floor, were also shops.' The Square appears to have been built by Richard Kyrke of Gwersyllt Hill towards the end of the 18th century. It was bought by the Borough Council in 1898 and was eventually re-developed (along with Birmingham Hall) into the Vegetable Market. Today, the site is occupied by the BHS store on Queen Street. This is not to be confused with the present day Queen's Square.*

Queen Street
Originally known as Stryt-y-Syfwr (*Trans.* Receivers street) after the time when the Receiver of the Lordship of Bromfield and Yale resided there. Later, the street took on the name of Lower Hope Street before being occasionally referred to as Queen Street in the late 18th century. By the 1830s, all other names appear to have been forgotten and it has retained the name Queen Street

Queen Street Welsh Congregational Church, c.1975.

ever since. The area to the west of this street was formerly known as Yspytty* (hospital) although the origins of this name are unknown.

Queen Street (Ebeneser) Welsh Congregational Church
Congregationalists first met in Wrexham in the 1790s in a room off Queen Street* where they remained until moving to Pentre Felin* in 1844. In 1863, they returned to Queen Street where they had built a new, neo-classical style church which stood on the site now occupied by the row of modern shops on the western side of Queen Street. Its foundation stone was laid on 14 July 1862 and it opened on 26 March 1863 (Minister Revd Owen Evans), housing the congregation that had previously worshipped in Pentre Felin Chapel.* The minister behind the building project was the Revd Rowland Williams (Hwfa Môn) but he was moved to Bethesda, Gwynedd, before the building was finished. In the 1872 survey it is shown as having seating for 550 people.

Interior Queen Street Welsh Congregational Church, c.1975.

Ebeneser closed in 1976 and was demolished in 1979 and a new chapel was built on Chester Road. It appears in the 1872 survey. The Religious Census of 1881 showed: Capacity 500; attendance (AM & PM) 258. The Religious Census of 1904 showed: Capacity 500; attendance (AM & PM) 405.

Congregationalists first met in Wrexham in the 1790s in a room behind the site of their 1863 Queen Street chapel. From there, they moved to Pentre Felin* in 1844.

Queen Victoria Statue, Parciau
To commemorate the reign of Queen Victoria (who died in 1901), WBC placed a commission with Henry Price,* a former student of the Wrexham College of Art* to produce a statue of the late Queen for sitting in front of the Guildhall,* facing Chester Street. Price had already been commissioned to produce a bronze statue of the Queen for the parade ground at Aldershot and the Wrexham statue was a duplicate of this. It was unveiled on 1 May 1905. In later years it was moved to its present site in front of the Community Centre in Parciau.* It was renovated during the major works carried out on the Parciau in 2000.

Queen's Head, Bath Street
A public house located in Bath Street* in the early part of the 19th century, which later changed its name to 'The New Mitre'* and was eventually demolished to make way for the Wrexham & Ellesmere Railway* viaduct in the 1890s.

Queen's Park Housing Estate
WBC had operated a very progressive housing policy since the end of the First World War. Many of the slum housing areas of the town had been cleared by 1939 and the residents re-housed in modern, 'garden village' style estates such as those at Acton, Spring Lodge and Maes-y-Dre. The abandonment of all corporation housing schemes during the period 1939–45 meant that by the time peace was restored there was a housing shortage in the town. Spearheaded by Aldermen Hampson and Jennings, the post-war council took steps to see what type of housing scheme would best meet the needs of the local population in the 1950s.

Based upon the tried and tested 'garden village' model and, in particular, the system of segregating housing and traffic pioneered at Radburn, New Jersey, the the Borough Surveyor (J.M. Davies), Borough Architect (H. Anthony Clark) and Professor Gordon Stephenson drew up detailed proposals. Later generations have looked back at the massive Queen's Park housing development with some disdain but, at the time, the proposals were both revolutionary and admired by all. A number of neighbourhoods would be developed on the area previously known as The Dunks, on either side of the river Gwenfro between Smithfield and Cefn Park. These neighbour-hoods would be self-supporting and the whole scheme encompassed not only houses but churches, schools, community centres, play areas and shops. The river Gwenfro was to be a central feature of the development and land left on both banks to create a riverside park and promenade. The housing developments were to make use of the natural contours of the land and thereby give the residents views over the town towards the mountains. All the houses were to have gardens and access to both front and rear. The laying out of numerous cul-de-sacs was thought to encourage community spirit and to reduce the danger to children from passing traffic.

The original plan to build 3,000 houses was very ambitious but, by the mid-1950s, the number of houses in the development had already reached 2,207. In about 1960, Alderman Herbert Jennings said of the development:

The Housing Committee is justly proud of its achievements in Queen's Park – an estate of 2,500 houses. Two shopping areas and a new proposed public house cater for the food and refreshments needs. A flourishing Community Association provides for the social and entertainment requirements at the Community Centre, Kingsley Circle. A new playing field has been laid out and developed at Hafod-y-Wern and a sports stadium is to be provided here also.

It is a pleasure to note that the spiritual needs of the community are served: religious activity flourishes and the Methodists, the Roman Catholics and the Church in Wales have all built new churches.

The Education Authority have built two new schools on the estate.

The development of the Queen's Park Estate has been especially satisfying to all who have been concerned in it. It is now entering into a period of completion and consolidation with the provision of more playing spaces for children, the building of more garages for the ever growing number of cars, and the completion of landscape and park areas. As finance and other conditions permit, I believe we shall progress towards completion of as good an estate and as happy a community as can be found anywhere.

The Queen's Park Youth Centre was built at a cost of £70,000 and opened by HRH the Duke of Edinburgh in 1965.

Queen's Park Methodist Church
Originally a mission church held in a barn in 1934, then in the hall of Hafod-y-Wern Junior School. Work commenced on a purpose built church in Harvard Way in the 1950s.

Queen's Square
Contrary to popular belief there was officially, no such location as Queen's Square in Wrexham until 1999 (there had once been a Queen Square*) but the area in front of the old Wrexham Library at the town end of Rhosddu Road, at its junction with Queen Street* and Lambpit Street,* was often referred to by this name. The re-development programme of the 1990s which culminated with the building of Henblas Square and the pedestrianisation of the town end of Rhosddu Road resulted in a large open, paved area being laid out in front of the Guildhall and along the side of the Old Library buildings during 1999. Following public consultation WCBC decided to name this area Queen's Square.

Queensway, Queen's Park
Laid out in the 1950s and 1960s as the major thoroughfare through the newly-developed Queen's Park housing estate.* It was named in celebration of the accession to the throne of Queen Elizabeth II in 1952. Some of the houses were built by Vanton Investments. The significant buildings on this road are: the Queensway Youth Centre (officially opened by HRH Prince Philip on 23 June 1965), Queensway Sports Centre* (officially opened by Barry Jones, MP, Parliamentary Under Secretary of State for Wales on 31 May 1975) and Gwenfro Schools* (opened in 1958).

R

Racecourse, The
Located on Mold Road, the Racecourse was developed for horse-racing involving the Wrexham Yeomanry Cavalry (see Denbighshire Hussars Imperial Yeomanry) by Sir Watkin Williams Wynn of Wynnstay. The first race was held at on 29 September 1807 for the Town Purse, valued at £60, which was won by Lord Stamford riding his filly *Belinda*. This meeting,

The Racecourse — the Pryce Griffiths Stand and the Turf, 2000.

which lasted for three days, became an annual event, usually in the first week of October, until 1825 when the meeting was reduced to two days (there had only been a two day meeting in 1823 due to a shortage of entries). In 1857, the event was reduced to one day, following the withdrawal of the support of Sir Watkin Williams Wynn and racing ceased altogether in 1858.

Racing was revived in 1867 as the Wrexham Autumn Sports, but the standard was very much lower and even included a donkey race. This annual meeting was stopped in 1872 and replaced by the Wrexham Races which operated under Jockey Club rules until 1876. The following year Sir Watkin granted the use of the Racecourse to the local militia which made it unavailable for racing. From 1890 until 1912, pony racing was organised at the Racecourse, under the British Pony and Galloway Racing rules, with Charles Murless* as the main driving force. *Wrexham Races – the forgotten Welsh racecourse*, Arthur N. Shone, a detailed account of the Racecourse was published in 1991. [Documents relating to racing DRO/DD/GR/261 & DD/WY/9061-2]

Wrexham Cricket Club used the Racecourse for its matches during the latter part of the 19th century and it was members of this club that formed Wrexham Football Club in 1872. The first football match, an internal game between members of the Wrexham club, was played on 5 October 1872. Since that date, with the exception of the period 1883–87, Wrexham AFC* have always played their home matches at the Racecourse.

The development of the Racecourse into the present day football stadium was a gradual process –

> The pitch was originally laid north–south but in 1902 it was turned through 90 degrees in time for the Wales v. England match and has remained on that axis ever since.
>
> The first cover was erected at the Plas Coch end in 1926 (extended in 1929) and during the 1930s a cover was erected along the Mold Road side which was linked to the Plas Coch section by a purpose-built stand, called the Plas Coch Stand.
>
> The Town End of the ground and the Ashfield side (north) were only provided with earth banks on which supporters could stand to get a better view of the games.
>
> In the late 1940s/early 1950s, the Town End bank was adapted to take concrete terracing.
>
> In 1962, the club bought the seats from the former Majestic Cinema* which were placed at the Town End to provide 1,000 seats and nicknamed 'The Pigeon Loft'.
>
> In the 1960s, a shelter was along the north side which lasted until 1972 when it was replaced by the Yale Stand.
>
> The Centenary Club was opened under the Yale Stand in October 1975 at a cost of £50,000.
>
> In 1978, the stand at the western end was demolished and replaced by the Border Stand, in honour of Border Breweries who were the freeholders of the Racecourse.
>
> In 1980, the Pigeon Loft was replaced by a modern cover for the Town End (Kop).

In 1985, the Mold Road Stand and the Plas Coch Stand were closed and grand plans to build a £40 million new stadium were seriously considered. Both stands were eventually demolished and the more realistic Pryce Griffiths Stand was built in their place.

During the 2000s, the Racecourse was the target of a protracted legal dispute between the owner, Mr Hamilton, and the Wrexham FC supporters. Hamilton wanted to redevelop the site and relocate the football club. Eventually, a consortium of local businessmen and club supporters were able to buy the Racecourse and thereby, hopefully, secure its future.

In 2008 plans were unveiled for the redevelopment of the Racecourse with an all-enclosed stadium and an 800 unit student village along Crispin Lane. The student village is nearing completion at the time of writing (2010).

In addition to horse-racing, cricket and soccer, the Racecourse has also played host to major boxing competitions, wrestling, pop concerts, international rugby union and rugby league matches (including pool matches for the 1999 Rugby World Cup and the 2000 Rugby League World Cup). In 2009, the Welsh rugby league side, Celtic Crusaders,* moved from south Wales to Wrexham, making the Racecourse its permanent home.

The area of the original racecourse that was not taken over by the football ground was eventually developed as the Denbighshire Technical College,* the Yale Technical Grammar School* and the North Wales Tennis Centre. Also on the site, and incorporated into the football ground, was the Turf Hotel, which gave Wrexham AFC the unique distinction of being the only club in the English Football League with a licensed public house in its grounds.

RAF Wrexham, Borras

The Air Ministry bought up land in Borras from the Gredington estate, taking fields from Borras Lodge, Borras Head, Borras Hall, Gourton Hall, Plas Goulbourne and Wrexham Golf Club in the early days of the Second World War. The first aircraft used the field as a Relief Landing Ground in 1940. In December 1940, Sir Alfred McAlpine's workmen moved in to build permanent

RAF Wrexham, 1943. Holt Road runs diagonally from the bottom of the photograph to half way up the right-hand side.

runways and the airfield was operational by mid summer, although not finished until October. Nº 96 Squadron arrived at Wrexham from RAF Cranage (flying 14 Defiants and 2 Hurricanes). The squadron was re-equipped with Bristol Beaufighters in 1942 and inspected in Wrexham by the Duke of Kent on 5 May. Nº 285 Squadron was also based in Wrexham at this time, flying Hudsons, Blenheims and Lysanders (on anti-aircraft co-operation duties). In 1943 it became a satellite training airfield to Cranage.

At the end of the war, RAF Wrexham became a base for packing spare parts for shipment overseas before being downgraded to 'care and maintenance'. In its latter years as an airfield, Borras (as it is known locally) was the home to Sir Jimmy McAlpine's* Beech Super King Air until the final runway was dug up in the quest for gravel.

RAF personnel were accommodated in hutments built on Plas Goulbourne* (the site of the present day Borras Park Schools*) and in Bryn Gryffydd.* Officers were accommodated in Cherry Hill.* One machine-gun position has survived in the form of a brick pill-box on Borras Road, opposite Walnut Tree Farm. Access to a large area around the airfield was restricted and the main guardhouse was located at the junction of Borras Park Road and Jeffreys Road.

Some of the detailed history of RAF Wrexham has been published in the series *Wings Across the Border*.

The original Ragged School shortly before demolition.

Ragged School
The boys' school was founded in July 1852 by Thomas Taylor Griffith* in a room close to the churchyard steps at Pont Tuttle* at a weekly rental of 1s-2d. The master's salary was 15s per week. Within weeks, the school had moved to new premises located in what had been the stable block of Bryn-y-Ffynnon House,* which was bought from the Wynnstay estate.* A girls' school was opened on the same site in 1856 but the numbers on their roll were substantially reduced by the regulation that all girls must have their hair cut short. These were Wrexham's first free schools. Both schools closed through lack of funds at the end of 1881.
    Headteachers:
        ? –1856 Robert Roberts
        1878–81 Mr & Mrs Mills

Raglan Arms, Lambpit Street
This public house was probably built in the 1850s, as the name almost certainly derives from Field Marshal Lord Raglan, who commanded the British forces in the Crimea from 1854–55. The pub was rebuilt in 1903 as part of the redevelopment of the Vegetable Market.* It was demolished in the 1980s to make way for the Henblas Square* re-development.

This photograph of the RWF Territorials marching into Central Station in July 1914 for their annual camp in Aberystwyth provides not only a clear view of the 'temporary' station building, but also the only view of the Ragged School (top right with the children outside watching the parade.

Railways
In 1844, the North Wales Mineral Railway Company* was formed with a view to constructing a railway from Brymbo, Ruabon and Minera to Chester, via Wrexham.

In 1845 the Shrewsbury, Oswestry and Cheshire Junction Railway Company was formed. Before any progress could be made by either company they amalgamated to form the Shrewsbury & Chester Railway Company* which eventually went ahead with the building of the railway from Chester to Shrewsbury, via Wrexham. The engineer for the Wrexham–Chester line and for the Minera branch was Alexander Ross and the contractor for the Chester–Wrexham line was Edward Betts.

The Wrexham, Mold * Connah's Quay Railway Company was formed in 1862 with its Wrexham terminus at the Exchange Station* (later extended to the Central Station*).

The Oswestry, Ellesmere & Whitchurch Railway (OE&WR) was established in 1861 and led to the forming of the Wrexham & Ellesmere Railway* in 1885, operating out of the Central Station.

Railway Inn (I), Railway Road
The building of the railway* line from Shrewsbury to Chester caused both a considerable disruption to the community of Rhosddu and an impetus to its growth. The building of railway sheds and cottages for railway workers in the village in the second half of the 19th century resulted in a growth in both employment and population. As a result of this the public house which was sited alongside the railway sheds took the name of the Railway Inn.

Railway Inn (II), Abbot Street
Very little is known about this public house which closed in 1920, at the same time as the Cross Keys,* Mount Street.

Railway Road, Rhosddu
A road which was originally part of Rhosddu Road until the arrival of the railway* in the mid 19th century. Isolated by the railway and situated alongside the Rhosddu railway sheds, it changed its name to Railway Road.

Rainbow Vaults, Hope Street
Located at N° 50 Hope Street, this public house was first mentioned c.1774 when it was known as the 'Rainbow Inn' and occupied N°s 50 and 51 Hope Street. Until 1818 it was the property of the Myddelton family. In April 1813, the Rainbow Inn formed part of the estate of Mrs B. Jones which was sold at the Lion Inn. The sale description stated:

> The Rainbow public house with large yard, stabling, brewhouse, and a convenient building with rooms over used as a cooper's shop situated in Hope Street occupied by Widow Thomas. Also a good front dwelling house adjoining with yard and part of a garden in the holding of Mrs Phillips except so much of a room in this last mentioned house as lies over part of the passage leading from Mrs Davies's house and subject to the road over and through the Rainbow Yard to and from Birmingham Square during the time of the holding of the Wrexham March fair as is now used and enjoyed. [DRO/DD/G/2827]

It appears in the 1833 survey.

A weighing machine, which was located in front of the inn, appears in the 1872 survey, although the 'Rainbow' itself is not shown. In the late 19th century serious consideration was given to the redevelopment of this site for a new Guildhall for Wrexham Council. In 1933, following the creation of Border Breweries (see Nag's Head Brewery), the Rainbow Vaults was converted into the Rainbow Stores, an off-licence retail outlet.

Randles, Edward *musician*
Born in Wrexham in 1763, he was the son of a butcher. Although blind, Edward Randles was taught the harp and the organ and was appointed organist at Wrexham Parish Church in 1788. Both he and his daughter Elizabeth* played the harp before King George III and Queen Charlotte. He died on 23 August 1820 in Wrexham.

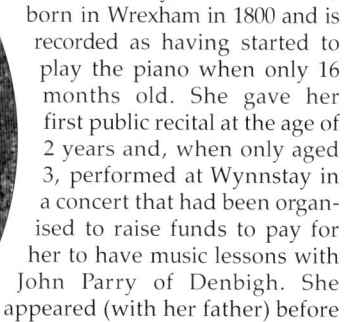

Randles, Elizabeth *musician*
The daughter of the blind harpist and organist Edward Randles and his wife Mary, Elizabeth was born in Wrexham in 1800 and is recorded as having started to play the piano when only 16 months old. She gave her first public recital at the age of 2 years and, when only aged 3, performed at Wynnstay in a concert that had been organised to raise funds to pay for her to have music lessons with John Parry of Denbigh. She appeared (with her father) before King George III and Queen Charlotte before her fourth birthday and the Prince of Wales offered to adopt her in order to ensure that her talent was developed to the full. She gave a concert at Cumberland Gardens in London at the age of 4. In 1807–08 she became part of a trio (with her father and John Parry) which toured Britain and gave a concert at the Hanover Square Rooms in London which was conducted by Sir George Smart, organist of the Chapel Royal. By the age of 14 she had mastered the harp, piano and organ. On the death of her father in 1820, she went to live in Liverpool where she died nine years later.

Elizabeth Randles.

Randles, Les *motorcycle racer*
Les Randles of Marford was the first winner of the Manx Amateur Road Race (now the Manx Grand Prix) in 1923. He rode a Sunbeam motorcycle to victory at an average speed of 52.71 mph. He also won the premier race the following year at an increased average speed of 56.71 mph.

Range Road, Hermitage
Named after the army firing ranges that were located in this area.

Ranscombe Crescent
A private housing development by Broseley Homes in the 1970s. The land was formerly part of Pant yr Ochain Farm* which was part of the Acton Park* estate. The origin of the name is unrecorded.

Raven, The, Hope Street
Also known as the 'Old Raven', this public house is first recorded in c.1699 and occupied part of the site of the present day New Look store. In 1746, the name was changed to the 'King's Head' (a name transfer from a public house located on the opposite side of the street) by Rowland Samuel and it remained licensed premises until about 1762 when it was converted into a shop and later, in c.1794, three shops. [DRO/963]

Rawlinson's Farm/Tenement
This was a farm included on the survey of the Acton Park estate carried out for Sir Foster Cunliffe in 1786. The farm was located in the townships of Acton and in Gwersyllt, between Chester Road and Wat's Dyke,* roughly the same site as the farm that became known as Tŷ Gwyn.* The field names were: *in Acton township* – Cae Fayen Mawr and Buchan [*Trans.* large and small ? field], Allt-y-Groes [*Trans.* hill of the cross], Brewin, Maes Acton [*Trans.* Acton field], Erw Pant rhan [*Trans.* part of the hollow acre], Little Meadow, Erw Fynnon [*Trans.* well field]; *in Gwersyllt* – Cae Edward Griffith [*Trans.* Edward Griffith's field]; Edard ap Edward's Croft, Pwll-y-Broen [*Trans.* possibly a mis-spelling for lamb's pool], Little Gorse, Cae Molly [*Trans.* Molly's field], Cae Croes Forth [*Trans.* crossroads field], Erw Coed [*Trans.* wood acre], Cae Tolgeth Têg [probably a mis-spelling of tylwyth têg, *Trans.* fairy field]. The last two fields were located on either side of Chester Road on the sites today occupied by Plas Acton Close and Plas Acton Garage. [FRO/D/AH/24]

Recreation Ground, Rhosddu
See William Jones Memorial Recreation Ground.

Rectors of Wrexham
The traditional title of Vicar of Wrexham was changed to Rector of Wrexham in 1971. (See St Giles Church)

Rectory, The, Westminster Drive
Following the sale of Beech Grove (the former Vicarage*/Rectory) on Chester Road, the Church in Wales bought this house from the Batho family in the 1980s and it became the Rectory.

Red Cow, The, (I) Beast Market
Located at the corner of Beast Market* and Seven Bridge Lane,* this public house survived from 1742 to at least 1828 but does not appear on the 1833 survey.

Red Cow, The, (II) Pen-y-Bryn
Originally called 'The Machine' (after the nearby public weighbridge), this was the property of Robert Griffith of Hafod-y-Bwch* in the early 19th century. It was also known as the Brown Cow.

Red Dragon, The, Prince Charles Road
A public house built by Border Breweries in the 1970s to cater for the Queen's Park housing estate. The name is taken from the trade mark of Border Breweries.

Red Lion, The, (I) High Street
Recorded by Norden in 1620 as being located on the south side of High Street, next to the High Cross.* Also, see The Lion, High Street.

Red Lion, The, (II) Kings Mills
Possibly the oldest public house in Wrexham, the Red Lion was built as a smithy in c.1492 and within six years had become an inn. The original building has survived as part of the present day public house.

The junction of Chester Street and Holt Street, showing the Red Lion Vaults on the corner and to the left a town house. Both premises were demolished to make may for the Wrexham Motor Company Garage and the Welch Fusilier public house.

Red Lion Vaults, The, Chester Street
Located on the eastern side of Chester Street just north of the junction with Holt Street and in the 1833 survey it is referred to as the Little Red Lion. At other times, it is referred to as the 'Old Red Lion'. In 1900, it was the property of John Jones* of the Island Green Brewery. In July 1919 it was sold to Bent's Brewery for £5,000. The pub was later demolished and a new building, re-named, the Welch Fusilier,* was built on the same site.

Red House
This was a property on Watery Lane, facing onto what was to become Bradley Road (opposite the junction of Belle Vue Road). It was owned by John Sparrow (died in 1847) and then Thomas Jones (died in 1866 – a George Jones of the Red House was buried in the Dissenters Burial Ground,* in 1860) before being bought by Benjamin Piercy* of Marchwiel Hall. Following his death it was sold by auction in September 1895. The land around it (which is usually referred to as the Red House Estate, was sold off for building at that time). The original farmhouse has survived and is now the premises of Glitz Dental Laboratories at 80 Bradley Road. [DRO/DD/DM/188/29; DRO/970; FRO/D/BC/ADDITIONAL FITZHUGH/11/37]

Reform Club, Chester Street
Once the Liberal Party Headquarters in Wrexham, this building was probably built in 1890 (from the date stone above the main entrance). It was visited by HRH Edward Prince of Wales (later Duke of Windsor) in 1934. In the 1970s, it became a discotheque before eventually being converted into flats called Tŷ Caer.

Regan, Rt Revd Edwin *Bishop of Wrexham*
Born in Port Talbot, south Wales on 31 December 1935, he was the son of James and Elizabeth Ellen Regan (née Hoskins). Educated at St Joseph's RC Primary School, Aberavon and Port Talbot Grammar School, he studied for the priesthood at St John's College, Waterford, Ireland, and Corpus Christi College, London. He was ordained as a priest in 1959 and was a curate in Neath (1959–66) before becoming the Adviser on Religious Education to the Archdiocese of Cardiff (1967–87). He was Chaplain to St Claire's Convent, Porthcawl (1967–71), Administrator of St David's Cathedral, Cardiff (1971–84) and the parish priest at Barry (1984–89) and Bridgend (1989–94). He is the Chairman of the Schools Committee of the Roman Catholic Hierarchy in England and Wales and member of the steering group for ICONS, a secondary schools programme for religious education. A fluent Welsh speaker, he was consecrated Bishop of Wrexham on 13 December 1994.

Regent House
This was built by E.G.M. Cape in c.1964, architect G. Raymond Jones, Anderson & Associates. Prior to this the site was occupied by four large terraced houses which, in 1951, were the premises of E.F. Tombs (dentist), the District Nurses' Home, the Denbighshire Technical College School of Music and the G. Trevor's Temperance Hotel.

Regent Street/*Stryt-y-Rhaglaw*
This street was originally part of Hope Street/Road. The street was laid out in the mid 19th century (it does not appear to have any name in the 1833 survey, but was almost certainly named after the Prince Regent, later King George IV). In certain early 20th century adverts, businesses located in this street give their address as Station Road.*

The site of the present day Grosvenor Precinct and Roxborough House was once open land known as the Orchard Field which belonged to Bryn-y-Ffynnon House.* One of the first important buildings to be constructed on this site was the English Wesleyan Chapel known as Bryn-y-Ffynnon Church* which was built in 1855–6. This chapel closed in 1889 and was then demolished to make way for a larger building with the capacity to seat 650 people. This was opened on 5 September 1890 and was in turn demolished to make way for the present building in the late 1960s.

The Wrexham County Museum* building was originally the Militia Barracks* built in about 1857. In 1879 they were converted into a Police Station* and Magistrates Court* (known as the County Buildings*) which function they served until closure in the 1970s. After a relatively short period as part of the Wrexham College of Art,* they became the property of WMBC in 1995 and were converted to house the County Museum.*

The Roman Catholic Pro-Cathedral of St Mary* and the Presbytery were built in 1857, the church replacing the Catholic chapel which had stood in King Street.*

The Wrexham Infirmary* was built in 1838 and served the town as a hospital until the opening of the Wrexham & East Denbighshire War Memorial Hospital* in 1926 when the building was adapted to accommodate the Denbighshire Technical College* until the 1950s. In recent years the building has been the Wrexham College of Art.

The narrow street which is today called Union Street,* leading to the former Wrexham Lager brewery site, was previously known as Cathrall's Lane and led through to Rhyd Broughton until it was truncated by the construction of the Shrewsbury–Chester railway line. The name was changed to Union Road in the late 19th century as this was the road leading to the Wrexham Poor Law Union Workhouse.*

To the west of the present day railway line ran a section of Wat's Dyke*. Both sides of Regent Street were once bounded here by common land known as Pwll-y-Wrach.* Grosvenor Road* was laid out through this land in 1869. One surviving photograph of the approach road to the railway station shows clearly a toll house near its junction with Regent Street and an open field on the site now occupied by the Royal Mail Sorting Office in which sheep are grazing. In the late 19th century this field (which extended as far as Gerald Street) was known as the Nurseries and was the location of the nursery belonging to Yeaman Strachan.* When the Denbighshire Technical College* was looking for a new site after the Second World War, the Nurseries site was a serious consideration.

On the corner of Duke Street* stood Capel Seion,* the Welsh Calvinistic Methodist Chapel opened in 1867. The Savings Bank,* a neo-classical building stood on Regent Street with its northern side on Egerton Street.*

On the corner of Regent Street and Caxton Place stood Caxton House, a red brick and terracotta building that was the offices of the Wrexham leader newspaper for many years. A fire in the 1950s seriously damaged the building and destroyed many of the newspaper's archives. In later years the building was used as offices by various businesses, including the legal practice of the former MP, Wil Edwards. Between Caxton House and the Royal Mail sorting office was Wrexham's first purpose-built motor garage, the Triplex. The garage and Caxton House were both demolished in 2003 to make way for a new development of seventy private apartments, built by the local company Gower Homes.

The Wrexham architectural practice of G. Raymond Jones, Anderson & Associates has had a marked impact upon the appearance of this street and were responsible for much of the redevelopment work including: Regent House, built by E.G.M. Cape in c.1964; the Grosvenor Shopping Centre, built by John Laing for Grosvenor Estates was completed in 1972; Imperial Buildings, built by John Laing for the Grosvenor Estates in the 1970s.

Regis Place
Named after the old township Wrexham Regis, this street of terraced houses, built by timber merchant and coach-builder Samuel Cooper (the father of Joseph Cooper who later lived at Bodhyfryd House*) in the early 19th century, ran parallel with Chester Street and was entered from Holt Street. Much of Regis Place (property belonging to Samuel Rogers Ltd of Charles Street) was demolished in 1932 as part of the WBC's slum clearance programme and the site now forms part of the modern People's Market. [Plans for cottages, dated 1912, DRO/1078 & 1048]

Registry Office
In 1881 this was located in John Bury's* office a N° 10 Temple Row. Sometime after 1921 this moved to Chester Street House (now known as the Old Registry*) in Chester Street, now the premises of Walker, Smith & Way, solicitors. In 1978 it relocated to N° 2 Grosvenor Road and is now in Tŷ Dewi, Rhosddu Road.

Religious Society of Friends
The activities of the Religious Society of Friends (The Quakers) in Wrexham date back to the early days of the sect and George Fox, the founder of the movement, visited the town in 1657. In 1660,

Two photographs illustrating not only two views of Regis Place but also two totally different life styles within a few yards of each other. The top picture shows industrial terraced housing while the lower picture shows a private house which may once have been the residence of local businessman Samuel Cooper. The tree in the second picture can also be seen at the far end of the terrace in the first picture.

Quaker James Fletcher (of Knowsley) visited the town 'to comfort the Friends in prison' and was himself arrested and detained for 16 weeks. Local Quakers are recorded as meeting 'in their own hired house' by 1661 and two years later Brian Sixsmith (a draper), William Lewis (a corvisor) and John ap Edward (a butcher) were fined for not attending the Parish Church. John ap John of Cefn Mawr was prosecuted at the Quarter Sessions in October 1663 for failing to attend church. He had once been a follower of Morgan Llwyd* but, after meeting George Fox, formed his own group of Quakers in the Cefn Mawr area. He became an evangelical preacher throughout Wales and was instrumental in securing 50,000 acres of Crown land in the American colonies where Welsh Quakers could settle to escape persecution; over 2,000 Welsh men and women crossed the Atlantic to settle in what was later to become Pennsylvania. He died in 1697. His fellow Quakers bought two newly-erected cottages in Holt Street, Wrexham, which were licensed for worship in July 1708. A piece of land was bought alongside the houses to serve as a Quaker burial ground.* The purchase was arranged by John James (a dyer) and Hannah Newton (a flax dresser) from Thomas Kynaston of Penley for £32-15s-0d. The upper storey was used for meetings and the lower floor let as tenements. By 1746, the Quakers appear to have ceased to worship in the town and the meeting house eventually became a

Presbyterian school before being demolished in the latter years of the 18th century.

In the 20th century, a small group of Friends began to meet at 39 King Street and in 1965 a purpose-built Meeting House was established on Holt Road, seating 80 people at a cost of £3,500. This building has recently been replaced by another purpose-built Meeting House on the same site.

Report on Education in Wales, 1847
See Blue Books.

Rhosddu
The name Rhosddu, referring to the area to the north of Wrexham town centre, means black moor and probably takes its name from the presence of coal and peat below the poorly drained surface. Several of the old field names in the neighbouring Stansty area indicate similar features e.g. Y Wern (*Trans.* swampy meadow), Erw Rhosydd (*Trans.* moors acre), Tirodd Duon (*Trans.* black lands), Cae-y-Rhos (*Trans.* moor field). In addition, the water-logged nature of the area is indicated in a survey of the Manor of Stansty Issa (*Trans.* lower Stansty) in 1707 which has a reference to a 'Causy thereupon' undoubtedly referring to a causeway lifting the road above the surrounding moor. Apart from one or two farmhouses and large villas, the first housing developments in the Rhosddu area stem from 1856, following the arrival of the railway and the sitting of goods and carriage sheds in the area. The engine sheds were located on the site of the Remploy factory on Railway Road* and the carriage shed on the site that was later the GPO depot and is now the car park of the Total Fitness centre. The railway cut the area in half, effectively severing the link between modern Rhosddu and Stansty. The population of the area was further enhanced with the opening of the Wrexham & Acton Colliery* in the late 1860s. As the area developed so did its facilities which gradually included a church (Rhosddu became a parish in its own right in 1886), a school, chapels and a public house.
[DRO/DD/WY/8950]

Rhosddu Colliery
See Wrexham & Acton Colliery.

Rhosddu Common
Also referred to as Rhos Stansty Common. This was located on the land later occupied by the Wrexham and Acton Colliery (now Rhosddu Industrial Estate in Rhosrobin).

Rhosddu County Primary School, Price's Lane
Opened in 1877 and originally known as Stansty School, it moved into new premises on Price's Lane on 15 April, 1915 (although the 1912 OS map shows the present school). During the Second World War a British restaurant operated at the school between 1941 and 1944. The schools operated as separate infant and junior schools until 1 September 1983 when they were merged to form Rhosddu CP School. In 2010 the school has a pupil population of 268. The school choir performed for HM The Queen and HRH Prince Philip at NEWI in 2003.

Headteachers:
Junior
	1877	Mr Davies
	1884	C.H. Wykes
	1910	W. R. Owen
	1936	J. B. Jones
	1954	William Taylor
	1977	J. Miles

Infant & Junior Schools merged 1 September 1983
Infants
	?	Mrs Roberts
	1897	Miss Thomas (Mrs Charles Edwards)
	1898	Miss J. Roberts (Mrs Felix)
	1909	Miss M. C. Jones (Mrs Walter Evans)
	1913	Miss E. A. Roberts
	1944	Miss V. E. Roberts
	1961	Mrs M. O. Henderson
	1977	Mrs E. Lawson
	1981	Mrs R. Jenkins

Infant & Junior Schools merged 1 September 1983
Primary
	1983	E. Ellis
	1996	Malcolm King

Rhosddu Farm
See Walnut Tree Farm.

Rhosddu Grange, Railway Road
This house and farm was located on the western side of Wat's Dyke and east of what is now New Road, Rhosddu. The property was once part of the Stansty Hall estate and belonged to the Edwards family. By 1620, the original house and farm was owned by the Hughes family of Yspytty* who remained there until *c.*1800 when it became the property of William Davenport. In the mid 19th century the property was bought by John Foulkes of Charles Street,* who demolished the original timber-framed house and built a new house which he called Alma Grange. Although there is no fixed date for this change it seems highly likely that it occurred shortly after the Battle of the Alma in 1854. Foulkes built other houses on the land *viz*: Ashfield,* Rhosddu Lodge,* Clermont Cottage* and Stansty Villa.*

Rhosddu Grange (or Alma Grange) was occupied by Elizabeth Saunders in 1851 and by 1881 was the home of Andrew Young, agent for the Wrexham & Acton Colliery.* In the 1930s, it was the home of Alderman William Thomas. In the early 1960s, the site was laid out as streets for private housing *viz*: Ffordd Meirionydd,* Ffordd Morgannwg,* Ffordd Caerfyrddin,* Ffordd Trefaldwyn* and Ffordd Môn.* The house has long since been demolished, but the name survives in Grange View, a terrace of houses in Price's Lane* and Grange Avenue* off East Avenue.* (See also Stansty Issa)

Rhosddu Halt
Opened by the Great Central Railway on 1 March 1917, this halt was sited in the fork of the Brymbo South Junction, just to the east of the road bridge as Colliery Road entered the Wrexham and Acton Colliery. It was closed in 1923.

Rhosddu Lodge (Stansty Lodge), 10 & 12 Weston Drive
This building should not to be confused with the Stansty Lodge that was located on the Mold Road. For a period, this house was referred to as Stansty Lodge, although it is generally accepted as Rhosddu Lodge.

In the mid 19th century, this property had been bought by John Foulkes of Charles Street, who appears to have demolished the original house and built the present day substantial house which then stood in its own extensive gardens. The house has the appearance of a typical late Regency/early Victorian villa with a number of neo-Elizabethan architectural features reminiscent of the local architect, Thomas Penson II.* Initially Foulkes may have lived here himself before moving to nearby Ashfield House,* but it is more likely that the first resident was local lawyer William Bennion, the father-in-law of John Foulkes, and the two households may well have exchanged houses in the mid 1840s. From 1851 to 1866, Rhosddu Lodge was leased to John Lewis, a local attorney. Foulkes died in December 1861 and the house was put up for auction in May of 1862 when the sale particulars included a description:

A Capital recently-erected DWELLING-HOUSE, Stables, Outbuildings, Ornamental Pleasure Grounds, Entrance Lodge,

Rhosddu Road, c.1960. With the exception of the old Library building (on the left behind the trees) everything in this photograph has changed and now forms the new Queen's Square. The pavement area on the left was named Coronation Walk after the visit of HM The Queen in 1953.

Rhosddu Road, c.1912. Garden Road is on the left and Cunliffe Street on the right.

Gardens, and Lands, containing altogether 6 acres 2roods 10 perches ... containing three excellent Entertaining Rooms on the Ground Floor, Kitchen, Back Kitchen, and Larder, and Washhouse, and Laundry, and six good Bedrooms; Stables for 4 Horses, Hay Loft, Coach House, Cow House, Piggery, and Granery; Entrance Lodge ... Excellent Pasture Land.

Whether the house was actually sold in 1862 is unrecorded but, by 1881, Elizabeth, the widow of the builder John Foulkes, had moved to live there from Ashfield. It was again put up for auction in July 1885, following the death of Elizabeth Foulkes two years earlier. Robert Walter Egerton, the son of Sir Robert Eyles Egerton,* and his wife Flora Augusta, were living at Rhosddu Lodge at the time of the First World War and his son, Lt Robert Randle Egerton, RE, died in Belgium on 16 November, 1914, aged 26. The house was later the home of J.A.W. Bates and then his son, Wrexham solicitor Joseph Henry Bates, whose widow lived there until her death in the 1950s. The former garden wall can still be seen alongside Stansty Road and turning the corner into Lodge Road, where the original drive entrance post can also be seen. In recent years the house has been divided into two and a number of streets were built in its gardens by local builder William Pemberton-Davies during the late 1950s/early 1960s. Lodge Road* takes its name from this house. The former stables and coach house at the rear of Rhsddu Lodge have survived and are now a dwelling named Lodge Court. Lodge Cottage on the corner of Stansty Road and Lodge Road was the entrance lodge for the house [DRO/DD/PL/168]

Rhosddu Methodist Chapel, Colliery Road
The Primitive Methodists built this chapel during the 1880s, with a schoolroom added in 1889. It served the area until it was closed in 1937, due to the poor condition of the building. It was rebuilt and re-opened in 1955. The Religious Census of 1904 showed: Capacity 150; attendance (AM & PM) 164.

Rhosddu Road
Rhosddu Road leads north-west from the present day Queen's Square to the junction of Walnut Street. Before the building of the railway in the 1850s, the road continued as far as the present day Railway Road before continuing north to rejoin what is now New Road close to Bryn-y-Glyn. The construction of the railway cut both the community and Rhosddu Road in two and led to the construction of New Road which linked Rhosddu Road with Rhosrobin.

Rhosddu United Methodist Free Church
The date when this congregation built a chapel in Rhosddu is unknown but the minister, the Revd Joseph Bentley, was living at N° 1 Cunliffe Street in 1881. The Religious Census of 1904 showed: Capacity 350; attendance (AM & PM) 239.

Rhosddu Welsh Baptist Church
See Garden Road (Calfaria) Welsh Baptist Church

Rhosddu Welsh Methodist Chapel
In 1887, a mission church from the Hill Street English Presbyterian Church was opened in the schoolroom, and was named Moriah.

Rhosnessney
This was the old Anglicised spelling of Rhosnesni* and was also used as the name of a small estate in the township of Erlas. Between 1709 and 1805 it was the property of a family named Benjamin and the house was rebuilt towards the end of the 19th century. The Benjamin family were also grocers and tallow chandlers in the town of Wrexham during the 18th century and also owned the estate of Hafod, a house and shop on Town Hill,* a large house 'in the churchyard at the back of the house last-

named, a large house and shop in Hope Street [on the site of the present day W. H. Smith] ... and various lands in the Town Fields'. The Benjamins were Nonconformists and some members of the family were buried in the Dissenters' Burial ground* in Rhosddu – John Benjamin (died 1703), Deborah Benjamin (died 1727), Margaret Benjamin (died 1753), Mary Benjamin (died 1718), Richard Benjamin (died 1763), Richard Benjamin (died 1740), Richard Benjamin (died 1751).

Rhosnesni
The origin of the name Rhosnesni is difficult to define. The word *rhos* is Welsh for moor but the meaning of the second and third syllables *nesni* is unclear. Palmer* suggests (quite logically) that they mean *nesa i ni* – closest to us, thereby translating the whole name as the moor closest to us. As Wrexham was surrounded by moors e.g. Rhosddu, Rhostyllen, Rhosrobin, it would seem logical that one would be seen as being the closest. W. O. Eddowes, who was born in the Beast Market in 1786, recalled: 'I remember Rhosnessney all a common. Sir Foster [Cunliffe*] enclosed it without an Act and divided it amongst the freeholders and planted all the trees in my time'. By the late 19th century the name had been applied to the settlement between Borras Road* and Holt Road,* most of which was in the south-eastern part of the township of Acton. Following the establishment of the Wrexham Rural District* in 1894 Rhosnesni came under its jurisdiction until 1935 when the boundary of the Wrexham Borough was extended. This alteration in the boundaries made it necessary to change of the name of Acton Road* (Rhosnesni) to Dean Road.*

The settlement grew up around the toll-gate on Holt Road (see Toll Gates) and was expanded in the late 19th century by the construction of a number of estate houses for the Acton Park* estate. This led to the building of a church, a chapel and the provision of a police station. Following the break up of the Acton Park estate, almost all of the land in Rhosnesni was bought by private developers and over a period of fifty years it has become an urban area. The opening of St David's School in 1957 marked the 'coming-of-age' of the settlement as an integral part of the Borough of Wrexham.

Rhosnesni High School/Ysgol Rhosnesni
Opened in September 2003 following the merger of St David's School* and The Groves School*. For twelve months, while major alterations were carried out to the former St David's School building, the pupils of the new school were accommodated at the former Groves School site. The school moved into the Rhosnesni Lane site in September 2004. The school serves the northern section of Wrexham town (Acton, Alexandra, Barker's Lane, Borras Park, Hafod-y-Wern, Rhosddu and Wat's Dyke schools) and the village school at Is-y-Coed). In 2010 it had 1,140 pupils on the roll.
Headteachers:

    2003–08   Bernard Knowles
    2008   D. Gareth Hughes

Rhosnesni Lane
Rhosnesni Lane appears to be one of the old routeways of the area, linking Rhosddu with the village of Rhosnesni. For most of its extent it was delineated on the north by the sandstone boundary wall of the Acton Park* estate, substantial sections of which can still be seen. In the early 20th century there were a few estate houses, the Gate Hangs High and some small cottages at the Rhosnesni end, with Park Farm* (on the site of the former Ray's Motors). In 1920, work began on building the Acton Park housing estate* inside the old Acton Park boundary wall. Shortly after this date, individual private houses began to be built along

This rather indistinct photograph of Rhosnesni Lane taken in the early 20th century shows two of the houses built by the Acton Park estate (right) and the only photograph showing the position of Park Farm house (on the left, behind the tree).

the lane, starting with Sunnyside (built by E.Ll. Rogers, Managing Director of Rogers & Jacksons* for 45 years) in *c*.1926. The house called Beechlands (now the site of a small development of private houses called the Beechlands) was once the home of G.W. Higginson (of the Wrexham Motor Company). The shops on the corner of Park Avenue* were built in the late 1950s by Mr & Mrs Edward Clarke (he was the son of Philip Clarke of Park Farm* and she was the daughter of E.Ll. Rogers) on an area of land that had previously been the location of the site offices for the builders of the Acton Park housing estate. The other two shops (now the off-licence and McColls) were built by Philip Clarke in the early 1930s.

Probably the most significant development on Rhosnesni Lane was the building of St David's School* in the mid 1950s.

The south side of the western end is dominated by the Nine-Acre Field,* once part of the Acton Park estate but, since the 1920s, the property of Wrexham Council. Despite several attempts to pass through plans for the residential development of this field (the original 1920s plans included a road cutting diagonally across this field linking Cooper's Lane* to Chester Road), it remains a much needed green space that was used for many years as playing fields by Grove Park School,* and the Groves School.*

Rhosnesni School/Rhosnesney Church of England School, Borras Road
This was believed to have been first established in a house in Borras Road (now Borras Park Road*) before a purpose-built National School was opened on the junction of Dean Road and Borras Road in 1870. The school was closed in 1971 and the pupils transferred to the newly-built Borras Park School.* The school buildings were then used as a playschool until the 1980s, after which they fell into a state of disrepair. The school was finally demolished and the site is now occupied by private houses. [DRO/ED/LB/101/9–11 & ED/MB/101/14]
Headteachers:

    1870   Miss Annie Pierce
    1871   Miss Eliza Broster
    1872   Miss Sarah McCreesy Harding
    1900   Miss F. M. Jackson (Mrs Butterworth)
    1908   Miss Holland
    1934   Gwilt Ll. Cathrall

Rhosnesni English Methodist Chapel, Rhosnesni Lane
Established as a Mission church by the Poyser Street Calvinistic

Methodist Chapel, the church was founded in 1919 and could accommodate 200 persons. [DRO/ND/1] The church building is of the pre-fabricated type which was popular in the late 19th/early 20th century and could usually be bought by mail order from a manufacturer that specialised in supplying buildings suitable for easy construction in a remote corner of the Empire.

Rhosrobin Chapel, opened in 1896, was a daughter church of Ebeneser in Rhosddu.

Rhosrobin Halt
Opened by the Great Western Railway on 1 September 1932, this halt was located between the Pandy road bridge and the junction with the Wheatsheaf/Gwersyllt Colliery branch line. The halt closed on 6 October 1947.

Rhyd Broughton Farm
Located above the junction of Berse Road and Pentre Broughton Road, this house still stands although now altered beyond all recognition and used as a residential home (with the former farm outbuildings being used as a veterinary practice. The property (and 45.4 acres) was sold to the industrialist Dyke Dennis* in 1926 for £5,000. In later years the farmhouse was the home of Mike Smith, the Welsh national soccer team coach.

Richards, JP, MP, Professor Robert *politician*
Born in 1884, the son of a mine worker, Rob Richards was educated at elementary school and Cambridge University. He became a lecturer at Glasgow University before being appointed Professor of Economics at UCNW, Bangor. He was elected Member of Parliament for Wrexham in 1922 and was appointed Under Secretary of State for India in the first Labour Government. He lost his seat in 1924, regained it in 1929 only to lose it again in 1931 after which he was appointed a tutor in economics at Coleg Harlech. He finally recaptured the Wrexham seat for Labour in 1935 and remained as MP until 1955. During the Second World War, he was the Regional Civil Defence Commissioner for Wales. He was a member of the 1945 mission to India to examine the question of independence.

He was never regarded as a good constituency MP and for long periods failed to visit Wrexham, residing at Brynglas, Llangynog in Montgomeryshire. He was a Justice of the Peace, a member of the Montgomeryshire Local Education Authority, the author of a number of books on mediæval Wales and a member of the Gorsedd of Bards of the National Eisteddfod. Much of his spare time was devoted to a study of birds. He was married but had no children. He died in December 1954.

Richmond Road, Little Acton
A development of private houses completed in two stages. The first phase (on the northern side of the street) was built by local builders H. R. & E. Roberts during the late 1950s/early 1960s. The second phase, which takes up most of the south side of the street was a continuation of the Cavendish Square development.* The land was once part of Cae'r Hen Dy (*Trans.* old house field) and Erw Coed Mawr (*Trans.* big wood acre), fields belonging to Little Acton Farm* and later, to the Acton Park* estate. There does not appear to be any local association with the street name.

Ridley View, Queen's Park
Built in the immediate post Second World War period as part of the first phase of WBC's Queen's Park housing development, it takes its name from the view eastwards either towards the local settlement of Ridley Wood or the more distant parish of Ridley in Cheshire.

Ridley Wood Close, Sontley Road
Part of a private development on land that was once part of the Ithens Farm* and, from the 1940s to the 1960s, Hermitage Camp.* Named after the local settlement of Ridley Wood.

Rink Cinema
See the Majestic Cinema.

Rivulet Road
Takes its name from its position alongside the Gwenfro River. The section east of Derby Road, leading to Happy Valley,* was not adopted by the local Council until the late 1990s.

Roberts, Aled Rhys *local politician & solicitor*
Aled Roberts was born in the Maelor Hospital,* Wrexham, on 17 May 1962. He was educated at Ysgol Y Ponciau, Ysgol Grango, Ysgol Rhiwabon, the University College of Wales, Aberystwyth and Christleton College of Law, Chester. He was employed as an articled clerk with Geoffrey Morris & Ashton in Wrexham and Mold before becoming an assistant solicitor and then a partner in the firm. He retired from the practice upon becoming Leader of WCBC in 2005, although he still acts as a consultant to the practice.

He joined the Liberal Party in 1978 and the Liberal Democrats upon the formation of that party in 1988 and was elected to represent the Ponciau ward on WCBC. He is the leader of the Liberal Democrat/Independent Alliance Group, was a member of the Executive Board (2001–03), Chair of the Children's and Young Persons Scrutiny Committee (2003–04) and the lead member for Corporate Governance (2005–08) and Children and Young People (2008 to date). He has been the Leader of the Council since March 2005. He was the Welsh Local Government Association spokesperson for Environment, Sustainability and Housing (2008 to date), member of the Welsh Ministerial Programme Board on Waste (2008 to date) and the Welsh Assembly Essex Implementation Board on Housing. He served as Mayor of Wrexham in 2003–04.

Aled Roberts was named Welsh Councillor of the Year in 2007 in the ITV Wales Politician of the Year Awards.

Roberts, Dr Caradog *musician*
Born in Rhosllanerchrugog in 1878, Caradog Roberts, after a brief career as an apprentice carpenter, graduated in music from Oxford in 1905 and became the youngest Welshman to gain a doctorate in music from Oxford. He was appointed Director of Music at Bangor University in 1914. He is best remembered for the many well-known hymn tunes that he wrote including *In Memoriam* and *Louvain* and the popular *The Lord is My Shepherd*. He died in 1935.

Roberts, David John *local politician*
Born at N° 17 Newtown, Gresford, on 26 November 1942, David Roberts was the son of Robert John Roberts, a master grocer who had served his time with Herbert Jennings.* He was educated at Gresford Primary School and Grove Park County School and intended training to become a teacher but, at the last minute, changed his mind and took a job as a progress chaser at De Havilland's at Broughton where he remained for a few years until being appointed as an Administrative Officer with Cheshire County Council. He is currently the Highway Planning Development Officer for Chester.

He was elected as a Liberal member for the Gresford & Bieston Ward of the Shadow WMBC in 1973, a seat which he retained until he retired from local government in 1996. He was also a Liberal member of Gresford Community Council from 1973–96. He served as Mayor in 1992–93, a year when the WMBC offices in Lambpit Street were opened and was present to host HM the Queen's visit to Overton's 700th Charter Anniversary in July 1993. As Deputy Mayor (1991–92) he met HRH Diana, Princess of Wales when she opened the King's Mills Visitor Centre.

David Roberts married Ann Love of Chester in 1966 and they have one daughter, and has lived all his life in Newtown, Gresford. Outside of his working and political life he has a variety of interests ranging from being a snooker referee (he presided over the 1973 and 1974 World Championships and the preliminary rounds of the 1976 World Championship) to competing in model aeroplane competitions throughout Britain and Europe and is a successful grower of geraniums.

Roberts, Peter *scholar & antiquary*
Born at Tai'n-y-Nant, Ruabon in 1760, the son of John Roberts clockmaker, Peter was educated at Wrexham Grammar School and St Asaph Grammar School. He matriculated to Trinity College, Dublin where he gained an MA. Poor health forced him to live in the south of France before becoming a tutor in Dublin. He was assigned a pension by two of his pupils which allowed him to return to Wales where he was appointed Vicar of Llanarmon Dyffryn Ceiriog. Living in Oswestry, he wrote a history of that town. In 1814 he became Vicar of Madeley in Shropshire and, four years later, Rector of Halkyn in Flintshire. He died on 30 May 1819. Among his published works are: *A Sketch of the Early History of the Cymry (700 BC–AD 500)*, *The Chronicles of the Kings of Britain* and *Cambrian Popular Antiquities*.

Roberts, OBE, Lt-Col Richard Conan *solicitor & clerk*
Born in Rhosrobin on 11 July 1879, Richard Roberts was articled to Hampden Poyser* of Poyser & Shuter in Wrexham and passed his final exams in 1900. He later started his own legal practice which, after taking his nephew in partnership, became Roberts & Russell (Bromfiled Chambers, 27 Rhosddu Road). He held a number of positions in local government and administration including: Clerk to WRDC; Clerk to the Joint Fever Hospital; Hon Sec of the Gresford Disaster Fund. He was appointed Clerk to the Magistrates of the Bromfield Bench in 1933, a position which he held until retiring in 1954. He was President of the Chester & North Wales Law Society and President of the Chester & North Wales Justices' Clerks Society.

He was commissioned as a captain in the Territorial Army during the First World War and saw active service in France before being posted to the War Office in London. He was then appointed legal adviser for the Wales Region of the Ministry of National Service. In 1919, he was involved in the training of disabled ex-servicemen and was appointed the first Director of National Service for Wales. He was awarded an OBE (Military) and, in 1922, was made a Knight of Grace of the Grand Order of St John of Jerusalem for his services to ex-servicemen. In the same year he stood as the Conservative candidate for Wrexham in the General Election, losing to Professor Robert Richards.*

He was a founder member of Wrexham Golf Club* and became Captain in 1926. He was appointed an Under-Sheriff of Denbighshire and Clerk to the Lieutenancy of Denbigh. During the Second World War he commanded one of the Wrexham Home Guard units.

Lt-Col Roberts was married to Gladys (she died in 1967) and lived at Bryn Eurys, N° 10 Acton Gate. He died on 30 November 1972. His portrait hangs in Wrexham Magistrates Court.*

Roberts, Alderman Robert C. *local politician*
Born in Wrexham, Robert Roberts was employed as a railway engineer by the Great Western Railway and British Railways all his working life until retiring in 1958. He was elected a Liberal councillor for the Acton Ward in 1950 and served as Mayor of Wrexham in 1961–62. He was elected an alderman in 1967. During his term of office as Mayor, the Acton Park housing estate was greatly expanded and Regent Street, between King Street and the General Station, was widened. His first wife, Hilda, died in June 1956 and he married Mary Elizabeth Williams in 1962. He had two sons. Robert Roberts lived at 186 Chester Road. He died at the War Memorial Hospital on 24 August 1969 and is buried in Wrexham Cemetery.

Roberts, JP, Walter *businessman & philanthropist*
Walter Roberts was the proprietor of an ironmongery business at N° 44 Hope Street, fondly remembered for the fascinating range of goods stocked and his shop sign which was a kettle (which can now be seen outside N° 2 Mount Street). He was a major figure among the local amateur dramatic societies and specialised in the production of pantomimes. His annual productions (in which he starred) began in 1907 and raised over £40,000 for the local

Roberts Square.

hospital and financed the establishment of the Pantomime Children's Ward at the War Memorial Hospital (a name continued at the Maelor Hospital). He was appointed a Justice of the Peace in 1927, a Freeman of the Borough of Wrexham on 20 October 1937 and a life governor of the Hospital. Walter Roberts was married to Doris and lived at The Gables, Percy Road. He died on 24 October 1942.

Roberts' Court, Beast Market
See Roberts' Square.

Roberts' Square, Beast Market
A small court development of seven dwellings located at the rear of St George's Crescent overlooking Eagles Meadow. It was demolished in 1932 as part of the Borough Council's slum clearance programme.

Robertson, Henry *industrialist*
He was born in Banff, Scotland in 1816, the youngest of the twelve children of Duncan and Christian (née Anderson) Robertson. His father was an official in the Inland Revenue service and died in 1831 when the family moved to Glasgow. Henry was originally intended for the ministry and gained a scholarship to Aberdeen University from where he graduated while only 19 years-of-age. A passion for engineering led him to take up employment in the Lanark-shire coal mines before becoming a pupil of the great railway engineer Robert

Stephenson who was building a railway from Glasgow to Edinburgh and on into England. Robertson was given the task of levelling the route across Shap Fell in Cumbria after which he set up his own business.

Henry Robertson came to Brymbo in about 1840/1 to report on the possibility of mineral development of the area on behalf of a Scottish bank. So impressive was his report that money was made available to him so that he could become involved in the development of the works. Robertson persuaded the Darby brothers to take over the management of the collieries and iron works and is regarded as having been responsible for the establishment of steel making at Brymbo. His main passion was, however, the construction of railways and he was a prime instigator behind North Wales Mineral Railway* (and the Brymbo branch – via the Moss Valley) and the Shrewsbury & Chester Railway* (for which he designed the Dee valley viaduct. He served as MP for Shrewsbury (three times) and Merioneth (once). He married Elizabeth, the daughter of William Dean of London in 1846 (she died in 1892) and had four children: Henry Bayer,* Elizabeth, Annie and Henrietta. Henry Robertson lived at various addresses in Chester and Shrewsbury before settling at Crogen, near Corwen and eventually building his own home at Palé Hall, Llandderfel, near Bala in 1871. During the latter years of his life he was chairman of the Vale of Llangollen Railway, the Broughton & Plas Power Coal Company, the Minera Lime Works, the Brymbo Steel Works, the Corwen & Bala Railway, the Wirral Railway Company, the Llangollen & Corwen Railway and the Brymbo Water Company. He died on 22 March 1888 and is buried at Llandderfel.

Henry Robertson.

Robertson, BA, Sir Henry Beyer *industrialist*
The son of Henry Robertson,* Sir Henry was born in Shrewsbury on 4 May 1862. He was educated at Winton House, Winchester, Eton and Jesus College, Cambridge, gaining a BA in 1884.

He joined his father's business in 1885 and, succeeded him in 1888. He acted as the host to Queen Victoria in 1889 when she stayed at Palé Hall during her visit to north Wales and was knighted in 1890 in recognition of his services and his father's achievements. He became the chairman of Brymbo Steel Works in 1891, a position which he held until his death in 1948. He, perhaps more than anyone, was responsible for the re-opening of the steel works after the shutd-own of 1931.

Sir Henry Beyer Robertson.

He was a Director of the Great Western Railway for over 50 years, Chairman of the River Dee Fishing Board, a Merion-ethshire County Councillor, High Sheriff and Deputy Lieutenant of Merionethshire and Chairman of the Quarter Sessions. He married Florence Mary Keates (she died in 1944) and they had seven children: Henry (see the Homestead*), Jean, Mary, Annie, Elizabeth, Duncan (see the Court*) and John.

Robinson, Colonel John *soldier*
John Robinson of Gwersyllt Ucha,* Wrexham, was the eldest son of Capt William Robinson (a Commissioner of Array) and grandson of Bishop Nicholas Robinson of Bangor. In November 1643, during the Civil War, he defended Holt Castle against the Parliamentary force commanded by Colonel Brereton. He then took part in the recapture of Hawarden Castle in December. Posted to Ellice's Regiment of Foot in January 1644 and then to Byron's Regiment of Foot, he served throughout the siege of Chester as a lieutenant-colonel and acted as a commissioner of surrender. On returning to Gwersyllt he found his home plundered and was forced to flee to Caernarfon Castle where he re-joined Byron and took part in the defence of that fortress. He again acted as a commissioner of surrender at Beaumaris Castle. He captured Lady Cheadle Fort, Beaumaris and was present at the fight at Y Dalar Hir. In 1648 he again took up arms for the King and marched to Beaumaris but arrived too late to be of any use and had to flee to Ireland. In 1651, he landed with the Earl of Derby's forces and was captured at Wigan. He managed to obtain his freedom and went into exile until the Restoration of 1660 when he was made vice admiral of North Wales, member of parliament for Anglesey and was nominated as a Knight of the Royal Oak. He died in March 1681, aged 65 and is buried in Gresford Parish Church where his memorial reads: 'Here lies John Robinson, who as a colonel of Charles the Martyr, vigorously maintained his cause. When he King fell, himself an exile, he abandoned not the exile Charles, with whom returning, he found to his delight at Gwersyllt, where he had left his property, destroyed by the hands of the rebels, an elegant edifice erected by those who had destroyed the former … His body, though formed of superior clay, yet being worn out, as well as ennobled by honourable wounds, was unable to retain beyond his 65th year of his age his soul, which aspired to heaven and surrendered it on the 15th March, 1680[1] of the Christian era'.

Robinson, BA, Ll.B, Frederick Victor *local politician*
Born in Croydon, Surrey, on 12 April 1911, Vic Robinson was the son of Irish parents – unusually his father was a Protestant and his mother a Roman Catholic. He spent much of his childhood in Upper Norwood and Bayswater where he was a pupil at St Stephen's School before moving to Ealing where he was a pupil at Ealing Central School for Boys. He joined the Great Western Railway Company as a junior clerk in the Divisional Engineering Office at Paddington. He passed his London Matriculation examinations in 1931 and became an external student at London University, graduating with a BA in history, while remaining in his job with GWR. The company sent him to work in Llanelli during the Second World War where he met Brenda Cole, the daughter of a local farmer, and they were married in 1945 (they had two daughters and one son). After a period of time working in Reading, he made a number of moves before settling in Penley in 1964 where he was a divisional manager with British Railways and his wife was the village postmistress. After retiring, he and his wife lived at Freestone House, Penley, where he embarked on a degree in law.

Vic Robinson first entered local politics as a parish councillor for Penley then became a member of the local community council where he was chairman for five years. He was also elected to represent Penley on WMBC and became Mayor in 1989. He retired from the Council in 1991. He died at his home on 8 April 1993 and is buried in the churchyard at Penley.

Roderic(k) Terrace, Salop Road
Located on the eastern side of Salop Road just below the entrance to Birch Street, this terrace of eleven houses is shown on the 1872 survey and was part of the Beechley House estate when that was sold in 1894. The sale particulars describe the houses as having a parlour, kitchen, back kitchen, pantry, three bedrooms and a yard with a substantial garden at the rear and a small flower garden at the front. The origin of the name is unknown.

Rogers, David *local politician*
Born in Wrexham on 19 October 1945, the son of Cyril and Melva Baines, David Rogers was educated locally until the age of 17. In 1966 he joined Lloyds Bank Ltd in London and was transferred to Wrexham in 1973, where he remained until he retired.

A socialist and active trade unionist, he joined the Labour Party in the early 1970s and was later elected Labour councillor for the Brynyffynnon ward on WMBC. Following the creation of WCBC he was elected to represent the same ward. He has served on a number of council committees and has chaired the influential Economic Development Committee during the recent redevelopment of Wrexham town centre. He was a member of Offa Community Council for twenty years, commencing in 1985, and a governor of various schools in the town. He was Mayor of Wrexham in 2004–05 when he felt privileged to take the salute when the 1st Bn, The Royal Welch Fusiliers marched through the town on their return from Iraq.

David Rogers married Jackie Jones (née Owen) in 1967 and they have two children, Simon and Samantha.

Rogers, Jonathan, GC, DSM *George Cross recipient*
Jonathan Rogers was born in Penycae, Wrexham on 16 September 1920. On 10 February 1964, he was serving as a Chief Petty Officer aboard HMAS *Voyager* of the Royal Australian Navy when his ship was in collision at Jervis Bay, off the Australian coast. With the ship sinking, Rogers kept up the morale of the junior ratings and organised the escape of many of the crew before choosing to remain on board with those who were injured and unable to leave the stricken ship. He encouraged them to meet their death with dignity and honour and upheld the highest traditions of the RAN. He was awarded a posthumous George Cross on 12 March 1965. CPO Rogers was already the recipient of the Distinguished Service Medal.

Rogers, Neil *local politician*
Born in 1949 and brought up in Southsea, collier's son Neil Rogers was educated at New Broughton Primary and Brynteg Secondary Schools. He became a process operative at Shotton Steel Works until 1973 when he joined Owens Corning on the Wrexham Industrial Estate.

He was elected a Labour member of Broughton Community Council in 1979 and in October 1986 became a Clwyd County Councillor representing the Broughton Ward. He served as chairman of the Libraries and Records Sub Committee and was chairman of the Labour group from 1991–96. Following the reorganisation of local government Neil Rogers became the Deputy Leader of WCBC in 1996 and Leader in 1998. He chaired the Policy Committee from 1996–98 and was elected Mayor in 2000. During his year of office he visited the Millennium Dome in London to see the work prepared by the youngsters from Wrexham schools and colleges, opened the refurbished Parciau* and presided over the first full march-past of the RWF since 1983.

Married to Eileen Prince of Southsea, he has a son and a daughter and lives in Cripps Avenue, Southsea.

Rogers & Jackson Ltd *ironmongers and builders merchants*
Founded in 1815, the company became Rogers & Jackson. A partner in the company towards the end of the 19th century was Alfred Ernest Owen* who later left them to seek work in the Midlands and became a partner in Rubery Owen.* At a later date the company became part of the Rubery Owen Group* and, after the takeover of the Wrexham firm of Powell Brothers & Whitaker* in 1927, was located in the Cambrian Works near the General Station. 'R&Js', as the company was known locally, was eventually taken over in the 1990s by the national wholesaler and retailer Builder Center. At various times the company had premises at Nº 30 High Street (Alfred Owen, ironmonger, 1886) – opposite the Market Hall, Nº 49 Hope Street – selling furniture, carpets, pottery, electrical goods, hardware, tools, mirrors, bathroom equipment, fireplaces, stoves, travel requisites, sports goods, cutlery, toys, prams, cycles and garden supplies (this building still stands with the company's date of foundation, 1815, displayed above the second floor windows), Priory Street, Chester Street and the former Penson's Theatre* in the Beast Market.

Roman Catholic School, Brook Street
This was opened in 1870 and demolished to make way for the railway in the 1890s. The proceeds from this compulsory purchase were used to assist with paying for the building of St Mary's RC Primary School* in Lea Road.

Romano, Grove Road
The only house to have been built on the southern side of Grove Road during the 19th century. Its exact details are unknown but it was built sometime after the 1872 survey on land that was previously part of the Grove Park estate. The appearance of the house would suggest that it may have been built to a design by James R. Gummow.* In the 1920s, the house was the home of Scotch draper William Alexander and his wife Rachel (née Stobo). He died there in 1932 and she died in 1946 and the house became part of the nurses' home for the Wrexham & District War Memorial Hospital. In the 1980s, the inner ring road was built through its grounds and the house was vacant by 1993 when it was bought by local builder Gordon Mytton who built a large extension on the rear and converted it into office accommodation. The house is a Grade II listed building.

Roose, MM, Leigh Richmond *footballer*
Born in Holt on 27 November, 1877 the son of a Presbyterian minister, Leigh Richmond Roose was educated at Holt Academy and the University College of Wales, Aberystwyth. Whilst an undergraduate he played in goal for both the college and Aberystwyth Town soccer teams before joining Druids in 1900. After commencing medical training at King's College Hospital, London he played for London Welsh and Stoke (travelling from London at the club's expense). He joined Everton in 1904, returned to Stoke in 1905, Sunderland in 1908, Huddersfield in 1911, Aston Villa in 1911 and Woolwich Arsenal in 1911. He represented Wales on 24 occasions. On the outbreak of war in 1914 Roose joined the 9th Bn, Royal Fusiliers and was reported missing, believed killed, on 7 October 1916. L/Cpl Roose had been awarded the Military Medal. Throughout his footballing career he had remained an amateur, an attitude which enabled him to volunteer to stand down from the Welsh side so that the reserve goalkeeper, Alf Edwards, could get a cap, a magnanimous gesture that was declined by the Football Association of Wales.

Rose & Crown, Chester Street
This was located adjacent to the corner of Chester Street and Lambpit Street, opposite the Seven Stars. A former private house – it was once the residence of the Revd Thomas Williams and the

Rose & Crown, Chester Street, c.1970.

Revd Robert Price, headmasters of Wrexham Grammar School* in the 18th century – this was converted into a public house at the beginning of the 19th century. It was demolished in the early 1970s as part of the redevelopment scheme for this area of the town and the licence was transferred to the new Cunliffe Arms* on Jeffreys Road.

Rose Grove, Queen's Park
This area of the Cefn Park* estate was requisitioned during the Second World War and temporary housing built in 1941 to accommodate Royal Ordnance Factory* workers. When the war was over these houses were utilised by WBC as temporary corporation housing and, in some cases, survived until the mid 1950s when they were known locally as 'Cardboard City'. The temporary houses were replaced by permanent houses, built by W.D. Stant on behalf of WBC, between the 1950s and 1960s. Most of the streets in this area were given the names of trees and shrubs. The land was bought by means of a compulsory purchase order from Lt-Colonel R. G. Fenwick-Palmer.*

Roseneath, Grove Park
This house was built at a cost of £14,000, by the engineer William Low* in 1864/5 and named after a part of the Duke of Argyll's estate which Low had surveyed as a young man. The plans for a Channel Tunnel were drawn up at this house in 1867 and Low's office here was known as the Channel Tunnel Office. Low moved to live in London in the early 1880s and, following his death in 1886, the house was bought by local solicitor Sir Evan Morris* who let it out to George Whitehouse. After Sir Evan's death in 1890, the house appears to have been let to J. T. Davies, the Managing Director of Cobden's Flour Mill* [DRO/DD/G/2832 & 2844] and following his death (on 8 January 1896) the contents were sold and the house was placed for auction by the executors of Sir Evan Morris in 1899. There appear to have been no takers and in 1906, the executors offered it to WBC for £5,000 as a possible new Guildhall;* they also suggested that the frontage on Rhosddu Road would make an ideal Police Station. Fearing accusations of being spendthrifts, the Council declined the offer and the house remained the property of the Morris family until it was bought by John Jones* (partner in the Island Green Brewery*) shortly before his death in 1912. In his will, Jones left the house and grounds to a charitable trust as a site for a new Wrexham infirmary. Problems arose with some restrictions on its use and with neighbours raising objections, he was obliged to buy up the adjacent property. In addition to the physical assets, John Jones also left the Trust £50,000 for the conversion of the house into a hospital.

During the First World War Roseneath was used as a military hospital and, in its final years, was incorporated into the War

Roseneath.

Above: the front which faced south onto Grove Park Road.

Below: the west front which faced west and overlooked the gardens. The four-square solidity of this house with a large number of windows in every room (including the attic) has an American feel about it and reflects the owner/designer's occupation as a civil engineer.

Memorial Hospital. The final traces of Roseneath vanished during the reconstruction of the War Memorial Hospital as Yale College in the 1990s.

Sale particulars, dated September 1899, describe the property as comprising: vestibule, entrance hall, dining room, drawing room, morning room, ante-room, butler's pantry, 3 principal bedrooms on the 1st floor (2 with dressing rooms with bath and H&C water), plus 3 other good bedrooms; 7 bedrooms on the second floor with lavatory, boxroom, house-maids' closets, etc. The basement comprised 2 kitchens, a scullery, 2 larders, beer and wine cellars, china and glass closet, servants' hall, housekeeper's room, coal cellar and out-offices. Outside there was a stable for 5 horses, a loose box with a loft and saddle room, a coach house, cleaning room, coachman's bedroom, large laundry, billiard room, lavatory, 2 other rooms, pleasure grounds with 2 conservatories, 2 vineries, a stove house, a melon house, a tool and potting shed and a walled kitchen garden. [DRO/DD/G/2856] (See also Wrexham and East Denbighshire War memorial Hospital; Wrexham Infirmary Trust)

Rosewood Avenue, Queen's Park
This was built in the immediate post Second World War period as part of the first phase of WBC's Queen's Park housing development. It was local authority policy at one time to name streets after trees and shrubs (See Acton Park housing estate).

Rossett Way, Little Acton
Built by Wrexham Borough Council in the early 1950s this development provided housing for the growing population of Little Acton which was caused by the expansion of Gresford Colliery.* It takes its name from the village of Rossett.

Rosier, GCB, CBE, DSO, RAF, Air Chief Marshal Sir Frederick
airman
Born in Wrexham on 13 October 1915, son of E. G. Rosier, a railway engine driver, Fred Rosier was educated at Grove Park School and played rugby for North Wales Schoolboys.

He received a Short Service Commission in the RAF in 1935 and served with 43 Squadron (Fighters) flying Hawker Fury aircraft at Tangmere 1936–39. He was a flight commander in 229 Squadron (Hurricanes) by May 1940 having helped form and convert the squadron from Blenheims. He first saw active service during the Second World War in France where he commanded a detachment of 229 Squadron at Vitry near Arras and was shot down by an Me109 receiving facial burns. Returning to active service by October 1940 he commanded 229 Squadron from RAF Northolt for the last 12 days of the Battle of Britain.

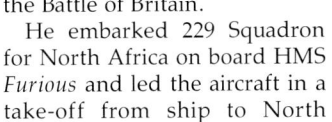

He embarked 229 Squadron for North Africa on board HMS *Furious* and led the aircraft in a take-off from ship to North Africa via Malta. Promoted to Wing Commander in 1941, he took charge of 262 Wing where he had joint operational control of the Desert Air Force's fighter squadrons. In November 1941 he spotted an Australian Tomahawk aircraft being forced down by enemy fighters and landed his single-seater to rescue the pilot. Having got Sgt Burney aboard he attempted to take-off but suffered a burst tyre and crashed the aircraft. Both he and Burney walked across the desert for four days, avoiding large enemy patrols, to reach safety with a Guards unit.

Rosier became the deputy commander of 211 Fighter Group and was awarded the DSO. Returning to the UK in 1943 he became OC 52 Operational Training Unit and then OC RAF Northolt.

His post-war appointments were numerous and varied as he rose to the highest echelons of the Royal Air Force: OC RAF Horsham St Faith 1947; Exchange Officer with USAF 1948–50; Instructor Joint Services Staff College, 1950–2; Grp Capt Operations at Central Fighter Establishment, 1952–4; Grp Capt Plans at Fighter Command 1955–6; ADC to HM The Queen 1956–8; Imperial Defence College 1957; Director of Joint Plans, Air Ministry, 1958; chairman Joint Planning Staff, 1959–61; AOC Air Forces Middle East, 1961–3; Senior Air Staff Officer, HQ Transport Command 1964–6; AOC-in-C, RAF Fighter Command 1966–8; UK Member Permanent Military Deputies Group, Central Treaty Organisation, Ankara 1968–70; Deputy C-in-C Allied Forces Central Europe 1970–3; Air ADC to HM The Queen 1972–3. Retiring from the RAF in 1973 he became a military advisor and director of the British Aircraft Corporation (Preston) Ltd., 1973–7 and and director of BAC Saudi Arabia. His awards included: DSO, 1942; OBE, 1943; Commander Order of Orange Nassau, 1947; CBE, 1955; CB, 1961; KCB, 1966; GCB 1972.

Air Chief Marshal Sir Frederick Rosier, GCB, CBE, DSO.

He was the chairman of the Polish Pilots Benevolent Fund and received the Polish Order of Merit in 1998. Sir Fred married Hettie Denise Blackwell of Wrexham in 1939, and they had three sons and one daughter. For the last few years of his life he lived as Sun Bank, Trevor, near Llangollen and died on 10 September 1998.

Rotary Club of Erddig
See Rotary Club of Wrexham Erddig.

Rotary Club of Wrexham
The Rotary Club of Wrexham was granted its charter in December 1928 and held its first meetings in the Wynnstay Arms Hotel, Yorke Street. Its first president was Sir Leonard Rowland and its first secretary was Arthur Hallett.
Presidents:

Sir Leonard B. Rowland*	1928–29	Pharmaceutical Retailer
Archdeacon Lewis Price	1929–30	Cleric
Frank P. Dodd	1930–31	Headmaster
John B. Stant	1931–32	Builder
Arthur Challoner*	1932–33	Builders Merchant
Leslie B. Sutcliffe	1933–34	Leather Manufacturer
Raymond S. Brock	1934–35	Medical Practitioner
Owen Evans	1935–36	Gas Supply
Charles Ll. Thomas	1936–37	Gentlemen's Outfitter
Norman D. Bird*	1937–38	Solicitor
James H. Fitzpatrick	1938–39	Journalist
Nicholas W. McCord	1939–40	Building Contractor
Thomas O. Pratt	1940–41	Hairdresser
Algernon Smith	1941–42	Photographer
Arthur Hallett	1942–43	Accountant
S. T. Boyce	1943–44	District Engineer
Reginald S. Holway	1944–45	Journalist
James A. Clarkson	1945–46	Accountant
James D. Batkin	1946–47	Brewer
Howell Williams	1947–48	Head Postmaster
Charles A. Knight	1948–49	Wine & Spirit Retailer
Thomas Lloyd Williams	1949–50	Department Store proprietor
Idwal Bryan Hughes	1950–51	Insurance Manager
George Vernon Price*	1951–52	Clerk WRDC
Harold J. Bennett*	1952–53	Headmaster
Arthur G. Camp	1953–54	Motor Vehicle Retailer
Colin M. Butterworth	1954–55	Estate Agent
Harold Jones	1955–56	District Manager Esso Petroleum
Francis F. Crowe	1956–57	Wholesale Fruiterer
Philip H. B. Derrick	1957–58	Footwear Retailer
John Stanley Jones	1958–59	Man. Director Dennis Ruabon
Harry Seddon	1959–60	Mgr. Water Co.
Richard A. Jones	1960–61	Regional Manager Wales Gas
C. Delme Jenkins	1961–62	Industrial chemist
John Raymond Morgan	1962–63	Gentlemen's Outfitter
Howel Glyn Jones	1963–64	Solicitor
Bryan Priestner	1964–65	Gentlemen's Outfitter
David E. M. Glynne Jones	1965–66	Vicar of Wrexham
Clifford Harris	1966–67	Borough Librarian
Percy Edwards	1967–68	Man. Director W. Phillips & Co.
Arthur McCartney	1968–69	Borough Public Health Inspector
Herbert Jennings*	1969–70	Grocery Retailer
Brinley Harris	1970–71	Manager Dept. of Social Security
Philip Walters*	1971–72	Town Clerk, WBC
Donald Dutton	1972–73	Grocery Retailer
Bill Moat	1973–74	Treasurer, WBC
T. A. Clark	1974–75	Accountant
Neville Scott	1975–76	Shoe Retailer
Deri O. Thomas	1976–77	Dental Practitioner
John Lomax	1977–78	Regional manager Wales Gas
Trevor Shone	1978–79	Bank Manager
Revd Gwynfryn LL. Davies	1979–80	Minister of Religion
Harry Bainbridge	1980–81	Building Society Manager
Hubert Davies	1981–82	Furniture Retailer
William Evans	1982–83	Travel Agency proprietor
John Crowe	1983–84	Wholesale Fruiterer
Des McGrath	1984–85	General Practitioner
Ralph Lawson	1985–86	Garage Proprietor
Tom Henderson	1986–87	Travel Agency Proprietor
Glyn Pryce	1987–88	Bank Manager
Rowland Cole	1988–89	Pharmaceutical Wholesaler
A. K. (Joe) Williams	1989–90	Electrical Wholesaler
Dennis Griffith	1990–91	Architect

David Gittins	1991–92	Building Contractor
Orlando Andrade	1992–93	Dental Practitioner
Richard Rawlings	1993–94	Insurance
Reginald Parrett	1994–95	Interior Designer
Arfon Pritchard	1995–96	Photographer
Norman Venner	1996–97	Restauranteur
W/Cmdr Brian Reader	1997–98	Royal Air Force Officer (retired)
Brian Paul	1998–99	Electrical Retailer
Revd Clive Tucker	1999–00	Education Administrator
George Cantrill	2000	Town Centre Manager
Gwilym C. Hughes	2000–01	Solicitor
W. Alister Williams	2001–02	Publisher
Anthony H. Thomas	2002–03	Accountant
Malcolm T. Brown	2003–04	Training Consultant
Michael Kagan	2004–05	Hotel Proprietor
Michael Brown	2005–06	Company Secretary
Brian Coles	2006–07	Structural Engineer
Pallavoor Anandaram	2007–08	Medical Consultant
Barney Parkinson	2008–09	Education
Pat Thomas	2009–10	Nursing Support Services
David Mason	2010–11	Armed Forces (Training)

The club has met at a number of venues over the years (including Stevens Café and Bacchus Wine Bar, Brook Street) but is currently based at its original meeting place, the Wynnstay Arms Hotel,* Wrexham. Meetings are held each Tuesday lunchtime.

Rotary Club of Wrexham Erddig

Founded in 1978 as a 'daughter' club of the Rotary Club of Wrexham. Originally called the Rotary Club of Erddig, it has held its meetings in a number of venues and currently meets at the Ramada Plaza Hotel each Thursday evening.

Presidents:

Gordon M'Cartney	1978–79	Local Authority
Clifford Jackson*	1979–80	Personnel
Elfed Whitley	1980-81	Industrial Chemist
Bob Rimmer	1981–82	Sales Representative
Edward Jones	1982–83	Fuel Wholesaler
Evan Martin	1983–84	Brewing
Emlyn Jones	1984–85	Further Education
Raymond Jones	1985–86	Architect
John Cooksley	1986–87	Chemical Engineer
Revd Reg Smith	1987–88	Cleric
Barry Williams	1988–89	Insurance Broker
Dan Evans	1989–90	Auctioneer
Nigel Rainsbury	1990–91	Supermarket Manager
Chris Jones	1991–92	Computer Services
Peter Lambert	1992–93	Architect
Terry Roberts	1993–94	Electrical Retailer
Philip Squires	1994–95	Packaging
John Rees	1995–96	Farmer
Barry Lloyd-Jones	1996–97	Accountant
Gwynn Evans	1997–98	Banker
Meirion Lansley-Jones	1998–99	Retailer
Malcolm James	1999–2000	Business Consultant
Graham Watson	2000–01	Surveyor
Harry Miller	2001–02	Engineering
Bob Baines	2002–03	Health & Safety
Graham Arthurs	2003–04	Consultant Anaeathetist
Viv Reeves	2004–05	District Judge
Peter Lambert	2005–06	Architectural Services
Trefor Roberts	2006–07	Primary Education
Godfrey Williams	2007–08	Environmental Consultant
Colin Rowlands	2008–09	Property Development
Tom Lewis	2009–10	Piano Tuning
Albert R. Ellison	2010–11	Manufacturing Electronics

Rotary Club of Wrexham Yale

Founded in 1998 as a 'daughter' club of the Rotary Club of Wrexham Erddig, this breakfast club was granted its charter in March 1999. It holds its meetings on Wednesday mornings at the Cross Lanes Hotel, Marchwiel.

Presidents:

Edgar Lewis	2000–01	Director of Education
Pamela Valentine	2001-02	Solicitor
Anne Roberts	2002–03	Education
Hywel Williams	2003–04	Local Government Administrator
Molly Yood	2004–05	Accountancy
Chris Burgoyne	2005–06	Banking
Alun Jones	2006–07	Electrical Engineering
John Savage	2007–08	Hospice Management
Medwyn Edwards	2008–09	Financial Advisor
Rita Hunt	2009–10	Nursing Administrator
Terry Wales	2010–11	Education

Rothesay Close, Croes Eneurys

Developed in the mid 1960s by local builders W. D. Stant on land that had once been part of Croes Eneurys Farm.* The street is named after Rothesay in Scotland.

Roundel Close

Built in the early 1980s on land that was previously part of Plas Goulbourne.* It is named after the roundel, the symbol of the Royal Air Force, presumably due to the street's close proximity to the former RAF Wrexham* airfield.

Rowland, Kt, JP, Sir Leonard Bromfield *local politician*

Born on 29 December 1862, at High Street, the son of pharmacist William Rowland,* Leonard Rowland was educated at Wrexham Grammar School,* Grove Park School* and Manchester College of Chemistry and Pharmacy, taking his finals in Edinburgh in 1886. He was apprenticed to his father and, after the death in 1891 of his elder brother, Langshaw, became the principal of the family pharmacy business. In 1928, the family business became L. Rowland & Company and he was Chairman and Director.

In 1906 he was the Speaker of the Wrexham Parliamentary Debating Society, and in 1928 was the founding President of the Rotary Club of Wrexham. He was a Justice of the Peace for Denbighshire (1918), an Income Tax Commissioner (1918), Worshipful Master of the Square and Compass Lodge of the Freemasons* (later the first Worshipful Master of the Bromfield Lodge*), President of the North Wales Chess Association, a regular contributor to the local press (under the pen-name 'Lux') and a keen lawn tennis player.

Elected a Borough Councillor by the narrow margin of 2 votes in 1908, he served as Mayor from 1915–19 for which service he was knighted in 1920. He retired from the Council in 1922.

he was married to Marguerite Lilian Bushby* and had five children. They lived at Whybro House, Chester Street (now the site of Ebeneser Chapel*) and at the White House, Bersham. Sir Leonard Rowland died on 18 December, 1939 and is buried in Wrexham Cemetery.*

Sir Leonard Rowland, Kt, in his Masonic regalia.

L. Rowland & Company Limited *chemists*
Founded by Edward Rowland, a farmer of Llwyn Onn,* Wrexham who bought an existing chemist and druggist business N° 42 High Street in 1810. In 1846 he moved to the premises at N° 9 High Street where he installed the shop front which still survives today. In 1841 the business is shown in the census as being headed by Mary Rowland (aged 45), a druggist, who was assisted by her children Thomas* and Edward. The company expanded and in 1928 became a private limited company known as L. Rowland & Company. In the 1940s it expanded into pharmaceutical wholesaling, later trading under the purchasing group brand name Numark. In 1964 the company moved into a new office and warehousing facility in Dolydd Road and by the 1990s was able to claim 'membership' of the élite Daily Post 100 biggest companies in the north-west. In December 1998 the firm was bought out by Phoenix Medical Supplies Ltd.

Rowland, MBE, JP, Lady Marguerite Lilian
Born in Llangollen in *c.*1870, the daughter of Thomas Bushby, she married Leonard Bromfield Rowland* and had five children. She was awarded the MBE in 1918 in recognition of her services during the First World War and was also presented with a diamond badge by the RWF. She was made a Justice of the Peace for the Borough bench in 1921. She died in 1939 and is buried in Wrexham Cemetery.

Rowland, JP, Thomas *local politician*
Born *c.*1821, Thomas Rowland was the son of William Rowland (died 27 January 1857), the proprietor of the Nag's Head Brewery.* He joined his father in the family business and, on retiring, sold it to H.K. Aspinall. He was elected a Tory member of WBC and served as Mayor in 1868 and 1881, was a Justice of the Peace and a churchwarden. He donated a font to St Mark's Church.* Thomas Rowland was a promoter of the Wrexham, Mold & Connah's Quay Railway Company.* His wife, Mary Ann Barlow was a native of Necton in Norfolk and they lived at The Groves* and later Oaklawn, Fairy Road* where he died on 15 January 1889. He is buried in Wrexham Cemetery.

Rowland, William *local politician*
Born 2 May 1822, the son of Wrexham chemist Edward Rowland of Llwyn Onn. His mother was Mary Langshaw of Chester. A druggist of N° 9 High Street, William Rowland was a 'Red' (Radical) councillor on WBC and served as Mayor in 1869–70. His brother Edward (died 1889), a partner in the family business, resided at Bryn Offa.* William Rowland was the father of Sir Leonard B. Rowland.* He died on 25 November 1878 at his home, Brooklands,* in Wrexham Fechan* and is buried in Wrexham Cemetery.*

Rowland's Cottages
These two cottages were sited off the north-west side of Holt Road, behind the main run of properties. They were demolished as part of the Borough slum clearance programme.

Roxburgh Place
Roxborough Place was located on the site of the present day Roxburgh House, off Regent Street. It was built by a Mr Young, a native of Roxburgh in Scotland. The entrance to the street was directly opposite Egerton Street. Originally, the street had eight small houses (numbered 1–8) along the western side and four larger cottages (numbered 9–12) along the eastern side. The street was demolished during the 1960s to make way for the new retail and office development in Regent Street.

Royal British Bowmen
This organisation was formed in 1787 by Sir Foster Cunliffe of Acton Hall. The society comprised many of the leading members of Wrexham society who actually took part in archery competitions held at various venues in country houses in the local area and one engraving that has survived shows the Bowmen meeting on the water meadows below Erddig Hall in 1822. Sir Foster Cunliffe's journal records:

About a year after we became resident in the country, Archery was introduced as a fashionable amusement. Sir Ashton Lever had the merit of being the first promoter of it. It seemed suited to the genius of the nation, and was followed eagerly in every part of the Kingdom and renewed the scenes of former times. Societies were formed under various denominations in different places, and none had the

A meeting of the Royal British Bowmen at Erddig, 1822.

honour of being composed of Ladies as well as Gentlemen except the Royal British Bowmen. Men may meet and may frame laws to keep themselves within the bounds of propriety, but without a due mixture of Ladies, their meetings will generally end in drunkenness ... a number of Ladies and Gentlemen of the neighbourhood met at Acton Feby 27th 1787 for the purpose of establishing a society to promote good neighbourhood thro' the medium of archery and under the influence of the British Bow, the most restful society was formed. There never was an Institution so auspiciously begun, and so happily conducted. It suited all ages, and had claims for all dispositions, there never was an instance of any one having said that they had passed an unpleasant day. It continued without relaxation during 7 years, and brought together a numerous and extensive neighbourhood, upon the easiest and most friendly footing. The harmony of the meetings was never interrupted, but the highest good humour displayed itself and it was not till after they had ceased that the full extent of their merit was known.

Seldom can those friends now meet, who formerly were certain of seeing each other once a fortnight. Formal invitations to dinner were then unknown. 'Come and dine with us, on such a day, and bring your Bow' was the mode of invitation. It was not necessary to be a shooter to enjoy these advantages, tho' certainly those who followed with keenness the noble art of Archery, had the greatest share of pleasure. I was amongst that number. I had the good fortune to gain several prizes, and so had my wife. In 1793, at the breaking out of the war with France, as most of the Gentlemen entered into some military employment, they laid down the Bow for the Musket, the modern for the Ancient Artillery at the last meeting, that they should be postponed till the return of Peace. At the close there were 66 Gentlemen members 40 of whom engaged in some Military occupation in defence of their country ... 8 were clergymen – 3 died and 15 were unoccupied and thus ended the most delightful society that every [sic] was established in any country whether it will ever be revived is very doubtful.'

The society was revived at Acton on 25 June 1819 when a meeting was held at Acton Park with 120 members and 16 guests present. Miss Emma Cunliffe, a passionate supporter of the 'Bowmen' kept a journal of their meetings between then and the 4 August 1826 when the last meeting appears to have been held, also at Acton. In the intervening years meetings were held in a large number of local houses including: Leeswood, Hawarden Castle, Hardwick, Ruabon Vicarage, Wynnstay,* Woodhouse, Pelton, Gresford Lodge,* Pen-y-Lan, Trefalyn, Erbistock, Edge, Gwersyllt Hall,* Broughton and Iscoed. The society had a tradition that an original song would be written and performed at each meeting. One of the members would be designated as 'Poet Laureate'; at the June 1819 meeting, this was Reginald Heber who wrote the following verses which were sung to the tune *Haste to the Wedding*.

> I warn you, ye ladies, who hope to subdue us,
> With eyes like the diamond & cheeks like the rose.
> The best of your glances can never pierce through us,
> Unless you come aided by quivers & Bows.
> For they that are seen
> In buff & in Green
> Have a grace, & a mien & a shape, & an air!
> *Chorus*
>
> Come see
> Critics in Archery!
> Who like our Archery lasses are fair?
> You've heard my young dears, of the little God Cupid
> Invok'd by your mothers, as tamers of hearts,
> But his arrows are blunt, & his aim is grown stupid
> Since you have been learning to scatter your darts!
> So swiftly they fly
> To the very bulls eye
> That, if Cupid had eyes, even Cupid might stare.
> *Chorus*
>
> Poor Venus has laid down her tandem of sparrows,
> Since time are so ticklish & taxes so high,
> But her presence is felt, mid your bows & your arrows
> It laughs on each lip & it beams on each eye.
> Mark! Mark! how the rose
> Of exercise glows!
> How sweetly those tresses are spread to the air.
> *Chorus*
>
> I've danced with the pretty, I've laughed with the witty
> With garlands of mirtle, & stockings of Blue
> But, where are the girls, in the court or the city
> Can fetter the heart my dear charmers like you?
> To the Arrow & Bow
> Such beauty you owe
> No rouge in the land with your blush can compare.
> *Chorus*
>
> We care not a rush, when assembled together
> Though dark & unfriendly the morning may be,
> Though the raindrop hangs damp on the point of the feather
> And drives us too soon from the turf & the tree.
> We may then shift the scene
> To the Bacon & Bean
> And the warmth of our Bosoms by Porter repair
> Come see
> Welch Hospitality
> And pray that the weather next month may be fair.

Royal Cambrian Lodge
There is a record of this lodge meeting at *The Feathers* in 1881.

Royal National Eisteddfod of Wales
See National Eisteddfod of Wales.

Royal Oak (I), High Street
This half-timbered building was formerly the premises of the clockmaker, Thomas Hampson. Until demolished in the mid 19th century it stood on the site now occupied by the Market Hall. It is sometimes referred to as *The Oak*.

Royal Oak (II), High Street
This public house has undergone a number of changes during its history. It first appears in the records for about 1780. It originally had a butcher's shop on High Street with the public house behind, accessed from a narrow passage. Its sign appears in J. M. W. Turner's painting of High Street, painted in *c*.1800. In 1841 the licensee was Sarah Harrison and in the 1880s, John Wilson (died 1889), whose brother was the licensee of the Walnut Tree Hotel. During and after the Second World War a number of Polish emigrés came to the Wrexham area and this pub became one of their regular meeting places and, consequently, it was nicknamed the 'Polish Embassy'. For a short time during the 1980s, the pub officially changed its name to the 'Embassy' but reverted to the Royal Oak in *c*.1995. It was shown in the 1833 survey.

Royal Observer Corps Headquarters, Borras
Built in 1960 as the headquarters for N° 17 Group Royal Observer Corps, this is the most significant reminder in the Wrexham area of the Cold War. Built of brick and reinforced concrete, with most of its accommodation below ground level, the building is not actually secured to the ground and, in the event of a nuclear explosion nearby, would 'bounce' without sustaining any serious damage. Reports from ROC posts throughout north Wales and the north-west of England were sent here for interpretation and, if necessary, forwarding to the defence forces. ROC posts maintained a check on not only passing aircraft (a hang-over from their role in the Second World War) but also monitored nuclear explosions (should they occur). The headquarters was operational until the ROC was ordered to stand-down in 1991. The property is now part of the Ty'n Twll Farm* estate and is rented out as a recording studio and to Wrexham Groundwork.

Royal Ordnance Factory, Marchwiel
Approved in August 1939, the massive Royal Ordnance Factory, Marchwiel, covered an area of *c*.1,730 acres (700 ha). Existing field boundaries and woodland were left in situ in an attempt to break up the outline of the site and hinder aerial reconnaissance. A casual glance at aerial photographs of the site clearly show that this attempt at concealment was non-effective. The site was chosen for a number of reasons:
1. high local unemployment
2. ground relief meant ease of building
3. distance from a large urban conurbation
4. distance from mainland Europe
5. good railway links

Built by McAlpine at a cost of £10.9 million, the factory began production of propellants in March 1941. The cordite section was supplied by three units producing nitroglycerine and two units producing nitrocellulose. To the south-west of the main factory complex were two smaller tetryl nitration plants. Employing 10,000 workers (many of whom were brought in to the area from other factories, most notably the ROF Waltham Abbey) the ROF had its own internal railway system which was powered by

Royal Ordnance Factory, Marchwiel. An RAF reconnaissance photograph of 2 April 1946, showing part of the giant works that were built during the Second World War. The concrete ROF roads stand out clearly. The river Clywedog can be seen meandering in the lower quarter of the photograph.

The straight section of road at an angle of 45° on the left-hand side of the photograph is now Bridge Road leading into Bridge Road North and then Abbey Road (undoubtedly named after Waltham Abbey in Essex) which leaves the photograph at top centre. Where Bridge Road meets Bridge Road North there is a slight kink in the road line where an old pre-ROF road goes off to the right. This is Redwither Lane (Road) by the Red Wither public house (which appears as a dull grey colour) and eventually joins up with Oak Road. [National Assembly for Wales]

Nº 26 Group Royal Observer Corps, Wrexham, in Parciau which was their headquarters from 1942–5.

diesel engines to avoid the danger of sparks igniting the munitions. One stop was at the Parkey Gate Station (at the east end of the North Marshalling Yard). The buildings were dispersed over a wide area, thereby reducing the danger of a chain-reaction explosion and also making bombing from the air almost impossible as a hit on one building would have little or no effect on any others. German *Luftwaffe* records show that the factory was photographed by a Heinkel *He*III in September 1940 but the ensuing raids in the area failed to hit the works. By the time the factory was fully 'on-line' the *Luftwaffe's* attention was being focussed elsewhere and, due to the design of the site, only saturation bombing – which the *Luftwaffe* was not equipped to carry out – could have inflicted serious damage.

The buildings were steel-framed with reinforced concrete and brick in-fill and most were only single-storey. The largest buildings in terms of height were those of the acid section which were three or four storeys high but internally open to the roof. They housed acid towers used for the concentration of sulphuric acid or de-nitrification of spent acids and were ventilated by means of large metal circular vents or louvred roofs.

Opposite Pentre Maelor was the nitro glycerine plant.

Workers at the ROF were subject to the Official Secrets Act and, such was their adherence to it, that few ever spoke about their work there. The workers wore the ROF badge of crossed bombs with the motto 'Front Line Duty'. Closed shortly after the end of hostilities, the bulk of the records of the ROF Marchwiel were destroyed almost immediately and the site was converted into the embryo Wrexham Industrial Estate. Today, many of the ROF buildings still survive. Some have been converted to modern industrial use while others stand isolated and empty. Proposals to expand the Industrial Estate in the near future could well lead to many more buildings disappearing from the landscape. (See also William Sylvester, GC and photograph overleaf)

Royal Ship Inn, Yorke Street
See Ship Inn.

Royal Visits
1642 – The first recorded Royal visit to Wrexham was that of King Charles I who arrived in the town on 27 September and addressed the people from a window of the Shire Hall in an attempt to raise support for the Royalist cause in the Civil War.

1642 – 7 October, Charles I returned to Wrexham and visited Sir Richard Lloyd's* house at Bryn-y-Ffynnon.*

1889 – The most noted of all Royal visits was that of Queen Victoria in 1889, during her tour of north Wales. On this occasion she visited a number of local sites, including Acton Park,* and, by way of acknowledging the reception which she had received from the Borough, knighted the Mayor, Evan Morris. [Photographs DD/DM/358/13–23; Documents DD/DM/343/7–8]

1903 – On Friday 8 May 1903, at 2 p.m., HRH George, Prince of Wales, and HRH Princess Mary of Wales (later King George V and Queen Mary), visited the town to unveil a memorial in the Parish Church to the men of the RWF who had lost their lives in the 2nd Boer War.

1923 – HRH Edward, Prince of Wales (later Edward Duke of Windsor), visited Wrexham on 2 November 1923 at 3.30 p.m. to lay the foundation stone of the Wrexham & East Denbighshire War Memorial Hospital.

1926 – HRH Prince Henry, Duke of Gloucester, came to the town on 9 June 1926 to to officially open the Wrexham and East Denbighshire War Memorial Hospital. He arrived at the Central Station and addressed the crowds from the balcony of the Wynnstay Arms Hotel in High Street and from the William & John Jones Hospital building.

1934 – HRH Edward, Prince of Wales, made a second visit to Wrexham on Friday 18 May 1934 as Patron of the National Council of Social Service.

1942 – HRH George, Duke of Kent, made an official visit to inspect RAF Wrexham and local ARP personnel on 5 May.

1953 – During her Coronation Tour of Britain, Queen Elizabeth II and Prince Philip visited Wrexham on 10 July 1953 and planted a tree in what was to become Coronation Walk, Rhosddu Road (outside the Guildhall Building).

1961 – On 7 July 1961, HRH Princess Alexandra visited the town to officially open the new Guildhall* building.

1963 – HRH Philip, Duke of Edinburgh visited Wrexham to officially open the Queensway Sports Centre.

1969 – In August 1969, during his tour of Wales after his investiture as Prince of Wales, HRH Prince Charles visited the Guildhall where he addressed the Council and later made a short speech from the balcony of Imperial Buildings (then the offices of WRDC).

1976 – 21 May 1976 HM The Queen and HRH Prince Philip visited Wrexham as part of the Silver Jubilee celebrations. After arriving by train and touring the town in the morning, the royal party had lunch at Hawarden Castle and opened the new creamery at Marchwiel in the afternoon, followed by Theatr Clwyd in the evening.

1977 – Official opening of Erddig Hall by HRH Charles, Prince of Wales.

1978 – Princess Alexandra opened the Kellogg's factory of the Wrexham Industrial Estate on 28 April.

1981 – After their wedding in 1981, the Prince and Princess of Wales visited the town and spent some time with schoolchildren at Bodhyfryd.

1982 – HRH Charles, Prince of Wales and Princess Diana of Wales came to Wrexham on 26 November to unveil the memorial to the miners killed in the Gresford Disaster* of 1934.

1986 – HRH the Duchess of Kent opened the first phase of the Maelor Hospital.*

1989 – HRH Charles, Prince of Wales visited Wrexham, 15 December.

1991 – HRH the Princess of Wales carried out the official opening ceremony of the Artificial Limb Unit at the Maelor Hospital on 30 July.

1991 – Opening of King's Mills Museum by HRH the Princess of Wales.

1998 – HRH The Duke of Kent opened the second phase of the Maelor Hospital.*

1998 – HM The Queen visited Wrexham on 6 March to officially open Wrexham Waterworld* while HRH Prince Philip went to the Wrexham Industrial Estate to open the extension to the JCB factory.

2001 – HRH The Prince of Wales was in Wrexham on 4 May, 2001 for a 'morale boosting' visit to the Welsh Rural Stress Helpline in offices in Trinity Street, an organisation set up to deal with the problems arising from the outbreak of foot and mouth disease in Wales.

2002 – HRH Princess Royal visits Wrexham

2003 – HM Queen and HRH the Duke of Edinburgh visit NEWI and Hightown Barracks on the 50th Anniversary of the Coronation tour, 5 June.

2005 – HRH Duchess of Gloucester visited NEWI to open the refurbished entrance hall at the Plas Coch Campus and the Nick Whitehead Theatre

2006 – HRH The Duke of Edinburgh opened the Wrexham Ramada Hotel on 2 March.

2007 – HRH Duke of Gloucester opened NEWI's re-furbished Regent Street campus, 11 April.

2007 – HRH Princess Royal opened new IMC premises at Wrexham Industrial Estate on Monday, 8 October.

2009 – HRH Princess Royal opened the Pharmacy department of the Maelor Hospital,* 30 July.

Royal Welch Fusiliers
Raised by Herbert of Chirbury in 1689 to serve in Ireland for the Protestant dual-monarchy of King William III and Queen Mary II against the Catholic King James I, the Royal Welch Fusiliers (RWF) have an unbroken record of service through to the present day. Originally designated the 23rd Regiment of Foot, the regiment has never been amalgamated with another regiment and has always been seen as a Welsh unit even before receiving the title The Welsh Regiment of Fusiliers in 1702 (the Royal prefix was added in 1712). For the last 125 years it has recruited its men mainly from north and mid Wales. The regiment has served in nearly every British campaign since 1689 and its battle honours include Peking 1900 where they served alongside the US Marines and, as a consequence, were allied to that force. In 1877, the RWF made Wrexham their permanent headquarters and the Barracks in Hightown became their Regimental Depot. During the First World War the regiment raised 42 battalions and lost over 10,000 officers and men killed. During the Second World War they lost over 1,300 officers and men killed. The Regimental War Memorial is in Bodhyfryd, Wrexham.*

The RWF has a peculiarity of dress in the Flash, a remnant of the ribbons used to tie up pig tails which were used to tie up the mens' hair, which is worn on the back of the collar. The regiment

The Royal Welch Fusiliers parade on Llwyn Isaf having been granted the Freedom of the Borough of Wrexham Maelor in September 1983.

is also unique in having its own Pioneers who, on ceremonial occasions, wear white aprons and carry axes; the Pioneers are also unique in being allowed to have full beards. The RWF has a regimental goat which is not a mascot but a full member of the regiment.

During the Second World War, the 9th Battalion RWF volunteered for airborne service and became the 6th Battalion The Parachute Regiment.

The regiment was granted the Freedom of the Boroughs of Wrexham (15 June 1946) and Wrexham Maelor (17 September 1983) which entitles them to march through the Borough with bayonets fixed, band playing and colours flying.

The spelling of the regiment's name was originally 'Welsh' then changed to the old English 'Welch' before reverting to 'Welsh' at the end of the 19th century. Such was the pressure from the regiment that the War Office was obliged to change the spelling back to 'Welch' in 1920.

As part of a defence review in 2008, the Royal Welch Fusiliers merged with The Royal Regiment of Wales to become 1st Bn, The Royal Welsh (The Royal Welch Fusiliers) and 2nd Bn, The Royal Welsh (The Royal Regiment of Wales).

Royal Welch Fusiliers War Memorial
Despite suggestions that it should be sited in High Street, the RWF War Memorial was erected on the corner of Grosvenor Road and Regent Street, in front of N° 1 Grosvenor Road (see Grosvenor Lodge). Designed and cast by the noted Welsh sculptor, Sir William Goscombe John, RA, it was a memorial to the 10,000 officers and men of the Royal Welch Fusiliers* who were killed or died in the First World War. However, since it was unveiled by Lt-General Sir Francis Lloyd, GCVO, KCB, DSO, Colonel of the RWF, on 15 November 1924, it has become a memorial to all members of the RWF who have been killed in any conflict since 1914. The figures on the memorial represent an 18th century fusilier passing the Colours into the hands of his 20th century counterpart. The inscription, which is taken from

The RWF War Memorial, Bodhyfryd, by Sir Goscombe John, one of the finest war memorials in Britain. [Geoffrey A. Jones]

the Welsh National Anthem, reads: *Pleidiol rwyf i'm Gwlad* (Trans. I am Loyal to my Country) and *Duw Cadw'r Brenin* (Trans. God Save the King). The overall height of the memorial is about 20 feet and the figures are about 10 feet.

In the mid 1960s, due to the increasing volume of traffic on the Grosvenor Road/Regent Street junction, the memorial was moved to its present site on land tucked between the junction of the original town end of Park Avenue* and Chester Street,* (originally known as Long Croft, a field that was part of the Bodhyfryd House estate). (See also Wrexham War Memorial)

Ruabon Road
Ruabon Road developed as a ribbon settlement beginning at the southern end of Pen-y-Bryn and gradually creeping out towards Felin Puleston.* In 1881, the 'town end' of the road was inhabited by a variety of proprietors of small businesses e.g. N° 1 – J. Simcock (salt dealer), N° 2 – John Jones (horse dealer), N° 8 – William Hodkinson (grocer) and artisans. As the street progressed south beyond Wellington Road, the residents moved up the social scale *e.g.* N°s 17 & 18, Holly Bank – the homes of Mrs Mary Rowland (the mother of Sir Leonard Rowland*) and the Revd Edward Jerman (minister of Hill Street Presbyterian Church*). The land to the west of the road, south of the junction with Wellington Road was called Cae Siac (Shack) and was developed by Hampden Poyser of Gwersyllt who, in 1897, laid out Poyser Street, leading off Ruabon Road, following the route of an unadopted track heading west towards Victoria Road. The shop premises of J.A. Mossford (monumental mason) on the corner of Poyser Street and the adjoining five shops were granted planning permission in 1900.

In 1872, there were no properties built alongside Ruabon Road beyond the Oak Tree* public house and Felin Puleston.* This situation changed following the laying out of the new Wrexham Cemetery* on land between the Wrexham–Shrewsbury railway, Bersham Road and Ruabon Road in 1876. Soon after this date individual private houses were built alongside the road and, by the end of the 19th century, new streets had appeared leading off Ruabon Road to both west and east. The land on the east side, between Fairy Road and N° 85 was owned in the late 19th century by Wrexham businessman William Henry Bosker, a successful local monumental mason who had previously lived in Lorne Street and saw a move to Ruabon Road as an expression of his upward social mobility. Where better for a high-class monumental mason to establish his business than close to the cemetery which was being featured as one of the main attractions of the town. He built N° 81 (now Charnwood, N° 85) in *c.*1890 as his own residence, and several of the houses between Charnwood and the corner of Fairy Road for members of his family. The row of properties on the east side was completed in 1910 when another monumental mason, J. W. Edwards* built South Grove.

Ruabon Road Cemetery
See Wrexham Cemetery.

Rubery Owen Group
After a period as a successful partner in the Wrexham company Rogers & Jackson*, Alfred Ernest Owen – an ironmonger, whitesmith, locksmith, bellhanger, tinplate worker, coppersmith, engineer and agricultural implement supplier – left Wrexham to seek his fortune in the Midlands. In 1905, he became a partner with John Tunner Rubery in Rubery, Owen & Company, a small engineering firm in Darlaston, specialising in the manufacture of light steel roofing. As the company expanded, it began to build cycle factories for the burgeoning Midlands cycle industry and this led to the manufacture of motor car components. The

company developed and put into production the manufacture of pressed steel chassis frames and constructed factories for several motor car manufacturers in the region. By 1910, John Rubery had decided to retire and Alfred Owen became the sole proprietor and, the following year, expanded into the manufacture of aircraft parts. The advent of the First World War boosted the company's output and profits, giving it a significant niche in an ever expanding market. The company eventually took over Owen's old Wrexham business, Rogers & Jackson and, in 1927, Powell Brothers & Whitaker.*

Alfred Owen of New Hall, Sutton Coldfield, died in 1929 and the company was left in the hands of his 21 year-old-son, Alfred George Beech Owen, who left Cambridge University to take over the position of Chairman and Managing Director and he was joined in due course by his brother William Beech Owen. Alfred was made a CBE in 1954 and knighted in 1961 for political and public services. In addition to his business interests he was Mayor of Sutton Coldfield, chairman of the Council of Dr Barnardo's Homes, vice chairman of the National Savings Movement, pro-chancellor of the University of Keele, Deputy Chairman of the Development Corporation for Wales and Deputy Lieutenant of Warwickshire. He died in 1975.

The Ministry of Aircraft production opened a Wrexham factory in 1941 on the site of the Abenbury Brickworks as a shadow factory for the production of propellors and fuselages. This was later taken over by Rubery Owen. Part of the original Wrexham site was bought by Wrexham Maelor Borough Council in March 1979 and Rubery Owen closed in March 1980. The site now forms the Whitegate Industrial Estate.

Rubery Way
Built by WBC on land that was originally part of Whitegate Farm.* This street was the access road to the Rubery Owen* factory.

Russell Grove
Laid out and built in 1930–1 as part of the Maes-y-Dre housing estate,* this street is commonly believed to have been named after William James Russell, Headmaster of Grove Park School from 1877–95 and Grove Park County School from 1895–1913. This is however incorrect. The street was originally to be called Russell Square and was to be one of three squares including Beaconsfield Square and Gladstone Square – all named after Prime Ministers. Only Russell Square went ahead (albeit with a partial change of name to Russell Grove). John Russell (1792–1878), the third son of the 6th Duke of Bedford, was Prime Minister 1846–51 and 1865–6.

Ruthin Road Cemetery
See Burial Ground, Ruthin Road.

Rutland Road, Whitegate
A private housing development that was partially laid out in the early inter-war period on land that was previously part of a smallholding. The south-west side of the street (backing onto Linden Avenue) was built shortly before the Second World War.

Rydal Court, Holt Road
A private housing development. Other than it is the name of a lake in Cumbria and a private school in Colwyn Bay, the reason behind the name is unknown.

S

St Anne's Roman Catholic Church, Prince Charles Road
Built to serve the new Queen's Park housing estate, this Byzantine style church was designed by architects Weightman & Bullen and opened in 1962.

St Anne's Roman Catholic Primary School, Prince Charles Road
Due to the threat of overcrowding at St Mary's RC Primary School* and the development of the large Queen's Park housing estate during the 1950s, it was decided by the Diocese of Menevia to build a second Roman Catholic primary school on Prince Charles Road, alongside the church of the same name. Plans were announced in 1954 but the school did not open until April 1967 when there were 50 children enrolled. In 2010, there were 315 children on the school roll. The first head teacher, Mrs Rebecca Angus, had previously taught at St Mary's RC Primary School.*

Headteachers
1967	Mrs Rebecca Angus
19 ?	Miss Marie Kennedy
19 ?	Brendan McDonald
1992	Mrs Marian Sumner
2000	Miss Rachel Molyneux
2008	Mrs Sharon Daltrey

St Christopher's Special School
This school was opened on a site next to Alexandra School (but accessed via a driveway off Park Avenue) on 4 October 1960 by Kenneth P. Thompson, Parliamentary Secretary to the Minister of Education. It could accommodate 100 pupils but initially only had 50 on the roll. A painting of St Christopher was presented to the school by Grove Park pupil Valerie Holmes. The school moved to the former Ysgol Morgan Llwyd buildings in the Hermitage in September 2000 and the new school premises were officially opened by Sir Alex Ferguson, CBE, (Manager of Manchester United FC) on 6 April 2001. In 2001 the school had a pupil population of 217 which had risen to 237 by 2010.

Headteachers:
1960–70	Miss Mona Edwards
1970–93	Derek S. Williams
1993–	Mrs Maxine P. Grant (now Pittaway)

St David's Church (Eglwys Dewi Sant), Rhosddu Road
Wrexham has always been regarded as an enclave of the English language within a Welsh speaking area but the campaign for a Welsh language Anglican church dates back to 1729 when a fund of £700 was made available to help pay for the construction of such a church but nothing came of it. Nonconformists worshippers were better catered for although even they only had six Welsh chapels amongst the fourteen chapels in the town. For many years those members of the Anglican church wishing to worship in Welsh did so at the Parish Church on alternate Sunday afternoons. This practice was ended by Canon Cunliffe* in 1838 when, bowing to local pressure from the English language congregation, the Parish Church became an exclusively English language church. In fairness, it must be pointed out that Cunliffe did make some efforts to establish an exclusively Welsh language church in the town but to no avail.

By 1871, the Welsh speakers were being catered for in St Mark's where they held a service each Sunday evening and, after 1875, an additional service was held on Sunday afternoons. Despite the fact that no English services were held at that church in the evenings, the regular congregation objected, stating that as English people had paid for the construction of the church they should have the exclusive use of it; if a Welsh language congregation wanted a church they should build one.

The arrival of the Revd David Howell as vicar in 1875 led to

St David's School, 1992.

both services being stopped and, for a time, the Welsh congregation held their services in the Town Hall before moving to the Savings Bank on Regent Street (The Religious Census of 1881 showed: Capacity 100; attendance (AM & PM) 55). In addition, a monthly Welsh communion service was held in the Parish Church at 8*am* on designated Sundays. Howell set up a fund to try and gather sufficient monies to build a Welsh church but by 1883 this had failed. In 1888 Howell offered to give part of the grounds of Llwyn Isaf as a site for a Welsh church and believed that such building would cost only £1,700. Plans were put into action whereby some unconsecrated land belonging to St Mark's church would be sold to the Wrexham, Mold & Connah's Quay Railway Company* and the money raised transferred to the Welsh church building fund. Once again, the congregation of St Mark's objected, stating that any funds raised from the sale of St Mark's land should be spent on that church to improve the heating and lighting. As the congregation had not bought the land (it was a gift from Sir Watkin Williams Wynn), and there were as many people attending services in the Savings Bank as were attending St Mark's, the Bishop and the Ecclesiastical Commissioners backed Howell and the money (some £1,650) was transferred.

The foundation stone of St David's was laid in the grounds of Llwyn Isaf by Sir Evan Morris (although an earlier stone had been laid by the vicar's daughter, Gwenllian) to commemorate Queen Victoria's visit to the town in 1889. A service was held in the unfinished building on St David's Day 1890 and it was consecrated on 28 July 1890. Designed by Howell Davies of Wrexham and built by J. Gethin of Shrewsbury, the church had seating for 248 persons. The final cost for its construction was in the region of £4,000. A lectern was presented by Alderman R. W. Evans in 1890. The Religious Census of 1904 showed: Capacity 300; attendance (AM & PM)158.

After the demolition of Church House* in the 1960s, the chancel of St David's was used for church meetings. It was demolished in 1987 and the site used by Lloyds Bank for modern office accommodation bearing the name Tŷ Dewi and later became part of the Yale College campus. Today, Tŷ Dewi is used as the Wrexham Register Office and also accommodates the Electoral Services of WCBC.

St David's Court
Named after St David's School which is located nearby.

St David's Crescent, Spring Lodge
This street was laid out in 1933 as part of the second phase of Wrexham Borough Council's Spring Lodge housing development.* The street was originally intended to be named Windy Ridge but this was changed almost immediately and the name of Wales' Patron Saint chosen instead.

St David's High School, Rhosnesni Lane. Opened in 1957 as the first purpose-built secondary modern school in Wrexham. Designed by the Denbighshire County Architect's Department and built on a 20 acre site by E. W. Gittins & Sons, Ltd., Johnstown, at a cost of £167,000. The school initially had 16 classrooms, 9 practical rooms and an assembly hall. Fears of subsidence led to the whole school being built on a series of concrete rafts. With an original pupil population of 545 at the time of its opening, St David's became a comprehensive school in 1974 and, shortly afterwards it became the largest school in the town. In 1991, some six acres of the school fields were sold as the site for a new private housing estate comprising Moorhead Close, Bickleywood Drive and Halstonwood Close. The school closed in July 2003 and merged with The Groves High School* to reopen as Rhosnesni High School* in September 2003. An illustrated history of the school was published in 2003 – *St David's School – a collection of pictures* by W. Alister Williams.

Headteachers:
1957–77	Gareth Vaughan Williams
1977–86	Emlyn R. Jones
1986–2003	Geoffrey E. Rate

St David's RC Chapel.

St David's Roman Catholic Chapel, King Street
Roman Catholics had been worshipping in Wrexham for some time, using rooms hired by the Revd John Briggs of Chester (later Bishop of Beverley) in Seven Bridge Lane* (near the Beast Market) and in Cutler's Entry* (off Charles Street) before Richard Thompson, the son of John Thompson (owner of the Ffrwd Colliery and iron master) bought, in 1828, land on King Street in order to build a small Roman Catholic chapel (in anticipation of the Catholic Emancipation Act which was passed in 1829). When the owner of the land discovered that it was to be used for a Catholic chapel he withdrew his offer to sell, claiming that the land could only be used for a residence. Thompson, then agreed to build a house on the site, purchased the land, and constructed a residence for a priest on the ground floor with a chapel above. The chapel was dedicated to St David and served as the place of worship for all the Catholics in Wrexham until 1857, when the same Richard Thompson paid for the building of St Mary's Pro-Cathedral. With the opening of St Mary's, the chapel was sold to the Nonconformist Church of Christ and by 1872 was a Baptist chapel.

From 1850 until 1907 Wrexham lay in the Roman Catholic diocese of Shrewsbury.

The succession order of priests was:
Resident Priests
1831–33	Revd D.L. Morton
1833	Revd John Tobin
1833–37	Revd John L. Collins
1837–39	Revd Joseph Kelly

Missionary Rectors
1839–47	Revd John Tobin
1847–50	Revd Joseph Jones (a former Methodist preacher)
1850	Revd Lewis Havard (?)
1851–53	Revd John Coulston
1853–57	Revd John Reah
1856	Revd James Ward (?)

St George's Crescent
This name was officially applied to the Beast Market in 1937 but is generally taken to refer to the properties on the north and west side of the area.

St George's Crescent, neither a crescent nor a link with St George.

St Giles' Boys Home, Rhosnesni Lane
This charitable organisation was run by the Church of England Waifs and Strays Society during the early part of the 20th century. Some of the money used to establish the home came from the bequest of local brewer John Jones* of Grove Lodge. Following a campaign lead by Harry Croom-Johnson,* plans were passed for new purpose-built premises on Rhosnesni Lane, the foundation stone of which records: 'To the glory of God and for the benefit of the children of the church this stone was laid by the Lady Harlech, November 28th 1913'. The completed building was dedicated by Archdeacon Fletcher on 4 June 1915. The first matron was Miss Holmes who retired in 1916 after 14 years in the post and was succeeded by Mr & Mrs J. J. Jones. The home vacated the premises in 1976.

In 1977, the building became the St Asaph Diocesan Resource Centre for education and some of the grounds (which had previously been used as a vegetable garden) were sold off for housing (see Lawson Close).

St Giles Crescent, Spring Lodge
Built in the early 1930s by WBC as part of the early phase of the Spring Lodge* housing estate, the street was named after the saint to whom Wrexham Parish Church is dedicated.

St Giles Home for Waifs and Strays
See St Giles Boys Home.

St Giles' Parish Church
Wrexham Parish Church is regarded as the town's crowning glory and is one of the finest examples of ecclesiastical architecture to be found in Wales. The original church was built

One of the earliest surviving photographs of Wrexham is this view of the Parish Church from Church Street taken in c.1850.

on the hill known as Bryn-y-Grôg (Hill of the Cross), overlooking the Gwenfro – not to be confused with the Bryn-y-Grôg on the way from Wrexham to Marchwiel. In the 1391 survey, mention is made of a site, called *capelle veterane* (Trans. old chapel) being let to four mercers of the town. This would imply that there had been an earlier church on a different site. Local historian, Derrick Pratt, contends (quite convincingly) that this site was possibly in Esclusham Detached, somewhere near the site of the Old Vicarage* at the top of Vicarage Hill.*

The building date of the original church is unrecorded but there are records stating that a church stood here in the 13th century – in 1220 the bishop of St Asaph gave the monks of Valle Crucis at Llangollen 'half of the [income of the] Church' of the town of Wrexham – the other half being given to them seven years later. No remains of this early building have survived. In 1247, Madog ap Gruffydd, Prince of Powys, bestowed upon the monks of Valle Crucis the patronage of the church of Wrexham. We do know that this church building had a tower of some description as records show that 'it was cast down on November 25, 1330'. A new church was then built on the same site and some parts of it survive in the present church and form the basis of the outline of the nave and aisles.

In about 1463, the tower of this second church was burned down (some records state that the whole building was destroyed by this fire) and, as a consequence, the greater part of the church was rebuilt during the latter half of the 15th century and the present tower, claimed as one of the 'Seven Wonders of Wales', and the chancel were added at the beginning of the 16th century (work appears to have still been continuing as late as 1520). The late 15th and 16th centuries were years of great investment in the parish churches of England but this did not apply so much in Wales. In the rich pastoral counties of England the great wealth generated by the wool trade resulted in large sums of money being invested in the local churches. Wrexham did not experience a period of economic boom so there was no reason for the local church to be the subject of a renovation programme so soon after it had been rebuilt. Consequently, one must reach the conclusion that this was the investment of a single individual rather than of the local community. There is some evidence to suggest that the ornamentation which resulted from this early Tudor work was financed by Lady Margaret Beaufort, the mother of King Henry VII. Her husband, Thomas Stanley, the 1st Earl of Derby, had strong connections with the Wrexham area (Stanley Street and Derby Road are named after his family). There is a great deal of symbolism both inside and outside the church building which indicate the influence of the Tudors: roses; portcullis; St James of Compostella (patron saint of Spain, the homeland of Queen Catherine of Aragon); St Catherine (perhaps another allusion to Catherine of Aragon); the figures of a young king and queen (possibly Henry VIII and Catherine of Aragon who were married in 1509) flanking a statue of St Giles.

In the 17th century, the Puritans had a dramatic effect on the internal decoration of the church but even they were not guilty of half the acts of 'vandalism' that are associated with them in popular myths. Even during the Interregnum of 1649–60 the church continued to serve the town as a place of worship, although some of the statuary and the font were removed.

At the beginning of the 18th century, the church received a number of generous gifts from Elihu Yale* of Plas Grono.* In 1819–22 new galleries were installed along both aisles and a triple-decker pulpit changed the nature of the church in an era when the sermon was the focus of attention and an expanding local population was being tempted into the Nonconformist chapels. The exterior of the church was restored by architect Benjamin Ferrey 1866–7 at which time pew rents were abolished and new seating was installed reducing the church's capacity to 1,350, from a previous maximum of 2,700. The interior was further restored by H. A. Prothero in 1901–3. A major restoration and conservation programme was carried out on the tower during the 1980s.

The church is dedicated to St Giles, although there is some evidence to suggest that it had originally been dedicated to St Mary and, before that, St Silin (both Silin and Giles can be translated into Latin as Aegidius). This may indicate that the origin of the church dates back to a time when Welsh churches were dedicated to Celtic saints many of whom (including St Silin) were not recognised by the Roman Catholic church. Certainly, by 1494, the church was known as 'the church of St Giles'.

Not all the parishioners were required to travel to St Giles in order to attend services and by the 19th century there were chapels elsewhere – Brymbo, Minera, Drelincourt, even the National School at Bersham was licensed for worship. In addition, several new churches were built – St Mark's* (off Regent Street), St John's* (Hightown), St James' (Rhosddu) and St David's* (Rhosddu Road). During the incumbency of David Howell* the parish was divided into four and three new parishes were formed at Esclusham (1879), Bwlchgwyn (1880) and Rhosddu (1886). Despite this, the Parish of Wrexham remained one of the largest in Wales, with a population of some 14,000 people in 1888 (more or less the same as it had been in 1865 before being broken up). In the 20th century, additional churches were opened in Rhosnesni (St John's*), Acton (St Margaret's), Queens Park (St Mark's), Poyser Street (St Michael's*).

Inside the church there are significant plaques and memorials to: Ann Wilkinson, wife of John Wilkinson*; Mary Myddelton* of Croesnewydd Hall* (by Roubiliac); Hugh Bellot, Bishop of

Chester*; Sir Foster Cunliffe* of Acton Hall*; the R.W.F.* (various campaigns); the Puleston family (of Hafod-y-Wern*); Sir Richard Lloyd* of Esclus Hall*; Sir Evan Morris.* The RWF Memorial window was unveiled to commemorate the regiments 300th anniversary in 1988. On either side of the chancel are carved heads that may represent Lady Margaret Beaufort and her husband Lord Derby.

The churchyard was substantially reduced in size in the 1890s when the Ellesmere railway line cut through its south side. The railway arches remained until demolished in the 1990s. The most notable tombs here are those of Elihu Yale* and the Palmer family of Cefn Park* which includes Sir Roger Palmer.* The grave of John Downman, RA,* was lost when the churchyard was levelled in 1904. The churchyard gates are the work of Robert Davies* of Croesfoel and date from 1720. They were restored in 1900 and again in the 1980s. The Religious Census of 1881 showed: Capacity 1,200; attendance (AM & PM) 1,258. The Religious Census of 1904 showed: Capacity 1,349; attendance (AM & PM) 1,577.

Vicars:
- c.1220 Alexander
- 1274 Cynwrig Fychan
- 1399 Richard ap Ieuan Lloit
- 1458 Sir Richard Tegen
- John (?) Gyffin (Kyffin ?)
- 1520 Hugh Puleston, LlB
- 1566 Hugh Sontley, BA
- 1598 Robert Lloyd, BD
- 1640 Rowland Owen, MA
- Morgan Llwyd* (non-episcopal vicar)
- 1649 Ambrose Mostyn, MA
- 1661 Rowland Owen, MA
- 1664 William Smyth
- 1684 Peter Wynn, MA
- 1686 Canon John Price, MA
- 1716 John Jones, MA
- 1731 Thomas Edwards, MA
- 1770 Dean William Davies Shipley, MA* (son of the Bishop of St Asaph). Non-resident for most of his incumbency.
- 1827 Canon George Cunliffe, MA,*
- 1875 Archdeacon David Howell, BD, FSA* (later Vicar of Gresford and Dean of St David's)
- 1891 Canon William Henry Fletcher, MA
- 1907 Canon Daniel Davies, MA, DD
- 1923 Archdeacon Lewis Oswald Hugh Pryce, MA (died in office)
- 1930 Canon Benjamin Davies, MA (died in office)
- 1941 Chancellor Robert Davies, MA (died in office)
- 1954 Chancellor D. E. M. Glynne Jones, MA
- 1966 Canon Llewelyn Hughes, BA

Rectors
- 1971 Canon Llewelyn Hughes, MA
- 1974 Canon J. Ivor Rees, BA
- 1976 Archdeacon Raymond S. Foster, BD, PhD, ThD
- 1984 Canon Barry Morgan, MA, PhD (later Bishop of Bangor and Llandaff, Archbishop of Wales 2003)
- 1986 Canon Barry Smith, MA
- 1996 Archdeacon Canon Malcolm Squires, BA
- 2002 Canon Geoffrey O. Marshall, BA
- 2010 Canon Professor Michael F. West, MA, Phd

A full history of this church, entitled *A History of the Parish Church of Wrexham*, was published in 1886 by A. N. Palmer* (reprinted 1984, Bridge Books, Wrexham). *The Parish Church of St Giles*, Wrexham a modern guide and brief history by W. Alister Williams was published in 2000.

St Giles' Schools, Poplar Road/Madeira Hill
(See also Dame Dorothy Jeffreys Free School, Beast Market for early history and Hughes Charity)
In 1881, the National Schools in the parish of Wrexham served to educate 800 pupils, the main building being in the Beast Market* (the former Dame Dorothy Jeffreys Charity School*). The vicar of Wrexham, David Howell,* organised an appeal to raise £4,000 to build a new school for boys which opened in 1885, at a total cost of £5,000, at the top of Madeira Hill, overlooking the valley of the Gwenfro and the Parish Church. Ten years later, a girls school was built between the boys school and Poplar Road at a cost of £4,363-7s-11d and the pupils of the National School for Girls (Tenters Square) moved in the following year.

On 3 March 1920, a war memorial was unveiled at the school to commemorate 100 old boys who had died in the First World War.

In 1921, when Job Mason,* who had been Headmaster of the Boys School for some 35 years was due to retire the school governors appointed a man from Stratford-upon-Avon as his replacement in preference to the senior assistant teacher who had served the school for 15 years. Fifty boys walked out of the school in protest and were soon followed by about 100 others, the whole group meeting in Erddig Park.* Following discussions, some were persuaded to return but the following morning 200 boys were still on strike and they marched to the Guildhall* in Chester Street carrying placards with slogans stating 'Strike boys. We do not want a stranger'. There they were spoken to by the Clerk to the Education Committee, E.C. Dowell, and then they paraded around the streets of the town. Despite the fact that the parents of the striking boys were notified that they were liable to prosecution if their sons failed to attend school the strike continued. The Education Committee met to re-consider their appointment to the headship but were told by the school managers that the best man had been chosen for the job, despite the fact that as a monoglot Englishman, he would be totally incapable of teaching Welsh. The managers added that they were unconcerned by the strike and that if parents were dissatisfied with the National School, they were free to send their children elsewhere. After several weeks a compromise was reached and the post was re-advertised with 'a knowledge of Welsh' being made a requirement of the post. The position was given to J. Jarvis Jones.*

The National School remained a Church School until 1953 when it became a Controlled School of the Local Authority. The opening of St David's Secondary Modern School* in 1957 saw the senior pupils being moved out of the National School which became a Junior Mixed School. In 1959 the school's name was officially changed to St Giles Primary School (taking its name from the saint to which the nearby Parish Church was dedicated). A new kitchen was opened in April 1959 and a large part of the old infant school was converted into a central hall/dining room. Further extensions in 1960 saw the building of indoor toilets and washrooms and two years later, central heating was installed. In 1964 an interior re-design was carried out when corridors were built to create separate classrooms. The closure of the adjacent Drill Hall led to the land being purchased by the local authority in 1968 and converted into a school playing field. In 1988, the former boys school underwent a major re-modelling by Clwyd County Council turning it into the excellent educational facility that it is today. Two years later a similar programme of modernisation was carried out at the infants school and the remodelled building was opened by the Bishop of St Asaph on 29 November 1990. In 2010 there are 299 pupils on the roll.

Among the notable old pupils of the schools are three mayors of Wrexham – Robert Roberts,* Herbert Hampson* and George Turner.*

The adjacent house, Poplar Cottage,* served as a school house for many years

Headteachers:
Boys
- 1886–21 Job Mason
- 1921–32 J. Jarvis Jones
- 1932–47 J.O. Price
- 1948–73 Joseph E. Brown

Girls & Infants

?	Miss McColl
?	Mrs Parker
1886–95	Miss Boston
1895–97	Miss Crebbin
1897–00	Miss Willens (Mrs Lindsay)
1900–01	Mrs Harris (temp)
1901–02	Miss Shatton
1902–06	Miss Light (Mrs Gordon Griffiths)
1906–24	Mrs Harris
1924–57	Miss M.M. Lloyd
1957–65	Miss Mabel Edwards
1966–80	Mrs Elaine Matthias
1980–89	Mrs Sheila Hughes
1990–	Mrs Anne Edmunds

Junior School

1973–89	Arthur Ellis
1989–2009	Philip A. Miller
2009–	Fraser Darlington

St James' Church, Rhosddu Road
The foundation stone for St James' Church, Rhosddu (designed by Wrexham architect William Turner) was laid on 30 September 1874 by Wrexham brewer Peter Walker* who had donated £400 towards the total building cost (1st phase) of £1,410. The church was opened in January 1876 but it was not consecrated until 22 April 1886. The ecclesiastical parish of Rhosddu was created by an order in Council of 1886 from a part of the old parish of Wrexham. The new parish incorporated Rhosddu, Acton, Stansty and Rhosnesni as well as parts of Gwersyllt and Gresford, an area of 3,300 acres with a population of 4,890. In later years, the Garden Village* area also became part of the parish of Rhosddu. The font was a gift from William Overton* to celebrate Queen Victoria's Golden Jubilee in 1887. The total cost of the building and the site was £2,583. A vicarage was built in 1888 at a cost of £1,600 (now part of WCBC Social Service Department's Cunliffe Centre) and a Church Room and School in 1889 at a further cost of £1,400) subscribed by Mrs Jackson of Chevet Hey.* The Religious Census of 1881 showed: Capacity 250; attendance (AM & PM) 427. The Religious Census of 1904 showed: Capacity 250; attendance (AM & PM) 263. The first vicar was David Stanley Davies, MA.

St James' Hall, Lord Street.

St James' Hall, Lord Street
Built on land belonging to the Revd T. Griffiths of Ruabon in about 1886, it is shown as being the property of Mr Edgar in 1897 (possibly James Edgar the Postmaster). It was the largest public hall in the area with a capacity of well over 1,000. This iron

St John the Baptist's Church. The building on the right of the photograph is the old 'tin' church which served the congregation in this area until St John's was built.

building was demolished in about 1906 to make way for a new sorting office for the Post Office in Egerton Street. Part of the building was re-assembled in Maesgwyn Road* where it became a dance-hall and later, a business premises.

St John's Ambulance Brigade
The Wrexham branch of this nationally known organisation was formed in 1927. The first ambulance vehicle was loaned to the Wrexham branch by a Cardiff branch. The first headquarters was sited at the junction of Rhosddu Road and Grove Road before moving into the Divisional Police Headquarters, then to the Maelor General Hospital, to the former Police Station on Prices Lane, Rhosddu, in the late 1990s and, more recently to a new purpose-built training centre on the Yale Business Park.

St John the Baptist's Church, Hightown
Built in 1908–9, by John Jones,* founder of the Island Green Brewery*, in memory of his wife, the Church of St John the Baptist cost of £8,509 and was consecrated by the Bishop of St Asaph on 29 July, 1910. It stood on the corner of King's Mills Road and Whitegate Road and was demolished in 1989–90. The east window, produced by Morris & Company and incorporating a design by Burne-Jones the noted Pre-Raphaelite artist, was

removed and placed in the Parish Church. The foundation stone of a schoolroom was laid by Mrs F.W. Morris in November 1927.

The Religious Census of 1904 showed: Capacity 180; attendance (AM & PM) 169.

Curates:
1910–15	Revd A.W. Rees
1915–17	Revd C. Mostyn Davies
1917–22	Revd J.R. Clarke
1923–25	Revd Dowell Ll. Jones
1925–28	Revd N.S. Baden-Powell
1928–34	Revd Hywel Davies
1934–35	Revd H.B. Evans
1935–44	Revd W.A. Lewis
1944–50	Revd A.R.W. Hughes
1950–58	Revd E.A. Grey
1958–59	Revd D.E. Lewis
1959–65	Revd H.J. Lloyd
1965–	Revd Glyn Conway

St John's Church, Rhosnesni
Church services were first held in Rhosnesni in the late 1860s, following the building of Acton Park Church School in 1868. The school building was adapted for use as the Rhosnessney School Church Mission. Some years later, Sir Robert A. Cunliffe* of Acton Park* paid for the construction of a Church Institute on the corner of Rhosnesni Lane* and Acton Road* (now Dean Road*). Following the passing of the 1902 Education Act, it became illegal to hold church services on school premises and services were transferred from Acton Park School to the Church Institute, the first being held there on 12 February 1905. Alterations were carried out to the building, including the addition of a bell, and it became known as the Rhosnessney Mission Church. The village War Memorial was erected in the grounds of the church but, due to it being made of wood, it had to be relocated inside the building in about 1928.

In 1971, the Rectorial Benefice of Wrexham was created and St John's became part of it. This building continued to serve the community of Rhosnesni until 1974 when the last service was held in the building on Good Friday. The site was later sold for £6,500. (See also St John the Evangelist's Church)

St John the Evangelist's Church, Rhosnesni
In the mid 1960s discussions commenced about the building of a new church in Rhosnesni to replace the Mission Church on Dean Road. Sites were considered in Acton Park, on Jeffreys Road and on Norfolk Road before the decision was made to build on land leased from WBC on the corner of Herbert Jennings Avenue and Borras Road. Designed by architect C.G. Gethin of Rhyl, the church was to have twelve sides representing the twelve apostles. Building work commenced in February 1974. The cost of building this church was £42,000 (estimated at £36,000) and it seats about 300. It was consecrated by the Bishop of St Asaph, the Rt Revd H. John Charles in April 1974. In 1981, St John's became the Vicar's Church for the Rectorial Benefice of Wrexham. A new church room was built alongside St John's in 1990 at a cost of £113,000.

St John's House, Chester Road
Built by John Jones,* solicitor and Mayor of Wrexham, this was later the home of Samuel Rogers (bought in 1920 for £1,700), before becoming a nurses' home for the War Memorial Hospital.* It was empty for many years before being adapted for use as a hostel for the homeless and is today (2010) run by the Wallich organisation.

St John's Road
Named after St John the Baptist's Church* which stood on the corner of this road at its junction with King's Mills Road until it was demolished during the 1980s.

This piece of canine sculpture was once positioned outside the front door of St John's House.

St Joseph's Convent, Derby Road
In 1960, the Sisters of St Joseph of Chambery became housekeepers at Bishop's House* to Bishop Petit.* In 1972, on the retirement of the bishop, the sisters moved into rented accommodation in Salisbury Road before moving to their present convent in Derby Road in 1973. The sisters work as teachers in local Roman Catholic schools, nurses and, more recently, minister to the parish.

St Joseph's Roman Catholic High School, Sontley Road
Work began on building Wrexham's first purpose-built Roman Catholic secondary school in 1958 on a site between Sontley Road* and Erddig Road,* across the way from the Bishop's House* and alongside Plas Derwen.* The school opened in September 1960. It was designed as a small secondary modern school with a maximum capacity of some 450 pupils. In September 1972, it became St Joseph's Roman Catholic Comprehensive School, taking many of the former pupils of the Convent Grammar School* in Grosvenor Road. It catered for pupils aged between 11 and 16 years and Sixth Form education was available at Yale VIth Form College* in Crispin Lane.

Headteachers:
John M. Cleary
John Thompson
John Kenworthy

St Joseph's Roman Catholic Secondary School, Sontley Road
See St Joseph's Roman Catholic High School.

St Margaret's Church, Chester Road
The original plans for the Garden Village estate had a church sited at the far end of Kenyon Avenue, close to the site of the present day Wat's Dyke School.* Due to the dramatic curtailment in the development of the estate, it was decided to build the church alongside the main Chester Road where it would also serve the recently established Acton Park housing estate.* Designed by T. Alwyn Lloyd, the architect for the Welsh Town Planning & Housing Trust, work began on St Margaret's in February 1928 and it was consecrated in December of the same year. Unlike the normal pattern of churches, St Margaret's has its altar at the western end. A chapel was later added on the southern side of the church and, in the late 1970s, a lounge was built at the eastern end. There is a large church hall at the rear of the building.

St Margaret's Way, Acton
Built in the 1960s as part of WBC's extension to the Acton Park* housing estate, this street was named after St Margaret's Church* which is located nearby.

Building the Wrexham, Mold & Connah's Quay railway extension into the Central Station. The congregation of St Mark's Church suddenly found itself located, not in a select, off town centre church, but in a church alongside major railway workings. The area seen here, extending along the side of Bryn-y-Ffynnon was known as The Walks before the railway came.

St Mark's Church, **(I)** St Mark's Road
St Mark's, like Bryn-y-Ffynnon Church,* was sited in part of the Orchard Field* which once belonged to Bryn-y-Ffynnon House.* By the 19th century, the land was part of the property of Sir Watkin Williams Wynn who presented it to the Church of England in 1858 for the purpose of building a new church to serve the centre of the ever-growing town of Wrexham. Sir Watkin made two conditions to the bequest *viz* – that no burials should take place in the yard of the new church and that the tree standing alongside the road which would lead to the church should not be removed. Both conditions were agreed to and the tree still survives in St Mark's Road* today.

Designed as a chapel of ease for the Parish Church of St Giles, by the architect Richard Kyrk Penson,* work on St Mark's commenced in 1856. The foundation stone was laid in August 1856 by Miss Cunliffe of Acton Hall and the building (which cost over £7,000) was consecrated on 21 May 1858. The chancel was 37 feet long, the nave 86 feet long and the transcepts 18 feet long. Inside, the roof was 65 feet above the floor of the church and, as a result of the poor acoustics a false ceiling (20 feet lower) had to be installed some years later. The spire, at nearly 200 feet, possibly the tallest in Wales, was completed on 5 June 1862 and became one of the features of the Wrexham skyline. The church was endowed, mainly by Miss Mary Anne Bennion of Beechley House* with four-fifths of the tithes of Minera. A large, unconsecrated part of the churchyard was sold in 1888 to the Wrexham, Mold & Connah's Quay Railway* and the monies raised were used to pay for part of St David's Church,* Rhosddu Road, much against the will of the congregation. The pulpit was of Caen stone and the font was a gift from the Mayor of Wrexham, Thomas Rowlands,* in 1863. The east window was a gift from Miss Anne Bennion (in memory of the Prince Regent – cost £450) and the west window was a family memorial to William and Elizabeth Overton.* A small window in the south aisle commemorated local solicitor Thomas Hughes (1803–63) and one in the north aisle was in memory of a cleaner who fell into a sewer and drowned.

When the church opened, it was intended that it would serve the poorer elements of the town's population and would seat 615 adults and 146 children in free pews. However, its location close to the commercial centre of the town and its proximity to

Above: The interior of St Mark's Church, c.1900.

St Mark's Church viewed from the west, c.1890.

important residential areas such as King Street and Grosvenor Road, led to its congregational make-up becoming very middle class, and passionately English. Despite campaigns to the contrary, St Mark's never became a parish church in its own right and its congregation were always looked down upon by those who attended services at St Giles. The first curate was James Clark Roberts, MA, who served the church from 1858–68. The Religious Census of 1881 showed: Capacity 700; attendance (AM & PM) 622. The Religious Census of 1904 showed: Capacity 700; attendance (AM & PM) 452.

After 1874, the church came under the direct control of the vicar of Wrexham and had no appointed curate-in-charge.

St Mark's was once described by Goodhart-Rendel as 'one of the best provincially designed town churches of its epoch'. During the 1930s, the interior was completely renovated. St Mark's acquired an enviable reputation for music, most notably, its choir. By the time the church closed in 1956, the attendance had dwindled to less than 100 and the repairs then required were estimated to cost £6,000. It was demolished in 1959 and a multi-storey car park now stands on the site and preserves the name. There were plans put forward for the site to be used as a new Wrexham Divisional Police Headquarters but this proposal was turned down in favour of a new building at Bodhyfryd* (see Police Headquarters*).

St Mark's Church, (II) Queens Park

In September 1956, the Bishop of St Asaph dedicated an oak cross on a open site in the new Queen's Park* housing estate where a new church was to be built. At the same time a fund was started which soon reached £15,000 – with the estimated cost of the new church being £28,000. Building work began almost immediately to a design by John L. Jones of L. W. Barnard & Partners. Taking the name of the town centre church that was closed in 1956, St Mark's Church in Queens Park was consecrated in 1957.

St Mark's Road

The original St Mark's Road was laid along the area previously known as The Walks, and extended from Hill Street, along the south side of St Mark's Church* to link into Cathrall's Lane* (later re-named Union Road*). The construction of Bradley Road* in 1881 cut across this road but both sections continued to be known as St Mark's Road. In 1887, plans were approved for the extension of the Wrexham, Mold & Connah's Quay Railway* from the Exchange Station* to a new terminus at Central Station* off Hill Street*. Although WBC had approved these plans almost immediately, matters were delayed by objections raised by the Quarter Sessions. The construction of the new railway line meant that St Mark's Road ceased to be a public thoroughfare and became a private access to the railway company's property. All that remains of this street today is a private access road leading east from Bradley Road to the rear of the Fire Station and a public road to the west of Bradley Road which was re-named Central Road.* The name St Mark's Road was then transferred to the short road which led from Regent Street* to the main gate of St Mark's Church, running along the side of County Buildings* (now Wrexham Museum). The church was demolished in the 1950s and the road now provides vehicle access to the St Mark's Car Park and pedestrian access to the Central Station.

St Mark's Terrace, Regent Street

St Mark's Terrace with the former Majestic Cinema building in the distance.

285

This short terrace of houses was located on the south side of Regent Street, to the west of Bryn-y-Ffynnon Church. It was demolished in the 1960s to make way for the new Regent Street shopping precinct.

St Mary's RC School

The first classes of a Roman Catholic school were held in Wrexham in 1840 when fewer than 50 pupils were taught in the priest's house in King Street.* In 1852, the school, which was growing in population, moved into the premises in Bank Street* which are now Marubbi's Café. Two years later they relocated to Yorke Street* and by 1856 were back in Bank Street where they remained for less than two months before moving back to King Street. By 1860, the school was located in Hill Street* and all records then come to an abrupt halt, so much so, that it appears likely that the school was closed for some years.

By 1867, Roman Catholic children were being educated in premises on the junction of Caia Road* and Mount Street.* An inspection report recorded that 'This school could hardly contain one half of the annual average which had been packed into it'. By 1870, the school was again on the move, this time to the east corner of Brook Street* and Vicarage Hill* where it was reported to have an 'excellent school house, well-ventilated and lighted and of ample dimensions' with a 'zealous and competent mistress'. The building of the Wrexham–Ellesmere Railway* viaduct at the rear of the premises during the 1890s meant that these premises were no longer suitable for use as a school and land was bought at the end of Tenters' Square* where, in 1893, the Earl of Denbigh laid the foundation stone of St Mary's Roman Catholic School. In 1952, the premises of the nearby Charity School* were bought and added to the school's accommodation and four years later a nursery school block was added. The shortcomings of these old buildings were highlighted in 1965 when a serious outbreak of dysentery occurred in the school and, despite a new annexe being built, the matter was not satisfactorily resolved until 1972 when all the pupils were moved into the newly vacated premises of the Convent Grammar School* in Grosvenor Road. The old buildings in Lea Road* were then demolished and a new school was built on the same site at a cost of £100,000 (built by E. W. Gittins & Sons). The school's motto is *Credu, Gobeithio, Caru* (Believing, Hoping, Loving).

St Mary's RC School, Tenters Square.

Headteachers:
1852–4	Mr Tierney
1854–7	Mr Cassidy
1857–60	Miss Law
1860	Mrs Parfitt
closed	
1867–8	George Raith
1868–77	Miss Elizabeth Christian
1877	Miss Kay (temp)
1877–9	Miss McCormack
1879–97	Sister St John

Juniors:
1897–1925	Sister Bernard
1925–43	Sister Trea

St Mary's RC Pro Cathedral and the Presbytery, c.1900.

1943–50	Sister Christina
1950–	Sister Norbert

Infants:

1896–1919	Sister Austin
1919–22	Sister Agatha
1922–5	Sister Seraphine
1925–54	Sister Aquinas
1954–	Sister Josephine
	Sheila Edwards

Primary:
  Michael Greany
  Mrs Katherine M. Jones

St Mary's Roman Catholic Pro-Cathedral, Regent Street
(See also St David's Roman Catholic Chapel)
Correctly named The Cathedral Church of Our Lady of Sorrows, this fine neo-Gothic building was built as the Roman Catholic parish church for Wrexham. It was designed in the Early Decorated style by the 23 year-old Edward Welby Pugin, the son of the renowned gothic revivalist architect Augustus Welby Pugin. It was built in 1857 by Richard Thompson of Stansty Hall* (originally from Wigan, he owned the Ffrwd Colliery) at a cost of some £9,000 as a memorial to his wife, Ellen, whose tomb lies inside. In 1957, the interior of the church, particularly the altar, was re-designed by Mold architect, F.C. Roberts.

In 1898, the diocese of Menevia was formed and St Mary's was consecrated as a Pro-Cathedral on 7 November 1907. In 1987, the Welsh Province of the Roman Catholic Church was re-organised and the Diocese of Wrexham* was created with St Mary's as the cathedral. The Religious Census of 1881 showed: Capacity 400; attendance (AM & PM) 640. The Religious Census of 1904 showed: Capacity 600; attend-ance (AM & PM) 520.

E.W. Pugin

Memorials within the cathedral include: the tomb of Ellen Thompson; memorial window donated by Lady Ffrench in memory of her parents, Richard and Ellen Thompson; memorial window in memory of Lord Ffrench and his wife Mary Ann (née Thompson); commemorative win-dow celebrating the silver jubilee of Bishop Francis Mostyn* (1898–1921); memorial window to Sisters Mary Augustine and Mary Regis of the Sisters of the Immaculate Conception; a memorial window to John Beirne,* Mayor of Wrexham and organist at the cathedral for 32 years; icon *Mother of God of Czestochowa*, gifted by the Wrexham Polish community; window in memory of St Richard Gwynn*; relic of St Richard Gwynn; icon of St Richard Gwynn; plaque in memory of F/Lt David S. A. Lord, VC, DFC,* who was formerly an altar server at the cathedral.

The parish hall which was built in 1913 is one of the largest in Wales.

The succession lists of priests is:

Missionary Rectors

1857–72	Canon Dr Edward F. Browne (died 17 July 1872)
1872–6	Canon Ambrose Lennon
1877–81	Canon William Hilton
1881–3	Very Revd Provost Hilton, VG
1883–95	Canon Henry Hopkins
1895–1900	Mgr Edward Henry Slaughter
1900–7	Canon John E. Quinn

Administrators (after 1907)

1907–14	Canon John E. Quinn
1914–47	Canon George Nightingale
1947–82	Adolph Andrew Evans
1982–90	Canon Cyril Schwarz
1990–99	Bernard Morgan
1999–	Revd Peter Brignall

St Michael's Church, Poyser Street
Built of Ruabon brick between 1910 and 1912 to a design by L. W. Barnard. Probably the most interesting feature of the interior was the east window which was designed by the firm of William Morris, the noted late 19th century designer.

Curates:

1912–13	Revd J.R. Evans
1913–17	Revd D.T. Silian Evans
1917–18	Revd D.M. Richards
1919–26	Revd H.I. Morgan
1926–30	Revd E. Parry
1930–33	Revd T. Gethin Roberts
1933–39	Revd Ivor Williams
1939–48	Revd D.H. Evans
1948–50	Revd Herbert Jones
	Revd R. Jones
1950–71	Revd T.R. Gittins

Vicars:

1971–74	Revd T.R. Gittins
1974–77	Revd Price Williams (part-time)
1977–80	Revd Philip Owens
1980–83	Revd A.G.M. Davies

St Peter's Church, Smithfield
Foundation stone of Church Hall was laid on 30 January 1955 by the Revd D.E.M. Glynne Jones, Vicar of Wrexham. Today the church is a furniture warehouse and the church hall serves as the Caia Park Council Rooms.

Sage, Lorna *author*
Lorna Stickton was born in Hanmer on 13 January 1943, Lorna Sage was educated at Hanmer School and the Girl's High School, Whitchurch and Durham University where she gained a 1st class degree. She later obtained an MA from the University of Birmingham. Married to Victor Sage at an early age she had one daughter and was divorced in 1974. She married Rupert Hodson in 1979.

Sage spent her entire working life as an academic at the University of East Anglia where she became professor of English in 1994. She was a noted book reviewer, working for learned publications on both sides of the Atlantic, and was the editor of

The railway bridge over Salop Road, demolished in the 1980s. In the distance Brooklands can be seen.

The Cambridge Guide to Women's Writing in English (published in 1999). She also wrote an autobiographical memoir *Bad Blood*, about her childhood in Hanmer, which won the Whitbread Biography Award in 2001 and was a finalist for the Whitbread Book of the Year.

Lorna Sage died on 11 January 2001.

Salop Road
Salop Road is a name given at various times to the road leading out of Wrexham, through Wrexham Fechan,* towards Marchwiel and eventually to Shrewsbury (Salop). It would seem that the name Salop Street/Road was officially applied to the road between Mount Street* and the Willow Bridge* in the early 19th century but, gradually, the name referred to the area as far as the Green Dragon* public house, replacing the name Wrexham Fechan. One can only guess at the reason for this change and it would seem likely that it occurred because the owners of the substantial new houses on the Wrexham Fechan road found the name Salop Road both easier to say and grander on the ear. To the indigenous population, the name Wrexham Fechan was applied to the road until well into the 20th century. Most of what is today recognised as Salop Road had been developed by the time of the 1872 survey with the exception of the area between the southern end of Roderick Terrace* and the corner opposite the Green Dragon.* This area, part of the Beechley* estate until sold in 1894, was built upon in the late 1890s and Birch Street* was laid out at the same time. [DRO/1003] Brooklands, a house almost certainly designed by J. R. Gummow* (it was the site of his father's house in 1833), was located on the west side of Salop Road on what is now the southern corner of St Giles Way.

Salop Road Wesleyan Methodist Chapel, Wrexham Fechan
Shown in the 1833 survey as being located on the west side of the street opposite the junction with Rivulet Road.

Salisbury Park Congregational Church.

Salisbury Park Congregational Church
Located at the junction of Salisbury Road and Percy Road. The Religious Census of 1904 showed: Capacity 600; attendance (AM & PM) 383. The Manse appears to have been at N° 31 Court Road.* Following the discovery of dry rot in the structure of the building, the chapel was demolished in 1980.

Salisbury Road (previously Salusbury Park)
This area was known as Groft Tudur and was the property of the Thelwall family of Wrexham. During the 18th century, Ann Thelwall married the Revd John Lloyd and their son, Colonel John Lloyd succeeded to the estates of the Salusburys of Galltfaenan and assumed the name Salusbury. It was in celebration of this connection that the area was re-named Salisbury Park (originally, and correctly, Salusbury Park). The large villa-style properties on the northern side of this road were built before the 1872 survey. The Gummow family* (architects) lived at N° 3 in 1881.

Salvation Army
The Salvation Army arrived in Wrexham in October 1881 and was designated the 226th Corps. They originally held meetings in the Public Hall* in Henblas Street and, for a time (before 1889), in the Temperance Hall (formerly Penson's Theatre* before moving to the premises of the old Hill Street Presbyterian Chapel* and later to the former Dame Dorothy Jeffreys Charity School* on the Beast Market* which they bought in 1885. In 1883 the press reported:

> In defiance of an order by the Corporation that they should desist from beating drums and tambourines and blowing cornets on the streets of the town to the annoyance of worshippers at churches and chapels, the Salvation Army continued their casual nuisance to the annoyance of the townspeople. At the public hall on Sunday evening the 'Captain' made a statement that they would not give in to the local authorities. The names of some of the local ring-leaders in the noise making were taken and legal proceedings will be taken against them.

The Army tried to gain permission from the Council to buy land at Yspytty* in 1902 but their proposals were turned down. The founder of the Salvation Army, General William Booth, visited Wrexham in August 1905.

The Salvation Army closed the doors on the Beast Market building (which was sold for £90,000) in December 1975 and temporarily moved to the Maes-y-Dre Community Centre until work was completed in 1977 on adapting the former Rogers & Jackson* offices in Garden Road,* Rhosddu into a new Citadel (at a cost of £150,000). This was officially opened in November 1977 by Lt-Col T. C. Jones of Coedpoeth, former OC Birmingham Division of the Salvation Army. The Religious Census of 1881 showed: Capacity 1,200; attendance (AM & PM) 1,922 The Religious Census of 1904 showed: Capacity 330; attendance (AM & PM) 183.

The Salvation Army Band was first formed in the late 19th century when instruments were purchased and allocated to six members who had no musical training whatsoever. After three months of practice the band made its first appearance with a repertoire of only two tunes. In the early 1900s musician David Watkins was appointed conductor and he transformed the band so that it played an ever-increasing role in the life of the Salvation Army in Wrexham. In 1915, John Young was appointed bandmaster, followed by Jack Duckett.

Samuel, JP, William Edge *Freeman & local politician*
Born in Wrexham on 21 February 1839, William Samuel is listed in the 1881 census (and on his gravestone) as a builder and contractor employing 26 men and 5 boys. Amongst many notable buildings, he built the National Schools* on Madeira Hill, the Victoria School in Brook Street,* Grove Park County School* and several houses on Fairy Road.* William Samuel married (1) Lucy (she died in 1876, aged 24) and (2) Hannah Wilson (born 1852, died 1952) and had three sons and three daughters. In 1881 he was living at N° 4 Carlton Villas, Sontley Road but later moved to Stratford House, Fairy Road.* He was elected to serve as a Conservative councillor for the East Ward of WBC on 1 November 1877, became Chairman of the General Purposes

Committee and served as Mayor of Wrexham in 1885. He was also Chairman of the Building Committee – in which role he was deeply involved in the building of the 'new Infirmary' (Croesnewydd Hospital) – and a member of the Wrexham Board of Guardians. In 1884, he was elected a member of the newly formed Denbighshire County Council, a position which he held until his death. He was elected Chairman of the County Council. In latter years he was a member of the Unionist Party. William Samuels was created an Honorary Freeman of the Borough of Wrexham, November 1911 and appointed a Justice of the Peace for the Wrexham Borough bench in 1889 and, later, for the County bench. He died at his home on 24 October 1917 and is buried in Wrexham Cemetery.*

Sandringham Road, Croes Eneurys
Built on land that had formerly been part of Croes Eneurys Farm,* by local builders Parker, Davies & Hughes Ltd. Work commenced in the late 1930s and the eastern side of the road was completed in 1938. The western side of the road was not built until after the Second World War. It was named after the royal residence at Sandringham. The parents of David S. A. Lord, VC* lived at Nº 22.

Sandway Road, Croes Eneurys
Sandway Road was laid out after 1934 on land that had previously been part of Croes Eneurys Farm* and developed by Parker, Davies and Hughes Ltd. Most of the houses had been built by the outbreak of war in 1939. It takes its name from the large deposits of sand which existed in this area, much of which was excavated and used in the building of the Croes Eneurys Estate.*

Sauvage, JP, Robert Freeman
Born in Ruabon in c.1856, Robert Sauvage was a partner in the tailoring firm of R. & T. Sauvage of Nº 1 Hope Street. He was created an Honorary Freeman of the Borough of Wrexham on 10 June 1931. He died on 25 April 1942.

Sauvage, Alderman Thomas local politician
Born on 10 March 1857, the son of James Sauvage, a grocer and draper of Rhosllanerchrugog, Thomas was educated at Wern School and a private school at Llwynenion before moving to the British School at Rhos then at Brook Street* in Wrexham. On leaving school he was apprenticed to a draper in Cefn for five years and was then employed by Robert Lloyd in Oswestry before opening his own business, in partnership with his brother Robert, in Church Street,* Wrexham. The business later moved to Nº 1 Hope Street.* Elected a Liberal member of WBC in 1901, Thomas Sauvage served as Mayor for four years – 1908 and 1919-21. He was elected an alderman in 1920, was a member of the Wrexham Board of Guardians and was appointed a Borough Justice of the Peace in 1915. Shortly before his death he became a Denbighshire County Councillor.

Thomas Sauvage married the daughter of William Garside, the manager of Plas Kynaston Colliery and for a time they lived in Cefn where he had a branch shop and served as a member of the local Parish Council. He later lived at Nº 14 King Street, Wrexham and was treasurer of the Salisbury Park Congregational Church.* He had four sons and two daughters. He died on 3 November 1922 while still in office as Mayor of Wrexham.

Savage, James singer
James Savage was born in Rhosllanerchrugog in about 1850. At the age of 16 he emigrated to the United States of America where he began to gain a reputation as a tenor of note. In 1870 he was heard by Lewis W. Lewis (Llew Llwyfo) who was touring with a party of choristers and was immediately offered a position as a tenor with the choir. Savage returned to Wales and entered the Royal Academy of Music where he won both the gold and silver medals in his second year. He was advised by Sims Reeves, perhaps the greatest tenor of the time, to become a baritone and joined the Carl Rosa Opera Company and then the English Opera Company. In 1890 Savage (or Sauvage as he had come to be known) again emigrated to America. In his latter years, he became a singing teacher.

Savings Bank
The Savings Bank was first established in 1832 at Nº 5 Temple Row. A purpose-built bank, it was erected in 1837 to a design by Edward Welch (See Infirmary) in the neo-classical style. It was located on the eastern corner of the junction of Regent Street* and Egerton Street.* Within the Savings Bank on Regent Street was a Penny Bank in 1881 whose treasurer was William Overton* and whose secretary was J. Horabin. The building was demolished in the mid 1890s to make way for the present Lloyds/TSB Bank building. On 1 April 1895, the Savings Bank moved into the premises of James & James, solicitors, in the Priory gatehouse* then later the Wrexham Gas Company offices in Regent Street and finally, in 1928, into purpose-built premises on the corner of Priory Street* and Hill Street.* In 1906 the Wrexham Savings Bank amalgamated with the Chester Savings Bank (when it held £75,615 on deposit).

In 1893, the Wrexham Savings Bank had as its president, Sir Watkin Williams Wynn and Vice-Presidents, the Ven Archdeacon David Howell, BD,* and Simon Yorke of Erddig Hall. The trustees at that time were: George Bate, J.R. Burton, David Davies, J.F. Edisbury,* William Overton,* Alfred Owen (see Rubery Owen), Benjamin Owen, W. Potter, Edward E. Rogers, W.J. Russell and the Revd Thomas Lloyd Williams. The treasurers were Messrs James & James. [Documents DD/DM/847/1-12, 14-19]

The Secretaries/Actuaries were:
- 1832 John Sadler (former wine merchant)
- 1833 John Farrar
- 1837 Bartholomew Dillon (former wine and spirit merchant, accountant, auditor of the Wrexham Union, accountant of the Wrexham branch of the North & South Wales Bank, schoolmaster) dismissed following legal prosecution, December 1842
- 1842 Thomas Tyndall (of West Bromwich, bank clerk in Wrexham)
- 1849 Anthony Dillon (manager of the Wrexham branch of the National Provincial Bank)
- 1854 John Bury (still in office in the early 1890s)
- c.1893 Richard Percy James (solicitor)

Saxon Street
Saxon Street was laid out prior to the sale of the Beechley and Kingsland estates in 1895. The land, formerly owned by the Bennions family of Beechley House,* was divided into numerous building plots prior to the sale. All the streets in the new development were to be named after royal dynasties of English monarchs. Saxon Street takes its name from the Saxon kings who ruled England until 1066.

Saxton, Judith romantic novelist
See Katie Flynn

Schools
In addition to the better-known schools which have their own entries, 19th century Wrexham had a number of private schools. In 1881 the following were recorded:

Old Vicarage School   Head Master, H. Poyner, MCP
Mrs Simms' Seminary, Wynnstay House,* King Street.
Mrs Wilson's Seminary, Grosvenor Road.*

Misses Simons' Seminary, King Street.*
Miss Liptrot's Seminary, 39 Erddig Road.*
Miss Edmund's Seminary, Boundary Street (Spring Road).*
Miss Humphrey's Seminary, Kingston House, Talbot Road.* (Boarding) also listed as Kingston House Ladies School.

Scott, John James *licensee & entrepreneur*
Born in Wensleydale, Jack Scott appears to have moved to Wrexham in the late 19th century from Anfield in Liverpool and became licensee of the Seven Stars* public house. He was the nephew of John Sunter, licensee of the Chester Street Vaults* and his first wife Abigail (died 1896) was the daughter of Fletchers, the clog makers of Charles Street.* Jack Scott was responsible for building a number of town centre properties. He built and operated the Empire Cinema* in Lambpit Street and bought and operated Edisbury's Mineral Water Factory in the Beast Market,* a share in the old Town Hall,* the Nelson Arms,* the Fleece,* the Hand Inn on Town Hill* and the Turf Hotel.* He was an officer in the Denbighshire Hussars Imperial Yeomanry* and captain of the Prince of Wales' Volunteer Fire Brigade.* A prime mover behind the introduction of the Pony and Galloway Races at Wrexham Racecourse* he also helped form the Wrexham Cycle Club, established an outside catering business based on the Seven Stars, was a keen pigeon fancier, hare courser, rifle shooter, and a pony and dog breeder. He died at his home in Craigmillar Road* in September 1946 and is buried in Wrexham Cemetery.*

Seion Welsh Calvinistic Chapel, Regent Street
See Seion Welsh Presbyterian Church, Regent Street.

Seion Welsh Presbyterian Church, Regent Street
This was located on the south-eastern corner of the junction of Regent Street and Duke Street on land bought from Thomas Taylor Griffiths for £1,085-15s-0d in July 1865. The site had previously been occupied by a wooden farm barn. The congregation moved to the new chapel in September 1867 from their previous chapel, also named Seion, off Abbot Street.* The twin towers of Seion were a major feature of the town's skyline for over 100 years and contained staircases which allowed the congregation access to the galleries. The dimensions of the chapel were: 27 yards long, 14 yards broad. It had seating for 800 people and £6,000 was spent on the building. In 1884, a schoolroom was built on Egerton Street. In 1951, the building was renovated and modernised according to plans drawn up by architect Professor Dewi Prys Thomas. The Manse was originally at Noddfa, Nº 27 Grosvenor Road* (the name was later changed to Awelon), which had been bought for £950 in 1920. This was sold for £1,800 in 1956 and a new Manse was bought for £3,650 at Nº 20 Park Avenue.*

By the late 1970s, there were a number of structural problems developing at Seion and it was decided to sell the site (which was in a prime town centre retail position) and to build a new church. The former girl's home at Llanelwy was bought in May 1979 and work on the new church began in December. The congregation moved out of Capel Seion at the end of May 1979 and moved, on a temporary basis, to Ebeneser in Rhosddu. Seion and the adjacent schoolroom were demolished shortly afterwards and the site is now a bakers and confectioners. The Religious Census of 1881 showed: Capacity 740 attendance (AM & PM) 401. The Religious Census of 1904 showed: Capacity 650; attendance (AM & PM) 500. [DRO/DD/DM/543/37–43 & ND/10/1–5]

Senior Society
One of the numerous friendly societies* in Wrexham, the Senior Society was founded in 1744 and, in its early days, occupied a

The twin spires of Seion Church were a significant feature of the Wrexham skyline until demolished in 1979.

cottage near the Red Cow* in Pen-y-Bryn. By 1808, they had sold this cottage and were meeting in The Black Lion* in Hope Street.

Sergeant-at-Mace
A Sergeant-at-Mace was first appointed in 1866, when the Borough Council was first given a mace. The first man to hold this post was David Higgins who was also the Borough's first Chief Public Health Inspector. Higgins was still in post in 1885 when he wrote to the Town Clerk to complain that his official uniform was too small for him and a new coat and gaiters were ordered.

Seven Bridge Lane
See Market Street. [DRO/1004]

Seven Stars, Chester Street
Palmer* found the earliest record of it as an inn to have been in 1769 when it was known as *The Star*, kept by John Edisbury. The present building was constructed by John James Scott,* licensee at the end of the 19th century (he had taken over the premises in the 1880s) and opened in 1890 with the name changed to *The Seven Stars*. The design was by Thomas Price of Liverpool and Dolgarrog and it was built by local builder and politician William Edge Samuel.* Mr Scott also built the adjoining red brick properties in Chester Street, linking the Seven Stars to the Old Registry* and The Empire Cinema* in Lambpit Street.* It was shown in the 1833 survey. (See *Around the 'Stars'* by Dorothy Scott).

Seven–Mersey Canal
Proposals were made in the late 18th century to build a canal from the Severn at Shrewsbury to the Mersey at Netherpool and an Act was passed for this purpose on 16 May 1793. Although never built, plans for this canal were drawn up in preparation for submitting the Bill to Parliament. The proposed course through the Wrexham area was north from the junction with the Montgomery Canal, passing to the west of Hafod-y-Bwch and between Plas Grono and Erddig Hall. The canal was then to pass between Bersham and Esless Mill* before turning north east, behind the College,* then east of Beeches Barn, Acton* and Hill House before dropping down to the Cheshire Plain after passing east of Borras Head House.* At the point where it turned north east, the canal was to be joined by a cut which flowed down from the Brymbo area, via Gough's House, Brymbo Hall,* Southsea and Lower Berse. [DRO/QSD/DC/4]

Shakerley, Bt, Colonel Sir Jeffrey *soldier*
Jeffrey Shakerley of Holme, Cheshire, was an ardent supporter of Charles I during the English Civil War.* He was present at the siege of Chester and the siege of Caernarfon and in the former, carried a message to the King from Rowton Moor by crossing the river Dee in a tub. He was created a baronet by Charles I. After the war he bought Gwersyllt Isa* from Capt Ellis Sutton so that he could live next to his friend and war comrade Colonel Robinson* of Gwersyllt Park.*

Sherwell Avenue
A private housing development by Broseley Homes in the 1970s. The land was formerly part of Pant-yr-Ochain Farm* which was part of the Acton Park* estate. The origin of the name is unknown.

Shields Court
This was built by the Wales & West Housing Association in the 1980s on land that had previously been the property of C.T. Clarke. All the streets in this development were named after members of the RWF who had been awarded the Victoria Cross, in this instance, Cpl Robert Shields, VC, 1827–1864. Born in Cardiff in 1827, Shields enlisted in the RWF on 9 April 1847 and served in the Crimean campaign. He bought his discharge in 1856 after which he was employed as a park ranger in London before emigrating to Bombay where he was employed as an overseer. He died in Bombay on 23 December 1864 and his burial place is not recorded. His citation reads:

> For volunteering, on 8th September 1855, to go to the front from the 5th parallel after the attack on the Redan, to bring in Lieutenant Dyneley, who was wounded and found afterwards to be mortally so.

Ship Inn, The Hope Street
This inn was known to have existed at the turn of the 19th century when it was the property of Thomas Evans who, in honour of the national hero of the time, re-named it 'The Nelson Arms'.* It was located on the same site as the main entrance of the present day QD Stores.

Ship Inn, Yorke Street
This is the only public house known to have stood on the west side of Yorke Street,* directly in line with the northern line of Temple Row.* It does not appear in the 1833 survey but, another public house, the Black Horse, is shown on almost exactly the same site. This would indicate that either the Black Horse Inn* moved premises and a new name was given to the old premises or the cartographer made an error. As the Black Horse came into existence at about this time, it would seem that the former explanation is the more likely. Appears in the 1872 survey and survived as the Royal Ship Inn until the demolition of the west side of Yorke Street in the 1960s. In the early 20th century the licensee was John Shone of Foster Road.

Shirehall, The
This building stood at the top of Town Hill on the site later occupied by the old Town Hall (demolished 1940). According to Palmer,* there were nine or ten shops on the ground floor and an open space where fish, fruit and vegetables were sold, with a 'series of solars or lofts, as well doubtless as a grand chamber for the Great and Quarter Sessions, and for the Lordship and Manor Courts' located above. It is mentioned in Norden's survey where it is described as the 'new hall' and it is estimated that it was built in the mid 16th century. Norden refers to it as 'The Common Hall' and 'The Hall of Pleas'.* This building would almost certainly have had the Lord's Prison located either in it or nearby. This Prison was known in Welsh as *Y Siambr Ddu* (The Black Chamber), described as 'a vile and filthy prison', and it is from this that Back Chamber Street took its name (See Back Chamber Street). The Roman Catholic martyr, Richard Gwyn* is believed to have been imprisoned here. In 1659, a levy of £450 was made on the county of Denbighshire to pay part of the costs of building a new Shirehall but, as much of the money was used to build a new Shirehall in Ruthin, the Wrexham building was only repaired. It was eventually demolished in 1713 and replaced by a new Town Hall* on the same site.

Shoe Inn, Bank Street
See The Horseshoe.

Shone, Isaac *local politician & civil engineer*
Born in Brymbo in 1835, Isaac Shone's father was the mineral agent to the Grosvenor Estate. Isaac established himself in Wrexham as a mining and civil engineer specialising in sanitary engineering. He married Jane, the daughter of William Pierce, tanner, of Wrexham. He worked in London for many years where he is best remembered for the Shone Drainage System, the Shone Ejector (which used compressed air to raise sewerage in low lying areas), which were installed into the Houses of Parliament and the Royal Courts of Justice, and the Shone Cuncta in Unum ventilation of sewers system. Having made his fortune, he returned to Wrexham in the 1860s where he lived for a short time at The Castle* in Pentre Felin (sometimes referred to as Pentre Felin House). He commissioned local architect J. R. Gummow* to design him a new house, Grosvenor Lodge* at N° 1 Grosvenor Road* which was completed in 1869.

Shone was a Liberal member of Wrexham Town Council and served as Mayor in 1878. His main claim to fame in Wrexham was the culverting of the Gwenfro* in Brook Street,* a scheme which he had intended to continue through to Tuttle Street.* His views for the future development of Wrexham were regarded by his fellow councillors as being too revolutionary and expensive and, as a consequence, he lost his seat on the Council. Shortly after this, in about 1882 he left the town and set up the civil engineering partnership of Shone and Ault in London where he remained until his death on 19 June 1918 aged 83 at his home, N° 5 Gwendolen Avenue, Putney. He is buried in Putney Vale Cemetery. He was the author of *Wrexham Municipality up to 1876*.

Shone, William *local politician*
Educated at Gwersyllt Church School, William Shone began his working life in his father's hackney carriage business. In 1901, he became a railway signalman and moved to Chester in 1907, Croesnewydd in 1913 and Wrexham in 1935. From 1935–54 he was a signalman, first class. He was the Chairman of the local

branch of the National Union of Railwaymen, a NUR Trustee (1947–50), President of the Co-operative Society (1952–3) and Secretary of the railway branch of the St John's Ambulance Brigade for 18 years. In 1946, he was made a Serving Brother of the Order of St John.

William Shone was elected to WBC in 1943 and was chairman of the Allotments Committee and the Housing Points Scheme Committee. He was elected Mayor in 1954 but, due to ill health, had to withdraw shortly before taking office. He was re-elected and eventually took up the office of Mayor in 1955. He lived at 27 Bertie Road and died in office on 1 March 1956, aged 66, and is buried in Wrexham Cemetery.* His wife's name was Elizabeth.

Shrewsbury & Chester Railway Company
The Board of the Shrewsbury, Oswestry & Chester Junction Railway Company first met on 30 June 1845 with W. Ormsby Gore acting as chairman. When the company merged with the North Wales Mineral Railway* in 1846 the new company became known as the Shrewsbury & Chester Railway Company. The directors (who included Henry Robertson*) immediately set about drawing up plans to complete the existing railway to Ruabon and then to link Ruabon with Shrewsbury. The line to Ruabon was opened in November 1846 and the renowned railway contractor Thomas Brassey began constructing the giant Dee valley viaduct (designed by Robertson) – 1,508 feet long, 147 feet high, with 19 stone arches each spanning 60 feet – at a total cost of £72,346 and a smaller viaduct over the Ceiriog valley – 849 feet long, 100 feet high and with 12 arches. The line was opened to traffic on 16 October 1848. On 1 September 1854, the Shrewsbury & Chester Railway became part of the Great Western Railway and was nationalised in 1948 as part of British Railways.

Shrewsbury Road
See King's Mill Road

Simons Fairground
The original Simon's Fair was established in the 19th century by John Simons. He died in his van on the Beast Market* in 1903, aged 74 and is buried in Wrexham Cemetery.* Originally, the business was a menagerie but, over the years, it gradually became a traditional fairground with steam powered rides and, at one time, was a travelling silent movie cinema. John Simons was succeeded by his son George, who was in turn succeeded by his son, also named George who was born in Wrexham and married Elizabeth Connell of Rhos, the daughter of another fun fair family. Although the Simons family travelled throughout north Wales, they always regarded Wrexham as their home and brought the fair to winter in the town. Throughout the 19th century and the first half of the 20th century, the fair was always located in the Beast Market but, with the redevelopment of that area in the 1970s, it moved to Eagles Meadow and is now located in the Bodhyfryd Car Park off Chester Road. The 'season' started in Ruthin in March and finished in Wrexham for Christmas. Numerous members of the Simons family are buried in Wrexham Cemetery.

Sinclair, AM, Karen *politician*
Born in Wrexham on 21 November 1952, and educated at Grove Park Girls School,* Karen Sinclair worked as a trained CAB adviser and in the local youth service for fourteen years, managing a house for people with learning disabilities.

She began her political career as a local councillor on Denbighshire County Council and the old Glyndŵr District Council. She became the Assembly Member for Clwyd South in 1999, represnting the Labour party. She served as Chief Whip and Cabinet Member for Business from 2003 to 2005 and was also a member of the Agriculture, Sustainability and Health and Social Services committees. Karen has always taken a keen and active interest in disability issues at the Assembly and led a wide-ranging investigation into the low numbers of British sign language interpreters in Wales and successfully lobbied the Assembly Government for £2.7m of extra funding to increase the numbers up to the European average. As Chair of the URBAN II West Wrexham regeneration project, Karen also helped oversee £16million of European and Assembly funding in the area to help local people overcome the barriers to employment, which included a new multi-million pound enterprise centre on the site of the former Brymbo steelworks.

A member of Unison, Karen lives in Llangollen and is married to Mike. They have two grown-up children, Helen and Thomas.

Sisson, William John *brewer*
Born in 1828, William Sisson was the son of John Sisson of Plas Coch, St Asaph (the agent for Lord Mostyn). Before moving to Wrexham in 1852, William lived at Llay Hall. He bought the Cambrian Brewery from Joseph Clark* which he operated until his death in 1904. He was a Director of the Wrexham, Mold & Connah's Quay Railway Co,* Chairman of the East Denbighshire Water Co,* Vice-President of the Wrexham Infirmary* and Manager of the National Schools.* He represented the South Ward on WBC from 1883–6 and was a staunch Conservative and Anglican. He married Miss Cornelia Elizabeth Harrison of Holywell and had ten children.

Skelland, J. Rodney *local politician*
The Conservative member for the Bronington ward, Rodney Skelland is the leader of the Conservative group on WCBC. He is a member of the Executive Board and lead member for Regeneration and Corporate Governance. He was Mayor in 2002–03. He lives in Willington, near Malpas.

Slaughter Houses
At one time, most butchers in the town would have operated their own small slaughter house. Following the Incorporation of the Borough in 1857 and the introduction of public health legislation during the mid and late 19th century, the provision of an official public slaughter house became a necessity. The first of these was opened in 1863 as part of the facilities provided at the WBC Depot* on Holt Road.

The last town centre slaughter house was located in Crescent Road (built before the Second World War on the site now occupied by the Foyer project building) and closed in the early 1990s.

Smith, Alderman Edward *local politician*
Born in Bangor on Dee in c.1834, Edward Smith was apprenticed to his uncle who was a draper in High Street, Wrexham. For a while, he worked in Liverpool before returning to the family business at Nº 26 High Street, which he in due course took over. His wife, Sophia Murless, was the sister of John B. Murless.* He was elected as a Conservative member of WBC in 1872, was elected Mayor in 1879 and became an Alderman. After retiring he resided at Esclus Hall and later moved to Reading.

Smithfield
The area of land known as Feather's Field, alongside the Beast Market, was purchased by WBC in 1873 and a Smithfield was built there in 1875 and, having taken a lease of the cattle market rights, moved to new premises in 1877. In 1955 a new building

was erected in the Smithfield for the exclusive purpose of selling attested cattle. The market eventually closed in the mid 1990s. The name Smithfield originates from the cattle market of that name in London and was one generally adopted for cattle markets throughout the country.

Smithfield Road
Smithfield Road appears as an unnamed and unsurfaced lane in the 1872 survey with just a few small properties on the south side, alongside Penson's Theatre.* The building of the Smithfield Market on the north side of the lane led to further residential development, starting with the refreshment house for the market by 1881. The bulk of the houses on this road were built in the early years of the 20th century. It takes its named from the adjacent cattle market.

Smithfield Road Presbyterian Church, Bernard Road
Opened in 1904, this church is now the Oasis Christian Centre.

Smiths' Court
One of the smallest and best concealed of the 19th century 'court' developments, this was accessed by a long passage from the northern side of Charles Street.

Smithy Close, Little Acton
The bungalows here are built on what was the orchard of Acton Smithy*

Smithy Lane, Little Acton
Named after the Acton Smithy* which stood near the junction with Chester Road. Smithy Lane was previously known as Heol Pwll-y-Kiln.*

Snowdon Drive, Tŷ Gwyn
A development by local builders H.R.&E. Roberts of private houses completed between 1961 and the mid 1970s. The larger detached houses, backing onto Chester Road were built by local developer John Parry in the early 1970s. The road takes its name from Anthony Armstrong Jones, who married HRH Princess Margaret on 6 May 1960 who became the 1st Earl of Snowdon in 1961. (See also Linley Place)

Soames Brewery
See Nag's Head Brewery and Frederick William Soames.

Soames, Frederick William *brewer & local politician*
Born in Blackheath, Kent, the son of Arthur Soames, Frederick was educated at Winchester School and learnt the brewery trade with Tetley & Company of Leeds. His father was a successful brewer and moved the family to Waltham Old Hall near Grimsby and later to Newark, Nottinghamshire. Arthur Soames bought the Nag's Head Brewery* in Wrexham from H. K. Aspinall in 1879 and gave it to his son who was then aged 21. A dynamic businessman, Frederick quickly expanded the brewery into the largest in the town (at the time of purchase the brewery had only 6 outlets which Soames eventually expanded to 120). He was elected to Wrexham Borough Council in 1890, representing the South Ward and served as Mayor of Wrexham in 1891. He did not stand for re-election to the council in 1893 and his second term of office as Mayor (1901–03) is therefore unusual in that he was elected from outside of the Council members.

Soames was the chairman of the Brewers' Association of North Wales, a partner in several maltings in Lincolnshire and chairman of Edisbury's North Wales Mineral Water Company, Wrexham. He was a Denbighshire County Councillor (representing Marchwiel), a Life Governor of Wrexham Infirmary, President of the Rhos Chess Club and President of Wrexham Football Club (he was the owner of the Racecourse* ground). He lived at Plas Fron, Roseneath* and, for many years, at Llwyn Onn* before building his own house Bryn Estyn Hall.* The uncle of Lady Baden-Powell, Frederick Soames was a keen supporter of the Boy Scout movement and paid for the construction of the Scout Hut at Rhosnesni (Lord Baden-Powell was a regular visitor to Bryn Estyn). He married the daughter of Henry West, QC, and they had a large family. Sadly, the First World War proved tragic for them and they lost their eldest son, Capt Henry Soames, MC, RFC (killed during a bombing test at Upavon in 1915), Lt Noel Soames (died in Egypt serving with the Cheshire Yeomanry), Capt Julian Soames (lost his leg) and their son-in-law (killed in action at Ypres with the Royal Welsh Fusiliers). He died 8 March 1926, aged 68 years, and is buried at Gresford Church. He was the great-uncle of Lord Soames of Zimbabwe.

Society of Friends
See Friends Meeting House and Quaker Burial Ground.

Sontley Road
In 1802, Sontley Road was called the Road from Coed-y-Glyn Bridge. [DRO/DD/WY/8352]

Spring Lodge Farm
Located in the area of the present day Spring Lodge Housing Estate*, with a frontage onto Holt Road* opposite the junction with Borras Road.* It had previously been known as Pwll yr Uwd* (until c.1804) and was part of the Hafod-y-Wern* estate. The house was described by Palmer* as being 'large and ancient, approached by an avenue from Holt Road, and was the head of a small estate which, in 1844, contained nearly 70 acres (extending from Holt Road to the Dunks* and from the present day Montgomery Road to Hullah Lane)'. The entrance to the 'avenue' was opposite Borras Road, in line with the present day Archers Way.*
Residents/Owners:

1580	Hugh Puleston.
1661	Hugh Puleston (died 1666, possibly the same man as the above Hugh Puleston).
1666	Mrs Jane Puleston (widow of Hugh Puleston).
1686	Robert Puleston (grandson of the above Hugh and Jane Puleston, he married Mary, daughter of Ambrose Lewis I).
1755	Mrs Potter was the owner (née Puleston).
1768	John Hughes, tenant (died 1775).
1788	John Hughes, tenant.
1811	Edward Holt (husband of Anne Maria Lloyd, the granddaughter of Ambrose Lewis III).
1859	Mr Lowe, tenant.
1919	Price H. Lloyd, tenant.

In 1919, the farm was sold for development to WBC for £3,700. It comprised 68 acres of land and the sale particulars described the buildings as a house with hall, dining room, drawing room, office, kitchen, scullery, dairy, 4 bedrooms, dressing room, 3 good attics. In addition, there was a cowhouse for 15 cows, stables for 5 horses, mixing house, loose box with loft, storehouse with loft, pigeries, boiler house, mens' loft, wood and poultry house, five bay hay shed. [DRO/DD/G/2886] Some of the land was developed in the early 1930s but the eastern section and the house survived until the late 1930s. Edward Clarke of Park Farm* recalled visiting the house at Spring Lodge in the early 1930s when the tenant was the agricultural threshing contractor Price Lloyd, 'It was a beautiful house, surrounded by mulberry trees, with a most beautifully sited grass tennis court.'

Today, the Spring Lodge Housing Estate* occupies almost exactly the site of the whole farm.

Spring Lodge Housing Estate
Commenced in the early 1930s (and developed in stages up until the outbreak of war in 1939), on what was previously Spring Lodge Farm,* as part of Wrexham's slum clearance programme. Spring Lodge provided new housing for the former residents of the Pentre Felin and Farndon Street areas of the town. The estate was designed by the Liverpool architects Lockwood, Abercrombie and Saxon. The second phase necessitated the demolition of the remaining buildings of Spring Lodge Farm and included the building of houses and flats.

Spring Gardens (1)
Located in Rhosddu, in the area now occupied by Spring Road,* Cunliffe Street,* Foster Road,* Acton Road and Garden Road, these ornamental gardens were the property of the Acton Park* estate. Although there is no record of their purpose or usage, they were almost certainly pleasure gardens which were let to residents of Wrexham who lived in properties with no gardens of their own. A study of the 1872 survey shows numerous small gardens, each laid out with paths, ornamental features, flower beds and summer houses. The proliferation of natural springs in the Wrexham area would suggest that the name derives from this source but it may have originated in London where the famous Spring Gardens were laid out in the early 17th century (and later became Vauxhall Gardens). These were one of the most popular leisure features in the capital and the Cunliffes may have 'borrowed' the name for their own 'pleasure gardens' in Wrexham. The Acton Park estate began to sell off some of the gardens in 1853 and by the end of the 19th century they had all be redeveloped as residential streets. The name is perpetuated in Springfield, Spring Road,* Garden Road* and Spring Gardens (2).*

Spring Gardens (2)
A new development of private houses built by Castlemead Homes in 2001 on land that was previously part of the Rogers & Jackson* site. The name is taken from the ornamental Spring Gardens* which were sited nearby until the late 19th century.

Spring Road
Spring Gardens in Rhosddu, the property of the Acton Park* estate began to be sold for development in 1853 and Spring Road takes its name from them. World Land Speed Record holder Parry Thomas* was born at Nº 6 where there is a commemorative plaque. Houses were still being built here in 1898.

Springfield, Rhosddu
A development by WBC of houses and flats on the site of what was previously Springfield Terrace* and the southern part of George Street.* The name comes from Spring Gardens* which were sited in this area in the early 19th century.

Springfield Terrace (1), Cunliffe Street
A terrace of eight houses on the north-west side of Cunliffe Street which appears in the 1872 survey. These houses were later demolished and replaced by a terrace of smaller houses in about 1900. The name comes from Spring Gardens* which were sited in this area in the early 19th century. Mr E. W. Gillet, who resided at No 3, was awarded the *Daily Herald* Order of Industrial Heroism for saving the life of a fireman who fell from a train into the path of another in November 1952.

Springfield Terrace (2), Garden Road
A small street of fourteen terraced houses located between Garden Road and George Street. The street was demolished by WBC and the Springfield* houses and flats built on the site. The name comes from Spring Gardens* which were sited in this area in the early 19th century.

Squire, Robert W. *local politician*
Born in London, Bob Squire served with the RAF Regiment during the Second World War. His family had been evacuated to Coedpoeth during the war and he joined them there on his demobilisation. He married Phyllis Williams of Coedpoeth and they had four sons and four daughters. He worked as a wines and spirits manager with Bass in Chester before joining the administrative staff of Brymbo Steel Works.

Bob Squire was elected an Independent member of WRDC (later WMBC), Coedpoeth Community Council and Clwyd County Council (of which he was chairman). Elected Mayor of Wrexham in 1985, he was also chairman of the governors at Penygelli Schools and a founder member of Coedpoeth Sports Club, where he ran the football team for many years. He lived in Heol Maelor, Coedpoeth and died in 1999.

Squire Yorke, Sontley Road
Built to service the new residential areas located on land that was formerly part of the the Erddig* estate. The public house, which opened in 1981, was named after Philip Scott Yorke* (1905–78), the last squire of Erddig, who inherited the estate in 1966. A former actor and travel courier, Philip Yorke never married and determined to give the estate to the National Trust. The sign on the Squire Yorke shows Philip riding his penny-farthing bicycle, something which he tried to teach HRH Prince Charles to do when he officially opened Erddig to the public in 1977. Philip Yorke is buried in Marchwiel Church.

SS *Wrexham*
Built in 1902 by Raylton Dixon of Middlesborough for a Danish shipping firm and originally named *Nord II*. It was 239 feet long with a beam of 35 feet and a draught of 20 feet and designed to operate in the ice of the Baltic Sea. In March 1905 it was sold to the Great Central Railway Company for £20,000, who used it as part of its North Sea fleet, sailing out of the Humber. It was re-named *Wrexham* to commemorate the purchase of the Wrexham, Mold and Connah's Quay Railway by the Great Central. During the First World War the *Wrexham* was requisitioned by the the government and carried supplies from Britain to Russia. On 19 June 1918, en route to Archangel, she struck an uncharted rock in the White Sea and was wrecked. All the crew were saved. The Great Central Railway received £99,311 in compensation for the loss.

Stabler Crescent, Garden Village
Built in the 1960s/70s by two developers, H.S. Elltoft of Acton Gate and Eric Roberts. This street is named after Alderman Arthur B.O. Stabler who was the Secretary of Wrexham Tenants Ltd the company that administered Garden Village.*

SS *Wrexham*.

Stage Coaches
Wrexham was a regular staging post for coaches travelling between Chester and Shrewsbury and on to London. Coaches bearing names such as *Nettle, The Swallow, The Oak, The Mail, Hirondelle, Mazeppa, Queen of Trumps* and others travelled along Chester Road and the Ellesmere Road (now King's Mills Road). A daily evening service was provided by the *Bristol New Royal Mail*. Other coaches heading for Oswestry and mid-Wales travelled out along Pen-y-Bryn and Ruabon Road. The first coaching station in Wrexham was the Feathers Inn* in Chester Street but later, Royal Mail coaches stopped at the Wynnstay Hotel in High Street. The last known stage coach service operated until shortly before the First World War, running twice weekly between Shrewsbury and Wrexham. One example of the coaches that operated through Wrexham is believed to have survived and is preserved in a Birmingham museum. An account of the coaches in Wrexham *Down the Road* was written by Charles S. T. Birch Reynardson.

Stanford, John *local politician*
Born in Cefn Mawr, John Stanford worked in the offices of Plas Kynaston Colliery before becoming the Manager of the Wrexham Coffee Tavern Company. He opened his own business at the Central Café, Nº 26 Hope Street. He was elected a member of WBC and served as Mayor in 1909 and was Chairman of the Markets Committee. He lived at Nº 19 King Street. He was a member of the International Order of Good Templars and a keen cricketer. Married to Annie (died 1922), John Stanford died at his home in July 1920 and is buried in Wrexham Cemetery.

Stanley Street
Laid out in the late 19th century and named after the the Stanley family of Knowsley (Earls of Derby) who had strong historical connections with the Wrexham area.

Stansfield, Sir Walter, CBE, MC, QPM *police officer*
Born 15 February 1919, the son of Frederick and Georgina Stansfield. He was educated at Chartres, Eure et Loire, France and the Heath Grammar School, Halifax. He joined the West Riding Constabulary in 1939 where he served until 1942 when he joined the Royal Artillery and was commissioned the following year. Due to his knowledge of French he served with Special Operations Executive (1943–45) and operated behind enemy lines in central France during the build up to D-Day and in the weeks following. He was awarded the Military Cross in 1945 and the French Croix de Guerre in 1947. At the end of the war he was appointed to the Allied Control Commission in Germany until 1946 when he was seconded to the Special Police Corps in Germany where he remained until 1950 when he re-joined the West Riding Constabulary. In 1956 he joined the Cyprus Police where he served until 1959 (awarded the Colonial Police Medal) when he again returned to the West Riding force. Promoted to Assistant Chief Constable in 1962 he became Chief Constable of the Denbighshire Force two years later. In 1967 he was appointed Chief Constable of the Derbyshire Police where he remained until his retirement. He was given the Queen's Police Medal in 1969, the Order of St John in 1974, made a Commander of the Order of the British Empire in 1974 and was knighted in the New Year Honours List of 1979. Married Jennie Margery Biggs in 1939, they had one daughter and lived at 84 Park Avenue. He was the joint editor of *Moriarty's Police Law* (1981 edition). Sir Walter died on 14 December 1984.

Stansty
One of the thirteen country townships of the old parish of Wrexham, Stansty should really be regarded as two townships – Stansty Ucha (*Trans.* upper Stansty) and Stansty Issa (*Trans.* lower Stansty). Stansty Issa has also been known as Stansty Abbatis (*Trans.* abbot's Stansty) – it was given to the Abbot of Valle Crucis Abbey by Gruffydd ap Madoc, Prince of Powys in 1254 – and Northcroft (also as early as 1254). The two townships were merged into one at the time of the Commonwealth. A list of the tenants of Stansty in 1314 has survived in the British Museum and is detailed in Palmer's* *History of the Thirteen Country Townships of the Old Parish of Wrexham*. The most important mediæval family in the township was that descended from Madoc ap Iorwerth ap David (died 1488) who assumed the Anglicised surname of Edwards in the 17th century. They owned most of the township and established the estate centred upon Stansty Hall.*

The township had an area of 577 acres and extended from Gwersyllt, across Wat's Dyke* (the line of the present day Crispin Lane*) to the boundary of Wrexham Regis in Rhosddu (roughly the line of the present day Cunliffe Street*/Garden Road*).

Stansty Close, Plas Coch Road
Built in the early 1970s on land that had previously been the garden of Stansty Villa.*

Stansty Hall/Park
The historical development of this property is complex and the understanding of it has been made even more difficult by the building and demolition of several houses on the land and the several uses of names of various buildings over the years. In the first edition of this encyclopaedia the history was completely confused.

The township of Stansty (which covers about 577 acres) is located north-west of Wrexham on either side of the Mold Road. In 1254, Gruffydd ap Madog, Prince of Powys, divided it into two parts, Stansty Ucha and Stansty Isaf, the latter of which he gave to the Abbot of Valle Crucis. Following the dissolution of the monastries in the mid 16th century, the two parts were reunited as one township although the two names were retained to identify two individual houses. According to A.N. Plamer, Plas Issa was built by David Edwards in 1577 and was located 'at the base of the triangle where Stansty Hall now [1903] stands'. This is certainly the house located in the north-east corner of the present day Stansty estate, close to the junction of Griffiths Road and Old Mold Road, the property which is today called Stansty Park. This house remained the centre of the Edwards family's estate until 1783 and still bears the date '1577'. After the death of John Edwards in July 1783 (buried in Gresford), the estate passed to Peter Edwards who died almost immediately and everything passed to Sir Edward Lloyd, Bt, of Pengwern, and from him to 1st Baron Mostyn who sold it in 1813 to another family named Edwards. They retained it for some fifteen years before selling it to the noted local industrialist and Roman Catholic benefactor Richard Thompson (see St David's RC Chapel and St Mary's RC Pro-Cathedral).

Stansty Hall.

Stansty Hall, c.1910.

Located near to Plas Issa, but slightly further into the Stansty estate, was another farmhouse called Plas Ucha, which also (after 1620) belonged to the original Edwards family. In the late 17th/early 18th century, this was known as the Crispin Inn which Palmer was convinced was an error in recording the correct name which he believed to be Crispinian (see also Crispin Lane). In later years, the name was simplified to the Crispin. In 1813, the house was sold to Mr Menlove and much of the land to Thomas Hayes. Sometime in the late 1820s, the house and land (of both Stansty Hall and Stansty Park) was bought by Richard Thompson who demolished the building and built a substantial new house on the site in 1830–2 which became known as Stansty Hall. The house had 9 bedrooms, a drawing room, music room, breakfast room, library and study as well as outbuildings and a walled garden on the north side. Thompson lived at Stansty Hall until 1855 after which it had various tenants and the ownership passed to Thompson's daughter Lady Anne Ffrench and then to Bishop Mostyn*. During the Great War, the house was occupied by various Army units and was then sold to Henry Dyke Dennis* of New Hall,* Ruabon. The house was demolished c.1924.

In 1907, Bishop Mostyn offered 50 acres at Stansty Park to the Wrexham Golf Club* with the clubhouse being located in Stansty Park (Stansty Isaf). The club remained here until 1923 when it moved to Borras and the house and land was bought by Henry Dyke Dennis. The iron railings and gates (by the Davies family* of Croesfoel), which stood at the Mold Road entrance, were saved when the house was demolished and can now be seen at Erddig.*

In 1947, the Dennis family sold all their property at Stansty and by the mid 1950s, it had been bought by Wrexham surveyor, auctioneer and estate agent, Kenneth Hugh Dodd.

The triangle of land between the Summerhill Road and Mold Road (in latter years forming part of the training ground for Wrexham FC* and then Lex XI football club ground) was originally called Crispin's Meadow.

A detailed history, *Stansty Hall*, by Quentin Dodd, is scheduled for publication in late 2010.

Stansty Lodge, Mold Road
Like its namesake Stansty Hall, Stansty Lodge (located on the Mold Road opposite the main entrance to Stansty Hall/Park*) is a property that has caused some confusion due to another house, Rhosddu Lodge,* also often being referred to as Stansty Lodge. This was once the centre of a sizeable estate and dates back to the 17th century when it was the home of Samuel and Jane Powell. They were followed by Mrs Jane Eyton (died 1729) and James (died 1760) and Martha Morgan. Their daughter inherited the property and it passed to her husband John Dymock of Little Acton* from whom it passed to the Garthewin estate in Llanfair Talhaiarn. In 1861, it was the home of local industrialist Richard Venables Kyrke who had moved there from Pendwyll Cottage in Broughton. By 1871, Kyrke had moved to live at Nant-y-Frith* and ten years later, Stansty Lodge was the residence of Thomas Henry Jones, Manager of the North & South Wales Bank in High Street (he was also the Borough Treasurer). The house was demolished during the 1980s and is now the location of Jones Brothers Farm Butchers.

Stansty Road/Lane
This road leads from the A541 Mold Road, opposite Stansty Park* to Rhosddu Road* close to the junction with Price's Lane.* Originally the road, as Stansty Lane, only reached from Stansty Park to Lodge Road, the remaining section being part of the original Rhosddu Road. In 1839 there were plans to build a tollgate house at the Stansty Park end of the road but these do not appear to have come to fruition. Two interesting houses were built on the south-west side, between Lodge Road and Railway Road, by John Foukes of Ashfield House* – Stansty Villa* and Claremont* (now N° 29, formerly known as Crossways). The council houses were built by WBC c.1937.

Stansty Villa, Stansty Road
This house was built by John Foulkes in 1842 (a small stone commemorative plaque can be seen on the south-west wall). By 1861, it was the home of retired wine merchant, George James Ihler and after his death, his spinster daughters lived there for many years. During the first half of the 20th century, the house was owned by local solicitor, Joseph Henry Bates of Rhosddu Lodge,* and was rented out to Major G.F. Hutton who had been a regular officer in the RWF and had also lived at nearby Ashfield House.* Following his death, the tenancy passed to his daughter, Miss Hutton, until her death in the early 1950s. In 1955, the house was sold to Mr & Mrs Smith who converted it into a children's home. Ten years later, former professional footballer Gren Jones and his wife Hazel bought the property and, in c.1968, opened Playland, a private playgroup here. They sold most of the garden for development and Stansty Close was built on the site. In 1978, the house and Playland were bought by Jackie Ryan.

Station Road
See Regent Street.

Steps, The, Well Square
A public house that stood on the south side of Well Square.* The building was demolished during the construction of the Wrexham & Ellesmere Railway* in the 1890s.

Stirling Avenue, Croes Eneurys
Built in the 1960s on land that was previously part of Croes Eneurys Farm.* In common with the other streets in this area, it was named after a royal residence, in this case, Stirling Castle in Scotland.

Stocks, Beast Market
Stocks were a system of legal punishment for minor offences. The convicted person was seated on a low bench with his/her ankles held securely by a wooden frame. This was designed to be a system of public display and humiliation of the offender. The Wrexham stocks were located on the south side of the Beast Market *and were removed during the 19th century.

Stockwell, GCB, KBE, DSO and Bar, **Gen Sir Hugh Charles** *soldier*
Born 16 June 1903, the son of Lt-Col H.C. Stockwell. Hugh Stockwell was educated at Marlborough and the Royal Military

College before being commissioned as a 2nd lieutenant in the RWF in 1923. He was appointed a brigade major in 1938 and lieutenant-colonel 1940. As a brigadier in 1942 he was given command of the 82nd West African Division (receiving a Mention in Despatches). In 1945 he took command of the Home Counties District and Eastern Command the following year with the rank of major-general. In 1947 he took command of 44th (Home Counties) Division (Territorial Army) followed by command of the 6th Airborne Division in Palestine (Mention in Despatches). He served as commandant of the Royal Military Academy, Sandhurst (1948-50), GOC East Anglian District and 3rd Infantry Division (1951–52), GOC Malaya (1952 with the rank of lieutenant-general), GOC I Corps BAOR (1954–56), military secretary to Secretary of State for War (1956). He was promoted to general in 1956 and became Adjutant General to the Forces (1959–60), Deputy Supreme Commander SHAPE (1960–63), ADC to HM The Queen (1959–62), colonel of the RWF (1952–65), colonel of the Malay Regiment (1954), colonel commandant of the Army Air Corps (1957–63), colonel commandant of the RAEC (1959). During the Suez War of 1956, Gen Stockwell was the GOC the ground forces. His decorations and honours include: GCB (1959), KBE (1949), DSO (1940), Bar to DSO (1957), GO Legion of Honour (France). chairman Inland Waterways Amenity Advisory Council, chairman British Waterways Board, President Kennet and Avon Canal Trust.

He married Joan Rickman, daughter of Charles Garrard of Warwickshire, 1931 and had two daughters. There is memorial plaque to him on Stockwell Grove.* He lived in Devizes, Wiltshire, and died on 27 November 1986. Biography, *The Life & Campaigns of General Hughie Stockwell from Norway through Burma to Suez* by Jonathon Riley, published in 2006.

Stockwell Grove
This road was laid out in the 1970s on land that had previously been part of the Hermitage army camp. It was named after General Sir Hugh Stockwell,* to whom a small memorial plaque exists near the junction with Norman Road – 'General Sir Hugh Stockwell, GCB, KBE, DSO, Colonel of the RWF, 1952–1965'.

Studio, The Chester Road
Built in the 1890s by Thomas H. Jones, R.A., a noted artist of Erddig Terrace, to a design by Gummow.* The building was situated on the corner of Grove Road and Chester Road. This was probably Wrexham's first purpose built artist's studio and in his prospectus, Jones described the main workroom as measuring 11' x 14', which was to be lit from above by means of a partly glazed roof. A waiting room 'finished with moulded ceiling with an enriched cornice. The walls will be relieved by well-chosen tints and finished below with well-finished oak panelled dado'. It had elaborately laid out grounds.

The building eventually became The Studio School, run by the Misses Davies of Foster Road, which later moved to Chevet Hey* in c.1932 and then (c.1938) to Belmont Road. In 1932, plans for converting The Studio into a dwelling were rejected. After the Second World War the building was used for a time as a piano manufactory and then became the Boy Scout Headquarters before being demolished.

Stokes' Court
A very small 'court' development on Pen-y-Bryn, opposite the Bowling Green Inn. It was accessed by a narrow passage. It appears on the 1872 survey.

Strachan, Yeaman *horticulturalist & local politician*
Born in Scotland in c.1831, Yeaman Strachan established a very successful nursery retail business in High Street (with the actual plant nurseries close to the Wrexham General Station (on a site that extended as far as Gerald Street and included the land now occupied by the Boy Scout Headquarters and the Post Office Sorting Office). In the 1881 census he is shown as employing 12 men and 4 boys. He married Mary Ann (died 1924), a native of Wrexham, and lived at Rosslyn Villa, Nº 6 Grosvenor Road. He was elected a Conservative member of WBC and served as Mayor in 1882. He was responsible for the design of the new Wrexham Cemetery* on Ruabon Road. He died at his home on 2 December 1891, aged 61, and is buried in Wrexham Cemetery.

Stratford Close
Built in 1964 as part of the third phase of the Acton Park housing estate,* this street was named after Stratford-upon-Avon to celebrate the 400th anniversary of the birth of William Shakespeare.

Stratford House, Fairy Road
It was built in 1876 for William Edge Samuel, JP, to an arts and crafts design by E.A. Ould. The initials W.E.S. appear above the front door. In 1925, the house was bought by Mrs Croom-Johnson (see Henry Croom-Johnson) who lived here until her death in the 1950s. It is a Grade II listed building.

Stryd-y-Bont Llwyd
(*Trans.* grey/brown bridge street) This was a section of the Chester Road, just to the north of the turning which has become the present day Bluebell Lane. The name is used in the plan of the Wrexham–Chester Turnpike dated November, 1827. The area in question later became the site of Gresford Colliery.*

Stuart Street
Stuart Street was laid out prior to the sale of the Beechley and Kingsland estates in 1895, formerly owned by the Bennion family of Beechley House.* All the streets in the new development were to be named after royal dynasties of English monarchs. Stuart Street, which merely acts as a link between Saxon Street and Norman Road, takes its name from the royal house of Stuart which reigned on the English throne from 1603 (King James I) until 1714 (Queen Anne).

Stuart Way
An extension to Stuart Street, this was built in the early 1960s.

Sun Brewery, Abbot Street
Located at the rear of the Sun Inn, Abbot Street on a site now occupied by the rear entrance to the New Look store (Hope Street) this brewery was owned by Thompson & Company and developed from the brew house of the Sun Inn.* It had cellars extending under Abbot Street* and Hope Street.*

Sun Inn, Abbot Street
Shown in the 1833 survey (See Sun Brewery), it closed in June 1955 when it was part of the Border Breweries chain of licensed premises. The last licensees were Mr & Mrs Richard Jones. The premises were later bought by the Littlewoods company, demolished and the site formed part of the rear entrance to their Hope Street store.

Sunday Opening
The referendum on Sunday opening of pubs of November 1975 resulted in public houses in the Wrexham area being permitted to open on Sundays on 9 November 1975 after 67.38% of the voters voted in favour. This was the first time that pubs had opened on Sundays since the passing of the Welsh Sunday Closing Act of 1881.

Sussex Gardens, Tŷ Gwyn

Sun Inn, Abbot Street, c.1955. [RCHBW]

Wrexham Baths, Tuttle Street. [Ken Jones]

A development of private houses completed by local builders H. R. & E. Roberts in the late 1960s on land that was previously part of Tŷ Gwyn Farm. Several of the streets in this estate are named after southern English counties but the reasoning for this is unknown.

Sutton Drive, Queen's Park
Developed immediately after the Second World War by WBC as part of the first stage of the Queen's Park* housing estate, the street was built on land that had previously been part of the Cefn Park* estate which had been bought by means of a compulsory purchase order from Lt-Col R.G. Fenwick-Palmer.* It is named after the local settlement of Sutton Green.

Swan Inn, Pen-y-Bryn
This building has had a licence since at least 1824. It is sometimes referred to as the New Swan Inn, to differentiate it from the Old Swan Inn in Abbot Street.* It appears in the 1833 and 1872 surveys.

Swimming Baths, Willow Road
The notion of providing public bathing facilities was first aired in Wrexham Borough Council in 1874 and a special Baths and Washhouses Committee was formed comprising councillors H. Davies, Bury and Roberts. An approach was made to Sir Watkin Williams Wynn (see Williams Wynn family) with a view to the Corporation buying part of the Orchard Field of Bryn-y-Ffynnon located at the bottom of Hill Street and constructing public baths on the site. The plan did not proceed, however, and the scheme was dropped. Had the scheme gone ahead, water for the baths would have been piped from the Gwenfro by the Workhouse (see Wrexham Poor Law Union). The matter was raised again in 1883 and two sites were considered: the Pentre Felin brewery, alongside Thornley Square* (price £2,000), and land to the north-west of the Old Three Tuns, alongside the Island Green Brewery* at Pen-y-Bont,* the property of the Wrexham & Ellesmere Railway Company.* The Council opted for the former and made an offer of £1,800 with an additional £700 for the six cottages in Thornley Square. The purchase was made but, before any progress could be made with developing the baths, the circumstances changed and there was a need for a much larger site capable of accommodating not only baths but various other public facilities deemed to be lacking in Wrexham.

In 1896, the Council proposed the purchase of the old Willow Brewery* which could be used, not only as a site for the public baths, but also as a site for an electricity generating station, a refuse depot and a depot for the stabling of horses and the

Girls Swimming Pool, 1957. [Ken Jones]

storage of equipment. Loans were raised (including £1,800 for the baths) in 1898 and work commenced on adapting the old brewery banqueting room. The Wrexham Baths were opened on 3 May 1901 by the Mayor of Wrexham, Thomas Jones,* having cost £4,330 to build.

The main part of the building comprised the swimming bath which was lined with white enamelled bricks with blue coping, measuring 60′ x 26′ 6″ and ranged in depth from 3′ 6″ to 6′ with a capacity of 50,000 gallons. It had a white Italian terrazzo floor and was surrounded by a promenade area with seventeen dressing cubicles made of pine. There was a diving board at the deep-end of the pool and a flight of steps led into the shallow end. The whole area was heated by hot-water pipes. In addition to the swimming pool, there were also seven Doulton enamel slipper baths, where residents of Wrexham, whose homes lacked proper bathing facilities, could take a bath. The whole building was lit by electric lighting. The baths were only to be open from April until October. The first baths attendant, David Jones of Barnfield (whose wife was employed to wash the towels), was appointed in June 1901. In 1904, water pipes were laid between the Bryn-y-Ffynnon well and the baths as the water in the wells on site had been found to be both unsuitable and unreliable.

The Wrexham Swimming Club (sometimes called the Willow Swimming Club) was formed almost as soon as the baths were opened and Herbert Wilson, a native of Liverpool who had opened a confectionery business in Wrexham in the 1890s, was appointed captain (later chairman). In February 1908 he and his wife, Jane, were appointed manager and manageress at the baths. At the time of his death in 1931, Wilson and his wife were on a joint salary of £160 per annum (plus house, fuel, heat, light and water). The second managers were Mr & Mrs Austin of Cheetham, Manchester, who were appointed on 2 March 1931.

A public gymnasium was opened on the upper floor of the premises in 1903. A proposal for a second plunge bath and additional slipper baths was made in November 1922 which was agreed the following month. The plans were modified so that the plunge bath would be an open-air pool but in 1924 it was decided that it should be covered as the Tuttle Street site was quite unsuitable for an open-air facility. On 15 October 1925, the new baths and laundry were opened by Alderman Taylor, JP, but, despite being 5 yards longer than the original pool, the new pool was too shallow for competitive swimming. Mixed bathing was permitted for the first time in 1928.

The public baths in Tuttle Street served Wrexham until 1970 when the new swimming baths were opened at Bodhyfryd. (See also Wrexham Waterworld)

Swimming Baths, Bodhyfryd
See Wrexham Water World.

Sycamore Road, Queen's Park
Built in the immediate post Second World War period as part of the first phase of WBC's Queen's Park housing development. It was local authority policy at one time to name streets after trees and shrubs (See Acton Park housing estate).

Sylfaen Hotel, Belmont Road
This private and commercial hotel opened in the early 1950s at N° 3 Belmont Road.*

Sylvester, GC, William George *George Cross recipient*
Born on 6 December 1914 at Chadwell Heath, Romford, Essex, William Sylvester was employed as a 'hillman' in the North Site of the Royal Gunpowder Factory, Waltham Abbey, Essex during the Second World War. On 18 January 1940, an explosion occurred in the factory at a time when Sylvester was purifying nitro-glycerine inside N° 2 Washing House which was located only 100 yards away. The Washing House sustained considerable damage with half the roof torn off, two thirds of the walls collapsed and all the hot water and air services were broken. Well aware of the acute danger in which he was in due to the possibility of the nitro-glycerine freezing (which would cause it to detonate), he remained at his post for two hours until the material had been processed and restored to a condition of stability. He was Gazetted with the Empire Gallantry Medal on 6 February 1940 and, with the institution of the George Cross as the highest civilian award for civilian gallantry in September 1940, the EGM was exchanged for a GC. With the opening of the Royal Ordnance Factory, Marchwiel* in 1941, William Sylvester moved from Waltham Abbey to Wrexham where he lived for the rest of his life. In later years he resided at N° 6 Overton Way,* Acton Park, where he died in 1995.

Sylvester Court
This street was laid out in the 1980s on land that had previously been the property of C. T. Clark, proprietor of the King's Mills Garage, and built by the Wales and West Housing Association. All the streets in this development were named after RWF who had been awarded the Victoria Cross, in this instance, Surgeon William Henry Thomas Sylvester, VC, MD, LRCS, LSA, who, as an Assistant Surgeon, was awarded the Victoria Cross for gallantry during the Siege of Sebastopol in 1855. Born at Long Street, Devizes, Wiltshire, he was trained as a surgeon at Mariscal University, Aberdeen, before being appointed an Assistant Surgeon on 3 March 1854. He saw service during the Crimean War and the Indian Mutiny before retiring in 1861 to become House Surgeon at Swansea Hospital and later Chief Medical Officer at Millbank Prison, London (with a private practice in Westminster). He died on 20 March 1920, at Paignton, Devon where he is buried. His citation reads:

> For going out on 8th September 1855, under a heavy fire in from of the fifth parallel Right Attack, to a spot near the Redan, where Lieutenant and Adjutant Dyneley was lying mortally wounded and for dressing his wounds in that dangerous and exposed situation. N.B. This officer was mentioned in General Simpson's despatch of 18th September 1855, for going to the front under heavy fire to assist the wounded.'

T

Talbot Inn, Hope Street/Queen Street
This was located at the junction of Hope Street and Queen Street. During the latter part of the 17th century and certainly until 1712, the property had belonged to the Kenrick family and it was in a barn (accessed from Queen Street) belonging to this inn that many dissenting groups held their meetings until 1762. Morgan Llwyd is believed to have held some of his early meetings there. After 1762, the barn was known as The Old Meeting House for many years. The first reference to The Talbot by that name was in *c*.1721.

The timber-framed Talbot was demolished in the early 20th century when the mock Tudor Talbot Hotel was built on the same site. For many years the hotel's activities were contained on the first and second floors with Burton's the tailoring shop occupying the ground floor. The hotel closed in April 1966 and, in recent years, the ground floor has been occupied by Dolland and Aitcheson (opticians). The name Talbot survives in a cellar bar in Queen Street.* The original building appears both in the 1833 and 1872 surveys.

Talbot Road, Salisbury Park
This road was laid out in the late 19th century on land that was once the property of the Thelwell family (see Salisbury Road*). There is no evidence of where this street name originates from although it would seem likely that several streets in this area of Wrexham (Salisbury Park, Trevor Street, Percy Road) were named after noted late mediæval or Tudor families, in this instance the Talbot family of Whitchurch. In the 1881 census Miss Humphrey's Seminary is shown as being located in this road and Evan Birkett Evans* ran a shop at N° 10 in 1883. A substantial part of the west side of the street is known as Cambridge Terrace.

Talbot Road Primitive Methodist Chapel
The congregation moved into this new chapel, named Mount Zion, in 1879, having previously been accommodated in a chapel in the Beast Market.* They moved to a new chapel in Poyser Street* in 1911. The Religious Census of 1881 showed: Capacity 200; attendance (AM & PM) 253. The minister in 1881 was the Revd H. Mowgetts and in 1886 the Revd A. C. Hall. The Religious Census of 1904 showed: Capacity 250; attendance (AM & PM) 149. In recent years this chapel has been the Church of Christ.

Tanat Way, Queen's Park
Built in the late 1940s as part of the first phase of WBC's Queens Park housing development. It is named after the Tanat valley in Montgomeryshire.

Tanner, Ambrose *soldier & victim*
Ambrose Tanner was a soldier who was shot down and killed in July 1716 outside the old Town Hall by a mob acting in support of James Stuart, the 'Old Pretender'.

Tanneries
For a substantial period of its history, Wrexham was renowned as a town specialising in the production of leather. Most businesses associated with this rather socially unpleasant trade were located either close to the Beast Market or close to ample sources of water, most notably the river Gwenfro.
Beast Market Tannery – Located just behind the National School* in the Beast Market,* and clearly shown on both the 1833 and 1872 surveys, this was a substantial tannery, the first recorded owner of which was William Poynton (formerly of The Walks*) who died in 1746. He was succeeded by his son, also named William (died 1766) and a memorial to both was erected in the south aisle of the Parish Church.* The business was then taken over by John Eddowes (whose wife was Mary Poynton) who already owned a tannery at 'Pentre'r felin newydd' (see below). Following the death of John Eddowes IV in 1812, the business was run by his widow Mary and brother William Owen Eddowes, who sold it in 1825 to William Pierce. Towards the end of the 19th century, the tannery was being run by Walter Jones of Charles Street. Of interest here is the fact that Elizabeth, the daughter of John Eddowes III, married James Gladstone of Liverpool and was the aunt of Prime Minister, the Rt Hon William Gladstone, MP. This tannery is clearly shown on both the 1833 and the 1872 surveys.
Pentre'r Felin Newydd Tannery – Located below the bridge at King's Mills, this tannery was founded by John Eddowes pre 1742 and inherited by his son John (the husband of Mary Poynton) and in turn by his grandson, also named John (who died in 1799) and great-grandson, John Eddowes IV (who died in 1812). (See also Cambrian Leather Works and Hugh Price & Company)

Tan-y-Bryn, Queen's Park
(*Trans.* below the hill) One of the last developments in WBC's Queen's Park* housing development.

Tan-y-Dre, Hullah Lane
(*Trans.* below the town) Built by WBC as part of the Queen's Park* housing estate.

Tapley, BEM, Alderman Joseph Harold *local politician*
Born in Chester on 25 October 1898 Harold Tapley began his working career in 1912 as a messenger boy with the General Post Office in Chester before moving to Oswestry in 1915. He served in the Royal Engineers from 1917–20 and saw active service in France where he was gassed. On being discharged from the army, he re-joined the GPO and moved to Wrexham. During the Second World War he was 'loaned' to RAF Fighter Command as an instructor in radio telegraphy and morse at Market Drayton. At the time of his retirement, he was the Supervising Postal and Telegraph Officer at Wrexham. He served on the Chester & North Wales District Council of the Union of Post Office Workers. He was a keen fisherman, badminton and tennis player and was responsible for laying out tennis courts in Acton Park, at the rear of the St Giles Home,* and behind St James' Church, Rhosddu. He was a sidesman at St Margaret's Church and a member of the Bromfield Lodge.*

He was elected to represent Acton Ward on WBC and became Mayor in 1968. He was elected an Alderman for the Acton Ward in 1970 and was awarded the British Empire Medal in 1955 for his services to the Post Office. Married to Doris Wilde of Oswestry, Harold Tapley lived at N° 24 Neville Crescent. He died on 19 September 1978. Tapley Avenue was named after him.

Tapley Avenue, Acton Park
Built by WBC in the 1950s as part of the third phase of the Acton Park housing estate,* this street was named after Alderman Harold Tapley.*

Taylor, John *local politician*
Born Cefn-y-Bedd in c.1878, the son of Richard and Jane Taylor of the Ffrwd public house, John was educated at Abermorddu and Caergwrle before commencing work at the Wilderness Brick & Terracotta Company in Gresford. In 1898 he began working for the Wrexham, Mold & Connah's Quay Railway* and remained with them through to the days of the Great Central Railway and the London & North Eastern Railway as a passenger train driver. He was a deacon at Trinity Church.*

John Taylor was elected a member of WBC in 1932 and became Mayor in 1942. He married Margaret, the daughter of George Thomas, a corn merchant of Caia Road.* He died on 12 September 1943, during his year of office as Mayor of Wrexham and is buried in Wrexham Cemetery*.

Taylor, Lawson *Town Clerk*
Bachelor Lawson Taylor was born in Burnley, Lancashire, c.1873, and was employed at the Town Clerk's office there between 1889 and 1905. He was appointed Wrexham's third Town Clerk in April 1906, succeeding Thomas Bury.* He was a founder member and secretary of the Association of Welsh Local Authorities and was appointed its honorary secretary in 1947. He retired in 1937 and died in 1947, when he was living with his niece at 52 Rhosnesni Lane and is buried in Wrexham Cemetery. Lawson Road* and Lawson Close* are named after him.

Telephone Exchange
The first recorded telephone exchange in Wrexham existed in the mid 1890s but its location is unrecorded. By 1900 an exchange

was operating in Nº 5 Argyle Street and there is still evidence of the telephone wire brackets on the back of the Westminster Buildings archway. The first 29 subscribers at the Wrexham Exchange were:

1. Broughton & Plas Power Coal Co. Ltd.
2. Vron Colliery Ltd. (Stansty Lodge)
3. C. K. Benson
4. Brymbo Steel Co. Ltd.
5. Charles Murless
6. unknown
7. Clark & Rea
7a. E. T. Clark
8. Robert Graesser
9. Williams & Co.
10. William Sillery
11. unknown
12. Poyser & Shuter
13. Wrexham Exchange Club
14. Acton, Bury & Acton
15. Williams, Thomas & Co.
16. John Little
17. Denbighshire County Police
18. George Dutton & Sons Co.
19. Rogers & Jackson
20. Evan Morris & Co.
21. Fire Station
22. Edward Evans
23. unknown
24. W. Wynn Evans
25. Vron Colliery Ltd. (Bradley Road)
26. Minera Mining Co. Ltd.
27. Westminster Brymbo Coal & Coke Co. Ltd. (Moss Valley)
28. Westminster Brymbo Coal & Coke Co. Ltd. (King Street)
29. Wrexham & Acton Colliery (Secretary)

At this time there were only 70 telephone subscribers in the town but by 1908 this had increased to 248. The telephone number Wrexham 1 was allocated to Cudworth & Johnson, engineers of Tuttle Street. On 15 February 1936 an automatic telephone exchange was opened at Nº 18 Grosvenor Road. Two modern extensions have been added to this exchange.

Temperance Hotel, Regent Street
See Maelor Hotel.

Templars' Avenue
Located on the north-west side of the Beast Market,* these ten terraced houses were cleared during the 1930s as part of the Borough slum clearance programme.

Temple Row
Temple Row is the terrace of properties located behind High Street, facing the Parish Church. The origin of the name is unknown, although interestingly, Palmer* makes no mention of it in his *History of the Town of Wrexham*. This would suggest that the name was not of ancient origin and might only have come into use in the late 19th century. There is no evidence to suggest that there was ever a Masonic Temple in this street.

Tenters Square
This is located near the top of Pen-y-Bryn and originally took its name from the practice of stretching woollen cloth on tenter hooks to prevent shrinkage during the manufacturing process. Tentering was usually carried out in an open space called a tenter field which, in the case of Wrexham, was probably on the upper south-east slope of the small valley formed by the river Gwenfro.* One of the town's pinfolds* was located in the centre of Tenter Square, as was a public urinal. Access to the 19th century Bridewell* and the National School* was through the square. During the 1990s a sports centre was developed on the site of the old Bridewell and this has now been redeveloped as 40 apartments, named Tenters Square, by Hawk Group of Wem.

Theatre Road
This road ran from the south-eastern corner of the Beast Market* across Eagles' Meadow.* It took its name from the Theatre Royal* (or Penson's Theatre*) which stood on the Beast Market junction. It was cleared as part of the Eagles' Meadow development of the late 1960s.

Theatre Royal
See Penson's Theatre.

Thirsty Scholar, The Egerton Street
See Egerton Arms.

Thomas Hampson, The
A new public house, developed by Witherspoons in the premises of the former HSBC bank in High Street.* Opened in November 2001. Now (2010) renamed the North & South Wales Bank* public house.

Thomas, BSc, John Richard *local politician*
John Richard Thomas was born in Llanaber near Barmouth in 1928. He was educated at Barmouth Primary School and Barmouth Grammar School before studying geography at the University College of Wales, Aberystwyth where he gained a BSc. He was appointed an assistant teacher of geography at Grango Secondary Modern School in Rhosllannerchrugog and moved to Ysgol Morgan Llwyd, Wrexham in 1965 where, within a few months, he was appointed Deputy Headteacher, a post which he retained until retiring in 1985.

He was elected a Plaid Cymru councillor for Rhosllannerchrugog on the Shadow WMBC in 1973 (the first Plaid Cymru councillor to serve on any Wrexham council). He was Chairman of the Leisure and Recreation Committee and was elected Mayor in 1981 when he was the first Welsh civic leader to meet Prince Charles and Princess Diana on their tour of Wales following their wedding.

Welsh speaker John Thomas was the Chairman of the Executive Committee for the National Eisteddfod* held in Wrexham in 1977 and for the Bro Maelor Urdd National Eisteddfod of 1995. In 1978 he was made a member of the Gorsedd. He was married to Mair Jones of Rhosllannerchrugog.

Thomas of Remenham, DFC, FIMechE, FRAeS, Baron *businessman*
William Miles Webster Thomas, was born in 1897, the only son of William Henry Thomas, a Cefn Mawr ironmonger and furnisher. He was educated at Acrefair School, Ruabon Grammar School for Boys and Bromsgrove School, Worcestershire. Showing a passion for engineering he was first employed as a 'premium pupil' with Bellis and Morcam, a Birmingham engineering firm. He served in an Armoured Car Squadron in East Africa before transferring to the Royal Flying Corps where he was commissioned. After qualifying as a pilot in Egypt, he flew on operations in Mesopotamia, Persia and Russia and was awarded the Distinguished Flying Cross 'for aerial combat and low ground strafing'. After the war he joined F. P. Raynham in air racing before taking up an appointment as a motoring journalist. In 1924, he was appointed a commercial adviser to William Morris and within three years was Sales Manager and a Director of Morris Motors eventually becoming Managing Director and Vice-Chairman in 1940. During the Second World War he controlled 63 factories and an aircraft repair establishment. He became Chairman of the Cruiser Tank Production Group and led a tank engine mission to the USA in 1942. He was knighted in 1943. After the end of hostilities he left Morris and became

Chairman of the Southern Rhodesian Development Co-ordinating Commission (1947) followed by the Colonial Development Corporation. He joined the nationalised British Overseas Airways Corporation (BOAC) as Vice-Chairman in 1948 and became Chairman the following year. He held this post during the difficult years following the intoduction of the Comet jet airliner and the subsequent crashes. In the mid 1950s he caused some questions to be asked in Parliament when he took on part-time positions as a director of H. Ferguson (Research) Ltd in Coventry and Monsanto Chemicals Ltd and he eventually resigned from BOAC and became Chairman of Monsanto in 1956 (serving until retirement in 1964). Between 1965 and 1970 he was Chairman and President of the National Savings Committee. He was also a Director and Chairman of Britannia Airways Ltd and a Director of Thomson Holdings. His autobiography *Out on a Wing: An Autobiography* was published in 1964. He was created a life peer in 1971. He married Hylda Nora Church in 1924 and had one son and one daughter. He died on 8 February 1980.

Thomas of Gresford, OBE, QC, LLB, MA, **Baron** *barrister & politician*
Martin Thomas was born in Wrexham, the son of Hywel and Olwen Thomas. His father was a police officer and the family lived at Oak Drive in Wrexham, Llangollen and Benjamin Road. He attended Acton Park School* and Grove Park School* where he was the captain of the Top of the Form team that won the national competition in 1953–4. He was a student at Peterhouse, Cambridge where he gained an LLB and an MA in classics. He was articled to the legal practice of Stanley Williams in Ruabon and practised as a solicitor in Wrexham before being called to the bar in 1967 when he became a barrister on the Wales and Chester circuit. In 1974 he was appointed a deputy circuit judge, became a recorder in 1976 and a Queen's Councillor three years later. He was a practising QC at Goldsmith Chambers, Goldsmith Buildings, Temple and a member of the Criminal Injury Compensation Board (1985–93).

Martin Thomas joined the Liberal Party in 1963 and was the party's candidate for the Wat's Dyke ward in the Wrexham Borough Council elections of the same year. In 1964 he became chairman of the Wrexham Liberal Association and in 1970 president. He stood for Parliament in the West Flint constituency on three occasions and for the Wrexham constituency in 1974, 1979, 1983 and 1987. In 1977, he became President of the Welsh Liberal Party. He was awarded the OBE in 1982 for his services to politics and was given a life peerage as Lord Thomas of Gresford in 1996. As a member of the House of Lords he is the Liberal Democrat spokesman on Wales (2004) and the Home Office (2004). He was the Liberal Democrat Shadow Attorney General (2004–06), Lord Chancellor (2006–07), Attorney General (2007–10), spokesperson for Justice (2007–10).

Outside of politics and the law, Lord Thomas is a keen supporter of rugby and rowing (President of Rex Rowing Club), President of the Friends of Gresford Church and the Maelor Hospital. President of the London Welsh Chorale and Vice President of the Llangollen International Eisteddfod and the Lloyd George Society. He was for many years the Chairman of local radio station Marcher Sound.

He married Nan Kerr in 1961 by whom he has four children; she died in 2000. He married Joan Margaret Walmsley (Baroness Walmsley of West Derby in the County of Merseyside), a fellow Liberal Democrat peer, in 2005. He lives at Glasfryn, Gresford.

Thomas, Alderman Thomas Francis *local politician*
Born in Morriston, Swansea, Thomas Thomas served as a petty officer in the Royal Navy during the First World War. During the Second World War he worked as the chief trade union official at the Royal Ordnance Factory,* Marchwiel, and was a member of the Whitley Council.

He was elected a Labour Councillor for the Cefn ward on WBC in 1945 and became Mayor in 1958. He was elected an Alderman in May 1964 and was a Director of the Wrexham Co-operative Society.* In later years he was in charge of the packing department at British Celanese on the Wrexham Industrial Estate.*

He was married to Ethel Hanney and they had two sons (one of whom was killed while serving in the Royal Air Force). He lived at 6 Ash Grove, Rhosnesni. Alderman Thomas died, aged 66, at the Maelor Hospital in January 1965, and is buried in Wrexham Cemetery.

Thomas, Vincent *musician*
Born in Wrexham Vicarage,* Vincent Thomas was the son of William Thomas, JP. He was educated at Grove Park School and was employed in Parr's Bank before returning to education in order to pursue a career in music, specialising in conducting. He made his debut at the Queen's Hall, London in 1898 and conducted a number of noted orchestras. He wrote several operas, including *Eos and Gwervil* (1902); *Gwenevere* (1903), *Enid* (1908) as well as shorter music pieces. He was deeply involved with the National Eisteddfod, both as a conductor and an adjudicator. He married Margaret Corsforth and had one son and one daughter. He died in London on 16 October 1940, aged 67.

Thomas' Brewery, College Street
Owned by Edward Thomas in 1799, this is the first recorded commercial brewery in Wrexham. After his death the business was taken over by Edward Crewe and later became the Albion Brewery*.

Thornley, Alexander Wylde *entrepreneur & philanthropist*
See Thornley Square, Mary Ann Square, the British Schools and Salisbury Park Church.

Thornley Square, Brook Street
Located on the south side of Brook Street opposite Well Street, this area of poor quality industrial housing was the subject of a compulsory purchase and demolition order in 1932 as part of the Borough slum clearance programme. It was named after Alexander Wylde Thornley.*

The Three Pigeons Inn, Hope Street
A public house on the site of the present day W. H. Smith store in Hope Street.* An illustration of the inn was printed by Thomas

Thornley Square, Brook Street, with the Wrexham Steam Laundry building on the left.

Painter* in 1863. It appears in the 1833 survey (see also Lion Hotel). In the early 19th century it was the property of Robert Griffith of Hafod-y-Bwch.*

Three Tuns, Town Hill
Shown in the 1833 survey located on the east side of Town Hill, this building was demolished to make way for the Wrexham & Ellesmere Railway* viaduct in the 1890s. The public house also appears in the Downman print of Bridge Street. [DRO/973]

Tiger Inn, Beast Market
Located on the end of Evans' Row* on the south-east corner of Farndon Street.* The site is now part of the road network in front of the present day Tesco store. In 1881 the licensee was Edward Rowland. It appears in the 1872 survey.

Tir Gwalchmai, High Street
Tir Gwalchmai (*Trans*. Gwalchmai's Land) was the name given to the area of High Street* close to the junction with Hope Street.* A. N. Palmer* found a reference to it in a deed of 1572 when it belonged to Sir Henry Salusbury, of Lleweni and did not seem to have any buildings on it. A 15th century document also refers to an area of land in High Street bounded on one side by the land of Gruffydd ap Gwalchmai. By 1620, the land had been built upon by Sir Henry Salusbury.

Tithe Barn, Farndon Street
A large tithe barn which belonged to the Thelwells of Blaen Iâl (from 1702–*c*.1828) is reputed to have stood on the west side of Farndon Street (somewhere opposite the present-day War Memorial Club) which was burned down shortly after 1843. The Thelwall family owned the tithes (having probably bought the rights from the Church) for the townships of Wrexham Abbot,* Wrexham Regis,* Abenbury Fawr,* Abenbury Fechan,* Gourton* and Bieston.* They were entitled to one-tenth of the value of all agricultural products, usually paid in kind and stored in this building.

Toll Gates
The first Turnpike Act in Britain was passed in 1663, but it was during the period 1750–70 that the majority of Acts were passed which enabled local trusts (companies) to charge a toll in exchange for building and maintaining a road. A General Turnpike Act was passed in 1773-74 to speed up the process through Parliament. In addition to a gate or bar which obstructed the road, the trusts usually built a small toll house where the toll-gate keeper (also known as a pikeman) lived. He would collect the toll ranging from $^{1}/_{4}$d (0.1p) for each head of cattle to 6d (2.5p) for a horse-drawn carriage.

The first Turnpike Act relating to the road from Wrexham to Mold was passed in 1756, establishing a turnpike road between the two towns. Originally, the first toll-gate after leaving Wrexham was located at the cross roads where Plas Coch Road and Berse Road met Mold Road, with the toll house sited on the south-west corner, thereby controlling access for any vehicles wishing to travel towards Mold from any of three routes. The tolls that were charged ranged from 4d–6d (1.6p–2.5p). In January 1845, all tolls were reduced by half, but in November 1848 they reverted to the original levels. A surviving poster of 1847 shows that the entire road produced £550 over and above the collection costs, and members of the public were invited to bid for the rights to collect the tolls. By 1850, there were plans in place to expand the turnpike network to reach from Wrexham to Brymbo and through Stansty to Rhosddu and Acton. As a result of this, in April 1850, it was resolved to move the toll-gate to a site nearer Wrexham town centre '…a Turnpike Gate, with proper conveniences, be erected upon and across the Road, at a certain place then and there agreed upon, between the Dispensary [Infirmary*] and the Wrexham Railway Station [Wrexham General Station*], in the township of Wrexham Regis.' This new gate was located on the Mold Road, just to the west of Cathrall's Lane (Union Street*) with the stone built toll house on the north side of the road.

The first Wrexham & Ruthin Turnpike Act was passed in 1758–59. The first toll-gate on leaving Wrexham was on Ruthin Road, just past the junctions with the present day Victoria Road and Bradley Road, with the toll house sited on the north side of the road, on the site of the present day newsagents shop.

The first Wrexham & Barnhill Turnpike Act was passed in 1781–82. The first toll-gates on leaving Wrexham were on Holt Road, at the junction with Borras Road, obstructing passage along both roads. The toll house, called Pwll-yr-Wydd* Gate, was sited between the two roads. There was a second toll-gate in Rhosnesni, at the junction of Holt Road and Acton Road (now called Dean Road*) opposite the present day Greyhound* public house. The toll house was a small, double-fronted brick house, once known as The Old Bar (from bar meaning barrier), which still survives on the corner of Holt Road and Dean Road.

Poster advertising the letting of tolls on the Wrexham–Mold road, 1847. [FRO/D/KK/824]

The Wrexham & Shrewsbury Turnpike Act was passed in 1751–52. The first toll-gate on leaving Wrexham was called King's Mills Turnpike and was sited on the present day King's Mills Road with the toll house on the south of the road on the site of Hightown Barracks.

The first Wrexham & Chester Turnpike Act was passed in 1755–56. The first toll-gate on leaving Wrexham was at the junction of what is now Box Lane but did not obstruct access to the main Chester Road. There is no evidence of a toll house at this site which may support the claim that Box Lane is so called because there was a toll-keepers box (similar to a sentry box) located at the Chester Road junction. There was a second toll-gate at Acton Smithy which controlled traffic along the Chester Road. Here there was a toll house sited on the south corner of the Chester Road and Pandy Lane junction.

In 1869, WBC petitioned Parliament to abolish all toll gates. In 1888, the newly-formed county councils assumed all responsibility for the turnpikes and the trusts were wound up. (See also Acts of Parliament)

Tongue, OBE, CPFA, IRRV, Sydney Frederick *Chief Executive*
Born in London on 13 February 1925, Sydney Frederick Tongue was educated at Tottenham Grammar School, from where he matriculated before spending five years serving in the Royal Air Force during the Second World War. He qualified as a Chartered Public Finance Accountant in 1954 and as a member of the Institute of Rating and Valuation in 1963.

He held a number of financial appointments in local government with Middlesex County Council, Edmonton Borough Council, Hemel Hempstead Development Corporation, Finchley Borough Council, Shorditch Borough Council and Newcastle-under-Lyme Borough Council before being appointed Treasurer to WRDC in February 1963.

In April 1974, he was appointed Deputy Chief Executive/Director of Finance to the newly-formed WMBC and, due to the illness of of Trevor Ll. Williams,* became Acting Chief Executive the following month. In May 1977 he was confirmed in the post of Chief Executive, a position which he held until retiring in 1988. During his service in Wrexham, Sydney Tongue supervised the merger of WBC and WRDC and was successfully involved with attracting new international and national companies to Wrexham following the loss of 18,000 jobs in the traditional industries of coalmining, textiles, steel, heavy engineering, brick-making and agriculture, By the time he retired in 1988, he had the satisfaction of seeing unemployment in the Wrexham area fall from 27% to 8%. He was the Public Works Loan Commissioner from 1968–72 and served as a specialist Industrial and Commercial Adviser to the House of Commons Select Committee on Welsh Affairs (1988–92).

He was awarded the OBE in June 1988 in recognition of his services to local government and success in attracting new employment to Wrexham. Sydney Tongue is married with three sons and continues to live in the Wrexham area.

Tower View, Queen's Park
Built in the immediate post Second World War period as part of the first phase of WBC's Queen's Park housing development on land that was previously part of the Cefn Park* estate. This street is named after the view of Wrexham Parish Church.

Town Clerks/Rural District Council Clerks/Chief Executives
The post of Town Clerk was created at the time of the Incorporation of the Borough of Wrexham in 1857. The first man to hold the office was John James,* a local solicitor, who had played a prominent role in obtaining the Charter for Wrexham. On the merging of WBC and WRDC in 1974, the post of Town Clerk was upgraded to that of Chief Executive Officer. Details of office holders can be found under the entry for each individual council.

The Town Hall in use as a bonded warehouse, c.1950.

Town Hall
Located at the top of Town Hill,* facing High Street. The *Aula placitorium* (Trans. Hall of Pleas) was the court house described in the 1391 survey as being 'in the middle of the forum* with shops built below, which is worth 50s. per annum'. In the 1562 survey it is called the *Aule ville* (Trans. town hall) and was built on Crown land at the top of High Street next to the High Cross which acted as 'The Common Hall' or the 'Hall of Pleas'.* This building is often referred to as the Shirehall.* The building commonly known as the Town Hall, was built in 1713 'at the expense of the County, and upon the site of the old building erected'. It comprised an open space on the ground floor with nine 'shop' spaces and a Grand Chamber above where the Great & Quarter Sessions were held, along with the manor courts of Wrexham Regis and, possibly, the manor courts of Bromfield and Yale. At the western end of the building a house was built for the County Treasurer. Much of the Town Hall was regularly leased out to other tenants. During the 1770s, the Town Hall was leased to the Yorkshire cloth traders who left in *c*.1788 when they built their own market (see Yorkshire Square*) below the Parish Church.* The development of Ruthin as the county town of Denbighshire, and the building of a Shirehall there, led to the decline of the Town Hall in Wrexham. The transfer of the Assizes to Ruthin in 1788 meant that little use was made of the Great Hall other than as an armoury for the Denbighshire Militia. One lessee of the ground floor, John Mellor, becoming concerned at the deterioration in the condition of the pillars, bricked up the open area and turned it into two warehouses.

In 1834, the Town Hall was described as '… a large brick edifice … the ground floor was formerly open, but is now enclosed between the pillars that support the upper storey: this consists of

Poster advertising the sale of the Town Hall.

a spacious and lofty room, formerly a court of justice, but now only used for public meetings, and as a depot for arms. A county house of correction, situated here, comprises seven wards for the classification of prisoners, who are allowed a portion of their earnings'. Sometime after 1841 (but before 1843), John Richards of Felin Puleston converted these warehouses into a spirit vaults for his business. Following the Incorporation of the Borough of Wrexham* in 1857, the Town Hall was put up for sale and bought by Messrs Painter & Overton of High Street, subject to the proviso that accommodation had to be provided for police and county business. In 1860, a judge had threatened to move his court to Llangollen because of the dreadful conditions prevailing in the Town Hall which he described as 'such a dirty hole which was almost as bad as the Black Hole of Calcutta'. The premises continued as a wine and spirit store for the remainder of its existence and became an official bonded warehouse.

Lesees and owners of the Town Hall:
- 1578 9 shops beneath the Shirehall – Robert Puleston
- 1619 9 shops beneath the Shirehall – Thomas Goldsmith, gent.
- 1628 9 shops beneath the Shirehall – John and David Edwards, gents. of Stansty Issa (sub-leased to George Manley, gent)
- 1658 believed to be vacant and in a state of disrepair
- 1661 Peter Edwards
- 1691 reverted to the Crown
- 1705 Peter Ellice (Croesnewydd), John Puleston (Pickhill Hall), John Puleston (Hafod-y-Wern), Thomas Pulford (Wrexham) during their tenure, the Shirehall was demolished and a new one built at the expense of the county of Denbighshire in 1713
- 1713 two storey building extension at south-west end of Hall – Philip Cross (corvisor), County Treasurer
- 1755 whole building – reverted to the Crown
- 1756 vacant space between the pillars and the house – Sir Lynch Salusbury Cotton, Bt, (Combermere and Lleweni)
- 1778 vacant space between the pillars and the house – Joseph Jackson, draper and John Mellor, merchant.
- 1806 whole building – John Mellor
- c.1829 whole building – Richard Roberts (Y Felin Puleston), smith
- 1841 whole building – John Richards
- 1843 whole building – William Overton
- 1857 whole building purchased from the Crown by William Overton and Thomas Painter. It later became the bonded warehouse of Thomas Williams & Co, wine & spirit merchants

In February 1940 the Borough Council accepted a tender from the Western Demolition Company and Contractors Ltd to demolish the Town Hall but the intervention of HM Office of Works caused the Council to go for the next lowest tender. The Town Hall was finally demolished in the spring of 1940 as part of a road improvement scheme and the actual demolition work was preserved on a private movie film (part of which is reproduced in the video *Wrexham a journey through time*). There is a rumour that the Nazi propagandist William Joyce, 'Lord Haw-Haw', broadcast that he had heard Wrexham had a Town Hall that needed demolishing, adding 'Don't worry, we'll do it for you', but there is no hard evidence to support this story.

The clock that appeared on the front of the Town Hall was purchased by local subscribers to commemorate the marriage of Sir Watkin Williams Wynn in 1852. This clock survived the demolition and was moved to its present site in Lord Street overlooking the bus station.

Town Hall Vaults, Back Chamber Street
As the name suggests, these licensed premises were located under the Town Hall and were accessed from Back Chamber Street.* Closed shortly before the demolition of the Town Hall in 1940, the licence was transferred to the new Acton Park Hotel,* Chester Road.

Town Hill
Originally known as both Glan-yr-Afon (the river bank) and Oswestry Road, this street has also been referred to as an extension of High Street. Palmer* records one reference to this street in 1670/71 as being known as Bridge Street. The name Town Hill appears to have come into common usage in the late 18th or early 19th centuries. Other than the Town Hall, the

Town Hill c.1910. The view looking towards the Hand Inn (built at the turn of the 20th century)

The railway bridge over Town Hill, demolished during the 1990s.

largest building in this street was the Hand Inn* which stood immediately behind the Town Hall* on the corner of Abbot Street.* The lower part of the street was dramatically changed in the 1890s when the construction of the Ellesmere railway led to the building of a railway bridge just below the junction of College Street. This railway bridge was demolished in 1995.

There are a number of interesting buildings located in this street.

N° 5: Formerly the premises of The Bon menswear shop, this timber-framed building was renovated during the 1970s, leaving much of the timber work and wattle and daub in-fill exposed. In the late 1990s, the shop was sold and became part of the One to Five public house.

N° 7: Formerly the premises of Cut, Shape & Face, this timber-framed building was extensively renovated during the early 1990s and the interior timber-framing was exposed and restored. In the front of the building is a large linen-fold panel with clear indications of the original floor level. Upstairs there is what may have originally been a priest hole.

N° 9: The premises formerly occupied by Dodman's shoe shop. This was once the Bull & Dogs* public house. It is a heavily altered timber-framed building with an 18th century brick frontage and a Victorian shop on the ground floor. Following extensive renovation work during the 1990s, much of the interior timber work was exposed along with some wattle and daub in-fill and the remains of wall paintings on the first floor.

Town Mill
See Abbot's Mill.

Town Well
This was located in the middle of Well Square* and was surrounded on three sides by a stone wall. The open eastern side gave access to steps leading down to the well itself. Before the establishment of piped water to the various properties in the town, this was the major source of fresh water and, according to A. N. Palmer,* produced up to 2,000 gallons per hour. The Revd George Cunliffe* wrote of the well in 1849:

> Here numbers of women and children resort hourly, even from the more distant parts of the town, for the purpose of fetching water, and also of carrying away all the gossip they can collect. Here the events of the day are discussed, magnified and distorted. Here many a frail pitcher is broken, and it had been far happier for some had they daily dipped their pail in the filthy brook than have sought the pure waters of the Ffynnon. About 30 feet below the well (on the south side of Well Square) there exists an old bath significantly called 'The Cold Bath', so cold indeed that few submit to the petrifying shock a second time. The refuse water of the well flows into this, and so passes off to the river. The bath is about 14 feet long, 10 feet wide and 5 feet deep. It is now in a dilapidated and dirty state, though full of water.

Palmer,* an industrial chemist by profession, twice analysed the water from the well and found it to be very hard but of 'considerable organic purity'. The construction of the Wrexham & Ellesmere Railway* in the 1890s led to the well being built over and the water diverted into a small, tiled chamber under one of the arches of the railway viaduct at the end of Well Place which can be accessed today by way of a small wooden door.

Townsend Avenue, Borras Park
A development of private houses built in the early 1960s by the London firm of Spinks & Denning on land that had previously belonged to William Clarke* and, pre-1918, to the Acton Park* estate. The origin of the name is unknown.

Townships of Wrexham
A township was a small mediæval communal or manorial sub-division of a parish. Traditionally, the old parish of Wrexham was divided into eighteen townships *viz*: Wrexham Abbot, Wrexham Regis, Esclusham Below, Esclusham Above, Minera, Bersham, Broughton, Brymbo, Abenbury Fawr, Abenbury Fechan, Bieston, Gourton, Burras Hovah, Burras Riffri, Acton, Stansty, Erlas, and Erddig. In addition to these, there were two other townships which appear in the 1391 survey (taken from a source dated 1289) but which later disappear, merging into their neighbours. These were Havat Wern (Hafod y Wern –44.5 statute acres), which name has survived, and Midun Hull (Midden Hill –158.5 statute acres). The location of this latter township is unrecorded but one can make an intelligent guess as to its situation by relating it to other known facts about the area.

A midden is a dung-hill or refuse-heap and, as such, is unlikely to have been located in the mediæval urban area of Wrexham. In the 13th century the Wrexham Maerdref* was administered by an official known as *maer-y-biswail* which translates as 'the bailiff of the dung-hill', a clear reference to the Midden Hill. It is a known fact that the area eastwards from Eagles' Meadow,* which was prone to flooding by the river Gwenfro, was highly prized for its deposits of both human and animal excreta in the days when such effluence was a valuable commodity used as a fertilizer. As late as the 1840s, residents of Wrexham were objecting to attempts to control the effluent in the Gwenfro, claiming that it would result in a devaluation of their land in the area of Eagles' Meadow. Townspeople wishing to dispose of sewerage in the days before sewers would have sought a convenient place to deposit it so that it would later be dispersed by water. The name Midden Hill' should be transcribed as Dung-hill Hill which would place it on a slope above a river. The only severe slope above a river in the immediate vicinity of the town centre (other than that below the Parish Church) is that located behind the shops on the south side of Charles Street. An examination of the surviving mediæval names for areas of Wrexham brings us to The Dunks,* an area to the east of the town, through which the Gwenfro flows and which, until very recently, regularly flooded in the winter. The origin of the name 'Dunks' is open to debate – it might have been a distortion of the word 'dung'. This would have been the area where the effluent deposited into the Gwenfro would have ended up. If this is a logical train of thought then it is but a small step to locate Midden Hill in the area between the the town centre and the 'missing' township of Hafod-y-Wern.

Trafalgar Close, Hermitage
Built in the 1970s, this small close of corporation owned flats took the name of the demolished Trafalgar Road* in Hightown.

Trafalgar Road
This street of terraced houses was built in the late 19th century and was located in Hightown, on the south side of King's Mills Road, leading to Napier Street. It was named after the battle of Trafalgar, 21 October 1805, fought between the British fleet under the command of Vice Admiral Horatio Viscount Nelson and the Franco-Spanish fleet under the command of Admiral Villeneuve. The street was demolished in the 1950s and the site is now occupied by Napier Square. The name was then transferred to the newly-built Trafalgar Close* on the Hermitage estate.

Nos 13–22 Trafalgar Road.

Transportation to the colonies
Thomas Clarke and George Fisher were found guilty of the burglary of the Cambrian Leather Works in 1844. They were sentenced to be transported for 10 years.

John Barton and Gomer Jones, stole 40lbs of roofing lead on 1 January 1853. They were tried and found guilty at the Denbigh Easter Quarter Sessions, 1853 and sentenced to be transported for seven years.

Travellers' Rest, King's Mills Road
In an early photograph, this noted public house appears to have been known as the Hightown and was a half-timbered building with a thatched roof. In addition to providing liquid refreshments for the local populace, it was also providing livery stable facilities. It was known locally as 'The Old Maids' (after the licensee Miss Turner who was assisted by Mrs Wood and Mrs Smith).

The pub was rebuilt in 1921 when the owner was Brig-Gen J.H. Lloyd, DSO, of Ellesmere and the licensee Miss Rachel Smith. It was later sold to Huntley & Mowatt (Island Green Brewery*) and then became part of the Border Breweries group. In the shippons which adjoined the original public house, church services were held by the congregation of St John's Church* after the 'tin' church had been moved and while the new church was being built in 1909–10.

'Treason of the Blue Books'
See Blue Books.

Trefalyn Hall, Rossett
Built c.1576, for John Trevor, Trefalyn Hall is regarded as being

The original Traveller's Rest which was replaced by the present building in 1921.

one of the finest brick Elizabethan houses in north Wales. Trevor was a member of the Brynkinalt Trevor family and had made his own fortune in London and as a soldier in the wars against France. He died in London in 1589 and was buried in Gresford Church. He was the father of Sir John Trevor (1563–1630) who built Plas Teg in 1610. The house remained in the ownership of the Trevors and their descendants until 1980 when it was sold and divided into private apartments.

Trefalyn Hall, c.1910.

Trem Eryri, Tŷ Gwyn Lane
Part of a Wain Homes development of 1989/90. There does not appear to be any logic in the name (*Trans*. Snowdonia view) as it would be impossible to see Snowdonia from this location.

Trem yr Eglwys, Coed-y-Glyn
(*Trans*. church view) Built in the 1970s on land that was previously part of Coed-y-Glyn.* The name is a reference to the Parish Church.

Trem-y-Nant, Coed-y-Glyn
(*Trans*. brook view) Built in the 1970s on land that was previously part of Coed-y-Glyn.* The name is a reference to the nearby river Clywedog.

Trevenna Way, Spring Lodge
Built in the mid 1930s as part of the second phase of the Spring Lodge* housing estate. The origin of the name is unknown and a search of Trevenna as a place name brings up two villages in Cornwall.

Trevor Street, Salisbury Park
Laid out in the late 19th century on land that previously part of Groft Tudur (Salisbury Park). Like other streets in this area (Salisbury Park, Talbot Road, Percy Road) it almost certainly takes its name from a noted family of late mediæval or Tudor times, in this case the Trevor's of Trefalyn (Rossett).

Trail's Court
A small court development of low quality terraced houses which was located on the southern side of Pentre Felin just east of the junction with Belle Vue Road.

Trevor's Commercial Hotel, Regent Street
Located opposite the Denbighshire Technical College* (now the Wrexham Art College) in the early 1950s.

Trevose, Chester Road
Built before 1900 by William Thomas, proprietor of Thomas & Son, gentlemen's outfitters of Hope Street. His son, Thomas, built Cherry Hill in Borras.* By 1951, it was the home of Mrs F. Roberts and became the home and surgery of dentist Derfel Thomas in the early 1960s.

Trident Way
Named after the Hawker-Sidley Trident passenger airliner – presumably, but inexplicably, because of its close proximity to the former RAF Wrexham*/Borras Airfield. This street was developed in the late 1970s on land that had previously been part of Plas Goulbourne Farm.

Trinity Presbyterian Church, King Street
(See also Hill Street Presbyterian Church) Built by the English Calvinistic Methodists of Hill Street, Trinity Church was designed by W. Beddoe Rees of Cardiff and built by T. Ll. Davies of Rhos. The schoolroom (intended to accommodate 250, with six classrooms) was officially opened by Mrs John Owens of Chester on Friday 8 November 1907 and the first service (which was held in the schoolroom) took place on Sunday 10 November. The church itself was officially opened on Friday 9 October 1908 by Mrs W.R. Evans of Ruthin and C. Tudor-Hughes of Wrexham with the first service two days later.

During the Second World War, the schoolroom was used as a reception centre for evacuees* from Liverpool, an extra classroom for Grove Park Girls School* and an emergency hospital for elderly ladies from London's East End (the latter remaining until June 1946).

A full history of this church was published in 1988 under the title *Trinity – A Town Centre Church* by Joan M. Hughes.

Trinity Street
Laid out in 1932, this street was named after Trinity Church* which stands at its northern corner. The premises of Chas Eames, which stood on the corner of Lord Street, was demolished in the 1960s and the present day Trinity House, designed by G. Raymond Jones, Anderson & Associates for Howel Glyn Jones, was opened in 1966.

Troon Close, Plas Goulbourne
Built in the early 1980s on land that was previously part of Plas Goulbourne Farm,* Troon Close is named after the noted golf course in Scotland, presumably because of the close proximity of Wrexham Golf Club.

Tryweryn Place, Queen's Park
One of the last developments in WBC's Queen's Park* housing development. it was named after the river Tryweryn near Bala.

Tudor Road, Hermitage
The first three houses in this private housing development were built in the 1920s. The street, in common with others in the area, takes its name from royal dynasties, in this case, the Tudors who ruled England and Wales from 1485 until 1603 (Henry VII, Henry VIII, Edward VI, Mary I, Elizabeth I).

Tunnels
One of the most prevailing beliefs in the town of Wrexham is the existence of numerous tunnels linking various notable buildings both inside and outside the town with the Parish Church. The best known tunnel theories state that there are tunnels linking Erddig Hall, Croesnewydd Hall, Bryn-y-Ffynnon (now demolished), Acton Park and the properties in High Street, Church Street and Town Hill with the Parish Church. It is usually claimed that these tunnels were constructed to enable people to escape from either their houses or the church in times of great danger.

To the best of my knowledge (and that of any other local historian) there is no validity in any of these claims. Some of the reputed tunnels would have been technically impossible to build (from Erddig such a tunnel would have to pass under two valleys) and all of them would have been extremely expensive to build and would have had no purpose. The origins of such tales are probably rooted in two facts.

1. Many large houses did have priest holes hidden within them where, during times of religious intolerance, Roman Catholic priests could be concealed.

2. Some country houses did have short tunnels built from the house to a location nearby (usually in the garden) which could be used as a secret means of escape, again in times of religious persecution. To date, there is no evidence of any such priest hole or tunnel being built in any of the houses mentioned above. Indeed, both Erddig Hall and Croesnewydd Hall were both built after the period of religious persecution had all but ended.

However, there is probably some truth in the old adage that there is no smoke without fire and the only factual origin that can be attributed to this tale is the presence of cellars under most of the older buildings in Wrexham, particularly in High Street, Church Street and Town Hill. Many of these cellars were, at one time, interlinking and this may have led to the belief that, if followed, they would eventually lead to the Parish Church.

Turf Hotel, Mold Road
This was rebuilt by Jack Scott* of the Seven Stars* in an effort to revive horse racing in Wrexham. Today, the Turf is the only public house on the grounds of a British football league club.

Turkey Paper Mills, Bersham
Built by Edward Bozeley in the early 19th century, the paper mill harnessed the water power from the river Clywedog. They were taken over by the Grevilles in the 1850s and specialised in the production of hand-made paper. On 26 March 1897 the works caught fire and, due to a faulty pump on the fire engine sent from Wrexham, the building was destroyed. In the enquiry which followed it was revealed that the fire engine had been directed to draw water from a new culvert which, unbeknown to those present, was heavily silted with sand and gravel. When this was sucked into the pump the engine stopped working. At the time of the fire, the paper company had just received a large order to produce banknote paper for the Indian government and also held a contract from the Stationery Office. The mills were rebuilt, but the last record of them operating is in 1911. The remains of the buildings can be seen near to Laurel Grove, just east of the road from Wrexham to Bersham.

Turner, George William *local politician*
George Turner was the founder and proprietor of Turners (Wrexham) Ltd, general wholesalers of Lord Street* (the site now occupied by the NatWest Bank). He was elected a member of WBC in 1944 and served as Mayor in 1951. He retired from local politics in 1957. He lived at Beverley Grange and Neenah, Horsley Lane, Marford. He married (1) 1912, Mabel Annie (died 1964) by whom he had two sons and two daughters, and (2) 1965, Mrs Myfanwy Jones. He was a director of Wrexham Football Club.* He died in January 1966.

Turner Close
The street was developed in the early 1980s on land that had once been part of the Plas Goulbourne Farm* estate and was named after the renowned English artist J. M. W. Turner who did once visit Wrexham and painted a picture of High Street which is now held in the Victoria and Albert Museum, London.

Turner's Yard
Located at the rear of N°s 23 & 24 Hope Street, The Fleece Inn* and the Green Man* public houses. It took its name from Richard Haighton Turner, the owner of the adjacent houses. [DRO/DD/G/2863]

Tuttle Bridge
A crossing of the river Gwenfro, this bridge is located at the foot of Madeira Hill.

Tuttle Street
Takes its name from Tothill or Twtil, the old name for a look-out, and was probably a reference to the top of Madeira Hill.* It runs from the junction of Mount Street and Yorke Street to the foot of Madeira Hill but, until at least 1831, extended to the top of Madeira Hill* to the area of Salisbury Park. Most of the western side of the street consisted of small terraced houses and the Nag's Head Brewery* while the eastern side had a mixture of terraced housing, the Nag's Head Vaults and the first Wrexham Public Baths and Swimming Pool.* The most significant house here was Plas Gwern.* (See also Wrexham Castle)

Twinning
WRDC signed a twinning partnership agreement with Kries Iserlohn in Germany on 17 March 1970 after twelve months of negotiation. In 1971, the Council of Europe awarded WRDC a prize for the best British Municipal Partnership, an award that was repeated in 1973. The creation of WMBC in 1974 led to this arrangement being continued and extended to cover the area of Markischer Kries and four years later both authorities were awarded a European Union flag of honour for promoting the European ideal.

Tŷ Gwyn Estate
See Tŷ Gwyn Farm.

Tŷ Gwyn Farm
(*Trans*. white house farm) Tŷ Gwyn Farm, which occupied the land now developed as the Tŷ Gwyn Estate, had a house which stood alongside Tŷ Gwyn Lane on what is now the south-western end of Hampshire Drive.* The earliest reference that Palmer* found to this farm was 1783, when it was part of the Acton Park* estate, the property of Ellis Yonge. The land, however, was certainly part of the Heol Pwll-y-Kiln* estate in the late 17th and early 18th centuries. The resident in 1869 was a Mr Jones and in 1881, Edward Randles, who was farming 111 acres and employing one labourer. The farm was bought for residential development by local builders H.R.&E. Roberts in the late 1950s. For some years the house was the home of the site manager and the farm buildings were used as the builder's yard. The last tenant was Mrs Lavinia Williams who moved out shortly before the house was demolished in the 1970s.

Tŷ Mawr
Recorded by Norden in his survey of 1620 as being a large house sited on the south side of High Street in the possession of Valentine Tilston.

Tŷ Meredith, Chester Street
The name 'Tŷ Meredith' was invented by A. N. Palmer* when referring to a large late Tudor town house which stood on part of the site now occupied by the People's Market (Mrs Dorothy Sunter Harrison, writing in her booklet *Around the Stars*, erroneously stated that Tŷ Meredith stood on the site now occupied by the Seven Stars public house). It was the town house of the Meredith family of Pentrebychan –until they purchased The Court* in 1616. It was later occupied by Owen Wynne (1771–80) and was demolished sometime during the very late 19th century. Palmer described it as being 'of considerable importance and before its front was modernised [*c.*1840] must have been very picturesque. Some of the rooms are still very quaint and over one of the fireplaces is a curious bit of carved oak panelling, which is worth looking at'.

In 1780, the tenancy of the house was taken by Richard Lloyd, the son of Thomas Lloyd, a mercer of High Street, and the nephew of William Lloyd of Plas Power.* His business as a flannel merchant was based in the house but, in about 1785, he established a small private bank in the front room. Known as Lloyd's Bank,* it flourished and was passed on to his son Richard. Richard (senior) acquired the Bryn Estyn estate in 1786. He was also the father of Sir William Lloyd.* Richard Lloyd (junior) was a leading figure in Wrexham society and was appointed High Sheriff of Denbighshire in 1824. He became bankrupt in 1849 and left Wrexham to live in Birkenhead where he died in 1860 and was buried in Wallasey churchyard.

The house was still standing when Palmer wrote his *History of the Town of Wrexham* in about 1890 but appears to have been demolished soon afterwards. Part of the site was redeveloped as three and four storey red-brick buildings divided into individual shops and the warehouse premises of the Wrexham Corn Mills.* In later years, during the 20th century, the premises were occupied by Thorne & Bessell (auctioneers), K. Hugh Dodd (auctioneers), G.R. Davies (corn merchants) and T.W. Davies

N. Whiting's shop on the corner of Tuttle Street and Phillips Place.

(wholesale grocers). These buildings were badly damaged by fire in the 1970s and were partially demolished and the site taken by the former Kwiksave store. Some of the remainder were demolished to make way for the People's Market in the 1980s. A section of these buildings survive as N⁰ˢ 45–47 Chester Street, located between the two entrances to the People's Market.

Owners and tenants:
1748–59	Thomas Hayman
1760–64	Richard Surridge (or Surwich)
1764–70	Revd John Yale
c.1771–80	Owen Wynne (of Llwyn)
c.1780–1814	Richard Myddelton Massie Lloyd (flannel merchant and banker)
1814–49	Richard Myddelton Massie Lloyd II (banker and High Sheriff of Denbighshire in 1824, bankrupted 1849)

Ty'n Twll Farm, Holt Road

Located in the old township of Bieston. From the mid 17th century until the end of the 18th century, Ty'n Twll (*Trans.* house in the hollow) was the property of the Shakerleys of Lower Gwersyllt after which it became the property of Sir William Lloyd* of Bryn Estyn.* In 1881 the farm appears to have been divided into two: (1) 129 acres tenanted by John Jones with his sons Ebeneser and John and (2) 24 acres tenanted by Henry Williams.

With the sale of the Bryn Estyn estate, Ty'n Twll passed into the ownership of the Wrexham brewer F. W. Soames, in whose family it remained until 1924 when it was sold to Albert John Jones, whose family had been tenants there since 1860. At the time of the sale the farm totalled some 80 acres. In 2001, the farm was owned by Raymond Jones, the grandson of Albert John Jones. The original house was replaced in about 1888. Some 7 acres of this farm were sold in 2000 for residential development by Redrow.

The main road to Holt used to take a different line. Coming from the Greyhound it followed the line of the present day farm drive at Ty'n Twll, passing the front of the house, before rejoining the modern road by Keeper's Cottage* at the foot of Keeper's Hill, then passing behind the modern Gredington Arms* public house. The land to the north of the old road (now one small field) was previously part of the Gredington estate, as was much of the land to the north of the Holt Road in the Llan-y-Pwll area.

U

Union Brewery, Tuttle Street

Owned by Charles Bate & Co, this brewery was founded in 1840 on land below the Parish Church* and was accessed from Tuttle Street. It was bought out by the Peter Walker Brewery of Burton on Trent in 1909 (the company operated by Sir Andrew Walker, brother of Peter Walker of Wrexham's Walker's Brewery*). It was sold to the Island Green Brewery* in 1927.

Union Hall, Henblas Street

This was shown in the 1833 survey. (See Birmingham Square)

The Regimental Band of the RWF leads a Colour Party of the United States Marines along Chester Street en route to lay up their Colour in the Parish Church, 1946. [Ann Edwards]

Union Street

Originally named Cathrall's Lane after Thomas Cathrall, a skilled ornamental plasterer who lived at Hope Cottage* (died 1881). This road led from the town to Rhyd Broughton and then towards Brymbo but was cut off by the construction of the Shrewsbury & Chester Railway* in the 1840s. Its present name derives from the fact that it once led to the Poor Law Union Workhouse.*

Union Vaults, Yorke Street

Located on the corner of Yorke Street and Mount Street. Also known as the Union Tavern, the property was sold in October 1905 and the front of the building was moved back to allow re-alignment of the corner of Yorke Street and Mount Street. This reconstruction allowed for the building of an interesting terracotta frontage which incorporated the name of the public house and the brewery. Although the name would suggest that the pub dated back to the early 19th century, by way of a celebration of the Act of Union with Ireland, there is no evidence that it existed before the mid-19th century. In recent years it became an Italian restaurant before becoming an Indian restaurant in the 1980s. It appears in the 1872 survey. (See Union Brewery) [DRO/DD/G/2874]

Union Workhouse

See Poor Law Union.

United Methodist Free Church, Rhosddu

The Religious Census of 1881 showed: Capacity 160; attendance (AM & PM) 62.

United States Army/Marine Corps

During the Second World War various detachments of the US Army were based at Wrexham.

'B' Company, 33rd Signal Corp Construction Battalion was formed at Camp MᶜCain, Mississippi, on 14 December 1942 and trained at Camp Van Dorn, Mississippi, until it moved to Camp Kilmer, New Jersey, from where it embarked aboard HMS *Andes*

on 8 February 1944. Docking in Liverpool on 19 February the company moved to Acton Hall, Wrexham where it remained until 26 June 1944 when it was moved to Downton prior to embarking on the SS *Joshua P. Lippencott* at Southampton on 6 July bound for France. The unit joined General Patton's 3rd Army and saw active service throughout the north-west Europe campaign moving through France, into Luxemburg and Belgium, and entering Germany at Minden on 3 March 1945. At the time of the German surrender the HQ and 2nd Platoon were at Hohenau, and 1st Platoon at Nuremburg in Germany. During the summer of 1945, this unit was withdrawn from Europe and posted to General Kruger's 6th Army in south-east Asia and were in Camp Angeles on the Philippines when the Japanese surrender was announced. They arrived back in the USA in November 1945.

Another unit based at Acton Hall was the 400th Armoured Field Artillery.

A motor pool detachment of black American servicemen were billeted in a variety of local homes including the Wrexham Vicarage* on Chester Road during the latter stages of the Second World War. As part of the U.S. Army's policy of racial segregation, these men were forbidden from mixing with their white compatriots.

The 83rd United States Army Hospital (OC Colonel F. G. Norbury) was stationed at Plas Power during 1944 and departed in June when it was part of the support force for the invasion of Normandy.

American units were also accommodated in huts in the area of Fenwick Drive,* Montgomery Road* and Eagles Meadow.*

Units of the United States Army Air Corps were stationed in the border area (the nearest being at RAF Poulton near Rossett) and many American pilots while on acclimatisation flights over the area used the tower of Wrexham Parish Church as one corner of their triangular navigation route.

The colours of the United States Marine Corps were laid up in Wrexham Parish Church at 12 noon on 12 September 1945 by Maj Harry W. Edwards, USMC, in recognition of the links between that unit and the RWF following the service of both in the Boxer Rebellion in China, 1900. A procession left the Guildhall in Chester Street headed by the band of the 2nd Bn, RWF and a detachment of the 21st Holding Battalion under Major W.R. Crawshaw, DSO. They were followed by four members of the USMC in dress uniform carrying the flag of the USA and the USMC standard. Then came the Macebearer and the Mayor and Mayoress (Cllr and Mrs J. W. Edwards*), the Town Clerk (Philip Walters*), the Town Councillors and representatives of the Red Cross, WVS, teachers, the Lord Lieutenant of Denbighshire.

Universal Supply Company, Hope Street
Owned by Thomas & Son in 1908, this shop sold 'gold and silver watches, chains and jewellery, clocks, cruets & cutlery, clothing, bedding, furniture and general miscellaneous goods'.

V

Vaughan, Rt Revd Francis John *Bishop of Menevia*
Born at Courtfield, Ross on Wye on 5 May 1877, the son of Colonel F. B. Vaughan, JP, DL, Francis Vaughan was a nephew of Cardinal Vaughan. He was educated at the Birmingham Oratory, Ushaw and the Sulpitian College in Paris and Rome. He became a curate in Port Talbot, then Rector of St Helen's Church, Barry Dock (1915–26) and was appointed Canon of the Cardiff Metropolitan Cathedral in 1922. Consecrated Bishop of Menevia on 8 September 1926 Francis Vaughan was the first bishop to live at Plas Tirion, Sontley Road which became Ty'r Esgob (Bishop's

Interior of the Vegetable Market, c.1972.

House). He died in office on 13 March 1935.

Vaults, The, High Street
Sited at N° 34 High Street these were spirit vaults located in the basement with cocoa rooms on the ground floor. In about 1823 they became the premises of Bartholomew Dillon, wine & spirit merchant, who was also the auditor of the Wrexham Union and accountant to the Wrexham branch of the North & South Wales Bank.* By 1833, his business had declined and he was then employed as a schoolmaster in King Street before being appointed as an actuary of the Wrexham Savings Bank* from which post he was removed in 1842.

Vegetable Market, Queen Street
This was a gradual development which began in the 1870s by the Market Hall Company which adapted the buildings known as Queen Square* and Birmingham Hall.* In 1898 the Borough Council bought the sites and as a result the area was extended and roofed over. A mock Tudor frontage was added on Queen Street, either side of an imposing entrance, and the area was then redesignated the Vegetable Market. The whole area was cleared during the 1980s (with the exception of the Queen Street frontage which survived into mid 1992) and the site is now occupied by the Henblas Square shopping precinct and WCBC offices.

Vernon Street, Rhosddu
This street was laid out in the 1890s and some of the houses were completed by 1896. It would appear that the street was named after Henrietta Vernon, the mother of the 1st Marquess of Westminster. Prior to the site's development, Wrexham AFC played Oswestry Town here on 7 September 1883, playing under floodlights powered by the Midland Electric Light & Power Company – one of the first football matches ever played under artificial lighting. Wrexham won the game 4–2.

The old Wrexham Vicarage in c.1895 when it was being used as offices for the construction of the Wrexham–Ellesmere railway. Behind the house is a station water tank and beyond that the gable end of the Brook Street British School.

(3) Beech Grove, Chester Road. This was built on the site of the 19th century house called Plas yn Llwyn* and was the home of the Batho family before the Second World War. The Church in Wales appears to have bought it for use as a vicarage in about 1939 and it became the Rectory in 1971. The church sold the house in the 1980s and it became Emral Guest House. During the Second World War, a motor pool of black American servicemen was billeted here as part of the US Army's policy of racial segregation. (See also Rectory)

Vicarage
(1) Located in the Bryn-y-Ffynnon area of the town, this three-storeyed brick house was built during the period that Thomas Edwards was Vicar of Wrexham (1731–70) and can be clearly seen in Buck's print of 1748. It stood opposite the junction of Abbot Street* and Vicarage Hill* and may have been built on the site of an earlier vicarage. It ceased to be used as a vicarage in 1826 and later became the property of Benjamin Piercy,* one of the prime movers behind the Wrexham & Ellesmere Railway Company.* In 1870, it was described as:

> a mansion house consisting of a kitchen about 5 yards square, with a small porch and scullery, a passage or hall, a laundry about 15 feet long by 10 broad, a sitting room built as a lean to, with no room over, two parlours, the larger ... square, the smaller 15 feet long by 10 broad, with lodging rooms and garrets and two cellars; also a brewing kitchen, a stable bay and coach house, and large garden fenced in with a stone and brick wall, the whole containing with the two cottages on north side of Well Street, 2 roods and 19½ perches.

It was sold to the Wrexham & Ellesmere Railway in 1880 for use as their company office, although an 1881 trade directory records a school (Head Master H. Poyner, MCP) at the Old Vicarage. The house became vacant before its demolition in 1897. Today, it is remembered in the name Vicarage Hill.* It is shown on both the 1833 and the 1872 surveys. It was while staying at the Vicarage as a guest of his father-in-law, the Revd Shipley, that Reginald Heber* wrote the famous Victorian missionary hymn 'From Greenland's Icy Mountains' which event is recorded by a plaque on Vicarage Hill.

(2) Llwyn Issa.*

These houses stood on Vicarage Hill between the Abbot Street junction and the railway bridge. The site is now occupied by student flats.

Vicarage Hill
Vicarage Hill takes its name from the old Wrexham Vicarage* which stood nearby. In 1844 it extended from Brook Street to Abbot Street then, in c.1877, was extended to link up with Priory Lane* (Street) and Hill Street.* A railway bridge was built across the street in the 1890s to carry the Wrexham–Ellesmere railway line (demolished in the 1990s). The large houses which stood on the east side of the street, just south of the Abbot Street junction, were originally thatched but had been re-roofed with slate by the early 20th century. These buildings were demolished in the 1970s and the site was left vacant until the late 1990s when, following the removal of the railway viaduct Snowdon Hall, a block of student flats, was built on the site. (See also Vicarage Hill Smithy).

Vicarage Hill Smithy
This property was sited immediately below the railway line on the south side of Vicarage Hill. In 1919 it consisted of two

smithies, each with one hearth and store sheds. [DRO/DD/G/2885] It was later converted into retail premises and was the Pink House (a ladies dress shop belonging to Miss Kathy Dougall*) and the premises of Bridge Books from 1979–85.

Vicars of Wrexham
See St Giles Church.

Victoria Brewery, Farndon Street
Established at the rear of the Cock* by John Morley in 1870, who appears to have gone bankrupt by 1879. The building was later converted into a flour mill. (See Victoria Mill)

Victoria Inn, Farndon Street
See The Cock and Victoria Brewery.

Victoria Hall, Brook Street
Housed in 1902 in the old British School,* the Victoria Hall Forward Movement Centre was first established in Belle Vue at what later became the Oddfellows Hall. The hall eventually became the offices of Aston & Son* and, in the past, has been a do-it-yourself and ironmongery shop and Scotts nightclub. The premises are currently (2010) vacant.

Victoria Mill.

Victoria Hall Forward Movement
A religious movement under the control of the Presbyterian Church. (See Victoria Hall) The Religious Census of 1904 showed: Capacity 1,100; attendance (AM & PM) 393. The Manse was located at Nº 13 Spring Road.

Victoria Mill, Farndon Street
The Victoria Brewery* was bought by John Allmond a grocer, tea dealer and corn miller (with retail premises in Hope Street and the Wilderness Mill in Gresford) who converted it into a flour mill. In 1895 the building was burned down but was re-built and was still operating at the outbreak of the First World War.

Victoria Place, Farndon Street
A small court development on the western side of Farndon Street,* backing on to Holt Street Buildings. It was shown on the 1872 survey.

Victoria Road
This road had existed as a quiet country lane until the 1880s when it was widened and made into an extension of Bradley Road,* thereby linking the growing town centre, Mold Road and the railway stations with Ruabon Road. House building along the

Welsh Methodist Church, Victoria Road.

road was a gradual process and was not completed until c.1905. It was named after Queen Victoria (1837–1901).

Victoria Road Welsh Wesleyan Methodist Church
Originally built as an 'iron' church in 1899. The Religious Census of 1904 showed: Capacity 80; attendance (AM & PM) 84.

Victoria Schools, Poyser Street
Following the transfer of responsibility for the British School in Brook Street from the managers to the Wrexham School Board* in 1898, plans were set in motion to build a new school on a 1.5 acre site in Cae Siac Field, Victoria Road.* The schools were designed by William Moss of Davies & Moss, Wrexham, and cost approximately £11,519 to build. They were officially opened by the Mayor of Wrexham on 1 January 1901. Following the implementation of the 1944 Education Act, the school became the Victoria Secondary Modern School and catered for pupils who had failed the 11-plus Entrance Examination for Grove Park Grammar School. In 1960 it became an infant and junior school. In 2010, the infant school had 142 on the roll and the junior school 228. They merged to become Victoria County Primary School in September 2010.

Headteachers:
Boys
1901–19   Charles Dodd*
1919–32   John Davies
1932–50   J. Jarvis Jones*
              C. R. R. Jones (served as acting headmaster during the Second World War)
Girls
1901–02   Miss Winifred Griffiths
1902–31   Miss Annie Elizabeth Wordsworth, OBE
              Miss F. E. Edwards (Mrs Purcell) (served as acting headmistress during the Second World War)

Juniors
1931–49 J. L. Mann
1950–66 Trevor E. Davies
1966–79 Edward D. Rydiard
1979–93 Miss Brenda Roberts, JP
1993–99 Philip Gallagher
1999–   John Hughes
Infants
1901–24 Miss A. Harris-Jones
1924–48 Miss F. K. Jones
1949–   Miss D. O. Jones
         Miss M. E. Humphreys
         Mrs Karen Davies
         John Hughes (acting)
Primary School
2010   John Hughes
Secondary Modern School
1950–60 Cerdyn Lloyd Thomas (became headmaster of Bryn Offa School*)

A detailed study of the setting up of the Victoria Board Schools is available in the *Transactions of the Denbighshire Historical Society*, Vol 46 (1997), 'A Board School: the Transfer of Responsibility and the Establishment of the Victoria Board Schools', by Gareth Vaughan Williams.

A memorial to those ex-pupils of the school who were killed in the First World War was unveiled by old boy Major Augustus Charles Herbert Benké, DSO, MC (later Governor of Pentonville, Walton and Wandsworth Prisons).

Victoria Evening School
Evening classes, run on a voluntary basis by Charles Dodd, were transferred to the Victoria Board Schools from the British Schools. In 1907 a paid headmaster was appointed to run the classes which continued for many years. During the 1920s the headmaster in charge was A. H. Jones who was under the overall control of the Wrexham Science and Art School.* Among the subjects taught in 1922 were: book-keeping, shorthand, home nursing, ambulance, arithmetic and English. Fees in that year were 5/- per term.

Village Court, Garden Village
A private housing development by local builders Harvey Homes in the late 1990s on land that was previously Garden Village Tennis Club. The name is a reference to the tennis club, using the words 'village' (as in Garden Village) and 'court' (as in tennis court).

Villiers Street, Rhosddu
This street was laid out in 1894 on land which had been part of the Red House estate. On the death of Benjamin Piercy* the land was sold off as building plots and most of the terraced houses here appear to have been built by 1900. The close proximity of these streets to the Cobden Flour Mill* undoubtedly attracted the developers to using the names of anti-Corn Law campaigners. This street was named after Charles Pelham Villiers (1802–98). A statues of him stand in front of the Agricultural Hall in Wolverhampton and in the Manchester Free Trade Hall.

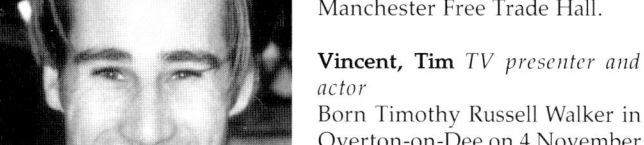

Vincent, Tim *TV presenter and actor*
Born Timothy Russell Walker in Overton-on-Dee on 4 November 1972, he was educated at Penley School and began acting at Theatr Clwyd in Mold. Aged 15, he was given the part of Billy

Tim Vincent

Ryan in Granada TV's children's drama series *Children's Ward* which he played for six series. He auditioned for the BBC children's programme *Blue Peter* and was given the job of presenter in 1993. Amongst other appearances, he has acted in *Dangerfield*, *Emmerdale*, presented *The Clothes Show* and appeared in the film *Sorted*. Since 2002, he has appeared on stage in *Bouncers* and *Lady Chatterley's Lover*. He has worked in the USA presenting *Phenomenon* and *Access Holly-wood*. In 2008, he was one of the contestants in the hit TV series *Dancing on Ice*.

Vogue Cinema, High Street
Opened on 26 July 1981 by Messrs Barry Flanagan (of the Hippodrome Cinema) and M. Roberts, the Vogue was a response to the upturn in interest in cinema during the 1970s. Located in rooms above the Jolly Tavern* in High Street, the Vogue was gutted by fire on 3 September 1986 and never re-opened. (*Ninety Years of Cinema in Wrexham*, Brian Hornsey, Privately published, 1990).

Vyrnwy Way, Queen's Park
Built in the late 1940s as part of the first phase of WBC's Queen's Park housing development. The street is named after Lake Vyrnwy in the Berwyn mountain range.

W

Waiters Arms, Yorke Street
Located on the east side of Yorke Street,* it appears in the 1872 survey. A headstone in the Burial Ground* on Ruthin Road records John Jones of the Waiters Arms, who died in 1836, and his wife Mary. [Lease DRO/1019]

Waithman, Robert *Lord Mayor of London*
He was born in Wrexham in 1764, the son of John and Mary (née Roberts) Waithman. His father, a joiner at the Bersham iron works, had originally hailed from Warton in Lancashire and had married Mary in Wrexham in 1761. John Waithman died in July 1764, aged 37, and was buried at the west end of Wrexham churchyard. Following the remarriage of his mother two years later, Robert was sent to live with an uncle in the Bath area. He received a basic education at a school owned by a Mr Moore which he left at the age of fourteen when he was sent to work in Reading from where he moved to London to take up employment with a linen draper.

By the time he was 22, Robert Waithman had opened his own business in the Fleet market which he later re-located to N[os] 103-4 Fleet Street (on the site of the present day Ludgate Circus). On 14 July 1787 he married his first cousin, Miss Mary Davies of Red Lion Street, Holborn. A very successful businessman, he amassed a large fortune and

Robert Waithman.

314

became involved in radical politics and was a regular debator at Fowler's Hall, advocating political reform and peace with the French revolutionary government. In 1796, he was elected to the Common Council of the ward of Farringdon Without where he was soon recognised as one of the leading orators. In 1812, he stood for election as the Member of Parliament for the City of London but was defeated. He won the seat in 1818, lost it in 1820, then regained it in 1826 and held it until his death some seven years later. A strong advocate of liberal policies, he was, however, opposed to free trade. He was elected an alderman of the City of London (representing Farringdon) on 4 August 1818. In the following year he was accused of obstructing the election of the Lord Mayor of London but was cleared of the charge and awarded costs. This event had no effect upon his continuing rise to prominence and in 1820 he was appointed Sheriff of London and Middlesex and, three years later, was elected Lord Mayor of London. The following year, his opponents published a successful political satire entitled *The Maxims of Robert, Lord Waithman, somewhile Chief Magistrate of London.*

Robert and Mary Waithman had a large family before she died in 1828. He died at his home in Woburn Place on 6 February 1833 and was buried in St Bride's Church, Fleet Street, where his memorial records him as being 'the friend of liberty, and of Parliamentary reform in its adverse days'. Another memorial, in the form of an obelisk, which was erected at the foot of Ludgate Hill, but has since been removed.

Walker, Peter *brewer & local politician*
Born in 1820, the eldest son of Peter and Mary (née Carlow) Walker of Auchinflower, Ayrshire. The family settled in Liverpool where Peter (senior) established a successful brewery. Aged 17, Peter was sent to train as a brewer to Joseph Clark* at the Cambrian Brewery* in Wrexham before returning to Liverpool to run the expanding wine and spirit business run by his father. From the 1840s, although still involved with the family business in Liverpool, he resided in Wrexham, most of the time at Coed-y-Glyn,* and when his brother (later Sir Andrew Barclay Walker, Bt, founder of the Walker Art Gallery and the Walker Engineering Laboratories) took over the running of Walker's Brewery in Warrington, Peter left the company. In 1860, he bought the small Willow Brewery* in Willow Road, Wrexham from Robert Evans (the father of R.W. Evans,* Mayor in 1892) which he expanded into one of the largest in the town.

Elected as a Tory member of WBC he served as Mayor in 1866 and 1867 but felt slighted when he was turned down for a further term in office and determined to move his brewery to Burton on Trent. He laid the foundation stone of his new premises on 17 February 1882 but died at his home Coed-y-Glyn, Wrexham on 13 April, aged sixty-two. The Willow Brewery closed down in 1865 and the business was transferred to Burton-on-Trent. Peter Walker, his two wives – (1) Agnes (his cousin) died in 1864 and (2) Jessie Crawford of Edinburgh who died in 1897 – and three of his children (Mary Jane, aged 1 year 5 months, William Carlaw, aged 7 years and Agnes, aged 7 years) are buried in the Ruthin Road Cemetery where his memorial obelisk is the only one still *in situ.** Another of his daughters, Elizabeth Anne, the wife of Richard Henry Venables Kyrke of Nant-y-Ffrith (the grandson of Richard Venables Kyrke* of Gwersyllt Hill), is buried in Wrexham Cemetery.*

Peter Walker presented the Parish Church with its pulpit in 1867 and, after his death, his executors complied with his wishes by contributing £1,000 towards the building of the National Schools* on Madeira Hill. He rebuilt the Salop Road Bridge –now known as the Willow Bridge*– at his own expense and gave £500 to the curates' augmentation fund at the Parish Church. At the time of his death he was the prospective Conservative candidate for Denbighshire. He was also one of the first to develop the Whitegate area of Wrexham when, in the 1880s he built Whitegate Farm* and two workmen's cottages off what is now Whitegate Road.*

Walker's Brewery, Willow Road
Peter Walker* bought the Willow Brewery* from Richard Evans in 1860 and rapidly developed it into the largest brewery in Wrexham by 1871, covering over 7,000 square yards. The brewery closed in September 1883, following Walker's decision to transfer his business to Burton-on-Trent which was a major economic blow to the town, particularly when one considers that the very large brewery that he built in Burton-on-Trent could easily have been built in Wrexham. The brewery buildings were bought by the Wrexham Corporation and accommodated the main council depot, workshops, stables, offices, refuse destructor, electricity generator, public baths,* public laundry, public swimming pool and assembly rooms. The premises were gutted by fire in the early 1970s and demolished shortly afterwards. The Walker company returned to Wrexham in 1909 when it bought the Union Brewery* in Yorke Street.

Walks, The, Bryn-y-Ffynnon
The Walks was a footpath which ran from Vicarage Hill* and Well Square,* along the back of the Island Green Brewery* and passed to the south of St Mark's Church.* It disappeared under the development of the Wrexham, Mold & Connah's Quay Railway during the 1880s. A terrace of poor quality housing, built just below the railway line, off Brewery Place, was also known as The Walks and was the subject of a compulsory purchase order in 1938 as part of the Borough slum clearance programme.

Walnut Street, Rhosddu
Developed in the late 19th century and named after the Walnut Tree* pub, it is located on the land of the former Walnut Tree Farm.*

Walnut Tree Farm, Rhosddu
The earliest records that Palmer* found of this farm are dated 1762 when it was the property of Robert Griffiths. In the early 19th century the farm was the property of Robert Griffith of Hafod-y-Bwch* and in 1844 had an area of just under 39 acres in fields on both sides of what is now Price's Lane* with a northern boundary following Wat's Dyke.* In 1861, the tenant was butcher and farmer, Thomas Price.

This farm, which also appears to have been known as Rhosddu Farm, gave its name to the Walnut Tree Hotel.*

Walnut Tree Hotel, Rhosddu Road
This public house stands on the site of what was originally (until the early 19th century) Rhosddu Farm* (see also Walnut Tree Farm), the property of the Griffiths (later Murhall-Griffiths) family. The hotel had been built by 1881 when the licensee was William Wilson (died 1884). During the Second World War the pub was the meeting place of the Walnut Hotel Air Raid Post and the Walnut Hotel Auxiliary Fire Squad. The Walnut Tree closed in 2010.

Walters, MBE, **Philip John** *Town Clerk & Freeman*
Philip Walters was born on 27 February 1906, at Gowerton, Swansea, the son of David Walters. He was educated at Gowerton County School and the University College of Wales, Swansea, where he studied law, gaining a 2nd Class Honours degree. In May 1929 he qualified as a solicitor, was articled to C. H. K. Newcombe, solicitors, in Swansea from 1924–29 and, on qualifying, was appointed part-time Clerk to the Gower Rural District Council.

He became the Assistant Town Clerk of Swansea in 1930 and the fourth Town Clerk of Wrexham in June 1937, a position which he held until his retirement in 1971. During the Second World War, he was appointed Food Executive Officer, National Registration Officer and Chief Billeting Officer for East Denbighshire. In the immediate post-war period, he was instrumental in developing the former Royal Ordnance Factory,* Marchwiel into the Wrexham Industrial Estate* and was closely involved with the negotiations which led to the purchase of land for the development of the new Queen's Park* Housing Estate and the expansion of the Acton Park Housing Estate.*

He was awarded the MBE in 1941 and in 1971 became the 25th person to be made a Freeman of Wrexham. He was the Secretary of the Association of Welsh Local Authorities, Captain of Wrexham Golf Club and served as President of the Rotary Club of Wrexham* in 1971–72. He was married to Jacqueline Harding of Swansea and lived at Gorwydd, Nº 9 Westminster Drive* and later at Gorwydd, Nº 5 Maes-y-Dre Road.* He died on 6 December 1984. Philip's Close in Borras is named after him.

Warburton-Lee, VC, Bernard Armitage Warburton *naval officer*

Born Bernard Armitage Warburton Lee at Broad Oak, Redbrook, Maelor on 3 September 1895, the son of Joseph and Eva Warburton Lee (the family name was changed to Warburton-Lee in 1919). He was educated at Malvern Link Prep School, Osborne College and Dartmouth Royal Naval College and passed out from HMS *Cornwall* in 1912. During the First World War he served on the light cruiser HMS *Hyacinth* and was involved in the hunt for and sinking of the German light cruiser *Koenigsberg* off the coast of East Africa before joining HMS *Cherwell* serving with the Grand Fleet in 1916. He served on destroyers for the remainder of the war and received a Mention in Despatches in 1918. He attended the RN College Greenwich and continued to serve on destroyers during the 1920s, gaining his first command, HMS *Sterling*, in 1925. He attended the Staff Course at the RN College, Greenwich in 1931 and Camberley in 1932, becoming a captain in 1936. This was followed by a period at the Imperial Defence College and promotion to flag captain and chief of staff to the vice-admiral Commanding the Reserve Fleet. In July 1939 he received the appointment of OC the 2nd Destroyer Flotilla, HMS *Hardy*, perhaps the pinnacle of achievement for an active naval officer and was destined to reach the very highest ranks of the Royal Navy. In April 1940 he was ordered to Norway and commanded the British naval forces at the first battle of Narvik on 10 April where he was killed and received a posthumous Victoria Cross. The citation for the VC reads:

> For gallantry, enterprise and daring in command of the Force engaged in the first Battle of Narvik, on the 10th April, 1940. On being ordered to carry out an attack on Narvik, he learned from Tranoy that the enemy held the place in much greater force than had been thought. He signalled to the Admiralty that the enemy were reported to be holding Narvik in force, that six destroyers and one submarine were there, that the channel might be mined, and that he intended to attack at dawn, high water. The Admiralty replied that two Norwegian Coast Defence Ships might be in German hands, that he alone could judge whether to attack, and that whatever decision he made would have full support. Captain Warburton-Lee gave out the plan for his attack and led his Flotilla of five Destroyers up the fjord in heavy snowstorms, arriving off Narvik just after daybreak. He took the enemy completely by surprise and made three successful attacks on warships and merchantmen in the harbour. The last attack was made after anxious debate. On the Flotilla withdrawing, five enemy Destroyers of superior gun-power were encountered and engaged. The Captain was mortally wounded by a shell which hit *Hardy's* bridge. His last signal was 'Continue to engage the enemy'.

The crippled HMS *Hardy* was then abandoned and Warburton-Lee died shortly after being brought ashore. He is buried in Ballangen New Cemetery, Narvik (British Plot 4, Row B, Grave 9).

Bernard Warburton-Lee married Elizabeth Campbell-Swinton in 1924 and had one son, Philip.

The most detailed account of his career appears in *Heart of a Dragon, the VCs of Wales and the Welsh regiments, 1914–82* by W. Alister Williams.

Bernard Warburton-Lee, VC.

Warburton-Lee's destroyer HMS Hardy.

Ward, Rt Revd John Aloysius *Bishop of Menevia*

Born on 24 January 1929, the son of Eugene and Hannah Ward (née Cheetham) John Ward spent part of his childhood in Wrexham and was a former pupil of St Mary's RC School.* He was later a student at Prior Park College, Bath and joined the Capuchin Franciscans at Pantasaph in 1945. Ordained a priest in 1953 he worked with the Diocese of Menevia Travelling Mission (1954–60) before becoming guardian and parish priest in Peckham, London. He was Provincial Definitor (1963–69), Director of Vocations (1963–69) and Delegate to the Secular Order of Franciscans (1966–69). Becoming Minister Provincial in 1969 he moved to Rome where he was appointed Definitor General of the order in 1970. Ten years later he was appointed Bishop Coadjutor of Menevia and, the following year, Bishop of Menevia. In 1983 he became Archbishop of Cardiff, a position which he held until 26 October 2001 when he resigned following accusations of having ignored warnings about paedophile priests in Cardiff.

Waring Court, Hightown

This was a development by the Wales and West Housing Association in the early 1980s on land that had previously been the property of C. T. Clark. All the streets in the development were named after RWF who had been awarded the Victoria Cross.

Lance Sergeant William Waring was born at Rock Terrace, Welshpool on 13 October 1885, the son of Richard and Annie Waring. He was educated at Christ Church Church of England School and the National School, Welshpool before taking up employment with a local poultry dealer. He enlisted in the Montgomeryshire Yeomanry in 1904 and was a sergeant on the outbreak of war in 1914. He saw active service in Egypt and Mesopotamia from March 1916–April 1918, transferring to the 24th Bn, RWF in 1917. He served in France and Flanders from May 1918 until his death in October. He was seriously wounded at Ronssoy in September and died of his wounds on 8 October 1918. William Waring is buried in Sainte Marie Cemetery, Le Havre (Division 62, Plot 5, Row 1, Grave 3). The citation for his VC reads:

> For most conspicuous bravery and devotion to duty at Ronssoy on the 18th September, 1918. He led an attack against enemy machine guns which were holding up the advance of neighbouring troops and, in the face of devastating fire from the flank and front, single handed, rushed a strong point, bayonetting four of the garrison and capturing twenty with their guns.
> Lance Sergeant Waring then, under heavy shell and machine gun fire, reorganised his men and led and inspired them for another 400 yards, when he fell mortally wounded.
> His valour, determination and leadership were conspicuous throughout.

Warren, Earls of
On 12 October 1282, King Edward I granted the *rhaglotries* of Wrexham, Marford and Yale to John, Earl of Warren who started building the castle at Holt as the centre of the lordship of Bromfield and Yale.* He passed the lordship on to his son, William de Warren in 1284 (died 1285) and the land passed to his son John, Earl of Warren. From John, the lordship passed, through a female line, to Edmund Fitzalan, the fifth Earl of Arundel.

Warrenwood Road
This road, which was laid out during the early 1960s, was on land that was once part of the Acton Park estate. It may have been the 'small Garden at Pwll-y-Warren [which I bought] from Lord Kenyon for £10 to build cottages' in 1803, that is recorded in the journal of Sir Foster Cunliffe*. The land in this area was sold by Sir Neville Cunliffe* in 1920 to Albert John Jones of Ty'n Twll Farm* and by him, in 1937, to William Clarke.* In 1958, it was sold to the London developers Spinks & Denning who built most of the eastern section of the Borras Park Estate.* It took its name from Parc-y-Cwning* which once covered much of this area.

Warwick Avenue, Whitegate
This was built by WBC in 1946–47 in the wake of the 1936 Housing Act on land that was previously part of Whitegate Farm.* The origin of the name is unknown.

Waterloo Close, Hermitage
A small cul-de-sac of flats developed by WBC as part of the Hermitage housing estate on land that was previously part of the Hermitage Camp.* All the streets on the development have military connections, in this case, named after the Battle of Waterloo, fought in Belgium on 18 June 1815, between the Allied forces under the command of the Duke of Wellington and the French forces under the command of Napoleon Bonaparte. Wrexham's local regiment, the RWF,* fought with great distinction at the battle.

Waterloo Tavern, Town Hill
See the Blue Bell.

Watery Road
Originally called Watery Lane (renamed in 1955), this is one of the old thoroughfares of Wrexham and was the route into the town from Croesnewydd. It takes its name from its position alongside the river Gwenfro and the mill race for the Pentre Felin Mill.* The old stone and thatched cottages that were built in this area were demolished in the early 20th century to make way for the superior terraced houses that now occupy the site.

Thatched houses on Watery Road, c.1895 with properties in Bellevue Road on the left.

Wat's Dyke
Wat's Dyke is an ancient earthwork, little more than a low grassy bank in many places (and missing altogther in others) which is believed to have been built by the Anglo-Saxons as a boundary or frontier between the territory conquered by them and the land to the west that was still under Welsh control. No exact date can be given for its construction and various dates between 640 and 750 are generally accepted. The dyke extends from near Flint in the north to the Morda brook near Oswestry in the south and incorporates a number of older hill forts (including Caer Estyn and Old Oswestry). The origin of the name is also unknown although it is believed to come from the Saxon name Wada who may have been the builder.

In the area of the town of Wrexham, Wat's Dyke came through the Alun valley, along the western boundary of what is now Garden Village and then followed the railway line to Wrexham Cemetery where it then cut across to follow the top of the valley of the Clywedog through part of Erddig Park (forming the boundary of The Court* and Green Park on the way), Middle Sontley and then on towards Ruabon. Much of the dyke was destroyed in the 19th and 20th centuries during the building of the railway, the cemetery and Green Park. The boundary fence between Crispin Lane* and the railway line follows almost exactly the line of Wat's Dyke. The name is often incorrectly written as Watt's Dyke.

Wat's Dyke School
Plans to build what was originally called Garden Village Infants School on 5.5 acres close to Wat's Dyke were revealed in 1961 but little progress was made until the dramatic expansion of the Croes Eneurys and Tŷ Gwyn areas in the 1960s and 1970s compelled the local authority to make further provision for primary school children in this area. The opening of the school was scheduled for 1976 but due to the bankruptcy of the builders,

did not take place until September 1977. Built to accommodate 180 children, Wat's Dyke now (2010) caters for 252 pupils. It is named after Wat's Dyke* which is located nearby.

Headteachers:
1977–98   John Dwyfor Williams, BEd
1998–   Robert Alun Evans, BEd

Wat's Dyke Way
The houses on the east side of this street are part of the original Garden Village Estate,* and a plaque between N°s 23 & 25 displays the date '1914'. Only some of the houses were built with cavity walls; whether this was because of brick shortages during the First World War or whether it was simply a cost-cutting exercise is unrecorded. The western side of the street (between Ffordd Estyn and Ael-y-Bryn) was mainly built by private developers in the mid 1960s. This street is located close to the ancient Wat's Dyke* earthwork from which it takes its name.

Wavell Avenue
Originally a street of three pre-fabricated houses, built shortly after the Second World War, Wavell Avenue was re-built as part of the Queen's Park* housing estate.

The street was named after Field Marshal Archibald Percival Wavell, PC, GCB, GCSI, GCIE, CMG, MC, LlD, DCL, 1st Earl Wavell of Cyrenaica and Winchester, Viscount Keven of Eritrea and Winchester (1889–1950).

Weale Court, Hightown
A development by the Wales and West Housing Association in the early 1980s on land that had previously been the property of C.T. Clark. All the streets in the development were named after RWF who had been awarded the Victoria Cross.

L/Cpl Henry (Harry) Weale was born at Nine Houses, Shotton on 2 October 1897, the son of John and Sarah Weale, was educated at St Ethelwald's School in Shotton and worked as a packer at John Summer's Steelworks. He enlisted in the 5th Bn, RWF (Territorial Force) in 1911 and was discharged in 1913 on joining the 3rd Bn, RWF (Special Reserve). Mobilised in 1914 he was on active service in France by November. Wounded in 1914 and 1915 and gassed in 1917, he was awarded the Victoria Cross for his action at Bazentin-le-Grand on 26 August 1918. The citation for his Victoria Cross reads:

> For most conspicuous bravery. The adjacent battalion having been held up by enemy machine guns, Lance Corporal Weale was ordered to deal with the hostile posts. When his Lewis gun failed him, on his own initiative, he rushed the nearest posts and killed the crew, then went for the others, the crews of which fled on his approach, this gallant non-commissioned officer pursuing them. His very dashing deed cleared the way for the advance, inspired his comrades and resulted in the capture of all the machine guns.

After being discharged in 1919, Harry Weale re-joined the 5th RWF and saw service in Ireland until 1922. He returned to his old job at John Summer's and later worked in Holywell and Rhyl. He married Susie Harrison of Rhyl in 1919 and they had four sons and one daughter. He died in Rhyl on 13 January 1959 and is buried in Rhyl Cemetery.

Weights & Measures
Before the advent of standardised weights and measures for the whole of the United Kingdom, each market town set the standard for the weights and measures in its area. In the case of Wrexham, the town was responsible for setting the weights and measures for the lordship of Bromfield and Yale and the northern part of the lordship of Chirk. An official would be appointed who would be responsible for looking after the various implements used in measuring capacity and weight. Any trader who wished to use the weights and measures would have to pay a fee to the official. It appears that these were in use until at least 1551, shortly after which date they became standardised throughout the country and the new national weights and measures were used by each market town.

Welch, Edward *architect*
Born in Overton in 1806, Edward Welch was a pupil of John Oates of Halifax. In 1828 he became a partner of Joseph Aloysius Hansom (of Hansom cab fame) and established a practice in York before moving to Liverpool. They designed a number of significant buildings throughout Britain but were declared bankrupt while work was being executed on their design for Birmingham Town Hall (1832–4). The partnership was then dissolved and Welch practised on his own from 1837–49. He later became an inventor and registered several patents dealing with the heating and ventilation of houses. He died in Southampton Row, London on 3 August 1868. His obituary in *The Builder* described him as '… a man of liberal and expansive ideas, and generously open to the merits and abilities of others, while modestly undervaluing his own'. In Wrexham, he is best remembered as the architect of the Savings Bank* on Regent Street (1837) and Rhosymedre Church (1836–7). Further afield, he designed: Beaumaris Gaol in Anglesey (1828–9); King William's College on the Isle of Man (1830–3); Victoria Terrace and the Bulkeley Arms Hotel, Beaumaris (1830–5); Bodelwyddan Castle (1830–40); Birmingham Town Hall (1832–4) and the Northern Hospital, Liverpool (1834).

Welch Entry, Queen Street
Recorded on the 1841 census, probably located between Lambpit Street and Henblas Street, this small street was occupied by skilled craftsmen (mostly shoe makers) and their families.

Welch Fusilier, Chester Street
Originally the site of the Red Lion,* this public house was re-built and enlarged in the 1930s by Bents Brewery. It was re-named the Welch Fusilier in recognition of the close association of Wrexham with the R.W.F.*

Well House, Well Square
This substantial three-storeyed house (plus an attic) stood in Well Square* and can be seen in both the 1833 and 1872 surveys of Wrexham. It was probably built in the first half of the 18th century and is first mentioned in the rate books in 1742. Built of brick with stone coynings and a slate roof, the house took its name from the Town Well* which was located opposite its front door. It had a small front garden which was located in that small detached section of the township of Esclusham* that covered the area now occupied by the eastern end of the Island Green* shopping precinct. The house itself was in the township of Wrexham Abbot.* The northern gable end of the house can be seen in a drawing of Well Square which was reproduced in A.N. Palmer's *History of the Town of Wrexham*. Adjoining the house, and a clear indication of its status in the town, was a cobbled yard edged on two sides by a barn, stable, coach-house and hay-loft. The first recorded occupant of the house was Edward James of Pen-y-Bryn, a currier, who was living there in 1744. He was married to Mary (died 1749 aged 29) and had one son and two daughters and was a churchwarden at the Parish Church.* He died 21 October 1772, aged 66, and the property passed to Thomas Edwards, a tanner of Pen-y-Bryn who lived at the 'Palace' in Pen-y-Bryn (probably a distortion of Plasdy or Plas and likely to have been the house known as Plas-y-Bryn*), a relative

Well Square.

of the Edwards family of Stansty.* He was also a churchwarden in 1776-7 and died in 1797 when the property passed to his eldest son, Thomas. Thomas Edwards, a wealthy man, was nicknamed 'The King' and lived at the house with his brother John, another currier and churchwarden (1807–08), who was nicknamed 'The Duke'. When the Wrexham & Ellesmere Railway Company* published their plans for the construction of the railway line through this part of Wrexham, they were obliged to buy the house and it was demolished in 1896.

Well Square
Well Square was an area close to the south of Hill Street (before that street was extended to link into the top of Vicarage Hill*) surrounding the Town Well.* The square could be accessed from the north via Bryn-y-Ffynnon Lane, an extension of Priory Street/Lane* (before it was demolished for the building of the Central Station*); from the west via The Walks;* from the east via Well Street* and from the south via Bath Street,* which linked it through to Brook Street.* The most prominent building here was Well House.* On the south side of the square was a public house called The Steps* (probably after the steps leading down to the Town Well) and, at the junction of Bryn-y-Ffynnon Lane, two cottages, one of which was called, according to Palmer,* the 'Fox and Goose'* and so may well have also have been a public house. It may be, however, that Palmer was mistaken and that this building was called the 'Fox & Dog'* which is shown on the 1833 survey. Palmer records that there was a plaque on the front of this building which bore the initials 'E.W.M.' and 'R.I.P.' and the inscription 'Blessed are they that trust in God. 1693'. The area was built over in the 1890s during the construction of the Wrexham & Ellesmere Railway* and now lies beneath the railway viaduct and the eastern end of the Island Green* shopping centre.

Wellington Place
See King Street.

Wellington Road, Pen-y-Bryn
Laid out in the mid 19th century, this short street was undoubtedly named after Arthur Wellesley, 1st Duke of Wellington (1769–1852), soldier, statesman and Prime Minister.

Wellswood Road, Barker's Lane
Built in the late 1970s by Broseley Homes. The origin of the name is unknown.

Welsh Baptist Church, Temperance Hall
The Religious Census of 1881 showed: Capacity 250; attendance (AM & PM) 106.

Welsh Entry, Queen Street
This was a narrow passageway between Ebeneser Chapel and the houses which stood to the north of it.

Welsh Guards Memorial, Bodhyfryd
An exact replica of the memorial to those Welsh Guardsmen killed during the Falklands War of 1982, erected at Fitzroy in the Falkland Islands, was officially unveiled at Bodhyfryd in June 2002 following a service in St Giles Church.

> IN MEMORY OF THOSE
> WELSH GUARDSMEN
> KILLED IN ACTION
> FALKLAND ISLANDS 1982
> 1ST BATTALION
> WELSH GUARDS
> G SQUADRON 22ND SAS REGIMENT
> YN ANGOF NI CHANT FOD
> WE WILL REMEMBER THEM

This memorial was produced (at a cost of £5,000) by Blackwells Stonecraft of Handbridge, Chester, the principal of which, Steve Blackwell is a resident of Llong, near Mold. Two former members of the company, John and Joseph Blackwell had both served in the Welsh Guards.

Wentworth Rise
Developed in the early 1980s on land that had previously been part of Plas Goulbourne Farm, this street of private houses was named after Wentworth golf course.

Wesleyan Day School
Founded in 1842 and accommodated in a chapel schoolroom. The location of this school is unrecorded but details were published in the *Report on the State of Education in Wales, 1847*:

'A school for boys and girls taught together by a master, in a room belonging to the Wesleyan chapel. Number of children, 85. Subjects taught – the Scriptures, the Wesleyan Catechism, reading, writing, and arithmetic. Fees, 1d. per week.

'I examined this school January 21. I found 39 scholars present, 16 of whom had been members of the school for more than two years, and many of them for more than four years. I heard 11

N°s 4–12 Wellington Road.

read a chapter of the Bible with ease. This appeared to be the extent of their attainments. None could write well, even upon a slate; none could work an easy sum of Addition of money; and none possessed a competent knowledge of Scripture. No one could tell me the meaning of the words *gospel* or *epistle*, although they all understand English.

'The master has never been trained to teach. He was formerly a cooper, and still follows that trade occasionally. His school is arranged on the British System; but he does not understand its operation. His pupils are undisciplined and noisy. There is no method of organization; the monitors are incompetent, and the children ignorant. No instruction is given in needlework, although a large proportion of the scholars are girls.

'The school-room is large, but ill lighted and dirty. The books and general apparatus are deficient.'

West Street, Rhosddu
Originally called Nelson Street, the name was probably changed to West Street to avoid confusion with the Nelson Street* which existed in Hightown. The name may originate from Lady Cecelie Victoria Cunliffe, wife of the 5th Baronet, whose maiden name was Sackville-West (see also Cunliffe Family and Price's Lane) but this seems unlikely as the street was still shown as West Street on the 1912 Ordnance Survey. More likely is the possibility that the street was re-named in the 1920s at the same time that a name was given to a new street on the opposite side of the railway lines, *viz* East Avenue. The name is a simple reference to the fact that the street is on the west side of the railway.

Westminster Buildings, Regent Street
Often referred to as Argyle Buildings, this property spans the archway leading from Regent Street to Argyle Street. It was built in 1875 by Wrexham engineer William Low* as a dowry for his daughter Alison (who married Dr Edwards-Jones). The contractor was W. E. Samuel* (who also built the North & South Wales Bank* building in High Street) and the cost was £6,000. There were originally two windows under the arch but these were bricked up, although their location can still be clearly seen. It served as the main entrance to the Wrexham Agricultural and Scientific Society Exhibition* of 1876. During the time of the Exhibition, the archway was secured by means of gates that had been loaned from Eaton Hall in Cheshire. The site had previously been occupied by a substantial town house which dated back to the 17th century, the occupants of which are given in some detail in A. N. Palmer's *History of the Town of Wrexham*. There is a memorial plaque to William Low under the arch.

Westminster Drive
The first part of this road, linking Maes-y-Dre Road* to Chester Road,* was laid out before the First World War but was seen as an extension of the former and not a road in its own right. In the 1930s, land was bought from Clarke Brothers (bakers of Yorke Street) to enable Chester Road to be linked through to the developing Park Avenue.* Some of the houses, e.g. Nos 12 and 14, were built before the Second World War but the majority, e.g. Nos 9, 15 and 17 (built by Charles Knight, manager of the Rainbow Stores in Hope Street) were built post-1945. Town Clerk Philip Walters* lived for a time at No 9. The Rectory moved from the former Vicarage* on Chester Road* to No 7 in the 1980s.

Westminster Temperance Hotel, Grosvenor Road
Located at Nos 7/9 Grosvenor Road, this hotel was owned by Mrs Voyce (1912) and Misses D. & D. Beirne (1951)

Westminster Private Hotel, King Street
This business first appears in a sale held in 1921 when it was bought by T.R. Voyce. It was situated on the north-west corner at the junction of King Street and Regent Street. Part of this building was also occupied by the Land Valuation Office. It was purchased by Denbighshire Education Committee on 28 November 1952 for use as a hostel for students of the Denbighshire Technical College.* It opened in 1953 and could accommodate 30 students. [DRO/DD/G/2899 & 1097]

Westwood, MA, LLD, **Rt Revd Dr William** *Bishop of Peterborough*
Born in Wrexham in 1925, Bill Westwood was educated at Grove Park Boys School* and Emmanuel College and Westcott House, Cambridge where he gained an MA. He served in the airborne forces from 1944–47 before entering the church and being appointed curate of Hull in 1952. Most of his clerical career was spent in East Anglia (Rector of Lowestoft, 1957; Vicar of St Peter Mancroft, Norwich, 1965; Rural Dean of Norwich, 1966; City Dean of Norwich, 1970; Bishop of Edmonton, 1975 and Bishop of Peterborough, 1984. He served in many important administrative positions within the Church of England and was honoured by being made a Freeman of the City of London in 1977 and given an Honorary LLD by the University of Leicester in 1991. He died suddenly in October 1999, shortly after his son had been the victim of a shooting incident in London.

White Bear, High Street
This half-timbered public house, also known as The Bear,* stood on the site now occupied by the Market Hall*.

White Bear Inn, Yorke Street
Located on the east side of Yorke Street* this inn appears in the 1872 survey.

White Horse Inn, Holt Street
This was located on the northern side of Holt Street, opposite the junction with Farndon Street. It was sold in July 1919. The site is now part of Bodhyfryd. [DRO/D/G/2887]

White Lion, Hope Street
Located at No 59 Hope Street, this public house was owned by Rowland Samuel (see also King's Head (II), Hope Street) from *c*.1742 until 1757 when it became a brazier's shop. In 1777, the premises were described as comprising '... a large shop, with parlour, kitchen and scullery, a large dining room, and seven lodging rooms, with a workshop and two large wine cellars'. It was licensed as a wine merchants in 1810 and, in 1832, was bought by Joseph Clark* (see Cambrian Brewery) as the Wine & Spirit Vaults. In 1841 the licensee was Edward Wilde. In 1893 it was Messrs Summers & Fitch's Vaults.

White Lion, Mount Street
This appears in the 1833 survey as being located on the north side of the street, almost opposite the Nags Head.* The licence for this public house was surrendered in 1889. There was a bowling green located at the rear of these premises.

Whitegate Farm, Whitegate Lane
This farm was located on the east side of Whitegate Lane (Road),* half way between the Ellesmere Railway line and King's Mills Road and was built by Wrexham brewer Peter Walker.* The property was up for sale by auction in November 1900 and by 1912 is listed in the Trade Directory as Whitegate Stud Farm. [DRO/DD/G/2861] The original farm house, which stands on the corner of Whitegate Road and Connor Crescent, is now Nos 18 & 20 Whitegate Road. Before the Second War Whitegate was a stud farm.

Whitegate Road
Named after Whitegate Farm* which was located nearby, it was

originally known as Whitegate Lane. This road was re-aligned after the construction of the road bridge over the Ellesmere Railway in the 1890s. It was partially widened in 1962. In 1961, the body of Janet Roberts was found outside the Hightown Bakery (then the school meals service kitchens) in Whitegate Road; she had been battered to death. Scotland Yard were called in to investigate the crime but it was solved by local police detective Charlie Matthews before the London detectives arrived in Wrexham. Terry Hughes was convicted of the murder and sentenced to life imprisonment. The Council houses on this road (Nos 2–12) were built in 1946–47, the remainder were built pre-war (G. F. Sumner & Sons being the main contractors).

Whitehouse, KCB, MICE, Sir George *railway engineer*
Sir George Whitehouse was born on 26 July 1857, the son of George Whitehouse, a schoolmaster of Wrexham. In later years his father became a prosperous coal merchant with premises in Regent Street. George (junior) attended the British School,* Brook Street and Grove Park School.* before becoming a student at King's College, London. He became a Member of the Institute of Chartered Engineers in 1892. In 1895 he became the Manager of the Uganda Railway Company and selected Nairobi as the company's headquarters. From 1904–9 he was Chief Engineer to the Argentine Railways and was later involved in railway developments in India, Mexico and Peru. Married to Florence Cecilia Hyatt, he spent his latter days at Sudbury in Suffolk and died on 17 November 1938.

Mrs White's Orphan Home
See Greystones.

Wilkinson, John *industrialist*
Born in Cumberland in 1728, the son of Isaac Wilkinson, an ironmaster, John was educated at the Dissenting Academy in Kendal. His father leased the Bersham Furnace, Wrexham in 1754 and moved to live at Plas Grono,* Erddig. John followed him into the iron industry and owned his own blast furnace at Bilston, Stafford-shire. He later joined his father's business and came to live at Wrexham Fechan* with his wife (who died in 1756 and was buried in Wrexham Parish Church*).

Isaac Wilkinson's business failed and he ceased trading in 1761 when the business was taken over by John and his brother William under the name of The New Bersham Company. By the mid-1770s, John was involved with James Watt in the manufacture of steam engines following the development at Bersham Iron Works* of a patent cannon boring machine. In 1792, he bought the Brymbo Hall* estate (c.500 acres) which contained rich deposits of both iron ore and coal. He built a lead smelting plant on the Minera-Chester Road, sank coal and ore pits at Caello and, eventually, moved his works from Bersham to Brymbo. His original furnace on the new site, 'Old Number One', is on record as being in production by 1796.

Wilkinson served as High Sheriff of Denbighshire in 1799. He died at his home at Hadley on 14 July 1808 and was buried in his garden at Castlehead. In 1828, his body was moved to inside Lindal Chapel in Cumbria. His property and business was inherited by his son, also named John. (see also The Court)

Wilkinson, William *industrialist*
The younger brother of John Wilkinson,* William was employed in the family iron works at Bersham* and, on the failure of the company, became a partner with John in the New Bersham Company. The brothers had irreconcilable differences which ended the partnership and William moved to France where he established a number of businesses by the mid 1790s. He was a shareholder in the Paris Water Works Company which set about providing the French capital with a modern supply of water. The contract for the provision of pipes for this company was given to John Wilkinson as a result of which he was accused of supplying the French government with cannon at a time when Britain and France were at war but no charges were brought against him. William married the daughter of James Stockdale of Carke in Lancashire and had two daughters. In 1797 he was living at The Court* in Wrexham then moved to Plas Grono.* He died in 1808 and was buried in the Dissenters Burial Ground,* Rhosddu Road on 5 March.

William Aston College, Mold Road.
See Denbighshire Technical College.

William & John Jones Charity Trusts
This charity was set up in accordance with the terms of the will of John Jones* of Grove Lodge, Wrexham. In his will, he specified that Dr Richard Williams (Bersham Lodge), Harry Croom-Johnson* (The Elms*) and Richard Geoffrey Williams, MRCS (Egerton House*), all medical practitioners, should be the Trustees and that two establishments should be set up, the first at the Claremont Hydro, Brighton Road in Rhyl, to provide a convalescent home by the sea (to be closed each year between 15 November and 15 April) and the second, on the Plas Gwyn estate in Minera, to provide a 34-bed convalescent home. These homes were to be available for the use of working class inhabitants of the parishes of Wrexham and Rhosddu but, if any vacancies existed that could not be filled from these two parishes, then residents could be taken from anywhere. Sufficient monies were to be set aside from his estate to allow for the annual running costs of both homes.

The Rhyl home was opened in 1915 with a total of 50 beds. Patients were admitted free of charge and, by 1953, 17,346 people had benefitted from a period of convalescence in Rhyl. During the Second World War, the home was requisitioned by the Ministry of Health between September 1939 and July 1948. It did not re-open until 1950.

The Minera Home was purpose-built and opened in 1918 with a capacity of 34 beds. By 1953, 4,877 patients had been admitted, again without any charge whatsoever. On the outbreak of war in 1939, the home was taken over as accommodation for evacuees. In 1951, it was found that the income from the fund was insufficient to meet the costs of running both homes and the

John Wilkinson.

Minera Home was sold to Denbighshire County Council who opened it as a residential home for the elderly on 14 November 1952. In 1958, the Claremont site was sold to Flintshire County Council and a new home was bought on East Parade, Rhyl. The Trust offices were located for many years at N° 51 King Street before moving to N°ˢ 44–46 Bridge Street in 1965. Today the Trust office is in College House* at the Parish Church.*
[DRO/DD/DM/379/1–19 & DRO/DD/DM/777]

William Jones Recreation Ground, Rhosddu
The land for this park (which is located alongside Garden Road) was given to the Corporation of Wrexham by local philanthropist and brewer, John Jones* of Grove Lodge, in memory of his brother, William Jones.* William died in 1904 and the park was laid out in 1907.

The 1881 Football Association of Wales Cup semi-final match, when Newtown White Stars beat Llanidloes 2–0 is recorded as having been played at the Recreation Ground, Rhosddu and Wrexham Football Club also played all their home matches on the Recreation Ground between 1883 and 1887. Whether this was the same ground (privately owned) as the William Jones Recreation Ground or another location is unknown.

Williams, Barrie Charles *local politician*
Barrie Williams was born on 25 February 1952 and brought up in Gwersyllt. He was educated at Holy Trinty School, Gwersyllt and Grove Park School, followed by Bingley College of Education where he gained a Certificate in Education. In September 1973 he began work at Sefton Park Secondary School, Liverpool but left teaching in 1977 and began a career in the transport industry as a driver with Crosville Motor Services. Quickly rising to Inspector he joined Midland Red (North) as a traffic controller in 1990 and now holds the same position with Arriva.

Elected as the Labour member for Gwersyllt on Clwyd County Council in 1985, he served as the Chairman of the Highways and Transportation Committee. On the re-organisation of local government in 1996 he became the member for Gwersyllt South-East on WMBC and was Chairman of the Transportation and Engineering Committee. He became Mayor in 1998 and presided over the opening of the long awaited St Giles Way section of the inner ring road. He also became the first Mayor to marry while in office and his wife, Suzanne Simcott, is a town councillor and former Mayor of Llangollen where they both live.

Williams, Cyril *local politician*
Cyril Williams is an Independent Councillor for Ruabon. He was Mayor in 1991.

Williams, Dr Daniel *divine & social benefactor*
Born in Wrexham *c*.1643, little is known of Daniel Williams' early life before he became a Presbyterian preacher at the age of 19. He served in Ireland between 1664 and 1687 where he was chaplain to the Dowager Countess of Meath and then minister of the Wood Street congregation in Dublin. In 1688 he was appointed minister of Hand Alley Presbyterian Church in Bishopsgate, London. In 1691 he succeeded Richard Baxter as the preacher at Pinner's Hall but was later removed from his post for his unorthodox views. He became the recognised leader of 'Three Denominations' in their dealings with the government and led their deputations to both Queen Anne and King George I. He was created a Doctor of Divinity by both Edinburgh and Glasgow in 1709. He died on 26 January 1715 and is buried at Bunhill Fields, London. Daniel Williams married twice but had no children.

In his will he left about £50,000 to charity which was mainly used to establish seven schools in north Wales– including one at Wrexham,* to set up scholarships for candidates to the Non-conformist ministry at Glasgow University and Carmarthen Academy and to establish the Dr Williams Library in Gordon Square, London, a centre for the study of Nonconformity in Britain. When the 1870 Education Act established universal elementary education, the trustees of the charity schools decided to use the funds to establish a boarding school for girls at Dolgellau which was to be known as Dr Williams' School.

Williams, Llŷr *musician*
Llŷr Williams is one of the most remarkable classical pianists to emerge onto the world stage in recent years. Born in 1976 in Pentre Bychan, he was educated at Ysgol Hooson in Rhos and Ysgol Morgan Llwyd, Wrexham. He read music at Queen's College, Oxford, graduating in 1998 with a 1st class degree and the prestigious Gibbs Prize in Music. He then gained a postgraduate scholarship to the Royal Academy of Music where he won numerous awards, including the Diploma of the RAM and was the Shinn Fellow from 2000–02, coaching singers and studying conducting.

Since completing his official academic studies, Llŷr Williams has made a significant impact as an international concert pianist appearing throughout the UK (BBC Promenade Concerts, Edinburgh Festival (winning the Critics Prize in 2002), Cardiff Singer of the World with various national orchestras and abroad (USA, Germany and France). Further awards include the Bortelli Buitoni Trust Award, the Oustanding Young Artist Award from MIDEM Classique and the Inter-national Artist Management Association and the 2009 Glyndwr Award for his outstanding contribution to the arts in Wales.

Llŷr Williams.

He has made a number of commercial recordings and was the subject of a Welsh-language documentary *Y Pianydd – Llŷr Williams* on S4C.

Williams, Malcolm *local politician*
Malcolm Williams was born in Llay on 28 December 1943 and educated at Llay Infant, Junior and Secondary Modern Schools. He was employed in the mining industry and as a production worker. He was elected a Labour member for both Llay Community Council and WMBC on 1 December 1977 (after 1996, WCBC) and became Mayor in 1990. He was the Chairman of the Planning Committee of WMBC and is currently a member of the Executive Board of WCBC. As Mayor he opened the North Wales Tennis Centre with John Marek,MP,* the Peoples Market with Joe Wilson, MEP, and the Welsh Games at the Queensway Sports Centre. Malcolm Williams lives in Llay.

Williams, Peter *industrialist*
Born at Old Pen-y-Bryn Farm, Pentre Broughton on 4 January 1855, Peter Williams was educated at Pentre Broughton school before becoming an apprentice at the Blast Pit in Brymbo. A badly broken leg ended his mining career and he returned to school where he studied science and engineering. Apprenticed in the fitting shop at Brymbo Steel Works* he soon displayed above average talent and, after further training at Kilmarnock, was involved in designing ejector pumps which were manufactured at Acrefair.

His career blossomed and he came to be regarded as an expert on the manufacture of steel and was appointed Managing Director of the Brymbo Steel Works in 1908. In 1914, he was appointed General Manager of the Normanby Park Steel Works at Scunthorpe. A fluent Welsh speaker, and staunch Liberal, Peter Williams was a lay preacher, Chairman of the local School Board, Chairman of the Parish Council, a Governor of the County School, Chairman Wrexham School of Science & Art* and a Magistrate. He died on 12 March 1919.

Williams, OBE, Trevor Lloyd *clerk*
Trevor Williams was born in Froncysyllte and began his working life as a teacher in Glyn Ceiriog and Corwen before becoming a student at Liverpool University where he graduated in law. He was articled to his brother, Stanley Williams, who had a legal practice in Bootle. On qualifying he joined Bootle Corporation as an assistant solicitor then moved to Essex County Council and Watford Borough Council before being appointed Deputy Town Clerk of Sutton and Cheam.

He was appointed clerk to WRDC in 1951, a position which he held until the authority amalgamated with WBC in 1974 and he became Chief Executive Officer of the new authority. He was awarded the OBE in 1967 and was made a Freeman of Wrexham Maelor in April 1978. Among the many positions which he held was that of Secretary to the North Wales Rural District Councils Association. Trevor Williams lived in Chirk.

Williams, Thomas Michael *local politician*
Born in Rhosrobin in April 1944, Michael Williams was educated at Gwersyllt Primary School and Yale Technical Grammar School before commencing work as a laboratory technician with the National Coal Board at Llay Hall Colliery. From there he went to British Steel as a computer programmer and then a personnel officer for a total of 23 years. In 1988 he was appointed the Director of Personnel at Sharp Electronics in Llay.

He was elected a Labour member of WRDC in 1967, representing the Gwersyllt North ward (he was then the youngest member of the Council) and a Justice of the Peace in 1968. He became the first Leader of WMBC in 1974 and served as Chairman of the Planning Committee. He was Mayor in 1978–79 (the youngest mayor, aged only 34) and served as Deputy Mayor in 1977. During his year of office as Mayor, the Freedom of the Borough was granted to the North Wales Police. He has served as the Chairman of the Federation of Industrial Development Associations and the National Association for Housing and Town Planning. Michael Williams retired from the Council in 1988 and is currently the Chair of the Betsi Cadwaladr University Local Health Board.* He married Willow Woodward (who served as Mayor in 1993 – see Willow Williams) in 1968 and they have two children and live in Summerhill.

Williams, William *Nonconformist minister*
Born at Cwmhyswn-ganol in Llanfachreth, Merionethshire in 1781, the son of William Probert, a carpenter and smallholder, William Williams was interested in religious matters as a child and, as a young man, worked with his father and started to preach at the age of 19. As an adult he attended school at Aberhafesp, Newtown, and in 1803 became a pupil at the Wrexham Academy (See Fairfield House) where his weakness in English meant that he gained very little. His reputation as a preacher, however, led to his being appointed a minister with the Independent congregations at Wern and Harwd in Minera and he was ordained on 28 October 1808.

He soon acquired a high reputation throughout Wales and he established new churches at Rhosllanerchrugog, Ruabon and Llangollen before moving to Liverpool in 1836. Failing family health and personal sickness led to his returning to Wern in 1839 and he died there on 17 March 1840 and is buried in the chapel cemetery. With John Elias and Christmas Evans, William Williams 'Y Wern' is regarded as one of the great figures of the Welsh Nonconformist movement. Although the chapel at Y Wern has been demolished, the burial ground still survives albeit very much overgrown.

Williams, CBE, LLB, Alderman William Emyr *local politician & Freeman*
Born in Merionethshire, *c*.1889, the son of Welsh Calvinistic Methodist minister, the Revd John Williams, BA, Emyr Williams moved to Wrexham as a child, living at Islwyn, Grosvenor Road, and was educated at Grove Park School. He gained a law degree from the University College of Wales, Aberystwyth and completed his articles with J.S. Lloyd of Wrexham, whom he later joined as a partner. During the First World War he was commissioned into the Royal Welsh Fusiliers and served in Egypt and Palestine.

He was elected a Borough councillor for the West Ward in 1922, served as Mayor in 1932 and was chairman of both the Finance and the Education Committees.

He married Mary, the daughter of J. E. Powell, JP, of Irvon, Wrexham, (See Powell Brothers & Whitaker) in 1927. Elected an alderman in 1935, he was made an Honorary Freeman of the Borough of Wrexham on 28 March 1951. He received an honorary degree of Doctor of Laws from the University of Wales in 1956. Emyr Williams chaired the committee that oversaw the production of A.H. Dodd's* *History of the Town of Wrexham* in 1957 and he served as President of the Association of Welsh Local Authorities. For many years he was the chairman of the Executive Committee of the National Eisteddfod and was a member of the Gorsedd of Bards with the bardic name Emyr Cyfeiliog. He was awarded the CBE in 1952. He had offices at Nº 56a Hope Street and lived at Nº 4 Foster Road.* He died at the War Memorial Hospital in July 1958 and is buried in Wrexham Cemetery.

Williams, JP, Alderman William Jonah *local politician & Freeman*
Born at Treuddyn in Flintshire in 1850, William Jonah Williams was educated at Treuddyn School and then at a private school in New Street, Mold. He entered the grocery trade in Mold with Henry Roberts & Son before moving to their Wrexham branch at Nº 1 Hope Street. He later worked in Liverpool and Warrington before returning to Wrexham to establish his own business on Town Hill in 1875 and later built the Central Stores on Bridge Street.

Jonah Williams was elected a Liberal member of WBC in 1901 and became Mayor in 1911 and 1912 and an Alderman in 1922. He was made an Honorary Freeman of the Borough in 1931. Outside of business and politics, he was appointed a Justice of the Peace in 1915, was a Trustee of the Dame Dorothy Jeffreys Charity* and a senior deacon at the Pen-y-Bryn Congregational Church. He was a passionate supporter of the National Eisteddfod (he was Mayor at the time of the 1912 Wrexham

Three of the great names in Welsh Nonconformity: L–R Christmas Evans, John Elias and William Williams (Y Wern).
[William Prydderch]

Built by Alderman Jonah Williams, the Central Stores stood on the corner of Bridge Street and Brook Street.

Eisteddfod) and was a keen Eisteddfod musician whose bardic name was Gwilym Terig. He married Sarah Jones of Hope Street in 1876 and they had six sons (one of whom was killed in the First World War) and six daughters. They lived at Fairfield House,* Erddig Road. William Jonah Jones died at his shop on 3 March 1937 and is buried in Wrexham Cemetery.

Williams, MBE, Willow *local politician*
Born in Gwersyllt in February 1944, Willow Woodward was educated locally at Holy Trinity and Bryn Alyn Schools and the Denbighshire Technical College* after which she was employed as a domestic bursar and catering officer at the Royal Holloway College, London. She married Michael Williams* in 1968 and has two sons.

Willow Williams was elected a Labour member of both Gwersyllt Community Council and WMBC (Gwersyllt West) in 1982. She has served as Chairman of the Community Council and Chairman of the Borough Housing Committee. Elected Mayor in 1993, her Mayoress was her mother, Mrs Marie Woodward (then aged 80). She retired from the Council in 1998 and lives in Summerhill. Outside of local politics, Willow has devoted a great deal of time to various voluntary agencies including Meals on Wheels, the Citizens Advice Bureau, Marriage Guidance, Wrexham Foyer and is currently Chairman of the Association of Voluntary Organisations in Wrexham. She was awarded the MBE in 2002.

Williams' Brewery
See Eagle Brewery.

Williams-King, Anne *soprano*
Born in Trefalyn Maternity Hospital, Rossett and brought up in Wrexham, Anne Williams-King began her musical career as a student at the Royal Northern College of Music, Manchester aged 17. As a teenager she had won the soprano prize and the David Lloyd Memorial prize at the National Eisteddfod of Wales. She was also the winner of the Belgian Bel Canto competition and gained the prestigious Peter Styvesant Scholarship to the London Opera Studio.

She made her professional debut in Paris at the Opera du Chatelet, followed by the role of Amelia in Verdi's *Un Ballo in Maschera* with the Welsh National Opera. Shortly afterwards, in 1985, she came third in the Cardiff Singer of the World competition which launched her international career.

She appears regularly as a principal singer with a wide variety of international orchestras and has made many TV and radio broadcasts. She has sung major soprano roles and all the British and many European opera houses including: the Royal Opera House, Covent Garden; Deutsche Opera am Rhein; Glyndebourne, Welsh National Opera; Scottish National Opera and English National Opera.

Anne Williams-King.

Married to David, Anne Williams-King lives in Penycae where she also works as a singer teacher.

Williams Wynn Family
Hugh Williams, DD (1596–1670) Rector of Llantrisant and Llanrhyddlad, Angelsey.

Sir William Williams, MP (1634–1700), 1st Baronet, son of Hugh Williams. A lawyer, he became Speaker of the House of Commons in 1680 and Attorney General in 1687 when he was knighted. He bought the Llanforda estate, Oswestry in 1675 and was created a baronet in 1688. He died 11 July 1700.

Sir William Williams, MP (1684–1740), 2nd Baronet, married Jane daughter of Edward Thelwall of Plas-y-Ward. He was High Sheriff of Montgomeryshire in 1705 and Merionethshire in 1706. He served as Member of Parliament for Denbighshire 1708–10.

Sir Watkin Williams (1692–1749), 3rd Baronet, inherited the Wynnstay* estate, Ruabon via his mother, which had previously been the property of Sir John Wynn of Watstay (see below), descendant of Sir John Wynn of Gwydir, who had married the heiress of Eyton Evans of Watstay. Sir Watkin adopted the additional surname Wynn. He was Member of Parliament for Denbighshire 1716–41 and 1742–9. He was an ardent supporter of the Stuart claim to the throne of England and The Cycle of the White Rose* met regularly at Wynnstay. He was passionately anti-Methodist. He died on 26 September 1749 as a result of a fall from his horse while hunting. He married (1) Ann, the daughter and heiress of Edward Vaughan of Llwydiarth and Llangedwyn, who brought a vast fortune to the Wynnstay estate; and (2) Frances, daughter of George Shackerley of Hulme in Cheshire.

Sir John Wynn, (d.1719) Baronet, married to Jane Evans of Watstay (Wynnstay), Ruabon.

Sir Watkin Williams Wynn, MP (1749–89), 4th Baronet, the eldest son of the 3rd Baronet and Frances Williams

Sir Watkin Williams Wynn (5th Baronet).

Wynn. He was Member of Parliament for Denbigh-shire 1774–89 and became custos rotulorum and Lord Lieutenant of Merionethshire in 1775. He was a patron of the arts and was friendly with Sir Joshua Reynolds (artist), Frederick Handel (composer) and David Garrick (actor). He was a prominent member of the Cymmrodorion Society of London and an ardent supporter of education in both Ruabon and London. During his childhood, the Wynnstay estate was further enlarged by the addition of the Mathafarn estate by purchase in 1752. He married (1) Henrietta Somerset, daughter of the Duke of Beaufort and (2) Charlotte, daughter of the Rt Hon George Grenville. He died in July 1789. He was offered an earldom which he declined.

Sir Watkin Williams Wynn, MP (1772–1840), 5th baronet, was born at Wynnstay, Ruabon. Educated at Oxford, he inherited the estate at the age of 17 years.

He represented Denbigh-shire in Parliament from 1796 until his death in 1840 and was Lord Lieutenant of Merionethshire and Denbigh-shire.

Passionately interested in military matters, he served in Ireland in 1798–9 where he commanded the Ancient British Fencible Cavalry,* a volunteer unit that he had personally raised from the Ruabon and Wrexham area in May 1794. The regiment fought at the battles of Newtown Barry and Arklow. It was disbanded on 2 May 1800. Sir Watkin also played a prominent role in the militia, yeomanry and volunteer movement in Denbigh-shire. He was ADC to King William IV, President of the Cymmrodorion Society of London from 1820 until his death. He married Henrietta Antonia Clive, daughter of the 1st Earl of Powis. He was offered an earldom but declined.

Cartoon of Sir Watkin Williams Wynn (6th Baronet) attired as a 'Prince in Wales'.

Sir Watkin Williams Wynn, MP (1820–85), 6th Baronet, son of the 5th Baronet, was born at St James's Square, London on 22 May 1820. He married his cousin Marie Emily, daughter of Sir Henry Williams Wynn, GCH, KCB, on 28 April 1852. He was offered a peerage in 1859 but, as his father and grandfather had been offered earldoms, he declined.

Sir Herbert Lloyd Watkin Williams Wynn, CB (1860–1944), 7th Baronet, nephew of the 6th Baronet. He married his cousin Louise Alexandra, the eldest daughter of the 6th Baronet, in August 1884 (divorced 1898, she died in 1911). He was Lord Lieutenant of Denbighshire. He died on 24 May 1944.

Sir Watkin Williams Wynn (1891–1949), 8th Baronet. He was obliged to sell large parts of the Wynnstay estate in 1947 in order to pay the death duties imposed on the demise of his father. Included in this sale was the house and contents of Wynnstay (the building being bought in 1947 by Lindisfarne School). He died on 9 May 1949 and was succeeded by his uncle as his son Watkin had been killed in an accident in January 1946.

Sir Robert William Herbert Watkin Williams Wynn, KCB, DSO, (1862–1951) 9th Baronet, uncle of the 8th Baronet. He married Elizabeth Ida Lowther of Swillington, Yorkshire.

Colonel Sir Owen Watkin Williams Wynn, CBE, FRAgS, (1904–1988) 10th Baronet. Born 30 November 1904, he was the son of the 9th Baronet. Educated at Eton and the Royal Military Academy, Woolwich, he was commissioned into the Royal Artillery in 1925 and served in the Royal Horse Artillery. He was the Adjutant to the 61st (Carnarvon & Denbigh Yeomanry) Medium Regi-ment, Royal Artillery (Terri-torial Army) 1936–40 and saw active service in France and was at the evacuation from Dunkirk, 1939–40. Captured in Singapore (having received a Mention in Despatches), he worked on the Siam and Burma Railway. Promoted to lieutenant-colonel, OC 361st Medium Regt, RA, 1946, he was the Hon Colonel of the 361st Medium Regt, RA, 1952–7. Retiring from the army he was the liaison officer for the Ministry of Agriculture (North Wales) from 1961–70, member of the Nature Conservancy Council for Wales 1963–6, a Justice of the Peace, Deputy Lieutenant of Denbighshire, 1947, High Sheriff of Denbighshire, 1954, Vice-Lieutenant of Denbighshire 1957–66, Lord Lieutenant of Denbighshire 1966–74, Lieutenant of Clwyd 1974–6, Lord Lieutenant of Clwyd 1976–79. CBE 1969, FRAgSc 1969. Married (1) 1939, Margaret Jean daughter of Col William Alleyne Macbean, RA (she died 1961), two sons (one of whom, 2Lt Robert Watkin Williams Wynn was killed in 1972 while serving in Northern Ireland; (2) 1968, Gabrielle Haden Matheson, daughter of Herbert Alexander Caffin. Died 13 May 1988.

Sir David Watkin Williams Wynn, DL, (1940–) 11th baronet, the second son of the 10th baronet, born 18 February 1940. He was educated at Eton and served as a lieutenant in the Royal Dragoons and a major in the Queen's Own Yeomanry. He married (1) 1968, Harriet Veryan Elspeth, daughter of Gen Sir Norman Tailyour, two sons, twin daughters. (2) Victoria Jane Dillon, twin sons. He was High Sheriff of Clwyd, 1990.

Williamson, JP, **Alderman Ralph** *local politician & Freeman*
Born in Macclesfield, Cheshire in 1851, Ralph Williamson and his wife Elizabeth (née Taylor, of Congleton, died 1934) moved to Wrexham where they established one of the most successful pork butchery businesses in the area with premises at N° 20 Town Hill (they later also had premises in Hope Street). He was elected a member of WBC and served as Mayor in 1897 and 1898 and an Alderman in 1903–20. He was made an Honorary Freeman of the Borough of Wrexham on 19 September 1923 and served as a Justice of the Peace for Denbighshire. He lived at West Grove, Ruthin Road. He died on 15 July 1932 and is buried in Wrexham Cemetery.* He had two daughters.

Willow Brewery
Owned by Richard Evans until its sale in 1860 to Peter Walker,* under whose guidance it developed into the largest brewery in Wrexham. Evans bought the Chester Street Vaults in the 1860s. The brewery was bought by WBC in 1898. (See Walker Brewery)

Willow Bridge
This bridge, which crosses the Gwenfro at the foot of Salop Road, was built by brewer Peter Walker* and opened in April 1877. It took its name from the nearby Willow Brewery.*

Willow House
This substantial property was located on the south side of the junction of Willow Road* and Madeira Hill.* It is shown in the 1833 survey of Wrexham (when it was the residence of J. Broster) and can clearly be seen, surrounded by laid out gardens, in the 1872 survey. In Buck's 1848 print of Wrexham, the house is shown on the extreme right and is annotated as being 'Mr Pulford's House' – probably John Pulford who died in 1768. It was then the residence of the Revd Thomas Pulford and later the property of Thomas Jones, then Thomas Stephenson and then Richard Greenhow (ironmaster). [DRO/DD/HB/350-2] Palmer*

Willow House, 'Mr Pulford's House' in c.1748. To the left is Y Bont Bren over the Gwenfro at the foot of Madeira Hill.

believed that it was the property that appears in Norden's Survey: 'George Goldsmith, and Maria his wife, hold by right of the said Maria ... two cottages and gardens in Wrexham Vechan, one barn, dovehouse and orchard there, and five closes or parcels of land called – 1. Y Kae Mayn [*Trans.* the stone field]. 2. – Errow gand [*Trans.* crooked acre]. 3. – Errow vechan [*Trans.* little acre]. 4. – Kaer kutt [*Trans.* hut field]. 5. – Yr hirdire [*Trans.* the long land]'. This last field name was used to describe the land now bounded by Sontley Road and Percy Road until the area was built upon in the late 19th century.

Ownership/Residence:

c.1612	George Goldsmith
c.1699	George Goldsmith (undoubtedly a descendant of the above), died December 1704. He was married to Ursula Pulford and their son, Richard Pulford Goldsmith, died in 1686/7.
1704	Alexander Pulford (possibly a nephew of George and Ursula Goldsmith). He was the father-in-law of the Revd John Appleton, master of the Wrexham Grammar School* and John Stephenton, of the Mitre Inn* in High Street. Died 1726.
1726	Revd Thomas Pulford (probably the son of the above Alexander Pulford). Headmaster of Wrexham Grammar School.* Died 1768.
1768	jointly owned by Mrs Elizabeth Stephenton and Thomas Wragg of Liverpool (daughter and son-in-law of above Alexander Pulford).
1769	Mrs Elizabeth Stephenton – when the property was described as comprising: 'that dwelling house ... the out-buildings, garden and orchard belonging to it, as well as those fields in Wrexham Regis, namely, Barn field, with the barn and the cottage standing upon it, the Hirdir, Cae'r cut, 'Penny giliad', and the crofts adjoining to it, and the Bronydd, and all that messuage, stables, garden and croft in Wrexham Fechan, in the occupation of John Woods (the Bridge House).
1780	let to Capt Thomas Jones (previously of The Court*). Died 1799 (shot in a duel at Ellesmere).
1799	Thomas Stephenton. Died 1825.
1827	Owned by Miss Thompson. Let to Mr Gronow.
1833	Thomas Broster.
1841	Catherine Jones
1843	Robert Humphreys Jones, solicitor.
c.1859	Owned by Richard William Evans* who opened a brewery here.
1860	Owner Peter Walker, who developed the existing brewery into the Willow Brewery.*

Following the closure of the Willow Brewery*, the whole site on both sides of Willow Road was sold to WBC; the house and its grounds formed part of the Corporation Depot. Today, all that remains of this property is the high retaining wall along the east side of Madeira Hill.*

Willow Road
This road ran W–E from the junction of Madeira Hill* and Tuttle Street,* along the southern side of the Gwenfro*, to Salop Road* near the Willow Bridge.* At its western end stood the town's first public baths and swimming pool. The gates, which can still be seen in the railings alongside the river, were where the council wagons dumped snow and other materials which had been cleared off the streets. On the southern corner with Salop Road stood the Bridge House Inn,* an interesting neo-Gothic building, demolished during the 1960s. Behind the Bridge House Inn was the Joy Centre* and Price's Candle Works.

Willow Road Brewery
See Willow Brewery.

Willow Road Depot
In 1895, WBC began to seek a suitable site in the town which could accommodate public baths, an electricity generator, a refuse disposal depot, stabling and warehousing for council vehicles and offices. The empty Willow Brewery,* with frontages on Tuttle Street* and Willow Road,* which covered over 7,000 square yards (including 4,500 square yards of buildings) fitted the bill ideally. It had an ample water supply from its own deep wells, the river Gwenfro* could be used to carry away the used water from the baths, the old brewery chimney and boilers could be used for heating the water and a refuse destructor could provide heat for the buildings. A resident engineer could service both the baths and the generator and a baths superintendent could act as caretaker for the whole site. Loans were raised to finance the purchase and the adaptation of the premises. The brewery site was bought for £8,200. The banqueting hall was converted into a swimming bath by contractor Gwilt Cathrall at a cost of £1,285. The depot was used by the Council until the buildings were demolished in the 1970s. Today, all that remains is the iron railing alongside the river Gwenfro. Set into the railing is a gate through which snow that had been gathered off the streets was dumped into the river.

Wilson Avenue
Built by WBC in the 1950s as part of the Queen's Park* housing estate.

This street was named after Field Marshal Henry Maitland Wilson, GCB, GBE, DSO (1881–1964), Supreme Allied Commander Mediterranean Theatre, 1944.

Wilson, KBE, DL Sir Donald Robert
Born on 6 June 1922, Donald Wilson was brought up at N° 56 Oak Drive and educated at Acton Park School* and Grove Park County School.* After service in the RAF during the Second World War he opened Wilson's Tyre Depot. In fifteen years had expanded it to 17 branches all over the country which he then sold to Dunlop and became a member of the board of that company.

In 1982 he was appointed Chairman of the Mersey Regional Health Authority and in 1985 Chairman of the Regional Chairmen's Group. In 1993, he moved to become chairman of the West Midlands Regional Health Authority. In 1986 he was knighted for his services to the National Health Service and in 1995 was created a Knight Commander of the Order of the British Empire. Sir Donald was a director of several companies and served as chairman of a number of organisations. In 1994 he was awarded an honorary fellowship by John Moores University, Liverpool and given an honorary doctorate of law by Liverpool University. Living in Pulford, he was also a Deputy Lieutenant of Cheshire. He died in 2001.

Wilson, MEP, BEd, Anthony Joseph 'Joe' *politician*
Born on 6 July 1937, the son of Joseph Samuel and Eleanor Annie Wilson (née Jones), Joe Wilson was educated at Birkenhead School, Loughborough College and the University of Wales. During his National Service between 1955–57 he served in the Royal Army Pay Corps. He had teaching posts in Guernsey and

Kent before being appointed a lecturer in Physical education at the Denbighshire Technical College* in 1969, a position which he held until being elected as the Labour Member of the European Parliament for North Wales in 1989. He married (1) 1959, Mary Sockett, one son and two daughters and (2) 1998, Sue Bentley. He lives in Ruabon Road, Wrexham.

Windermere Road, Little Acton
A development by local builders H.R.&E. Roberts of private houses completed c.1959 on an estate that was originally known as the Edgby Park Estate. The land was once part of Cae'r Hen Dŷ (*Trans.* old house field), Erw Coed Mawr (*Trans.* big wood acre) and Pritchard's Croft, fields belonging to Little Acton Farm* and later to the Acton Park* estate.

Windsor Drive
A development of private houses built in the 1930s, all with names that have some relationship with the Royal family. This street was named after HRH Edward, the Duke of Windsor, the eldest son of King George V and Queen Mary (1894–1972). He succeeded to the throne in 1936, as King Edward VIII but abdicated in favour of his brother who became King George VI.

Woodland Grove, Queen's Park
Developed immediately after the Second World War by WBC as part of the first stage of the Queen's Park* housing estate. The street was built on land that had previously been part of the Cefn Park* estate which had been bought by means of a compulsory purchase order from Lt-Col R.G. Fenwick-Palmer.*

Woodlands, Chester Road
A substantial private house built opposite the Nine-Acre Field* in the late 19th century, possibly by Richard Phennah after whose death it was sold in October 1919. In later years it was the home of Alexander Reid, a Scotch draper with business premises in King Street, and H. Coskerie (1951). The house comprised an entrance hall, morning room, dining room, drawing room, kitchen, landing, four bedrooms and a bathroom. It was demolished in the late 1990s and a small block of private flats named Llys Awelon was built on the site.

Woodbine Farm/Cottage, Cefn Road
Originally called The Hullah, this farmhouse stood close to the junction of Sutton Drive* and Cefn Road* and was part of the Cefn Park* estate. In 1881 it was a farm of 16 acres occupied by Mary Ann Bithell, a widow. An attractive, solid looking, stone house it was taken over by Cartrefle College as the Principal's house and was later used for student accommodation. The house was demolished in the 1990s and the Plas Rhosnesni Residential Home was built on the site.

Woolley, John Brian *athlete*
Born in Wrexham in 1937, Brian Woolley was a pupil at Acton Park School* and Grove Park County School* where he gained the honour of being *Victor Ludorum* in 1953, 1954 and 1955 and gained a Welsh Schools Under-19 Rugby cap. In 1955 he became the British Amateur Athletics Championship Junior Long Jump Champion. During National Service with the RAF he became RAF Middle East Command Long Jump and Sprint Champion (1956–7) and played rugby for the RAF Middle East Command. As an undergraduate at Loughborough University, he became a member of the Welsh Track and Field team at the Commonwealth Games of 1958 and was British Inter-Counties Long Jump Champion. The following year he became the British Universities Athletic Union Long Jump Champion and a member of the Great Britain Athletics team. From 1959–61 he was the Welsh Games Long Jump Champion, becoming the first Welshman to clear 24 feet. He qualified for the Commonwealth Games in 1962 but had to withdraw due to injury.

Brian Woolley became a teacher and lecturer in physical education, latterly at the North East Wales Institute on Deeside. Married to Mary, they had two children. He died in 1992.

Workhouse
See Poor Law Union.

Wren's Nest, Rhosddu Road
This was the home of Wrexham Mayor, Stanley Craig.* His son, Peter Craig, was severely handicapped and, as a consequence, Stanley Craig gave the house to Wrexham for use as a residential home. Today the house accommodates Greystones Achievement Through Endeavour (GATE) and the Haulfryn Resource Centre.

Wrest, Percy Road
The home of Robert Henry Done,* Wrest was located on the corner of Hillbury Road and Percy Road. It was offered for sale in October 1901. [DRO/DD/G/2865]

Wrexham (the origins of the name)
The origin of the name Wrexham are lost in the mists of time. A variety of theories have been propounded by local historians, some of which are fanciful, some too simplistic while others have the ring of scholarship if not documented proof about them.

The basic name has existed since the Middle Ages and is almost certainly Anglo-Saxon or Old English in origin. There have been a variety of spellings e.g. Wristlesham (1161), Wrechessam (1202), Wrettesham (1236), Wrychtesham (1284), Wryghtlesham (1319), Wrightesham (1326), Wryghtesham (1347) and Wryxham (1439), some of which may truly reflect the dialect of the time while others are simply a strangers efforts to interpret an unusual sounding name. Noted Wrexham local historian, Derrick Pratt, introduced a new theory in the 1970s which seems to answer all the questions raised by earlier interpretations. The first element of Wrexham is simply the Old English 'wyrtha' – a workman or wright as in 'wheelwright' or 'shipwright'. The 8th century 'wyrtha' gave the personal name 'Wrhytel'. The second element *viz* 'ham' derives not from the Anglo Saxon word meaning a dwelling place, a house, village or collection of dwellings, but rather from the Old English 'hamm' meaning an enclosure, a meadow or a water meadow. Put both elements together and you get a name which means 'a workman's or wright's meadow'. In mediæval times Wrexham was divided into Wrexham Fawr* and Wrexham Fechan.* If we apply Mr Pratt's translation to these names then they would mean simply the wright's large meadow and the wright's small meadow. As these townships were divided by the river Gwenfro then we should perhaps go one step further and substitute 'water meadow' for 'meadow'.

The Welsh versions of the name Wrexham – Gwrexham (1254), Gregsam (1291), Gwrecsam and Wrecsam (present day) – are simply variations on the English name and not translations.

Wrexham Abbot
The original town of Wrexham, bounded in the west by Wat's Dyke, in the north by Acton Park, in the east by Spring Lodge and Hafod-y-Wern and in the south by the river Clywedog, was divided into two townships *viz* Wrexham Abbot and Wrexham Regis.* The origin of this division dates back to the 13th century. In 1220, the abbey of Valle Crucis near Llangollen, was granted lands, comprising the rectorial tithes, in the area of Wrexham, Bersham and Acton by Bishop Reyner of St Asaph. In 1247, Madog ap Gruffydd Maelor, lord of Dinas Bran, granted the abbey the vicar's tithes. Part of this land grant developed into the

The Wrexham & Acton Colliery, Rhosddu. Note the wooden headgear.

township of Wrexham Abbot. By 1315, the township was subdivided into 12 tenancies, each of whom had to pay their tithes at the Abbot's manorial court house (see The Court). In addition, the township had a mill where all corn had to be ground (see Pentre Felin).

In 1535, the manor derived the following income from the township:

Rents of assize	£14-2s-8d
Farm of the mill	£5-0-0
average annual profits of the court	£2-13s-4d

In 1537, Valle Crucis Abbey was dissolved and the manor of Wrexham Abbot came under the direct control of the Crown. Almost immediately, it was leased to Sir William Pickering of Oswaldkirk in Yorkshire for a period of 21 years and, in return, the King received annual rents of £4-8s-10d (for the manor house), £5-0s-0d (for the mill) and £5-0s-0d (for the tithes). Following the death of Henry VIII, the lease was renewed by Edward VI and in 1574, it passed to Hester, the daughter of Sir William. She married Edward Wotton who was knighted in 1603. Three years later, King James I granted the township of Wrexham Abbot to Sir Edward for 130 years. In 1651, the lease was held by Lady Margaret Wotton and remained in her control until 1651 when it was sequestered by Parliament and sold to Michael Lea, gentleman, and John Lawson, grocer, of London. In about 1663, Henry Wynn, bought the manor of Wrexham Abbot and it became an important part of what was to become the Wynnstay estate. A map of Manor of Wrexham Abbot, prepared for Sir Watkin Williams Wynn* in 1802 is preserved in the Denbighshire Record Office. [DRO/DD/WY/8352]

Wrexham Academy

An independent educational establishment which opened in 1791. The first principal was Revd Jenkin Lewis of Penybryn Independent Chapel,* and instruction took place at Penybryn Chapel. In 1811 Dr George Lewis, a surgeon and dissenter took over as principal. the Academy moved to Llanfyllin in 1816. One notable pupil was the Madagasgar missionary David Griffiths of Gwynfe, Carmarthenshire.

Wrexham & Acton Colliery, Rhosddu

The Wrexham & Acton Colliery (sometimes called Rhosddu Colliery) was located to the west of the main Wrexham–Chester railway line and to the east of the Wrexham-Bidston railway line, on the site now occupied by the Rhosddu Industrial Estate.* It was reached along Colliery Road.* The two shafts at the colliery were sunk in 1868 and 1869 to a depth of approximately 1,050 feet and the first coal is believed to have been raised in 1870. The mine had several seams, including Main Seam (7 feet thick), Brassey Coal (4 feet thick) and Crank Coal (21 inches thick). The company eventually became part of the United Wrexham & Westminster Collieries Ltd with Henry Dennis* as Chairman and Managing Director. By 1901, the Wrexham & Acton Colliery was employing 855 men (721 underground and 134 on the surface). By 1914, this had risen to a peak of 976 (813 underground and 163 on the surface). The mine was eventually closed in 1924, solving the manpower shortages at Gresford Colliery* which was also owned by the same company. One colliery engine house, constructed of red brick, has survived in Rhosddu Industrial Estate and can be seen alongside the A483, Wrexham bypass.* [DRO/DD/DM/910/1]

The known managers were:
- 1891 Jonathan Dodd (died 1893)
- 1893 John Newton (previously manager of the Ffrwd Colliery, died 1912)
- 1912 Edward Jones (temporary)
- 1912 John Edwards (previously manager of Hafod Colliery*)
- ? J. Walker Steele
- ? William Jones (previously assistant manager at Hafod Colliery,* he remained until closure in 1924)

Wrexham Agricultural & Scientific Society Exhibition, 1876

This was one of the most significant art and industrial exhibitions held anywhere in Britain (outside of London) during the 19th century. From the beginning, the proposals showed that the town intended to put on a large exhibition and it was decided that the initial plan to use the Public Hall* and the Vegetable Market* was too short-sighted. Mining engineer William Low* offered the use of a large piece of land at the rear of some buildings which he had recently erected on Hope Street. The temporary building covered an area

The art hall at the Wrexham Agricultural & Scientific Exhibition, 1876.

The medallion struck for the Wrexham Agricultural & Scientific Exhibition, 1876.

from Egerton Street* to Argyle Street* and from the back of Hope Street to Rhosddu Road.* The main entrance, which was in Hope Street, through the archway in Westminster Buildings,* was closed off by means of two large gates loaned by the Duke of Westminster from his estate at Eaton Hall. The foyer was lined with statuary and tropical plants and the walls decorated with tapestries. In the Grand Hall (which measured 50 yards by 25 yards) were displayed paintings by old masters including Van Dyke, Rubens, Raphael, Holbein and Rembrandt. Here a resident orchestra and pipe organ played throughout the exhibition. Other displays included examples of industrial products (bricks, mineral waters and steam engines), modern paintings and ancient craftwork dating from Roman and pre-Roman Britain. Manuscripts were loaned by national museums including a 12th century copy of the works of the Venerable Bede. A special medallion was struck to commemorate the event.

Wrexham & District Electric Supply Company Ltd.
The Wrexham & District Electric Supply Co Ltd was incorporated in December 1889 as a limited company with a registered office at Yspytty, Nº 72 Queen Street, Wrexham. Its nominal capital was £20,000 of £5 shares. Only 115 of these shares were ever issued and nothing was ever paid up or credited as being paid up on them. The Company was established to obtain powers to supply electricity to Wrexham and to set up generating centres in and around the town. In 1892 it was taken to court for the non-payment of £105 (two years rent) to Sir Watkin Williams Wynn and, as the company was declared to have no goods or chattels of value, a petition was served to wind it up on 1 August 1893. [DRO/DD/DM/910/9]

Wrexham & District Electric Tramway Company
(See also Wrexham & District Horse Tramway) The Wrexham & District Electric Tramway Company was a subsidiary of the British Electric Traction Company. The original plans for the company's tramway network were submitted to WBC in December 1898 when the proposed routes were:

1. Turf Hotel (Mold Road) – Regent Street – Hill Street – Vicarage Hill – Brook Street – Bridge Street – Pen-y-Bryn – Ruabon Road.
2. Turf Hotel (Mold Road) – Regent Street – Hope Street – High Street – Yorke Street – Mount Street – Salop Road – King's Mills Road – Hightown Barracks.

For some reason, the second route was never developed and the emphasis switched to the first route which was extended to Johnstown. The track and overhead lines were laid between Pen-y-Bryn, Wrexham and Johnstown in 1903 and ten tramcars were ordered from the Brush Electrical Company of Loughborough. On Saturday 4 April 1903, the first trams commenced operating between the New Inn, Johnstown and Pen-y-Bryn. Within a few months the track had been extended to the Turf Hotel on Mold Road and up Gutter Hill as far as Duke Street in Rhos.

The company's first General Manager was Mr King who, on his death in 1906, was succeeded by A.A. Hawkins. A Depot/Garage was constructed close to the New Inn in

Wrexham & District Electric Tramway, c.1918.

Johnstown and another at Maesgwyn Road,* Wrexham (both premises still survive; that at Johnstown still has the tram lines entering the front door). During the First World War, women were employed as drivers and conductresses. The expansion of the motor bus services during the 1920s led to the eventual closure of the tram service on Thursday 31 March 1927. Sections of tramway can still occasionally be seen when road surfaces are lifted in the town centre of Wrexham.

Wrexham & District Horse Tramway
This company commenced operating on 7 October 1876, running two-horse double-decker trams from Johnstown to Ruabon Road (near the junction with Empress Road). When the tollgate on Ruabon Road was abolished, the track was extended to Pen-y-Bryn. The company offices were located in Temple Row in 1881 and had a shed in Johnstown and a smaller shed at Packsaddle Bridge. It was taken over by Frederick Llewelyn Jones in 1884 and he ran it (utilising three tramcars) until the service was withdrawn in April 1901. (See also Wrexham & District Electric Tramway)

Wrexham & District Volunteer Training Corps
See Denbighshire Volunteer Regiment.

Wrexham & East Denbighshire War Memorial Hospital
Following a public meeting held in the summer of 1918, this hospital was built in conjunction with the William & John Jones* Hospital Trust which made available £50,000 of the initial cost of £100,000. Intended as a memorial to the men of Wrexham and East Denbighshire who were killed in the First World War, the hospital's foundation stone was laid by HRH Edward, Prince of Wales on 2 November 1923. The official opening was carried out by HRH Prince Henry, Duke of Gloucester, on 9 June 1926. The hospital replaced the Wrexham Infirmary.*

A new nurses' home, called Plas yn Llwyn* was opened in 1934 and Roseneath* was converted into wards for ENT patients in 1935, followed shortly afterwards by an Outpatients Department (1939) and two new wards in 1940 – Mason and Evington (the latter named after Mrs W. V. Evington who had paid £10,000 for their construction). Romano,* a 19th century villa on Grove Road was taken over as a nurses home shortly after the Second World War. The hospital was taken over by the Regional Hospital Board in 1948. In 1955 the hospital's Memorial

The plans for the proposed Wrexham & East Denbighshire War Memorial Hospital, less than half of which was actually built.

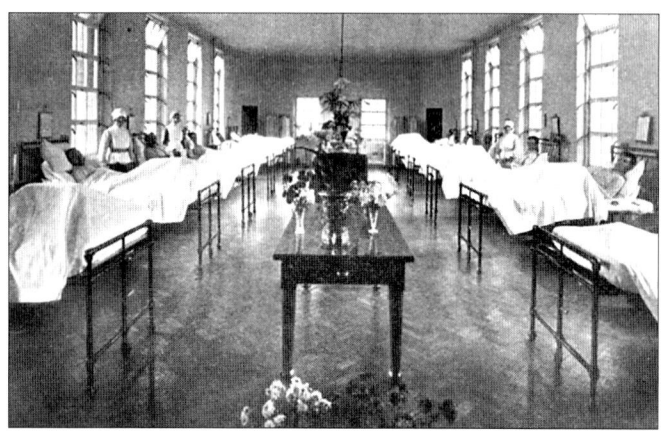

The Pantomime Ward at the War Memorial Hospital, paid for by donations from the Walter Roberts pantomime productions.

Chapel was built with public donations totalling £10,000, organised by the Rotary Club of Wrexham,* the foundation stone being laid by the Bishop of St Asaph. In 1979 the Community Dental Centre was moved into the hospital grounds from its former home at Nº 1 Grosvenor Road. Both nurses homes were closed in the 1980s and the larger of the two was demolished and the site used for Nightingale House Hospice.* With the building of the Maelor Hospital, the War memorial Hospital closed in the spring of 1986 and, after a period when it was empty and in danger of being demolished to become a supermarket, it became the new home of Yale College.* (See also Wrexham Infirmary Trust and John Jones)

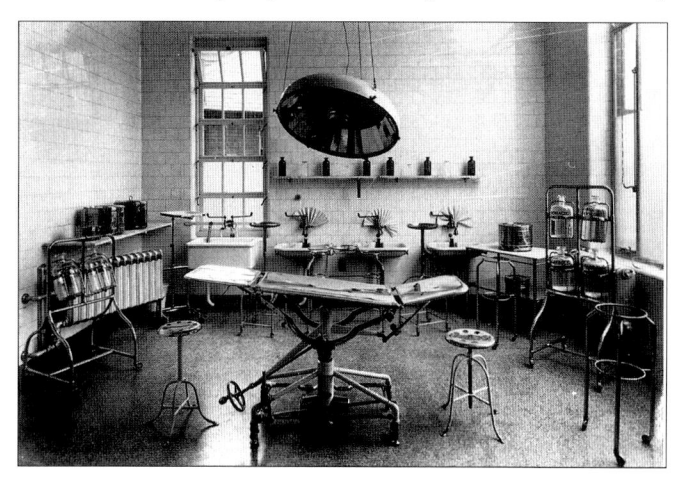

Wrexham & East Denbighshire Water Company

Established by Act of Parliament in 1904, the Wrexham & East Denbighshire Water Company had previously been known as the Wrexham Waterworks Company and took on the works established by that company since 1863.*

In 1921, the company began to draw supplies from the Park Day Level at Minera and a filter station was established at Legacy to deal with this new source of water which was of particular value in times of drought. During the drought of 1933, an additional pump was installed in the Speedwell Shaft which pumped water from the lower workings of the Minera Mines into the Park Day Level.

In 1928, the company established its first chlorination equipment at Minera, Legacy and Packsaddle. This led to the construction of a water tower at Legacy which was commissioned in 1934.

In 1951, the W&EDWC were granted permission to abstract up to 6 million gallons of water per day from the river Dee at Sesswick. The company took over the water works which had been built by the Ministry of Works for the Royal Ordnance Factory* at Marchwiel which gave them a pumping station on the Dee and a treatment works at Llwyn Onn as well as several miles of water mains.

In July 1952, the W&EDWC took over the Ruabon Water Company and the Ruabon Reservoir Company which brought two reservoirs at Penycae under its control. In October of 1953, the Cefn, Acrefair & Rhosymedre Water Undertaking became the subject of a compulsory purchase order which gave the company four additional reservoirs (of which only two, Cefn-y-Fedw and Sugn-y-Pwll, are still in use). In July 1955, it took over the Brymbo Water Company and with it the impounding reservoirs at Pendinas, Nant-y-Ffrith and Llyn Cyfnwy together with two filter stations. A new filtration system and pumping station were built at Penycae in 1956.

On 1 April 1960, the company took over the Garth and Fron

The theatre at the War Memorial Hospital. c.1924.

water companies which gave it an additional three small reservoirs, a hydraulic ram house and a pumping station at Tan-y-Cut Wood. At this time a new pumping station was set up at Oerog Springs.

On 1 April 1964, the W&EDWC took over the water under-taking of the Llangollen Urban District Council which included an intake on the Vivod stream, a pumping station near the Horseshoe Falls and a filtration works at Berwyn and several small reservoirs.

Work was carried out between 1969 and 1971 to build an aqueduct to bring additional water supplies from the Abersychnant stream to the Pendinas reservoir.

On 1 January 1974, the company took over the remaining water supply companies in the Wrexham area namely those belonging to the Maelor Rural District Council, the WRDC plant at Llantysilio and that part of the water undertaking of the Ceiriog Rural District Council lying within the Dee catchment area.

With effect from 1 April 1974, the W&EDWC became agents for the supply of water from the Welsh National Water Development Authority in accordance with the Water Act of 1973.

The Company's head office was at 21 Egerton Street, Wrexham.

The viaduct over the Clywedog just south of King's Mills.

Wrexham & Ellesmere Railway

The Wrexham & Ellesmere Railway (W&ER) story began in 1861 when the Oswestry, Ellesmere & Whitchurch Railway (OE&WR) was established. In 1864 the Wrexham, Mold & Connah's Quay Railway* (WM&CQR) received approval for a line between Wrexham Exchange Station and Whitchurch and work began but was abandoned in 1873. The return of Benjamin Piercy* to the Wrexham area in 1881 revived interest in the possibility of a railway and, in conjunction with Henry Robertson* of Brymbo Hall, plans were made to link Wrexham with Ellesmere after the OE&WR had reached that town and the W&ER was established in 1885. Wrexham Central Station* was linked to the Exchange Station* in 1887 by the WM&CQR and the contract to build the line to Ellesmere was awarded to local engineer John Woolley. Woolley died in 1891 and the contract was awarded to Davies Brothers of Wrexham. The W&ER set up offices in the Old Vicarage* next to the Central Station and the first sod was cut on 11 July 1892. Shortly afterwards 600 men commenced work on the viaduct that was to carry the line across the town and which was to change the face of the south-east section of Wrexham beyond all recognition. At first, work was slow and the line was not opened to traffic until 2 November 1895. The line never really lived up to the expectations of its developers although it provided an important link between Wrexham and mid Wales through the operations of the Cambrian Railways Company. It eventually closed in 1965. Over the next twenty years the railway bridges were removed and, in the late 1990s, that part of the viaduct which had been built through the churchyard of St Giles was demolished as part of the re-development and landscaping of the valley of the Gwenfro and the construction of the St Giles Link Road. Two full and detailed articles on the W&ER were published in the *Transactions of the Denbighshire Historical Society*, Vol 47 & 48 (1998 &1999) 'Memories of the Wrexham & Ellesmere Railway: A Personal Odyssey', Parts 1 & 2, by Derrick Pratt.

Wrexham & Minera Extension Joint Railway

A small railway line that ran northward from Brymbo, through Coed Talon, to Mold and, despite its name, it never came any nearer to Wrexham than Brymbo.

Wrexham & North Wales Bank, Chester Street

See Lloyd's Bank* and Tŷ Meredith.*

Wrexham Association for Detecting and Prosecuting of Felons

A single document survives in the Denbighshire Record Office referring to this organisation which was established by the leading citizens of the Wrexham area in November 1810.

Whereas divers burglaries, felonies, and larcenies have been committed, and the offenders have too frequently escaped justice for want of immediate pursuit and

The viaduct over the Gwenfro, just north of King's Mills.

effectual prosecution. We, whose names are hereunto subscribed, have entered into articles of agreement, for the apprehending and prosecuting of any offender or offenders, guilty of the undermentioned crimes; and being determined to the utmost of our power, to bring all such to condign punishment, do offer the following rewards for information which shall lead to conviction.

> Burglaries & highway robbery £5-5-0
> Stealing any horse, mare or gelding £5-5-0
> Stealing cattle, sheep or pigs £2-2-0
> Stealing poultry £1-1-0
> Breaking into, or stealing any goods or chattels out of any outbuildings £2-2-0
> Robbing a garden, orchard or fishpond £2-2-0
> Stealing corn, peas, beans, grass, potatoes, hay, turnips, or any grain or pulse whatsoever; or of stealing or damaging any plough, waggon, cart or other implements of husbandry £2-2-0
> Breaking or stealing any gate, fence, pale, rails, posts, lead, iron, copper, brass etc., etc. £1-1-0.

The signatories included every prominent name in the Wrexham area, headed by Sir Watkin Williams Wynn.*

Wrexham Bailiwick
See Wrexham Commote.

Wrexham Barracks
See Hightown Barracks.

Wrexham Baths, Bodhyfryd
See Wrexham Waterworld

Wrexham Bicycle Club
The first cycle club in north Wales, this was formed in 1877 and originally met at the Temperance Hall (formerly Penson's Theatre* in the Beast Market*) but later moved to the Lion Hotel* in High Street. The Club's first captain was Ernest Groom who was appointed after winning a race from Wrexham to Chester and back with a time of 51 minutes. The club changed its name to the Wrexham Cycle Club in the 1880s so as to allow the owners of tricycles to join. The original rules forbade cycling on a Sunday and, as a result, a breakaway group, called Wrexham Star was formed but this did not last long. The club closed in 1887 but was revived shortly afterwards with Sir Robert E. Egerton* as President and a membership of over 100. They were responsible for organising the annual town carnival, the proceeds of which were given to the Infirmary.* The club was still going in 1911 but probably disbanded with the outbreak of war in 1914.

Wrexham Board of Poor Law Guardians
See Poor Law Guardians.

Wrexham Borough Council
The original Borough of Wrexham (post 1857) was divided into four wards in 1876 (North, South, East, West), each of which had one alderman and three councillors. The present day locations of the original boundaries of the Borough are: a line heading north on the western side of the Great Western Railway line, then north-east along the northern side of Garden Road, along Cunliffe Street and Acton Road to Price's Lane and Croes Eneurys Farm. East from Croes Eneurys Farm, through Acton Park to Overton Way then south through Central Avenue and Park Avenue. East along Camberley Drive to Bickley Wood Drive then south-east along Deva Way to Abenbury. West to King's Mills then along the northern side of the river Clywedog to Felin Puleston and completing the circuit by going north along the western side of the Great Western Railway.

On 1 April 1935, Wrexham Town Council took over the parishes of Abenbury Fawr, Acton, Bieston, Bersham, Broughton, Erlas, Erddig, Gwersyllt, Marchwiel and Stansty from the Rural District Council. This added some 6,000 people to the population of the Borough. Two new wards were added, Wat's Dyke and Acton, and membership of the council was increased from 28 to 36. An attempt to further expand the borough in 1967 was unsuccessful. Wrexham Borough Council merged with part of Wrexham Rural District Council, Maelor Rural District Council and part of Hawarden Rural District Council in 1974 to form Wrexham Maelor Borough Council.

Wrexham Borough Council Town Clerks
1857–79   John James* (part time)
1879–06   Thomas Bury* (part time)
1906–37   Lawson Taylor*
1937–70   Philip John Walters, MBE*
1970–74   John Phillips Hughes, LlB*

Wrexham Borough Council Depot, Holt Road
This was located on the right hand side of Holt Road, roughly where Montgomery Road is located today. It was opened in the 1860s.

Wrexham Borough Electricity Undertaking
Inaugurated in 1900, it set up its generating plant in Willow Road* (see Wrexham Swimming Baths) in the former Willow brewery buildings. It had the capacity to generate 950 kilowatts of electricity which had to be supplemented with a supply from the North Wales Power Company. By 1948, when the electricity industry was nationalised, the total capacity available was 6,450 kilowatts and the whole supply was taken over by the Merseyside and North Wales Electricity Board (MANWEB) who maintained a district office in Willow Road for many years.

Wrexham Borough Sewerage Works,
In about 1869, the Borough Council leased Hafod-y-Wern Farm from Mr Davies-Cooke of Gwysanau, near Mold and converted it into a sewerage works. The house was used as the residence of the manager, Lieut-Col Alfred Jones, VC. When the lease expired in the 1890s, the Corporation moved the works out to Five Fords Farm in Marchwiel.

Wrexham Brick & Tile Company, King's Mills
See The Bricky, Abenbury

Wrexham Bypass, A483
For many years traffic travelling through Wrexham along the A483 had caused considerable congestion problems in the town centre, with vehicles originally travelling the length of Chester Road/Street, along High Street and up Pen-y-Bryn and Ruabon Road then, after the establishment of the first stage of the inner ring road, along Chester Road, Grove Road, Grosvenor Road, Bradley Road, Victoria Road and Ruabon Road. As early as 1950, proposals were considered for a new road (part of the Manchester–Swansea Trunk Road) bypassing the town of Wrexham and linking Gresford to the A5 near Newbridge. In 1956 the estimated cost of building this new road was £1.5 million. It was not until April 1972 that work began on the bypass (by this time it was reduced to a road of 4 miles, linking Gresford with the old A483 at Croesfoel) at an estimated cost of £2,797,080. The road was built by Sir Alfred McAlpine & Son Ltd. Further extensions were made to the bypass in the 1980s when, by means of a fly-over, it was continued southward from Croesfoel to link up with the A5. A second fly-over took it over the Gresford roundabout and allowed it to be extended, down the Wilderness into the Alyn valley to link up with the A55 near Chester.

Wrexham Castle, Erddig Park
The earthwork remains of a 12th century motte and bailey castle

can be seen in Erddig Park, on a promontory overlooking the river Clywedog and Black Brook. An outer ditch, 37 yards wide and 27 feet deep, separates the 'castle' from the remainder of the promontory and a second ditch, 39 yards wide, separates the bailey from the motte. Wat's Dyke* runs along the western side of the bailey. The motte (the mound on which a wooden or stone tower would have been built) stands some 19 feet above the bailey (the enclosed courtyard). The earliest reference to a castle at Wrexham appears in the Cheshire Pipe Roll of 1161 when Robert de Monte Alto (Mold) and Simon fitz William paid £16-18s (£16.90) for 'equipment for the castellan of Wristlesham' during the struggle against Gwynedd. In 1391 the court precedents records that 'the tenantry of Bromfield were convicted of divers insurrections and rebellions against the lord earl of Surrey' – possibly during the rebellion of Madog ap Llywelyn in 1294–95 – which included the burning of a castrum (castle) de Glyn (until the late 17th century this section of the Clywedog valley lay in the 'lords park of Glyn', from which we get the modern name of Coed-y-Glyn*). The 'castle' is also mentioned in the 16th century Harlean MSS 473 in the British Library: 'By Wrexham within a quarter of a myle toward Ruabon, in a Park Glyn standeth the ruyens of a castle great which somtymes was the chief house of the prince of Brimfelde'.

Of interest here is the name Twt Hill, which is usually applied in north Wales to fortified positions, usually castles e.g. at Rhuddlan and Caernarfon. It is generally believed that Tuttle Street in Wrexham takes its name from a distortion of the term Twt Hill. This being the case, it would suggest that there was another fortification somewhere not too far from Tuttle Street. It would be strange, however, if there were no folk memory of the existance of such a castle. This could only be explained by the fact that the castle may have only existed for a relatively short period and was then replaced by a more significant building. The fact that no development took place at the top of Madeira Hill,* in the area now occupied by St Giles' School, until the mid 19th century, and there is no record of any building in this area before this period, would suggest that the possible site for a castle would be on the opposite, or northern side, of the Gwenfro valley. This would make the site of the Parish Church a likely contender and the fact that the church was moved there from an earlier site close to Island Green, would explain the disappearance of any memory of a castle. If this supposition has any validity, it would explain why references are made in mediaeval documents to a 'castrum de Glyn' (the site in Erddig) and the 'castellan of Wristlesham' (perhaps the site above the Gwenfro.

Wrexham Cemetery

The need for a new cemetery to replace the existing Burial Ground* on Ruthin Road was evident by the early 1870s. A 10-acre plot of land was bought in Hightown for £1,202-7s-0d but objections led to it being sold to the War Office as the site for the new Hightown Barracks. In its place a 5-acre plot at Cae'r Clefion* was bought in 1874 and laid out as a cemetery at a total cost of £5,000. The landscaped grounds (which may at one time have been used for some form of extractive industry) were laid out by local horticulturalist and politician Yeoman Strachan. The chapels and lodge were designed by the Borough Surveyor William Turner. The land was consecrated and the first burial took place in April 1876 (Ethel Irene Pritchard, aged 11, of Edernion, Ruabon Road, Grave 03450). The official opening took place on 3 July 1876. In 1888 the cemetery was expanded on the town side and, in the early 20th century a further 12-acres were bought from the Ruabon Charities. The details of all burials in this cemetery are available on a computerised database held by WCBC.

With no further land available to develop this cemetery, plans

The entrance to Wrexham Cemetery, Ruabon Road.

were made to acquire land in Bryn Offa for a new public cemetery. Tests found this land to be unsuitable and land was purchased at Pandy where a new cemetery was opened in 2009, officially named Wrexham Cemetery Plas Acton Road.

Wrexham Civic Society

This was founded on 1 November 1972 by the former Town Clerk of Wrexham, Philip Walters,* who became its first Chairman and was succeeded by Tudor Owen in 1983. The society has six aims:
  i) to encourage high quality architecture and planning.
  ii) to preserve buildings of distinction and historic interest.
  iii) to protect the beauty of the countryside.
  iv) to eliminate and prevent ugliness, whether from bad design or neglect.
  v) to stimulate interest in the good appearance of town and country.
  vi) to inspire a sense of civic pride.

Among the society's successes are: the restoration of the Acton Park gates, the creation of conservation areas in the town, preservation orders for a large number of trees, the establishment of annual awards in recognition of contributions to the environment. The society has sponsored commemorative plaques to be placed on notable buildings in the town e.g. on A.N. Palmer's home in Bersham Road.*

Wrexham Commote

Commote, Raglotry and Baliwick were different names used at different periods for the mediæval judicial, accounting and administrative district, centred upon Wrexham, that comprised the ancient townships of Wrexham, Ruabon, Marchwiel, Erbistock and part of Bangor-is-y-coed. The chief officer of a commote was the raglot (known in Welsh as the rhaglaw) who resided in Wrexham Castle,* the motte and bailey castle in Erddig Park.* Such an official was still functioning in 1388 but, by 1401, had been replaced by the ringgild and the provost.

Wrexham Corn Mills, Chester Street

Brothers Thomas and Ben Jones of Trevor opened a grocery business in Wrexham in the late 19th century. When Ben died, a third brother, Hugh, joined the business which operated as 'H.&T. Jones'. They bought land which had formerly been part of the site of Tŷ Meredith* in Chester Street (now the site of the People's Market and the former Kwiksave store) where they built a large warehouse for their corn merchants business. They also opened shops in High Street and Queen Street before transferring all their retail grocery trade to premises on the site of the Lion Hotel* (now W.H. Smith) in Hope Street. Thomas Jones* became Mayor of Wrexham in 1899.

Wrexham County Borough Council
Following the reorganisation of local government in 1996, the new unitary authority of Wrexham was established by merging together the former Wrexham Maelor Borough Council with part of Glyndŵr District Council. The new authority's headquarters were based at the Guildhall, Wrexham.

Wrexham County Borough Council (Chief Executive Officer)
1996–2003	Derek Griffin*
2003–	Isobel Garner*

Wrexham Cycle Club
See Wrexham Bicycle Club.

Wrexham Dispensary
See Dispensary.

Wrexham Fawr
(*Trans.* greater or upper Wrexham) This was the mediæval term used to describe that area of the town of Wrexham north of the river Gwenfro (or on the left bank), including the town centre and most of what was later called Wrexham Regis.

Wrexham Fechan
(*Trans.* little or lower Wrexham) This was a term used to describe that area of the mediæval town south (or on the right bank) of the river Gwenfro as far as Coed-y-Glyn,* including (after 1660) part of what was termed Wrexham Regis. In latter years, the name Wrexham Fechan was given to the street between Mount Street* and Salop Road.* By the late 19th century the name was only applied to the street between the Willow Bridge* and Bryn-y-Cabanau Road.*

Wrexham Fechan Farm
According to the the 1790 Hafod-y-Wern* estate rental, it belonged to Bryan Cooke and was let to Thomas Berry. Its location is not recorded but may have been the land shown on the 1833 survey, located between Wrexham Fechan,* the south bank of the river Gwenfro and the road to Shrewsbury, held by Miss Potts.

Wrexham Fever Hospital
See Croesnewydd Hospital.

Wrexham Football Club
Wrexham Football Club was founded at the Turf Hotel* on 28 September 1872 by members of Wrexham Cricket Club. They played their first match on the cricket ground at the Racecourse on 5 October. The club joined the Football Association of Wales in 1876 and, in the first international match (Scotland v. Wales) two Wrexham players got their first caps. The team played in the first Welsh Cup Final in 1878 at Acton Park,* captained by Charles Murless.* Between 1882 and 1887 Wrexham played their home games at the Recreation Ground, Rhosddu (see William Jones Memorial Recreation Ground) before returning to the Racecourse where they have played ever since. In 1883 they entered the Football Association Cup competition for the first time but, following controversy over a goal in a match against Oswestry, disorder broke out at the Racecourse, as a consequence of which, Wrexham were expelled from the FA. In order to re-enter the competition, the original club was wound up and a new club, Wrexham Olympic, was founded and played under that name for three seasons before reverting to its original name. The club has played in the Football Combination League, the Birmingham & District League and in the Football League (firstly in the 3rd Division (North) in 1921). During the Second World War they palyed in the Regional League (West) before returning to the 3rd Division (north) at the end of hostilities. In 1960, the club was demoted to the 4th Division of the Football League, returning to the 3rd Division almost immediately and then being demoted again and in 1966 end up at the bottom of the Football League. During the 1970s the club climbed to the 2nd Division. During the 1980s, the team was again relegated to the 4th Division and they were almost forced to apply for re-election to the Football League. In 1993, the club managed to gain promotion but, by the turn of the Millennium, financial difficulties and clashes with the Chairman, Alex Hamilton, brought the club to a new all-time low. In 2004, the club was placed in financial administration and was given a 10-point deduction and it was again relegated. In 2007, the club was relegated from the Football League to the Conference National League.

A number of detailed histories of the club, the Welsh Cup and players have been published. (See also the Racecourse)

Wrexham 41 Club
The founding meeting of the Wrexham 41 Club was held at the Trevor Arms Hotel, Marford on 11 April, 1958. The founder members were: Creswell A. Lee, John Rowley, Bob Johnson, Oswald Jones, Tom Rowbottom, Gordon Parker, Ron Williams.

Presidents:
1958–59	Creswell A. Lee
1959–60	John Rowley
1960–61	Oswald Jones
1961–62	Ron Williams
1962–63	Robert Johnson
1963–64	Tom Rowbottom
1964–65	A. Parker
1965–66	John Cragg
1966–67	Bill Moat
1967–68	R. Bingham
1968–69	Peter Bond
1969–70	Hughie Jones
1970–71	Don Dutton
1971–72	E. Pryce
1972–73	John Cotter
1973–74	Neville Cheetham
1974–75	Orlando Andrade
1975–76	Tom Henderson
1976–77	Mike Darlington
1977–78	Selwyn Mattox
1978–79	Oliver Silvester
1979–80	Ivor Morgan
1980–81	Derek Price
1981–82	Ralph Byrne
1982–83	Emrys Jones
1983–84	Ralph Morgan
1984–85	Brian Davies
1985–86	Mike Williams
1986–87	Gwilym Hughes
1987–88	Gary Evans
1988–89	Bill Armitage
1989–90	Nigel Rainsbury
1990–91	Mike Shelley
1991–92	Paul Weston
1992–93	Stan Rogers
1993–94	Tom Lewis
1994–95	Albert Ellison
1995–96	Colin Rowlands
1996–97	Hywel Williams
1997–98	Dave Adamson
1998–99	Anthony O'Toole
1999–00	Alan Goring
2000–01	Gerry Craddock
2001–02	John Yoxall
2002–03	Roger Dutton*
2003–04	Tom Lewis
2004–05	Stan Rogers
2005–06	Robert Thompson
2006–07	Derek Price
2007–08	Dan Evans
2008–09	Vaughn Rawson
2009–10	Gwyn Edwards
2010–11	Steve Mackreth

Wrexham General Station
See General Station.

Wrexham Golf Club
The first golf club in Wrexham was established in 1902 on Bluebell Farm, Pandy, on land that was part of the Acton Park* estate (9-hole). The first President was Sir Foster Cunliffe.* Preparations for the sinking of Gresford Colliery caused them to look around for a new course in 1907. Another golf club had been founded in Gwersyllt Park* in 1905 (9-hole) but, by 1906, problems with the lease caused the members to look elsewhere and, through the good offices of Bishop Mostyn* they were offered a 50-acre site in Stansty Park by Lady Anne Ffrench. The two clubs joined together at the 9-hole Stansty course where they remained until 1923 when they moved to Borras and built an 18-hole course. The outbreak of the Second World War and the construction of RAF Wrexham* at Borras next to the golf course resulted in the reduction of the course to 9 holes. Eventually, some of this land was regained from the Air Ministry and more land was bought to enable the present 18-hole course to be laid out and formally opened in 1951. A detailed history of the club, *Wrexham Golf Club Its History Since 1906*, has been published.

Wrexham Golf Club, Stansty Park, c.1910.

Wrexham Grammar School, Chester Street.
The will of Edward Jones of Plas Cadwgan (dated 7 January 1580) states 'In case a benefice or living of £30 yearly at the least, be obtained from the Bp of St Asaph, it is to be for finding a free school at Wrexham, and my Exors to give £18 to the use thereof, over and above the £18 heretofore bequeathed by Dr David ap Edwarde late vicar of Ruabon.' When this school was actually founded is unrecorded but, the death of Alderman Valentine Broughton of Chester resulted in a bequest being made of £6-13s-4d per annum 'forever' 'towards the maintenance of the schoolmaster for the time being in the town of Wrexham, for the education of youth in good condition and learning there.' In addition, he also left £3-6s-8d to the choisters of Wrexham Parish Church but this was eventually also paid to the schoolmaster which would suggest that there was already a schoolmaster in Wrexham and that the Grammar School had been founded before Broughton's death on 18 June 1603.

The precise location of the original building is unknown but Norden's Survey of 1620 makes reference to a barn in 'the Lambpint' being 'adjacent to the schoolhouse'. As 'the Lampint' was a name for the area bounded by Chester Street, Lambpit Street and Queen Street, this would suggest that the original building was sited in roughly the same area as the later Grammar School building as shown in the 1833 and 1872 surveys. The only

The Wrexham Grammar School building at the end of the 18th century. A watercolour by Moses Griffith.

pictorial reference of the early building is an illustration by Moses Griffiths which is now held by the National Library of Wales. Until *c*.1800 the school was no more than a room with no dwelling house attached, then the building was demolished and the building which stood on the site until the 1970s was constructed. In 1812, the school suffered greatly following the withdrawal of £60 from the annual £101 grant given by the Dame Dorothy Jeffreys Charity. In 1817 the balance of £41 was also cancelled. The school never recovered from this loss of funding and struggled to survive throughout the 19th century. The *Report on the State of Education in Wales, 1847,** stated:

> There is no account of the origins of this school. It is supported by endowments set apart respectively 'for the education of youth in good erudition and learning,' and 'for schooling poor boys of the parish of Wrexham.' The subjects of instruction and the objects of the charity are left unlimited. The present income of the charity amounts to £18. The school buildings comprise an excellent residence, with a garden adjoining, for the master, and two school-rooms capable of accommodating 190 scholars. The present master enjoys the benefit of these advantages, and receives £14 per annum from the endowment, on condition of his teaching six pupils gratuitously in any subjects which they may desire to learn, the pupils to be nominated by the trustees. It appears, however, that no scholars are at present taught upon the foundation, and that none have been nominated by the trustees since the

The Wrexham Grammar School c.1850, viewed from Chester Street. This building later became the Guildhall.

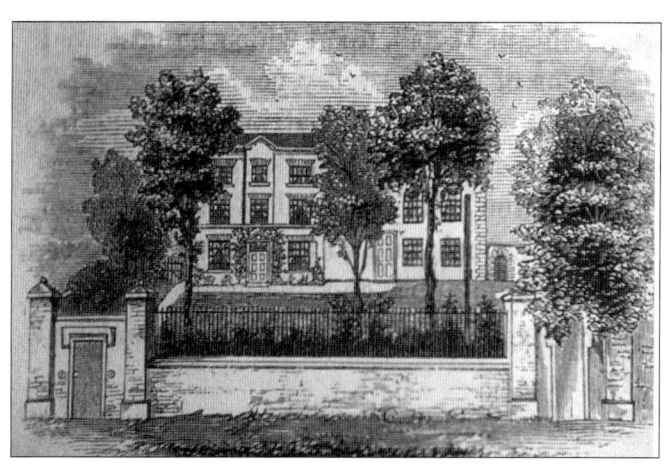

appointment of the present master.

I visited this school January 28. It is taught by a master and two ushers. There are at present 7 boarders, 3 day-boarders, and 35 day-boys: 20 of these receive a plain English education in what is called the *lower school*; those in the *upper school* learn also French and the classics. The terms for day-boys vary from 6 to 10 guineas per annum, according to the age of the pupils. As these terms exclude the poor, and the master has hitherto received no charity scholars upon the foundation, the school, in its present state, appeared to be beyond the purpose of this enquiry. It is considered by the inhabitants to be conducted in an efficient manner.

It eventually closed in 1880 when its traditions were taken over by Grove Park School.* In 1883 the premises were sold to WBC for £2,500 and were adapted for use as municipal buildings taking the name The Guildhall.* Some of its notable ex-pupils were: Morgan Llwyd* (the theologian) Thomas Pennant of Whitford (the scientist and topographical writer) and Thomas Gee of Denbigh (the publisher and politician).

The school is clearly marked in both the 1833 and 1872 surveys, the latter including a floor plan.

Schoolmasters:

A comprehensive list of the schoolmasters is not available. In his diligent searches through the parish and other records of the area, A.N. Palmer* uncovered several references to schoolmasters, *etc.*:

Maddocks   Usher of Wrexham School. Died 1657.
Jeffrey Williams   Usher of Wrexham School *c*.1664
Jeffrey Williams   Schoolmaster. Died 1683
Ambrose Lewis   Headmaster of Wrexham School *c*.1662–78 (possibly later). Died 1698/9
Stephen Jones   Schoolmaster of Wrexham. Died 1686.
John Stoddart   Schoolmaster *c*.1690.
Thomas Upton   Master of the Grammar School, *c*.1707. Died 1708.
William Lloyd   Head Schoolmaster. Died 1715.
Revd Richard Appleton   Headmaster of Wrexham Grammar School, Sept 1723.
John Roberts   Usher of Wrexham Grammar School. Died 1724/5.
Mr Pulford, MA   Headmaster, 1729.
Revd William Lewis   Headmaster. Died 1743/4.
Revd Thomas Williams, BA   Master, 1748. Died 1757.
Revd Robert Price, MA   Headmaster, 1756–68. Died 1811.
Mr Jones   Master at the Grammar School, Usher of the Latin School, 1769–70.
Revd Charles Anson Tisdale   Headmaster 1770–2.
David Richards   Assistant Master, 1770. Known as Dafydd Ionawr.
Revd Edward Davies, BA   Headmaster, 1772–1804. Died 1811. Lived at Holt Street House.
Revd James Smedley   Headmaster (ex-Westminster School), 1804–09.
Revd Samuel Norman   1809–13.
Revd John Kendal   Headmaster 1809–38. Buried in the Burial Ground,* Ruthin Road. His headstone was extant in 2001.
Revd David Roberts   Schoolmaster 1838–43.
Joseph Floater   Headmaster. 1843–68(?). He died on 14 August 1868 and is buried in the Burial Ground,* Ruthin Road. His headstone was extant in 2001.
Revd Thomas Kirk, MA   Headmaster 1868–80 (resigned).

Wrexham Improvement Bill, 1851

This Bill was drawn up on 5 November 1851 for presentation to Parliament. The proposer was R. Humphries Jones of Wrexham. The purpose of the Bill was to grant powers for improving paving, lighting, watching, watering, cleansing and draining in the town. Particular attention was paid to the laying of new sewers through Eagles' Meadow in place of the open sewers and the river Gwenfro which had previously been used for the disposal of sewerage. [DRO/QSD/DI/2-3, 6] Wrexham Maelor

Wrexham Infant School

Founded in 1831, the location of this school is unrecorded but some details have survived, taken from the *Report on the State of Education in Wales, 1847*:

A school for infants of both sexes, taught together by a mistress with one assistant, in a loft set apart for the purpose. Number of children, 125. Subjects taught – the Scriptures, Parry's First Catechism, reading, and grammar. Salary of mistress, £25; assistant £10.

I visited the school January 22. It is held in a loft above a cooper's workshop, which was dirty and cold. There is no play-ground for the infants, except the adjoining yard, filled with timber and cooper's tools, which make it very dangerous for infants. The room was ill supplied with apparatus. The stock of books is very small. There were none of the materials usually employed in infant schools for awakening the interest of young children.

I found only 39 children present, 100 being absent in consequence of a heavy fall of snow. The mistress was confined at home by a severe illness. The school was conducted by the assistant. Seven of the children present could read with ease; upon other subjects they were ignorant. Only 4 could answer very easy questions from Scripture, and 14 were ignorant of the alphabet; but in the absence of the mistress the children were seen to disadvantage, the assistant not possessing the peculiar skill required in managing an infant school.

It was stated that the mistress has conducted a school for 16 years, and has been trained for that purpose at a school in Chester.

Wrexham Infirmary

In 1836 a building fund was established to pay for an infirmary to replace the Dispensary* which operated in Yorke Street.* The following year a three-day bazaar held in the Town Hall netted £1,053 and work commenced on a new building on Mold Road.* The land upon which it stands was once a field belonging to Bryn-y-Ffynnon House. The original sandstone building in the classical style was designed by Edward Welch. The Infirmary was completed in 1838 and included a dispensary and consulting

Wrexham Infirmary (now the Art School) set amid rural tranquility.

Wrexham Lager Brewery c.1948, clearly displaying the Ace of Clubs trade mark. The Bavarain-style building on the right is now all that remains of what was once a flagship industry in Wrexham.

room. The first ward for in-patients, named the Victoria Ward, was opened in 1840. Thomas Taylor Griffith, one of the prime movers behind the scheme and consultant surgeon at the new hospital, paid £105 for the stone used on the Regent Street frontage of the hospital and also contributed over £300 towards its upkeep. Originally, annual subscribers paying 1 guinea or donating 10 guineas were entitled to become governors of the Infirmary and could recommend up to 12 persons each year for treatment (inclusive of one in-patient for whom an additional 10/6d would have to be paid towards board). Doctors visited the Infirmary on three days each week and there was a full-time house surgeon. The Matron had to be unmarried and aged between 30 and 50. In addition to her medical duties, she was also required to do all the cooking. Each ward was to be cleaned daily by the nurses and each week they would be scrubbed with soap and water. Patients had to provide their own linen and medicine bottles and all bandages had to be returned for re-use. Those patients who were fit enough were expected to assist with the nursing, washing, ironing and general cleaning of the wards.

By 1860, the Infirmary was dealing with over 2,000 patients each year and, since opening, had admitted over 41,000 people. Several extensions were carried out to the building during the 19th century with the Jubilee Wards being added in 1888. The Infirmary served as the Wrexham hospital until 1926 when the Wrexham & East Denbighshire War Memorial Hospital* was opened. Shortly after this date the Infirmary was taken over by the Denbighshire Technical College* (which had previously been the Wrexham School of Science and Art*) and a further programme of expansion of the buildings took place. The opening of the new Denbighshire Technical College at Plas Coch in 1953 led to the Infirmary becoming the home of the Wrexham School of Art which still occupies the building today albeit under its present title of the North Wales School of Art & Design.

When first opened, the Infirmary had a garden surrounding the building and access from Regent Street was through gates in a high sandstone wall. The wall and the surrounding gardens were cleared as part of a road widening scheme on the junction of Bradley Road and Regent Street. Hope Villa (now the Lager Club) was purchased at the end of the 19th century and converted into a hostel for the nursing staff. The hospital's first motor ambulance was bought in 1922.

Wrexham Infirmary Trust
This was established in the will of local brewer and philanthropist, John Jones* of Grove Lodge* who bought Roseneath* in 1912 and gave it and £50,000 to a trust for the establishment of a new infirmary in Wrexham. There were immediate problems with the bequest caused by legal limitations on the use of the house and land at Roseneath and, shortly before his death, John Jones gave instructions for the purchase of neighbouring properties in order to bypass these objections. The original trustees were: John Oswell Bury,* Richard Williams, Canon Davies (Vicar of Wrexham), Harry Croom-Johnson* and Richard Geoffrey Williams.

Wrexham Lager Beer Company
A group of Manchester businessmen, many of whom were of German origin, established the Wrexham Lager Beer Company (with registered offices in Manchester) in 1881, building a specialist brewery in Central Road, Wrexham because of the quality of the Pant-y-Golfen spring in Maesgwyn which was very similar to that of the water in Pilsen. Built in the Bavarian style, the new brewery began production in 1883. Despite the high quality of the product, the Wrexham Lager Brewery was unable to generate sufficient sales to make it a viable concern and it went into liquidation in September 1892. Immediately, the Company Chairman, Robert F. Graesser* (who had already played an important role in saving the company a few years earlier) bought up the shares and, having cleared all debts, was able to carry on trading. The company is often credited with being the first British lager producer but this is not correct as the Austro-Bavarian Brewery of Tottenham had brewed lager in 1881, but had gone out of production in 1894.

Graesser's next major step in developing the company was to get Wrexham Lager supplied to the White Star shipping line which greatly expanded the market. In 1922 the company bought the Cross Foxes* pub in Abbot Street and, in 1938, 23 local Beirne pubs. In 1949, the company was bought by Ind Coope and Allsopp who instituted a major expansion of the brewery and began producing other brands of lager. In 1961 Ind Coope merged with Ansells and Tetley and the Wrexham brewery underwent another major modernisation programme. In 1978, they revived the name Wrexham Lager Beer Company but changes in customer demands and the streamlining of production on a national scale led to the decline of the brewery and it eventually closed on 4 April 2000.

Wrexham 'Links'
Notable people with family or short-term links with the

Wrexham area:

Sir Robert Armstrong-Jones, MD, FRCS, FRCP, CBE, – educated at Grove Park School* in the 1870s. Grandfather of Anthony Armstrong-Jones, 1st Earl of Snowdon. (See also Snowdon Drive).

Jeff Crowe, New Zealand cricketer – grandson of John Crowe of Wrexham who emigrated to New Zealand. His family ran the well-known Wrexham fruit and vegetable wholesale business Crofruit.

Martin Crowe, New Zealand cricketer – grandson of John Crowe of Wrexham (see Jeff Crowe above).

Russell Crowe, actor and Academy Award winner – grandson of John Crowe of Wrexham (see Jeff Crowe above).

Surg-Maj Thomas Hale, VC – awarded the Victoria Cross for his gallantry during the Indian Mutiny. He was a pupil at Wrexham Grammar School.*

Henry James – author, was a pupil at Ruabon Grammar School.

Lt-Col Alfred Stowell Jones, VC, soldier and engineer, awarded the Victoria Cross for his gallantry during the Indian Mutiny – manager of the Hafod-y-Wern Sewage Farm* during the late 19th century.

Sir Henry Lunn – educated at Grove Park in the 1870s, he founded the travel agency Lunn-Poly.

Ray Milland, (Reginald Truscot Jones) Academy Award winning actor – attended Victoria School.

Richard Nixon, President of the United States of America was descended from the Puleston family of Hafod-y-Wern.*

Thomas Pennant – the noted botanist and topographer, was a pupil at Wrexham Grammar School.*

Rt Hon Enoch Powell, MP – the controversial Conservative politician was the nephew of Wrexham Mayor Ethel Claire Breese.*

John Prescott – Deputy Prime Minister in the Labour government of 1997–2010, attended school in Acrefair and his family came from Chirk.

Dr Joseph Priestly – the renowned scientist, married Mary Wilkinson, the sister of ironmaster John Wilkinson,* in Wrexham Parish Church* on 23 June 1762.

Peter Sissons, TV journalist – a descendant of Wrexham brewer William Sisson* (see Cambrian Brewery).

H.G. Wells – science-fiction writer, was a teacher at Holt Academy.

Wrexham Literary Institute, Temple Place
Mentioned in the *Wrexham Advertiser*, 1 July 1851. This organisation provided a reading room and library containing 'nearly 1,000 volumes in every walk of literature. Open weekly upon Monday Evening, from 7 till 9 o'clock.' The patron was Sir Robert H. Cunliffe, Bt, of Acton Park.*

Wrexham Maelor Borough Council
Wrexham Maelor Borough Council (WMBC) was established in 1974 following the reorganisation of local government and the consequent merger of Wrexham Borough Council, part of Wrexham Rural District Council, Maelor Rural District Council and part of Hawarden Rural district Council. The council's main offices were located in the Guildhall in Wrexham with various departments accommodated elsewhere e.g. at the former MANWEB offices in Rhostyllen.

Wrexham Maelor Borough Council (Chief Executive Officer)
1974–77	Trevor Lloyd Williams, OBE*
1977–88	Sydney F. Tongue, OBE*
1988–95	Robert J. Dutton, OBE*
1995–96	Nick Dawson*
1996	Chris Leech*

Wrexham *Maerdref*
Under the Welsh princes each commote (see Wrexham Commote) contained a maerdref (*Trans.* bailiff's township) which was the agricultural centre with a prime function of supporting the prince's itinerant court on its circuit of the realm. The *maerdref* of Wrexham comprised the townships of Wrexham Fawr* and Wrexham Fechan* which were administered by the *maer y biswail* (*Trans.* bailiff of the dung hill). After 1282, these two townships were reorganised to form a provostry administered by a provost.

Wrexham Market Hall Company
The Wrexham Market Hall Company was responsible for the building and operating of the three market halls (Butchers, Vegetable and Butter) in the town between 1848 and 1898 when they were sold to WBC for just over £50,000. The company's office was on High Street, in the entrance building to the Butcher's Market. [DRO/DD/W/547–605]

Wrexham Museum
Originally built, to a design by local architect Thomas Penson,* as the Militia Barracks* in 1857. The decision to build new barracks in Hightown (see Hightown Barracks) in the 1870s made this building redundant and it was converted into the town police station and court buildings. The opening of the new Divisional Police Headquarters* at Bodhyfryd led to the police leaving the building. The opening of the Law Courts at Bodhyfryd made the building redundant once again. For a period of some twenty years it was taken over by the Wrexham College of Art & Design until 1995 when it was handed over to WMBC for use as the new town museum. The creation of the unitary authority of WCBC on 1 April 1996 meant that the new museum would serve the whole county of Wrexham. Much of the essential redevelopment of the building was carried out during 1996–7 following a substantial National Lottery grant. The A.N. Palmer Local Studies Centre was opened by the Mayor of Wrexham on 3 August 2002. Following further Lottery funding, Wrexham Museum is currently (2010) undergoing major redevelopment.

A small Wrexham Town Museum had existed in the Wrexham Library* on Queen Square until that building was closed upon the opening of the new library on Llwyn Isaf and a Heritage Centre was located on King Street. (See also County Buildings)

Wrexham, Mold & Connah's Quay Railway Company
The WM&CQ Railway was incorporated by an Act of Parliament dated 7 August 1862. The company's first directors were: Thomas Barnes, Richard Champion Rawlins, Richard Kyrke Penson,* William John Sissons and Charles Hughes.*

The completion of the Wrexham, Mold & Connah's Quay Railway (WM & CQR) was announced on 26 August 1865 with a temporary station built in Wrexham. Unfortunately, the Railway Inspector, Colonel Yolland was far from satisfied with the standard of the contractor's work on both the track and the platforms and goods shed in Wrexham. For these and other reasons he refused to allow the line to open. A Stationmaster was appointed shortly afterwards (to reside at a house called The Crispins – see Crispin Lane) and before the end of the year four further staff were employed. The line opened unceremoniously to goods traffic on New Year's Day 1866. Colonel Yolland gave his approval for passenger traffic in April and the line was formally opened on 1 May.

The Wrexham 'terminus' was sited alongside the Great Western Railway's Wrexham General station (to which it was linked by a footbridge) but was a much more subdued affair. The contractor for the construction of the WM&CQR was Benjamin Piercy* and the Resident Engineer was his brother Thomas.

The Wrexham, Mold & Connah's Quay Railway branch from the Exchange Station, under the Bradley Road bridge, towards the Central Station.

On 1 November 1887, the line was extended into Wrexham, terminating at the Central Station, and the old station on Mold Road was renamed the Exchange Station. In 1897 the WM&CQR went into receivership and was effectively taken over by the Great Central Railway on 1 January 1905. In 1923, the Great Central became part of the London & North Eastern Railway. The most westerly signalbox of the old WM&CQR was located near Crispin Lane, just outside the Exchange Station in 1908. It was eventually dismantled and moved to Loughborough where it now forms part of the Great Central Railway.
[DRO/QSD/DU/1/6–7]

Wrexham Exchange Stationmasters: (these are only a few of the Stationmasters and the dates are not those of their appointment).

1868	F.G. Whitwham
1876	Mr Fisher
1878	Thomas Cartwright
1883	Edward G. Roberts
1895	J.C. Jones (died 1915)

A full and very detailed history of this company *The Wrexham, Mold & Connah's Quay Railway*, by James I.C. Boyd was published by Oakwood Press in 1991.

Wrexham Exchange Station, the original 'terminus' of the Wrexham, Mold & Connah's Quay Railway.

Wrexham Muslim Association
In September 2010, the Wrexham Muslim Association purchased the former North Wales Miners Institute* on Grosvenor Road and commenced conversion of the building into a mosque. It is intended that the mosque will have a prayer hall that can accommodate about 800 worshippers, a madrasah school, a library, a day centre, function rooms, a community hall and funeral services.

Wrexham Parochial Charities
The monoies raised by the charities were to be divided into twenty parts and distributed as follows:

Brymbo School	8 parts
Minera School	6 parts
Poor apprentices	2 parts
Distressed poor (not on relief)	2 parts
Expenses	2 parts

Wrexham Philharmonic Society
Recorded as existing in 1886, this society's officials were: president – A. Peel; conductor – Revd C. Hylton Stewart, MA; secretary – W.A. Bayley of Nº 51 Hope Street. Practices were held each Tuesday evening. It would seem that this society was responsible for organising the annual Wrexham Music Festival in the 1880s.

Wrexham Provostry
See Wrexham Maerdref.

Wrexham Public Library
Wrexham's first public library was opened in the Upper Assembly Room of the Town Hall in 1878. The first Librarian appears to have been R. Gough (1881). Following the purchase of the old Grammar School by the Corporation, the Library was moved to that site in 1884. Books were supplied by public donation and from a £25 annual grant given by the Wrexham Working Men's Hall Trust and £10 from the Lady Cunliffe Memorial Fund.

In 1903, the Scottish-American millionaire philanthropist, Andrew Carnegie, pledged £4,000 towards the building of a purpose-built library in Wrexham with an additional £300 for furnishings. Three possible sites were considered: adjoining St Mark's Church,* Ysbytty* and Guildhall Square* in Chester Street. The Borough Council eventually decided to have the Library built on Guildhall Square next to the Guildhall with a view to it forming part of a new municipal complex. The Carnegie fund administrators declined the site on the grounds that it was not their role to provide funds for subsidised civic buildings. The plans were re-drawn and the library was to remain in Guildhall Square but as a separate building. The Council then approached Sir Robert Cunliffe,* trustee of the defunct Wrexham Working Men's Club* with a request that he release £950 from the trust for inclusion in the library project. Sir Robert declined, but added that he would be willing to contribute if the library were built on the Ysbytty site. Despite the objections of many councillors who felt that they were being dictated to, the conditions were accepted.

Two cottages at the end of Lambpit Street were demolished to allow access to the site and the foundation stone of the library was laid on New Year's Day 1906 by the Mayoress. The building opened to the public on 15 February 1907 by Sir Foster Cunliffe.* The architect was Vernon Hodge of Teddington. The building included both lending and reference libraries as well as a large lecture hall (which later became the town museum). The building was enlarged in 1951–2 (at a cost of £6,641).

A new 1,900 square metre library was built on Llwyn Isaf between June 1971 and December 1972 at a cost of £176,000, to a design by James A. Roberts of Birmingham. It was officially opened by former local MP James Idwal Jones on 24 January 1973 (although it had been in use since December 1972). An extension was built on to the library to accommodate the Wrexham Arts Centre which was officially opened on 21 January 1974 by the former Head Librarian Clifford Harris, FLA, JP. The 1907 Library was adapted for other use by the local authority and is now the Information Systems Department of WCBC.

Wrexham Ramada Hotel, Ellice Way
Built by the QN Hotels Group, the Wrexham Ramada Hotel opened for business in January 2006 and was officially opened by HRH the Duke of Edinburgh on 2 March 2006.

Wrexham Regis
Wrexham Regis is the name applied to the ancient township area of Wrexham which was under the control of the Crown. It comprised most of the area which is today contained by a line linking together the northern bank of the river Clywedog (from the bridge in Erddig Park) – King's Mills – Abenbury Road – the northern bank of the river Gwenfro – Prince Charles Road – part of Deva Way – Archer's Way – Borras Road – Camberley Drive – Park Avenue – Rhosnesni Lane – Spring Road – Garden Road – Maesgwyn Road – the railway line entering Wrexham Central station – the northern side of Abbot Street – High Street – Yorke Street – Tuttle Street – Madeira Hill – Erddig Road – Sontley Road – the northern edge of the Coed-y-Glyn housing estate – Erddig Road until it reaches the northern bank of the river Clywedog in Erddig Park and 'completes the circle'.

Wrexham Rhaglotry
See Wrexham Commote.

Wrexham Round Table (N° 305)
A meeting to consider the formation of a Wrexham Round Table was held at the Wynnstay Arms Hotel* on 5 December 1950, called by Ralph Berens of Chester Round Table. A chairman, treasurer and secretary were appointed from the 18 persons present. At the third meeting, on 15 January 1951, the 24 persons present were designated the 24 founder members. The inaugural meeting was held on 12 March in the ballroom at the Wynnstay Arms when, in addition to the 24 founder members, there were also 50 Round Tablers present from other clubs, 7 Rotarians, Ralph Berens, Philip Walters* (Wrexham Town Clerk and Past Chairman of the Swansea Round Table) and the Mayor of Wrexham. The first officers were: Chairman – R. Creswell Lee; Vice-Chairman – Neville Cromar; Hon Treasurer – John Morgan; Hon Secretary – Peter Kirby; Council Members – Peter Bond, John Davies, Alec Henderson, Bill Scarrat, Don Wilson and Frank Wingett.

Chairmen:

1951–2	R. Creswell A. Lee
1952–3	W. N. Cromar
1953–4	John C. Davies
1954–5	R. D. Wilson
1955–6	William B. Scarrat
1956–7	Peter W. Bond
1957–8	Tom E. Henderson
1958–9	William W. Moat
1959–60	Neville M. Scott
1960–1	Donald R. Dutton
1961–2	G. D. Evans
1962–3	J. Peter Kirby
1963–4	A. Selwyn Mattox
1964–5	F. Neville Cheetham
1965–6	Peter D. Bird
1966–7	G. R. Jones
1967–8	D. B. Edwards
1968–9	Gwilym C. Hughes
1969–70	Ralph Byrne
1970–1	G. William Armitage
1971–2	John Rees
1972–3	E. David Gittins
1973–4	Ronald A. Davies
1974–5	Michael H. Williams
1975–6	Gordon A. McCartney
1976–7	Peter Walford
1977–8	Gwynne Belton
1978–9	Dan Evans
1979–80	Robert G. Thompson
1980–1	Paul H. Dempsey
1981–2	Paul Weston
1982–3	John A. Yoxall
1983–4	William T. Ellis
1984–5	Anthony J. O'Toole
1985–6	H. Ian Williams
1986–7	Les J. Crates
1987–8	Roger T. Dutton*
1988–9	D. J. Adamson
1989–90	Paul J. Christian
1990–1	H. R. Davies
1991–2	Peter Byrne
1992–3	D. Preece
1993–4	Anthony J. O'Toole
1994–5	P. Stappleton
1995–6	C. Stapely/P. Byrne
1996–7	M. Williams
1997–8	Richard A. P. Williams
1998–9	Gwyn Edwards
1999–00	Nigel Byrne
2000–01	Jonathan Sharples
2001–02	Richard B. Williams
2002–03	R.A.P. William
2003–04	Jonathan Sharples
2004–05	P. Byrne
2005–06	A. Williams
2006–07	R.B. Williams
2007–08	S. Pearson
2008–09	A. Williams/P.I. Price
2009–10	P.I. Price
2010–11	T.J. Mitchell

Wrexham Rugby Club
Formed in November 1925 at a meeting held at the Imperial Hotel, Regent Street, G.C.S. Mowatt was elected President, E.G. Mort Club Captain and J. Bloor Vice-Captain. Membership fees were 10/6 (playing) 7/6 (non-playing). The club originally played at Huntroyde, using the outbuildings of the Green Dragon Hotel as changing rooms. Their first match was against Chester Training College which Wrexham won 15-6. In 1926, they moved to play at The Hermitage,* Percy Road* where they remained until the outbreak of war in 1939 when the military took over the ground. In 1946 Wrexham Rugby Club amalgamated with Wrexham Cricket Club, Men's Hockey Club and Ladies Hockey

Club to become Wrexham Sports Club. In 1971, a squash club was added. The club is now housed at Bryn Estyn Lane. Delwyn Griffiths was Secretary for over 20 years and compiled a detailed history of the club. [DRO/NTD/981]

Wrexham Rural District Council
Wrexham Rural District Council (WRDC) was established in accordance with the Local Government Act of 1894. The first meeting was held in the Boardroom of the Wrexham Poor Law Union* on 10 January 1895. In accordance with the Local Government Act of 1929 and the County of Denbigh Review Orders of 1934 and 1935, parts of the Rural District were transferred to WBC on 1 April 1935 and, at the same time, parts of the Llangollen Rural District were transferred to Wrexham Rural District. The Rural District covered an area of 72,370 acres. The population was served by 52 councillors who were elected every three years and, at the time of its amalgamation with WBC in 1974, the headquarters was Imperial Buildings (the former Imperial Hotel*) in Regent Street. The parishes which formed the Rural District in 1974 were: Abenbury, Allington, Bersham, Broughton, Brymbo, Burton, Cefn, Erddig, Erbistock, Esclusham Above, Esclusham Below, Gresford, Gwersyllt, Holt, Is-y-Coed, Llay, Llangollen Rural, Llantysilio, Marchwiel, Minera, Penycae, Rhosllanerchrugog, Ruabon and Sesswick.

Clerks
1895–11   J. Oswell Bury*
1912–19   R.C. Roberts, OBE*
1919–46   G. Vernon Price, MBE*
1946–74   Trevor Ll. Williams, OBE*

Chairmen:
1895–99   Capt B.T. Griffith-Boscawen
1899–04   Arthur E. Evans
1904–07   George Cromar
1907–09   Joseph Edwards
1909–11   Charles Morris
1911–13   John Allen
1913–37   Sir H.L.W. Watkin Williams Wynn, Bt, CB
1937–9   E.A. Cross, MBE,CA, JP
1939–41   Professor J. Share Jones, MBE, MD, DVSc, MSc, FRCVS
1941–3   Robert Edwards
1943–5   John Edwards, JP
1945–6   James Lee, CA (died in office, January 1946)
1946   Gethin Davies, CA, JP (January to April only)
1946–8   Peter George, JP
1948–50   W. F. Humphreys, CA, JP
1950–2   Edward Boden, CA, JP
1952–4   Emmanuel Williams, CC, JP
1954–6   William Charles, MBE, JP
1956–8   G. Leyland, JP
1958–60   R.D. Jones, JP
1960–2   G. W. Matthews, JP (died in office January 1962)
1962–4   Ivor Griffiths, JP
1964–6   George Richards, CC, JP
1966–7   E. Davies, JP
1967–9   John Griffiths, CC, JP
1969–71   H.E.C. Fey
1971–2   Mrs E.M. Massee
1972–3   V. Lloyd Parry
1973–4   Walter Hughes

Wrexham School Board
Following the passing of the 1871 Education Act, School Boards were to be established wherever it was felt that the provision for elementary education was inadequate. In November, WBC passed a resolution to set up such a board which received Department of Education approval in December. It was to comprise of seven elected members. The nominees were: Revd Canon Dr Edward F. Browne (RC priest); Walter Jones (CofE); J. Pryce Jones (Headmaster Groves Academy, Nonconformist); John Beale* (Mayor); Charles Hughes* (publisher, Hughes & Son, Nonconformist); F. L. Heaton (doctor, CofE); Charles Roche (proprietor leather works, Nonconformist); John Lewis (solicitor, CofE); George Bradley* (Nonconformist); William Overton* (CofE); T. B. Acton (solicitor, CofE); Ald John Jones* (CofE); T. T. Griffiths (CofE); Ald William Rowlands (CofE); Dr D. E. Williams (CofE); Revd T. Kirk (Headmaster, Wrexham Grammar School, (CofE); John Beirne* (RC). Following a series of meetings, these names were reduced to the required number: Mr Lewis, Mr Heaton, Ald Jones, Mr Pryce Jones, Mr Charles Hughes, Mr Charles Roche, Canon Browne, all of whom were deemed elected. The composition of this Board was intended to lay the pattern for future members, comprising 3 Anglicans, 3 Non-conformists and one Roman Catholic and, whenever possible, public elections were to be avoided in favour of uncontested nominations. However, these good intentions did not survive for long and in March 1871 the resignation of Canon Browne led to the contested election of William Overton in his place.

The role of the School Board was to oversee and regulate the operation of schools within the Borough. The members were often responsible for ensuring the attendance of pupils at school, the appointment of teaching staff, investigation of complaints and the drawing up and execution of plans for the building of new schools. For full details on the election and operation of the Wrexham School Board see the series of articles in the *Transactions of the Denbighshire Historical Society* by Gareth Vaughan Williams, commencing in Vol 40 (1991).

Wrexham School of Science and Art, Chester Street.
This was founded by WBC following their unsuccessful attempt to persuade the authorities to locate the University College of North Wales in Wrexham. It was originally housed in rented rooms (£30 per annum) in Argyle Street* in 1888, teaching courses in building and machine construction, solid and plane geometry, shading from models, shading from the cast, freehand drawing and model drawing. Classes in chemistry and mathematics were held in Grove Park School.* In 1892, dairy classes were started in conjunction with the University College of North Wales, Bangor. The school moved into new buildings in Guildhall Square,* erected at a cost of £1,100 in 1894 and was funded by WBC,* Denbighshire County Council and the Department of Science and Art in London. Students were fee paying. In 1907 the school came under the control of the Denbighshire Education Committee. In 1914 plans were in place to have a Technical Department attached to Grove Park School and the necessary machinery was purchased and a professor was appointed to take charge. The outbreak of war in August led to everything being placed on hold and, very soon, the machinery was requisitioned for use in a munitions factory.

The School remained in the Guildhall Square buildings until the establishment of the Denbighshire Technical College* in 1927. One of its former students, Henry Price, sculpted the statue of Queen Victoria* which now stands in The Parciau*.
Principals:
1892–1922   Walter Fuge, FSAM (Arlunydd Maelor)

Wrexham Steam Laundry
Located in Brook Street/Lea Road in the premises now occupied by Rollings motor factors.

Wrexham War Memorial
The majority of the citizens of Wrexham mistakenly believe that the RWF War Memorial in Bodhyfryd is the memorial to the town's dead in two World Wars. In fact, the town has two war memorials erected after the First and Second World Wars. The first, a memorial bearing the names of all those from the Borough of Wrexham who were killed in the Great War, can be seen in the north aisle chapel of the Parish Church which became known as the War Memorial Chapel. A Book of Remembrance was completed and placed in situ in 1953. The second, taking the

form of bronze plaques displaying the names of all the men from Wrexham who were killed in the Great War were placed in the entrance porch to No. 1 Grosvenor Road.* These were moved to the War Memorial Hall in the 1950s and placed alongside further plaques, this time in stone, with stained-glass panels, which record the names of all those from the town and district who died in the Second World War. Each year, on Remembrance Sunday, wreaths are placed on all three memorials, although, because of its prominent position, the main ceremony always takes place at the RWF Memorial.

Also sited in Bodhyfryd are the Normandy Veterans Memorial,* the Burma Star Association Memorial (unveiled in 1995, it was designed by a student of the Welsh College of Horticulture and incorporates and a terracotta Burma Star, plants from the Far East and a series of wooden railway sleepers to represent the Burma railway) and the Korean Veterans Memorial.*

The Welsh Guards Falklands Memorial was erected at Bodhyfryd in 2002.*

Wrexham Water Works Company
This was established in 1863 with a capital of £15,000 for the purpose of bringing piped water from the stream at Pentrebychan to the town of Wrexham. The Company promoted a Bill through Parliament which became the Wrexham Waterworks Act of 1864. The first directors were: John Dickenson, Edward Davies, Joseph Clark, John Clark, John Beale and Peter Walker.

The original works established by the Company were an abstraction reservoir sited below Pentrebychan Hall* and a storage reservoir and slow sand filters at Packsaddle Bridge on the Ruabon Road which were opened on 11 January 1867. The water was conveyed to Wrexham through an 11 inch pipe which, although renewed in parts, is still in use.

Following additional powers that were granted in 1874, an impounding reservoir, drawing water from Ruabon Mountain, was built at Cae Llwyd in 1876/7 and opened in 1878. This supplied water not only to Wrexham but also to a large part of east Denbighshire and a small part of Flintshire (most notably the area around Gresford, Marford, Rossett, Llay and Burton).

By an Act of 1880, the Wrexham Waterworks Company's area was extended to cover part of Cheshire and additional parts of Flintshire and a reservoir was built at Marford Hill in 1882. Three filters and a new reservoir were then added at the Gronwen Filter Works in 1884/5 and a fourth filter was added in 1911. At this time the company offices were located in Charles Street.

In 1895, the original 1867 works, with the exception of the abstraction reservoir, were closed and replaced by new facilities which included a covered service reservoir on the site of what is now the Packsaddle Depot of the Wrexham & East Denbighshire Water Co.

Between 1895 and 1902, two boreholes were sunk at Talwrn and a pumping station was constructed which was originally powered by steam. In 1904, work began on another impounding reservoir at Tŷ Mawr, Bronwylfa which was opened in 1908. The Act of Parliament which granted the right to build this reservoir also changed the Company's name to the Wrexham & East Denbighshire Water Company.* [DRO/DD/DM/212/1–41]

Wrexham Waterworld, Bodhyfryd
The Wrexham Swimming Baths at Bodhyfryd, completed in May 1970 probably caused more controversy than any other building in the town centre. Its parabolic roof raised many objections because of the design, cost and difficulty of building. The building housed three pools (1) main pool – 33.5 metres in length with two shallow ends at (50cms) and a deep centre (210cms) (2) learners pool – depth ranging from 50cms to 94cms (3) diving pool – 12.2 metres square and 3.8 metres deep, with a concrete diving stage at 1, 3 and 5 metres and spring boards at 1 and 3 metres.

The Wrexham Swimming Baths were closed to the public and were officially re-opened by HM The Queen in 1998 after a major refurbishment programme in which the whole interior of the building was re-built and the name was changed to Wrexham Waterworld. The new facility has a six lane, 25-metre competition pool, learner and function pools, a 65-metre slide, a bubble pool and rapids river ride.

Wrexham Workhouse
See Poor Law Union.

Wrexham Yeomanry Cavalry
See Denbighshire Hussars Imperial Yeomanry.

Wright, Noel I. *local politician*
Welsh speaker Noel Wright was the Labour councillor for the Cefn ward of WMBC from 1974 until his death in December 1990, aged 80 years. He was Chairman of the Housing and Health Committee, was responsible for naming the People's Market and was Mayor in 1976. During the Second World War he served in the Royal Tank Regiment. Married to Doris, he had three children and lived at 34 Heol Cefnydd, Cefn Mawr.

Whybro House, Chester Road
This house, located in Chester Street, was the home of Sir Leonard Rowland.* The house was demolished and the site is now occupied by Ebeneser Welsh Congregational Chapel.*

Wyndham Gardens, Queen's Park
Built in the immediate post Second World War period as part of the first phase of WBC's Queen's Park housing development, the origin of the name is unknown.

Wrexham Waterworld.

Wynn, Sir Watkin Williams*
See Wynn Family.

Wynn Avenue, Rhosddu
One of the early streets of council houses developed by WRDC in the 1920s. The name almost certainly comes from Sir H.L.W. Watkin Williams Wynn, Bt,* who was then chairman of WRDC.

Wynne, JP, George Frederick *industrialist & inventor*
George Frederick Wynne was born in *c*.1853 in Stafford, the eldest son of George Frederick and Margaret Wynne. His father was a ladies boot and shoe manufacturer. By 1861, the family had moved to Chester where the father was the proprietor of a boot and shoe manufactuary, employing 150 people, later specialising in the making of shoes for infants. George joined his father in the family business but left to become a school teacher in Chester then an engineer with the Gorlon foundry in Manchester in 1874. He came to Minera in 1878 as assistant secretary to the Minera Mining Co, living at Plas Gwyn, eventually becoming the Company Secretary of the Minera Mining Co which he liquidated in 1897. He formed the United Minera Mining Co in 1897 (from the Minera Mining Co and the New Minera Mining Co) which closed in 1914 and he bought the waste heaps, smelting buildings and all the rights and set up. He then set up the Minera Mines Gravel & Concrete Co in 1917 and the Record Vanner & Slimer Co (through which he designed and manufactured automatic ore-dressing and separation machinery) in 1917, and the Infallible Exposure Meter Co.

In addition to his normal work in the mining business, Wynne was a gifted amateur inventor, holding patents for a variety of mining machines and drills. He also had a particular interest in the field of photography, designing one of the earliest successful actinometers (1893), print meter (1897) and an exposure meter (1914) all of which he eventually manufactured and marketed through his own Wrexham-based company, the Infallible Exposure Meter Co (established in 1917).

He married a Minera-born lady named Winifred in 1878 and invested heavily in land in the parish of Minera, most notably farms at Cwtoia, Pantywyll, Ty Brith, Tan-y-Graig, Pen-y-Graig, Pen-y-Palment, Pink, Tan-y-Rhiw and Bronheulog, as well as Plasgwyn, Smelt Cottages, the Five Crosses beerhouse and the Old Chapel. Further afield he owned Plas-y-Coed (Esclusham), cottages at New Bridge, Coed-y-Felin estate (Brymbo), Deio Isaf (Corwen) and land at Marton in Shropshire. In his later years, lived at a bungalow named 'Kingsley' after the author Charles Kingsley.

Wynne was appointed a Justice of the Peace for Denbighshire in 1912 and was a member of the Freemasons. He died in 1933.

A Wynne's Infallible Exposure Meter.

Wynnstay Arms Hotel, Yorke Street
Originally a small inn called *The George* (recorded in the first quarter of the 18th century). In 1702 the landlord was listed as John Edwards who was also a smith. By 1723 the inn had been greatly enlarged and the name was changed to *The Eagles* (or *The Three Spread Eagles*) when the property was owned by the Williams Wynn family of Wynnstay Hall, Ruabon (the three spread eagles being part of their arms). It was known by this name in 1730 and is referred to as The Eagles as late as 1822, well after the date when it had become commonly known as *The Wynnstay Arms*. The hotel was the meeting place for The Cycle,* a pro-Jacobite secret society established with the aim of restoring the house of Stuart to the throne of England. One of The Cycle documents suggests that the landlord in 1773 was a man named Daniel Porter (junior). During the 18th and early 19th centuries a bull-baiting post was positioned in the street outside *The Eagles* where, on a weekly basis, tethered bulls were baited by dogs. It was shown in the 1833 survey as the Wynnstay Arms. In 1841, the innkeeper was Richard Johnson and by 1859, Mrs Elizabeth Johnson. By 1864 John B. Murless* was the tenant and he was followed by his son Charles.*

At the end of the 19th century, the hotel occupied three floors (as well as a basement and attics) comprising:

Ground floor: Lounge, Smoke Room, Bar Parlour, Commercials Dining Room, Commercials Writing Room, Service Room, Commercials Lounge, Coffee Room. On the Yorke Street side of the arched entrance were a Tap Room, Bar, Ladies Room, Smoke Room, Luggage Room, Ladies Waiting Room, Boots Room, Saddle Room as well as a carriage and Motor Shed and Stables for 27 horses.18 Loose Boxes, several Stock Rooms, Sale Room, Bottling Stores and Offices
First Floor: Ball Room, Upper Sale Room, Sitting Room, Meeting Room, Manager's Apartment, 33 Bedrooms, 6 Bathrooms.
Second Floor: 42 Bedrooms, 6 Bathrooms.
There was also a Mezzanine Floor which housed 14 Staff Bedrooms and two Bathrooms.
[DRO/DD/DM/286/19 & in Liverpool Record Office, Edmund Kirby Collection, inclusive of floor plans]

During the 1960s, the hotel was sold and plans were made for its complete demolition. Pressure was brought to bear on the owners to preserve the building and by way of a compromise, the outer wall, facing High Street was retained while the remainder of the building was demolished and replaced by a modern hotel with a large car park at the rear. The old coaching entrance from Yorke Street was converted into the hotel's main street entrance. At the same time, the hotel's name was changed to the Wrexham Crest Hotel, in order to conform with the group identity. In May 1985, the hotel was sold by Crest Hotels to the Burtonwood Brewery who revived the name the Wynnstay Arms Hotel and in March 1999, the company completed a major refit and modernisation programme as a result of which the whole of the ground floor facing out onto High Street became the Cuprum Bar. In 2010, it was bought by the Lloyds Hotel Group, owned by Stephanie and David Booth and featured in the BBC Wales television series *New Hotel Stephanie*.

The hotel has been the birthplace of many local organisations including The Cycle of the White Rose,* Freemasonry, the Football Association of Wales, the Rotary Club of Wrexham* and Wrexham Round Table.*

Wynnstay Brewery, Yorke Street
Located at the rear of the Wynnstay Arms Hotel* it was owned by John* and Charles Murless.*

Wynnstay House
This is one of two buildings which made up Wynnstay Place in King Street.* Wynnstay House was sited on the western corner of King Street and Regent Street and was a private school in 1881 (see Schools).

Wynnstay Place
See King's Street.

Wynnstay Arms Vaults, Yorke Street
Also known as the Wynnstay Vaults, it appears in the 1872 survey. (See Wynnstay Arms Hotel)

Y

Y Wern
(*Trans.* the marsh) Developed by WBC in the 1950s as part of the Queen's Park* housing estate. It takes its name from the marshy nature of the area which was known as The Dunks* and which was, for many years, prone to flooding by the river Gwenfro. Prior to this area being built upon, a great deal of preparatory work had to be carried out as the land was very water-logged and soft and, in some areas, had the consistency of quick-sand.

Yale, Elihu *entrepreneur and benefactor*
Born in Boston, Massachusetts on 5 April 1649, Elihu Yale was the second son of David Yale, a prosperous merchant in the city and a descendant of the Yales of Plas-yn-Iâl and Plas Grono,* Wrexham. The family returned to Plas Grono in 1651 before settling in London. Elihu was educated at a private school run by Dr William Duggard and was, for a short time, employed by his father. Sent to India in 1671, he remained in the sub-continent until 1699 and had a very successful career. This included a period as Governor of Fort St George from 1687 until 1692 when he was accused of corruption in his dealings relating to his brother Thomas. He returned to London a very wealthy man and spent the last 22 years of his life between Plas Grono and Queens Square, London. He married Catherine Hynmer, a widow with four children, in 1680 and it was she who provided the initial finance for his business interests in India. They had four children before separating. Yale died in London on 8 July 1721 and was buried in Wrexham Parish Churchyard on 22 July.

He is best remembered for his generosity to many organisations including Wrexham Parish Church, the Society for the Propagation of the Gospel, a Welsh prayer book and the Connecticut College (which took his name). On 11 June 1718, he sent the college two trunks of textiles (which were to be sold at a profit), 417 books, a portrait and the arms of King George I – total value about £1,162. As the largest single benefactor of the college, the authorities adopted the name Yale College. In 1721, he sent the college further goods to the value of £562.

His epitaph reads:

Born in America, in Europe bred, In Africa travell'd and in Asia wed, Where long he liv'd and thriv'd; in London dead. Much good, some ill, he did; so hope all's even And that his soul thro' mercy's gone to Heaven. You that survive and read this tale, take care, For this most certain exit to prepare: Where blest in peace, the actions of the just Smell Sweet, and blossom in the silent dust.

Biographies include: *Elihu Yale, The American Nabob of Queen Square*, Hiram Bingham, New York, 1939; *Elihu Yale, The Great Welsh American*, Wrexham Area Civic Society, 1991.

Yale College of Wrexham, Grove Park
(For early history see Yale Grammar Technical School)
After protracted discussions the former Wrexham & East Denbighshire War Memorial Hospital* building and site in Grove Park was bought in 1993 as the new home for the former Yale VIth Form College which was to become a tertiary college under the name Yale College. In addition to the hospital site, the college acquired the former Grove Park Boys County School buildings and site, the Bersham Road site and Grove Park Road which passed through the middle of the campus was made private. In the old hospital grounds a second phase development was carried out, costing £14 million, built by Pochin with Wrexham architects TACP of Grosvenor Road. Following the threat of legal action by Yale University in America (see Elihu Yale) the Wrexham college was obliged to change its name from Yale College to the Yale College of Wrexham in 2000. In 2001 the number of students on the roll was 2,850 full-time and 8,500 part-time.

Principals:
  1993–2002   Emlyn R. Jones
  2002–   Paul Croke

Yale Grammar Technical School, Crispin Lane
The first purpose-built technical grammar school in the area, Yale was opened in the late 1950s in temporary accommodation erected at the rear of the Denbighshire Technical College on Mold Road.* A new building, designed by the Denbighshire County Architects Department, was built on Crispin Lane and the school's name was changed to Yale High School. By Christmas 1964, the 4th and 5th year pupils were moved into the upper floor of this new building and were followed by the remainder of the school in early 1965 a total of 390 students (which had grown to 470 by 1966). At the first Speech Day to be held under the new name, the guest speaker was Professor Brewster of Yale University. In 1972, Denbighshire Education Auhority adopted comprehensive education throughout the county and Yale became a VIth Form College supplying A-level

Elihu Yale, benefactor of Yale University and Wrexham Parish Church.

One of the most significant areas of change in Wrexham during the 1990s was that which was once called Grove Park. The closure of the Wrexham & East Denbighshire War Memorial Hospital and the relocation to the site of Yale College led to a major investment in buildings which are clearly visible in this aerial photograph. The former War Memorial Hospital main entrance can be seen centre left with the former Grove Park County School for Boys centre right and Grove Park County School for Girls top right. Top left is the Nightingale House Hospice. [TACP]

courses for all the comprehensive schools in Wrexham. first occupied in 1964 and officially opened in 1965. In 1993 the college again embarked upon a period of re-organisation as it was incorporated and passed out of the control of the local authority. It took over the further education courses being run by the North East Wales Institute and absorbed the former NEWI technical training site in Bersham Road. Recognised as a tertiary college, the name was again changed to Yale College. (See also Yale College of Wrexham)

Headmasters/Principals:
- c.1959   Bruce Brown
- 1974   Eifion Ellis
- 1987   Emlyn R. Jones

Yale Grove, Acton
Built in the early 1920s as part of the first phase of the Acton Park housing estate,* this street was named after the lordship of Bromfield and Yale. (See Lordships of Bromfield and Yale)

Yale Hospital
This opened in November 1988 as a private acute medical/surgical hospital.

Yarwood Drive, Barker's Lane
This was built in the late 1970s by Broseley Homes. The origin of the name is unknown.

York Terrace, Lambpit Street
A row of three small houses built in Lambpit Street in 1892/3 by John Scott of the Seven Stars* as lodgings for commercial travellers and the artistes appearing at the Hippodrome* and later the Empire* theatres. The site is now occupied by the Guildhall* offices.

Yorke Family
Simon Yorke I (1696–1767) – John Mellor of Erddig Hall* died in 1733 and left his estate to his nephew, Simon Yorke, the son of Simon and Anne Yorke (née Mellor). Simon married heiress Dorothy Hutton in 1740 and they had one son and one daughter. Simon died in 1767.

Philip Yorke I, MP, FSA, (1743–1804) was the only son of Simon and Dorothy Yorke and was educated at Wanstead and Hackney followed by Eton and Cambridge University. He was called to the Bar at Lincoln's Inn. He married Elizabeth, the daughter of Sir John Cust of Belton House, the Speaker of the House of Commons, in July 1770 and they had eight children. He inherited his uncle's estates at Newnham and was financially very secure. Much of his time and money was spent improving his estate at Erddig and he became Member of Parliament for Helston in Cornwall and for Grantham (although he rarely visited either constituency and never spoke in Parliament). He was the author of *The Royal Tribes of Wales* which was published in 1799. Elizabeth died in 1779 and in 1782 he married Diana Meyrick with whom he had six more children. He died in 1804. His biography, *Philip Yorke I (1743–1804) Squire of Erthig* by Eric Griffiths, was published in 1995.

Simon Yorke II (1771–1834), the eldest son of Philip and Elizabeth Yorke, he married Margaret Holland of Terydan in 1807. They had six children including Simon Yorke III and General John Yorke (of Plas Newydd, Llangollen).

Simon Yorke III (1811–94), he married Victoria Cust, his cousin and the goddaughter and lady-in-waiting of Queen Victoria. They had two sons and two daughters.

Philip Yorke II (1849–1922), the son of Simon and Victoria Yorke, he married Annette Fountayne, daughter of Sir Richard Puleston of Emral in 1877. They separated almost immediately and she died in 1899. Philip married Louisa Matilda Scott of Wiltshire in 1902 and they had two sons, Simon (IV) and Philip (III). Philip was a Justice of the Peace for Denbighshire and was elected Mayor from outside of the Council in 1896.

Simon Yorke IV (1903–66), a life-long bachelor, he became something of a recluse and died intestate in 1966.

Philip Yorke III (1905–78), the last Squire of Erddig. A Cambridge graduate he had hopes of becoming a priest but eventually became an actor and stage manager with his own company the Country Theatre Players, which toured Britain. In later years, he became an organiser of European tours and a travel guide. He succeeded to the Erddig estate in 1966 and, in his latter years lived at Tai Clawdd, Ruabon. An amiable eccentric, he decided to give Erddig to the National Trust in order to save it from the ravages of time, the National Coal Board and future death duties. He died while attending a church service and was buried in the family vault in Marchwiel Church on 7 July 1978. (See Squire Yorke public house) His biography, *Philip Yorke, Last Squire of Erddig* by Geoffrey Veysey, was published in 2002.

Philip Yorke III, the last 'Squire of Erddig'.

Yorke Street

The name of this street has caused some contention since Palmer published his *History of the Town of Wrexham* in 1893. In that work, Palmer stated: 'I have never found the street, now known as 'York Street' called by that name before the year 1780. It has

Yorke Street, c.1930. The whole of the left-hand side of this street was cleared in the 1960s, thereby opening up an unobstructed view of the Parish Church. Visible in this photograph are the Royal Ship Inn (left), the Wynnstay Arms Hotel (top), the Black Horse Inn (right) and S. Parrott, gents hairdresser).

been supposed that York Street was named after Yorkshire Square, towards which it led, but the latter is mentioned for the first time in the rate books in 1786, while the name of the former occurs, as we have seen, in 1780'. Palmer then continues to refer to the street as 'York' rather than 'Yorke' Street. The 1833 survey shows the name spelt without an 'e' whereas the 1872 survey clearly shows the spelling of the name with an 'e' which implies that the street was named after the Yorke family of Erddig Hall. This is likely to be the origin of the name as the Yorke family came into possession of the Erddig estate in 1716 and the name only appears to have been changed some fifty years later, at least six years before Yorkshire Square* was built. For most of the 18th century it was referred to as the Street Below the Churchyard or, sometimes, the Street Below the Eagles (as the Wynnstay Arms Hotel* was once known). Earlier still it had been known as Swine Market Street or *Marchnad-y-Moch*. The current practice of spelling it as Yorke Street and then translating this as Stryt Efrog would therefore appear to be a mistake; it should either be York Street/*Stryt Efrog* or Yorke Street/*Stryt Yorke* (or perhaps, more interestingly, using the old name *Marchnad-y-Moch*).

Like many of the main thoroughfares in Wrexham, Yorke Street was most noted for a number of public houses which were situated there. Commencing down the eastern side there was the Wynnstay Arms Hotel* and the Wynnstay Arms Vaults,* followed by the Hop Pole Inn,* the Waiters' Arms,* the White Bear Inn,* the Black Horse Inn* (still surviving) and the Union Vaults* on the corner of Mount Street.* On the western side of the street, (which was demolished as part of a road-widening scheme in the 1967) was the Ship Inn.* Between Yorke Street and Temple Row, on the site now occupied by the grassy bank below the churchyard, stood two rows of what can best be described as tenement buildings which were accessed from Temple Row* or via passages from Yorke Street. [Deeds to properties in this street can be found in DRO/DD/CP/543, 545–6, 548–9, 552]

Yorkshire Hall
See Public Hall.

Yorkshire Square
This was located off Tuttle Street, below the Parish Church. Land which belonged to William Edwards, a tanner of Pen-y-Bryn* was used in 1788 to build a square of small one storied shops around an open space for the use of the Yorkshire cloth dealers who visited the town for the annual March Fair (See Markets & Fairs). Prior to this date, the dealers had rented space in the Town Hall.* Sometime before 1824, the dealers moved from Yorkshire Square to Birmingham Square* which came to be known for a time as New Yorkshire Square. The shops were then converted into cottages which were of a very poor quality and which were described in the 1849 Board of Health Report:

> Here are altogether 35 tenements with one privy, and that in a state quite unapproachable. The court is occupied by dung pits and collections of filth, and in parts sodden with ordure. The privy of these cottages drains into a succession of open pools of soil, which extend at the back of other cottages, and into a public way opening from Tuttle Street. The sickness here is severe, and the mortality 38·2 in 1,000.

This appears in the 1833 survey as Old Yorkshire Square, in the 1841 census as Old Yorkshire Hall and in the 1872 survey as Yorkshire Square. Prior to the Great Reform Act of 1832, the owners of Yorkshire Square (primarily residents of Huddersfield) were entitled to twenty-eight votes in the Denbighshire County election.

Young Women's Christian Association (YWCA)
This was established as a club for female munitions workers in Wrexham during the First World War and became the Wrexham Girls' Club in 1919. Its main purpose at that time seems to have been to provide a respectable place for young women to take their boyfriends to a dance. In about December 1919, it was taken over by the Young Women's Christian Association, with a salaried organiser, and the club was closed to boys on three evenings each week when classes were held in needlework, etc.

In May 1920, following a bazaar which raised £500 and a grant from the Welsh Division of the YWCA, premises were built on land belonging to Miss Allington-Hughes. Dancing was allowed to continue on two evenings each week until 1925 when the increasing popularity of the pastime resulted in an increased provision and as a result of this the evening classes declined. The 2nd Wrexham Girl Guides Company was attached to the club (which was becoming known as the Blue Triangle Club, taken from the badge of the YWCA) and the situation continued unchanged until 1932 by which time the club was running at a loss. Lady Rowland* who had been the President and Mrs Aston, the Hon Secretary, resigned. The new committee under the leadership of Mrs C. P. Williams (President) and Miss K. Allington-Hughes (Patron) reorganised the club, did away with the salaried post, and established a Dinner Hour Club. In 1933 a new and larger social centre was established in Argyle Street and in April 1934, the Pioneers were started (for girls aged between 11 and 16 years) and from 1935 the Club greatly increased in popularity. [DRO/DD/G/223/2]. By 1951, the YWCA was accommodated in premises in Hill Street.

Ysgol Bodhyfryd
Opened as Wrexham's first Welsh language junior school, Bodhyfryd was originally accommodated in premises off Park Avenue, in the area that came to be known as Bodhyfryd. The school later moved to premises on Range Road. In 2001 there were 303 pupils on the roll and in 2010, 280.

Headteachers:
    Miss Beryl Syvell
    Miss M.J. Davies
    Arwel Gwynn Jones
    Dafydd Roberts
    Geraint Jones

Ysgol Clywedog/Clywedog High School
This school opened in September 2003 following the reorganisation of secondary education in Wrexham prompted by the fall in pupil

Mrs Olwen Berwyn Davies and some of the first pupils at Ysgol Bodhyfryd.

numbers. Bryn Offa School, the Groves High School and St David's School were closed and the pupils merged into two new schools, Rhosnesni High School* and Ysgol Clywedog. In September 2004, Ysgol Clywedog moved into the former the Groves High School buildings in order that the premises at Bryn Offa could be refurbished, remaining there until Easter 2005. The school serves the southern section of Wrexham town (Gwenfro, St Giles, Victoria schools) as well as the villages of Bwlchgwyn, Coedpoeth, Marchwiel, Minera and Rhostyllen. In 2010, there were 898 pupils on the roll.

Headteachers
   2003–07   Mrs Janette Smith
   2007   Dr David Kirby

Ysgol Morgan Llwyd, Stockwell Grove

Ysgol Morgan Llwyd, Wrexham's first Welsh language secondary school, opened in September 1963 in part of the Victoria School with 36 children accommodated in two classes. The school moved to temporary accommodation at the old Hermitage* army camp. The school eventually acquired purposed-designed buildings in 1974, officially opened by Cllr Gwilym Parry. However, due to the school's success in attracting new pupils, problems arose with overcrowding and it moved to the former Cartrefle College* site in September 2000 and was officially opened by the Welsh First Secretary, Rhodri Morgan, on 9 March 2001. In October 2001 it had 730 pupils on the roll. By 2010 this had risen to 763.

Headteachers:
   1963   Mrs Rhiannon Grey-Davies (Deputy Head, acting Head)
   1964   W.J. Davies (February)
   1980   R. Alun Charles
   1987   Edward Williams
   2000   Hugh Foster Evans

Ysgol Plas Coch, Plas Coch Road

Opened in September 1992 as Wrexham's second Welsh language junior school. In 2001 it had 239 children on the roll. By 2010, this had fallen to 202.

Headteachers:
   1992   G. Jones
   2009   Osian Jones (acting)

Yspytty

The area of land bounded by Queen Street and Hope Street was formerly known as Yspytty or Spytty (from the Welsh *yspyty* meaning hospital) although the origin of this name is unknown. Slightly further north, the area of Llwyn Isa,* where the Guildhall is now located was sometimes referred to as Upper Yspytty or Yspytty Ucha. [DRO/NTD/92] A house located in Queen Street was also known by this name and existed in the early 17th century when it was the property of the Puleston family of Hafod-y-Wern.* The original house, of half-timber construction with a thatched roof, was probably built by a wealthy Stansty farmer named Hughes in the early 17th century. He does not appear to have lived in the property but to have let it out to various tenants including:

John Lewis (attorney of Wrexham) of The Lodge, Rhosddu, who used it as his business premises until 1742. He died in July 1762 and was buried in Rhosddu.

Thomas Hayman (attorney of Wrexham) from 1742–47 when he moved to Tŷ Meredith* in Chester Street. He married Eleanor Puleston of Pickhill Hall and their daughter Anne was Privy Purse to Princess Caroline of Wales.

Yspytty was bought by Vincent Price a Wrexham surgeon. He completely rebuilt the house in brick and sandstone and had a large, landscaped garden extending behind the properties on Lambpit Street. He lived there for a short time until his death in 1786.

In 1789 it was bought by John Evans a mercer and clothier with a shop at N°s 36–7 High Street. He died in 1796 and the house was left to Watkin Hayman. He died three years later and his widow continued to live at the house until her death in 1805 when it was inherited by John Burton, the nephew and heir of John Evans. On his death in 1813, the property passed to his daughter Mary Ann and from her, by her marriage to the Revd John Pearce, minister of the United Presbyterian Chapel* in Chester Street. He was, unusually for a cleric, something of an entrepreneur, and by 1824 appears to have been operating a bank at the house (he was also later involved in mining and was joint owner of the Southsea & Broughton collieries). He remained in the house until at least 1853 when he was declared bankrupt. He died in 1857 and the house was sold to John Lewis, a solicitor. There is no record of the house after 1893. The site was later occupied by the Glynn Cinema* and the Old Library* and is now the site of the Guildhall* offices on Lambpit Street.*

Yspytty Croft

A small piece of land (of just over 1 acre) on the right hand side of Rhosddu Road, sold to Mr Buttal (of Grove Park*) by Sir Foster Cunliffe* of Acton Park* in 1786 for £146. A field opposite it (of just over 3 acres), called Cae Gron (*Trans.* round field), was sold by Sir Foster to Mr Davies Cooke in 1789 for £216. [FRO/D/AH/24]

Z

Zoedone Mineral Works, Pentre Felin

This business was established in the 1880s and located in the former Abbot's Mill* in Pentre Felin. In the 1890s, it became the Aerated Beverage Buffet Company. It used water drawn from a well on the premises. A.N. Palmer* first came to Wrexham to take up employment as a chemist with this company. The whole site was offered for sale in May 1903 and was bought by Evan Birkett Evans* as new premises for his leather company, Hugh Price & Company.* [DRO/DD/G/2869]

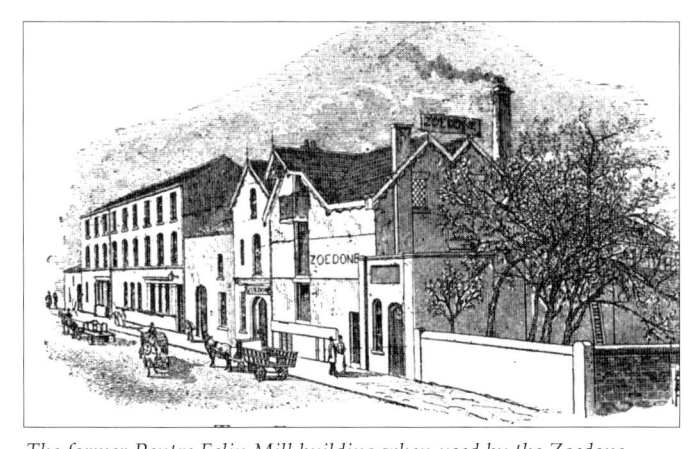

The former Pentre Felin Mill building when used by the Zoedone Mineral Works in the 1880s. This later became the Hugh Price & Company leather works.

SELECT BIBLIOGRAPHY

Bagshaw, John	*Broughton Then and Now*, 1992, Bridge Books, Wrexham.
Belton, Gwynne	*Grove Park Schools — a collection of pictures*, 1997, Bridge Books, Wrexham.
Bingham, Hiram	*Elihu Yale — the American Nabob of Queen Square*, 1939, New York.
Brown, Roger L.	*David Howell, a Pool of Spirituality*, 1998, Gee & Son, Denbigh.
Bodlander, A., *et al*	*Marcher Railways. The railways of Wrexham and Oswestry, a photographic history,* 2008, Bridge Books, Wrexham.
Boyd, James I C	*Wrexham, Mold and Connah's Quay Railway*, Oakwood Press, Oxford, 1991.
Byrne, Kathryn	*St Mary's Cathedral, Wrexham, the Story of a Catholic Community*, 2007, Bridge Books, Wrexham.
	The Story of Bishop's House (Plas Tirion), Wrexham, Diocese of Wrexham, Wrexham, 2009.
Byron, Arthur	*History of the Jeffreys and Byron Families*, privately published 1982.
Chaloner, Joan	*Wrexham Hospitals, a pictorial record,* 2005, Bridge Books, Wrexham.
Christiansen, Rex	*Forgotten Railways North and Mid Wales*, 1984, David & Charles, Newton Abbot.
Cust, A. L.	*Chronicles of Erthig on the Dyke*, n.d., John Lane, London.
Davies, Gareth, *et al*	*Who's Who of Welsh International Soccer Players*, 1991, Bridge Books, Wrexham
Davies, Glyn	*Minera — The History of an Industrial Parish*, 1964, Private, Wrexham.
Dempsey, Thomas	*Richard Gwyn — Man of Maelor: Martyr or Traitor?* 1970, Bolton.
Dodd, A. H.	*A History of Wrexham, Denbighshire*, 2nd Ed., 1989, Bridge Books, Wrexham.
	The Industrial Revolution in North Wales, 3rd edition reprint, 1990, Bridge Books, Wrexham.
Dodd, C.	*Wrexham Scholars.* n.d. Private.
Edge, Mike	*Wrexham Bus Companies — a collection of pictures*, 2000, Bridge Books, Wrexham.
Edwards, Ifor	*Davies Brothers Gatesmiths*, 1977, Welsh Arts Council, Cardiff.
Ellis, Tom	*Ater the Dust has Settled*, 2004, Bridge Books, Wrexham.
Garland, Ian	*A History of the Welsh Cup, 1877–1993*, 1993, Bridge Books, Wrexham
Garnett, Oliver	*Erddig, Clwyd*, 3rd Ed., 2001, The National Trust, London
Gilpin, Dennis	*Rhosllannerchrugog, Johnstown, Ponciau and Penycae — a collection of pictures*, Vols. 1 & 2, 1991 & 1992, Bridge Books, Wrexham.
Glover, Brian	*Prince of Ales — The History of Brewing in Wales*, 1993, Alan Sutton, Stroud.
Griffiths, Eric	*Philip Yorke I (1743–1804) — Squire of Erthig*, 1995, Bridge Books, Wrexham.
Gummow, J. R.	*Hints on House Building, 1874,* Wrexham.
Helm, P. J.	*Jeffreys*, 1966, Robert Hale, London.
Hubbard, Edward	*The Historic Buildings of Wales: Clwyd (Denbighshire and Flintshire)*, 1986, Penguin Books, London.
Hughes, D.	*Bishop Sahib: A Life of Reginald Heber*, 1986, Churchman.
Hughes, H. Ellis	*Eminent Men of Denbighshire*, n.d. *c.*1946, The Brython Press, Liverpool.
Hughes, Joan M.	*Trinity A Town Centre Church*, 1988, private, Wrexham.
James, Arnold J. *et al*	*Union to Reform, 1536–1832*, 1986, Gomer, Llandysul.
	Wales at Westminster, 1800–1979, 1981, Gomer, Llandysul.
Jenkins, John, *et al*	*Who's Who of Welsh International Rugby Players*, 1991, Bridge Books, Wrexham.
Jones, Beryl M. etc	*Wrexham Breweries and Inns*, 2001, Bridge Books, Wrexham.
Jones, Geoffrey A. *et al*	*Images of Wrexham. The County Borough through the camera lens*, 2007, Bridge Books, Wrexham.
Jones, Ioan D.	*Brymbo Steel Works — a collection of pictures*, 1991, Bridge Books, Wrexham.
Jones, John	*Wrexham and its Neighbourhood*, private, 1868, Railton Potter, Wrexham.
Jones, Peter	*Wrexham — a complete record, 1872–1992*, 1992, Breedon Books, Derby.
Jones, Richard, *et al*	*History of Gas Production in Wales*, 1978, Wales Gas.
Jones, Tim	*Rioting in North East Wales, 1536–1918*, 1997, Bridge Books, Wrexham.
Jones-Mortimer, H. M. C.	*A List of the Names and Residences of All the High Sheriffs of the County of Denbigh from 1541 to 1970*, 1971, Private.
	A List of the Names and Residences of All the High Sheriffs of the County of Flint from 1541 to 1970, 1964, Private.
Kelly, Ithel	*The North Wales Coalfield — a collection of pictures*, Vol.1, 1990, Bridge Books, Wrexham.
Kidner, R. W.	*The Cambrian Railways*, 1992, The Oakwood Press, Oxford.
Lerry, G. G.	*Mayors and Town Clerks of Wrexham* (unpublished typescript).

	Henry Robertson, Pioneer of Railways into Wales, Woodalls, Oswestry, 1949.
	Collieries of Denbighshire — Past and Present, private, n.d. c.1946, Wrexham.
Lloyd, Thomas	*Lost Houses of Wales*, 2nd Edition 1989, Save Britain's Heritage, London.
Lloyd, Sir William (Ed. George Lloyd)	*Narrative of a journey … to the Boorendoo Pass in the Himalaya Mountains … 1840*, Private, London.
Mason, Margaret	*Alexandra, 1910–1999 — the story of a much loved school*, 1999, Wrexham County Borough Council, Wrexham.
Matthias, K., *et al*	*A Wrexham Collection*, 1998, Bridge Books, Wrexham.
Mayo, Patricia Elton	*The Making of a Criminal, 1969*, Weidenfeld & Nicolson, London.
Milne-Tyte, Robert	*Bloody Jeffreys — The Hanging Judge*, 1989, Andre Deutsch, London.
Owen, Bryn	*History of the Welsh Militia and Volunteer Forces — Denbighshire & Flintshire Regiments of Militia*, 1997, Bridge Books, Wrexham.
Palmer, Alfred N.	*A History of the Town of Wrexham*, 1893, Woodall, Minshall and Thomas, Wrexham.
	A History of the Thirteen Country Townships of the Old Parish of Wrexham, 1903, Private, Wrexham.
	The Town Fields and Folk of Wrexham in the Reign of James Ist, 1883, Private, Wrexham.
	John Wilkinson and the Old Bersham Ironworks, 1899, Private, Wrexham.
	A History of Ruabon, 1992, Bridge Books, Wrexham.
	A History of Holt, Isycoed and Bangor Isycoed, 1991, Bridge Books, Wrexham.
	A History of the Parish Church of Wrexham, reprint, 1984, Bridge Books, Wrexham.
	A History of the Parish of Gresford, reprint, 1987, Bridge Books, Wrexham.
Perrin, Dennis	*A History of Acton Park School*, Acton Park Schools, 1998, Wrexham.
Phillips, Alan	*Military Airfields of Wales*, 2006, Bridge Books, Wrexham.
Pratt, Derrick, *et al*	*Wings Across the Border, Vols 1, 2 & 3*, 1998, 2002, 2005, Bridge Books, Wrexham.
Pritchard, T. W.	*Remembering Ruabon/Cofio Rhiwabon*, 2000, Ruabon Field Club, Ruabon.
Reynardson, Charles S. T. Birch	*Down the Road or Reminiscences of a Gentleman Coachman*, 1887, Chapman & Hall, London.
Rees, Cynthia	*A History of the Parish of Marchwiel*, 1998, Bridge Books, Wrexham.
Rees, T. Mardy	*A History of the Quakers in Wales*, 1925, Spurrell & Son, Carmarthen.
Schoolong, KBE, Sir W.	*Alliance Assurance, 1824–1924*, 1924, Private, London.
Scott, Dorothy	*Around the Stars*, Wrexham, 1987, Private, Wrexham.
Shone, Arthur N.	*Wrexham Races — The Forgotten Welsh Racecourse*, 1991, Snowy Publications, Wrexham.
Smith, David J.	*Action Stations 3. Military Airfields of Wales and the North-West*, 1981, Patrick Stephens, Cambridge.
Southern, D. *et al*	*Wrexham Railways — a collection of pictures Vols 1 & 2*, 1992 & 1993, Bridge Books, Wrexham.
Steen, Gerald	*Wrexham Trams and Buses, 1903–33 — A Personal Memoir*, 1978, GS Publications, Wrexham.
Thomas, D. Aneurin	*The Welsh Elizabethan Catholic Martyrs*, 1971, UWP, Cardiff.
Tucker, Norman	*North Wales in the Civil War*, reprint ,1992, Bridge Books, Wrexham.
	Denbighshire Officers in the Civil War, n.d. Private. Colwyn Bay.
	Royalist Officers of North Wales, 1642–1660, 1961, Private, Colwyn Bay.
Parry, DSO, Col. Ll. E. S. *etc.*	*Historical Records of the Denbighshire Hussars Imperial Yeomanry*, 1909, Woodall, Minshall, Thomas & Co., Wrexham.
Williams, C. J.	*Industry in Clwyd — An illustrated history*, 1986, Clwyd Record Office, Hawarden.
	Metal Mines of North Wales — a collection of pictures, 1997, Bridge Books, Wrexham.
Williams, Gwyneth	*Wrexham and District — a portrait in old picture postcards*, 1990, S. B. Publications, Market Drayton.
Williams, W. Alister	*Old Wrexham — a collection of pictures Vols 1–5*, 1981–91, Bridge Books, Wrexham.
	The Parish Church of St. Giles, Wrexham, 2000, Bridge Books, Wrexham.
	VCs of Wales and the Welsh Regiments, 1984, Bridge Books, Wrexham.
	Heart of a Dragon, the VCs of Wales and the Welsh Regiments 1854–1902 & 1914–82, 2007/2008, Bridge Books, Wrexham.
Williamson, Stanley	*Gresford: The Anatomy of a Disaster*, 1999, Liverpool University Press, Liverpool.
Veysey, Geoffrey	*Philip Yorke Last Squire of Erddig*, 2002, Bridge Books, Wrexham.
——	*1841 Census for Wrexham Town*, Clwyd Family History Society, Gwernymynydd, 1998.
——	*A Descriptive Account of Wrexham, Its History, Trade, and Commerce*, n.d., Robinson, Son & Pike, Brighton.
——	*A Complete Record of the Royal Visit to Wales 1889* Woodhall, Minshall, and Co., Oswestry & Wrexham, 1889.
——	*A Street Atlas of Wrexham, 1872*, Bridge Books, 1998, Wrexham.
——	*Bennett's Directory — Wrexham & District*, 1912.
——	Britain's Original Lager Brewery, The story of Wrexham Lager Brewery, n.d.,Wrexham Lager Brewery, Wrexham.
——	*Crockers Wrexham Directory and Postal Guide for 1881–1882*, nd, W. C. Crocker, Shrewsbury.
——	*Elihu Yale, the Great Welsh American*, 1991, Wrexham Area Civic Society, Wrexham.

―― *Holt — A Pictorial History* — 1999, Holt Local History Society, Holt.
―― *The Official Commercial Directory for Wrexham and District*, various issues (published annually), *Wrexham Leader*, Wrexham.
―― *The Wrexham Directory*, various issues (published annually), Selwyn Mattox, Wrexham.
―― *Wrexham Directory, 1886*, 1981, Clwyd Record Office, Hawarden.
―― *Wynnstay & The Wynns, A Volume of Varieties*, Oswestry, 1876.